ISBN 978-1-5281-9049-7
PIBN 10997447

1 MONTH OF
FREE
READING

at
www.ForgottenBooks.com

By purchasing this book you are eligible for one month membership to ForgottenBooks.com, giving you unlimited access to our entire collection of over 1,000,000 titles via our web site and mobile apps.

To claim your free month visit:

www.forgottenbooks.com/free997447

English
Français
Deutsche
Italiano
Español
Português

www.forgottenbooks.com

Mythology Photography **Fiction**
Fishing Christianity **Art** Cooking
Essays Buddhism Freemasonry
Medicine **Biology** Music **Ancient
Egypt** Evolution Carpentry Physics
Dance Geology **Mathematics** Fitness
Shakespeare **Folklore** Yoga Marketing
Confidence Immortality Biographies
Poetry **Psychology** Witchcraft
Electronics Chemistry History **Law**
Accounting **Philosophy** Anthropology
Alchemy Drama Quantum Mechanics
Atheism Sexual Health **Ancient History**
Entrepreneurship Languages Sport
Paleontology Needlework Islam
Metaphysics Investment Archaeology
Parenting Statistics Criminology
Motivational

REPORTS

OF

CASES DECIDED

BY THE

ENGLISH COURTS,

WITH

NOTES AND REFERENCES TO KINDRED CASES AND AUTHORITIES.

BY

NATHANIEL C. MOAK,

Counsellor at Law.

VOLUME XXXII.

CONTAINING

11 CHANCERY DIVISION, pp. 701-972.
3, 4, 5, 6, 7 PROBATE DIVISION.

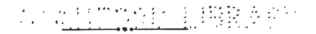

ALBANY, N. Y.:

WILLIAM GOULD & SON,

LAW PUBLISHERS AND BOOKSELLERS.

1883.

359787

JUDGES.

LORD HIGH CHANCELLOR.

Right Hon. LORD CAIRNS,[1] appointed 1874.
Right Hon. LORD SELBORNE,[2] " 1880.

LORDS OF APPEAL IN ORDINARY.

Right Hon. LORD BLACKBURN, appointed 1876.
Right Hon. LORD GORDON,[3] " "
Right Hon. WILLIAM WATSON,[4] " 1880.

PRIVY COUNCIL, JUDICIAL COMMITTEE.

(APPOINTED UNDER 34 & 35 VICT., CH. 91: USUALLY SITTING.)

Right Hon. Sir JAMES W. COLVILE.[5]
Right Hon. Sir BARNES PEACOCK.
Right Hon. Sir MONTAGUE E. SMITH.[6]
Right Hon. Sir ROBERT P. COLLIER.
Right Hon. Sir RICHARD COUCH.[7]

1 Retired with Earl of Beaconsfield's administration, April, 1880: 15 L. J., 227.
2 Appointed under Gladstone's administration, April, 1880 15 L. J., 227.
3 Died August 21, 1879: 15 L. J., 115.
4 Appointed to fill vacancy of Lord Gordon, April, 1880: 15 L. J., 115, 234.
5 Died December 7, 1880 : 15 L. J., 595, 602.
6 Resigned December 21, 1881 : 16 L. J., 607, 622 ; 72 L. T., 168.
7 Appointed January 26, 1881, in place of Sir James W. Colvile : 16 L. J., 49, 58.

SUPREME COURT OF JUDICATURE.

COURT OF APPEAL.

Ex officio Members.

The Right Hon. the LORD HIGH CHANCELLOR (President).
The Right Hon. the LORD CHIEF JUSTICE of England.
The Right Hon. the MASTER OF THE ROLLS.
The Right Hon. the LORD CHIEF JUSTICE of the Common Pleas.
The Right Hon. the LORD CHIEF BARON of the Exchequer.

Ordinary Members.

Right Hon. Sir WILLIAM MILBOURNE JAMES,[1]	appointed 1870
Right Hon. Sir GEORGE MELLISH,[2]	" "
Right Hon. Sir RICHARD BAGGALLAY,	" 1875.
Right Hon. Sir GEORGE WM. W. BRAMWELL,[3]	1876.
Right Hon. Sir WILLIAM BALIOL BRETT,[4]	"
Right Hon. Sir RICHARD PAUL AMPHLETT,[5]	"
Right Hon. Sir HENRY COTTON,[6]	1877.
Right Hon. Sir ALFRED HENRY THESIGER,[7]	"
Right Hon. Sir GEORGE JESSEL,[8]	1881.
Right Hon. Sir NATHANIEL LINDLEY,[9]	" "
Right Hon. Sir JOHN HOLKER,[10]	" 1882.
Right Hon. Sir CHARLES SYNGE CHRISTOPHER BOWEN,[11]	" "
Right Hon. Sir JOHN DAVID FITZGERALD,[12]	" "
Right Hon. Sir EDWARD FRY,[13]	1883.

---

1 Died June 7, 1881: 16 Law Jour., 258; 71 Law Times, 105.

2 Died June 16, 1877 12 Law Jour., 372.

8 Retired September 1, 1881: 71 L. T., 333; 16 L. J., 411.

4 Appointed Master of the Rolls, April 5, 1883: 18 L. J., 183, 203.

5 Retired on account of ill health, October, 1877: 63 L. T., 417.

6 Appointed June, 1877, in place of Lord Justice MELLISH: 12 Law Jour., 386.

7 Appointed November, 1877, in place of Lord Justice AMPHLETT· 12 L. J., 631. Died October 20, 1880: 15 L. J., 507, 508, 518, 527; 69 L. T., 419, 433.

8 Promoted to Court of Appeal, September 10, 1881· 16 L. J., 397. Died March 21, 1883: 74 L. T , 375, 390.

9 Promoted from Court of Common Pleas, October 29, 1881: 71 L. T., 409. Sworn in November 1, 1881: 72 L. T., 12.

10 Died May 24, 1882 : 17 L. J., 275 ; 73 L. T., 71.

11 Appointed from Queen's Bench to Court of Appeal, in place of Sir JOHN HOLKER, June 1, 1882 : 73 L. T., 87 ; 17 L. J., 289.

12 Appointed June 5, 1882· 73 L. T., 104 ; 18 L. J., 318.

13 Appointed to Court of Appeal, from Chancery Division, April 5, 1883. 18 L. J., 133, 203 74 L. T., 401.

HIGH COURT OF JUSTICE.

CHANCERY DIVISION.

Right Hon. the LORD HIGH CHANCELLOR (President).

Right Hon. Sir GEORGE JESSEL,[1] Master of the Rolls, appointed 1873
Right Hon. Sir WILLIAM BALIOL BRETT,[2]   "   1883.
Hon. Sir RICHARD MALINS,[3] Vice-Chancellor,   "   1866.
Hon. Sir JAMES BACON,   "   "   1870.
Hon. Sir CHARLES HALL,[4]   "   "   1873.
Hon. Sir EDWARD E. KAY,[5]   "   "   1881.
Hon. Sir EDWARD FRY,[6]   Justice of the High Court,   "   1877.
Hon. Sir JOSEPH W. CHITTY,[7]   "   "   "   " . 1881.
Hon. Sir JOHN PEARSON,[8]   "   "   "   1882.

QUEEN'S BENCH DIVISION.

Right Hon. Sir ALEXANDER JAMES EDMUND COCKBURN,[9] Bart., G.C.B.,
    Lord Chief Justice of England, appointed 1859.
Right Hon. Sir JOHN DUKE COLERIDGE,[10] Lord Chief Justice of England,
    appointed Dec. 1, 1880.

Hon. Sir JOHN MELLOR,[11]   appointed 1861.
Hon. Sir ROBERT LUSH,[12]   "   1865.
Hon. Sir WILLIAM V. FIELD,   "   1875.
Hon. Sir HENRY MANISTY,   "   1876.
Hon. Sir CHARLES SYNGE CHRISTOPHER BOWEN,[13] "   1879.
Hon. Sir FORD NORTH,[14]   "   1881.
Hon. Sir JOHN HOLKER,[15]   1882.
Hon. Sir CHARLES DAY,[16]   "

1 Promoted to Court of Appeal, September 10, 1881: 16 L. J., 397. Died March 21, 1883: 74 L. T., 375, 390; 18 L. J., 159, 166, 180.

2 Appointed Master of the Rolls, from Court of Appeal, April 5, 1883: 10 L. J., 188, 208.

3 Retired March 19, 1881: 16 L. J., 137, 146.

4 Resigned October 13, 1882: 17 L. J., 541.

5 Appointed March 30, 1881: 16 L. J., 147.

6 Appointed April 30, 1877, under the act of April 24, 1877 12 Law Jour., 251.

7 Appointed September 6, 1881: 71 L. T., 321, 323; 16 L. J., 397.

8 Appointed and sworn in, October 24, 1882: 17 L. J., 541, 566.

9 Died November 20, 1880: 15 L. J., 576, 589; 15 Am. L. Rev., 134.

10 Appointed to fill vacancy occasioned by death of Lord COCKBURN.

11 Resigned June 11, 1879: 14 Law Jour., 365; 67 Law Times, 127.

12 Died December 27, 1881: 72 L. T., 145, 173; 16 L. J., 624; 17 L. J., 6.

13 Appointed June 11, 1879: 14 Law Jour., 365; 67 Law Times, 127—transferred to Court of Appeal, June 1, 1882.

14 Appointed in place of Mr. Justice LINDLEY, promoted to Court of Appeal. Sworn in November 1, 1881. 72 L. T., 1, 12.

15 Appointed January 10, 1882: 17 L. J., 15, 33 ; 72 L. T., 181. Died May 24, 1882: 17 L. J., 275, 73 L. T., 71; 73 L. T., 87; 17 L. J., 289.

16 Appointed June 5, 1882 18 L. J., 319 ; 73 L. T., 91.

COMMON PLEAS DIVISION.

Right Hon. LORD COLERIDGE,[1] Lord Chief Justice of the Common Pleas, appointed 1873.

Hon. Sir WILLIAM ROBERT GROVE, appointed 1871.
Hon. GEORGE DENMAN,   "   1872.
Hon. Sir NATHANIEL LINDLEY,[2]   "   1875.
Hon. Sir HENRY CHARLES LOPES,   1876.
Hon. Sir J. C. MATHEW,[3]   1881.
Hon. Sir HENRY MATHER JACKSON,[4]   "   "
Hon. Sir LEWIS W. CAVE,[5]   "

EXCHEQUER DIVISION.

Right Hon. Sir FITZ-ROY KELLY,[6] Lord Chief Baron, appointed 1866.
Hon. Sir ANTHONY CLEASBY,[7]   appointed 1868.
Hon. Sir CHARLES EDWARD POLLOCK,   "   1873.
Hon. Sir JOHN WALTER HUDDLESTON,   "   1875.
Hon. Sir HENRY HAWKINS,   1876.
Hon. Sir JAMES FITZ-JAMES STEPHEN,[8] "   1879.

COURT OF APPEAL IN BANKRUPTCY.

The Ordinary Judges of the Court of Appeal.

PROBATE, MATRIMONIAL, DIVORCE AND ADMIRALTY DIVISION.

Right Hon. Sir JAMES HANNEN (President), appointed 1872.
Right Hon. Sir ROBERT J. PHILLIMORE,[9]   "   1876.
Right Hon. Sir CHARLES PARKER BUTT,[10]   "   1883.

CHIEF JUDGE IN BANKRUPTCY.

Hon. Sir JAMES BACON, Vice-Chancellor.

JUDGE OF THE COURT OF ARCHES.

LORD PENZANCE, appointed 1875.

---

1 Appointed to fill vacancy occasioned by death of Lord COCKBURN.
2 Promoted to Court of Appeal, October 29, 1881. 71 L. T., 409.
3 Appointed March 1, 1881: 16 Law Jour., 103.
4 Appointed March 1, 1881: 16 L. J., 103. Died March 12, 1881: 16 L J., 113.
5 Appointed March 26, 1881, to fill vacancy occasioned by death of Mr. Justice JACKSON: 16 Law Journal, 123.
6 Died September 18, 1880. 15 Law Jour., 459; 69 Law Times, 359, 367.
7 Resigned January, 1879. 14 Law Jour., 15; 66 Law Times, 191.
8 Appointed January, 1879, in place of Baron CLEASBY: 14 L. Jour., 34; 66 Law Times, 191.
9 Retired March 21, 1883: 74 L. T., 383.
10 Appointed March 26, 1883: 74 L. T., 383; 18 L. J., 109, 181.

TABLE OF CASES

REPORTED IN THIS VOLUME.

C A S E S

DETERMINED BY THE

PROBATE, DIVORCE, AND ADMIRALTY DIVISION

OF THE

HIGH COURT OF JUSTICE, ·

AND BY THE

C O U R T   O F   A P P E A L

ON APPEAL FROM THAT DIVISION,

AND BY THE

ECCLESIASTICAL COURTS,

XLI VICTORIA. ·

———— • • ————

[3 Probate Division, 1.]

Nov. 26, 1877.

[IN THE COURT OF APPEAL.]

*SOTTOMAYOR, Otherwise DE BARROS v. DE BARROS (). [1

Nullity of Marriage—Consanguinity—Marriage illegal by the Law of Domicile.

The petitioner and respondent, Portuguese subjects domiciled in Portugal, and first cousins to each other, came to reside in England in 1858, and in 1866 they went through a form of marriage before the registrar of the district of the city of London. In 1873 they returned to Portugal, and their domicile throughout continued to be Portuguese. By the law of Portugal a marriage between first cousins is illegal, as being incestuous, but may be celebrated under a Papal dispensation :

Held, reversing the decision of the court below, that the parties being by the law of the country of their domicile under a personal disability to contract marriage, their marriage ought to be declared null and void.

Simonin v. *Mallac* (2 Sw. & Tr., 67 ; 29 L. J. (P. M. & A.), 971,) distinguished.

APPEAL by the petitioner from the decision of Sir R. Phillimore, dismissing a petition to have her marriage declared null and void. The facts are fully stated in the report of the case in the court below ().

(¹) Reversing 20 Eng. Rep., 605.   (²) 2 P. D., 81 ; 20 Eng. R., 605.

2] *July 28. *Inderwick*, Q.C., *Dr. Tristram* and *Bayford*, for the appellant: The law of the place governs the forms and ceremonies requisite to a valid marriage, *Conway*, *otherwise Beazley* v. *Beazley* ('); but the cases carry the rule no further. This case is governed in principle by *Brook* v. *Brook* ('), where a marriage between a man and his deceased wife's sister, both being domiciled British subjects, was held invalid, though solemnized in a country where such marriages are lawful. *Steele* v. *Braddell* (') lays down the principles as to minors. They are under no incapacity to marry in England, Scotland, or Ireland, but in England and Ireland consents are required, and in Scotland not. A marriage between English and Irish minors in Scotland was therefore held good, the consents being only a part of the forms and ceremonies. *Warrender* v. *Warrender* (') lays down the same principle, that the *lex loci* is looked to so far only as relates to the forms and ceremonies.

[COTTON, L.J.: In the case of *Brook* v. *Brook* (') the parties were under an incapacity imposed by our own statute law. A case where, on the ground of a foreign law, we are asked to declare a marriage bad, which would have been perfectly good if the parties had been English subjects, seems to be in a different position.]

The cases referred to establish the principle that a marriage between two persons who by the law of the country of their domicile cannot intermarry is void wherever it is solemnized.

Willis, Q.C., and *Jacques*, for the Queen's proctor: According to the law of England, the validity of a marriage is determined by the *lex loci contractus*, subject to two exceptions, that if a domiciled Englishman applies to the courts of his own country, they will not recognize his marriage if forbidden by our law, and that a marriage which, by the general consent of Christendom, is incestuous, will be deemed invalid, though allowed by the law of the place where it was solemnized. In *Brook* v. *Brook* (') the *lex loci* is treated as governing the solemnization and the capacity of the parties to contract. That a marriage generally looked upon as incestuous would not be recognized is admitted, 3] but this is not *such. The other exception is illustrated by the *Sussex Peerage Case* ('), where the marriage was valid according to the laws of Rome, where it was celebrated, but the application was made to the courts of our own

(') 3 Hagg. Eccl., 639.   (') Milw. Ir. Eccl. Rep., 21.
(') 9 H. L. C., 193.   (') 2 Cl. & F., 488, 530.
(') 11 Cl. & F., 85.

country, where such a marriage was illegal under the provisions of the Royal Marriage Act.

[JAMES, L.J.: Does your argument involve this—that if the Duke of Sussex had acquired real estate in France, and become domiciled there, his children could have inherited ?]

No; the consequences of the marriage must be determined by the law of the domicile. The courts of any country may decline to give to a marriage the full effect which it would have had if conformable to their own law, and yet decline to declare that the parties have been living in concubinage: Burge, Foreign and Colonial Law, i, pp. 184, 188.

[JAMES, L.J.: Those passages appear hardly consistent with *Brook* v. *Brook* (¹).

BAGGALLAY, L.J.: Suppose the parties had gone to Madrid, would they be treated by the courts of Madrid as legally married ?]

The courts of Madrid must give effect to the *lex loci contractus.* · *Simonin* v. *Mallac* (²) governs the present case. *Conway* v. *Beazley* (³) comes within the principle of *Brook* v. *Brook* (), which is quite consistent with *Simonin* v. *Mallac* (²). The question is discussed in Burge, Foreign and Colonial Law, i, p. 195. *Warrender* v. *Warrender* (⁴) does not apply, for it was a case of divorce, which depends on the domicile. [Wharton on Conflict of Laws, ss. 160, 161, and *Ruding* v. *Smith* () were also referred to.]

Inderwick, in reply, referred to Story, Conflict of Laws, s. 183.

Cur. adv. vult.

Nov. 26. The judgment of the Court (James, Baggallay, and Cotton, L.JJ.,) was delivered by

COTTON, L.J.: This is an appeal from an order of the Court of Divorce, dated the 17th of March, 1877, dismissing a petition presented by Ignacia Sottomayor, praying the court to declare *her marriage with the respondent [4 Gonzalo de Barros to be null and void. The respondent appeared to the petition, but did not file an answer or appear at the hearing; and by direction of the judge the Queen's proctor was served with the petition, and appeared by counsel to argue the case against the petition.

There were several grounds on which the petitioner originally claimed relief, but the only ground now to be consid-

(¹) 9 H. L. C., 193.
(²) 2 Sw. & Tr., 67; 29 L. J. (P. M. & A.), 97.

(³) 3 Hagg., 639.
(⁴) 2 Cl. & F., 488, 530.
(⁵) 2 Hagg. Cons, Rep., 371.

ered is that she and the respondent were under a personal incapacity to contract marriage. The facts are these: The petitioner and respondent are Portuguese subjects, and are and have always been domiciled in that country, where they both now reside. They are first cousins, and it was proved that by the law of Portugal first cousins are incapable of contracting marriage by reason of consanguinity, and that any marriage between parties so related is by the law of Portugal held to be incestuous and therefore null and void ; but though not proved, it was admitted before us that such a marriage would be valid if solemnized under the authority of a Papal dispensation.

In the year 1858 the petitioner, her father and mother, and her uncle, De Barros, and his family, including the respondent, his eldest son, came to England, and the two families occupied a house jointly in Dorset Square, London. The petitioner's father came to this country for the benefit of his health, and De Barros for the education of his children and to superintend the sale of wine. De Barros subsequently, in 1861, became manager to a firm of wine merchants in London, carrying on business under the style of Caldos Brothers & Co., of which the petitioner's father was made a partner, and which stopped payment in 1865. On the 21st of June, 1866, the petitioner, at that time of the age of fourteen years and a half, and the respondent, of the age of sixteen years, were married at a registrar's office in London. No religious ceremony accompanied or followed the marriage, and although the parties lived together in the same house until the year 1872, they never slept together, and the marriage was never consummated. The petitioner stated that she went through the form of marriage contrary to her own inclination, by the persuation of her uncle and mother, on the representation that it would be the means of 5]   preserving her father's Portuguese property *from the consequences of the bankruptcy of the wine business.

Under these circumstances the petitioner, in November, 1874, presented her petition for the object above mentioned, and Sir R. Phillimore, before whom the case was heard, declined to declare the marriage invalid and dismissed the petition, but did so, as we understand, rather because he felt himself bound by the decision in the case of *Simonin* v. *Mallac* (¹), than because he considered that on principle the marriage ought to be held good. If the parties had been subjects of Her Majesty domiciled in England, the marriage would undoubtedly have been valid. But it is a well-recog-

(¹) 2 Sw. & Tr., 67; 29 L. J. (P. M. & A.), 97.

nized principle of law that the question of personal capacity to enter into any contract is to be decided by the law of domicile. It is, however, urged that this does not apply to the contract of marriage, and that a marriage valid according to the law of the country where it is solemnized is valid everywhere. This, in our opinion, is not a correct statement of the law. The law of a country where a marriage is solemnized must alone decide all questions relating to the validity of the ceremony by which the marriage is alleged to have been constituted; but, as in other contracts, so in that of marriage, personal capacity must depend on the law of domicile; and if the laws of any country prohibit its subjects within certain degrees of consanguinity from contracting marriage, and stamp a marriage between persons within the prohibited degrees as incestuous, this, in our opinion, imposes on the subjects of that country a personal incapacity, which continues to affect them so long as they are domiciled in the country where this law prevails, and renders invalid a marriage between persons both at the time of their marriage subjects of and domiciled in the country which imposes this restriction, wherever such marriage may have been solemnized. In argument several passages in Story' s Conflict of Laws were referred to, in support of the contention that in an English court a marriage between persons who by our law may lawfully intermarry ought not to be declared void, though declared incestuous by the law of the parties' domicile, unless the marriage is one which the general consent of Christendom stamps as incestuous. It is hardly possible to suppose *that the law of England, or [6 of any Christian country, would consider as valid a marriage which the general consent of Christendom declared to be incestuous. Probably the true explanation of the passages in Story is given in *Brook* v. *Brook*, by Lord Cranworth (), and by Lord Wensleydale ('), who express their opinions that he is referring to marriages not prohibited or declared to be incestuous by the municipal law of the country of domicile.

But it is said that the impediment imposed by the law of Portugal can be removed by a Papal dispensation, and, therefore, that it cannot be said there is a personal incapacity of the petitioner and respondent to contract marriage. The evidence is clear that by the law of Portugal the impediment to the marriage between the parties is such that, in the absence of Papal dispensation, the marriage would be by the law of that country void as incestuous.

(') 9 H. L. C., at pp. 227, 228.   (') 9 H. L. C., at pp. 241, 242.

The statutes of the English Parliament contain a declaration that no Papal dispensation can sanction a marriage otherwise incestuous; but the law of Portugal does recognize the validity of such a dispensation, and it cannot in our opinion be held that such a dispensation is a matter of form affecting only the sufficiency of the ceremony by which the marriage is effected, or that the law of Portugal, which prohibits and declares incestuous, unless with such a depensation, a marriage between the petitioner and respondent, does not impose on them a personal incapacity to contract marriage. It is proved that the courts of Portugal, where the petitioner and respondent are domiciled and resident, would hold the marriage void, as solemnized between parties incapable of marrying, and incestuous. How can the courts of this country hold the contrary, and, if appealed to, say the marriage is valid? It was pressed upon us in argument that a decision in favor of the petitioner would lead to many difficulties, if questions should arise as to the validity of a marriage between an English subject and a foreigner, in consequence of prohibitions imposed by the law of the domicile of the latter. Our opinion on this appeal is confined to the case where both the contracting parties are, at the time of their marriage, domiciled in a country the laws of which prohibit their marriage. All persons are legally bound to 7] take *notice of the laws of the country where they are domiciled. No country is bound to recognize the laws of a foreign state when they work injustice to its own subjects, and this principle would prevent the judgment in the present case being relied on as an authority for setting aside a marriage between a foreigner and an English subject domiciled in England, on the ground of any personal incapacity not recognized by the law of this country.

The counsel for the petitioner relied on the case of *Brook* v. *Brook* (¹) as a decision in his favor. If, in our opinion, that case had been a decision on the question arising on this petition, we should have thought it sufficient without more to refer to that case as decisive. The judgment in that case, however, only decided that the English courts must hold invalid a marriage between two English subjects domiciled in this country, who were prohibited from intermarrying by an English statute, even though the marriage was solemnized during a temporary sojourn in a foreign country. It is, therefore, not decisive of the present case; but the reasons given by the Lords who delivered their opinions in that case

(¹) 9 H. L. C., 193.

strongly support the principle on which this judgment is based.

It only remains to consider the case of *Simonin* v. *Mallac* ('). The objection to the validity of the marriage in that case, which was solemnized in England, was the want of the consent of parents required by the law of France, but not under the circumstances by that of this country. In our opinion, this consent must be considered a part of the ceremony of marriage, and not a matter affecting the personal capacity of the parties to contract marriage; and the decision in *Simonin* v. *Mallac* (') does not, we think, govern the present case. We are of opinion that the judgment appealed . from must be reversed, and a decree made declaring the marriage null and void.   *Judgment reversed.*

Solicitors for petitioner: *Tamplin, Taylor & Joseph.*
Solicitor for respondent: *J. P. Poncione.*

(¹) 2 Sw. & Tr., 67; 29 L. J. (P. M. & A.), 97.

See 11 Eng. Rep., 874 note.

The principal case below, is reported 19 Am. Law Reg. (N.S.), 76, 87 note.

See another decision on merits, 5 Prob. Div., 94, post, p. 336.

In this country the weight of authority is that a marriage which is valid by the law of the place where it is celebrated, unless contrary to the prohibitions of natural law, is valid everywhere, though such marriage be expressly forbidden by the law of the domicil of the parties.

Thus where, by a judgment of divorce and the statute of the State, the defendant was forbidden to marry again during the life of the plaintiff, and the defendant took with him, from his State to another where his marriage was not forbidden, a woman and there married her, after which he and the woman to whom he was so married returned to the State of their domicile and there resided : Held, the marriage was legal and valid, though the parties resorted to another State to consummate it with intent to evade the law of their domicile.

California : See Elliot v. Wohlfrom, 54 Cal., 384.

Canada, Lower : 3 Rev Crit., 23.

Canada, Upper : Harris v. Cooper, 31 U. C. Q. B., 182.

Illinois : Roth v. Ehman, 14 Chic. Leg. News, 293, 21 Am. Law Reg. (N.S.), 589, 595 note.

Irish : Steele v. Braddell, Milward, 1.

Kentucky : Stevenson v. Gray, 17 B. Monroe, 193.

Maryland : See Garner v. Garner, 56 Md., 127, 26 Alb. L. J., 274.

Massachusetts : See Com. v. Lane, 113 Mass., 458, 18 Amer. R., 509, 521 note ; Loud v. Loud, 129 Mass., 14.

New Jersey : See Yorston v. Yorston, 32 N. J. Eq., 495.

New York : Van Voorhis v. Brintnall, 86 N. Y., 18, 21 Am. Law Reg. . (N.S.), 9, 22 note, reversing 23 Hun, 264, overruling Marshall v. Marshall, 2 id, 238, 4 Thomp. & Cook, 449, and Thorp v. Thorp, 23 Alb. L. J., 213, 47 N. Y. Superior Ct. R., 80, 60 How. Pr., 295, and distinguishing Copsey v. Ogden, 11 N. Y., 228, and Haviland v. Halsted, 34 id., 643 ; Thorp v. Thorp, 23 Daily Register, 41 Ct. Appeals, reversing 47 N. Y. Superior Ct. R., 80, 60 How. Pr., 295 ; Moore v. Hegeman, 27 Hun, 68, 14 Chic. Leg. News, 322 ; Kerrison v. Kerrison, 8 Abb. N. C., 444, 60 How. Pr., 51 ; Matter of Webb's Estate, 1 Tuck., 372.

See People v. Baker, 76 N. Y., 88–9.

North Carolina : See Williams v. Oates, 5 Ired., 535 ; State v. Kennedy, 76 N. C., 251.

Pennsylvania : Van Storch v. Griffin, 71 Penn. St. R., 240, 244.

Tennessee : Dickinson v. Dickson, 1 Yerg., 110.

See State v. Bell, 7 Baxt., 9.

United States: Ponsford *v.* Johnson, 2 Blatchf., 51.

Virginia: See, however, in this State, Kinney *v.* Com., 30 Gratt., 858.

Though if a court of the State where the parties are domiciled should, after acquiring jurisdiction, for such reason declare the marriage null, the judgment would be binding on the courts of the State where the marriage took place: Roth *v.* Ehman, 14 Chicago Leg. News, 293, 21 Am. Law Reg. (N.S.), 589, 595 note.

[3 Probate Division, 8.]

Jan. 22, 1878.

[IN THE COURT OF APPEAL].

8]   *THE CYBELE (O.519). ().

Salvage—Her Majesty's Ships—Vessel belonging to Ramsgate Harbor—Board of Trade —Harbors and Passing Tolls Act, 1861 *(24 & 25 Vict. c. 47), Pt.* VII.—*Merchant Shipping Act,* 1854 *(17 & 18 Vict. c. 104), ss.* 484, 485.

Under the Harbors and Passing Tolls Act, 1861, the harbor of Ramsgate and the property and powers of its trustees were transferred to the Board of Trade. In a suit for salvage remuneration for services rendered by a vessel belonging to the harbor and vested in the Board of Trade under the provisions of the act:

Held, affirming the decision of the judge of the Admiralty Court, that the vessel was not a ship belonging to Her Majesty within the meaning of the Merchant Shipping Act, 1854, ss. 484, 485; and therefore that the Board of Trade were not precluded from recovering salvage in respect of its services, and that the claims of the commander and crew might be adjudicated upon without the consent of the admiralty.

THIS was an appeal from a judgment of Sir R. Phillimore, the judge of the Admiralty Court (').

The action was brought by the owners, master, and crew of the Ben Achie against the steamship Cybele for salvage remuneration. The steam-tug Vulcan and the lifeboat Bradford, both of which belonged to Ramsgate Harbor, assisted in saving the ship. The owners of the Cybele having appeared, the Board of Trade, as the owners of the Vulcan and the Bradford, were added to the suit, in order to have their claim for salvage services against the Cybele adjudicated.

The defendants demurred to the claim of the Board of Trade in respect of the Vulcan and Bradford, on the ground that it was contrary to the provisions of the Merchant Shipping Act, 1854.

The pleadings are given fully in the previous report (').

The Merchant Shipping Act, 1854 (17 & 18 Vict. c. 104), s. 484, enacts that "In cases where salvage services are rendered by any ship belonging to Her Majesty, or by the commander or crew thereof, no claim shall be made or al-

(') Affirming 21 Eng. Rep., 609.   (') 2 P. D., 224; 21 Eng. R., 609.

lowed for any loss, damage, *or risk thereby caused to [9 such ship, or to the stores, tackle, or furniture thereof, or for the use of any stores or other articles belonging to Her Majesty supplied in order to effect such services, or from any other expense or loss sustained by Her Majesty by reason of such services."

Section 485 provides that "No claim whatever on account of any salvage services rendered to any ship or cargo, or to any appurtenances of any ship by the commander or crew or part of the crew of any of Her Majesty's ships shall be finally adjudicated upon unless the consent of the admiralty has first been obtained, such consent to be signified by writing under the hand of the Secretary of the Admiralty."

By the Harbors and Passing Tolls Act, 1861 (24 & 25 Vict. c. 47), Pt. vii, s. 22, it is enacted that "The Harbor of Ramsgate and the soil thereof, and all propert , real and personal, vested in the trustees of the said harbor, or in any person in trust for the purposes of the said harbor, with their actual and reputed appurtenances, subject to all leases, contracts, charges, or other liabilities affecting the same, shall be transferred to and are hereby vested in the Board of Trade."

Sir R. Phillmore overruled the demurrer, being of opinion that the Vulcan and Bradford were not Her Majesty's ships within the meaning of the clause in the Merchant Shipping Act, and awarded £1,200 to the owners, officers, and crews of the Vulcan and the Bradford, without requiring any evidence of the consent of the admiralty.

From this judgment the defendants appealed.

W. G. F. Phillimore (*Myburgh* with him), for the defendants, contended that the two vessels being vested in the Board of Trade for public purposes were Her Majesty's ships. He referred to *Cargo ex Woosung* ( ), *The Thetis* ([2]), and to the Harbors and Passing Tolls Act, 1861, s. 28, which gives the Board of Trade a percentage on the salvage payable on any ship or wreck brought into Ramsgate Harbor.

Clarkson, and *Wood Hill*, for the plaintiffs, were not called on.

JAMES, L.J.: I am clearly of opinion that these are [10 not Queen's ships within the meaning of the act. The Board of Trade merely took the harbor and the boats, like an ordinary corporation, using the harbor and the harbor boats, as an ordinary harbor corporation, for harbor purposes; and I really cannot see that the learned judge could

[1] 1 P. D., 260; 17 Eng. Rep., 559.　　　　[2] 3 Hagg. Ad., 14, at p. 61.

have come to any other conclusion than the one at which he arrived. The appeal must, therefore, be dismissed with costs.

BAGGALLAY, L.J.: I am of the same opinion. These are boats simply employed for commercial purposes—the steam-tug and the lifeboat of the harbor—for performing the ordinary harbor services; they are not under the special control of Her Majesty, nor do they perform the services of the Queen's ships.

THESIGER, L.J.: I am of the same opinion. It is unnecessary to give an exact definition of the term "Her Majesty's ships," though I agree with the other members of the court in considering that the term is used in the ordinary and natural sense. It is not intended to include every case in which every department of Her Majesty's service thinks proper to use a vessel for that service.

Appeal dismissed.

Solicitors for defendants : *Pritchard & Sons.*

Solicitor for owners and crew of the Vulcan and Bradford : *The Solicitor for the Board of Trade.*

[3 Probate Division, 11.]

Jan. 25, 1878.

[IN THE COURT OF APPEAL.]

11]   *THE PECKFORTON CASTLE (').

Collision—Sailing Regulations—Articles 12 and 17—Ships crossing—Ship overtaking.

A ship and a bark were both on the port tack. The bark was the windward vessel, and had the wind three points free. The ship was close hauled, and when first sighted by the bark was approaching her on her lee beam:

Held, affirming the decision of the judge of the Admiralty Court that the ships were crossing each other, and that it was the duty of the bark, being the windward vessel, to get out of the way of the other.

The definition of an "overtaking ship" in *The Franconia* (2 P. D., 8; 19 Eng. R., 547,) questioned.

THIS was an appeal from a judgment of Sir R. Phillimore, the judge of the Admiralty Court (').

The action was brought by the owners of the German bark August against the owners of the ship Peckforton Castle, of Liverpool, to recover damages in respect of a collision which occurred between the two vessels on the 6th of July, 1877, in the channel, near the Lizard. There was a counter-claim by the owner of the Peckforton Castle, laying the blame of the collision on the August. There was some conflict of

(') Affirming 21 Eng. Rep., 607.   (') 2 P. D., 222; 21 Eng. Rep., 607.

evidence as to the exact course of the ships and the direction
of the wind, but, according to the view which the court
took of the evidence, when the ships approached each other,
the August was heading about E.; and the Peckforton Castle
was on her starboard beam, standing in a North Easterly
direction, and the wind was about N.W. The Peckforton
Castle, being the fastest sailer of the two, ran into the August
on her starboard beam, about her main rigging. The facts
are more fully stated in the judgment of the court.

Under these circumstances the plaintiffs contended that
the Peckforton Castle was an "overtaking" ship, within the
meaning of the 17th article of the Sailing Regulations, and
ought to have kept out of the way of the August; and the
owners of the Peckforton Castle contended that the ships
were "crossing," and that the case *was covered by [12
the 12th article ('); and as both ships had the wind on the
same side, the August, being the windward ship, ought to
have kept out of the way of the Peckforton Castle.

Sir R. Phillimore was of opinion that the August was to
blame, and from that decision the plaintiffs appealed.

Jan. 21. *Milward*, Q.C. (*Clarkson* and *C. Hall* with him),
for the plaintiffs: The result of the evidence is that when
the two ships approached each other the Peckforton Castle
was two or three points abaft the beam of the August, and
was therefore an overtaking ship. The plaintiffs rely on the
definition of an overtaking ship in *The Franconia* (*), where
Brett, J.A., delivering the judgment of the Court of Appeal,
said that when two ships are on the same course, and the
hinder ship is in such a position that she cannot see either
of the side lights of the forward ship, the hinder ship, if she
is going faster than the other is an overtaking ship. That
was the case in the present instance.

Butt, Q.C., and *Myburgh*, for the defendants: Considering the course of the two ships, and the direction of the
wind, it was impossible for the Peckforton Castle to have
overtaken the August, if she had been, when first sighted,
two or three points abaft the beam of the August. The result of the evidence is that the two ships were crossing each

(') The 12th article is as follows:
" When two sailing ships are crossing so
as to involve risk of collision, then, if
they have the wind on different sides, the
ship with the wind on the port side shall
keep out of the way of the ship with the
wind on the starboard side, except in the
case in which the ship with the wind on
the port side is close-hauled and the other
ship free, in which the latter ship shall
keep out of the way; but if they have the
wind on the same side, or if one of them
has the wind aft, the ship which is to
windward shall keep out of the way of the
ship which is to leeward."

(*) 2 P. D., at p. 12; 19 Eng. R., 547.

other.   Even if the Peckforton Castle was a little abaft of
the August they were still crossing ships within the meaning
of the 12th rule.

Milward, Q.C., in reply.

Cur. adv. vult.

Jan. 25, 1878.   The judgment of the court was delivered by
BAGGALLAY, L.J.: Shortly after noon on the 6th of July
13]   last *the German bark August and the British ship
Peckforton Castle came into collision in the English Channel
near the Lizard.

The bark was passing up channel on a voyage from South
Carolina to Bremerhaven, and the ship was proceeding in
ballast from Rotterdam to Cardiff.

An action of collision was at once instituted by the owners of the August against the owners of the Peckforton Castle, which was met by a counter-claim of the latter; the
action came on for trial, and on the 31st of the same month
the judge of the Admiralty Court held that the August was
alone to blame.   From that decision the present appeal is
brought.   It is the common case of the plaintiffs and of the
defendants that at the respective times when each vessel
was first seen from the other, the August was on the port
tack, heading E. or nearly so, and had the wind at least
three points free; it is further agreed that for at least half
an hour before the collision the Peckforton Castle was close
hauled and on the port tack, but there is much conflict of
evidence as to the direction of the wind and the consequent
course of the Peckforton Castle, and also as to various other
circumstances of the case.   It was, however, admitted in the
Admiralty Court, and has been admitted in the argument
before us, that the real question at issue is whether the 12th
or the 17th article of the Regulations for preventing collisions at sea is applicable to the circumstances of the present case.

The plaintiffs assert that the Peckforton Castle was first
seen from the August about half-past eleven; that the wind
was then, and continued until after the collision, to be from
N. to N. by W.; that the Peckforton Castle, when so first seen,
was three points on the starboard quarter of the August,
distant about three miles, and heading between E.N.E. and
N.E. by E., that is, at an angle of from two to three points
from the course of the August, which was E.; that each
vessel continued on her course until just before the collision,
the speed of the Peckforton Castle being considerably in excess of that of the August; that under such circumstances

the Peckforton Castle was an overtaking vessel, within the meaning of the 17th Article of the Regulations, and as such bound to keep out of the way of the August, but neglected to do so.

The defendants, on the other hand, insist that the wind was *from N.W. to N.W. by N.; that the Peckfor- [14 ton Castle, which, during the forenoon had been on the starboard tack, heading W. by S., went on the port tack at 12 o'clock, and that thenceforth her course was between N.N.E. and N.E. by N., or inclined at an angle of from five to six points to that of the August; that the August was first seen from the Peckforton Castle about 12.15, being then four points on the port bow, and distant about a mile and a half; that, under such circumstances, the August and Peckforton Castle were crossing vessels, within the meaning of the 12th Article of the Regulations, and the August being to windward, was bound to keep out of the way, and not having done so was alone to blame.

The defendants further assert that at no time was the Peckforton Castle three points on the starboard quarter of the August as seen from that ship, and that if she had been so situate with the wind from N.W. to N.W. by N., a collision between the two vessels could not possibly have occurred if each had continued on her course. Having regard to the two views so put forward by the parties, we are of opinion that the question of fact, upon the solution of which the decision of this appeal must depend, is that of the direction of the wind; if this be ascertained, the course of the close hauled ship lying within six points of the wind can be readily determined. [His Lordship then shortly referred to the evidence adduced on both sides, and proceeded:] We are satisfied upon this evidence that the wind, at and near the place where the collision occurred, was for some time previously to and for some time after the collision from N.W. to N.W. by N., as alleged by the defendants.

Now one effect of our having arrived at this conclusion as to the direction of the wind, in the face of the positive statement of so many witnesses who were on board the August, is to materially lessen the value which we might otherwise have been disposed to attach to their evidence upon other matters as to which there is a conflict of testimony, but in our opinion it is unnecessary to enter into any particular consideration of these other controverted matters.

It being established that the direction of the wind was from N.W. to N.W. by N., the course of the Peckforton Castle on her *port tack must have been, as alleged by [15 the defendants, between N.N.E. and N.E. by N., inclined therefore at an angle of at least five points to that of the August, and it was utterly impossible for the Peckforton Castle to have been ever seen from the August three points on the starboard quarter of the latter, or indeed in any direction abaft her beam ; the statement of the master of the Peckforton Castle appears to be substantially correct, that after he went about, his ship was pretty broad on the starboard bow of the August.

The ship and the bark were consequently crossing vessels with the wind on the same side, and the bark being to windward was bound to keep out of the way ; this she neglected to do, and we agree with the learned judge of the Admiralty Court in thinking that she was alone to blame.   The gentlemen who have given us their assistance as nautical assessors concur in the views which we have expressed, but they are further of opinion that the August was guilty of a breach of the well recognized rule of navigation, that a ship having the wind free should give way to one close hauled, this view was probably taken by the judge of the Admiralty Court, and by the Elder Brethren who assisted him, but we prefer to base our decision against the plaintiffs upon the ground that they disobeyed the directions given in article 12.

The appeal must be dismissed with costs.

His LORDSHIP then added :   The judgment which I have just read is the judgment of the court.   I desire, however, to add a few observations with reference to that portion of Mr. Milward's argument which was based upon the judgment in the case of *The Franconia* (¹).

Mr. Milward, in support of his contention that the Peckforton Castle was overtaking the August, and relying upon the evidence of his own witnesses, that she was three points on the starboard quarter of the latter, claimed the benefit of the definition of an overtaking vessel suggested by Lord Justice Brett in delivering the judgment in the case of *The Franconia* (²).   What Lord Justice Brett said was as follows: "Can we then form a definition *of the difference between crossing ships and overtaking ships ?   It seems to me that this may be a very good definition—I will not say that it is exhaustive, or that it may not on some occasion be found to be short of comprising every case, but I think it is a very good rule—that if the ships are in such a position, and are on such courses, and at such distances, that if it were night the hinder ship could not see any part

16]

(¹) 2 P. D., 8; 19 Eng. R., 547.   (²) 2 P. D , at p. 12; 19 Eng. R., 547.

of the side lights of the forward ship, then they cannot be said to be crossing ships, although their courses may not be exactly parallel. It would not do, I think, to limit the angle of the crossing too much, but a limit to that extent, it seems to me, is a very useful and practical rule. And then if the hinder of the two ships is going faster than the other she is an overtaking ship.''

In the Franconia case that vessel was two points on the quarter of the Strathclyde. Mr. Milward's argument was this : If the Peckforton Castle was three points on the starboard quarter of the August she could not, had it been night, have seen any of the side lights of the August, and she was accordingly an overtaking vessel, and the 17th, and not the 12th article of the Regulations was applicable. This would have been a very effective, if not a conclusive, argument, if it had been established that the Peckforton Castle was three points on the starboard quarter of the August. But we have held that the Peckforton Castle was not three points on the starboard of the August, or in any direction abaft her beam, and the question whether the definition is accurate or not is not of importance in the present case.

I desire, however, to state that, without expressing any dissent from the definition, which I am bound to say I at the time thought satisfactory, it was not in my opinion necessary for the decision of the Franconia case. I am unwilling to be considered as giving it an unqualified assent. The arguments in the present case have caused me to entertain some doubt upon the subject, and I desire to reserve to myself the right of reconsidering it when the circumstances of any case before us may require it.

It is occasionally a matter of considerable difficulty to decide whether a particular vessel is crossing, overtaking, or approaching another, within the intent and meaning of the several articles of the Regulations, and the court whose duty it is to decide such *questions must act upon the [17 view taken by it of the circumstances of the case under consideration, and with a due regard to the usual matters provided for by the 19th article, as well as to those recognized rules of navigation which, though not expressed, or not fully expressed, are nevertheless of general application.   ·

JAMES, L.J.: I also desire to add that the result of the argument induces me to come to the conclusion that I doubt whether the definition laid down in *The Franconia* (') can

(') 2 P. D., at p. 12; 19 Eng. R., 547.

be laid down as a rule to be so generally applicable as appears to have been intimated in that case.

THESIGER, L.J.: With regard to the definition referred to, after what has fallen from the other members of the court, I have only to add that I am not prepared in a case like the present to express the opinion that that definition ought not to be adopted as a convenient rule of navigation. I only desire to reserve my assent to it until the occasion arises when it will have to be considered more fully whether the test given by it can be in all cases equally applied.

Appeal dismissed.

Solicitor for plaintiffs: *T. Cooper.*
Solicitors for defendants: *Gregory, Rowcliffes & Rawle.*

[3 Probate Division, 18.]

Nov. 13, 1877.

18]   *THE ENGLISHMAN (O. 180).

Collision—Regulations for Preventing Collisions at Sea, Art. 9—Merchant Shipping Act, 1873 (36 & 37 Vict. c. 85,) s. 17.

A French trawler and a schooner came into collision in the English Channel in the morning before sunrise. The trawler was proceeding at a speed of from two to three knots an hour. She had her trawl on deck and was about to let it go. A white light was exhibited at her masthead, but no side lights were exhibited. At the hearing of an action of damage to recover for the damages sustained in the collision, the court found that the collision was caused by the absence of any look-out on board the schooner.

It was then submitted that the trawler had infringed the Regulations for Preventing Collisions at Sea by not exhibiting the regulation side-lights, and by reason of such infringement was in fault, within the meaning of the 17th section of the Merchant Shipping Act Amendment Act, 1873:

Held, that the trawler had infringed the Regulations by not exhibiting the Regulation side-lights:

Held, also, that, as in the absence of a look-out on the part of the schooner, the neglect of the trawler to observe the regulations as to lights could not by any possibility have contributed to the collision, the section had no application, and the schooner was alone to blame for the collision.

THIS was an action of collision instituted on behalf of the French fishing smack L'Étoile against the schooner Englishman and her owners defendants intervening. The action was brought to recover damages in respect of a collision which occurred between the two vessels before sunrise on the morning of the 27th of November in last year, south of the Kentish Knock lightship.

The statement of claim alleged that at daybreak the L'Étoile, a lugger of 42 tons register, was sailing close-hauled on the port tack, proceeding slowly through the water with a bright light exhibited at her masthead, and that those on board her were just about to let out their trawl-net when the Englishman was seen about a mile distant on the port-bow, and that although a flare-up was burnt and a light shown on board the L'Étoile the two vessels came into collision, the stem of the Englishman striking the L'Étoile nearly amidships on the port-side.

The defendants in their statement of defence and counter-claim alleged that before sunrise on the day of the collision the Englishman was heading northeast on the starboard tack with the Regulation side-lights burning and a good look-out kept; that in these *circumstances the [19 L'Étoile was for the first time observed under the bows of the Englishman, and immediately afterwards the collision occurred; and that the L'Étoile had no lights except a hand or binnacle-light inclosed in something like a box on deck, and had not her side-lights fixed and burning as required by law.

By way of counter-claim the defendants repeated the allegations before set out in the statement of defence and counter-claim, and alleged that the Englishman had been damaged in the collision.

The plaintiffs in their reply admitted that the L'Étoile had no side-lights burning.

Nov. 12.   The action was heard before the judge and two of the Elder Brethren of the Trinity Corporation.

Witnesses were examined orally in court on behalf of the plaintiffs and the defendants.   It was proved in evidence that at the time of the collision the L'Étoile was proceeding at a speed of from two to three knots an hour, and that her trawl-net was on her deck, and some of her crew were getting it ready to be lowered into the water.   The result of the evidence on the other portions of the case appears from the judgment.   After hearing the evidence the court intimated its opinion that the collision had been caused by the absence of a look-out on board the Englishman.

The question whether the L'Étoile was not also to blame under the provisions of the 17th section of the Merchant Shipping Act, 1873, was then argued.

Milward, Q.C.., and *E. C. Clarkson*, for the plaintiffs.

Butt, Q.C., and *W. G. F. Phillimore*, for the defendants: The L'Étoile at the time of the collision was not stationary or attached to her nets within the meaning of the 9th Article of the Regulations for Preventing Collisions at Sea: *The Esk* ('); *The Jennie S. Barker* ('). She was, therefore, just

(¹) Law Rep., 2 Ad. & E,, 350.   (²) Law Rep., 4 Ad. & E., 456.

as any other sailing vessel of her size in motion bound to exhibit the fixed Regulation side-lights, and not having done so she must be deemed in fault under the provisions of 36 & 37 Vict. c. 85, s. 17. Even though a white light was shown as pleaded by the L'Étoile and not seen by the look-out on board the Englishman, it by no means follows that 20] the *port side-light of the L'Étoile would have escaped being noticed. Consequently the omission to exhibit such light might possibly have contributed to the collision ; and this being the case, the L'Étoile, under the provisions of the section must be held liable for a moiety of the damage arising out of the collision : *The Fanny M. Carvill* (¹).

Clarkson, in reply : The 17th section of 36 & 37 Vict. c. 85, can only apply where the neglect to observe the Regulations for Preventing Collisions could in the special circumstances of the case before the court have by any possibility contributed to the collision. On the evidence in the present case the white light of the L'Étoile was not seen from the Englishman, it is reasonable therefore to conclude that the side-lights of the L'Étoile if exhibited would not have been seen. How, then, can the neglect to exhibit such lights by any possibility have contributed to the collision ?

Cur. adv. vult.

Nov. 13. Sir Robert Phillimore : This is a case arising out of a collision between a small French fishing lugger called the L'Étoile, of 42 tons register, and a three-masted schooner called the Englishman, of 183 tons register. The exact time of the collision is a matter of dispute. On the one hand, on behalf of the L'Étoile, it is stated to have been about seven o'clock in the morning, and on the part of the Englishman, to have been at about half-past five in the morning. The evidence is conflicting in this as in other cases, and the right time would be somewhere between these two periods. The collision took place, at all events, on the morning of the 27th of November, in last year, nine or ten miles distant from the Kentish Knock. The direction of the wind is undisputed, it being S. S. W. The weather is stated on the part of the L'Étoile to have been clear, and to have been overcast but clear in the statement on the part of the Englishman. The L'Étoile was close hauled on the port tack, heading to the westward, and was getting her trawl out. At this time she was proceeding, as it appears on the evidence, at a speed of from two to three knots an hour. Her trawl-net 21] was on the deck, and was being attended to *by a por-

(¹) 44 L. J. (Adm.), 84.

tion of the crew, who were getting it ready. The master of the L'Étoile ordered her side-lights to be taken in and a globular white light to be exhibited at the masthead. There were also, as it appears from the evidence, two small white lights used by the crew on deck while they were getting the net ready. Those on board the L'Étoile saw the lights of the Englishman a mile off on their weather bow, and then they showed one or two white lights and a flare-up, but no heed was taken by the English vessel, which ran into the French vessel and struck her port side amidships. There is no question that the latter was not seen or heard of before the time of the collision. The preliminary act, filed on behalf of the defendants, says the L'Étoile was first seen under the bows of the Englishman. According to the evidence she was neither seen nor heard of until the jibboom of the Englishman had run between the masts of the L'Étoile. The Englishman appears to have had the wind on her starboard quarter. Now, there has been a great discussion on a very important subject, namely, whether the Englishman had or had not a proper look-out, and of course it was her duty, having the wind free, to get out of the way of the French vessel. I considered this matter, and the various other parts of the case, with the Elder Brethren, and we arrived at the clear conclusion that the fair result of the evidence, taking into consideration all the circumstances, and the demeanor of the witnesses, was that there was the want of a look-out on board the Englishman. Nor, indeed, was it stoutly contended, nor could it be that that was not the case. The question remains to be decided with respect to the liability of the French vessel for disobedience to the Regulations for Preventing Collisions at Sea, and that leads to the consideration of the 17th section of the Merchant Shipping Act, 1873, which enacts as follows:

If in any case of collision it is proved to the court before which the case is tried that any of the Regulations for preventing collision contained in or made under the Merchant Shipping Acts, 1854 to 1873, has been infringed, the ship by which such Regulations has been infringed shall be deemed to be in fault, unless it is shown to the satisfaction of the court that the circumstances of the case made departure from the Regulation necessary.

Now the Regulations respecting the lights to be carried by *vessels fishing with trawl-nets are to be found in the [22 9th article of the Regulations for Preventing Collisions at Sea, which provides that "open fishing boats and other open boats shall not be required to carry the side-lights required for other vessels;" . . . The L'Étoile was not an open fishing boat, but a decked boat. The next clause of the same 9th article is as follows: "Fishing vessels and open boats, when at anchor, or attached to their nets and stationary, shall exhibit a bright white light." It is therefore clear that, unless this vessel was attached to her net and stationary, it was not her duty to exhibit a white light, but that it was her duty to exhibit the Regulation side-lights. We have no doubt, upon this part of the case, that the vessel was not attached to her net, and was not stationary. It was said that, as she was just preparing to put down her net, it would be too harsh a construction of the rule to consider her not to be stationary. I think the principle laid down by me in the case of *The Esk* ([1]), in the analogous instance of one vessel having an anchor overboard, but not holding, applies in this case. In that case I said as follows:

> The object of the Regulations, so far as their bearing on the present case is concerned, with respect to carrying lights, is to furnish the means of apprising other vessels whether the vessel carrying them be stationary or in motion, in order that the coming or meeting vessel may direct her course in consequence, and give the vessel carrying colored lights and in motion a wider berth than she would give if that vessel carried an anchor-light and was stationary. This is the principle which underlies these rules; it is possible, no doubt, to draw fine distinctions between vessels which have just actually raised their anchor off the ground and those which are in the very act of doing so; but practically the true criterion as to the application of the Regulation must be, whether the vessel be actually holden by and under the control of her anchor or not. The moment she ceases to be so, she is in the category of a vessel under way, and must carry the appointed colored lights.

I am of opinion that the principle of that decision applies to the present case, and that the rule of navigation to which I have referred has been infringed by the French vessel on this occasion. It remains to be considered what is the legal result of this infringement; it being, in our judgment, clearly proved that the collision in this case was caused, as I have said, by the want of a look-out on the part of the Englishman. The clause of the statute I have read has been the subject of very careful judicial consideration, 23] *both in this court and on appeal to the Judicial Committee of the Privy Council, which affirmed the judgment which I delivered in the case of *The Fanny M. Carvill* ([2]). There is no doubt that there is a difficulty in applying the principle laid down in the judgment in that case to all the cases coming before the court, but, as I infer from the language of the judgment, the true principle to be applied is this, that the party guilty of an infringement of the regulations has the burthen cast upon him of showing that the infringment could not possibly have contributed to the collision. Therefore in this case, I have to consider, looking

([1]) Law Rep., 2 Ad. & E., 350.   ([2]) 44 L. J. (Adm.), 34.

to all the circumstances of the case, whether the absence of
the side lights of the L'Étoile could have possibly contributed to the collision. In the present case there was the want
of a look-out. The French vessel had a white light visible
a mile distant at least; she had a flare-up shown, and neither
white light or flare was seen, and indeed those on board the
English vessel knew nothing of the approach of the French
vessel until the shock of the collision. On this point it is
not immaterial to observe that the blow was upon the
weather bow. The question would then arise, did the absence of the red light of the L'Étoile contribute to the collision? After much consideration we think that it did not;
that the collision was the consequence of no look-out on
board the Englishman, and that the side lights of the L'Étoile
would have been unseen as much as the masthead light.
The absence of lights, in our judgment, could not have contributed to the collision; therefore the 17th section of the
Merchant Shipping Act, 1873, does not apply, and the English vessel is alone liable for the damage which in our opinion was unquestionably caused by the want of a look-out on
board that vessel.

Solicitors for plaintiffs: *Lowless & Co.*
Solicitors for defendants: *Shephard & Skipwith.*

[3 Probate Division, 24.]

Nov. 16, 1877.

*THE SKIBLADNER (S. 502, Liv.).   [24

*Salvage—Services Rendered by putting Hands on board Vessel Infected with Yellow
Fever—Amount of Award.*

Two Norwegian barks, both bound to England, fell in with each other on the high
seas, about 3,000 miles from Liverpool; one of the barks was in distress, her first
mate having died, and her master, her second mate, and one of the crew being sick
with yellow fever. The other bark was short-handed, but her mate, with the consent of her master, went on board the distressed vessel and succeeded in navigating
her to Liverpool. During the voyage, the master, the second mate, and two of the
crew died. On the arrival of the vessel at Liverpool an action of salvage was instituted against her. At the hearing of the action, the value of the salved property
was taken at £5,135 13s. 2d.
    The court awarded £600 to the mate who had gone on board the distressed vessel,
£100 to the owners of the salving vessel, £50 to her master, and £150 amongst the
remaining plaintiffs.

THIS was an action of salvage, instituted on the 16th of October, 1877, on behalf of the owners, master, and crew of the
Norwegian bark Hirundo, against the Norwegian bark Skibladner, her cargo and freight.

The statement of claim, so far as material, was in substance as follows:

The Hirundo is a bark belonging to Porsgrund in Norway, of 332 tons register. She left Tonala in Mexico in the month of August, 1877, with a cargo for Queenstown for orders. She had a crew of eight hands, all told, her usual comple-. ment being nine, but one having deserted.

About 10 A.M. of the 26th of August, being in latitude 36° N. and longitude 70° W., those on board the Hirundo saw the Skibladner. The Skibladner is also a Norwegian bark of about 360 tons register, and was bound from Fernandina in Florida to Liverpool.

The master of the Hirundo went in his boat on board the Skibladner, and there learnt that the first and second mates and the master's wife were sick with yellow fever, and that the master was so weak that he had not been able to write up the log or take an observation since he left port. The said master asked the master of the Hirundo to keep company with him till the afternoon, and take an observation for him.

An observation was accordingly taken, and the longitude was chalked up on a blackboard and put over the side of the Hirundo, but the Hirundo lost sight of the Skibladner.

About 8 A.M. of the 1st of September, being in latitude 37° 53' N., longitude 68° 54' W., those on board the Hirundo saw a vessel about four miles ahead, laying to, with all sails set and shaking, her main topsail aback, and two Nor-25] wegian *flags hoisted upside down and tied in the middle with string as signals of distress, one at her mainmast head and the other at the gaff peak. The wind was light, and the Hirundo steered towards the vessel, and when she was recognized as the Skibladner, lay to. A boat was then sent from the Skibladner to the Hirundo, manned by two men.

The steward of the Skibladner, who was one of the two men in the boat, before coming on board asked permission from the master of the Hirundo to do so, after warning him that the fever which had broken out was worse. When they came on board the boat's crew stated that the master's wife had died in the night when they had parted company, and that the first mate had died on the 28th of August, that the second mate and one seaman were very ill with the fever, that the master was very sick, and they had no one to navigate, and were unable to navigate the Skibladner, but were by the master's orders keeping her in an easterly course, and they asked that some one might be sent to navigate

her. The master of the Hirundo said that he was short-
handed, and could not spare a navigator, as he had only
one besides himself, but he offered to go on board to see the
captain.

The master of the Hirundo accordingly went on board the
Skibladner, and saw her master, and was by him asked to
send some one to navigate the Skibladner, and the master
of the Hirundo thereupon returned to his vessel and requested Osman Osmandsen, the only mate of the Hirundo,
to take charge of and navigate the Skibladner. The said
mate was the only person in the Hirundo who besides her
master could navigate a ship. The master was seriously
ruptured, and was also under apprehension that he might
have caught the infection from having been on board the
Skibladner, and the Hirundo was already short-handed.
For all these reasons, both the master and the said Osman
Osmandsen were unwilling that the latter should leave the
Hirundo, but, for the sake of saving the lives of those on
board the Skibladner and the Skibladner herself, it was arranged that the said Osman Osmandsen should go.

The said Osman Osmandsen, accompanied by the master
of the Hirundo, accordingly went on board the Skibladner.
They found the master of that vessel very ill of yellow fever,
and the said Osman Osmandsen was requested by the said
master of the Skibladner to stay on board and navigate the
ship to England, on the ground that he, the said master of
the Skibladner, was so ill that he did not expect to recover.
On the said Osman Osmandsen promising to do so, the master said that he could lie down in peace. The Skibladner
had then nine hands on board, all told, out of her original
complement of ten, but of these the master, second mate,
and one seaman were ill with the fever, and unable to
work. There was also a passenger on board—a landsman—
who was also ill.

The master of the Hirundo, who came on board with the
said Osman Osmandsen, instructed him as to the medicines
to be given to the sick, and went away, promising to keep
the Hirundo ahead and show a light, and to speak the Skibladner next morning. This was done. The Hirundo then
sailed away, and was lost sight of.

The said Osman Osmandsen steered the Skibladner a
course for Liverpool, taking one watch, and the said steward
the other. The said Osman Osmandsen regularly visited the
sick men, and administered to them the medicines which had
been recommended.

*On the 5th of September the second mate of the   [26

Skibladner died.   On the 6th her master and the sick seaman died, and on the same day the said Osman Osmandsen
was taken seriously ill.   The next he was delirious and
unable to leave his berth.   The third day he recovered sufficiently to be able to do duty, though still requiring medicine
for some days.

The weather had been fine up to the 11th of September,
but on that day the wind increased, and as the Skibladner
was so short-handed, the fore and main top-gallant sails
were split by the violence of the wind before they could be
stowed.   During all the time the said Osman Osmandsen
had, in addition to his duties as commander and officer, to
work as an ordinary seaman.   The said passenger was not
able to render any assistance.

On the 14th an able seaman, who had been with the steward in the boat, was taken ill with the fever, and on the 17th
he died.

On the 11th of October the Skibladner arrived off the Great
Ormeshead, and was taken in tow by a tug.   On the same
day a Liverpool pilot came on board, and the Skibladner
was anchored in the Mersey.

The defendants tendered by act in court £515 as sufficient
salvage remuneration for the plaintiffs' services, and submitted to the judgment of the court on the allegations in the
statement of claim.

Nov. 16.   The action was heard before the judge, assisted by two of the Elder Brethren of the Trinity Corporation.

It was agreed that the value of the Skibladner should be
taken at £2,500, and the value of her freight and cargo at
£2,635 13s. 2d.

W. G. F. Phillimore and *Barnes*, for the plaintiffs, referred to *The Active* (').

E. C. Clarkson, for the defendants: In awarding salvage
remuneration in this case the court ought not to lose sight
of the circumstance that the services of Osman Osmandsen
were rendered entirely in cold latitudes, and that, therefore,
he actually ran little or no danger of infection from the yellow fever on board the Skibladner.

SIR ROBERT PHILLIMORE :   This is, in the judgment of the
court, a case of most meritorious salvage.   It is impossible
to praise too highly the gallantry of this man Osman
Osmandsen, or to doubt that the preservation of the lives of
27]   those on board the *Skibladner was due to his courage

(') 14 Jur., 606.

and skill. The navigation of this vessel to Liverpool, a distance of about 3,000 miles, took more than forty days. However, it is unnecessary to go over the facts of the case in detail. It is enough to state that the case is one of extraordinary merit. The danger from infection from the yellow fever that had attacked the ship was, in my opinion, by no means over when Osman Osmandsen went on board, and indeed it has been pointed out to me by the Elder Brethren that if the vessel had been in port she would still have been detained in quarantine some days. Looking at all the circumstances, I have to consider whether, the value of the property salved being £5,135, the tender of £515 is a sufficient salvage remuneration for the services rendered. Now, I am of opinion that it is not, and I shall award £900. The great service in this case no doubt was rendered by Osman Osmandsen, and I shall award to him £600. The master of the Hirundo parted with one of his navigators, and he was in very bad health himself. In these circumstances, the consequences of assisting the Skibladner as he did might have been serious to his own vessel. Taking all this into consideration, I shall award £100 to the owners of the Hirundo, and £50 to her master, which will leave £150 to be divided among the crew, according to their rating.

Solicitors for plaintiffs: *Bateson & Co.*
Solicitors for defendants: *Stone & Fletcher.*

[3 Probate Division, 28.]

Nov. 27, 1877.

*THE CARGO ex SARPEDON (O. 435).　　　[28

Salvage—Contribution—Rules of Supreme Court, Order xvi, *Rule* 18—*Non-liability of Shipowners for Life Salvage in cases where no Property belonging to them has been Salved.*

The C., a Spanish steamship, fell in at sea with the S., an English steamship, with signals of distress flying and entirely helpless from injuries sustained in a collision with a third vessel. The passengers of the S. and a quantity of specie, which had formed part of the cargo of the S., having been taken on board the C., attempts were made by the master and crew of the C. to tow the S. into safety. These attempts were ineffectual, and ultimately, after the master and crew of the S. had gone on board the C. the S. was abandoned, and her passengers, master, and crew were landed in safety at an English port. Afterwards the specie was arrested in an action of salvage instituted at the suit of the owners, master, and crew of the C., who claimed in the action to recover for life salvage and for salvage services rendered to the S. and the specie. The owners of the specie appeared as defendants, and served a notice on the owners of the S. calling upon them to contribute to the remuneration claimed by the plaintiffs. Thereupon the owners of the S. appeared. At the hearing of the action the court awarded salvage remuneration to the plaintiffs for the services rendered, but reserved all questions as to the liability of the owners of the S. The owners of the specie then moved the court to declare that such portion of the sum awarded as was awarded for life salvage ought to be recouped to the owners of the specie.

The court refused the motion on the ground that no property belonging to the owners of the S. having been salved they could not be held personally liable to pay any portion of the sum awarded.

THIS was an action of salvage instituted on the 17th of October, 1876, on behalf of the owners, master, and crew of the Calderon, a Spanish steamship, against specie forming part of the cargo of the English steamship Sarpedon. The owners of the specie appeared as defendants, and the plaintiffs delivered a statement of claim, which set forth *inter alia* the following facts :

The Calderon, bound on a voyage from Lisbon to London, at daylight on the 4th of September, 1875, and about eighty-five miles southwest of Ushant, came in sight of the Sarpedon, an iron steamship of about 1,556 net tons register. The Sarpedon, which was manned by a crew of seventy-three hands, all told, and had on board her fifteen passengers and eight boxes of specie, in addition to other cargo, had been in collision with another steamer called the Julia David, and had received such injuries in the collision that her passengers and crew, expecting her to sink at once, had left her and taken to such of her boats as were available. Signals of distress were hoisted on board the Sarpedon, and the Calderon took on board the passengers and specie, 29] together with a number of letters from the *Sarpedon, and the master of the Sarpedon requested the Calderon to take the Sarpedon in tow. Two hawsers were passed from the Sarpedon to the Calderon and were made fast on board the Calderon, and the Calderon endeavored to tow the Sarpedon but the Sarpedon having become unmanageable, the hawsers had to be cut to prevent a collision with the Calderon. Another attempt was afterwards made to tow the Sarpedon, but after the hawsers had been made fast a second time between the two vessels it became necessary again to cut them, and ultimately, after about six hours had been spent in fruitless efforts to tow the Sarpedon, the crew of the Sarpedon were taken on board the Calderon, and the Sarpedon was abandoned with her engine-room full of water and four feet of water in her after hold, about seventy miles to the southwest of Ushant. The Calderon then proceeded to Falmouth, and there landed the passengers, master, and crew of the Sarpedon.

The defendants, in their statement of defence, admitted

that the facts stated in the statement of claim were substantially true, and alleged that the value of the specie saved was £28,000.

On the 16th day of January, 1877, the action came on to be heard, and the judge, after hearing counsel for the plaintiffs and the defendants, directed the hearing to be adjourned, and on the 19th of January the defendants applied to the court by motion and obtained leave to issue a notice addressed to the owners of the Sarpedon pursuant to Order XVI, Rule 18, of the Rules of the Supreme Court, 1875. Accordingly, the owners of the specie served on the owners of the Sarpedon a notice alleging, *inter alia*, that the action had been brought by the plaintiffs against certain specie forming part of the cargo of the Sarpedon and the owners of the specie, to recover remuneration for services rendered by the said plaintiffs on the high seas to the steamship Sarpedon, to the said specie, and to the master, crew, and passengers of the Sarpedon, at the request and by the direction of the master of the Sarpedon; that the defendants claimed against the owners of the Sarpedon that they should contribute to the remuneration so claimed by the plaintiffs, and that the question of such remuneration should be determined between the plaintiffs, the owners of the specie, and the owners of the Sarpedon; and that if the owners of the Sarpedon wished to dispute their obligation to contribute to the amount of remuneration claimed by the plaintiffs, they must appear in the action [1].

*On the 5th of February, the owners of the Sarpedon [30 appeared in the action, and on the 12th of February the court ordered that the notice served upon them by the owners of the specie should be treated as a pleading.

The owners of the Sarpedon on the 2d of March filed an answer, which alleged *inter alia* substantially as follows:

The services of the plaintiffs were rendered by the plaintiffs under an agreement made by the master of the Sarpedon, as agent for the owners of the Sarpedon, and the owners of her cargo, whereby the master of the Sarpedon employed the plaintiffs to render salvage assistance to the Sarpedon, her cargo, master, and crew, upon the terms that the plaintiffs were to be paid salvage for these services if and so far

---

[1] The notice further alleged that the owners of the specie claimed to be indemnified by the owners of the Sarpedon against the claim of the plaintiffs in the action, on the ground that the collision with the Julia David had been caused by the improper navigation of the Sarpedon.

Owing, however, to the Court of Appeal having decided that the Julia David was alone to blame for the collision, the question of the right of the owners of the specie to be indemnified never came before the court.

as their services should prove successful, and that the owners
of the Sarpedon were not to be liable in respect of any of the
plaintiffs' services, whether for life salvage, or otherwise,
unless the services of the plaintiffs should prove successful
in saving the Sarpedon or some part thereof. The services
of the plaintiffs were not successful in saving the Sarpedon
or any part thereof, but the Sarpedon and all her cargo, except the specie saved, was wholly lost.

The owners of the Sarpedon are not liable to the plaintiffs
for any salvage in respect of any services rendered to the
Sarpedon, or her cargo, or in saving the lives of the master
and crew of the Sarpedon, and the said specie alone having
been saved, such specie and its owners are alone liable for
saving the lives of the master and crew of the Sarpedon.
The owners of the Sarpedon deny liability to contribute to
the remuneration claimed by the plaintiffs.

The plaintiffs and the owners of the specie filed separate
replies to the answer of the owners of the Sarpedon, and in
such replies joined issue on so much of such answer as is
above set out.

May 5.   The issues raised on the original pleadings of the
plaintiffs and the owners of the specie again came on to be
heard, together with the issues raised on so much of the answer of the owners of the Sarpedon as is above set out.

On the case being called on, it was with the consent of the
court agreed between the counsel for the different parties to
the action that the question of the liability of the owners of
the Sarpedon to pay or contribute towards the payment of the
plaintiffs' costs, and whatever sum the court should award
as salvage remuneration in the action, should be reserved
31]   until the Court of *Appeal had given its decision in an
appeal from this court in an action of damage entitled *The
Julia David* (O. 408), which action had been instituted on
behalf of the owners of the Sarpedon against the Julia David
for the recovery of the damages sustained by the Sarpedon
in the collision referred to in the statement of claim.

Cohen, Q.C., and *G. Bruce*, for the plaintiffs.

Butt, Q.C., and *W. G. F. Phillimore*, for the owners of
the specie.

E. C. Clarkson, for the owners of the Sarpedon.

SIR ROBERT PHILLIMORE: The facts of this very meritorious case of salvage are admitted, and are not the subject
of controversy. It has been agreed, after a great deal of
discussion, that the only questions which it is incumbent on

the court to day to decide are, what amount of salvage remuneration shall be paid in consequence of the saving of
life, and the saving of the specie, and also whether any, and
what amount of salvage remuneration shall be awarded on
the ground of a separate engagement ineffectual, but still
performed to the utmost efforts of the salvors to save the
ship herself considered apart from the specie, and the lives
of the passengers, master, and crew of the Sarpedon.

It has also been agreed that the question as to the contribution which it is contended should be made by the owners
of the Sarpedon to the owners of the specie shall stand over
until the decision of the Court of Appeal, on the merits of
the collision between the Sarpedon and the Julia David be
arrived at.   I have already said that this is a case of very
meritorious salvage, eighty-eight lives and £28,000 of specie
were saved at the risk of the lives of the persons who rendered the services in question.   The Spanish vessel which
rendered these services to the English vessel was a very
costly instrument—if I may use such an expression—for she
and her cargo were worth £53,000.   She went out of her
way considerably, almost two days' steaming, to take these
English people whose lives had been so saved into an English port, and it would be difficult, I think, to describe a
service with more ingredients of merit than there are in this
case.   I have no doubt whatever that but for the succor
which the Calderon afforded *those eighty-eight lives [32
and £28,000 worth of specie would have been lost.

I shall make an award of £4,000 as the salvage remuneration for these services, and I am of opinion that it would be,
in the circumstances of this case, drawing too fine a line to
attempt to establish a distinction between the saving specie
and the lives, and the services rendered to the ship, and I
shall, therefore, not make any separate award of salvage
remuneration for the engagement, as it has been called,
which was ineffectual, to save the ship herself.

The question of contribution will stand over, as I have
already said, until the Court of Appeal has given its decision as to the merits of the collision with the Julia David.
The apportionment of the award, which the court has just
made, between the owners, master, and crew of the Calderon will also stand over (').

On the 7th of August, the Court of Appeal delivered judg-

(') On the 29th of May, the court apportioned the £4,000 awarded to the plaintiffs, as follows: To the owners of the
Calderon £3,000, to the master of the Calderon £250, and to the officers and crew
of the same vessel £750 to be divided
among them according to their respective
ratings on board thereof.

ment in the action of damage which had been instituted by
the owners of the Sarpedon against the Julia David, and
pronounced that the Julia David was alone to blame for the
collision between her and the Sarpedon.

Nov. 13. *W. G. F. Phillimore*, on behalf of the owners
of the specie, moved the judge in court to determine how
much of the sum awarded for salvage to the plaintiffs, and
subsequently paid to them by the owners of the specie, was
for life salvage, and how much for salvage of specie, and to
declare that the sum awarded for life salvage ought to have
been paid to the plaintiffs by the owners of the Sarpedon,
and further to order the owners of the Sarpedon to recoup to the owners of the specie the sum paid by them
in respect of life salvage and costs to the plaintiffs. He stated
that the owners of the specie had paid to the plaintiffs the
whole amount awarded for salvage remuneration, and the
plaintiffs' costs in the action, and contended that on the admitted facts of the case the services of the plaintiffs in
saving the lives of the passengers, master, and crew of the
Sarpedon were rendered under a salvage agreement, which,
33]   *if not expressly made with the master of the Sarpedon, must be implied from the Sarpedon having hoisted signals of distress, and that consequently, as the owners of the
Sarpedon were liable *in personam*, under such salvage agreement, it would be clearly inequitable if the amount of life
salvage remuneration in the case should be entirely borne
by the owners of the specie : *The Medina* (').

E. C. Clarkson, for the owners of the Sarpedon, opposed
the motion. He referred to 17 & 18 Vict. c. 104, s. 458, and
The Cargo ex Schiller (').

Cur. adv. vult.

Nov. 20. SIR ROBERT PHILLIMORE : The court has already awarded the amount of salvage remuneration due in
this case, namely, £4,000 upon £28,000 of specie, being part
of the cargo belonging to the Sarpedon. The Sarpedon herself was abandoned at sea in a sinking condition, and has
not been recovered, but eighty-eight persons were taken
from on board of her and saved by the Calderon, a Spanish
vessel. It may be observed, in passing, that these persons
were "persons belonging to" the lost ship, on the construction put on the 458th section of the Merchant Shipping Act,
1854, by the Judicial Committee of the Privy Council in the
case of *The Fusilier* ('). The owners of the specie have

(') 1 P. D., 272; 17 Eng. R., 570; 2   (') 1 P. D., 473 ; 18 Eng. R., 453; 2 P.
P. D., 5; 19 Eng. R., 544.   D., 145; 21 Eng. R., 566.
                        (') B. & L., 341.

cited the owners of the Sarpedon, the lost vessel, and now call upon them to contribute to the payment of the £4,000 awarded by the court. It was first contended on behalf of the owners of the specie that the master of the Sarpedon had expressly contracted with the master of the Calderon to save the lives in question. I am of opinion that this contention is not in accordance with the facts of the case.

Secondly, it was contended that the master of the Sarpedon was bound to contract, and did contract by implication, with the master of the Calderon for the saving of these lives. In support of this proposition the case of *The Medina* () was cited.

The circumstances of that case were very peculiar. The captain of the ship which had gone to pieces contracted, on behalf of 550 *pilgrims who were left on a rock just [34 six feet above the water, to take them off for the sum of £4,000. The case was transferred to this court from the Exchequer Division of the High Court of Justice. I considered the contract to be a salvage contract, and reduced the amount to £1,800, on the ground of the unreasonableness of the amount extorted, as I thought it to be, by intimidation. That case cannot, in my opinion, be considered as supporting the demand of the owners of specie in the case before me. I consider it to be now a fixed principle of salvage law that, in the absence of any special contract, some property in the ship or cargo must be saved in order to found the liability of the owners of the ship or cargo to the payment of salvage remuneration. It has been pertinently asked in this case: If the specie as well as the ship had been entirely lost, would the owners of the lost specie have been liable to contribute to the salvage to which, it is argued, the owners of the lost ship are liable? The principle was much discussed in the case of *The Fusilier* (²), already adverted to, but the case of *The Cargo ex Schiller* (³) appears to me to have a direct bearing upon the question now before me. In that case the Schiller had been lost, but specie to a large amount, part of her cargo, had been recovered by divers. I considered the cargo was liable to pay salvage remuneration, and made an award of £500. The sentence was appealed from, and affirmed by two out of three of the judges of the Court of Appeal. Lord Justice Baggallay's judgment contained several passages which perfectly bear upon the present case. After affirming the liability of the cargo to pay salvage, he says:

(¹) 1 P. D., 272; 17 Eng. R., 570; 2 P. D., 5; 19 Eng. R., 544.   (²) B. & L., 341.
          (³) 1 P. D., 473; 18 Eng. R., 453; 2 P. D., 145; 21 Eng. R., 566.

In the terms of the section, it is a liability to pay "a reasonable amount of salvage;" but is this to be construed as a general personal liability to be enforced against the owners under any circumstances, whether the ship and cargo are lost or not, or as a liability capable of being enforced against, and therefore limited to the value of, the property, whether ship or cargo, saved from destruction?

After an argument, in which the latter construction is upheld, he says:

Upon the consideration of these several sections of the act, I am of opinion that the liability to pay a reasonable amount of salvage to life salvors is imposed upon owners of cargo as well as upon owners of the ship, and that such liability 35] *is not a general personal liability to be enforced in any circumstances, whether the ship and cargo are lost or not, but a liability limited to the value of the property saved from destruction.

I am of opinion that the owners of the lost ship are not personally liable to pay salvage, and I therefore reject the prayer of the owners of the specie to determine how much of the sum awarded by me was for salvage of life, and how much for salvage of the specie, and to declare that the owners of the Sarpedon ought to recoup to the owners of the specie the sum they have paid in respect of life salvage.

Nov. 27. The case was again mentioned, and the court, after having heard counsel for the owners of the Sarpedon in support of an application for costs, and counsel for the owners of the specie in opposition thereto, condemned the owners of the specie in the costs incurred in the action by the owners of the Sarpedon other than the costs of the application.

Solicitors for plaintiffs: *Clarkson, Son & Greenwell.*
Solicitors for owners of the specie: *Toller & Sons.*
Solicitors for owners of the Sarpedon: *Pritchard & Sons.*

[3 Probate Division, 39.]

Jan. 11, 1878.

39]   *THE SARAH (M. 506; J. 513; L. 543, Liv.).

Salvage—Services rendered in setting Salvors in Motion—Amount of Award.

A steam-tug, having a vessel in tow, saw a ship ashore and went out of her way to inform, and informed, another steam-tug of what she had seen. The other steam-tug thereupon proceeded to the stranded ship and towed her into safety. In an action of salvage instituted on behalf of both steam-tugs against the ship:

Held, that the owners, master, and crew of both steam-tugs were entitled to salvage remuneration.

THREE actions of salvage were instituted against the ship Sarah, her cargo, and freight. The first action was instituted on behalf of the mate and two of the crew of the steam-tug Great Western; the second action on behalf of the owners, master, and the rest of the crew of the same vessel ; and the third action on behalf of the owners, master, and crew of the steam-tug Kingfisher.

Two separate statements of claim were delivered; from which it appeared that the actions were brought to recover in respect of services rendered to the Sarah and her cargo on the 14th and 15th of October in last year, when the Great Western having in consequence of information from the Kingfisher, proceeded to the Middle Mouse bank, and there found the Sarah on shore and temporarily left by her master and crew, had put the plaintiffs in the first action on board her, and ultimately succeeded in getting her off the bank and towing her into the Mersey in safety.

The 3d, 4th, 5th, and 6th paragraphs of the statement of claim delivered in the second and third actions were in terms as follows :

3. On the 14th day of October last, at between 10 and 10.30 A.M., it being then nearly low water, with a moderate gale from W.S.W. increasing, and a heavy sea running, the Great Western was about abreast of the Orme's Head, on the look-out for vessels.

4. Under these circumstances the steam-tug Kingfisher came up and spoke the Great Western, and gave information that a vessel was ashore on the Middle Mouse.

5. In order to give this information, the Kingfisher, which was in attendance upon a vessel she had engaged to tow to Liverpool, was obliged temporarily to leave the said vessel and to go out of her way a distance of some miles, and but *for her having done this those on board the tug Great   [40 Western would in all probability not have known the position and danger of the Sarah, and between the time of giving the said information and the Sarah being towed off, as hereinafter mentioned, no other tug was in the neighborhood.

6. The Great Western at once, acting on the above information, proceeded towards the Middle Mouse, arriving there about noon.

The 24th, 25th, and 26th paragraphs of the same statement of claim contained allegations to the effect that the mate, seaman, and fireman of the Great Western, who had been put on board the Sarah and were the plaintiffs in the first action, were wrong in instituting a separate action, and that they were bound as to the amount of remuneration 'they were entitled to recover for their services by a custom existing in the port of Liverpool, whereby the master and crew rendered, but reserved all questions as to the liability of the owners of the S. The owners of the specie then moved the court to declare that such portion of the sum awarded as was awarded for life salvage ought to be recouped to the owners of the specie.

The court refused the motion on the ground that no property belonging to the owners of the S. having been salved they could not be held personally liable to pay any portion of the sum awarded.

THIS was an action of salvage instituted on the 17th of October, 1876, on behalf of the owners, master, and crew of the Calderon, a Spanish steamship, against specie forming part of the cargo of the English steamship Sarpedon. The owners of the specie appeared as defendants, and the plaintiffs delivered a statement of claim, which set forth *inter alia* the following facts:

The Calderon, bound on a voyage from Lisbon to London, at daylight on the 4th of September, 1875, and about eighty-five miles southwest of Ushant, came in sight of the Sarpedon, an iron steamship of about 1,556 net tons register. The Sarpedon, which was manned by a crew of seventy-three hands, all told, and had on board her fifteen passengers and eight boxes of specie, in addition to other cargo, had been in collision with another steamer called the Julia David, and had received such injuries in the collision that her passengers and crew, expecting her to sink at once, had left her and taken to such of her boats as were available. Signals of distress were hoisted on board the Sarpedon, and the Calderon took on board the passengers and specie, 29] together with a number of letters from the *Sarpedon, and the master of the Sarpedon requested the Calderon to take the Sarpedon in tow. Two hawsers were passed from the Sarpedon to the Calderon and were made fast on board the Calderon, and the Calderon endeavored to tow the Sarpedon but the Sarpedon having become unmanageable, the hawsers had to be cut to prevent a collision with the Calderon. Another attempt was afterwards made to tow the Sarpedon, but after the hawsers had been made fast a second time between the two vessels it became necessary again to cut them, and ultimately, after about six hours had been spent in fruitless efforts to tow the Sarpedon, the crew of the Sarpedon were taken on board the Calderon, and the Sarpedon was abandoned with her engine-room full of water and four feet of water in her after hold, about seventy miles to the southwest of Ushant. The Calderon then proceeded to Falmouth, and there landed the passengers, master, and crew of the Sarpedon.

The defendants, in their statement of defence, admitted

that the facts stated in the statement of claim were substantially true, and alleged that the value of the specie saved was £28,000.

On the 16th day of January, 1877, the action came on to be heard, and the judge, after hearing counsel for the plaintiffs and the defendants, directed the hearing to be adjourned, and on the 19th of January the defendants applied to the court by motion and obtained leave to issue a notice addressed to the owners of the Sarpedon pursuant to Order xvi, Rule 18, of the Rules of the Supreme Court, 1875.   Accordingly, the owners of the specie served on the owners of the Sarpedon a notice alleging, *inter alia*, that the action had been brought by the plaintiffs against certain specie forming part of the cargo of the Sarpedon and the owners of the specie, to recover remuneration for services rendered by the said plaintiffs on the high seas to the steamship Sarpedon, to the said specie, and to the master, crew, and passengers of the Sarpedon, at the request and by the direction of the master of the Sarpedon ; that the defendants claimed against the owners of the Sarpedon that they should contribute to the remuneration so claimed by the plaintiffs, and that the question of such remuneration should be determined between the plaintiffs, the owners of the specie, and the owners of the Sarpedon ; and that if the owners of the Sarpedon wished to dispute their obligation to contribute to the amount of remuneration claimed by the plaintiffs, they must appear in the action ([1]).

*On the 5th of February, the owners of the Sarpedon [30 appeared in the action, and on the 12th of February the court ordered that the notice served upon them by the owners of the specie should be treated as a pleading.

The owners of the Sarpedon on the 2d of March filed an answer, which alleged *inter alia* substantially as follows :

The services of the plaintiffs were rendered by the plaintiffs under an agreement made by the master of the Sarpedon, as agent for the owners of the Sarpedon, and the owners of her cargo, whereby the master of the Sarpedon employed the plaintiffs to render salvage assistance to the Sarpedon, her cargo, master, and crew, upon the terms that the plaintiffs were to be paid salvage for these services if and so far

---

([1]) The notice further alleged that the owners of the specie claimed to be indemnified by the owners of the Sarpedon against the claim of the plaintiffs in the action, on the ground that the collision with the Julia David had been caused by the improper navigation of the Sarpedon. Owing, however, to the Court of Appeal having decided that the Julia David was alone to blame for the collision, the question of the right of the owners of the specie to be indemnified never came before the court.

as their services should prove successful, and that the owners
of the Sarpedon were not to be liable in respect of any of the
plaintiffs' services, whether for life salvage, or otherwise,
unless the services of the plaintiffs should prove successful
in saving the Sarpedon or some part thereof.   The services
of the plaintiffs were not successful in saving the Sarpedon
or any part thereof, but the Sarpedon and all her cargo, except the specie saved, was wholly lost.

The owners of the Sarpedon are not liable to the plaintiffs
for any salvage in respect of any services rendered to the
Sarpedon, or her cargo, or in saving the lives of the master
and crew of the Sarpedon, and the said specie alone having
been saved, such specie and its owners are alone liable for
saving the lives of the master and crew of the Sarpedon.
The owners of the Sarpedon deny liability to contribute to
the remuneration claimed by the plaintiffs.

The plaintiffs and the owners of the specie filed separate
replies to the answer of the owners of the Sarpedon, and in
such replies joined issue on so much of such answer as is
above set out.

May 5.   The issues raised on the original pleadings of the
plaintiffs and the owners of the specie again came on to be
heard, together with the issues raised on so much of the answer of the owners of the Sarpedon as is above set out.

On the case being called on, it was with the consent of the
court agreed between the counsel for the different parties to
the action that the question of the liability of the owners of
the Sarpedon to pay or contribute towards the payment of the
plaintiffs' costs, and whatever sum the court should award
as salvage remuneration in the action, should be reserved
31]   until the Court of *Appeal had given its decision in an
appeal from this court in an action of damage entitled *The
Julia David* (O. 408), which action had been instituted on
behalf of the owners of the Sarpedon against the Julia David
for the recovery of the damages sustained by the Sarpedon
in the collision referred to in the statement of claim.

Cohen, Q.C., and *G. Bruce,* for the plaintiffs.
Butt, Q.C., and *W. G. F. Phillimore,* for the owners of
the specie.
E. C. Clarkson, for the owners of the Sarpedon.

SIR ROBERT PHILLIMORE: The facts of this very meritorious case of salvage are admitted, and are not the subject
of controversy.   It has been agreed, after a great deal of
discussion, that the only questions which it is incumbent on

the court to day to decide are, what amount of salvage remuneration shall be paid in consequence of the saving of life, and the saving of the specie, and also whether any, and what amount of salvage remuneration shall be awarded on the ground of a separate engagement ineffectual, but still performed to the utmost efforts of the salvors to save the ship herself considered apart from the specie, and the lives of the passengers, master, and crew of the Sarpedon.

It has also been agreed that the question as to the contribution which it is contended should be made by the owners of the Sarpedon to the owners of the specie shall stand over until the decision of the Court of Appeal, on the merits of the collision between the Sarpedon and the Julia David be arrived at. I have already said that this is a case of very meritorious salvage, eighty-eight lives and £28,000 of specie were saved at the risk of the lives of the persons who rendered the services in question. The Spanish vessel which rendered these services to the English vessel was a very costly instrument—if I may use such an expression—for she and her cargo were worth £53,000. She went out of her way considerably, almost two days' steaming, to take these English people whose lives had been so saved into an English port, and it would be difficult, I think, to describe a service with more ingredients of merit than there are in this case. I have no doubt whatever that but for the succor which the Calderon afforded *those eighty-eight lives [32 and £28,000 worth of specie would have been lost.

I shall make an award of £4,000 as the salvage remuneration for these services, and I am of opinion that it would be, in the circumstances of this case, drawing too fine a line to attempt to establish a distinction between the saving specie and the lives, and the services rendered to the ship, and I shall, therefore, not make any separate award of salvage remuneration for the engagement, as it has been called, which was ineffectual, to save the ship herself.

The question of contribution will stand over, as I have already said, until the Court of Appeal has given its decision as to the merits of the collision with the Julia David. The apportionment of the award, which the court has just made, between the owners, master, and crew of the Calderon will also stand over (¹).

On the 7th of August, the Court of Appeal delivered judg-

(¹) On the 29th of May, the court apportioned the £4,000 awarded to the plaintiffs, as follows: To the owners of the Calderon £3,000, to the master of the Calderon £250, and to the officers and crew of the same vessel £750 to be divided among them according to their respective ratings on board thereof.

ment in the action of damage which had been instituted by
the owners of the Sarpedon against the Julia David, and
pronounced that the Julia David was alone to blame for the
collision between her and the Sarpedon.

Nov. 13.   *W. G. F. Phillimore*, on behalf of the owners
of the specie, moved the judge in court to determine how
much of the sum awarded for salvage to the plaintiffs, and
subsequently paid to them by the owners of the specie, was
for life salvage, and how much for salvage of specie, and to
declare that the sum awarded for life salvage ought to have
been paid to the plaintiffs by the owners of the Sarpedon,
and further to order the owners of the Sarpedon to recoup to the owners of the specie the sum paid by them
in respect of life salvage and costs to the plaintiffs.   He stated
that the owners of the specie had paid to the plaintiffs the
whole amount awarded for salvage remuneration, and the
plaintiffs' costs in the action, and contended that on the admitted facts of the case the services of the plaintiffs in
saving the lives of the passengers, master, and crew of the
Sarpedon were rendered under a salvage agreement, which,
33]   *if not expressly made with the master of the Sarpedon, must be implied from the Sarpedon having hoisted signals of distress, and that consequently, as the owners of the
Sarpedon were liable *in personam*, under such salvage agreement, it would be clearly inequitable if the amount of life
salvage remuneration in the case should be entirely borne
by the owners of the specie : *The Medina* (').

E. C. Clarkson, for the owners of the Sarpedon, opposed
the motion.   He referred to 17 & 18 Vict. c. 104, s. 458, and
The Cargo ex Schiller (').

                                      Cur. adv. vult.

Nov. 20.   SIR ROBERT PHILLIMORE :   The court has already awarded the amount of salvage remuneration due in
this case, namely, £4,000 upon £28,000 of specie, being part
of the cargo belonging to the Sarpedon.   The Sarpedon herself was abandoned at sea in a sinking condition, and has
not been recovered, but eighty-eight persons were taken
from on board of her and saved by the Calderon, a Spanish
vessel.   It may be observed, in passing, that these persons
were "persons belonging to" the lost ship, on the construction put on the 458th section of the Merchant Shipping Act,
1854, by the Judicial Committee of the Privy Council in the
case of *The Fusilier* (').   The owners of the specie have

(') 1 P. D., 272; 17 Eng. R., 570; 2   (') 1 P. D., 473; 18 Eng. R., 453; 2 P.
P. D., 5; 19 Eng. R., 544.   D., 145; 21 Eng. R., 566.
                        (') B. & L., 341.

cited the owners of the Sarpedon, the lost vessel, and now call upon them to contribute to the payment of the £4,000 awarded by the court. It was first contended on behalf of the owners of the specie that the master of the Sarpedon had expressly contracted with the master of the Calderon to save the lives in question. I am of opinion that this contention is not in accordance with the facts of the case.

Secondly, it was contended that the master of the Sarpedon was bound to contract, and did contract by implication, with the master of the Calderon for the saving of these lives. In support of this proposition the case of *The Medina* (') was cited.

The circumstances of that case were very peculiar. The captain of the ship which had gone to pieces contracted, on behalf of 550 *pilgrims who were left on a rock just [34 six feet above the water, to take them off for the sum of £4,000. The case was transferred to this court from the Exchequer Division of the High Court of Justice. I considered the contract to be a salvage contract, and reduced the amount to £1,800, on the ground of the unreasonableness of the amount extorted, as I thought it to be, by intimidation. That case cannot, in my opinion, be considered as supporting the demand of the owners of specie in the case before me. I consider it to be now a fixed principle of salvage law that, in the absence of any special contract, some property in the ship or cargo must be saved in order to found the liability of the owners of the ship or cargo to the payment of salvage remuneration. It has been pertinently asked in this case: If the specie as well as the ship had been entirely lost, would the owners of the lost specie have been liable to contribute to the salvage to which, it is argued, the owners of the lost ship are liable? The principle was much discussed in the case of *The Fusilier* ('), already adverted to, but the case of *The Cargo ex Schiller* (') appears to me to have a direct bearing upon the question now before me. In that case the Schiller had been lost, but specie to a large amount, part of her cargo, had been recovered by divers. I considered the cargo was liable to pay salvage remuneration, and made an award of £500. The sentence was appealed from, and affirmed by two out of three of the judges of the Court of Appeal. Lord Justice Baggallay's judgment contained several passages which perfectly bear upon the present case. After affirming the liability of the cargo to pay salvage, he says:

(') 1 P. D., 272; 17 Eng. R., 570; 2 P. D., 5; 19 Eng. R., 544.   (') B. & L., 341.
    (') 1 P. D., 473; 18 Eng. R., 453; 2 P. D., 145; 21 Eng. R., 566.

something, would delay the wife in obtaining redress as to the main object of the suit, because the respondent refuses to give her the means of obtaining a decision on a totally distinct and incidental question.

This is a result so obviously unreasonable that the court is bound to avoid it, unless constrained by the clearest language to adopt it. It was urged that where authority is conferred by the Legislature to vary settlements (23 & 24 Vict. c. 144, s. 5), the power is given to do so "after" a ·final decree, and that it is to be presumed that this word was used advisedly with the object of giving a larger power than existed with regard to maintenance. But I cannot draw this inference. No reason was suggested, or has occurred to my mind, why such a distinction should be made. I rather infer that the word "after" is used as the equivalent of the word "on" in the earlier enactment.

I am of opinion, therefore, that I have jurisdiction to entertain this petition. The only question which remains is, whether the petitioner, by her delay, has by the practice of the court precluded herself from instituting these proceedings. By the 95th rule it is directed that applications to the court to exercise the authority given by the 32d section and other sections which are mentioned, are to be made in a separate petition, which must, unless by leave of the judge, be filed as soon as by the said statutes such application can be made or within one month thereafter. If the 32d section is to be construed in connection with the 96th rule 52] the petitioner has not made her application within *one month after the earliest time at which it might have been made. But assuming as I do that I have the power, I think it is a case in which I ought to give leave to the petitioner to make her application at a later period. The objection was not taken by the respondent until all the expense and delay of the investigation of his means had been incurred, and it is not shown that any prejudice has accrued to the respondent by the petition for maintenance not having been presented fourteen days sooner.

I shall therefore make an order on the respondent in accordance with the registrar's report.

Solicitors for petitioner : *Shaen, Roscoe & Massey.*
Solicitors for respondent: *Brooks, Jenkins & Co.*

See 26 Eng. R., 522 note ; New York Code Civil Procedure, §§ 1766, 1769.

[3 Probate Division, 60.]

June 7, 1878.

[IN THE COURT OF APPEAL.]

*THE GENERAL STEAM NAVIGATION COMPANY v. THE [60
OWNERS OF THE STEAMSHIP OCEANO.

THE OCEANO.

[1877 G. 422.]

Collision—Crossing Ships—Rules for Navigation of the Thames, rule 29.

Where one of two steamers in the Thames was steering parallel to the shore and
the other was steering in an oblique course across the stream:

Held, that they were crossing vessels, so that under the 29th of the rules of 1872
for the navigation of the Thames, the one which had the other on her own starboard
was bound to keep out of the way of the other.

The Velocity (Law Rep., 3 P. C., 44) considered.

THIS was an appeal by the plaintiffs, the owners of the
steamship Virgo, from a judgment of Sir R. J. Phillimore,
pronouncing both ships to blame for a collision between the
Virgo and the Oceano.

The collision took place in clear weather soon after noon
on the 29th of December, 1877. The Oceano was going up
the Thames in the Hope reach below Gravesend against an
ebb tide, and was proceeding along the river on the northern
side of the mid-channel. A little below the Ovens buoy the
Oceano starboarded her helm to avoid a brigantine which
was coming down the river, there not being room, as the
witnesses on behalf of the *Oceano stated, to pass on [61
the north side of the brigantine. She did not then resume
her former course but steadied, and continued going obliquely across the river until the collision with the Virgo
took place near the southern shore.

The Virgo was a steamship coming down the river on the
southern side of the mid-channel along the Gravesend reach.
She had to deflect her course in order to avoid another vessel, but had resumed her course along the southern shore
some time before the collision took place.

The collision took place about the meeting of the two
reaches, which are at a considerable angle to each other, so
that if each vessel had been proceeding along the middle
line of the stream their courses would have been nearly at
right angles to each other.

When a collision was imminent the Virgo stopped her engines and put her helm hard a-port, and it was contended

on the part of the Oceano that this caused the collision. The Court of Appeal, however, came to the conclusion that the only effect of this manœuvre was to diminish the violence of the collision.

The result was that the stem of the Virgo struck the Oceano on the starboard side and so injured her that she filled.

Sir R. J. Phillimore held both vessels to blame and gave judgment accordingly. The plaintiffs appealed. The case was heard before the Court of Appeal, with nautical assessors.

May 28, 31. *Butt*, Q.C., and *E. C. Clarkson*, for the appellants.

Milward, Q.C., and *Dr. Phillimore*, contrà.

[*The Velocity* (¹); *The Ranger and The Cologne* (²); and *The Esk* (); and the Rules for the Navigation of the Thames, issued in 1872, rule 29, were referred to.]

Cur. adv. vult.

June 7. The judgment of the Court (James, Baggallay, and Bramwell, L.JJ.) was delivered by

JAMES, L.J.: In this case the learned judge from whom this appeal is brought, by and with the advice and concurrence of his nautical assessors, pronounced both the ships, the Oceano and the Virgo, to blame, and made the consequential order thereon.

62] *But except in the general allegation that a collision in broad daylight in an unobstructed and wide channel of the river Thames was very disgraceful, and the general statement that both ships had time enough each to get out of the way of the other, we are not informed as to what particular wrongful act or wrongful omission the court below finds to have been established by the evidence against either of the litigant ships.

There are two distinct issues to be determined. Was the Oceano to blame? the burthen of proof on that issue being on the Virgo. Was the Virgo to blame? the burthen of proof on that issue being on the Oceano.

On the first issue the skilled assessors whose assistance we have, unhesitatingly pronounce their concurrence with the finding of the court below. They advise us that, irrespectively of any special rule of navigation, the Oceano was clearly and very much in the wrong. The Oceano was proceeding up the river in the Hope reach below Gravesend against an ebb tide, and was, when the movements began which ultimately led to the collision, near the Essex shore,

(¹) Law Rep., 3 P. C., 44.   (²) Law Rep., 4 P. C., 519.   (³) Law Rep., 3 P. C., 436.

as near which as the ship could conveniently go was the
proper and ordinary course for her to take. A little below
the Ovens buoy, she had to deflect her course in order to
pass a brigantine, the William, which was going down the
river. At this time, the Virgo was going down the river,
and according to the usual and normal course was going as
near the Kent shore as she conveniently could. She also
had to deflect her course to pass some craft at anchor.
Both ships were thereby brought nearly into the mid-stream.
At the time the Oceano manœuvred to clear the brigantine
she must have been very near the north shore, because according to the Oceano's own case she could not then have
safely gone between the brigantine and that shore. When
she had cleared the brigantine, her proper course then would
have been to have ported her helm so as to bring her back
to her original course, and to have proceeded in that course
along the waterway which was open and clear before her.

Our assessors are of opinion that there was nothing which
she saw, or could have seen in the position or course of the
Virgo, to require or justify her in not taking that course.
But instead of that she continued in the direction which she
had assumed in *order to clear the brigantine, ob-   [63
liquely across the channel, until she came into collision with
the Virgo, close to the Kentish shore. Moreover, when she
was approaching the Virgo, she took no precaution, she did
not, as she ought to have done, ease or stop, or reverse her
engines until it was too late, until she was warned by the
whistle of the other ship, and when it was too late to do
anything.

Further than this, our assessors have also pointed out that
the Oceano clearly violated the special rules of navigation enacted for the river Thames. By the 29th of those rules it is,
amongst other things, provided that "if two vessels under
steam are crossing so as to involve risk of collision, the
vessel which has the other on her own starboard side shall
keep out of the way of the other." And our assessors
are of opinion that the ships were crossing ships, and that
the Oceano being the crossing ship which had the other
on her starboard side, was under an obligation to keep clear
of the other vessel. It was suggested to us that the decision
of the Privy Council in *The Velocity* (¹) had established that
the rule as to crossing ships did not apply to the river
Thames. It is difficult to conceive how a decision of the
Privy Council on the general maritime rules in 1869, could
be held so to nullify an express provision in the local legis-

(¹) Law Rep., 3 P. C., 44.

lation promulgated in the year 1872, specially and exclusively for the regulation of the navigation of the Thames
itself. It may be convenient further to notice that there
seems to be a great misapprehension, induced probably by
the language of the marginal or head-note of the case, as to
what was really decided by that case. It seems to have been
considered that it was laid down generally that the rule as to
crossing ships could not be applied in a winding and crowded
river like the Thames. What was decided really was, that
in such a river the particular direction taken for a moment,
or a few moments, in rounding a corner or avoiding an obstacle, was not such an indication of the real course of the ship
as to justify another ship in saying, "I saw your course, I
saw that if you continued in that course we should be crossing
ships, and I left to you, therefore, the entire responsibility
of getting out of my way under the rule." And all that
was really decided was, that in the particular part of the
Thames, and under the particular circumstances which the
64   *court had to deal with in that case, a vessel was not
by that rule exonerated from the consequences of her omission to do what good seamanship required her to do. And
this is made quite clear in the subsequent case of *The Ranger* (') in which the *Velocity* case was carefully examined,
and in the particular circumstances of that case followed.

In the case we have to deal with there were no special circumstances to interfere with the application of the rule. If
ever there is a case of crossing ships, it must surely be when
one ship is going obliquely up and across the channel, and
the other is going down the same channel. And that their
courses were so crossing as to cause danger of collision is
proved by the fact that they did come into collision. Our
assessors' conclusion that the Oceano was to blame is one in
which we entirely concur with them, and with the finding
of the court below.

There remains the other question. Was the Virgo to
blame? Our assessors, after a very careful examination of
the evidence, are unable to find any proof of this. The
Virgo was' keeping her course, as she well and properly
might, near the south shore. She, in order to pass the craft
at mooring, went out into the mid-stream, and then slightly
ported to recover her course. There was nothing at that
time to induce her or to call on her not to do this. She in
good time eased and stopped her engines when she saw the
Oceano approaching, and at the very last moment she ported
hard. No doubt in doing this she did not literally comply

(') Law Rep., 4 P. C., 519

with the rule as to keeping her course, viz., doing nothing. But our assessors are of opinion, and we see no reason for differing from them, that this last porting, when in the very jaws of the peril, was not only not blamable, but was forced on her by the right and duty of self-preservation under such circumstances. And, in fact, this last porting, so far from contributing to the mischief, diminished it. Considering the size and power of the ships which came into collision, the blow was a singularly light one. That it was so slight is, in the judgment of our assessors, mainly to be attributed to the Virgo having so ported and having previously taken the timely precaution of diminishing, and, as far as could be, stopping her way through the water.

*In concurring with the conclusion of our assessors [65 we have not been unmindful of the very just observations which have been made to us on the evidence of the master of the Virgo. There is no doubt that, in saying that he saw the Oceano porting after she had starboarded to clear the brigantine, he said that which was not the fact. Whether he imagined that he saw, or thought after the collision that he recollected that he saw, the Oceano do what he expected she would have done, or whether it is an absolute misstatement, it is not necessary to say. But disregarding that evidence, and if necessary disregarding the whole of his evidence, there is sufficient in the facts otherwise proved and patent to compel us to come to the conclusion, differing in this respect from the court below, that the Oceano has not proved, that which it was for her to prove, that the Virgo was to blame.

We must therefore vary the order appealed from, and pronounce that the Oceano was to blame, and that the Virgo was not to blame, and condemn the Oceano in the whole damage and the cost of the suits, both below and in this court.

Solicitor for appellants : *W. Batham.*
Solicitors for respondents : *Lowless & Co.*

[3 Probate Division, 71.]

June 25, 1878.

71] .*In the Goods of* CHARLES APTHORP WHEELWRIGHT, deceased.

Executrix—Universal Legatee—Remuneration.

H. P. W., sole executrix and universal legatee, renounced her rights as such to the grant of letters of administration, which was accordingly made to G. W., one of the next of kin. Upon the death of G. W., intestate and insolvent, H. P. W. was allowed to retract her renunciation as universal legatee, and take a grant of letters of administration *de bonis non.*

THE Rev. Charles Apthorp Wheelwright died, having by his will appointed his daughter, Henrietta Pretyman Wheelwright, sole executrix, and named her universal legatee.

The daughter, by reason of illness, renounced her right to the grant in both characters, and letters of administration, with the will annexed, were, on the 22d of January, 1859, granted at the Peterborough District Registry to the Rev. George Wheelwright, a son of the testator, who intermeddled in the estate, and died on the 7th of December, 1875, intestate and insolvent. Some other property, of the value of about £200, having recently accrued to the testator's estate,

Pritchard, for Henrietta Pretyman Wheelwright, moved the court to allow her to withdraw either her renunciation to the grant as executrix or as universal legatee. The words of the statute (20 & 21 Vict. c. 77, s. 79), that upon renunciation the rights shall cease, only apply to her as executrix, and there is nothing except rule 50 to prevent the court from allowing her to withdraw her renunciation as universal legatee. The enforcing of that rule is in the discretion of the court: *In the Goods of Gill* (¹); *In the Goods of Badenach* (²).

SIR J. HANNEN (President): She has not renounced her beneficial rights as universal legatee. Let her take the grant in that character.

Solicitors: *Cobbold & Wolley.*

(¹) Law Rep., 3 P. & D., 113; 7 Eng. R., 348.   (²) 3 Sw. & Tr., 465.

[3 Probate Division, 72.]

May 29, 1878.

*S. v. A., otherwise S.   [72

Nullity—Non-consummation—No structural Defect.

Wilful wrongful refusal of marital intercourse is not in itself sufficient to justify the court in declaring a marriage null by reason of impotence.

When, after a reasonable time, it is shown that there has been no sexual intercourse, and that the wife has resisted all attempts, the court, if satisfied of the *bona fides* of the suit, will infer that the refusal arises from incapacity, and will pronounce a decree of nullity of marriage.

THIS was a suit for nullity of marriage by reason of the alleged impotence of the wife. The parties were married on the 8th of August, 1868, and lived together until the month of September, 1877. The other facts sufficiently appear in the judgment.

Dr. Spinks, Q.C., and *Searle*, appeared for the petitioner, and relied upon the case of *G.* v. *G.* (¹).

Inderwick, Q.C., and *Bayford*, for the respondent: The application is not *bona fide*. The petitioner married her, in spite of her deformity, to obtain a small sum of money which she then possessed, and now seeks to get rid of her, not because she is malformed, which is not true, but because of her deformity (²).

SIR J. HANNEN (President): I am of opinion that this petition must be dismissed. It is a case in which the medical evidence established that each of the parties is perfectly capable of sexual intercourse, and the questions are, whether there has in fact ever been sexual intercourse between them, and if not, whose is the fault?

I have nothing to rely on but the evidence of the two parties. The petitioner alleges that the respondent would not allow him to have intercourse with her, such is the effect of his statement; and the respondent alleges that she did allow him on the first occasion that he chose, that she was always ready and willing at all times afterwards; and that on one occasion, and on one occasion only, he made an attempt which approached, if it did not actually reach positive consummation.

It is to be borne in mind that the ground upon which the *court proceeds in these cases is the physical inca- [73 pacity of the parties. A wilful wrongful refusal of marital intercourse is not in itself sufficient to justify the court in declaring a marriage to be null by reason of impotence.

(¹) Law Rep., 2 P. & D., 287.

(²) The respondent was hump-backed and diminutive.

However much we may revolt from the idea of a man using
force to compel his wife to have intercourse with him—and
such a feeling is one which probably is much stronger at the
present day than in past times—no case has gone the length
of saying because a man naturally abstains from using force,
that therefore the refusal, if it be a merely wilful refusal on
the part of the wife, will justify him in coming to the court
and asking that it shall be declared that the marriage is void.
Recent cases only establish this in advance of previous decisions, viz., that where a woman is shown not to have had
intercourse with her husband after a reasonable time for
consummation of the marriage, if it appears that she has abstained from intercourse, and resisted her husband's attempts, the court will draw the inference that that refusal
on her part arises from incapacity. In the case of *G.* v. *G.* (¹)
the evidence of Dr. Farr, was to this effect,—"The result of
my examination is, that sexual intercourse is practically impossible. There are means by which, in my opinion, her
condition may be remedied; but in order that they should
succeed it is necessary that she should lend herself to them."
So that it being necessary that she should submit to some
physical treatment, Lord Penzance, under the circumstances,
was satisfied of the practical impossibility arising from the
physical condition of the woman. In another case, a case
of *P.* v. *L., falsely called P.* (²), the evidence was as in the

---

(¹) Law Rep., 2 P. & D., 287.
(²) Decided the 3d of May, 1873, by Sir
J. Hannen. The substance and effect of
the pleadings and evidence in this case
were as follows: The petition alleged
the marriage of the parties on the 5th of
February, 1866, at Christ Church, Lee, in
Kent, cohabitation until May, 1872, and
the incapacity of the respondent, and her
refusal to submit to remedies. The answer denied the incapacity and refusal.
The petitioner said at the time of my marriage I was thirty, and the respondent
eighteen. I attempted to consummate the
marriage, but there appeared to be an
obstruction. She screamed and became
hysterical, and afterwards complained of
pain and suffering. In appearance she
seemed to be a child, and not a woman.
I made other attempts, but she resisted
me and on one occasion hit me in the face.
She also threatened to drown herself.
In 1869 she left me. After a time I discovered where she was living, and persuaded her to return. We lived together

until 1872, when she left me and refused
to return.
Dr. Hicks, M.D., said that at the request of the petitioner, he examined the
respondent some time ago. The hymen
was unchanged, and the parts were rather
smaller than usual. She refused to submit to remedies. (There was also other
medical testimony to the same effect.)
She refused to be again examined by him
or to submit to any remedies, and said
that when she married she had no idea
that there would be sexual intercourse—
that she had no sexual desire.
The petitioner's sister and friends were
called, with whom petitioner and respondent had stayed, and who tried to reason
with her, but to no purpose. She said it
was like the beasts of the field. She also
admitted to them that there had been no
consummation.
The medical report upon the husband
showed that his condition was normal.
Dr. Spinks, Q.C., and *Searle,* appeared
for the petitioner. The respondent did
not appear.   *Decree nisi.*

*case of *G.* v. *G.* (¹) that intercourse between the par- [74
ties was practically impossible. There was no physical impossibility in the grosser sense of that expression, but it was
proved to my satisfaction that the respondent was not really
and truly in nature a woman—that she remained a child incapable of understanding the nature of the act: and that
therefore being entirely free from the passions of women in
that respect she resisted the action of her husband as though
it were something unnatural. Those cases are totally different from the present. In the present case it is sufficient for
me to say the medical evidence is complete, that the respondent's physical condition is in all respects suitable for connection, and as a matter of fact is such as would have been
presented if there had been sexual intercourse, as she says
there was on one or two occasions several years ago. That
she has not the appearance of a married woman who has
been accustomed to habitual sexual intercourse is consistent with either case.

In such a state of things, there being no proof except the
evidence of the two parties, what is there to lead me to a
conclusion in favor of the petitioner? I find nothing tending to corroborate his statement. It has been said that no
motive has been suggested for the husband taking these proceedings. It is of course very difficult to penetrate men's
minds, but taking his own statement, I must say that it
does not impress me in favor of his case. It must be obvious to everybody that the fact that a woman *on the [75
first night of the marriage only should have refused her
husband access to her would be a totally insufficient ground
for his at once asserting that he "was a stupid for having
married her." Supposing it were true that she had refused,
he should have waited for another occasion, and should
have trusted to the effect of their associating together as
man and wife to produce a change in her feelings. But, on
the other hand, an expression of that kind is quite consistent with a feeling of regret that he had entered into a marriage with a person whose appearance might not present the
usual attractions of a bride.

This being the state of things, viz., the woman alleging
that he did on that night have connection with her, her condition being consistent with such statement, and there being
nothing upon which I can rely as corroborating his evidence
rather than hers, it is my duty to take into account the fact
that it is only after nine years' living together as husband
and wife that he institutes these proceedings. I do not say

(¹) Law Rep., 2 P. & D., 287.

that he ought to have done what it is alleged he originally said—that he ought to have taken these proceedings the next day—but he ought to have done so after a reasonable time. The law has indicated what is a reasonable time in requiring three years' cohabitation, by which is meant, that three years is a sufficient time to ascertain whether it is a mere coyness on the part of the woman or whether there is any physical incapacity. But he has lived with the respondent such a length of time that the conditions of her existence are changed, for nine years is a considerable period in anybody's life. It was his duty, if he felt he was subject to the wrong which he says he was, to have instituted these proceedings at a much earlier period, in order that it might have been judicially determined whether or no there had been a valid marriage between them. Without saying that the delay would in itself be a bar to the proceedings, I am bound to take it into account, in arriving at the conclusion whether or not the absence of ordinary conjugal intercourse is to be attributed to the man or the woman. The letter that has been written by the brother makes no impression whatever on my mind. Her allegation that the marriage was consummated on the first night was put forward by the solicitor promptly. The letter is the 76] letter of a somewhat illiterate person, and the *obvious meaning of it is, that she alleges that the fault was not hers but the man's, and whether or no the brother was right in the use of his expression about the marriage being "consummative," if the letter is looked at with unprejudiced eyes, all that the brother intended to say was, that the state of things which existed between them was alleged by the wife not to be her fault but the fault of the husband.

I therefore come to the conclusion that the petitioner has failed to make out his case, and the petition must be dismissed with costs.

Petition dismissed with costs.

Solicitor for petitioner : *J. M. Weightman.*
Solicitors for respondent : *Robinson & Co.*

[3 Probate Division, 76.]

May 27, 1878.

[IN THE COURT OF APPEAL.]

In the Goods of THARP.

THARP v. MACDONALD.

[1877 T. 4.]

Probate—Will of Married Woman—Separate Estate—Savings from Allowance to Wife of Lunatic—Judicature Act, 1873, s. 24, subs. 7.

When the will of a married woman is tendered for probate on the ground that she had separate property, and the probate is contested, if the court is satisfied that there is separate property, it has power to grant probate of all such property as the testatrix had power to dispose of without deciding what that property is. But it is in general the duty of the court, so far as the evidence and pleadings enable it to do so, to decide judicially of what such property consists.

And, *semble*, where the will is made under a power, if the court has all persons interested before it, it ought to decide the question not only whether there is a power, but whether it is well executed.

The savings of an annual allowance for her separate maintenance, paid to the wife of a lunatic living apart from her husband, under an order in lunacy, are her separate property, although the order does not expressly state that the allowance is for her separate use.

THIS was an appeal from an order of Sir R. J. Phillimore, made on the 8th of November, 1877.

Lady Hannah Charlotte Tharp was married in 1815 to Mr. John *Tharp. A settlement was made on their mar- [77 riage, but no power being given to the wife over the property settled, it did not affect the question in the present action.

On the 17th of January, 1816, Mr. Tharp was found lunatic by inquisition. By an order of the Lord Chancellor, dated the 24th of December, 1819, it was ordered that £4,000 a year should be allowed out of the income of the estate of Mr. Tharp "for the separate maintenance of his wife payable quarterly." The principal part of the lunatic's estates being in the West Indies subsequently became valueless, and on the 4th of November, 1826, another order was made in the matter of the lunacy, directing that instead of £4,000 a year, an allowance of £300 "should be paid to Lady Mary Tharp out of the lunatic's English estates by half quarterly payments." It was not expressly stated in either of the orders that the allowance was to be for the separate use of Lady Hannah Tharp. This allowance the testatrix received till the time of her death. The only other source of income of Lady H. Tharp was an annuity of £500 payable under a letter dated the 24th of April, 1822, from Lady Elizabeth Gavin, a relative of Lady Hannah Tharp living in Scotland, to her daughter, the Marchioness of Breadalbane, which was as follows :

"Since writing the above, it appears that Lady Hannah Tharp, from the total ruin of Mr. Tharp's estates in the West Indies, is without a possibility of having anything to subsist on, and in the event of his death would have no jointure. I wish her to receive from what I shall leave you £500 annually till she marries."

Under this letter, which was proved as a will, Lady Hannah Tharp after Lady E. Gavin's death received the annuity of £500 during the remainder of her life.

Lady Hannah Tharp died on the 3d of May, 1876, at Edinburgh, her husband being still alive and a lunatic domiciled in England.   At the time of her death she had accumulated considerable savings out of her income amounting to about £20,000.   She made a will, dated the 29th of January, 1869, and six codicils, the last of which bore date the 11th of April, 1876, by which she appointed John Macdonald her executor.   A very small portion of her property was in England, almost all being invested in the 78]   *names of her trustees in Scotch securities and stocks. The trustees in June, 1877, commenced a suit of multiplepoinding in the Scotch court for the purpose of ascertaining the title to the assets in Scotland.   The committee of Mr. Tharp then commenced the present action in the Probate Division of the High Court of Justice to which Macdonald was made defendant, claiming that the will and codicils should be pronounced invalid, and that administration should be granted to the plaintiff as committee of her husband.

Macdonald, by his defence, maintained the validity of the will and codicils on the ground that Lady Hannah Tharp had property to her separate use, and by way of counter-claim, claimed that the will and codicils might be admitted to probate.

Sir R. Phillimore being of opinion that Lady Hannah Tharp, living apart from her husband by reason of the lunacy, had a right to accumulate savings out of the income allowed her by the court as separate estate, made an order directing probate of the will and codicils limited to such effects as she had power to dispose of and had disposed of accordingly, but without referring specially to any of the funds.   From this order the plaintiff appealed.

Inderwick, Q.C., and *Dr. Swabey* (*R. A. Bayford*, with them), for the plaintiff : There is no proof that there is any separate property in respect of which the probate can be granted. With respect to the allowances made by the court in the lunacy, it is not stated in the orders that the allowances are to be for Lady H. Tharp's separate use. *Brooke* v. *Brooke* ('), and *Barrack* v. *McCullock* ('), relied on by the other side, are not in point. Therefore the savings are not the separate property of the testatrix. Neither is there any proof that the savings of the annuity under the Scotch will are separate property. That question is now under litigation in the Scotch court. At all events the grant of probate was irregular in not deciding what part of the property is separate property. In fact the judge refused to go into that question. Before the passing of the Judicature Act, 1873, the *judge of the Probate Court used to hear evidence, [79 and consider what separate property there was, although the practice was not clearly settled: *Haddon* v. *Fladgate* ('), *Re Elliott* ('). So also in the case of a will of a married woman made under a power, the court considered the question whether there was a power, although it had no power to determine the question whether the power was well executed. And now the Judicature Act, 1873, s. 24, subs. 7, gives full power to every Division of the High Court to decide all questions between the parties, so that all matters may be finally determined and multiplicity of legal proceedings avoided. This power has been exercised by the Probate Division in a recent case of *Pledger* v. *Mant* ('), in which the judge heard and decided the question whether certain property was part of the separate estate of a married woman. That has not been done in the present case, and the plaintiff will have to take proceedings in the Chancery Division to determine what is separate property.

Southgate, Q.C., and *G. Browne*, for the defendants, were not called on.

JESSEL, M.R.: This is an appeal from a decision of Sir Robert Phillimore, and it raises some questions of importance as to the practice of the Court of Probate, and also as to the right of the deceased Lady Hannah Charlotte Tharp to dispose by will as her separate estate of very considerable property. The executor propounded a will, which was no doubt perfectly valid, to dispose of the separate estate of the lady, if she had any. The committee of the husband,

(') 25 Beav., 342.　　　　　　　(') 1 Sw. & Tr., 48.
(') 3 K. & J., 110, at p. 120.　　　(') Law Rep., 2 P. & M., 275.
　　　　　　　(') Unreported.

who is a lunatic, opposed probate, and claimed grant of administration on the ground that she really had no separate estate, and therefore the contest between the parties really was whether there was any separate estate authorizing the Court of Probate to grant probate to the executor in the form in which it seems it is usually granted, "of such personal estate and effects as she had power to dispose of." Now, the point as to the practice of the Probate Court is this: No doubt the old Ecclesiastical Court was in the habit of 80] granting probate of a testamentary *appointment of a married woman, without deciding the question as to whether the appointment was a valid one or not. In the Ecclesiastical Court, when there existed a power which enabled a married woman to dispose of property, and there was a question whether the power was well executed or not, the practice was to grant probate of the instrument in order to enable the Court of Equity, which as a general rule was the proper court to decide upon the sufficiency of the execution, to decide the question. The Ecclesiastical Court was in this position, that it could not finally decide the question for itself. If it entertained the question, and decided to refuse the probate, it prevented the Court of Equity from deciding it. So that in one way it would have finally decided the question, whereas by adopting the other way they left the question of the effect of the probate to be decided by the Court of Equity, and accordingly this practice, which was affirmed by the Privy Council in the case of *Barnes* v. *Vincent* ([1]), sprung up. In all cases where it was a mere question of the sufficiency of the execution of the power, there the court being satisfied that there was a power capable of being exercised, and there was some ground for disputing or fairly disputing the question as to the validity of its exercise, granted the probate in order to enable a court of competent jurisdiction to decide the real question between the parties.

With regard to the question immediately before us, which is not a question of the grant of probate of a will of a married woman who has merely exercised a power, but where the allegation is not that she had a power properly so called, but had merely a right of testamentary disposition, as one of the incidents of property belonging to her for her separate use, it appears to me that different considerations arise. As far as I am aware, and I have asked for information which I do not possess myself, it does not appear that this exact question came before the court previous to the passing

([1]) 5 Moo. P. C., 201.

of the Probate Act—that is, previous to the establishment
of the Probate Court as distinguished from the old Ecclesiastical Court.

Three cases have been cited to us before the Probate
Court, in all of which the judges decided that, as a fact, a
married woman *had some separate property.   The [81
three decisions—two of them reported, namely, *Haddon* v.
Fladgate(') and *Re Elliott*('), and one of them unreported
—were made by three different judges who have sat in the
Probate Court and have all actually decided the question
that there was some property settled to the separate use.
That seems to have been the position of matters at the time
of the passing of the Judicature Act.   As regards' two of
them, they were decisions before the Judicature Act, and as
regards the other, which is unreported, it was a decision
after the Judicature Act.

The question, therefore, is whether there was any established practice in the Court of Probate as to what should be
done in the case of an allegation merely of the existence of
separate estate.   If there were any established practice at
all, I should suppose it would have been in accordance with
the decisions which I have referred to, before the Judicature
Act: but as I understand from the learned registrar who
has given us his assistance in this case, there really was no
established practice as regards cases relating merely to the
property given to the separate use of the married woman.

That being so, I wish to consider whether the Judicature
Act has made any difference, and, in addition to that, what
is the most convenient course to pursue.   Of course, I take
it in all these cases it is not sufficient that the judge should
have jurisdiction; there is always another question whether
he should exercise the jurisdiction conferred upon him or
not.   Now, if we look at the 6th and 7th sub-sections of the
24th section of the Judicature Act, 1873, I think it is plain
that the meaning of the Legislature was this, that whenever
a subject of controversy arises in an action which can conveniently be determined between the parties to the action,
the court should, if possible, determine it so as to prevent
further and needless litigation.   That is the effect of the sections, although not the exact words of them.

Now, in the case of a contest in the Probate Division as
to whether a married woman had separate property or not,
it is obvious that there can be but two parties to that contest
—the surviving husband and the executors propounding
the testamentary *instrument of the married woman [82

(') 1 Sw. & Tr., 48.   (') Law Rep., 2 P. & M., 275.

for probate. If the property is not settled to her separate use it belongs to the husband, and if it is it belongs to the executors, to be distributed according to the will, and in such contest in every court the executors would be entitled to represent, and would be the only persons entitled to represent, the legatees claiming under the testamentary instrument. Therefore, we have a suit so constituted that every person is before the court whose interests can be affected by the decision of the judge in that suit. But, in addition to that, it appears to me that the decision of the question is absolutely involved in the granting of probate. The probate is granted of something which the married woman has power to dispose of. It is not too much to assume that the judge, somehow or other, is satisfied that she has something to dispose of, because, unless there is power or unless there is separate property, she has nothing to dispose of, the property being the husband's. I leave out of consideration the singular case of a will *ex consensu viri*, which is another exception. That being so, the natural thing for the court to do is to decide the question between the parties, it being an element in the conclusion at which the judge arrives that probate shall be granted. It does not appear to me that the decision in *Barnes* v. *Vincent*(') has anything whatever to do with the question we have to decide, and for these reasons: first of all, as I said before, it was decided at a time when the then Court of Probate, being an Ecclesiastical Court, was a court of very limited jurisdiction, and could not decide the question of the sufficiency of the execution of the power; and, secondly, because in the case of testamentary powers it may happen, and it frequently does happen, that other persons besides the executors are entitled to be heard in addition to the husband or his legal personal representative; so that, in such a case you have not necessarily all parties before the court. If you had, I think the same reason which now enables the court to decide all questions arising in controversy between the parties fairly arising out of the suit, would apply to enable, and more than enable, to justify the court in deciding the question of the valid execution of the power. If it had before it the only parties who were interested in the decision, it seems to me that the right 83] course would be not *to leave it open for the decision of another court, but for the court itself to decide and thus to carry out what appears to me to be the principles of the Judicature Act. But in the case of separate estate, all the parties being necessarily before the court, if there is

(') 5 Moo. P. C., 201.

sufficient evidence before the court of the existence of separate estate, it appears to me that the fact of there being such separate estate, ought to be then decided.   But it does not follow that the court is bound to decide as to every scrap of separate estate or as to the details of what it consists.   It may happen that the court, being satisfied that there is separate estate, finds it difficult, from want of evidence or from questions of foreign law being involved, to decide as to the existence of other portions of separate estate.   In that case it does not appear to me that the court is bound to wait for the decision of those questions, but may properly grant probate, leaving those other questions which cannot then be conveniently decided to be decided at a future period.   I limit my observations as to the duty of the court to decide questions, to those questions which are ready to be and can be conveniently and properly decided between the parties to the pending suit.

Now, applying those considerations to the case before us, what have we here? Lady Hannah Charlotte Tharp was for many years living separate from her husband by reason of the confirmed lunacy of her husband.   The husband was under the care of the persons intrusted by sign manual with the care of lunatics, and was living under medical supervision, which necessarily made a complete separation between the husband and the wife.   The wife was living alone in a house of her own.   The Lord Chancellor in the first instance, and subsequently the Lords Justices for the time being intrusted with the sign manual, directed that a sum of money should be paid annually to the wife for her separate maintenance.   The actual form of the order I take to be immaterial.   The first order simply directed the consignees to pay the money for her separate maintenance, and that was carried out by the payment to her.   The subsequent order of Lord Justice James directed the payment to be made to her, but that does not appear to me to be material.   The substance of the order was that there should be an annual sum allowed her for her separate maintenance *out of the [84 husband's estate.   Was this money her separate property in the sense of being settled to her separate use?   I think it was; in fact I should have said I have no doubt it was.   It cannot be pretended that she was under any liability to expend it in any particular way for her maintenance.   She might have bought furniture, or horses, or carriages, or things which would last for many years, intending to enjoy the things so purchased from year to year.   She might have determined to buy in one year things which were to be paid for in the next, or to be paid for over a series of years. She might have bought a piano upon the well-known system by which the payments are distributed over a very considerable period of time. Is there any doubt or question that that property so acquired would have been her own separate property? In fact, in equity we are familiar with the two forms of allowance for maintenance. One is where the allowance is a sum certain for maintenance, that means that the sum is to be paid to the guardian or person entitled to receive the maintenance absolutely; and the other is where it is intended that no more shall be paid than that which is actually required, the form is to allow a sum not exceeding such a sum for maintenance. That is to avoid the inconvenience of having to call upon the payee to refund. In my opinion it is impossible to suppose that it was intended by the persons making these orders that there should be any refunding on the part of the receiver of the amount which she actually expended in the course of the year. As regards the right of the husband, his right was bound by the order of the judge, who had the control over the affairs of the lunacy precisely to the same extent as if the husband himself had been sane and made the allowance upon the same terms. That being so, there is authority precisely going to the extent that an allowance to the wife for her maintenance living separate from her husband becomes separate property and cannot be recovered by the husband during his lifetime, or by his representatives after his decease. It appears to me, therefore, that the only difference, if difference it be (and I am not sure there is a difference), between myself and the learned judge below, is that I think it clearly proved that this was property settled to the separate use of the wife, whereas he may perhaps have thought it was proved only *prima facie*, subject to rebuttal.

85] *That being so, it seems to me that the granting of the probate was right. As to the form of it, it appears to be the settled practice that where one power is proved you grant the probate not only with reference to that particular power, but extend it to all the other powers possessed by the married woman. Following the analogy, if you found that the married woman had some estate settled to her separte use, you would grant probate generally to all property that she had power to dispose of, and which was settled to her separate use. Therefore it does not appear to me to be necessary to go further.

But in this instance another question has been raised; and following out the principles which I have enunciated, if I

thought that question ready for decision, I should certainly
now give my opinion upon it, so as to settle all matters between the parties; and then I think it would be convenient,
if the court had come to a decision upon all questions between the parties, that the order should recite what had
been decided so as to conclude the parties, or if they did not
elect to be concluded, to enable them to appeal from the
order, or from so much of the order as contained what they
thought was an erroneous recital.

The second question is this. It appears that Lady Elizabeth Gavin, a relative of the testatrix, wrote a letter dated
the 24th of April, 1822, to her daughter, which, as the law
then stood was a good will. [His Lordship read the letter.]
Now, if this were an English woman domiciled in England,
looking at the circumstances of the case that, at the date
when the letter was written, Lady Hannah Tharp was living
separately from her husband, who was an incurable lunatic,
and that the letter recites that she was without a possibility
of anything to subsist upon, I should say that that annuity
was left her for subsistence, and, consequently, would be
for her separate use; but, inasmuch as it does not appear
that Lady Elizabeth Gavin was domiciled in England, or
that the will must be construed according to English law, I
think that in the absence of evidence it would be improper
to express a final opinion as to the effect of the bequest
contained in that letter, and it must be left for the court in
Scotland to decide. If there were no other means of deciding it, I think it might not have been improper for the case
to have stood over to *have further evidence adduced   [86
before the Court of Probate as to the domicile of Lady Elizabeth Gavin, and also as to the law of Scotland if the domicile should be proved to be Scotch. I find that on the 20th
of June, 1873, there was a multiplepoinding action raised in
the Scotch court, which is now pending, which will in fact
determine this very question, for almost the entirety of the
property of this lady is situate in Scotland, and the Scotch
court will therefore decide it directly, and it appears to me
more convenient than the English court deciding it; because
if it turns out to be a Scotch domicile you will have a Scotch
court deciding upon the Scotch law, and seems to me a
better course where it can be pursued than sending it from
England to the Scotch court for the Scotch court to determine as to the law. It seems to me that the most probable
result will be that it is a Scotch domicile, and, therefore,
looking to these circumstances, it seems to me it is more
convenient to let the Scotch action proceed and the matter

be determined there, and that we are not called upon to decide this additional question which it is not absolutely necessary to determine in order to affirm the grant of probate by the judge of the Court of Probate.

Under all the circumstances, it appears to me that the judgment of the court below should be affirmed.

BAGGALLAY, L.J., after referring to the pleadings in the suit, and to the order in lunacy, proceeded as follows: It appears to me impossible, having regard to the various decisions upon similar questions, to do otherwise than to hold that, so far as any portions of the accumulations of the allowance made to the testatrix for her separate maintenance were concerned, they were within the jurisdiction of the Court of Probate—that they were separate estate, in respect of which she had power to dispose not only in her lifetime, but by her will, and that as regards such property her will was a testamentary document which ought to have been admitted to probate.

An argument has been raised before us to the effect, if I rightly understand Mr. Inderwick's argument, that Sir R. Phillimore ought to have found in form and in terms that she had separate estate within the jurisdiction. I certainly 87]   read the order made *by the learned judge in the action as involving that statement. In the course of the argument before him, Mr. Inderwick having asked him to find as a fact that there was a *prima facie* case of separate estate made out, there being an accumulation from her separate property, Sir Robert Phillimore is stated to have used these words: "Certainly I find that I grant probate upon this ground, that, *prima facie*, she had a separate estate and power to bequeath it, and then I confine probate to such effects as she is found to have the power of disposing of." That is to say, having regard to the orders made in the lunacy, directing the payment of these sums of money to Lady Hannah Tharp for her separate estate, and to the payments made under them, there was a *prima facie* case, and no case to rebut it nor any attempt to rebut it by evidence to the contrary effect. I think that Sir Robert Phillimore did in effect find that there was separate estate, and finding that there was separate estate he made the order against which the present appeal is brought.

As far as regards the other separate estate alleged to have resulted from the accumulation of the £500 a year which this lady seems to have enjoyed under a certain letter addressed by Lady Elizabeth Gavin to her daughter, who was interested in her estate, requesting her to pay £500 a year to this lady for the rest of her life, or until she should marry again, which was, in the result, for the rest of her life, I do not think we are called upon to express any opinion upon it. I think it would be very undesirable that the matter should come before the Scotch court with the expression of any opinion of ours upon it. The accumulations from the other fund are sufficient to support the order which Sir Robert Phillimore made.

BRAMWELL, L.J.: I think that this order should be affirmed. Upon the question whether there was any separate personal estate arising from the husband's money I shall say nothing, except that it seems to me that Mr. Inderwick's admission in the course of his argument, if that she had died indebted her creditors would have had a right to it, is almost fatal. I say no more upon that, and I say nothing about the property got from the Scotch lady.

I wish, however, to say that I have some doubt whether the *learned judge upon the case presented to him [88 could, and consequently whether he did, adjudicate finally upon the question of there being separate estate, so as to bind the parties to the litigation. I have no doubt, if the question had been properly presented to him, he would have had jurisdiction to do so, because every one of the divisions, and every judge, has now jurisdiction under the Judicature Act to do that which might be done by any other division or any other judge, and it seems to me that if the action could have been brought in the High Court for the purpose of having a declaration as to the title to this property, such a case as that might have been presented to the learned judge of the Probate Court, and he might have adjudicated upon it. But I have a doubt as to whether he could have done it upon the present materials, for this reason—all that is asked on behalf of the defendant is that probate of the will might be granted. Now the 7th sub-section of section 24 says that the High Court of Justice "shall have power to grant, and shall grant either absolutely or on such reasonable terms and conditions as to them shall seem just, all such remedies whatsoever as any of the parties thereto may appear to be entitled to in respect of any and every legal or equitable claim properly brought forward by them respectively in such cause or matter." Now the legal and equitable claim brought before the Probate Division was the right to probate as it seems to me. The section then goes on to say, "so that as far as possible all matters *so* in controversy," not "all matters in controversy between the parties," but "so in controversy," and therefore you

must look to what the claim is, in order to see whether there
is a controversy before you can determine upon what it is
the learned judge can adjudicate. I doubt very much
whether he could have adjudicated upon this case finally
between the parties. Possibly if the pleadings had contained
a prayer for a declaration as to' the rights he might have
done it, but I doubt very much whether he could have done
it upon the pleadings as they stand, and I doubt, with all
respect, whether he has done so. I doubt whether it would
not be competent for any of Mr. Inderwick's clients to say,
"There is no adjudication against me with respect to any
particular property, and I am at liberty, therefore, to contest generally that it decides the case as to any particular
89] *property at all." But it would obviously be very
convenient that there should be an adjudication as to the
particular property because, supposing the learned judge to
do what he seems to have thought he was bound to do and
no more, that is to say, to grant probate, if there was a
prima facie case made out upon the case presented to him,
this inconvenience follows,—that one tribunal half hears the
question, if I may so say, and half decides it, holding that
there is a *prima facie* case; and another tribunal is to re-
hear that half, and to hear the other half to decide finally
between the parties. It is obviously an inconvenience attended with expense for no good that I can see. But there
is this to be said in favor of what the learned judge has done
here, that in no one of the cases, where there has been an
adjudication orally by the judge as to the rights between
the parties, has the decree been drawn up in such a way as
in my opinion to form an estoppel. All that has been done
is to say that probate should be granted. I am satisfied
that the judge was right in granting probate, and I doubt
very much, upon the question presented by the pleadings
and otherwise, whether more could have been done by the
learned judge in the court below.

JESSEL, M.R.: The order may be drawn up in this form:
This court being of opinion that the savings of the allowance made to the testatrix under the lunacy form part of
her separate estate, affirm the order of Sir R. Phillimore,
without prejudice to any question as to the savings of the
£500 annuity.

Solicitors: *Bridger & Collins; Frere, Forster & Frere.*

[3 Probate Division, 90.]

Feb. 25, 1878.

*THE PRINCETON (O. 55, Liv.).   [90

Collision—Compulsory Pilotage in the Mersey—Mersey Docks Consolidation Act, 1858 (21 & 22 Vict. c. xcii), s. 128—Merchant Shipping Act, 1854 (17 & 18 Vict. c. 104), s. 388.

A duly qualified Liverpool pilot having been employed to pilot a ship from sea into the Mersey and take her into dock, piloted her over the bar, but owing to the state of the tide being unable to dock her that day, anchored her in a clear berth in the river. The pilot remained in charge of the ship, and the next day the state of the weather being such as to render it unadvisable to take her into dock that day, she remained at anchor. In the course of that day, and whilst the pilot was in charge, the ship dragged her anchor and came into collision with a bark. In an action instituted by the owner of the bark against the ship the court decided that the collision was caused solely by the negligence of the pilot in charge of the ship:

Held, that the owners of the ship were not answerable for the damage, for it was occasioned by the fault of a pilot acting in charge of the ship within a district where the employment of such pilot was compulsory by law.

THIS was an action of damage instituted on the 26th of January in this year, on behalf of the owner of the Dutch bark Twee Zusters against the American ship Princeton.

The statement of claim contained the following allegations:

1. About 4.15 A.M. on the 25th of January, 1878, the Twee Zusters, of 375 tons register, was lying at anchor in a proper berth in the river Mersey. Her proper anchor lights were duly exhibited and burning brightly, and a proper watch was kept.

3. At such time the ship Princeton, which had been lying at anchor at a distance of about 150 fathoms and to the eastward and southward, was observed to have broken her sheer and to be driving partly athwart the tide, and to be approaching the port-bow of the Twee Zusters. Chain was thereupon paid out on both anchors, and the helm of the Twee Zusters was hard a-ported; but notwithstanding the Princeton drove foul of and carried away the jibboom and cathead of the Twee Zusters, and did other damage.

4. During the following flood the Princeton, although nearer to the Twee Zusters than on the previous flood, kept clear of the Twee Zusters, but at about 6 P.M., the tide being ebb and running about three knots an hour, and the wind being a gale from N.W. to N.N.W., and the Twee Zusters lying head up the river with a sheer to the westward, the Princeton, which had previously been observed to be ranging about, again broke her sheer and started, driving athwart the tide, and drove down upon the port-bow of the

Twee Zusters, and although the helm of the Twee Zusters
was put hard-a-port, the Princeton with her starboard side
struck the Twee Zusters on the port-bow and did her considerable damage.

9. The said collisions and the damages consequent thereon
were occasioned by the neglect or default of those on board
the Princeton.

91] *The defendants, the owners of the Princeton, delivered a statement of defence and counter-claim. Such
statement denied the material fact alleged in the statement
of claim, and, after setting forth the defendant's version of
the facts and stating that the defendant's ship was in charge
of a duly qualified pilot, proceeded as follows:

10. The said collisions were occasioned by the negligence
of the plaintiff or of those on board the Twee Zusters.

11. The defendants further say that if and so far as the
said collisions or either of them respectively were or was
occasioned by any neglect on the part of those on board the
Princeton, such collisions respectively were solely occasioned
by some default or incapacity on the part of the said pilot,
who was a duly qualified pilot acting in charge of the
Princeton within a district where the employment of such
pilot was compulsory by law, within the true intent and
meaning of s. 388 of the Merchant Shipping Act, 1854, and
not by any neglect on the part of the master or crew of the
Princeton.

By way of counter-claim the defendants rely upon the
matters hereinbefore alleged, and say that by reason of the
said collisions they have suffered great loss and damage.

Feb. 22, 23, 25. The case was heard before the judge,
assisted by two of the Elder Brethren of the Trinity Corporation.

Butt, Q.C., and *Myburgh*, appeared for the plaintiff.
Milward, Q.C., and *E. C. Clarkson*, for the defendants.

Witnesses on behalf of the plaintiff and the defendants
were examined orally in court. The following facts were
proved by the witnesses called on behalf of the defendants:

The pilot who was on deck and in charge of the Princeton
on the occasion of both the first and the second collision,
and who remained in charge of her until she was taken into
dock, was taken on board off the Orme's Head, in order to
pilot her into the Mersey and into dock, and having taken
charge of her, piloted her into the river, and brought her
to anchor on the evening of the 24th of January, on the ebb

tide, about an hour after high water. If the Princeton had arrived in the river before high water that evening she would have been docked that tide. On the 25th of January the weather was so rough that the master of the Princeton, after consultation with the pilot, determined not to dock on the morning tide. The Princeton was taken into dock on the 26th of January. The pilot of the Princeton was paid for two extra days' detention in the river.

SIR ROBERT PHILLIMORE: One of the vessels that came into collision in this case was the Twee Zusters, a Dutch vessel of 375 tons register, and heavily laden. She had anchored on the *23d of January in this year, in a proper [92 berth, in the river Mersey, to the westward of mid-river, and had dropped both her anchors, the starboard one with forty-five fathoms of chain and the port one with sixty fathoms of chain. The other vessel was an American ship called the Princeton, of no less than 1,349 tons register, and laden with a cargo of cotton. Previous to the collision she was lying in a proper berth abreast of the Bramley-Moore Dock, where she had dropped her starboard bower anchor with seventy fathoms of chain. The Twee Zusters had anchored twenty-four hours earlier than the Princeton. It was admitted, and was proved by the evidence in this case, that in coming to anchor neither of the vessels gave the other a foul berth, there having been at that time at least a distance of a cable's length between them ; but, nevertheless, they came into collision twice. It is admitted that whichever of the two vessels was to blame for the first collision was to blame for the second, because the giving of a foul berth, which caused the first collision, was the occasion of the second collision. The first collision occurred by the jibboom of the Twee Zusters coming into contact with the starboard side of the Princeton, and, on the evidence, it is plain that the collision must have been caused by one of the two vessels dragging on the ebb tide ; the wind at the time blowing in the opposite direction to the set of the tide.

The main question which the court has discussed with the Elder Brethren is, which of the two vessels dragged? After careful consideration of the evidence, which is contradictory on the point, we think that on the whole it establishes that the Twee Zusters remained at her anchors, and that the Princeton drove down upon her. We are clearly of opinion that the pilot in charge of the Princeton ought to have let go the second anchor as a precaution which the state of the weather imperatively demanded. We think

that the collision was caused by the dragging of the an- ·
chor of the Princeton, to prevent which proper measures
were not taken.   I therefore pronounce the Princeton alone
to blame.

Butt, Q.C., on behalf of the plaintiff, then submitted that
as no evidence had been given to prove that any report had
been made to the pilot that the Princeton was dragging, that
the master and crew of the Princeton were to blame for the
93]   collision, and *that the defendants had not proved the
11th paragraph of the defence.

SIR ROBERT PHILLIMORE :   The Elder Brethren are
clearly of opinion that the pilot of the Princeton ought
himself to have seen that the Princeton was dragging her
anchor and to have ordered the second anchor to be dropped.   I decide, therefore, that the collisions were solely
attributable to the negligence of the pilot in charge of the
Princeton.

The question whether the pilot of the Princeton had been
at the time of the collisions in charge of the Princeton by
compulsion of law was then argued by counsel.

Butt, Q.C., and *Myburgh*, for the plaintiff :   The only
enactment now in force which deals with the question of
compulsory pilotage in the Mersey is the Mersey Docks
Consolidation Act, 1858, and the combined effect of the
128th, the 130th, and the 138th sections of that act (') is, that
the masters of all inward bound vessels other than coasting
vessels in ballast or under the burden of 100 tons, are bound
94]   by compulsion of law to employ a licensed *pilot to

(') 21 & 22 Vict. c. xcii, s. 128 :
"The pilot in charge of any inward
bound vessel shall cause the same (if
need be) to be properly moored at anchor in the river Mersey, and shall pilot
the same into some of the wet docks
within the port of Liverpool, whether
belonging to the board or not, without
making any additional charge for so
doing, unless his attendance shall be
required on board such vessel while at
anchor in the river Mersey, and before
going into dock, in which case he shall
be entitled to receive five shillings per
day for such attendance."
Sect. 130 : "In case the master of
any inward bound vessel other than a
coasting vessel in ballast or under the
burden of one hundred tons shall refuse
to take on board or employ a pilot, such
pilot having offered his services for that
purpose, such master shall pay to such

pilot . . . the full pilotage rates which
would have been payable to him if he
had actually piloted such vessel into
the port of Liverpool."
Sect. 138 : "If the master of any
vessel shall require the attendance of
a pilot on board any vessel during her
riding at anchor, or being at Hoylake
or in the river Mersey, the pilot so
employed shall be paid for every day
or portion of a day he shall so attend
the sum of five shillings and no more,
provided that the pilot who shall have
the charge of any vessel shall be paid
for every day of his attendance whilst
in the river ; but no such charge shall
be made for the day on which such
vessel, being outward bound, shall
leave the river Mersey to commence her
voyage, or being inward bound shall
enter the river Mersey."

pilot them into the Mersey, or into dock, but that they are
not bound to employ any pilot at all on any day after the
day of their arrival in the river.   In the case of an inward
bound vessel, the compulsion to employ a pilot ceases as
soon as the vessel has been brought to an anchor, or at least
at the end of the day of her arrival in the river, and the employment of a pilot does not again become compulsory until
the vessel is actually in motion on her way to her dock:
The Annapolis ('); *The Woburn Abbey* (').   It is in evidence that the pilot of the Princeton was paid the extra sum
of 5s. a day in respect of his detention on board the Princeton after she had come to her berth.   This extra payment
was made in pursuance of the provisions of the first part of
the 138th section above referred to, and it is clear from the
judgment of the Judicial Committee of the Privy Council in
the recent case of *The City of Cambridge* ('), that the provisions with respect to extra payments in that section relate
to voluntary pilotage only.

The policy of the law is not in favor of compulsory
pilotage, and statutes relating to it must be strictly construed.   If the contention of the defendants that pilotage
was compulsory in this case is a right contention, it would
equally hold that however long the Princeton might have
remained in the river without docking, so long her owners
would be exempted from all liability provided she was
placed under the charge of a qualified' pilot, all of whose
orders were obeyed.

Milward, Q.C., and *E. C. Clarkson*, for the defendants:
It is unnecessary for the defendants to contend that however long might have been the interval between the Princeton's entering the river, and her going into dock, her owners
would still be successful on a plea of compulsory pilotage.
It is enough for them to show that in the present case the
pilot of the Princeton was employed to perform an entire
duty, to pilot' the Princeton into the Mersey and take her
into dock, and that the collisions occurred during the performance of that duty.   It cannot be that the defendants
are to be held liable because through accidental circumstances the actual docking has not been completed as soon
as it otherwise would have been.

*It is clear, on the evidence, that it was from acci- [95
dental circumstances that the Princeton was not docked on
the day of her arrival in the river.   She was prevented from
being docked before the collision by the lateness of her ar-

(¹) Lush., 295. (³) Law Rep., 5 P. C., 451; 9 Eng. R.
(²) 38 L. J. (Adm.), 28. 256.

rival on the 23d of January and the state of the weather on the morning of the 24th of January. There is, therefore, a strong analogy between the circumstances of this case and those of the case of the *City of Cambridge* ('). In the present case the detention of the Princeton in the river was a step in her progress into dock, and the Princeton being still *in itinere* to her dock it must follow that she had not at the time of these collisions ceased to be liable to compulsory pilotage.

Myburgh, in reply.

SIR ROBERT PHILLIMORE: I must take as facts to which the law is to be applied in this case that a duly qualified Liverpool pilot was taken on board the Princeton under an engagement to pilot that vessel to her mooring place, and subsequently to take her into dock, and that in the discharge of that engagement the pilot had moored her for the night, meaning to take her on the next day into dock. That on the next morning the weather was such as in his judgment to render it unsafe to proceed that day into dock, and that he so advised the master, and, in consequence, the vessel did not go into dock. On that day the collisions happened. The question arises, whether, having regard to the provisions of the Mersey Dock Consolidation Act, 1858, and especially to the provisions of the 128th and the 138th sections, the Princeton remained under the charge of her pilot by compulsion of law during the interval between coming to anchor and docking.

It is not necessary that I should do more than refer to the cases of *The Annapolis* (') *The Woburn Abbey* (') and *The City of Cambridge* ( ), in support of the view I take. Looking at the principle to be extracted from those cases, and giving a reasonable interpretation to the 138th section of the act of Parliament I have referred to, I am of opinion that 96]   the Princeton was, when the *collision occurred, still under the charge of a compulsory pilot who had been taken on board by compulsion of law. To hold otherwise would be, in my opinion, to put a harsh construction on the statute. The ship was *in itinere*, and in her progress to dock, at the time when she came into collision with the Twee Zusters. There was no discontinuance of the engagement of the pilot, or the substitution of a voluntary for a compulsory service.

The circumstances of the case are, it must be remembered, that this vessel was compelled to remain where she was by

(¹) Law Rep., 5 P. C., 451 ; 9 Eng. R.,   (²) 38 L. J. (Adm.) 28.
256.   (⁴) Law Rep. 4 A. & E., 161 ; 5 P. C.,
(³) Lush, 295.   -   451 ; 9 Eng. R., 256

vis major. If she could have gone into dock, but did not do so, I am not prepared to say I should consider that she was entitled to the immunity which I am of opinion in the circumstances she is entitled to. My decision in this case entirely depends on the special facts before me. I think that the pilot was still in charge of the vessel at the time of the collisions. With regard to the contention that the sum of 5*s.* a day received by the pilot was a voluntary pilotage charge, that argument has already been disposed of by the judgment of the Judicial Committee of the Privy Council in the case of *The City of Cambridge*(¹), and the reception of it would not affect the construction I put upon the act. I pronounce that the Princeton was under the charge of a pilot taken on board by compulsion of law and employed under compulsion of law at the time the collisions with the Twee Zusters happened. There will be no costs on either side.

Solicitors for plaintiff: *Bateson & Co.*
Solicitors for defendants: *Duncan, Hill & Dickinson.*

(¹) Law Rep., 4 A. & E., 161 ; 5 P. C., 451 ; 9 Eng. R., 256.

See 18 Eng. Rep., 82 note ; Matter of the Matthew Cay, 5 Prob. Div., 49, post, p. 289

Where the employment of a pilot is compulsory, neither the vessel nor its owner is liable for his negligence.

Otherwise, if not compulsory: The Killarney, Lush. Adm., 427.

Under the English statutes in relation to compulsory pilotage in the port of Liverpool, an owner of a vessel is not relieved from liability for damage to freight unless a pilot was in charge under the act, and was actually and necessarily engaged in the discharge of his duty. Where, therefore, a vessel had left its dock at Liverpool in charge of a pilot, and anchored in the river Mersey to finish loading and to receive coal for a voyage to New York ; and while at anchor an accident oc-

curred causing the loss: Held, that the owner was not excused from liability by said statutes : Guiterman v. Liverpool, etc., 88 N. Y., 358, reversing 9 Daly, 119.

A butcher employed a licensed drover to drive home a bullock, which he had purchased, from Smithfield market. The drover's boy, by his negligent driving, allowed the bullock to run into a shop, whereby damage was done to the goods therein. Held, that the owner of the bullock was not liable for the damage so done : Milligan v. Wedge, 12 Ad. & Ell., 737, 4 Per. & Dav., 714, Arn. & Hodges, Q. B., 73.

As to liability of a vessel for pilotage of a pilot offering his services but not employed: Schooner Small, 8 Ben., 523.

[3 Probate Division, 97.]

Feb. 26, 1878.

97]   *THE WILLIAMINA proceeded against as THE WIL-HELMINA (O. 184).

Collision—Admission of Liability—Reference to Registrar and Merchants—County Courts Admiralty Jurisdiction Act, 1868 (31 & 32 Vict. c. 71), s. 9—Certificate for Costs.

The defendants in an action for damage, before any statement of claim had been delivered, admitted their liability for the damage proceeded for, and by consent the question of amount was by an order of court referred to the registrar and merchants to report thereon. At the reference before the registrar the plaintiffs claimed as damages £295 18s. 1d. The registrar reported to the court that there was due to the plaintiffs £199 18s. 6d.

Afterwards the plaintiffs moved the judge to condemn the defendants in the costs of the action and of the reference. Evidence was given on affidavit in support of the motion to the effect that the plaintiffs at the time their action was instituted were liable to a claim for salvage in respect of services rendered to their vessel after the collision, and that subsequently and before the reference £60 had been paid and accepted in settlement of such claim:

Held, that the court had jurisdiction to certify that the case was a fit case to be tried before it, and that the proper order to be made was that the plaintiffs should have the costs of the action, but that each party should bear their own costs of the reference.

[3 Probate Division, 145.]

April 16, 1878.

145]   *THE CLEOPATRA (D. 364).

Salvage—Derelict—Amount of Award—Apportionment.

A vessel constructed entirely for the purpose of conveying the obelisk known as Cleopatra's Needle from Alexandria to England, was, with the obelisk on board her, abandoned in the Bay of Biscay by her master and crew, and by the steamship employed to tow her to England, and the next day was found floating on her beam ends about ninety miles northeast of Ferrol by another steamship, which succeeded in towing her into Ferrol in safety.

Subsequently an action of salvage was instituted to determine the amount of salvage remuneration to be paid to the salvors for the services rendered, and bail was given in the action in the sum of £5,000. By the consent of all parties, the judge in court fixed the value of the property salved at £25,000.

At the hearing of the action, the court awarded £2,000 as salvage remuneration to the plaintiffs, and on a subsequent application apportioned the award as follows: £1,200 to the owner of the salving vessel ; £250 to her master, and the residue to be distributed among her crew according to their rating, and services as salvors.

THIS was an action of salvage, in which the plaintiff, John Dixon, the owner of the Cleopatra and the contractor for the conveyance of the obelisk known as Cleopatra's Needle from Egypt to the Thames, claimed that the court should adjudicate upon a dispute between himself and the owner, master, and crew of the steamship Fitzmaurice, with respect to the salvage remuneration to be awarded for salvage services rendered in October last, when the Cleopatra, with the obelisk on board, had been found by the Fitzmaurice derelict in the Bay of Biscay, and had been taken in tow by that vessel and towed in safety into the port of Ferrol.

On the 30th of November the owner, master, and crew, of the Fitzmaurice appeared in the action, and on the 19th of December Mr. Dixon, who had in the meantime delivered a statement of claim, put in bail to answer judgment in the sum of £5,000.

On the 5th of April the salvors delivered their statement of defence. Such statement of defence, after alleging that at the time of the services rendered the value of the Fitzmaurice, her cargo, and freight, was £10,778 or thereabouts, and setting forth the details of such services proceeded, in substance, as follows:

40. By the services of the defendants the Cleopatra and the Needle on board her were saved from total loss, and the plaintiff has been enabled to earn the *freight or the [146 reward payable to him for the carriage of the Needle from Alexandria to England.

41. The said services were of a very difficult and arduous nature, and in rendering them the Fitzmaurice and her master and crew incurred great danger.

43. The said Needle was and is of great value. The freight or reward payable to the plaintiff for the carriage of the Needle to England, amounted to the sum of £10,000.

44. The plaintiff admits that he is liable to the defendants in respect of all their services, including their services to the Needle itself.

Mr. Dixon, in his reply, admitted the 44th paragraph of the statement of defence, but denied the truth of the allegations contained in the 43d paragraph, and alleged in substance that he had contracted at his own expense and risk to transport the obelisk to London and erect the same uninjured in a vertical position in one piece, together with certain adjuncts, on a site to be agreed upon on or before the 1st of January, 1879; that on, and not before the due completion of the above contract, he was to be paid a consideration of £10,000; that at the time of the services rendered by the salvors, he had incurred expenses in or about the transportation of the obelisk, amounting to the sum of £6,983 13s. 3d., and that the total cost of transporting and erecting the obelisk in accordance with the terms agreed on, would amount to the sum of £15,000 or thereabouts.

On the 5th of March, counsel on behalf of the salvors moved the judge in court to order an appraisement of the Cleopatra and the obelisk, and after some discussion it was arranged, with the consent of counsel, that the question as to the value of the vessel and the obelisk should be referred to the judge, who thereupon directed that the value thereof for the purposes of the action, should be taken at the sum of £25,000.

March 30 ; April 1.   On these days the action was heard before the judge, assisted by two of the Elder Brethren of the Trinity House.

Witnesses were examined orally in court.

Sir Henry James, Q.C., and *E. C. Clarkson*, for the owners, master, and crew of the Fitzmaurice.

Butt, Q.C., *G. Bruce* and *Hollams*, for Mr. Dixon.

The result of the evidence can be gathered from the judgment.

Cur. adv. vult.

147]   *April 6.   SIR ROBERT PHILLIMORE :   In this case, in order to avoid confusion between the term plaintiff and defendant, it is proper to observe that the action is brought by the owner of the salved property, seeking, under the 460th section of the Merchant Shipping Act, 1854, to have the salvage services rendered to his property adjudicated upon by the court.   The Fitzmaurice, a screw steamship of 297 tons register, was proceeding on her voyage from Middlesborough to Valencia with a cargo of pig iron, and a crew of sixteen hands, when on the 15th of October, 1877, between five and six in the evening, about ninety miles northeast of Ferrol, a port on the northwest coast of Spain, her look-out reported some object floating to leeward, apparently the wreck of a vessel.   The weather was very heavy, and there was a very high sea running at the time.   The Fitzmaurice made towards the object, which was discovered to be the Cleopatra lying on her port beam ends, and abandoned by her crew.   The Cleopatra was a vessel built in compartments, about ninety-five feet long from stem to stern, the breadth of her beam being fifteen feet.   The obelisk on board her weighed 187 tons.   The Cleopatra was constructed entirely for the purpose of conveying the obelisk from Egypt to England.   She was, as described in the ninth paragraph of the statement of defence, "like a ship's boiler with a bridge in the middle."   There was ballast con-

sisting of railway iron weighing about twenty tons, which
was put in merely to trim the ship fore and aft.

According to the evidence of the captain of the Cleopatra,
she had been towed by the steamer Olga from Alexandria
to about 132 miles N.N.E. of Cape Finisterre. The weather,
previously to the 14th of October, had been extremely tempestuous, and on that day the Olga was obliged to cast off
the tow rope of the Cleopatra. The Cleopatra had rolled
and pitched so much that it was with great difficulty that
the iron rails were partially replaced. She made no water.
Her captain said that he stood by her to the very last moment,
and abandoned her only on the 15th of October, when he
saw the greatest danger threatening himself and his crew.
On Monday morning the boat of the Cleopatra was hauled
by means of ropes to the side of the Olga, and her crew were
put in safety on board that vessel. It is a most melancholy
incident in the case *that the Olga during the night [148
had sent a boat with six men to the Cleopatra, all of whom
were lost, and the boat apparently missed the ship, and must
have been swamped in the tremendous sea that was then running. Those on board the Olga, concluding the Cleopatra to
have foundered, went on to Falmouth.

It was about six o'clock in the evening of the 15th that
the Fitzmaurice came up to the Cleopatra, which was then
lying on her port beam ends, and, to use the expression of
the master of the Fitzmaurice, with her bridge continually
" swashing into the water " every roll she made. The master ordered the chief officer to get the boats ready, but he
remonstrated so strongly upon the danger that would be incurred that the order was recalled, and there were no volunteers for the service that night. The Fitzmaurice steamed
close up to the Cleopatra, and kept her in sight all night.
About six o'clock next morning a boat was got ready, but
the crew were very reluctant to embark in her. At last
three of them, with the chief officer, volunteered, and a boat
was put overboard, in which they pulled round the Cleopatra. There was a very heavy sea. The Cleopatra was
continually "slapping her bridge into the water," and was
on her beam ends as on the night before. Two of the men
rowed and two made ready to jump on her bridge, which
was their only chance of getting on board her, on account of
the peculiar construction of her deck. After a series of vain
attempts for upwards of an hour and a half, the chief officer
at last succeeded in getting on board the Cleopatra. A deep
sea line was then got on board the Cleopatra, and fastened
to the hawser of the Fitzmaurice. The difficulty of the op-

eration was greatly enhanced by the fact that the Cleopatra had a circular as well as a rolling motion. This was a consequence of her rudder head being broken off, and the chain having become entangled. According to the evidence she went round all the points of the compass four times in fifteen minutes. To this difficulty was added another. A portion of the tow line of the Cleopatra was hanging under water fast to a shackle low down in the stem of the Cleopatra, with a chain bridle attached to it. Both these impediments to the navigation of the Cleopatra were overcome by the skill and courage of the salvors, who, being lashed by a rope to the rail, were often wholly submerged in the water in the pro-
149] cess of clearing away these *obstacles from the stem and stern of the vessel. No less than three times volunteers were mustered on deck to perform these services, which at last being completely successful, and two hawsers having been made fast to the Fitzmaurice, the Fitzmaurice, after undergoing various minor misadventures, brought the Cleopatra in safety to Ferrol on Wednesday, the 17th of October, about 9 P.M., making fifty-two hours' service from the time the Cleopatra was first seen at 5.30 P.M. on Monday the 15th of October, and a towage of ninety-three miles.

A good deal has been said on the subject of the nominal plaintiff's but real defendant's position in this court. It is not denied that so far as this case is concerned he is to be considered as owner of the salved property with all the liabilities incident to it. Much eulogy has been bestowed by counsel on both sides upon his generous patriotism in securing for his native country, perhaps at considerable expense to himself, this interesting historical monument. I have no doubt that Mr. Dixon deserves all the praise which has been given him, and I hope that measures will be taken to make good any pecuniary loss which he may incur in consequence of this suit ; but I cannot allow any consideration of the kind to influence my award of salvage. The salvors have done bravely and well a difficult and dangerous work, and have a right to be well remunerated. The principles upon which such remuneration is awarded are well known in this court, but having regard to the arguments of counsel it may be as well to re-state them in this instance. Perhaps the language of that experienced and learned judge, Sir John Nicholl, in the case of *The Clifton* (¹) contains as good a summary of these principles as can be found. In delivering judgment in that case he said :

(¹) 3 Hagg., 117, 120.

Now salvage is not always a mere compensation for work and labor ; various circumstances upon public considerations, the interests of commerce, the benefit and security of navigation, the lives of the seamen, render it proper to estimate a salvage reward upon a more enlarged and liberal scale. The ingredients of a salvage service are, first, enterprise in the salvors in going out in tempestuous weather to assist a vessel in distress, risking their own lives to save their fellow creatures, and to rescue the property of their fellow subjects ; secondly, the degree of danger and distress from which the property is rescued—whether it were in imminent peril, and almost certainly lost, if not at the time rescued and preserved ; *thirdly, the degree of labor and skill which the salvors incur [150 and display, and the time occupied. Lastly, the value. Where all these circumstances concur, a large and liberal reward ought to be given ; but where none or scarcely any take place, the compensation can hardly be denominated a salvage compensation, it is little more than a mere remuneration *pro opere et labore.*

The peculiar character of the property salved presented some difficulty in the application of the last of these elements of salvage remuneration. In ordinary cases the marketable value of the property salved is easily ascertained. It is estimated, and, if necessary, appraised by skilled persons. It cannot be said perhaps with strict truth that this obelisk has no marketable value. In the affidavit of Mr. Burrell, the owner of the Fitzmaurice, now before me, which has not been answered, it is credibly stated that Glasgow and other great cities, to say nothing of the towns in America, would be willing to give large sums for the possession of this remarkable monument of antiquity; but still the marketable value of it for the purposes of this action was not easily ascertained. It was agreed by both parties, without any suggestion from me, that the value of the property salved should be fixed by the court.

Apart from the consideration of the mere immediate marketable value, I have had to bear in mind the æsthetic, if I may use the term, value of the object. Its antiquity is undoubted, at least I am informed the inscriptions testify to its existence not less than sixteen hundred years before the birth of our Lord. It was transferred from On to Alexandria by the Emperor Augustus, and obtained its name of Cleopatra's Needle in honor of that memorable queen. To appraise the value of such an object as so much granite would be as absurd as, in the case of the salvage of a painting by Raffaelle or of a sculpture by Michael Angelo, to estimate the value at the cost of the canvas and frame in the former, or of the mere marble in the latter, case. The obelisk is an object which if once lost could never be replaced. It is a unique historical monument; within eighteen inches of the height of the Luxor Obelisk in the Place de la Concorde at Paris, which is said to have cost the French Government not less than £80,000. Taking these things into consideration I fixed the value, on which I have now to make my award, at £25,000.

Bearing in mind that the property was wholly abandoned 151] by the *owner, and that it was saved by great courage, labor, and skill, exhibited in circumstances of considerable peril, and that in the opinion of the Elder Brethren if the Cleopatra had been struck in her derelict state she would certainly have been sunk, besides occasioning great peril to the ship that came in contact with her, I think I shall do right in awarding the sum of £2,000, with costs.

April 16. *E. C. Clarkson*, on behalf of the salvors, moved the judge in court to apportion the sum of £2,000 awarded for salvage in the action.

Hollams, on behalf of Mr. Dixon, applied that leave be given to pay the total amount awarded into the hands of the salvors' solicitors for distribution.

SIR ROBERT PHILLIMORE: I shall make the following apportionment in this case: I award £1,200 to the owner of the Fitzmaurice and £250 to the master of that vessel. There will then remain £550, and this sum is to be divided in shares among the remaining salvors in proportion to their ratings on board the Fitzmaurice.   Double shares are to be allotted to the chief mate and the crew of the boat which first boarded the Cleopatra, with the exception of the man who was slung over the bows of the Cleopatra, and succeeding in clearing away the tow rope by which the Cleopatra had previously been towed.   To this man three shares are to be given.   The total amount of the award may be paid to the solicitors for the salvors for distribution according to the apportionment.   There will be no order as to the costs of this application. ·

Solicitors for Mr. Dixon : *Argles & Rawlins.*
Solicitors for the salvors: *Gellatly, Son & Warton.*

[3 Probate Division, 152.]

June 25, 1878.

152]   *THE NELLY SCHNEIDER.   (1877. W. 294.)

Co-ownership—Sale of Ship in invitum of a Majority of Part-owners—The Admiralty Court Act, 1861 (24 Vict. c. 10), s. 8.

Since the passing of the 8th section of the Admiralty Court Act, 1861, the court has a discretionary power to order the sale of a vessel proceeded against in an action of co-ownership, notwithstanding that the sale is opposed by the majority of the co-owners.

THIS was an action of co-ownership instituted on behalf of John Williams, John Swainson, and William Swainson, against the British vessel Nelly Schneider. An appearance in the action was entered for the remaining part-owners of the vessel, who gave bail to answer judgment in the action. The statement of claim, after stating that the plaintiff, John Williams, was owner of nine sixty-fourths of the Nelly Schneider, and each of the two remaining plaintiffs owners of one sixty-fourth share therein, contained allegations to the effect that in the year 1876, during the building of the Nelly Schneider, the plaintiff, John Williams, had applied to Joseph Fisher, one of the defendants, to be appointed master of the vessel ; that Joseph Fisher was the intended managing owner of the Nelly Schneider, and had promised to appoint John Williams master, provided that the said John Williams would purchase and become the owner of nine sixty-fourth shares in the vessel and find purchasers for three other sixty-fourth shares therein ; that the plaintiff, John Williams, agreed to these terms, and having himself purchased and become owner of nine sixty-fourth shares of the vessel, and procured the plaintiffs, John Swainson and William Swainson, and one of the defendants each to purchase, and become owners of one sixty-fourth share of the vessel respectively, was duly appointed master of the vessel ; but after the vessel had made divers voyages under his command had been wrongfully, and against the wishes of the plaintiffs, John and William Swainson, discharged by the said Joseph Fisher from his employment, though the said John and William Swainson had purchased and become owners of their respective shares in the vessel upon the faith and understanding that the plaintiff, John Williams, was to be her master.

*The statement of claim then proceeded as follows: [153

5. The defendant, Joseph Fisher, has sent the Nelly Schneider upon a voyage not approved of by the plaintiffs.

6. In consequence of the wrongful discharge of the plaintiff, John Williams, he claims and is proceeding in this court for the recovery of damages against the Nelly Schneider.

7. Accounts relating to the ownership and earnings of the Nelly Schneider are outstanding and unsettled between the plaintiffs respectively and the said Joseph Fisher as managing owner of the Nelly Schneider.

8. The plaintiffs respectively do not approve of the Nelly

Schneider being employed otherwise than under the command of the plaintiff John Williams.

The statement of claim concluded by claiming that, in the event of the Nelly Schneider not being brought back to this country pursuant to the bond given in the action, such bond be declared forfeited, and all necessary relief thereon given to the plaintiffs; that the defendants might be ordered to bring the Nelly Schneider back to this country upon the completion of her present voyage; that she might be sold by the marshal and the proceeds of sale divided among her owners in the proportions to which they might be entitled thereto; and that the accounts between the plaintiffs and the defendant, Joseph Fisher, might be referred to the registrar and merchants, and the defendants and their shares in the proceeds of the sale of the vessel condemned in any sums reported due to the plaintiffs respectively.

The defendants, in their statement of defence, denied the allegation in the statement of claim with respect to the terms under which the plaintiff, John Williams, had been appointed master of the Nelly Schneider, and alleged that the discharge of such plaintiff had been done rightfully and for reasonable cause, and, further, that there were no co-ownership accounts relating to the Nelly Schneider outstanding and unsettled, other than such accounts as would be regularly rendered at the end of the then next half year, whilst no application had been made before the institution of the action for any accounts to be rendered or settled.

The 5th paragraph of the statement of defence was in terms as follows:

The defendants submit that this action, except so far as it sought and seeks bail for the safe return of the Nelly Schneider should be dismissed with costs.

On the 3d of April, 1878, an action of wages and disburse-
154]   ments *against the Nelly Schneider, entitled the *Nelly Schneider*, 1877, W. No. 285, being the proceedings referred to in the sixth paragraph of the above-mentioned statement of claim, came on to be heard before the judge in court, and after the plaintiff John Williams, and the above-mentioned John and William Swainson had been called as witnesses, and given evidence in support of the plaintiff's case therein, was adjourned by the court for the purpose of a compromise being arrived at. The evidence then given by the plaintiff, John Williams, in effect went to establish the

truth of the allegations contained in the statement of claim in the present action, whilst the evidence given by John and William Swainson proved in substance that, when they had taken shares in the Nelly Schneider, they had done so under the understanding that the plaintiff was to be the master of the vessel, and that it was contrary to their wishes for him to have been dismissed from his employment as master.

April 4. The present action came on to be heard before the judge in court.

Butt, Q.C., and *E. C. Clarkson*, for the plaintiffs.

Milward, Q.C., and *Bucknill* (*W. G. F. Phillimore* with them), for the defendants.

The plaintiff, John Williams, was called as a witness, and proved that the evidence given by him in the above-mentioned part-heard action of wages and disbursements against the Nelly Schneider was true.

The counsel for the plaintiffs then submitted that the circumstances of the case required that the court should exercise the power conferred on it by the 8th section of the Admiralty Court Act, 1861 (24 Vict. c. 10), and decree a sale of the whole ship in the event of the defendants not being willing to purchase the plaintiffs' shares at a valuation.

The counsel for the defendants declined to consent to such an order being made.

SIR ROBERT PHILLIMORE: The court has full power to decree a sale of the ship, but it will be very reluctant to do so at the instance of part-owners not possessing a majority of shares. In *the present case I think it will be to [155 the interest of all parties to the action that some arrangement should be come to between them. The course suggested by the counsel for the plaintiffs does not seem to be an unreasonable course to adopt, and I shall make this decision in this case: I shall order that a valuation of the shares now held by the plaintiffs in the vessel be made; that a copy of such valuation be filed in the registry, and that thereupon the defendants have the option allowed them of purchasing such shares at the amount fixed by the valuation. If the defendants do not exercise this option within a fortnight, the ship must be appraised and sold by the marshal.

April 5. *Bucknill*, on behalf of the defendants, stated to the court that the defendants were not prepared to exercise the option of purchasing the plaintiffs' shares of the vessel at a valuation.

E. C. Clarkson, on behalf of the plaintiffs, applied for an order of appraisement and sale.

SIR ROBERT PHILLIMORE: The plaintiffs' application must be granted. The vessel will be appraised and sold when she comes back to England after her return from her present voyage.

June 25. The judge, with the consent of the counsel for the plaintiffs and the defendants, directed a warrant to issue for the arrest of the Nelly Schneider, and decreed that she should be appraised and sold.

Solicitors for plaintiffs : *Stokes, Saunders & Stokes.*
Solicitors for defendants : *Ingledew, Ince & Greening.*

As to partition of vessels, see 14 Eng. Rep., 443 note.

Where no other relation exists between the shareholders of a steamboat than that which arises from the joint ownership, they are not partners, nor is their liability to be measured by the rules of law peculiar to partnership relation. Where one of the shareholders sells out his interest in a steamboat, and the bill of sale, in accordance with the acts of Congress, is duly acknowledged and recorded, it is valid notice to all past and subsequent creditors with whom the owners may have contracted: Adams v. Carrol, 85 Penn. St. R., 209.

A., B., C. and D. purchased a steamboat of E. and F., who held a policy upon the property, which they assigned to the parties with the assent of the insurer. D. afterwards sold his interest to A., B., and C., but did not assign his interest in the policy. Held, that A., B., and C., though owners of the whole property insured at the time of the loss, could not recover for the share of D. Part owners of vessels are tenants in common of their several interests: Walker v. Fireman's Ins. Co., 2 Handy, 256.

Where H., P., B. and A., contributed each an equal sum to be expended by H. in building a steamboat, with the understanding that these sums with such credit as he could obtain would enable H. to get her out, and that she should then be run in his name until her debts were paid out of her net earnings, and that he should then convey three-fourths to P., B., and A., retaining one-fourth himself, but that, meanwhile, they should have no interest in her; and there was no agreement to repay the advances in case the enterprise failed, the transaction constitutes a partnership from the beginning, and P., B., and A., are liable for the unpaid debts contracted in building the boat: Lape v. Parvin, 2 Disney (Ohio), 560, 4 Warden Law Gaz., 202.

[3 Probate Division 156.]

July 8, 1878.

156]   *THE HENRY COXON (1878, M. 11).

Evidence—Collision—Non-admissibility in Evidence of log kept by Mate who has subsequently died—Deposition before Receiver of wreck—Merchant Shipping Act (17 & 18 Vict. c. 104) s. 448.

Two vessels, the H. and the G., came into collision on a Saturday; on the Monday morning following the mate of the H. made an entry in the ship's log of the circumstances of the collision. The master of the H. afterwards made a deposition relating to the collision before a receiver of wreck, under the Merchant Shipping Act, 1854, s. 448.

On the hearing of an action of damage brought against the H. by the owners of the G., it was proved that the master and mate of the H. had died, and it was sought to render the entry in the log and the deposition evidence on behalf of the H.:

Held, that the documents were not admissible.

THIS was an action instituted on behalf of the owners of the steamship Gange against the owners of the Henry Coxon, for the recovery of damages arising out of a collision between the two vessels on Saturday, the 12th of January, 1878, in Sea Reach in the river Thames.

July 6, 8. The action was heard.

After the witnesses called for the plaintiffs had been examined, one of the owners of the Henry Coxon was examined as a witness on behalf of the defendants, and gave evidence to the effect that, subsequently to the collision the Henry Coxon, having on board her the master and all the crew who had been on board her at the time of the collision, with the exception of the second engineer, had been despatched on a voyage to Riga ; that she was known to have left Riga, homeward bound, on the 12th of June, 1878, and to have passed Copenhagen on the 15th of that month, but that nothing since had been heard of her, except that one of her boats had been picked up.

The second engineer of the Henry Coxon was also examined as a witness on behalf of the defendants. He stated that he had been below at the time of the collision ; that the log of the Henry Coxon was in the handwriting of the first mate, who had been on deck at the time of the collision, and that the entry in it relating to the collision had been made on the Monday morning after the *collision, and had [157 been signed by the witness after it had been signed by the first mate.

Counsel for the defendants tendered the entry in question as evidence in the action. They also proposed to put in the deposition of the master of the Henry Coxon, taken on the 15th of January in this year, before the receiver of wreck, at the Custom House in London, in pursuance of the 448th section of the Merchant Shipping Act, 1854, 17 & 18 Vict. c. 104.

Butt, Q.C., and *E. C. Clarkson*, for the defendants : The entry in the log relating to the collision is a contemporaneous entry made by a deceased person in the execution of his duty, and in the course of business : *Price* v. *Earl of Torrington* ([1]) ; Taylor on Evidence, p. 596, 7th ed.

The Admiralty Advocate (*Dr. Deane*, Q.C.), *Webster*, Q.C.,

([1]) Salk., 285 ; 1 Sm. L. C., 328 (7th ed.)

and *W. G. F. Phillimore,* for the plaintiffs: The entry in the log relating to the collision is not a contemporaneous entry, and is not shown to be confined to a narrative of facts known to the person making it of his own knowledge. It would be most dangerous to extend the doctrine laid down in the case of *Price* v. *Earl of Torrington* (') to such documents as ships' logs; *Smith* v. *Blakey* ('). The cases of *Nothard* v. *Pepper* ('), and *The Little Lizzie* ('), clearly show that the master's deposition is not evidence which can be received.

Butt, Q.C., in reply.

SIR ROBERT PHILLIMORE: I have fully considered the questions of evidence which have been raised in this case. The Henry Coxon made a voyage subsequent to that on which the collision in question in this action occurred, and since then she has never been heard of. It must, therefore, be concluded that she has perished with all hands; her crew on the voyage on which she was lost consisted of the same 158]   crew who were on board her at the *time of the collision, with the exception of one man, the engineer in charge of the engines, who was not on deck at the time of the collision. In these circumstances the log of the vessel which has perished is tendered by the defendant's counsel as being evidence in the action on the authority of various cases, the earliest of which was, I think, the case of *Price* v. *Earl of Torrington* ('); and it is contended that inasmuch as the entries in this log were made by the first mate of the Henry Coxon who was on board her when she started on the voyage on which she must have been lost, and were entries made by him in the course of his duty, and contemporaneously with the occurrence of the facts to which they relate, the court ought to admit them as evidence in this case. Now, I think upon the whole, though the question is not without difficulty, that the principle to be gathered from the authorities which have been referred to is adverse to the admission of the log. I am not satisfied that the log can be considered in the light of a contemporaneous instrument. The collision took place on the Saturday, and the entry which the defendant's counsel have referred to appears not to have been made until the following Monday morning. I think it was to the interest of the person who made the entry relating to the collision to represent that the collision took place in con-

---

(') Salk. 285; 1 Sm. L. C., 328 (7th ed.)   in force at the date when the case of *No-*
(') Law Rep. 2 Q. B., 326.   *thard* v. *Pepper* (17 C. B. (N.S.), 39) was
(') 17 C. B. (N.S.), 39. The 449th sec- decided, is repealed by the Merchant
tion of the Merchant Shipping Act, 1854, Shipping Act, 1876, s. 45.
(') Law Rep., 3 A. & E., 56.

sequence of the bad navigation of the Gange and not of his own vessel. There is another matter to consider. It seems to me that the authorities point to this, that entries in a document made by a deceased person can only be admitted as evidence, on the grounds on which it is sought to make this log admissible, where it is clearly shown that the entries relate to an act or acts done by the deceased person and not by third parties. Now we all know as a matter of common knowledge in these proceedings, that it is the duty of the mate to enter not only the manœuvres that were executed on board his own ship, and all the matters relating to her navigation, but also to state what was the cause of the collision, and whether it was in consequence of the manœuvres and navigation of the other ship, and that which is set down in the log with respect to one of these sets of facts is ordinarily so inextricably mixed up with that relating to the other set, that it is difficult, if not impossible, to separate *them so as to disentangle the parts of the entry re- [159 lating to what was done by the vessel on board which the log was kept from those parts which relate to what was done by the other vessel. I think that this case does not come within the principle of the cases where evidence of this kind has been admitted. The question is one of extreme difficulty, but I think in the circumstances I must rule that this log is not admissible as evidence.

The defendants have also tendered in evidence the deposition made by the master of the Henry Coxon before the receiver of wreck in London. Now I know of no principle under which it would be admissible, on the contrary, I hold it to be quite clear that it is inadmissible. I do not, however, consider that the matter is *res integra*. The case of *Nothard* v. *Pepper* (¹) has been cited, and I think that that case is in point, and that it is my duty to follow it. It is certainly true that in that case the party whose deposition was sought to be put in evidence was alive at the time of the trial, while the master of the Henry Coxon must be presumed to be dead. In my opinion, however, that circumstance cannot affect the decision I ought to pronounce. On the authority of the case I have referred to I must refuse to admit this deposition as evidence.

Solicitors for plaintiffs: *Gellatly, Son & Warton.*
Solicitors for defendants: *Cooper & Co.*

(¹) 17 C. B. (N.S.), 39.

[3 Probate Division, 160.]

July 9, 1878.

160]   *THE PAPA DE ROSSIE (W. 181).

Taxation of Costs—Costs between Solicitor and Client—Refusal of Registrar to disallow Costs alleged to have been incurred through Negligence of Solicitor.

On a taxation between solicitor and client of the costs of a cause, objections were taken on behalf of the client to charges occasioned by the postponement of the trial and the amendment of the pleadings, on the ground that the postponement of the trial and the amendment of the pleadings had been rendered necessary by the negligence of the solicitor; the registrar refused to disallow the items, on the ground that it was not within his province as taxing master to inquire into the question of negligence :

Held, on motion in court to review the taxation, that the ruling of the registrar was right.

ON the 3d of July, 1877, an action of necessaries instituted on behalf of James Wright against the Papa de Rossie was, after having been called on for hearing before the judge in court, compromised upon the terms that the plaintiff should have judgment for the amount sued for in the action, and that each party thereto should bear his own costs.

On a subsequent day the London agents of the solicitor, who had been originally retained by the plaintiff to conduct the suit on his behalf, and had acted therein up to the settlement of the action, brought in the plaintiff's costs for taxation, and the assistant registrar having, in taxing such costs, allowed certain items to the allowance of which the plaintiff objected, another solicitor who had been retained for the plaintiff in relation to the taxation, on the 1st of March in this year carried in the following objections to the taxation :

The solicitor for the plaintiff objects to the allowance by the assistant registrar of the items in the two bills of costs of Mr. ——, formerly the plaintiff's solicitor, of and relating to the postponement of the trial of this cause on the 20th of June, 1877, and of the amendment of the reply, on the ground that such postponement and amendment were rendered necessary by the negligence or default of the said Mr. ——; that the affidavits used on the taxation raised this objection, and the facts are not disputed ; and it is submitted that the question whether or not Mr. —— is entitled to charge such items against his client, the plaintiff, is a fit and proper matter to be dealt with by the said assistant registrar on the taxation.

On the 1st of April in this year, the assistant registrar,

having *taken the objections to the taxation into con- [161
sideration, decided that he ought to adhere to the view he
had expressed on the taxation,—that a charge of negligence,
even if it could be sustained, was not a ground for disallow-
ing any costs necessarily incurred, but alleged to have been
rendered necessary by such negligence, it being beyond his
province as taxing officer to inquire into and decide such
charge.

July 9th. *Muir*, on behalf of the plaintiff, moved the
judge in court to direct the assistant registrar to disallow
the costs incurred in respect of the matters mentioned in the
plaintiff's objections to taxation,—and to review his taxation
upon such principles as the court should lay down. He referred to Rule 26 of the Rules of the Supreme Court (Costs).

E. C. Clarkson, on behalf of the solicitor who had brought
in the costs for taxation, opposed the motion. If a solicitor
has been guilty of negligently conducting the affairs of a
client, the proper remedy of the client is by an action of negligence against the solicitor.

SIR ROBERT PHILLIMORE: In a case of this kind I should
have thought it obvious that the proper course for the client
to take would be to bring his action against the solicitor for
negligence. If the plaintiff is liable to pay certain costs incurred by reason of the negligence of his solicitor, and brings
his action against the solicitor, he will be entitled to recover
damages. In the absence of any authority in support of the
motion, I can only say that I am of opinion that the registrar decided rightly in this case.

Solicitors for plaintiff: *Ingledew & Co.*

Solicitors for the solicitor opposing the motion: *Fielder &
Sumner.*

[3 Probate Division, 162.]

July 9, 1878.

*THE THEODOR KÖRNER (B. 114). [162

*Practice—Inspection of Documents—Reports of Survey procured for the Purposes
of Future Litigation—Damage to Cargo—Admiralty Court Act, 1861 (24 Vict.
c. 10), s. 6.*

The defendant in an action of damage to cargo is not entitled to obtain from the
plaintiff inspection of reports of surveys in possession of the plaintiff written and
prepared solely for the purpose of the action.

ON the 26th of March in this year, at the request of Messrs.
Begbies, Ross & Gibson, of London, a surveyor of shipping
surveyed the German ship Theodor Körner for the purpose

of ascertaining the cause of certain alleged damage to a portion of a cargo of wheat which she had brought from New York, and was then discharging in the London Docks, and the same day made his report of survey in writing. The next day the vessel was surveyed by another surveyor of shipping, who on that date made his report of survey in writing.

On the 8th of April an action under the 6th section of the Admiralty Court Act, 1861, was instituted on behalf of Messrs. Begbies, Ross & Gibson against the Theodor Körner, and on the 1st of July a statement of claim was delivered in the action. It appeared, from allegations in the statement of claim, that the plaintiffs were indorsees of the bills of lading of the cargo of wheat which the Theodor Körner had brought from New York ; that the vessel arrived in London in the month of March ; and that the said cargo of wheat when delivered to the plaintiffs was delivered greatly damaged and deteriorated.

On or about the 18th of June the plaintiffs filed an affidavit of discovery. In such affidavit one of the plaintiffs deposed as follows: "I object to produce" (the reports of survey made by the two surveyors) "on the ground that they are documents written and prepared solely for the purpose of proceeding in the action. "

July 9. *E. C. Clarkson*, on behalf of the defendants, the owners of the Theodor Körner, moved the judge in court to direct the plaintiffs to give the defendants' solicitor inspection of the reports of survey referred to in the above-men-
[63] tioned affidavit. He relied *on the case of *Martin* v. *Bulchard* ('), where, in a similar case, the Common Pleas Division had granted inspection.

[SIR ROBERT PHILLIMORE referred to the case of *Bustros* v. *White* (').]

Myburgh, on behalf of the plaintiffs, opposed the motion, on the ground that the documents, the inspection of which was sought, were privileged, under the authority of the decision of the Court of Appeal in the recent case of the *Southwark and Vauxhall Co.* v. *Quick* (').

SIR ROBERT PHILLIMORE: I do not see how, having regard to the language of the plaintiffs' affidavit, I can grant the motion. The affidavit states in effect that the plaintiffs have in their possession these two reports of survey, but that they object to produce them, on the ground that the documents in question were written and prepared solely for

(') 36 L. T. (N.S.), 732. (') 1 Q. B. D., 423.
(') 3 Q. B. D., 315 ; 28 Eng. R., 285.

the purpose of proceeding in this action. This being so, I am of opinion if I did grant the motion I should be disregarding the principle, in accordance with which the Court of Appeal decided the case of the *Southwark Waterworks Co.* v. *Quick* (¹). This I cannot do. The motion must therefore be rejected.

Solicitors for plaintiffs : *Plews & Irvine.*
Solicitors for defendants : *Thomas Cooper & Co.*

(¹) 3 Q. B. D., 315 ; 28 Eng. R., 285.

[3 Probate Division, 164.]

July 19, 1878.

[IN THE COURT OF APPEAL.]

*THE FRANCONIA (H. 347, 1877).   [164

THE HAMBURG-AMERIKANISCHE PACKETFAHRT-ACTIEN-
GESELLSCHAFT V. BURRELL and Others.

Limitation of Liability—Non-liability of Shipowners in respect of Crew-Space in Spar-decked Steamer—Meaning of Gross Tonnage without any Deduction of Engine Room Space—German Ship—Order in Council of 26th of June, 1873—Merchant Shipping Act, 1854 (17 & 18 Vict. c. 104), ss. 21, 22, 28—Merchant Shipping Act, 1862 (25 & 26 Vict. c. 63), ss. 54, 60—Merchant Shipping Act, 1867 (30 & 31 Vict. c. 124), s. 9.

The owners of a German steam vessel instituted an action under the Merchant Shipping Act, 1862, s. 54, to limit their liability for damages occasioned by a collision. The vessel had three decks, and her crew were berthed below the spar deck. By Order in Council, dated the 26th of June, 1873, made under s. 60 of the same act, it was directed that German steamships measured after the 1st of January, 1873, should be deemed to be of the tonnage mentioned in their registers in the same manner, and to the same extent, as the tonnage denoted in the certificate of registry of British ships was deemed to be their tonnage. In the register of this ship the crew space was deducted :

Held, by the judge of the Court of Admiralty, that in estimating the tonnage for the purpose of limitation of liability the crew space must be deducted.

Held, by the Court of Appeal, that the Order in Council of the 26th of June, 1873, did not make the certificate of registry conclusive evidence of the tonnage or of the propriety of deducting the space solely appropriated for berthing the crew.

Held, further, that under the Merchant Shipping Act, 1854, s. 21, subs. 4, a closed-in space, solely appropriated to the berthing of the crew, is to be excepted in estimating the tonnage only when it is on the upper deck, and not when it is between the spar deck and the tonnage deck.

Held, also, that the crew space cannot in the case of a foreign, any more than of a British, ship, be deducted under the "Merchant Shipping Act, 1867," s. 9, unless the provisions of that section as to inspection by a surveyor appointed by the Board of Trade, and the other conditions therein contained, have been complied with ; and therefore, that, as in the present case these conditions had not been complied with, the space appropriated for berthing the crew must not be deducted.

THIS was an action instituted on the 20th of November, 1877, on behalf of the owners of the German ship Franconia, to limit their liability, under the provisions of the 54th section of the Merchant Shipping Act, 1862, in respect to damage occasioned by a collision between the Franconia and the steamship *Strathclyde*(').

165] *The plaintiffs, by their amended statement of claim, after admitting that the collision with the Strathclyde, though occurring without the actual fault or privity of the plaintiffs, had been caused by the negligence of those on board the Franconia, and alleging that the gross tonnage of the Franconia, without deduction on account of engine room, was 3098.45 tons, claimed *inter alia* that it might be declared that they and the ship Franconia were not answerable in damage on account of the collision in respect of loss or damage to ships, boats, goods, ι. d other things to an aggregate amount exceeding £8 for each ton of the Franconia's gross tonnage, without deduction on account of engine room, such aggregate amount according to the above estimate of the tonnage being £24,788.

On the 21st of December, 1877, the judge in court pronounced that the plaintiffs were entitled to limited liability as claimed, and were answerable in damages in respect of loss or damage to ships, goods, and merchandise, on the occasion of the collision, to an amount not exceeding £24,788.

On the 26th of February, 1878, before any further step had been taken in the action, the plaintiffs, having been advised that an error had been made in calculating the gross tonnage of the Franconia without any deduction for engine room at 3098.45 tons, and that such error had arisen by reason of it having been erroneously supposed that, for the purposes of the action, the spaces solely appropriated to the berthing of the crew on board the Franconia ought to form part of and be included in the tonnage, applied by counsel to the judge in court for leave to make such re-amendments in the statement of claim as would bring the question of the extent of the plaintiffs' liability again before the court. The judge in court gave the plaintiffs leave to amend their statement of claim, and in due course to enter the action afresh for a rehearing.

On the 2d of March the plaintiffs re-amended their statement of claim, by alleging throughout that the gross tonnage of the Franconia, without deduction on account of engine room, was 2944.12, instead of 3098.45 tons, and by inserting £23,553 instead of £24,788, as the amount to which they claimed to limit their liability.

166]   *From the certificate of registry of the Franconia, it

(') 2 P. D., 163 ; 21 Eng. R., 581.

appeared that she was an iron screw steamer, brig rigged, with engines of 360 horse-power nominal, and was entitled to carry the German flag, and to all the rights, qualities, and privileges of a German ship; that she had been entered on the ship's registry, kept in pursuance of the law of the German Empire, on the 30th of May, 1874 ; that her tonnage measurement was taken by virtue of the order for ship's measurements of the 5th of July, 1872 (*Gazette of the Empire*, p. 270), and in full compliance therewith on the 28th of May, 1874, at Hamburg ; and that the following was the amount of such tonnage measurement:

	Registered British tons.
(*a*) Space under the measurement deck . . .	2228.03
(*b*) Space above the measurement deck :	
One space between decks	848.01
One round house	15.99
One other erection	6.42
Gross capacity of the ship	3098.45
From this is to be deducted :	
(1) Berths of crew which are between decks . .	154.33
(2) Spaces taken up by engines and boilers as well	
as by the fixed coal bunkers	833.08
Net capacity of the ship	2111.04 (¹)

It was established in evidence that the Franconia had three decks, the uppermost of which was a spar deck extending from stem to stern ; that the whole of the space on board her appropriated to the berthing accommodation of her crew, including the *master, was below the spar deck, and [167 between it and the main or tonnage deck ; that she had no break, poop, or any other permanent closed-in space on the upper deck available for or appropriated to the accommodation of her crew ; and that there was not permanently cut in any beam or cut in or painted in or over the doorway or

(¹) The original admeasurement of the Franconia made by the officials of the customs at London was also put in evidence. This document, dated the 4th of March, 1876, was headed "Certificate of British Tonnage," and stated that the true registered tonnage of the Franconia admeasured agreeably to the mode directed by the Merchant Shipping Act, 1854, was 1952.62 tons, and that her principal dimensions and tonnage were as follows:

As per German measurement, dated		
at Hamburg the 30th of May,		
1874	3098.45	gross tonnage.
Allowance for power . .	991.50	British measurement.
	2186.95	register tonnage.
Crew space	154.33	German measurement.
	1952.62	

hatchway of any place occupied by seamen or apprentices, or appropriated to their use, the number of men which it was constructed to accommodate, with any words whatever indicating the number of men it was constructed or intended to accommodate ; and that no such words are cut or painted in any part of the ship.

May 14, 1878. The plaintiffs applied to vary the judgment by substituting £23,553 for £24,788.

W. G. F. Phillimore, and *Stubbs*, for the plaintiffs : The 54th section of the Merchant Shipping Act, 1862, provides that the amounts beyond which shipowners seeking a limitation of their liability shall not be answerable shall depend upon "the tonnage" of the wrongdoing vessel, and in the case of steamships the meaning of the word "tonnage" is defined by the same section to be "the gross tonnage without deduction on account of engine room." Up to the recent decision of the Court of Session in the case of *Burrell* v. *Simpson* () it had always been the practice for plaintiffs in causes of limitation of liability to consider the gross tonnage without deduction of engine room referred to in the section to be the gross capacity of the ship without any deduction either on account of engine-room, or on account of spaces solely appropriated to the crew, and to calculate the limit of their liability accordingly. Having regard, however, to the decision in that case, the plaintiffs submit that the court would be disregarding the provisions of the section if it did not hold the tonnage of the Franconia, for the purposes of the action, to be the number of tons apparent on the nation alcertificate of registry of that vessel as her tonnage capacity, after such part of the tonnage space, denoted in such certificate to be space solely appropriated to the crew as did not exceed one-twentieth of her remaining tonnage, had alone been deducted. 168] The defendants will probably *contend that, inasmuch as the Franconia is a spar-decked steamer and her crew are berthed above her tonnage deck and below her spar deck, whilst the steamer before the court in *Burrell* v. *Simpson* (¹) could not from her size have had three decks, the decision in that case cannot afford any guide in the present. The plaintiffs, however, rely upon that case as laying down a principle applicable to all steamships, whatever may be the number of their decks. "The tonnage" defined in the 54th section of the Merchant Shipping Act, 1862, as "the gross tonnage without deduction on account of engine room" can

(¹) 4 Sess. Cas. (4th Series), p. 177.

only mean the "register tonnage" plus the allowance for
engine room space, that is to say, the tonnage without deduction on account of engine room, ascertained as directed
by such of the provisions of the Merchant Shipping Act,
1854, with regard to tonnage measurements as are applicable. Now, the regulations with regard to the tonnage measurement of all vessels are contained in the 20th, 21st, 22d
and 23d sections of the Merchant Shipping Act, 1854, and of
these sections the 23d section, relating to an allowance to be
made for the space occupied by the propelling power in
steamers, is inapplicable, inasmuch as in order to ascertain
the tonnage of the Franconia for the purposes of the action,
no such deduction is to be made from her gross tonnage.
Of the remaining sections, s. 20 declares that, in applying
the rule contained in the 21st section, the second deck from
below shall in ships like the Franconia be deemed the tonnage deck ; and s. 21 lays down a rule of tonnage measurement called rule 1 (applicable to the Franconia and nearly
all other ships), under which, by means of a computation as
therein directed, the tonnage capacity of the spaces both below and above "the tonnage deck" is to be estimated. It
is further provided by the same section that the tonnage
under the tonnage deck shall be deemed to be the register
tonnage of the ship "subject to the additions and deductions
hereinafter mentioned." These words "additions and deductions" can only refer to the allowance for engine room
space in s. 23, which is not to be deducted in this case, and
to the provisions of s. 21, sub-sections 4 and 5. Of these sub-
sections, subs. 4 must be construed as providing that, in calculating the tonnage of spar-decked as well as all *other [169
vessels, all spaces solely appropriated to the berthing of the
crew either above or below the tonnage deck are not to be
taken into account, except when the tonnage of such spaces
exceeds one-twentieth of the remaining tonnage of the ship,
and then only the excess over such one-twentieth of the remaining tonnage is to be added. The provisions with regard
to the crew space on board British ships contained in the
9th section of the Merchant Shipping Act, 1867, applying as
they all do to all such ships, whether spar-decked vessels
or not, clearly show that this construction of the 21st section
of the Merchant Shipping Act, 1854, is the right one. The
Franconia is a German ship and her tonnage capacity has
been measured in Germany as required by the Order in
Council of the 26th of June, 1873, made in pursuance of the
60th section of the Merchant Shipping Act, 1862, and is de-

noted on her certificate of registry ('). The court therefore
170] *cannot look behind the tonnage measurements apparent on such certificate, but must apply the directions
contained in the 21st section to such measurements, instead
of to the measurements which would if she had been a British ship have been taken under the same section.

E. C. Clarkson (*Butt*, Q.C., with him), on behalf of the
defendants: The case of *Burrell* v. *Simpson* (') is only material as an authority that, where in computing the tonnage
of a steamer "crew space" has been properly deducted according to law, then the owners of such steamer on claiming
a limitation of their liability under the Merchant Shipping
Act, 1862, are entitled to the benefit of that deduction. The
defendants, however, deny that, in the case of a spar-decked
steamship, any deduction whatever is to be made on account
of "crew space" below the spar deck. Under the Merchant
Shipping Act, 1854, the liability of shipowners for damage
done by their vessels, whether sailing vessels, or steam ves-

('') The following are the material portions of this Order in Council:

Whereas by the Merchant Shipping
Act Amendment Act, 1862, it is enacted
that whenever it is made to appear to
Her Majesty that the rules concerning the
measurement of tonnage of merchant ships
for the time being in force under the principal act have been adopted by the government of any foreign country, and are
in force in that country, it shall be lawful for Her Majesty by Order in Council
to direct that the ships of such foreign
country shall be deemed to be of the tonnage denoted in their certificate of registry or other national papers, and thereupon it shall no longer be necessary for
such ships to be remeasured in any port
or place in Her Majesty's dominions, but
such ships shall be deemed to be of the
tonnage denoted in their certificates of
registry or other papers in the same manner, to the same extent, and for the same
purposes, in, to, and for which the tonnage
denoted in the certificate of registry of
British ships is to be deemed the tonnage
of such ships.

And whereas it has been made to appear to Her Majesty that the rules concerning the measurement of tonnage of
merchant ships now in force under the
Merchant Shipping Act, 1854, have been
adopted by the government of His Majesty the German Emperor, with the exception of a slight difference in the mode

of estimating the allowance for engine
room, and such rules are now in force in
that country, having come into operation
on the 1st day of January, 1873, Her Majesty is hereby pleased by and with the
advice of her Privy Council to direct as
follows:

.   .   .   .   .

2. As regards steamships: that merchant ships belonging to the said German
Empire which are propelled by steam or
any other power requiring engine room
the measurement whereof shall after the
said 1st day of January, 1873, have been
ascertained and denoted in the registers
and other national papers of such steamships testified by the dates thereof shall
be deemed to be of the tonnage denoted
in such registers or other national papers
in the same manner, and to the same extent, and for the same purpose, in, to, and
for which the tonnage denoted in the certificate of registry of British ships is
deemed to be the tonnage of such ships;
provided nevertheless that if the owner
or master of any such German steamship
desires the deduction for engine room in
his ship to be estimated under the rules
for engine room measurement and deduction applicable to British ships instead of
under the German rule, the engine room
shall be measured and the deduction calculated according to the British rules.

(') 4 Sess. Cas. (4th Series), p. 177.

sels, depended on the value of the ship and her freight, the
value of no part of the hull, or of the machinery, being deducted. It was then determined that the law should be
altered, and in order to relieve steamship owners from being
at a disadvantage compared with the owners of sailing ships
of the same tonnage, owing to the great value of the machinery in steamers, the Legislature provided that steamship
owners, instead of being liable in proportion to the value
of such machinery, should be liable according to the space
that machinery occupied. The reason for such a change of
the law is apparent. But what reason can there be for in-
ferring that space occupied for the berthage of the crew is
not to be taken into consideration in estimating the tonnage
on which the limited amount of £8 per ton is to be paid?
The word gross tonnage is advisedly used in the 54th section
of the Merchant Shipping Act, 1862, and obviously means
the entire tonnage of the *ship without any deduc-   [171
tion at all, and it is only *ex majori cautelâ* that the words
"without deduction on account of engine room" are added.
The Order in Council of the 26th of June, 1873, is invalid
and *ultra vires*. It appears by the recitals in the Order in
Council itself that a condition precedent, the performance of
which alone could enable the Queen in Council to put the
provisions of the 60th section of the Merchant Shipping Act,
1862, in force with regard to German ships, has not been fulfilled. The Order in Council does not recite that the rules
as to measurement adopted by the German Empire are identical with the rules laid down in the Merchant Shipping
Act, 1854, with respect to the measurement of British ships.
But on the contrary, it is stated on the face of the order,
that there is a difference with regard to estimating the engine
room space between the German rules and the English rules.
This objection is a substantial one, for it can be shown that
owing to this difference the tonnage of the Franconia, denoted on her certificate of registry, is not the same by 150
tons, as her register tonnage would be if she had been measured under the Merchant Shipping Act, 1854.. Even if the
court should be of opinion that the tonnage measurements
denoted in the certificate of registry of this German ship are
prima facie binding, the court, if it is of opinion that the
tonnage has been erroneously computed, will order the vessel to be remeasured, in accordance with the rule contained
in s. 21 of the Merchant Shipping Act, 1854 (17 & 18 Vict.
c. 104).

Stubbs, in reply.

Cur. adv. vult.

May 28. SIR ROBERT PHILLIMORE: The Court desires to express its obligation to counsel for the valuable assistance they have rendered to it by their arguments in this case. The owners of the Franconia, having admitted their liability for damage done to the defendants, have in a suit for the limitation of that liability under the Merchant Shipping Amendment Act, 1862, s. 54, stated erroneously, as they contend, the tonnage of the Franconia to be 3,098 tons and a fraction. They now claim to have this error rectified by reducing the tonnage to a fraction over 2,944 tons, the effect of which is to lessen their liability by about 154 tons; and a question of some difficulty and novelty is raised, 172] *whether, for the purpose of estimating the tonnage for which the plaintiffs in this suit are liable, the space solely appropriated to the berthing of the crew is or is not wholly or in part to be deducted.

The section just referred to, after limiting the liability for personal injury to an aggregate amount of £15, and in the case of damage to goods in an aggregate amount of £8 for each ton of the ship's tonnage, proceeds as follows:

Such tonnage to be the registered tonnage in the case of sailing ships, and in the case of steamships the gross tonnage without deduction on account of engine room: In the case of any foreign ship which has been or can be measured according to British law the tonnage as ascertained by such measurement shall, for the purposes of this section, be deemed to be the tonnage of such ship.

The Franconia is a steamship. The question is what is the meaning of the term gross, applied to the tonnage? In order to ascertain the meaning of this term, regard must be had to various sections of the Merchant Shipping Acts.

The 20th section of the Merchant Shipping Act, 1854, 17 & 18 Vict. c. 104, enacts that—

Throughout the following rules the tonnage deck shall be taken to be the upper deck in ships which have less than three decks, and to be the second deck from below in all other ships.

Now the Franconia has three decks, and therefore her tonnage deck will be the second deck from below.

By the 21st section of the same act, the tonnage is to be ascertained in a particular way as provided by rule 1 in the same section. By subs. 3 of this section, the register tonnage is to be ascertained by a computation from the areas as therein stated. But the tonnage so ascertained is to be subject to the additions and deductions thereinafter mentioned. To these I will presently refer.

In subs. 4 of the same section, it is provided that

If there be a break, a poop, or any other permanent closed in space on the upper deck, available for cargo, or stores, or for the berthing or accommodation of passengers or crew, the tonnage of such space shall be ascertained,"—in the manner there mentioned—"and shall be added to the tonnage under the tonnage-deck, ascertained as aforesaid, subject to the following provisos; first, that nothing shall be added for a closed-in space solely appropriated to the berthing of the crew, unless such space exceeds one-twentieth of the remaining tonnage of the ship, and in case of such excess the excess only shall be added; . . ."

*Then there follows another provision in regard to [173 deck passengers, which does not concern this case.

These clauses apply to the register tonnage of all ships. The 23d section introduces a new proviso as to steamships and enacts that—

In every ship propelled by steam . . . . an allowance shall be made for the space occupied by the propelling power, and the amount so allowed shall be deducted from the gross tonnage of the ship, ascertained as aforesaid, and the remainder shall be deemed to be the register tonnage of such ship.

And then follow rules for estimating the deduction. Gross tonnage is, I think, to be ascertained under the provisions of the 21st section above referred to, and one of these provisions is, under subs. 4, to deduct the space solely appropriated to the berthing of the crew, so far as it does not exceed one-twentieth of the remaining tonnage of the ship.

I return now to the 54th section of the Merchant Shipping Act, 1862, which enacts that the tonnage shall be "the registered tonnage in the case of sailing ships, and in the case of steamships the gross tonnage without deduction on account of engine room."

It is to be observed that this act of 1862 provides that it shall be construed with and as part of the Merchant Shipping Act, 1854.

The contention that according to the language of the 54th section of the Merchant Shipping Act, 1862, the tonnage of the steamer is to be taken without deduction either for engine room or for berthage is, I think, erroneous, because the words "gross tonnage" in this statute ought to have the same construction as clearly must be put on them when used in the 23d section of the Merchant Shipping Act, 1854.

I agree with the opinion expressed by the Lords of Session in the recent case (1876) of *Burrell* v. *Simpson* (¹).

In that case the Lord President says (²):

What is meant here, I apprehend, by gross tonnage without deduction of engine room means just the actual tonnage without deduction of engine room, or in other words, the contrast between a sailing ship in this clause and a steamship is this, that in the case of a sailing ship the registered tonnage is to be taken; in the case of a steamship it is not to be the registered tonnage, but what is called the gross tonnage without the deduction of engine room which, if deducted, would *make it the registered tonnage. In short it is the [174

(¹) 4 Sess. Cas. (4th Series), p. 177.　　　　　(²) At p. 184.

want of the deduction of engine room that makes this gross tonnage instead of being registered tonnage.

It has been contended, admitting the law to be as I have stated it is, that in this case, inasmuch as the Franconia is a spar-decked ship, there is no closed-in space solely appropriated to the berthing of the crew, according to the true meaning of the words in the 4th sub-section of the 21st section of the act of 1854, but I am unable to adopt this opinion. Having regard to all the provisions in the 20th, 21st, and 23d sections, I think that the deduction from the tonnage in cases of closed-in spaces is applicable to the berthing space provided in a spar-decked ship.

Lastly, with regard to the argument respecting the certificate of registry of this German vessel.

The 60th section of the Merchant Shipping Act, 1862, provides that the Queen may, by Order in Council, direct that when the English rules for the measurement of tonnage of merchant ships have been adopted by a foreign government, the ships of such foreign country shall be deemed to be of the tonnage denoted in their certificates of registry to all intents and purposes as if they were British ships. These measurement rules were extended to Germany by an Order in Council dated the the 26th of June, 1873.

It has been contended that the Order in Council referred to is, on the face of it, invalid, inasmuch as it contains the words: "with the exception of a slight difference in the mode of estimating the allowance for engine room," thereby exceeding the authority conferred upon it by the statute. I am not inclined to put so rigid a construction upon the Order in Council, which in all substantial respects complies with the directions of the statute. Upon the whole I am of opinion that the plaintiffs are entitled to the reduction of the tonnage measurement which they claim. It only remains to observe that the plaintiffs admit that they have claimed to deduct about seven tons in excess of the number of tons they are empowered to deduct under the provisions of subs. 4 of rule 1, and that, consequently, they benefit of these seven tons must be given to the defendants.

The defendants appealed.

_____

July 19.   *Butt*, Q.C., *Clarkson*, and *Raikes*, for the appellants : *This crew space cannot be deducted under the act of 1854. The 21st section, subs. 4, provides for crew space on the upper deck not being included, but in subs. 5, relating to spar-decked ships, there is no provision made for deducting any space between decks. It is evident that

the ship in *Burrell* v. *Simpson* (') was not a spar-decked
ship, and the point did not arise. The deduction cannot be
made under the act of 1867, s. 9, for the conditions of that
section have not been complied with. The Order in Council
is *ultra vires*. A foreign certificate of registry is evidence
of the measurements, but it cannot be used to decide the
question whether a certain space has been properly deducted from the tonnage, which is a question of law. Section 60 of the act of 1862 does not make the certificate
conclusive evidence of the tonnage.

Benjamin, Q.C., *Phillimore*, and *Stubbs*, contrà: The
meaning of "gross tonnage" under the act of 1854 is shown
by *Burrell* v. *Simpson* ('), which shows that the crew space
is to be deducted under that act.

[JAMES, L.J.: I cannot see that the construction of s. 21,
subs. 4, was discussed in that case.]

Unless crew space is to be deducted, there is nothing to
satisfy the plural word "deductions" in s. 21, subs. 3, there
being only one other deduction. Then by the Order in
Council the certificate of registry is evidence of the tonnage;
it gives the whole tonnage and the amount deducted; and
the certificate being made conclusive as to the registered
tonnage the deductions must be taken to have been properly
made. It is urged that this ship has not complied with the
conditions which entitle the owners of a ship to deduct crew
space under s. 9 of the act of 1867. The answer to that is,
that being a German ship she could not literally comply
with them; and that it must be understood that the Legislature did not intend a foreign ship to be subject to the condition of being surveyed by a surveyor appointed by the
Board of Trade. The Order in Council makes the registry
conclusive evidence of the tonnage, and the court cannot go
behind it.

JAMES, L. J.: I am of opinion that the order of the learned
judge cannot be sustained. He appears to have proceeded
on the *case of *Burrell* v. *Simpson* (), but when that   [176
case is considered, it is really no authority upon the question, because the point which is raised here, as to the difference between a closed-in space between decks and a closed-in
space above the upper deck, was never before the court at
all, and I gather from the absence of all reference to it that
the crew space there was a crew space which was clearly
within s. 21, subs. 4 of the act of 1854, and that the only
point really in controversy in that case was, whether in a
steamship the gross tonnage mentioned in s. 54 of the act of

(') 4 Sess. Cas. (4th Series), p. 177.

1862 was to be taken as the tonnage, with the deductions which have to be made in a steamship other than engine-room, or whether it was to be gross tonnage without any deduction whatever; and no question arose as to whether the space in question was one which ought to be excluded under s. 21. I have not heard anything in answer to the arguments of Mr. Butt, which pointed out that there was a very distinct provision in the act of 1854 that, where the crew were lodged on the upper deck, the closed space which would otherwise be charged should not, if appropriated for the convenience of the crew, be included for the purposes of tonnage, and that then, under subs. 5, the whole measurements between the decks are to be taken without any deduction. I therefore have no doubt that, upon the construction of that first act of Parliament, no deduction ought to have been made for the berths of the crew below the spar deck. After that act came the act 30 & 31 Vict. c. 124, which makes provision for the better security and health of English seamen, and contains (s. 9) very detailed provisions, requiring certain things to be done, certain inscriptions to be put on a beam and on the doors, a certain quantity of air to be secured to each seaman, and so on, and requires that the ship shall be inspected and certified, and when that is done, when those provisions are all complied with, then there shall be a further allowance for the space occupied by the sailors' berths, the allowance being made expressly subject to the performance of all those conditions, and being made by way of bounty to the shipowners for making provisions for the health of the seamen. It is not pretended that those conditions have been complied with, or can have been complied with, by the respondents' ship in this case. It does not 177] *appear that the ship ever was examined by a surveyor. The fact is proved that it had not got the proper announcement (at all events on the beam) of the accommodation provided for the seamen. The ship, therefore, has not brought herself within the last act of Parliament, and cannot be allowed the deductions given by that act.

Mr. Benjamin contends that if an English certificate of registry had shown the gross tonnage and the amount of registered tonnage, deducting the tonnage of the berths, the register would be conclusive evidence that all the provisions of the act of Parliament had been complied with, and that the court would have been precluded from going behind it, even on the most conclusive evidence that there had been some mistake made or some error committed by some of the parties, and that under 25 & 26 Vict. c. 63, s. 60, and the

Order in Council, the effect of the German certificate of registry is the same. I cannot agree with that argument. The certificate of registry is, no doubt, *prima facie* evidence of the tonnage, and the 60th section of the act of 1862 enables the Queen in Council to give the same effect to the certificate of registry of a foreign ship. All it authorizes the Queen in Council to do, and all the Queen in Council has done, as was very well put by Mr. Benjamin in his argument, is that it has authorized all our people to accept the measurements made by the Germans exactly in the same way as if they had been made in England.

All we have got before us, then, is that the gross tonnage is so much, that the actual measurement of the room occupied by berths is so much, and the actual measurement of the room occupied by engine, boilers, and coal bunkers is so much, that is to say, those measurements, as actual measurements, are to be taken as the true measurements. This is all that the order in council does, and I quite agree with the judge below in the opinion that this order was not *ultra vires*. But the legal result of those measurements, that is to say, whether the crew space is to be deducted, is something beyond the power which is given to the Queen in Council to declare. We take the German certificate to be true, and therefore take the actual crew space to be 154 tons. The question whether it is or is not to be deducted is a question of English law, to be determined by an English court upon the act of *Parliament, and not to be determined [178 by an Order in Council giving a certain recognition to the German certificate.

I am of opinion, then, that we are bound to hold, upon the construction of the act of Parliament, that the berths between decks are not to be deducted for the purposes of this suit.

BRETT, L.J.: I cannot agree with the judgment of the learned judge of the Admiralty Court, except that I agree with him in the view that the Order in Council is not *ultra vires*. I cannot adopt the argument of Mr. Butt upon that point, and I think it is not *ultra vires* for the reason given by the learned judge of the Admiralty Court, viz., that it is substantially in accordance with the statute. That Order in Council is to have a certain effect, which is stated in ss. 60 & 61 of the act of 1862. By s. 60 the result is that the certificate of registry of a German ship is to be accepted in our courts, and the German ship shall thereupon be deemed to be of the tonnage denoted in those certificates, "in the same manner, to the same extent, and for the same pur-

poses in, to, and for which the tonnage denoted in the certificates of registry of British ships is deemed to be the
tonnage of such ships."

Mr. Benjamin argues that if this were a British register, it
would be conclusive. I cannot agree with that. I know of
no law which says that the register is to be conclusive for
all purposes. I apprehend you are entitled to look behind
the register, and to see whether the provisions of the act of
Parliament, on which and in virtue of which the register
was made, were complied with. I think that a German certificate is no more conclusive than a British certificate would
be. We are only to consider it as determining the tonnage
in the same manner and to the same extent as if it was a
British register. We should be entitled to see whether a
British register was made according to the act of Parliament
which authorizes it to be made. Therefore the question
comes to be whether in this case the register is made according to the provisions of the act of Parliament, or would have
been so made if it had been a British ship.

Now, it is said, first, that the crew space ought to be
deducted by virtue of the statute of 1854. It seems to me
that this particular crew space cannot be deducted under
that act.

179] *I agree that the 21st section applies to the measurements both of steamships and sailing ships, and that if
you have a crew space brought within the terms of s. 21, it
is to be deducted before you arrive at the gross tonnage of
the ship. I think that s. 23 gives to a steamship, besides
the deductions which are given in s. 21, another deduction,
that is for the engine room, and that therefore a steamship,
under ss. 21 and 23, is entitled to deduct, in order to get at
her registered tonnage, such crew space as is provided for in
s. 21, and also the engine space under s. 23. The question,
therefore, is whether, in order to arrive at the gross tonnage
in the present case, you ought to deduct the crew space. It
seems to me that this cannot be done under s. 21 of the act
of 1854, for this simple reason, that the crew space is not on
the upper deck.

It is said that the Scotch case of *Burrell* v. *Simpson* (')
decides that it does not signify, under the act of 1854,
whether the crew space is on the upper deck or between
decks. A Scotch decision is to be treated with great respect,
but is not a binding authority, and supposing the Scotch
court to have decided that point, if we differed from it we
should be entitled to decide differently. But I cannot

(') 4 Sess. Cas. (4th Series), p. 177.

think that the Scotch court did decide that point. If the crew space there was a space on the upper deck, it clearly came within the terms of s. 21, and from the absence of all discussion on the point it is to be inferred that it was so, and the only question appears to have been whether the terms of s. 54 of the act of 1862 prevented its being deducted, and I entirely agree with the Scotch court in saying that they did not.

Then it is said that this space can be deducted under the act of 1867, for that it could have been so deducted if this had been a British ship. The answer to that seems to me to be that if this had been a British ship this space could not have been deducted, because it is clear upon the facts that this case was not brought within the act of 1867. That there was no cutting in the beam may be considered a trifle, but there is a much more material fact that there has been no survey and allowance by the proper officer whom the Engglish Legislature has trusted with this duty, that is to say, a surveyor of the Board of Trade. The English Legislature has not thought fit to intrust any ordinary surveyor with the *power of giving these certificates, but only an [180 authorized surveyor of the Board of Trade, and therefore this crew space is not brought within the act of 1867.

It is said, as I understand, that we may apply to this ship the rule in the act of 1867, without compliance with the conditions, because it is a foreign ship. It seems to me if we did that we should legislate. If the Legislature in passing the act of 1867 has overlooked the cases of foreign ships, we cannot help that. Those who think they have overlooked it inadvertently must go to the Legislature and get the act of Parliament altered. We have only to construe the act.

The result is that the gross tonnage in the present case is the gross tonnage, without deducting either crew space or engine room.

COTTON, L.J.: The question we have to decide is what, under the act of 1862, s. 54, is to be considered the gross tonnage of a steamship without any deduction on account of engine room. For that we are thrown back on the act of 1854, s. 23, which is the first section that mentions steamships, and provides that in cases of steamships a deduction is to be made "from the gross tonnage of the ship ascertained as aforesaid" for the space occupied by the propelling power. The gross tonnage there referred to is to be ascertained under s. 21; and the question is, whether that section allows for all ships a deduction for the crew space, except where the crew space is in some erection on the upper deck? And in our opinion it does not. There are two sub-divisions of s. 21 bearing on the point. Subs. 4 deals with the case of there being a poop or other closed-in space on the upper deck, without reference to the question whether it is a spar deck or not. It does not refer to the case of a closed-in space above the tonnage deck, but simply to a closed-in space on the upper deck, whichever that may be, and provides for the measurement of that space, subject to a proviso that no addition is to be made for a closed-in space solely appropriated to the berthing of the crew, unless it exceeds a certain amount. The whole sub-division, in my opinion, only applies to the case where there is a provision made for the berthing of the crew on the upper deck. Then 181] sub-division 5 deals with *the case with which we have here to deal—the case of a vessel having a spar deck—but there is no exception made of a space between the spar deck and the tonnage deck, which is appropriated for the crew.

A case in the Court of Session was referred to, and of course we should regard with the greatest respect any opinion expressed by the judges there, but it is not shown whether the ship in that case was a ship which had a spar deck, with accommodation of the crew between that and the tonnage deck, or was a vessel which had accommodation for the crew on the upper deck; and until it is shown that the former was the case, we cannot consider the judges as having expressed an opinion upon the point which arises here.

Then we come to the question whether, under the Order in Council made under s. 60 of the act of 1862, the certificate of registry is conclusive. It was not contended that, if the matter turned upon the act of 1854 without the act of 1862, the Franconia could rely upon that certificate as being conclusive that the crew space ought to be deducted, because it appeared on the face of the certificate that the crew space was between decks; and of course it must depend upon the true construction of the act of Parliament, not upon the certificate, whether or no crew space can properly be deducted. But, in my opinion, the true effect of the section of the act of 1862 and the Order in Council is this, that the measurement is to be taken as sufficient, and that when Her Majesty is satisfied that a foreign nation has adopted our principle of measurement, the ship need not be measured when any question arises as to the proper measurement in this country; but it was never intended that where a question arises whether, upon the true construction of an English act of Parliament, a certain deduction ought to be made, and a reign certificate treats it as a deduction which ought to be made, that certificate should be binding upon the courts in this country.

The court, then, must, without regard to the certificate, decide the question whether the Franconia is entitled, under the act of 1867, to deduct the crew space. I need not add anything to what has been said by the Lords Justices on that question. The deductions to be allowed under that act are subject to certain *stipulations and conditions. [182 It may or may not be an oversight that those conditions are such that a foreign ship cannot, except under very special circumstances, get the benefit of the act; but the foreign ship is coming here to get the benefit of the limit of liability afforded by an English act of Parliament, and if it is to get the benefit of that it must take it of course with all the burdens imposed by the act. One of these burdens is that the crew space, if between decks, is to be counted in, unless certain things are done as required by the act. Those things have not been done in the present case, and we are unable to say that the Franconia is entitled under the act of 1867 to deduct crew space when she has not complied with the requisitions of that act, when she has not got the necessary certificate of survey, or the proper words put up showing that proper accommodation had been provided for the crew.

Solicitors for plaintiffs: *Stokes, Saunders & Stokes.*
Solicitors for defendants: *Gellatly, Son & Warton.*

See note 19 Eng. R., 367 ; Harris *v.* Owners of the Franconia, 20 id., 446 ; The Franconia, 21 id., 581.

[3 Probate Division, 182.]

July 30, 1878.

THE ANDALUSIAN (L. 339, Liv.).

Limitation of Liability—Meaning of Recognized British Ship—Merchant Shipping Act, 1854 (17 & 18 Vict. c. 104), ss. 2, 19, 106, 516—Merchant Shipping Act, 1862 (25 & 26 Vict.), c. 63, s. 54.

A newly built vessel, exceeding fifteen tons burden, on being launched, ran into and damaged a passing ship. The owners of the damaged ship thereupon instituted an action in this court against the newly built vessel to recover for the damage done to their ship, and this court pronounced the vessel proceeded against solely to blame for the collision. Afterwards an action of limitation of liability was instituted by the owner of the newly built vessel, a natural born English subject, who therein claimed a declaration that he was entitled to a limitation of liability in respect of damage occasioned by the collision.

At the hearing of the action it appeared that the newly built vessel, though registered as a British ship at the time of the institution of the action, was not so registered at the time of the collision:

Held, that the vessel was not a "recognized British ship" when the collision occurred, and that her owner was not entitled to have his liability limited.

THIS was an action of limitation of liability instituted in the month of July in this year, on behalf of the owner of the Andalusian, against the owners of the ship Angerona, 183] the owners of her cargo, *and her master and crew, for the purpose of obtaining *inter alia* a declaration that the plaintiff was entitled, under the provisions of the Merchant Shipping Acts, to a limitation of his liability in respect of the damages arising out of a collision which took place on the 14th of July, 1877, when the Andalusian, on being launched from the plaintiff's shipbuilding yard on the Cheshire side of the river Mersey, ran into and damaged the Angerona as the latter vessel was passing down the river in tow of a tug.

The statement of claim, after stating that the plaintiff was a natural born English subject, and at the time of the collision was the sole owner of the steamship Andalusian, and setting out the facts relating to the collision, and that in consequence of the same the Angerona and her cargo was damaged, and certain personal effects of her master and crew were lost and damaged, alleged *inter alia* in substance as follows :

5. An action—1877. Letter A, No. 342, Liverpool District Registry—was brought in the Probate, Divorce, and Admiralty Division of this court by the owners of the Angerona, the owners of her cargo, and her master and crew, against the plaintiff, as owner of the Andalusian, for the recovery of damages in respect of the loss of or damage to the Angerona and her cargo, and the said personal effects ; and on the 7th day of August, 1877, judgment was given in the said action, and the plaintiff was thereby condemned in the damage proceeded for and in costs, and the usual reference to ascertain the amount of the said damage was ordered (').

6. The plaintiff is apprehensive that other claims may be made upon him in respect of loss of goods on board the Angerona at the time of the said collision.

7. The said collision was occasioned by the improper navigation of the Andalusian.

8. No loss of life or personal injury was occasioned by the said collision.

9. The said collision happened without the actual fault or privity of the plaintiff.

10. At the time of the said collision the Andalusian had been built as and for a British ship, and all the measurements necessary for the purpose of her registration (except

(') See *The Andalusian*, 2 P. D., 231; 21 Eng. R., 615.

crew space) had been made before she was launched, but
she was not actually registered till the 24th of September,
1877. The plaintiff had not, at the time of the said collision,
been guilty of any breach or non-observance of any of the
provisions of the statutes then in force relating to the measurement and registration of British ships.

11. Since the said collision the Andalusian has been completely measured and registered in accordance with the
provisions of the said statute ; and the plaintiff has in all respects complied with such provisions.

12. The gross tonnage, as finally registered, of the Andalusian, with *deduction for crew space, but without   [184
deduction on account of engine room, is 1722.52 tons.

13. The plaintiff hereby offers to pay into court, in respect of his liability for loss of or damage to the said ship
Angerona and her boats, and the goods, merchandise, and
other things on board her at the time of the said collision,
the sum of £13,780 3s. 3d., being the aggregate amount of
£8 per ton for each ton of the gross tonnage of the Andalusian, without deduction on account of engine room, together
with such interest thereon as the court shall direct, for distribution among such persons as shall establish their claims
in respect of such loss or damage.

The statement of claim then claimed a declaration of limitation of liability in the usual form applicable to the case.

The defendants, in the 1st paragraph of their statement
of defence, denied that the launch, then or afterwards called
the Andalusian, was a ship within the meaning of the Merchant Shipping Act, 1862, on the 14th of July, 1877, and
after stating in paragraph 2 that the plaintiff was the builder
of the launch, and had on the said 14th of July, 1877, the
control and management of it, and of the operation of
launching it, alleged in so much of the 3d and subsequent
paragraphs of such statement of claim as is material in substance as follows :

3. The launch, through the negligence of the plaintiff or of
his servants, came into collision with and damaged the ship
Angerona and her cargo, and the personal effects of her
master and crew, at the time and in the circumstances stated
in the statement of claim. The damage so done was not
caused by improper navigation of the launch within the
meaning of the Merchant Shipping Act, 1862.

4. At the time of the said collision and damage the launch,
which was intended to be a steamship, had in her no engines,
boilers, or machinery, had no masts, yards, or sails, or

other means of propulsion or navigation, and was in many other respects incomplete and unfinished, and could not have been used as a ship. It had no master or crew on board it.

5. At the time aforesaid the launch had not been surveyed as required for a ship by the Merchant Shipping Act, 1854, and it had not been and could not have been measured for the purpose of calculating its tonnage, and it had no tonnage within the meaning of the Merchant Shipping Act, 1862.

6. Judgment in the action referred to in the statement of claim was recovered against the plaintiff, and not *in rem* against the launch.

8. The defendants do not admit any of the allegations in paragraphs 9, 10, 11 and 12 of the statement of claim, except that the launch was not registered till the 24th of September, 1877.

The plaintiff delivered a reply, joining issue on the 1st, 2d, and 5th paragraphs of the statement of defence, and 185] alleging, with *respect to the 4th paragraph of the statement of defence, that the Andalusian was ready to receive her engines, boilers, machinery, masts, yards and sails, then ready to be placed in her, and that she was not, otherwise than admitted, incomplete or unfinished.

July 24. The action was heard before the judge in court.

Witnesses for the plaintiff were examined orally in court, and the register of the Andalusian was put in. No witnesses were called for the defendants. The plaintiff was called as a witness on his own behalf, and stated that he was a natural born British subject, and the owner of the Andalusian, but that he had not had any direction or control over the operation of launching her. The result of the evidence given by the other witnesses can be gathered from the judgment.

Sir J. Holker, A.G., *Butt*, Q.C., and *E. C. Clarkson*, for the plaintiff: If the Andalusian at the time of the collision was "a British ship" within the provisions of the 54th section of the Merchant Shipping Act, 1862, and if the damage done by her was done by her in the course of navigation, the court will, without doubt, hold that the plaintiff is entitled to have his liability for such damage limited in accordance with the provisions of that statute. The first question then is—Was the Andalusian on the 14th of July, 1877, " a ship" within the meaning of the Merchant Shipping Acts? This question must clearly be answered in the affirmative.

The interpretation clause (s. 2) of the Merchant Shipping Act, 1854, which act is to be construed as part of the Merchant Shipping Act, 1862, defines the term "ship" as including every vessel used in navigation not propelled by "oars," and must certainly extend to a vessel such as the Andalusian was when the collision occurred. At that time she was complete, with the exception of her masts and sails and such of her steam machinery as could not have been placed on board her until after she had been launched. Indeed, even an unfinished vessel in the builder's yard has been decided to be a "ship": *Ex parte Hodgkin* ([¹]). With regard to the question whether the Andalusian at the date of the collision was a British ship, and therefore a ship to which the provisions of the 54th section of the Merchant *Shipping Act, 1862, could apply, it will, no doubt [186 be contended on behalf of the defendants that, as the Andalusian was not in fact registered when the collision happened, her owner must be excluded by the operation of the Merchant Shipping Act, 1854, ss. 19, and 516, from the right given to owners of British ships of limiting their liability. But these sections are not applicable to the present case. The 54th section of the Merchant Shipping Act, 1862, is in terms extended to "any ship whether British or foreign." In the first place, these words, if taken in their ordinary meaning, would surely include the Andalusian, for when the damage in this case was done that vessel belonged to the plaintiff, a natural born British subject qualified to own a British ship under the 18th section of the Merchant Shipping Act, 1854; and in the second place, the provisions of that act, enacting that a ship belonging to British subjects shall not be recognized as a British ship unless registered as thereby required, must only have been intended by the Legislature to apply to cases where registration was necessary, and had been omitted through the default of the shipowner. Now, as the 23d section of the Merchant Shipping Act, 1854, requires that the engine room space should be deducted, in order to arrive at the registered tonnage in steamships, the Andalusian, having been as a matter of necessity launched without her engines, could not have been put on the register before the collision and the plaintiff was guilty of no default whilst she remained unregistered. He in fact placed her on the register as soon as it was practicable for him to do so, and she was on the register at the date of the institution of the action. To hold that in such a case the limitation of the shipowner's liability is taken away would

([¹]) Law Rep., 20 Eq., 746; 15 Eng. R., 593.

be straining the words of the 54th section of the Merchant Shipping Act, 1862. Moreover, it is not unimportant to notice that that section does not refer to the "registered tonnage," but only to the gross tonnage of steamers. If the Legislature had meant to confine the section to registered British steamers, why should it not have done so in express terms?

The damage or loss in respect of which the plaintiff asks to limit his liability in damages, was damage or loss caused by reason of the improper navigation of the Andalusian, 187] without the actual *fault or privity of the plaintiff. Damage by reason of improper navigation, though including damage occasioned by whatever is improperly done with a ship during the course of a voyage: *Good* v. *London Steamship Owners' Association* (¹) is not confined to such damage, but extends to anything improperly done with a ship in motion on the water, and is therefore an expression rightly describing the damages sustained by the defendants in this case: *Laurie* v. *Douglas* (²).

Benjamin, Q.C., and *Myburgh*, for the defendants: The 516th section of the Merchant Shipping Act, 1854, provides that the ninth part of that act, relating to the limitation of ·the liability of shipowners in respect of damage caused by improper navigation, shall only apply to such British ships as are within the meaning of the same act "recognized British ships," an expression which is by the 19th section exclusively confined to such British ships required to be registered, i.e., employed in British waters and above fifteen tons burden, as have obtained registration. It therefore follows that inasmuch as the 54th section of the Merchant Shipping Act, 1862, which is now the ruling enactment with regard to the limit beyond which the liability of shipowners coming within it shall not extend, is to be read as incorporated with the ninth part of the Merchant Shipping Act, 1854, the only proper construction to be put on the provisions contained in such 54th section is that shipowners, who are owners of unregistered British ships required by law to be registered, are excluded from the benefits and privileges conferred by it. This construction is borne out by the provisions of the 106th section of the Merchant Shipping Act, 1854, and the judgment in the recent case of the *Union Bank of London* v. *Lenanton* (³), where the effect of placing a ship belonging to British subjects on the register, was much discussed. It is clear, then, that if the contention of the defendants on this

(¹) Law Rep., 6 C. P., 563.   (²) 15 M. & W., 746.
(³) 3 C. P. D., 243; 30 Eng. R., 189.

point is right, the plaintiff cannot, as the Andalusian was not registered until after the collision, claim the relief he seeks. It is, however, contended that as it was always intended to register her, and as she was in fact registered before the commencement of the action, it would be wrong for the court to hold *that the plaintiff has not brought [188 himself within the statute. It is, however, submitted that this contention must fail, for the power of claiming a limitation of liability under the Merchant Shipping Acts is a power restricting the right of obtaining compensation from a wrongdoer, and the conditions under which it has been conferred by the Legislature ought for that reason to be strictly construed. It is quite immaterial that the Andalusian was actually registered before the commencement of the action, for the right of the defendants to be recouped the damage done to their property accrued the moment the wrongful act was done, and the case can only be treated as if the compensation to which the defendants were entitled had been paid at that time. Moreover, the provisions of the 54th section of the Merchant Shipping Act, 1862, require that the amount beyond which a claimant shall not be answerable shall be ascertained with reference to the registered tonnage of the wrongdoing vessel, and at the time of the accident the Andalusian had no registered tonnage. It was never intended that the expression "damage done by improper navigation" should extend to include damage done by a vessel in motion from the land into the water.

Sir J. Holker, A.G., in reply.

Cur. adv. vult.

July 30. SIR ROBERT PHILLIMORE: On the 14th of July, 1877, the Andalusian, a vessel in the imperfect and unfinished state of equipment, which is termed a launch, having been built in a building yard on the Cheshire side of the river Mersey, was launched into that river, and brought into collision with a ship called the Angerona, which ship brought an action against the Andalusian, in this court, and I pronounced that the Andalusian was to blame for the collision. The Andalusian now brings an action for limitation of her liability under the Merchant Shipping Acts, and this action is opposed on behalf of the Angerona, upon the grounds— first, that the Andalusian was not a ship; secondly, that she was not used in navigation at the time of the collision; and, thirdly, that she was not a British registered ship.

The court is much indebted to the able and ingenious arguments of the Attorney-General and Mr. Benjamin, upon

189] all these *points. By the 2d section of the Merchant
Shipping Act,·1854, it is enacted that "ship shall include
every description of vessel used in navigation, not propelled
by oars." I am disposed to consider that a ship of this
character, in the imperfect state of a launch, might be included under this provision. The 18th section of the same
act provides that "no ship shall be deemed to be a British
ship unless she belongs wholly to owners of the following
description." It is only necessary to mention one category,
namely, "natural born British subjects." The Andalusian
is proved to have been the property of a natural born British
subject, and therefore is, in one sense, a British ship. The
last and most important question remains to be considered.
At the time of the collision this launch-ship had not her engines and boilers, and other portions of her machinery on
board, and was not in a condition to be registered, and as a
matter of fact, was not registered.

By the 19th section of the same statute, it is enacted that
"every British ship must be registered in manner hereinafter mentioned," with certain exceptions which it is not
necessary to mention, and it is further enacted that "no
ship required 'to be registered shall, unless registered, be
recognized as a British ship." The 54th section of the Merchant Shipping Act, 1862, limits the liability of shipowners
with reference to the registered tonnage of sailing ships and
the gross tonnage of steamships, without deduction on account of engine room ; and the 516th section of the Merchant
Shipping Act, 1854, provides, that nothing in that part of
that act which relates to limitation of liability, shall be construed to extend to any British ship not being a recognized
British ship within the meaning of the act. It has been
contended by the Attorney-General, that these sections
should not be construed to deprive a vessel, such as this
launch—not yet ripe for registration, but intended to be
registered when the proper time has arrived, of the benefits
of this limitation of liability ; that it would be very harsh to
put this construction upon the sections ; that this launch is
not a ship "required to be registered " because at the time
of her being launched, she was not ready for registration,
inasmuch as a launch cannot, and, in this instance, did not,
take place with all the machinery on board which it is necessary she should have at the time of registration ; that she
190] is not an offender against the *law by reason of not
having been fully registered, and that being owned by a
British subject and intended to be registered, she might be
recognized as a British ship.

After much consideration, I am unable to arrive at this conclusion. It is in the first place, to be remembered, that the limitation of liability is a creature of statute law; that upon general principles of jurisprudence and natural equity, as I think Dr. Lushington more than once said, the sufferer is entitled to a *restitutio in integrum* at the hands of the wrongdoer; that it is not a question of the launch being liable to a penalty for necessary non-registration, but a question whether she is entitled to a privilege which operates severely upon the sufferer, unless she brings herself strictly within the plain meaning of the provisions of the statute. Now, it appears to me, that however unfortunate it may be that the collision should have happened before the privilege of limitation of liability accrued, I think that it has so happened, and that with respect to this privilege at least, the Merchant Shipping Acts, from beginning to end, treat a registered British ship as the only recognized British ship entitled to this privilege. I must, therefore, reject the claim of the plaintiff in this suit, and there must be judgment for the defendants with costs.

Solicitors for plaintiff : *Duncan, Hill & Dickinson.*
Solicitors for defendants : *Simpson & North.*

[4 Probate Division, 1.]

Nov. 18, 1878.

[IN THE COURT OF APPEAL.]

1]   *NIBOYET V. NIBOYET.

Divorce—Foreigner—Jurisdiction—20 & 21 Vict. c. 85, ss. 27, 31.

The court has jurisdiction to grant a divorce against a foreigner.

A marriage was solemnized at Gibraltar between a Frenchman and an English woman. The husband resided for several years in England, but being a consul for France he retained his domicile of origin. The wife presented a petition for a divorce, alleging adultery committed in England, and desertion. The husband appeared under protest and prayed to be dismissed:

Held, reversing the decision of Sir R. J. Phillimore (by James and Cotton, L.JJ., Brett, L.J., dissenting), that the court had jurisdiction to grant a divorce.

APPEAL from an order of Sir R. J. Phillimore dismissing a petition for a divorce.

The question was, whether the court had jurisdiction to receive a petition for divorce presented by a wife, her domicile of origin being English, the marriage having been celebrated at Gibraltar, and the alleged adultery having taken 2] place in England; the *domicile of the husband, who was a consul for France, having been and continuing to be French, although he was residing in England.

Sir R. J. Phillimore dismissed the petition on the ground that the court had no jurisdiction as against a foreigner.

The facts of the case are fully stated in the report in the court below ('), and in the judgments of the judges in the Court of Appeal.

July 16, 19, 1878. *Inderwick*, Q.C., and *Swabey*, for the petitioner: There is no case in which a natural born subject of the Queen has been refused a divorce on any question of domicile. The divorce might not be recognized in some other countries, but such divorces are constantly granted in every Protestant country. The wife being domiciled here is entitled to a divorce *valeat quantum*. The husband and wife were in this country; the offence was committed here, and they are entitled to the benefit of the law of this country: *Brodie* v. *Brodie* (²); *Ratcliff* v. *Ratcliff* (³); *Firebrace* v. *Firebrace* (⁴); *Deck* v. *Deck* (⁵). If every natural born subject can under ss. 27 and 31 of the act 20 & 21 Vict. c. 85, present a petition, she must have a right to a divorce: *Bond* v. *Bond* (); *Le Sueur* v. *Le Sueur* (⁶); *Simonin* v.

(¹) 3 P. D., 52.
(²) 2 Sw. & Tr., 259.
(³) 1 Sw. & Tr., 467.
(⁴) 47 L. J. (P. A. & D.), 41.
(⁵) 2 Sw. & Tr., 90; 29 L. J. (P. M. & A.), 129.
(⁶) 2 Sw. & Tr., 93; 29 L. J. (P. M. & A.), 143.
(⁷) 1 P. D., 139; 17 Eng. R., 442.

Mallac ( ); *Sottomayor* v. *De Barros* ('). The question could not have arisen formerly because the canon law was the same all over the world. The statute 23 Hen. 8, c. 9, as to citation out of the jurisdiction, did not apply if the defend ant had appeared. In *Lindo* v. *Belisario* ('), the court de cided the question. *Donegal* v. *Donegal* () may have been collusive in its origin. In *Shaw* v. *Attorney-General* ('), and *Lloyd* v. *Petitjean* ('), the court assumed jurisdiction. No doubt in many of these cases the parties did not appear, but that cannot have given the court jurisdiction. It must be admitted that much of the reasoning in *Shaw* v. *Gould* () is against the petitioner, but all the Lords did not concur in the reasoning. *The observations in *Warrender* v.   [3 *Warrender* (') are strongly in favor of the petitioner.

Gorst, Q.C., and *Greenwood*, for the Queen's proctor : It is clear that every husband and every wife in every country cannot apply to this court for a divorce. One at all events must be domiciled here, and the wife's domicile is that of her husband, so that here both are foreigners. *Deck* v. *Deck* () is the only case in which the court has pronounced for a divorce between persons not domiciled here. But the courts of one country ought not to make orders affecting the personal status in another country of a person not dom iciled here. Even if English subjects by origin domiciled abroad can be divorced here, it does not follow that this court will interfere against a person who has never been domiciled here. In *Bond* v. *Bond* ("), the court is said to have followed *Deck* v. *Deck* ('), but that is not so. *Brodie* v. *Brodie* (''), referred to in *Manning* v. *Manning* (''), is in favor of the respondent ; and so is *Wilson* v. *Wilson* (''). *Sot tomayor* v. *De Barros* (') was a very strong case. The doubts as to the wife's domicile raised in *Dolphin* v. *Robins* (") were not shared by all their Lordships. *Pitt* v. *Pitt* (") shows that there cannot be a divorce granted unless the parties are domiciled here. *Yelverton* v. *Yelverton* (") and *Tollemache* v. *Tollemache* (") show that the court has no jurisdiction in such cases.

Inderwick, Q.C., in reply.   *Cur. adv. vult.*

(') 2 Sw. & Tr., 67; 29 L. J. (P. M. & A.), 97.
    (') 3 P. D., 1.
    (') 1 Hagg. Cons., 216.
    (') 3 Phillim., 597.
    (') Law Rep., 2 P. & D., 156.
    (') 2 Curt. Cons., 251.
    (') Law Rep., 3 H. L., 55.
    (') 2 Cl. & F., 488.
       (") 1 Sw. & Tr., 574.

(') 2 Sw. & Tr., 90; 29 L. J. (P. M. & A.), 129.
    (") 2 Sw. & Tr., 93 ; 29 L. J. (P. M. & A.), 143.
    (") 2 Sw. & Tr., 259.
    (") Law Rep., 2 P. & D., 223.
    (") Ibid, 435; 4 Eng. R., 663.
    (") 7 H. L. C., 390.
    (") 4 Macq., 627.
       (") 1 Sw. & Tr., 557.

Nov. 18. JAMES, L.J.:   This case was argued and decided
in the court below, and. has been argued before us, exclusively on one question, viz., whether an English court has
or has not jurisdiction to dissolve the marriage tie between
persons not domiciled in England, the dissolution of such a
marriage being the real and avowed object of the petitioner in
the suit.   That such should be the avowed object of the suit,
4]   and that the parties should be *desirous of having the
opinion and decision of the court on that question, does not
preclude the court from seeing, or enable the court to avoid
seeing, what the real question raised by the pleadings is.
The petitioner after alleging the marriage at Gibraltar, alleges
desertion for two years, and upwards, without reasonable
excuse, and adulterous intercourse committed and continued from the year 1867 down to the institution of the proceedings, at and in the neighborhood of Sunderland, in the
county of Durham, and therefore in England.   The prayer
is, that the court would be pleased to decree the dissolution
of the marriage, but to that is added the usual prayer for
general relief, the exact words are, "such other and further
relief in the premises as to this honorable court may seem
meet."   I read these words as being in substance such further or other relief.   The respondent appeared under protest,
and pleaded to the jurisdiction in substance, that he was by
birth and domicile a Frenchman, and that, although he had
resided in England from the year 1862 to the year 1869, and
afterwards from the year 1875 to the commencement of the
suit, he so resided in the discharge of his duties in the consular service of his own government.   And he sums up
thus : "During the whole period of the respondent's absence
from France aforesaid, he retained his French domicile, and
has not now and never had any domicile in England.   By
reason of the premises, this honorable court has not had any
jurisdiction to dissolve the marriage of the respondent with
the petitioner."   And he prayed to be dismissed from all
further observance of justice in this suit.   But whether the
respondent is or is not right in his contention that the court
has no jurisdiction to dissolve the marriage, the plea to the
jurisdiction must fail if the petitioner be entitled to any relief whatever in the suit, on the facts stated in her petition.
Can there be any doubt that before the English act of
Parliament transferring the jurisdiction in matrimonial
causes, from the church and her courts to the sovereign and
her court, the injured wife could have cited the adulterous
husband before the bishop, and have asked either for a restitution of conjugal rights or for a divorce *a mensa et thoro*,

and in either case for proper alimony? The jurisdiction of the Court Christian was a jurisdiction over Christians, who, in theory, by virtue of their baptism, became *members [5 of the one Catholic and Apostolic Church The church and its jurisdiction had nothing to do with the original nationality or acquired domiciles of the parties, using the word domicile in the sense of the secular domicile, viz., the domicile affecting the secular rights, obligations, and status of the party. Residence, as distinct from casual presence on a visit or *in itinere*, no doubt was an important element ; but that residence had no connection with, and little analogy to, that which we now understand when we endeavor to solve, what has been found so often very difficult of solution, the question of a person's domicile. If a Frenchman came to reside in an English parish his soul was one of the souls the care of which was the duty of the parish priest, and he would be liable for any ecclesiastical offence to be dealt with by the ordinary, *pro salute animæ*. It is not immaterial to note that dioceses, and states or provinces, were not necessarily conterminous. The Channel Islands, which are no part of England, are in the diocese of Winchester, and the Isle of Man is in the province of York ; and many similar cases might be found on the continent. And although the laws of the state somtimes interfered by way of coercion, regulation, or prohibition, with the Courts Christian, the latter acted *proprio vigore*, and they administered their own law, not the law of the state, and they administered it in their own name and not in the name of the sovereign. The language of the act creating the existing court strikingly illustrates this, when it enacts that all jurisdiction vested in or exercised by any Ecclesiastical court or person in England, &c., shall belong to and be vested in Her Majesty. It was not previously vested in her, although she had appellate jurisdiction as supreme Ecclesiastical judge. If before that act had passed, the facts alleged in this petition had occurred, and the injured wife had applied to the Bishop of Durham for such relief in the matter as was then competent to him, is it possible to conceive any principle on which the guilty husband could demur to the ordinary's jurisdiction? The wrong done in his diocese, the offending party openly and scandalously violating the laws of God and of the church in his diocese, why should he decline to interfere? What could it be to him whether the offender was born in any other diocese or born in any other country, Christian, heathen, or Mahometan, and had *not in the eye of the [6 secular court abandoned his domicile therein? And what

principle of international law could there have been to create
the slightest difficulty in the way of a decree for restitution,
for separation *a mensa et thoro*, or for alimony? The wrongdoer has elected to reside within the local limits of the
jurisdiction of the Church Court, and neither the Court of the
State nor the Church or State Court of his own country
has any ground for alleging that the Church Court appealed
to is usurping a jurisdiction, when it by Ecclesiastical monition, declaration, and censure, compels the offending
party to give proper redress or declares the offended party
to be thenceforth relieved from the obligation to provide for
or to adhere to the bed and board of the other; which was
what the decree of divorce *a mensa et thoro* really amounted
to.   If I were asked to define, and it were necessary to define, what in the particular case of matrimonial infidelity
constituted a matter matrimonial in England at the time
when the act was passed, I should define it to be a case of
infidelity where the matrimonial home was in England—the
matrimonial home in which the offended husband ought to
be no longer bound to entertain the unchaste wife, or in
which the chaste and offended wife ought to be no longer
bound to share the bed and board of the polluted husband
—the matrimonial home, the purity of which was under the
watch and ward of the church there.   I will give two illustrations of my meaning.   It appears to me impossible to suppose that an English court would lose its jurisdiction or not
have jurisdiction because the guilty party consorted with
his or her paramour outside the territorial limits of the diocese or on a journey.   And, on the other hand, I do not think
that an English court ought to have exercised or would
have exercised jurisdiction in the case of a French matrimonial home by reason of an act of infidelity done during
a visit, or in transit to or through the English diocese.   The
proper court in that case would have been a French court.
I arrive, therefore, at the conclusion that the facts stated in
the petition would have constituted a matter matrimonial in
England, in which some jurisdiction would, but for the
passing of the act, have been vested in and exercised by an
Ecclesiastical court or person in England, and that such
jurisdiction now belongs to and is vested in Her Majesty.
7]   This appears to me sufficient to dispose *of the plea
which denies all jurisdiction whatever in the subject-matter
of complaint.

But the same considerations appear to me also sufficient
to dispose of the question which was discussed and considered in the court below, viz., whether the court can under

the English statute decree a dissolution of the tie. The act
was passed expressly "to constitute a court with exclusive
jurisdiction in matters matrimonial in England, and with
authority in certain cases to decree the dissolution of a marriage." I read that as "in certain of *such* cases" "in certain of *such* matters matrimonial" in England. And that
is followed by the 27th section which is quite universal in
its language. "It shall be lawful for any husband . . . .
it shall be lawful for any wife." That universality is of
course to be limited by the object and purview of the act,
and is to be read thus: "And in any such matrimonial matter in England it shall be lawful for any husband or wife,
&c." And except such limitation I am unable to find any
limitation which on any principle of construction ought to
be implied. Of course it is always to be understood and implied that the Legislature of a country is not intending to
deal with persons or matters over which, according to the
comity of nations, the jurisdiction properly belongs to some
other sovereign or state. But I do not find any violation of
that comity in the Legislature of a country dealing as it may
think just with persons native or not native, domiciled or
not domiciled, who elect to come and reside in that country,
and during such residence to break the laws of God or of
the land. I am unable, more especially, to imply any limitation of the authority of the court by reference to the principles of law which were at the passing of the act in the
course of development in the American courts, where it is
now settled that the jurisdiction is to be determined by the
domicile of the complaining party at the time of the complaint brought. No such principle had then been established
or recognized in any court in this kingdom, and on the con-
in one very important division of the realm, Scotland, the
Scotch courts had exercised jurisdiction in entire disregard
of any such principle. That fact was present to the English
Legislature with full knowledge of certain very painful and
embarrassing consequences resulting from it. But the Legislature did not think it necessary or *fit to make any pro-   [8
vision in that behalf. A Scotch divorce *a vinculo* between
persons not Scotch by domicile was held to be void in England as to an English marriage. But so far as Scotland was
concerned, and so far as any consequences of the divorce
would have to be determined by the Scotch courts, the divorce was to all intents and purposes valid and effectual.
It is very inconvenient and very distressing that two people
should be husband and wife in one country and not husband
and wife in another, that their marriage should be a lawful

marriage in one and bigamous in another, that they should
be compellable by the laws of a Christian country to a cohabitation which by the laws of another Christian country
would be an adulterous intercourse. And if we could find
in the general application of the, law as laid down by the
American authorities a satisfactory escape from the difficulty, we should be sorely tempted to strain the construction of the English statute to bring it into harmony with
that law. But I do not find any such satisfactory solution
in that law. In the first place it appears to me to be a violation of every principle to make the dissolubility of a marriage depend on the mere will and pleasure of the husband,
and domicile is entirely a matter of his will and pleasure.
It would be very desirable no doubt that a judicial decree
of dissolution of a marriage affecting the status of husband
and wife, a decree *in rem*, should be if possible recognized
by the courts of every other country according to the principles of international comity. But is such a result possible ? Would any French court recognize the dissolution of
a French marriage because the French husband had been
minded to establish his domicile in England ?

In England a divorce *a vinculo* is only granted under certain conditions, and with very careful precautions and stringent regulations to prevent its being the result of collusion
between the parties. But supposing the collusion to assume
the form of an abandonment of the English domicile, and
the establishment of a new domicile in some country where
a divorce can be obtained, almost if not quite, by mutual
consent and arrangement ? Would an English court, or
ought it to recognize such a dissolution of the marriage tie
and allow the English wife, whose original domicile would be
restored thereby to return to this country and contract a
9]   *valid marriage here. Moreover a dissolution of the
marriage for adultery is only one of the modes by which the
status or alleged status of husband and wife is judicially
determined. A decree of nullity of a pretended marriage is
quite as much a decree *in rem*, and has all the consequences.
How would it be possible to make domicile the test of jurisdiction in such a case ? Suppose the alleged wife were the
complainant, her domicile would depend on the very matter
in controversy. If she was really married her domicile
would be the domicile of her husband, if not married then
it would be her own previous domicile. If domicile is required to give jurisdiction, that requisite could not be supplied by the negligence or consent of the party; and a decree
for dissolution would always be liable to be opened by a

fresh litigation raising the question—often a most difficult question—of the domicile.

I find myself unable to arrive at the conclusion that the domicile of the complaining party ought to determine the existence of the limits of the jurisdiction given by the English statute to the English court. The only limitation which I can find is the limitation of the jurisdiction to those matters which come under the category of matrimonial matters in England, to every one of which the English law, with all its consequences, so far as England is concerned, must be applied. I have endeavored to ascertain what such a matter is, and I have arrived at the conclusion that the present case comes within that category. It is a misfortune that that law with its consequences may not be recognized in another country, but that misfortune inevitably arises from an irreconcilable conflict of laws produced by the irreconcilable views of different Christian communities as to the dissolubility or indissolubility of the marriage tie, or the sufficiency of the grounds for a dissolution. I do not think that I am overruling any English case in holding that on the facts stated in this petition the wife is entitled to the relief she asks, or in laying down that where and while the matrimonial home is English, and the wrong is done here, then the English jurisdiction exists and the English law ought to be applied.

BRETT, L.J.: In this case the wife filed a petition praying for a dissolution of her marriage on the ground of alleged adultery and *desertion by her husband. The peti- [10 tion in form prayed for a dissolution of the marriage. It contained also in the usual general terms an alternative prayer "for such other and further relief in the premises as to the court may seem meet." The material facts stated in the different pleadings, as the facts on which the parties relied, were that the parties were in 1856 married at Gibraltar according to English form, that the wife was English by birth, the husband French by birth, that the husband had from 1862 to 1869 acted as French vice-counsel at Sunderland, and from 1875 to 1876 and until he was cited to appear in this suit, as French consul at Newcastle. The adultery was committed in England. The wife was resident in England. The petition was served in England. The husband was residing in England. But the husband had never been domiciled in England. The husband appeared under protest and pleaded to the jurisdiction. No one appeared for the husband at the hearing, but the Queen's proctor, by direction of the court, intervened and submitted for argument two propositions or questions: (1) Whether, it being admit-

ted by the petitioner that the respondent has a French domicile, this court has any jurisdiction as a matter of general
law? (2) If it has not jurisdiction as a matter of general
law, whether the particular circumstances of this case give
it jurisdiction? In discussing these propositions all the arguments in the court below were confined to the question
whether the court had jurisdiction to grant a dissolution of
the marriage. The judgment was given on that question
alone. The arguments of counsel before us were all pointed
at that question alone. That was the only relief really desired or really demanded in either court. That being so, it
appears to me, though I say it with great deference, that we
ought, as matter of decision, to deal with that question alone;
dealing with the jurisdiction of the court in other matters
only in case and so far as that jurisdiction may seem to us
to assist in determining whether the court had or had not
jurisdiction to grant a dissolution of marriage under the circumstances of this case. The arguments preferred in support of the appeal and in favor of the jurisdiction were:
First, that the husband though not completely domiciled
in England was *bona fide* and more than casually resident
in England, and that such residence made him liable to the
11] jurisdiction of any court exercising *jurisdiction in
matrimonial causes in England; secondly, that his mere
presence in England when charged with a matrimonial offence gave jurisdiction to the English court; thirdly, that
the mere application to an English court of a person claiming its decree against another for an alleged matrimonial
offence gives jurisdiction to the court. It was argued from
these propositions that the mere fact of the statute constituting a court with power to grant divorce gave the court
jurisdiction to entertain the prayer for divorce as against
this respondent, if the case could be brought within any
of these propositions. But it was further argued, fourthly,
that upon the true construction of the terms of the statute
it in terms enacts jurisdiction over all persons, English or
foreign, and that an English court must obey the statute
The decision must in the end depend upon the construction
of the statute, because before it no court in England had jurisdiction to grant divorce; but as preliminary to the decision it seems desirable to consider the matter according to
some general principles. As has been frequently pointed
out, a decree of dissolution of marriage cannot be the judicial declaration of a mere consequence agreed between the
parties for the breach of a contract, as in ordinary cases of
breach of contract, or a mere compensation or individual

remedy for the breach of a private duty as in an action
for damages, but can only be a judicial sentence of the
law of the country in and for which the court is acting,
by which such court assumes to alter not only the relation between the parties but the status of both. Marriage is the fulfilment of a contract satisfied by the solemnization of the marriage, but marriage directly it exists
creates by law a relation between the parties and what is
called a status of each. The status of an individual, used
as a legal term, means the legal position of the individual
in or with regard to the rest of a community. That relation
between the parties, and that status of each of them with
regard to the community, which are constituted upon marriage, are not imposed or defined by contract or agreement
but by law. The limitations or conditions or effects of such
relation and status are different in different countries. As
that relation and status are imposed by law, the only law
which can impose or define such a relation or status (i.e.,
relative position) so as to bind an individual, is the law to
which such individual is *subject. The power of a law [12
which enacts restrictions on or grants relaxations of the
personal condition of individuals is territorial, i.e., limited.
The meaning of that is, that it is only binding on the natural
born subjects of the lawgiver or on those who have otherwise become his subjects. By the universal comity of nations foreigners do not by their mere sojourn in a country
make themselves subject to its personal laws, other than its
police or correctional law, or laws expressly enacted to bind
all who are in fact within its territorial limits. By the universal independence of nations each binds by its personal laws
its natural born subjects and all who may become its subjects. By the universal consent of nations every one who
elects to become domiciled in a country is bound by the
laws of that country, so long as he remains domiciled in it,
as if he were a natural born subject of it. It follows then
from the nature of the subject-matter, that laws which, for
certain enacted or predicated causes, as distinguished from
causes agreed upon between the parties, alter the personal
relations of individuals to each other, or their relation to
the community, can only bind the natural born subjects of
the enacting country or foreigners who have become domiciled in it; but they may, consistently with principle and
the universal consent of nations, bind both of these. The
law then which enables a court to decree an alteration in the
relation between husband and wife, or an alteration in the
status of husband or wife as such, is as matter of principle

the law of the country to which by birth or domicile they owe
obedience. The only court which can decree by virtue of such
law is a court of that country. Another mode of considering
the subject, or another line of argument is this.   A judgment
or decree determining what is the status of an individual is a
judgment or decree *in rem.*   It is, therefore, if binding at all,
not only a binding judgment as between the parties to the
suit, but is to be recognized as binding in all suits and by
all parties.   Such a judgment, where the jurisdiction of the
court which made it is recognized, is treated as binding and
final, not only by all the courts of the same country but by
the courts of all countries.   The jurisdiction of the courts of
a country in which people have elected to be and are in fact
domiciled is in all countries admitted, and the judgment or
decree *in rem* of the courts of a country in which people are
13]   domiciled *is therefore treated as binding in all countries.   But the jurisdiction of a country exercised, whether
by legislation or by its courts, over the personal status of the
subjects of another country who are merely present in it, or
are merely sojourning in it, or are merely cited to it, is not
admitted by the country of which such people are subjects
or by other foreign countries. If, therefore, the courts of
any country should assume, by a decree of divorce or any
other decree determining the relation or the status of a married person, to alter that relation or status of a foreigner not
domiciled, the decree would not be recognized as binding by
the courts of any other country.   Then the relation or status
of a married person, would be one in the country of the court
making the decree, and another in all other countries.   That
is to say, a man or woman would be treated as married in
one country and not so in another ; or married people might
be enjoined to live together in one country and to live apart
in another.   No court ought to assume or presume to place
people in so deplorable a position, unless forced to do so by
the express law of the country whose law it is administering.
Another general consideration seems to be as follows.   The
status of marriage is the legal position of the married person as such in the community or in relation to the community.   Which community is it which is interested in such
relation ?   None other than the community of which he is a
member, that is, the community with which he is living as a
part of it.   But that in fact is the community in which he is
living so as to be one of the families of it.   That is the community in which he is living at home with intent that among
or in it should be the home of his married life.   But that is
the place of his domicile.   It follows that upon principle

the only law which should assume to alter his status as a married man is the law of the country of his domicile; the only court which should assume to decree such alteration is a court administering the law of that country. The country or society of his birth is not interested in his marriage status so long as he is domiciled elsewhere.

From all these considerations it seems that the only court, which on principle ought to entertain the question of altering the relation in any respect between parties admitted to be married, or the status of either of such parties arising from their being *married, on account of some act which by [14 law is treated as a matrimonial offence, is a court of the country in which they are domiciled at the time of the institution of the suit. If this be a correct proposition, it follows that the court must be a court of the country in which the husband is at the time domiciled; because it is incontestable that the domicile of the wife, so long as she is a wife, is the domicile which her husband selects for himself, and at the commencement of the suit she is *ex hypothesi*—still a wife. The case of an adulterous husband deserting his wife by leaving the country of his domicile and assuming to domicile himself in another, might seem to raise an intolerable injustice; but we cannot help thinking that in such case, if sued by his wife in the country in which he had left her, he could not be heard to allege that that was not still the place of his married home, i.e., for the purpose of that suit, of his domicile. So much for the principle, if there were no authorities. It is very right, however, to consider the decisions of the courts of other countries, and very necessary to consider the decisions of the courts of our own country; the decisions in our own country before the statute being, it should be observed, necessarily decisions as to the extent to which English courts, or the English Legislature acting as if judicially, recognized the decisions of foreign courts. Now the American authorities seem clear, and they are of great importance, because the American courts have been called upon oftener than any others to consider and deal with the subject. The results of American decisions seem to be most ably collected and stated in Mr. Bishop's elaborate, and, in my opinion, admirable treatise on Marriage and Divorce. "When parties," he says at § 709, "resort to the courts of a foreign state or country without a change of domicile, for the purpose of obtaining a divorce to which they would not be entitled by the laws of their own country, the divorce, as we shall hereafter see, will be treated at home as invalid. The true principle is undoubtedly that the foreign tribunal had no proper jurisdiction over the subject-matter, being one of status, with which the courts of the parties' domicile are alone competent to deal." At § 721: "The tribunals of a country have no jurisdiction over a cause of divorce wherever the offence may have occurred, if neither of the 15] parties has an *actual *bona fide* domicile within its territory; nor is this proposition at all modified by the fact that one or both of them may be temporarily residing within reach of the process of the court, or that the defendant appears and submits to the suit." At § 740: "The place where the offence was committed, whether in the country in which the suit is brought or a foreign country, is quite immaterial." At § 741: "The domicile of the parties at the time the offence was committed, is of no consequence; the jurisdiction depends upon their domicile at the time the proceeding is instituted and judgment rendered." At § 745: "It is immaterial to this question of jurisdiction, in what country or under what system of divorce laws the marriage was contracted." These extracts, which seem to me, after minute reference to the cases on which they are founded, to correctly state the effect of a multitude of American decisions, given by judges of the highest authority, make it clear that in America the only court which can decree any alteration in the relations between married people or in the status of either of them as a married person, is the court of the country in which they are domiciled at the time of the institution of the suit. This is also laid down by Story in his treatise on the Conflict of Laws, ch. 5, s. 110: "As to the constitution of the marriage, as it is merely a personal consensual contract, it must be valid everywhere if celebrated according to the *lex loci;* but with regard to the rights, duties, and obligations thence arising, the law of the domicile must be looked to." It is equally clear that the decisions in Scotland are to the contrary. The Scotch courts will entertain a suit for divorce, and decree a divorce at the instance of either party who has been resident for a certain period in Scotland, though neither party is Scotch and neither is domiciled in Scotland. This view of the courts of Scotland was, however, distinctly denied to be the law of England in *Rex* v. *Lolley* ('). Lolley and his wife were both English; the husband was domiciled in England; the marriage was in England; the husband committed adultery in England and Scotland; the wife instituted a suit against him in Scotland for a divorce; the Scotch court decreed a divorce; Lolley afterwards, and

(') 2 Cl. & F, 567 n.

during the lifetime of the lady who had procured this decree, married another woman in *England. He was [16
tried in England for bigamy, and was convicted. The case
was argued before all the judges, and the conviction was
confirmed, because they held that the Scotch court had no
jurisdiction recognized in England to grant the first divorce,
which was therefore to be treated in England as null and
void. This decision was treated by Lord Brougham in *Mc-
Carthy* v. *De Caix* (¹) as a decision that no sentence of a
foreign court can annul a marriage made in England. But
it has since been shown that it only amounts to a decision
that the Scotch court had, in the view of the English law,
no jurisdiction where the parties were not domiciled in
Scotland, though they were for a time resident there. The
elaborate judgment of Lord Brougham in *Warrender* v.
Warrender (²) is a long criticism to show that this was all
that was necessary to be decided in Lolley's case, that if it
decided more it was wrong, and that the true and only condition of jurisdiction was domicile. In the case itself, Sir
G. Warrender was married in England ; the adultery charged
against his wife was abroad ; the husband was domiciled
in Scotland at the institution of the suit ; the wife was not
in Scotland ; it was held by the House of Lords that the
Scotch court had jurisdiction, on account of the domicile
of the husband and because the domicile of the husband
was the domicile of the wife. In *Conway* v. *Beazley* (³) it was
held by Dr. Lushington that where the first husband was
English, was married in England, and was not domiciled
in Scotland, a sentence of divorce in Scotland was void because the Scotch court had no jurisdiction. But he clearly
indicated his opinion that if the husband had been domiciled
in Scotland the sentence there would have been binding
everywhere. In *Yelverton* v. *Yelverton* (⁴), in a suit for restitution by the wife, the marriage was in Scotland, the husband was Irish, and had never been domiciled in England ;
the wife was resident in England. The English court held
that it had no jurisdiction, on the ground that, at the time
of the commencement of the suit the husband was not domiciled in England. In *Firebrace* v. *Firebrace* (⁵) Sir James
Hannen acted, in a suit for restitution of conjugal rights, on
the *authority of that rule, which he said was laid [17
down in *Yelverton* v. *Yelverton* (⁴). He declined jurisdiction, on the ground that at the commencement of the suit

(¹) 2 Cl. & F., 568 n.   (³) 3 Hagg. Ecc. Rep., 639.
(²) 2 Cl. & F., 488.   (⁴) 1 Sw. & Tr., 574.
                    (⁵) 47 L. J. (P. D. & A.), 41.

the husband was not domiciled in England.   In *Tollemache* v. *Tollemache* (') a suit for divorce was instituted in England by a husband domiciled at that time in England.   The defence of the wife was that she had been previously divorced in Scotland.   But the Scotch sentence was passed when the husband was not domiciled in Scotland.   The court in the second suit held that the first divorce was void because there was no domicile in Scotland, but granted a divorce in the suit before it because there was domicile in England.   In *Ratcliff* v. *Ratcliff* (') the marriage was in India and the adultery in India, but at the institution of the suit the husband was domiciled in England.   Lord Campbell, Martin, B., and Cresswell, J., held that the domicile gave jurisdiction.   The opinion of Lord Penzance seems clear from what he said in *Wilson* v. *Wilson* ('), as cited in the judgment of the present case.   "Now it is not disputed that if the petitioner was domiciled in England at the time the suit was commenced, this court has jurisdiction; but whether any residence in this country short of domicile, using that word in its ordinary sense, will give the court jurisdiction over parties whose domicile is elsewhere, is a question upon which the authorities are not consistent.   It is the strong inclination of my own opinion that the only fair and satisfactory rule to adopt on this matter of jurisdiction is to insist upon the parties in all cases referring their matrimonial differences to the courts of the country in which they are domiciled."   But then there are English cases which are or seem to be to the contrary.   In *Simonin* v. *Mallac* (') the suit was for a decree of nullity instituted by the wife.   Both husband and wife were French, and were domiciled in France.   The marriage was in England, solemnized according to English, but not according to French, formalities.   The marriage was void according to French law, which was stated to be applicable to its subjects marrying abroad.   The English court entertained the suit because the marriage was in England, and held it bind-18] ing *because it was solemnized in due English form. It may, having regard to the French law, if it was as stated, be at least doubtful whether the suit was well decided.   But as the question was whether there ever was a valid marriage, that is to say, whether the contract to marry was ever carried out, the country in which the alleged marriage was solemnized had jurisdiction.   In *Deck* v. *Deck* (') the suit

(¹) 1 Sw. & Tr., 557.   (³) Law Rep., 2 P. & D., 441.
(²) 1 Sw. & Tr., 467.   (⁴) 2 Sw. & Tr., 67; 29 L. J. (P. M. & A.), 97.
          (⁵) 2 Sw. &. Tr., 90; 29 L. J. (P. M. & A.), 129.

was by the wife for a divorce for adultery and desertion. Husband and wife were English, and the marriage was in England, but the husband was domiciled in America. He had there married another woman. The court entertained the suit, and granted a divorce. The ground of the decision was that both parties were English, and therefore bound by the Divorce Act. This at the utmost only shows that the act applies to English subjects, whether domiciled or not, and does not show that it is applicable to foreigners not domiciled. But I respectfully differ from the decision. In *Callwell* v. *Callwell* (¹) the suit was by the husband for a divorce. Husband and wife were Irish; the marriage was in Ireland, the adultery was in England and on the continent. The husband was not domiciled in England. Cresswell, J., Willes, J., and Hill, J., doubted as to jurisdiction, but entertained the suit on the ground that the wife had appeared without protest, and therefore was too late to plead to the jurisdiction. This decision must be supported on a rule of pleading which is recognized in one of the stages of *Wilson* v. *Wilson* (²) as still in force. It is, unless as matter of pleading, inconsistent with the cases above cited. In *Brodie* v. *Brodie* (³) the husband was Australian and domiciled in Australia. The marriage and adultery were in Australia. The court entertained the suit. The judgment was: "We say nothing as to what the effect of the evidence might be in a testamentary suit; we think that the petitioner was *bona fide* resident here, not casually or as a traveller. After he became resident here his wife was carrying on an adulterous intercourse in Australia. He is therefore entitled to a decree *nisi* for a dissolution of the marriage." If this was held to be a domicile, it is consistent with all the cases; if it is to be taken as a decision that there can be a minor *species of domicile sufficient for one purpose and not [19 for another, I know of no authority or ground of reason for such a distinction. I cannot agree with it. I do not think that cases arising before the Ecclesiastical courts in which, a matrimonial offence being alleged against subjects or against domiciled foreigners, the question arose whether by reason of their temporary sojourn in one of the dioceses they might be served with process in that diocese, are applicable. Such questions did not raise the point of the general jurisdiction of the law of the country, but rather a question of procedure within an admitted jurisdiction of such law.

(¹) 3 Sw. & Tr., 259.   (²) Law Rep., 2 P. & D., 435; 4 Eng. R. 663.
(³) 2 Sw. & Tr., 259.

On the grounds, then, of the nature of the subject-matter of
the suit, of the nature of the judgment given in such suit,
of the interest of the country in which the dispute arises, of
the comity due to other nations, of the immense mischief of
a judgment of such a nature being given under circumstances
which will prevent it from being recognized everywhere, and
of the preponderance of authority in Egland, I am of opinion
that, unless the statute has otherwise enacted, the domicile of
the husband in England at the institution of the suit is, according to the true construction of the statute, the fact which
gives jurisdiction to the English Divorce Court to decree
divorce; that with such a domicile the court has jurisdiction
over a foreigner as well as over an English subject; that without such domicile the court has ho jurisdiction, though the
party is an English subject. The same rule, I confess, seems
to me to apply, for the same reason, to its power to grant any
relief which alters in any way that relation between the
parties which arises by law from their marriage. It applies, therefore, as it seems to me, to suits for judicial separation and to suits for the restitution of conjugal rights. I
do not think it does apply to suits for a declaration of nullity of marriage or in respect of jactitation of marriage. I do
not think that the statute binds the court to entertain and
exercise a jurisdiction in matters over which, according to
the comity of nations, as interpreted by English judges,
and acted upon by the English Parliament in its quasi judicial legislation, the English law ought not to assume authority. It is true that the words of the statute are general;
but general words in a statute have never, so far as I am
aware, been interpreted so as to extend the action of the
20] statute beyond *the territorial authority of the Legislature. All criminal statutes are in their terms general;
but they apply only to offences committed within the territory or by British subjects. When the Legislature intends
the statute to apply beyond the ordinary territorial authority of the country, it so states expressly in the statute, as
in the Merchant Shipping Act, and in some of the Admiralty
Acts. If the Legislature of England in express terms applies its legislation to matters beyond its legislatorial capacity, an English court must obey the English Legislature,
however contrary to international comity such legislation
may be. But unless there be definite express terms to the
contrary, a statute is to be interpreted as applicable and as
intended to apply only to matters within the jurisdiction of
the Legislature by which it is enacted. In this statute there
are no such definite express terms. It may be observed,

moreover, that the preamble confines the purview of the
statute to English matrimonial causes. It does not say to
British causes, but to English causes. It thus limits the
statute and the action of the court to a part only of Her
Majesty's dominions or subjects. It cannot be confined
to matrimonial offences committed in England, or it would
not reach the case of a matrimonial offence committed abroad
by a domiciled English husband or wife. Yet it is confined
to an English matrimonial cause. It seems to me to follow
that it is confined to a matrimonial offence committed by persons domiciled in England. I am of opinion that, upon principles of law, irrespective of the terms used in the statute
which are relied on, the court had no jurisdiction, and that
the statute did not by any terms used in it give jurisdiction
in this case. I am therefore of opinion that the judgment
should be affirmed.

COTTON, L.J.: The facts on which this case comes before
us have been already sufficiently stated, and it is unnecessary for me to repeat them. I agree with the judge of the
Court of Divorce that the fact of the respondent having in
1863 presented a petition to that Court of Divorce seeking
for a dissolution of his marriage with his wife, the present
petitioner, which was in 1865 dismissed, does not give that
court jurisdiction. The question is, whether, independently
of that circumstance, the Court of Divorce has jurisdiction
*to make a decree against a respondent not domiciled [21
in England. In considering this question it must be remembered that the respondent has been a resident in this country, not casually or as a traveller, but for several years, and
that the adultery—the breach of the matrimonial contract
on which the petitioner bases her claim for relief—was committed in England. Moreover, the respondent was resident
in England at the time when the petition was presented and
was served in England with the process of the court; and
the question is, not whether the respondent was liable to
be called on to defend himself in the court, but whether
the court has under the circumstances jurisdiction as
against a person duly cited to appear before it to make the
decree prayed—that is, jurisdiction over the subject-matter
of the suit. The decision depends on the true construction
and effect of the act 20 & 21 Vict. c. 85. In any court in
England that is the only question, for it has been long established that aliens coming into this kingdom are bound
by its statutes if on their true construction applicable to
them. The petition contains a prayer for general relief, but
the only question argued, and that which we have to decide

is, whether the Court of Divorce has jurisdiction to dissolve
the marriage.   I shall, however, for the purpose of arriving
at a decision on this point, first consider whether the court
has jurisdiction to grant the petitioner any relief at all.
The preamble of the act recites that it is expedient to establish a court with exclusive jurisdiction in matters matrimonial in England; and s. 6 vests in Her Majesty all
jurisdiction exercised by any Ecclesiastical court in England, and directs that this shall be exercised by the new
court established under the act.   Has this court jurisdiction
to entertain a petition for restitution of conjugal rights or for
a judicial separation presented by one of two married persons
against the other where both are resident though not domiciled in England, and where the breach of the matrimonial
compact has been committed in England either by refusal to
cohabit or by adultery?   A judgment for either of these objects is, in my opinion, not open to the objection mainly relied
on in support of the judgment of the court below, namely,
that a decree for dissolution would alter the status of the
spouses, and that this depends on the law of their domicile,
22]   and ought to be left to the *courts of the country where
that may be.   If we are to consider the question of public
policy, assuredly every state has an interest in taking measures to secure that all residents within its local limits shall
faithfully perform the obligations of the marriage contract.
But the question is as to the effect of the act.   The complaint
of the injured party in the case which I have supposed would,
in my opinion, be a matrimonial matter arising in England,
and therefore one for the decision of which the court was
constituted.   Moreover, the Diocesan courts, whose jurisdiction is vested in the Court of Divorce, looked to the residence not to the domicile of the respondent for the purpose
of deciding whether a suit could be entertained; and I see
no reason for supposing that an Ecclesiastical court, acting
pro salute animæ, would have declined to interfere against
an offending husband or wife in respect of an act committed
within the local limits of its jurisdiction, because the parties
though resident within those limits were domiciled elsewhere.
There is, in my opinion, no sufficient reason for limiting the
right and liability to sue and be sued in the Court of Divorce
to persons domiciled in England; and my opinion is, that
under the circumstances of this case the Court of Divorce
has jurisdiction to entertain a petition for judicial separation against the respondent.   If so, has it under s. 27 jurisdiction to entertain a petition for dissolution of marriage?
In my opinion it has.   That section is in the most general

terms. It gives to any husband or any wife power under certain circumstances to present a petition for dissolution ; and s. 31, subject to certain exceptions not applicable to the case which we are now considering, gives the petitioner, on proof of his or her case, a right to a decree for dissolution. No doubt the words "any husband and any wife" must be subject to some limitation. They cannot be considered as giving to a husband or wife resident and domiciled abroad a right to petition against a wife or husband, neither resident nor domiciled here ; but, in my opinion, this section gives to any husband or wife, who under the earlier provisions of the act would have a right to apply to the court for relief, power to present a petition for the remedy given by ss. 27 and 31 ; and I am of opinion that the court cannot on the reasonable construction of the act disclaim jurisdiction to entertain a *petition under s. 27 against [23 the respondent, without holding that the court has no jurisdiction to give the petitioner any relief in the matter. I have already stated my opinion that the court has jurisdiction to entertain a petition in such a case as the present against the respondent for judicial separation ; and the result, in my opinion, is that he cannot successfully dispute the jurisdiction of the court to decree a dissolution of his marriage. It is, however, necessary to deal with the argument that the effect of a decree maintaining the jurisdiction of the court in this case may be that, inasmuch as status depends on the law of the country of domicile, the respondent and the petitioner, though in this country no longer husband and wife, may in other countries be still so regarded. It is true that this may be the result, but the question before us is what on the true construction of the act is the jurisdiction of the court—in other words, what is the relief given by the act to the wife as against her offending husband. I cannot hold that the difficulties which may arise from a decree for dissolution are sufficient to prevent the court from acting on what, in my opinion, is the true construction of the act.

Warrender v. *Warrender* (¹) was much referred to during the argument, but that case cannot in any way be relied on as a decision in favor of the petitioner's right to sue here, because in that case, in which there was a divorce in the Scotch court, the domicile of the parties was Scotch. But Lord Lyndhurst in that case, on the assumption that the decree of a Scotch court would not in England affect the personal status of persons who, though domiciled in Scotland, were married in England, deals with the argument

(¹) 2 Cl. & F., 488.

1878   Niboyet v. Niboyet.

based on this objection in a passage which may usefully be referred to. He says (¹) that if these difficulties arise on the true construction of the act of Parliament, it is for the Legislature to amend the matter by legislation, and not for the court to do so apart from its ordinary rules in construing statutes.

In support of the view that the Court of Divorce has no jurisdiction over a person resident but not domiciled in England, cases have been referred to in which the court has relied on the domicile of the defendant as giving jurisdiction against a person not resident here. But these cases are not 24] authorities that there is no jurisdiction *against a person resident though not domiciled here. In each case the decision must be taken with reference to the facts before the court, and a decision that to give the court jurisdiction as against a respondent not resident in England it is necessary to prove that his domicile is in this country, does not establish that where there is residence in England there must also be domicile here. It is unnecessary to refer to all the cases which have been cited or referred to during the argument. I will, however, refer to one or two of them. In *Yelverton* v. *Yelverton* (²), which was a case relied upon as supporting the judgment under appeal, the respondent was not domiciled in England or resident here ; and the decision in effect was that the court had no jurisdiction to cite him—that is, no jurisdiction over him personally, he not being resident here, and that the fact of his not being resident here was pointedly before the learned judge when he gave his judgment appears from a passage of the report (³) : "Major Yelverton is not an Englishman ; he never had a residence in England, nor was he ever guilty of any misconduct towards the plaintiff in England ; and from the passage which I have read from the report of *Carden* v. *Carden* (⁴), I infer that Dr. Lushington would have held that there was no jurisdiction unless evidence had been given of some residence in England. That foundation was laid in every case that was cited, and I cannot treat any one of them as an authority for overruling Major Yelverton's protest." In *Tollemache* v. *Tollemache* (⁵), another case relied upon, the court, on the petition of the husband, granted a decree of divorce after a decree for divorce obtained by him in Scotland, but did so not on the ground that the decree of the Scotch court was void in Scotland, but because, assuming that the decree ob-

(¹) 2 Cl. & F., at p. 560.   (³) 1 Sw. & Tr., at p. 590.
(²) 1 Sw. & Tr., 574.   (⁴) 1 Curt., 558.
                (⁵) 1 Sw. & Tr., 557.

tained in Scotland was sufficient to enable the divorced wife to marry in that country, which assumes that the Scotch court had jurisdiction, it did not give the petitioner—the man who was domiciled in England—a personal capacity to marry there. That is in effect that the decree of the Scotch court for divorce, though effectual there, was of no effect in England. In *Tovey* v. *Lindsay* (¹) the House *of Lords [25 did not pronounce any final decision, and the question was whether a wife, who was residing in England and living separate from her husband under the provisions of a deed of separation, could be cited to appear in Scotland where her husband was domiciled. It was a question of jurisdiction over the person of the defendant, not over the subject of the suit.

In my opinion there is no authority—certainly none binding on this court—for holding that in this case the court has no jurisdiction to decree a dissolution. I think that on the true construction of the act the court ought to entertain the petition, and that the judgment dismissing the petition on the ground of want of jurisdiction ought to be reversed.

Protest overruled and action remitted.

Solicitors for petitioner : *Chapman, Turner & Prichard.*
Solicitor against petition : *Queen's Proctor.*

(¹) 1 Dow., 117.

See 11 Eng. R., 878 note ; 10 Abb. N. C., 838 note ; 16 Amer. Law Reg. (N.S.), 65–78, 193–204 ; 26 Alb. L. J., 447, 467 ; 21 Am. Law Reg. (N.S.), 595 note ; 11 Cent. L. J., 201, 26 Am. Rep., 27 note.

The rule that the domicile of the wife follows that of the husband, is inapplicable to a case of divorce, where the parties are actually living in different jurisdictions : Dutcher v. Dutcher, 39 Wisc., 651 ; Mellen v. Mellen, 10 Abb. N. C., 329, 338 note ; Hunt v. Hunt, 72 N. Y., 218, affirming 16 Hun, 622.

See Kennedy v. Kennedy, 87 Illinois, 250 ; Burlington v. Swanville, 64 Maine, 78.

In many of the States it is held that a court in one State cannot adjudge to be dissolved, and at an end, the matrimonial relation of a citizen of another State domiciled and actually abiding there throughout the pendency of the judicial proceeding without a voluntary appearance by the defendant, and with no actual notice to him thereof, and without personal service of process on the defendant within the state of the court ; People v. Baker, 76 N. Y., 83.

English : Briggs v. Briggs, 5 Prob. Div., 163, post, p. 383, 11 Cent. L. J., 46 ; Id., 201 note.

Indiana : Hood v. State, 56 Ind., 263, 26 Am. R., 21, 27 note.

Kansas : See Lewis v. Lewis, 15 Kans., 181.

Massachusetts : Sewall v. Sewall, 122 Mass., 156.

Michigan : Wright v. Wright, 24 Mich., 180.

See Platt's Appeal, 80 Penn. St. R., 501.

Minnesota : State v. Armington, 25 Minn., 29.

See Morey v. Morey, 27 Minn., 265.

New Jersey : Doughty v. Doughty, 27 N. J. Eq., 315, 28 id., 581.

· **New York :** People v. Baker, 76 N. Y., 78 (reversing 15 Hun, 256), distinguishing Kinnier v. Kinnier, 45 N. Y., 535 ; Hunt v. Hunt, 72 id., 217 ; Cheever v. Wilson, 9 Wall., 108, and Pennoyer v. Neff, 95 U. S., 714 ; Stanton v.

Crosly, 9 Hun, 370, 375 and cases cited; People v. Smith, 13 id., 414.

Pennsylvania: Platt's Appeal, 80 Penn. St. R., 501 ; Love v. Love, 10 Phila., 453.

Though such a judgment is not void as to the plaintiff. It cannot be attacked by him or his grantor: Elliot v. Wohlfrom, 55 Cal., 384.

A wife who has appeared in a suit for divorce, brought by her husband against her in another State, in which a decree is rendered in his favor, and who subsequently executes a release reciting the divorce therein obtained, and for a pecuniary consideration discharging all her claims against him and his estate, cannot, after his subsequent marriage and cohabitation with another woman, maintain a libel for divorce therefor against him in this State, on the ground that the court in the other State had no jurisdiction of his libel, without proving that he went to that State for the purpose of procuring a divorce : Loud v. Loud, 129 Mass., 14.

Where the statute requires residence for a specified time as a condition of suing for divorce, the residence must be actual and bona fide, *animo manendi* : Dutcher v. Dutcher, 39 Wisc., 651.

The statute of Wisconsin requires that the *plaintiff* shall have been a resident of the State for one year, no matter how long the defendant may have been : Dutcher v. Dutcher, 39 Wisc., 651·

So in **Missouri**: Pate v. Pate, 6 Mo. App., 49.

In **Iowa**: Whitcomb v. Whitcomb, 46 Iowa, 437.

In **Michigan**: Wright v. Wright, 24 Mich., 180.

In **Tennessee**: Gettys v. Gettys, 3 Lea, 260.

Where a soldier of English origin married a Scotswoman in Scotland, and after living with her there for one year and two months, deserted her in Ireland where he had moved with his regiment and disappeared, the Lord Ordinary held that the court had no jurisdiction to entertain an action of divorce, at the wife's instance, on the ground of the desertion : Appleby v. Appleby, 19 Scot. L. Repr., 602.

A judgment of divorce in another State may be declared void on account of fraud : Doughty v. Doughty, 27 N. J. Eq., 315, 28 id., 581.

Jurisdiction of the person of a defendant in an action for divorce may be acquired by a court of the State in which he or she is a domiciled citizen, by such proceedings in the nature of service of process as the law of the State has made equivalent to personal service within its jurisdiction ; so long as the citizen retains that relation to the State, he owes it allegiance and is subject to its laws, and this subjection he cannot throw off by a temporary or prolonged absence from the State. A judgment of divorce, therefore, rendered by the court of another State against a domiciled citizen thereof, upon a substituted service of process such as the law of the State has authorized in the case of an absent defendant, is valid *in personam* so as to affect a dissolution of the marriage contract, and is conclusive upon the defendant in the courts of this State, although he was not within the territorial jurisdiction during the progress of the suit, and did not appear therein : Hunt v. Hunt, 72 N. Y., 218, affirming 9 Hun, 622.

Where a guilty party in a case of divorce marries again without leave of court during the life of the other party, and afterwards obtains such leave, a continued cohabitation in the belief that the marriage already solemnized is or has become legal, does not render it so : Thompson v. Thompson, 114 Mass., 566.

Where by statute an illegitimate daughter was made legitimate and made " capable to inherit and transmit any estate as fully as if she had been born in lawful wedlock," held that by the act the daughter became for all purposes of inheritance the lawful child and prospective heir of her father, and vested with the same inheritable blood as if born to him on that day in wedlock : McGunnigh v. McKee, 77 Penn. St. R., 81.

The act of a State legislature declaring that " A." was thereby constituted a legal heir of B., confers no capacity upon A. to acquire property beyond the State passing the act : Barnum v. Barnum, 42 Md., 253.

[4 Probate Division, 26.]

July 9, 1878.

*THE LADY DOWNSHIRE (1876, H. 297.)   [26

Damage—Mersey Sea Channel Act, 1874 (37 & 38 *Vict. c.* 52), *sec.* 1, *sub-sect.* 2
—Infringement by Possibility contributing to Collision—The Merchant Shipping Act. 1873 (36 & 37 *Vict. c.* 85), *s.* 17.

It is provided by 37 & 38 Vict. c. 52, s. 1, that all vessels having two or more
masts shall, whilst lying at anchor in the sea channels leading to the river Mersey,
exhibit two white lights, and that any general Regulations for preventing Collisions
at Sea for the time being in force under the Merchant Shipping Acts shall be construed as if this regulation were added thereto. A vessel failing to exhibit lights
as required by this section is liable to be held in fault under the 17th section of the
Merchant Shipping Act, 1873, for the provisions of the 1st section of 37 & 38 Vict.
c. 52, are to be regarded as virtually incorporated with the Regulations for preventing Collisions at Sea, made under the Merchant Shipping Acts.

THIS was an action of damage instituted on behalf of
the owners of the three-masted schooner or brigantine, Edward John, of 137 tons register, against the steamship Lady
Downshire.

The statement of claim alleged, in effect, that on Friday,
the 12th of May, 1876, the Edward John was at anchor in
the Crosby channel in the river Mersey, with an anchor
light duly exhibited, *when the Lady Downshire came   [27
up the channel with her masthead light and her side lights
open, and rapidly approaching ran into the Edward John,
striking her violently on the starboard bow and causing her
to sink ; that the Lady Downshire was to blame for not keeping clear of the Edward John, and for neglecting to keep a
good look-out, and to observe the 16th article of the Regulations for preventing Collisions at Sea.

The statement of defence alleged that, on the day of the
collision, the Lady Downshire, with a good look-out, was
proceeding up the Crosby channel in charge, by compulsion
of law, of a duly appointed Liverpool pilot, and whilst so
proceeding, a white and green light was seen about a point
or a point and a half on the starboard bow, apparently about
two miles off ; that shortly afterwards the green light disappeared and a red light was seen ; that there being but one
white light the lights seen were supposed to be the masthead
and side lights of a steamship, and upon the red light being
seen the helm of the Lady Downshire was, by order of the
pilot, put hard a-port and her engines stopped and reversed,
when it was seen that the white light was on board the Edward John and the colored lights were those of another vessel, and although the helm of the Lady Downshire was kept

hard a-port and her engines were kept reversing her port
bow came into collision with the starboard bow of the Edward John; that the collision was occasioned by the neglect
of the Edward John to exhibit two bright lights in pursuance
of the provisions of 37 & 38 Vict. c. 52, s. 1, but that if any
blame was attributable to the Lady Downshire, it was wholly
attributable to the neglect or default of her pilot.

Witnesses were examined orally in court on behalf of the
plaintiffs. The evidence of the witnesses proved that the
collision occurred within the limits within which, under
the provisions of 37 & 38 Vict. c. 52, a vessel of the description of the Edward John ought when at anchor to have exhibited two bright lights, that the Edward John, at the
time of the collision, was in charge of a Liverpool pilot;
and that such pilot had informed the master of the Edward
John that he ought to exhibit two bright lights, but that the
master had answered that he had only one anchor light on
board. No witnesses were examined on behalf of the defendants.

28]   *Milward*, Q.C., and *W. G. F. Phillimore*, appeared
for the plaintiffs.

Butt, Q.C., and *E. C. Clarkson*, for the defendants.

SIR ROBERT PHILLIMORE: The first question to be determined in this case is, whether 37 & 38 Vict. c. 52, s. 1, is or
is not brought within the 17th section of the Merchant Shipping Act, 1873. The former act, entitled an Act to make
Regulations for preventing collisions in the sea channels
leading to the river Mersey, enacts in the first section, that—

Any general Regulation for preventing Collisions at Sea for the time being in
force under the provisions of the Merchant Shipping Acts, shall be construed as
if the following regulations were added thereto.

And then there follow two sub-sections, the first of which
contains provisions as to the course to be taken by steamships and vessels in tow of steamships "when navigating
in the sea channels or approaches to the river Mersey, between the Rock lighthouse and the furthest point seawards,
to which such sea channels or approaches respectively are
for the time being buoyed on both sides." The second sub-
section provides as follows:

Every ship at anchor in the said sea channels or approaches, within the limits aforesaid, shall carry the single white light prescribed by Article 7 of the
General Regulations for Preventing Collisions at Sea, made under the authority
of the Merchant Shipping Acts Amendment Act, 1862, at a height not exceeding
twenty feet above the hull, suspended from the forestay, or otherwise, near the
bow of the ship where it can be best seen; and in addition to the said light all
ships having two or more masts shall exhibit another similar white light, at
double the height of the bow light, at the main or mizzen peak, or the boom
topping lift, or other position near the stern, where it can be best seen.

It has been admitted in this case, and is proved by the evidence, that the collision occurred within the sea channels of the river Mersey, within the meaning of these words as they are used in the sub-section to which I have just referred. It has also been admitted that the plaintiffs' vessel, the Edward John, was a three-masted brigantine, and ought, according to the direction in such sub-section, to have carried two lights, whereas she only carried one on her fore-stay, though that was a light of considerable power. On these admitted facts, it has been contended by the counsel for the plaintiffs, that according to 37 & 38 Vict. c. 52, that act is not incorporated with the Merchant Shipping Acts; *and that con- [29 sequently it is not open to the defendants to contend that the Edward John by the absence of a second light has brought herself within the 17th section of the Merchant Shipping Act, 1873, whereby it is provided as follows:

If in any case of collision it is proved to the court before which the case is brought that any of the Regulations for preventing collision contained in or made under the Merchant Shipping Acts, 1854 to 1873, has been infringed, the ship by which such regulation has been infringed shall be deemed to be in fault, unless it is shown to the satisfaction of the court that the circumstances of the case made departure from the regulation necessary.

Now, after giving my best attention to the arguments on both sides, I am of opinion that the words of the 17th section of the Merchant Shipping Act, 1873, "Regulations for preventing collisions contained in or made under the Merchant Shipping Acts, 1854 to 1878," do refer to and include the regulations contained in 37 & 38 Vict. c. 52. Consequently, as it is admitted that the Edward John, by exhibiting only one anchor light, infringed one of such last-mentioned regulations, and as we are of opinion that on the result of the evidence the want of a second light was such an infringement of the regulation as might by possibility have contributed to the collision, I must pronounce that the Edward John is to blame for the collision, unless I think it has been shown to my satisfaction that the circumstances of the case made departure from the regulation necessary. Now I am of opinion that no such circumstances are shown in this case. The pilot was perfectly aware of the law and told the master to put up two lights. The master said he had no second light, and could not exhibit it. I am therefore of opinion that the Edward John must be holden to blame under the statute, no sufficient reason being given for her non-compliance with 37 & 38 Vict. c. 52. The question remains whether the Lady Downshire, the vessel proceeded against, is also to blame for the collision. [His Lordship then proceeded to comment on the evidence with regard to the manœuvres taken by the Lady Downshire, and coming to the conclusion that she had been guilty of negligent navigation, pronounced both vessels to blame for the collision.]

Solicitors for plaintiffs : *Lowless & Co.*
Solicitors for defendants : *Stokes, Saunders & Stokes.*

---

4 Probate Division, 30.]

Aug. 7, 1878.

30]   *THE SOPHIA COOK (Liv. 1878, V. 306).

Bottomry—Practice—Interest.

A bottomry bond on ship, freight, and cargo provided for payment of a bottomry loan, together with interest at 8 per cent., at or before the expiration of five days after the arrival of the ship at her port of discharge. The bond further provided that an additional premium of 10 per cent. on the loan should become payable if default was made in payment. The ship having arrived at her port of discharge, default was made in payment of the bond, and a suit was instituted by the bondholder against ship, freight, and cargo, to recover the amount of the loan and interest, and the additional premium of 10 per cent :

Held, that the additional premium of 10 per cent. could not be enforced against the cargo, but that the bondholder was entitled to interest at 4 per cent. from the date when the bond became payable until payment.

THIS was an action of bottomry instituted on behalf of the assignee of a bottomry bond on·the brigantine Sophia Cook, of Halifax, Nova Scotia, her cargo and freight, against the said vessel, her cargo and freight. The proceedings were carried on in default against the ship, but an appearance in the action was entered on behalf of the owners of cargo.

The statement of claim, after alleging, *inter alia*, that the Sophia Cook having received damage on a voyage from New York to Goole, and put in to Philadelphia for repairs and supplies, and there borrowed on bottomry the sum of $4,515 43c. to pay for such repairs and supplies, proceeded in the 3d and 5th paragraphs thereof in substance as follows :

3. By a bond or instrument of bottomry, dated the 3d day of May, 1878, the master of the Sophia Cook did, in consideration of the sum of $4,515 43c. advanced to him by one John Smith, of Halifax, Nova Scotia, bind himself, the Sophia Cook, her freight and cargo, to repay the said sum of $4,515 43c. with a bottomry premium thereon of 8 per cent., amounting to $361 23c., at the exchange of $4 92c. to the pound sterling, at or before the expiration of five days after the arrival of the Sophia Cook at her anchorage in the port of discharge, with an additional premium of 10 per cent. on

the sum advanced, if the said sum and premium should not be paid within the said period of five days. But in case of the loss of the Sophia Cook such an average as should by custom become due on the salvage was alone to be paid.

5. The Sophia Cook, after such bond given, proceeded on her voyage, and arrived, on or about the 13th of June last, safely at her anchorage in the port of Goole, being her port of discharge, bringing her cargo and earning freight. The said period of five days expired on the 18th of June last, without payment being *made of the sum due under [31 the said bond, and the plaintiff is and was at the date of the issue of the writ in this action entitled to sue for and receive the said sum of $4,515 43c., and $361 23c., amounting at the exchange aforesaid to the sum of £991 3s. 10d., and the said additional premium of 10 per cent. on the sum advanced amounting to $451 54c., or, at the exchange aforesaid, to the sum of £91 15s. 6d.

The defendants in their statement of defence admitted the validity of the bottomry bond save so far as it purported to bind the cargo to an additional premium of 10 per cent., and alleged that the master of the vessel had no authority to bind the cargo-owners to the payment of such additional premium. The action was heard on affidavits before the judge in court.

In an affidavit made by the plaintiff it was stated in effect that in fixing the amount of maritime interest payable on a bottomry bond the prompt payment of the bond on the termination of the risk was a material consideration, and that in practice the masters of vessels obtained loans on bottomry at lower rates of premium in cases where they allowed a claim to be inserted in the bond providing for the payment of an additional rate of premium if delay should occur in payment of the money due on the bond.

W. G. F. Phillimore appeared for the plaintiff: The question whether the court will assist the plaintiff in obtaining payment of the additional premium referred to in the statement of claim cannot be considered as settled. In the case of *The D. H. Bills* (¹) the court refused, as against the owners of cargo, to give effect to a provision in the bottomry instrument in that case, which stipulated that in default of prompt payment of the principal money and maritime interest due on the bond £10 per cent. interest until payment should be paid. In the subsequent case of *The Cargo ex Vineland* (²), where the cargo-owners did not ap-

(¹) See note (a) at end of case.   (²) Not reported. [July 23, 1878, M. 180.]

pear at the hearing, the court pronounced for the principal money due on a *respondentia* bond with maritime interest, and additional interest exceeding 4 per cent. per annum in respect of the time since the bond fell due. It is in the interest of shipowners that no undue restriction should be placed on the terms on which money can be obtained on bottomry.

E. C. Clarkson, for the defendants: In the case of *The* 32] *Cargo *ex Vineland* (¹) the-cargo owners did not appear, and the case cannot be considered as an authority.

SIR ROBERT PHILLIMORE: I cannot allow the additional premium of 10 per cent. The practice in the registry is to allow interest at 4 per cent. from the date of the instrument of bottomry becoming payable until payment thereof, and I cannot sanction any additional allowance.

I adhere to the rule I acted upon in the case of *The D. H. Bills* (').

Solicitors for plaintiffs: *Bateson & Co.*
Solicitor for defendants: *Carr.*

(¹) Not reported. [July 23, 1878, M. 180.]   (') See note (a) below.

(*a*) June 25, 1878.

THE D. H. BILLS (1878, B. 150).

IN this case the master of the American ship D. H. Bills, in consideration of a loan on bottomry, executed an instrument of bottomry on ship, freight and cargo. The material portions of such instrument of bottomry were substantially as follows:

At or before the expiration of three days after the ship D. H. Bills should have arrived at Newport, Monmouth, aforesaid, and before the unloading of any part of the said cargo, pay free of any average whatever, to the said Messrs. Howard, Fox & Co., or their assigns, the sum of £1,295 British sterling, together with the further sum of £161 17s. 6d. British sterling for bottomry premium thereon at the rate of £12 10s. percentum, making together the sum of £1,456 17s. 6d. British sterling: and also, in case default should be made in payment of the said last-mentioned sum at the time aforesaid, pay to Messrs. Howard, Fox & Co., or their assigns, interest for the same sum at the rate of £10 percentum per annum from the time aforesaid, until payment of the said sum.

After the safe arrival of the D. H. Bills at Newport, Monmouthshire, default was made in payment of the sums due on bottomry at the time specified, and the plaintiff instituted this action against the D. H. Bills, her cargo and freight, and thereon claimed to recover the above-mentioned sum of £1,456 17s. 6d., and an additional sum of interest at the rate of 10 per cent. per annum from the time at which, according to the instrument of bottomry, payment ought to have been made, until payment thereof.

An appearance in the action was entered for the owners of the cargo on board the D. H. Bills.

The action was heard.

W. G. F. Phillimore, on behalf of the plaintiff, moved for judgment in the action.

J. P. Aspinall, for the defendants, did not dispute the right of the [33 plaintiff to payment of the sums lent on bottomry, together with maritime interest for the same, but submitted that the master of the D. H. Bills had no authority to bind the cargo-owners to the payment of the 10 per cent. interest claimed in respect of delay in payment.

SIR ROBERT PHILLIMORE : The defendants in the case have taken an objection to the court making any order which might render them liable for the payment of the additional interest at 10 per cent., which the master of the D. H. Bills has agreed should be paid. The practice in the registry in bottomry cases is, I am informed, to allow interest at the rate of 4 per cent. from the date from which the amount secured on bottomry ought to have been paid until payment thereof. To this rate of interest the plaintiff will be entitled. Subject to the observations I have made, I pronounce for the validity of the instrument of bottomry in this case.

Solicitors for plaintiff: *Clarkson, Son & Greenwell*.
Solicitors for defendants : *Waddilove & Nutt.*

[4 Probate Division, 33.]

Nov. 22, 1878.

THE TIRZAH (1878, L. 267).

Merchant Shipping Act, 1878 (36 & 37 *Vict.* c. 85), s. 17—*Infringement of Regulations for preventing Collisions at Sea.*

Where in a case of collision between ships, it is proved that the Regulations for preventing Collisions at Sea have been infringed by one of the ships, and that such infringement might possibly have caused or contributed to the collision, the ship guilty of such infringement will be held to blame, unless it is shown to the satisfaction of the court that the circumstances of the case made a departure from the regulations necessary.

A brig of 239 tons, beating to windward on the starboard tack at night, encountered such rough weather as to render it justifiable in the opinion of the court that her side lights should be removed from the place where they were usually carried in the fore-part of the vessel to the after-part near the taffrail, and the lights were so removed. In this latter position the lights were obscured to the extent of a point, or a point and a half, on either bow. The brig came into collision with a bark on the opposite tack:

Held, that the circumstances of the case did not justify the brig in carrying the lights so as to be obscured as above-mentioned, and that the brig must be deemed to be in fault under the 17th section of the Merchant Shipping Act, 1878.

THIS was an action of collision instituted on behalf of the bark Duke of Wellington against the brig Tirzah.

The statement of claim alleged in substance as follows :

2. About half-past twelve A.M. of the 28th day of August, 1871, the Duke of Wellington was off Orfordness ; the wind was west south-west; the weather was *very clear, [34 but very dark, the tide was ebb ; the Duke of Wellington, under all plain sail, except mainsail and foretop gallantsail, was heading north-west and making from three to four knots an hour, the regulation lights were duly exhibited, and a good look-out was being kept on board her.

3. In these circumstances those on board the Duke of Wellington saw a vessel without lights from a quarter to half a mile off and about three points on her starboard bow. This vessel, which was the Tirzah, was watched, but no light could be seen. Suddenly the Tirzah showed a red light very close to the Duke of Wellington, whereupon the Duke of Wellington was put hard a-port and the spanker sheet and lee main braces were let go. But before the Duke of Wellington could pay off enough the Tirzah came into collision with her; the two vessels striking on their port bows, and much damage being done to the Duke of Wellington.

4. Those on board the Tirzah broke Articles 2 and 5 of the Regulations for preventing Collisions at Sea.

5. The collision was caused by the breach of the articles stated in the last paragraph hereof, or otherwise by the negligence of the defendants, or of those on board the Tirzah.

The defendants delivered a statement of defence and counter-claim. The defence was in substance as follows:

1. Shortly before 0.30 A.M. on the 28th day of August, 1878, the brig Tirzah, of 239 tons register, of which the defendants were owners, manned by a crew of eight hands all told, whilst on a voyage from Archangel to London with a cargo of oats, was in the North Sea off Orfordness.

2. The wind at such time was about west by south, blowing a strong breeze, and the weather was clear, and the Tirzah was sailing close-hauled on the starboard tack, and was proceeding at the rate of about one knot and a half per hour, with her regulation sailing lights properly exhibited, and with a good look-out being kept on board her.

3. At such time the green light of a vessel, which proved to be the Duke of Wellington, was seen at the distance of about one mile from the Tirzah, and bearing about three points on her port bow. The Tirzah was kept close-hauled by the wind in the expectation that the Duke of Wellington would keep out of the way, but the Duke of Wellington approached and rendered a collision imminent, and although she was loudly hailed, and the helm of the Tirzah was put hard down to ease the blow, the Duke of Wellington with her stem struck the port bow of the Tirzah, and did her considerable damage.

4. Save as hereinbefore appears, the defendants deny the truth of the several allegations in paragraphs 2 and 3 of the statement of claim.

5. The defendants deny the truth of paragraphs 4, 5, and 6 of the statement of claim.

7. The Duke of Wellington improperly neglected to take proper measures for keeping out of the way of the Tirzah.

8. The collision was caused by the negligent and improper navigation of the Duke of Wellington.

By way of counter-claim the defendants repeat the several averments made in the defence, and claim a declaration that they were entitled to the damage sustained by them by reason of the said collision.

*Nov. 21, 22, 1878. The action was heard before [35 the judge, assisted by two of the Elder Brethren of the Trinity House.

Witnesses on behalf of the plaintiffs and defendants were examined orally in court.

It appeared from the evidence that before the passing of the Merchant Shipping Act, 1873, the Tirzah usually carried her side-lights on stanchions placed on the quarter just before the taffrail, and that the lights so placed had been passed as efficient by the officers of the Board of Trade. After the passing of the Merchant Shipping Act, 1873, the officers of the Board of Trade had ordered the lights to be placed in the fore-part of the vessel, and they had been so placed accordingly, and from that time the lights, in ordinary weather, had been carried in the fore-part of the vessel. On the night in question, the weather being rough and the spray breaking over the bows of the Tirzah, her master removed the lights from forwards and placed them on the stanchions on the quarter. The lights, when so placed, were obscured to the extent of a point or a point and a half on either bow. The rest of the evidence, so far as material, can be gathered from the judgment.

Butt, Q.C., *W. G. F. Phillimore*, and *Stokes*, for the plaintiffs: There is evidence that the side-lights of the Tirzah were obscured to the extent of a point or so on either bow; if so, the Tirzah infringed the Regulations for preventing Collisions at Sea, in such a manner as might by possibility have contributed to the collision, and must be held to be in fault under the 17th section of the Merchant Shipping Act, 1873: *The Magnet*(') ; *The Fanny M. Carvill* (').

E. C. Clarkson, and *Myburgh*, for the defendants: No questions upon the 17th section of the Merchant Shipping Act, 1873, can arise in this case, for the two vessels were

('') Law Rep., 4 A. & E., 417.　　　　　('') 44 L. J. (Adm.), 34.

approaching each other in such a direction that the side lights of the Tirzah would, if there had been a proper look-out on board the Duke of Wellington, have been seen. If, therefore, there was any infringement of the regulations on the part of the Tirzah, such infringement could by no possibility have contributed to the collision : *The English-* 36] *man* ('). *Again, if the Tirzah did infringe the Regulations for preventing Collisions at Sea, the infringement was justified by the circumstances of the case, the state of the weather having rendered it necessary that the lights of the Tirzah should be removed aft.

Butt, Q.C., in reply :   It is impossible to say that the obscuration of the lights of the Tirzah could by no possibility have contributed to the collision.   Assuming it was necessary that the lights of the Tirzah should be removed aft, it cannot have been necessary that they should have been so placed as to be obscured.

SIR ROBERT PHILLIMORE : This is a case of collision which happened between twelve and one in the morning of the 28th of August, and about ten miles from Orfordness. The direction of the wind was stated to be west southwest or west by south, and the weather was clear but dark.   It appears that there was a strong and heavy sea, and at the time the tide was ebb.   The vessels that came into collision were the bark Duke of Wellington and the brig Tirzah. The Duke of Wellington was by far the larger ship, being 794 tons register, and the Tirzah was only 239 tons register. The Duke of Wellington was bound from South Shields to Carthagena, with a crew of sixteen hands, and a cargo of coal and coke.   Between twelve and one o'clock she says that she had all her plain sail set, except mainsail and fore-top gallantsail, and was heading north-west, making three to four knots an hour.   No question arises as to her lights, which were admitted to be proper.   She says she saw a vessel without lights from a quarter to half a mile off, and about three points on her starboard bow ; and that the vessel was watched.   There is no doubt it was the Tirzah, but no light could be seen.   Suddenly she appeared close to the Duke of Wellington, who could not pay off soon enough, and the two vessels struck together on their port bows.

Now the Tirzah's case is, that she was close-hauled on the starboard tack, and was under her topsails courses, jib, and trysail, proceeding, as she says, at the rate of about one and a half knots an hour, and that she saw the green

(') 3 P. D., 18; *ante*, p. 16.

light of the Duke of Wellington at a distance of about a mile, and about three points on her port bow. She was kept close-hauled by the wind, expecting *the Duke [37 of Wellington would keep out of the way, but the Duke of Wellington approached, and a collision took place. There is no dispute on this part of the case that the Duke of Wellington was a vessel on the port tack, and the Tirzah was on the starboard tack, therefore it was the duty of the former vessel to keep out of the way. The Duke of Wellington was unable to discharge this duty, she says, on account of the insufficiency of the red light of the Tirzah, and the 17th section of the Merchant Shipping Act, 1873, has been invoked in her favor. This section provides,

If, in any case of collision, it is proved to the court before which the case is tried that any of the regulations for preventing collision contained in or made under the Merchant Shipping Acts, 1854 to 1873, has been infringed, the ship by which such regulation has been infringed shall be deemed to be in fault, unless it is shown to the satisfaction of the court that the circumstances of the case made departure from the regulation necessary.

Now this section has undergone much discussion, both in this court and before the Judicial Committee of the Privy Council, and the result of the cases is to establish the law to be that in any case where an infringement of the regulations could by any possibility have caused or contributed to the collision, the ship infringing the regulation is brought under the section to which I have referred. Now, in this case, the Tirzah did usually carry her lights forward, and at eight or ten o'clock of the night previous to the collision they were removed aft, and, as I understand, fixed close to the taffrail.

One of the questions that I have put to the Elder Brethren of the Trinity House is, whether, having regard to the state of the weather the act of the master in shifting the lights was justifiable, and they are of opinion that it was, and in that I agree. The lights were, however, unfortunately placed aft in such a position as unquestionably to infringe the regulations, to what extent is perhaps doubtful, but we think the obscuration must have been to the extent of a point or a point and a half on either bow.

The second question arises in this state of things: could such an infringement of the regulations by possibility have contributed to the collision? That is evidently a question for the Elder Brethren, who have assisted me with their nautical skill, and, in their opinion, the question must be answered in the affirmative.

*Another question, which is, perhaps, the most [38

important question in this case, then arises, with regard
to the last branch of the same section, namely : were there
in this case any circumstances which made a departure
from the regulations necessary? It appears, on the evidence, that before the passing of the act of 1873, the officers
of the Board of Trade in Dublin passed the lights of the
Tirzah as efficient and properly placed, although they were
then in the same position as they were after they had been
shifted on the night of the collision. It also appeared in
evidence that soon after the passing of the act in question
the lights of the Tirzah were again inspected, and, under
the orders of the Board of Trade inspectors were placed forward, and were from that time, as a general rule, carried in
the fore-part of the vessel. Now it has been argued, with
considerable acuteness, that the Tirzah was constrained, by
the state of the weather, to remove her lights from the position forwards in which they had been up to eight or ten
P.M. in the evening before the collision, and in which they
were placed by the direction of the officers of the Board of
Trade; and that the placing of the lights in their original
position aft was the best makeshift that could be adopted
in the emergency. After giving much consideration to this
argument, I have arrived at the conclusion that it does not
offer a sufficient excuse for the infringement of the regulations that this vessel was in such rough weather as to render it justifiable or necessary that her lights should be
removed from forward to aft. It seems to the court that, if it
was necessary to place the lights aft, proper places ought
to have been provided in the after-part of the vessel, so that
the lights, when carried aft, would have been visible according to the regulations. Such places were not provided; I
must, therefore, under the provisions of the statute, hold
that the Tirzah is deemed to be in fault for the collision.

Solicitors for plaintiffs: *Stokes, Saunders & Stokes.*
Solicitors for defendants: *Cooper & Co.*

[4 Probate Division, 39.]

Jan. 29, 1879.

*THE CONSTITUTION (1879, O. 40).   [39

Jurisdiction—Salvage—National Vessel of War commissioned by Government of Foreign State.

A vessel of war commissioned by the government of a foreign state, and engaged in the national service of her government, was stranded on the coast of England. She had a cargo of machinery on board her, alleged to belong to private individuals, of which her government had for public purposes charged itself with the care and protection. Important and efficient salvage services were rendered to the ship and her cargo. A suit was instituted on behalf of certain of the salvors against the ship and her cargo. The court refused to order a warrant to issue for the arrest of the ship or cargo, and held it had no jurisdiction to entertain the suit.

THIS was an action of salvage instituted on behalf of the owner, master, and crew of the British steam-tug Admiral against the United States frigate Constitution and her cargo, for the recovery of salvage remuneration for services rendered to the property proceeded against.

On the 27th of January counsel on behalf of the plaintiffs applied ex parte to the judge in court to order a warrant to issue for the arrest of the Constitution, and for a warrant to arrest her cargo.

The affidavit to lead warrants made by the owner of the Admiral was, so far as material, as follows:

On the 17th day of January instant, I received a telegram from Lieutenant Viry, Swanage Station, to the following effect:

"American frigate Constitution ashore on Bollard Point. Send strongest tug immediately. Two if possible."

I thereupon despatched my tug Admiral to the assistance of the vessel Constitution, and she rendered important and efficient salvage services to the ship Constitution and her cargo, and was instrumental in getting the vessel off the ground.

After the salvage services were completed, I, on the 21st of January instant, received the following letter from the consular agent at Portsmouth:

"United States of America.
"Consular Agency, Portsmouth.
"20th January, 1879.

"Mr. George Drover,—If you have any claim to present against the U.S. frigate Constitution, please put it in writing, and bring it to my office as early as possible to-morrow forenoon. If you cannot come, forward it to me by return post. The ship sails soon.

"I am, sir, your obedient servant,
"C. E. McCheane, U.S. Consular Agent."

*In reply to this letter, I, on the 21st instant, sent the following tel- [40 egram:

"Impossible my coming Portsmouth. I claim £1,500 services rendered by my tug Admiral. You no doubt are aware my tug was the means of towing Constitution off. Malta and the three other tugs could not move ship, but when we-commenced towing, ship immediately came off.   Please wire reply immediately, as I leave shortly for London."

Afterwards, on the 23d instant, I received a sum of £200 in recognition of the services rendered by my said tug, accompanied by the following letter :

> " United States of America.
>   " Consular Agency, Portsmouth.
>   " 22d January, 1879.
>
> " Mr. George Drover, Cowes.
> " Sir,—I am instructed by the captain of the U.S. frigate Constitution, on behalf of the United States Government, to forward to you a check for £200, in recognition for the services rendered to that vessel upon the occasion of her stranding on Bollard Point by your tug Admiral, and by the master and crew of that tug.   I shall be obliged to you to settle with the master and crew accordingly.
> " It may prevent some misconception on your part if I inform you the value of the Constitution and cargo, principally empty casks and machinery, on board her does not exceed £12,000.   My government are happy that the services, with the important co-operation of H.B.M. tug Malta, were rapidly and easily successful.
>   " I am, sir, your obedient servant,
>   " C. E. McCheane, U.S. Consular Agent."

Such sum of £200 is entirely inadequate and insufficient compensation for the services rendered, and on the 25th instant I returned the said sum to the consular agent, accompanied by the following letter :

>   " January 25th, 1879.
>   " Constitution.
> " McCheane, Esq.
> " Sir,—Herewith please find check received to-day for £200.   I cannot think of accepting so small a sum.   I am willing to refer the matter to the Admiralty Court.   If you wish to communicate with me, please address letter to care of Clarkson, Son & Greenwell, 24 Carter Lane, Doctor's Commons, London.   I shall be there Monday morning, 10 o'clock.
>   " Yours truly,
>   " George Drover."

The frigate Constitution had on board her at the time of the services a valuable cargo, consisting principally of machinery belonging to private individuals, exhibitors at the Paris Exhibition, and was on a voyage from Havre to New York.   I am informed and believe that the value of the vessel Constitution and her cargo amount to considerably over £12,000.

On the 28th of January instant, I received a further letter from the American consulate to the following effect :—" Your favor of the 25th instant returning the check for the £200 has been received.   This award for the services of your tug Admiral to the Constitution was made advisedly, and is considered by competent and disinterested experts as ample and liberal, and my information is that it is final.   Check will remain at my office till noon of the 15th of February next, when, you having failed to call for it, its amount will be forwarded by me to the United States Navy Department.   The said vessel Constitution and the 41] *cargo on board her are now lying off Portsmouth, and will leave immediately for New York."

Applications have been made by my solicitors to the American Legation, and I am unable to obtain sufficient compensation for the services of the said tug without the aid and process of this honorable court.

The judge ordered the motion to be adjourned, and directed that notice thereof should be given in the meantime to the Secretary of State for Foreign Affairs ; to the Minister of the United States in London, and to the commander of the Constitution (¹).

Jan. 29.   Notice in pursuance of the above-mentioned order having been given, the motion was renewed.

The following letter from the Minister of the United States, which had been received by the solicitors retained in the case on behalf of the Government of the United States, was read to the court:

Legation of the United States.
London, January 28th, 1878.

Messrs. Thomas Cooper & Co., Solicitors, &c.

Gentlemen,—The accompanying notice marked *A*, having been left at this Legation with the janitor after the office was closed last evening, I shall be obliged to you to instruct counsel to be present in court to-morrow morning to inform the Right Honorable the Judge of the Admiralty Court that the ship against which the warrant has been applied for by the owners, master, and crew of the steam-tug Admiral is the United States national ship of war Constitution, regularly commissioned by the Government of the United States, and that the Constitution at the time of the alleged salvage services was engaged in the national service of the United States for public purposes, and in pursuance of a special act of Congress passed in that behalf.

You will please also instruct counsel to inform the judge that the so-called cargo consists of property of which the United States Government has for public purposes charged itself with the care and protection.

Under these circumstances, I, as the representative of the Government of the United States, cannot recognize that the High Court of Justice has any jurisdiction whatever in this case.

I am, respectfully yours,

John Welsh.

Jan. 27.   *The Admiralty Advocate* (*Dr. Deane*, Q.C.), on behalf of Her Majesty's Government: Her Majesty's Government recognize the character of the Constitution as a public vessel belonging to a sovereign state, and protests against the court exercising jurisdiction.

Milward, Q.C., and *W. G. F. Phillimore*, in support [42 of the motion :   No doubt that the Constitution is a national ship of war of the government of a foreign state, but it has never been decided that such a ship is free from a maritime lien for salvage.   Indeed, there are dicta in the recent case of *The Charkieh* (²) strongly in favor of the liability to arrest in such a case extending to all ships whether public or private.   Even although the court should decide in favor of the immunity of the Constitution herself from arrest, the question would still remain whether the plaintiffs have not a right to require the court to assist them in enforcing their claim against the cargo on board.   There is no evidence in the case that that cargo has ceased to belong to private individ-

(¹) With the assent of the judge the   take the requisite steps to carry out this
solicitors for the plaintiffs undertook to   order.
(²) Law Rep., 4 A. & E., 59; 6 Eng. R., 400.

uals; and this being so, the mere fact that it has for a time been taken charge of by the United States Government cannot prevent a lien for salvage attaching which this court must recognize. It is one thing to hold that the public ship of a friendly nation is by comity free from arrest in our ports, but it is going very much further to assert that her extra-territoriality shall in all circumstances be so complete that no civil or criminal process of the courts of the country whose waters she has entered can be executed on board her. Suppose a British subject to be improperly confined on board of a foreign ship of war in our waters, is it to be assumed that the courts of this country are powerless to set him at liberty? (¹) Opinions of Attorney-Generals of the United States, vol. i, pp. 25, 47; *The Santissima Trinidad* (²).

[SIR ROBERT PHILLIMORE: The last mentioned case refers to prize property. Prize property is property of a peculiar character, and has always been treated as subject to peculiar considerations.]

The very question raised in the present case, as to the liability of the owners of the cargo of a foreign national vessel of war to pay salvage, must have been decided in the case of *The Prins Frederik* (³), if the foreign government con-
43]   cerned there had not *ultimately submitted to an arbitration, and it is curious, assuming the exemption of public vessels from local jurisdiction to be really so extensive as that now claimed, that throughout the report of that case there should be found nothing either in the arguments or the observations of Lord Stowell to lead to the conclusion that the warrant which had issued in that case had been wrongly extracted. It has always been considered that the greatest encouragement should be given to shipowners to render salvage services to vessels in danger, and it cannot be to the real interest of foreign governments that no tribunal should exist before which claims for assistance rendered to foreign public ships can be brought: *The Exchange* (⁴).

E. C. Clarkson, for the Minister of the United States of America: The Government of the United States have possession of the property against which the plaintiffs ask that a warrant should issue, and such property cannot be arrested without a violation of the implied undertaking under which the Constitution came within the jurisdiction of this

---

(¹) Report of the Royal Commission on Fugitive Slaves, 1876, p. xxxi (Memorandum by the Lord Chief Justice of England).

(²) 7 Wheaton, 283.
(³) 2 Dodson, 451.
(⁴) 7 Cranch, 116.

country: *The Exchange* ('). It is unnecessary to dilate upon the evils which might possibly flow from an attempt to execute the process of the court in such a case as the present. They are indeed sufficiently obvious; for example, suppose the process of this court for delivery of the property on board the Constitution should be resisted. The question, moreover, ought not to be treated as if there was no remedy to the plaintiffs except through the procedure of this court. There is a well-known remedy open to salvors who have rendered salvage services to the ships belonging to the governments of foreign sovereign states, but that remedy is not to be found in an application to this court. The remedy in such cases is a representation to the proper department of Her Majesty's Government through whom any remuneration really due for the alleged service might be obtained.

The Admiralty Advocate: Her Majesty's Government have a right to prohibit the issue of the warrants prayed for in this case. The plaintiffs have not been able to bring forward any precedent in favor of their application; nor have they shown any reason why the property which they ask to have arrested should be more *liable to seizure by [44 process out of this court than any other property of a foreign government brought into this country under the implied assent of the Crown: *Nathan* v. *Virginia* (*).

Milward, Q.C., in reply.

Cur. adv. vult.

SIR ROBERT PHILLIMORE: On Monday last an application was made to this court to allow a warrant to issue, and to be served upon a ship of war belonging to an independent state at amity with Her Majesty. The court directed the case to stand over, and suggested that it would be proper that notice should be given to his Excellency the Minister of the United States in this country, and also to the Secretary of State for Foreign Affairs. The court has had reason to congratulate itself that it took that step, because the result has been that it has had the advantage of hearing the opinion of counsel on behalf of the United States Government, and also the opinions of the law officers of the Crown. Now it appears from the affidavit to lead the warrants in this case, that on the 17th of January a telegram was sent from Swanage Station to the owner of the Admiral at Cowes to the following effect: "American frigate Constitution ashore on Bollard Point. Send strongest tug immediately.

(') 7 Cranch, 116.   (*) 1 Dallas, 81 n.

Two if possible," and that the tug Admiral was sent in consequence; and that the ship was got off the point on which
she had stranded. Afterwards the consular agent for the
Un te   States wrote to the owner of the Admiral as follows :d

> If you have any·claim to present against the U. S. frigate Constitution, please
> put it in writing and bring it to my office as early as possible to-morrow fore-
> noon. If you cannot come, forward it to me by return post. The ship sails
> soon.

In reply to this letter the owner of the Admiral on the
21st of January sent the following telegram. [His Lordship
here read the telegram in question.] Afterwards, on the
23d of January, the owner of the Admiral received a sum
of £200, in recognition of the services of his vessel accompanied by the following letter. [His Lordship here read
the letter of the United States Consular Agent at Portsmouth as above set out.] The owner of the Admiral being
45]   dissatisfied with this amount of remuneration *returned
the £200 which had been sent to him, and subsequently
made the application now before the court. The question
is therefore raised whether the court has any jurisdiction in
the case. And here I must also say that the Minister of the
United States of America has written a letter which has
been read to the court, and is in the following terms. [His
Lordship here read the letter of the American Minister
above set out.] Now, it is admitted, and, indeed, it could
not be denied, that if I were to exercise the jurisdiction
prayed for in this case, I should be doing that for which
there is no legal ground or precedent. It is clear upon all
the authorities which are to be found in the case of *The
Charkieh* (') that there is no doubt as to the general proposition that ships of war belonging to a nation with whom
this country is at peace are exempt from the civil jurisdiction of this country. I have listened in vain for any peculiar circumstances to take this case out of that general
proposition. It has happened to me more than once, since
I have had the honor of sitting in this chair, to have been
requested by foreign states to sit as arbitrator and to make
an award in cases—one of collision, and two of salvage. If
a similar request had been made to the court in this case, I
would have gladly undertaken the duty sought to be imposed upon it; but I have now only to consider whether
there is any authority for the proposition that when a
foreign state refuses to waive the privilege which it possesses, it is competent to this court, nevertheless, to treat it

(') Law Rep., 4 A. & E., 59, 96.

as an individual, and serve civil process on its property. I am clearly of opinion that it would be very wrong and improper in me to assent to this application on the part of the owner of the steam-tug. I see no distinction in this case between refusing the warrant prayed for the ship and that for the cargo, and I refuse it equally in both cases. I think it unnecessary to go into the cases cited—*The Charkieh* (¹) and other cases—because they are distinguishable from the present, inasmuch as the principal points decided in *The Charkieh* (¹) were that the Khedive of Egypt was not an independent sovereign, and that his ship had been treated as a vessel of commerce and not of war. That case is materially different from the one now before the court. It has been alleged that great hardship will ensue *from [46 the decision of the court, inasmuch as it will expose foreign ships to great difficulty in future if necessity should arise for salvage services to be rendered to them. To that I must answer that it would be improper to suppose that any foreign government would not remunerate the services of salvors, taking proper means to ascertain what these services were. I have no reason to suppose that such would not be the case. Be that as it may, I have to discharge my duty, which is to say, that in the absence of precedent and principle, I cannot consent that any warrant shall issue from this court, and I must dismiss the case.

Solicitors for plaintiffs : *Clarkson, Son & Greenwell.*
Solicitor for the American Minister : *Cooper & Co.*

(¹) Law Rep., 4 A. & E., 59, 96.

[4 Probate Division, 60.]

Dec. 18, 1877.

*NOAKES v. NOAKES and HILL.   [60

Settlement—Injunction to restrain dealing with the Property.

A petitioner had obtained a decree *nisi* for dissolution of his marriage. Before an order could be obtained to vary the post-nuptial settlement, the respondent was about to sell or otherwise dispose of some of the property. The court granted an injunction to restrain her from dealing with it.

THIS was an application for an injunction. On the 30th of June, 1877, the petitioner obtained a decree *nisi* for dissolution of his marriage by reason of the respondent's adultery. There had been a post-nuptial settlement in favor of the respondent, which the petitioner was desirous should be varied, but the proper time for obtaining an order to that effect had not arrived, viz., when the decree would be made absolute.

Bargrave Deane, on an affidavit that the respondent was about to sell the property included in the settlement, moved for an injunction. He referred to the Judicature Act, 1873, s. 25, subs. 8, and Order LII, rule 4.

THE PRESIDENT : Let an injunction issue to restrain the 61] *respondent from dealing with any property which she may claim under this alleged settlement, and ordering, if the sale of the property should have taken place, that she bring into court the money received from such sale.

Solicitors for petitioner : *Glennel & Fraser.*

Solicitors for respondent and co-respondent : *Nash & Field.*

[4 Probate Division, 61.]

Feb. 19, 1878.

LAWFORD (Otherwise DAVIES) v. DAVIES.

Nullity—Irregular Marriage in Scotland—Twenty-one Days' Residence in Scotland—Mode of Computation.

Two persons domiciled in England arrived in Scotland about 4 A.M. of the 1st of July, 1870, remained there until the 21st following, and between 11 and 12 A.M. of that day contracted a marriage by declaration before a registrar :

Held, that they had not lived in Scotland for twenty-one days next preceding the marriage, and that therefore it was invalid.

THIS was a petition for a declaration of nullity of marriage by reason of informality.

The petitioner Miss Lawford, and John Augustus Jackson Davies, intending to contract a clandestine marriage, left London for Scotland by the train which was timed to pass Berwick-upon-Tweed at 4 A.M. of the 1st of July, 1870, and they arrived at Edinburgh about 6 A.M. of that day. After remaining in Scotland until the 21st of July following, they between 11 and 12 o'clock A.M. of that day contracted a marriage by declaration before the registrar at No. 51 Cockburn Street, Edinburgh. The petitioner prayed for a declaration of nullity of marriage, on the ground that the parties, being at the time domiciled in England, had not lived in Scotland for twenty-one days next preceding the marriage (¹).

(¹) 19 & 20 Vict. c. 96, s. 1: "After the thirty-first day of December, 1856, no irregular marriage contracted in Scotland, by declaration, acknowedgment, or ceremony shall be valid, unless one of the parties had at the date thereof his or her usual place of residence there, or had lived in Scotland for twenty-one days next preceding such marriage ; any law, custom, or usage to the contrary notwithstanding."

The respondent appeared in the suit, but filed no answer.
Dr. Spinks, Q.C., and *Dr. Tristram*, appeared for [62 the petitioner.

The evidence as to the facts was taken when the case was adjourned for proof of the Scotch law.

Mr. John Blair Balfour, an advocate of the Scotch bar, was called to prove the law of Scotland applicable to the case.

There had been, he said, no judicial decision upon the statute, but by analogy from the law in other cases, the requisite twenty-one days had not been completed. In Bell's Commentaries, vol. ii, p. 178 (5th ed.), the law is thus stated : "1. By a decision of the House of Lords, confirmed in subsequent cases in the Court of Sessions, the settled rule for computing the period of death-bed deeds" (made sixty days before the grantor's death) "is that the *terminus a quo*, the day or date of the deed, must be excluded, and the sixty days reckoned independently of it. 2. The day does not run from noon to noon (as it does in navigation reckoning), but consistently with the common understanding of the country, from midnight to midnight. The sixty days are in a case of bankruptcy, precisely as in the case of a death-bed, to be held as exclusive of the day on which the deed is made, and as expiring the moment the sixtieth day from the bankruptcy begins, according to the maxim '*dies inceptus pro completo habetur*.'" According to this rule of computation, the parties had lived in Scotland only nineteen days and two half days before the marriage, which is therefore invalid.

Mr. Wm. McIntosh, of the Scotch bar, who was also called as a witness, was of the same opinion.

THE PRESIDENT: This being a matter depending upon the construction of a statute dealing with marriages in Scotland, the evidence of Scotch lawyers is properly admissible. I see no reason why I should not act upon Mr. Balfour's statement of the law, which is exceedingly clear, and I therefore find that the parties had not lived in Scotland for twenty-one days next preceding the marriage, and that therefore the marriage is invalid.

Decree nisi for nullity of marriage, with costs.

Solicitors for petitioner : *Lawford & Waterhouse.*

[4 Probate Division, 63.]

March 26, 1878.

63]   *FIREBRACE V. FIREBRACE.

*Restitution of Conjugal Rights—Respondent abroad—Jurisdiction—Service of
Proceedings.*

A wife's remedy for matrimonial wrongs must be usually sought in the place of her
husband's domicile.

The English Divorce Court has not jurisdiction against a foreigner, after he
has quitted this country, for not rendering conjugal rights to his wife while he
was here.

The provisions of the 42d section of 20 & 21 Vict. c. 85 (for service out of Her
Majesty's dominions) do not apply to suits for restitution of conjugal rights.

THIS was a suit for restitution of conjugal rights, and
raised various questions as to the jurisdiction of the court.
The facts are fully stated in the judgment.

Henry Matthews, Q.C. (*Searle*, with him), appeared for
the petitioner.

Dr. Spinks, Q.C. (*Gorst*, Q.C., and *Bayford*, with him),
for the respondent.

THE PRESIDENT : This suit, by Isabella Firebrace against
her husband, Robert Firebrace, was commenced on the 9th
of February, 1872, for restitution of conjugal rights. The
respondent appeared under protest, and afterwards by act
on petition submitted to the court that it had no power to
entertain the suit, or to make any order thereon, on the
ground that he had left England before its institution, and
that from the time of so leaving England he had been out of
the jurisdiction of the court, and had no home or place of
abode within its jurisdiction, and that the court had no
power to order its process to be served on the respondent
personally or otherwise, and therefore prayed that the said
petition should be dismissed.

The argument of the case has been from time to time postponed at the request of the parties, and I had hoped that
the decision of the court would not be called for; but as
I am informed that no settlement has been come to, I am
requested to give my judgment, which I accordingly now
proceed to do.

The material facts of the case are these. The respondent's
64] *father, William Firebrace, was a native of Barbadoes,
and held a commission, first in a West Indian regiment and
afterwards in the 58th regiment of the line. The said William Firebrace accompanied his regiment to various places
in England, Ceylon, and Scotland, down to 1841, when he

Firebrace v. Firebrace.   1878

retired from the service and at once proceeded to Australia, where he settled, taking with him his wife and family, including the respondent, who had been born in 1828, at Newport, in the Isle of Wight. The said William Firebrace never had an English domicile, and he retained his domicile of origin until he acquired a domicile of choice in Australia, which he retained until his death in 1856. From the time when the respondent accompanied his father and mother to Australia in 1841, he remained there assisting his father in his business and afterwards carrying on business for himself until 1866, with the exception of a short visit to England in 1856.

The first question discussed before me was the domicile of the respondent. It appears to me clear, upon the facts above stated, that down to 1866 the respondent's domicile was Australian, derived, in the first instance, from his having as a minor acquired the domicile chosen by his father, and continued by his own act in establishing himself in the colony.

A more difficult question arises as to the effect of his coming to England in 1866. He had married the present petitioner in 1858 at Melbourne, she being a native of the colony and domiciled there. He alleges that he came to England temporarily for the benefit of his health, which had suffered from a recent accident, and that he at first proposed to leave his wife in Australia during his absence, but that he subsequently determined to bring her with him, thinking that change of scene and society might enable her to shake off habits of intemperance which he states she had contracted. From the time of his arrival in England in July, 1866, down to the time of his leaving in 1872, the respondent never had any permanent abode in this country, but resided in hotels, furnished apartments, and houses taken for short terms of a few months only. He alleges that during the whole time he looked upon Australia as his home, where he still continues to hold property, never having held any property in England except money at his bankers and a few shares of trifling value in joint *stock companies. He further alleges [65 that as his health grew stronger he thought of returning to Australia, and in August, 1868, formed the determination, of which his wife was aware, of leaving England as soon as it could be conveniently arranged to return to Australia, and that it was only in consequence of facts coming to his knowledge, upon which he instituted a suit for dissolution of his marriage on the ground of his wife's adultery, that he abandoned his intention to return to Australia at that time.

That suit was commenced in May, 1869, and was heard in 1872, during which time the respondent was obliged to come from Scotland and reside in England, for the purpose of complying with an order of this court which the petitioner had obtained that she should have access to her children, and that they should not be removed from the jurisdiction. The petitioner, on the other hand, alleges that her husband before leaving Australia sold his property there, and came to England intending to reside there permanently.   She further says that on several occasions the respondent has spoken to her about purchasing an estate in England ; that after their return to England, and whilst they were living at Tunbridge Wells, he took her to see an estate in the neighborhood consisting of an old house and some land, and that he expressed his intention, if he purchased the property, of rebuilding the house, and that after some discussion he determined not to make the purchase.   The mother of the respondent has made an affidavit in the case, and states that her son came for a time to England in 1866 in consequence of an accident he had received, but that she never heard him say, nor does she believe it to be the fact, that he ever contemplated remaining permanently in England ; on the contrary, she has often heard him say that he wished and intended, as soon as he prudently could do so, to return to Australia, all his property being there.

Upon a consideration of the evidence on the one side and on the other, I come to the conclusion that it is not established that the respondent ever abandoned his Australian domicile and acquired an·English domicile. · In the first place, as I have already stated, it appears to me clear that the domicile of the respondent's father was never English. It was first West Indian, and, secondly, Australian.   His 66]   taking service in the British army in no way *affected his domicile.   Secondly, the fact that the respondent was born in England does not affect his domicile, the domicile of the child being that of the father at the time of the child's birth.   These propositions were involved in the decision of the House of Lords in *Udny* v. *Udny* ('). It follows, therefore, that the respondent did not by coming to England in 1866 acquire an English domicile, unless it was his intention to do so.   If he intended to abandoned his Australian domicile of choice without a fixed intention of acquiring another, his domicile of origin would revive, and that was West Indian, not English.   But in fact there is nothing which shows that he had abandoned his Australian domicile.   The bulk of

(') Law Rep., 1 H. L., Sc., 441.

his property remains in Australia, and as against his own statement and that of his mother that he always intended to return thither, there is nothing but the wife's statement that on some occasions he contemplated, but never carried out, the purchase of property in England. The wandering life which he led down to the time of his instituting his suit against his wife strongly confirms his contention that he never intended to acquire an English domicile. Further, it appears that he left England with his children immediately after his suit was commenced, and only returned under compulsion, and finally, on the conclusion of that suit, and before the present suit was commenced, he quitted this country, and has never since returned. Even supposing, therefore, that he ever did contemplate acquiring an English domicile, he abandoned it before the commencement of this suit; and that abandonment will not be the less operative because his motive was to avoid the liability to proceedings in this court. I find, however, as a fact that he never did acquire an English domicile.

This being so, the case of *Yelverton* v. *Yelverton* (¹) is a direct authority on the question now before the court. There Sir Cresswell Cresswell says: "This is a court for England, not for the United Kingdom, or for Great Britain, and, for the purpose of this question of jurisdiction, Ireland and Scotland" (and I may add the colonies), "are to be deemed foreign countries equally with France or Spain. If this be so, this is a suit against a *foreigner who is not and [67 was not at the commencement of this suit within the Kingdom of England, who never had any residence in England" (by which, as the context shows, the learned judge meant other than a temporary one), "who never owed obedience to the laws of England, except during the period of his temporary sojourn here, and who is not said to have done anything in England contrary to those laws."

This passage is literally applicable in all respects to the present case, but it may be said that the facts show that the respondent has done something contrary to the English law by refusing while in England to render his wife conjugal rights, and I will deal with the point as if this had been stated in the petition.

In the first place, although Sir Cresswell Cresswell alludes to the absence of any allegation of any past breach of English law as a fact in the case, the authorities he cites do not advert to that circumstance as being of importance. And the learned judge sums up the effect of the authorities thus:

(¹) 1 Sw. & Tr.; 586 ; S. C., 29 L. J. (P. M. & A.), 40.

"Unless some ground can be discovered for saying that Major Yelverton was domiciled in England according to the law as laid down by Lord Lyndhurst, by Boullenois, and by Story, he was not subject to the jurisdiction of this court." Thus showing that he rests his judgment on the want of an English domicile in Major Yelverton. No decision has been brought to my notice where the jurisdiction of this court has been asserted against a foreigner after he had quitted this country for not rendering conjugal rights to his wife while here ; and it appears to me that the court has not jurisdiction in such a case.

The domicile of the wife is that of the husband, and her remedy for matrimonial wrongs must be usually sought in the place of that domicile. It is not, however, inconsistent with this principle that a wife should be allowed in some cases to obtain relief against her husband in the tribunal of the country in which she is resident though not domiciled. What these cases may be, it is unnecessary now to determine, and I abstain from discussing this question, as I believe it will shortly be raised before me in another case now pending ; but it appears to me that the particular relief now sought by decree for restitution of conjugal rights does not, where the husband had quitted the jurisdiction before suit, present an exception to the rule above stated. 68] In such a suit the wife *does not seek a remedy by a change in her own status or right. In suits for divorce and judicial separation the primary object is to free the wife in whole or in part from the obligation of marriage. In a suit for restitution of conjugal rights the primary object is to control the husband. She asks that her husband shall in the future be compelled by the process of the court to take her back to live with him in a common home. In other words, she prays that the English law shall be put in force against him, but as the obligation of a foreigner to obey the laws of this country lasts no longer than the time during which he is within its jurisdiction, the tribunals of this country cannot call upon him to obey those laws after the obligation has ceased.

The difficulty, amounting in most cases to an impossibility, of enforcing the decree of the court in the circumstances of the present case lends additional force to the arguments against the existence of the jurisdiction. Suppose the case of a citizen of the United States deserting his wife while in England and returning to his own country where a suit for restitution of conjugal rights cannot be maintained. It is obvious that he could not be required to return to his wife in this country. All that he could be called upon to do would be to receiver her in his own. The court must necessarily be powerless in most cases to enforce such a decree. And even if the remedy by sequestration of the property of the husband could be resorted to, it would be a singular anomaly that this court should by this or other process endeavor to compel him to observe in his own country a course of conduct which he could not by the laws of that country be called upon to adopt. For these reasons, as well as upon the authority of *Yelverton* v. *Yelverton* ('), I am of opinion that this suit cannot be maintained.

It is to be observed that in *Yelverton* v. *Yelverton* (') Sir Cresswell Cresswell entered into an elaborate investigation of the question whether the petition in a suit for restitution of conjugal rights could be served out of the jurisdiction, and he gives his reasons (based on the nature of the jurisdiction of the Ecclesiastical courts to which suits of this kind formerly belonged) for holding that it could not be so served unless the respondent had a residence in England; but he appears to have assumed that the *42d [69 section of 20 & 21 Vict. c. 85, authorized service abroad of a petition for restitution of conjugal rights where the court has jurisdiction to entertain the suit. His attention does not appear to have been called to the fact that the 42d section speaks only of such petitions, which by reference to the 41st section will be seen to be a petition in a suit either for a decree of nullity, judicial separation, dissolution of marriage, or jactitation of marriage, and not a petition for restitution of conjugal rights. Whether this was intentional, as has been contended before me, or accidental, I cannot take upon myself to say, but the fact remains that no power is given by the act to serve such a petition out of the jurisdiction. Whether any proceeding like that by "ways and means" of the Ecclesiastical court could be resorted to may be open to question. The effect of the 42d section, however, does not appear to me of importance in the present case, as I think it clear that it does not extend the jurisdiction of this court as to persons. It only gives to the court where its jurisdiction already exists greater facility of serving its process. But, for the reasons I have stated, I am of opinion that this court had not jurisdiction over Mr. Firebrace after he left this country, and, therefore, that the present suit cannot be maintained.

Solicitors for petitioner: *Simpson, Hammond & Co.*
Solicitors for respondent: *Sladen & Mackenzie.*

(') 1 Sw. & Tr., 586; S. C., 29 L. J. (P. M. & A.), p. 40.

[4 Probate Division, 69.]

Jan. 14, 1879.

SANSOM V. SANSOM.

Costs—Alimony—Sequestration of Pension—Form of Order.

. The court in enforcing payment of alimony and costs will authorize sequestrators
to receive portions of a civil service pension.
Willcock v. *Terrell* (Law Rep., 3 Ex. D., 323) followed.

THE petitioner had, in 1877, obtained a decree of judicial
separation with costs, and an order for payment of permanent alimony at the rate of £139 a year. The respondent
had not paid any portion of the costs or alimony, and had
gone to reside at Boulogne, so that it was useless to issue
either a writ of attachment or execution.

70] *Subsequently it was discovered that in July, 1875,
the respondent had been awarded a pension of £402 a year
for services in the legal department of the government.

An order *nisi* attaching this pension was accordingly made
and served upon the respondent, and on the 5th of November, 1878, he having appeared before the President, and notice having been given to Her Majesty's paymaster-general,
the following order was made, viz.:

"Upon hearing counsel for the petitioner, and the solicitor for the respondent, and upon reading the affidavits of
. . . . I do order that the yearly pension, amounting to the
sum of £402 4s. 5d., authorized by a minute of Her Majesty's
Treasury, and dated . . . . and payable monthly at the
office of the paymaster-general to the respondent, shall be
and shall henceforth stand charged with the payment of the
sum of £71 8s. 2d., being the amount of the petitioner's
costs of this suit directed to be paid pursuant to order dated
. . . . and the sum of £416 5s. arrears of alimony ordered
to be paid pursuant to an order dated . . . . And I do
further order that one half of the said monthly instalments
of the pension shall be paid in respect of the amount of alimony to the petitioner or to . . . ., her trustee, and in respect of the costs to . . . ., her solicitors, until the said costs
and arrears of alimony now due, and in the meantime to become due, and the costs of this application, amounting to
the sum of £18 12s. 8d., shall be satisfied, and that from
and after the payment of such costs and all arrears of alimony, one-third of the said monthly instalments of the pension shall be paid to the petitioner or to . . . ., her trustee,
in satisfaction of the order for alimony dated . . . . And

Branford v. Branford.   1879

I direct the paymaster-general to pay such proportions of the said monthly instalments of the pension as they become payable to the petitioner, her trustee, or her solicitors in pursuance of this order.

"Dated this   day of   1878.

".James Hannen."

Bowen moved the court to vary this order by omitting therefrom all direction to or order on Her Majesty's paymaster-general. Such an order is *ultra vires: Crispin* v. *Cumano* (').

Ambrose, Q.C., and *Searle*, contrà, cited *Willcock* [71 v. *Terrell* (').

THE PRESIDENT: When I made the order complained of, I intended that it should be in accordance with the terms of the order in *Willcock* v. *Terrell* ('), and it must be varied accordingly (').

Solicitor for petitioners: *F. Deakin.*
Agents for the Solicitor of the Treasury: *Hare & Fell.*

(') Law Rep., 1 P. & D., 622.
(') Law Rep., 3 Ex. D., 323.
(') The order was accordingly altered as follows: It is ordered that the said order be varied by omitting therefrom all direction to or order on Her Majesty's paymaster-general to pay or cause to be paid to the said petitioner or her trustees the proportions of the pension payable to the said respondent, and that the said respondent, his solicitor, his banker, or agent, be and each of them is hereby restrained from receiving the proportions of such pension now 'due or hereafter to become due, and that . . . . the trustee of the said petitioner do receive the said proportions of such pension in the place and in the stead of the respondent.

[4 Probate Division, 72.]

April 8, 1879.

*BRANFORD v. BRANFORD & SHEPPERD, and the [72 QUEEN'S PROCTOR intervening.

Evidence—Communications between Attorney and Client—Privilege—Divorce.

After the trial of a petition for divorce; the Queen's Proctor intervening and charging the petitioner with adultery, counsel on behalf of the Queen's Proctor proposed to ask a solicitor who had acted for the petitioner at the former trial whether the petitioner before such trial had not confessed to him that he had been guilty of a matrimonial offence:

Held, that the question was inadmissible, the communication being privileged.

IN this case the petitioner had obtained a decree *nisi* by reason of the respondent's adultery with the co-respondent, and subsequently the Queen's Proctor obtained leave to intervene, and alleged, amongst other things, that the petitioner had himself been guilty of adultery. This and the other issues raised by the Queen's Proctor came on for trial

before the president and a common jury. In the course of
73] the action, Mr. Rudland, who was *one of the partners in the firm of solicitors who had acted for the petitioner
in the former trial, was called on behalf of the Queen's Proctor, and asked whether, on the day before that trial the petitioner had made a communication to him as to his having
been guilty of a matrimonial offence. The question was objected to by the petitioner's counsel.

Gorst, Q.C. (*Bargrave Deane*, with him): The question
is put on behalf of the Queen's Proctor, acting as a public
officer, and if this were a criminal suit it would be admissible. Suits of this nature are quasi-criminal.

Inderwick, Q.C. (*Keogh* with him): The Queen's Proctor
is in only the same position as one of the public. It has
been decided by the House of Lords in *Mordaunt* v. *Moncreiffe* (¹) that a matrimonial cause is a civil proceeding.

THE PRESIDENT: I think the point taken by the Queen's
Proctor is concluded by the decision in the House of Lords
that proceedings of this kind are not criminal, and if not
criminal then they must be civil, for there cannot be quasi-
civil or quasi-criminal cases. In civil actions the rule is well
established that in order to protect persons who are threatened with legal process, communications between them and
their solicitors with reference to those matters are privileged.
The evidence must therefore be rejected.

Solicitors for the petitioner: *Saunders & Co.; Queen's
Proctor.*

(¹) Law Rep., 2 H. L., Sc., 374; 10 Eng. R., 57.

See 26 Alb. L. J., 24; 36 Am. Rep.,
631 note; 1 Whart. Ev., §§ 587–9; 1
Greenl. Ev., §§ 238–245; Weeks on Attorneys, §§ 151–171; 1 Macn. & Gord.,
627, Little, Brown & Co.'s Ed.; 3 Hare,
122 note, Banks's Ed.; N. Y. Code,
Civil Proc., §§ 835–6.

The facts which make communications privileged must be proved, and
the burden lies on him who seeks to
exclude them as evidence because they
are privileged: Earle *v.* Grant, 46 Vt.,
113.

In order to make communications to
counsel privileged they must be made
to them confidentially as counsel, the
relation of attorney and client must exist at the time, and the communication
must be made for the purpose of obtaining advice in regard to legal rights.
A general retainer in the matter as to
which advice is sought is not necessary, but the attorney must be counsel in that matter and the communication made to him as such: Earle *v.*
Grant, 46 Vt., 113.

All communications made by a client
to his counsel with a view to professional advice or assistance, are privileged whether such advice relates to a
suit pending or contemplated, or to any
other matter proper for such advice or
aid.

English: Carpmael *v.* Powers, 1 Phill.
687, 4 N. Y. Leg. Obs., 260; Garland
v. Scott, 3 Sim., 396, 398 note, Banks's
Ed.; Greenhough *v.* Gaskell, Cooper's
Chy. Temp., Brougham, 96; Walsing-
ham *v.* Goodrick, 3 Hare, 122; Man-
ser *v.* Dix, 1 K. & J., 451; Wilson *v.*
Northampton, etc., 30 Week. Repr.,
988.

Maine: Sargent *v.* Hampden, 38
Me., 581.

New York: Britton *v.* Lorenz, 45 N. Y., 51, 56–7; Bacon *v.* Frisbie, 80 id., 394, 36 Amer. R. 627, reversing 15 Hun, 26; Root *v.* Wright, 84 N. Y., 72, reversing 21 Hun, 344, 347–9; Williams *v.* Fitch, 18 N. Y., 546; Yates *v.* Olmsted, 56 id., 632, reversing 65 Barb., 43, 462; Coveney *v.* Tannahill, 1 Hill, 33; Rogers *v.* Lynn. 64 Barb., 373; Cairns *v.* Platt, 36 N. Y. Super. Ct. R., 361.

United States, Circuit and District: Matter of Aspinwall, 10 Bankr. Reg., 448, Blatchf., J.

The rule prohibiting an attorney from disclosing communications made by a client, is not confined to communications made in contemplation of, or in the progress of an action or judicial proceeding, but extends to those made in reference to any matter which is the proper subject of professional employment: Root *v.* Wright, 84 N. Y., 72, 38 Amer. R., 495; Clark *v.* Richards, 3 E. D. Smith, 89.

The rule of exclusion applies to every attempt to give the communication in evidence without the assent of the person making it; and so, includes a case where the evidence is sought to be given without such consent against a third person: Bacon *v.* Frisbie, 80 N. Y., 394, 36 Amer. R., 627, 631 note.

It is not essential to bring the case within the statutory prohibition that a fee be paid at the time of the communication, or that a suit was pending or contemplated; if the communication was in the course of any professional employment, related to the subject matter thereof, and may be supposed to have been drawn out in consequence of the relation of the parties to each other, it is entitled to protection as a privileged communication: Bacon *v.* Frisbie, 80 N. Y., 394, 36 Amer. R., 627, 631 note.

An attorney-at-law employed to draw an assignment of a mortgage acts as an attorney and not as a notary merely; and the court should not permit him as a witness to testify against his client as to disclosures made to him by the latter in the course of such employment: Getzlaff *v.* Seliger, 43 Wisc., 297.

But see Machette *v.* Wanless, 2 Colorado, 170.

It has been held that an attorney cannot be compelled on a supœna *duces tecum* to *produce* the papers of his client intrusted to him or to state the contents: Coveney *v.* Tannahill, 1 Hill, 33; McPherson *v.* Rathbone, 7 Wend., 216.

Counsel will be excused from producing deeds in their possession and which they have received in their character as counsel; and from testifying as to their *contents:* Kellogg *v.* Kellogg, 6 Barb., 116; Jackson *v.* Denison, 4 Wend., 558; McPherson *v.* Rathbone, 7 id., 217.

When valuable papers, upon which the liberty of a client depends, are intrusted to counsel, it is his duty not only to return them when the relation of attorney and counsel ceases, and to observe the secrets confided to him with absolute fidelity, but also to abstain from wilfully doing or saying anything through which such papers, or the knowledge of their existence, can be used by any one to the prejudice of his client. This duty of secrecy is not extinguished by the fact that the client, without satisfying the claims of his counsel to compensation, has substituted another attorney or counsel in his place: Matter of Habna, 11 Abb. N. C., 423.

See another case, 87 N. Y., 521.

When communications are made to an attorney by either of two or more parties in the presence of the other, while employed as their common attorney to give advice as to matters in which they are mutually interested, the rule prohibits him from testifying to such communications in an action between his clients and a third person: Root *v.* Wright, 84 N. Y., 72, 38 Am. R., 495.

Declarations made to an attorney with reference to his employment in the cause fall under the same privilege, although the attorney declines the engagement: Sargent *v.* Inhabitants, 38 Maine, 581.

A correspondence between a district attorney representing the United States and the Attorney-General, is confidential in its nature, and cannot be given by third persons, United States *v.* Six Lots, 1 Woods 264.

In Woburn *v.* Henshaw, 101 Mass., 193, it was held that a party who offers himself as a witness, cannot refuse to answer questions as to a conversation with his counsel, on the ground that it is a privileged communication.

See also Com. v. Nichols, 114 Mass., 285, 287, 19 Am. Rep., 846, and note p. 848.

The contrary is held in *Ohio* in *criminal* cases : Duttonshofer v. State, 34 Ohio St. R., 91.

But see under statute of that State in *civil* cases, King v. Barrett, 11 Ohio St. R., 261.

In *Indiana* such evidence is inadmissible : Bigler v. Reyher, 43 Ind., 112.

Communications which passed between defendant and his agents for the purpose of being communicated by his agents to his legal adviser, held to be privileged : Reid v. Langlois, 1 MacN. & Gord., 627.

Letters written by a defendant, after the institution of the suit, to an unprofessional agent abroad, "confidentially and in reference to the defence of the defendant"; held not privileged : Kerr v. Gillespie, 7 Beav., 572.

It seems that when such a communication is sought to be proved, in an action to which the person making it is not a party, an objection thereto by the party against whom it is offered will lie, on the ground of public policy. Bacon v. Frisbie, 80 N. Y., 394, 36 Am. R., 627, 631 note.

The privileged relation of attorney or counsel and client, can only exist for lawful purposes ; and hence if the client confide to them a criminal design, or they be present when a wrong, either public or private, is done by their client, their knowledge thus acquired is not privileged : Coveney v. Tannahill, 1 Hill, 33 ; People v. Blakesley, 4 Park., 176 ; Bank v. Mersereau, 3 Barb. Chy., 598 ; People v. Mahon, 1 Utah, 205 ; Queen v. Hayward, 2 Cox's Cr. Cas., 23 ; Reg. v. Farley, Id., 82 ; Cutts v. Pickering, Nels. Chy., 81.

See Francis's Case, 1 City Hall Rec., 121.

Contrà, Com. v. Moyer, 25 Alb. L. J., 92, Phila. Quarter Sess.

A solicitor for a prisoner is bound to produce a document when the prisoner is charged with an offence in respect of such document : Reg. v. Bunn, 9 Cox's Cr. Cas., 281.

On a trial for murder, an attorney employed by the prisoner on the day of the alleged murder to draw for him certain papers, viz., a lease and receipt, cannot be compelled to testify to the drawing of such papers by him, or to the contents thereof, nor as to the state of either of the papers when delivered to the prisoner ; where such papers are not in any manner necessarily connected with the perpetration of any crime, and they cannot, of themselves, in any way aid in the commission of any fraud or crime : Graham v. People, 63 Barb., 469.

On a trial of one for murder, the attending physician of deceased is competent to testify to the symptoms of deceased. and as to what he had learned concerning his condition while attending him : Pierson v. People, 18 Hun, 239, 79 N. Y., 424.

Communications made by the client to counsel are not privileged if made in the presence of all the parties to the controversy, and this exception includes a case where the communications were made by the plaintiff's assignor in trust for creditors, in the presence of the defendant, to the attorney employed to draw the papers between them.

New York : Whiting v. Barney, 30 N. Y., 330, 337, 339–342, reversing 38 Barb., 393 ; Britton v. Lorenz, 45 N. Y., 51, 56–7 ; Hibbard v. Haughian, 70 id., 54, 61–2 ; Coveney v. Tannahill, 1 Hill, 33 ; Sherman v. Scott, 2 Civil Proc. R., 366 ; Woodruff v. Hurson, 32 Barb., 557 ; Prouty v. Eaton, 41 id., 460 ; Shafer v. Mink, 14 North West. Repr., 126, Sup. Ct., Iowa.

An attorney or counsel is not a competent witness to testify as to facts communicated to either by his client in the course of the relation subsisting between them, but may be examined as to the mere fact of the existence of the relation : Chirac v. Reinicker, 11 Wheat., 280.

An attorney cannot excuse himself from stating as a witness how he obtained possession of a paper which is the basis of his client's suit, upon the ground that he might be violating professional confidence if required to testify : Allen v. Root, 39 Tex., 589.

A request to an attorney, or employing him to defend an action, is not a privileged communication, and may be proved by the evidence of the attorney. He may be required to testify who employed him, and under whose direction he acted : Eickman v. Troll, 12 N. W. Repr., 347, Sup. Ct., Minn. ;

Mulford *v.* Muller, 1 Keyes, 34, 3 Abb. Dec., 330.

An attorney may be called against his client to prove the existence of a paper deposited with him by his client, and that it is in his possession, with a view to enable the party calling him to resort to secondary evidence : Coveney *v.* Tannahill, 1 Hill, 33 ; Brandt *v.* Klein, 17 Johns., 335 ; Jackson *v* McVey, 18 id., 830 ; Mitchell's Case 12 Abb. Pr., 249, 29 Barb., 622 ; Peck *v.* Williams, 13 Abb. Pr., 68 ; Hibbert *v.* Knight, 2 Exch., 11, 6 N. Y. Leg. Observer, 294, explaining Marston *v.* Downes, 6 C. & P., 381.

See McPherson *v.* Rathbone, 7 Wend., 217.

The privilege of counsel does not extend to the concealment of the *subject* discussed, but only to the discussion. Counsel was required to answer as to what affairs of the bankrupt were discussed in a particular conversation, though excused from the statement of the conversation.

Privilege of counsel will not justify counsel in refusing to answer with whom he had conversation in relation to affairs of bankrupt, though it will excuse him from stating the conversation had.

Privilege of counsel cannot be set up as an excuse for not answering whether "a particular paper ever came under witness' observation," or whether "witness drew, or directed to be drawn, a certain deed from the bankrupt," or whether "at a certain date witness received certain checks drawn to the order of the bankrupt," or "what disposition was made of such checks."

Acts and things which have come to witness' knowledge, by reason of his position as counsel, may be inquired about, and the witness required to state all the information he has in regard to them which was not communicated to him by the bankrupt, or by some one through the bankrupt's direction : Matter of Aspinwall, 10 Nat. Bank. Reg., 449.

An attorney employed by one to draw his will, is a competent witness to prove communications upon the subject by deceased to him : Sanford *v.* Sandford, 5 Lans., 495–7.

If an attorney or counsel having drawn a will, or advised testator upon it, accepts a retainer to contest its probate, he cannot claim a privilege from testifying as a witness at the instance of the proponents : Sheridan *v.* Houghton, 16 Hun, 628, 6 Abb. N. C., 234, 84 N. Y., 643.

An attorney is bound to disclose, when called as a witness by the adverse party, the contents of a notice, which he received, to produce a paper in the hands of his client : the privilege of the client only extends to exclude the disclosure of any fact communicated confidentially to the witness in the character of his attorney : Spenceley *v.* Schulenburgh, 7 East, 357, 3 Smith (Eng.), 325.

A communication made by a client to his attorney, in respect to a matter concerning his case, is privileged. But this privilege does not extend to and excuse an attorney from testifying in regard to an agreement or settlement made by him with the opposite party at the request of his own client : Thayer *v.* McEwan, 4 Bradw. (Ills.), 416 ; Ford *v.* Tennant, 32 Beav., 162 ; Gore *v.* Bowser, 5 De Gex & Smale, 30.

Instructions given by a party to his attorney, not in the presence of the opposing party, in respect to a settlement of matters in dispute, are inadmissible in behalf of the party *giving* them: Childs *v.* Delaney, 1 Thomp. & Cook, 506.

An attorney for the plaintiff in a judgment, when called by the defendant on the trial of an issue on *scire facias*, to revive the judgment in favor of the plaintiff's representatives, may be permitted to testify to an alleged admission of payment made to him by his client after judgment recovered, and before execution was issued, the authority of the attorney to issue execution and to satisfy the judgment continued, and though the communication was made as a guide to him in issuing or withholding the execution. Such communication is not confidential and privileged : Clark *v.* Richards, 3 E. D. Smith, 89.

An attorney is not restrained by any rule of law from giving evidence of a conversation between him and his client touching the justice of his suit after a writ of inquiry, executed on an interlocutory judgment, and a compromise thereupon ; for the purpose of the suit having been obtained, the communication could not be said to have been made by way of instruction for conducting his cause: Cobden *v.* Kendrick, 4 T. R., 431.

So any statement by the client after the relation of attorney and client has ceased: Mandeville *v.* Gurnsey, 38 Barb., 225; Marsh *v.* Howe, 36 id., 649.

[4 Probate Division, 73.]

Nov. 18, 1877.

In the Goods of GRACE HASTINGS.

Administration—Next of Kin—Lunatic—Grant to a Stranger.

The sole next of kin of an intestate was lunatic. Her committee renounced, and H. K. L., a stranger in blood, applied for grant of letters of administration. The Masters in Lunacy, and next of kin of the lunatic, approved of the application. The court, upon the consents of the next of kin being filed, ordered the grant to be made to H. K. L.

GRACE HASTINGS, late of Lyndham, in the county of Oxford, died on the 20th of February, 1877, intestate, a spin-74] ster, without *parent, leaving her sister, Elizabeth Hastings, her sole next of kin, and only person entitled in distribution to her personal estate. Elizabeth Hastings was of unsound mind, and Thomas Smallhorn, of Lyndham, had been appointed committee of her estate and effects.

The Masters in Chancery objected to a grant to Thomas Smallhorn, on the ground that if he were also administrator he would have to render the accounts to himself. He therefore renounced his right.

Bayford moved that the grant of administration be given to Henry Kent Lockwood. He is a stranger in blood to the deceased, but is a person in whom in her lifetime she had great confidence. Moreover, the Masters in Lunacy approve of the grant being made to him, and so do the next of kin of the lunatic.

THE PRESIDENT: The consents of the next of kin of the lunatic must be filed, and then the grant may be given to the applicant.

Solicitors: *Walters, Young & Co.*

[4 Probate Division, 76.]

Jan. 22, 1878.

In the Goods of RULE.   [76

Foreign Will—Probate abroad of Copy—Form of Grant in this Country.

R., domiciled in Mexico, made a will according to the law of Mexico. The proper court there decreed probate of a Spanish translation and not of the original:

Held, that the grant in this country must be made upon the production of an English translation of the Spanish copy, and not of a certified copy of the original.

On the 9th of October, 1875, John Richard Rule, domiciled at Panchuca, in Mexico, executed a will according to the law of Mexico, and appointed John Potts and Thomas Horncastle executors. The will was written in English. He died at Panchuca on the 28th of April, 1876, and on the 24th of May following the will was formally opened before the civil judge, and after a Spanish translation of it had been made it was deposited in the archives of the Mexican court. On the 29th of May the judge decreed that the Spanish translation duly verified be notified to the executors for their acceptance and oath, and sent to England as notice to the legatees. This decree was registered in Mexico on the 3d of June following.

Mr. Horncastle executed a delegation of his office upon Mr. Potts, who died on the 27th of November following, and on the 16th of February, 1877, Mr. E. A. Gibson was appointed by the judge in Mexico executor for and on behalf of the heirs.

Upon Mr. Gibson applying for letters of administration (with the will annexed), limited to the property in this country, the registrars refused to make the grant until a copy of the original will was obtained from Mexico.

Searle moved for grant of letters of administration (with will annexed) upon production of a translation into English of the Spanish translation of the original will. The court acted upon the Spanish translation, and not upon the original will: *In the Goods of Deshais* ([1]); *In the Goods of Clarke* ([2]).

THE PRESIDENT: The certified translation of the [77 original will is the proper document upon which I must act. The courts of this country give credit to a foreign tribunal for having duly investigated the facts upon which it

([1]) 4 Sw. & Tr., 13, 15; S. C., 34 L. J. (P. M. & A.), 58.
([2]) 36 L. J. (P. M. & A.), 72.

proceeded, and in this case I find that the foreign court has recognized the existence of a will in a particular form as contained in a Spanish or alleged Spanish translation of the original will. That, therefore, is the only document on which I can proceed, and upon that document being translated into English I shall act upon it. I grant administration, with the will so translated annexed.

Solicitors for all parties: *Boltons, Robins & Busk.*

[4 Probate Division, 77.]

March 12, 1878.

In the Goods of WILLIAM BRIDGER.

Will of Married Woman—Executrix—Chain of Representation.

The administrator (with will annexed) of the estate of a married woman does not as such represent an estate of which she was executrix.

E. C. S., surviving executrix of W. B., made, while covert, a will, and appointed J. S. her executor. J. S. was also solely entitled to all the estate of E. C. S., of which E. C. S. had no disposing power:

Held, that J. S., as administrator (with will) of E. C. S., did not represent W. B. Grant of letters of administration (with will) *de bonis non* of W. B. given to R. F., a residuary legatee under that will.

WILLIAM BRIDGER, late of Bishopsgate Street Within, in the city of London, died on the 28th of May, 1864, having made his will, dated the 14th of April, 1862, and thereof (amongst others) appointed his wife, Ellen Charlotte Bridger, executrix, and named Rosa Feast a residuary legatee. Ellen Charlotte Bridger survived her co-executors, and intermarried with John Stanley. During her second marriage she, by virtue of the powers vested in her by her marriage settlement with Stanley and of all other powers her enabling, made her will, and thereof appointed John Stanley sole executor, and devised and bequeathed to him all estates vested in her as trustee or mortgagee. He was also the sole person entitled to her personal estate, over which she had no disposing power. She died on the 12th of June, 1876, 78] and on the *11th of July following letters of administration in the form referred to in the judgment, with her will annexed, were granted to John Stanley.

Part of the estate of William Bridger remained unadministered.

Jan. 29, 1878. *Searle* moved for a grant of administration (with will) *de bonis non* of the personal estate and effects of William Bridger to Rosa Feast, one of the residuary legatees named in the will. *Cur. adv. vult.*

March 12, 1878. THE PRESIDENT: William Bridger died in May, 1864, having made his will, of which he appointed his wife (with others) executrix. She proved this will, and survived the other executors.

She afterwards married John Stanley, and during coverture with him made a will under certain powers vested in her, and appointed her husband, John Stanley, sole executor, who was the sole person entitled to the personal estate over which she had no disposing power. She died on the 11th of July, 1876, and thereupon letters of administration, with her will annexed, were granted to John Stanley.

Administration to the unadministered estate of Bridger is now asked by Rosa Feast, daughter of Bridger, and one of the residuary legatees under his will.

The question is, whether this is necessary or can be granted, having regard to the fact that administration of the effects of Ellen Charlotte Stanley, formerly Bridger, with her will annexed, has been granted to John Stanley.

The question appears to me to be one of construction. What is the meaning of the language of the grant which has been made? The grant recites that Ellen Charlotte Stanley having during her coverture with John Stanley, by certain powers and authorities given to and vested in her by an indenture of the 28th of March, 1866, and all other powers and authorities her enabling, made and executed her last will and testament bearing date the 12th of April, 1875, and thereof appointed her husband, John Stanley, sole executor, and that the said John Stanley, as the lawful husband of the said deceased, was the sole person entitled to her *personal estate over which she had no dis- [79 posing power, and concerning which she had died intestate, and proceeds as follows: "And be it also known that at the date hereunder written letters of administration, with the will (a copy whereof is hereunto annexed) of the personal estate of the said deceased, were granted to the said John Stanley."

This language appears to me to apply only to the personal estate which belonged to the deceased in her own right, and not to personal estate which was vested in her as executrix. The appropriate language to carry the estate of an executrix will be found in the form of probate of a married woman's will, including an executorship belonging to her, which recites that "administration of all such personal estate as she by virtue of the aforesaid indenture had a right to appoint or dispose of, and has in and by her said will appointed or disposed of accordingly; and also so far as concerns all such personal estate and effects as vested in her, the said deceased, as sole executrix of the will of the said E. B., but no further or otherwise, was granted by the court to the said C. D."

In the absence of language to this effect, the administrator of the estate of a married woman deceased, with the will annexed, takes only as an administrator of an executrix, that is, he has no privity or relation with the original testator, and in no way represents him. This appears to me to be the true view of the case upon principle, and is not inconsistent with the authorities.

In *In the Goods of Martin* (') A. died leaving a will, by which he appointed his wife sole executrix. She proved the will, and afterwards married B., and during her coverture made a will in execution of a power, and appointed B. her sole executor. Thus far the facts are precisely the same as in the present case. Upon the death of B.'s wife, he took out limited probate of her will, and also administration of the rest of her effects. It was held that he was entitled as representing the whole of his wife's personal estate to administration of the unadministered effects of A. This decision proceeds on the assumption that neither the limited probate of the wife's will, nor the administration of the rest of her estate, carried with it the administration of the unad-80] ministered effects of *the first testator, and that therefore a fresh grant was necessary as to them, of which the court considered the husband was the proper grantee.

It appears to me that in the present case the administration granted to J. Stanley, with the will of his wife annexed, did not carry with it more than the limited probate and the *cæterorum* grant did in the case cited, and that therefore a further grant is required as to the unadministered effects of Bridger. To whom that grant is to be made is not in question here, as, if a grant is necessary, J. Stanley consents to it being made to the present applicant, the residuary legatee.

In the Goods of John Hughes (') Sir Cresswell Cresswell held that the will of a married woman made under a power, and appointing executors, did not continue the chain of representation from a former will, of which the married woman was executrix. In the case of *In the Goods of Richards* (') Lord Penzance followed the decision in *In the Goods of Martin* ('), and by implication held that the chain of repre-

---

(') 3 Sw. & Tr., 1; S. C., 32 L. J. (P. M. & A.), 5.
(') 4 Sw. & Tr., 209; S. C., 29 L. J. (P. M. & A.), 165.
(') Law Rep., 1 P. & D., 156.

sentation was not continued by the will of a married woman appointing an executrix to whom administration of the rest of her effects was also given, and administration of the unadministered effects of the original testator was accordingly granted.

I, therefore, hold that the chain of representation is broken in the present case, and that administration of the unadministered effects of Bridger, deceased, must be granted to the present applicant, as residuary legatee.

Solicitors for all parties: *Gush & Phillips.*

[4 Probate Division, 81.]

April 16, 1878.

*In the Goods of ISAAC DIXON.　　　　[81

Will—Construction—Legal Heirs—Residuary Legatees.

I. D., by his will, gave all his property to A. H. for life, and then "the whole" .... to his "legal heirs and theirs forever":

The court *held,* that both his realty and personalty were given to his co-heiresses, and therefore made the grant to M. T., one of the co-heiresses, as one of the residuary legatees.

ISAAC DIXON, late of Cockermouth, in the county of Cumberland, grocer, made his will, bearing date the 5th of September, 1868, and thereby gave the whole of the income of his estate and effects to his aunt, Ann Hill, for life, with the following further devise and bequest : "The whole after her decease, after funeral expenses, medical attendances, and trustees' necessary expenses, and reasonable remuneration goes to my legal heirs, and theirs forever."

He died on the 15th of January; 1870, and his property at his death consisted of a freehold house and personalty under the value of £600.

Administration with the will annexed had been granted to Ann Hill, who died in May, 1876. On the 20th of March, 1877, application was made for a grant of administration *de bonis non* with will annexed to Martha Todhunter as one of the residuary legatees referred to in the will. The court directed notice to be given to the next of kin, which having been done,

March 12, 1878. *Bayford* renewed the application : Miss Todhunter, as one of the co-heiresses of the testator, is, under the words "legal heirs," entitled to the grant as one of

the residuary legatees : *De Beauvoir* v. *De Beauvoir* (¹);
Jarman on Wills, vol. ii, p. 73, 3d ed.

Dr. Tristram, for the next of kin : There is nothing in
the will to show that the testator knew that he was disposing of real estate. The gift, therefore, is either void for uncertainty, or "heirs" should be construed as next of kin :
82] *Thomason* v. *Moses* (²); *Williams on Executors,
6th ed., p. 1032 ; *In re Philps' Will* (³); *In re Steeven's
Trusts* (⁴).

Cur. adv. vult.

April 16, 1878. THE PRESIDENT: In this case the deceased, Isaac Dixon, died on the 15th of January, 1870, possessed of real and personal estate. By his will, dated the
5th of September, 1868, he appointed certain persons trustees and managers on behalf of his aunt, Ann Hill. The
will proceeds: "I hereby give and bequeath to the said
Ann Hill the whole of my income, that is or can be derived
from my estate and effects, for her maintenance and support, and the use of what household furniture might be
necessary for her comfort after my decease, as long as she
lives ; the stock-in-trade and remaining portion of the furniture to be sold, and the money derived therefrom, with all
other moneys recoverable belonging to the estate, to be
placed by the above trustees to the best advantage and security of their ability and belief, the whole after her decease,
after funeral expenses, medical attendances, and trustees'
necessary expenses and reasonable remuneration, goes to my
legal heirs and theirs forever."

The question is, whether, on the true construction of the
words "my legal heirs and theirs forever," the co-heiress
took as residuary legatee of the personalty as well as realty
and would, therefore, be entitled in that character to a grant
of administration with the will annexed?

This being a mixed fund there is no doubt that the heir of
the testator would take the realty. The question then arises
whether there is anything to show that the testator intended
by the same words to designate different persons to take
the realty and the personalty. In some circumstances the
word "heirs" may undoubtedly be considered in a wider
sense than that technically given to it by the English law,
and may mean those entitled to take either by inheritance
or succession, but it is a fixed principle of construction, applicable to all instruments, that the person whose words are

(¹) 3 H. L. C., 524.   (³) Law Rep., 7 Eq., 151.
(²) 5 Beav., 77.   (⁴) Law Rep., 15 Eq., 110; 5 Eng. R., 746.

to be interpreted must be presumed to have used them in their true legal signification, unless the contrary appears from the context taken in connection with the facts to which the *document relates. I have looked in vain for [83 anything in this will to show that the testator meant by the words "legal heirs and theirs forever" other persons than those properly fulfilling the description of heirs. That the testator was an illiterate person, probably ignorant of the true meaning of legal phraseology, might assist the court if it had to choose between conflicting presumptions, but there is here nothing to show that the testator had in his mind an intention that his property, which he deals with as one entire fund, should be distributed in different directions. The case appears to me to be directly within the authority of *De Beauvoir* v. *De Beauvoir* ('), the effect of which is clearly stated in the following passage of the judgment of Lord St. Leonards (then Lord Chancellor), at p. 557: "As far, therefore, as the authorities go with respect to personal estate, whether the gift be an immediate gift, or whether it be a gift in remainder, the cases appear to me to be uniform—to give to the words the sense which the testator has himself impressed upon them—that if he has given to the heir, though the heir would not by law be the person to take that property, he is the person who takes as *persona designata*. It is impossible to lay down any other rule of construction." In the present case the testator died leaving co-heiresses. This, however, makes no difference in the construction to be put on the will. *De Beauvoir* v. *De Beauvoir* (') is an authority that the use of the word "heirs" in the plural will not by itself affect the presumption that the testator intended to designate his proper legal heir, and the case of *Mounsey* v. *Blamire* (') shows that co-heiresses take as legatees under a bequest to "my heir," if there be no context to explain it otherwise.

I therefore grant administration, with the will annexed, to the applicant, as one of the residuary legatees of the testator; the costs of both parties to be paid out of the estate.

Solicitors for heir-at-law: *Bell, Brodrich & Gray.*
Solicitors for next of kin: *Speechley & Co.*

(') 3 H. L. C., 524.   (') 4 Russ. Ch. Cas., 384.

[4 Probate Division, 84.]

May 4, 1878.

84]   *SMITH & KIRK v. HOPKINSON.

Costs—Payment out of real Estate.

The testatrix by her will directed that her testamentary expenses be paid out of her real and personal estate. The personal estate being insufficient, the court ordered payment of the costs of suit out of the real estate upon conditions assented to by all parties.

MARY MARIA NIGHTINGALE, late of Wheatcroft, in the parish of Crich, in the county of Derby, spinster, made a will dated the 26th of February, 1875, whereby she devised to the defendant and his children two small farms subject to the payment of certain annuities, and bequeathed the residue of her personal estate after certain specific legacies amongst the plaintiffs and others. By a will dated the 6th of January, 1877, she revoked the gift of part of one of the farms, which she devised instead to the plaintiff Smith and his wife, and she appointed both plaintiffs executors, and directed amongst other things that her "just debts, funeral, and testamentary expenses be paid and discharged out of her real and personal estate." The instructions for the latter will were given by the testatrix to the plaintiff Smith, and the will was prepared by his direction, and at the wish of the testatrix kept secret from the defendant. She died on the 22d of March, 1877, and probate of the latter will was opposed by the defendant on the ground that it was not duly executed, and by reason of incapacity and undue influence. The issues were tried before the President by a special jury, when a verdict was found for the plaintiffs, and the court pronounced for the will.

Mellor, Q.C. (*Bayford*, with him), for the defendant, asked that his costs might be allowed out of the real estate, the personal estate being insufficient.

Inderwick Q.C. (*Powles*, with him), for the plaintiffs, offered no opposition, provided that the costs be paid ratably upon the shares of each devisee.

THE PRESIDENT: The circumstances of the case would 85]   justify *an order for payment out of the personal estate, and, as the parties consent, I order payment ratably out of the real estate.

Solicitors for plaintiffs: *Johnson & Weatherall*, for G. Cursham, Ripley.

Solicitor for defendant: *E. Warriner*, for W. B. Hextall, Derby.

[4 Probate Division, 85.]

July 7, 1878.

In the Goods of WILLIAM BELL.

Executor according to Tenor.

A testator gave to W. F. B. and H. H. W. all his real and personal estate to apply the same, "after payment of debts," to the payment of legacies.

The court granted probate to W. F. B. and H. H. W. as executors according to the tenor.

THIS was an application for grant of probate to executors according to the tenor.

William Bell, late of Yatton Lodge, Rudgwick, in the county of Sussex, Esq., deceased, died, having made his will bearing date the 16th of November, 1877.

By the will the testator gave "all my real and personal estate . . . (except what I otherwise bequeath and devise by this my will) unto William Fry Buchanan . . . and the Rev. Henry Hoyle Winwood, upon trust to pay and apply the rents, interest, and annual produce thereof to the following purposes." Then followed a series of bequests in paragraphs, numbered 1, 2, 3, &c. Paragraph 5 contained a gift of residue "after payment of my lawful debts and liabilities;" and paragraph 6 also contained a similar devise and bequest "after payment of my lawful debts and liabilities."

Searle moved the court to grant probate of the will to Mr. W. F. Buchanan and the Rev. H. H. Winwood, as executors according to the tenor. Their duties are to pay the debts and legacies, and to hand the residue to the residuary legatee: *Pickering* v. *Towers* ('); *In the Goods of Fry* (*); *In the Goods of Adamson* (').

THE PRESIDENT: I think that by the true construction of the *will these gentlemen are appointed to collect [86 the assets and pay the debts and legacies, and that therefore probate should be granted to them as executors according to the tenor.

Solicitors : *Bowker, Peake, Bird & Collins.*

(') 2 Lee, 401.   (*) Law Rep., 3 P. & D., 253 ; 14 Eng.
(') 1 Hagg., 80.   R., 704.

[4 Probate Division, 86.]

Feb. 18, 1879.

In the Goods of JOHN SEE.

Administration—Executor not Competent—20 & 21 Vict. c. 77, s. 73.

The sole executrix and universal legatee, having died in the testator's lifetime, and the next of kin being abroad, the court granted letters of administration with the will annexed, to the guardian of persons entitled in distribution.

JOHN SEE, late of No. 4 Princess Street, in the parish of Marylebone, bricklayer, deceased, died on the 28th of November, 1878, having made his will bearing date the 8th of December, 1877, and thereof appointed his wife sole executrix and universal legatee. She died in his lifetime.

The testator had two children, one of whom, viz., Ann Elizabeth See, also died in his lifetime, leaving three children minors. The testator's other child, John Allanby See, was in America and could not be found. The testator's property consisted of (amongst other things), a leasehold house, and an immediate representative was necessary to receive the rent and pay the ground rent.

Searle moved the court for a grant of letters of administration with the will annexed to George Thurston See, as guardian of the children of Ann Elizabeth See. The case is within the provisions of the 73d section of 20 & 21 Vict. c. 77. There is no executor competent to take probate. *In the Goods of Sawtell* ('), *In the Goods of Pine* (').

THE PRESIDENT: I think the guardian is entitled to the grant under the 73d section.

Motion granted.

Solicitors: *Smith, Fawdon & Low.*

(') 2 Sw. & Tr., 448.   (') Law Rep., 1 P. & D., 388.

[4 Probate Division, 87.]

May 8, 1878.

87]   *D'ALTON v. D'ALTON.

Children—Custody—The Mother a Roman Catholic and the Father a Protestant.

Although the wife may have obtained a decree of judicial separation, the court will not give her the custody of the children if she intends to bring them up in a religion different from that of their father, and different from that in which they have been educated during the cohabitation of their parents.

A husband and wife having been Roman Catholics, the husband afterwards became Protestant, and placed the children at a Protestant school. The wife filed a petition for judicial separation, but withdrew it and returned to live with her husband on his promise that the children should be educated as Roman Catholics. He broke the promise, and she subsequently filed another petition and obtained a judicial separation.

Upon an application by the wife for custody of the children that they might be educated as Roman Catholics, the court rejected the application, and gave the custody to a third person, with full access by both parents.

THE petitioner and respondent were married in November, 1867, and there were issue of the marriage two boys who, at the time of this application, were respectively nine and seven years of age. At the time of the marriage both husband and wife were members of the Roman Catholic Church, but the husband afterwards became a Protestant, and in 1875 placed the children at a Protestant school kept by Miss Ballard, where they had ever since remained. Subsequently in May, 1875, the wife filed a petition for judicial separation, but withdrew it a month afterwards and returned to live with her husband, upon his promise to allow the children to be educated as Roman Catholics. This promise was not kept, and upon the husband being again guilty of misconduct the wife filed another petition, and obtained a decree of judicial separation by reason of her husband's cruelty and adultery.

She then made an application for the custody of the children of the marriage.

Cur. adv. vult.

Jan. 21, 1878. THE PRESIDENT: This case has given me very great anxiety, and it is with much hesitation that I have arrived at the conclusion which I am about to state. In the unfortunate circumstances which have arisen between the parties to this suit, the sole difference between the parents with regard to the children *being now apparently the [88 question of religion, I have to consider what is most for the benefit of their offspring, whose interests are of paramount importance upon this application.

If these parents had been of the same religion I should have given the custody of one, and possibly of both, of the children, at any rate for the present, to the mother, upon the principle that she ought not, by reason of the wrongful act of the father, to be deprived of the comfort and society of them. But as she avows that her main object is to bring them up as Roman Catholics, I have to consider, first of all, whether she has any right to insist upon this? and, secondly, whether it is for the interests of the children that she should so bring them up?

With regard to the rights of the petitioner, the principle

which guides the court is, that the innocent party shall
suffer as little as possible from the dissolution of the marriage, and be preserved, as far as the court can do so, in the
same position in which she was while the marriage continued
—first, by giving her a sufficient pecuniary allowance for her
support; and, secondly, by providing that she should not
be deprived of the society of her children unnecessarily.
As it has been put by one of my predecessors, "the wife
ought not to be obliged to buy the relief to which she is entitled, owing to her husband's misconduct, at the price of
being deprived of the society of her children." But it is to
be remembered that if the marriage had contined undis-
solved, and the husband and the wife had continued to live
together, she would would not have been able to control the
husband otherwise than by her example and influence, as
to the religious education which should be given to their
children. Does then the fact that a judicial separation has
been granted to her confer upon her a new right in this respect? and does not the answer to that question afford the
foundation for the judgment which I ought to pronounce?

It has been very naturally argued that weight ought to
be given to the husband's written promise as to the religious
education of the children, but in considering its legal effect
I feel I must not give way to the strong feeling of sympathy
which that document naturally creates in my mind, as the
husband, whatever promise he may make to the wife upon
89] the subject, is always, in *point of law, entitled to
retract it. A much more favorable impression would undoubtedly have been left upon my mind with regard to Mr.
D'Alton if he had simply avowed that he had altered his
mind, and now retracted his promise; and if that promise
had only recently been given and immediately retracted, it
might have had the effect of leading me to think that this
zeal of his with regard to his children's religious education
was only affected for the purpose of annoying his wife.
But I am bound to say that when I look at the dates I do
not think I can fairly act upon that assumption. The promise was made in 1875, and assuming it was sincerely given,
Mr. D'Alton may have been willing to make even so considerable a sacrifice as that of the question of the children's
religious education, for the purpose of bringing about a
reconciliation with his wife, and I can easily imagine that
as time passed on his feeling might have altered, and that,
notwithstanding the promise, he might afterwards insist on
their being brought up as Protestants.

It appears then that at some time or other, he says the

day after the promise (I hope for his sake it was not exactly so) but at some time afterwards, and long before the cohabitation ceased, he had given directions that the children should no longer be brought up as Roman Catholics, and that therefore while he possessed the full right to exercise his paternal authority, he caused the children to be brought up as Protestants. As this state of things was brought about by the husband while he had the right to exercise his privileges as a father, and continued so long before the institution of this suit, I cannot say that it is in the interest of the children that they should now have their course of education interrupted, and be sent to an establishment where they may be brought up in the Roman Catholic religion. That they were born and baptized in that faith must not weigh with me when I regard their tender age at the time when the change was made, as they were not of an age when it is possible to conceive that the doctrines of the Roman Catholic Church had become so implanted in their minds that it would do them permanent injury to be educated in the faith of the Protestant Church, to which they have now been accustomed for more than two years.

*I have, therefore, come to the conclusion that I am [90 not entitled to give these children to the mother for the avowed purpose of having their course of religious instruction changed by their being brought up in the Roman Catholic religion, and, that I must refuse to give her the custody of them. On the other hand acting, as I have said, upon the principle that she is to be injured as little as possible in her maternal rights, I should allow as large an intercourse with her children as the circumstances admit; nor do I intend to give the husband the custody in the ordinary sense of the word, which would enable him to do what he pleased, under any circumstances, without reference to the wife. She must have access to them at all convenient times, but not exceeding that which is customary, at the school where they are placed. The children are boarders at a school against which the mother has no complaint to make, except that they are there brought up as Protestants. I see no reason therefore to remove them, and I commit the custody to Miss Ballard for the present until further order, with liberty to the father and mother to have access to them from time to time. I need not specify the times the father is to have access, as if there is any difficulty it can be arranged at the registry.

It is desirable in the interest of these children that they should not be troubled with their parents' dissensions, nor be made the depository of their parents' grievances, the one against the other; and if either parent should make use of the access to influence the children against the other parent I should interfere to deprive the disobedient party of all right of access.

The result is that I order the children to be restored to the custody of Miss Ballard, with access on the part of both parents in the manner I have specified.

Order accordingly.

From this order the petitioner appealed, and the appeal was argued before the full court (¹).

May 8. The petitioner appeared in person.

91] *McCall*, for the respondent, referred to *Symington v. Symington* (¹) and in *Re Meades* (²).

SIR R. J. PHILLIMORE: This is an appeal from the judgment of the Judge Ordinary, with respect to the custody and education of two boys, the children of the parties. The wife has obtained a judicial separation from the husband on the ground of his adultery and cruelty, and so far as sympathy is concerned in the matter it is impossible not to feel it for the petitioner who has addressed the court to-day. The decision of the Judge Ordinary was that the two boys, one of the age of nine and the other of the age of seven years, shall be placed in a school belonging to the Church of England and there educated, access being given to both parents on proper conditions. The wife made an application to the Judge Ordinary which she has renewed to day, to the effect that she should have the sole custody of the children, on the ground that the father was originally a Roman Catholic, and that the children have been brought up in the Roman Catholic faith, and that the statement of the husband, now that he has become a member of the Church of England, is insincere on his part, and made for the purpose of depriving her of the custody of her children.

In all these painful cases it appears to me that the first duty of the court is to consider what is for the benefit of the children. That should be the paramount consideration with the court, and I am of opinion that the Judge Ordinary was correct in the judgment which he formed, both with regard to the facts of the case and the law applicable to it. He held that it was for the interest of these children, looking at all the facts, that they should be educated as to a great

(¹) The President, Sir R. J. Phillimore, and Mr. Justice Lopes.

(²) Law Rep., 2 H. L., Sc., 415.

(³) 5 Ir. Rep., Eq., 98.

degree they have been for several years in the place where the father had placed them, and that the course of their education there ought not to be interrupted or disturbed. There was no evidence of the alleged insincerity of the father with respect to his religious belief. The custody of the cildren is not absolutely given to him; it is vested in the schoolmistress. Both parents have all reasonable opportunity given to them of access to their children, and the decision of the Judge Ordinary that the boys should be brought up in the religion which their *father pro-   [92 fesses and has professed for some time, was a proper decision.

My opinion therefore is that the order should be undisturbed and should be affirmed by us.

LOPES, J.: It is for the interest of the children in this very painful case that the decision of the Judge Ordinary should not be disturbed.

It cannot be doubted that the exact object which the petitioner has in view in obtaining the custody of the children is to bring them up as Roman Catholics. It is urged that the respondent has adopted the Protestant faith for the purpose of annoying the petitioner, and not upon conviction. I cannot see that the evidence supports that contention, and I unhesitatingly say that I think the court, in the particular and painful circumstances of the case, has adopted a wise course. It has given the custody of the children neither to the father nor to the mother, but to Miss Ballard, the schoolmistress, and they are to be educated in the way they have according to the evidence been educated for some years past, and in the faith professed by the father, with, it is observed, the fullest access by the mother. The children are also to spend their holidays with both parents. I think the order should not be disturbed.'

THE PRESIDENT: I have nothing to add.

Judgment affirmed, and appeal dismissed.

The petitioner *in person.*
Solicitor for respondent: *M. S. A. D'Alton.*

See 27 Eng. Rep., 739 note ; 15 Cent. L. J., 23 281; 16 Western Jur., 436–448, excellent article by Hon. Seymour D. Thompson.

The parents are the natural guardians, and *prima facie* entitled to the custody, of their minor child, as well as chargeable with the obligation of its support : Chapsky *v.* Wood, 26 Kans., 650.

The general rule is that the father is entitled to the custody of his infant children, but it is a mistake to suppose that the father has an absolute natural right to the custody of the infant : Heinemann's Appeal, 96 Penn. St. R., 112 ; Matter of Watson, 11 Abb. N. C., 215.

The mother of an illegitimate child is its natural guardian, and entitled to its custody until deprived of that right by a lawful guardian : Bustamento v. Analla, 1 New Mexico, 255.

In determining as to the custody of children as between their father and mother, the opportunities that will be afforded for their nurture, education and support, and the promotion of their well-being, together with their attachments and desires should be considered : Matter of Watson, 11 Abb. N. C., 215 ; State v. Kirkpatrick, 54 Iowa, 373.

When a court is asked to appoint a guardian of the person of a child it will investigate the circumstance and act according to a sound discretion, the primary object being the good of the child : Heinemann's Appeal, 96 Penn. St. Rep., 112 ; Bustamento v. Analla, 1 New Mexico, 255.

It is the duty of a court, whenever the custody and possession of minor children is sought by habeas corpus, to inquire whether the surroundings of the child are such as make for its highest welfare, and then to do for it that which such welfare compels : Bullen v. Cantwell, 15 Cent. L. J., 369, Sup. Ct., Kans.; State v. Grigsly, 21 Amer. Law Reg. (N.S.), 803, Sup. Ct., Ark.

It is the duty of a court, whenever the custody and possession of minor children is sought, to make such order for their care and custody as the best interests of the children may require, and to that end it may commit them to the custody of other than a parent ; and this, notwithstanding the fact that in a decree of divorce they were committed to the care and custody of either father or mother. Such a decree may bind the parties inter sese, but does not conclude the court as to the best interests of the children : Matter of Bort, 25 Kans., 308.

It appeared that a father neglected to provide medical treatment for his wife and three children, all of whom died : Held, that the court properly appointed a guardian for the two remaining minor children : Heinemann's Appeal, 96 Penn. St. Rep., 112.

The fact that a child is willing to remain in defendant's custody is entitled to but little weight : Bustamento r. Analla, 1 New Mexico, 255.

A child is not in any sense like a horse or other chattel, subject matter for irrevocable gift or contract : Chapsky v. Wood, 26 Kans., 650.

While the mere gift of a child is revocable, yet if reclamation is sought, the courts will consider the welfare of the child, in determining whether to sustain the right and award possession to the parent. If reclamation be sought immediately after the gift, and the pa rent be not obviously an unfit person by reason of immoralities, etc., the courts will, as a rule, consider the child's welfare as promoted by a return to its parent, and will pay little attention to prospective advantages of wealth, social position, or otherwise, held out on the other side ; but if, on the other hand, reclamation is not sought till after the lapse of many years, till the child has formed other ties, and a different direction has been given to its course of life, then the courts may properly give weight to the condition of the child's present surroundings, and all advantages which a continuance in those surroundings may reasonably be expected to give.

In such cases three rights or interests are to be regarded : first, that of the parent ; second, that of those who have for years discharged all the obligations of parents ; and third, and chiefly, that of the child : Chapsky v. Wood, 26 Kans., 650 ; James v. Chisborn, 63 Geo., 335 ; Bustamento v. Analla, 1 New Mexico, 255.

Where a parent gives or surrenders his child to another for nurture and adoption, the court, looking to the best interests of the child, should refuse to direct its re-delivery to the parent: 26 Alb. L. J., 26, 44 ; Matter of Scott, 8 U. C. Pr. Rep., 58 ; Matter of Walker, 3 Vict. Rep. (Law), 38 ; Matter of Moore, Irish Rep., 11 C. L., 1 ; Matter of Turner, 25 L. T. Rep. (N.S.), 907 ; Matter of Moorehead, 30 Pittsb. Leg. Jour. (13 N. S.), 130, 133, Orphan's Court.

In habeas corpus proceedings between parents to recover the custody of a child, the mere fact that the child is in a foreign jurisdiction by the procurement of the defendant, will not deprive the court of jurisdiction, nor be a sufficient excuse for not producing the child in obedience to the writ: Rivers e. Mitchell, 13 Repr., 106, to appear in 55 or 56 Iowa.

The court will order a mother residing abroad to deliver up, within a certain time, infant sons above

D'Alton v. D'Alton.   1878

the age of seven years residing with her, to the custody of the father in England, or to concur with him in such steps as may be necessary, before the foreign tribunals have the custody of such infant children directed to be made to him: Hope *v.* Hope, 2 Equity R., 1065, 19 Beav., 237, 4 De Gex, M. & G., 328.

See S. C., 8 De Gex, M. & G., 731.

The court may require the party to whom children are awarded to give bonds, with sureties, not to remove the children from the State, and may allow the father to visit and take them out riding, etc., on giving similar bonds not to take them out of the county, and to return them to their custodian the same day: Matter of Bort, 25 Kans., 308.

Where a decree of divorce is granted upon the application of the husband for the reason of the adultery of his wife, she ceases, whether or not the decree awards the custody of the children to the father, to have any right to the care, control, education or companionship of the minor children; and the court has no jurisdiction, after final judgment, to enjoin upon the husband or the children the company of the woman who has violated her marriage vows: Crimmins *v.* Crimmins, 64 How. Pr., 108.

In Scotland it is still held that a wife, living apart from her husband, is not entitled to retain the custody of a child of the marriage; and averments of cruelty, which would be relevant in an action of separation and aliment, are not a relevant answer by her to a petition by the husband for the custody of the chi'd: Bloe *v.* Bloe, 19 Scot. L. Repr., 595.

That the wife is not bound by her agreement that her husband should keep the possession of their children, does not affect the husband's right to make a conveyance dependent upon the observance of the conditions imposed by him in a deed of trust to another for her benefit: Owsley *v.* Owsley, 78 Ky., 257.

A decree of divorce rendered in the State of Wisconsin on service by publication, so far as it attempted to fix the custody of the minor children who were then residents of the State of Iowa, is without jurisdiction and void: Kline *v.* Kline, 57 Iowa, 386.

Where a decree of separation from bed and board has been entered in favor of a wife against her husband, without any provision for the maintenance of the wife, she cannot afterwards have the decree changed so as to make such provision, by showing that the husband's pecuniary circumstances are such that an allowance of alimony would be proper: Erkenbrach *v.* Erkenbrach, 68 How. Pr., 194, 4 Month. L. Bull., 54.

Where, by the terms of a decree granting a wife an absolute divorce from her husband, the care, custody and education of the children of the marriage are given to the wife, and it is adjudged that the husband shall pay her a certain sum *per annum*, for her support and maintenance, and for the support, maintenance and education of the children, the court has power afterwards, when the burden of maintaining and educating the children has ceased, to reduce the allowance to the wife, by deducting from it the amount which, upon the evidence on which the court acted in fixing it, was allowed for for the support and education of the children: Kerr *v.* Kerr, 9 Daly, 517.

Where the decree in an action for divorce awards the custody of a child to one parent, it cannot be transferred to the other in a collateral action, but only by a change in the decree obtained by direct proceedings for that purpose: Jennings *v.* Jennings, 56 Iowa, 288.

Though such a modification will, in a proper case be made: Sherwood *v.* Sherwood, 56 Iowa, 608.

[4 Probate Division, 115.]

March 31, 1879.

[IN THE COURT OF APPEAL.]

115] *THE SWANSEA v. THE CONDOR (1878, P. 16).

*Collision—Inevitable Accident—No Light—Neglect of Rule—Costs of Successful
Appeal.*

An action for damages by collision in the Thames was brought by the owners of a
barge against the owners of a steamer. The steamer had been obliged to alter her
course in order to avoid another barge, and the barge with which the collision took
place was last of three in tow of a tug, and did not carry a light as directed by the
rules of the Thames Conservancy; but there was no evidence that the want of a
light contributed to the collision:
  Held, reversing the decision of the Admiralty Court, that the steamer was not to
blame, and that she might have acted differently if the barge had carried a light.
  The action was dismissed without costs, but, *semble,* that in successful admiralty
appeals the appellants will have the costs of the appeal.

THE plaintiffs were the owners of the barge Swansea, which
at midnight on the 20th of October, 1877, was going up the
Thames below London Bridge, the last of three barges in
116] tow of a steam *launch. The launch carried the regulation lights, but the Swansea had no light. The Condor,
a steamer of 434 tons register, was coming down the river
towards the south shore. Her engines had been stopped,
but in order to clear a barge they were turned slowly ahead
and her helm was starboarded. In order to clear the launch
and the three barges the Condor's helm was then ported and
the engines were reversed, but her bow struck the Swansea
on the port side and did damage for which this action was
brought. The other facts of importance in this case are
stated in the judgments.
    The action was tried before Sir R. J. Phillimore, judge of
the Admiralty Court, and two Elder Brethren of the Trinity
House, on the 20th of June, 1878.
    Milward, Q.C., and *Phillimore,* for the plaintiffs.
    Butt, Q.C., and *Clarkson,* for the defendants, the owners
of the Condor.
    SIR R. PHILLIMORE: This is a case of collision which
happened about midnight or later on the 24th of October,
1877, in the river Thames, opposite the Aberdeen Steam
Wharf.
    The vessels which came into collision were the Swansea, a
dumb barge in tow of a tug called the Jane, and a steamship
called the Condor. The stem of the Condor went into the
port midships of the Swansea, abaft her beam, and did her

considerable damage. The state of the weather may be
taken, both on the admissions of the Condor and on the
general result of the evidence, to have been what is well
known and often described in this court as "clear but
dark," and the pilot of the Condor, in his evidence, states
distinctly that it was a night on which lights could be seen at
a reasonable distance. The main defence was, as it appears,
and as I think was hardly denied by the counsel for the
Condor, that looking to the crowded state of the river and
other circumstances, the collision was the result of unavoidable accident. In the first place, I have consulted the Elder Brethren on the nautical points of the case, of which
there are several which present themselves, more for their
opinion than for mine; and we have no doubt whatever that
the Jane with her three barges, two immediately astern of
her and one immediately astern of the two, was properly
navigated on the north side of the mid-channel, with this
*one exception, that she disobeyed the rule of the [117
Thames Conservancy, which was binding on her, and which
is in these words: "The person in charge of the sternmost
or last of a line of barges, when being towed, shall exhibit,
between sunset and sunrise, a white light from the stern of his
barge." There was a clear infringement of this rule here, for
no such light was exhibited from the stern of the last barge.
The defence that the parties were ignorant of the existence of
the rule, and that it was generally not observed is, in my judgment, not valid, and I should be very sorry that anything I
should say should by any possibility lead to the conclusion
that the court would listen to such a defence as this. But
under the 17th section of the Merchant Shipping Act, 1873 (36
& 37 Vict. c. 85), the court is at liberty to consider whether the
disobedience to the rule I have referred to did or did not contribute to the collision in this case. The Elder Brethren are
very clearly of opinion, and I agree with them, that it did not
contribute to the collision. What is necessary for the decision of this case may be stated in a few words. The Condor's engines had been stopped previous to clearing a single
barge that was lying about mid-river. Those on board the
Condor, it appears from the evidence, had seen the lights of
the tug Jane with barges in tow crossing her bows. Now,
if the pilot of the Condor had not set her engines on, as he
did, until the tug and the barges which the tug was towing
had passed clear of her, there would have been, in the judgment of the Elder Brethren, in which I agree, no collision.
The collision was caused by the Condor going ahead before
the tug got clear. The Elder Brethren are also of opinion

that the tug Jane was quite right in going full speed, as by
so doing the chance of a collision was lessened. I must,
therefore, pronounce the Condor alone to blame for the collision.

Judgment for the owners of the Swansea.

The owners of the Condor appealed. The appeal was
heard on the 31st of March, before James, Baggallay, and
Bramwell, L.JJ., and two nautical assessors.

Butt, Q.C., and *Clarkson*, for the owners of the Condor:
The barge ought to have carried a light, otherwise it might
118]   not be *possible to see how many barges were being
towed.   The Condor could not have done otherwise than she
did.   The collision was, perhaps, unavoidable, and in that
case the action ought to have been dismissed without costs.
It is said that the tug, having these barges astern, could not
stop, but vessels in such a position cannot complain of other
vessels.

Milward, Q.C., and *Phillimore*, for the owners of the
Swansea: It is admitted that the rule as to the last barge
carrying a light is not usually followed, and it is clear
that the want of a light did not in any way cause the collision.   The best thing the tug could do was to go on and
try to clear the Condor, and the tug is not to blame for not
stopping.

JAMES, L.J.:   Having had the opportunity of considering
this case with our nautical assessors, who have very carefully read the evidence, and have heard the representations
made, we find ourselves unable to concur with the judgment
given in the court below, bearing in mind the state of the
river, and the fact that the Condor was obliged to do something to get out of the way of a barge which was there in
mid-channel, and that the Condor did nothing, in our opinion, except the very smallest thing that could be done, to
give her headway to get away from the barge.   There was
nothing that was bad seamanship, or negligent, or improper
in the conduct of the Condor in getting away from the first
barge as she did, which, however, did bring her into the
place where the collision occurred with the steamtug and
barges which were going up the river—and it is not an immaterial thing to consider—going up the river at full speed
—as great a speed as the tug could go with a strong flood
tide, and at two or three knots an hour in addition.   Then,
the Condor was placed in this additional difficulty by a matter in which we cannot agree with the decision of the court

below—that was the absence of the light. It is quite clear that the steamtug, with its train of barges, in coming up the river in the way I have said, did violate the express rule of navigation of the Thames by not having a light on the stern of the barge which should have carried it; the object of which must be to give everybody having anything to do with the navigation of the river notice of what it is they are likely to come into collision with. If *the barge had shown [119 that light, it is impossible to know what would have been the conduct of the master and pilot of the Condor on seeing that light, and knowing that the tug and the barges were coming full speed up the river, incapable of stopping themselves. If the steamtug had been, like the Condor, a vessel without the burden of barges behind, it seems to me to be as much the duty of the steamtug to stop as of the Condor; their duty would have been the same with regard to one another—that is, with reference to the Condor and the steamtug. But though the steamtug could not stop, there was no notice given to the Condor that that was the state of things; there was nothing to inform the Condor of the fact that there was a train of barges behind the tug, and, in the absence of that intimation, the circumstances were so likely to throw the Condor into a difficulty that I cannot consider that we ought to hold the master of the Condor to blame for not having done that which he might have done; or, rather, for having done that which he probably would not have done, if he had known what the state of things was, and if he had had that full information which he ought to have received from the tug and barges, by the exhibition of that light which plainly by the rules ought to have been exhibited.

BAGGALLAY, L.J.: I am of the same opinion. It appears to me that the Condor was in a position of very considerable difficulty. The navigable portion of the stream is very narrow at that point, and there were a number of barges about. There being a strong adverse tide she had occasion to keep her engines going to a certain extent, in order to overpower the tide and to steer properly. I am unable to take the same view that was taken in the court below as to the absence of a proper light on the stern of the last barge in the tow, and it appears to me that, having regard to all the circumstances, the Condor adopted a reasonable course, and the accident was the result of circumstances which could not have been avoided by her. In point of fact, she might have a right to assume, seeing only the lights on the steamtug and no other light indicating where the tow ended—she might fairly assume that there were only one or two barges at the stern of the steamtug ; and had there been no more, 120] the accident would not *have occurred, for the first two barges passed by safely, and it was only the additional barge which had no light on it that was struck. I agree, therefore, with James, L.J., that the judgment of the court below should be reversed.

BRAMWELL, L.J.: I am of the same opinion. Mr. Milward was unable to show why it was wrong for the Condor to put way on her as she did, and I could not think it was wrong in itself, unless she had some reason to suppose that there was something for her to run against, and I cannot see there was such a reason.

Butt, Q.C., and *Clarkson*, asked for the costs of the appeal.

Milward, Q.C., and *Phillimore*, contended that there ought to be no costs of a successful appeal: *The Marpesia* (').

JAMES, L.J.: With regard to the question of costs in this case, it is quite clear that there has been a general impression in the profession that the old rule of the Court of Privy Council should be followed, and there is color for that in the decisions which the registrar has handed up to us ; and it appears that this court in a particular case decided in that way. We think that requires great consideration, and we doubt whether it can be right that there should be one rule as to costs in one branch of the High Court of Justice, and another rule in another branch of the High Court of Justice. I think, in future, the rule will be that the costs in every case follow the result, as in other branches of the High Court, but we certainly are not prepared to apply that rule for the first time in this case of the Condor unless the occasion itself were a right one. I am not satisfied with the evidence given on behalf of the Condor, and on the general facts of the case and all the circumstances, and with regard to the former decisions of this court, I think we should dismiss the action without costs. I think, however, that it may be considered as settled that there will be no difference in future in the rule as to the costs.

Action dismissed without costs.

Solicitors for the Swansea: *Waltons, Bubb & Co.*
Solicitor for the Condor: *W. Batham.*

(') Law Rep., 4 P. C., 212 ; 3 Eng. R., 92.

[4 Probate Division, 121.]

Feb. 24, 1879.

*THE ROBERT DIXON (1879, J. 173). (')   [121

Salvage—Towage Contract—Counter, claim.

A tug under contract to tow a ship is not entitled to salvage remuneration for res‑
cuing the ship from danger brought about by the tug's negligent performance of her
towage contract.

A tug agreed to tow a ship from Liverpool round the Skerries for a fixed sum.
The tug imprudently towed the ship in bad weather too near a lee shore, and the
weather becoming worse during the performance of the agreed towage service, the
hawser parted, and the ship was placed in a position of danger, and was com‑
pelled to let go her anchors to avoid being driven on shore. From this position she
was rescued by the tug, having been compelled to slip her anchors and chains, which
were lost:

Held, that the tug was not entitled to claim salvage remuneration, and that her
owners were liable to pay for the loss of the anchors and chains.

THIS was an action of salvage instituted on behalf of the
owners of the steamtug Commodore against the ship Robert
Dixon.

The statement of claim alleged in substance as follows :

The steamtug Commodore is a first class tug, belonging to
the port of Liverpool.

The Robert Dixon is a ship of 1,368 tons register, be‑
longing to the port of New York, and is of the value of
£11,000.

On the 18th day of March last, the Commodore having
been engaged to tow the Robert Dixon from Liverpool to
the Skerries for a sum of £49, passed her 12-in. hawser on
board and paid out the full scope of it (ninety fathoms), and
towed the vessel out of dock and down the river, crossing
the bar at about 5.30 P.M.

At this time the wind was from the northward; a strong
breeze, the sea moderate, and the vessel was being towed
three-quarter speed or five to six knots an hour on a W. by
N. ¼ N. course.

Shortly before 10 P.M. the wind was increasing consider‑
ably and the sea rising, and at about 11, the wind still in‑
creasing, and the ship sagging to leeward owing to her being
light, she was hauled up to N.W. by W., and at about
11.30 to N.W., being then abreast of Point Lynas, a strong
gale blowing and the ship pitching very heavily.

At 12.30 the course was altered again to N.W. ¼ N.; it
was then blowing a whole gale, and the ship laboring heav‑

(') Affirmed 5 Probate Div., 54, *post*, p. 292.

ily, the tug towing her at about a knot and a half an hour, and at about 1 A.M. the hawser parted on board the ship, owing to its having been made fast in a negligent and improper manner. The Skerries bore at the time W. by S., distant eleven miles, Point Lynas S., distant nine miles, and the Ormes Head S.E. by E., distant about nineteen miles.

The tug then hailed the ship to wear round with her head to the eastward, but the channel pilot on board replied that·that was impossible, and that they were drifting in rapidly, and hailed the tug to come and take hold of them again.

122] *Between that time and 2.30 A.M., the tug made several efforts to get hold of· the vessel, but she could not succeed in getting hold, and at the time aforesaid, the ship having drifted to within three miles of the shore off Bull Bay, she was hailed by the tug to let go her anchors, which she did.

After the ship's anchor had been let go she dragged to leeward, and the tug was hailed to go and take off those on board of her, but owing to the sea that was running it was impossible for the tug to get near the ship which was then within two miles of the shore, and still drifting to leeward.

The tug hailed the vessel to get her own hawser ready, and after several attempts a heaving line was got on board, the ship's hawser got over her port bow and made fast, and the tug then went ahead with the scope of about thirty fathoms in a northerly direction, stopped the vessel from dragging further, and held her up to her anchors until about 4.30 o'clock.

٭ At this time a heavy squall·from the northward struck the tug, canting her with her head inshore, and obliging her to slip the hawser. The ship at this time had drifted so far as to shut in the Skerries light, and was still drifting in towards the shore.

At about 5 A.M. the tug got close under the stern of the vessel, and a life-line was passed, and one of the tug's life buoys hauled on board.

The ship was then hailed to get in her hawser, but it appeared that several of the crew refused to work; an attempt was, however, made by some of them, but given up in about an hour ; a line was then made fast to the hawser; and the hawser was let go from the ship and hauled on board the tug by means of her screw-winch. It was then about 9.30 o'clock. The tug commenced towing ahead, and so continued till 12 o'clock.

The tug then proceeded to tow the vessel . . . . until she had a good offing about seven miles N.W. of the Skerries, when the tug let go. It was then about 6.30 P.M.

By means of the above-mentioned services, the tug rescued the vessel and those on board her, from a position of imminent peril; the said services were wholly beyond the scope of those which the tug had agreed to render, and in performing them those on board the tug displayed great courage and skill, incurred considerable risk both to the tug and themselves; the tug herself sustained damage to the amount of about £150 and was detained for ten days in repairing the same, and also lost a hawser, certain lines, ropes and life buoys, of the value of about £70.

But for the said services the said vessel must have gone ashore and become a total wreck, and the lives of those on board would probably have been lost.

The defendants, the owners of the ship Robert Dixon, by way of defence and counter-claim alleged in substance as follows:

The Commodore had towed the Robert Dixon into the port of Liverpool, and the master of the Robert Dixon had promised to let the Commodore have the tow out on the usual terms. On the forenoon of the 18th of March one of the plaintiffs, or one of the managers for the owners of the Commodore, urged the master of the Robert Dixon to allow his vessel to be towed to sea that day. The master of the Robert Dixon refused because the weather was threatening. Afterwards on the same day the master of the Commodore came to the master of the *Robert Dixon, and urged [123 him to go to sea that day, and offered if the Robert Dixon would do so that he would put the ship round the Skerries for the rate to the Skerries, and would provide a towing hawser without charge. On these terms the master of the Robert Dixon agreed to be towed to sea that day.

The towing hawser provided by the Commodore was old and worn out, and was not reasonably sufficient for the purpose. The Robert Dixon was in ballast trim, and was towed on a course which, having regard to the trim of the vessel and the state of weather was an unsafe and an improper course. Those in charge of the Commodore, although requested by those on board the Robert Dixon to tow further from the land, for a long time improperly neglected so to do, and the Robert Dixon was by reason of such neglect suffered to drift far to leeward.

During the night the wind increased and the sea rose, and

when at last the Commodore began to tow the ship to windward the hawser parted. The hawser was properly made
fast, and was not made fast in a negligent and improper
manner.

After the hawser had parted the Robert Dixon was drifting in towards the shore, and the Commodore negligently
omitted to make proper efforts to get hold of the Robert
Dixon.

The starboard anchor of the Robert Dixon was let go,
which brought the ship's head to wind, and the ship's hawser was then passed to the Commodore, but was cut adrift.
Shortly afterwards the port anchor of the Robert Dixon was
let go, and both chains were payed out to the full length,
when the ship was brought up, and she lay securely at her
anchors. The Commodore rendered no assistance during
the night.

At daylight the Commodore came round on the ship's
quarter, and those on board endeavored to create a panic
amongst the crew of the Robert Dixon by hailing them to
leave the ship.

In the forenoon the wind and sea moderated, and the ship's
hawser, which had got foul, was cleared, and given to the
Commodore, in order that she might hold the ship up to her
anchors, and the crew of the Robert Dixon manned the
windlass, and tried to get one of the anchors. The Commodore did not bring the ship up to her anchors, and after
towing a little while the master of the Commodore said that
if the Robert Dixon did not at once slip her anchors he
would leave her. The crew of the Robert Dixon, being unable to weigh the anchors without the assistance of the tug,
were compelled to slip both anchors. About 1 P.M. the cables were slipped, and the Commodore proceeded with the
Robert Dixon in tow.

The Commodore about 6.30 cast off, when the Robert
Dixon proceeded on her voyage under sail.

At the time the agreement to tow was entered into the
weather was dirty and threatening, and although the wind
and sea afterwards increased, the change of weather was
only what the parties contemplated at the time the agreement was entered into, and nothing occurred to change the
character of the services agreed to be rendered.

The defendants deny that the Commodore incurred any
risk as alleged, or sustained damage and loss as alleged, and
they deny that the Robert Dixon was in a position of imminent peril, or of peril, or was rescued from a position of imminent peril as alleged.

*If the Commodore did incur any risk, or damage, [124 or loss, it was by reason of the negligence and improper conduct of those in charge of the tug, and if the Robert Dixon was at any time in a position of peril, the peril was occasioned by the negligence and improper conduct of those in charge of the Commodore, and the Commodore did nothing to rescue her from such position.

Save as hereinbefore admitted the defendants deny the claim, and they say that the plaintiffs did not perform any service in the nature of salvage service, and if they did they have by reason of their misconduct forfeited all claim to salvage remuneration.

The defendants have paid into court the sum of £49, the sum agreed to be paid for the services rendered, and they say the plaintiffs are not entitled to any further sum.

COUNTER-CLAIM.

By way of counter-claim the defendants say that the master of the Commodore agreed with the master of the Robert Dixon for reward to tow the Robert Dixon from Liverpool round the Skerries, and to provide a fit and proper towing hawser for the service. The master of the Commodore took the Robert Dixon in tow on the terms of the said agreement, but he towed her in a negligent and improper way, and towed her with a towing hawser which was unfit and improper for the said service, and the owners and master of the said tug were guilty of negligence in providing such unfit and improper towing hawser, and by reason of the premises the said towing hawser broke when the Robert Dixon was on a lee shore, and it was necessary for those on board the Robert Dixon to let go both anchors to prevent the ship drifting on shore, and afterwards the master of the Commodore neglected and refused to enable those on board the Commodore to get the anchors, and threatened to leave the Robert Dixon unless the chains were slipped, and those on board the Robert Dixon, being unable to get the anchors, were compelled to slip the chains, whereby the chains and anchors were lost. Those on board the Commodore further negligently and improperly cut a towing hawser of the Robert Dixon, and damaged it to the extent of £40. On her arrival at her port of destination, the Robert Dixon being without anchors and chains, her master was compelled to employ a tug at an expense of £40. The value of the anchors and chains lost as aforesaid was about £375.

The defendants claim the said sum of £375, and the said several sums of £40, amounting together to £455.

The plaintiffs by their reply denied the principal averments in the defence, and as to the counter-claim alleged as follows :

The plaintiffs admit the agreement therein set forth, and say that during the performance of the same both the ship and tug encountered dangers, and the tug performed services wholly beyond the scope of the contemplated employment, and entitling the plaintiffs to salvage remuneration.

Feb. 20, 21, 24. The case was heard by the judge assisted by two of the Elder Brethren of the Trinity Corporation. Witnesses on behalf of the plaintiffs and defendants were 125] examined orally *in court, and the depositions of witnesses examined abroad on commission on behalf of the defendants were put in and read.

The evidence on behalf of the plaintiffs and defendants supported the allegations in their respective pleadings. Among other witnesses who were examined were pilots from the Liverpool pilot boats, who described the course taken by the Commodore.

The defendants proposed to give evidence in support of the items of the counter-claim, but on the counsel for the plaintiffs objecting to evidence as to these details being given at the hearing, the court directed that in case the counter-claim should be sustained, the items should be referred to the registrar assisted by merchants.

Butt, Q.C., and *Potter*, for the plaintiffs : The steamtug was not guilty of any negligence, and she incurred risks and performed duties which were not within the scope of the towage contract made with the master of the Robert Dixon.

Milward, Q.C., *G. Bruce*, and *F. W. Raikes*, for the defendants : The towage agreement entered into by the master of the Commodore, was entered into with full knowledge that, owing to the state of the weather, something more than ordinary towage service was required. Moreover, the danger from which the plaintiffs claim to have rescued the Robert Dixon was occasioned by the improper and negligent navigation of the steamtug, and in consequence the plaintiffs are not entitled to claim as salvors : *The Minnehaha*('). The slipping of the anchors and cables and the losses consequent thereon were caused by the negligence of the tug, and must be borne by the plaintiffs.

Butt, Q.C., in reply.

Sir Robert Phillimore : There are certain propositions which are agreed upon, or cannot be denied, relative to this

(') Lush., 335.

case, which it may be convenient to state before I proceed
to pronounce my decision upon the merits of the case itself.
This vessel, the Robert Dixon, a ship of 1,368 tons register,
at the time when the plaintiffs allege that the salvage service commenced, was off Bull Bay, within a quarter of a
mile of the shore.   There is no doubt, *first, that she   [126
was in a position of considerable danger, the wind blowing
directly upon the shore; and, secondly, that she could only
be rescued from that danger by the help of steam power;
nor can it be doubted, as matter of law, that if the vessel,
that came up to her and whose services were refused, or any
other vessel except the Commodore had towed her out of
that position, such vessel would have been entitled to salvage. The defence raised here, however, is not that the
Commodore did not perform what would have been in its
general character salvage service, but it is alleged that having regard to the circumstances under which the agreement
of towage was entered into, nothing occurred to change the
character of the services agreed to be rendered, and that if
the Robert Dixon was brought into a position of peril, it
was owing to the negligence of the plaintiffs.

The Commodore was engaged as a tug to tow this large
sailing vessel clear of the Skerries, and she impliedly contracted of course to find adequate power, knowledge, and
skill, for the performance of this service.   The vessel, however, came into the position of danger, which I have mentioned, and the Commodore now makes a claim in this court
in the character of a salvor, because she says that that danger was the consequence of supervening circumstances over
which she had no control.   In answer to this claim, the
defendants have raised two points, the first of which is the
breaking of the hawser by which the Robert Dixon was
being towed.   With regard to this, looking to all the circumstances of the case, namely, that it was patent to the
master of the Robert Dixon that the hawser was chafed;
that the master's attention was drawn to it, and he refused
to allow his hawser to be used; that the river pilot saw it,
and was of opinion that it was inadequate; and that it had
been used from five to one o'clock, when a heavy sea came
on suddenly; I do not think, and the Elder Brethren agree
with me, that the contention that the master of the Commodore was to blame for having attempted to tow the vessel
with an improper hawser can succeed.

The second point which raises a more serious question
remains, and is this, namely, whether the tug, if she had
pursued a proper course, would have been compelled to

place the sailing ship in a position of danger. It is impor-
127] tant to remember that the weather *had been bad for
some time, and that at the time when the towing was begun
it was seen to be very doubtful. Now, the course the tug
ought to have pursued was a north-west course; the course
she says she pursued is thus stated in the statement of
claim : " The wind was from the northward, a strong breeze,
the sea moderate, and the vessel was being towed three
quarter's speed, or five to six knots an hour, on a W. by
N.½N. course." It appears from the evidence of the master
of the tug himself that he received orders from the pilot to
steer a W.N.W. course. The contention on the part of the
defendants with regard to this part of the case is, that,
according to the evidence, the master of the tug steered a
course which brought him inside the pilot-boat No. 6,
although to have gone outside the pilot-boat would have
been a course of, comparatively speaking, perfect safety,
and a course that at the same time two other vessels pursued. Now the master of the tug says that at eleven o'clock
he put the vessel's head to N.W. by W. of his own accord.
Unfortunately, it was too late to regain the ground he had
lost, and this necessitated the vessel being placed in a position of considerable danger. Now, it is a matter very much
for the Elder Brethren of the Trinity House to advise the
court on a point of this description—as to whether there
was a want of common prudence and skill in going to leeward ; and as to whether it was consistent with common
prudence to have taken that course in the then state of the
weather ; and they are clearly of opinion that it was not,—
that it was an imprudent course to have pursued. The consequence was that the sailing vessel was driven within a
mile and a quarter of the shore, and was pla e in a position of jeopardy resulting from the imprudence of this navigation on the part of the tug. That being the opinion of
the Elder Brethren, it is impossible to come to any other
conclusion than that the Commodore did not act as a salvor,
but, on the contrary, was to blame. We are, however,
clearly of opinion that though the master acted imprudently
he acted in good faith, and we have no reason to believe,
nor is it suggested, that he endeavored to induce the crew
to leave the vessel, or that he purposely placed her in a
position of danger, or in any way intentionally miscon-
128] ducted himself. We think that he did not *give
that skill and prudence which he tacitly contracted to give
when he engaged to tow the vessel. It may be as well to
refer to the very careful language used by the Judicial

Committee of the Privy Council in the case of *The Minne-haha* (¹), in the following passage :

Whether the circumstances in each particular case are sufficient to turn tow-age into salvage must often be a subject of great doubt, as it is in the present case ; but there is one point upon which their Lordships can entertain no doubt, and upon which they are surprised that any doubt should have been thrown at the bar. If the danger from which the ship has been rescued is attributable to the fault of the tug ; if the tug, whether by wilful misconduct or by negligence, or by the want of that reasonable skill or equipments which are implied in the towage contract, has occasioned or materially contributed to the danger, we can have no hesitation in stating our opinion that she can have no claim to salvage. She never can be permitted to profit by her own wrong or default. When it is remembered how much in all cases—how entirely in many cases—the ship in tow is at the mercy of the tug ; how easily, with the knowledge which the crews of such boats usually have of the waters on which they ply, they may place a ship in their charge in great real or apparent peril ; how difficult the detection of such a crime must be, and how strong the temptation to commit it, their Lordships are of opinion that such cases require to be watched with the closest attention, and not without some degree of jealousy.

I am of opinion, after receiving the advice of the Elder Brethren, that this case is brought within the scope of these observations of their Lordships of the Privy Council, in this case of *The Minnehaha* (¹), and that the tug "materially contributed to the danger" in which this vessel was placed. It remains only to consider the other part of this case, namely, the part of the counter-claim by which the defend-ants claim to be reimbursed for the loss occasioned by reason of the Robert Dixon having been obliged to slip both her anchors. Inasmuch as I am of opinion that the loss of these anchors and chains was a consequence of the impru-dent navigation of the tug, I must refer the matter to the registrar and merchants to ascertain their value, and the amount of the loss which was so caused. I must pronounce for the tender, and for the damages claimed by way of counter-claim in respect of the loss of the anchors and chains, subject to a reference to the registrar and mer-chants.

Solicitor for plaintiffs: *Ayrton.*
Solicitor for defendants: *Neal.*

(¹) Lush., 335, at p. 348.

[4 Probate Division, 157.]

March 22, 1879.

[IN THE COURT OF APPEAL.]

157] *CHAPMAN v. THE ROYAL NETHERLANDS STEAM NAVIGATION COMPANY (1876, C. 381).

Ship—Collision—Limitation of Liability of Shipowner—Mode of ascertaining Amount when both Ships to blame—Merchant Shipping Act, 1862 (25 & 26 Vict. c. 63), s. 54—Claim of Owners of Cargo and Crew—Priority.

In an action of collision in the Admiralty Division, where both ships have been injured and both ships have been held to blame, and have accordingly been condemned to pay the moiety of each other's damage, and either of the parties to the collision has applied to have his liability limited under the Merchant Shipping Act, 1862, s. 54, no set-off is allowed between the two amounts for which they are liable in damages, until the limitation of liability imposed by that statute has been applied.

The S. and V. came into collision, both ships were damaged, but the V. was sunk, with her cargo, and lost. In an action by the owners of the V. and counter-claim by the owners of the S., both ships were held to blame and condemned to pay the moiety of each other's damage. Under this judgment the damage payable by the S. was £14,000, and that payable by the V. was £2,000. The owners of the S. then brought an action in the Chancery Division for limitation of their liability, and paid into court £5,212, the aggregate amount of £8 a ton on her registered tonnage:

Held (Brett, L.J., dissenting), that the owners of the V. must prove for £14,000 against the fund in court, and must pay the £2,000 in full to the owners of the S.

The judgment of Jessel, M.R., on this point reversed:

Held, also, by Jessel, M.R., that the owners of the V. and the owners of the cargo, or the underwriters in their place, and the master and crew of the same ship, must prove *pari passu* against the fund in court in respect of the moiety of their respective losses.

THIS action was brought by the owners of the steamship Savernake to limit their liability in respect of the damage arising out of a collision between the steamships Savernake and Vesuvius on the 7th of April, 1876, in consequence of which the Vesuvius was totally lost with the whole of her cargo.

The defendants, the Royal Netherlands Steam Navigation Company, were the owners of the Vesuvius, and the other defendants, Messrs. Van Stolk, were the owners of a portion of her cargo.

The parties agreed upon a special statement for the opinion of the court, in which the following facts were stated :

On the 22d of April, 1876, the defendants, the Royal Netherlands Company commenced an action in the Probate, 158] Divorce, and *Admiralty Division against the present plaintiffs and the ship Savernake for damages to the Vesuvius by reason of the said collision.

The present plaintiffs defended the action, and put in a

counter-claim against the owners of the Vesuvius in respect
of damage sustained by the Savernake in the collision.

The action was tried on the 24th of July, 1876, before Sir
R. Phillimore, the judge of the Court of Admiralty, when
judgment was pronounced deciding that the collision was
occasioned by the fault of the master and crew of the Savernake, and also of the master and crew of the Vesuvius, and
that the damage arising therefrom ought to be borne equally
by the owners of the two ships; and by the said judgment
the owners of the Savernake were condemned in a moiety of
the claim of the owners of the Vesuvius, and the owners of
the Vesuvius were condemned in a moiety of the counter-
claim of the owners of the Savernake in respect of their
damages; and the damages were referred to the registrar
of the Admiralty Division to assess the amount thereof, and
no order was made as to costs.

The present action was commenced in November, 1876, in
the Chancery Division by the owners of the Savernake, who
claimed a declaration that the plaintiffs were not answerable
in damages, in respect of loss or damage to the Vesuvius and
her freight and cargo, to an aggregate amount exceeding £8
for each ton of the gross register tonnage of the Savernake,
without deduction for engine room.

In pursuance of an order of the Master of the Rolls, the
plaintiffs, on the 29th of December, 1876, paid into court
£5,212 3s. 5d., being the amount of the £8 per ton on the
tonnage of the Savernake, together with interest from the
time of the collision.

On the 8th of May, 1877, the judge of the Court of Admiralty stayed all proceedings in the action in the Admiralty
Division; and on the 25th of June, 1877, the usual judgment in actions for limitation was made in the action in the
Chancery Division, and certain inquiries were directed as to
the persons entitled to claim distributive shares in the fund
in court.

The persons claiming to prove against the fund in court
were, 1. The Royal Netherlands Company; 2. Messrs. Van
Stolk; and *3. The master and crew of the Vesuvius, [159
in respect of their clothes and private effects.

The questions for the judgment of the court were:

1. Whether the defendants, the Royal Netherlands Company, were entitled to prove against the fund in court, which
then amounted to £5,238 4s. 7d., for the full amount of the
losses and damages sustained by them by reason of the collision—or (if the court should adopt the judgment of the
Admiralty Division) for one moiety only of the said losses

and damages—less the moiety of such damages as should
be found to be payable by them to the plaintiffs as owners
of the Savernake, and to be paid pro rata with the other
claimants out of the fund in court in respect of one or other
of the amounts so proved for.

2. Whether, in the event of the damages being calculated
according to the latter basis, the losses and damages sustained by the plaintiffs by reason of the collision should be
ascertained by the Chief Clerk or in the Admiralty Division
before the chief clerk's certificate was made or otherwise.

3. Whether the defendants, Messrs. Van Stolk, and the
other owners of the cargo of the Vesuvius, were entitled to
be paid out of the fund in court the full invoice value of the
goods belonging to them in priority to the claim of the defendants, the Netherlands Steam Navigation Company, and
the master and crew of the Vesuvius.

4. Whether the master and crew of the Vesuvius were
entitled to be paid out of the said fund in court pro rata
with the other claimants.

5. Whether the underwriters of the cargo of the Vesuvius
who may have paid for a total loss of the goods insured by
them were entitled to prove in their own names, and themselves to receive out of court the amount of the fund which
might be apportioned in respect of the goods insured by
them.

The whole loss sustained by the owners of the Vesuvius
was taken to be £28,000 ; and the total loss sustained by the
owners of the Savernake was taken to be £4,000.   No question arose as to the limitation of liability of the owners of the
Vesuvius, as the sum of £4,000 was far below £8 on each ton
as her registered tonnage.

The first question was argued first.

160]   *Davey, Q.C., Webster, Q.C., and E. C. Clarkson,
for the plaintiffs, the owners of the Savernake, contended
that there ought to be no set-off between the amounts for
which the owners of the two ships were liable, until the total
liability of the Savernake as limited by the Merchant Shipping Act, 1862, s. 54, had been ascertained.   Therefore the
owners of the Vesuvius must first pay into court £2,000,
being the moiety of damage due from them, and then prove
against the fund in court, £5,238 4s. 7d., for the difference,
which would leave them £3,238 4s. 7d.

Holl, Q.C., and Phillimore, for the owners of the Vesuvius, contended that the Vesuvius being adjudged to pay
£2,000, and the Savernake £14,000, the balance of that
amount, £12,000, was the amount in respect of which the

owners of the Vesuvius were entitled to prove against the fund in court, which would give them the whole of the fund.

Chitty, Q.C., and *Stubbs*, for the owners of the cargo of the Vesuvius.

JESSEL, M.R.: I will first of all give my view of what the meaning of the thing is, and then I will see how far that view is consistent with the well-known forms and precedents.

When two ships come into collision, and both are in fault, one or the other can recover damages, and only one of the two, because the result of the action is that either the plaintiff or the defendant is to win something. That is the meaning of it. The consequence of the collision is that damage being done to one or both vessels, the owners of one vessel can recover something from the other. The admiralty rule in such a case is to take the amount of damage done to each vessel, to add them together, and to halve the amount, so that each owner is *inter se* to bear half, and then to ascertain who is to pay to the other, and the monition finally issues for the balance. That is all that is ever recovered in the action. That is the substance of it. The one party who wins, recovers from the other party who loses, damages by reason of the collision. The mode of arriving at the amount of damages is what I have stated; by reason of our very curious procedure and very curious rules of law, it is an odd mode, but the substance is, in my opinion, what I have stated.

*Now, let us look at what the Merchant Shipping [161] Act, 1862, s. 54, provides: "Where any loss or damage is by reason of the improper navigation of such ship as aforesaid caused to any other ship or both, they are not to be answerable in damages" beyond a certain amount. What, then, were they answerable for before the Judicature Act passed? They were answerable for the balance. The other side could not have got from the admiralty judge a monition for more than the balance. Although the form of the judgment states the rule in the way I have mentioned, when you come to examine it in fact it resulted in an order for the balance and nothing more. Since the Judicature Act is there any distinction?

If there is, it is entirely in favor of the same view, because, since the Judicature Act, these things are no longer raised by cross causes, but by counter-claim. There is really only one judgment. What is to be done on that judgment? What is the duty of the judge? I think it is as plain as plain can be that that which was formerly called set-off is now a matter of right and duty, a right in the first party to pay, and a duty in the judge to grant.

I think that is perfectly clear when you look at the act of Parliament which is for the purpose of enabling the court to do complete justice. Is it complete justice to make one side pay and leave the other side without paying? The 24th section of the Judicature Act, 1873, subs. 3, says: "The said courts respectively, and every judge thereof, shall also have power to grant to any defendant in respect of any equitable estate or right, or other matter of equity, and also in respect of any legal estate, right, or title claimed or asserted by him, all such relief against any plaintiff or petitioner, as such defendant shall have properly claimed by his pleading, and as the said courts respectively, or any judge thereof, might have granted in any suit instituted for that purpose by the same defendant against the same plaintiff or petitioner." Nothing can be wider. The same "relief" shows clearly it may be in diminution of the plaintiff's claim, it may be in excess of the plaintiff's claim, but, though it is no longer to be a cross action, the judge is to do complete justice between the parties.

Then the 3d rule of Order XIX says: "A defendant in 162] an *action may set off or set up, by way of counter-claim against the claims of the plaintiff, any right or claim, whether such set-off or counter-claim sound in damages or not, and such set-off or counter-claim shall have the same effect as a statement of claim in a cross action, so as to enable the court to pronounce a final judgment in the same action, both on the original and on the cross claim." And Order XXII, rule 10, says: "Where in any action a set-off or counter-claim is established as a defence against the plaintiff's claim, the court may, if the balance is in favor of the defendant, give judgment for the defendant for such balance, or may otherwise adjudge to the defendant such relief as he may be entitled to upon the merits of the case."

Now, I am asked to make that word "relief" mean where he wins altogether. I decline to accept any such interpretation. It may be in diminution of the plaintiff's claim, as it is in the 3d sub-section of the 24th section of the act of 1873. The result, therefore, is this, that where it says, "The court may adjudge what the defendant is entitled to," it means, "the court shall," and consequently where the question in the action is, who is to pay damages on account of the collision, the court is bound to see who is to pay on the balance and to order for it. Therefore, the result under the Judicature Act is the same as the practical result was before the Judicature Act, by reason of the judge only issuing the monition for the balance. The total result, therefore, is this, that the mode of calculating the damages is what I have stated, but the damages are calculated as the damages arising from the collision, payable by one party to the other, which is the balance in case both vessels are damaged. Of course in the case of one vessel being damaged only, there is only one payment in respect of that one vessel.

That, I think, is the fair view of the act of Parliament, not two losses, not two separate independent actions, and two separate independent rights, but the loss arising from the collision ; and if you look at the act of Parliament you will find that there is nothing said about the person entitled to recover. It is only a limitation of the amount that the owner of the vessel is liable to pay. It appears to me a fallacy to say that the owner of that vessel is entitled to recover from the owner of the other ; on the *con- [163 trary, he is liable to pay the balance (that is the substance of the case), and not entitled to recover.

Although it is true that you may have, by reason of some defective procedure, or some difficulty in reaching the owner of the other vessel, a difficulty in making your demand effectual, it appears to me that is the substance of the matter, and all the rest is mere form. That being so, I am of opinion that as between the owners of the two vessels the amount payable as damages to the owners of the Saver-nake is the difference or balance of the two moieties ascertained in the way I have indicated. So far as they are concerned, they have a right to prove, and as I have already said, it does not make the owners of the Savernake liable to pay beyond the £8 per ton, nor was it intended that they should pay more.

Now as regards the intention of the Legislature, I think that is plain : originally the limit of the shipowner's liability was the value of the vessel, but there was inconvenience about that, and instead of that this tonnage value was substituted ; the theory being, that when the owner of the vessel (and when I say owner of the vessel I mean owner of the vessel and freight) gave up all he was entitled to, he should not pay more. That is the theory of the Legislature, and when you look at it in that light, it is quite clear he is not to be in a position to receive compensation for damage to his vessel, and at the same time not to pay compensation for damage to the vessel of other people ; he is not to put money into his own pocket ; clearly he is to get no profit, and he is to give up his vessel and freight, and that will be the result according to the decision I have arrived at. It seems to me to be in accordance with the substance of the enactment, and also with the history of the legislation.

July 19. On this day the remaining questions were argued before the Master of the Rolls.

Holl, Q.C., and *Phillimore*, for the owners of the Vesuvius.

Chitty, Q.C., and *Stubbs*, for the owners of the cargo, referred to *The Milan* (').

JESSEL, M.R.: It does not appear to me that there is 164] any question *of priority at all. What I am now dealing with is not that which has been lost through the negligence of the owners, because that is the other half, and, as Dr. Lushington says in *The Milan* ('), "The admiralty rule as applied to the owner of cargo would appear to rest upon the considerations I have just mentioned, that abstract justice might give a remedy to him against the owner of each vessel in proportion to the culpability of each ; but as it is impossible, where both of these are in fault, strictly to apportion the blame, by an equitable though arbitrary rule, or, as it has been called, a *judicium rusticorum*, the opposing ship is made liable to one half only of the damage, and the innocent owner of cargo is left, as to the other half, to sue the owner of the ship on board which his goods were carried. I do not see injustice in this arrangement : on the contrary its purpose is equity."

It appears to me that decides both questions. First of all, what can the owner of the one ship claim against the other ship ? he can only claim half the damage (in this case there is no question as to the damage), therefore he can, as against the owners of the other ship, in no case get more than half the damages, and if he can never get more, he cannot prove for more, because it is impossible to allow a man to prove for a larger sum than he is entitled to be paid. The dividend in that case might be considerably more than 10s. in the pound, and he cannot get more than he is entitled to. Instead of valuing the other ship, and paying in the value of ship and freight, we have an arbitrary tonnage rate fixed to represent the value of the ship for this purpose, and it appears to me plain that his proof cannot exceed that.

The next question is the question of priority as between him and other claimants. There is no priority claimed against other owners of cargo, but it is said, as between owners of

(') Lush., 388.   (') Lush., at p. 401.

cargo and owners of ship, that the owners of cargo should get a priority or preference as against the other ship. Why ? This is a sum divisible between the owners of ship and the owners of cargo, because, as regards this sum, it is the ship the proceeds of which I am dealing with (or the sum paid in lieu of proceeds) which was to blame. It is on account of the negligence of that ship that this sum is recovered. It is not a sum which is lost by *reason of any negli- [165 gence on the part of the shipowner, that is the other half, and as to that, the owners of the cargo will have a right of action against the shipowner, a right of action which I do not interfere with, but that right of action does not give them any lien as far as I know, or at least it does not exist by common law or statute against the other shipowner.

It appears to me, therefore, that as far as this fund is concerned there is no priority.

The order made by the Master of the Rolls was as follows :

This court doth declare that the defendants the Royal Netherlands Steam Navigation Company are entitled to prove for the moiety of the loss and damage sustained by them, less a moiety of the loss and damage sustained by the steamship Savernake, and to be paid in respect of such balance *pari passu* with the other claimants out of the fund in court ; and doth declare that the defendants the owners of the cargo of the Vesuvius are entitled to prove in respect of a moiety only of the value of their goods and merchandise and *pari passu* with the defendants the Royal Netherlands Steam Navigation Company, and the master and crew of the Vesuvius ; and doth declare that the underwriters may prove in their own names and receive out of court the amount of the fund apportioned in respect of the goods insured by them on their proving that they have paid for a total loss. And it is ordered that the inquiries directed by the judgment of the 25th of June, 1877, stand over till the loss and damages have been assessed in the Admiralty Division, and that the plaintiffs pay the costs of the questions.

From this judgment, so far as it related to the answer to the first question as to the amount for which the Royal Netherlands Company were entitled to prove, the plaintiffs appealed.

The appeal was heard on the 6th of November, 1878.

———

Davey, Q.C., *Webster*, Q.C., and *Clarkson*, for the plaintiffs ; There is no right of set-off in such a case as this. The judgment of the Admiralty Court condemns each party in the whole amount to which they are liable to pay to the other. Before the Judicature Act there would have been a separate action and a separate judgment in each case : *The North American* ('). It is true that where both ships were found to be in fault, a monition issued out of the Admiralty

(') Swab., 466 ; Lush., 79.

Registry to pay the balance, but the monition was not the judgment, but a process to enforce it. The principal and cross cause were quite independent, and the evidence in one was not admissible in the other without special leave, and 166] all *the pleadings and procedure were distinct: Pritchard's Digest (¹); *The Singapore* (²). The practice was intended merely to prevent circuity of action. If instead of bringing a cross cause the defendant had lain by and brought a cause of damage afterwards for the damage to his ship, he would have been entitled to judgment, although his conduct for so doing might have been visited with costs: *The Milan* (³); *The Aurora* (⁴); *The Calypso* (⁵). This was the practice to which the limitation of liability under 25 & 26 Vict. c. 63, s. 54, had to be applied. The object of the act was to create a fund out of which all parties having a claim for damages against the defendant's ship should be paid proportionally. It was not intended to alter the rights of the defendants against the plaintiffs. Nor has any alteration been made by the Judicature Act. Each judgment still has its full effect, although they are combined in one final judgment: *Wahlberg* v. *Young* (⁶). It was still in the power of the defendants if they had pleased to bring a separate action instead of claiming damages by counter-claim. If the contention of the defendants is to prevail, the owners of the Savernake will have to pay exactly the same damages to the Vesuvius as if the Savernake had been alone to blame, which cannot be just, and would, in fact, be overruling the judgment of the admiralty judge of the Court of Admiralty.

Holl, Q.C., and *Phillimore*, for the defendants, the owners of the Vesuvius: Before the passing of the Judicature Act, when both ships were liable for damages the monition was for payment of the balance. It is erroneous to say that the practice was introduced merely to avoid circuity of action. It was based upon the rule that where there was joint default and joint loss, the damages must be apportioned between them. In fact, the damages were thrown into hotchpot, and divided between the parties. The damages of one were never assessed independently of the other. It was on the same principle as the mutual credit clauses in the Bankruptcy Acts. If it appeared that both ships were in fault, and the defendant did not bring in his cross claim, the judge would not compel the money found due in the original action

(¹) Page 591.   (⁴) Lush., 327.
(²) Law Rep., 1 P. C., 378.   (⁵) Swab, 28.
(³) Lush., 388.   (⁶) 45 L. J. (C.P.), 783.

to *be brought into court till the defendant had made [167 his claim. The whole matter was one of broad principle to apportion the damages between the two ships, and was treated as one question, although technically there were two suits. The monition was the final judgment; it was the judicial act determining the rights of the parties. The monition for payment by one party would not be issued without payment by the other. The limitation of liability introduced by the Merchant Shipping Act could not take effect till after their mutual liabilities were assessed and the balance ascertained. The ship which has to pay the balance does not need the protection of the act, except for the balance payable by her: *The Woodrop Sims* (') ; *De Vaux* v. *Salvador* (*) ; *Hay* v. *Le Neave* (*) ; *The Seringapatam* ('). Under the Judicature Act, in all cases where the parties proceed by claim and counter-claim the judgment is only for the balance: Order XXII, rule 10 ; *Staples* v. *Young* ('). Therefore, whatever doubt there may have been under the old practice, the defendants are clearly entitled under the present practice to prove against the fund for the whole of the balance.

Chitty, Q.C., and *Stubbs*, for the owners of the cargo of the Vesuvius.

Davey, Q.C., in reply.

Cur. adv. vult.

1879. March 22. BAGGALLAY, L.J.: The question involved in this appeal has arisen under the following circumstances :

On the 7th of April, 1876, a collision took place between the steamship Savernake, belonging to the plaintiffs, and the steamship Vesuvius, belonging to the defendants, the Royal Netherlands Steam Navigation Company.

On the 22d of the same month an action for damages was commenced in the Admiralty Division by the owners of the Vesuvius against the Savernake and her owners ; the owners of the Savernake defended the action, and put in a counter-claim against the owners of the Vesuvius.

The action was tried on the 24th of July, 1876, before the judge of the Admiralty Division, who held both vessels to blame, *and condemned the owners of each in a [168 moiety of the losses and damage sustained by the other, and it was referred to the registrar of the Admiralty Divi-

(¹) 2 Dods. Adm. Rep., 83.   (³) 2 Shaw's Sc. App., 395, at p. 403.
(²) 4 Ad. & E., 420.   (⁴) 3 Wm. Rob. Adm. Rep., 38.
                        (⁵) 2 Ex. D., 324.

sion, assisted by merchants, to assess the amount of such damage respectively.

The owners of the Savernake thereupon availed themselves of the provisions of the Merchant Shipping Acts, and commenced the present action in the Chancery Division, claiming a declaration that they were not answerable in respect of loss or damage to the Vesuvius and her freight, and the goods, effects, and merchandise and other things on board the said ship, to an aggregate amount exceeding the sum of £5,064, being the amount of £8 per ton on the registered tonnage of the Savernake, and for relief consequent on such declaration. The defendants in the limitation action are the Netherlands Steam Navigation Company and the owners of a portion of the cargo which was on board the Vesuvius at the time of the collision.

By an order of the Master of the Rolls dated the 9th of December, 1876, leave was given to the plaintiffs to pay into court to the credit of the action the sum of £5,212 3s. 5d., being the amount of the aforesaid sum of £5,064, together with interest thereon at 4 per cent. per annum from the time of the collision, and on the 29th of December, 1876, the sum of £5,212 3s. 5d. was paid into court pursuant to such order.

By the same order the defendants, the owners of the Vesuvius and the defendants the owners of her cargo, were restrained from further prosecuting the proceedings commenced by them in the Admiralty Division against the owners of the Savernake in respect of the collision, until judgment in the present action or further order, without prejudice to the continuation of the proceedings in the said Division in respect of the counter-claim of the Savernake.

On the 25th of June, 1877, judgment was given by the Master of the Rolls in the limitation action, and a declaration of limitation of the liability of the owners of the Savernake, as claimed by them, was made, and inquiries were directed for the purpose of ascertaining who were the persons entitled to the fund so paid into court and its accumulations, and in what proportions it ought to be distributed amongst the persons who should be found entitled, and the injunction awarded by the order of the 9th of December, 169] 1876, *was continued until further order against the defendants the owners of cargo, and all claimants other than the defendants the Steam Navigation Company.

It would appear that the effect of these proceedings in the present action has been to leave the damages, in which the owners of the two ships have been respectively condemned, to be assessed by the registrar and merchants under the order of the Admiralty Division of the 24th of July, 1876.

In the course of the prosecution of the inquiries so directed by the Master of the Rolls, the defendants the Steam Navigation Company, as owners of the Vesuvius, claimed to prove for the full amount of the loss and damage sustained by them by reason of the collision—or in the alternative to prove for one moiety of such losses and damages—less the moiety of such damages as should be found to be payable by them to the plaintiffs in respect of the losses and damages sustained by the plaintiffs, and to be paid pro rata with the other claimants out of the fund in court, in respect of the amount for which they should be held entitled to prove.

On the 13th of July, 1878, the claims so asserted by the plaintiffs, together with certain other questions which had arisen in the course of the proceedings, were brought under the consideration of the Master of the Rolls, upon an agreed statement of facts. The first of the alternative claims of the Steam Navigation Company does not appear to have been pressed, at any rate it has not been supported in argument before us, and it is clearly untenable; the second was opposed by the plaintiffs, who insisted that the company ought to prove for a moiety, when ascertained, of the amount of damage sustained by the Vesuvius, without deducting a moiety of the amount of damage sustained by the Savernake. If this contention of the plaintiffs were to prevail, it would leave them in a position to assert their claim against the owners of the Vesuvius for the amount, when ascertained, in which such owners have been condemned in respect of the damage occasioned to the Savernake by the improper navigation of the Vesuvius.

The Master of the Rolls decided in favor of the second of the alternative claims of the company, and from that decision the present appeal is brought.

*The owners of the Vesuvius have not asserted any [170 claim to a limitation of their liability.

The question involved in the appeal is one of considerable importance, not only to the parties interested in the present action, but also as affecting the principle upon which the liabilities of shipowners are to be measured, in cases where both ships are held to blame in respect of a collision, and the owners of one or both claim a limitation of liability under the provisions of the Merchant Shipping Acts.

If the contention of the respondents is well founded, the plaintiffs, as the owners of the Savernake, instead of having their liability limited to £8 per ton upon the registered tonnage of the ship, will also lose the amount in which the owners of the Vesuvius have been condemned, and will be exactly in the same position as regards the amount of loss they will have to bear as they would have been in had they been held alone to blame, that is to say, they will have to pay the £8 per ton and bear the loss of all the damage done to their own ship. The owners of the Vesuvius, on the other hand, by reason of their escaping the payment of the amount in which they have been condemned, by deducting it from the amount in which the owners of the Savernake have been condemned, and proving for the balance only, will obtain payment in full of so much of the amount in which the owners of the Savernake have been condemned as is equal to the amount in which they have themselves been condemned. The claimants, in respect of cargo, &c., are also benefited by the decision of the Master of the Rolls, inasmuch as the proportionate parts of the fund paid into court to which they are entitled will be increased in amount by a reduction of the proof of the owners of the Vesuvius, and we consequently find them siding with the company in opposing the appeal. Now, it certainly strikes one as improbable that such an apparently inequitable result should be in accordance with a true construction of the Merchant Shipping Acts, but if such be their true construction we are bound to adopt and act upon it, however inequitable in our opinion the result may be. The question, therefore, for present consideration is whether the true construction of the acts is that which the Master of the Rolls has adopted.

With all respect for that learned judge, and for Lord 171] Justice *Brett, who is of opinion that the appeal should be dismissed, I think that the view contended for by the plaintiffs is more in accordance with the true construction of the Merchants Shipping Act, 1862, upon which, as it appears to me, the whole question turns.

The 54th section of that act, so far as it is applicable to the case we are now considering, may be conveniently stated in the following terms: "Where by reason of the improper navigation of any ship, but without the actual fault or privity of its owners, loss or damage is caused to any other ship or to any goods on board such other ship, the owners of such first-mentioned ship shall not be answerable in damages in respect of such loss or damage to an aggregate amount exceeding £8 per ton of their own ship's tonnage."

The aggregate which is so limited to £8 per ton is made up of (1) damages in respect of the loss or damage to the other ship, and (2) damages in respect of the loss, or dam-

ages to the goods on board such other ship ; but, as regards
both classes of damages, they are to be in respect of loss or
damage occasioned by the improper navigation of the ship,
whose owners claim the benefit of limited liability. What,
then, are the damages to which the owners of the Vesuvius
would be entitled in respect of the loss or damage occasioned to that ship by the improper navigation of the Savernake, if no claim to limited liability had been made by the
owners of the Savernake ? It appears to me that the damages to which, upon this hypothesis, the owners of the Vesuvius would be entitled would be a moiety of their claim in
the admiralty action, as assessed under the order of the
24th of July, 1876, or under any substituted jurisdiction.
It may be, and possibly is, quite true that after the assess-
ment of the amounts in which the owners of the ships were
respectively condemned, the Admiralty Division would order the owners of the Savernake, which had admittedly sustained less damage than the Vesuvius, to pay to the owners
of the Vesuvius the difference between the amounts of the
two assessments ; but that would be mere procedure adopted
for convenience only, and to avoid the circuitous course of
reciprocal payments ; the amount of damage occasioned to
each ship by the improper navigation of the other could not
be altered by the order for payment *of the balance [172
by the one condemned in the larger amount. And it is in
respect of the damage occasioned to one ship by the improper
navigation of the other, as such damage would be ascertained
independently of the provisions of the Merchant Shipping
Acts, that limited liability is given by those acts, and not in
respect of the ultimate balance, which under the procedure of
any court having jurisdiction may be payable on the final
winding-up of all matters of account arising out of the collision.

But our attention has been directed in the course of the
argument to the practice of the court, as constituted previously to the passing of the Judicature Acts of setting off,
in cases of collision in which both ships were held to blame,
the amounts in which the owners of the ships were respectively condemned, and of issuing a monition for payment of
the balance by the owners of the ship condemned in the
larger amount, and it has been contended on behalf of the
respondents that such balance, being the amount which
could have been so ultimately recovered by the owners of
the ship that had sustained the greater amount of damage,
should be treated as the amount of damages provable by
them in a limitation suit.

It is immaterial, in my opinion, to consider the various steps in the proceedings of the Admiralty Court which would have preceded the issuing of a monition for the payment of a balance under such circumstances as have been referred to in argument, though cases have been cited on the subject by the one side and the other. I will assume, for the purpose of the few remaining observations which I have to make, that the practice was as it has been represented by the counsel for the respondents, and as I have endeavored to concisely describe it. It sufficiently illustrates the nature of the argument founded upon it, though exception may be taken to the form in which it has been presented.

But in what respect did the practice of the Admiralty Court, of issuing a monition for the payment of the balance after the sums which each party was liable to pay to the other had been ascertained, differ in principle from that which might and probably would be adopted by the Admiralty Division under similar circumstances, and to which attention has been directed? Then, as now, convenience dictated the form in which the ultimate order should be 173] *made, but such ultimate order was for the purpose of giving effect to rights previously declared after the pecuniary results of such declaration had been ascertained. It appears to me that under the provisions of the Admiralty Jurisdiction Act, 1861 (24 Vict. c. 10), and the recent Judicature Acts, the Court of Admiralty, previously to the last mentioned acts coming into operation, and the Admiralty Division from that time, acquired the power of doing directly what the Court of Admiralty previously to the act of 1861 had done or endeavored to do indirectly; that is to say, the power, after the amounts in which the owners of each ship were liable to the owners of the other had been ascertained, of securing that the owners of one ship should not receive the amount coming to them, without ample provision being made that they should in return pay or account for the amounts of their own liability, and in no better way can such provision be made than by setting off the one amount against the other, and ordering payment of the balance, and for that purpose and for no other, as it appears to me, have monitions or orders for payment of the balance been from time to time made.

I am of opinion that the order of the Master of the Rolls should be reversed, and that an order should be made, declaring that the owners of the Vesuvius ought to prove for the amount of one moiety of the loss or damage sustained by their ship by reason of the improper navigation of the

Savernake, when such amount shall have been assessed in manner directed by the order made in the Admiralty Division on the 24th of July, 1876 ; and that the costs should follow the result.

BRETT, L.J.: This was an appeal from an order of the Master of the Rolls, dated the 19th of July, 1878, made upon a question of law raised before him, in and by a statement of facts agreed upon by the plaintiffs and the defendants, in an action to limit the liability of the plaintiffs in respect of the losses and damages arising out of a collision between two steamships. The questions as stated in the case, were, (1.) Whether, under the circumstances set forth, the defendants, the Royal Netherlands Steam Navigation Company, are entitled to prove against the sum of £5,238 4s. 7d. paid into court, for the full amount of the losses and damages they have *sustained by reason of the said col-   [174 lision—or for one moiety only of the said losses and damages —less the moiety of such damages as should be found to be payable by them to the plaintiffs as owners of the steamship Savernake.   (2.) Whether, in the event of the defendants' claim being calculated according to the latter basis, the losses and damages sustained by the plaintiffs by reason of the said collision should not be ascertained by the chief clerk or in the Admiralty Division before the chief clerk's certificate is made or otherwise.

The order of the Master of the Rolls was as follows :— "This court doth declare that the defendants, the Royal Netherlands Steam Navigation Company, are entitled to prove for one moiety of the loss and damage sustained by them, less a moiety of the loss and damage sustained by the steamship Savernake, and to be paid in respect of such balance *pari passu*, &c.   And it is ordered that the inquiries directed by the judgment dated the 25th of June, 1877" (the judgment in the limitation action), "do stand over until the loss and damages which the plaintiffs and the defendants the Royal Netherlands Steam Navigation Company have sustained have been assessed in the Admiralty Division."

It is difficult from these statements to ascertain the exact question which we have to determine. That can only be eliminated from a consideration of the facts which have happened and the course of the litigation.

A collision having occurred between the steamship Savernake, belonging to the plaintiffs, and the steamship Vesuvius, belonging to the defendants, the latter brought an action in the Admiralty Division against the Savernake. The owners of the Savernake, the present plaintiffs, defended that action, and put in a counter-claim in respect of the damage sustained by the Savernake in the collision.

This action was tried in the Admiralty Division, and both vessels were pronounced to be in fault, and the damages were referred to the registrar and merchants. Actions were threatened or were anticipated on behalf of certain owners of cargo on board the Vesuvius. Then the owners of the Savernake commenced an action in the Chancery Division to limit their liability in respect of all claims to £8 a ton. ·175] Under an order made in that action the *owners of the Savernake paid into court the sum of £5,212 3s. 5d., the aggregate amount of £8 per ton on the proper tonnage of the Savernake, with interest, and an inquiry was directed to ascertain the persons entitled to claim upon the said sum, and the manner in which the same should be distributed among the persons found to be entitled. For besides the owners of the Vesuvius the owners of the cargo on board her also made claims. In the course of the inquiry thus ordered, a question arose as to the amount in respect of which the owners of the Vesuvius would be entitled to prove, for the purpose of obtaining their proportion of the distribution. It was alleged that the damage to the Vesuvius amounted to about £28,000, and the damage to the Savernake to about £4,000.

The owners of the Vesuvius claimed to prove on the following footing: Damage to Vesuvius, £28,000; owners of Vesuvius entitled to be paid in respect of such damage, £14,000. Damage to Savernake, £4,000; owners of Savernake entitled to be paid, or to deduct in respect of such damage, £2,000. Therefore, owners of Vesuvius, if there were no limitation, would be entitled to receive £12,000. Therefore they are in the limitation of liability suit entitled to prove for £12,000.

The owners of the Savernake contended that the proof should be as follows: Damage to Vesuvius, £28,000; Vesuvius, if there were no limitation, would be entitled to be paid £14,000; but by reason of the limitation given to the Savernake are only entitled to be paid to the extent of £5,200, or, in other words, Savernake only liable to pay £5,200. Damage to Savernake, £4,000; owners of Savernake entitled to receive in respect of such damage, £2,000. Therefore, if there were no other claimants, the owners of the Savernake would have to pay £3,200. Therefore in the limitation suit the owners of the Vesuvius can only prove for £3,200.

The Master of the Rolls decided in favor of the view presented by the owners of the Vesuvius, and his order carries out that view. The appeal is against that order. Our decision must depend upon what is the true application to such a case of sect. 54 of the statute 25 & 26 Vict. c. 63 (Merchant Shipping Amendment Act, 1862), by which, omitting inapplicable matter, it is enacted that the owners of any ship shall not, where any loss or damage is by reason of the improper navigation of such ship caused to any other *ship, "be answerable in damages in respect of loss [176 or damage to ship, goods, merchandise, or other things . . . to an aggregate amount exceeding £8 for each ton of the ship's tonnage." The case to which we have to apply this enactment is that of a collision between two ships, a claim and a counter-claim in the Admiralty Division, a judgment thereon that both vessels were to blame, and a limitation action in the Chancery Division by the owners of the vessel which was the less injured of the two. The same question might have been raised by a petition in the admiralty for a declaration of limitation of liability. No difficulty in the application of the statute in question can arise, except where both vessels are pronounced to be in fault. At the time of the passing of the act of 1862 the difficulty therefore could only have arisen in respect of a decision given, or to be given, in a suit in the Admiralty Court. Since the passing of the Judicature Act of 1873, s. 25, subs. 9, it may arise in respect of a decision in other Divisions of the High Court. But the Merchant Shipping Amendment Act, 1862, must be interpreted, I think, as it would have been on the day after it came into operation. I therefore, with deference, think it better not to discuss the effect of the procedure under the Judicature Act. Whatever was the effect of the Merchant Shipping Act, 1862, upon the rights of parties before the Judicature Act must be, in my opinion, its effect now. The Judicature Acts did not alter rights, but only procedure.

In order to interpret the Merchant Shipping Act, 1862, or to apply it, it seems to me necessary to consider what at the time of the passing of the act the course of procedure in the Admiralty Court in a cause of damage was. In case of a collision a cause was instituted by the owners of one of the ships, a warrant was issued, either the ship proceeded against was seized, or her owners, without waiting for such seizure, entered an appearance upon giving bail to or paying into court the amount for which the cause was instituted. If the ship was seized, bail might be given to the ascertained value of the ship, if that was less than the sum for which the cause was instituted, or to the amount for which the cause was instituted if the value of the ship was greater than that. The cause then proceeded; the owners of the ship proceeded against might or might not institute a 177] cross cause; if they did not, the single cause *proceeded to hearing. If the question of joint blame was raised by proper pleadings in that cause, the court would in that suit give judgment either that the defendant's ship was solely to blame, or that both ships were to blame; and the court in and by such judgment, unless the amount was admitted, would refer to the registrar and merchants the amount of damage done to the plaintiff's ship. In the former case the plaintiff would eventually be entitled to recover the whole amount of damage done to his ship, in the latter case the half of such amount. After the report of the registrar to the court the plaintiff applied to the court for "an order for the payment" of the money due to the plaintiff. If the defendant had paid money into court the order was to pay to the plaintiff the amount due out of the fund in court, and upon such "order for payment" the plaintiff obtained a check from the registrar. If the defendant and sureties had given bail, the "order for payment" was an order on the defendant and his bail to pay the amount on a particular day. If the amount was not paid on that day the "order for payment" was enforced by "monition" to pay it on a particular day, and on neglect by "attachment." But in general before the Judicature Acts the defendants in a suit instituted in respect of a collision did at some time, sooner or later, institute a cross cause. To the cross cause thus instituted the original plaintiffs sometimes appeared and sometimes did not appear. If they appeared they in their turn gave bail. If they did not appear, and their ship could not be seized, the cross cause could not for the time proceed, yet the court before 1862 had no power to stay the proceedings in the first cause. This was decided in several cases—as in *The Seringapatam* ([1]); *The Heart of Oak* ([2]); *The Carlyle* ([3]); *The North American* ([4]). The first case proceeded to judgment, that is to say, to the judgment which declared the liability, and it further proceeded to the inquiry thereupon by the registrar and merchants. And the court could no direct an inquiry as to the amount of damage done to the defendant's ship so as to allow the defendant to deduct the half of such amount from the amount due to the plaintiff. That was decided in *The Seringapa-* 178] *tam* ([1]). *The court, therefore, allowed the inquiry to proceed as to the amount of damage suffered by the

([1]) 3 Wm. Rob. Adm. Rep., 41 n.   ([3]) 30 L. T. [O.S.], 278
([2]) 29 L. J. (Adm.), 78.   ([4]) Sw., 466.

plaintiff's ship, and issued "an order for payment" against
the defendant and his bail.   But the court by anticipation
refused to issue a "monition" to the defendant and his
bail, to pay to the plaintiff the loss or damage suffered by
the plaintiffs' ship; for, instead of making the "order for
payment" an order to pay to the plaintiff, it ordered "the
amount to be paid into court under the decree not to be
paid out till the plaintiff should consent to a deduction in
respect of the damage done to the defendant's ship."   Thus,
in *The North American* and *The Tecla Carmen* ('), where
there was no appearance to the cross-action, the court
refused to stop the proceedings in the first action, or to refer
the damage done to both vessels; but after the report of
the registrar on the amount of damage done to the plaintiff's vessel refused to make "an order for payment" to the
plaintiff, until decree should be given in the cross action,
and ordered the amount reported due by the registrar to be
paid into the registry.   It is obvious that the Court of Admiralty was struggling to effect in these cases, as the result
of the litigation, that only one payment should, in fact, be
made, and that such payment should be a payment of the
balance between the amounts of the two damages.   But the
court could not interfere until the moment when it was
asked to enforce the decree it had been obliged to make,
that is to say, until it was called upon to issue a "monition
to pay."   That it refused to do.   The difficulty in proceeding, which the court so evidently considered to be just,
namely, so as to make the suit end in one payment only,
and that a payment of the balance, was met by the enactments contained in sect. 34 of the Admiralty Court Act,
1861 (24 Vict. c. 10).   "The High Court of Admiralty may,
on the application of the defendant in any cause of damage,
and on his instituting a cross cause for the damage sustained by him in respect of the same collision, direct that
the principal cause and the cross cause be heard at the same
time and upon the same evidence; and if in the principal
cause the ship of the defendant has been arrested on security given by him to recover judgment, and in the cross
cause the ship of the plaintiff cannot be arrested, and security *has not been given to answer judgment there- [179
in, the court may, if it think fit, suspend the proceedings
in the principal cause until security has been given to answer judgment in the cross cause."   The court after that
statute could, if the defendant instituted a cross cause,
force the plaintiff to appear to it, and insist that both causes

(') Lush., 79.

should be heard together. This could be for no other purpose than to arrive directly at the result which had been
sought, and which was probably arrived at indirectly, in
the cases of *The Seringapatam* (') and *The North American* ('). The same result was now procured, whether there
was at the commencement of the litigation only one cause or
a cause and a cross cause. Before the litigation ended there
was a cause and a cross cause. But in such circumstances
the two causes, though tried together and upon the same
evidence, were distinct and separate causes just as they had
been before: *The Calypso* ('). Each, therefore, proceeded
by separate pleadings and resulted in form in separate
judgments as to liability. In each there was, if the proceedings were formally drawn out, a judgment or decree
which declared that both ships were to blame, and ordered
a reference to the registrar and merchants to ascertain the
amount of damage suffered in each cause by the plaintiff's
ship. Whether the registrar would thereupon in form hold
two separate references, I know not. I doubt much whether
he ever did. He would, in strictness, I presume, make a
report in each case, though I should think he never did.
It may even be that "an order for payment" would be made
in each suit, though I much doubt it. But it seems to me
impossible to suppose that more than one "monition" ever
issued. It cannot be that the Court of Admiralty ever
issued two "monitions," so as uselessly and ridiculously to
force both the parties to pay and receive the moneys
awarded to one of them, thereby both paying and receiving
an identical sum. There must have been one "monition"
only, and that must have been to pay the balance only, upon
which monition, if disobeyed, one attachment alone could
issue. One party only was made to pay; one party only was,
or may well be said to have been, made liable in damages.

180] *The question then is how to apply the 54th section
of the Merchant Shipping Amendment Act, 1862, to such a
procedure. The limitation of liability is applicable as well
to cases in which the defendant's ship is solely to blame as
to cases in which both ships are to blame. It was therefore,
when the statute was passed, applicable to claims enforced
by a common law action, as well as to claims enforced in the
admiralty, only that the complication arising from action
and cross action in which both ships should be held to blame
could only arise in the admiralty, for upon such a finding
in the common law actions neither party would be liable to
pay any damages. Again, the limitation might be required

(') 3 W. Rob., 41 n.   (') Lush., 79.   (') Sw., 28.

either when the only claim against the defendant was by the
owner of the other ship, or where there were several persons
claiming against him.   In the former case, if the action were
at common law, the amount of the verdict was, I have no
doubt, upon the evidence given, confined to the limitation
amount, the verdict being practically the last step in the
cause other than mere administrative steps taken as matter
of course by the successful party.   If the suit were in the
Admiralty Court, and the defendant's ship declared solely
to blame, there must have been an inquiry by the court,
that is, by the registrar and merchants, as to the amount of
damage suffered by the plaintiff's ship; and if that amount
was greater than the limitation amount, the "order for payment" must have been confined to such amount.   But if in
either court there were several claims in different actions
against the defendant, or if several claims were apprehended, the defendant, as against all those actual or apprehended claimants, might proceed in Chancery by a bill, or,
after the Admiralty Court Act, 1861, in the Admiralty by a
petition for a declaration of the amount of his liability, and
for an injunction to stay actions, and for an order as to the
distribution of such amount ratable amongst the several
claimants.   This power was given to the Court of Chancery
formerly by the statute 53 Geo. 3, c. 159, sect. 7, afterwards
by the Merchant Shipping Act, 1854, pt. ix, sect. 514.   It
was given to the Court of Admiralty by the Admiralty Court
Act, 1861, s. 13.   This application by a shipowner was, it
must be observed, made in a different action or suit from
the collision action or suit, and was made as between the
shipowner and parties who *who were not parties to   [181
any one collision action or suit.   The limitation suit, or
petition, might be commenced before or after the judgment
as to liability in an admiralty suit, and so far as I can see,
if before execution, before or after judgment in a common
law action.   The claim for a limitation of liability, as against
several or aggregate claims, could not be made by any means
in any of the suits brought in the admiralty for compensation by reason of the collision, or in any action at law
brought to recover such compensation.   And that being so,
it seems to me to follow that every such suit or action must,
if not stopped by injunction at an earlier stage, have proceeded to judgment as if no statute limiting the liability existed.   How, then, could the statute affect such suit or action
if allowed to proceed?   Only after judgment and before execution.   Suppose, then, a cause in the admiralty by the
one shipowner against the other, and a cross cause, and

judgment in each declaring that both ships were to blame, and ordering inquiry as to the amount of damage suffered by the ship proceeded against. And suppose such inquiry or inquiries held, and report or reports made as to the amount of damage suffered by each ship. If there were no Limitation of Liability Act the one party would obtain an "order for payment" of the balance, and the other party would obtain no order for payment, or at the most one party alone would obtain a " monition," and that would be a monition to pay the balance. But, then, suppose other claims are made or apprehended against him who would have to· pay such balance, and he thereupon in a suit instituted by him, or in a petition presented by him, claims a declaration of limitation of liability. He must claim a declaration to be answerable in damages in respect of all claimants only to the extent of £8 per ton in the aggregate. How would that affect the "order for payment" already obtained against him? It cannot alter it. The Court of Chancery could not direct the Court of Admiralty to alter its order already properly made in a cause properly before it. The Court of Admiralty could not on the petition alter its order previously given in the cause. There is no such power mentioned in the statutes giving the power to declare the limitation. Upon such a petition, or in such a suit, the court is directed to declare the amount of limitation, and to distribute such amount among the claimants. There is no other direction. 182]   *The amount of one claim is, in the case supposed, already settled. There is no power to unsettle that amount. In such a state of circumstances, therefore, the amount of the shipowner's claim would be the amount already ascertained by the inquiry before the registrar as the amount to be paid and recovered, which would be the balance ascertained without reference to the limitation of liability.

If this would be the result where the application, by bill in chancery or by petition in admiralty, was made after the judgment declaring liability was given in the collision causes, could the result be different, ought it to be held to be different, where the application for limitation is made before such judgment is given ? Upon such application for limitation the court may or may not, "as it thinks fit," the statute says, restrain further proceedings in the collision causes. The present case is an instance. The Master of the Rolls has not stayed all further proceedings in the collision causes, but on the contrary, has directed further proceedings in the limitation cause to stand over, until the loss and damages which the plaintiffs and defendants the Royal Netherlands Steam Navigation Company have sustained have been assessed in the Admiralty Division. But if the court in the limitation cause does not restrain further proceedings in the collision causes, it cannot give any direction as to the form of proceeding in those causes. Then the proceedings in those causes must follow the ordinary form. In such case, therefore, of cause and cross cause, and decrees or judgments therein declaring both ships to blame, the inquiry or inquiries before the registrar must proceed in ordinary form, and .then the amount of loss or damage suffered by the vessels must be ascertained, and so the right to payment in favor of the party to be paid be ascertained, and the amount which he is entitled to be paid be ascertained, all in ordinary form. Then the court acting in the.limitation suit interferes and distributes the limitation amount. It seems to me impossible that the court could in such case distribute upon a different amount than that thus ascertained. Where, therefore, the limitation action or application by petition is instituted after the judgment in a damage cause or causes, or where either of them is instituted before such judgment, but no order is made to *stay any proceeding in the dam- [183 age causes, the 54th section of the Merchant Shipping Act, 1862, to be invoked as against several claimants, cannot prevent the more successful party from ascertaining in the usual way, and according to the usual rules, the amount of loss or damage primarily due to him. In such cases the phrase "answerable in damages" is applicable to the last proceeding only of the whole litigation, that is to say, to the distribution of the limitation amount among all parties. And if in such cases it would and could be applicable only to the last proceeding, it seems to me to follow that it ought only to be applied to the same last proceeding in all cases. If so, where the Court of Chancery in a limitation suit, or the Court of Admiralty on petition, thinks right to stop the proceedings in the admiralty collision causes before the balance of the two losses is ascertained, and to ascertain itself the balance, it is bound, it seems to me, to ascertain such balance according to the ordinary rules, and not to apply the 54th section until after such balance is ascertained, and it is about to perform the last act, namely, to distribute the limitation amount.

It is suggested that by such a construction the plaintiff in the limitation cause, that is, the defendant in one of the collision causes, is deprived of his right to obtain a deduction in respect of the damage done to his ship. But it does not seem to me that such objection is well founded. He does obtain such deduction; such deduction is made in order to arrive at the ratable amount in respect of which the other shipowner's share of the distribution is to be paid to him. The amount for which such other shipowner is to prove is the balance between his loss and the loss of the plaintiff in the limitation cause. It is not this but the other construction which would, as it seems to me, work relative if not direct injustice. The owner of cargo in the one ship suing the other ship in the admiralty, where both ships are pronounced to be in fault, can recover only half the loss or damage done to his cargo: *The Milan* ([1]). But no deduction can be made from that half. Suppose, then, by way of example, cross causes by the two ships, and also a cause by owner of cargo against the ship claiming limitation.

184]   *Let the limitation amount of the ship B. be £2,000. Let the damage to ship A. be £6,000.
Half damage to A. is £3,000.
Damage to ship B. is £2,000.
Half damage to B. is £1,000.
Damage to cargo in ship A. is £6,000.
Half damage is £3,000.
Upon the construction of the Limitation Act adopted by the Master of the Rolls,
Ship A. would prove for £2,000.
Cargo in ship A. would prove for £3,000.
But by force of the limitation statute neither could recover payment of the whole of his loss. The fund to distribute being £2,000, ship A. would recover £800.
Cargo in ship A. would recover £1,200.
But upon the opposite construction ship A., though damaged to the extent of £6,000, the half damage being £3,000, would only be entitled to say that ship B. was liable to pay her £2,000. Ship B. damaged to £2,000 would claim £1,000. Ship A. would prove only for £1,000. The cargo in ship A. would still prove for £3,000; the fund to be distributed being still £2,000 ship A. would only recover £500. Cargo in ship A. would recover £1,500. The Limitation Act was passed solely in favor of ship B. Why, without any advantage whatever to ship B., should it be construed as thus to alter the relative rights of ship A. and the cargo in ship A.? A statute, for purposes of public policy derogating to the extent of injustice from the legal rights of parties, should be so construed as to do the least possible injustice. This statute whenever applied must derogate from the direct right

([1]) Lush., 388.

of the shipowner against the other shipowner. Upon the construction suggested by the appellants it would derogate also from his relative rights as regarding other parties. It should be so construed as to derogate as little as possible, consistently with the phraseology, from the otherwise legal rights of the party. It seems to me that the phrase of "answerable in damages" may be, and therefore on this last rule of construction ought to be, applicable to the last step in litigation, that is to say, to the damages which but for this section would be ultimately payable by the person seeking its protection. It need *not and therefore ought [185 not, to be applied until the last stage is reached. If so, it leaves untouched all the precedent steps necessary to ascertain the amount of that last payment, which but for it would have to be made. In the present case, therefore, it is not to be applied until the balance, which would otherwise be payable to the owners of the Vesuvius, is ascertained by the same rules as it would be ascertained irrespective of the Limitation Act. That result is effected by the order of the Master of the Rolls. In my opinion that order is right, and ought to be affirmed.

In consequence of the arguments used before us I have given reasons for my judgment more technical than those given by the Master of the Rolls for his; I however entirely agree with him in the larger reasons given by him for his judgment.

COTTON, L.J.: The facts of the case have been fully stated by Lord Justice Baggallay, and it is unnecessary for me to repeat them.

The appeal is against so much of an order of the Master of the Rolls as declares that the defendants the Steam Navigation Company are entitled to prove for one moiety of the loss and damage sustained by them, less a moiety of the loss and damage sustained by the steamship Savernake, which was the ship belonging to the plaintiffs in this suit, and against the directions consequential on that declaration.

The plaintiffs, the owners of the Savernake, commenced an action to obtain the protection given by the 514th section of the Merchant Shipping Act, 1854.

Under an order of the Master of the Rolls the plaintiffs paid into court the sum fixed by sect. 54 of the Merchant Shipping Act of 1862, as the amount of their liability, and are entitled to the benefit of that section.

When an action is commenced and money paid into court under sect. 54, to which I have just referred, the liability is, under the act of 1862, provided for by proof against the fund paid into court.

The acts provide that the sum paid into court shall be the limit of the statutory liability for the loss or damage by reason of the improper navigation of the ship. The effect of the 186] order of the *Master of the Rolls is to deprive the owners of the Savernake of the amount of half the damage occasioned to their vessel, for which the owners of the Vesuvius were by the order of the 24th of July, 1876, in the Admiralty Court condemned or declared to be liable, and it does so for the purpose of satisfying a portion of the amount of the damage sustained by the Vesuvius by reason of the improper navigation of the Savernake, which under the acts referred to is to be provided for solely out of the fund in court. This is apparently against the words and meaning of the Merchant Shipping Acts, and the provision therein contained limiting the liability of the owners of the Savernake; and certainly is so, if the amount assessed as half the damage to the Vesuvius is the damage for which the owners of the Savernake would, independently of the act, be answerable. But it is attempted to support the order appealed from by urging that in the Admiralty Court a monition to enforce payment in such cases is issued only for the balance of the moiety of the loss sustained by the greater sufferer, after deducting the moiety of the loss sustained by the other vessel. This, in fact, is the case, and on this it is contended, and I understand this was the view of the Master of the Rolls, that the action and cross action in the Admiralty Court, and all the proceedings therein up to and including the monition, are means taken to ascertain one set only of damages, viz., that to which the greater sufferer is entitled, that being the balance mentioned in the monition. I am unable to agree with this view. The monition would have been preceded by the decree of the 24th of July, 1876, in which both vessels were declared to be in fault, and each was condemned in a moiety of the claim of the owners of the other vessel. A monition is, according to the practice of the Admiralty Court, the first step in the process to enforce payment, not the declaration of liability; and though it issues only for the balance of the sums for which the parties have been declared liable each to each, yet this, in my opinion, is done only as a matter of convenience to work out the result of the cross claims, and to avoid process being issued by each party against the other. It is said that the monition is the judgment. This depends on the meaning in which that word is used. It is so in the sense of being the order on which process to enforce payment is issued, but in my *opinion it is not so in the sense of being the [187 order of the court, which declares and establishes the liability. What takes place is, in my opinion, like what frequently occurs in proceedings in the Court of Chancery, where parties have cross claims against each other, the amount of which depends upon accounts or inquiries to be taken or made in chambers. In such cases the decree declares the liability of each, the necessary accounts to ascertain the amount are directed, and the decree on further direction directs payment of the balance only. It is suggested that there will be a difficulty if the owners of the Vesuvius proceed in the Court of Admiralty, not only to have the amount of the damage sustained by each ship ascertained, but to obtain a monition for payment, that this would be for the balance of one half of the loss sustained by each vessel, and that they must be admitted to prove for this balance. Looking to the form of the order of the Master of the Rolls, it can hardly be supposed that he intended the proceedings in the Court of Admiralty to be carried on till the monition for payment was obtained. But if a monition were obtained in this case, it would not be right, if the view which I take is otherwise correct, that it should be for the balance of half the damage sustained by the Vesuvius, after deducting half the damage sustained by the Savernake. For under the circumstances there can be no set-off, as the owners of the Savernake have claimed the benefit of the limited liability given by the act, which leaves to the owners of the Vesuvius a right to be paid a dividend only on the damage sustained by that ship, while they, the owners of the Vesuvius, remain liable in full.

For these reasons I agree with Lord Justice Baggallay that the order appealed from must be reversed, and that the defendants, the owners of the Vesuvius, must rank against the fund in court for the entire amount of the moiety of the damage to which they have been declared entitled.

Solicitors for plaintiffs : *T. Cooper & Co.*
Solicitors for defendants : *Pritchard & Sons; Stokes, Saunders & Stokes.*

[4 Probate Division, 191.]

Dec. 17, 1878.

191]   *THE JACOB LANDSTROM (1878, K. 5).

Practice—Salvage—Salvors having different Interests—Refusal to consolidate—
Tender in both Actions.

In a case where two actions of salvage were instituted, on behalf of plaintiffs having adverse interests against the same vessel, to recover salvage reward in respect
of services rendered on the same occasion, the court, on the plaintiffs refusing to
consent to a consolidation order, allowed the defendants to make a single tender in
respect of the claims in both actions.

ON the 8th of December, 1877, an action of salvage, entitled *The Jacob Landstrom*, 1877, O. No. 397, was instituted on behalf of the owners, masters, and crews of the
smacks Emblem, Welcome, Young Pheasant, and Reindeer, against The Jacob Landstrom, her cargo, and freight ;
and on the 4th of January, 1878, another action of salvage,
entitled *The Jacob Landstrom*, 1878, K. No. 5, was instituted on behalf of the owners, master, and crew of the
steamtug Harwich, the master and crew of the life-boat
Springwell, and the owners, masters, and crews of the
smacks Volunteer and Albatross, against the Jacob Landstrom, her cargo and freight.   Separate appearances were
entered in each action, and statements of claim in each
action were delivered respectively on the 24th of December,
1877, and on the 23d of January, 1878.

The statement of claim delivered in the first above-mentioned action, alleged that on the 3d of December, 1877, the
Emblem and the Welcome had found the Jacob Landstrom ashore on the Long Sand and abandoned, and that
the next day, the Young Pheasant having in the meantime
come up, the plaintiffs had succeeded at high water in
backing the Jacob Landstrom off the sand.   That afterwards the Volunteer and the Albatross came up, having on
board the mate of the Jacob Landstrom, and that under
his instructions the plaintiffs subsequently rendered further
services to the Jacob Landstrom.

The statement of claim delivered in the second above-
mentioned action, after alleging that the plaintiffs in such
action had, between 4 and 5 A.M. of the 3d of December,
1877, found the Jacob Landstrom on the Long Sand, and
burning flares, and that the life-boat Springwell had taken
192]   off the master and crew *of the Jacob Landstrom,
and started in tow of the Harwich to Harwich harbor, leav-

ing the Albatross in charge of the Jacob Landstrom, by the desire of her master, proceeded, in the 8th, 10th, and 11th paragraphs, substantially as follows:

8. Several smacks came up and hailed the Albatross, and hearing she had charge of the Jacob Landstrom sailed away. Two Colchester (') smacks, however, stayed by, and their crew, though warned, proceeded to get on board the Jacob Landstrom, whereupon some of the Albatross' crew again went on board the Jacob Landstrom and endeavored to prevent their doing damage. As the tide and sea rose all were obliged to leave.

10. On the morning of the 4th the Volunteer, with the mate of the Jacob Landstrom and an agent acting for her at Harwich came up to the Albatross, and the two waited till 11 A.M., when it was high water. The wind was N.E. and it was fair weather, but there was a very heavy sea. The Colchester smacks which were laying-by, were again warned by the agent and the mate of the Jacob Landstrom not to interfere. Two other Colchester smacks now came up (').

11. At the top of high water the Jacob Landstrom floated off with the assistance of the sails, which had been set aback, and the plaintiffs from the Volunteer and Albatross went on board her and proceeded to navigate her, though they were much interfered with by the men from the four Colchester smacks, some of whom, though repeatedly warned, pressed on board her.

The defendants in the action, 1877, O. No. 397, on the 28th of February gave notice to the plaintiffs in both actions, that the judge in court would be moved to order that the two actions should be consolidated, or that, in the event of either of the plaintiffs objecting thereto, the defendants should be at liberty to make a tender in court in the action, 1878, K. No. 5, of a sum that they might deem sufficient to satisfy the claims for salvage in both actions. A similar notice of motion was also given in the action 1878, K. No. 5.

March 5. The two motions came on to be heard together.

E. C. Clarkson appeared for the defendants in support of the motion.

W. G. F. Phillimore for the plaintiffs in the action entitled the *Jacob Landstrom*, 1878, K. No. 5, refused to con-

(') The smacks mentioned in these paragraphs were the Emblem, Welcome, Young Pheasant, and Reindeer.

sent to the two actions being consolidated, and contended
that the practice of the court required that the defendants,
193] if they were of opinion that *both sets of plaintiffs
were entitled to remuneration as salvors, should make a
separate tender in each action.

Stubbs, for the plaintiffs in the action entitled the *Jacob
Landstrom,* 1877, O. No. 397, also opposed the motion on
the same ground.

SIR ROBERT PHILLIMORE: The first question that comes
before the court is as to the power of consolidation. It is
hardly necessary to say that it has always been considered
a power incident to the whole case to order actions to be
consolidated both in the case of wages and other suits.
That is already laid down by Dr. Lushington in the case of
The William Hutt ('), where Dr. Lushington said:

> "But according to my knowledge the universal practice of the court has been
> to consolidate actions where the decision of each action depends on precisely the
> same facts, and in salvage suits the court has gone further, consolidating actions
> where there are several sets of salvors not rendering precisely the same services.
> The power of consolidating actions is most beneficial. But for this power the
> owners of a ship would often be vexed by a host of different actions arising out
> of one matter, as in a case of collision by all the several owners of cargo in the
> vessel run down, and the court could afford no relief, having no power to order
> the evidence in one action to be taken as evidence in another."

I perceive that in the case of *The Melpomene* ('), decided
by myself in 1873, I ordered two cases to be consolidated
where the application was on behalf of the plaintiffs and
resisted by the defendants. Nevertheless, the more recent
practice of the court has been not to force consolidation
where the parties object to it and maintain that their interests are different. But although in these cases the court has
not compelled consolidation, it has always held it to be in
its power to condemn the party refusing to consolidate in
costs. In the present case I do not direct a consolidation of
the actions, but there remains the further question whether
it is not competent to the owners of the salved property to
make one tender, and on the whole I am of opinion that it
is quite clear that there are cases in which it would be impossible to make a separate tender in each action. Take
the case of a derelict and two salvors setting up separate
claims. It would be impossible for the owner to know what
194] the services were. He would know *the value of the
vessel and of the cargo, but it would be impossible for him
to ascertain the separate value of the services rendered by
each. It is therefore quite clear that there must be cases in
which it would be unjust to call upon the owner of the

(') Lush., 27.   (') Law Rep., 4 A. & E., 129; 7 Eng. R., 366.

property to make a separate tender.   I am of opinion that the present case falls within the category of such cases.   I order a single tender for the whole services rendered to the ship, the defendants to elect, if they choose, in which action it is to be paid in (¹).

Solicitors for plaintiffs in action K. No. 5, 1878 : *Tatham, Oblein & Nash.*

Solicitors for plaintiffs in action O. 397, 1877 : *Lowless & Co.*

Solicitors for the owners of the Jacob Landstrom : *Stokes, Saunders & Stokes.*

(¹) The following order was drawn up in action 1877, O. No. 397 :

March 5. The judge having heard counsel on both sides in this action and in action 1878, K. No. 5, made no order upon the defendants' application to consolidate, counsel for the respective plaintiffs objecting to such consolidation; but he nevertheless gave leave to the said defendants to make a tender in one of the said actions in respect of the claim in both actions.

In obedience to this order the solicitors for the owners of the Jacob Landstrom brought the sum of £320 into court as a tender, and served on the respective solicitors for the plaintiffs in each action a notice of tender, which *mutatis mutandis* was in the following form :

" We, Stokes, Saunders & Stokes, in pursuance of an order of the judge on the 5th of March in this action, hereby tender to the plaintiffs in this action and in action O. No. 397, the sum of £320 in satisfaction of their respective claims for salvage, together with the taxed costs.

" April 30, 1878."

On the 6th of May, 1878, the solicitors for the plaintiffs in the action, 1878, K. No. 5, accepted the tender, and on the 29th of June, on the plaintiffs in the action, 1877, No. O. 397, objecting to the amount of the tender being paid out of court, unless the whole or a portion thereof was paid to them, obtained an order from the registrar that the statements of claim in the two actions should be exchanged between the plaintiffs thereto, and that supplementary pleadings should be entered into on the question as to the disposal of the amount tendered.   Subsequently, on the 2d of December, the owners of the Jacob Landstrom and their bail were dismissed by the registrar from the two actions and from all further observance of justice therein.   On the 17th of December the solicitors for the owners of the Jacob Landstrom applied to the judge that the amount brought into court as a tender should be paid to them for the use of their parties, and the judge granted the application ; the solicitors for the respective plaintiffs having consented thereto.

[4 Probate Division, 195.]

Jan. 14, 1879.

*THE POMMERANIA (1879, O. 6).   [195

Practice—Substituted Service—Discontinuance—Rules of the Supreme Court, Order XXIII, *rule* 1.

A written notice by plaintiff's solicitors " we are instructed to proceed no further with the action " is a sufficient notice of discontinuance within Order XXIII, rule 1.

Foreign shipowners commenced an action in this country in respect of a collision at sea, and then discontinued the action.   An order was made afterwards for leave

to serve a writ, in an action respecting the same collision, issued against them
at the suit of the defendants in the former action, by way of substituted service
upon the solicitors who acted in the former action as the solicitors for the foreign
shipowners.

Upon its appearing that the solicitors had ceased to act for the foreign shipowners,
the order was set aside.

THIS was an action of damage *in personam*, instituted on
behalf of the owners of the British bark Moel Eilian, against
the owners of the German ship Pommerania, to recover damages sustained in a collision between the two vessels in the
English Channel, in the month of November last.   The writ
in the action was taken out on the 7th of January in this
year, by Messrs. Pritchard & Sons, who on the same day
applied in the registry for leave to serve the same, by way
of substituted service, on Messrs. Stokes, Saunders & Stokes,
and in support of their application, brought in an affidavit
alleging, *inter alia*, as follows :

The defendants in this action are the owners of the steamship Pommerania,
and in the month of November last, commenced an action *in rem* in the admiralty section of the Probate, Divorce, and Admiralty Division of this court against,
and arrested the bark Moel Eilian.   The said action is still pending, and bail
has been given therein for the Moel Eilian.

The said plaintiffs in the said action *in rem*, and who are the defendants in this
action, as I am informed and verily believe, are all of them resident in the empire of Germany, and legal service of the said writ cannot be effected upon them
personally; but Messrs. Stokes, Saunders & Stokes, have acted and are still acting as the solicitors of the said defendants the plaintiffs in the said action *in
rem ;* and I verily believe that service of the writ issued in this action upon the
said Messrs. Stokes, Saunders & Stokes, would effectually bring this action to
the knowledge of the said defendants.

The registrar having heard counsel, granted the application, and on the 8th of January, substituted service of the
196]   writ, together *with a copy of the above-mentioned
affidavit and of the registrar's order was duly made on
Messrs. Stokes. Saunders & Stokes.

W. G. F. Phillimore, on behalf of Messrs. Stokes, Saunders & Stokes, moved the judge in court, to set aside the
service of the writ and the order permitting substituted service, and all subsequent proceedings in the action, and to
direct that the costs of and incidental to the motion, might
be ordered to be paid by the plaintiffs.   He relied on an
affidavit in which one of the members of the firm of Messrs.
Stokes, Saunders & Stokes, deposed to the following statements :

On the 27th November, 1878, I, being instructed to do so on behalf of the
underwriters of the Pommerania, issued a writ *in rem*, 1878, O. No. 356,
against the owners of the vessel, Moel Eilian and her freight, indorsed with a
claim for damages for the loss of the Pommerania and her cargo, by collision
with the Moel Eilian.

Upon the said 27th day of November, 1878, the said Moel Eilian was arrested upon a warrant taken out by us in the aforesaid action, and on the same day, Messrs. Pritchard & Sons, solicitors, entered an appearance on behalf of the owners of the Moel Eilian, and bail was given in the said action.

The appearance demanded the delivery of a statement of claim. But before any statement of claim was delivered I was instructed on behalf of the aforesaid underwriters to discontinue proceedings.

Accordingly, on the 3d of January, 1879, I gave the defendants notice in writing of discontinuance, by writing to Messrs. Pritchard & Sons, a letter in the words and figures following :

"31 Great St. Helen's, E.C., 8 January, 1879. " Moel Eilian.

"Dear Sirs,—We are instructed to proceed no further with this action. We presume you do not require a formal order dismissing it. Yours truly, " Stokes, Saunders & Stokes."

I received no answer to the said letter.

I have never had any instructions from the owners of the Pommerania, nor have I acted in their behalf or in their name, except in bringing and discontinuing the aforesaid action. I am not now instructed or acting on behalf of the aforesaid underwriters, and I have no authority to act on behalf of either owners or underwriters.

The collision in the case occurred on the high seas.

E. C. Clarkson, for the owners of the Moel Eilian, referred to Rule 171 of the Admiralty Court Rules of 1859.

SIR ROBERT PHILLIMORE : I think that the letter, the contents of which are set out in the affidavit in support of the motion, was such a notice in writing as is provided for by Rule 1 of Order XXIII *of the Rules of the Su- [197 preme Court. The action, instituted on behalf of the owners of the Pommerania against the Moel Eilian, having therefore been wholly discontinued on the 3d of January, the subsequent order of the 8th of January, permitting substituted service of the writ in the action against the owners of the Pommerania, must have been made by the registrar in ignorance of the real facts of the case. The motion now before the court must be granted with costs.

Solicitors for owners of the Moel Eilian : *Pritchard & Sons.*

Solicitors for owners of the Pommerania : *Stokes, Saunders & Stokes.*

See Mr. Stewart's note, 33 N. J. Eq., 259.

Where defendant is served with the summons and is a non-resident, the question whether any additional papers shall be served upon him is simply a question of practice for the court.

The satisfaction of a judgment entered upon personal service on a defendant may be vacated, and a new execution authorized, on motion, without notice thereof to the defendant.

"After service of the first process upon the party, it is simply a matter of practice whether any and what notice should be given him of any subsequent proceedings in the cause :" Suydam v. Holden, Selden's Notes, Oct. 1853, p. 16 (p. 170, 2d ed.). The case reported, 11 Abb. Pr. (N.S.), 329 note, is not this case below as is erroneously stated in the second edition of Selden's Notes.

Where a creditor resided out of the

State, an imprisoned debtor was discharged without notice to him, the court holding "A person out of the State is to be considered, as to the purpose of a service under this act, as not to be found :" Matter of Williams, Col. & Caines, 114.

Where the defendant in an action at law brought a suit in equity in the same circuit court against the non-resident plaintiff in that action, to restrain its further prosecution ; held, that service of the subpœna in the equity suit upon the attorney for the plaintiff in the action at law, was a sufficient service to confer jurisdiction : Segee v. Thomas, 3 Blatchf., 11.

The defendant to a bill of revivor had appeared to the original bill by his solicitor, but before the filing of the bill of revivor had gone out of the jurisdiction. The court ordered that service of the subpœna to appear, on the solicitor, should be good service on the defendant : Norton v. Hepworth, 1 MacN. & Gord., 54, and cases cited in note by Mr. Perkins, Little, Brown & Co.'s Ed.; Hope v. Hope, 4 De Gex, M. & G., 341–3, affirming 19 Beav., 237.

Service of a subpœna to answer, upon a defendant out of the jurisdiction, may be authorized to be made upon a person within the jurisdiction, whom the defendant has authorized to act for him in the suit': Murray v. Vipont, 1 Phill. Chy., 520, and cases cited by Mr. Dunlap in note, p. 522, Banks & Co.'s Ed.

An action is *pending* in a court for all purposes of that suit, though judgment has been recovered therein, so long as such judgment remains unsatisfied : Wegman v. Childs, 41 N. Y., 159 ; Ulshafer v. Stewart, 71 Penn. St. R., 170.

See Porter v. Kingsbury, 77 N. Y., 168–9.

Service of motion papers by the defendant's attorney to set aside an attachment and an order for publication, made upon the plaintiff's attorney some four years after the entry of judgment in the action, was held sufficient : Drury v. Russell, 27 How. Pr., 130.

See also Pitt v. Davison, 3 Abb. Pr. (N.S.), 406, 37 N. Y., 242.

Service of a writ abroad, when service was subsequently admitted in correspondence, has been held valid : Nichol v. Gwyn, 1 Sim., 390.

Where an infant is a non-resident, special directions must be given as to the manner of service of an order that he procure a guardian to be appointed, if any notice thereof shall be deemed requisite : Knickerbacker v. DeFreest, 2 Paige, 304.

The principle, on which substituted service is ordered is, that there is reasonable ground to suppose that the service will come to the knowledge of the defendant : Hope v. Hope, 4 De Gex, M. & G., 328, affirming 19 Beav., 237.

The rule that process cannot be served out of the jurisdiction, does not extend to an order which may be allowed to be served out of the jurisdiction : Davidson v. Marchoness, 2 Keen, 509, 514–6 ; Hawkins v. Hall, 1 Beav., 75.

And so a notice : Johnson v. Nagle, 1 Molloy, 240.

See Cameron v. Cameron, 2 Myl. & Keen, 289 ; Parker v. Lloyd, 5 Sim., 508.

An order for the appearance of a *non-resident* infant defendant must be obtained and published, or served in the same manner as in the case of adult defendants ; and if the infant does not appear by guardian within twenty days after the expiration of the time limited in the order, the complainant may apply to the court to appoint a guardian *ad litem* to appear and answer for such infant : Ontario Bank v. Strong, 2 Paige, 301.

The entry of judgment, though without jurisdiction and void, so far terminates the functions of the attorney that another attorney may issue an execution thereon ; if a new attorney be employed and issue execution, such issue is a complete *substitution*, so that subsequent service of papers for a motion to vacate the judgment, with a stay of proceedings meanwhile, is properly made upon such new attorney : Ward v. Sands, 10 Abb. N. C., 60.

Congress has power to authorize the Supreme Court to fix by rule the manner of serving process. A rule providing for service of process upon an attorney is valid, and jurisdiction of his client can be thus acquired : Levinson v. Oceanica, etc., 17 Alb. Law Jour., 285.

[4 Probate Division 197.]

March 18, 1879.

THE HANKOW (1879, B. 250).

Ship—Damage—Compulsory Pilotage—6 Geo. 4, c. 125, s. 59—Merchant Shipping Act, 1854 (17 & 18 Vict. c. 104), ss. 353, 370, 376—Port of London.

The master of a vessel belonging to the port of London and bound up the Thames, on a voyage from Australia to London with passengers on board, is required by law to employ a licensed pilot within the limits of the port of London.

[4 Probate Division, 204.]

April 8, 1879.

*THE MARY HOUNSELL (1879, O. 83). [204

Ship—Damage—Pilot Cutter in tow of sailing Vessel—Regulations for preventing Collisions at Sea, Articles 2, 5, 8—Merchant Shipping Act, 1873 (36 & 37 Vict. c. 85), s. 17.

A brigantine with a cutter towing astern came into collision with another brigantine in the Bristol Channel after dark. Both brigantines had the regulation side lights exhibited, but the cutter had only a white light exhibited at her masthead, and the brigantine towing the cutter was sailing close-hauled on the starboard tack whilst the brigantine which came into collision with her was going free:

Held, that the Regulations for preventing Collisions at Sea had been infringed by the cutter, and that the vessel towing her was to be deemed in fault for the collision by virtue of the provisions of the 17th section of the Merchant Shipping Act, 1873 (1).

THIS was an action of damage instituted on behalf of the owners, master, and crew of the brigantine Bessie against the brigantine Mary Hounsell.

The statement of claim contained the following material allegations:

1. Shortly after 6.30 P.M. on the 23d of February, 1879, the Bessie, of 187 tons register, was off Barry Island.

2. At that time the wind was about north northwest, the weather was cloudy but clear. The Bessie was sailing close-hauled on the starboard tack under all plain sail, heading about west by north, and making from four to five knots an

(1) Since the decision of this case an Order in Council (gazetted the 19th of August, 1879), has been issued, which is to come into force in September, 1880. The 9th article of the order provides as follows:

"A pilot vessel, when engaged on her station on pilotage duty, shall not carry the lights required for other vessels, but shall carry a white light at the masthead, visible all round the horizon, and shall also exhibit a flare-up light or flare-up lights at short intervals which shall never exceed fifteen minutes.

"A pilot vessel, when not engaged on her station on pilotage duty, shall carry lights similar to those of other ships."

hour, with a pilot cutter sailing in tow of her. The regulation lights of both vessels were duly exhibited and burning
brightly, and a good look-out was being kept.

3. In these circumstances those on board the Bessie observed the red light of a sailing vessel, which afterwards
proved to be the Mary Hounsell, about 1¼ miles distant, and
about one point on the port bow. As the Mary Hounsell
approached and got near the Bessie, the latter was kept as
205] close to the wind as she could be *got. The Mary
Hounsell when about a cable's length off, altered her course,
appeared to be starboarding her helm, opened her green light,
and caused danger of collision ; and, though she was loudly
hailed to port her helm and the helm of the Bessie was
ported, struck with her stem the port bow of the Bessie,
doing her so much damage that she shortly afterwards went
down.

4. A good look-out was not kept on board the Mary
Hounsell.

5. The Mary Hounsell improperly neglected to keep out
of the way of the Bessie.

The defendants, the owners of the Mary Hounsell, delivered the following statement of defence and counter-claim :

Shortly before 6.45 P.M. on the 23d day of February, 1879,
the brigantine Mary Hounsell, of 160 tons register, was in
the Bristol Channel, near Barry Island.

The wind at such time was about northeast by north, and
not about north northwest, as alleged in the statement of
claim ; the weather was dark but clear, and the Mary Hounsell was on the port tack, sailing full and by, and heading
about east by south half south, and proceeding at the rate of
about four knots per hour through the water. Her proper
regulation sailing lights were duly exhibited and burning
brightly.

At such time three lights, apparently the red and green
lights and masthead light of a steamer, were seen at the distance of about from a mile and a half to two miles from the
Mary Hounsell, and bearing about half a point on her starboard bow. These lights proved to be the red and green lights
of the Bessie, and a white light at the masthead of a vessel
which she had in tow. The Mary Hounsell was kept full
and by on the port tack. The Bessie shut in her red light,
leaving her green light open on the starboard bow of the
Mary Hounsell. The Bessie with the said vessel in tow
approached, and under a port helm caused immediate danger of collision, and although the helm of the Mary Houn

sell was put hard down, the Bessie with her port bow came into collision with the starboad bow of the Mary Hounsell, and did the Mary Hounsell considerable damage.

The Bessie and the vessel she was towing did not duly observe and comply with the regulations as to lights, but carried improper and deceptive lights.

The statement of defence contained other charges of negligence against the Bessie, and alleged that the collision was occasioned by negligence on the part of the Bessie, and that the defendants relied by way of counter-claim on the several statements and allegations therein contained. At the hearing witnesses were called on behalf of the plaintiffs and the defendants in support of their respective cases. The pilot who was on board the Bessie gave evidence to the effect that he was not licensed by any pilotage authority, and would have had to give up charge to any duly licensed pilot; that the cutter towing astern of the Bessie had been hired by him and other unlicensed pilots, but at the time of the collision *had only one man on board and that no flares [206 had been shown from her before the collision. The result of the remainder of the evidence appears from the judgment.

Butt, Q.C., and *W. G. F. Phillimore*, for the plaintiffs: The cutter is a pilot cutter, and it was necessary under the provisions of the 8th article of the Regulations for preventing Collisions at Sea, that the cutter should exhibit a white light at her masthead. If the Mary Hounsell had had an efficient look-out it must have been apparent to those on board her that the white light on the pilot cutter was not shown from the Bessie: *The Marmion* ('); *The Esk and Gitana* (').

Milward, Q.C., and *E. C. Clarkson*, for the defendants: The cutter was not a licensed pilot cutter, and the pilots belonging to her were unlicensed pilots. She was therefore not a pilot vessel within article 8 of the Regulations for preventing Collisions at Sea. Moreover that article does not apply to pilot vessels in tow of other vessels, and probably only to pilot vessels when actually engaged in the service of supplying pilots, and in this case, the pilot cutter had got rid of all her pilots. The court must find that the Bessie was in fault under the 17th section of the Merchant Shipping Act, 1873. She was in intendment of law one vessel with the pilot cutter, and ought not to escape the consequences of the neglect of the latter vessel to exhibit side lights.

Phillimore, in reply, referred to *The Columbus* (').

(') 1 Asp. Mar. Law Ca., 412.   (') Law Rep., 2 A. & E., 350.
(') 2 Hagg., 178 n.

SIR ROBERT PHILLIMORE: I am of opinion that the
Bessie, with the pilot cutter attached to her by a rope, must
be considered, in the application of the Regulations for preventing Collisions at Sea, as one vessel. And I am of opinion
—and the Elder Brethren agree with me—that the white light
which the pilot vessel carried might possibly have misled the
Mary Hounsell. The next question is whether there has
been in this case any infringement of any of the articles of the
Regulations for preventing Collisions at Sea. Now, whether
the 5th or the 8th article of the Regulations applies, it appears to the court that a conclusion must be drawn equally
207]   *hostile to the case set up on the part of the Bessie.
For, on the one hand, if the 5th article of the Regulations
applies, or, in other words, if this cutter was a sailing ship
under weigh, or being towed, she falls under the express
provision of that article which declares that a sailing ship
under weigh or being towed shall never carry a white masthead light; but if, on the other hand, the article to be applied
is the 8th article of the Regulations, which declares that sailing pilot vessels shall not carry the lights required for other
sailing vessels, but shall carry a white light at the masthead
visible all round the horizon ; then it must be observed,
that that article, in the opinion of the court, contemplates
not a vessel being towed by another vessel, but an independent vessel ; and in that case, the white light would not
be misleading. In the result it appears to the court that
the cutter and the Bessie both infringed the Regulations for
preventing Collisions at Sea, the cutter, by showing a white
light when she was being towed, and the Bessie, by allowing herself to proceed under the circumstances in such a
manner that a white light of the cutter and the side lights
of the Bessie appeared to an approaching vessel to be all
three exhibited from the Bessie.

This being so, the court has to consider whether there has
not been in this case such an infringement on the part of
the Bessie of the Regulations for preventing Collisions at
Sea, as would render her liable to be deemed at fault within
the provisions of sect. 17 of the Merchant Shipping Act,
1873, which enacts—

If in any case of collision it is proved to the court before whom the case is
tried, that any of the regulations for preventing collisions contained in, or made
under the Merchant Shipping Acts, 1854 to 1873, have been infringed, the ship
by which such regulation has been infringed, shall be deemed in fault, unless
the circumstances of the case made departure from the regulation necessary.

There are no circumstances in this case that made a departure from the regulation necessary ; and it has been held by

the Judicial Committee of the Privy Council, that a vessel is to be deemed in fault under the section, in any case where the infringement of the regulations could by possibility have been contributory to the collision: *The Fanny M. Carvill* (¹). I have already said that, in my opinion, the white light of the pilot cutter was a misleading *light, [208 and I must therefore pronounce the Bessie in fault for towing the other vessel exhibiting a white light.

The next question is this, whether the Mary Hounsell is not also to blame, and after conference with the Elder Brethren on this point, we are all of opinion that the story told by the Bessie is the true story, and that she was close-hauled on the starboard tack, and that the Mary Hounsell had the wind free and ought to have got out of the way, which she did not do. I therefore pronounce both vessels to blame.

Solicitors for plaintiffs: *Stokes, Saunders & Stokes.*
Solicitors for defendants: *Ingledew, Ince & Greening.*

(¹) 44 L. J. (Ad.), 34.

[4 Probate Division, 208.]

March 4, 1879.

THE EUDORA (1879, S. 79).

Practice—Bottomry—Arrest before Bond payable.

Where the holders of a bottomry bond, on ship and freight payable seven days after the arrival of the ship, being apprehensive that her cargo would be discharged forthwith, and their security diminished, instituted a bottomry suit, after the arrival of the ship and before the expiration of the seventh day, and arrested the ship, the court, on the application of the owners of the ship, who had paid the amount of the bond and interest into court, condemned the plaintiffs in costs.

THIS was a motion on behalf of the owners of the ship Eudora, the defendants in an action of bottomry instituted against the Eudora and her freight, to direct the Eudora, which had been arrested in the action on the 22d of February, 1879, to be released without bail, and to condemn the plaintiffs in damages, and in the costs of the motion, and all costs incurred by the institution of the action.

March 1. *E. C. Clarkson*, on behalf of the defendants, brought on the motion, and the court, with the consent of *Myburgh*, counsel for the plaintiffs, ordered the vessel to be released on the amount of the bond and interest being paid, and adjourned the rest of the motion.

March 4. The motion was renewed. *Clarkson*, for the defendants, in support of the motion, referred to a stipula-
209] tion in the *bottomry bond providing that if the advance on bottomry and the bottomry premium should be paid at or before the expiration of seven days after the safe arrival of the vessel at London the bond should be void, and to affidavits which alleged that the vessel arrived safely at London on the 22d of February, 1879, and that the amount of the bond and the maritime interest thereon was tendered out of court to the plaintiffs' solicitors on the 27th of February. He contended that at the time of the institution of the action and the arrest of the vessel no cause of action existed.

Myburgh, for the plaintiffs, in opposition to the motion, referred to statements on affidavits that the bondholders had communicated with the persons interested in the vessel, but had received no intimation that the bond would be met when due, and that they had been apprehensive that the vessel would have been discharged before the expiration of seven days from her arrival, and the security for payment of the bond thereby diminished. The plaintiffs were warranted by the settled practice of the court in instituting the action, and arresting the vessel, without waiting until the bond became payable: *The Jane* ('); *The San Jose Primeiro* (').

SIR ROBERT PHILLIMORE: I think this is not a case for damages, but so much of the motion as asks that the plaintiffs be condemned in costs must be granted.

Solicitors for plaintiffs: *Hollams, Sons & Coward.*
Solicitors for defendants: *Lowless & Co.*

(') 1 Dod., 461.　　　　　　　　　　(') 3 L. T. (N.S.), 513.

[4 Probate Division, 210.]

March 11, 1879.

210]　　　　　*THE CECILIE (1879, E. 18).

Bottomry—Jurisdiction—Bottomry Bond not providing for Payment of Interest.

The master of a Danish vessel being without funds or credit at Hamburgh, in order to obtain necessaries to enable his vessel to proceed on a voyage to Africa and back to London, obtained a loan on the security of instruments by which he pledged his vessel and bound himself for the repayment of the sum advanced within six days after the arrival of the vessel in London. No stipulation was made for interest of any kind:

Held, in an action of bottomry instituted against the vessel, that the instruments were valid bottomry bonds, and that the holders were entitled to payment out of the proceeds of the vessel of the sum advanced together with 4 per cent. interest from the time when the bonds became due.

THIS was an action of bottomry instituted on behalf of Elliot's Metal Company against the Danish schooner Cecilie.

The statement of claim, so far as material, alleged as follows:

The Cecilie, a schooner of 126 tons register or thereabouts, belonging to the kingdom of Denmark, being about to proceed on a voyage from Hamburgh to Africa and thence to the port of London, funds were required to refit and repair the said vessel.

The master of the Cecilie being without funds or credit at Hamburgh, and being unable to pay the expense of the repairs and the necessary disbursements of the schooner at Hamburgh so as to enable her to prosecute her voyage, was compelled to resort to two several loans, together equal to £265 17s. 6d. sterling British money, on two bottomry bonds of the said vessel or schooner for the purpose of enabling him to pay the said expenses and disbursements, which sum Wilhelm Rodewaldt, of Hamburgh, at the request of the master by public advertisement and private contract with the said master, advanced to the said master, and accordingly the said master by two several bonds of bottomry by him duly executed bound himself and the said schooner and her appurtenances, to pay unto the said Wilhelm Rodewaldt, his assigns, or order, or indorsees, the said sums within six days after the arrival of the Cecilie at the port of London from the said intended voyage from Hamburgh to Africa.

The Cecilie subsequently proceeded on her voyage from Hamburgh to Africa, and thence to the port of London, and duly and safely arrived at the said port of London on the 23d day of December, 1878.

The two several bonds in paragraph 2 herein mentioned were duly indorsed and assigned by the said Wilhelm Rodewaldt to the plaintiffs.   ·

The bonds or instruments referred to in the statement of claim were both in the same form, and the following is a notarial translation of one of them:

I, the undersigned captain of the Danish vessel named the Cecilie, hereby acknowledge *for myself and my heirs, the duplicate being valid as a single [211 acknowledgment, that I am indebted to Mr. Wilhelm Rodewaldt, for provisions and equipment of the said vessel and for the prosecution of her voyage from Hamburgh to Africa and back to London, in the sum of 2,739 marks and 35 pf., wherefore I pledge my ship and appurtenances, and bind myself to pay the above sum within six days after my arrival in London or wheresoever else I may put in ; said payment to be prompt and uncontested according to the law of exchange in all parts.

No appearance was entered on behalf of the owners of the Cecilie, and the averments in the statement of claim having been verified by affidavit, counsel on behalf of the plaintiffs, on the 4th of March last, moved the judge in court to pronounce for the validity of the bonds with interest and costs, and to order the ship to be sold. So much of the motion as asked the court to pronounce for the validity of the bonds was opposed on behalf of material men, who claimed in respect of necessaries supplied to the Cecilie, and the court ordered a sale of the vessel, but directed that the rest of the motion should stand over; all questions of priority and of the validity of the bonds being reserved.

March 11. The motion was again called on.

Butt, Q.C., and *H. R. Hodgson*, for the plaintiffs, in support of the motion: The bonds put in suit in this case are valid bottomry bonds. They were given by the master in a foreign port where he was without funds or credit, and it must be presumed from the language used that they were given for necessary charges to enable the ship to proceed on the voyage on which she was then engaged. All the other essentials of a bottomry contract are present in this cause, for it is apparent on the face of the bonds that the money was lent on the security of the ship, and was only to be repaid in the event of the ship not being lost on the voyage. The words "my arrival," must be construed as in the case of *Simonds* v. *Hodgson* (¹) to mean "my arrival with the ship," or "my ship's arrival." It is true that the bonds do not provide for the payment of maritime interest, but that circumstance is immaterial, whereas in the present case the contract entered into is subject to sea risk. In the recent 212] case of *The Elpis* (²) *this court held that a bond in form very similar to the bonds signed by the master in the present case was a valid bottomry bond.

E. C. Clarkson, for the material men, contrà: The bonds in this case are in an unusual form. The bonds are to become payable not only on the safe arrival of the ship at London, but at any intermediate port. Further, the bonds do not provide for the payment of interest, and it is almost impossible to conceive that the lender could have intended the loan to be subject to maritime risk, without making some stipulation for the payment of interest or premium to compensate him for such a risk. The instruments are not

(¹) 3 B. & Ad., 50.   (²) Law Rep., 4 A. & E., 1; 5 Eng. R., 546.

expressly declared to be subject to maritime risk, and having regard to the whole transaction as appearing on the face of the instruments, it is reasonable to conclude that the transaction is not really a bottomry transaction.

SIR ROBERT PHILLIMORE : I am not convinced by Mr. Clarkson's argument ; on the contrary, I am satisfied that on the authority of precedents and decided cases, I must hold that the instruments in respect of which this action is brought are valid bottomry bonds. I, therefore, pronounce for their validity. The plaintiffs will be entitled to payment out of the proceeds of the ship of the amount due on the bonds; and also, in accordance with the practice of the court, to the payment of interest on the same at the rate of 4 per cent. from the date when the bonds became due until payment thereof.

Solicitors for plaintiffs : *Harrisons.*
Solicitors for material men : *Waltons, Bubb & Walton.*

[4 Probate Division, 213.]

May 13, 1879.

*THE ANDERS KNAPE (1879, C. 111).　　　[213

Salvage—Service in the Nature of Pilotage rendered to Foreign Vessel which had received Damage.

A fishing smack fell in near the Long Sand buoy with a foreign steamship. The steamship had been on the sands near the Kentish Knock light-ship, but had got off with some damage to her rudder, and had a signal for a pilot hoisted. The master of the smack boarded the steamship and piloted her to the entrance of Harwich harbor :

Held, that the owners, master, and crew of the fishing smack were entitled to salvage remuneration.

When a person goes on board of a vessel in distress, and pilots her into harbor, he is entitled to salvage remuneration, unless it is established that he has contracted to render the services for pilotage remuneration only.

THIS was an appeal from the City of London Court in an action of salvage instituted on behalf of the owners, master, and crew of the smack Faith, against the Swedish steamship Anders Knape, of 401 tons register.

The action was heard in the City of London Court on the 10th of March last, when *Bucknill* appeared for the plaintiffs, *Myburgh* for the defendants, the owners of the Anders Knape. In an affidavit of value filed on behalf of the plaintiffs, the value of the Anders Knape was stated to be £2,335.

It appeared from the proceedings in the court below that

the master of the Faith was called as a witness for the plaintiffs, and gave evidence that on the morning of the 14th of
February, between 7 and 8, he and five others, forming the
crew of the Faith, were in the Faith near to the Long
Sand buoy. The weather was very hazy, and between 12
and 1 they fell in with a steamship having a flag hoisted
for a pilot, which proved to be the Anders Knape. The
master of the Anders Knape hailed the smack, and the
master of the smack went alongside. The following is the
account given by the master of the smack of what then
took place :

> I said, "Captain, what do you want ?" He said, "Come up." I went on deck,
> and after I went on deck he said, "Are you a pilot ?" I said, "No, I am not a
> pilot." He says, "Can you take charge of my ship ?" I says, "Where are you
> bound to, captain ?" He says, "No, no." He would not tell me. He talked,
> and all he kept saying was, "Are you a pilot ?" I repeatedly told him I was not
> 214] *a pilot, that he would get no pilots there where we were. It happened
> so that we stood talking about it for a long time, and I told him if he did not
> require my assistance I should leave him. And he turned round and took hold
> of my shoulder, and said, "No, you shall not leave. I want you, and you shall
> stop," and he refused to let me get into the boat. I considered that he gave me
> charge then. He says, "You say that you can take my ship to Harwich. Then
> take her to Harwich." And I did, and I told the man to port the helm. The
> ship's head was then into the southwest, which was quite contrary to the way
> we wanted to go to Harwich, and the captain left me then. The ship answered
> the helm very slowly. There was a fresh wind—what we call a fresh wind.
> There was a good deal of sea.

The master of the smack added that he piloted the steamship to the entrance of Harwich harbor, and then a Trinity
House pilot boarded her and took her into the harbor. The
wheather at the time was so thick that he could scarcely see
three times the length of the vessel.

On cross-examination the witness was asked what flag the
smack had exhibited, and he produced the flag which had
been flying at the masthead of the smack ('), and spoke to
the following conversation between himself and the master
of the Anders Knape :

> The captain says, "You have got a pilot's flag up ?" I said, "No, captain,
> the vessel is close to you, you can see that is not a pilot flag I am sure."

In answer to the learned judge of the court below, the
witness gave the following answers :

> *Mr. Commissioner Kerr:* About that flag. Do fishermen use that flag ?—
> We have got only that flag belonging to the vessel.
> Why should you use a flag at all ?—We use that. I will tell you what we
> used it for once since I have been in the vessel. It was the fore-part of this
> winter. There was a schooner standing on the Long Sand. We hoisted that
> and warned the man off, or he would have gone on and lost her.

(¹) The flag was a square flag, red and white, with a small blue border.

Why was it up on this particular morning ?—We hoisted that because we see the steamship coming.

Why did you hoist it.   It is very like a pilot flag ?—We hoisted it to let him know if he wanted any assistance he could have it.

The master of the Anders Knape was examined through an interpreter, on behalf of the defendants, and gave, *inter alia*, the following evidence:

On the night of the 13th, and the morning of the 14th of February, we got aground, and got off again about three in the morning ; and without assistance *anchored in eleven fathoms of water, and waited till daylight.   We [215 were making water, but were able to keep under the water by means of our donkey engines.   At first I intended to go to Dover, but feared that night might come on before we got there, and put back for Harwich, when I made up my mind to go to Harwich.   We had a signal for a pilot.   We afterwards saw the fishing smack.   The smack had a flag flying.   [*The flag produced by the master of the Faith was referred to.*]   I cannot say if that was the flag.   The flag was white and red.   The smacksman came on board.   The second mate speaks English.   I asked the smacksman if he was a pilot, and he told me that he was a fisherman.   Then I asked him if he could pilot me into Harwich, and he answered "Yes."   The rudder was not repaired at Harwich, and the steamer afterwards came to London with the rudder in the same state it was in when she went into Harwich.   The rudder went a little heavy that was all.   We had been near the light-ship and had read the name of the light-ship, "The Kentish Knock," on the side.   We knew perfectly well where we were.

The learned judge of the court below dismissed the action with costs, on the ground that he was satisfied on the facts that the service rendered was pilotage service and nothing else.   He also stated that in his opinion the flag which the smack was flying was to all intents and purposes a pilot flag, and that the services were offered and accepted solely as those of a pilot.

From this decision the plaintiffs appealed.

On the 13th of May the appeal was heard.

E. C. Clarkson, appeared for the appellants: The plaintiffs are entitled to be rewarded as salvors.   The condition of the Anders Knape was one requiring salvage assistance, and the master of the Faith, even if he had been a licensed pilot, could not have been compelled to take charge of her for mere pilotage reward: *The Hedwig* (¹) ;   *The Bomarsund* (²) ;   *The Æolus* (³) ;   *The Frederick* (⁴) ;   *The Little Joe* (⁵).

Myburgh, for the respondents: The master of the Anders Knape had no signals of distress hoisted, but only made the usual signal for a pilot, and required no more than pilotage assistance.   The damage to the Anders Knape was very slight and she was in no way disabled.   The mas-

(¹) 1 Spks., 23.   (³) Law Rep., 4 A. & E., 29 ; 5 Eng. R., 565.
(²) Lush., 78.   (⁴) 1 Wm. Rob., 17
                         (⁵) Lush., 88.

ter of the Faith really came on board in the capacity of a
pilot, and he rendered no services other than pilotage services: *The Columbus* ('); *The Enterprise* ('). Though no
216]   *tender has been made, the respondents have always
been prepared to pay a liberal pilotage remuneration.

Clarkson, in reply.

SIR ROBERT PHILLIMORE: This is a case about which I
admit I was exceedingly doubtful in the course of the argument. I have referred to the case of *The Frederick* (*)
which is cited in the case of *The Æolus* ('), and in which Dr.
Lushington said:

> "It has been urged in the argument for the owners that pilots are not to con-
> vert their duties into salvage services. This may be a correct position under
> ordinary circumstances ; at the same time, it is to be observed that it is the
> settled doctrine of this court that no pilot is bound to go on board a vessel in
> distress to render pilot service for mere pilotage reward. If a pilot being told
> he would receive pilotage only, refused to take charge of a vessel in that con-
> dition, he would be subject to no censure ; and if he did take charge of her he
> would be entitled to a salvage remuneration."

Now, the facts of the case are these. This foreign vessel
the Anders Knape had been on the sand, and had sustained
some damage to her rudder. She was, therefore, in a condition in which salvage services might be rendered to her.
The master of the smack, who is one of the plaintiffs in this
case, says that he went on board this vessel, and was told
by her captain that the rudder was broken and that the
ship had been aground. A considerable quantity of evidence has been produced as to whether the master of the
smack contracted as a salvor, or whether he contracted as a
pilot. It has been well put by Mr. Myburgh that there are
grounds for contending that he contracted to act as a pilot,
but the evidence of the captain of the Anders Knape is distinctly the other way. He says that the master of the
smack told him that he was a fisherman, and that he could
conduct the ship into Harwich—that is to say, if he wished
it; that he could help him to go into a port of refuge. Supposing nothing had been said ; supposing the master of the
smack had gone aboard the Anders Knape without saying
anything at all, and the captain of the Anders Knape had
said "I want to go to Harwich," and thereupon the master
of the smack had proceeded to put the vessel in a right
direction, could it be doubted that the master of the smack
217]   would have thereby rendered a salvage *service,
looking to the state of the ship and looking to the fact that
the master of the smack had been asked to take her to Har-

(¹) 2 Hagg., 178 n.   (³) Law Rep., 4 A. & E., 29; 5 Eng
(²) 1 Wm. Rob., 17.   R., 565.

wich? I am of opinion that the facts of the case are brought within the ruling in the judgment of Dr. Lushington in the case of *The Frederick* (¹) to which I have referred. I think that this was a case in which a pilot would have been subject to no censure if he had refused to take charge of this vessel as a pilot, and if he had taken charge of her would have become entitled to a salvage remuneration, unless he had expressly contracted otherwise in the circumstances. Although I admit that the distinction between what is pilotage and what is salvage is a nice one, upon the whole, I am of opinion that a salvage service was rendered in this case, and that some salvage remuneration should be awarded, and I shall award £30 with the usual costs. There will be leave to appeal.

Solicitors for appellants: *Lowless & Co.*
Solicitors for respondents: *Stokes & Co.*

(¹) 1 Wm. Rob., 17.

[4 Probate Division, 217.]

May 14, 1879.

THE HEBE (1879, O. 49).

Salvage—Derelict—Quantum of Remuneration.

Salvors having by meritorious services rendered at the risk of their lives salved a derelict vessel, her cargo and freight, valued together at £750, the court awarded £360 as salvage remuneration.

THIS was an action of salvage instituted on behalf of the owners, masters, and crews of four fishing smacks and a steamtug, against the owners of the Hebe, and the cargo lately laden therein together with the freight due for the transportation thereof.

The following allegations contained in the statement of claim were admitted by the defendants:

The Concord, Deerhound, Paul, and Mary Ann, are four smacks belonging to the port of Colchester each carrying six hands. Their tonnage according to builder's measurement is as follows: Concord, forty tons, Deerhound, thirty tons, Mary Ann, forty tons, Paul, thirty-five tons.

The Harwich is a steamtug belonging to the port of Harwich of sixty horse power. She was manned by a crew of seven hands.

*On the morning of Friday, the 24th of January, [218 1879, the four smacks were cruising off the coast of Essex in order to render assistance to vessels in distress. The wind was blowing strong from E.N.E. with snow squalls and there was a very heavy sea.

About 6.30 A.M. those on board the Concord saw rockets in the direction of the Heaps Sand, and shortly afterwards in the direction of Clacton-on-Sea. They proceeded towards the sand and got near it about 9 A.M. As they did so, they saw a vessel on the sand and also saw the Clacton-on-Sea life-boat with fourteen or fifteen rescued sailors in her. About the same time the Deerhound came up. The crews. of the two smacks manned the Concord's boat with six hands, three from each, and those in the boat pulled towards the life-boat found that the rescued sailors were the master and crew of the stranded vessel, asked if they should take charge of her, and were requested by her master to do so. The stranded vessel was the Hebe, and from the violence of the gale she had lost all her boats.

The Mary Ann and Paul had now come up. The Concord's boat proceeded to try and reach the Hebe, but the wind and weather were so violent that they had to return to the smacks. The tide was now about half flood. After waiting an hour three smacks' boats started all doubly manned, six in the leading boat and four in each of the others, keeping close together in case of accident to the leading boat, and with difficulty and danger succeeded in reaching the Hebe.

The Hebe, which belongs to the port of Bergen in Norway, is a three-masted ship of about 400 tons and was laden with a cargo of deals and battens. Her crew had cut away all her masts before leaving her. They had gone off in such a hurry as to leave many of their clothes on deck. The sea frequently made a clean breach over her and was washing about the loose articles on the deck.

The smacksmen cleared away the ropes and gear, put the clothes of the crew into the round house and got the anchors and chain ready in the event of her coming off. They had great difficulty in preventing their boat from being knocked to pieces against the sides of the Hebe.

About 12 noon the Hebe began to move, and about 12.30 she floated. One of the hawsers was then got on deck so that she might be taken in tow by one of the smacks, but it was found that the sea was too heavy for towage, and the smacksmen were compelled to let the Hebe drift till she got into seven or eight fathoms of water and then bring her up. The Concord was sent to Brightlingsea the nearest telegraph station to telegraph to Harwich for a tug.

The other smacks remained by the Hebe with ten of the smacksmen on board. The night was a rough and dangerous one. The smacksmen had only one boat with them which they had during the night to haul on to the Hebe's deck and lash to the rail. They also lighted and fixed two anchor lights.

About 9 A.M. of Saturday, the 25th, the Harwich which had started after receiving the telegram came up. The weather had somewhat moderated, and the smacksmen on board the Hebe were able to get the anchor. About 11 A.M. the Harwich began to tow, the Deerhound being made fast astern with two hawsers in order to steer her as she could not otherwise have been navigated, and about 4 P.M. the Hebe was brought into Sheerness harbor, safely anchored with two anchors, and delivered to the receiver of wreck. The plaintiffs at the same time specially delivered to the receiver a chronometer, a quadrant, three gold chains, and some other articles found on board the Hebe.

*The Hebe was a derelict when the plaintiffs first [219 went on board her, and neither the master nor any of the crew of the Hebe ever returned to her while the aforesaid services were being performed.

At the hearing it appeared that the Hebe, at the time she was stranded, was on a voyage with cargo from Norway to London, and it was agreed that the value of the Hebe, her cargo and freight should, for the purposes of the action, be taken to be £750.

W. G. F. Phillimore, for the plaintiffs.
J. P. Aspinall, for the defendants.

SIR ROBERT PHILLIMORE: This is a very meritorious salvage service. There is no reasonable doubt that but for the promptitude and courage of the salvors the vessel and her cargo would have been entirely lost, and they ought to receive a very large reward. Unfortunately the value of the property salved is only £750. I shall award to the salvors £360 together with costs.

Solicitors for plaintiffs: *Goody & Stock.*
Solicitors for defendants: *Ingledew, Ince & Greening.*

[4 Probate Division, 219.]

July 15, 1879.

[IN THE COURT OF APPEAL.]

THE BYWELL CASTLE (1878, L. 256).

LONDON STEAMBOAT CO. v. BYWELL CASTLE (Owners of).

Ship—Navigation—Collision—Porting—Wrong Manœuvre—Extreme Danger.

It is wrong to port the helm when a collision is apprehended and the other ship is on the starboard bow.

But where one ship has by wrong manœuvres placed another ship in a position of extreme danger, that other ship will not be held to blame if she has done something wrong, and has not been manœuvred with perfect skill and presence of mind.

THIS was an appeal from a judgment of the Court of Admiralty finding both ships to blame for a collision between them.

The Bywell Castle, a screw steamer of 891 tons register, was after dark on the evening of the 3d of September, 1878, coming down Galleons Reach in the Thames with tide, keeping in or to the north of the middle of the stream, and, ac-

220]   cording to her case, *she did not alter her course, or altered it very slightly, until immediately before the collision, when she stopped and ported her helm.

The Princess Alice, a paddle-wheel steamer of 158 tons register and 220 feet long, had come up the river under the south shore till near Tripcock's Point. She then, according to her case, starboarded her helm so as to keep close to but clear a powder hulk which was moored just above Tripcock's Point, and then cross to Bull Point on the north shore, when she was struck on the starboard bow by the Bywell Castle, in consequence of the porting of the helm of the Bywell Castle. According to the case of the Bywell Castle, the Princess Alice went over from Tripcock's Point towards the north shore beyond midstream, then starboarded her helm in order to go up Galleons Reach, and continued under a starboard helm so as to come round and under the bows of the Bywell Castle. The Princess Alice was struck on the starboard bow and soon afterwards sank. More than 500 of her passengers and many of the crew, including the captain, were drowned. The other material facts of the case are stated in the judgments given below.

An action was brought by the London Steamboat Company, owners of the Princess Alice, against the owners of the Bywell Castle, and there was a counter-claim by the owners of the Bywell Castle.

The action was tried before Sir R. Phillimore and two Elder Brethren of the Trinity House.

Dec. 11, 1878. *R. E. Webster*, Q.C., *Phillimore*, and *Stubbs*, for the Princess Alice.

Butt, Q.C., *Clarkson*, and *Myburgh*, for the Bywell Castle.

SIR R. PHILLIMORE, after stating the facts of the case and the result of the evidence: It appears to us that when the Princess Alice was on a parallel course with the Bywell Castle, red light to red light, if their respective courses had been continued, they would have passed at a safe distance from each other; but when a very short distance, variously stated at from 100 to 400 yards, intervened between the two vessels, the master of the Princess *Alice ordered [221 the helm to be put hard a-starboard, by which he brought his vessel athwart the bows of the Bywell Castle, and this fearful collision ensued. The Captain of the Princess Alice having been unfortunately among the number of those who were drowned, it is impossible to ascertain the motive which induced him to give this order, but I may say that the Elder Brethren strongly incline to the belief that he was misled by seeing the green light of the tug Enterprise. There is, however, no trustworthy evidence on this point. It appears to us, moreover, that the Princess Alice was navigated in a careless and reckless manner, without due observance of the regulations respecting look-out and speed. In our opinion the Princess Alice is to blame for this collision. It remains to be considered whether the Bywell Castle in any way contributed to it. She appears to have been navigated with due care and skill till within a very short time of the collision. But the evidence certainly establishes that having seen the green light of the Princess Alice, she hard a-ported into it. There is no doubt that this was not only obviously a wrong manœuvre, but the worst which she could have executed. The only defence offered for it is that it was executed so very short a time before the collision. There have been several cases decided in this court, in which it has been holden that a wrong manœuvre taken at the last moment had really no effect upon the collision, on account of the proximity of the two vessels, and I have consulted anxiously with the Elder Brethren whether the wrong action of the Bywell Castle can be placed in this category. They are of opinion that if the obviously wrong order of hard a-porting had not been given and obeyed, though the Princess Alice might have received some injury, she would not have sunk, and the lives of her crew and passengers would probably have been saved.

I am bound, therefore, to pronounce both vessels to blame for this collision.

Damage to be paid for by the vessels equally.

The owners of the Bywell Castle appealed, and the appeal was argued before James, Brett, and Cotton, L.JJ., assisted by two nautical assessors.

Butt, Q.C., *Clarkson*, and *Myburgh*, for the Bywell Castle.

R. E. Webster, Q.C., and *Phillimore*, for the Princess Alice.

222] *JAMES, L.J.: Upon the point which is first to be considered, namely, whether the Princess Alice was in fault or not, we have the direct finding of the judge of the Court of Admiralty, and of the Trinity Masters who assisted him, they finding in distinct terms that the Princess Alice was once in a parallel course with the Bywell Castle, red light to red light, and that if their respective courses had been continued they would have passed at a safe distance from each other; but that when a very short distance, variously stated at from 100 to 400 yards, intervened between the two vessels, the master of the Princess Alice ordered the helm to be put a-starboard, by which he brought his vessel athwart the bows of the Bywell Castle. That was the finding of the judge and the Trinity Masters, who heard all the evidence, and all the comments made, and many of the defences that have been suggested to us on the evidence. They came to that conclusion, and it would require a great deal to satisfy me, that we, sitting as a Court of Appeal, could, on any considerations suggested to us, overrule that finding. My own opinion, moreover, is that the evidence is in support of it. Then with regard to the general conduct of the Princess Alice—on which I have not heard a comment made in support of her—the court says, "It appears to us, moreover, that the Princess Alice was navigated in a careless and reckless manner, without due observance of the regulations respecting look-out and speed." That is not to be questioned. Therefore, upon the first issue, whether the Princess Alice was to blame, there can be no doubt that we must affirm the judgment of the court below. The judge of the court below then says that the Bywell Castle "appears to have been navigated with due care and skill till within a very short time of the collision," and I understand our assessors to agree with those in the court below, that all the manœuvres of the Bywell Castle up to the time of the collision were executed with due care and skill. Then there comes the very last thing that occurred on the part of the Bywell Castle, which is that she, in the very agony, just at the time when the two ships were close together, hard a-ported. The judge and both of the Trinity Masters were of opinion that that was a wrong manœuvre. I understand our assessors to agree in that conclusion, but they advise us that it could not, in their opinion, have had the *slightest appre- [223 ciable effect upon the collision. That view, if adopted by us, and I think that it should be adopted, would be suffi- cient to dispose of the case upon the question of contribu- tory negligence. But I desire to add my opinion that a ship has no right, by its own misconduct, to put another ship into a situation of extreme peril, and then charge that other ship with misconduct. My opinion is that if, in that moment of extreme peril and difficulty, such other ship happens to do something wrong, so as to be a contributory to the mischief, that would not render her liable for the damage, inasmuch as perfect presence of mind, accurate judgment, and promptitude under all circumstances are not to be expected. You have no right to expect men to be something more than ordinary men. I am therefore of opin- ion that the finding of the court below, that the Bywell Castle was, for the purposes of the suit, to be considered to blame, must be overruled, and that the Princess Alice was alone to blame.

BRETT, L. J.: In this case the Admiralty Court has found that both ships were to blame, and there are, practically, cross appeals. The judgment of the Admiralty Court is made to depend on four principal findings, some of which are findings of fact, and the others are judicial opinions as to the manœuvres which were employed or ought to have been employed. The four principal findings seem to be these: First, that at one moment these ships had come on to courses which might be called parallel courses, red light to red light, so that if the respective courses had been continued they would have passed at a safe distance from each other. That is a finding in favor of the Bywell Castle. The ap- peal of the Princess Alice is practically against that finding. The next principal finding is that the Princess Alice was going at full speed, and that the Bywell Castle was going at something like half speed. The third finding is that the Bywell Castle, up to a very short time before the collision— which, taken in conjunction with the evidence and the first finding, seems to mean, up to the time of putting her helm hard a-port—was navigated with due care and skill. That

is a finding in favor of the Bywell Castle, which is challenged
224] by the appeal of the Princess Alice. The *fourth
finding is that though up to that moment the Bywell Castle
was right, and although the red light of the Princess Alice
had been on her port bow, she did wrong in ordering her
helm hard a-port. That is the finding against the Bywell
Castle.

Now, having in the judgment of the Admiralty Court four
distinct findings, we are asked to review them; but we
ought not, in accordance with the rules that govern the
Court of Appeal, to overrule any one of these findings unless we are convinced that it was wrong. Therefore, applying that rule to the findings which are in favor of the Bywell
Castle, we must consider whether we can say that the Admiralty Court was wrong in holding that at some particular
moment these vessels were on parallel courses, red light to
red light, and that up to the time of the order being given
to put the helm hard a-port the Bywell Castle had been
navigated with due care and skill. So far from being able
to say that the court was wrong, it seems, on the balance of
evidence, tested by the probabilities of the case, that the findings were right. But there was this suggestion—very well
put by Dr. Phillimore in the course of the argument—that
both ships were going round Tripcock's Point on the south
shore of the river in parallel circles, and he said that a vessel
going up the river on the ebb tide may pass on the inner
circle when coming round such a point; and if she did
so the other vessel ought to keep on the outer circle, the
one coming up the stream on the southern circle, and the
other going down the northern circle. If so, at the first moment of sighting each other, the ship coming up the river
would show her red light, but not as she came round the.
circle; it is obvious that she would then show her green
light, and then they ought to pass starboard side to starboard side. But there is another course which a vessel
coming up the river and approaching such a point may take
if she wishes to cheat the tide; she can go, not as has been
said, on a straight course to the other side without turning
up into the next reach, but she can come round the point
with a slightly starboard helm so as to take her across to the
north side of the reach, not coming in a straight line to
the next point, but nearer to the north shore, and so cheat
the tide. Now, that she may do, and not only is that what
she may do, but, on the whole, with ebb tide, it is more than
225] probable that that is *what she would ·do. With
regard to a vessel going down such a reach, the course will

be to go as near as possible down the centre of the stream ; and if no other vessel is coming up, she will not port her helm, but will round Tripcock's Point, keeping out in the tide, and therefore, when going down Galleons Reach, she will, for her own advantage, not port her helm at all. Those being the probabilities, we have the evidence here on the one side and on the other. No doubt the Princess Alice did come close round Tripcock's Point, and her case is that she did take, or intend to take, a course which is not improbable, coming close round the magazine, and keeping on the south side ; and that, under those circumstances, she did show her green light to the Bywell Castle on the starboard bow and that the Bywell Castle showed her green light as she was coming down. But the evidence on the other side is, that the Princess Alice came close to Tripcock's Point, but did not straighten herself up the river, so as to run by the powder magazine ; and that when she passed by the stern of it she was going directly towards the north side. She would, therefore, and did show her red light to the Bywell Castle before coming up to the point, and after clearing the point, and after clearing the powder magazine, so that finally it came ahead of the Bywell Castle. That is what the Bywell Castle says did happen—that the red light drew across the river to the north side, and came ahead of her. That would, it seems to me, fully indicate to the Bywell Castle that the Princess Alice was going a course which would take her across to the north side, and this is an answer to the argument that the Bywell Castle ported without having any regard to the Princess Alice. That is a very unlikely thing for her to do, but if she saw this red light passing on until it came ahead of her it is not unnatural that she should slightly port her helm. It seems a natural and proper thing to do that which she says she did, and for the reason which she gives, there being no reason why she should do that for any other purpose. Therefore the argument that she executed a wrong manœuvre fails. I agree with the finding that it was not wrong. Then the Princess Alice would naturally keep on her course until she got more to the north, as it is said she did. It has been argued if she was then under a starboard helm, though she got on to the port bow of the *Bywell Castle, that the Bywell Cas- [226 tle nevertheless ought to have starboarded or kept straight down the reach. It seems to me that that is to propound a most dangerous rule, that if vessels are coming round a point, one under a starboard helm, if she crosses so that her red light is on the port bow of the other, she shall have a

right to keep her helm to starboard. It seems to me that
the rule that both ships ought to pass port side to port
side applies, and it would be dangerous to hold the contrary.
It was the duty of the Princess Alice, if under a starboard
helm, to ease off at once so as to pass port side to port side.
According to the evidence and to the argument before us
she did not do that. It seems to me that not only could I
not legally say that the finding of the court below was
wrong, but, taking the evidence and the probabilities, I
should have decided in the same way, that the red light of
the Princess Alice had got on the port side of the Bywell
Castle, and that it was her duty to ease off. I cannot indeed have a doubt that the Princess Alice was in the wrong.
She was in the wrong for not keeping on the port side of the
Bywell Castle, having once got there, and she was also in
the wrong in going at the time at full speed; therefore she
was twice in the wrong. Then, if that be so, of course
she was still more wrong if, instead of easing her starboard helm, she kept on that helm, and if she did ease,
she was still more wrong in putting the helm again to
starboard. If she was on the port side of the Bywell
Castle, by her wrong act she put the Bywell Castle's captain into an extreme difficulty, in being close to him showing him a green light on his port bow. The next question
is whether the Bywell Castle being put into that difficulty
did what was wrong. It is said that she did so in two instances. But what is the wrong that the court is bound to
find she did? Not merely that she did a wrong thing, but
that she was guilty of a want of that care or skill which
she ought to have shown under such difficult circumstances.
I am clearly of opinion that when one ship, by her wrongful act, suddenly puts another ship into a position of difficulty of this kind, we cannot expect the amount of skill
as we should under other circumstances. The captains
of ships are bound to show such skill as persons of their
position with ordinary nerve ought to show under the circumstances. But any court ought to make the very great-
227] est *allowance for a captain or pilot suddenly put
into such difficult circumstances; and the court ought not,
in fairness and justice to him, to require perfect nerve and
presence of mind, enabling him to do the best thing possible.
What the pilot did was to give the orders to stop and to put
the helm hard a-port; and the order to stop was carried out.
He says that he gave the order not only to stop, but to
reverse. I agree that if he had time to do it he ought to
have done it. There was some dispute as to who did give

the order, and it is said that if he did give the order it was not obeyed. But whichever order was given we must consider the circumstances. He was not called upon to give the order to stop and reverse until the other ship had done the wrong thing. Where did she do it? She did it close to him, and the first order was to stop or to stop and reverse, the next to put the helm a-port. Whichever it was, the court has not found that there was any wrong order as to the stopping or reversing, though it has found that the order to port was wrong. We are, however, advised that the order to put the helm hard a-port had no practical effect as to the collision. If that be so, of course it follows that the last wrongful act of the Princess Alice was done so near to the other that it was impossible by any manœuvre to avoid the collision. If the fact of ordering the helm hard a-port had no effect upon the collision, it is immaterial whether it was given or not. Even if it had an effect and was wrong, we have come to the conclusion that the captain of the Bywell Castle was suddenly put into an extremely difficult position, and assuming that a wrong order was given, that it ought not under the circumstance to be attributed to him as a thing done with such want of nerve and skill as entitles us to say that by negligence and want of skill the Bywell Castle contributed to the accident. Therefore, though agreeing with all the other findings as to the Princess Alice, we must come to a different opinion as to the last finding, the result of which is that we must hold the Princess Alice solely to blame.

COTTON, L.J.: After the very full way in which Brett, L.J., has entered into the case it is unnecessary for me to say more than that I have come to the same conclusion, but I wish to add *a few words. There are in this case [228 two questions to consider. First, was the judge of the court below right in finding that the Princess Alice was in fault? We here are only dealing with the evidence which was brought before the judge of the court below, who had the benefit of seeing and hearing the witnesses. We have not had that opportunity of testing the evidence; and that in this case is of very considerable importance, because a great deal of the argument on behalf of the Princess Alice consisted in commenting on alleged discrepancies in the evidence of the witnesses for the Bywell Castle, and asking us, practically, to discredit their evidence. In such a case, in order to overrule the finding of a judge of the court below, we ought to be satisfied that his finding cannot upon the

evidence be sustained. This in the present case I cannot
say, because on the evidence which we have heard I should
have arrived at the same conclusion a's the learned judge of
the court below. [His Lordship then commented on the evidence, and concluded that he agreed with what in substance
was the evidence on behalf of the Bywell Castle, that the
Princess Alice going over to the point on the north shore
had got on the port bow of the Bywell Castle, and that she
did alter her course by starboarding and hard a-starboarding
her helm.] On the other point, that the Bywell Castle did
not contribute to the accident, by hard·a-porting before the
collision, I agree with the view expressed by Brett, L.J.
Our assessors tell us that it could not in any way have been
contributory to the accident which in their opinion was then
inevitable. Even if the collision had not been unavoidable
at the time when the helm of the Bywell Castle was put
hard a-port, I should·not have held that vessel liable. For
in my opinion the sound rule is, that a man in charge of a
vessel is not to be held guilty of negligence, or as contributing to an accident, if in a sudden emergency caused by the
default or negligence of another vessel, he does something
which he might under the circumstances as known to him
reasonably think proper ; although those before whom the
case comes for adjudication are, with a knowledge of all the
facts, and with time to consider them, able to see that
the course which he adopted was not in fact the best. In
this case, though to put the helm of the Bywell Castle hard
229] a-port was not in fact the best thing to be *done, I
cannot hold that to do so was under the circumstances an
act of negligence on the part of those who had charge of
that vessel.

Judgment for the Bywell Castle.

Solicitors for Bywell Castle: *Newman, Stretton & Hilliard.*
Solicitors for Princess Alice: *T. Cooper & Co.*

[4 Probate Division, 229.]

March 3, 18, 1879.

In the Goods of TEODORO UZUAGA Y FERNANDEZ, Deceased.

Administration—Bond—Sureties abroad.

Administration bond allowed to be executed by foreigners resident abroad, upon proof that the administrator was unable to obtain sureties resident here, that the deceased had no debts unpaid, and that the person on whose behalf the letters of administration were applied for was solely entitled to the estate in this country.

THE deceased, by his will, dated the 30th day of July, 1861, appointed his brother sole executor and universal legatee, who died in the testator's lifetime. The deceased died on the 27th of July, 1873, a bachelor, without parents, leaving a sister his sole next of kin.

The deceased was a native of Cuba, and died domiciled there, and his sister, who was also a native of Cuba, and domiciled and resident there, had, by power of attorney, appointed Alezo Uzuaga to collect the property of the deceased in this country, which consisted of £5,957 11s. 4d. on deposit account in the Bank of England.

Alezo Uzuaga was also a foreigner, and unable to obtain two sureties resident in England.

Searle, moved the court to allow the administration bond to be executed by two friends of the applicant resident in Paris. The affidavits show that the applicant is unable to obtain sureties resident here, and that the sister is by decree of the proper court at Cuba solely entitled to the money, and there is an opinion of a French advocate that the sureties might if necessary be sued in France on the bond: *In the Goods of Reed* (¹); *In the Goods of Houston* (²).

*The court refused the application.   (230

Searle, again moved the court upon an affidavit showing also that all the deceased's debts in Cuba had been paid, and that there were no debts in this country.

SIR J. HANNEN: I think the case of *In the Goods of Houston* (²) is now a direct authority. I can make no distinction between that case and this, and must therefore grant the application. But the sureties must justify.

Solicitors: *Druce, Sons & Jackson.*

(¹) 3 S. & T., 439.   (²) Law Rep., 1 P. & D., 85.

[4 Probate Division, 230.]

May 16, 1879.

THE QUEEN'S PROCTOR V. FRY.

Baptisms in India—Evidence.

In an action to determine the right to letters of administration, the issue being as to the legitimacy of certain persons, copies of registers of baptisms in India were admitted in evidence.

THIS was an action to obtain revocation of a grant of letters of administration, and another grant to the Crown, on the ground that the deceased had died intestate and without any known relations. The issues in the action were whether Miss Ceta Howard and Miss Jessie Howard were the legitimate children of Sir Simon Howard.

Bowen (*The Attorney-General*, with him), for the Crown, tendered in evidence copies of entries of baptisms in India. The original registers are in India, but the copies tendered have been transmitted to the India Office and are deposited there. The question has been decided as to entries of marriages: *Ratcliff* v. *Ratcliff and Anderson* (¹); *The Peerless* (²).

Dr. Spinks (*H. D. Greene*, with him), for the defendant, contended that there was a distinction in this respect between the records of marriages and baptisms.

SIR J. HANNEN: I am of opinion that there is no distinction between the two classes of documents. Both are kept by order of the Government of India, and the same 231]   public reasons which *render it desirable that the one should be kept, apply equally to the other.

The documents were admitted accordingly.

Solicitor for plaintiff : *The Queen's Proctor.*
Solicitors for defendant : *Vallance & Vallance.*

(¹) 1 S. & T., 467.   (²) 1 Lush., 42.

[4 Probate Division, 232.]

April 29, 1879.

*MANSEL v. THE ATTORNEY-GENERAL.   [232

*Legitimacy—Pleadings—Amendment—Jurisdiction—Citation to see Proceedings
—Legitimacy Declaration Act (21 & 22 Vict. c. 98).*

In a petition under the Legitimacy Declaration Act the petitioner may allege that
he claims real estate, and may also state how he claims it, but he cannot allege, or
pray for a declaration, that he is entitled to such estate to the exclusion of some
other person, e.g., by reason of the illegitimacy of the person.

A petitioner alleged that he claimed real estate as heir-at-law of his father, and
that E. B. M. also claimed to be such heir-at-law. Leave to cite E. B. M. was refused on the ground that E. B. M. was not interested in disputing the only facts
which the court was competent to determine, i.e., the legitimacy of the petitioner or
the marriage of his parents.

The court has power to amend the pleadings at any time, and, if necessary, to
order allegations to be reinserted which it had previously directed to be struck out.

[5 Probate Division, 5.]

May 28, 1879.

5]   *THE PASITHEA (1879, K. 82).

Salvage—Practice—Two Actions against the same Property—Costs.

In a case where the defendants, in two actions of salvage instituted against the same property, were ordered to pay only one set of costs, to be apportioned between the plaintiffs in the two actions, the court directed that the apportionment should be made according to the amounts of the plaintiffs' respective bills of costs.

Two separate actions of salvage were instituted against the Pasithea, one by the owners, master, and crew of the smack Prince of Wales, and the other by the owner, master, and crew of the steamtug Harwich; an application to consolidate the actions was made before hearing, and, the plaintiffs objecting to the consolidation, no order was made. The action was now heard.

Butt, Q.C., and *W. Phillimore*, appeared for the owner, master, and crew of the Harwich.

Nelson, for the owners, master, and crew of the Prince of Wales.

E. C. Clarkson and *Cottingham*, for the defendants, the owners of the Pasithea.

The JUDGE awarded £50 to the owners, master, and crew of the Prince of Wales, and £600 to the owner, master, and crew of the Harwich, and ordered that the defendants should only pay one set of costs, to be apportioned between the plaintiffs according to the amounts of their respective bills of costs, observing that the apportionment of the costs according to the amounts of the taxed costs of the plaintiffs, as directed in the case of *The Sarah* (') had been found to be inconvenient in practice.

Solicitors for the Harwich: *Tatham & Co.*
Solicitors for the Prince of Wales: *Lowless & Co.*
Solicitors for defendants: *Stocken & Jupp.*

(') 3 P. D., 39, at p. 42.

[5 Probate Division, 6.]

July 1, 1879.

*THE EMPUSA (1878, C. 297).   [6

Limitation of Liability—Costs—Claim in respect of a Loan on Security of Freight —Merchant Shipping Act, 1862 (25 & 26 Vict. c 63), s. 54.

Although the plaintiff in an action for limitation of liability is ordinarily liable to pay the costs of the action, yet, if the defendants raise unnecessary issues on which they fail, he is entitled to the costs of those issues, and he will not be ordered to pay the costs occasioned by a dispute between rival claimants to the proceeds in court.

The master of the ship C., bound from Philadelphia to Antwerp, obtained at Philadelphia from M. a loan of money on freight upon the security of an instrument signed by him, by which it was stipulated that the loan should be repaid after arrival of the C. at Antwerp or other intermediate port at which the voyage should end, and that if there should be no payment of freight the loan should not be paid back.

The C., whilst on the course of her voyage to Antwerp, came into collision with another ship and sank, and her cargo was lost. The collision was occasioned by the negligence of those in charge of the other ship, and her owners instituted an action for limitation of their liability. In such action a sum of money was awarded out of the proceeds paid into court to the owners of the C. for loss of freight. M. claimed a portion of this sum in respect of his loan :

Held, that his claim was well founded.

Semble, where in an action for limitation of liability a sum of money is awarded as compensation for loss of freight to the owners of a vessel run down by the plaintiff's ship, the holder of a bottomry bond on the freight of the vessel run down is entitled to claim, in respect of the loan on bottomry, a portion of the sum awarded for loss of freight.

ON the 26th of September, 1878, the British steamship Empusa came into collision with the ship Commerce in the English Channel off Hastings. In consequence of the collision, the Commerce was sunk and her cargo was lost or damaged, and two of her crew were drowned. The owners of the Empusa instituted a suit for limitation of liability. The statement of claim stated that the collision was caused by the negligence of those on board the Empusa, and occurred without the actual fault or privity of the plaintiffs, that the sum of £8 per ton, calculated on the gross tonnage of the Empusa, amounted to £8,805, and that the plaintiffs were ready to bring that sum, together with interest thereon from the date of the collision, into court, and such further sum in respect of the loss of the lives of the two men who were drowned, as the court might direct.

*The owners of the Commerce and the owners of her [7 cargo entered separate appearances and delivered separate statements of defence. The statement of defence delivered by the owners of the Commerce alleged that the master of the Empusa, who was one of the plaintiffs, was on board at the time of the collision and that the plaintiffs neglected to provide a proper and efficient crew for the Empusa, and that the collision was caused or contributed to by their neglect, and happened with the actual fault or privity of the plaintiffs respectively. The statement of defence delivered on behalf of the owners of the cargo stated that the owners of the cargo did not admit that the collision occurred without the actual fault or privity of the plaintiffs, and submitted that while the claims for loss of life remained unsettled the ·plaintiffs were not entitled to judgment, unless they paid into court or gave bail for the full amount of £15 per ton on the gross tonnage of the Empusa.

On the 11th of January, 1879, the action came on for hearing. and witnesses were examined *viva voce.*

Webster, Q.C., and *Myburgh,* for the plaintiffs.

Milward, Q.C., and *E. C. Clarkson,* for the owners of the Commerce.

Stubbs, for the owners of the cargo of the Commerce.

Witnesses were examined on behalf of the plaintiffs to establish that the master of the Empusa was below at the time of the collision, and that the vessel was properly manned.

SIR ROBERT PHILLIMORE: The only question before me in this case is as to the applicability of the 54th section of the Merchant Shipping Act, 1862, that is to say, whether it is shown to the court that there was any actual fault or privity on the part of the owners of the Empusa. The exposition of the law contained in the case of *The Obey* (¹) appears to me to be directly in favor of the plaintiffs. I must therefore reject the defence.

No doubt, as a general rule, the plaintiffs in an action for limitation of liability are liable to pay the costs of the proceedings, but in this case the defendants, the owners of the Commerce, have raised special issues which have rendered 8] it necessary that the plaintiffs *should call witnesses, and these issues have been decided against the defendants, and I cannot do justice without giving to the plaintiffs the extra costs occasioned by those special issues. The plaintiffs will be entitled to a decree of limitation of liability on the usual terms, on payment into court of the amount of £8 per ton of the tonnage of the Empusa, together with interest, and the costs of the action other than the costs occasioned by the issues unnecessarily raised by the defendants, and on giving bail for or paying into court the sum of £1,000 in respect of the claims for loss of life, and

(¹) Law Rep., 1 A. & E., 102.

also undertaking to pay into court any additional sum for which they may hereafter be pronounced liable in respect of such claims.

In pursuance of this decision, the owners of the Empusa, on the 14th of February, brought into court the sum of £8,940 13s. 8d., and on the 20th of February the further sum of £1,000.

The usual reference then took place, and the registrar made his report. In his report he disallowed a claim made on behalf of the Cassa Marittima of Genoa, and questions having arisen between the Cassa Marittima and the owners of the Commerce with reference to this claim, the judge, on hearing counsel for the owners of the Commerce and the Cassa Marittima, ordered the facts relative to such questions to be stated in a special case. The following case was stated accordingly :

On the 24th day of August, 1878, Elijah Nickerson, master of the British ship Commerce, then lying in the port of Philadelphia, requested from the agent of the Cassa Marittima of Genoa a loan of £598 1s. 4d. upon the security of the freight of the said ship to be earned on a voyage from Philadelphia to Antwerp.

The said loan was granted, and the said Elijah Nickerson signed the following instrument.

"Fifteen days after arrival at the port of Antwerp or other intermediate port at which shall end the voyage of my vessel denominated the ship Commerce, I promise to pay to the order of the Cassa Marittima of Genoa the sum of five hundred and ninety-eight pounds one shilling and fourpence sterling, value received as loan on freight for the last expenses necessary to the undertaking of the voyage from Philadelphia to Antwerp, Belgium, on the conditions of the regulations of the Cassa Marittima, of which I have received a copy, ship and freight being in accordance with such regulations liable for repayment with priority over every other credit."

On the back of this instrument were printed the regulations of the said Cassa Marittima, a copy of the same is annexed hereto and is to form part of this case.

*The sum of £598 1s. 4d. secured by the said bill was [9 not actually advanced in full by the Cassa Marittima to the said master, but such sum was and is the aggregate amount of the actual advance made by the Cassa Marittima to the said master, and the premium and interest on such actual

advances which premium was retained by the Cassa Marittima pursuant to regulation 13 of the said regulations.

The said loan was duly made, and the Commerce sailed
in due course on her destined voyage from Philadelphia to
Antwerp, but on the 26th day of September, while off Hastings, in the English Channel, the Commerce was run into
and sunk by the steamship Empusa, and with her cargo
and freight was totally lost.

The plaintiffs, who are owners of the steamship Empusa,
admitted their liability for the damages occasioned by the
said collision, and brought this suit to limit such liability
in the manner provided by the statute in that behalf, and
obtained a decree therein on payment into court of the
amount of their statutory liability, and all claims in respect
of the loss or damage occasioned by the said collision were
referred to the registrar and merchants to report thereon.

Amongst other claims, the defendants, the owners of the
Commerce, claimed the sum of £2,148 13s. 6d. as damages
for the loss of the freight to be earned by the said ship on
the said voyage from Philadelphia to Antwerp, and were
allowed the sum of £2,088 in respect of such freight, being
the amount of such freight less the expenses of completing
the voyage.

The Cassa Marittima of Genoa also claimed the sum of
£598 1s. 4d. as the damages they had sustained by reason
of the loss of the freight, which was pledged to them as security for the said advance, and their claim was disallowed
by the registrar on the ground, among others, that the owner
of the ship was the only person who could recover in respect of the freight, and that the Cassa Marittima were not
entitled to claim in competition with the owners of the Commerce, that vessel having been lost.

The Cassa Marittima of Genoa contend that they are entitled to prove for the loss of the freight so far as it was
pledged to them, and that the defendants are not entitled
to recover as part of their damages the freight which would
have to be paid to the Cassa Marittima if the Commerce had
arrived at Antwerp, and that, the said freight having been
allowed by the registrar as part of the claim of defendants,
the owners of the Commerce, such owners ought to hold and
receive the same as trustees for the Cassa Marittima, and
are under an obligation to pay a proportion thereof to the
said Cassa Marittima, or to allow the Cassa Marittima to
receive the same out of court.

The questions for the opinion of the court are:—First.
Whether the Cassa Marittima, as against the owners of the

Commerce, are entitled to prove against the fund paid into court by the plaintiffs for the said sum of £598 1s. 4d. as damages occasioned in respect of the said collision.

Second. Whether, if the Cassa Marittima are not entitled to prove for the said sum as damages against the fund paid into court by the plaintiffs, they are entitled as against the defendants, the owners of the commerce, to receive payment of the said sum out of court, or to an order that the said defendants, out of the moneys recovered by them as damages in respect of the loss of the said freight, should pay to the said Cassa Marittima the said sum for which the freight was pledged.

Third. Or, in the alternative, that the Cassa Marittima are entitled to receive *out of the fund in court applicable [10 to the payment of damages for loss of freight, or from the defendants, the owners of the Commerce, the same proportions of the sum of £598 1s. 4d. as the total sum apportioned in respect of the loss of freight bears to the whole freight of of the said ship.

CASSA MARITTIMA, GENOA.

Rules for Loans on Freight (').

The loans which the Cassa Marittima agree to make on freight must be subject to the following rules:

1. Any owner desirous to obtain a loan on freight from the Cassa Marittima must make his request in accordance with the printed form which will be given him for the purpose.

3. The loan can never exceed a third of the whole freight the vessel may make.

4. The owner or the captain before he can obtain a loan must produce the bills of lading signed by the shipper in proof of not having received any previous advances on the freight.

5. The loan must be repaid within fifteen days after the arrival of the ship in the port to which she is bound, or wherever the voyage may terminate, and the vessel and freight will be liable to the repayment of the loan with priority over every other credit.

6. In the event of the vessel on arrival at the port of destination being ordered by the shipper of the cargo to any other port, the amount of the loan must be repaid to the agents of the Cassa Marittima, and a further loan may be asked, which the agents have power to grant or decline.

9. A receipt will be given by the captain or owner when

('){ } Only such of the rules as are material are set out.

the loan is made, signed in accordance with the above rules, or with any others that may be established.

11. Loans shall always be made in gold, and shall be repaid in gold, at the current rate of exchange on London at the port where the vessel discharges, or to the Cassa Marittima in Genoa.

12. Loans shall always be exempt from any contribution to either general or particular average.

13. The premium and interest on the sums granted in loan on freight according to the list must be always retained on the loan itself, and in case of a total loss, if there be no payment of freight, either total or partial, the sums received as loan shall not be paid back, except that which has been taken beyond the third part of the freight.

15. The owner or captain shall not take any other advances upon the same freight at the port of loading, or in such case hold themselves bound to return the present loan, even though the vessel be lost.

16. The captain shall give immediate notice on arrival at the port of discharge to the Cassa Marittima in Genoa, or to their agents at the nearest port, incurring otherwise the penalty of 10 per cent. on the amount of the loan.

May 31. The special case came on for argument.

Myburgh, for the Cassa Marittima: It is not necessary, 11] in order *to support the claim now made, to contend that the claim could be enforced in an action of bottomry against the Commerce or her master. The bond operates as an assignment of freight, and when, as in the present case, there is a fund in court representing freight, the Cassa Marittima, as the assignees of freight, are entitled to claim on the fund. Moreover, if the Cassa Marittima cannot enforce the bottomry bond, it is the wrongful act of the Empusa that has disabled them, just in the same sense as the wrongful act of the Empusa has prevented the Commerce earning her freight, and both claims ought to be dealt with on the same principles. [He referred to *The Dante* (¹).]

[SIR ROBERT PHILLIMORE: I think there is no doubt that the loan was a loan on bottomry.]

E. C. Clarkson, for the owners of the Commerce: No doubt the instrument signed by the master of the Commerce was an instrument of bottomry, and was subject to maritime risk. It is expressly stipulated on the face of the instrument that the repayment of the loan should be made after the arrival of the Commerce at Antwerp or any intermediate

(¹) 2 Wm. Rob., 427.

port. It would be contrary to all the principles by which
the contract of bottomry has been considered to be governed
to hold that, although this risk has gone against the bondholder, yet the amount lent should still be paid back. Not
only has there been no arrival of the Commerce at any port
at all, but it is by no means certain that, even if no collision
had occurred, the voyage would have been completed in
safety. Any damage which the Cassa Marittima can be
said to have sustained by the collision must therefore be too
remote to give a right to any share of the fund in court.
The master of the Commerce would scarcely have paid a
bottomry premium, or, what is the same thing, have allowed
it to be retained on the loan, if he had contemplated that
the Cassa Marittima were not to run the risk of his vessel
being lost by sea perils.

Myburgh, in reply.

SIR ROBERT PHILLIMORE: This is a case for which there
is no legal precedent, but it is one that is to be decided on
general principles of equity; and I decide that the Cassa
Marittima is *entitled to receive out of the fund in   [12
court applicable to the payment of damages for loss of
freight the same proportion of the £598 1s. 4d. as the total
sum apportioned in respect of the loss of freight bears to
the whole freight of the ship. The actual apportionment
will be made by the registrar.

In pursuance of this decision the following order, omitting immaterial parts, was drawn up in the registry:

The judge having heard counsel on both side on the special case filed herein,
pronounced that the Cassa Marittima was entitled to £181 6s. 7d. out of the
amount reported by the registrar as recoverable in respect of the total freight of
the vessel Commerce, and he directed the costs relating to the said special case
to be costs in the action.

July 1. *W. Phillimore*, on behalf of the owners of the
Empusa, moved the court to vary so much of the order
drawn up in pursuance of the above mentioned decision as
condemned the owners of the Empusa in the costs of and
incident to the special case, on the ground that such costs
were extra costs over which the owners of the Empusa had
had no control, and which had been merely incurred for the
purpose of settling a dispute confined to claimants on the
fund in court. The owners of the Empusa were no parties
to the special case stated as to the claim of the Cassa Marittima, and had no notice that costs would be asked for
against them. They admit that by the practice of this court
and that of the Chancery Division, they will have to pay the
costs of the action, but by the costs of the action must be

understood only the costs of obtaining the decree of limitation of liability, and the ordinary expenses of the distribution of the fund in court, such as the expense of the usual advertisements, &c. To use the language of the court in the case of the *African Steamship Co.* v. *Swanzy* ('), the owners of the wrongdoing vessel are not liable to bear the expense of "adverse litigation occasioning costs over which the plaintiffs have no control." The case of the *African Steamship Co.* v. *Swanzy* (') has been recently followed by this court in the case of *The City of Buenos Ayres* (').

Myburgh, for the Cassa Marittima of Genoa: None of the costs of and incident to the special case were improperly 13] incurred; *they were all occasioned by the wrongful act of the Empusa, and it was for the court to say in its discretion by whom they should be borne. The court has exercised its decision rightly.

E. C. Clarkson, for the owners of the Commerce.

SIR ROBERT PHILLIMORE: On consideration I have come to the conclusion that the order I made on a former occasion, condemning the owners of the Empusa in the costs of and incident to the special case, was wrong, and I must therefore rescind it. In these actions of limitations of liability it is sometimes difficult to draw a line of demarcation with respect to what costs may be and what costs may not be considered as costs for which the owners of the wrongdoing vessel are to be rendered liable. On the whole, however, and looking at all the circumstances, I am satisfied that this is not a case in which I ought to saddle the owners of the Empusa, though they are the plaintiffs in the limitation of liability suit, with the extra costs of determining the points of law which have been raised between the owners of the Commerce and the Cassa Marittima as to the loan on freight. Indeed, if I were to do so, I do not think my decision could be brought within any established principle. I must, therefore, rescind that part of my former order which relates to costs. The order I shall make instead of the part thus rescinded will be that the Cassa Marittima and the owners of the Commerce will each bear their own costs of and incident to the special case.

Solicitors for the Cassa Marittima: *Cooper & Co.*

Solicitors for owners of the Commerce: *Clarkson, Son & Greenwell.*

Solicitors for owners of the Empusa: *Lowless & Co.*

(') 25 L. J. (Ch.), 870.   (') 1 Asp. Mar. Law Cases, 169.

[5 Probate Division, 14.]

July 18, 1879.

*THE MARY (1879, O. 166).   [14

Damage—Liability of Tug for negligent Navigation where the Vessel in tow is in charge of a Pilot by compulsion of Law—Merchant Shipping Act, 1854 (17 & 18 Vict. c. 104), s. 388.

Where a steamtug towing a vessel under a towage contract is so negligently navigated as to come into collision with a vessel belonging to third parties, the owners of the steamtug are liable for the damage done, even if at the time of the collision the vessel in tow was in charge of a duly licensed pilot by compulsion of law whose default solely occasioned the collision.

THIS was an action of damage brought by the owners of the steamtug Sussex against the bark Mary, to recover the damages sustained in a collision between the two vessels on the 30th of April last. At the time of the collision, which happened in Sea Reach in the river Thames, the Sussex and another tug called the Rambler were proceeding up the river towing the Desdemona, a large sailing ship of 1,400 tons register, and the Mary was working down on the starboard tack. There was on board the Desdemona a duly licensed Trinity pilot, who was in charge of her by compulsion of law.

The statement of claim, after setting forth the circumstances in which according to the case of the plaintiffs the collision had occurred, attributed the collision solely to the neglect and default of those on board the Mary.

The 5th, 6th, 7th, and 8th paragraphs of the statement of defence were so far as is material in substance as follows:

5. Those on board the Desdemona and the tugs failed to keep a good look-out.

6. Those on board the Desdemona and the tugs, and in particular those on board the Sussex, neglected or omitted to take proper measures in due time to keep clear of the Mary.

7. Those on board the Desdemona and the tugs, and in particular those on board the Sussex, starboarded their helms at an improper time.

8. Those on board the tugs, and in particular those on board the Sussex, wrongfully neglected or omitted to slacken speed when approaching the Mary.

The defendants by way of counter-claim repeated the allegations in the statement of defence, and alleged that the Mary had suffered damage by the collision.

15] *A reply was delivered on behalf of the plaintiffs
containing, *inter alia*, the following paragraphs:

The plaintiffs further, in reply to the said counter-claim,
say that if and so far as the said collision was occasioned by
any neglect or default on the part of the Desdemona or of
the said tugs, it was occasioned solely by some fault or incapacity of a pilot in charge of the Desdemona and of the said
tugs, who was a qualified pilot within a district where the
employment of such pilot is compulsory by law, and not by
any negligence on the part of the plaintiffs or their servants.

The plaintiffs further, in reply to the said counter-claim,
say that the said tugs were employed by the Desdemona
and were under the orders of those on board the Desdemona,
and that the allegations in the said counter-claim, charging
the Desdemona and the Rambler with having caused or contributed to the said collision, are immaterial and irrelevant.

The action was heard on the 10th and 11th of June last,
together with an action of damage (1879, B. No. 171) brought
by the owners of the Desdemona against the Mary to recover the damages the Desdemona had sustained by reason
of the Sussex having been driven against her in consequence
of the same collision.

After hearing the evidence of witnesses called on behalf
of the owners of the Sussex, the owners of the Desdemona
and the owners of the Mary, the court came to the conclusion that the Sussex had not made proper endeavors in time
to get out of the way of the Mary, and that no blame whatever attached to the Mary, and consequently dismissed the
Mary from both suits against her with costs, and pronounced
that the Sussex was solely to blame for the collision.

On the application of counsel, the court directed that the
questions of law and fact raised on the pleadings, as to the
liability of the owners of the Sussex in respect of the damages claimed by the owners of the Mary by way of counter-
claim, should be reserved.

July 8. The questions of law and fact reserved were
argued.

Butt, Q.C., and *W. Phillimore*, for the defendants.

E. C. Clarkson, for the plaintiffs.

The authorities cited in argument are referred to in the
judgment.

                              Cur. adv. vult.

July 18. Sir Robert Phillimore: In this case the
steamtug Sussex has been found alone to blame for the col-
16] lision with the *bark Mary. It is now contended that

the Sussex, the wrongdoer, is exempt from responsibility to the injured ship upon the ground that the Desdemona, the ship which the Sussex, in conjunction with another tug was towing, had a pilot on board by compulsion of law. To this defence two answers have been made: (1.) That the immunity of the ship towed does not extend to the tug. (2.) That it is not proved by trustworthy evidence that the collision was solely occasioned by the fault or incapacity of the pilot acting in charge of the ship, and therefore that the 388th section of the Merchant Shipping Act, 1854, does not apply to this case.

First, as to the question of law, to use the language of Dr. Lushington in *The Protector* ('): "But the great principle that a wrongdoer is responsible to the injured party, saving in the excepted cases, continues unaltered." The burden of proof lies upon the party claiming the exemption. It is necessary to bear in mind the distinct relations subsisting between the ship and her tug and the ship and her pilot. Perhaps a close attention to this distinction will remove the difficulty which the language of some of the earlier reported cases on this subject is supposed to have created.

The root of the exemption in the case of compulsory pilotage is that the pilot is not the servant of the owner of the towed ship, but a person forced upon him by the statute; but the relation of the owner of the ship to the tug is very different. The tug is his servant voluntarily taken and employed by him for the occasion. The law implies, when the tug is employed, a contract between the owner or master of the tug and the owner of the ship to the effect that the tug will obey the directions of the shipowner and act as his servant; but this contract does not affect third parties, and the principle which exonerates the ship in the case of the pilot does not apply to the tug.

It has been said, indeed, in various cases, that the tug and the vessel she has in tow are to be regarded as one vessel, but this rule has only been laid down for the purpose of rendering a ship in tow subject to the rules of navigation applicable to steamers; in that sense only can they be treated as one vessel. The master *of the tug has a [17 separate contract and a separate responsibility from the pilot. In one sentence, it is by the exercise of free will that the ship takes the tug; by compulsion of law that she takes the pilot.

It has been contended, however, that my predecessor, Dr. Lushington, ruled in the case of *The Duke of Sussex* (') that

(') 1 W. Rob., 45, at p. 57.   (') 1 W. Rob., 270.

the exemption of compulsory pilotage extended to the tug, but I think that a careful examination of this case does not lead to that conclusion; the case was decided in 1841, when the 55th section of the 6 Geo. 4, c. 125, was in force, which did not contain the words "compulsory by law." The case is reported in the first volume of William Robinson's Reports, p. 270, and much more fully and accurately in the first volume of the Notes of Cases, p. 161; and it appears that Dr. Lushington, following a decision of the Court of Exchequer, decided that if the pilot was taken on board, whether by compulsion or not, the owner of the ship was exonerated from responsibility. Dr. Lushington seems to have been much impressed by the mischievous consequences which would follow from holding that the tug was not as much under the control of the pilot as the tow, and the chief object of his judgment seems to have been to refute the contrary opinion. He appears to have had the same object in the subsequent decision in *The Christina* (¹), delivered in 1848.

Looking to all the circumstances of this decision, I am of opinion that the case of *The Duke of Sussex* does not furnish a precedent for the case now before me; and I am fortified in this opinion by a subsequent decision of the same learned judge in *The Ticonderoga* (²), in the year 1857. In that case Dr. Lushington said (at p. 216):

I take the true meaning of the plea to be that the Ticonderoga was in the service of the French Government ; that the steamer was attached to her, and she was compelled, by the order of the government, to employ her in all the proper duties which could attach to a steamer. . . . The blame having been imputed to the steamer, let us consider whether the Ticonderoga can or cannot be made responsible for the damage which has been done. Now, that the steamer was engaged in the service of the Ticonderoga, and that the steamer took the Ticon-18] deroga into *mischief, there can be no doubt whatever. We must recollect that this is a proceeding *in rem*. . . . Let us see what cases there are in which the court does not hold a vessel responsible for the damage done ; there is one case, and one only, that I am aware of, and that is where a pilot is taken on board by compulsion. On what principle is the owner in that case relieved from paying the damage done? On the principle of compulsion. The principle that the man is not the servant of the owner, but is forced upon him by act of Parliament. Was this steamer taken by compulsion, or was it not? What species of compulsion is it which is averred on behalf of this American vessel that is to relieve her from the responsibility which the maritime law of the world attaches to the wrongdoer? Entering into a stipulation with the French Government. It is impossible to contend that because a person has entered into a voluntary contract by which he is finally led into mischief, that that can relieve him from making good the damage which he has done.

Upon the whole, I am of opinion that the Sussex is not exonerated from the consequences of her wrongful act by reason of the Desdemona having on board a pilot by compulsion of law.

(¹) 3 W. Rob., 27.   (²) Swa., 215.

Having expressed my opinion on the question of law, it is perhaps necessary to deal with the question of fact, but I think it right to state that my recollection of the opinion of the Trinity Masters, as well as a re-perusal of the evidence, leads me to the conclusion that the damage was, as a matter of fact, occasioned not solely by the fault or incapacity of the pilot, but that the master of the ship and the tugs were, as Sir John Nicholl said in *The Girolamo* ('), in *pari delicto ;* and that I do not think there is any trustworthy evidence that the pilot's orders were obeyed.

Upon both grounds of law and fact I pronounce judgment in favor of the Mary.

Solicitors for owners of the Sussex : *Lowless & Co.*

Solicitors for owners of the Desdemona : *Mercer & Mercer.*

Solicitors for owners of the Mary : *Cooper & Co.*

(') 3 Hagg., 169, at p. 176.

[5 Probate Division, 24.]

May 2, 1879.

*HUTLEY and Another v. GRIMSTONE and Another.   [24

Pleading—Undue Influence—Party propounding last Will—Right to begin.

In a testamentary suit the party propounding the last will is entitled to begin. So also is a party who alleges only undue influence, in opposition to the validity of a will.

THE plaintiffs propounded a draft of a will, dated the 19th of June, 1867, of Stephen Hutley, who died on the 13th of November, 1877. The defendants alleged that that will had been revoked by a will dated the 27th of January, 1872, which they propounded ; and the plaintiffs, in their reply, alleged that the will propounded *by the defendants [25 had not been duly executed, and that the deceased was not, at the time of its execution, of sound mind, memory, and understanding. Upon these pleadings the defendants claimed the right to begin.

Dr. Deane, Q.C., *Serjt. Ballantine, Dr. Swabey,* and *W. Ballantine,* were counsel for the plaintiffs.

Inderwick, Q.C., and *Jeune,* for the defendants.

SIR J. HANNEN : I had occasion yesterday (') to deal with a portion of this subject, and I then held that it lies

(') The case referred to was that of *Keays* v. *Adams and another,* in which the plaintiff, as executor, propounded a will dated the 21st of December, 1877, and two codicils, dated respectively the 5th of March, and the 12th of April, 1878, and the defendants pleaded only that

the codicils were procured by undue influence.

Serjt. Parry and *Bayford,* were counsel for the plaintiff, and

Hy. Matthews, Q.C., *Inderwick,* Q.C., *Waddy,* Q.C., and *Searle,* for the defendants.

upon the party who pleads the affirmative issues impeaching a will to begin, for though there would be some proof of the will necessary beyond that raised by the issues, yet the parties have not by the pleadings required the proof, and it is only needed by the court.

This, however, raises a somewhat different question, because here I understand the defendants allege that all other wills, of course including that of 1867, were revoked by what they say was the last will of January, 1872.

As far as my experience extends, it has been the practice of the court to grant the right to begin to the person propounding the last will; and it is based upon reasons of convenience, which the court is entitled and bound to consider. A testator often executes numerous wills, and the court might be engaged in investigating the validity of a series, all of which would be of no importance whatever if the last will were established to be the true will; if the inquiry begins at any other point in the series, much time and labor might be thrown away, and it might be still necessary to investigate the last will. For these reasons I think the defendants are entitled to begin.

Solicitor for plaintiffs: *A. G. Ditton.*
Solicitors for defendants: *Paterson, Snow & Bloxham.*

See 22 Eng. Rep., 739 note; Pierce on R. R. (ed. 1881), p. 187.

The test by which to determine who has the right to begin, is to be found in the answer to the question, "which party should have a verdict, if no evidence were given?" and this is ordinarily to be determined by the pleadings alone: Katz v. Kuhn, 8 Daly, 168–170.

It was held in Katz v. Kuhn, 9 Daly, 166, 168–170, that though on the pleadings plaintiff had the affirmative, defendant at the commencement of the trial could admit plaintiff's case and his right to the judgment demanded in the complaint, unless an affirmative defence be established, and if he did so, defendant was entitled to open and close. This case is not, we think, good law.

The party holding the affirmative of the issues raised by the pleadings has the right to begin, and is entitled to the concluding argument. If plaintiff is required to give any evidence on any question, he is so entitled; if not, but the defendant, on the issues, is required to give the first evidence, he is entitled to the affirmative.

Illinois: In this State defendant was held entitled to the defence, though plaintiff's damages are not liquidated: Chicago, Burlington, etc., v. Bryan, 90 Ills., 127.

Indiana: Hyatt v. Clements, 65 Ind., 12; Kirkpatrick v. Armstrong, 79 id., 884.

Iowa: Delaware, etc., v. Duncombe, 48 Iowa, 488.

New York: Murray v. New York, etc., 85 N. Y., 236, 9 Abb. N. C., 309, reversing 19 Hun, 350; Hunter v. American, etc., 4 id., 794; Smith v. Sergent, 67 Barb., 243; Penhryn, etc., v. Meyer, 8 Daly, 61; Opper v. Carlton, 9 id., 157, 159; Katz v. Kuhn, Id., 166.

See Claflin v. Baere, 16 N. Y. Weekly Dig., 47, 8 Ohio L. J., 289; Howard v. Hayes, 47 N. Y. Super. Ct. R., 89.

North Carolina: Stronach v. Bledsoe, 85 N. C., 473.

In an action against a principal and surety upon an obligation which showed on its face the suretyship, the principal answered by a general denial and the surety by pleas in confession and avoidance only : Held, that the plaintiffs were entitled to open and close : Kirkpatrick *v.* Armstrong, 79 Ind., 384.

The fact that the complaint alleges facts not essential for plaintiff to aver or prove, and that the same are denied by the answer, does not deprive defendant of the right to open and close : Murray *v.* New York, etc., 85 N. Y., 236, 9 Abb. N. C., 809, reversing 19 Hun, 350.

In an action on a note, the answer admitted its execution, and that it was indorsed by the payee to plaintiff, but alleged that this indorsement was only for the purpose of prosecution, and that the payee was the true owner. Held, that defendant did not hold the affirmative ; and also that such a question cannot be raised for the first time at the close of the case, and after plaintiff has given much evidence as to the consideration paid for the note : Gifford *v.* Waterman, 16 N. Y. Weekly Dig., 140.

An error of the court in refusing to allow the plaintiff to open the case to the jury, is not cured at a later stage of the trial by allowing him the closing address : Penhryn, etc., *v.* Meyer, 8 Daly, 61.

In some States the denial of the right to open the case and to the concluding argument is held to be a matter of right, and as matter of law to entitle the injured party to a reversal :

Illinois : Chicago, Burlington, etc., *v.* Bryan, 90 Ills., 127.

New York : Murray *v.* New York, etc., 85 N. Y., 236. 9 Abb. N. C., 809, reversing 19 Hun, 350 ; Hunter *v.* American Popular, 4 id., 794 ; Penhryn, etc., *v.* Meyer, 8 Daly, 61 ; Opper *v.* Carlton, 9 id., 157, 159.

North Carolina : Stronach *v.* Bledsoe, 85 N. C., 473, 474.

In others, to be a matter of discretion and not to be cause for reversal.

Iowa : Goodpaster *v.* Voris, 8 Iowa, 339 ; Delaware, etc., *v.* Duncombe, 48 id., 493.

Minnesota : See State *v.* Beebe, 17 Minn., 242, 250.

The right of review by an appellate court in a criminal action is limited to exceptions taken on the trial to decisions of the court, and to errors appearing upon the face of the record.

It seems, that where justice has been perverted by practice *dehors* the record, or the accused has been injured by any circumstance occurring on the trial, not the subject of legal exception, the legal remedy of the party aggrieved is by a motion for a new trial : Walsh *v.* People, 88 N. Y., 458.

The error book was supplemented by an affidavit of the prisoner's counsel, to the effect that while the colloquy was going on between the counsel and the court, the photograph was examined by jurors who had not before done so : Held, that although the court might have interfered and prevented such examination, its omission to do so when attention was called to the subject did not constitute legal error : Walsh *v.* People, 88 N. Y., 458.

Remarks made by counsel in summing up to a jury are *dehors* the record, and their propriety or impropriety cannot therefore be passed upon, on error, by the Supreme Court : Fulmer *v.* Com., 97 Penn. St. R., 503, 508.

Interruptions of an argument may be made for the purpose of stating objections and making motions : Morrison *v.* State, 76 Ind., 385.

If the argument goes beyond the evidence, objection must be made at the time, and the specific grounds of objection stated. None not so stated will be available on appeal : Morrison *v.* State, 76 Ind., 335.

Where a defendant on his trial for murder identified three letters by a witness, and then handed them to the judge to be marked and preserved until they should be used, but afterwards offered in evidence only two of them, it was held improper and irregular in the State's attorney to make any allusion to the third letter, in his closing remarks, wondering what it contained and that it should not have been allowed ; but that if no objection was made to the remarks at the time, and no exception taken, it was not sufficient to authorize a reversal : Bulliner *v.* People, 95 Ills., 896.

If a party claim that an assertion by the opposite counsel is improper, the proper practice is for the defendant, by his counsel, to move the court to restrain the prosecutor, or to have withdrawn or corrected any misstatement which has been made : Morrison *v.* State, 76 Ind., 885.

If the law be misstated in a material

respect likely to prejudice, the opposing counsel should apply for a special instruction correctly stating the law : Commissioners, etc., *v.* Kiser, 26 Kans., 279, 283.

As a general rule the interference of the court with counsel, when opening a case to the jury, is a matter of discretion, the exercise of which is not the subject of exception : Walsh *v.* People, 88 N. Y., 458.

It is exceedingly difficult to lay down a rule beyond which counsel shall not be allowed to travel in their argument to the jury, and the presiding judge should not be severe in arresting the argument because it may seem to him that the inference is forced, the analogy unnatural, or the argument illogical ; yet counsel should not be allowed to comment, in their address to the jury, on evidence which was offered and excluded, and the court should arrest such argument on objection being made: Sullivan *v.* State, 66 Alabama, 48.

Misstatements of counsel in their argument to the jury may be a ground for setting aside a verdict, but a presumption will obtain in favor of the action of the trial judge in refusing a new trial therefor : Wickersham *v.* Timmons, 49 Iowa, 267.

Where in a criminal prosecution the attorney for the State, against defendant's objection, indulges in language calculated to excite prejudice in the mind of the jury, the fact that the trial court neglected to rebuke such language, will not alone be sufficient ground for a reversal, if the case be otherwise correctly tried, and it appears that, under the law and the evidence, no other result than a conviction was possible without misbehavior of the judge: State *v.* Zumbunson, 7 Mo. App. Rep., 526.

It is the duty of the district court to interfere of its own motion in all cases where counsel in argument in jury trials state pertinent facts not before the jury, or use vituperation and abuse predicated on alleged facts not in evidence, calculated to create prejudice against a prisoner: State *v.* Gutekunst, 24 Kans., 252.

So, promptly to suppress any attempt on the part of counsel for the people to bring irrelevant matters into a case,

merely for the purpose of exciting the prejudices of a jury: Earll *v.* People, 99 Ills., 125.

Where one is put upon trial for a grave crime involving his liberty or life, it is highly improper for the prosecutor to do or say anything, the only effect of which is to inflame the passions or arouse the prejudices of the jury against the accused, without throwing any light on the case : Earll *v.* People, 99 Ills., 123.

It is the duty of the court, on the trial of one where his life or liberty is involved, to stop the State's attorney in his closing argument when he assumes facts not proved and urges them for a conviction. Such conduct is unfair to the accused, and he should be protected by the court. When such unfairness is gross, a judgment of conviction in a doubtful case should be reversed : Fox *v.* People, 95 Ills., 71.

The remark of the attorney-general, that "if the juries don't punish crime, the people will rise up, and should rise up and punish it," is reprehensible, and he should have been rebuked by the court in the presence of the jury.

Law officers are under peculiar obligations to set an example of respect for the law, and not to say or do anything which will tend to beget or encourage lawlessness : Scott *v.* State, 7 Lea (Tenn.), 232.

The prosecuting attorney in his closing argument to the jury, in referring to the evidence of defendant who had testified in his own behalf, said " It was incumbent on him to show how these things were. Did he tell us how she was hurt ? It was incumbent on him to prove how she was hurt, and the preponderance of testimony is in favor of conviction and against the defendant, and upon such evidence they must convict." Held error, for which the judgment should be reversed : State *v.* Mahley, 68 Mo., 815.

The trial court having failed to instruct the jury upon a material point, the prosecuting attorney in his closing argument undertook to supply the omission, and in doing so, against the defendant's objection and without interruption by the court, used language which was calculated to mislead the jury, and which the record seemed to show did mislead them. Held error, and judgment reversed: State v. Reed, 71 Mo., 200.

The court permitted counsel for one of the parties, in argument to the jury, to read and comment upon matter not in evidence, nor relevant to the issue, and which was prejudicial to the opposite party; held an irregularity or an abuse of discretion which prevented a fair trial, and for which the verdict should be set aside and a new trial ordered: Union, etc., v. Cheever, 36 Ohio St. R., 201.

Defendant's counsel having tendered in evidence a deed of assignment by the plaintiff of his estate, declined, where an objection to its reception was suddenly withdrawn, to put it in:

Held, that the plaintiff's counsel was entitled to comment forcibly to the jury on such a course, but not to ask them to accept as true that the plaintiff had assigned his estate, and was therefore entitled to be believed as a disinterested witness, nor any other facts deducible from the contents of the deed: Challacombe v. Wiggins, 7 Vict. L. R. (Law), 330.

Not every indiscreet remark made by the prosecuting attorney in the presence of the jury will be ground for new trial: State v. Guy, 69 Mo., 430; State v. Stark, 72 id., 37; State v. Baber, 74 id., 292, 298; Morrison v. State, 76 Ind., 334.

A statement that on a former trial the defendant had been convicted, made in the hearing of the jury by the prosecuting attorney to opposing counsel, in reply to a remark by the latter calculated to elicit such remark, and remarks of the same character made by a witness in the course of his examination in fixing certain dates, are not sufficient causes for reversing the judgment: Shepherd v. State, 64 Ind., 43.

Where counsel stated in his argument to the jury that a verdict for a certain amount had been rendered in the cause upon a former trial, and on being rebuked by the court, saying such a remark was highly improper and had nothing to do with the case, apologized by saying, "this is a matter of record;" held not sufficient cause for reversal: Goldman v. Wolff, 6 Mo. App. R., 490, 497.

It is not ground for a new trial that the prosecuting attorney made an illogical argument or a misstatement of the law: Morrison v. State, 76 Ind., 335.

Where the prosecuting attorney said in his argument to the jury, "Malice may bud and bloom in a man's heart almost in a moment, or in a short time:" Held, this was no ground for a reversal: State v. Estes, 70 Mo., 427.

See also State v. Stark, 72 Mo., 37; State v. Baber, 74 id., 292, 298.

Reading to the jury on the second trial of a cause the judgment of the court setting aside a former verdict for the improper admission of evidence, and commenting on such evidence and on the judgment, though improper, is not a ground for a new trial: Powell v. Wark, 4 Pugsley & Burb. (New Brunsw.), 15.

In general, arguments of counsel to the jury should be confined to the evidence and the principles of law claimed to be applicable thereto; but in discussing these, the motives to duty, the causes that may be supposed to control human action under different circumstances, and the probabilities or reasonableness of this or that theory as tested by human experience, necessarily may be considered. The court should see that the line of argument is kept within reasonable bounds, and not suffer one to be convicted or prejudiced on account of real or imaginary crimes for which he is not being tried. But except for a palpable abuse of discretion in this respect, manifestly tending to an improper conviction, there should be no reversal: Bulliner v. People, 95 Ills., 396.

Where the State's attorney, in his concluding speech to the jury in a criminal case, improperly asserts his own belief in the guilt of the accused, and asserts facts bearing on the question of guilt which are not in evidence, but in another portion of his speech he told the jury they should acquit unless they believed from the evidence, beyond a reasonable doubt, that the defendant's guilt was established, and the court instructed the jury that they should disregard any mere assertions of the State's attorney when of opinion of guilt or matter of fact, but decide the case solely on the evidence and the law; it was held this instruction should be deemed to have had the effect to destroy the force of the improper remarks made by the State's attorney: Kennedy v. People, 40 Ills., 488.

Upon the trial of an indictment for murder, the district attorney, while opening the case, handed to the jury a photograph which he stated was a likeness of the deceased, a young girl : the prisoner's counsel thereupon objected ; the court replied, in substance, that the objectionable act had been done and could not be recalled :

Held, that an exception was untenable: Walsh v. People, 88 N. Y., 458.

The court has and may exercise a large discretion in limiting the arguments of counsel, and may impose a reasonable restriction to be determined from the character and circumstances of the case on trial : 8 Cr. Law Mag., 619 ; 14 Cent. L. J., 45 ; 21 Amer. Law Reg. (N.S.), 625.

Connecticut: State v. Hoyt, 47 Conn., 519, 535-7.

Illinois: White v. State, 90 Ills., 117.

Mississippi: Lee v. State, 51 Miss., 566.

Missouri: State v. Linney, 52 Mo., 407.

New York: People v. Cook, 8 N. Y., 77 ; Elwell v. Chamberlain, 81 id., 621.

North Carolina: State v. Collins, 70 N. C., 307.

Ohio: Weam v. State, 24 Ohio St. R., 584.

If the court limit the time for counsel to sum up to an unreasonably short time, so as to deprive the party of the right to be heard by his counsel on his whole case, a new trial will be awarded : 8 Crim. Law Mag., 619 ; 14 Cent. L. J., 45 ; 21 Amer. Law Reg. (N.S.), 625.

California: People v. Kenan, 13 Cal., 581 ; People v. Chew, 6 id., 636.

Connecticut: State v. Hoyt, 47 Conn., 519, 537.

Georgia: Hunt v. State, 49 Ga., 255.

Illinois: White v. State, 90 Ills., 117.

Indiana: Lynch v. State, 9 Ind., 541.

Virginia: Wood v. Com., 3 Leigh, 749.

The refusal of a court to hear argument of counsel as to the admissibility of evidence, is not per se error : Olive v. State, 11 Neb., 4.

As to how far and when a party may have a new trial on account of the negligence or mistake of his own attorney: 16 Western Jurist, 281.

As to when the court will refuse to receive or will strike from the files a brief because unnecessarily abusive of other party or counsel : Stager v. Harrington, 27 Kans., 474.

[5 Probate Division, 26.]

July 25, 1879.

26] *BETTS and Another v. DOUGHTY and Others, and DOUGHTY and Others, Intervening.

Will—Testatrix prevented by Force and Threats from altering it—Amendment of Pleadings.

M. A. D., the testatrix, in 1853 made her will, by which she gave her property equally between the plaintiffs, defendants, and interveners. In an action by the plaintiffs propounding this will, it appeared that in 1874 she gave instructions for another will, which would have deprived the plaintiffs of all interest in her estate.

In the course of the plaintiffs' case some evidence was given tending to show that the testatrix was prevented by force and threats from executing the proposed will.

The court allowed the pleadings to be amended by adding statements to that effect, and praying for a declaration that the plaintiffs held their shares as trustees for the defendants and interveners.

THE plaintiffs propounded a will dated the 14th day of July, 1853, of Mary Ann Doughty, who died on the 6th day of December, 1878. The defendants alleged that the will

was not duly executed, that the deceased was not of sound
mind, memory, and understanding, that the will was procured by undue influence, and that the deceased did not
know and approve of the contents. The will left the property, in the events which had happened, equally between
the plaintiffs who were children of her sister and the defendants, and interveners, who were respectively children
of two of her brothers. The interveners by their statement
of claim supported the will.

In 1874, the deceased had given instructions for a will by
which she divided her property equally between the defendants and the interveners, excluding the plaintiffs altogether.
The draft of this proposed will had been approved by the
deceased, who was at that time residing with the plaintiffs
and remained with them until her death.

The action came on for hearing before a special jury, and
in the course of the plaintiffs' case it appeared that the clerk
of the solicitor who prepared the proposed will, attended with
it at the house of the plaintiffs, for the purpose of getting it
executed, but was not allowed to see the deceased; she was
told by the plaintiffs that if she executed the will she could
no longer reside in their house. She was then about eighty
years of age.

*Inderwick, Q.C. (Witt, with him), for the defend-   [27
ants, asked for leave to amend the statement of defence, by
adding as follows:

6. That after the making of the said alleged will of the
14th day of July, 1853, the said deceased was prevented by
the force and threats of the plaintiffs from executing a further will prepared by and under her instructions, whereby
the plaintiffs would have been deprived of all interest under
the said alleged will.

The defendants claim—

"That the court will declare that the plaintiffs are trustees
of the shares devolving on them by the said will of the
14th day of July, 1853, for the defendants and for the interveners."

Dr. Spinks (Bayford, with him), for the interveners, supported the application.

Sir H. James (Pritchard and Frere, with him), for the
plaintiffs, contrà.

THE COURT allowed the amendment, and adjourned the
hearing to enable the parties to produce further evidence
for and against the facts alleged in the amendment.

The parties afterwards came to terms before the close of
the adjournment, and no further evidence was therefore

given, and the court only pronounced for the validity of the will propounded by the plaintiffs.

Solicitors for plaintiffs : *Pritchard & Sons.*
Solicitors for defendants : *White, Barrett & Co.*
Solicitors for interveners : *Combe & Wainwright.*

[5 Probate Division, 35.]

Nov. 18, 1879.

35]   *THE CARTSBURN (1879, K. 191).

Damage—Claim to Indemnity by the Owners of Defendant's Vessel against Owners of the Tug towing the Vessel—Rules of the Supreme Court, Order XVI.

In an action of damage between two vessels, the court has jurisdiction, under Order XVI, to determine whether or not the defendants' vessel is entitled to indemnity against a tug by which she was being towed at the time of the collision.

A collision took place between the vessels S. and C. The C. at the time was being towed by a tug. The owners of the S. instituted an action of damage against the C., and alleged in their statement of claim that the collision was caused by the negligence of the C. and her tug, or of one of them. The owners of the C. obtained leave to issue a notice to the tug that they claimed to be entitled to indemnity, and the court made an order that the owners of the tug be at liberty to appear and defend, being bound by any decision the court might come to as to the cause of the collision.

At the hearing the owners of the tug appeared, but the defendants did not, and the court pronounced that the C. was alone to blame for the collision, and that her owners were not entitled to indemnity over against the owners of the tug :

Held, on motion on behalf of the owners of the C. to rescind so much of the judgment as pronounced that the owners of the C. were not entitled to indemnity, that the court had not exceeded its jurisdiction.

THIS was an action of damage instituted on behalf of the owners of the bark Slavia against the ship Cartsburn.

The owners of the Cartsburn having entered an appearance, their solicitors took out a summons applying for leave to issue a notice against the owner of the Leader, a steam-tug, in tow of which the Cartsburn was at the time of collision, claiming indemnity from him in respect of the damage proceeded for in the action. By an order made on the summons on the 10th of June last the judge in chambers granted the leave applied for.

On the 14th of June the plaintiffs delivered their statement of claim, and therein alleged that on the evening of the 4th of May, 1879, the Slavia, whilst lying at anchor in Penarth Roads, was run into and damaged by the Cartsburn as that vessel came into the roads in tow of the Leader, and that the collision was occasioned by the neglect of the Cartsburn and the Leader, or of one of them. On the 18th

ɔf June the following notice, bearing date the 14th of
*June, was, together with a copy of the statement of [36
claim, served by the defendants' solicitors on the owner of
the Leader.

Take notice that this action has been brought by the plaintiffs against the defendants' ship the Cartsburn for damage
alleged to have been sustained by the plaintiffs by a collision between the plaintiffs' bark Slavia and the Cartsburn.
The defendants, the owners of the Cartsburn, claim to be
indemnified by you against liability in respect of the said
alleged damage, on the ground that the liability of the
Cartsburn in respect of the said alleged damage, if any,
arises from the negligence and improper navigation of the
master and crew of the tug Leader, in tow of which tug the
Cartsburn was, and that the Leader was owned and possessed by you and was being navigated by your servants.
And take notice that if you wish to dispute the plaintiffs'
claim in this action as against the Cartsburn or the said defendants, you must cause an appearance to be entered for
you within eight days after service of this notice.   In default
of your so appearing you will not be entitled in any future
proceeding between the defendants and yourself to dispute
the validity of the judgment in this action, whether obtained
by consent or otherwise.

On the 25th of June the owner of the Leader entered an
appearance.

June 27.   *W. Phillimore*, on behalf of the owners of the
Cartsburn, in pursuance of notice of motion served on the
plaintiffs and on the owner of the Leader, applied to the judge
to give directions as to the mode of having the questions in
the action determined.

E. C. Clarkson, for the plaintiffs, opposed the motion.

SIR ROBERT PHILLIMORE: I am of opinion that the application of the defendants is one that ought to be granted.
The present case is, I think, one of those very cases to which
the provisions of the 24th section of the Judicature Act,
1873, and the rules contained in Order XVI of the Rules of
the Supreme Court, must have been intended to apply.
Moreover, the leave of the court has been already obtained
for the owner of the Leader to appear in the suit, and he
has entered an appearance.   I shall order that the owner of
the Leader be at liberty to appear and defend, being bound,
as between him and the defendants, the owners of the
Cartsburn, by·any decision the court may come to in the
action.   *Application granted.*

On the 28th of June, on application on behalf of the owner
37] *of the Leader, the judge ordered that the order should
be varied by adding the words "as to the cause of collision."
The order as amended was, omitting immaterial parts, in
terms as follows :

The judge having heard counsel for the plaintiffs and the defendants, owners
of the Cartsburn, ordered that Andrew Bain, owner of the steamtug Leader, be
at liberty to appear and defend, being bound as between him and the said defendants by any decision the court may come to in this action as to the cause of
collision.

On the 19th of July the owner of the Leader delivered to
the plaintiffs a statement of defence. . The statement of defence alleged in substance that at the time of the collision
the Leader was towing the Cartsburn under an agreement
to tow her into Penarth Roads, and was proceeding to the
middle of the roads to bring up there ; that the Cartsburn,
though previously directed to do so, neglected to follow the
Leader round the stern of a bark anchored near the Slavia,
and ultimately came into collision with the Slavia, notwithstanding that those on board the Leader did all they could
to bring the Cartsburn round, and that the collision was not
caused by any default or neglect on the part of those on
board the Leader, but by the neglect or default of those on
board the Slavia.

On the 30th of July the solicitors for the plaintiffs gave
notice of trial to the owners of the Cartsburn and the owner
of the Leader.

On the 6th of August the action was heard('), and witnesses having been examined orally in court on behalf of the
plaintiffs and the owner of the Leader, the court made an
order which, so far as material, was as follows :

The judge having heard counsel for the plaintiffs and for the owner of the
Leader, pronounced the collision in question in this action to have been occasioned solely by the fault or default of the master and crew of the vessel Cartsburn, and for the damage proceeded for, and condemned the owners of the
said vessel Cartsburn and their bail in the said damages, and in costs. The
judge further pronounced that the defendants, the owners of the Cartsburn,
were not entitled to any contribution or indemnity against the owner of the
steamtug Leader in respect of the said damages or costs, and he condemned the
said defendants and their bail in the costs incurred by the co-defendant.

Subsequently the solicitors for the owners of the Cartsburn
38] *gave notice that the judge in court would be moved
that so much of the judgment in the action as declared
that the defendants, the owners of the Cartsburn, were
not entitled to any contribution or indemnity against the
owner of the Leader, or decided anything as between the

(¹) The owners of the Cartsburn did not appear either by counsel or in person.

said defendants and the owner of the Leader, or gave directions consequential upon such declaration or decision, be struck out.

In support of the motion an affidavit was filed which, *inter alia*, alleged that with the exception of the statement of claim no other pleading in the action was delivered to the owners of the Cartsburn either on behalf of the plaintiffs or of the owner of the Leader, and that the owner of the Leader did not serve the solicitors of the owners of the Cartsburn with any notice of trial.

Nov. 4. The motion was heard.

W. Phillimore, for the owners of the Cartsburn, in support of the motion : The court had no power at the trial to decide any question as to the liability of the owner of the Leader to indemnify the owners of the Cartsburn. The object of bringing in a third party, under the provisions of Order XVI of the Rules of the Supreme Court, is merely to insure that the judgment in the action against the original defendant should be binding on the third party whether he appears or not. [He referred to the form of notice given in Appendix B to the Rules of the Supreme Court.] No question can be tried in the action which is not a common question as between the plaintiff and defendant, and the defendant and the party brought in : *Benecke* v. *Frost* (¹). The owners of the Cartsburn might wish to show that the liability of the owner of the Leader as against them depended on a question of contract, but by the judgment as it now stands they are precluded from doing this. This could never have been intended. The only defence which it was competent for the owner of the Leader to make in this action was that the plaintiffs could not recover against the owners of the Cartsburn : *Horwell* v. *London Omnibus Co.*(²). At any rate the owners of the Cartsburn had not proper notice that the question of the Leader's liability to them would be tried in the action.

Myburgh, for the owner of the Leader : The notice [39 of the 14th of June was issued at the instance of the owners of the Cartsburn, and the subsequent order giving the Leader liberty to appear and defend was also granted on their application, therefore the owners of the Cartsburn cannot now be heard to complain of what they have caused to be done. The liability of the Leader in respect of the collision was "a matter relating to or connected with the original subject of the cause" within the meaning of the Judicature Act,

(¹) 1 Q. B. D., 419.	(²) 2 Ex. D., 365.

respect likely to prejudice, the opposing counsel should apply for a special instruction correctly stating the law : Commissioners, etc., *v.* Kiser, 26 Kans., 279, 283.

As a general rule the interference of the court with counsel, when opening a case to the jury, is a matter of discretion, the exercise of which is not the subject of exception : Walsh *v.* People, 88 N. Y., 458.

It is exceedingly difficult to lay down a rule beyond which counsel shall not be allowed to travel in their argument to the jury, and the presiding judge should not be severe in arresting the argument because it may seem to him that the inference is forced, the analogy unnatural, or the argument illogical ; yet counsel should not be allowed to comment, in their address to the jury, on evidence which was offered and excluded, and the court should arrest such argument on objection being made : Sullivan *v.* State, 66 Alabama, 48.

Misstatements of counsel in their argument to the jury may be a ground for setting aside a verdict, but a presumption will obtain in favor of the action of the trial judge in refusing a new trial therefor : Wickersham *v.* Timmons, 49 Iowa, 267.

Where in a criminal prosecution the attorney for the State, against defendant's objection, indulges in language calculated to excite prejudice in the mind of the jury, the fact that the trial court neglected to rebuke such language, will not alone be sufficient ground for a reversal, if the case be otherwise correctly tried, and it appears that, under the law and the evidence, no other result than a conviction was possible without misbehavior of the judge : State *v.* Zumbunson, 7 Mo. App. Rep., 526.

It is the duty of the district court to interfere of its own motion in all cases where counsel in argument in jury trials state pertinent facts not before the jury, or use vituperation and abuse predicated on alleged facts not in evidence, calculated to create prejudice against a prisoner : State *v.* Gutekunst, 24 Kans., 252.

So, promptly to suppress any attempt on the part of counsel for the people to bring irrelevant matters into a case,

merely for the purpose of exciting the prejudices of a jury : Earll *v.* People, 99 Ills., 125.

Where one is put upon trial for a grave crime involving his liberty or life, it is highly improper for the prosecutor to do or say anything, the only effect of which is to inflame the passions or arouse the prejudices of the jury against the accused, without throwing any light on the case : Earll *v.* People, 99 Ills., 123.

It is the duty of the court, on the trial of one where his life or liberty is involved, to stop the State's attorney in his closing argument when he assumes facts not proved and urges them for a conviction. Such conduct is unfair to the accused, and he should be protected by the court. When such unfairness is gross, a judgment of conviction in a doubtful case should be reversed : Fox *v.* People, 95 Ills., 71.

The remark of the attorney-general, that "if the juries don't punish crime, the people will rise up, and should rise up and punish it," is reprehensible, and he should have been rebuked by the court in the presence of the jury.

Law officers are under peculiar obligations to set an example of respect for the law, and not to say or do anything which will tend to beget or encourage lawlessness : Scott *v.* State, 7 Lea (Tenn.), 232.

The prosecuting attorney in his closing argument to the jury, in referring to the evidence of defendant who had testified in his own behalf, said " It was incumbent on him to show how these things were. Did he tell us how she was hurt ? It was incumbent on him to prove how she was hurt, and the preponderance of testimony is in favor of conviction and against the defendant, and upon such evidence they must convict." Held error, for which the judgment should be reversed : State *v.* Mahley, 68 Mo., 315.

The trial court having failed to instruct the jury upon a material point, the prosecuting attorney in his closing argument undertook to supply the omission, and in doing so, against the defendant's objection and without interruption by the court, used language which was calculated to mislead the jury, and which the record seemed to show did mislead them. Held error, and judgment reversed: State v. Reed, 71 Mo., 200.

The court permitted counsel for one of the parties, in argument to the jury, to read and comment upon matter not in evidence, nor relevant to the issue, and which was prejudicial to the opposite party; held an irregularity or an abuse of discretion which prevented a fair trial, and for which the verdict should be set aside and a new trial ordered: Union, etc., v. Cheever, 36 Ohio St. R., 201.

Defendant's counsel having tendered in evidence a deed of assignment by the plaintiff of his estate, declined, where an objection to its reception was suddenly withdrawn, to put it in:

Held, that the plaintiff's counsel was entitled to comment forcibly to the jury on such a course, but not to ask them to accept as true that the plaintiff had assigned his estate, and was therefore entitled to be believed as a disinterested witness, nor any other facts deducible from the contents of the deed: Challacombe v. Wiggins, 7 Vict. L. R. (Law), 380.

Not every indiscreet remark made by the prosecuting attorney in the presence of the jury will be ground for new trial: State v. Guy, 69 Mo., 430; State v. Stark, 72 id., 37; State v. Baber, 74 id., 292, 298; Morrison v. State, 76 Ind., 334.

A statement that on a former trial the defendant had been convicted, made in the hearing of the jury by the prosecuting attorney to opposing counsel, in reply to a remark by the latter calculated to elicit such remark, and remarks of the same character made by a witness in the course of his examination in fixing certain dates, are not sufficient causes for reversing the judgment: Shepherd v. State, 64 Ind., 43.

Where counsel stated in his argument to the jury that a verdict for a certain amount had been rendered in the cause upon a former trial, and on being rebuked by the court, saying such a remark was highly improper and had nothing to do with the case, apologized by saying, "this is a matter of record;" held not sufficient cause for reversal: Goldman v. Wolff, 6 Mo. App. R., 490, 497.

It is not ground for a new trial that the prosecuting attorney made an illogical argument or a misstatement of the law: Morrison v. State, 76 Ind., 335.

Where the prosecuting attorney said in his argument to the jury, "Malice may bud and bloom in a man's heart almost in a moment, or in a short time:" Held, this was no ground for a reversal: State v. Estes, 70 Mo., 427.

See also State v. Stark, 72 Mo., 37; State v. Baber, 74 id., 292, 298.

Reading to the jury on the second trial of a cause the judgment of the court setting aside a former verdict for the improper admission of evidence, and commenting on such evidence and on the judgment, though improper, is not a ground for a new trial: Powell v. Wark, 4 Pugsley & Burb. (New Brunsw.), 15.

In general, arguments of counsel to the jury should be confined to the evidence and the principles of law claimed to be applicable thereto; but in discussing these, the motives to duty, the causes that may be supposed to control human action under different circumstances, and the probabilities or reasonableness of this or that theory as tested by human experience, necessarily may be considered. The court should see that the line of argument is kept within reasonable bounds, and not suffer one to be convicted or prejudiced on account of real or imaginary crimes for which he is not being tried. But except for a palpable abuse of discretion in this respect, manifestly tending to an improper conviction, there should be no reversal: Bulliner v. People, 95 Ills., 396.

Where the State's attorney, in his concluding speech to the jury in a criminal case, improperly asserts his own belief in the guilt of the accused, and asserts facts bearing on the question of guilt which are not in evidence, but in another portion of his speech he told the jury they should acquit unless they believed from the evidence, beyond a reasonable doubt, that the defendant's guilt was established, and the court instructed the jury that they should disregard any mere assertions of the State's attorney when of opinion of guilt or matter of fact, but decide the case solely on the evidence and the law; it was held this instruction should be deemed to have had the effect to destroy the force of the improper re-of 1873, was, to adopt the words of the Master of the Rolls in the case of *The Swansea Shipping Co.* v. *Duncan* ('),

to prevent the same question being tried twice over, where there is any substantial question common as between the plaintiff and defendant in the action, and as between the defendant and a third person ; and in such a case the third person is to be cited to take part in the original litigation, and so as to be bound by the decision on that question once for all.

If the Cartsburn were to be allowed now to raise an issue between herself and the steamtug as to the facts of the collision, the result would be precisely what it was the intention of the Legislature to obviate. The case would substantially be heard twice over. With regard to the technical point of procedure that has been raised, I cannot see that there has been any material departure from the course prescribed by Order xvi, Rules 17, 18, 20, and 21.

The order of the 27th of June, giving to the owner of the Leader liberty to defend, the notice of trial of the 30th of July, addressed to the owner of the Leader, as well as to the defendants, and the statement of defence of the owner of the Leader, imputing blame to the Cartsburn, which was filed on the 2d of August, were sufficient notice to the owners of the Cartsburn that they would have to meet at the trial the 42] cases set up both by the Slavia *and by the Leader. They did not choose to appear. It would seem as if they meant, in the event of the Slavia being found to blame to have the advantage of the finding of the court and, on the other hand, if the Cartsburn was found to blame, to deny that she was affected by the sentence. I dismiss this application with costs.

Solicitors for plaintiffs : *Ingledew, Ince & Greening.*
Solicitors for owners of the Cartsburn : *Fielder & Sumner.*
Solicitors for owner of the Leader : *Clarkson, Son & Greenwell.*

(') 1 Q. B. D., 644, at p. 649.

[5 Probate Division, 42.]

August 11, 1879.

[IN THE CONSISTORY COURT OF LONDON.]

THE RECTOR, CHURCHWARDENS AND BURIAL BOARD OF
THE PARISH OF ST. GEORGE'S, Hanover Square, v. HALL
AND LORD GEORGE PAGET.

Mortuary—Faculty—Costs.

The rector, churchwardens and burial board of an urban parish applied for the
grant of a faculty to authorize the erection of a parochial mortuary with a post-
mortem room attached, in a consecrated burial ground situate in a populous part of ·
the parish, and closed for burials by Order in Council.   The court being of opinion
that the petitioners had made out their case for the establishment of a mortuary on
the site proposed, directed that a faculty should issue for the erection of the mortuary, but directed that certain conditions to be specified in the faculty should be imposed with respect to the manner of using the mortuary.

[5 Probate Division, 49.]

Nov. 26, 1879.

*THE MATTHEW CAY (1879, B. No. 106).   [49

*Practice—Damage—Defence on Merits and on Ground of Compulsory
Pilotage—Costs.*

Where the defendants in a collision suit raise a defence on the merits, and also set
up a plea of compulsory pilotage, and the court dismisses the suit on the ground that
the plea of compulsory pilotage is established, each party to the suit will, in accordance with the practice prevailing in the Court of Admiralty before the Judicature
Acts, be left to bear his own costs.

THIS was an action of damage instituted on behalf of the
owner of the paddle steamer Wye against the owners of the
steamship Matthew Cay.   The statement of defence alleged
that at the time of the collision the Matthew Cay, in tow of
a steamtug, bound on a voyage from Bristol to Cardiff, was
proceeding down the river in charge of a duly licensed pilot,
and after setting out the circumstances under which according to their case the collision occurred proceeded, so far as
material, as follows:

The collision was caused by the negligent navigation of
the Wye.

Save as herein admitted, the defendants deny the truth of
the several allegations in the statement of claim, and the
defendants deny it to be the fact that the Matthew Cay or
her tug respectively were or was guilty of all or any of the
acts of negligence alleged in the statement of claim.

32 ENG. REP.   19

If and so far as the collision was occasioned by any improper or negligent navigation of the Matthew Cay or her tug, it was solely occasioned by some fault or incapacity of the pilot of the Matthew Cay, who was a qualified pilot acting in charge of the Matthew Cay, within a district where the employment of such pilot was compulsory by law, and whose orders were obeyed by the masters and crews of the Matthew Cay and her tug.

Nov. 22. The action was heard before the judge, assisted by two of the Elder Brethren of the Trinity House.

Witnesses were examined in court on behalf of the plaintiff and the defendants. The several witnesses called on behalf of the defendants gave evidence as well in support of the allegations in the statement of defence that the Wye and not the Matthew Cay was alone to blame for the collision, as of the alternative defence that the Matthew Cay was, at the time of the collision, subject to compulsory pilotage, and had on board and in charge of her a duly licensed Bristol pilot, whose default or neglect solely occasioned the colli-

50]   sion; and the court pronounced that the *Matthew Cay was only to blame for the collision, but that the pilot of the Matthew Cay was at the time of the collision acting in charge of her by compulsion of law, and that the collision had been solely occasioned by his default or neglect, and dismissed the action.

Milward, Q.C., and *E. C. Clarkson,* for the defendants, applied for the costs of the action, or in the alternative, for the costs of the issues on which they had succeeded. It is admitted that by the practice of the Court of Admiralty the action would have been dismissed without costs, but this is not the rule of practice in the three Common Law Divisions, and if the action had been brought in one of those divisions the defendants would have been held entitled to at least some of the costs asked for. It is not right that there should be one rule as to costs in one branch of the High Court of Justice, and another rule in other branches of the same court: *The Condor* (¹).

Bompas, Q.C., and *Myburgh* for the plaintiff, opposed the application, on the ground that the practice of the Court of Admiralty had been founded on a right principle, and had been sanctioned by the Court of Appeal since the coming into operation of the Judicature Act, and that as the costs were in the discretion of the court, Rules of the Supreme Court, Order LV, the court, in the exercise of that discre-

(¹) 4 P. D., 115, at p. 120.

tion, would consider that the proper order to make would
be to dismiss the action without costs: *The Daioz* (¹) ; *The
General Steam Navigation Co.* v. *The London and Edinburgh Shipping Co.* (²).

Cur. adv. vult.

Nov. 26.   SIR ROBERT PHILLIMORE: This is a case in
which the defendants pleaded, by way of defence, both the
merits and compulsory pilotage.   The court was of opinion
that the plaintiff was right on the question of the merits,
and the defendants were right on the question of compulsory pilotage, and the matter stood over for the consideration of the court as to what order it should make with respect
to costs.   Now the recent *decisions of the Court of   [51
Appeal have not left the question of costs in a very satisfactory state.   The decision of that court in the case of *The
Daioz*(¹) was in 1877, and the Master of the Rolls in giving
the judgment of the court in that case said, "The rule acted
on in the Admiralty Court in cases like the present, was that
when the owners of a vessel were relieved from liability on
the ground of compulsory pilotage, no costs were given on
either side, and the same rule ought to apply in the Court
of Appeal; there will therefore be no costs, either in the
court below or in the Court of Appeal."   That was in a case
where compulsory pilotage was pleaded.   Then there is another case, a later case, which turned on the question of inevitable accident.   I refer to the case of *The Condor* (³) in 1879.
In that case Lord Justice James is reported to have said that
it required great consideration "whether it could be right
that there should be one rule as to costs in one branch of
the High Court of Justice and another in another branch of
the High Court of Justice," and to have said afterwards,
"I think, however, that it may be considered as settled that
there will be no difference in future in the rule as to costs."
That was with regard to the question of costs in cases of inevitable accident.   It appears to me that I must follow the
rule laid down in the case of *The Daioz* (¹), and I think it
would be found, upon inquiry, to work a great injustice if
that rule was to be changed.   I say nothing about the rule
in cases of inevitable accident; but where compulsory pilotage is pleaded by way of defence, together with a defence
as to the merits of the collision, I do not see how the owner
of a vessel which suffers wrong is to know, when the action
is brought, either that there is a pilot on board, or that he
is a duly licensed pilot, or that the crew did or did not obey

(¹) 3 Asp. Mar. Law Cas., 477.   (²) 2 Ex. D., 467, at p. 469.
                    (³) 4 P. D., 129.

his orders, or did not contribute by their own negligence to the collision. There are many circumstances which seem to take the practice with regard to costs as applied to cases where compulsory pilotage is pleaded out of that rule, which, according to the decision in the case of *The Condor* ('), might be laid down in cases of inevitable accident. Until better instructed I shall, in cases where the defence of compulsory pilotage is set up as well as a defence on the merits, 52] and the defendants succeed in establishing *the defence of compulsory pilotage, adhere to the ruling laid down in the case of *The Daioz* ('), and, therefore, I shall dismiss the case without costs on either side.

Solicitors for plaintiff: *Luard & Shirley.*
Solicitors for defendants: *Ingledew, Ince & Vachell.*

(') 4 P. D., 120.   (') 3 Asp. Mar. Law Cas., 477.

[5 Probate Division, 54.]

Dec. 8, 1879.

[IN THE COURT OF APPEAL.]

54]   *THE ROBERT DIXON (1879, J. 173).

Salvage—Towage Contract—Counter-claim for negligent Towage.

A tug under contract to tow a ship is not entitled to salvage remuneration for rescuing the ship from danger brought about by the tug's negligent performance of her towage contract.

A tug agreed to tow a ship from Liverpool to the Skerries for a fixed sum. The tug imprudently towed the ship in bad weather too near a lee shore, and, the weather becoming worse during the performance of the agreed towage service, the hawser parted and the ship was placed in a position of danger and was compelled to let go her anchors to avoid being driven on shore. From this position she was rescued by the tug, having been compelled to slip her anchors and chains, which were lost:

Held (affirming the decision of the judge of the Admiralty Court), that the tug was not entitled to claim salvage remuneration, and that her owners were liable to pay for the loss of the anchors and chains.

Semble, if a tug receives positive directions from the ship she is towing as to the course she is to steer, she is bound to obey them; and if the ship gets into danger in consequence of such directions the tug is not liable.

THIS was an appeal from a judgment of the judge of the Admiralty Court, Sir R. Phillimore (').

The action was brought by the owners of the steamtug Commodore against the ship Robert Dixon for salvage.

The statement of claim, the statement of defence and counter-claim, and the effect of the evidence are fully set out in the previous report. The principal facts established

(') 4 P. D., 121; *ante*, 191.

by the evidence adduced by the respective parties, were shortly as follows:

On the 13th of March, 1879, the tug Commodore, having been engaged to tow the Robert Dixon from Liverpool to the Skerries for the sum of £49, towed the vessel out of dock and down the river, crossing the bar at about 5.30 P.M. At this time the wind was from the northward with a strong breeze, the sea moderate, the course taken being W.N.W. which direction was indicated to the master of the tug by the master of the Robert Dixon at the commencement of the voyage. The two vessels were taken inside the Pilot Boat No. 6, which was moored off the coast; and it was *alleged by the defendants that the safe course would [55 have been to keep outside that boat. At 11 P.M., the sea rising and the wind increasing to a gale, the tug hauled up to N.W. by W. and afterwards to N.W., and at 12.30 again altered the course to N.W.½N. At 1 o'clock the tug's hawser parted, and after some ineffectual attempts had been made by the tug to get hold of the Robert Dixon again, during which the ship drifted to leeward within three miles of the shore off Bull Bay, she was hailed by the tug to let go her anchors, which she did. The ship however dragged her anchors and drifted towards the shore into a dangerous position. The gale continued all night and the ship continued drifting, but in the morning about 9.30 o'clock the tug succeeded in getting hold of the ship's hawser and towed her to a safe offing about seven miles N.W. of the Skerries, but the Robert Dixon was obliged to slip both her anchors.

The owner of the tug claimed salvage for these services, and the owners of the Robert Dixon put in a counter-claim claiming damages for the loss of their anchors and chains, which they alleged to have been caused by the negligent and improper towage of the Commodore.

The judge of the Admiralty Court held that the ship was placed in a position of danger by reason of the tug imprudently towing her in bad weather too near a lee shore; and that the tug, having materially contributed to the danger in which the vessel had fallen, could not claim salvage remuneration; and he also held that the defendants were entitled to recover compensation under their counter-claim for the loss of their anchors and chains.

From this judgment the plaintiffs appealed. The arguments on the appeal related entirely to the effect of the evidence.

Webster, Q.C., and *Potter*, for the plaintiffs.

Milward, Q.C., *G. Bruce*, and *F. W. Raikes*, for the defendants, were not called on.

JAMES, L.J.: It appears to us, and the assessors who have assisted us, not only that it is impossible for us to say, as we should have to do if we overruled the judgment ap-
56]   pealed from, *that there was not sufficient evidence before the judge of the Admiralty Court to warrant his finding, but that if the case came for the first time before us as a new matter the evidence would not warrant any other conclusion. Whether the evidence establishes that the tug acted in violation of any positive directions from the ship during the voyage it is not necessary for us to give an opinion, because if it be true that no directions were given to the tug apart from the general directions at the commencement of the towage, it comes to this, that the master of the tug was acting as it was his duty to do on his own discretion to take the ship on a safe course to the Skerries, allowing for possible contingencies and a change of weather. It appears to our assessors and to me that the tug ought not to have taken a course inside the inshore pilot boat. That boat was purposely moored where it was in order to be inside the usual tracks of the ships, and I think the tug ought not to have gone inside the boat. If so the decision of the judge of the Admiralty Court is warranted by that fact alone ; and the tug did by its want of skill and prudence—for I see no reason whatever to attribute to the master any intention to make salvage—bring the ship into a position of danger by which the injury occurred. Therefore upon the main point whether the tug is entitled to salvage I am of opinion that it is not so entitled, and I also think that when an accident happens, and the original danger is found to have occurred through want of skill, the loss occasioned by the accident, as the loss of the anchors was in this case, is properly attributable to the want of skill which caused the original danger. It might have been different if the accident had happened from the want of power in the ship. It was suggested in the present case that the accident happened through the drunkenness of the crew, but the evidence in support of that charge is far too shadowy for the court to attach any importance to it. Therefore, on both points, the appeal must be dismissed.

BAGGALLAY, L.J.: I am of the same opinion. This is an action of salvage for services performed by a tug which was at the time under contract of towage from Liverpool to the Skerries. The suggestion made by the plaintiffs is that the ship met with a misfortune beyond the control of the tug,

and the tug was used *for salving the ship. *The Min-* [57
nehaha (') lays down clearly under what circumstances a
towage contract can be turned into a salvage. "If the danger from which the ship has been rescued is attributable to
the fault of the tug; if the tug, whether by wilful misconduct or by negligence, or by the want of that reasonable
skill or equipment which are implied in the towage contract, has occasioned or materially contributed to the danger, we can have no hesitation in stating our opionion that
she can have no claim to salvage. She can never be permitted to profit by her own wrong or default." The principles there stated have been universally recognized. The
only question here is whether the danger into which the
ship was brought was fairly attributable to the fault of the
tug; I do not say to the wilful misconduct of the master of
the tug—that charge has been negatived by the judge of
the Admiralty Court and I do not suggest it—but by his
negligence or want of skill. I think that it was so attributable. I am persuaded that the course made by the tug
was not the safe course, and that she continued in it too
long, and so got the ship into a dangerous position.

BRETT, L.J.: The plaintiffs being under a towage contract, bring this action, in which they assert that the towage
service was altered into salvage; and it seems to me that
the plaintiffs are in this position, that it lies on them to
show that the change occurred without any want of skill on
their part, but by mere accident over which they had no
control. The burden of proof on both the affirmative and
the negative issues is on the plaintiffs, that is, both that
there was an inevitable accident beyond their control, and
that they showed no want of skill. In that proof, in my
opinion, they fail; and I think they fail mainly on their
own evidence, and that it is not necessary to rely on the evidence of the defendants' witnesses.

On the plaintiffs' own evidence, it appears that when the
licensed pilot left the ship she was left in the command of
the captain with the assistance of a channel pilot, and the
command remained in the captain during the whole of the
transaction. I think it is proved by the plaintiffs' witnesses
that the captain did *direct the general course to be [58
taken by the tug. I am very much inclined to think that a
tug is bound to obey the orders of the captain, and if the
captain had insisted on the tug keeping that course, the tug
would have been bound to obey; certainly, the captain
could not have complained of the tug obeying him. But

(') Lush., 335, 349.

1879   The Robert Dixon.

here, on the plaintiffs' own showing, the only evidence was that at the beginning of the towage the tug was directed to tow the ship in a particular course. I assume that to have been the right course; but on the way the weather became threatening. Assuming that no further order was given by the captain, it was the duty of the tug to use reasonable care and skill, and unless she was ordered to the contrary, she had the command of the course.

The weather became more and more threatening; the ship sagged to the leeward more than she ought. Then the tug ought to have altered her course and kept more off the shore, so as to avert the danger. But undoubtedly the master of the tug, by reason of negligence—I do not for a moment accuse him of anything worse—allowed the ship to get too much to leeward and to come to a place where she ought not to have been. They went inside the inshore pilot boat, and they ought to have gone outside it. The assessors of the judge of the Admiralty Court and our assessors all agreed that the ship ought not to have been in that position. Therefore, unless the master of the tug can clear himself by showing that he acted upon orders from the ship, he cannot excuse himself from the charge of negligence, and the burden lies on him to do so. He may have done right when he changed his course towards the north, but then it was too late. It was too late then to draw the ship away from the shore. The result is that the plaintiffs have not shown that the danger was not incurred through their want of care. If so, this towage service was never changed into salvage. Whether they were entitled to towage under their contract is not now before us, but certainly they are not entitled to salvage. In the counter-claim the burden of proof is also on the plaintiffs. For it being proved that the ship was brought into a dangerous position on a lee shore by their fault, unless they can show that it was the fault of the ship's crew that they were obliged to 59] slip their anchors, the plaintiffs are liable *for the loss. In my opinion they have failed in discharging themselves of this burden also, and they must therefore be held liable for the loss.

Judgment affirmed.

Solicitor for plaintiffs: *Ayrton.*
Solicitor for defendants: *J. Neal.*

[5 Probate Division, 59.]

Jan. 26, 1880.

[IN THE COURT OF APPEAL.]

THE CARTSBURN (1879, K. 191).

Claim for indemnity—Notice to Third Party—Rules of Supreme Court, Order XVI.

A collision took place between the ship S. and the C., which was being towed by a tug. The owners of the S. brought an action against the owners of the C., alleging the collision to have been occasioned by the negligence of the C. and her tug, or one of them. The owners of the C. obtained leave to serve notice on the owner of the tug that they claimed to be entitled to indemnity, and the court made an order that the owner of the tug should be at liberty to appear and defend, "being bound as between him and the defendants by any decision the court may come to in this action as to the cause of collision." At the hearing the owner of the tug appeared, but the defendants did not, and the judge of the Admiralty Court pronounced that the collision was occasioned by the default of the master and crew of the C., and condemned the owners in damages and costs, and declared that they were not entitled to indemnity from the owner of the tug :

Held, on appeal, that the order giving the owner of the tug liberty to appear and defend did not put matters in train for trying any issue between him and the defendants, and that so much of the judgment as negatived the right to indemnity by the owner of the tug must be struck out.

THIS was an appeal by the owners of the Cartsburn from a judgment of the judge of the Admiralty Court, Sir R. Phillimore ([1]).

Jan. 13, 14. *Cohen,* Q.C., and *W. G. F. Phillimore,* for the appellants : The notice here was given under Order XVI, and the object of bringing in a third party under that order is merely to insure that the judgment in favor of the plaintiff shall be binding on him, but not to decide questions as between the third party and the defendant. No pleadings were delivered as between the owners of the Cartsburn and the Leader, nor were any directions *given under [60 which an issue between them could be tried. *Treleven* v. *Bray* ([2]) shows the restricted effect of Order XVI. In order to try the question between defendants the proceedings should have been taken under s. 24, subs. 3 of the Act of 1873. The rules 17–21 of Order XVI, all refer to questions in the action.

[COTTON, L.J.: Is it not a question in the action whether the tug was in fault ?]

No, for it makes no difference to the plaintiffs whether the Cartsburn or the tug was in fault. In *Walker* v. *Balfour* ([3]) a question was tried as between the defendant and a

([1]) 5 P. D., 35; *ante,* p. 282.   ([2]) 1 Ch. D., 176.

([3]) 25 Weekly Rep., 511.

third party, but in that case there were pleadings between them. Here no pleading by the third party had been served upon the appellants. The rules state that the object is to bind the third party ; nothing is said about binding the defendant. The only defence which the owner of the Leader could set up in this action was that the plaintiffs could not recover against the Cartsburn: *Horwell* v. *London General Omnibus Co.* ('). The proceeding was one in which the appellants were not bound to appear, for they knew that they had no defence as against the plaintiffs, and to bind the appellants by this decision in their absence is a miscarriage of justice.

Myburgh, and *Raikes*, for the owner of the Leader: In the pleadings of the Cartsburn there was an admission of no defence. The only question to be tried was between the Cartsburn and the Leader, and the application of the 28th of June was for the purpose of having that question tried, and that order was served by the owners of the Cartsburn on the owner of the Leader. The owners of the Cartsburn had notice of trial, they knew that the pleadings were complete, and they might have seen all the pleadings that there were.

[JAMES, L.J.: How do you show that they knew that a question between you and them was going to be tried ?]

Witnesses had been examined *de bene esse* before the trial for the purpose of throwing the blame on the Cartsburn, and it was default of the owners of the Cartsburn not to appear at the trial. The judge and the counsel for the plaintiffs [61] and for the owner of the *Leader all understood the order of the 28th of June as intended to settle the whole matter, and the owners of the Cartsburn must have known that the proceedings were conducted on that footing.

Cohen, Q.C., in reply.

Jan. 26, 1880. The judgment of the Court (James, Baggallay, and Cotton, L.JJ.,) was delivered by

JAMES, L.J.: The facts of this case are fully set forth in the report of the case in the court below, and it is not necessary therefore to restate them.

The applicants, the proprietors of the ship Cartsburn, gave notice in the court below and have repeated it here as follows: "That so much of the judgment of the 6th of April, 1879, in this action as declares that the defendants, the owners of the Cartsburn, are not entitled to any contribution or indemnity against the third party Andrew Bain, or decides

('·) 2 Ex. D., 365, 377.

anything as between the said defendants and the said Andrew Bain, or gives directions consequential upon such declaration or decision, be struck out, and that the said Andrew
Bain pay the costs of and incidental to this application."
We are of opinion that to a considerable extent the motion
ought to have been acceded to in the court below, and
ought to be acceded to here.   We have arrived at that
conclusion from these considerations, that there was no
litis contestatio established, no issue joined, and no trial
had as between the Cartsburn and the Leader, and therefore that any adjudication between them is erroneous as being *coram non judice*, and ought to be removed from the
judgment.

The third party in this case was brought in under the usual
notice given by leave of the court, which after stating the
object of the action, and that the defendants claimed indemnity from the owner of the Leader, proceeded : "And take
notice that if you wish to dispute the plaintiffs' claim in this
action as against the Cartsburn or the said defendants, you
must cause an appearance to be entered for you within eight
days after the service of this notice.   In default of your so
appearing, you will not be entitled in any future proceeding
between the defendants and yourself to dispute the validity
of the judgment in this action whether obtained by consent
or otherwise."   That evidently refers *to a future pro-   [62
ceeding which might be taken by the owners of the Cartsburn against the owner of the Leader, on the ground that,
if the plaintiffs succeeded, that success was due to some
fault of the Leader ; but there is nothing in that notice, and
there is nothing consequent on it, which amounts to a claim
by the Cartsburn against the Leader for indemnity or otherwise.   There was no claim, no action brought, and nothing
equivalent to any action by the owners of the Cartsburn
against the owner of the Leader, and nothing was done
which could enable the Cartsburn to recover in the action.
If the owners of the Cartsburn could not recover in the action, and could not obtain judgment against the owner of
the Leader, it seems to follow that the owner of the Leader
could not have been entitled to any judgment as between
him and the Cartsburn.   So it stood upon the notice.   Then
when the owner of the Leader appeared in court upon the
notice, an order was made on the 28th of June, which was
as follows: "The judge, having heard counsel for the
plaintiffs and the defendants, owners of the Cartsburn, ordered that Andrew Bain, owner of the steamtug Leader, be
at liberty to appear and defend, being bound as between

him and the said defendants by any decision the court may
come to in this action as to the cause of the collision." Now
it probably was intended by that order to put the matter in
course of investigation, not only as between the plaintiffs
and the other parties, but as between the owners of the
Cartsburn and the owner of the Leader; but the order did
not proceed to do what was necessary to effectuate that intention. It was quite competent to the court either to have
directed the owners of the Cartsburn to have brought in a
claim, or to have done something equivalent to bringing in a
claim by which, when the matter had been disposed of as
between the plaintiffs on the one hand and the owners of the
Cartsburn and the Leader on the other, any subsequent
question as between the owners of the Cartsburn and the
owner of the Leader might have been put in course of investigation. But no such proceeding was directed, no issue
was directed to be joined, no issue of fact was settled which
was to be tried between those parties themselves after the
plaintiffs' case had been disposed of, and the plaintiffs of
course had a right to have their case finally heard and dis-
63] posed of independently *of any consequential case
which might have to be determined as between the owners
of the Cartsburn and the Leader.

We think therefore that so much of the judgment as pronounced that the defendants the owners of the Cartsburn
were not entitled to any contribution or indemnity against
the owner of the Leader in respect of the said damages and
costs, and as condemned the said defendants and their bail
in the costs incurred by the co-defendant, must be struck
out of the judgment as being a matter which was not properly before the court for determination.

The appellants contended before us that we ought to go
further, and under that part of the notice of motion which
asks that whatever decides anything between the said defendants and Andrew Bain may be struck out of the judgment, we ought to interfere with that part of the finding
which pronounces the collision in question in this action to
have been occasioned solely by the fault or default of the
master and crew of the Cartsburn. That declaration we are
not in a condition to interfere with. It is a finding as between the plaintiffs and the defendants, and is the finding
upon which the judgment against the Cartsburn is pronounced; and if there was anything wrong in that finding
in point of fact, as being contrary to the evidence, or not
supported by the evidence, or if there was anything wrong
in the trial by which the judgment was arrived at, the only

mode of obtaining relief from that would be by a regular appeal against the judgment, or by something in the way of a motion for a new trial. But it is as it stands a finding between the plaintiffs and the Cartsburn, and we cannot interfere with it in the absence of the plaintiffs, who are not before us. It is a judgment as between the plaintiffs and the defendants, the owners of the Cartsburn, and it was obtained in the presence, whatever may be the effect of it, of the owner of the Leader, who was called upon to intervene, and take part in the trial. Whatever may be the consequences of that under the circumstances is not before us for determination. The finding is a finding between the plaintiffs and the Cartsburn which we cannot alter, though we might strike it out ; and it is to be observed that if the finding as to the cause of the collision is struck out, there is nothing to bind the Leader at all, because the only thing by which the Leader was to be bound was the decision of *the court in this action as to the cause of the colli- [64 sion. Therefore that part of the judgment must remain. We simply strike out the adjudication that the owners of the Cartsburn were not entitled to any contribution or indemnity, and the direction condemning them in costs, leaving the rest of the judgment as it stands. The whole difficulty arose apparently from some mistake or misapprehension of the court as to what the meaning of the order of the 28th of June was, and we think there should be no costs upon either side either in the court below or here.

Judgment accordingly.

Solicitors for the Cartsburn : *Fielder & Sumner*.
Solicitors for the Leader: *Clarkson, Son & Greenwell*.

[5 Probate Division, 73.]

Feb. 25, 1880.

[IN THE COURT OF APPEAL.]

*THE SIR CHARLES NAPIER (1879, F. 208).   [73

Wages—Set-off and Counter-claim—Loss of Ship caused by Negligence of Master —Payment by Underwriters—Amount payable on Total Loss.

In an action of wages by master against shipowner, the defendant, by way of set-off and counter-claim, claimed damages for the loss of the ship by the negligence of the plaintiff. Reply, that the ship was insured against a total loss, and that the underwriters had paid or agreed to pay to the owners the whole amount payable by them on a total loss :

Held, on demurrer, that the reply was bad, because the plaintiff had not pleaded that the money had been actually paid to the defendant, or that the counter-claim had been brought without the authority of the underwriters.

ACTION by the master against the owner of the ship Sir Charles Napier for the recovery of wages and disbursements.

Set-off and counter-claim: that whilst the defendant was sole owner of the Sir Charles Napier, and the plaintiff was in command, the plaintiff so neglected his duty as master and conducted himself so negligently, that by his negligence the ship was wrecked and totally lost, and claiming damages for such loss.

Reply, *inter alia*, that the vessel was fully insured on behalf of her owners, of whom the defendant was one, by policies of insurance against a total loss, and became on the occasion mentioned in the counter-claim a total loss; that the underwriters paid or agreed and became liable to pay to the owners of the vessel, of whom the defendant was one, the whole amount of money payable by and in the policies of insurance in the event of a total loss, and that the defendant could not without the privity and authority of the underwriters maintain any set-off or counter-claim against the plaintiff in respect of the loss of the ship.

Demurrer.

Dec. 16, 1879. *E. C. Clarkson*, for the defendant: The allegations in the reply, even if they could be substantiated by evidence, would be no defence to the defendant's counter-claim. It was the invariable practice in the Court of Admiralty to allow the defendants in a cause of master's wages 74] to set off any damages *which had been sustained by them by reason of the plaintiff's negligence. Why should a different rule be applied since the passage of the Judicature Act? The counter-claim of the defendant arises out of his contract with the plaintiff. The negligence of the plaintiff is a breach of that contract. If the principle contended for by the plaintiff were to be upheld, underwriters must necessarily be made parties in nearly every action of damage in this court, but it is well known that they are never made parties in such actions, and indeed have no independent right of action, and cannot sue in their own names for damage to the property insured: *Simpson* v. *Thomson* (¹).

Hilbery, for the plaintiff: It must be taken as admitted upon this demurrer that the defendant is claiming the damages he seeks as a trustee for the underwriters, and that he has not any authority from them to maintain his counter-claim against the plaintiff. This being the case, it becomes obvious that the court has no jurisdiction over the counter-claim. Whatever may have been the practice of the Court

(¹) 3 App. Cas., 279; 24 Eng. R., 138.

of Admiralty it is now provided by the 24th section of the Judicature Act, 1873, that the defendant in an action can only have such relief by way of counter-claim as ought to have been given in the Court of Chancery in a suit instituted before the passing of that act.   According to the principles administered by the Court of Chancery the defendant in the circumstances alleged in the reply would have been debarred from any counter-claim : *Bristowe* v. *Needham* (¹); *London, Bombay and Mediterranean Bank* v. *Narraway* (²); *Clark* v. *Cort* (³); *Rawson* v. *Samuel* (⁴); *Watson* v. *Mid Wales Ry. Co* (⁵).   If the defendant has been paid or is entitled to receive the amount of the policies in this case, he is in the same position with regard to any damages for the loss of the ship he may recover from third parties as if such damages had been recovered by him as an executor of, or a trustee for the underwriters : *North of England Insurance Association* v. *Armstrong* (⁶). [He also referred to the Rules of the Supreme Court, Order XVI, rule 7 ; Order XIX, *rule 3; Order XXII, rule 10 ; and *Fair* v. *M'Iver* (⁷) ;   [75 *Macdonald* v. *Carington* (⁸).]

Clarkson, in reply.

SIR ROBERT PHILLIMORE: It appears to me that there is a fallacy running through the plaintiff's argument.   It assumes that the claim made by the defendant for damages for the loss of his ship by the negligence of the plaintiff, is a claim made by the defendant in a representative capacity. Now I cannot see my way to decide that the claim made by the defendant by way of set-off and counter-claim is a claim by him in any other capacity than that of a shipowner, the same capacity in which he is sued.   Some confusion seems to have arisen from the proper distinction not having been drawn between what was a matter of set-off before the Judicature Act, and what may now be included under counter-claim.   Several cases have been cited in support of the proposition that the defendant is not entitled to claim by way of counter-claim any damage in a representative capacity, and I do not indeed understand that the principle involved in these cases is disputed ; but it has been contended, and I think rightly contended, on behalf of the defendant, that they are not applicable in a case like the present case, where the set-off or counter-claim arises out of the

(¹) 7 M. & G., 648.
(²) Law Rep., 15 Eq., 93; 5 Eng. R., 736.
(³) Cr. & P., 154.
(⁴) Cr. & P., 161.
(⁵) Law Rep., 2 C. P., 593.
(⁶) Law Rep., 5 Q. B., 244.
(⁷) 16 East, 130.
(⁸) 4 C. P. D., 28; 31 Eng. R., 382.

personal contract between the master and the shipowner. I must sustain the demurrer with costs.

Judgment for the defendant.

From this judgment the plaintiff appealed. The appeal was heard on the 25th of February, 1880.

Hilbery, for the plaintiff.

E. C. Clarkson, for the defendant, contended that the reply did not allege that the money had been paid to the defendant by the underwriters, but only that they had paid or agreed to pay it. This ought to be taken as against the pleader—that the money had not yet been paid, and therefore that the relation of trustee had not been constituted. Nor was there any distinct allegation that the counter-claim was brought without the privity of the underwriters.

Hilbery, in reply, submitted that the allegations in the 76] reply *were sufficiently distinct; but if the court should be of a contrary opinion, he asked leave to amend.

JESSEL, M.R.: This is an appeal from a decision of Sir R. Phillimore allowing a demurrer to a portion of the reply. I am very loth to allow demurrers of this description, which do not go to the merits of the action, and only raise subsidiary questions. Still it is our duty to decide the question which is brought before us. This being an action against the owner of a ship for wages earned by the master, the defendant raises a defence and counter-claim on the ground that the vessel was lost by the plaintiff's negligence. To this set-off and counter-claim the plaintiff replies that the owner was fully insured, and that as he is entitled to recover his loss from the underwriters, the loss is no defence to the action for wages. And he says that he is entitled to judgment personally against the defendant, but that the defendant, if successful, would not be entitled to judgment for himself but on behalf of the underwriters for whom he is a trustee; so that there would be two judgments, and not one only as required by Order XIX, rule 3, and Order XXII, rule 10. If the pleading had sufficiently alleged the facts, I might have thought there was force in the plaintiff's contention; but in the pleading there is no allegation of the fact of payment by the underwriters. The allegation is, that the underwriters "have paid or agreed and become liable to pay" to the owners the whole amount payable under the policies of insurance, and as the pleading must be taken in the sense least favorable to the pleader, it does not appear that the defendant has lost his right of action against the plaintiff, for it is not shown that the relation of trustee and *cestui que trust* has actually arisen between the defendant and the underwriters.

Another defect in the pleading is, that it is not distinctly alleged that the counter-claim was brought without the privity or authority of the underwriters. It must also be borne in mind that a set-off and counter-claim are not the same thing, and that a matter may be an answer to one but not to the other. I am therefore of opinion that the judgment of Sir Robert Phillimore allowing the demurrer must be affirmed with costs.

*With respect to the application for leave to amend,   [77 if the plaintiff should be prepared with an affidavit that the defendant has actually received the money, and that the counter-claim was made without the authority of the underwriters, he may be allowed to amend.

JAMES and COTTON, L.JJ., concurred.

Judgment affirmed.

Solicitors for plaintiff: *F. W. & H. Hilbery.*
Solicitor for defendant : *Wynne.*

[5 Probate Division, 77.]

Feb. 25, 1880.

[IN THE COURT OF APPEAL.]

THE CONSETT (1877, R. 376).

Practice—Action of Damage by Owners of Ship and Owners of Cargo—Costs of Reference.

The costs of the reference as to damages in an action of damages do not follow the costs of the action, but are in the discretion of the judge as the costs of a fresh litigation.

Where, therefore, an action had been brought by the owners of a ship and the owners of the cargo against another ship for collision, and both ships had been held to blame, and the judge afterwards gave the plaintiffs the owners of the cargo the costs of the reference, the Court of Appeal refused to interfere with his order.

APPEAL from an order of the judge of the Admiralty Court, Sir R. Phillimore (¹).

The action was brought by the owners of the ship Jessore, her master and crew, and the owners of her cargo, against the steamship Consett claiming damages for a collision between the two ships. The judge held that both ships were to blame, and that the damage must be borne equally by the owners of the two ships; and directed the usual reference, but made no order as to costs.

The plaintiffs accordingly took in their claims, which were

(¹) 5 P. D., 52; *ante*, p. 292.

supported by affidavits, and the registrar reported, *inter alia*, that the owners of the cargo of the Jessore ought to be allowed £15,094 2s. 10d., but he made no report as to how the costs of the reference ought to be borne.

The owners of the cargo of the Jessore then moved the 78]   judge in *court to order the costs of the reference and of their affidavits to be paid by the owners of the Consett, and his Lordship made the order asked for ; but gave leave to the defendants to appeal from· his decision.

;   The defendants accordingly appealed.

E. C. Clarkson (*Webster*, Q.C., with him), for the defendants :   The same rule ought to be followed in the reference as to the amount of damages as at the trial of the action, and no costs ought to be allowed to the owners of the cargo any more than to the owners of the ship which carried it :   *The Hibernia*(').   It is true that in the case of *The City of Manchester* (') the judge of the Admiralty Court acted on a different rule, and gave the owners of the cargo costs of the action, but that decision was contrary to the principle usually followed in the Court of Admiralty.

Butt, Q.C., and *Myburgh*, for the plaintiffs, were not called on.

JESSEL, M.R.:   I think that this appeal cannot succeed. Under the Judicature Act the costs are subject to the discretion of the judge, that is, of course his judicial discretion. When the trial takes place and there are cross claims, and both parties claim the full amount of damages, and the judge holds both to blame, he may well act upon the rule that there shall be no costs.   But the investigation before the registrar is a new litigation.   It may be stopped at the outset by the defendants tendering a reasonable sum, or it may be carried on to the end and great expense incurred, and the judge will exercise his discretion as to the costs just as if, instead of a reference, there had been a fresh action on the judgment.   He may make the defendants pay all the costs, or he may say that the pla ntiff's claim has been unreasonable and extravagant and réfuse to give any costs.   In any case the costs are in his discretion as in a fresh litigation. In this case he has exercised that discretion, and we cannot interfere with it.   Therefore the appeal must be dismissed with costs.

JAMES and COTTON, L.JJ., concurred.

Solicitors for plaintiffs : *Gregory, Rowcliffes & Rawle.*
Solicitors for defendants : *Cooper & Co.*

(') 2 Asp. Mar. Law Cas., 454.   (') 5 P. D., 3.

[5 Probate Division, 79.]

May 24, 1876.

*SANTO TEODORO V. SANTO TEODORO. [79

English Marriage—Foreign Husband—Stipulation for an English Residence by Wife—Jurisdiction of Court.

An English lady consented to marry the eldest son and heir of a Neapolitan nobleman, on condition of their always having, after marriage, a residence in England, and of their residing there six months, at least, in each year. The marriage was celebrated in August, 1854, in England. There were five English trustees of the marriage settlements, which contained a proviso that they should be construed according to the law of England. A few months after the marriage a London residence was taken and furnished by the parties, which they occupied for six months in each year, with two or three exceptions, from 1855 to 1872, living for the remainder of the year in apartments in the palace of the husband's father, at Naples, or at other places on the continent. In 1872, the lady separated from her husband in consequence of his cruelty and adultery, and she continued up to the hearing to reside in their London residence.

In 1878 the husband's father died, when he succeeded to his title and estates and palace at Naples, and since then he had resided sometimes at Naples, but principally at other places on the continent. The petition and citation were served on the husband at Paris, and he had entered no appearance:

Held, that the court had jurisdiction to dissolve the marriage.

THIS was a petition by the Duchess de Santo Teodoro, of 36 Lowndes Street, Hyde Park, London, for a dissolution of her marriage with the Duke de Santo Teodoro, a Neapolitan nobleman, by reason of his adultery and cruelty.

The petition and citation were served on the respondent in Paris, and he had entered no appearance.

Dr. Spinks, Q.C., and *Dr. Tristram*, for the petitioner.

Dr. Spinks, Q.C., in opening the case, after stating shortly the facts he should prove, directed the attention of the court to the fact that the respondent was a Neapolitan nobleman, and that as his property and his palace were in Italy, and as since the petitioner separated from him in 1872, owing to his marital misconduct, he had resided at Naples, but principally at other places on the continent, he could not be said to have now an English domicile or residence. The petitioner, however, was an English subject and only agreed to marry the respondent on his promising that *they [80 should have a permanent residence after marriage in England, and should reside in England six months in the year at least. The marriage was celebrated in England with a view to such residence in England. The stipulation as to residence had been adhered to from 1855 up to their separation in 1872, and since that time the petitioner had continued

him and the said defendants by any decision the court may
come to in this action as to the cause of the collision." Now
it probably was intended by that order to put the matter in
course of investigation, not only as between the plaintiffs
and the other parties, but as between the owners of the
Cartsburn and the owner of the Leader; but the order did
not proceed to do what was necessary to effectuate that intention. It was quite competent to the court either to have
directed the owners of the Cartsburn to have brought in a
claim, or to have done something equivalent to bringing in a
claim by which, when the matter had been disposed of as
between the plaintiffs on the one hand and the owners of the
Cartsburn and the Leader on the other, any subsequent
question as between the owners of the Cartsburn and the
owner of the Leader might have been put in course of investigation. But no such proceeding was directed, no issue
was directed to be joined, no issue of fact was settled which
was to be tried between those parties themselves after the
plaintiffs' case had been disposed of, and the plaintiffs of
course had a right to have their case finally heard and dis-
63] posed of independently *of any consequential case
which might have to be determined as between the owners
of the Cartsburn and the Leader.

We think therefore that so much of the judgment as pronounced that the defendants the owners of the Cartsburn
were not entitled to any contribution or indemnity against
the owner of the Leader in respect of the said damages and
costs, and as condemned the said defendants and their bail
in the costs incurred by the co-defendant, must be struck
out of the judgment as being a matter which was not properly before the court for determination.

The appellants contended before us that we ought to go
further, and under that part of the notice of motion which
asks that whatever decides anything between the said defendants and Andrew Bain may be struck out of the judgment, we ought to interfere with that part of the finding
which pronounces the collision in question in this action to
have been occasioned solely by the fault or default of the
master and crew of the Cartsburn. That declaration we are
not in a condition to interfere with. It is a finding as between the plaintiffs and the defendants, and is the finding
upon which the judgment against the Cartsburn is pronounced; and if there was anything wrong in that finding
in point of fact, as being contrary to the evidence, or not
supported by the evidence, or if there was anything wrong
in the trial by which the judgment was arrived at, the only

mode of obtaining relief from that would be by a regular appeal against the judgment, or by something in the way of a motion for a new trial.   But it is as it stands a finding between the plaintiffs and the Cartsburn, and we cannot interfere with it in the absence of the plaintiffs, who are not before us.   It is a judgment as between the plaintiffs and the defendants, the owners of the Cartsburn, and it was obtained in the presence, whatever may be the effect of it, of the owner of the Leader, who was called upon to intervene, and take part in the trial.   Whatever may be the consequences of that under the circumstances is not before us for determination.   The finding is a finding between the plaintiffs and the Cartsburn which we cannot alter, though we might strike it out ; and it is to be observed that if the finding as to the cause of the collision is struck out, there is nothing to bind the Leader at all, because the only thing by which the Leader was to be bound was the decision of *the court in this action as to the cause of the colli-   [64 sion.   Therefore that part of the judgment must remain. We simply strike out the adjudication that the owners of the Cartsburn were not entitled to any contribution or indemnity, and the direction condemning them in costs, leaving the rest of the judgment as it stands.   The whole difficulty arose apparently from some mistake or misapprehension of the court as to what the meaning of the order of the 28th of June was, and we think there should be no costs upon either side either in the court below or here.

Judgment accordingly.

Solicitors for the Cartsburn : *Fielder & Sumner*.
Solicitors for the Leader: *Clarkson, Son & Greenwell*.

[5 Probate Division, 73.]

Feb. 25, 1880.

[IN THE COURT OF APPEAL.]

*THE SIR CHARLES NAPIER (1879, F. 208).   [73

Wages—Set-off and Counter-claim—Loss of Ship caused by Negligence of Master —Payment by Underwriters—Amount payable on Total Loss.

In an action of wages by master against shipowner, the defendant, by way of set-off and counter-claim, claimed damages for the loss of the ship by the negligence of the plaintiff.   Reply, that the ship was insured against a total loss, and that the underwriters had paid or agreed to pay to the owners the whole amount payable by them on a total loss :

Held, on demurrer, that the reply was bad, because the plaintiff had not pleaded that the money had been actually paid to the defendant, or that the counter-claim had been brought without the authority of the underwriters.

more particularly in consequence of his having formed an
improper intimacy with an opera singer, with whom adultery was charged. She had since continued to reside at
36 Lowndes Street, Hyde Park, and the respondent had resided apart from her at different places on the continent.

The respondent's father died in 1873, when he succeeded to
his estates in Italy, and to his palace at Naples. Between
1871 and the date of the petition he had committed adultery
with the opera singer at Naples, Milan and Paris.

The petitioner gave evidence as to her family, her position
and fortune, that she accepted the respondent on the condition of their having an English home, and that she always
resided there for six months in the year, that the marriage
was celebrated in England, and the house No. 36 Lowndes
Street, Hyde Park, taken for them in 1855, that they furnished it, and shared with Mrs. Locke the larger proportion
of the expenses of the establishment, and resided together
there for about six months in the year from 1853 to 1872,
with two or three exceptions, and that she had continued
to reside there, separate from her husband, ever since.

SIR R. J. PHILLIMORE interposing, said, I am quite satisfied at present, that the Duke is subject to the jurisdiction
of the court.

83] *Dr. Spinks*, Q.C., also produced the marriage settlement, and referred the court to the clause in it providing
that it should be construed according to the laws of England.

SIR R. J. PHILLIMORE: The contract is made in England,
there is a long cohabitation in England, the husband has
been served.

The petitioner having proceeded with and concluded her
evidence, Mrs. Locke corroborated her, and other witnesses
were examined in support of the charges of cruelty.

The deposition of witnesses taken on commission at Naples, Florence, Milan, and Paris, were put in and read,
proving the respondent's adultery at those places.

SIR R. J. PHILLIMORE: The petitioner's counsel I do not
think I need trouble further. The evidence of adultery is
plain and indisputable. The evidence in regard to cruelty
requires more consideration; but on the whole I am satisfied
that the cruelty was of that kind which the law requires in
order to give a wife the right of separation from a husband,
viz., that it rendered cohabitation unsafe and insecure. That
cruelty was condoned by a subsequent cohabitation of the
Duchess with her husband, but it has been revived by subsequent adultery, which is proved beyond all doubt. The

petitioner in this case is entitled to a decree *nisi*, with costs, against her husband.

Solicitors for petitioner : *Baxters & Co.*

See *ante*, p. 133 note.

[5 Probate Division, 84.]

Dec. 4, 5, 1879.

*SMEE and Others v. SMEE and the CORPORATION   [84
OF BRIGHTON.

Will—Capacity—Delusions—Burden of Proof.

A man may be capable of transacting business of a complicated and important kind, involving the exercise of considerable powers of intellect, and yet may be subject to delusions so as to be unfit to make a will.

But if the delusions under which a man labors are such that they could not reasonably be supposed to have affected the dispositions made by his will, the will would be valid.

Banks v. *Goodfellow* (Law Rep., 5 Q. B., 549) followed.

The burden of proving capacity to make a will rests upon those who propound the will, and, *a fortiori*, when it appears that the testator was subject to delusions.

THE defendant, the widow of William Ray Smee, deceased, propounded a will dated the 21st day of June, 1859, of the deceased, and the other defendants propounded a later will of the 12th day of April, 1867. The plaintiffs alleged that the deceased was not of sound mind, memory, and understanding at the date of execution of either of the wills.

The deceased was for many years secretary to the committee of treasury of the Bank of England, and in November, 1852, met with a severe railway accident, in consequence of which he, in 1854, resigned his appointment. In the same year he married the defendant Mrs. Smee. By the will of 1859 he left his property, subject to the payment of some small legacies, to his wife absolutely, and named her sole executrix ; and by the will of 1867 he gave her the property for life or widowhood, and devised and bequeathed the residue to the corporation of Brighton towards forming a public library in the Royal Pavilion at Brighton. The deceased managed his own affairs down to the time of his death, and took an active part in politics, and amongst other things wrote an able pamphlet on the repeal of the malt tax. He had been left by his father a life interest in a sum of £18,000, and it appeared that in the early part of February, 1859, if not sooner he was laboring under insane delusions as to this and other matters. The following is one of the memorials pre-

pared and sent by the deceased, which illustrates the character of the delusions :

"To Her Most Gracious Majesty Victoria, Queen of Great
85] *Britain and Ireland.—The humble memorial of William Ray Smee, of No. 2 St. Edmund's Terrace, Regent's
Park, London, showeth,—

"1. Until a very recent period your memorialist thought
himself to be the eldest child of Mr. William Smee, of the
Bank of England, and his conduct as a son was dutiful, con-
siderate, and affectionate.

"2. Memory, however, has now brought a knowledge of
circumstances which renders this supposed parentage more
than doubtful, and induces him to think he is in some way
connected with your Majesty's family.

"3. Your memorialist, when quite young, remembers
walking with Master Alfred Smee and the nurse. There was
a crowd of people looking at some show. They all at once
turned to her, and demanded to know which was the prince,
and on being told your memorialist, they escorted him home
with loud hurrahs.

"4. King George IV came to see your memorialist when
living at Camberwell. He was but a little boy. The King
walked into the parlor from the garden. His Majesty took
a chair, balanced it on one leg, looked under, round, and up
and down the chair, then fixing his eyes upon him, said,
after a little pause, somewhat contemptuously, 'What do
you call this ?' 'A chair.' The King, still keeping his eyes
fixed, replied, 'This thing a chair ; a chair, do you call it ?'
Astonished, your memorialist asked, 'Can you not sit upon
it ?' The King seemed moved, did not again speak, but
sat down, took him upon his knee, and heard him read.
Some time afterwards Mrs. Smee came in, when the King
with much feeling patted your memorialist upon the head,
and said, 'Poor boy, poor boy, get on with your learning ;
a great destiny is preparing for you, although you do not
know it.'

"5. Your memorialist at this period was remarkable
for the quickness and rapidity with which he acquired
knowledge. He was at the top of the school, and at the
end of the half-year all the boys escorted him in triumph.
The master said he had never met with a boy more full of
promise.

"6. When your memorialist became about eleven years
of age his proficiency at school ceased. Every morning Mr.
86] William *Smee administered to him drugs that made

him very sick, and during the day deprived him of his proper quantity of nourishment, and prohibited him from eating any animal food.

"7. When this conduct first commenced, a lady spoke to your memorialist as he was standing in the road opposite his house. Her kind words and manner are now distinctly remembered; she asked him whether he had enough to eat. He wished to screen Mr. William Smee, and did not like to tell a stranger how sadly he was treated, and replied he had. But on leaving her, felt very sorry for what he said.

"8. This concealment, so kindly meant, was most of all disastrous to your memorialist, as he then received less and less, lost his memory and strength, and became half an idiot; subsequently more food was given him, and he partly recovered; yet, when again sent to school he was a totally changed boy, very nervous, and learning very slow.

"9. When about thirteen years of age your memorialist came to live in the Bank of England, and he was again drugged with medicines administered by Mr. William Smee. At school he sat for weeks doing nothing, and your memorialist remembers a visit from a gentlemen (and although not certain, yet he thinks he was addressed as Sir Henry Alford), who heard him read, and who appeared satisfied on finding he could not comprehend what he read. Yet this gentleman seemed anxious and uncomfortable, and said the memory, artificially taken away, might come back, and if so he was ruined.

"10. Within six months of this period he was called away from school to be introduced to a gentleman whom Mr. William Smee merely called 'a great man.' Your memorialist met him in Finsbury Circus, and all three walked up and down there, and the 'great man' asked all sorts of questions about him in his presence. He was dressed not like a gentleman but a well-to-do mechanic. On a sudden, the 'great man' exclaimed, 'I am discovered; see if the gentleman just past turns back.' He turned, 'I must be off,' he said, 'I must not be seen again,' and he disappeared, walking at a very rapid pace. Your memorialist now remembers much of the conversation, and regrets to say the great man in the mechanic's dress had the well-known face of the Duke of Wellington.

*"11. About a year from this time a gentleman [87 called upon your memorialist and said a sum of money was coming to him, and required him to appoint a trustee. With great form, Mr. William Smee was appointed; but

your memorialist has never received either principal or interest, and there is no mode of getting it except by public trial,
and it may be better to go without even a very large sum
of money than bring these circumstances before the world.

"12· Your memorialist, thus continually drugged and
deprived of his fortune, became at seventeen years of age
a mere tool in the hands of Mr. William Smee,—made completely ignorant of the past; and all his ideas and previous
views in life have been thus taken away, and he was compelled to accept the situation in Mr. Smee's department of
the Bank of England.

"13· When eighteen years of age, Mr. William Smee
came quite excited to your memorialist and said, 'There is a
report a prince is a clerk in my department, and he is
employed in the annuity office.' Your memorialist observed
he was engaged in that office, and should be glad to know
his name. Mr. William Smee seemed embarrassed, and
made no answer. That evening he was again drugged, and
until a few days ago all knowledge of the circumstance
was oblitered.

"14· Thus was your memorialist made like a youth born
at eighteen years of age. His mind a blank, yet it became
a creative mind, and even then, if left alone, he would have
made friends and would have risen in the world. But this
was not permitted, and your memorialist constantly found
himself thwarted by some unknown hand. Many instances
of this could be mentioned. Two schemes of public importance, which required two acts of Parliament to complete
them, were suppressed, and the only reason your memorialist
had given him was that they would be allowed to go before
the House of Commons with his name attached.

"15· About seven years ago your memorialist met with
a railway accident, which made him very ill, and compelled
him to give up his situation as secretary to the committee of
treasury at the Bank of England, and obliged him to live
much in the country. It, however, caused blood to flow
from the head, and this has, at length, so far relieved the
88] brain that memory, which *it was thought might
return, has actually done so. Mr. William Smee was perfectly aware this result might happen, for four years before
his death, when walking with him, he said, as if thinking
about it, 'As soon as I perceive he knows I shall die.'

"16· Mr. William Smee in his last illness, when alone
with your memorialist, made many strange remarks, three
of which ought to be mentioned. First, he said, every
trouble experienced by him has been made to happen by

deep design for a great object. Second, that the railway accident would cause him to become abler and better than he had ever been for reasons he knew nothing about. Here Mr. William Smee paused and seemed absorbed in thought. After a few minutes he addressed your memorialist thus,— 'William, you are a man of the highest character, and I now perceive this knowledge cannot be kept from you.' Third, and, wonderful to relate, one morning, Mr. William Smee, with a manner and a look that can never be forgotten, exclaimed—these are his exact words—' Extraordinary and unheard of means have been adopted to keep him down, or he must have come to the throne.'

"17. These observations would indicate that disease and great age had impaired the faculties of Mr. William Smee. Your memorialist tried to established this, as he wished to upset the will made at this period. But all those who had opportunities of judging were of opinion his mind was even clearer and stronger than before his illness.

"18. Your memorialist is a person probably not unlike your Majesty's family. In Paris on two occasions he was told he belonged to the Royal Family of England, and his denial was hardly believed. Even in London he has more than once been taken for the Duke of Cambridge.

"19. Throughout life your memorialist has been distinguished by good temper, kindness of disposition, and a certain bonhommie; but the foregoing circumstances, the knowledge of which has only come very gradually within the last few days, have greatly pained and wounded him, neither has he any means of ascertaining whether everything is yet known to him.

"20. Your memorialist is now about forty-three years of age, and although he hopes now to become, with respect to his brain, *like other men, yet he is in very delicate [89 health and has a sensitive mind.

"Your memorialist, therefore, humbly prays your Majesty to be graciously pleased to take some notice of him, and to cause the remainder of his days to be passed in honor and amid the charms of the best society ; and your memorialist, as in duty bound, will be forever grateful.

"William Ray Smee.

"December 22, 1859."

After the memorial to her Majesty became known to his family, and his claims upon his father's property as a trust fund for him were treated lightly by them, the deceased kept aloof from them, and his nephew stated that in an

interview which he had with the deceased in March, 1877,
the deceased stated in respect of the imaginary trust fund
that it would be found at the Bank of England after his
death.   In the box which contained the will of 1867 were
also found copies of the memorial in the deceased's handwriting.

Dr. Deane, Q.C., *Searle*, and *Rigg*, appeared for the
plaintiffs.

Sir H. S. Giffard, S.G., *Grady*, and *Bayford*, for Mrs.
Smee.

Inderwick, Q.C., and *Finlay*, for the Corporation of
Brighton.

THE PRESIDENT, in summing up the case to the jury, said :

The period of the testator's life with which you have to
deal is from 1852 down to 1867, the period within which he
made the two wills in question.

In 1852 he met with the accident on the railway, but the
consequences of that accident, grave as they were, do not
appear to have manifested themselves for a considerable
time afterwards.   He married in 1854, and it has not been
suggested that he was not at that time capable of contracting
marriage.   In 1858 his father died.   Whether his father's
death had anything to do with exciting the morbid condition
of his mind does not appear, and is immaterial to the inquiry,
but upon that occasion he manifested delusions which it is
not disputed possessed his mind from that time forward—it
is said even down to his death ; at any rate, long after 1867.

It is important to bear in mind the nature of the deceased's
90] *delusions.   He had an idea that he was the son of
George IV; that when he was born a large sum of money
was placed in his father's hands in trust for him ; that he
was robbed by his father by the diversion of a large part of
that trust fund from him to his brothers; and that all that
his father really had to give to his brothers was a sum of
£1,000 each, the rest of the property (about £50,000) left by
his father and divided by will between his children, being
part of the imaginary trust fund, to which the deceased
believed he alone was entitled.

He made a will in June, 1859, and a later will in April, 1867.
By the later will, with which you have first to deal, he left
his property to his wife for life, and after her death to found
a free public library for the use of the people of Brighton.
The question is whether that will can be deemed to be the
will of a sane man.

The law on the subject is this.   The fact that a man is
capable of transacting business, whatever its extent, or how-

ever complicated it may be, and however considerable the powers of intellect it may require, does not exclude the idea of his being of unsound mind. A man may be a good carpenter, and yet his mind be tainted with insanity to such an extent as to render him irresponsible for a crime on the ground that he did not know the nature of the act. A very few years ago there was a man in Bethlehem Hospital who had been acquitted of crime as being insane, but who painted pictures of considerable value. His insanity in no way interfered with his skill as a painter. All the arguments, therefore, addressed to you on the subject of the testator's capacity to deal with complex subjects, to write pamphlets, and to make calculations, have nothing to do with the question whether or no he was of unsound mind with reference to the making of his will. He was admittedly of unsound mind, as shown by that which is a most conclusive symptom and evidence of it, namely, the presence of delusions—that is to say, ideas which you cannot conceive any rational man to entertain.

Then arises another question, as to which undoubtedly there has been a difference of opinion between eminent authorities. A few years ago (¹) it was generally considered that if a man's mind were *unsound in one particular, the mind [91 being one and indivisible, his mind was altogether unsound, and therefore that he could not be held capable of performing rationally such an act as the making of a will. A different doctrine subsequently prevailed, and this I propose to enunciate for your guidance. It is this. If the delusions could not reasonably be conceived to have had anything to do with the deceased's power of considering the claims of his relations upon him and the manner in which he should dispose of his property, then the presence of a particular delusion would not incapacitate him from making a will.

But you should specially bear in mind that any one who questions the validity of a will is entitled to put the person who alleges that it was made by a capable testator upon proof that he was of sound mind at the time of its execution. The burden of proof rests upon those who set up the will, and, *a fortiori*, when it has already appeared that there was in some particular undoubtedly unsoundness of mind, that burden is considerably increased. You have, therefore, to be satisfied from the evidence that has been offered by those who propounded the will of 1867, and the earlier will also, that the delusions under which the deceased labored

(¹) See *Waring* v. *Waring*, 6 Moo. P. C., 341; *Smith* v. *Tebbitt*, Law Rep., 1 P. & D., 398, and cases there cited.

were of such a character that they could not reasonably be supposed to affect the disposition of his property.

This is an extremely delicate and difficult investigation, and may be illustrated by reference to the physical world. There might be a little crack in some geological stratum of no importance in itself, and nothing more than a chink through which water filters into the earth; but it might be shown that this flaw had a direct influence upon the volume, or color, or chemical qualities of a stream that issued from the earth many miles away. So with the mind. Upon the surface all may be perfectly clear, and a man may be able to transact ordinary business or follow his professional calling, and yet there may be some idea through which in the recesses of his mind an influence is produced on his conduct in other matters. You have to say whether or not the flaw or crack in the testator's mind was of such a character that, though its effect may not be seen on the surface of the document before you, it had an effect upon him when dealing with the disposition of his property, and making the 92]   bequest to the Corporation of *Brighton. He had an idea that he was the son of George IV, and it is for you to say whether that idea might not have had an effect upon his mind when he was considering what he should do with his property? It is perfectly clear that the testator was thoroughly of unsound mind in one particular, and it is for you to say whether the character of his unsoundness does not show a possibility and probability of connection between his will and the delusions under which he suffered, namely, that he was connected with the man who had taken such deep interest in the town of Brighton. Unless your minds are satisfied that there is no reasonable connection between the delusion and the bequests in the wills, those who propound the wills have not discharged the burdens cast upon them, and your verdict must be against them. The case is different, but only in degree with regard to the earlier will, as that will, being in favor of his wife, appears to be unconnected with his delusions. The capacity required of a testator is, that he should be able rationally to consider the claims of all those who are related to him, and who, according to the ordinary feelings of mankind, are supposed to have some claim to his consideration when dealing with his property as it is to be disposed of after his death. It is not sufficient that the will upon the face of it should be what might be considered a rational will. You must go below the surface and consider whether the testator was in such a state of mind that he could rationally take into consideration, not merely the amount and nature of his property, but the interest of those who by personal relationship or otherwise had claims upon him.

In dealing with the matter you must consider the testator's relations with reference to his brothers. He believed that they had by the fraud of his father been put in possession of two-thirds of property which belonged to him. His brother Alfred, in a latter in reply to one from the testator, in which the claim was first hinted at, treated the matter somewhat lightly, and it appeared from the evidence of Mr. Alfred Hutchinson Smee that there was in consequence a coolness between them, and that for many years they ceased to visit each other. If that were the state of his mind, believing that he had been defrauded by his brother of two-thirds of a sum of about £50,000, it will be for *you [93 to say whether his delusion can be treated as wholly unconnected with the will, in which he left all of his property to his wife for life and nothing under any contingency to his brothers or sisters. The subject as I have said is difficult and delicate, but it is one of which I have no doubt the best solution is to be found by the verdict of a jury. It being conceded that the testator was undoubtedly of unsound mind, are you satisfied that when he made either of the wills he was capable of dealing with the subjects before him entirely free from the delusions under which he suffered? If the evidence does not satisfy you as to this, your verdict should be against the will.

The jury having found that the deceased was not of sound mind when the wills were executed, his Lordship pronounced against both wills and allowed the costs of the plaintiffs and widow only out of the estate.

Inderwick, Q.C., asked for the costs of the corporation of Brighton also.

THE PRESIDENT: I am of opinion that the corporation of Brighton cannot be considered to blame for having raised the question as to the deceased's sanity. But that is not sufficient to entitle them to costs. I cannot allow them their costs, but I do not condemn them in costs.

Solicitor for plaintiffs: *T. H. Devonshire.*
Solicitors for corporation of Brighton: *Tilleard & Co.*
Solicitor for defendant: *J. Anderson Rose.*

See 27 Eng. R., 417 note; 21 Amer. Law Reg. (N.S.), 670 *et seq.*

The mere fact that a testator believed in spiritualism or has a delusion is not sufficient to invalidate his will, provided such belief or delusion did not contribute to produce the will or any particular devise or bequest in it: La Beau v. Vanderbilt, 3 Redf. Surr. R., 384, 388–390; Brown v. Ward, 53 Md.,

376, 86 Amer. R., 422; Matter of Smith's Will, 52 Wisc., 543; Frank Leslie's Will, 15 N. Y. Weekly Dig., 56, Mem. 27 Hun, 475; 1 Redf. on Wills (4th ed.), 74 *et seq.*, Redf. Cases on Wills, 367.

See Robinson *v.* Adams, 62 Maine, 369; Canada's Appeal, 47 Conn., 450.

A will made by one who is the victim of insane delusions, with regard to the property of which he seeks to dispose, though his memory and power of reasoning are unimpaired, will not be admitted to probate: Brinton's Estate, 13 Philadelphia, 234; Boyd *v.* Ely, 8 Watts, 73.

Partial insanity, in the absence of fraud or imposition, will not avoid a contract, unless it exists with reference to the subject of it at the time of its execution; but, in cases of fraud, it may be considered in determining whether a party has been imposed upon: Mc-Nett *v.* Cooper, 13 Fed. Repr., 586.

Where a delusion is taken advantage of, or operates to produce a result, an act which is the offspring of it cannot stand: 1 Redf. on Wills (4th ed.), 68, § 20; Robinson *v.* Adams, 62 Maine, 369, 898-9; Bell *v.* Lee, 28 Grant's (U.C.) Chy., 150.

In Greenwood *v.* Cline, 7 Oregon, 27, the court said: "It is said that fraud and undue influence are not ordinarily susceptible of direct proof, and in a majority of cases can only be inferred from the nature of the transaction or from the relations of the parties to each other. In Marsh *v.* Tyrrel, Sir John Nicholl said: 'The ground for imputing it must be looked for in the conduct of the parties and in the documents, rather than in oral evidence. The necessary inferences to be drawn from that conduct will afford a solid and safe basis for the judgment of the court.'"

In Greenwood *v.* Cline, 7 Oregon, 32-3, the court said: "But the evidence goes further, and shows an attempt to influence the mind of the testatrix by means of pretended spiritualism.

"After the death of the testatrix's husband, Mrs. Cline was very solicitous to have her mother go to Salem and live with her, but the testatrix was not disposed to comply with her wishes in that respect. On one occasion Mrs. Cline went out to visit her mother and told her that her father's spirit had ridden out with her in the stage, and that he was very anxious that she should move to Salem and live with her. About this time it also appears that the testatrix was in the habit of attending spiritual seances in company with the Clines, at the house of Mr. Lawson, who had been the attorney of Mrs. Cline during and since the settlement of her father's estate. Mrs. Cline, Lawson and his wife were avowed spiritualists. Mrs. Lawson claimed to be a spiritual medium, and on one occasion, when the testatrix was present, a pretended letter was produced, purporting to come from the deceased husband 'Uncle Billy Greenwood,' as the witness called him. This letter undertook to advise the testatrix about matters in this world in regard to her son William.

"It said that Mr. Greenwood, in looking back into the world, thought William was rather a rough character and liable to squander her property, that she ought to get it all out of his hands if she could and place it in such 'condition or fix' that he could not get hold of it. George Roland, a witness, says Lawson exhibited this letter to him the next day and read it to him, and wanted to know if it did not sound like 'Uncle Bill Greenwood talked.' Witness replied that it did sound like 'Uncle Billy.'

"This witness says Mrs. Greenwood appeared rather nervous over the matter and was anxious to have a manifestation from Mr. Greenwood. He also says that he saw the testatrix and the Clines there on several different occasions and that there was always some manifestation from Mr. Greenwood, and the witness says he met Mrs. Greenwood going there on another occasion, on which she told him that Mrs. Lawson was going to develop some more for her.

"Mrs. Cline admits that she and her mother were at Lawson's on one occasion when a communication was received purporting to come from her deceased father, but pretends that she did not know what it was: that she gave but little attention to the matter. She claims, however, that it produced no impression upon her mother except that of disgust, that she looked upon Mrs. Lawson as a humbug, and Mr.

Lawson as too smart a man to be so easily duped.

"We are left in doubt by the testimony as to whether the testatrix became a believer in the doctrine of spiritualism or not.

"Some of the witnesses say that she did, while others claim that she did not. The question, therefore, does not arise in this case whether the will of a spiritualist can be maintained when it appears to be the 'direct and obvious offspring of spiritual communications and influences.' This transaction does show however that there was an evident attempt, by means of these pretended spiritual communications, to produce an improper impression upon the mind of the testatrix in regard to her son William, the object of which was to impress upon her mind that William was a bad character; that he was not only faithless but dishonest, and would squander her property upon lewd women and in saloons, if she did not place it in such 'condition or fix' that he could not get hold of it. In consequence of this impression, about this time or shortly thereafter, we find her taking away from him the land she had given him when a boy, with the understanding at the time that it was to be his, and upon which he had made valuable improvements and held for seventeen years. This was given to Mrs. Cline free from rent."

"W. lived for years in unlawful relations with a woman who shared his his home, and who claimed to be a spiritualistic medium and to have daily communications with his deceased wife, whose memory he greatly revered; during this time she acquired great influence over him, and controlled him to a large degree in the management of his business affairs; at the same time he was addicted to the use of alcoholic liquors to such excess that he became very much debilitated in mind and body; previous to his death he conveyed large portions of his property, for the consideration of 'one dollar and friendship,' to the woman with whom he had been living in adulterous intercourse:

Held, that the conveyances should be set aside, on the ground that they were procured by undue influence": Leighton v. Orr, 44 Iowa, 679.

The court (pp. 689–690) said : "The

unlawful relations existing between these parties, the influence the defendant must have obtained, the confidential relations that must have existed between them, the confidence necessarily reposed may be well likened to that existing between friend and adviser, physician and patient, or many other relations in life that beget confidence. It matters not what the relation is, if confidence is reposed and influence obtained. Transactions based thereon or obtained thereby, will be jealously watched and guarded by courts of equity, and set aside unless the beneficiary shows the *bona fides* of such transaction : 1 Kerr on Fraud and Mistake, 150–1–2 and 183.

"In Bayless v. Williams, 6 Coldwell, 542, this doctrine was held applicable to a contract or conveyance of real estate, where friendship and gratuitous service performed for the plaintiff by the defendant was the only confidential relation that existed between them.

"In Lyon v. Home, 6 Equity Cases (Law Reports), 655,—case in principle much like this,—it was held the burden was on the defendant to support the deeds or gifts, and that he should satisfy the court they had not been obtained by reason of confidence reposed or undue influence.

"The defendant in that action was somewhat celebrated as a spiritualist. The plaintiff sought him and thrust her gifts upon him, in consequence however of directions received, as she supposed, through the defendant from her deceased husband. It is true nothing of that kind is shown in the case at bar, but the legal principle announced in the case is not placed on that ground. Nor was there in that case, as in this, any illegal or immoral relations existing between the parties, and the influence thereby engendered the onus or burden of supporting the deeds or gifts was on the defendant."

Mr. Bigelow on Fraud, 272, says : "It is also to be observed that one who prevails over another through spiritualistic means, to obtain a gift of property, may be compelled to restore or make good the property so obtained. In the case cited, a widow of advanced years was induced by the defendant, acting as a spiritual medium, to adopt him as her son, to transfer to him a large amount of property, to make her will in his favor, and to settle upon him a large reversionary interest. Having afterwards instituted a suit to set aside these gifts, it was held that the relation existing between the parties implied the exercise of dominion by the the defendant over her mind ; and the latter having failed to show that the gifts were the pure, voluntary and well-understood acts of the plaintiff, she was entitled to judgment. The burden of proof rests upon the defendant in such cases, just as in those of attorney and client, guardian and ward, and the like."

In Lyon v. Home, L. R., 6 Eq. Cas., 655, A., a widow, aged seventy-five, within a few days after seeing B., who claimed to be a "spiritual medium," was induced, from her belief that she was fulfilling the wishes of her deceased husband, conveyed to her through the medium of B., to adopt him as her son, and transfer £24,000 to him ; to make her will in his favor ; afterwards to give him a further sum of £6,000, and also to settle upon him, subject to her life interest, the reversion of £30,000 (these gifts being made without consideration, and without power of revocation). Held, that the relations proved to have existed between them implied the exercise of dominion and influence by B. over A.'s mind ; and, consequently, that as B. had failed to prove that these voluntary gifts were the pure, voluntary, well-understood acts of A.'s mind, they must be set aside.

In this case the court (pp. 674-681) said : "Then as regards the law, the question is not as to the validity of a will, but whether two gifts, one to the amount of £30,000 actually transferred, and the other to the amount of £30,000 in reversion, each irrevocably and without consideration, supported by deeds, are or are not to be upheld.

"On this I will first of all refer to what has been said in two cases by Lord Eldon and Lord Cottenham.

"In Hatch v. Hatch, 9 Ves., 292, 296, Lord Eldon said : ' This case proves the wisdom of the court in saying, It is almost impossible in the course of the connection of guardian and ward, attorney and client, trustee and cestui que trust, that a transaction shall stand purporting to be bounty. The court cannot permit it except quite satisfied that

it is an act of * * * a rational consideration, an act of pure volition uninfluenced, and that inquiry is so easily baffled in a court of justice, that, instead of the spontaneous act of a friend, uninfluenced, it may be the impulse of of a mind misled by undue kindness or forced by oppression. Therefore, if the court does not watch these transactions with a jealousy almost invincible, in a great majority of cases it will lend its assistance to fraud.'

"Lord Cottenham, in Dent v. Bennett, 4 Myl. & Cr., 269, 276, which was the case of a medical man, observed : ' It was argued upon the authority of the civil law and of some reported cases, that medical attendants were, upon questions of this kind, within that class of persons whose acts, when dealing with their patients, ought to be watched with great jealousy. Undoubtedly they are ; but I will not narrow the rule, or run the risk of in any degree fettering the exercise of the beneficial jurisdiction of this court, by any enumeration of the description of persons against whom it ought to be most freely exercised.

"The relief—as Sir S. Romilly says in his celebrated reply in Huguenin v. Baseley, 14 Vesey, 873,—' the relief stands upon a general principle applying to all the variety of relations in which dominion may be exercised by one person over another.'

"Huguenin v. Baseley was the case of a minister of religion.

"The question then arises, was the relation of the defendant to the plaintiff during these transactions at all analogous to those which are referred to by Lord Eldon and Lord Cottenham ? I answer that it has been proved to be so. At the outset, the result of the evidence of Mrs. Pepper, Mrs. Denison, and Mrs. Sims, is, that the plaintiff was greatly attached to her husband ; that her husband had told her that a change would take place in seven years from his death, and that they would meet ; that she consequently expected her own death in the autumn of 1866, and was told that if she became a spiritualist that need not be, but he would come to her ; that she took to reading books on spiritualism, among others, the ' Incidents in my (defendant's) life,' and became desirous of meeting the defendant. Then Mr. Burns proves the letter of September, 1866, in which she writes with reference to the defendant:" 'I am a firm believer in all he states in his book, and consider him highly favored by the most High God.' Besides this, the plaintiff is proved to have been superstitious and eminently affected by dreams and visions, particularly by the vision of the golden-haired boy. I am satisfied in spite of what she said on cross-examination, that she was deeply impressed with that vision, and felt it as reality. Moreover, she had been told by her father that she would adopt a son, and it was with a mind saturated with all this, that she sought the defendant because of that which she terms 'his strange gift.' I have read from his answer the defendant's account of himself.

"On the 2d of October, according to the answer, the incidents in the defendant's life were alluded to. On the 4th he called on the plaintiff, and became acquainted with her antecedents, birth, parentage, marriage, wealth and other circumstances. He was then told by the plaintiff 'that previous to her late husband's death he told her a change would come over her in seven years, and that she thought it meant her death, but that now she thought the event to occur was that she was to meet and adopt the defendant.'

"On the 7th, £30,000 is alluded to and £24,000 promised. The plaintiff is represented by the defendant as saying, 'Why, I have seen you in visions these many years, and the only difference was that your hair was lighter, more of a golden yellow, than it now is —many years ago, even before you could have been born. Why, even my father before he died told me I should adopt a son.' With reference to this, we find in one of defendant's letters a communication signed with the initials 'M. G.,' as betokening her father, which is as follows : The spirits say, 'Dear Daniel, be patient and hopeful; you are recovering, and, with care, will have many years of usefulness on earth. Your mother, my darling Jane, is well, and we are near her at all times.' At this same interview of the 7th of October, the defendant tells us there came sounds known as rapping. A call for the alphabet was made, and the following sentence, or words nearly

similar, spelt out : 'Do not, my darling Jane, say ' Alas ! the light of days forever fled ;' the light is with you. Charles lives and loves you.' This is the defendant's own account. Whether there were or were not what are called maifestations before the 7th, there were certainly manifestations then and on the 8th, and manifestations far beyond any admitted by the defendant ; 'on the 11th,' says the defendant, 'I called at her request, and we went to the city in a cab. There were no manifestations. The plaintiff sat very near me with my hands in hers, under her shawl, all the way to the city. On this occasion the £24,000 was transferred, and the defendant spoken of by the plaintiff at the banker's and broker's as her adopted son.' This without more is, in my judgment, enough to throw upon the defendant the *onus* of proving that the plaintiff's acts were the pure, voluntary, well-understood acts of her mind, unaffected·by the least speck of imposition or undue influence, or as Lord Eldon has expressed it, 'acts of rational consideration, of pure volition uninfluenced.' But the case does not stop here. The defendant states himself to be what is called 'a medium.' Mr. Wilkinson casually saw the plaintiff and the defendant sitting at a table, and the defendant acting as a medium, and it is to be inferred that this was nothing unusual or uncommon, not only from this circumstance but from Mrs. Tom Fellowes' affidavit, in which she says she went by the plaintiff's appointment to meet the defendant at the plaintiff's lodgings, 'and he came accordingly, and after a short time we all three sat at the table for a seance, the plaintiff asking the defendant to seat himself at his own place at the table and to begin to call the spirits ;' and from Mrs. James Fellowes' affidavit, in which she says, after alluding to her introduction to the defendant, that the plaintiff said to him 'let us have a manifestation,' but he said he could not, as he had a bad headache and must leave.

"I am aware that the defendant has been cross-examined as to these and other parts of these affidavits and of the extent to which he has contradicted them, but Mrs. James Fellowes and Mrs. Tom Fellowes were cross-examined, and I am satisfied that they are both witnesses of truth, and in every sense, as regards memory and otherwise, quite reliable. I am satisfied, too, that much more occurred on Sunday, the 7th of October, 1866, in the shape of manifestations and communications, than the defendant admits. Even on his own admission, what did occur, had reference to the plaintiff's husband. I am satisfied that the representations made by the plaintiff to Mrs. Tom Fellowes in the defendant's presence were according to the facts, and that Mrs. Tom Fellowes is accurate when she says in the seventh paragraph of her affidavit : ' On this occasion the plaintiff was very open and communicative in telling me, in the presence of the defendant of her disposition of her property, and he continually checked her, saying it was unnecessary to go into minute particulars, and the plaintiff said she wished Plessy (meaning myself) to know exactly what she had done, as she had only obeyed her husband's commands as communicated by his spirit through the mediumship of the defendant. He, however, then denied that he had himself had anything to do with the matter. I remember, also, that on this occasion the defendant asked me whether ' I had never lost any one very dear to me, into whose presence I should like to be brought again.' I cannot take the defendant's denial so referred to, to mean more than that the communications from the plaintiff's husband were not caused by any act or volition of the defendant, this being in truth consistent with what he represents as his 'strange gift.' Then the defendant, in his cross-examination, swears that he has seen spirits ; that he has conversed with them orally ; that in his presence tables and chairs have -been moved bodily, in violation of the rules of gravity, and that he himself has floated in the air ; and on being asked how the spirits communicate to a medium, when they communicate by knocking, he says : ' Strange sounds are heard like a rapping sound. The alphabet is called or pointed out in some instances, and when a sound is given, that indicates that that letter is to be written down. I have no alphabet to be used for this purpose, they can be called orally as well as pointed out. We go through A, B, C, D, and so on, and when the right letter is arrived at, the spirit gives a knock. The

knocks are both affirmative and negative, one signifies ' no,' and three ' yes,' but you can arrange that as you please.'
    " Add to this the antecedents of the plaintiff and defendant, the defendant's letters from which I have read extracts, the page from the destroyed book, and the book B in his handwriting ; then consider that a woman past seventy, within eleven days after first seeing the defendant, mentioned 30,000 pounds and actually transferred 24,000 pounds to him, and followed this gift by a will in his favor, then a gift of £6,000 and then of a reversionary interest in £80,000 more, and assuredly there is proof of transactions which ought to be watched with what Lord Eldon termed ' a jealousy almost invincible,' proof which throws on the defendant the whole onus of supporting such gifts. I have already read the defendant's statements and explantions from his answer and affidavits with reference to the book B (I have read extracts from the book itself). I am altogether dissatisfied with those statements and explanations. The contents of the book disproves them. It is said, however, that the plaintiff's desire to be introduced into the society in which the defendant moved, prevailed much with her ; that her testimony is not to be relied on ; that there is not only what defendant has sworn to, but Mr. Wilkinson's answer, and evidence of many witnesses besides his to which weight is due ; that the plaintiff professed herself to be ' a medium ;' that she still deals in spiritualism ; that the defendant was under her influence, not she under his ; that she had the advantage of independent advice—Mr. Hall's, Mr. Jenkins', Mr. Wilkinson's ; that she is a person of business habits and business knowledge ; that the letters, commencing with that of the 10th of October, 1866, were entirely her own, and that she herself had stated and admitted to Mr. Wilkinson and other persons, that the transactions were not connected with spiritualism. I agree that she did so state to Mr. Wilkinson and other persons. I have said that I cannot rely on her testimony. She seems to have had to do with spiritualism in connection with this very suit, but her desire to be introduced into the society in which the defendant moved, was clearly not such an induce-

ment as to account for what she did, or the main inducement; and when it is said that the defendant was under her influence, not she under his, I disagree entirely. The facts I have recapitulated, the letters I have read, the defendant's appearance here in court, the antecedents of both parties, and the statements in the defendant's answer of what occurred when and after he and the plaintiff quarrelled, led irresistibly to widely different conclusions.

"As to the plaintiff's admissions and statements that the transactions were unconnected with spiritualism, for some months she was as anxious as the defendant to support the gifts. I may say, obstinately desirous of supporting them. From her oral communications with Mr. Wilkinson (these commenced on the 12th of November, after her conversation with Mrs. Tom Fellowes), she was aware of the danger of referring what she did to spiritualism. These circumstances and her peculiar character, and the knowledge or suspicion that her sanity might be questioned, sufficiently account for what she said and did as deposed to by the various witnesses. Besides which, the defendant was generally present, and by no means unaware of the value of anything which might be deemed confirmatory. I am satisfied that the statements and admissions to the effect that the transactions had nothing to do with spiritualism, were not according to the fact.

"As to the plaintiff's professing to be a medium, she said this and almost anything which occurred to her, from time to time, as seeming likely to make her of importance to those with whom she was conversing. But the defendant has been proved to be the person who acted as the 'medium.' There is no proof of the plaintiff's having so acted, nor do I believe she did. True it is, however, that she has business habits and a knowledge of business, but obviously a limited capacity, very limited as compared with the defendant's, and though I disregard her statements as to her letters and think her quite able of herself to have composed the letters she wrote to Mr. Wilkinson; the letter of the 10th of Oct., beginning 'My dear Mr. Home,' and ending 'yours very truly and re-

spectfully, Jane Lyon,' is at singular variance with what she said at the banker's and the broker's the day after, with reference to the adoption of the defendant as a son, and with what the defendant represents her as having said to himself, both on the 11th and at the interview on the 7th of October. This letter has not been satisfactorily explained or accounted for. As to the independent advice, the relation between the plaintiff and the defendant remained unaltered throughout.

"He was in constant communication with her. Both parties expected that what was being done would be questioned by the husband's relations. Sanity was talked of. Precautions were taken that questions of the kind might be met if raised; nothing like a power of revocation was ever suggested, though this would have added much to the validity of the deeds and to the control of the plaintiff over the defendant, and, besides, I think it a just and sound observation that all that was done was much more by way of caution against what others might do, than by way of protection to the plaintiff against her own folly and infatuation. There had been acts of confirmation in Bridgman v. Green, 2 Ves. Sen., 627. But Lord Chief Justice Wilmot said: 'In cases of forgery, instructions under the hand of the person whose deed or will is supposed to be forged, to the same effect as the deed or will are very material; but in cases of undue influence and imposition they prove nothing, for the same power which produces one, produces the other, and, therefore, instead of removing such an imputation it is rather an additional evidence of it.' In Huguenin v. Baseley, 14 Ves., 273, 296, there was the answer of the solicitor who prepared the deed, but with reference to this, Lord Eldon said: 'There is in this case an attempt to show why there was not a power of revocation, and that is a part of the transaction, one of the most liable to objection. The evidence and answer of the attorney go to this distinctly, that she informed him she was to have all her affairs arranged. He was struck with the circumstance of her making an irrevocable deed, and told her that she should make a will,' and in another part of the judgment he said, 'I am bound to look at all the circumstances that led to the execution of a voluntary instrument, and to observe that the attorney did not state this improvident act to the brother of this lady, or, as Lord Chief Justice Wilmot said, go and talk both to the grantor and grantee upon it.' There was no suggestion of a power of revocation or of communication with any of the husband's relations, or any question asked or inquiry made of the defendant, and on the 19th of January, 1867, when the last of the deeds was being read over and executed, the defendant says (this being his account, varying from the plaintiff's) : 'She afterwards called me to her, and kicking a footstool from under the table, pointed for me to kneel there. I did so, close to her, and she put her left arm around my neck, and fondled my cheek while they were reading the parchment.' I have already said that in my opinion the onus of supporting the gifts and deeds rests entirely on the defendant ; to this I now add, for the reasons I have given and having regard to the facts and evidence I have gone through, that in my judgment he has not made or proved such a case as is requisite for their support. There must, therefore, be a declaration in the usual form, that the gifts and deeds are fraudulent and void ; there must be the necessary transfers and assignments to the plaintiff, and an account against the defendant."

In Robinson v. Adams, 62 Maine, 370, 399–400, 404–6, the court held that " if the testatrix believed that the spirit of her deceased husband directed or dictated the will and codicil and acted under that belief, they are void."

" Where a grantor is shown to be insane on a particular subject, or with reference to a particular person, *and the deed is an act referable to that state of mind, no more need be proved in order to vacate the deed.* In such a case the rule of equity that a grantor must be proved to have been of unsound mind or under undue influence at the very time the deed impeached was executed, is not applicable. It is sufficient to invalidate any instrument executed for an inadequate consideration by a person of weak intellect, to show that the person in whose favor it was executed held a situation of confidence with respect to the maker of

such instrument": Jones v. Jones, 21 Amer. Law Reg. (N.S.), 666, 668–9, 1 Amer. Law Mag., 101, 29 Pittsb. Leg. Jour., 387, 39 Leg. Int., 52, Supreme Court, Penn.

" Evidence tending to show that the testator was of feeble mind, and believed in ghosts and supernatural influences, had some tendency to show unsoundness of mind, or that weakness of mind which would be easily imposed upon by the exertion of undue influence": Woodbury v. Obear, 7 Gray, 470.

The maxim of the law, "once insane presumed to be always insane," is not an unqualified one.

Neither observation nor experience shows us that persons who are insane from the effects of some violent disease, do not usually recover the right use of their mental faculties. Such cases are not unusual, and the return of a sound mind may be anticipated from the subsiding or removal of the disease which has prostrated their minds. If, therefore, the proof in a proceeding to annul a deed made by a person to his prejudice when he is alleged to have been insane, only shows a case of insanity directly connected with some violent disease, the party alleging the insanity must bring his proof of continued insanity to that point of time which bears directly upon the contract impeached, and not content himself with proof of insanity at an earlier period : Turner v. Rusk, 53 Md., 65.

A person of full age, who has been insane, may, after he has sufficiently recovered his reason to understand the character of his act, file a bill in equity to annul a deed or contract to his prejudice made by him when he was of unsound mind and incapable of contracting : Turner v. Rusk, 53 Md., 65.

In an action to set aside a deed on the ground of fraud and undue influence, it appeared that as the grantor who was seventy years of age, and who formerly had been a strong and vigorous man, had become and was at the time physically weak and his mind so impaired as to require the assistance of others in his business affairs, and that he was unable to care properly for his own interests. Defendant, who was a nephew of M., employed S., a neighbor, with whom M. was on intimate terms, to procure the deed, agreeing to pay $1,000 therefor. S. had the deed drawn by an attorney without the knowledge of any other person, he giving instructions as to its terms ; he brought the attorney with the deed to his residence, then brought M. there, and the deed was executed and acknowledged before the attorney, who was a notary. M. had declared that he intended to give the farm to defendant, but at other times had said that his nephews and nieces were alike to him and should share equally in his property. The deed conveyed the grantor's farm, reserving a life estate, and provided for the payment of $500 to each of two sisters of the grantee. M. on his return home stated in answer to inquiries that he had signed no paper in regard to his affairs, and when questioned afterwards, emphatically denied that he had executed a deed. About fifteen months after the execution of the deed M. was adjudged a lunatic in proceedings *de lunatico.* Neither the defendant nor S. were called as witnesses. Held, that the evidence justified a finding of undue influence : Rider *v.* Miller, 86 N. Y., 507.

The law must not be so administered as to encourage dishonest people to cultivate the depraved habits and appetites of others, for greater facility in overreaching them : Storrs *v.* Scougale, 48 Mich., 388.

When a man is addicted to a habit which enfeebles his intellect and his power of self-protection, a person who spends day after day in driving hard bargains with him cannot obtain their enforcement in equity if he does not make a very clear showing of open dealing : Storrs *v.* Scougale, 48 Mich., 388.

A party is not bound by a contract entered into when his mental condition is such as to preclude any fair or reasonable exercise of the reasoning faculties : Kilgore *v.* Cross, 1 McCrary, 144.

The question in determining whether a gift has been made, is not what the donor had contemplated or intended but whether his intentions were carried into effect ; and to accomplish this, an intelligent will directing or assenting to the act done, is essential : Duncombe *v.* Richards, 46 Mich., 166.

A sale of land for an exorbitant price may be set aside in equity, even though the purchaser bought with full knowledge of its value, if the vendor has compelled the sale by taking advantage of the possession of a fictitious claim against him : Storrs *v.* Scougale, 48 Mich., 888.

A dissolute spendthrift of 25 gave a mortgage on all the real estate to which he was entitled as his father's heir, to a man who knew all about the circumstances, to secure the payment of an alleged loan of $5,000, for which he gave his note, and which was made up of the following items : $1,000 in cash; a former due bill of $47 given up ; $199 interest credited, on a previous mortgage ; $110.85 paid as premium upon an insurance policy assigned to the mortgagee ; $556.75 withheld by the latter to pay annual premiums thereafter as they should fall due; and $3,200 as the purchase price of 160 acres of land worth but little more than $1,000, and which the mortgagee required him to buy as a condition of lending him any money, though he had no use for the land and knew nothing about its value. Held, an unconscionable transaction which a court of chancery could not sustain, and that the mortgagor should have leave to reconvey the land, though his mortgage should be held good for the $1,000 paid, the amount of the due-bill, indorsement upon the previous mortgage debt, and the premiums paid upon the insurance policy, with interest from the date of each payment, conditional that the policy be reassigned to the mortgagor : Butler *v.* Duncan, 47 Mich., 94.

Where undue influence is alleged, mental incapacity in connection with proof of influence is a circumstance entitled to more or less weight, according to all the circumstances of the case : Wilson's Appeal, 11 Weekly Notes (Penn.), 333, 39 Leg. Int., 110.

Where a person whose mind is enfeebled by disease or old age, is so placed as to be subjected to the influence of another person, and makes a voluntary disposition of property by gift in favor of such person, the court requires proof of the fact that the donor understood the nature of the act, and that the act was not done through the influence of the donee.

Where it is obvious that a gift made

by such person is intended to operate as a will, it presents an additional reason for imposing upon the donee the burden of showing, convincingly, the validity of the act: Haydock v. Haydock, 34 N. J. Eq., 570.

Against the consequences of mistaken judgment or mere imprudence and folly, on the part of one making a contract, courts can grant no relief. But the acts and contracts of persons who are of weak understanding and who are thereby liable to imposition, will be held void in courts of equity, if the nature of the act or contract justifies the conclusion that the party has not exercised a deliberate judgment, but has been imposed upon, circumvented or overcome by cunning artifice or undue influence: Kilgore v. Cross, 1 McCrary, 144.

A note executed to a bank by a father, to take up two notes of his son on which the names of the father and of others were forged as indorsers, will be cancelled in equity, when it appears that the information of the forgery was suddenly sprung upon the father at a private interview between him and the officers of the bank, one of whom was a lawyer, brought about by the bank, no opportunity being given the father to consult with friends or obtain legal advice, and his state of mind being little short of mental aberration: Coffman v. Lookout Bank, 5 Lea (Tenn.), 232.

Where there is great weakness of mind in a person executing a conveyance of land, arising from age, sickness, or any other cause, though not amounting to absolute disqualification, and the consideration given for the property is grossly inadequate, imposition or undue influence will be inferred, and a court of equity will, upon proper and reasonable application of the injured party, interfere and set the conveyance aside: Moore v. Moore, 56 Cal., 89; Kester v. Bahr, 1 Luz. Leg. Reg. Rep., 262; Haydock v. Haydock, 34 N. J. Eq., 570.

Where the grantor stands in such a relation to the grantee as to be likely to be under her influence, a conveyance may be set aside though no fraud or moral wrong could be imputed to the grantee; and although it is probable, from the circumstances of the case, that if the contents and legal effect of the instrument had been fully explained to the grantor by an independent legal adviser, the grantor would still have executed the deed, though probably with some modifications in the details: Irwin v. Young, 28 Grant's (U.C.) Chy., 511.

See also Lavin v. Lavin, 27 Grant's (U.C.) Chy., 567.

For an article upon "Legal Responsibility in old age," by Dr. George M. Beard, see 2 Medico Legal Papers, 185–235.

See also Wilson v. Mitchell, 12 Weekly Notes (Penn.), 441.

For an article upon "Drunkenness," as affecting testamentary capacity, by Dr. Stephen Rogers, see 2 Medico Leg. Papers, 62–76.

In order to avoid an instrument on account of drunkenness merely, the maker must have been in such a state of drunkenness as not to know what he was doing, or the consequences of his own acts: Hewitt's Appeal, 55 Md., 509; Kahl v. Schoben, 35 N. J. Eq., 461.

See Bell v. Lee, 28 Grant's (U.C.) Chy., 150.

In some cases, undue influence will be inferred from the nature of the transaction alone; and in all cases, a court of equity exercises its benign jurisdiction, to set aside instruments executed between parties, in which one party is so situated as to exercise a controlling influence over the will, conduct and interests of another: Sears v. Schafer, 6 N. Y., 268; Cherbonnier v. Evitts, 56 Md., 295.

Illinois: Anderson v. Irwin, 101 Ills., 411.

Maryland: Cherbonnier v. Evitts, 56 Md., 276, 294.

New Jersey: Haydock v. Haydock, 34 N. J. Eq., 570.

New York: Sears v. Schafer, 6 N. Y., 268.

So insanity: Anderson v. Irwin, 101 Ills., 411.

Undue influence may be found, where any relation of mutual confidence, such as attorney and client, clergyman and parishioner, physician and patient, parent and child, exists between the parties at the time of the transaction.

Attorney and client; principal and agent.

Kansas: Yeomans v. James, 27 Kans., 195.

Maryland: Kerby v. Kerby, 57 Md., 345.

New Jersey: Haydock v. Haydock, 34 N. J. Eq., 570.

Parent and child.

Maryland: Kerby v. Kerby, 57 Md., 345.

Missouri: Miller v. Simonds, 72 Mo., 669.

New York: Coleman v. Phelps, 15 N. Y. Weekly Dig., 483.

A voluntary conveyance by a child to its parent while still under the paternal roof, is presumptively void. The burthen is on the parent to show, in the clearest and most satisfactory manner, that it is in every particular worthy of receiving the sanction of a court of equity: Miller v. Simonds, 72 Mo., 669.

One who places himself in the position of a confidential adviser of a person who seeks his aid to escape from threatened criminal proceedings and to settle charges brought against him, is a trustee, and has the burden of showing good faith in any bargains or transfers which he may meanwhile make with the person who thus relies upon his advice: Storrs v. Scougale, 48 Mich., 388.

The mere relation of father and son does not *per se* create a presumption of fraud or undue influence in a mutual dealing, but may do so when connected with other facts showing inequality or controlling influence: Carpenter v. Soule, 88 N. Y., 256; Corvee v. Cornell, 75 id., 101.

As to the relation of

Uncle and nephew: Held valid: Eakle v. Reynolds, 54 Md., 305.

Successive transfers of property, consisting of mortgages, were procured by a nephew from his uncle within a few days before the latter's death, and while he was in an enfeebled condition. The uncle was 82 years old, had made his home with his nephew, and was said to be estranged from his other near relations. He was a temperate and thrifty bachelor who had little society. The nephew was neither temperate nor thrifty. Held, that as the assignments were made on the donor's death-bed, and in the absence of all near relations except the beneficiary, they were open to suspicion, and on a bill to set them aside, the beneficiary

had the burden of showing their fairness: Duncombe v. Richards, 46 Mich., 166.

Concubinage: Held valid: Hewett's Appeal, 55 Md., 509.

Where a legacy is left to the draftsman of a will who is at the time, and for many years prior thereto has been, the legal adviser of the testator, it rests upon him to establish affirmatively that the testator acted with full knowledge of all the surrounding circumstances, and to prove that the transaction is free from all fraud or undue influence on his part: Post v. Mason, 26 Hun, 187; Matter of Rea, 88 Leg. Int., 420; Cheatham v. Hatcher, 30 Gratt. (Va.), 56.

A person propounding a will prepared by himself, without the assistance of any third person and under which he takes a benefit, is bound to give clear and convincing evidence that the testator knew and approved of the clause under which he takes the benefit; this principle applies even in the case of a near relative of the testator. In the absence of such evidence, probate of that portion of the will may be refused and granted of the remainder: Hegarty v. King, L. R., 7 Ir., 18; Matter of Rea, 88 Leg. Int., 420.

See Wilson v. Mitchell, 12 Weekly Notes (Penn.), 441.

Courts of equity always watch with suspicion, transactions between persons standing in a fiduciary relation to each other, in matters of gift and contract; and although such transactions are not treated as altogether void, yet the burden of proof is upon the party holding the relation, to show that the influence necessarily arising from the confidence thereby reposed has not been abused. And hence it is, that in gifts *inter vivos* between such persons, it is incumbent on the donee to show, that it was the free and voluntary act of the donor.

But there is an obvious difference between a gift, whereby the donor strips himself of the enjoyment of his property while living and a gift by will, which takes effect only from the death of the testator.

The fact that a party is largely benefited by a will prepared by himself, or in the preparation of which he takes an active part, is nothing more than a suspicious circumstance, of more or less weight, according to the facts of each particular case.

Such facts and circumstances are to be considered by the jury in determining the question of fraud : Griffith v. Diffenderffer, 50 Md., 466.

Fraud or undue influence in procuring one legacy in a will does not invalidate other legacies not so procured : Harrison's Appeal, 48 Conn., 202.

Where the issue is as to the fact of undue influence in procuring a will, and it appears that the undue influence was confined to a single legacy in the will, the jury may find under that issue the will void as to that legacy and valid as to the others: Matter of Harrison's Appeal, 48 Conn., 202.

Where a will is assailed on the ground of fraud and undue influence, if it is proposed that the jury shall find whether such fraud and undue influence affect the whole will or certain parts of it only, and what parts, there ought to be a separate issue framed presenting directly that question to the jury: Griffith v. Diffenderffer, 50 Md., 466.

Where an alleged testator is shown by evidence to be weak in mind, whether arising from age, bodily infirmity, great sorrow or other cause tending to produce such weakness, though not sufficient to produce testamentary incapacity, and the person whose advice has been sought and taken, receives a large benefit under the instrument propounded as a will, it must be shown affirmatively that the alleged testator had full understanding of the nature of the disposition contained in it (Trew v. Clarke, 30 P. F. Smith, 170, distinguished) : Boyd v. Boyd, 16 id., 283, followed.

Every man who draws a will under such circumstances as those specified above, is required to prove, affirmatively, all the circumstances connected with the drawing of the will, and must make it appear that the alleged testator was laboring under no mistaken apprehension as to the value of his property and the amount he was giving to his confidential adviser : Cuthbertson's Appeal, 97 Penn. St. R., 163 ; S. P., Wilson's Appeal, 11 Weekly Notes (Penn.), 333–5, 39 Leg. Int., 110.

The fact that one of the parties to a contract is old, and is the grandfather and the employer of the other, does not raise a conclusive presumption of such an inequality between them as imposes upon the latter the burden of proving affirmatively that no deception was practised, no undue influence used, and that all was fair, open, voluntary and well understood. While these relations are, as matter of fact, consistent with weakness and confidence on the one side, and strength and undue influence on the other, this is not necessarily presumable from the relations themselves, and it must be shown in order to impose the burden : Corvee v. Cornell, 75 N. Y., 91.

The influence of a person standing in a fiduciary relation to the testator may lawfully be exerted to obtain a will or legacy, so long as the testator thoroughly understands what he is doing, and is a free agent : Matter of Rea, 38 Leg. Int., 420.

A solicitor prepared a will, by which a large part of the testator's property, real and personal, was given to himself. It appeared that the will was made according to instructions given by the testator, and that the solicitor had not obtained the gifts by any undue influence, misrepresentation, or suppression of fact. Held, reversing the decision of Vice Chancellor Stuart, that the gifts could not be impeached in equity : Hensden v. Weatherill, 2 Eq. R., 783.

See also Wilson v. Mitchell, 12 Week. Notes (Penn.), 441.

A testator, eighty years of age but possessed of mental and physical vigor, left the bulk of his estate to one daughter, whose husband was his confidential adviser, the scrivener of the will, and trustee and co-executor under it : Held, that in the absence of any evidence showing undue influence, or that the testator had not full knowledge of his estate and its disposition, no presumption arose against the validity of the will. Held, further, that there were no facts which, if submitted to a jury, would justify a verdict against the validity of the will : Harrison's Appeal, 12 Weekly Notes (Penn.), 17, 39 Leg. Int., 218 ; Stokes v. Miller, 10 Weekly Notes (Penn.), 241 ; Wilson v. Mitchell, 12 id., 441.

Mere mental weakness will not authorize a court of equity to set aside an executed contract, if such weakness does not amount to inability to comprehend the contract, and is unaccompanied by evidence of imposition or undue influence : Pickerell *v.* Morss, 97 Ills., 226–8.

Illinois : Pickerell *v.* Morss, 97 Ills., 220, 226 and cases cited.

New York : Children's Aid *v.* Loveridge, 70 N. Y, 387 ; Coit *v.* Patchen, 77 id., 533.

If the testator has sufficient intelligence to comprehend the condition of his property, his relations to those who are or may be the objects of his bounty and the scope and meaning of the provisions of his will, and if it is his free act, it will be sustained.

Canada, Upper : Thompson *v.* Torrance, 28 Grant's Chy., 253.

Connecticut : Canada's Appeal, 47 Conn., 450.

Iowa : Webber *v.* Sullivan, 12 N. W. Repr., 319.

Kentucky : 1 Ken. L. J., 412.

New York : Matter of Frank Leslie's Will, 15 N. Y. Weekly Dig., 56, Mem. 27 Hun, 475 ; Dougall *v.* Gates's Will, 14 N. Y. Weekly Dig., 501, Mem. 26 Hun, 670.

Pennsylvania : Wilson *v* Mitchell, 12 Weekly Notes (Penn.), 441 ; Harrison's Appeal, 12 id., 17, 39 Leg. Int., 218 ; Matter of Whittaker's Will, 39 id., 272.

Wisconsin : Matter of Lewis's Will, 51 Wisc., 101.

An instruction to the jury " that if, at the time of executing the deed in question, the grantor had mind to know and comprehend that he was making a deed and thereby conveying the land described in it to his son, and had an object in so doing which he comprehended, then he was of sound mind," is not a correct definition of mental soundness : Schuff *v.* Rawson, 79 Ind., 458.

The weakness of mind shown by vacillation, shiftlessness, improvidence, occasional despondency and a religious hobby, does not in itself render one incompetent in any such sense as to make business dealings with him *prima facie* fraudulent : West *v.* Russell, 48 Michigan, 74.

Influence to be undue, must have induced the testator to reach a wrong conclusion. If the conclusion reached is the result of erroneous conviction engendered in the mind of the testator

on his own motion, it may possibly be that he is of unsound mind ; but it cannot be said undue influence has been exercised : Webber *v.* Sullivan, 12 N. W. Repr., 319, Sup. Ct., Iowa.

Undue influence of that kind which will affect the provisions of a testament, must be such as subjugates the mind of the testator to the will of the person operating upon it, and in order to establish this, proof must be made of some fraud practised, some threats or misrepresentations made, some undue flattery, or some physical or mental coercion employed, so as to destroy the free agency of the testator ; and these influences must be proved to have operated at the very time of making the will : Stokes *v.* Miller, 10 Weekly Notes (Penn.), 241.

Pennsylvania : Stokes *v.* Miller, 10 Weekly Notes, 241.

A party seeking to avoid a will on the ground of undue influence, must show that the testator was subjected to such influence as amounted to a moral coercion.

New York : Children's, etc., *v.* Loveridge, 70 N. Y., 387, 394 ; Coit *v.* Patchen, 77 id., 533 ; Dougall *v.* Gates, 14 Weekly Dig., 502, Mem. 26 Hun, 670.

Pennsylvania : Estate of Woods, 13 Phila., 236.

The opinion of the jury as to the fairness of distribution of an estate, cannot be substituted for the will of the testator : Webber *v.* Sullivan, 12 N. West. Repr., 319, Sup. Ct., Iowa.

When parties, having legal capacity therefor, enter into a contract resting upon a valid consideration, such contract cannot be ignored by the court, simply because it appears unreasonable or absurd that one of the parties should have entered into the arrangement : Barnes *v.* Gragg, 28 Kans., 51.

Where there was no evidence tending to show that the mind of the testator had been "blunted or dimmed" by the use of drugs so as to render him easily influenced, an instruction to this effect is properly refused : Webber *v.* Sullivan, 12 N. West. Repr., 319, Sup. Ct., Iowa.

The burden of proof is on the contestants to establish undue influence ; and the fact that the will is unjust or unreasonable, is not evidence that such influence was exercised: Webber v. Sullivan, 12 N. West. Repr., 819, Sup. Ct., Iowa.

Testamentary capacity is the normal condition of one of full age, and the affirmative is with him who undertakes to call it in question, and this affirmative must be stablished not in a doubtful but in a reasonable manner : Grubbs v. McDonald, 91 Penn. St. R., 236 ; Matter of White's Will, 4 N. Y. Month. Law Bull., 16, Livingston, Surr. Kings Co., and cases cited ; Griffith v. Diffenderffer, 50 Md., 466.

On a bill to set aside a deed for the grantor's incompetency, the burden of proving incompetency is upon the complainant, whose case fails if the evidence is so evenly balanced as to leave the question in doubt : Gibbons v. Dunn, 46 Mich., 146.

Where one who has the burden of showing fair dealing is evasive in his testimony, he increases the burden, and it is no excuse that he was afraid of being entrapped by counsel : Duncombe v. Richards, 46 Mich., 166.

It is not enough, to deny probate to a will, that it does not appear affirmatively that it was read over to or by the testator before he executed it, where it does not also appear that it was *not* read over to or by him then, and it further appears that he was then capable of reading it, and fully understood its contents, which were in accordance with his instructions, and there is no proof of fraud or imposition : Kahl v. Schober, 35 N. J. Eq.,461.

A conclusion that the testator was unduly influenced by his wife, is not justified by the fact that their relations before marriage were of an improper character : Frank Leslie's Will, 15 N. Y. Weekly Dig., 56, Mem. 27 Hun, 475.

Where evidence of undue influence is offered, it must be shown that such influence was exercised at the time of making the will, or it is properly rejected : Webber v. Sullivan, 12 N. W. Repr. 319, Sup. Ct., Iowa.

Where a will is assailed on the ground of false representations instilled into the mind of the testator, it must appear that such representations were made for the purpose of influencing the testator in making his will : Griffith v. Diffenderffer, 50 Md., 466.

To invalidate a will on the ground of undue influence, there must be affirmative proof of the facts from which such influence is to be inferred. It is not sufficient to show that the party benefited by the will had the motive and opportunity to exert such influence. If not proven directly, the circumstances from which it is inferred must be such as to lead justly to that conclusion : Matter of Gibson's Will, 14 Chic. Leg. News, 408, Surrogate Kings Co., N. Y.; Cudney v. Cudney, 60 N. Y., 62.

To set aside a deed made by a married woman on the ground of duress or undue influence, where it appears from the proof that she was a lady of good intelligence and capacity, in full possession of her mental faculties, and the deed shows upon its face that she appeared with her husband before a justice of the peace and solemnly acknowledged it to be her act, requires the clearest and most satisfactory evidence: Linnenkemper v. Kempton, 58 Md., 159.

In the following cases undue influence was held, under all the circumstances, not to be established : Estate of Woods, 13 Phila., 236 ; Matter of Boyer, Id., 255 ; Shaw v. Ball, 55 Iowa, 55.

In the following to have been established: Matter of Thompson, 13 Phila., 403 ; Smith v. Hickenbottom, 57 Iowa, 733.

The burthen of proof is upon one alleging mental incapacity to make a valid contract, unless it is shown that the party contracting was insane *prior* to the date of the contract, when the burthen is shifted, and claiming under the contract must prove that it was executed during a lucid interval : McNett v. Cooper, 13 Fed. Repr., 586.

Declarations and acts of the testator after the execution of a will, claimed to have been obtained by fraud or undue influence, are admissible for the purpose of showing that he did not understand that he had executed it : Canada's Appeal, 47 Conn., 450; Rider v. Miller, 86 N. Y., 507.

Declarations made by parties who afterward become legatees in a will, before the execution thereof, are not admissible to affect the validity of the will : Matter of Ames, 51 Iowa, 596.

The declarations of an executor, who is a legatee and party to the record, is not admissible where other legatees may be affected by the declarations: Matter of Ames, 51 Iowa, 596.

Declarations of a legatee made after the execution of the will, tending to show undue influence in procuring it, are not admissible to affect its validity: Matter of Ames, 51 Iowa, 596.

The contrary has been held in New York: Horn v. Pullman, 10 Hun, 471, 72 N. Y., 270.

On the issues whether an instrument offered for probate as a will was executed when the testator was of sound and disposing mind, whether it had been revoked by the testator, and whether he was unduly influenced to revoke it, evidence was admitted of the declarations of the testator made after he erased his signature to the will, to the effect that a certain person (through whose influence, it was contended, that the will was revoked) told him to erase his name, and that he felt he had to do as this person said. The jury were instructed that these declarations were not evidence to prove facts, but to show the condition of the testator's mind at the time, and what his testamentary capacity was. The jury found in favor of the will, and that it had not been revoked. Held, that the party objecting to the will had no ground of exception : May v. Bradlee, 127 Mass., 414.

Any evidence which tends to prove the precise mental condition of the testator, and to place him before the jury just as he was when the will was made, is admissible ; and for this purpose the declarations of a testator may, in some cases, be the most satisfactory proof. It is a common practice to admit such testimony under issues involving testamentary capacity, and upon the same grounds it ought to be received under issues of fraud and undue influence ; provided they are made sufficiently near in time, as to justify a reasonable inference that the mental condition which they are intended to denote, existed at the time of the execution of the will. Declarations made by a testatrix of her testamentary intentions some months before the execution of her will and codicil, and before any improper influences are supposed to have operated upon her, are admissible. Evidence of this character may be offered either to rebut the charges of

fraud and undue influence, by showing that the will is consistent with the long cherished wishes of a testator ; or that it is contrary to well settled convictions of what he thought was a just and proper disposition of his property among others standing in the same natural relation with those benefited by the will. The weight to be given to such testimony is a question for the jury : Griffith v. Diffenderffer, 50 Md., 466.

On the issues whether an instrument offered for probate as a will was executed when the testator was of sound and disposing mind, and whether it had been revoked by the testator through the undue influence of a third person, evidence was admitted to show the condition of the testator's mind at the time of a conversation between the testator and the person, a woman, through whose influence it was contended that the will was revoked, in which the testator said he was going to make a will and leave this person a certain sum, and that that person replied that she wanted the whole or nothing. Held, that the evidence was admissible on both issues : May v. Bradlee, 127 Mass., 414.

Where the declarations of a testator made after the execution of his will, are made so remote as not to constitute a part of the res gestæ, they cannot be offered under issues of fraud and undue influence as independent evidence to prove the charge of fraud, or to show the external acts of undue influence, or attempts to influence the testator to make a will in a particular direction : Griffith v. Diffenderffer, 50 Md., 466.

On a bill to set aside transfers of mortgages made on the grantor's deathbed, and claimed by the transferee to have been made as a gift, testimony that the donor, though shown to be a prudent and sensible man, had confidentially disclosed to inferiors and strangers what he intended to do with his property, can give little support to a suspicious case ; nor can testimony that he had once handed over to the transferee a box of mortgages, saying, " I give you all my personal paoperty," —there being no reason to suppose that he afterwards considered himself divested of the property, or that the supposed donee considered himself owner ;

nor can testimony that after the transfers were made, the donor was heard to say that the donee should have his property when he was done with it: Duncombe v. Richards, 46 Mich., 166.

. Where undue influence is alleged in procuring the execution of a will while the testator was incapacitated by reason of sickness, statements of the testator made a considerable time prior to the execution of the will, to the effect that he intended to make such disposition of his property as was done by the will, are admissible: Dye v. Young, 55 Iowa, 433.

See Kennedy v. Kennedy, 87 Ills., 250; Burlington v. Swanville, 64 Maine, 78.

Evidence of declarations made by a decedent, and tending to show a change of mind in regard to the disposal of his property, and an actual alteration thereof, are admissible in proceedings to contest his will, to corroborate the testimony of a witness as to the existence and contents of a later will, and the rejection of such evidence is irreconcilable with the admission of evidence offered by the proponents to disprove such testimony, and is prejudicial to the contestants: Hope's Appeal, 48 Mich., 518.

Where the contestant of a will produced several witnesses and proposed to prove by them what· decedent, a short time before his death, said and did with reference to his children, and calling for his will demanded it of the party in whose favor it had been made, who refused to produce it, stating that decedent was crazy, and to pay no attention to him: Held, such testimony should have been admitted, as bearing upon the question whether he procured the devise to himself by fraud or undue influence: Matter of Hollingsworth's Will, 12 N. W. Repr., 590, Sup. Ct., Iowa. -

Declarations of a grantor cannot be admitted to impeach his deed, while his declarations in support of it are admissible as against himself or those claiming under him: Kerby v. Kerby, 57 Md., 345.

In determining whether a testator has been induced by undue influence, or fraud, to execute a will, the state of his feelings towards the persons to whom he has given his property may be inquired into, and upon such inquiry his declarations and acts before and after the execution of the will may be proved. Such declarations and acts will have less weight as they are remoter from the time of such execution, but the jury are to determine as to their weight: Canada's Appeal, 47 Conn., 450.

Upon the trial of an action to set aside a will on account of the alleged mental unsoundness of the testator and the use of undue influence, it is not error to exclude evidence of conversations of the testator which do not tend to prove either unsoundness of mind or the exercise of undue influence: Vance v. Vance, 74 Ind., 370.

As bearing upon the issue of undue influence in obtaining a will, it is competent to show that a son, who was the principal legatee, had the whole charge of the decedent's business for several years preceding her decease, had been her confidential adviser and assistant; that he had lived with her; that the other children of the decedent were subject to suspicions in her mind; that the son, for these reasons, had every opportunity for undue influence; that a very large share of her income was used by him in his own interest; that decedent, on some occasions, spoke of her income being eaten up with interest, insurance and taxes; and that on one occasion, at least, a friend, who had called to see the mother at her request, was by the son denied admission: Porter v. Throop, 11 N. W. Repr., 174, 47 Mich., 313.

On a question of undue influence, proof of litigation between the testator and contestant is admissible: Canada's Appeal, 47 Conn., 450.

So, on proof of such fact, the inference may be forcible that the person in whose favor the will was made, used a feeling against the contestant for poisoning the testator's mind against him: Porter v. Throop, 11 N. W. Repr., 174, 47 Mich., 313.

Undue influence over a testator must be satisfactorily established, by other evidence than his declarations, although they are admissible to show the extent and effect of such influence.

The will in this case sustained, but not the codicils, they being held to have been executed while the testator was suffering under senile dementia: Rusling v. Rusling, 35 N. J. Eq., 120.

A commission of lunacy finding one incompetent as of a given date prior to the finding, is competent evidence of such prior incompetency : Rider v. Miller, 86 N. Y., 507 ; Estate of Dyre, 12 Phila., 156.

Though not conclusive : Estate of Dyre, 12 Phila., 156 ; Colegate's Estate, 35 Leg. Int., 90.

On a bill to set aside a conveyance for inadequate consideration, the fact that the land transferred had been held under a tax title only is relevant ; the purpose of the inquiry is to find out how the amount paid compares with the market value of the interest sold : West v. Russell, 48 Mich., 74.

Where the validity of a will was contested on the ground of undue influence and want of testamentary capacity, the caveators proved by a witness that the propounder (surviving wife of testator) was crying while sitting on the bed whereon her deceased husband was lying, and said that the caveators "did not treat her with any respect, and if the will stood, they would treat her like a dog ;" it was held error to exclude the testimony of the propounder in rebuttal, under the circumstances of this case : Gilmore v. Gilmore, 86 N. C., 301.

On the issue whether an instrument offered for probate as a will was executed when the testator was of sound and disposing mind, a medical expert was interrogated, and answered upon a hypothetical case based on the evidence, as to whether the testator was or was not of sound mind, and as to whether he was able to transact the general and ordinary business of life. He was then asked whether, assuming the facts stated to be true, the testator was competent to make a will. Held, that the judge presiding at the trial might properly refuse to allow this question to be put : May v. Bradlee, 127 Mass., 414.

A non-professional witness may be asked whether the acts and declarations of the testator, testified to by such witness, seemed to him rational or irrational.

Minnesota : Pinney's Will, 27 Minn., 280.

New York: Rider v. Miller, 86 N.Y., 507 ; Matter of Ross, 87 Id., 514.

The examination of non-professional witnesses must be limited to their con-clusion from the facts to which they have testified ; they may not express their opinions on the general question whether the mind of the testator was sound or unsound : Matter of Ross, 87 N. Y., 514 ; Eckler v. Eckler, 14 N. Y. Weekly Dig., 218, Mem. 26 Hun, 391 ; Pinney's Will, 27 Minn., 280.

In an issue as to whether testamentary capacity has been impaired or destroyed by sickness, a non-expert who was well acquainted with the testator, both in sickness and health, and who had the care of him in sickness, may be allowed to testify that he saw no difference between his mental condition in sickness and in health: Screvin v. Zack, 55 Iowa, 28.

On the issue whether an instrument offered for probate as a will was executed when the testator was of sound and disposing mind, a person who had been the guardian of the testator for many years, while he was under guardianship as an insane person but who was not an expert, was asked by the party propounding the will, whether he had, while guardian, observed anything which led him to infer in his own mind that his ward was crazy. The judge allowed the question to be put, with the explanation that the question was, whether the witness ever observed any fact which led him to infer that there was any derangement of intellect : Held, that the party objecting to the will had no ground of exception : May v. Bradlee, 127 Mass., 414.

Where, however, there is an infraction of this rule, the decree will not be reversed, "unless it appears to the appellate court that exceptant was necessarily prejudiced thereby :" Code, § 2545 ; Matter of Ross, 87 N. Y., 514.

It is not the expression of an opinion for a witness to testify, by way of illustrating the imbecility of age, that defendant "talked like a child :" Smith v. Hickenbottom, 57 Iowa, 733.

It has been held, that where the defence of insanity is interposed in behalf of one charged with crime, it is not error to permit the prosecution to ask witnesses, whether expert or lay, whether in their opinion the defendant knew the difference between right and wrong: Guiteau v. United States, 2 Colorado Law Repr., 497, 1 Mackey, 498, 561.

In the following States a non-professional witness may give an opinion as to the sanity or insanity of another, but this can only be done in connection with their statements of the particular conduct and expressions which form the basis of their judgment. Their opinions are not receivable in answer to hypothetical questions, or upon statements of facts deposed to by other witnesses.

Maryland: Kerby v. Kerby, 57 Md., 845.

Mississippi: Wood v. State, 58 Miss., 741.

Missouri: State v. Klinger, 46 Mo., 229 ; State v. Erb, 74 id., 204–5.

Pennsylvania: Dickinson v. Dickinson, 61 Penn. St. Rep., 401 ; First National, etc., v. Wirebach, 12 Weekly Notes (Penn.), 150, 158.

In Michigan, an old acquaintance of the testator may be asked, " Having reference to the extent of her (decedent's property) at the time of making this will, in your opinion, decedent had sufficient mental capacity to take into consideration the state of her property, the amount of it, and the relation of her children to her, so as to be competent to make this will." Also, " From what you know of decedent, from your acquaintance with her from the time you first knew her up to 1875, what could you say about her mental ability to comprehend and understand a disposition of her property, and her ability to make her will to the extent of this paper here"—the will : Porter v. Throop, 11 N. W. Repr., 174, 47 Mich., 813.

Where an acknowledging officer, when summoned to attest the transfer of property procured by the transferee under suspicious circumstances, neglects to carefully investigate the condition of things in the beneficiary's absence, his testimony that the donor seemed to be in full possession of his faculties, is less satisfactory than if he had taken such precaution : Duncombe v. Richards, 46 Mich., 166.

[5 Probate Division, 94.]

Aug. 6, 1879.

94] *SOTTOMAYER, Otherwise DE BARROS, v. DE BARROS (The Queen's Proctor Intervening).

Marriage—Different Domiciles—Lex loci contractus.

The validity of a marriage in England must, though the domicile of one of the parties may be foreign, be decided according to the law of England.

Marriage is based upon the contract of the parties, but is a status arising out of the contract to which each country is entitled to attach its own conditions, both as to its creation and duration.

G. B., a Portuguese, but domiciled in England, married in England I. S., a Portuguese lady, domiciled in Portugal. They were first cousins, and by the law of Portugal first cousins are, except by dispensation from the Pope, incapable of contracting marriage:

Held, by the English Divorce Court, that the marriage was lawful :

Held, also, that ignorance of the parties, as to the effects of Portuguese law upon the validity of the ceremony, could not affect the validity of the marriage.

THE facts of this case and the arguments of counsel are set forth in the judgment.

Inderwick, Q.C., and *Bayford*, appeared for the petitioner.

Sir J. Holker, A.G., *Willis*, Q.C., *Gorst*, Q.C., and *Jacques*, for the Queen's Proctor.

After the hearing and arguments of counsel the court took time to consider its judgment.

Aug. 6. THE PRESIDENT: In this suit the petitioner prayed that her marriage with the respondent might be declared null and void, on the ground that she and the respondent were natives of Portugal, and at the time of the marriage domiciled in Portugal, that they were natural and lawful first cousins, and that, according to the law of Portugal, first cousins are incapable of contracting marriage on account of consanguinity.

The respondent entered an appearance, but did not file any answer.

The case came on for hearing before Sir R. Phillimore, who directed that the papers should be sent to the Queen's Proctor, in order that he might, under the direction of the Attorney-General, instruct counsel to argue the question whether the petitioner had shown a sufficient ground for a decree of nullity.

*First. By reason of the incapacity of the parties to [95 contract marriage in 1866.

Secondly. By reason of fraud.

Thirdly. By reason of the petitioner's want of intention to contract a marriage, and of her ignorance of the effect of the ceremony.

On the 7th of November, 1876, the Queen's Proctor obtained leave to intervene in the case, and filed pleas.

On the 30th of January, 1877, it was ordered by consent of the parties that the questions of law referred to the Queen's Proctor for argument be heard before the questions of fact, without prejudice to either party.

The case accordingly came on for argument before Sir R. Phillimore on the 17th of March, 1877, when the learned judge stated that he was satisfied that the petitioner perfectly understood she was about to contract a marriage, and that it could not vitiate the marriage that she had an erroneous view of its future consequences, and refused to set it aside on the ground of incapacity, of age, or collusion, or fraud; and further held that the marriage having been contracted in England, and being valid by English law, could not be declared null on the ground that the parties were incapacitated from entering into it by the law of Portugal.

The arguments and judgments will be found reported in 2 P. D., 81. On appeal this judgment was reversed.

The arguments and judgment in the Court of Appeal will be found in 3 P. D., 1. The case was accordingly remitted to this division in order that the questions of fact raised by the Queen's Proctor's pleas should be determined. The Queen's Proctor by these pleas alleged: First. Collusion;

Secondly. That the petitioner and respondent were lawfully married ; Thirdly. That the marriage was not procured by fraud ; Fourthly. That the petitioner intended to, and did contract, a lawful marriage, and was not ignorant of the effect thereof ; Fifthly. That the petitioner and respondent cohabited as man and wife ; Sixthly. That the petitioner and respondent at the time of their marriage were domiciled 96] *in England. It was objected on behalf of the petitioner that the Queen's Proctor was not entitled to intervene on any ground but that of collusion.

This depends on the construction to be put on the 7th section of 23 & 24 Vict. c. 144.

By that section it is enacted that, during the period between the decree *nisi* and the decree absolute, "any person shall be at liberty to show cause why the decree *nisi* should not be made absolute by reason of the same having been obtained by collusion or by reason of material facts not brought before the court."

This part of the section does not apply because no decree *nisi* has been pronounced, but the section proceeds, "and at any time during the progress of the cause, or before the decree *nisi* is made absolute, any person may give information to the Queen's Proctor of any matter material to the due deicsion of the case, who may thereupon take such steps as the Attorney-General may deem necessary, and if from any such information, or otherwise, the Queen's Proctor shall suspect that any parties to the suit are, or have been, acting in collusion for the purpose of obtaining a decree contrary to the justice of the case, he may, under the direction of the Attorney-General, and by leave of the court, intervene in the suit, alleging such case of collusion, and retain counsel, and subpœna witnesses to prove it."

In this case information was given to the Queen's Proctor of matter material to the due decision of the case, amongst other things, that facts tending to show that the parties at the time of the marriage were not domiciled in Portugal, but in England, which were not brought before the court, could be proved ; and he therefore took the directions of the Attorney-General on the subject, and, suspecting that the parties were acting in collusion, he, under the direction of the Attorney-General and by the leave of the court, intervened in the suit. Having so done, the question is whether he may plead anything besides collusion ?

This question was decided in the affirmative in the case of *Dering* v. *Dering* ([1]). There the intervention was after de-

([1]) Law Rep., 1 P. & D., 531.

cree *nisi.* But in the case of *Drummond* v. *Drummond* (¹) the same *question had arisen before the decree *nisi*, [97 and Sir C. Cresswell held that the Queen's Proctor was entitled to plead other pleas besides collusion ; and the same course was allowed in *Boardman* v. *Boardman* (²).

I therefore hold that the Queen's Proctor is entitled to set up other defences in addition to that of collusion, and I proceed to give my findings on the several issues raised by the Queen's Proctor's pleadings.

The first of these is whether the petitioner and respondent are guilty of collusion ?

I am of opinion that this charge is not established.

The second is whether the parties were lawfully married ?

It was not disputed that a ceremony of marriage was gone through which was valid according to the law of England. Whether it was valid according to the law of Portugal, and the effect of its invalidity by that law, will be considered hereafter.

The third issue is whether the marriage was procured by fraud ?

I am of opinion that the evidence which was given before Sir R. Phillimore, as well as that which has been adduced before me, clearly establishes that the marriage was not procured by fraud.

Fourthly, whether the petitioner intended to contract a lawful marriage, or was ignorant of the effect thereof ?

The evidence leaves no doubt on my mind that the petitioner intended to contract a lawful marriage, and was not ignorant of any fact the knowledge of which could be material to the constitution of a valid marriage.

On this point I may refer to the evidence of Mr. Miller, a solicitor who was consulted by the father of the respondent with regard to the marriage before its celebration, and he says that, being struck with the youth of the parties, he saw them on the subject both separately and together, and that he ascertained that they both wished it.

That they were ignorant of the effect of the Portuguese law on the ceremony is most probable, but this ignorance cannot affect the validity of the marriage.

*The fifth issue is whether or not the petitioner and [98 respondent cohabited as husband and wife ?

I do not give any opinion on this question, as I consider it immaterial for the purpose of this cause : *Simonin* v. *Mallac* (³).

The sixth issue is the important one on which the argu-

(¹) 2 Sw. & Tr., 269.   (²) Law Rep., 1 P. & D., 233.   (³) 2 Sw. & Tr., 67.

ments have chiefly turned, namely, whether or not the petitioner and the respondent were, or either of them was, at the time of the marriage domiciled in England?

With regard to the petitioner, as she was a minor at the time of the marriage, her domicile was that of her father. His domicile was Portuguese down to the time of his coming to England in 1858, and I am not satisfied that he had at that time or at any time afterwards mental capacity to change his domicile. I therefore find that the domicile of the petitioner at the time of the marriage was Portuguese.

With regard to the respondent, he was also a minor, and his domicile was therefore the same as his father's, whom I shall call Gonçalo de Barros, though he was sometimes called Caldas. This person formerly carried on the busi of wine grower and exporter in Portugal. In 1858 he came to England, bringing with him the whole of his family. Here he set up in business as a wine merchant and importer. In 1860 he took a lease of a house in Dorset Square for twenty-one years.

On the 31st of July, 1861, an agreement was entered into for the formation of a partnership for twenty years between the brother of Gonçalo de Barros and his sister and sister-in-law, as wine importers and merchants, under the style of Caldas Brothers, of which partnership Gonçalo was to be manager at a salary of £500 per annum, with the option of becoming a partner. The business was to be and was carried on at 9 Catherine Court, St. Swithin's Lane. The firm of Caldas Brothers failed in 1865, but Gonçalo de Barros continued to reside in London, and his son the respondent, being still a minor, set up in the wine business. It is said by one of the witnesses that Gonçalo de Barros lived "privately" in London at the time, by which it would seem to be meant that he followed no business, but it is probable that the business of the son was regarded as the business of both. In 1868, in 99] *the course of some legal proceedings which were instituted in Portugal, Gonçalo de Barros informed his solicitor that his domicile was English, and instructed him to collect evidence in support of this assertion, which was done.

In 1870, Gonçalo de Barros died in London, never having quitted England since his coming here in 1858. Evidence was given that he frequently said during this period that he meant to remain in England; and, on the other hand, the only evidence besides that of the petitioner and her mother offered to rebut the inference to be drawn from the facts above stated was that of one witness, that Gonçalo frequently said that he should return to Portugal "as soon as his affairs were settled." It is evident, however, that this is not the language of a man who has become the manager of a business at a salary of £500 a year; and, even assuming the correctness of the witness' memory, such declarations cannot outweigh the evidence of the facts I have stated: *Doucet* v. *Geoghegan* ('). From these facts I draw the inference that the father of the respondent, at the time he became the manager of the wine business, had adopted England as his place of permanent residence, with the intention of remaining there for an unlimited time; in other words, . that he became domiciled here.

It follows, therefore, that the respondent's domicile was English. There is abundant evidence that the respondent himself, after he came of age, continued to look upon England as the place of his domicile, and this may, perhaps, have some reflex effect in considering which place his father had chosen as his domicile; but as the time of the marriage is the important point in the case, I do not think it necessary to dwell on the evidence of the respondent's subsequent intentions.

The question then arises, What is the law applicable to such a case? It is clear that the judgment which has been already given by the Court of Appeal is not applicable to such a state of facts. The language of the Court of Appeal is explicit. "It was pressed upon us in argument that a decision in favor of the petitioner would lead to many difficulties, if questions should arise as to the validity of a marriage between an English subject and a foreigner, in consequence of prohibitions imposed by the law of the domicile *of the latter. Our opinion in this appeal is con- [100 fined to the case where both the contracting parties are at the time of their marriage domiciled in a country the laws of which prohibit their marriage."

This passage leaves me free to consider whether the marriage of a domiciled Englishman in England, with a woman subject by the law of her domicile to a personal incapacity not recognized by English law, must be declared invalid by the tribunals of this country. Before entering upon this inquiry, I must observe that the Lords Justices appear to have laid down as a principle of law a proposition which was much wider in its terms than was necessary for the determination of the case before them. It is thus expressed: "It is a well recognized principle of law that the question of personal incapacity to enter into any contract is to be decided by the law of domicile;" and again, "As in other contracts, so in

('¹) 9 Ch. D., 441; 26 Eng. R., 226.

that of marriage, personal capacity must depend on the law
of domicile." It is of course competent for the Court of
Appeal to lay down a principle which, if it formed the basis
of a judgment of that court, must, unless it should be disclaimed by the House of Lords, be binding in all future
cases. But I trust that I may be permitted without disre-
spect to say that the doctrine thus laid down has not hitherto been "well recognized." On the contrary, it appears
to me to be a novel principle, for which up to the present
time there has been no English authority. What authority
there is seems to me to be the other way.

Thus in the case of *Male* v. *Roberts* (¹) the contract on
which the defendant was sued was made in Scotland. The
defence was that the plaintiff was an infant. But Lord Eldon held the defence bad, saying, "If the law of Scotland
is that such a contract as the present could not be enforced
against an infant, that should have been given as evidence.
The law of the country where the contract arose must govern
the contract."

Sir E. Simpson, in the case of *Scrimshire* v. *Scrimshire* (²),
when dealing with this subject, says, "This doctrine of trying contracts, especially those of marriage, according to the
laws of the country where they are made, is conformable to
what is laid down in our books, and what is practised in all
civilized countries." And again (p. 413), "These authori-
101] ties fully show *that all contracts are to be considered according to the laws of the country where they are
made. And the practice of civilized countries has been conformable to this doctrine, and by the common consent of
nations has been so received."

This is the view of the subject which is expressed by
Burge, vol. i, c. 4, p. 132, and by Story, Conflict of Laws,
s. 103; and Sir C. Cresswell, in *Simonin* v. *Mallac* says (³):
"In general the personal competency of individuals to contract has been held to depend on the law of the place where
the contract was made." If the English reports do not furnish more authority on the point, it may perhaps be referred
to its not having been questioned.

I cannot but think, therefore, that the learned Lords Justices would not desire to base their judgment on so wide a
proposition as that which they have laid down with reference to the personal capacity to enter into all contracts.
In truth, very many and serious difficulties arise if marriage
be regarded only in the light of a contract. It is indeed
based upon the contract of the parties, but it is a status

(¹) 3 Esp., 163.   (²) 2 Cons., 412   (³) 2 Sw. & Tr., 67.

arising out of a contract to which each country is entitled
to attach its own conditions, both as to its creation and duration.   In some countries no other condition is imposed
than that the parties, being of a certain age and not related
within certain specified degrees, shall have contracted with
each other to become man and wife; but that in these countries marriage is regarded not merely as a contract is clear,
since the parties are not at liberty to rescind it.   In some
countries certain civil formalities are prescribed : in others a
religious sanction is required.   If the subject be regarded
from this point of view, the effect of the recent decision of the
Court of Appeal has only been to define a further condition
imposed by English law, namely, that the parties do not both
belong by domicile to a country the laws of which prohibit
their marriage.   But, as I have already pointed out, that judgment expressly leaves altogether untouched the case of the
marriage of a British subject in England, where the marriage
is lawful, with a person domiciled in a country where the
marriage is prohibited.   With regard to such a marriage, all
the arguments which have hitherto been urged in support
of the larger proposition, that a marriage good by the law
*of the country where solemnized must be deemed   [102
by the tribunals of that country to be valid, irrespective of
the law of the domicile of the parties, remain with undimin-
ished effect.   They cannot, I think, be stated with greater
accuracy and force than by Sir Cresswell Cresswell in *Simonin* v. *Mallac* ('), and as I certainly could not express myself
so well, I shall adopt the language of that learned judge as
my own, without introducing the qualification which the
decision of the Court of Appeal has created.   But before
quoting the language of that very eminent judge, I must observe that the Court of Appeal has distinguished the present
case from that of *Simonin* v. *Mallac* ('), on the ground that
there the incapacity arose from the want of consent of parents, and that the "consent of parents required by the law
of France must be considered a part of the ceremony of marriage."   Certainly Sir C. Cresswell did not base his judgment on that ground.   After observing that a distinction
might be drawn between an absolute and a conditional prohibition, he proceeds : "But taking the decree of the French
court in the suit there instituted as evidence that by the law
of France this marriage was void, we again come to the
broad question, is it to be judged of here by the law of England or the law of France ?   In general the personal competency or incompetency of individuals to contract has been

(¹) 2 Sw. & Tr., 67.

held to depend upon the law of the place where the contract
is made. But it was and is contended that such a rule does
not extend to contracts of marriage, and that parties are
with reference to them bound by the law of their domicile."
Then, after reviewing the authorities, he says: "It is very
remarkable that neither in the writings of jurists, nor in the
arguments of counsel, nor in the judgments delivered in the
courts of justice, is any case quoted or suggestion offered to
establish the proposition that the tribunals of a country
where a marriage has been solemnized in conformity with
the laws of that country, should hold it void because the
parties to the contract were the domiciled subjects of another country where such a contract would not be allowed."
And later on the following passage occurs, which is especially applicable to the present case: "Every nation has a
right to impose on its own subjects restrictions and prohi-
103]   bitions as to entering into marriage *contracts, either
within or without its own territories; and if its subjects
sustain hardships in consequence of those restrictions, their
own nation only must bear the blame. But what right
has one independent nation to call upon any other nation
equally independent to surrender its own laws in order to
give effect to such restrictions and prohibitions? If there
be any such right, it must be found in the law of nations—
that law to which all nations have consented, or to which
they must be presumed to consent for the common benefit
and advantage, and which would be for the common benefit
and advantage in such a case as the present? The observ-
ances of the law of the country where the marriage is celebrated, or of a foreign country? Parties contracting in any
country are to be assumed to know or to take the responsibility of not knowing the law of that country. Now the law
of France [in this case read Portugal] is equally stringent
whether both parties are French or one only. Assume then
that a French subject comes to England and there marries
without consent a subject of any foreign country, by the laws
of which such a marriage would be valid; which law is to
prevail? To which country is an English tribunal to pay the
compliment of adopting its law? As far as the law of nations
is concerned, each must have an equal right to claim respect
for its laws. Both cannot be observed; would it not then be
more just, and therefore more for the interest of all, that the
law of that country should prevail which both are presumed
to know and to agree to be bound by? Again, assume that one
of the parties is English, would not an English subject have
as strong a claim to the benefit of English law as a foreigner

to the benefit of foreign law?''   ''The great importance of
having some one certain rule applicable to all cases, the
difficulty, not to say impossibility of having any rule applicable to all cases, save that the law of the country where a
marriage is solemnized shall, in that country at least, decide whether it is valid or invalid, the absence of any judicial
decision or dictum, or of even any opposite opinion of any
writer of authority on the law of nations, have led us to the
conclusion that we ought not to found our judgment in this
case, on any other rule than the law of England as prevailing amongst English subjects.''

This was the opinion of Sir C. Cresswell, Channell, B.,
and *Keating, J., constituting the full court, whose [104
decisions at that time were only subject to review by the
House of Lords.   The Court of Appeal has indeed, without
alluding to the arguments of these very eminent judges, now
overruled their opinion to some extent.   But Cotton, L.J.,
has expressed his concurrence in their views, so far as is
necessary for the purposes of the present case.   He says,
''No country is bound to recognize the laws of a foreign
state when they work injustice to its own subjects, and this
principle would prevent. the judgment in the present case
being relied on as an authority for setting aside a marriage
between a foreigner and an English subject domiciled in
England, on the ground of any personal incapacity not
recognized by the law of this country.''

Numerous examples may be suggested of the injustice
which might be caused to our own subjects if a marriage were
declared invalid, on the ground that it was forbidden by the
law of the domicile of one of the parties.   It is still the law in
some of the United States that a marriage between a white
person and a ''person of color'' is void.   In some States
the amount of color which will incapacitate is undetermined ;
in North Carolina all are prohibited who are descended from
negro ancestors to the fourth generation inclusive, though
one ancestor of each generation may have been a white person (Pearson on Marriage, sect. 308).   Suppose a woman
domiciled in North Carolina, with such an amount of color
in her blood as would arise from her great grandmother being a negress, should marry in this country, should we be
bound to hold that such a marriage was void?   Or suppose
a priest or monk domiciled in a country where the marriage
of such a person is prohibited were to come to this country
and marry an English woman, could the court be called on
at the instance of the husband to declare that the marriage
was null and to give a legal sanction to his repudiation of

his wife ? Mr. Dicey, in his excellent treatise on Domicile, p. 223, answers these questions in the negative, and places these two cases under this head : "A marriage celebrated in England is not invalid on account of any incapacity of either of the parties, which though enforced by the law of his or her domicile is of a kind to which our courts refuse recognition."

105] *But on what principle are our courts to refuse recognition if not on the basis of our laws? If this guide alone be not taken, it will be free to every judge to indulge his own feelings as to what prohibitions by foreign countries on the capacity to contract a marriage are reasonable. What have we to do, or, to be more accurate, what have English tribunals to do with what may be thought in other countries on such a subject? Reasons may exist elsewhere why colored people and whites should not intermarry, or why first cousins should not. But what distinction can we properly draw between these cases, and why are they not both to be regarded in the same light here, namely, that as they are alike permitted by our laws we cannot recognize their prohibition by the laws of other countries as a reason why we should hold that such marriages cannot be contracted here.

Of the cases cited on the argument the only one which I think necessary to mention is that of *Mette* v. *Mette*('), where Sir C. Cresswell held that a domiciled English subject could not marry his deceased wife's sister at the place of her domicile, although by the law of that place the marriage would be good. But Sir C. Cresswell had himself pointed out in *Simonin* v. *Mallac*(') the difference between controversies arising in the country where the marriage was celebrated and those arising elsewhere ; and his judgment in that case showed that he considered that the law of the place of celebration must prevail before the tribunals of that place.

Before concluding, I wish to direct attention to the statute law on the subject of the marriage of first cousins. The statute of 32 Hen. 8, c. 38, after reciting that the See of Rome had usurped the power of making that unlawful which by God's law was lawful, and the dispensation whereof they always reserved to themselves as in kindred or affinity between cousins german, and all because they would get money by it and keep a reputation for their usurped jurisdiction, enacts that "all and every such marriages as within this Church of England shall be contracted between lawful persons as by this act we declare all persons to be

(') 1 Sw. & Tr., 416.   (') 2 Sw. & Tr., 67.

lawful that be not prohibited by God's law to marry" shall be valid.

*This statute and all the marriage acts which have [106 since been enacted are general in their terms, and therefore applicable to, and bind, all persons within the kingdom. In the weighty language of Lord Mansfield, "the law and legislative government of every dominion equally affects all persons and all property within the limits thereof, and is the rule of decision for all questions which arise there:" *Campbell* v. *Hall* (¹).

Where is the enactment, or what is the principle of English law, which engrafts on this statute the exception that it shall not apply to the marriage in England of cousins german, who by the law of another country were prohibited from marrying without the dispensation of the pope? And, further, I would ask what is the distinction between the prohibition of a marriage, unless the consent of a parent be obtained as in *Simonin* v. *Mallac* (²), and the prohibition of a marriage unless the dispensation of the pope be granted, as in this case? And if there be a distinction, which I am unable to perceive, why is greater value to be attached by the tribunals of this country to the permission of the pope than to that of a father?

For the reasons I have given, I hold that the marriage between the petitioner and the respondent was valid, and I dismiss the petition.

Solicitors for petitioner: *Tamplin & Co.*
The Queen's Proctor.

(¹) Cowp., 208. (²) 2 Sw. & Tr., 67. See *ante*, page 1, 7 note.

[5 Probate Division, 106.]

Nov. 6; Dec. 2, 1879.

JENNER V. FFINCH and Others.

*Will—Revocation by Implication—Parol Evidence of Intention—Execution—
Presence of Testatrix—Costs.*

If upon the face of a testamentary document and the facts known to the testatrix at the time of its execution, it is doubtful whether the testatrix intended altogether to revoke a former will, the court will admit parol evidence to ascertain the intention.

In such a case the doubts having been caused by the condition in which the testatrix had left her testamentary papers, the court allowed the costs of *all par- [107 ties out of the estate, including, besides the costs of the executors propounding the former will, the costs of legatees named in it.

A testatrix signed a document in the presence of two witnesses, who twenty minutes afterwards subscribed the document in an adjoining room. The door was open, but the testatrix was not aware that they were signing:

Held, that the document was not duly executed.

THE plaintiff Constance Elizabeth Jenner propounded a
will dated the 2d of February, 1879, of Emma Selina
Loring, late of No. 2 Sydney Place, Bath, spinster, who
died on the same day. The defendants, Messrs. Ffinch,
Stamp, and Jameson, after pleading (amongst other things)
that the paper writing propounded by the plaintiff is not
testamentary, also propounded a will dated the 10th of
July, 1876, of which the testatrix had appointed them executors. The Rev. Edward H. Loring and others, parties
cited, pleaded that previous to the execution of the will of
the 2d of February, 1879, and on the same day the testatrix executed another document containing the words, "I
wish the will I made destroyed," and that this and the
other document of the same date together constituted the
last will.

The wills of the 10th of July, 1876, and of the 2d of February, 1879 (which are more fully referred to in the judgment), were in many respects inconsistent with each other,
and together disposed of much more property than the testatrix possessed.

The following are the bequests in the will of the 10th of
July, 1876:

All watches, &c., orna-ments of the person, books, manuscripts, carriages, &c., and stable furniture	To cousin Constance E. Jenner.
Plate, &c. . . .	Hector MacNeal.
£5,000	Edw. Henry Loring.
£1,000	Hector MacNeal.
£1,000	Walter Loring MacNeal.
£500	Lisette Caroline Drury.
£500	Alice Mary Master.
£100	Wm. Norman Winckworth.
£200	Amabel E. Skipper.
£200	Ethel Rosine Jukes Keele.
108] *£500	L. A. H. Butcher.
£25	Fanny Reekes.
£25	E. Hunt.
£500	J. F. Halstead.
£1,000	North Devon Infirmary.
£1,500	To augment the stipend of the Vicar of Holy Trinity, Barnstaple.
All my share and interest in which my grandmother, Mrs. Jameson, has a life interest	To my cousin Constance Eliz. Jenner.
Residue . . .	Hector MacNeal.

The following are the bequests in the will of the 2d of February, 1879 :

All watches, &c., ornaments of the person, books, manuscripts, carriages, &c., and stable furniture	Constance E. Jenner.
All Loring plate . .	Hector MacNeal.
£10,000	Edwd. Hy. Loring.
£1,000	Arthur H. Loring.
£1,000	Walter Loring MacNeal.
£500	Lisette Caroline Drury.
£500	Alice Mary Master.
£100	Wm. Norman Winckworth.
£200	Amabel E. Skipper.
£200	Ethel Rosine Jukes Keele.
£100 for life , .	Fanny Reekes.
£400	J. F. Halstead.
All mother's money	Cousin Constance Eliz. Jenner.

The testatrix died possessed of property amounting in value to about £18,000, and it will be seen that by the first will the legacies in money amounted to about £12,000, and by the second will to about £14,000. The document containing the words, "I wish the will I made destroyed," was not attested until shortly after it was signed by the testatrix, and when the witnesses did sign, they did not sign in the actual presence of the testatrix.

*Dr. Deane, Q.C., and *Middleton*, for the plaintiff : [109 The last will is inconsistent with the first. It exhausts all the property, and alters all the legacies in the first will. The first will is therefore revoked by implication : *Dempsey* v. *Lawson* (').

Inderwick, Q.C., and *Searle*, for the defendants : A will duly executed can only be revoked by another will showing within itself an intention to revoke the former. The court cannot look beyond the documents themselves. These two wills are not upon the face of them inconsistent with each other, and must therefore be admitted to probate.

Phillimore, for Loring : The document with the words, "I wish the will I made destroyed," was duly executed. The court will infer from all the circumstances that the document was executed in the presence of the testatrix : *Birks* v. *Birks* (*); Williams on Executors, 8th ed., p. 170.

Lawrence, Q.C., and *Meyrick*, appeared for Messrs. MacNeal ; and *J. F. Skipper*, for other legatees.

Cur. adv. vult.

(') 2 P. D., 98; 20 Eng. R., 620. (*) 4 S. & T., 23.

1879. Dec. 2. THE PRESIDENT: Emma Selina Loring, the deceased in this case, died on the 2d of February, 1879. She had made a will on the 10th of July, 1876, by which she left her watches, jewels, trinkets, ornaments, wearing apparel, books, manuscripts, carriages, harness, and stable furniture to her cousin Constance Elizabeth Jenner; and her plate and plated articles to her cousin Hector MacNeal; and the following legacies: to her cousin E. H. Loring £5,000, to Hector MacNeal £1,000, to her cousin Walter MacNeal £1,000. Then followed a number of pecuniary legacies to friends, servants, and charities, and she bequeathed "all the share and interest which shall belong to me at my death in which my grandmother Mrs. Jameson now has a life interest to my cousin Constance Eliz. Jenner, and she bequeathed the residue of her personal estate to the said Hector MacNeal for his own use and benefit," and she appointed the defendants executors.

In the same house in which the testatrix was lying "sick unto death," her grandmother Mrs Jameson was also resid-
110] ing, but *unable from infirmity to communicate with the testatrix otherwise than by writing. On the 1st of February she wrote a letter to the testatrix, reminding her of the necessity of making her will, and advising certain dispositions "as the MacNeals are so well off." Shortly after this the testatrix dictated to her cousin Constance, the plaintiff, who was assisting in nursing her, the following words: "I wish the will I made destroyed." This having been reduced to writing was signed by the testatrix in the presence of the plaintiff and Carlotte May, the nurse, but they did not attest it at the time. An interval of twenty minutes or half an hour elapsed before the witnesses put their names to the paper, and they did so in the adjoining dressing room, though with the door open, yet out of sight of the testatrix and without her being conscious that they were engaged in any act connected with the paper she had herself signed. In no sense can it be said that the witnesses signed in the presence of the testatrix, and this document is therefore inoperative as a testamentary instrument.

After signing the paper expressing her wish that her will should be destroyed the testatrix again dictated to her cousin, who at her dictation wrote as follows: [The judge here read the document of the 2d of February, 1879.] It will be seen on examination that the legacies made in this paper are some of them to the same persons and for the same amount as in the former will; some for larger amounts and others for smaller, while a few are omitted. This paper was duly executed by the testatrix in the presence of two witnesses who duly attested it. It is clear that this document must be admitted to proof as testamentary, but the question remains whether it is to be admitted to proof alone or together with the will of July, 1876.

It was submitted by counsel for the plaintiff that the case was governed by that of *Dempsey* v. *Lawson* ('), and that it followed from that decision that the paper of the 2d of February, 1879, should alone be admitted to proof.

I do not, however, think that *Dempsey* v. *Lawson* (') is an authority upon the point which is raised for consideration on this occasion. In *Dempsey* v. *Lawson* (') I relied solely on the contents of the second instrument, taken in connection with the *earlier one, and with the facts [111] with reference to which the second was made, and which therefore might afford a guide to the testatrix's meaning.

In the present case, although I think that the will of the 2d of February, 1879, does contain some internal evidence of the intentions of the testatrix that it should be in substitution of the first, I think it desirable, if I can properly do so, to have recourse to external evidence to show whether or not the testatrix intended the last instrument to constitute her sole will, and so by implication to revoke the first. This makes it necessary that I should consider the question which I advisedly left undetermined in *Dempsey* v. *Lawson* ('), whether such external evidence is admissible, and under what circumstances.

By the Wills Act (1 Vict. c. 26, s. 20), it is enacted that "No will or codicil or any part thereof shall be revoked otherwise than aforesaid (i.e., by marriage), or by another will or codicil executed in manner hereinbefore required." This leaves untouched the question what will being duly executed will revoke an earlier one. I think it clear that no express words of revocation are necessary. The authorities appear now to establish that revocation by implication is sufficient. On this point I refer to what I said in *Dempsey* v. *Lawson* ('). The question what instruments are to be admitted to probate, as together or separately constituting the testator's last will, is solely for the Court of Probate as it was formerly for the Ecclesiastical Court.

In considering this question the Prerogative Court did in some circumstances admit parol evidence with respect to the factum of the instrument, in order to investigate *quo animo* the act was done by the testator.

The subject was very fully considered by Sir H. Jenner in

(') 2 P. D., 98; 20 Eng. R., 620.

Thorne v. *Rooke* ('), and he came to the conclusion that
where there is something on the face of the instrument raising doubt or ambiguity as to whether it was intended by
the testator to be in substitution for or addition to a previous
will, the court is justified in having recourse to external
evidence to ascertain the testator's intentions.   In the case
before him the learned judge thought there was no such
112]   doubt or ambiguity, but the cases of *Methuen* v.
Methuen ('), commented on and not disapproved of by Sir
H. Jenner, may be referred to as showing what doubt arising on the face of the instrument, and taken in connection
with the facts known to the testator, will be sufficient to
justify the admission of external evidence.

There the testator having made one codicil, under which
his wife and daughters took certain benefits, after the marriage of one of the daughters made a codicil in which, after
reciting that he had made a provision for this daughter,
proceeded to make dispositions in favor of the wife and
daughters differing from those in the first codicil.   There
was nothing making it absolutely impossible that the testator
meant their disposition to be cumulative, but, as Sir H. Jenner points out, it did appear that if both the codicils had
been acted upon "the property of the deceased would not
have been equal to the payment of all the legacies that had
been given."

It was upon this state of facts that Sir J. Nicholl said:
"The first instrument remains uncancelled and there are no
revocatory words in the second.   It is contended that the
court has no power to inquire further, but the same rules
do not apply in a case relating to the factum of the will
which would apply if the inquiry were concerning the construction of it.   In the Court of Probate the whole question
is one of intention.   The *animus testandi* and the *animus
revocandi* are completely open to investigation in this court.
It is admitted that if there is doubt on the face of the instrument the court may admit parol evidence."

The same learned judge's remarks to the same effect in
Greenough v. *Martin* (') may also be referred to.

Accepting then as correct Sir H. Jenner's limitation of
the power of this court to admit parol evidence to those
cases in which the instrument itself (in connection with the
facts known to the testator) gives rise to doubt, I proceed
to consider in what respect the instrument of the 2d of February, 1879, taken in connection with the state of the testator's family and the nature and extent of her property, gives

(') 2 Curt., 799.   (') 2 Phill., 416.   (') 2 Add., 239, 243.

rise to doubt whether she intended it to be an addition to her previous will.

In the first place there is that element of doubt which was *present in the case of *Methuen* v. *Methuen* (¹), [113 which was pointed out by Sir H. Jenner as justifying parol evidence, namely, that the property of the testatrix would be wholly insufficient to meet the legacies if those given by the last instrument are to be considered cumulative to those given by the first. Can anything be more improbable than that the deceased lady intended to dispose of property substantially twice as much as she possessed? It is not impossible in some circumstances that a testator might contemplate dying worth more than he possessed at the time of making his will, but there is nothing in this case to suggest the probability of this testatrix contemplating such a contingency.

There is also the further fact that some of the dispositions of the instrument of the 2d of February must have been intended as in substitution for and not in addition to the dispositions of the first. I refer especially to the bequest to the present plaintiff in these words, "all my mother's money to my cousin, Constance Elizabeth Jenner." It was not disputed that this includes the same property as the testatrix had by her first will given to the plaintiff under the description of the share and interest, &c., "in which her grandmother had a life interest."

These and some minor matters such as the repeated gift appearing on the face of the instrument of the carriages, books, &c., to the plaintiff, and the gift of "all the Loring plate" to Captain MacNeal, appear to me to give rise to that amount of doubt which justifies the court in having recourse to external evidence, in order to ascertain whether the testator intended this instrument to be an addition to her will or in substitution for it in whole or in part.

But when external evidence is admitted in this case, it becomes clear beyond the possibility of doubt that the testatrix did not intend this document to be an addition to the will, but did intend it to be in substitution for it, for she was under the impression that she had effectually put an end to her will by directing it to be destroyed. The changes in the disposition of the first will effected by the second to the disadvantage of the MacNeal family were no doubt made in consequence of her grandmother's letter. It is clear therefore, when the external facts are looked at, that she

(¹) 2 Phill., 416.

114] *intended the paper of the 2d of February to be her sole will, and by it, and by no other instrument, intended to dispose of her property. I therefore hold that by implication it revoked the will of 1876, and that it alone should be admitted to probate.

The litigation having arisen from the state in which the deceased left her testamentary papers, and the interests of the parties represented at the hearing being different, the costs of all parties must be borne by the estate.

Solicitors for plaintiff: *Collyer-Bristow & Co.*
Solicitors for defendants: *Clarke, Woodcock & Ryland.*
Solicitors for interveners: *Bowlings, Foyer & Horderer;
J. B. C. Huxham; Pike & Son; Barnard & Co.*

See 4 Eng. Rep., 680 note; 28 Amer. R., 595 note.

Whether it is essential to the validity of a will that the testator affix his signature *before* the attesting witnesses affix theirs, *quære?* Matter of Lewis's Will, 51 Wisc., 101, 113.

On the execution of a will, the witness must in some way, either by word or act, be informed by the testator personally, or by some one speaking for him, in his presence, that the document is his will. A mere tacit signing by the testator with attestation by the witnesses is not enough: Estate of Fusilier, 1 Myrick, 40.

There being no room for the signature of the testator or witnesses at the foot of the single page on which a will was written, the testator signed by writing his name transversely along the left-hand margin, near the top and running downwards as far as the commencement of the second line of the will.

The names of the attesting witnesses were written above the will and opposite to portion of the testator's signature: Held to be a good execution: Matter of Collins, L. R., 3 Ir., 241.

The signature of the testator must be at the *end* of the will, and no material clause must follow it: Sisters, etc., *v.* Kelly, 67 N. Y., 410, reversing 7 Hun, 290.

And must be finished: Matter of Gilbert's Will, 1 Pugsley & Burb., 525.

Where a will appears to have received only a partial signature by attesting witness, as, for instance, the first name or initials; and the last name does not definitely appear to have been actually traced (either with ink or pencil), the execution of the will is imperfect, and probate should be denied: Matter of Winslow, 1 Myrick, 124.

Where a witness signed his Christian name only to a will; held, that the will was not duly executed, the evidence showing that the witness by writing his Christian name had not completed his intention to attest. In order to establish the validity of an attestation by a Christian name, it must be shown that such name, designation, or mark, was used by the witness to identify himself, and with a completed intention of thereby attesting the will: McConville *v.* McCreesh, L. R., 3 Ireland, 73.

The testator having determined to modify a previous will, and the instrument prepared conformably to his instructions having been placed before him for execution, in the presence of two witnesses attending at his request, he signed it at the foot, and was seized with death as he was in the act of signing in the margin: Held, that the provision of the statute requiring the attestation of the subscribing witnesses had not been complied with, and that the instrument was not valid as a last will and testament, not being complete at the testator's decease. The testator being still occupied in authenticating the instrument at the moment of the attack; held, under the circumstances, there was no testamentary declaration or rogation of the witnesses.

A will must be perfect at the testator's decease, and if not then a perfect instrument, it cannot take effect. There is no will until all the statutory ceremonies are completed. The mere intention to have them performed is not sufficient, but the intention must be effectuated in fact.

The act of the witnesses is just as essential as the act of the testator. The request to the persons summoned as witnesses is revocatory till acted on. Death revokes it. At the time the witnesses sign, they must sign under a present existing request, and when death intervenes before their signature has been accomplished, they cannot sign after the testator's decease so as to give effect to the instrument.

Whether one dies intestate or testate, is immutably fixed at the instant of death : Vernam v. Spencer, 3 Bradford, 16.

A subscribing witness is, either (1) one, who being present at the execution of the instrument, at that time, and at the request of the party, attaches his signature to it; or, (2) one who, though not present at the execution of the instrument, yet subsequently in the presence of the party, who acknowledging the signature request him to sign, affixes his signature to it. But one, though present at the execution of the instrument and a witness of the signature, does not become a subscribing witness by subsequently affixing his signature to it, of his own motion, and in the absence of and without request on the part of the party : Huston v. Ticknor, 10 Am. Rec., 659.

The execution of a will is to be judged of by the law as it stood at the time of its *execution*. Where the statute at that time required that it should be executed in the presence of two witnesses, it required two witnesses *then* competent. If one was then incompetent and continued so till her death, the estate passes to the heirs, and cannot be divested by subsequent legislation before probate : Camp v. Stark, 81 Penn. St. (Sup.), 235.

The attestation of a will is sufficiently proved if it be shown to have been subscribed by the witnesses in the conscious presence of the testator. No formal request need be proved : Matter of Allen's Will, 25 Minn., 39.

After the will was signed by the testator, who was sitting up in bed, in a small bedroom, it was taken into an adjoining room, placed on a table and there subscribed by the witnesses, the door between the rooms being open, and the table so situated that the testator could see the witnesses subscribing, if he chose to do so, without materially changing his position: Held, that this was a subscription in the testator's presence : Will of Meurer, 44 Wisc., 393, 28 Amer., 591 ; Amber v. Weishar, 74 Ills., 110; Matter of Allen's Will, 25 Minn., 39.

See Butler v. Benson, 1 Barb., 527.

See cases cited by Mr. Stewart in note, 31 N. J. Eq., 242.

Otherwise where, though a door was partly open, the testator could not see the subscribing witnesses sign : Mandeville v. Parker, 31 N. J. Eq., 242, and Mr. Stewart's note ; Matter of Downie's Will, 42 Wisc., 66 ; Doe v. Therrean, 1 Pugsley & Burb., 389 ; Ruddon v. McDonald, 1 Bradf., 352.

But see, in New York, Lyon v. Smith, 11 Barb., 124.

Where the subscription of the witnesses takes place in a different room from that in which the testator is, he must be proved to have been in a position where he could have seen the witnesses as they subscribed their names : Norton v. Bazett, Deane & Swabey, Ecc. R., 259.

A will signed by the attesting witnesses in the same room where the testatrix lay in bed with the curtains closed, and her back to the attesting witnesses, who deposed to her utter inability to have turned herself so as to have drawn aside the curtains ; held, not to have been signed by the witnesses in the presence of the testatrix : Tribe v. Tribe. 1 Robert. Ecc., 775.

A decedent went into a store to execute his will. His brother James was there, and also Mr. Harrison and Mr. Miller. James said to Harrison in the hearing of the decedent, "My brother has been making his will, and I would like to have you witness it," to which Harrison replied, "All right." The decedent, James and Harrison then went into a small inclosure or desk, with glass around the top, so that persons inside of it were visible to others in the store. James said to Harrison, "This is my brother's will, I would like to have you witness it," whereupon decedent signed it, and Harrison, who saw him sign it, also signed as a witness. James then stepped out of the inclosure, and going to Miller, who was engaged at a counter about ten feet away, said, "Mr. Miller, Mr. Harrison has been kind enough to witness my brother's will, now I want you to," and then Miller went into the inclosure where decedent remained (Harrison having stepped out to make room for Miller) and signed his name to the will as witness. Before James asked Miller to sign, the latter did not know that decedent was signing his will, although he surmised so, because James had told him, a few weeks before, that his brother was coming there to execute his will, and that he (James) would like him (Miller) and Harrison to witness it. Miller testified that he thinks decedent heard James request him to witness the will. Miller did not see decedent sign, nor hear him acknowledge his signature to the will. Held, that there was no publication of the will by decedent in Miller's presence, and therefore that there was no execution of it in compliance with the statute: Ludlow v. Ludlow, 35 N. J. Eq., 480.

An acknowledgment by the testator of his signature and execution of the will, is equivalent to the actual seeing by the witness of the physical act of subscription: Hoysradt v. Kingman, 22 N. Y., 372; Robinson v. Smith, 13 Abb. Pr., 359; Miller v. Mott, 36 N.Y., 496.

In order to constitute a due acknowledgement of the signature of a will under section 9 of the Wills Act of 1837, it is necessary that the attesting witness should actually see the signature of the testator at the time of the acknowledgment. And *semble*, that though the testator should say "This is my will," or even "My signature is under there," and the witnesses do not actually see the signature, there could be no sufficient acknowledgment: Blake v. Blake, 51 Law Jour. Rep. N.S. (Chy.), 377, approving Hudson v. Parker, 8 Robert. Ecc., 25, and dissenting from Gwillim v. Gwillim, 3 Swabey & Tr., 200; Beckett v. Howe, L. R., 3 P. & Div., 1.

See also Matter of Summers, 2 Robert. Ecc. R., 295.

In *New York*, it is held that where the testator has already subscribed a will, the statute does not require that the subscribing witness should be shown the *signature* of the testator to the will at the time of the acknowledgment of its execution: Willis v. Mott, 36 N. Y., 486.

Where the subscription to a will was not made by the testatrix in the presence of the attesting witnesses, nor either of them; neither was it acknowledged by her to them, or either of them; and to one of the attesting witnesses there was no declaration by the testatrix or any one, in her presence, that the instrument was her will: Held, that the requirements of the statute in respect to execution were neither formally nor substantially complied with: Baker v. Woodbridge, 66 Barb., 261.

Where the testator had affixed his signature to a will, and on producing it asked the witnesses to witness his will, and they signed as such: Held, insufficient; that the testator should have called the attention of the witnesses to the fact that he had signed or subscribed that document, and that it was his will: Matter of Taney, 1 Myrick, 210; Lewis v. Lewis, 11 N. Y., 220; Chaffe v. Baptist, etc., 10 Paige, 85; Sisters, etc., v. Kelly, 67 N. Y., 409.

But see Baskin v. Baskin, 36 N. Y., 418, affirming 48 Barb., 200; Willis v. Mott, 36 N. Y., 486; Haynes v. Haynes, 33 Ohio St. R., 598; Coffin v. Coffin, 23 N. Y., 9.

The deceased came into a store where two persons were, produced a paper, and said: "I have a paper that I want you to sign." One of the persons took the paper and saw what it was and the signature of the deceased. The testator then said: "This is my will: I want you to witness it." Both persons thereupon signed the paper as witnesses under the attestation clause. The deceased then took the paper and said, "I declare this to be my last will and testament," and delivered it to one of the witnesses for safe keeping. At the time when this took place, the paper had the name of the deceased at the end thereof.

Held, that there was no sufficient signing of the will by the deceased in the presence of the witnesses, nor a sufficient acknowledgment to them that he had done so, to satisfy the requirement of the statute, and that the paper was not entitled to be admitted to probate: Mitchell v. Mitchell, 16 Hun, 97, affirmed 77 N. Y., 596, distinguishing Baskin v. Baskin, 36 id., 416.

A testatrix having pointed to her will, which she had previously signed, and expressed her satisfaction at its contents, and by *gestures* intimated that she had signed the same, and that she wished two persons present together to attest the will ; held, to have duly acknowledged her signature: Matter of Davies, 2 Robt. Ecc. Rep., 337.

Testator came, with his will in his pocket, to the house of his brother Jeremiah, who lived with his daughter Isabel, and said, "Jeremiah I want you and Belle to witness my will." He then asked for a pen and ink, put his hand in his pocket, took out the will and signed it. It was then signed by the brother and daughter under the usual attestation clause, and he then put it in his pocket and carried it away: Held, that there was a sufficient publication of the will : Darling v. Arthur, 22 Hun, 84 ; Turnure v. Turnure, 35 N. J. Eq., 437.

A testator signed his will in the presence of one attesting witness.

Some weeks after, the testator, with that attesting witness, attended at the house of another person, and informed him that the will, which he then produced, had been signed by him and the first witness ; and at the testator's request, this person signed his name as a second attesting witness, in the presence of the testator and the previous attesting witness:

Held, that there was no attestation to satisfy the statute ; and administration granted as upon intestacy : Matter of Lacey, 6 Wy., Webb & A'B. (Ins., Ecc. & Mat.), 44.

A testator who is so blind that he can do little more than distinguish night from day, is capable of acknowledging his signature to his will: Matter of Mullen, Irish Rep., 5 Eq., 309.

A request to sign as witnesses may be communicated by signs, or implied from the acts of the parties : Hutchings v. Cochrane, 2 Bradf., 295 ; Obenwaelder v. Schorr, 8 Mo. App., 458; Turnure v. Turnure, 35 N. J. Eq., 437.

No formal attesting clause is necessary. The request to sign as a subscribing witness need not be a *direct* request : Matter of Crittenden, 1 Myr-

ick, 50, 54; Obenwaelder v. Schorr, 8 Mo. App., 458.

Where all the circumstances show the design of the testator to execute his will, his knowledge of the character of the instrument, and the purpose for which the witnesses attend, his signing the instrument, and acknowledging it to be his will, his observing the witnesses sign and then taking the executed paper into his own possession without objection or comment, sufficiently establish and imply a request to the attesting witnesses to join in the necessary formalities : Matter of Cochrane's Will, 2 Bradf., 295 ; Turnure v. Turnure, 35 N. J. Eq., 437.

Where a will prepared by the counsel of decedent, pursuant to her directions, was handed to her by one of the subscribing witnesses, who stated that he came "to witness her signing her will," and the testatrix having read it declared it to be her will, signed it, and both witnesses subscribed their names in her presence ; held, that there was sufficient evidence of a *request* to the witnesses to attest the instrument : Matter of Cochrane's Will, 2 Bradf., 295 ; Turnure v. Turnure, 35 N. J. Eq., 437.

A request to a witness to subscribe the will, made by a third person in the hearing of the testator, is, in law, the request of the testator, if he is conscious and does not dissent therefrom : Cheatham v. Hatcher, 30 Gratt. (Va.), 56 ; Etchison v. Etchison, 53 Md., 348 ; Bundy v. McKnight, 48 Ind., 502.

See Kingsley v. Blanchard, 66 Barb., 317.

Though this would not be a proper acknowledgment of a prior signature by the testator : Matter of Summers, 2 Robert. Ecc. R., 295.

Although, when a man is well and strong, a declaration made by a third person in his presence that an instrument is his will, on a request by such person to the witnesses to sign it, may be assumed to be the acts of the testator ; yet, where the testator is at the end of a sickness which has lasted over eleven years ; when he is within a few hours of his death, and very feeble, and able to speak but faintly, such assumption cannot be made, unless his adoption of the acts of such person be clearly proved : Heath v. Cole, 15 Hun, 100.

An attending witness to a will being unable to write, instead of attesting by a mark,' procured another person to write her name, she holding the pen while her name was being written: Held, a good attestation : Bell v. Hughes, L. R., 5 Ir., 407.

One of the witnesses to a will may write the signature of his associate witness to the will when such associate witness is unable to write, and may then write his own name as a witness that such illiterate witness has attested the execution of the will by his mark ; Matter of Derry, 1 Myrick, 202.

In *Canada*, when a will is subscribed by two witnesses in the presence of the testator, such subscription is valid, though not in the presence of *each other :* Crawford v. Curragh, 15 U. C. Com. Pl., 55.

So in *Ireland :* Sullivan v. Sullivan, L. R., 3 Ir., 299.

In *New York :* Hoysradt v. Kingman, 22 N. Y., 372 ; Willis v. Mott, 36 id., 486.

The positive evidence of one witness that a will was properly executed will not be overcome by the non-recollection of the other : Morris v. Porter, 52 How. Pr., 1, 5.

Mere failure of memory on the part of the subscribing witnesses will not defeat a will if the attestation clause and other circumstances are sufficient to prove its execution: Rugg v. Rugg, 21 Hun, 383, 10 N. Y. Weekly Dig., 401 ; Will of Meurer, 44 Wisc., 393 ; Morris v. Porter, 52 How. Pr., 1 ; Remsen v. Brinckerhoff, 26 Wend., 325 ; Haynes v. Haynes, 33 Ohio St. R., 598 ; Abbott v. Abbott, 41 Mich., 540 ; Allaire v. Allaire, 37 N. J. Law, 312, affirmed 39 id., 113 ; Young v. Bonner, 27 Gratt. (Va.), 96 ; Settle v. Aikman, 28 U. C. Q. B., 337 ; Crawford v. Curragh, 15 U. C. Com. Pl., 55 ; Brinchley v. Still, 2 Robert. Ecc., 162 ; Matter of Lewis's Will, 51 Wisc., 113 ; Ela v. Edwards, 16 Gray, 9 ; Webb v. Dye, 18 W. Va., 376.

Though the due execution of a will cannot be assumed in the face of positive evidence to the contrary or in the absence of all proof on the subject, except perhaps in case of ancient wills, merely because it purports to be the will of the testator, and the attestation is in due form : Haynes v. Haynes, 33 Ohio St. R., 598.

An executor of a will is a competent witness to prove its execution, though not a subscribing witness : Rugg v. Rugg, 83 N. Y., 592, 21 Hun, 383.

The evidence of an attesting witness impeaching a will, though it will not be positively rejected, is to be received with the most scrupulous jealousy : Young v. Barnes, 27 Gratt. (Va.), 96 ; Cheatham v. Hatcher, 30 id., 96 ; Webb v. Dye, 18 W. Va., 376.

See Obenwaelder v. Schorr, 8 Mo. App., 458.

A will appeared attested by two marksmen, both of whom died before it was propounded ; no fourth person was present at its execution. The whole will was in the handwriting of the testator. It was proved that the witnesses were in his employment at the date of the will, and that they were illiterate persons. Probate was granted : Clark v. Clark, L. R., Ir., 306, affirmed 5 id., 47.

Testatrix having duly executed her will under an *assumed* name, subsequently altered the will by erasing that name and signing her true name ; but the witnesses did not subscribe the will as altered. Probate was granted of the will as it originally stood, as the court considered the *assumed* name might be regarded as the mark of the testatrix : Matter of Redding, 2 Robert. Ecc., 339.

Where two papers identical in form and language are each on the same day signed, witnessed and published as the last will of the testator, the second paper does not affect a revocation of the first : both are the same will : Odenwaelder v. Schorr, 8 Mo. App., 458.

It is the general rule that two or more testamentary instruments, executed at the same time, by the same testator, are to be construed together and viewed as one will, and must be admitted to probate as such. Where a will is executed in duplicate, each is a complete will, and it would be unnecessary to admit to probate and record both duplicates. Where the petition for the probate of a will does not properly describe it as having been executed in duplicate, and one of the duplicates is thereupon admitted to probate, the probate is irregular, but will not be revoked for that reason, as the irregularity does not affect the validity of the will, or the competency of the proof thereof : Matter of Crossman's Will, 3 N. Y. Civ. Proc Rep., 65.

[5 Probate Division, 116.]

Feb. 10, 1880.

*_In the Goods of_ BLEWITT, Deceased.   [116

Will—Interlineations—Attestation by Initials.

The initials of a testatrix and the attesting witnesses in the margin of the will opposite interlineations are sufficient to render the interlineations valid.

SARAH BLEWITT, late of No. 43 Chelsham Road, Clap-
ham, in the county of Surrey, widow, died on the 27th of
December, 1879. On the day before her death she executed
her will, and after it had been duly attested two interlineations were made, the one giving an additional legacy and
the other appointing another executor. The testatrix then,
in the presence of the witnesses who had attested the will,
signed her initials in the margin of the will opposite the interlineations, and the witnesses added their initials.

Bayford, for the executors, asked for the direction of the
court as to the interlineations.

S. Stephens, for the legatee, asked for probate with the
interlineations. The statute has been sufficiently complied with : _In the Goods of Wingrove_('); _In the Goods of
Hinds_('); _In the Goods of Amiss_('); _In the Goods of
Christian_(').   _Cur. adv. vult._

Feb. 10. THE PRESIDENT : Two interlineations were introduced into the will after execution and attestation, but
the testatrix signed with her initials in the margin against
these interlineations, and the witnesses subscribed their initials in attestation of this signature of the testatrix. The
Wills Act, s. 21, enacts that "no . . . . interlineation or
other alteration made in any will after the execution thereof
shall be valid . . . . unless such alteration shall be executed in like manner as is required for the execution of
the will, but the will with such alteration as part thereof
shall be deemed to be duly executed if the signature of
*the testator and the subscription of the witnesses be   [117
made in the margin," &c.

The only question, then, is, whether the signature and subscription by initials only are sufficient.

A mark is sufficient though the testator can write : _Baker
v. Dening_(').

Initials, if intended to represent the name, must be

(¹) 15 Jur., 91.   (³) 2 Rob., 117.
(²) 16 Jur., 1161.   (⁴) 2 Rob., 111.
                    (⁵) 8 Ad. & E., 94.

equally good.   The language of the Lord Chancellor in
Hindmarsh v. *Charlton* (¹), seems equally applicable to the
testator's signature as to the witnesses' subscription : " I
will lay down this as to my notion of the law that to make
a valid subscription of a witness there must either be the
name or some mark which is intended to represent the
name ;" and Lord Chelmsford says, "The subscription
must mean such a signature as is descriptive of the witness, whether by a mark or by initials, or by writing the
name in full."

In *Christian's Case* (²) the initials of the witnesses were
held sufficient, although if merely placed to attest the alteration they will not serve as an attestation to the will itself :
Re Martin, deceased (³).

I am therefore of opinion that the interlineations against
which the initials of the testatrix and the witnesses are
placed, should be admitted to proof.

Solicitor for executor : *G. S. Warmington.*
Solicitor for legatee : *R. Hewlett.*

(¹) 8 H. L. C., 160, at p. 167.   (²) 2 Rob., 110 ; S. C., 7 N. C., 265.
          (³) 1 Rob., 712 ; S. C., 6 N. C., 694.

[5 Probate Division, 138.]

March 9, 1880.

138]   *ANSDELL V. ANSDELL, SLEDDALL and CROCKETT.

*Settlements—Variation—Retrospective Operation of Matrimonial Causes
Act, 1878.*

An ante-nuptial settlement having been executed a decree *nisi* was afterwards obtained for dissolution of the marriage of the parties, and before the decree was made
absolute the Matrimonial Causes Act, 1878, was passed, allowing the court, notwithstanding that there are no children of the marriage, to exercise the powers vested in
it by 22 & 23 Vict. c. 61, s. 5 :
Held, that the court had jurisdiction to vary the settlement though there was no
issue of the marriage.

THIS was an application to vary an ante-nuptial settlement.
Prior to the marriage of the petitioner and respondent the
petitioner had settled a policy of insurance upon the respondent, upon the trusts hereinafter referred to in the
judgment.   A decree *nisi* in the suit was pronounced on
the 9th of May, 1878, dissolving the marriage by reason of
the respondent's adultery.   On the 27th of May following
the act, 41 Vict. c. 19 (the Matrimonial Causes Act, 1878),
s. 3 (¹), came into operation, and on the 12th of November
following the decree *nisi* was made absolute.

(¹) This section is set forth in the judgment.

*The usual petition was afterwards filed for vari- [139
ation of the settlement, and the registrar reported that,
assuming the court had the necessary jurisdiction, the respondent's interests under the settlement ought to be extinguished.

March 2. *Middleton*, for the respondent, in objection to
the report: There being no children of the marriage the
court has no jurisdiction in this case under 22 & 23 Vict.
c. 61, s. 5 (¹), and the Matrimonial Causes Act, 1878, gives the
court no power, as the settlement was executed and the suit
commenced before the passing of that act. An act is only
retrospective where it affects practice and procedure and
not rights. At the time of the passing of the latter act the
respondent had a right to the settlement, and the court is
asked to extinguish that right by reason of some offence
committed before the date of the act. The offence must be
subsequent: *Hitchcock* v. *Way* (²); *Charlesworth* v. *Holt* (³).

Inderwick, Q.C., and *Pritchard*, for the petitioner: The
act is remedial, and therefore retrospective in its operation,
unless there is in the act a clear intention to the contrary:
Page v. *Bennett* (⁴); *The Ironsides* (⁵); *Binns* v. *Hey* (⁶);
Maxwell's Construction of Statutes, 201. The words of the
act itself show that a retrospective operation was intended,
as it permits the court to exercise the powers of the previous act.

Cur. adv. vult.

March 9. THE PRESIDENT: This was a suit by a husband for dissolution of marriage. A decree *nisi* was pronounced on the 9th of May, 1878, and this decree was made
absolute on the 12th of November, 1878. The petitioner by
his marriage settlement assigned to trustees a policy on his
own life for £1,000 for the benefit of the wife for her life or
widowhood, and after her death or second marriage without
child or issue of deceased child by the said marriage to the
husband's next of kin, and the petitioner covenanted with
the trustees to keep up the policy. There were no children
*of the marriage. After the dissolution of the mar- [140
riage the petitioner consented to an order being made by the
court that he should pay to the respondent £150 per annum
during their joint lives, so long as she should remain unmarried and lead a chaste life, and the petitioner presented

---

(¹) This section is set forth in the judgment.

(²) 6 Ad. & E., 943.

(³) Law Rep., 9 Ex., 38; 12 Eng. R., 315.

(⁴) 29 L. J. (Ch.), 398.

(⁵) 1 Lush., 458.

(⁶) 1 D. & L., 661.

a petition for the variation of the settlement by extinguishing the interest of the respondent in the policy.

Assuming that I have power to grant the prayer of this
petition, I think it just and reasonable that I should do so,
but it is contended that the court has not such power. This
depends on the construction to be put on the 5th section of
22 & 23 Vict. c. 61, and the 3d section of 41 Vict. c. 19.

By the first of these it is enacted that the court after a
final decree of . . . . dissolution of marriage may inquire
into the existence of ante-nuptial . . . . settlements made
on the parties whose marriage is the subject of the decree,
and may make such orders with reference to the application
of the whole or a portion of the property settled either for
the benefit of the children of the marriage or of their respective parents as to the court shall seem fit.

It was held in the case of *Corrance* v. *Corrance* (¹) that
the court had no power to deal with marriage settlements
under this section, unless there were issue of the marriage
living at the time of the application to the court for alteration of the settlements. If the law had remained unaltered
I must, on the authority of this case, have rejected this petition, because there are no children of the marriage which
has been dissolved, but by the 3d section of the Matrimonial
Causes Act, 1878 (41 Vict. c. 19), which came into operation
on the 27th of May, 1878, it is enacted that " the court may
exercise the powers vested in it by the provisions of s. 5 of
22 & 23 Vict. c. 61, notwithstanding that there are no children of the marriage."

It was contended that this enactment does not give the
court power to deal with this marriage settlement, because
the decree *nisi* was pronounced before the act came into
operation, and that it would be giving a retroactive effect
to the enactment if the prayer of this petition was granted,
141] and that it did not appear *that the section was intended to have a retrospective operation. Several cases
were cited illustrative of the well known maxim referred to
by Lord Coke in 2 Inst., 292, " Nova constitutio futuris for-
mam imponere debet, non præteritis."

Little assistance can be derived from these authorities in
determining in the particular case, whether the Legislature
intended that the new enactment should be operative with
respect to pending litigation. The general rule no doubt is
that the law, as it existed when the action was commenced,
must decide the rights of the parties in the suit, unless the
Legislature expressed a clear intention to vary the relation

(¹) 1 P. & D., 495.

of the litigant parties to each other: *Hitchcock* v. *Way* (¹).
The question in each case must be whether the intention of
the Legislature is clearly manifested. It is a rule in the
construction of statutes that the natural and ordinary meaning must be given to the language of an act of Parliament,
unless it would lead to some manifest absurdity, or injustice
which it cannot be presumed the Legislature intended.
Here the language of the section is peculiar, it does not pur-
port to give a new power, but says that the court may exercise its existing powers notwithstanding the absence of the
conditions on which they had been held to depend. This
has more analogy with a legislative interpretation of the
fifth section, than a "nova constitutio." The court is still
acting under the authority of that section, and I cannot see
that this leads to any injustice to the respondent. But if
the coming into operation of the third section of the later
act is to be regarded as making a new point of departure, it
did not alter the law, applicable to the proceedings which
were then pending against the respondent. These were
solely for dissolution of the marriage, and the new enactment merely enlarges the consequences which might follow
on a future final decree for dissolution, when the time should
arrive for the court to exercise its discretion in determining
what would be fit to be done in the circumstances of the
case. Proceedings for variation of the settlement are totally
distinct from those for the dissolution of the marriage. It
is only after a final decree of dissolution that the court can
be set in motion by a new petition to inquire into the existence of settlements and to order a *different appli- [142
cation of the settled property. In the present case this new
enactment came into force before the final decree. The
court was therefore armed with this enlarged power long
before the present proceedings were commenced or would
have been commenced.

On these grounds I am of opinion that the court is entitled to make the order asked for, and conceiving it to be
fit and just to do so, I confirm the registrar's report and extinguish the respondent's interest in the policy.

Solicitors for petitioner: *Pritchard, Englefield & Co.*
Solicitors for respondent: *Ayrton & Briscoe.*

(¹) 6 Ad. & E., 952.

[5 Probate Division, 142.]

April 6, 1880.

BAKER V. BAKER.

Dissolution of Marriage—Lunatic Petition—Committee.

The lunacy of a husband or wife is not a bar to a suit by the committee for the dissolution of the lunatic's marriage.

Such a suit may be instituted by the committee of the estate of the lunatic.

THIS was a demurrer to a petition by John Alfred Baker, of the City of Bristol Steam Saw Mills proprietor, the committee of the estate of William Baker, a person of unsound mind, so found by inquisition, and of the said William Baker, by the said John Alfred Baker, his guardian.

The petition alleged the marriage of William Baker with Gertrude Blanche Baker, the respondent; their cohabitation; that there had been no issue of the marriage; that the respondent had committed adultery; and that the petition is presented by the leave and under the direction of the right honorable the Lords Justices, and the petition prayed for a dissolution of the marriage and further and other relief.

The respondent, in her answer, denied the adultery, and alleged: 2. That the petitioner is not parmanently insane. 3. That the petition is bad in substance.

The points for argument were:

1. That the petition does not allege that the petitioner is permanently insane, nor that there is no prospect of his recovering within a reasonable time.

143]   *2. That it is not competent to the petitioner during his lunacy to present a petition to this court for a dissolution of his marriage, and that the court cannot proceed to hear and determine the matters alleged, or to pronounce a decree of dissolution of marriage thereon.

March 6.   *Dr. Deane*, Q.C., and *Bayford*, in support of the demurrer: *Mordaunt v. Moncrieff* (¹) does not apply. That was the case of a lunatic respondent.   In *Woodgate v. Taylor* (²), as appears by the note to the case reported in 30 Law Journal, P. & M., 197, the Lords Justices were of opinion that it was not proper for the committee of a lunatic to petition for a dissolution of the marriage, but that the proper remedy was a judicial separation. *Bawden v. Bawden* (³) also do

(¹) Law Rep., 2 P. & D., 112; S. C., on appeal, Law Rep., 2 H. L., Sc., 374; 10 Eng. R., 57.

(²) 2 Sw. & Tr., 512; 30 L. & J. (P. & M.), 197.

(³) 2 Sw. & Tr., 417; 31 L. J. (P. & M.), 94.

not apply as those were suits for judicial separation. In such cases no affidavit is necessary from the petitioner, but the 41st section of the first Divorce Act imperatively requires it in suits for dissolution of marriage. A man does not necessarily wish for a dissolution of his marriage because his wife has committed adultery. It is a question for him alone whether he so feels the wrong, and he alone ought to decide. Unless there is, which there is not, something in the act which shows that the Legislature intended to give the power to another person to sue on behalf of the husband the court ought not to proceed to give a remedy which is irrevocable. Besides the suit is by the committee of the estate, whereas the committee of the person, if any one, is the proper party to sue.

Inderwick, Q.C., and *Searle*, in support of the petition: In construing the act, there is no difference between a petitioner and respondent, and the same principles are applicable to a suit either for dissolution of marriage or judical separation. If the petitioner can ask for any he can ask for all the relief which the court can give. The words of the statute (s. 27) are quite general and apply to "any husband" and "any wife" resident or domiciled here: *Niboyet* v. *Niboyet* ('). In *Parnell* v. *Parnell* ('), and *Portsmouth* *v. *Portsmouth* ('), the marriage was annulled [144 in a suit in behalf of a lunatic. The question of personal option may well be left to the Lords Justices to consider on behalf of the lunatic. In many cases as, e.g., where there are settlements, a judicial separation would be a very inadequate remedy for a wife's adultery. In *Wells* v. *Cottam* (') a marriage was set aside against the wish of both husband and wife.

Dr. Deane, Q.C., in reply.

Cur. adv. vult.

April 6. THE PRESIDENT : the first named petitioner in this case is the committee of the estate of William Baker, a lunatic, and he prays that the marriage of the lunatic may be dissolved on the ground of his wife's adultery.

The petition alleges that it is presented by the leave and under the direction of the Lords Justices, and that the said William Baker is a person of unsound mind so found by inquisition, and that there is no present prospect of his recovery.

The respondent has denied the adultery, and has also demurred to the petition on the grounds that it does not

(¹) 4 P. D., 22.   (²) 1 Hagg. Eccl., 355.
(³) 2 Hagg. Con., 169 ; S. C., 2 Phillim., 158.   (⁴) 3 Sw. & Tr., 364, 593.

allege that the petitioner (by which is meant the said William Baker) is permanently insane, nor that there is no prospect of his recovering within a reasonable time : and further, that it is not competent for the petitioner during his lunacy (by which is meant the committee during the lunacy of the said William Baker) to present a petition for dissolution of the marriage, and that the court cannot proceed to hear and determine the matter alleged in the petition, or to pronounce a decree of dissolution therein, and lastly, that the action being for personal relief, ought not to be brought by the committee of the estate.

The broad question raised upon this demurrer is, whether it is competent for any one to institute on behalf of a husband, who is incapacitated by insanity from giving his assent to it, a suit for the dissolution of the lunatic's marriage.

This most important question was touched upon, though not decided, in the case of *Mordaunt* v. *Moncrieff* (¹) before 145] the House *of Lords. It now becomes necessary to determine whether or not there is a distinction between the case of a lunatic being made a respondent in a suit for dissolution of marriage, and that of the committee of a lunatic bringing such a suit on the lunatic's behalf—whether or not to the proposition that a lunatic may be sued in such an action it is a corollary that a lunatic may sue.

The learned judges who took part in the case of *Mordaunt* v. *Moncrieff* (¹) in its several stages all agreed that the answer to the question there raised must be sought exclusively in the act of Parliament by which the Divorce Court was established; and the same remark applies with equal force to the point now under consideration. The conflicting views taken on the subject of the application of the statute to the case of a lunatic respondent may be thus summarized. Those who thought that proceedings could not be taken against an insane person argued thus. The Legislature has instituted a new tribunal and new proceedings for the determination of questions not hitherto cognizable by English law. The statute requires the parties or entitles and empowers them to do certain things, partly in the interest of the parties themselves, partly in the interest of the public, which can only be done, or effectually done, by sane persons: yet no provision is made in case of the respondent being insane. The inference to be drawn from this state of things is that the new procedure was not intended to apply to the case of a respondent being a lunatic, and that such a case must be

(¹) Law Rep., 2 H. L., Sc., 374 ; 10 Eng. Rep., 57.
(²) Law Rep., 2 P. & D., 112 ; on appeal, Law Rep., 2 H. L., Sc., 374 ; 10 Eng. R., 57.

left to be dealt with, as it must have been before the act, by application to the House of Lords, which is still open to all persons for whom the act does not afford a remedy. On the other hand, those who hold that the proceedings might be maintained against a lunatic respondent argued thus: true it is the Legislature has instituted a new tribunal and new proceedings for the determination of questions not hitherto cognizable by English law, but this tribunal and these proceedings are not criminal, but civil, and therefore, though no provision is made for the case of a lunatic respondent, by analogy to other civil proceedings, a lunatic respondent is liable to be sued, and the fact that the insanity may preclude an effectual defence being set up must be regarded as a misfortune resulting *from ther espondent's condi- [146 tion, and does not affect the petitioner's right to sue, any more than the death or insanity of a material witness for the defendant.

The latter of these two contentions prevailed in the House of Lords, and I am of course bound, not only by the actual decision, but by the principles on which it proceeded, and if those principles embrace not only the case of a lunatic respondent, but that of a lunatic petitioner, I must apply them in the present instance.   It is remarkable that all those judges who thought that proceedings could be maintained against a lunatic were also of opinion that they might be maintained on behalf of a lunatic; while, on the other hand, those who thought that the proceedings could not be maintained against an insane person were of opinion that the proceedings could not be taken on behalf of such a person.

In *Mordaunt* v. *Moncrieff* (¹) the judges consulted were asked the specific question, whether proceedings for dissolution of a marriage could be instituted or maintained on behalf of a husband who before the proceedings were instituted had become incurably insane.

Mr. Justice Brett says: "There are acts specifically required to be done by a petitioner which make the procedure more clearly in language applicable to the case of an insane petitioner."   I shall for convenience adopt the expression "insane petitioner" used by the learned judge, but it is to be observed that in this and analogous cases the committee of the lunatic is the petitioner.

Mr. Justice Keating says: "Looking to the words of the statute, it is difficult to suppose the Legislature ever contemplated a lunatic being a petitioner;" and, after stating his opinion that suits before the act for nullity or judicial sepa-

(¹) Law Rep., 2 H. L., Sc., 874; 10 Eng. Rep., 57.

ration could have no application to a proceeding for dissolution of marriage, he concludes, "I answer your Lordships'
question, therefore, by saying that a lunatic cannot be a
petitioner for a dissolution of his or her marriage."

In the court below (') the learned judge had expressed his
view more fully on this point, and I refer to his judgment
for an explanation of the grounds of his opinion.

The language of Lord Penzance has a direct application
to the present case, because he argues, from what he con-
147]   ceives to be the *impossibility of distinguishing the
cases of a lunatic petitioner and a lunatic respondent, that
the proceedings under the act could not apply to the latter,
while he admits that if these proceedings can be taken
against a lunatic, they may also be taken on behalf of such
a person.   He says('): "It is to be observed at the outset
that there are no words applicable to the case of lunacy,
either of the petitioner or of the respondent.   If suits were
intended to be entertained by and against such persons, it
would be reasonable to look for some provisions by which
their friends or relations might act for them and protect
their interests.   But there are none such, nor indeed any
special provisions or machinery for the conduct of such suits.
If the statute applies to lunatics at all, it deals with them
in all respects like other persons.   Accordingly, the lunatic
petitioner must present a petition and accompany it by an
affidavit sworn by himself as to the truth of its allegations.
On this s. 41 is express."

On the other hand, the Lord Chief Baron says('): "The
alternative question propounded by your Lordships, whether
a petition for a dissolution of marriage can be preferred on
behalf of a lunatic husband or wife seems to me to involve
many considerations essentially different from those which
arise in the present case; but I think, as a matter of law, a
committee or guardian may lawfully sue by petition under
the act."   And in this opinion Denman, J., and Pollock, B.,
concurred; and it was intimated that Sir Samuel Martin,
who had heard the arguments, but had since retired from
the bench, also shared the opinion of those learned judges.

Turning to the speeches of the learned lords who took part
in the decision of the case, I find that Lord Chelmsford abstained from expressing an opinion on the point now arising
for my determination.   He says: "The alternative question
submitted to the judges, whether proceedings for the dissolution of a marriage can be instituted on behalf of a lunatic

(¹) Law Rep., 2 P. & D., 112.   (²) Law Rep., 2 P. & D., at p. 129.
(³) Law Rep., 2 H. L., Sc., 383; 10 Eng. Rep., 57.

husband or wife is unnecessary to be determined, and as it
involves considerations very different from those which apply to the cases where the respondent is a lunatic, and as
there may be conditions annexed by the act to the presenting a petition for a divorce with which a lunatic may be unable *to comply, I should not like to express any [148
opinion without hearing a fuller argument upon the question than was necessary upon the hearing of this appeal."

Lord Hatherley, however, clearly indicates that his opinion is that proceedings might be taken on behalf of a lunatic petitioner. He says: "Great stress has been laid in the
court below, as well as in some of the opinions delivered in
your Lordships' House, on the supposed incompatibility of
the enactments with the supposition of any principal respondent, or, indeed, any petitioner being a lunatic or a person incapable from insanity of acting on his or her own
behalf. The 41st section, for instance, is pointed out as regards the petitioner, which requires him or her to verify the
petition by affidavit. But be it observed that this section
applies to petitions, in suits for nullity, judicial separation,
or jactitation of marriage, as much as to those for divorce *a
vinculo*. Now the suits for nullity, judicial separation, and
jactitation of marriage had long been cognizable in Ecclesiastical Courts, and suits for nullity as in the *Portsmouth
Case* ('), often proceeded on the insanity of him who applied
for a decree. All these are now transferred to the new court,
and are directed by the 22d section of the act to be conducted as heretofore with regard to procedure, and this 41st
section cannot be taken to have stayed such suits from proceeding by the simple fact of requiring an affidavit, which,
in the *Portsmouth Case* ('), for instance, could not have been
made."

It appears from these quotations that the weight of opinion, though not amounting to judicial decision, largely pre-
ponderates in favor of these proceedings being maintainable.

This being the state of the authorities upon the question,
the duty of determining the question in the first instance
now devolves upon me.

No one can feel more strongly than I do the difficulty of
administering the law of divorce where one of the parties is
insane. One of the peculiarities of that law is, that the public is deemed to be interested in the full disclosures of the
relation of the litigants to one another, and of the conduct
of the complaining party. This was so strongly felt, that as
the first act did not *arm the court with sufficient [149

('¹) 1 Hagg. Eccl., 355.
32 ENG. REP.   24

power to investigate the petitioner's antecedents, a public officer was afterwards authorized to intervene in the proceedings.

To allow the suit to proceed against an insane ,person is an abandonment of the most obvious and, in most cases, the only means of obtaining that information which the Legislature has considered the public welfare requires. With regard to the interests of a respondent, although the proceedings are not criminal, yet the same principles of justice and humanity which introduced into the criminal law the provision that no insane person can be-called upon to answer a charge of having committed a crime when sane, seem equally applicable to proceedings against a respondent, and especially a woman for dissolution of marriage on the ground of adultery. These arguments cannot be more forcibly expressed than they are in the judgment of the Lord Chief Baron, but he and the judges who concurred in his opinion, as well as Lord Hatherley, considered that those arguments must yield to what they deemed the plain provisions of the act of Parliament, that a petitioner should be absolutely entitled to a decree of dissolution of marriage upon proving certain facts, though the respondent might be precluded by mental incapacity from offering any defence.

The difficulties which are presented in the case of a lunatic petitioner are indeed different in character, but they do not appear to me to be more formidable than those to which I have adverted in the case of a lunatic respondent. If the proceedings are in the one case to be put on the same footing as other civil proceedings, I can see no reason why they must not be so in the other. If an insane respondent must defend herself as best she may by means of a guardian *ad litem*, I do not see where the act has indicated that an insane petitioner may not institute a suit for divorce through his committee, as he might sue for the breach of an ordinary contract. The only provision which has been pointed to as having such an effect is the 41st, which requires the petitioner to verify his or her petition by affidavit, so far as he or she is able to do so, but, as Lord Hatherley has pointed out, this section is equally applicable to suits for nullity and judicial separation, which could undoubtedly, before 150] the act of 1857, be *instituted on behalf of a lunatic by his committee. It cannot be supposed that it was intended, by the mere provision that the facts should be verified by the petitioner's affidavit, to prevent for the future such suits being instituted. I entertain no doubt that I have power in such cases to allow the husband's committee, who would in fact be the petitioner on the lunatic's behalf, to make the required affidavit, and that is what has been done in this case without objection on the part of the respondent.

Another argument has been urged to which undoubtedly great moral weight must be allowed, that the right to sue for a divorce is personal and cannot be exercised by any but the individual himself who has been wronged. He might, if he were sane, condone his wife's offence, he might be conscious of matrimonial offences committed by himself which would legally debar him from from obtaining a decree, which his conscience might therefore prevent his asking for. But these arguments are equally applicable to suits for judicial separation, which it is conceded may be maintained on behalf of lunatics. It has however been urged, and for this the great authority of Lord Stowell has been invoked, that in these cases the lunatic, if he recovered his senses, might forgive his wife and take her back, whereas in case of dissolution the mischief, if he should regard it as such, might be irreparable, for his divorced wife might have married some one else, but this argument should rather be addressed to the discretion of the Lords Justices, without whose consent these proceedings cannot be taken, than urged on this occasion, for it is to be observed that proceedings for judicial separation would in some cases be productive of as great a personal hardship to a lunatic husband as a dissolution of his marriage. Though insane on some subjects he might be capable of deriving comfort and advantage from the society of his wife, and might be willing to overlook her frailty in consideration of her kindness to himself or his children. Yet there is only the exercise of the discretion of the Lords Justices to prevent such a husband having an erring, but perhaps still beloved, wife, for ever debarred from access to him. I should add that the probability of a husband forgiving his wife's adultery is not to be regarded as remote. It is a fact of every day occurrence, as the records of this court abundantly show.

*On the other hand it cannot be denied that, if [151 reasons of expediency are to be regarded, great wrong might arise from holding that no proceedings for divorce can be maintained against the adulterous wife of a lunatic. She might be left in possession of property settled on her by her husband, which she and her paramour might enjoy to the exclusion of the lunatic. She might exercise powers of appointment in favor of the paramour or the children of her and his adultery, a spurious offspring might be foisted upon her husband and his family, by which the devolution of estates or titles might be diverted in favor of illegitimate objects. These evils would only be avoided by a dissolution of the marriage.

The consideration which has most pressed upon me in support of the respondent's contention is this: It is well known that it is a part of the religious faith of all Roman Catholics and of many members of the Church of England that the bond of marriage is indissoluble. It is certainly startling that if a member of the Roman Catholic or of the Anglican Church, believing in his conscience that the dissolution of a marriage is unlawful in the sight of God, should have the misfortune to become insane, the committee of his estate might be authorized on account of some question of money to obtain a decree dissolving his marriage. And I do not feel that this consideration is satisfactorily disposed of by the fact that the Lords Justices have a discretion in the matter, for how can they or any human tribunal determine what might be the conscientious conviction of any one on such a subject? But this and all other considerations of a like kind appear to me to be overpowered by the decision of the House of Lords, which seems to amount in substance to this, that as proceedings for divorce are civil, though no provision for the case of lunatics is contained in the act, recourse must be had in such a case to the ordinary forms of civil courts where lunatics are litigants. I am unable to see any distinction between the cases of lunatic petitioners and lunatic respondents, and I adopt the language of Lord Penzance, "I say lunatic petitioners as well as respondents, for there is no distinction made in the act. The words throughout are quite general, and there is no middle ground between the two opposite opinions that these words include lunatics or exclude them all together."

152] *For these reasons I am of opinion that the judgment of the House of Lords is, by necessary implication, binding on me in the present occasion, and I must therefore hold that the insanity of a husband or wife is not a bar to a suit by the committee for the dissolution of the lunatic's marriage.

It only remains for me to consider the minor questions which were raised on the argument.

First, it is said that it is not alleged in the petition that William Baker was incurably insane, or that he will not recover within a reasonable time. But what more can be said on such a subject than that there is no present prospect of his recovery? This is equivalent to saying that there is no present prospect that he will recover within a reasonable or any other time, although it cannot be alleged that it is impossible that he may after some unknown and unascertainable period be restored to reason.

No application has been made to me to postpone the trial for the purpose of being informed whether there is a probability of the lunatic at some future time being sane, but the demurrer is based on the assumption that while he remains insane the suit cannot be maintained. If the court is to hold its hand till all hope is extinguished it must wait till the Greek Kalends.

Another point which the learned counsel for the respondent has taken is, that the right to institute a suit for dissolution of marriage, if it exist at all, belongs not to the committee of the estate but to the committee of the person. I think that this is not a question of law, but for the discretion of the Lords Justices. They probably considered that, as all litigation involves liability to costs, it belonged rather to the keeper of the purse than of the person, to control the proceedings by which they would be incurred.

Solicitors for petitioner: *Thomas White & Sons.*
Solicitors for respondent: *Surr, Gribble & Bunton.*

See 10 Eng. R., 77 note, *post*, p. 471.

At common law marriage with an insane person is a nullity, because of inability to assent: Smith *v.* Smith, 47 Miss., 211 ; Ward *v.* Dulaney, 23 id., 414.

Occasional spells of insanity before marriage, and ultimate permanent insanity several years afterwards, together with evidence of hereditary taint in the family of the defendant, do not warrant a divorce: Smith *v.* Smith, 47 Miss., 211.

By the statutes of Mississippi neither insanity nor idiocy of either party at the time of the marriage is ground for divorce ; but, in addition thereto, the other party must have been at the time of the marriage ignorant of such disability. This, and the provision that the issue of such marriage shall not thereby be bastardized, are the only changes the statute makes in the common law: Smith *v.* Smith, 47 Miss., 211.

Insanity occurring after marriage is not ground for divorce: Wertz *v.* Wertz, 43 Iowa, 534.

Where a bill is filed in the name of an insane wife, against her husband, for a divorce, while she is in close con-finement in another State, beyond the jurisdiction of our courts, it matters not who advised the filing of the bill, she can give no consent to the proceedings, and everything done in her name and the decree of divorce will be invalid, and may be set aside on bill filed by her conservator. Whether there is fraud in fact or not, the law will presume fraud, from the unequal position of the parties, and that will vitiate the decree.

Where a party is unable, in consequence of mental weakness, to protect himself, equity will lend its aid that no injustice may be done. It will protect such party against his own acts, as well as those of others done in his name : Bradford *v.* Abend, 89 Ills., 78.

The fact that both parties were insane when a petition was filed under statute of 1873, c. 371, § 3 (which provided that an absolute divorce may be decreed upon the petition of one divorced *nisi*), is not a conclusive reason for dismissing the petition ; and the fact that the divorce *nisi* was obtained while they were sane, does not make it a matter of course that an absolute divorce should be granted ; and a statement of facts agreed by the guardians, does not free the court from its duty to dispose of the case as public policy and the interests of the parties require: Garnett *v.* Garnett, 114 Mass., 379; S. C., 19 Am. R., 369.

On a bill for divorce, the defence of insanity at the time of the adultery was held not to be established. Depravity of character and abandoned habits, in themselves, are not evidence of insanity: Hill *v.* Hill, 27 N. J. Eq., 214, 216–8.

[5 Probate Division, 153.]

April 22, 1880.

153]   *HARVEY, Otherwise FARNIE, v. FARNIE.

Marriage in England—Divorce in Scotland—Validity.

The English Divorce Court will recognize as valid the decree of a Scotch court dissolving the marriage of domiciled Scotch persons, though the marriage was solemnized in England and the woman was English prior to her marriage.

Semble, in some cases the English Divorce Court might recognize as valid the decrees of a foreign court dissolving the marriages of English persons.

THIS was a petition for declaration of nullity of marriage. The respondent, Henry Brougham Farnie, a domiciled Scotchman, married on the 13th of August, 1861, in England, an English woman. After their marriage they resided in Scotland until 1863, when the wife obtained a decree from a Scotch court for dissolution of the marriage by reason of his adultery. On the 31st of May, 1865, his former wife being still alive, he married the petitioner at All Souls Church, Marylebone. These facts having been proved,

Benjamin, Q.C., *Ffooks,* Q.C., *Inderwick,* Q.C., *Bayford* and *Ffooks,* for the petitioner: The second marriage is null and void. The Scotch court could not annul an English marriage. This was decided in *Lolley's Case* ('). That case has never been overruled, and has been recognized or followed in *Tovey* v. *Lindsay* (*); in *McCarthy* v. *De Caix* (*); in *Birtwhistle* v. *Vardill* (*); *Dolphin* v. *Robins* (*); *Shaw* v. *Gould* (*); *Shaw* v. *The Attorney-General* (*); *Pitt* v. *Pitt* (*). In *Warrender* v. *Warrender* (*) the head-note is wrong, but that case does not apply, as there the marriage was Scotch.

Dr. Deane, Q.C., *Winch* and *Ward,* for the respondent, were not called upon.

THE PRESIDENT: In this case the respondent, a Scotchman by birth and domiciled in Scotland at the time of his 154]   marriage, *married an English woman on the 13th of

(¹) Russ. & Ry., 237.
(²) 1 Dow., 117, 124.
(³) 2 Russ. & My., 614.
(⁴) 2 Cl. & F., 571; 7 Cl. & F., 895.
(⁵) 7 H. L. C., 390, 413, 414, 419.
(⁶) Law Rep., 3 H. L., 55, 70.
(⁷) Law Rep., 2 P. & D., 156.
(⁸) 4 Macq., 627.
(⁹) 2 Cl. & F., 488.

August, 1861, at Cardigan, and immediately after his marriage returned with her to Scotland. He remained domiciled there until after the year 1863, when his wife obtained in a Scotch court a decree for divorce *a vinculo* upon the ground of his adultery. After the dissolution of the marriage he contracted a second marriage with the petitioner in England in the year 1865, and the petitioner now seeks to have it declared that this marriage was null because the respondent had a wife living at the time—in other words, that the Scotch divorce was inoperative at least as to England—and therefore that the first wife must be held by an English court to be the respondent's true wife.

The argument which has been addressed to me amounts to this: that because the marriage was celebrated in England, it was indissoluble in Scotland, or indissoluble except for some cause for which it could have been dissolved in England.

But it must be remembered that for the purposes now under consideration a Scotchman is in precisely the same position as any foreigner, and although when he comes into this country without changing his domicile, he is bound to pay obedience to the English law, and amongst other things, can only contract a marriage here in accordance with its requirements: yet from the moment that he leaves this country and goes back to his own, he owes no further allegiance to the English law, and from that time forward his rights and duties and status can only be regulated by the law of the country of his domicile so long as he remains there.

In this case the respondent married an English woman, but that has no bearing upon this question, because it is clear that the wife acquired the domicile of her husband. This is not a mere fiction; it is the literal and absolute fact. A woman when she marries a man does in the most emphatic manner elect to make his home hers; and, accordingly, when the respondent returned to his native country with his wife they took with them, so to speak, their status of married persons and entirely withdrew themselves from the English jurisdiction; they took with them everything connected with the marriage, except the superfluous evidence of the parish register, and from that time forth while the man remained in Scotland, the place of his domicile, English *law had nothing whatever to do with him. [155 The Scotch court, therefore, was possessed of the entire subject with which it had to deal. Both the man and the woman were there, and their status was, as I have said, transferred to that country, because the marriage was entered into with a view to its obligations being discharged in the Scotch home.

By the law of Scotland a marriage of this kind, although celebrated in England, can be dissolved by the Scotch courts : *Warrender* v. *Warrender* ('). The principles of that decision have been fully expounded by Lord Brougham, at pages 532–35 of his judgment, and need no justification from me. Is this court then bound to recognize the dissolution of the marriage by the Scotch court where the contract was celebrated in England ? From the time when the husband and wife left this country their connection with England ceased. While they remained in the country of the husband's domicile they were subject only to the laws of that country, and a sentence of the court before which the question of dissolving the marriage could alone be brought is like a judgment *in rem*. It was not merely a decision *inter partes*, but operated upon the status itself ; it unmade that status, and rendered the husband—who up to that time had been a married man—an unmarried man, and accordingly into whatever country he might afterwards go he carried with him that status of an unmarried man, which had been constituted by the only court of competent jurisdiction before which it had been brought, or before which it could then be brought.

It is perfectly true that in some cases we do not recognize the status derived from the country of the domicile where such status would interfere with our views of the interests of our country, or our subjects, or of morality and the highest justice. I refer, for example, to the status of slavery, but a decree of divorce has never been put upon any such grounds. It would always have been impossible for us to do so with consistency, not only now since the constitution of this court, but also previously, inasmuch as divorces could even then have been obtained here, although not by an appeal to the ordinary tribunals. Where, as in this case, the divorce is decreed by the court of the country where the 156] *parties were domiciled, we have nothing to do with the grounds upon which the tribunals of that country may proceed in declaring what shall entitle the man or woman to have his or her marriage dissolved.

It appears to me, therefore, upon general principles that we are bound to recognize the change of status brought about by a decree of divorce in another country, where that decree applies to the domiciled subjects of that country. But though these are the general principles which govern

(¹) 2 Cl. & F., 488.

the subject, I might be bound by some particular provision of the municipal law of England to proceed not in accordance with the generally received principles of jurisprudence, but upon some special ground applicable to England alone. That there is no statute law upon the subject is clear, and the only case which has been referred to, as having the effect of compelling me to decide contrary to the principles which it appears to me to govern this subject, is *Lolley's Case* (¹).

It is somewhat remarkable that the exact words of the decision in that case have been lost sight of. The judges held the conviction right, being unanimously of opinion "that no sentence or act of any foreign country or any state could dissolve an English marriage *a vinculo matrimonii*, for grounds on which it was not liable to be dissolved *a vinculo matrimonii* in England." This judgment like every other must be taken with reference to the facts upon which it proceeded, and if so considered amounts to no more than this: that no sentence or act of any foreign country or state could dissolve an English marriage such as the one then before the judges, that is to say, the marriage of two English persons domiciled in England who had not changed their domicile at the time when the aid of the Scotch court was invoked to dissolve the marriage. Putting that construction upon the decision there is nothing to challenge remark, and yet although the language of the resolution is most carefully guarded it has been frequently assumed, and by Lord Brougham particularly, that the judges decided that an English marriage (whatever may be the true meaning of that term) could not be dissolved at all except in England. But the judges said nothing of the kind. They said merely that no foreign court can dissolve an English *marriage [157 for grounds on which it was not liable to be dissolved *a vinculo matrimonii* in England. The judges therefore who framed that sentence did not consider that it could be laid down as law that a marriage could not be dissolved in England at all. It would have been an idle form of words to use if they had not considered that the law of England provided means of obtaining divorce *a vinculo matrimonii*, although not by the ordinary tribunals, yet by the peculiar and exceptional proceeding before the House of Lords. And further their decision leaves open for consideration this most important question, whether an English marriage could not be dissolved by the decree of a foreign court, provided it proceeded only upon such grounds as would have been recognized as sufficient for dissolving the marriage in England.

(¹) Russ. & Ry., 237.

Much may be said in favor of our recognizing in such circumstances the decree of the foreign court. For assuming that we protect the interests of society in England against the dissolution of the marriage of English persons abroad for some cause for which it could not be dissolved here— there seems no reason why, by the comity of nations, we should not recognize the decree of a foreign court which proceeded upon principles in accordance with the English law. Where the parties have not gone abroad for the purpose of defrauding the English law, but, being abroad, have sought only such a remedy as they might have obtained in England, why should not we recognize the sentence of the foreign court? Many illustrations might be given of hardships from acting upon any other principle. These have been so strongly felt that in the American courts it is now established that a wife can acquire a domicile apart from her husband for the purpose of instituting a suit against him for divorce. In such a case, if the substance is looked at and not the form, it does not matter whether it is said that a wife can acquire a separate domicile for that purpose, or that residence short of domicile under certain conditions shall entitle the wife to institute a suit for divorce. But it might equally be a hardship upon a husband that he should be obliged in all cases to go to the place of his domicile to seek a remedy for the wrong done to him abroad. His residence there might be under conditions which would make it practically impossible for him to come back to England. He 158] *might have married a woman in a foreign country, where though not the place of his domicile he might have his only means of subsistence. All the evidence of her guilt might be there, and to require him to come back to England for the purpose of seeking a remedy might be in effect to deny it to him altogether. Such a case is not now before the court. I am merely calling attention to the fact that the qualification of the judges in *Lolley's Case* (¹) points to this, that there may be some instances in which an English marriage may be dissolved by a foreign court if the proceedings be upon a ground for which the *vinculum* might have been dissolved in England.

Lord Brougham, who was counsel in *Lolley's Case* (¹), felt very strongly the hardship of the sentence passed upon his client, and most persons would now agree that it was unduly severe, because the man apparently had acted upon advice that had been given him. And, inasmuch as English persons could go across the border and contract a valid

(¹) Russ. & Ry., 273.

marriage which would have been invalid if contracted in England, he might very well not be able to perceive the distinction between that and going across the barder to get a marriage dissolved, and yet Lolley was sentenced to seven years' transportation because he did not see that distinction. Lord Brougham, therefore, under the influence of his feelings, disparaged this case whenever he had the opportunity, and he also, as it would seem, misconceived it, for he constantly represented it as deciding something more than it did. For instance, in the case of *McCarthy* v. *De Caix* (¹) he says, it is "fully established by the opinion of the twelve judges who solemnly decided it after argument that no proceeding in a foreign court could operate to dissolve or affect a marriage celebrated in England." Instead of using the words the judges had used—"an English marriage"—he uses the expression, "a marriage celebrated in England," and he also leaves out the qualification and represents them to have decided that no proceeding whatsoever in a foreign court could operate to dissolve a marriage contracted in England. He further says that Lord Eldon was under a misapprehension as to *Lolley's Case* (²): "I find," he says, "from the note of what fell from Lord Eldon on the present appeal, that his Lordship *labored under considera-   [159 ble misapprehension as to the facts in *Lolley's Case* (²), he is represented as saying he will not admit that it is the settled law, and that therefore he will not decide whether the marriage was or not prematurely determined by the Danish divorce. His words are, that 'without other assistance I cannot take upon myself to do so.'" It is probable that Lord Eldon at that time, namely, in 1831, was aware of what the real decision was in *Lolley's Case* (²), and that he had freed himself from the error he had been led into by Lord Brougham. For Lord Brougham states (at p. 620) that he had furnished Lord Eldon with a note of *Lolley's Case* (²) when the case of *Tovey* v. *Lindsay* (²) was being argued before the House of Lords. What that note was we see in 1 Dow's Reports, p. 127. It was in these words that the judges "were unanimously of opinion upon the points reserved that a marriage solemnized in England was indissoluble by anything except an act of the Legislature." I have shown that this is incorrect.

In *McCarthy* v. *De Caix* (¹) Lord Brougham took the opportunity of showing that *Lolley's Case* (²) from his point of view was a *reductio ad absurdum*. But it appears from

(¹) 2 Russ. & My., 617.   (²) Russ. & Ry., 273.

(²) 1 Dow., 117, 131.

Lord St. Leonards' observations in the case of *Geils* v. *Geils* (')
that he was counsel in the case of *McCarthy* v. *De Caix* (')
for the successful representative of the husband.   And he
says (p. 262), "My recollection enables me to say that the
question of the effect of the divorce was not argued in that
case, but the Lord Chancellor took up the point, and upon
the strength of *Lolley's Case* ('), he held that an English
marriage could not be dissolved by a Danish court, and that
our law could not recognize a dissolution."   I have not the
pleadings in that case before me, but it is evident that the
bill had been so framed that it did not raise this point which
Lord Brougham took, for if it had necessarily raised the
question it is inconceivable that Lord St. Leonards would
not have taken it.   But be that as it may, it amounts simply
to this, that Lord Brougham upon a misconception of what
the judges had decided in *Lolley's Case* ('), insisted that it
was still law and that it led to these conclusions, which it
160]   was perfectly plain from what he said *in *Warrender* v. *Warrender* (') he thought absurd.   What he really
thought of *Lolley's Case* (') as he understood it, and as it
has been interpreted before me to day, is clear from his
observations in *Warrender* v. *Warrender* (').   Lord Lyndhurst, while he condemned what he termed the dangerous
and precipitate course of Lord Brougham in speaking of the
decision in *Lolley's Case* ('), agreed with Lord Brougham
that the Scotch court had jurisdiction to dissolve a marriage
which had been celebrated in England between a domiciled
Scotchman and an English woman.
    In the case of *Geils* v. *Geils* (') Lord St. Leonards takes
the point which I have already indicated to be the turning
point in this case, for when dealing with the case of a domiciled Scotchman marrying an English woman in England
(which is the case here) he says "The marriage is both an
English and a Scotch marriage" (to which the reporter has
added the scarcely necessary note, "English in point of
celebration and Scotch in point of substance").   It appears
from another report of this case (') that the proceeding in
the Scotch court was for a cause for which the marriage
could not have been dissolved in England, for it was by a
wife for adultery alone.   Adultery only was alleged in the
pleadings, though in some proceedings in England she had
accused him of cruelty also.

(¹) 1 Macq. H. L., 259.   (⁴) 2 Cl. & F., 488.
(²) 2 Russ. & My., 617.   (⁵) 1 Macq., 254, at p. 259.
(³) Russ. & Ry., 273.   (⁶) 20 L. T. (O.S.), 145.

In *Conway* v. *Beasley* (¹) this subject was brought before Dr. Lushington, than whom no one was more competent to form and express an opinion upon it. The decision there was that where a domiciled Englishman marries an English woman in England, if a decree of divorce be pronounced by a Scotch court while the domicile of the parties remains English, it will not be recognized in an English court as a dissolution of the marriage. This was in accordance with *Lolley's Case* (²) as I understand it. But Dr. Lushington expressly refused to treat *Lolley's Case* (²) as an authority for the proposition which has been contended for on behalf of the petitioner. He says (p. 643): "Cases have been cited in which it is alleged that a final decision has been pronounced by a very high authority upon the operation of a Scotch divorce upon *an English marriage—that it [161 has been determined that a marriage celebrated in England cannot be dissolved by the Scotch tribunal—that the contract remains forever indissoluble. The authorities principally relied on for establishing that position are the decisions of the twelve judges in *Lolley's Case* (²), and the decision of the present Lord Chancellor on a very recent occasion. If these authorities sustained to its full extent the doctrine contended for, the court would feel implicitly bound to adopt it; but I must consider whether in *Lolley's Case* (²) it was the intention of these very learned persons to decide a principle of universal operation absolutely and without reference to circumstances, or whether they must not, almost of necessity, be presumed to have confined themselves to the particular circumstances that were then under their consideration." He concludes (p. 653), "My judgment, however, must not be construed to go one step beyond the present case, nor in any manner to touch the case of a divorce *a vinculo* pronounced in Scotland between parties who, though married when domiciled in England, were at the time of such divorce *bona fide* domiciled in Scotland, still less between parties who were only on a casual visit in England at the time of their marriage, but were, both then and at the time of the divorce, *bona fide* domiciled in Scotland."

In *Maghee* v. *McAllister* (³) the question in this cause came before the Irish Lord Chancellor Blackburne. The only difference in the facts was that the wife was an Irish woman married to a domiciled Scotchman in England, but

(¹) 3 Hagg. Eccl., 639.   (²) Russ. & Ry., 273.
(³) 8 Ir. Ch. Rep., 604.

in my judgment the original domicile of the wife is irrelevant upon the ground I have already mentioned. *Maghee
v. McAllister* (¹) is therefore a direct decision on the question
now before the court. The Lord Chancellor, after considering all these cases, Lolley's amongst the rest, says, p. 607:
"The case of *Munro* v. *Munro* (²) establishes that a marriage between a Scotchman and an English woman, though
celebrated out of Scotland, is a Scotch marriage, so as to
have the effect of legitimising children born before the marriage according to the rule of the Scotch law. The opinions
of Lord Brougham and Lord Lyndhurst in *Warrender* v.
162]   *Warrender* (³), *of Lord St. Leonards in *Geils* v.
Geils (⁴), of Dr. Lushington and Mr. Justice Storey, appear
to be that a marriage such as this is a Scotch marriage ;"
and in giving his final judgment, he says (p. 609): "The
first marriage was celebrated in England between an Irish
woman and a Scotchman. He had not changed his domicile
at the time of the marriage. He returned to Scotland with
his wife, and she became a domiciled Scotch woman, and
amenable to the jurisdiction of the Scotch court. The case
of *Warrender* v. *Warrender* (³) is expressly in point ; and,
acting on that case and *Munro* v. *Munro* (²), I am bound to
hold the marriage to have been a Scotch marriage, notwithstanding *Lolley's Case* (⁵). It was held in that case that a
marriage celebrated in England, the parties being both English, could not be dissolved by the Scotch courts. The parties in that case were not domiciled in Scotland, and had
gone there merely for the purpose of getting rid of the marriage."

For the reasons I have given, and on the authorities I
have referred to, I am of opinion that the resolution in
Lolley's Case (⁵) is only applicable where the facts are similar, namely, where the parties, both at the time of the marriage and of the divorce, are domiciled English, and that it
does not apply to a case where the parties are domiciled
Scotch, or where the husband is a domiciled Scotchman, and
during the continuance of that domicile his marriage is dissolved by the competent court of jurisdiction in Scotland.
In my judgment that is a good divorce everywhere, since it
actually changes the status of the man, so that he may afterwards go to any other country in the condition of an unmar-

(¹) 3 Ir. Ch. Rep., 604.   (³) 2 Cl. & F., 488.
(²) 7 Cl. & F., 842.   (⁴) 1 Macq. H. L., 259.
                    (⁵) Russ. & Ry., 237.

ried man, free to contract another marriage. For these reasons my judgment must be in favor of the respondent.

Solicitor for petitioner: *S. A. Tucker.*
Solicitor for respondent: *J. S. Ward.*

Affirmed 6 Probate Division, 35, *post*, p. 489.

[5 Probate Division, 163.]

May 11, 1880.

*BRIGGS v. BRIGGS.   [163

Marriage—Divorce in America—Bigamy.

Two English persons married in England. The husband afterwards went to Kansas, in the United States, and, after an interval of a year, presented a petition and obtained a divorce by reason of his wife's desertion. He then married again. The wife had received no notice of the petition:

Held, that his domicile at the time of the divorce was English; and that, therefore, the divorce was null and void, and he had committed bigamy.

Quære, whether the domicile of the wife is the domicile of the husband, so as to compel her to become subject to the jurisdiction of the tribunals of any country in which the husband may choose to acquire a domicile.

THIS was a petition by Mrs. Sarah Priscilla Briggs for dissolution of marriage with her husband, the respondent, George Mills Briggs, on the ground of his adultery and desertion.

There was no appearance by the respondent.

April 4.   *Searle*, for the petitioner.

The facts and arguments sufficiently appear in the judgment.

Cur. adv. vult.

May 11.   THE PRESIDENT: The petitioner, Sarah Priscilla Briggs, seeks the dissolution of her marriage with the respondent, on the grounds of his desertion, bigamy, and adultery.   The marriage took place at Birmingham in 1862. Both the parties were domiciled English subjects.   In 1868 the respondent, being in difficulties, left this country to avoid his creditors, and went to the United States.   After attempting to establish himself in business at Cleveland, in Ohio, he, as he himself says, at the sight of one of his creditors, fled 2,000 miles farther west, and took up his residence in the State of Kansas, and there, on the 9th of June, 1873, procured a divorce from his wife on the ground of her desertion.   On the 25th of September in the same year he went through a ceremony of marriage with Emma Helsby, with whom he has ever since cohabited.

It is not essential for the petitioner's purpose to establish the charge of desertion, as either the Kansas divorce is valid, in which case her marriage is already dissolved; or it is in-164] valid, and she is *entitled to succeed in this suit on the ground of her husband's bigamy and adultery. In this state of things a decree of this court, whichever way it may be, will satisfy the object she has in view, by defining her position with regard to her husband, and enabling her, if so disposed, to contract a fresh marriage. It is only of importance, on public grounds, that the judgment of the court should be based on principles which may be safely applied to future cases.

The first question which has to be considered is, whether or not the respondent, at the time of the institution of his suit for divorce had acquired a domicile in the State of Kansas. This is undoubtedly a question of difficulty on which opinions may differ.

In the first place, it is clear that the respondent did not voluntarily seek a new home. He left this country through fear of his creditors. The letters to his wife, which have been produced, show that he had not, down to the summer before he commenced proceedings for divorce, abandoned the idea of returning here if, as he hoped, he could pay his debts. Writing in June, 1872, he says: "How dare I return to England unless I could pay my creditors;" and he adds that if he had a sum of money he had left with his wife, and which he requests her to bring to him, he "could soon be a rich man, and could return to England and enjoy his and her declining years in peace and plenty;" and in a later letter he says his real design was to have returned, feeling certain he could make money in America. "If I had not had a strong head and strong mind, my heart would have broken, or I should have gone mad at the prospect, as I now see it, of being probably compelled to end my days here;" and in another letter he says, "I am building up all my hopes on being able to return to England in four or five years, and cannot do so except by practising the most strict economy," and other statements to the same effect occur in his letters. These passages seem strongly to indicate an "animus revertendi."

The onus of proving an intention to abandon the domicile of origin lies on those who assert it. In the present case though the respondent has not entered an appearance to the petition, he has given evidence under a commission issued at the instance of his wife, and he does not allege that he 165] had acquired a Kansas *domicile, he merely swears that he had been resident in Kansas twelve months before March, 1873, when he filed his petition for divorce, and it appears from the proceedings and from the evidence of an expert that this is all that is required by the law of Kansas to give the courts of that state jurisdiction. It is of course possible that after writing the letters I have quoted, and before March, 1873, he had formed the fixed intention of remaining in Kansas, but as I have said it lies on him to prove this, and he has not attempted to do so. In these circumstances it appears to me that it is not established, that at the time of commencing proceedings for divorce he had freed himself from the restrictions of the English law by abandoning his English domicile and acquiring a domicile in Kansas.

If this be a correct view of the facts the law applicable to the subject is abundantly clear. This was an English marriage within the meaning of *Lolley's Case* ('), and it is governed by the resolution of the judges, that "no sentence or act of any foreign country can dissolve an English marriage *a vinculo matrimonii*, for grounds on which it was not liable to be dissolved *a vinculo matrimonii* in England." Here the marriage was dissolved on the sole ground of the desertion of the wife, for which it could not have been dissolved in England. It follows that in the courts of this country, whatever may be the case in Kansas, it must be regarded as a subsisting marriage, and the connection which has since been formed by the respondent by marriage with another woman must be treated here as bigamous and adulterous.

This view of the facts renders it unnecessary for me to determine whether I ought to act upon the doubt expressed by Lord Westbury in *Pitt* v. *Pitt* ('), viz., "whether the domicile of the husband is to be regarded in law as the domicile of the wife, either by construction or by attraction, so as to compel the wife to become subject for the purposes of divorce to the jurisdiction of the tribunals of any country in which the husband may choose to acquire a domicile," a doubt, however, which Lord Kingsdown stated he did not share.

I am also relieved from the necessity of considering the effect of the wife, as she alleges, not having received notice of the *proceedings in the Kansas court, the lax prac- [166 tice of that court having been satisfied by the oath of the husband that he had posted to his wife in England a notice

(') Russ. & Ry., 237, at p. 239.   (') 4 Macq., 640.

. of his petition, and by publication of the notice in a Kansas newspaper during three weeks.

This practice of the Kansas court certainly illustrates in a remarkable manner the injustice which Lord Westbury points out may be done to a wife by allowing the husband to choose his own forum ; Lord Kingsdown's opinion, on the other hand, seems in accordance with the conclusions of foreign, and especially American, jurists on this subject.

For the reasons I have stated I pronounce a decree *nisi*, on the ground of bigamy coupled with adultery, and condemn the respondent in costs.

Solicitors for petitioner : *Letts Brothers*.

[5 Probate Division, 166.]

April 13, 1880.

THE SAVERNAKE (1876, O. 275).

Collision—Practice—Both Ships to blame—Costs of Reference.

An action of damage was brought by the owners of the ship V. against the ship S., and the owners of the S. claimed damages by way of counter-claim against the V. At the hearing of the action the court found both ships to blame for the collision, condemned the owners of each ship in a moiety of the damage sustained by the other, referred the question of damages to the registrar and merchants and made no order as to costs. Afterwards the owners of the S. brought their counter-claim into the registry. No tender was made by the owners of the V., and the registrar struck off less than one-ninth of the amount claimed, but made no recommendation as to the costs of the reference :

The court, on the application of the owners of the S., condemned the owners of the V. in the costs of and incident to the reference.

THIS was an action of damage instituted on behalf of the owners of the steamship Vesuvius against the steamship Savernake. The owners of the Savernake defended the suit, and claimed damages by way of counter-claim against the owners of the Vesuvius, and on the 24th of July, 1876, the court pronounced that both vessels were to blame for the collision in respect of which the action was brought ; condemned the owners of each in a moiety of the losses and damages sustained by the other, referred the question of 167] *damages to the registrar and merchants and made no order as to costs.

In November, 1876, the owners of the Savernake commenced an action in the Chancery Division for the purpose of having their liability for the damage to the Vesuvius, and her cargo, in consequence of the collision, limited under the Merchant Shipping Act, 1862, s. 54, and on the 29th of December, 1877, they paid into court in that action £5,212 3s. 5d.,

being £8 per ton on the tonnage of the Savernake, together
with interest.

On the 8th of May, 1877, the judge of the Court of Admiralty stayed all proceedings in the action in the Admiralty
Division, pending the decision of the action for limitation of
liability in the Chancery Division.

On the 25th of June, 1877, judgment was given in the limitation of liability action in the Chancery Division, when
a declaration limiting the liability of the owners of the
Savernake, as claimed by them, was made, and inquiries
were directed for the purpose of distributing the amount
paid into court amongst those persons who should be found
entitled.

By an order of the Master of the Rolls made in the limitation of liability action on the 19th of July, 1877, it was declared, *inter alia*, that the owners of the Vesuvius were
entitled to prove for the moiety of the loss and damages sustained by them less a moiety of the loss and damage sustained by the owners of the Savernake, and that the inquiries,
directed for the purpose of the distribution of the amount
paid into court, should stand over till the loss and damages
in respect of which the owners of the Savernake were liable
had been assessed in the Admiralty Division.

So much of the last mentioned order, as declared that the
owners of the Vesuvius were entitled to prove for the moiety
of the loss and damage sustained by them, less a moiety of
the damage sustained by the owners of the Savernake, was
reversed by the Court of Appeal on the 22d of March, 1879,
and that court declared that the owners of the Vesuvius
were entitled to prove against the fund in court for the
amount of one moiety of the loss or damage sustained by
their vessel in the collision, and that the amount for which
they were so entitled to prove should be ascertained in the
admiralty registry, as directed by the *order of the   [168
judge of the Admiralty Court made on the 24th of July,
1876 (').

On the 22d of July, 1879, the owners of the Savernake
brought in their counter-claim amounting to £957 6s. into
the admiralty registry. No tender was made by the owners
of the Vesuvius, and on the 10th of November, 1879, the
registrar reported that there was due to the owners of the
Savernake for their moiety of the damages, pronounced for
by the order of the judge of the Court of Admiralty on th

(') See *Chapman* v. *The Royal Netherlands Steam Navigation Co.*, 4 P. D., 157.
It did not appear at the hearing of the
motion that at that time any proceedings
had been instituted in the Admiralty
Registry to ascertain the amount of damage sustained by the Vesuvius.

24th of July, 1876, the sum of £848 13s. together with interest, but made no recommendation as to how the costs of the reference should be borne.

April 13. *Myburgh*, on behalf of the defendants the owners of the Savernake, moved the judge in court to condemn the owners of the Vesuvius in the costs of and incident to the reference.   The court has a discretion as to how the costs of the reference are to be borne, and it is now settled law that that discretion must be exercised without any reference to the nature of the judgment pronounced at the hearing of the action, and solely according to the result of the litigation before the registrar: *The Consett* ('). In the present case the counter-claim brought in by the owners of the Savernake was not an exorbitant one, and no tender was made by the owners of the Vesuvius before the registrar. The discretion of the court ought therefore to be exercised in favor of the owners of the Savernake, and the costs they ask for given to them.

E. C. Clarkson, for the plaintiffs the owners of the Vesuvius, contrà.

SIR ROBERT PHILLIMORE: In this case I must follow the decision of the Court of Appeal in the case of *The Consett* (').   The application will therefore be granted and with costs.

Solicitors for owners of the Vesuvius : *Pritchard & Sons*.
Solicitors for owners of the Savernake : *T. Cooper & Co.*

(¹) 5 P. D., 77.

[5 Probate Division, 169.]

Feb. 19, 1880.

169]   *THE TALCA (1880, R. 32).

Restraint—Bail for safe Return—Jurisdiction.

The court has jurisdiction to arrest a vessel in an action of restraint at the suit of a part owner holding a minority of shares, notwithstanding that the vessel is about to proceed on a voyage approved of by a minority of the part owners, and is being employed under a charter entered into by the ship's husband, appointed to act on behalf of all the owners.

THIS was an action of restraint instituted on behalf of John Nicholas Richardson, the owner of eight sixty-fourth shares in the vessel Talca, against that vessel.   The writ was indorsed as follows: "The plaintiff, as owner of eight sixty-fourth shares in the vessel Talca, being dissatisfied with the management of the said vessel, claims that the owners shall give him a bond in £625 for the value of the plaintiff's said shares in the said vessel." On the 11th of February in this year a warrant to arrest the Talca was applied for in the registry, and an affidavit to lead warrant made by the plaintiff was brought in. From such affidavit it appeared that the plaintiff was the owner of eight sixty-fourth shares in the ship; that on the 16th day of January, 1880, he attended a meeting of the owners of the vessel, when it was resolved by a majority of the owners to send the vessel to the west coast of South America, and he thereupon gave notice that he would not be liable in any way for the debts of the said intended voyage. Subsequently, on the said 16th day of January, he wrote Messrs. L. & G. Tullock, the managers of the vessel, the following letter:

Swansea, January 16, 1880.

Confirming the verbal notice I gave at the meeting of owners to-day, I shall decline for the reasons stated to participate in any way with the projected voyage, or with any outlay in respect thereof, or with any outlay whatever upon the vessel on and from this date ; and, further, I shall require approved security for her safe return, equal to the amount I have at stake in her, before she leaves this port.

On the 29th of January, not having received any reply, he wrote a further letter, which was as follows:

I notice "Talca" is entered outwards for loading, please, therefore, to send me the required security, as per my letter of the 16th inst., to save unpleasant *results. If I do not hear from you by return, I shall consult a solicitor, [170 and you will unnecessarily involve my co-owners in law costs.

An appearance was entered for. the remaining owners of the Talca, and their solicitors, on the 17th of February, gave notice that the judge in court would be moved on behalf of the defendants to order the release of the Talca and to condemn the plaintiff in the costs of the release.

In support of the motion an affidavit was filed, in which one of the members of the firm of Messrs. L. & G. Tullock deposed in substance as follows:

On or about the 10th day of February, 1879, my firm were appointed managers of the said bark, and from that time to the present time I have acted as the manager of the said bark under the appointment aforesaid.

In the month of November last, at a time when the said vessel was about due in London on a voyage from the United States, I, as such manager as aforesaid, procured a freight for the said vessel for a voyage to Valparaiso and back at 22s. 6d. per ton on the outward passage, and 50s. or 55s. according as the ship should discharge in the United Kingdom or on the continent, for the homeward passage. The charterers of the said ship for the said voyage to Valparaiso and back are Messrs. Duncan, Fox & Co., of Liverpool, and formal charterparties were made and signed by them and me for the same voyage on or about the 28th day of the said month of November.

The ship commenced loading the cargo of coal at Swansea, to be taken out to Valparaiso under the outward of the said two charterparties, on or about the 31st day of January last, and on the 11th day of February instant she finished loading the said cargo.

On the same day that the said ship finished loading the said cargo, she was arrested in this action.

I have no interest in the said ship except as manager, and my right to the management of her has not been disputed during the twelve months that I have had the management, either by the above named plaintiff or by any other owner.

The said plaintiff gave me no warning that I was not to charter the said vessel for the voyage in question, or for any other voyage ; and I *bona fide* entered into the said charterparties as the agent or representative of the owners of the said ship generally.

E. C. Clarkson, for the defendants, in support of the motion : In the circumstances of this case the defendants are entitled to have the vessel released without bail. This is not the usual case of a part owner dissenting to the proposed employment of a vessel before any charterparty has been entered into. Here the charter complained of was made more than a month before the plaintiff expressed any dissatisfaction, and was signed by the ship's husband, who had been regularly appointed by the owners generally, and who 171] *in so signing acted as the agent of the plaintiff, as well as of the other part owners.

G. Bruce, for the plaintiff. The right of a part owner holding a minority of shares in a vessel to institute an action of restraint and arrest the vessel is undoubted, and the court is bound, on sufficient proof being adduced that the plaintiff objects to the manner in which the vessel is being employed, to order that security for the safe return of the vessel be given by the remaining part owners in the amount of the plaintiff's interest in the vessel: *The Appollo* ('). This is no hardship on the defendants, for if the court makes the order for security, the plaintiff, though not liable for the expenses of the voyage on which the vessel is engaged, will not be entitled to any share of the profits of the adventure. As soon as the plaintiff knew of the intended employment of the vessel he objected. He cannot be prejudiced by what was done without his knowledge. All the facts of the case are before the court on affidavit, and the plaintiff asks, not only that the motion should be dismissed with costs, but also that the present should be treated as the hearing of the action, and that the court should order that the defendants should give the security for safe return claimed by the writ.

Clarkson, in reply.

SIR ROBERT PHILLIMORE : I am of opinion that on principle a release of the vessel can only be granted on bail being put in to the amount of the plaintiff's shares. I do not think that the right of the plaintiff to arrest the vessel is in

(¹) 1 Hagg., 306.

any way affected by the fact that the ship's husband, who negotiated the charterparty to which the plaintiff objects, was appointed by the whole body of the co-owners without objection on the part of the plaintiff. The motion must be dismissed with costs.

As all the facts of the case are before me, and as the plaintiff's counsel has applied for an order that the defendants give security for the safe return of the vessel, I shall make that order now in order to prevent further delay and expense.

Solicitor for plaintiff: *J. Davies.*
Solicitors for defendants: *Pritchard & Sons.*

[5 Probate Division, 173.]

April 21, 1880.

*THE FANCHON (1880, S. 067).   [173

Mortgage—Mortgagor's right to charter Ship.

Where a beneficial charterparty has been entered into by a mortgagor in possession of a ship, the mortgagee cannot object to the charterparty being carried out simply upon the ground that the effect of carrying out the charterparty will be to remove the ship out of the jurisdiction of the court, and to render it difficult for him to enforce his mortgage security.

THIS was an action of mortgage instituted on behalf of one of the members of the firm of Messrs. Smith, Payne & Smith, bankers, of London, the transferee of a mortgage on twenty sixty-fourth shares of the British colonial vessel Fanchon, against that vessel. On the 7th of April, when the vessel was arrested, she was under charter to Messrs. Hagan & Co., ship-brokers, of London, and a member of that firm entered an appearance as an intervener in the suit and gave notice that the court would be moved on his behalf to release the vessel immediately, and condemn the plaintiff in costs.

The motion was grounded on an affidavit made by the intervener and by a member of the firm of shipbrokers who had effected the charter as agents for the ship-owners. This affidavit contained, *inter alia,* the following allegations:

On the 19th day of March the Fanchon arrived at Queenstown on a voyage from Boston in the United States with a cargo of grain, and was ordered to Hull, where she arrived on the 25th of March. The agents of her owners had been instructed after the arrival of the vessel at Queenstown to find outward employment for her, and on the 31st of March they chartered her to Messrs. Hagan & Co. to carry a cargo of cliff stone from Hull to Philadelphia. It is difficult to procure charters from Hull to the ports of the United States, and many ships sail from Hull to those ports in ballast, and the charter under which the Fanchon was so chartered was the most advantageous which could be pro-174] cured for the *vessel, which could in no way be damaged or deteriorated by performing it. The plaintiff's mortgage became due on the 6th of April, and on the same day the plaintiff sent a ship-keeper on board her. The discharge of the inward cargo of the Fanchon was completed about the 9th of April, whilst the vessel was under arrest, and the loading of the outward cargo under the charter in question commenced about the 10th of April, and she would be fully loaded and ready to proceed on her outward voyage on the 19th of April. Neither the agents for the ship nor the charterers had any previous knowledge that the plaintiff intended to arrest the vessel.

A copy of the charterparty was annexed as an exhibit to the above mentioned affidavit. The charter contained the ordinary stipulations, and provided that the Fanchon should load in the customary manner at Hull about 700 or 800 tons, at captain's option, of cliff stone, and proceed to Philadelphia alongside such pier or wharf where she could lie afloat as ordered and deliver the same on being paid freight at the rate of 12s. sterling per ton invoice freight in full of all port charges and pilotage as customary.

It was stated in another affidavit filed in support of the motion that there was little doubt that if the ship was detained under arrest till the mortgaged shares were sold the buyers of the cliff stone at Philadelphia would reject it on its arrival there.

An affidavit, in which the manager of Messrs. Smith, Payne & Co. deposed, *inter alia*, as follows, was filed in opposition to the motion.

The mortgage proceeded on in the action was duly transferred for value to the plaintiff on behalf of Messrs. Smith, Payne & Smith, but the amount thereby secured was not due until the 6th day of April, 1880, and the plaintiff was therefore not entitled to take possession of the vessel under the said mortgage until that day. Upon that day the plaintiff duly took possession by his authorized agent, and he was in possession when the proceedings in this court to enforce the said mortgage were commenced, and when the vessel was arrested.

The Fanchon is a vessel belonging to Yarmouth, Novia Scotia, and no owner or part owner of the said vessel is resident within the jurisdiction of the court, and having reference to the circumstances hereinafter mentioned, I am informed and believe that should the vessel be allowed to leave this country before the plaintiff's mortgage is satisfied the plaintiff's security will be in peril, and it will be extremely doubtful and uncertain when he will have an opportunity of enforcing his claim. The plaintiff's claim on the said security amounts to upwards of £1,000.

As regards the charter referred to in the affidavits in support of the motion, I am informed and believe that it is not a charter for any profitable employment of the ship, but a mere charter for ballast for the purpose of taking the vessel 175] back *to America out of the jurisdiction of this court with as little loss as possible, and I am informed and believe that the freight payable under such charter is not a profitable or proper freight except for that purpose, and that the said freight will barely pay the expenses of the voyage back to America.

A further affidavit in opposition was brought in, in which it was stated that notice that the plaintiff intended to take possession of the Fanchon was served on one of the officers in charge of the Fanchon on the 3d of April, 1880 ; that the broker of the Fanchon was informed on the 8th of April that the persons shipping the outward cargo of cliff stone on board the Fanchon would do so at their own risk ; and that it was believed that during the negotiations between the agents for the ship and the agents for the charterers, the latter had been informed that the plaintiffs were about to take possession of the Fanchon.

An affidavit filed in reply on behalf of the intervener, stated that if the Fanchon had proceeded in ballast to the United States she would have made a loss of £50, whilst under the charter she would earn £480.

April 21.   The motion was now heard.

E. C. Clarkson, and *J. P. Aspinall*, for the intervener: There is no proof that by the performance of the charterparty in this case the security of the mortgage will be in any way depreciated or diminished.   On the contrary, the result of the evidence is that the charterparty is the most beneficial charterparty that could in the circumstances be procured.   Consequently the charterers are entitled to have the vessel released, for it is settled law that unless it can be proved that the engagements of the mortgagors as to the employment of the ship entered into whilst the mortgagee is out of possession would impair the mortgage security, the mortgagee is bound by them to the same extent as the mortgagor: *Collins* v. *Lamport* (¹) ; *Johnson* v. *Royal Mail Co.* (²) ; *The Innisfallen* (³).

Moreover, in this case the agent of the owner had no notice when he effected the charter that the mortgagee intended to take possession of the ship, and have her placed under arrest.

*[They also referred to the Merchant Shipping Act, [176 1854 (17 & 18 Vict. c. 104), s. 70.]

Butt, Q.C., and *W. G. F. Phillimore*, for the plaintiffs: In considering what engagements of a mortgagor are binding on his mortgagee, it cannot be that the sole question to be decided is whether the charter if carried out will leave a margin of profit.   There must be a further question whether the charterparty was entered into *bona fide* or for the purpose of prejudicing the rights of the mortgagee.   The circumstances in which the charter in this case was effected are suspicious.   The loading of the outward cargo began during the time the vessel was under arrest, and after the day when it must have been known that the mortgage money was due, whilst it certainly cannot be contended that the charter is a very profitable one. It must, moreover, be remembered that the vessel belongs to a colonial port, and that if the arrest is taken off and she is allowed to leave the jurisdiction, not only will the legal right of the plaintiff to enforce his mortgage by a suit *in rem* be interfered with, but he will probably be put to much greater expense in realizing his security than if the mortgaged shares were sold whilst the arrest continued.

Clarkson, in reply.

SIR ROBERT PHILLIMORE : This case is not without difficulty, and after some consideration I have arrived at the following conclusion. The case relied upon as containing the law upon the subject is that of *Collins* v. *Lamport* ('), in which judgment was delivered by Lord Chancellor Westbury in 1865, and the passage which has been referred to more than once in the argument, and which I must mention again, is this :

As long therefore as the dealings of the mortgagor with the ship are consistent with the sufficiency of the mortgagee's security, so long as those dealings do not materially prejudice and detract from or impair the sufficiency of the security comprised in the mortgage, so long is there parliamentary authority given to the mortgagor to act in all respects as owner of the vessel, and if he has authority to act as owner he has of necessity authority to enter into all those contracts touching the disposition of the ship which may be necessary for enabling him to get the full value and benefit of his property.

Therefore the proposition of law governing the case is that 177] the *mortgagor has full power to deal with the ship, provided he does not materially impair the value of the mortgagee's security. I take it that it lies on the mortgagee to satisfy the court that this charterparty would materially prejudice his security ; and I am not satisfied on reviewing the evidence that he has discharged this burden of proof. I think that he has failed to show that the carrying the charterparty into effect would impair his security. It is a case in which the principle laid down in *Collins* v. *Lamport* (') applies, and I must order the release of the vessel. I do not think it is a case for costs.

Solicitors for plaintiffs : *Waltons, Bubb & Waltons.*
Solicitors for intervener : *T. Cooper & Co.*

(') 34 L. J. (Ch.), 196.

[5 Probate Division, 177.]

June 29, 1880.

THE SILESIA (1880, V. 019).

Salvage—Agreement set aside as inequitable—Costs.

Where, in the opinion of the court, a salvage agreement is exorbitant, the court will refuse to enforce it.

In a case where the master of a disabled ship at sea about 340 miles from Queenstown, requested assistance from a mail steamer, and agreed in writing to make his owners responsible to the extent of £15,000, provided the master of the mail steamer would tow the disabled ship to Queenstown, and the service was performed, the court declined to enforce the agreement, and awarded to the salvors by way of salvage reward £7,000, in addition to a sum sufficient to cover penalties which had become payable by the owners of the mail steamer by reason of the vessel deviating to perform the service.

THIS was an action of salvage instituted on behalf of the owners, master, and crew of the steamship Vaderland against the steamship Silesia, her cargo and freight.

The statement of claim alleged in substance as follows:

1. The Vaderland is a screw steamship of 2,748 tons register, fitted with engines of 300 horse power, working up to 1,800 horse power, and at the time of the services hereinafter stated was on a voyage from Antwerp to Philadelphia laden with a general cargo, and carrying mails and 274 passengers. She was carrying the mails under a subsidy from the Belgian government, and was under heavy penalties both for delay and deviation. She was manned by a crew of seventy-six hands, including H. E. Nickels her master; and was of the value of £50,000. Her cargo was worth £20,000, and the freight and passage-money she was earning amounted to £2,700.

*2. At about 8 o'clock on the morning of the 26th of [178 March, 1880, the Vaderland was in the North Atlantic Ocean in about latitude 49° 34' N. and longitude 15° 38' W., and was proceeding on her said voyage when those on board her sighted a large steamship flying signals of distress. The course of the Vaderland was immediately altered, and she bore down towards such vessel.

3. The wind at such time was fresh from the eastward, and there was a heavy westerly swell.

4. The Vaderland reached the distressed vessel, which proved to be the screw steamship Silesia in a disabled condition, rolling dangerously in the trough of the sea, and the Vaderland steamed as close as possible to the Silesia, and her engines were stopped. It was then about 10 A.M.

5. Shortly afterwards C. Ludwig, the master of the Silesia, came on board the Vaderland, and stated as the facts were that the Silesia was on a voyage from New York to Hamburg laden with a general cargo and specie, and carrying passengers and mails, and that her main shaft had broken five days previously, and that she was quite disabled and required assistance and to be towed to Queenstown.

6. The master of the Vaderland, considering the number of persons on board the Silesia, and the danger to which they and the Silesia and her cargo were exposed, and notwithstanding the heavy responsibility he would incur by deviating from his voyage with the Vaderland, which was one of a regular line of steamers carrying as aforesaid the mails and passengers, agreed with the master of the Silesia to tow the latter to Queenstown, but only upon the terms that £15,000 should be paid for the service. To these terms the master of the Silesia agreed, and they were reduced into writing and signed by the masters of the Silesia and the Vaderland respectively.

7. All hands on board the Vaderland were thereupon engaged in making preparations for towing the Silesia, and a wire tow-rope from the Silesia was hauled on board the Vaderland, and there made fast.

8. The Vaderland then commenced to tow the Silesia, but at about 12.45 P.M. the tow-rope parted.

[In the 9th, 10th, 11th, 12th, and 13th paragraphs the operations attending the towage service were detailed.]

14. The various operations stated in the last seven paragraphs were performed with difficulty, and were attended with danger to the Vaderland and those on board her, as there was still a heavy swell and danger of fouling and collision was experienced. Those of the crew of the Vaderland who tended the hawsers incurred considerable risk of personal injury from breaking of hawsers.

15. During the 28th fog prevailed. At about 6 P.M. on that day the ships were off Galley Head, on the coast of Ireland. At 10 P.M. a pilot was taken on board the Vaderland, and the Vaderland continued to steam towards Queenstown, but very slowly until daylight reappeared. The lead was kept constantly in use.

16. At 6.10 A.M. on the 29th of March the fog lifted and Daunt's Rock Lightship was seen ahead and speed was increased. At 7.20 A.M. the fog being very dense the hawsers were slipped, and the two vessels were brought safely to anchor in ten fathoms of water.

*17. The Vaderland steamed up the harbor of [179 Queenstown, and the Silesia was towed up by some steamtugs.

18. The Vaderland then took on board a fresh supply of coal, and resumed her voyage.

19. By the said services the Silesia and her cargo and specie and those on board her were saved from a position of great danger.

21. The Vaderland in rendering the said services had tow-ropes damaged entailing a loss to her owners of upwards of £60. She also consumed about 245 tons of coal extra, of the value of £225, and incurred other expenses ('). She deviated *from her voyage and lost six days, and she incurred [180 great risk of being damaged by collision with the Silesia, and of getting her propeller fouled by the tow-ropes and of so becoming disabled.

(') The following are particulars of the expenses referred to in this paragraph, delivered pursuant to order :

	£	s.	d.
Insurance on steamship Vaderland during time occupied in rendering the salvage services	50	0	0
Wages paid to the master, officers, and crew of the Vaderland during same time	90	0	0
Provisions for crew and passengers of the Vaderland during same time	132	0	0
Extra coals consumed during same time	225	0	0
61 gallons oil consumed during same time	12	4	0
Damage done to the Vaderland's hawsers	60	0	0

Port charges in Queenstown—

	£	s.	d.			
Telegrams	3	9	9			
Boat coming to Roches' Point	2	0	0			
Pilotage from sea	8	12	6			
Harbor dues	4	3	7			
Cost of arresting Silesia	5	3	8			
Miller, Ship Chandler	16	5	2			
Boat hire of officers	0	6	0			
Pilotage to sea	4	10	0			
Agency and commission	5	18	9			
Master's expenses	4	0	0			
				54	4	0

Expenses in Queenstown—

	£	s.	d.			
Telegrams respecting Silesia	0	3	6			
Interpreter	0	5	0			
Messrs. Allen, costs in Admiralty Courts	25	7	2			
Sundry cab hire	0	10	0			
Agency and commission	1	6	8			
				27	11	11

Penalties due to the Belgian Government for deviation and delay	1155	0	0
Estimated loss of Vaderland's earnings	1000	0	0
Estimated loss on charter of s. s. Hevelius	2000	0	0
	£4806	0	4

The plaintiffs claimed, 1, the sum of £15,000 salvage pursuant to the said agreement. 2. In the alternative such an amount of salvage as the court might think fit to award.

The statement of defence, after requiring the plaintiffs to prove their allegations as to the mail contract of the Vaderland, and the alleged penalties therein, and alleging in effect that the allegations in the statement of claim as to the weather, and the difficulty of the services rendered by the Vaderland were exaggerated, proceeded in the 3d and 6th paragraphs substantially as follows:

3. The agreement pleaded in paragraph 6 of the statement of claim was as the defendants submit an inequitable one, and was only signed by the master of the Silesia under compulsion, and because the master of the Vaderland threatened to leave the Silesia and proceed upon his voyage unless the said agreement was signed by the master of the Silesia. The master of the Silesia at the time when the said agreement was being discussed repeatedly stated that the sum demanded was in his opinion much too large, and proposed to the master of the Vaderland that the amount to be paid for the services to be rendered should be left to be settled between the owners of the two vessels.

6. Except that the Vaderland deviated from her voyage and lost four days, the defendants deny the several allegations in paragraphs 19 and 21 of the statement of claim. They deny that the plaintiffs have any claim under the agreement, but they submit to pay such an amount of salvage as the court upon consideration of all the circumstances may deem just.

The values of the Silesia, her cargo, passage-money, and freight were agreed as follows: The Silesia, £49,000; her cargo, £56,000; specie, £958; passage-money and freight, £2,640; in all, £108,598.

June 23, 24. The action was heard before the judge, assisted by two of the Elder Brethren of the Trinity House. Witnesses were examined orally in court on behalf of the plaintiffs and the defendants. The result of their evidence, so far as the same is material to this report, appears from the judgment. The agreement referred to in the 6th paragraph of the statement of claim was put in. The following is a copy of such agreement:

"At Sea, 20th 8, 80, on board the Steamer Vaderland.
"We have this day made agreement as follows: Captain Nickels engages to
181]   assist the Silesia with broken shaft and disabled, and *tow her to Queens-

town to anchorage.   For this service Captain Ludwig makes the company responsible for the above mentioned service for the sum of £15,000.

(Signed) '' C. Ludwig.
(Signed) "H. E. Nickels.

'' Witness to the above signatures.

(Signed) '' T. Weberney, Chief Officer."

With respect to the item in the particulars relating to the Helvelius, evidence was given on behalf of the plaintiffs that in order to make up for the derangement of the service caused by the detention of the Vaderland, they had cancelled a charterparty under which the plaintiffs' steamship Hevelius was engaged, and had employed her in the mail service.

It was agreed between the plaintiffs and defendants that, in the event of the court deciding against the salvage agreement set up by the plaintiffs, the owners of the Silesia would pay any sum not exceeding the sum of £1,155, which the owners of the Vaderland might be forced to pay to the Belgian government in respect of the penalties referred to in the 1st paragraph of the statement of claim.

Butt, Q.C., and *E. C. Clarkson*, for the plaintiffs : There is no authority for holding that salvage agreements will be set aside merely because the amount agreed to be paid is more than the court itself would have awarded.   Indeed, the true principle would seem to be that a salvage agreement will only be set aside where it is shown that the master of the salved vessel has signed it under compulsion.   In the recent case of *The Medina* ('), where a salvage agreement was signed by the master of a steamship employed in carrying pilgrims in the Red Sea, it was obvious on the evidence that if the master had refused to sign the agreement he would have taken upon himself the responsibility of allowing the pilgrims under his charge to be exposed to imminent peril of death.

In the present case the passengers on board the Silesia were in no danger of their lives, even in the unlikely case of the master of the Vaderland refusing on request to take them on board the *Vaderland.   In fact, the master of the   [182 Silesia was under no pressure whatever to accept the assistance of the Vaderland, but was merely in the same position as the master of every valuable vessel which is in want of salvage assistance.   In these circumstances the court will be loth to interfere with an agreement come to between two perfectly competent parties.   If the court should be of opinion that the agreement ought to be set aside, the plaintiffs, the owners of the Vaderland, are clearly entitled to be recom-

(') 1 P. D., 272,· 17 Eng. R., 507; 2 P. D., 5, 19 Eng. Rep., 544.

pensed for the expenses occasioned to them by the necessity they were under of getting another ship to take the place of the Vaderland. The expenses they so claim to recover are in this instance what they estimate as their loss on the charter of their steamship Helvelius. In considering the amount of responsibility which the master of the Vaderland undertook when he entered into the agreement, it must not be forgotten that he was under instructions from his owners not to render salvage assistance to vessels not belonging to them, unless to save life.

Webster, Q.C., and *W. G. F. Phillimore*, for the defendants: The agreement cannot be supported. It is true that the lives of the crew and passengers of the Silesia were in no immediate danger, and so far the present case differs from that of *The Medina* ('), but it is idle to say that the master of the Silesia was under no compulsion to sign the agreement, it being in evidence that he was told that unless the agreement was entered into the Vaderland would go away and leave him. Moreover, the amount specified in the agreement is so grossly exorbitant in relation to the services rendered that the court will, on that ground alone, refuse to assist in carrying it out : *The Helen & George* ('). Whatever may have been the instructions given to the master of the Vaderland from his owner, the bills of lading and policies of that vessel are so framed as to admit of assistance being given to vessels in all situations.

Butt, in reply.

SIR ROBERT PHILLIMORE: This is a case of salvage service of very considerable merit, and upon that point there is no dispute whatever. The only question for this court to 183] decide is, whether, *having regard to all the principles on which salvage remuneration is awarded, the sum of £15,000, which was the sum agreed upon between the two masters, is so exorbitant as to induce the court to set the salvage agreement in this case aside. The short history of the case is this : the Vaderland, a screw steamship of 2,748 tons register, with engines of 300 horse power, working up to 1,800 horse power, was on a voyage from Antwerp to Philadelphia laden with a general cargo, and carrying mails and 274 passengers. That there were these passengers on board is a most important element in this case. The mails were carried under a subsidy with the Belgian government, and the owners of the Vaderland were under penalties not to deviate or delay. The Vaderland had a crew of seventy-six hands, and her value, added to the value of her cargo

('), 1 P. D., 272, 17 Eng. R., 507; 2 P. D., 5, 19 Eng. R., 544.   (') Swa., 368.

and freight, was £72,000.   The vessel to which the salvage services in this case were rendered was the Silesia, and she had sixty-two passengers on board with a crew of ninety-five hands, and was 3,150 tons gross register, and with her cargo and freight was of the value of about £108,000.   The Silesia was going from New York to Hamburg, and at the time when the accident happened she had got within 340 miles or thereabouts of Queenstown.   On the morning of the 21st of March in this year the Silesia broke her propeller or screw shaft in the stern tube, and the consequence of that was that she became utterly inefficient so far as her steam power was concerned.   The weather was fine and the sea was smooth, but after tossing about for four or five days, and when only about seven miles from the place at which the accident happened, she hoisted signals of distress, and on the 26th of March the Vaderland bore down upon her. What passed between the two masters it is better to state in their own words, both having regard to the importance of the principles involved and the great value of the salved ship herself.   The statement of Captain Nickels of the Vaderland is as follows:

Ludwig, the captain of the Silesia, asked me to tow him into a safe port. I said I could not do it, because I had instructions from my owners. Then he said, What am I to do, I cannot steer the ship? After a little while I said I will break my instructions for £20,000. He said that was rather too much, and mentioned £12,000. I said I would not run the risk for that money; then he made an offer for £15,000, and I said yes.

*Captain Ludwig's account is this :   [184

Captain Nickels took me into his room, and I said I had been trying to sail for five days, but having the wind against me I could make no way. I thought I had better not try any longer, and I requested him to tow me. Nickels said he had instructions not to tow any ship as they had been taken in before, except for a certain sum of money, and then to give him a written agreement. I asked what he wanted. I said we had a case a couple of years ago and we had to pay £4,000 for it, and £5,000 would be about the money. He said, no, £20,000. I said I was astonished, as it was an enormous sum, and they would never pay so much. I insisted on £5,000, and he insisted on £15,000. I thought it was a great sum, and he threatened to leave me unless I signed for £15,000.

[His Lordship here read the agreement.]
The Vaderland took the Silesia in tow, and in about three days they accomplished 340 miles, and at the end of six days the Vaderland had again reached the vicinity of the spot where she had fallen in with the Silesia.   That was the time she lost, and it was very strongly contended on her behalf that she had rendered herself liable to penalties under the mail contract by the deviation she had made from the course of her voyage.   On this point I may observe that the question as to these penalties has been made the subject of

an arrangement between the parties.   Therefore so far this
question is disposed of.   The master of the Vaderland referred in his evidence to instructions given him by his owners not to deviate from his voyage or delay the ship to render
any assistance to vessels other than those belonging to his
owners, except for saving life.   On the other hand, the bills
of lading and policies of insurance of the Vaderland provide
for liberty to the ship to "assist all vessels in all situations."
I do not think that the instructions to the master of the
Vaderland can be pressed as affording any guide to the
court in ascertaining the amount of remuneration to be
awarded for the services rendered.

There is a large sum mentioned as the estimated loss on
the charter of the screw steamer Helvelius, which was employed in consequence of the derangement of the service in
which the Vaderland was employed.   The loss on this head
I do not estimate at more than £500.

The question the court has to consider is whether the salvage agreement is an agreement which is so exorbitant
185]   that, in accordance *with decided cases and the principles on which they are founded, the court ought to set it
aside.   And here I should say that in order to assist the
court in arriving at a conclusion upon this subject, it is
necessary to consider, and I have considered carefully with
the assistance of the Elder Brethren of the Trinity House,
whether the owners of the Silesia, if present, would or would
not have been justified in calling for the assistance of the
Vaderland and in accepting the terms which the captain of
the Vaderland asked.   After the best consideration of this
case, and considering the principles of other analogous
cases, I have come to the conclusion, and the Elder Brethren
agree with me, that the sum specified in the agreement is so
exorbitant that the court ought to exercise its equitable
jurisdiction and not to assist in the carrying of it into effect.
Looking to all the circumstances of the case, I have come to
the conclusion that the proper sum to award in this case will
be £7,000 to cover everything but the penalties.   The question of costs must stand over for argument.

June 29.   *E. C. Clarkson*, on behalf of the plaintiffs,
moved the judge in court to condemn the defendants in the
costs of the action.   The general result of the action is in
the plaintiffs' favor, and the court in its discretion ought to
give them the costs they ask for.   If the defendants had not
intended to dispute the right of the plaintiffs to a sufficient
award of salvage they ought to have tendered the amount

they considered the plaintiffs were entitled to. It is true that the plaintiffs have failed on one issue, but the extra costs of that issue are merely nominal. The same witnesses would have been called even if the agreement had not been set up.

W. G. F. Phillimore, for the defendants: The court ought to make no order as to the costs of the action. This was the course pursued in the case of *The Medina* ('), where, as in this case, the defendants made no tender.

[He also referred to *The City of Manchester* (').]

SIR ROBERT PHILLIMORE: I think upon the principle on which this court and the Court of Appeal acted in the case of *The Medina* ('), I must order that each party to   [186 the suit shall bear his own costs.

Solicitors for plaintiffs: *Hollams, Son & Coward.*
Solicitors for defendants: *Lowless & Co.*

(') 1 P. D., 272, 17 Eng. R., 509; 2 P. D., 5, 19 Eng. R., 544.
(') 5 P. D., 3; 19 Eng. R., 544.

[5 Probate Division, 186.]

June 18, 1880.

THE CRAIGS (1880, C. 063).

Salvage—Derelict—Amount of Salvage Award—Apportionment.

A derelict vessel was found in the North Atlantic Ocean, 800 miles from land, in a seriously damaged condition, and was navigated into Queenstown by salvors, who incurred great risk and hardship in rendering the service. The value of the derelict was £5,100. The court awarded £2,300 as salvage reward.

THIS was an action of salvage instituted on behalf of the owners, master, and crew of the screw steamship Teutonia, against the ship Craigs, her cargo and freight.

The paragraphs of the statement of claim describing the nature of the salvage services, the circumstances in which they were rendered, and the expenses incurred in rendering them were, so far as material, as follows:

The Teutonia is a screw steamship of 2,693 tons register, of which the plaintiffs were the owners, and at the time of rendering the services hereinafter mentioned, the Teutonia was bound on a voyage from New Orleans to Liverpool, laden with a general cargo and horses, and manned by a crew of fifty-two hands.

At about 4 A.M. on the 25th day of February, 1880, the Teutonia, in the prosecution of her said voyage, was in the North Atlantic Ocean, in about latitude 48° N., and longitude 27° W., and about 800 miles to the westward of Queenstown. The wind at the time was north-easterly, and there was a heavy swell running. In these circumstances a vessel was fallen in with apparently in distress or abandoned.

The Teutonia was stopped, and her chief officer and a boat's crew proceeded to, and with risk and difficulty succeeded in boarding, the vessel. She proved to be the ship the Craigs of Greenock, 1,148 tons register, laden with a full cargo of pitch pine, and bound from Pensacola to Greenock. The Craigs had been abandoned by her crew, and was found to be in a disabled condition. She had lost her rudder. Her main yard was carried away in the slings, her two lower topsails were gone, and her upper fore and main topsails were split, and others of her sails were about the decks torn in pieces, the main hatch was broken, and the fresh water tank was found to be full of salt water, the bulwarks 187] · were *smashed in on both sides, and the port pump was out of order, and it was estimated that there was about 4 ft. 6 in. of water in the hold.

The mate returned to the Teutonia and reported to the master the state of the Craigs, and the master determined to attempt to tow the Craigs to the nearest port. He accordingly sent some of the plaintiffs on board the Craigs, and at 6 A.M. the Teutonia steamed close to the Craigs, and, with considerable risk to the Teutonia, the steel hawser of the Craigs was passed to the Teutonia, and bent on to her ten-inch Manilla hawser, and made fast on board.

At about 7.30 A.M. the Teutonia commenced to tow the Craigs, but the Craigs having lost her rudder, sheered about a great deal, and after being towed for some time the hawser parted and carried away some of her head gear. The mate then returned to the Teutonia, and consulted with the master, and determined to attempt to sail the Craigs into port. Some stores and water, and a boat belonging to the Teutonia, were put on board the Craigs, and the plaintiffs McAdam, Graham, and Percival, able seamen, having volunteered to go with the mate, were put on board the Craigs, and at about 10.15 A.M. the Teutonia proceeded on her voyage, leaving the plaintiffs William Putt Couch, Lawrenson, Shiel, Hebe, Royal, Heidstrom, McAdam, Knowles, Pan, Mallon, Graham, and Percival on board the Craigs.

The salvors on board the Craigs proceeded to get the Craigs under command by getting up steam in the donkey engine to work the starboard pump, the port pump being out of gear, and then attempted to refix a temporary rope rudder which had been left by the crew of the Craigs, which however proved useless, whereupon the chief officer and the carpenter proceeded to construct a jury rudder of wood.

About this time it was found that the Craigs had 7 ft. 6 in. of water in the hold instead of 4 ft. 6 in. All hands worked till dark, and the night watches were kept by two hands in a watch.

On the 26th of February the Craigs, still drifting to the northward and eastward, was in latitude about 48° 2′ N., and longitude 26° 34′ W., the salvors were employed securing the bowsprit and head gear, and in setting up and securing other gear, and in the construction of the jury rudder. Towards midnight it blew a fresh gale from N.W., with heavy squalls backing to S.W. On the 27th the wind was a fresh breeze from the N.W., and on the·28th the Craigs encountered strong variable winds with heavy squalls, the decks being filled with water, the ship being in an unmanageable condition. The jury rudder was completed, but owing to the heavy weather it could not be shipped, and in securing it to the deck the boatswain Shiel received a severe injury to his ankle. The donkey pump was kept going, and the crew constantly employed in attempting to get the ship under command.

On the morning of the 29th of February the donkey feed pump became choked with salt, and the pumping in consequence was stopped for four hours, and the ship made five inches of water per hour. A heavy gale was blowing from the W.S.W., with a high sea, and the Craigs was laboring heavily in the trough of the sea. The Teutonia's boat was stove in, and the plaintiff Royal was washed off the house on deck, and severely injured.

On the 1st of March the gale increased to a hurricane from the W.S.W., and the water in the hold increased to eight feet, notwithstanding the donkey pump was constantly pumping. The gale continued during the 2d, and the donkey *boiler became salted, and caused the pump to [188 be stopped for ten hours, during which time the water in the hold increased to fifteen feet. On the 3d the gale continued and varied N.W. to S.W. The water in the hold was reduced to twelve feet, when the donkey engine broke down, and the crew turned to work the pump by hand, until in about five hours the donkey engine was repaired and at work again.

On the 4th of March the gale continued to blow from the south-westward, and the carpenter repaired the port pump, and it was started. On the 5th the gale continued, and the ship still drifted to the northward, and could not be got on to the other tack, and the crew became exhausted, having been up day and night. On the 6th the fresh water was nearly finished, and a temporary condenser was fitted by the carpenter and donkey engine man.

On the 7th the heavy gale and high sea continued, and, whilst working at the rudder, the plaintiff McAdam was washed overboard by a sea, and was rescued with difficulty. The ship had by this time drifted into about latitude 51° 25' N., and longitude 19° 11' W. During the afternoon the gale moderated somewhat, and the ship was got on to the starboard tack. The gale increased again in the evening with a high cross sea, which caused the Craigs to labor heavily and ship a great deal of water, and the same weather was experienced during the 8th.

On the 9th the weather moderated, and the sea commenced to go down. The wooden jury rudder was got overboard, and, by means of gudgeon chains, was fixed in position against the sternpost, and by steering chains to the quarters, and the ship was got under steerage command by noon. The ship at this time was in about latitude 52° 19' N., and longitude 17° 30' W., and from the 10th to the 15th the Craigs experienced head winds from the S.E. and moderate weather.

On the 16th, with a heavy breeze and a high sea, the wind shifted to the N.W., and took the ship aback, and the chain gudgeons of the rudder parted. Sheers were rigged, and the rudder hove up, and the gudgeons were repaired, and on the 17th the rudder was re-shipped and secured, notwithstanding the heavy sea and laboring of the ship. At about 3 P.M. a heavy sea struck the ship and carried away a steering gear bolt. At about 6 P.M., the ship heading E.N.E., and drifting to the north-eastward, an unsuccessful attempt was made to wear-ship.

On the 18th of March the wind was blowing a fresh gale from S.S.E. with a high sea, the ship laboring heavily, and making about four inches of water per hour. The ship was with great difficulty got round to the southward, being at the time in about latitude 52° 12' N., and longitude 13° 52' W. The provisions were found to be running short, in consequence of which the crew was put upon short allowance.

On the 20th a sudden shift of wind to N.W. caught the ship aback and displaced the rudder. The rudder was refixed, but about midnight the ship took a sudden sheer, and became unmanageable before the wind, and on the 21st finding the ship still unmanageable, the rudder was hove up and enlarged, and was then refixed. At about noon the steamship Iowa was spoken, and provisions and other things were obtained.

On the 22d the wind blew strongly from the S.E., and continued from that quarter during the 23d and 24th, freshening to a gale. The plaintiff, William Putt Couch (the mate), was ill from the 21st to the 23d. On the 25th a heavy sea *struck the rudder, and carried away the lower gudg- [189 eon, and started a steering gear bolt, but at daylight the rudder was hove up and repaired.

During the 26th, 27th, 28th, and 29th, the weather was moderate and the vessel was worked to the southward by wearing: the latitude on the 26th being about 51° 47′ N., the longitude 13° 49′ W.

At about 10 A.M. on the 30th, the south-west coast of Ireland was sighted. At 3 P.M. a pilot was obtained. During the night a strong W.S.W. gale was experienced, and the ship was hove to.

On the 31st, at daylight, the ship stood in for the land, and shortly afterwards the starboard steering chain was carried away by the sea, but a preventer chain was fitted. At noon a steamtug was engaged for £15 to tow the Craigs into Monkstown, and at 4 P.M. the Craigs was brought up by her anchors in Monkstown Reach in Queenstown Harbor.

By the said services the Craigs and her cargo were rescued from total loss.

In rendering these services the plaintiffs on board the Craigs incurred great hardships, and ran very great risk of losing their lives. The mate never had his clothes off except once for the purpose of changing them, and never had any regular rest. Shiel had his ankle crushed and severely injured, and Royal received a hurt in his side, and McAdam was nearly drowned as aforesaid. The said services were very skilfully rendered.

The master of the Teutonia in parting with his chief officer and boatswain and carpenter and nine men took upon himself great responsibility, and himself and the crew who remained on board the Teutonia incurred much extra labor by reason of her being short handed.

The owners of the Teutonia incurred great risk of loss or damage to the Teutonia, and of becoming liable to the owners of the cargo of the Teutonia by reason of her being left short handed, and by reason of the Teutonia taking the Craigs in tow the owners of the Teutonia suffered damage.

In rendering the said services the plaintiffs the owners of the Teutonia have incurred the following losses and expenses, viz.,—for provisions £8 3s. 4d., for the small boat of the Teutonia £20, for stores supplied as aforesaid by the

Iowa £21 5s. 1d., and for expenses at Queenstown, including towage, pilotage, and provisions, £52.

The defendants, the owners of the Craigs, her cargo, and freight, paid into court and tendered to the plaintiffs the sum of £1,800. This tender was rejected, and the defendants delivered a statement of defence, admitting in substance that the plaintiffs had rendered the services in the statement of claim mentioned.

June 18. The action was heard before the judge, assisted by two of the Elder Brethren of the Trinity House. No witnesses were called, either on behalf of the plaintiffs or the defendants. It was agreed that the value of the property salved should, for the purposes of the case, be taken as £5,100.

190] *Butt*, Q.C., and *E. C. Clarkson*, appeared for the plaintiffs: The services in this case are so meritorious that the court ought to award to the salvors a moiety of the value of the property salved, and in addition direct that the expenses incurred in rendering the services should be paid: *The Rasche* (¹).

W. G. F. Phillimore, for the defendants: The tender made by the defendants is a most liberal one, and the court ought to pronounce for it: *The Andrina* (²).

SIR ROBERT PHILLIMORE: This is an action of salvage to recover for salvage services rendered to a derelict vessel of very considerable value. The services lasted about thirty-five days, and were rendered to a ship and cargo of the value of over £5,000. One circumstance to bear in mind in this case is that the vessel was laden with a full cargo of pitch pine, and therefore was not so likely to perish at sea; she had not a cargo of iron, as in the case of *The Rasche* (¹) to which I have been referred. It is not necessary, after the full statement made by counsel and looking to the fact that the salvage service is not disputed, to repeat the averments in the statement of claim. I will just state a summary of what is admitted to have been in every respect the true condition of the vessel. She had lost her rudder, her mainyard was carried away, her two lower topsails were gone, and her upper fore and main topsails were split, and other sails were about the decks torn in pieces. The main hatch was broken and the fresh water tank was found to be full of salt water, the bulwarks were smashed on both sides, and the port pump was out of order, and it was estimated that there was about 4 feet 6 inches of water in the hold. It is diffi-

---

(¹) L. R., 4 A. & E., 127; 7 Eng. R., 364.   (²) L. R., 3 A. & E., 286.

cult to describe a vessel in a worse condition than that in which she is admitted to have been. What happened was this: an attempt was made to tow her, and it was found that the towing was extremely difficult and inconvenient. The chief mate and others of the crew of the Teutonia volunteered to go on board the vessel and take her to her destination 800 miles off. During the time they were on board these salvors suffered considerable hardships and were exposed to great peril. Altogether the case constitutes a case *of very great merit. The question is whether the [191 tender of £1,800 is sufficient. Looking to all the circumstances of the case I shall increase the tender to £2,300. .

Butt, Q.C.: Will your Lordship apportion the award among the plaintiffs?

SIR ROBERT PHILLIMORE: The court has always found it of great assistance in these cases that the counsel for the plaintiffs should state to the court a scheme for the apportionment.

Butt, Q.C.: The apportionment might be as follows: £500 to the owners of the Teutonia, £100 to the master of the Teutonia, £1,550 to be divided among the actual salvors, and the remainder of the award, £150, to the rest of the crew of the Teutonia.

SIR ROBERT PHILLIMORE: I will apportion the award in the manner the counsel for the plaintiffs suggests. The award of £500 to the owners of the Teutonia is to cover all expenses, and the £1,550 awarded to those of the crew of the Teutonia who volunteered to remain on board the Craigs is to be divided amongst them according to their rating, any substitutes amongst them to share as if they had had the rating of A. B.'s.

Solicitor for plaintiffs: *Wynne.*
Solicitors for defendants: *Waltons, Bubb & Walton.*

[5 Probate Division, 192.]

Feb. 24, 1880.

*THE AFRIKA (1879, B. 306).   [192

*Salvage—The Merchant Shipping Act, 1854 (17 & 18 Vict. c. 104), s. 182—
Agreement for Apportionment of Salvage.*

The 182d section of the Merchant Shipping Act, 1854, does not prevent seamen who are entitled to recover salvage remuneration from entering into an arrangement through their solicitor for the apportionment of the amount due to them.

Where the owners of a ship have received a lump sum in respect of services rendered by their ship, master and crew, and have paid over to the crew a portion of

such sum, which the crew, acting under the advice of their own solicitor, have accepted in settlement of their claims for salvage, the court will not, where the portion
so paid over is not extravagantly small, disturb the settlement in the absence of
fraud or concealment.

THIS was an action for distribution of salvage carried on
on behalf of four able seamen and two freemen who formed
part of the crew of the steamship Durham, against the owners of the steamship Durham. The Durham is a vessel of
1,827 tons gross register, and in March, 1879, when in the
Gulf of Finland, and manned by a crew of twenty-seven
hands, all told, she rendered salvage services to the steamship Afrika. The statement of claim described at some
length the services rendered by the Durham and her crew
to the Afrika, and then proceeded as follows:

13. The defendants have received for and in respect of the
said services, the sum of £3,000, as and for salvage reward
for the services rendered as aforesaid, to the Afrika, her
crew and cargo, and before its ascertainment or receipt, they
paid to the plaintiffs £12 10s. each on account of the sums
due to them in respect of their services aforesaid, but the
defendants, though requested by the plaintiffs so to do, have
wholly refused to pay to the plaintiffs, or any of them, any
further sum or sums as their equitable proportion of the
said sum of £3,000, and there still remains due and owing
from the defendants to the plaintiffs, a large sum as such
proportion as aforesaid, and the plaintiffs are unable to obtain the same without the assistance of this honorable court.

The plaintiffs claim—

1. Judgment pronouncing that the plaintiffs are entitled
to an equitable proportion of the said sum of £3,000 in respect of their services aforesaid, and for such sum beyond
the said sums paid to the plaintiffs respectively as aforesaid,
as to the court shall seem just.

The defendants delivered a statement of defence, of which
the 5th, 6th, and 9th paragraphs were in substance as follows:

5. The defendants admit that the plaintiffs took their fair
part with the other members of the crew of the Durham, in
193] and about the rendering of the services *in the statement of claim mentioned, save certain extra services which
were rendered by certain members of the crew of the Durham
other than the plaintiffs, and they admit that the services
rendered to the Afrika were necessarily of an arduous nature
and attended with some exposure and risk, and that by
these services the Afrika, her cargo, and crew, were saved.

6. In answer to the 13th paragraph, the defendants admit and allege that they have received the sum of £3,000 and no more, as and for salvage reward for and in satisfaction of all claims for all the said services rendered to the Afrika, her crew and cargo, by the Durham, her master and crew, and they say that the plaintiffs and certain other members of the said crew of the Durham, namely, J. W. Good, T. Wilkinson, and A. Anderson, instructed Messrs. Singleton & Martinson, solicitors, to act as their solicitors, and to apply on their behalf to the defendants for the payment of their respective shares of the said salvage, and authorized the said solicitors to settle their respective claims in respect of the said salvage with the defendants, and that after the said sum of £3,000 had been finally ascertained and settled as the total amount of salvage in respect of the said services, and after such sum had come to the hands of the defendants or their agents, and after the said plaintiffs and their said solicitors had full knowledge thereof, the said plaintiffs and the said J. W. Good, T. Wilkinson, and A. Anderson, by their said solicitors agreed with the defendants to accept from the defendants the sum of £132 10s., in settlement of the claims of the plaintiffs, and the said J. W. Good, T. Wilkinson, and A. Anderson respectively, for and in respect of the said salvage and their costs; and the sum of £132 10s. was on the 8th day of July, 1879, accordingly paid by the defendants, and received by the said solicitors acting on behalf and with the authority of the plaintiffs and the said J. W. Good, T. Wilkinson, and A. Anderson, in settlement of their said respective claims for salvage and costs. The defendants crave leave to refer to the authority in writing given by the said plaintiffs to the said solicitors, and to the receipt for the said sum of £132 10s.

9. Save as herein admitted, the defendants deny the truth of the said 13th paragraph.

The plaintiffs demurred to the 6th paragraph of the statement of defence.

J. P. Aspinall, for the plaintiffs, in support of the demurrer, contended that it was apparent on the pleadings that the plaintiffs had received an inadequate amount in respect of the services they had rendered, and that the agreement referred to in the paragraph demurred to amounted to a stipulation by the plaintiffs to abandon their right to salvage, and was illegal and void under the provisions of s. 182 of the Merchant Shipping Act, 1854: *The Rosario* ('); *The Enchantress* (').

(') 2 P. D., 41; 20 Eng. R., 579.   (') Lush., 93.

E. C. Clarkson, for the defendants, contrà.

194] *SIR ROBERT PHILLIMORE: This is a case of distribution of salvage. A steamship called the Durham rendered salvage services in 1879 in the Gulf of Finland to a
ship called the Afrika, and £3,000 has been accepted as the
total sum of salvage remuneration for such services, and
paid over to the owners of the Durham. Certain of the crew
have brought the present action, in which they claim such
portion of this sum as is due to them, and the owners of the
Afrika, who have appeared to defend the suit, rest their
case upon the 6th paragraph of the statement of defence.
[His Lordship here read the paragraph.] This paragraph
is demurred to, principally upon the ground that it sets up
an agreement to accept a certain sum in respect of salvage
remuneration, contrary to the provisions of the 182d section
of the Merchant Shipping Act, 1854, which renders it unlawful for any seaman to abandon any right he may have or
obtain in the nature of salvage, and declares that any agreement to do so shall be wholly inoperative. Now it has been
urged by counsel for the plaintiffs that the court must hold
that any agreement, of any sort or kind by which a solicitor
is to receive a certain sum in respect of salvage services in
lieu of the sum which might be awarded by the court as salvage remuneration, is invalid, and that any arrangement of
that kind is wholly inoperative. I think that to hold thus
would be to draw an unwarrantable conclusion from the
words of the section. In my opinion, therefore, the demurrer cannot be allowed. I should not, however, take the
course of rejecting the demurrer if by so doing I was preventing the plaintiffs traversing the facts alleged in the 6th
paragraph of the statement of defence. On this point I
think it necessary to refer to the law laid down in the *Enchantress* ([1]), and I take the law as laid down in that case to
be perfectly clear. In that case Dr. Lushington said:

> I conceive a duty is hereby imposed upon me to decree, upon application
> made, what in my judgment is an equitable apportionment of salvage, unless I
> am barred by one or two circumstances—either an equitable agreement between
> the parties, or an equitable tender.

Dr. Lushington goes on to say: "I will consider the
present case in both ways. First, was there an equitable
195] agreement *made between the parties?" Now, in
the present case the terms of the agreement are not yet before the court for its consideration, and will only be before
it when the matter is properly brought before it at the hearing, when one of the questions to be determined will be

([1]) Lush., 93.

whether the agreement, having been made by solicitors and approved by the parties, was, having regard to all the circumstances, an equitable agreement. On the one hand, I think it is competent for the defendants to set up the defence they have set up in the 6th paragraph of the statement of defence, to the effect that, irrespective of any question whether the agreement was or was not equitable, it was an agreement with the defendants, and that the plaintiffs' solicitors received the £132 10s., and that that sum was accepted by the plaintiffs; in other words, I conceive it was perfectly competent for the defendants to plead in the manner they have pleaded. On the other hand, I conceive it was equally competent for the plaintiffs to have alleged that, admitting the fact that the solicitors did make the agreement in question, nevertheless, having regard to all the circumstances, the agreement was one of those inequitable agreements, either fraudulent or illusory, which the court has always felt itself competent to look into, and, if necessary, revise. Taking that view of the law, I reject the demurrer in this case, and I wish it to be understood that I do so upon the grounds I have stated.

An amended reply was afterwards delivered, of which the following is the material part:

3. As to paragraph 6 of the statement of defence the plaintiffs further say that if the agreement in the said paragraph mentioned was made and if the sum of £132 10s. was paid to the said solicitors in the said paragraph mentioned under the said agreement, as in the said paragraph alleged (which the plaintiffs do not admit) the plaintiffs' part of the said sum, that is to say, £12 10s. each, was less than the just and equitable share of the said sum of £3,000, due to the plaintiffs in respect of the said salvage services, and the said solicitors received the said part in settlement of the claims of the plaintiffs in ignorance of the just rights of the plaintiffs, and the said agreement and receipt limited the proportion of the said sum of £3,000, due to the plaintiffs, and surrendered without any consideration whatsoever, the just rights of the plaintiffs to the remaining part of their fair share, and were and are inequitable and inoperative as against the plaintiffs.

*The defendants delivered a rejoinder joining issue [196 on the 3d paragraph of the amended reply, and demurring to the same paragraph upon the ground, *inter alia*, that the said paragraph did not contain any good or sufficient ground for avoiding the agreement and settlement and payment pleaded in the 6th paragraph of the statement of defence.

Feb. 24. The action and the demurrer to the reply came on to be heard.

Witnesses were examined orally in court on behalf of the plaintiffs and the defendants. The result of their evidence can be gathered from the judgment.

Milward, Q.C., and *Aspinall*, for the plaintiffs, submitted that the agreement set up in the 6th paragraph of the statement of defence was so inadequate, that the court would disregard it and award a further sum to the plaintiffs.

E. C. Clarkson, and *Phillimore*, for the defendants, contended that even although the amount received by the plaintiffs should be considered less than would have been awarded by the court, yet the arrangement, having been made in good faith and by competent advisers on behalf of the plaintiffs, ought not to be disturbed.

SIR ROBERT PHILLIMORE: I am of opinion that the agreement in this case does not militate against the provisions of the 182d section of the Merchant Shipping Act, 1854. The question before me is not whether if the plaintiffs had been plaintiffs in an action of salvage the court would have awarded them more or less than the sum which they have agreed to accept, but whether any good ground has been shown for the court interfering with the arrangement that has been made. No doubt if any fraud or concealment had been shown the court would not hesitate to have the whole case re-opened, but in my opinion no evidence has been offered tending to show any fraud or concealment or any disreputable conduct in order to induce the plaintiffs to sign a receipt. Throughout the whole transaction they were assisted by a solicitor, who appears to have acted in perfect good faith, and indeed there is nothing extravagantly wrong in the settlement itself. In these circum- 197] stances *it would, in my opinion, be wrong to allow the matter to be re-opened. I must therefore dismiss the action with costs.

Solicitor for plaintiffs : *H. C. Coote.*
Solicitors for defendants : *Rollit & Sons.*

[5 Probate Division, 197.]

Feb. 27, 1880.

[IN THE COURT OF APPEAL.]

THE PARLEMENT BELGE (1878, O. 60).

Public Vessel—Exemption from Arrest—Trading by Public Vessel.

As a consequence of the absolute independence of every sovereign authority and of the international comity which induces every sovereign state to respect the independence of every other sovereign state, each state declines to exercise by means of any of its courts any of its territorial jurisdiction over the person of any sovereign or ambassador, or over the public property of any state which is destined to its public use, or over the property of any ambassador, though such sovereign, ambassador, or property be within its territory:

Held, therefore, reversing the decision of the Admiralty Division, that an unarmed packet belonging to the sovereign of a foreign state, and in the hands of officers commissioned by him, and employed in carrying mails, is not liable to be seized in a suit *in rem* to recover redress for a collision, and this immunity is not lost by reason of the packet's also carrying merchandise and passengers for hire.

THIS was an appeal on behalf of the Crown from a decision of Sir R. J. Phillimore([1]).

1879. Dec. 11, 12, 13, 20. *Sir H. S. Giffard*, S.G., the Admiralty Advocate (*Dr. Deane*, Q.C.), and *A. L. Smith*, for the appeal: This is a public ship, and apart from the convention she is not liable to seizure. She belongs to the King of the Belgians in his public character, and if she was trading contrary to her public character that is a question which cannot be raised by a private foreigner though our government might have a right to complain. The property of one sovereign is not subject to seizure in the territories of another, and that the vessel is not armed makes no difference. The carrying arms is only the most usual proof that a ship belongs to the government and is employed for public purposes. *The Exchange*([2]) was a strong case, but it has always *been accepted. Any property of a sovereign [198 is protected: *Vavassear v. Krupp*([3]). The goods on board may not be protected, but that does not affect the ship: *The Prins Frederik*([4]); *Briggs v. The Light-ships*([5]). This ship is employed by the King of the Belgians, officered by him, and carries his flag. She has been invited to the ports of this country under the belief that irrespective of the treaty she would not be subject to our laws. Moreover, she has been declared by the Crown to be a public ship, and

([1]) 4 P. D., 129. ([2]) 9 Ch. D., 351; 26 Eng. R., 166.
([2]) 7 Cranch, 116. ([4]) 2 Dod., 451.
([5]) 11 Allen (Mass.), 157.

this declaration is conclusive. The court cannot go behind the declaration of the Crown as to the political status either of persons or things. The Crown determines what is an independent government. The Crown declares a blockade, and many other cases may be put. It is argued that this gives the Crown a power inconsistent with the constitution, but that is not so.

[BRETT, L.J.: Can Her Majesty give to a private ship privileges not recognized by international law?]

It is not necessary to say that she can, but Her Majesty's declaration that the ship is a public ship is conclusive. The international law is part of the common law of England, *Triquet* v. *Bath* ('), and by international law a public ship is free from arrest. The general language of acts of Parliament however large is construed *salvo jure reginæ*.

[*Webster*, Q.C.: That is not disputed.]

Then the question is, whether Her Majesty can recognize, and by recognizing affirm, the political character of a thing so as to free it from the ordinary jurisdiction of the courts. Every person residing here is subject to the laws of this country, and the proposition in Viner's Abridgment, Prerogative, T. 7, 8, that the Queen cannot give a foreigner an exemption from being impleaded here is not disputed, but if by a principle of international law a person having a particular character is not liable to be so impleaded the Queen's recognition of him as having that character is conclusive in all her courts.

[BRETT, L.J.: I do not feel clear that if Her Majesty chose thus to recognize as ambassador a person who had not been sent by any foreign government he could claim the privileges of an ambassador.]

199] *JAMES, L.J.: How can any municipal court try that question? I apprehend that we should be bound to act on the representation of the foreign office.]

The appellants merely use the treaty in the present case in order to get rid of the argument that the ship is not a public ship because of her trading. Were it not for that they would simply rely on her being a public ship.

[BAGGALAY, L.J. Suppose the conditions in Article X of the treaty were broken, is the ship still privileged?]

Yes, until the treaty is abrogated for breach it remains in force : Kent Comm. I, 183.

[JAMES, L.J.: Would a treaty that all Belgian ships should have the privileges of Belgian ships of war be binding?]

(') 8 Burr., 1478.

It is not necessary to say that it would, but only that the allegation that the ship is a public ship is conclusive. As to her being a public ship, the question is now what is the purpose for which she is used? The distinction is not between public ship of war and private ship of war, but between public ship and private ship. The law is summed up in 1 Phill. Int. Law, 404, 2d ed. According to that, what is the evidence of the character of the ship—armament, or commission? No doubt commission. A transport or troop-ship commanded by an officer holding a commission from government is a public ship, though unarmed; a privateer though armed is not. A vessel belonging to a sovereign in his public capacity is a public ship whether armed or not: *Briggs* v. *The Light-ships* ('). In the case of *The Constitution* ('), a public vessel, though carrying cargo, was held privileged. An armed frigate belonging to a government is undoubtedly privileged—but suppose her steam launch, which is not armed, ran down a vessel, she certainly would also be privileged as part of the fleet. Trading cannot take away the privilege, for if so it would take away the privilege from a man of war: *The Santissima Trinidad* (').

Webster, Q.C., and *Phillimore*, contrà: This vessel was in fact mainly employed as a trading vessel. The fact of a vessel being in the possession of the sovereign of a country does not *necessarily make her a public vessel, and [200 she is not so if she is employed in carrying goods and passengers for hire. The privilege is by international law confined to vessels which form part of the armed force of a country: *The Exchange* ('). The reasoning in which case (') is inconsistent with the idea that the court went only on the public character of the vessel apart from her being armed. In *United States* v. *Wilder* (') general average was enforced against goods of the United States, it being held that the property of a sovereign is not exempt from process. Halleck's Int. Law, p. 176, ed. 1878, and Phill. Int. Law, vol. i, 2d ed., p. 343 *et seq.*, support this contention. The opinion of Lord Stowell set out in the report of 1876 by the Royal Commission on Fugitive Slaves, p. lxxvi, is in terms which imply that he did not consider a public ship to stand on the same footing as a ship of war. Being owned by a sovereign is not sufficient to give privilege to a ship, and, unless carrying mails is such a public service as to give privilege to ships employed in it, this is not a ship employed for a public

(') 11 Allen (Mass.), 157, 165, 186.   (⁴) 7 Cranch, 116.
(') 4 P. D., 39.   (⁵) 7 Cranch, 116, at p. 142.
(') 7 Wheat., 283.   (⁶) 3 Sumn., 308, 313.

purpose. No vessel employed in carrying on a mere commercial enterprise has ever been held privileged. Again, this is not a suit properly speaking against the owners, there is no personal citation to them, it is a proceeding *in rem* to perfect an inchoate maritime lien, *The Bold Buccleugh* ('); and this is no breach of the privilege if any exists.

[JAMES, L.J.: According to your argument any one may seize the ship of a foreign sovereign unless he will appear and defend, which is derogatory. The distinction between giving a remedy against the sovereign and giving a remedy seems unsubstantial.]

The courts have treated the difference as substantial. In *The Ticonderoga* (') there was a collision while the vessel was engaged in the French service, and in an action *in rem*, after the determination of the charterparty, a remedy was enforced against the ship, which shows that there may be a right against the ship which is suspended, for there the ship could not have been proceeded against at the time.

[BRETT, L.J., referred to *The Athol* (').]

201]   *The Solicitor-General says this is the first attempt to attach a vessel under these circumstances, but until the case of *The Exchange* (') it was doubtful whether even a ship of war had the privilege.

[JAMES, L.J.: That is mere matter of history. You admit it to be settled that she has such a privilege.]

· The observations of Lord Stowell in *The Prins Frederik* (') show that at that time he did not consider it any absurdity to suppose that a ship of war could be arrested. The freedom from arrest is of modern growth and ought not to be extended. Ships of war stand on a different footing from other public vessels, the expeditions on which they are sent may be of the most important immediate consequence to the country. Moreover they are under martial law, and if they were to be held subject to civil law there would be a conflict: Ortolan de la Diplomacie de la Mer, 2d ed., bk. ii, c. 10, 211, 217. In *Morgan* v. *Lariviere* (') the title to property was decided upon adversely to a foreign government.

[JAMES, L.J.: There was a trustee who could be sued here.

BAGGALLAY, L.J.: The observations on page 433 show that the case is no authority for the present case.]

In *Gladstone* v. *Musurus Bey* (') there was a decision against a foreign sovereign.

(¹) 7 Moo. P. C., 267.

(²) Swa., 215.

(³) 1 Wm. Rob., 374.

(⁴) 7 Cranch, 116.

(⁵) 2 Dods., 451, 484, 485.

(⁶) Law Rep., 7 H. L., 423; 12 Eng. R., 52.

(⁷) 1 H. & M., 495; 32 L. J. (Ch.), 155.

[JAMES, L.J.: There again the property was in trustees.]
The case of *Vavasseur* v. *Krupp* (¹) has been referred to,
but there the ships were not in use in this country, and the
object of the action was to deal with property in the absence
of the owner. In *Taylor* v. *Best* (²) an action against several defendants, one of whom was privileged, having been
allowed to go on to replication, the privilege was not allowed.
There also Jervis, C.J., said that if the suit could proceed
without proceeding against the person of the ambassador it
could go on, and the same principle was laid down in the
Maddalena Steam Navigation Co. v. *Martin* (³). In *The
Santissima Trinidad* (⁴) it is laid down that the question
whether a ship is a public ship must be *tried by the' [202
court, and that the property of a sovereign may be seized
by a proceeding *in rem*. The case of *Briggs* v. *The Light-
ships* (⁵) is distinguishable, for the suit was not an admiralty
suit *in rem*, but a suit to enforce a statutory local lien which
could not be enforced without personal citation. The *United
States* v. *Wilder* (⁶) shows that this makes a difference. It
is said that as a man cannot sue his own sovereign, so by
the comity of nations he cannot sue a foreign sovereign ; but
the rule is not coextensive in the two cases. If the ship is
not a ship of war the proceeding *in rem* is allowable, though
a foreign sovereign be the owner: *Prioleau* v. *United
States* (⁷) ; *The Marquis of Huntley* (⁸) ; *The Cybele* (⁹) ; and
Bynkershoek favor this view.

[THE COURT intimated that the effect of the convention
need not be argued at present.]

Sir H. S. Giffard, S.G., in reply : The respondents refer
to Bynkershoek, but do not cite him, for he proves too much ;
he maintains that ships of war can be seized, a doctrine
which all the text-writers repudiate : Wheaton's Int. Law,
199, ed. Lawrence. The case of *The Santissima Trinidad* (⁴)
is treated of in *Briggs* v. *The Light-ships* (⁵), and explained
by the court. It was a question of prize or no prize, which
by the consensus of nations is remitted to the prize courts.
The privilege depends on the immunity of the sovereign, not
on anything peculiar to a ship of war, though it seldom
arises as to anything else, because hardly anything belonging to a sovereign in his public capacity, except a ship of
war, ever goes wandering into the jurisdiction of foreign
courts. As regards the distinction between proceedings *in*

(¹) 9 Ch. D., 351 ; 26 Eng. R., 166.   (⁵) 11 Allen (Mass.), 157.
(²) 14 C. B., 487 ; 28 L. J. (C.P.), 89.   (⁶) 3 Sumn., 308.
(³) 2 E. & E., 94 ; 28 L. J. (Q.B.), 310.   (⁷) Law Rep., 2 Eq., 659.
(⁴) 7 Wheat., 283.   (⁸) 3 Hagg., 246.
(⁹) 3 P. D., 8 ; *ante*, p. 8.

rem and *in personam*, it is difficult to understand an action against a thing. A proceeding *in rem* is only a mode of suing the owners. Precisely the same argument was used in the case of *The Exchange* (¹) as here, that there was nothing derogatory to the dignity of a sovereign in a pro eed ng *in rem* against his property, but it did not prevail. c*Wads-*
203] *worth* v. *Queen of Spain* (²) and *De Haber* v.*Queen of Portugal* (³) support the view that a proceeding against property is a mode of suing the owner.

[JAMES, L.J.: But for the Admiralty Court Act, 1861 (24 Vict. c. 10), this ship could not have been proceeded against in the Admiralty Court, as the collision did not take place on the high seas. It would be rather singular if an English statute, passed only for the more convenient distribution of business, were to be held to affect the rights of a foreign sovereign.]

Cur. adv. vult.

1880. Feb. 27. The judgment of the Court (James, Baggallay, and Brett, L.J.,) was delivered by

BRETT, L.J.: In this case proceedings *in rem* on behalf of the owners of the Daring were instituted in the Admiralty Division, in accordance with the forms prescribed by the Judicature Act, against the Parlement Belge, to recover redress in respect of a collision. A writ was served in the usual and prescribed manner on board the Parlement Belge. No appearance was entered, but the Attorney-General, in answer to a motion to direct that ju gment with costs should be entered for the plaintiffs, and that a warrant should be issued for the arrest of the Parlement Belge, filed an information and protest, asserting that the court had no jurisdiction to entertain the suit. Upon the hearing of the motion and protest the learned judge of the Admiralty Division overruled the protest and allowed the warrant of arrest to issue. The Attorney-General appealed. The protest alleged that the Parlement Belge was a mail packet running between Ostend and Dover, and one of the packets mentioned in article 6 of the convention of the 17th of February, 1876, made between the sovereigns of Great Britain and Belgium ; that she was and is the property of his Majesty the King of the Belgians, and in his possession, control, and employ as reigning sovereign of the state, and was and is a public vessel of the sovereign and state, carrying his Majesty's royal pennon, and was navigated and employed by and in the possession of such government, and was officered by officers

(¹) 7 Cranch, 116. (²) 17 Q. B., 171. (³) 17 Q. B., 196.

of the Royal Belgian navy, holding commissions, &c. In answer it was averred on affidavits, which were not contradicted, that the packet boat, *besides carrying let- [204 ters, carried merchandise and passengers and their luggage for hire.

Three main questions were argued before us : (1.) Whether, irrespective of the express exemption contained in article 6 of the convention, the court had jurisdiction to seize the Belgian vessel in a suit *in rem ;* (2.) whether, if the court would otherwise have such jurisdiction, it was ousted by article 6 of the convention ; (3.) whether any exemption from the jurisdiction of the court, which the vessel might otherwise have had, was lost by reason of her trading in the carriage of goods and persons. In the course of the argument we desired that it might, in the first instance, be confined to the first and third questions, reserving any further argument on the second question to be heard subsequently, if necessary. We have come to the conclusion that no such argument is necessary. We, therefore, give no opinion upon the second question. We neither affirm nor deny the propriety of the judgment of the learned judge of the Admiralty Division on that question.

The proposition raised by the first question seems to be as follows : Has the Admiralty Division jurisdiction in respect of a collision to proceed *in rem* against, and, in case of non-appearance or omission to find bail, to seize and sell, a ship present in this country, which ship is at the time of the proceedings the property of a foreign sovereign, is in his possession, control, and employ as sovereign by means of his commissioned officers, and is a public vessel of his state, in the sense of its being used for purposes treated by such sovereign and his advisers as public national services, it being admitted that such ship, though commissioned, is not an armed ship of war or employed as a part of the military force of his country ? On the one side it is urged that the only ships exempted from the jurisdiction are armed ships of war, or ships which, though not armed, are in the employ of the government as part of the military force of the state. On the other side it is contended that all movable property, which is the public property of a sovereign and nation used for public purposes, is exempt from adverse interference by any court of judicature. It is admitted that neither the sovereign of Great Britain nor any friendly sovereign can be adversely personally impleaded in any *court of this [205 country. It is admitted that no armed ship of war of the sovereign of Great Britain or of a foreign sovereign can be seized by any process whatever, exercised for any purpose, of any court of this country. But it is said that this vessel, though it is the property of a friendly sovereign in his public capacity and is used for purposes treated by him as public national services, can be seized and sold under the process of the Admiralty Court of this country, because it will, if so seized and sold, be so treated, not in a suit brought against the sovereign personally, but in a suit *in rem* against the vessel itself. This contention raises two questions: first, supposing that an action *in rem* is an action against the property only, meaning thereby that it is not a legal proceeding at all against the owner of the property; yet can the property in question be subject to the jurisdiction of the court? Secondly, is it true to say that an action *in rem* is only and solely a legal procedure against the property, or is it not rather a procedure indirectly, if not directly, impleading the owner of the property to answer to the judgment of the court to the extent of his interest in the property?

The first question really raises this, whether every part of the public property of every sovereign authority in use for national purposes is not as much exempt from the jurisdiction of every court as is the person of every sovereign. Whether it is so or not depends upon whether all nations have agreed that it shall be, or in other words, whether it is so by the law of nations. The exemption of the person of every sovereign from adverse suit is admitted to be a part of the law of nations. An equal exemption from interference by any process of any court of some property of every sovereign is admitted to be a part of the law of nations. The universal agreement which has made these propositions part of the law of nations has been an implied agreement. Whether the law of nations exempts all the public property of a state which is destined to the use of the state, depends on whether the principle, on which the agreement has been implied, is as applicable to all that other public property of a sovereign or state as to the public property which is admitted to be exempt. If the principle be equally applicable to all public property used as such, then the agreement to exempt ought to be implied with regard to all such public 206] *property. If the principle only applies to the property which is admitted to be exempt, then we have no right to extend the exemption.

The first question, therefore, is—What is the principle on which the exemption of the person of sovereigns and of certain public properties has been recognized? "Our king," says Blackstone (B. 1, c. 7), "owes no kind of subjection to any other potentate on earth. Hence it is that no suit or action can be brought against the king, even in civil matters, because no court can have jurisdiction over him. For all jurisdiction implies superiority of power; authority to try would be vain and idle without an authority to redress, and the sentence of a court would be contemptible unless the court had power to command the execution of it, but who shall command the king?" In this passage, which has been often cited and relied on, the reason of the exemption is the character of the sovereign authority, its high dignity, whereby it is not subject to any superior authority of any kind. "The world," says Wheaton, adopting the words of the judgment in the case of *The Exchange* ('), "being composed of distinct sovereignties, possessing equal rights and equal independence, all sovereigns have consented to a relaxation in practice, under certain peculiar circumstances, of that absolute and complete jurisdiction within their respective territories which sovereignty confers." "This perfect equality and absolute independence of sovereigns has given rise to a class of cases in which every sovereign is understood to waive the exercise of a part of that complete exclusive territorial jurisdiction which has been stated to be the attribute of every nation." "One of these is the exemption of the person of the sovereign from arrest or detention within a foreign territory. Why have the whole world concurred in this? The answer cannot be mistaken. A foreign sovereign is not understood as intending to subject himself to a jurisdiction incompatible with his dignity and the dignity of his nation." By dignity is obviously here meant his independence of any superior authority. So Vattel, Lib. 4, c. 7, s. 108, speaking of sovereigns, says: "S'il est venu en voyageur, sa dignité seule, et ce qui est dû à la nation qu'il représente et qu'il gouverne, le met à couvert de toute insulte, lui *assure des respects et toute sorte [207 d'égards, et l'exempte de toute juridiction."

In the case of *The Duke of Brunswick* v. *The King of Hanover* ('), the suit was against the king. There was a demurrer to the jurisdiction. Lord Langdale in an elaborate judgment allowed the demurrer. He rejected the alleged doctrine of a fictitious extra-territoriality; he admitted that there are some reasons which might justify the exemption of ambassadors which do not necessarily apply to a sovereign, but he nevertheless adopted an analogy between the cases of the ambassadors and the sovereign, and allowed

(') 7 Cranch, 116.   (') 6 Beav., 1.

the demurrer on the ground that the sovereign character is
superior to all jurisdiction. "After giving to the subject,"
he says ('), "the best consideration in my power, it appearing to me that all the reasons upon which the immunities of
ambassadors are founded do not apply to the case of sovereigns, but that there are reasons for the immunities of sovereign princes, at least as strong if not much stronger than any
which have been advanced for the immunities of ambassadors; that suits against sovereign princes of foreign countries must, in all ordinary cases in which orders or declarations of right may be made, and in requests for justice,
which might be made without any suit at all; that even the
failure of justice in some particular cases would be less prejudicial than attempts to obtain it by violating immunities
thought necessary to the independence of princess and nations, I think that on the whole it ought to be considered as
a general rule, in accordance with the law of nations, that a
sovereign prince resident in the dominions of another is exempt from the jurisdiction of the courts there."

From all these authorities it seems to us, although other
reasons have sometimes been suggested, that the real principle
on which the exemption of every sovereign from the jurisdiction of every court has been deduced is that the exercise of
such jurisdiction would be incompatible with his regal dignity—that is to say, with his absolute independence of every
superior authority. By a similar examination of authorities
we come to the conclusion, although other grounds have
sometimes been suggested, that the immunity of an ambas-
208] sador from the jurisdiction of the courts of *the
country to which he is accredited is based upon his being
the representative of the independent sovereign or state
which sends him, and which sends him upon the faith of his
being admitted to be clothed with the same independence of
and superiority to all adverse jurisdiction as the sovereign
authority whom he represents would be.

The reason of the exemption of ships of war and some
other ships must be next considered, and the first case to be
carefully considered is, and always will be, *The Exchange* (').
It is undoubted that the decision applies, in fact, only to
the case of a ship of war. Yet, in considering what was the
principle on which the judgment was founded, there are
some important circumstances to which attention must be
directed. The plaintiffs filed their libel against the schooner
Exchange, found in an American port, and prayed for the
usual process to attach the vessel, and that she might be

(') 6 Beav., 1, at p. 50.   (') 7 Cranch, 116.

restored to her owners. Upon this libel the usual process
in a cause of restitution was issued and executed, that is to
say, the vessel was detained. There was no appearance in
the suit. Then the usual proclamations issued for all persons to appear and show cause why the vessel should not
be restored to the owners. No person appeared. Then the
Attorney-General of the United States appeared and filed a
suggestion. In this it must be noticed that the vessel is not
described as "an armed ship of war," but as "a certain
public vessel belonging to his Imperial Majesty, and actually
employed in his service." It certainly is to be remarked
that those who conducted this case with unusual ability,
deliberately, in stating the cause of objection, rested the
claim of exemption not on the fact of the vessel being an
armed ship of war, but on the fact of her being one of a larger
class, namely, "a public vessel belonging to a sovereign,
and employed in the public service." It is upon the suggestion so pleaded, that the court gives judgment. It is
right, however, to say that the fact of the vessel being an
armed ship of war was before the court, and that the judgment frequently uses that phrase, though by no means
invariably. It is impossible within reasonable bounds to
set out the elaborate judgment of Marshall, C.J., and the
court. The reasoning seems to be as *follows: The [209
ship is within the territorial jurisdiction of the United States
—*prima facie* the Court of the United States has jurisdiction. But all nations have agreed to certain limitations of
their absolute territorial jurisdiction—as, for instance, they
have abjured all personal jurisdiction over a foreign sovereign
within their territory, and this on account of his dignity, and
all personal jurisdiction over foreign ministers, and, says
the judgment, this is on the same principle; and all jurisdiction over a foreign army passing through the territory.
Is the same immunity to be held to apply to ships of war?
The judgment answers, Yes, and upon the same principle:
i.e., that to hold otherwise would be inconsistent with the
dignity—that is to say, the recognized independence of the
foreign sovereign. After dealing with the case of private
foreigners and merchant vessels in a foreign country, the
judgment continues, "But in all respects different is the
situation of a public armed ship; she constitutes a part of
the military force of her nation, acts under the immediate
and direct command of her sovereign, is employed by him
in national objects. He has many and powerful motives for
preventing those objects from being defeated by the interference of a foreign state. Such interference cannot take

place without affecting his power and dignity. The implied
license therefore under which such vessel enters a friendly
port may reasonably be construed, and it seems to the court
ought to be construed, as containing an exemption from the
jurisdiction of the sovereign within whose territory she claims
the rites of hospitality."

The Prins Frederik (¹) seems to us to be worthy of great
attention. An armed ship of war belonging to the King of the
Netherlands was arrested on a claim for salvage. The case
was elaborately argued upon the question of jurisdiction.
An argument of the closest and most forcible reasoning, to
which we see no answer, was presented by Dr. Arnold, the
admiralty advocate (see p. 466). "There is a class of things,"
he says, "which are not subject to the ordinary rules applying to property, which are not liable to the claims or de-
mands of private persons, which are described by civilians
as *extra commercium*, and in a general enumeration are by
210] them denominated *sacra religiosa, publica *publicis
usibus destinata*. These are things which are allowed to
be, and from their nature must be, exempt and free from all
private rights and claims of individuals, inasmuch as if these
claims were to be allowed against them, the arrest, the
judicial possession and judicial sale incident to such proceedings would divert them from those public uses to which
they are destined. Ships of war belonging to the state are
included in this class of things, by their nature and of
necessity arising from their nature. The same inconvenience
which would arise from such proceedings in the courts of
their own country, would equally arise if such vessels could
be arrested and detained in a foreign port. There is another
point of view. It is the interest and duty of every sovereign
independent state to maintain unimpeached its honor and
dignity." The point and force of this argument is that the
public property of every state, being destined to public
uses, cannot with reason be submitted to the jurisdiction
of the courts of such state, because such jurisdiction, if
exercised, must divert the public property from its destined
public uses; and that, by international comity, which
acknowledges the equality of states, if such immunity,
grounded on such reasons, exist in each state with regard
to its own public property, the same immunity must be
granted by each state to similar property of all other states.
The dignity and independence of each state require this
reciprocity. It was this reasoning which induced Sir William Scott to hesitate to exercise jurisdiction, and so to act

(¹) 2 Dod., 451.

as to intimate his opinion that the reason could not be controverted. The case has always been considered as conveying his opinion to have been to that effect. Such was the view of Lord Campbell, who in *De Haber* v. *The Queen of Portugal* (') says that the difficulties suggested by the argument were in the opinion of Sir William Scott insuperable. But if so, he assented to an argument which embraced in one class "all public property" of the state, and treated "armed ships of war" as a member of that class.

In the case of *The Athol* (') Dr. Lushington certainly extended the immunity from jurisdiction to a troop-ship, which was not an armed ship of war, though she was employed in a sense as part of the military force of the country. The reason of his judgment *was in terms that in [211 cases of tort or damage committed by vessels of the Crown, the legal responsibility attaches to the actual wrongdoer only. That is in effect to say that the vessels of the Crown cannot be touched.

We come next to the important case of *Briggs* v. *The Light-ships* ('). By the Massachusetts Statute it was enacted that "any person to whom money is due for labor and materials furnished in the construction of a vessel shall have a lien upon her, which lien may be enforced by petition to the superior court praying for a sale of the vessel. The petition may be entered or filed, a process of attachment issue against the vessel, and notice be given to the owner thereof to appear and answer to the petition." This enactment gave a statutory lien on the vessel, to be enforced by process of a court. It is a more extensive lien than the common law possessory lien in respect of work done on the vessel, as it is not lost by loss of possession. It is to be enforced by the same process as a maritime lien. It is therefore in effect an enactment which applies the incidents of a maritime lien to a new subject-matter, viz., a claim for work and labor in the construction of a vessel. It follows that upon the point raised in that case the reasoning must be as applicable to every maritime lien, and the means of enforcing it, as to that similar statutory lien. Now, in that case the plaintiffs filed a petition and prayed an attachment and sale of the vessel. The court thereupon issued process of attachment and ordered notice to be given to the United States by service on their attorney. The vessel was attached and notice given accordingly. The United States appeared specially and pleaded to the jurisdiction, that at the time of the filing of the petition the vessels were the public property of

(') 17 Q. B., 171.   (') 1 Wm. Rob., 374.   (') 11 Allen, 157.

the United States and in their possession, and held and
owned by them for public uses, and as instruments employed by them for the execution of their sovereign and
constitutional powers, and, therefore, not subject to the process or jurisdiction of the court.   The question, therefore,
was whether the court had jurisdiction to take possession
of the vessels in order to sue them if necessary, and to give
notice to the government that if they had any objection to
such sale they must appear?   Every step in that case was
212]   the same as *in the case of *The Exchange* ('), and as
in the present case.   The objection to the jurisdiction as
pleaded was in substance the same as that pleaded in the
case of *The Exchange* (') and in the present case.   The vessels, however, were not ships of war, or vessels employed in
the military service of the state.   They were like the Parlement Belge—vessels which were the public property of the
state and in their possession, and held and owned by them
for uses treated by them as public.   It is obvious that all
the arguments which have been used in the present case
on behalf of the plaintiffs might have been, and almost
certainly were, used in that case.   But the court gave
judgment declining the jurisdiction.   "It is said for the
petitioners" (says the judgment at p. 165) "that these light
boats were not intended for military service.   But after they
had once come into the possession of the United States for
public uses, they were subject to the exclusive control of the
executive government of the United States, and could not
be interfered with by state process.   The immunity from
such interference arises, not because they are instruments
of war, but because they are instruments of sovereignty.
These reasons have satisfied us that there is no principle
upon which the courts of this commonwealth can entertain
jurisdiction of these petitions."   The judgment then reviews
many cases, amongst others *The Marquis of Huntley* ('), in
which Sir John Nicholl treated "government stores" in
charge of a lieutenant, but on board a ship which was only
chartered by government, as beyond his jurisdiction, though
the ship and freight were within it, *The Schooner Merchant* ('),
in Florida, in which it was held that the "mails" could
not be arrested or detained for salvage.   *The Thomas A.
Scott* ('), in which a "transport ship" owned by the United
States, but not commissioned, was held to be beyond jurisdiction.   The judgment ends thus: "The exemption of a
public ship of war of a foreign government from the juris-

(¹) 7 Cranch, 116.   (³) Marvin on Wreck and Salvage, s. 122.
(²) 3 Hagg., 246.   (⁴) 10 L. T. (N.S.), 726.

diction of our courts depends rather upon its public than upon its military character." The reasoning of that careful judgment is the reasoning of the Admiralty advocate in the case of *The Prins Frederik* ('). The *ground of [213 that judgment is that the public property of a government in use for public purposes is beyond the jurisdiction of the courts of either its own or any other state, and that ships of war are beyond such jurisdiction, not because they are ships of war, but because they are public property. It puts all the public movable property of a state, which is in its possession for public purposes, in the same category of immunity from jurisdiction as the person of a sovereign, or of an ambassador, or of ships of war, and exempts it from the jurisdiction of all courts for the same reason—viz., that the exercise of such jurisdiction is inconsistent with the independence of the sovereign authority of the state.

The judgment of Lord Campbell in *De Haber* v. *The Queen of Portugal* (') seems to the same effect, though the decision may fairly be said to apply only to a suit directly brought against the sovereign. But he relies on the Statute of Anne with regard to ambassadors, and says, "Can we doubt that in the opinion of that great judge (Lord Holt) the sovereign himself would have been considered entitled to the same protection, immunity, and privilege as the minister who represents him." And he cites the statute thus: "It has always been said to be merely declaratory of the law of nations recognized and enforced by our municipal law, and it provides that all process whereby the person of any ambassador or of his domestic servants may be arrested, *or his goods distrained or seized* shall be utterly null and void." The italics are as written by Lord Campbell. And further, citing *The Prins Frederik* ('), he says, "Objection being made that the court had no jurisdiction, a distinction was attempted that the salvors were not suing the King of the Netherlands, and that being in possession of and having a lien upon a ship which they had saved, the proceeding might be considered *in rem.* But Lord Stowell saw such insuperable difficulties in judicially assessing the amount of salvage, the payment of which was to be enforced by sale, that he caused representation to be made to the Dutch government, who very honorably consented to his disposing of the matter as an arbitrator." The decision therefore is that the immunity of the sovereign is at least as great as the immunity of an ambassador, but as the statute declares that the law is, and always has been, not *only that an [214

(') 2 Dod., 451.	(') 17 Q. B., 171.

ambassador is free from personal suit or process, but that his goods are free from such process as distress or seizure, the latter meaning seizure by process of law, it follows that the goods of every sovereign are free from any seizure by process of law.

The latest case on the point seems to be the case of *Vavasseur* v. *Krupp* (¹) before this court. The question was whether the English court had jurisdiction to order "shells" belonging to the Mikado of Japan to be destroyed, supposing they were an infringement of the plaintiff's patent. All the judges held that there was no such jurisdiction. "I suppose," says James, L.J., "that there is a notion that in some way these shells became tainted or affected through the breach or attempted breach of the patent, but even then a foreign sovereign cannot be deprived of his property because it has become tainted by the infringement of somebody's patent. He says, 'It is my public property, and I ask you for it.' That seems to me to be the whole of the case." Brett, L.J., said, "The goods were the property of the Mikado. They were his property as a sovereign—they were the property of his country." "I shall assume, for this purpose, that there was an infringement of the patent, yet the Mikado has a perfect right to have these goods; no court in this country can properly prevent him from having goods which are the public property of his own country." And Cotton, L.J., says, "This court has no jurisdiction, and in my opinion none of the courts in this country have any jurisdiction to interfere with the property of a foreign sovereign, more especially with what we call the public property of the state of which he is sovereign, as distinguished from that which may be his own private property. The courts have no jurisdiction to do so, not only because there is no jurisdiction as against the individual, but because there is no jurisdiction as against the foreign country whose property they are, although that foreign country is represented, as all foreign countries having a sovereign are represented, by the individual who is the sovereign."

The principle to be deduced from all these cases is that, as a consequence of the absolute independence of every sovereign authority, and of the international comity which induces every sovereign state to respect the independence 215] and dignity of every *other sovereign state, each and every one declines to exercise by means of its courts any of its territorial jurisdiction over the person of any sovereign or ambassador of any other state, or over the public

(¹) 9 Ch. D., 351; 26 Eng. R., 166.

property of any state which is destined to public use, or over the property of any ambassador, though such sovereign, ambassador, or property be within its territory, and, therefore, but for the common agreement, subject to its jurisdiction.

It is said, however, that there are authorities inconsistent with the view that this is a part of international law. The case of *The Santissima Trinidad* (') is relied on. But, as was pointed out in the judgment in *Briggs* v. *The Lightships* ('), the former case is one depending upon a well known doctrine of the law of prize, viz., that property captured in breach of the laws of neutrality is held by the prize courts of the neutral state not to be lawful prize. In the case of the *United States* v. *Wilden* (') it would be uncandid to say that there are not expressions of Story, J., which are in favor of the contention that the immunity from jurisdiction is confined to ships and materials of war. But in that case the right which was adverse to the United States Government was a possessory lien for general average. The remedy of the shipowner was in his own hands. He required no assistance from any process of any court, as would also be the case in a lien for freight. As a decision, therefore, the case is not in point, because the United States were plaintiffs voluntarily seeking the assistance of the Massachusetts tribunal. But it seems to us sufficient to say that we do not consider the observations of Story, J., to countervail effectually the arguments and decisions in the other cases which have been cited. There is then the opinion of the learned judge of the Admiralty Division, expressed in the case of *The Charkieh* ('). The decision is, of course, not in point, because the case was decided on the ground that the Khedive was not an independent sovereign. But there is a careful consideration in the judgment of the question whether the ship would have been liable to the jurisdiction of the court, in proceedings *in rem* in respect of a collision, if the Khedive had been a sovereign prince. The conclusion is that she would have been. Such an opinion deserves *respect-   [216 ful attention. We are not quite sure whether we correctly appreciate the grounds of the opinion. The learned judge agrees that "an ambassador is personally exempt from the service of all process in a civil cause and from any action which renders such service necessary;" and that "the law as to the privileges of an ambassador applies with equal

(¹) 7 Wheat., 283.   (⁴) Law Rep., 4 A. & E., 59; 6 Eng.
(²) 11 Allen (Mass.), 157.   R. 400.
(³) 3 Sumn., 308.

force to the sovereign." "But," he continues, "it remains
to be considered whether there may not be a proceeding *in
rem* against property of the sovereign or ambassador which
is free from the objections fatal to the other modes of procedure." He then says "that he would be prepared to hold
that proceedings *in rem* in some cases may be instituted
without any violation of international law, though the owner
of the *res* be in the category of persons privileged from personal suit." This is an intimation of an opinion not yet
conclusively formed that proceedings *in rem* are a legal procedure solely against property, and not directly or indirectly
against the owner of the property. But then he says that a
proceeding *in rem* cannot be instituted against the property
of a sovereign or an ambassador, if the *res* can in any fair
sense be said to be connected with the *jus coronæ* of the
sovereign, or the discharge of the functions of the ambassador. From this one would infer that no personal process
can issue against a sovereign or an ambassador ; that no
process *in rem* can issue against any property which can in
any fair sense be said to be connected with the *jus coronæ*,
but that such process might issue against other property of
a sovereign or an ambassador. But then he says that "it is
by no means clear that a ship of war to which salvage services have been rendered may not *jure gentium* be liable to
be proceeded against in a Court of Admiralty for the remuneration of such services." Yet such proceedings are undoubtedly by means of process *in rem*, and it can hardly be
denied that a ship of war is property connected with the *jus
coronæ*. "I am disposed to hold," he says, "that in case
of salvage or collision the *obligatio* attaches *jure gentium*
upon the ship whatever be her character, public or private."
If this includes a ship of war it seems to us difficult to understand how it is not inconsistent with the principle of the
judgment in the cases of *The Exchange* (') and *Briggs v.
217] The Light-ships* ('). If it does not *include a ship
of war, the distinction between other processes and the process *in rem* is not always an answer in the claim of immunity. But then the learned judge expresses an opinion
that in the case before him there was a nearer goal at hand,
because it was idle to contend that the ships were not trading vessels to all intents and purposes, though, when engaged
in their regular employment they carried mail-bags. This
seems to intimate that the ships then in question were not
public ships at all. We cannot think that this judgment
discloses any final opinion of the learned judge, either as to

(') 7 Cranch, 116.   (') 11 Allen (Mass.), 157.

the limits of the nature of the property which is exempt or
as to the whole nature of the action *in rem* with regard to
the question under discussion.   Having carefully considered
the case of *The Charkieh* (¹) we are of opinion that the proposition deduced from the earlier cases in an earlier part of
this judgment is the correct exposition of the law of nations,
viz., that as a consequence of the absolute independence of
every sovereign authority and of the international comity,
which induces every sovereign state to respect the independence of every other sovereign state, each and every one
declines to exercise by means of any of its courts, any of its
territorial jurisdiction over the person of any sovereign or
ambassador of any other state, or over the public property
of any state which is destined to its public use, or over the
property of any ambassador, though such sovereign, ambassador or property be within its territory, and therefore, but
for the common agreement, subject to its jurisdiction.

This proposition would determine the first question in the
present case in favor of the protest, even if an action *in rem*
were held to be a proceeding solely against property, and
not a procedure directly or indirectly impleading the owner
of the property to answer to the judgment of the court.
But we cannot allow it to be supposed that in our opinion
the owner of the property is not indirectly impleaded.   The
course of proceeding, undoubtedly, is first to seize the property.   It is, undoubtedly, not necessary, in order to enable
the court to proceed further, that the owner should be personally served with any process.   In the majority of cases
brought under the cognizance of an Admiralty Court no
such personal service could be effected.   Another course
*was therefore taken from the earliest times.   The [218
seizure of the property was made by means of a formality
which was as public as could be devised.   That formality of
necessity gave notice of the suit to the agents of the owner
of the property, and so, in substance, to him.   Besides
which, by the regular course of the admiralty, the owner
was cited or had notice to appear to show cause why his
property should not be liable to answer to the complainant.
The owner has a right to appear and show cause, a right
which cannot be denied.   It is not necessary, it is true, that
the notice or citation should be personally served.   But unless it were considered that, either by means of the publicity
of the manner of arresting the property or by means of the
publicity of the notice or citation, the owner had an opportunity of protecting his property from a final decree by the

(¹) Law Rep., 4 A. & E., 59; 6 Eng. R., 400.

court, the judgment *in rem* of a court would be manifestly contrary to natural justice. In a claim made in respect of a collision the property is not treated as the delinquent per se. Though the ship has been in collision and has caused injury by reason of the negligence or want of skill of those in charge of her, yet she cannot be made the means of compensation if those in charge of her were not the servants of her then owner, as if she was in charge of a compulsory pilot. This is conclusive to show that the liability to compensate must be fixed not merely on the property but also on the owner through the property. If so, the owner is at least indirectly impleaded to answer to, that is to say, to be affected by, the judgment of the court. It is no answer to say that if the property be sold after the maritime lien has accrued the property may be seized and sold as against the new owner. This is a severe law, probably arising from the difficulty of otherwise enforcing any remedy in favor of an injured suitor. But the property cannot be sold as against the new owner, if it could not have been sold as against the owner at the time when the alleged lien accrued. This doctrine of the Courts of Admiralty goes only to this extent, that the innocent purchaser takes the property subject to the inchoate maritime lien which attached to it as against him who was the owner at the time the lien attached. The new owner has the same public notice of the suit and the same opportunity and right of appearance as the former 219] owner would have had. He is *impleaded in the same way as the former owner would have been. Either is affected in his interests by the judgment of a court which is bound to give him the means of knowing that it is about to proceed to affect those interests, and that it is bound to hear him if he objects. That is, in our opinion, an impleading. The case of *The Bold Buccleugh* (¹) does not decide to the contrary of this. It decides that an action *in rem* is a different action from one *in personam* and has a different result. But it does not decide that a court which seizes and sells a man's property does not assume to make that man subject to its jurisdiction. To implead an independent sovereign in such a way is to call upon him to sacrifice either his property or his independence. To place him in that position is a breach of the principle upon which his immunity from jurisdiction rests. We think that he cannot be so indirectly impleaded, any more than he could be directly impleaded. The case is, upon this consideration of it, brought

(¹) 7 Moo. P. C., 267.

within the general rule that a sovereign authority cannot be personally impleaded in any court.

But it is said that the immunity is lost by reason of the ship having been used for trading purposes. As to this, it must be maintained either that the ship has been so used as to have been employed substantially as a mere trading ship and not substantially for national purposes, or that a use of her in part for trading purposes takes away the immunity, although she is in possession of the sovereign authority by the hands of commissioned officers, and is substantially in use for national purposes. Both these propositions raise the question of how the ship must be considered to have been employed.

As to the first, the ship has been by the sovereign of Belgium, by the usual means, declared to be in his possession as sovereign, and to be a public vessel of the state. It seems very difficult to say that any court can inquire by contentious testimony whether that declaration is or is not correct. To submit to such an inquiry before the court is to submit to its jurisdiction. It has been held that if the ship be declared by the sovereign authority by the usual means to be a ship of war, that declaration cannot be inquired into. That was expressly decided under very trying circumstances in the *case of *The Exchange* ('). Whether the ship [220 is a public ship used for national purposes seems to come within the same rule. But if such an inquiry could properly be instituted it seems clear that in the present case the ship has been mainly used for the purpose of carrying the mails, and only subserviently to that main object for the purposes of trade. The carrying of passengers and merchandise has been subordinated to the duty of carrying the mails. The ship is not in fact brought within the first proposition. As to the second, it has been frequently stated that an independent sovereign cannot be personally sued, although he has carried on a private trading adventure. It has been held that an ambassador cannot be personally sued, although he has traded; and in both cases because such a suit would be inconsistent with the independence and equality of the state which he represents. If the remedy sought by an action *in rem* against public property is, as we think it is, an indirect mode of exercising the authority of the court against the owner of the property, then the at-. tempt to exercise such an authority is an attempt inconsistent with the independence and equality of the state which is represented by such owner. The property cannot upon the

('') 7 Cranch, 116.

hypothesis be denied to be public property; the case is within the terms of the rule; it is within the spirit of the rule; therefore, we are of opinion that the mere fact of the ship being used subordinately and partially for trading purposes does not take away the general immunity. For all these reasons we are unable to agree with the learned judge, and have come to the conclusion that the judgment must be reversed.

Appeal allowed.

Solicitors for plaintiffs: *Lowless & Co.*
Agents for Treasury Solicitors: *Hare & Fell.*

[5 Probate Division, 221.]

April 23, 1880.

[IN THE COURT OF APPEAL.]

221] *THE CITY OF MANCHESTER (1878, O. 372).

Collision—Action by Owners of Cargo—Both Vessels to blame—Costs.

The owners of a cargo laden on board a vessel which had been sunk in a collision with another vessel brought an action of damage against the owners of such other vessel. The judge of the Admiralty Division pronounced that both vessels were to blame for the collision, gave the plaintiffs half their damages from the defendants, and condemned the defendants in the costs of the action. The decision that both vessels were to blame was upheld by the Court of Appeal:

Held, that, as the plaintiffs had failed on the issue that the vessel carrying the cargo was not to blame, no costs ought to have been given.

THIS was an action by the owners of a cargo carried on board the Moselle against the owners of the ship City of Manchester, which had run into and sunk the Moselle. The statement of claim alleged that the collision was caused by the negligence of the defendants or of their servants on board the City of Manchester, and was not caused or contributed to by the negligence of any of those on board the Moselle. The defendants, by their statement of defence, denied these allegations and alleged that the collision was occasioned by the negligent and improper navigation of the Moselle.

Sir R. Phillimore, on the 25th of April, 1879, pronounced judgment, finding both vessels to blame, and ordered the owners of the City of Manchester to pay the plaintiffs half their damages. On the 20th of May a supplemental order was made, giving the plaintiffs their costs of the action (¹).

The defendants appealed from the judgment and the supplemental order. The plaintiffs gave notice that they should contend that the City of Manchester alone was to blame,

(¹) 5 P. D., 3.

and that the defendants might be condemned in the whole damage.

Butt, Q.C., and *E. C. Clarkson*, for the defendants.

Phillimore, and *Stubbs*, for the plaintiffs.

THE COURT (James, Baggallay, and Bramwell, L.JJ.) agreed with the court below in holding that both vessels were to blame.

*Butt, Q.C., for the defendants, on the order as to   [222 costs: It is settled that as regards damages the same principles are applied whether the plaintiff is owner of the ship or of the cargo, and the same rule ought to hold as to costs. Now in the case of an action between the owners of two vessels as to a collision, if both vessels are to blame, neither party gets costs, and the same rule ought to be followed in an action by the owner of the cargo on board one of them. If the plaintiffs cannot get the whole of the damages from the defendants, why should they get the whole costs? The plaintiffs' case partially fails; they come for the whole damages and get only half; they should bear the costs of the part of their case which fails.

Phillimore, contrâ: This is an appeal for costs, and will not lie.

[JAMES, L.J.: Where costs are given with regard to the conduct of the parties there is no appeal; but where a general rule is laid down and costs given according to it an appeal will lie.]

This is a separate interlocutory order, and ought to have been appealed from within twenty-one days.

[JAMES, L.J.: It must be treated as part of the decree, otherwise there was no jurisdiction to make it.]

Then, on the merits, the case is this: a man sues for £1,000, the defendant insists that nothing is due, and the plaintiff recovers £500, can he be deprived of costs?

[BRAMWELL, L.J.: If he sued in respect of two causes of action which are severable, and succeeded on one, but failed on the other, he could not get full costs.]

This is hardly that case, for if the owner of a cargo sues a shipowner, and the shipowner is to blame, the plaintiff must recover something, and what he is to recover is a mere question of quantities. The case of *The Milan* ([1]) was carefully considered and is a leading authority, and the court will not readily depart from what was done in that case. The Judicature Act, 1873, s. 25, subs. 9, provides that in cases of collision where both vessels are in fault the admiralty rule shall be followed.

([1]) Lush., 388.

[JAMES, L.J.: That enactment was only intended to exclude the common law rule as to contributory negligence.]

The Consett (') is in the plaintiffs' favor.

223] *JAMES, L.J.: The order as to costs which is under appeal can only be sustained on the ground of its being part of the decree, for if the case had been disposed of by a final judgment the court would have had no jurisdiction to make a subsequent order. There is, therefore, no ground for the objection that this is an interlocutory order which must be appealed from within twenty-one days. The learned judge in the court below did not deal with the costs in this case as being within his judicial discretion, but as being subject to a universal rule, that where in a case of collision the owners of the cargo on board one vessel recover damages against the owner of the other vessel they are entitled to full costs, although in consequence of the vessel by which the cargo was being carried being to blame the plaintiffs only recover half the damages sustained. I cannot agree with this as a general rule, and I think that such a rule would tend to encourage unnecessary litigation. The owners of the cargo here embarked in a litigation in which they asserted that the defendants were to blame, and that the ship carrying the cargo was free from blame. There were, therefore, two issues; whether the defendants were to blame and whether the carrying ship was to blame. And it appears probable that the greater part of the costs was occasioned by the contention that the carrying ship was not to blame, in which contention the plaintiffs failed. The strict course then would be to give the plaintiffs the costs of the issue on which they succeeded, and to make them pay the costs of the issue on which they failed, but, to avoid the expense of such apportionment, the right course will be to discharge the order so that the plaintiffs will get no costs in the court below. The appellants will pay the costs of the appeal, except so far as they have been increased by the cross appeal.

BAGGALLAY, L.J.: The judge of the court below has not treated this as a case of discretion as to costs, but has gone upon a general rule which he considered to be laid down in the case of *The Milan* ('). I am of opinion, therefore, that an appeal lies. As to the costs of this particular action, if I were called upon to deal with them as a matter of discre-
224] tion, I should say that justice *requires that costs should not be given to either party. At the same time I do not say that in every case the owner of the cargo is in the same position as the owner of the carrying ship. It might

(') 5 P. D., 52.   (') Lush., 388.

be just to say that in the present case the plaintiffs should have the costs of the action, except so far as they have been increased by the claim on which they fail, and that they should pay the costs occasioned by that claim. But this substantially would lead to the same result.

BRAMWELL, L.J.: I cannot consider it right that because the owner of the cargo recovers something he should therefore receive the whole of his costs without regard to his having failed in a part of his contentions. Suppose the owners of the City of Mancester had admitted that they were to blame, but denied that the other ship was free from blame, and had tendered half the damages, if the action had gone on the plaintiffs ought to have paid the whole costs upon its being decided that the other ship was also to blame. In a recent case, where a plaintiff recovered only nominal damages, he was ordered to pay the whole costs.

Appeal allowed.

Solicitors for plaintiffs : *Stokes, Saunders & Stokes.*
Solicitors for defendants : *Gellatly, Son & Warton.*

[5 Probate Division, 224.]

June 8, 1880.

THE AMPTHILL (1880, S. 0639).

Co-ownership—Receiver—Judicature Act, 1873 (36 & 37 *Vict. c. 66), s. 25,
sube. 8—Discretion.*

The court will appoint a receiver in a co-ownership suit where circumstances exist which in the opinion of the court render such a course just and convenient.

THIS was a co-ownership action instituted on behalf of the owner of a moiety of the bark Ampthill against the Ampthill and against the owner of the remaining moiety of that vessel.

The indorsement on the writ stated that the plaintiff claimed the appointment of a receiver to collect general average contributions due to the owner of the said bark, and the general and particular average due under certain policies of insurance thereon, and also a settlement of accounts between the plaintiff and the defendant and contribution by the defendant to the outstanding *debts and liabilities [225 of the bark, and a settlement of disputes in respect of the employment thereof, and a sale of the defendant's shares in the said bark to provide for the contribution aforesaid.

A motion was made on behalf of the plaintiff, that the

plaintiff should be appointed receiver without remuneration. In support of the motion an affidavit was filed which
contained statements to the effect that the defendant had
acted as managing owner of the Ampthill ever since the
plaintiff had purchased his interest in the vessel; that in
1879 the vessel being in want of necessary repairs the money
to pay for such repairs was borrowed from bankers on the
security of a bill of exchange drawn by the defendant on
and accepted by the plaintiff, and of the deposit of certain
title-deeds of the plaintiff; that the bill of exchange had
been dishonored, and was still unpaid, and that the plaintiff
was liable to the bankers for the whole amount of the bill.
The affidavit also stated that a sum of about £223 for general average contribution in respect of sea damage sustained
by the Ampthill was due to her owners, and that there were
also due to her owners certain sums for average contributions payable by insurance associations in which the Ampthill had been insured.

E. C. Clarkson, for the plaintiff: The court ought to exercise the power of appointing a receiver recently conferred
on it by the 25th section of the Judicature Act, 1873. If
the court thinks the plaintiff ought not to be appointed receiver he is willing to consent to the appointment of any
person the court may think fit to appoint.

G. Bruce, for the defendant: It is quite unusual to appoint a receiver in cases of this kind, and the only result of
the appointment of a receiver will be to complicate the proceedings. Every legitimate end will be answered if the
court makes the usual decree for a sale of the ship and directs the accounts to be taken by the registrar. No charge
has been made against the conduct of the defendant as
managing owner, and as managing owner he has all the
powers of a receiver.

E. C. Clarkson, in reply.

SIR ROBERT PHILLIMORE: The only question I have to
consider is whether the present case is a proper one for the
226] *exercise of the power which the court now undoubtedly possesses of appointing a receiver under the 25th section of the Judicature Act, 1873, and it seems to me that
where an action of co-ownership is brought by the owner of
one moiety of a vessel against the owner of the other moiety,
such a case is one where the appointment of a receiver would
be both just and convenient. The course I shall take is
this, I shall appoint an independent person who, as receiver,
will collect all sums due to the owners of the Ampthill, and
pay whatever he may collect into the registry. His duties

will be the ordinary duties of a receiver, and he must apply
to the court if any difficulty should arise. The registrar
will fix the amount of security to be given by the receiver (¹).

Solicitors for plaintiff: *T. Cooper & Co.*
Solicitors for defendant: *Stokes & Co.*

(¹) The following is the order which
was drawn up:
June 8. The judge having heard
counsel on both sides appointed John
Hedley, of Blyth, in the county of
Northumberland, shipowner, upon his
first giving security to the satisfaction
of the registrar, to receive, collect, and
get in from the owners or underwriters
of the late cargo of the bark Ampthill,
and from the underwriters on the said
bark and her freight, all outstanding
debts and liabilities for general average, contribution, freight, or claims for

general and particular average on
policies of insurance effected on the
said bark or her freight or cargo and
due to the owners of the said bark, and
all other moneys, if any due or owing
to the joint owners of the said bark
from any person whatsoever, and ordered that the said receiver should pass
his accounts every three months, and
pay over the balance into the Bank of
England to the credit of this action,
with liability to apply to the court if
necessary for instructions from time to
time.

[5 Probate Division, 227.]

May 4, 1880.

*THE HJEMMETT (1880, O. 75).   [227

*Towage—Jurisdiction of County Court having Admiralty Jurisdiction—County
Courts Admiralty Jurisdiction Act, 1868, 31 & 32 Vict. c. 71, s. 8.*

A tug having entered into a contract to tow a ship from A. to B. for a specified
sum, the ship, during the performance of the agreed towage, was injured by collision, and the tug was detained nearly three days in attendance on the ship. In an
action of towage instituted by the owner of the tug in a county court, and transferred to this court, this court held that it had no jurisdiction to award, in addition
to the sum agreed to be paid for towage, any remuneration for the delay.

THIS was an action of towage instituted in the City of
London Court, on behalf of the owners of the steamtug
Vivid against the foreign bark Hjemmett. The suit was
transferred to this court under the 6th section of the County
Courts Admiralty Jurisdiction Act, 1868.

The following particulars of the plaintiff's claim in the
action were furnished in pursuance of an order of this court
of the 26th of February last:

The plaintiffs entered into an agreement on or about the
26th of December, 1879, to tow the bark Hjemmett from Sea
Reach to London for the sum of £13. During the towage
the Hjemmett collided with a steamer. The Vivid arrived
at Gravesend at 6.30 of the 26th of December with the
Hjemmett in tow, and would have proceeded to London in
pursuance of the agreement. The captain of the Hjemmett

declined however to allow the plaintiffs to proceed with the towage of the vessel to London until he had cleared away the wreck and part of the damage the Hjemmett had sustained from colliding with the steamer. The master of the Hjemmett accordingly brought up at Gravesend for the purpose, as he stated, of clearing the wreckage away, and detained the plaintiffs' tug Vivid in attendance on the ship from 6.30 P.M. of the 26th of December, 1879, until 9 A.M. of the 29th of December, 1879.

The plaintiffs, in addition to the sum of £13, the agreed amount of towage, claim from the defendants such reasonable sum for compensation as the court may award for the detention of their tug from 6.30 P.M. of the said 26th of December, 1879. The plaintiffs estimate this detention at the sum of £18, being three days, and detention or demurrage at the rate of £6 per day, being the usual rate of demurrage for a tug of the description of the Vivid, and thus claim the said sum of £18 in addition to the said sum of £13, the agreed amount of towage,

The owners of the Hjemmett appeared as defendants, and tendered £13.

228] *May 4. The action came on to be heard before the judge in court. No pleadings were delivered, and no witnesses were called either on behalf of the plaintiffs or of the defendants. The statement of facts contained in the plaintiffs' particulars were admitted, except the statement therein contained to the effect that the master of the Hjemmett had detained the Vivid. With respect to the detention of the Vivid at Gravesend, it was however admitted that the Vivid had remained there in attendance on the Hjemmett for the time specified in the particulars. It was also admitted that the Vivid had afterwards, on the 29th of December, taken the Hjemmett in tow at Gravesend, and had ultimately towed her to London.

E. C. Clarkson, for the plaintiffs: The contract made by the owners of the Vivid was to tow the Hjemmett direct from Sea Reach to London, and it must be taken to have been an implied term of this contract that any extra service which the Vivid might render during the towage should be compensated for by an additional towage remuneration. By remaining for three days in attendance on the Hjemmett at Gravesend the Vivid did render such an extra service, and her owners are entitled to receive an equitable compensation in respect thereof.

Phillimore, for the defendants: The owners of the Vivid

have done no more than they contracted to do. They contracted that the Vivid should tow the Hjemmett from Sea Reach to London for £13, and the contract has been performed. If it had been the intention of the owners of the Vivid to claim for detention during the towage they ought to have made an express stipulation to that effect.

E. C. Clarkson, in reply.

SIR ROBERT PHILLIMORE: I wish it to be understood that in deciding this case I am not expressing any opinion as to what decision the court might have arrived at, if the present action had been an action of salvage to recover salvage remuneration for salvage services arising out of the performance of a towage contract. The questions which might then have to be considered would be two,—first, whether there having been a valid agreement *to take   [229 a vessel in tow from one place to another, the fact of the ship in tow having been delayed from accident releases the tug from her contract. This question, however, in the circumstances of this case does not arise, as the Vivid admittedly fulfilled her contract and took the Hjemmett from Sea Reach to London. The second question, and the only question which arises in the present case is, whether such a delay as occurred in the present case renders it necessary that the tug should be paid an additional remuneration beyond the sum agreed to be paid for towage. Now the contention on behalf of the tug is, that owing to the Hjemmett having been delayed at Gravesend, a separate service beyond the original towage contract, or a sort of subsidiary service, has been performed by the plaintiffs, and that some remuneration in respect of that service should be awarded in this action. I do not, however, think that I have the power in an action of towage to make an award in respect of such a service, and I must therefore dismiss so much of the claim of the plaintiffs as claims any remuneration beyond the sum of £13. The tender of £13 must be upheld, and I must condemn the plaintiffs in all the costs of the action incurred since the tender was made.

Solicitors for plaintiffs : *Lowless & Co.*
Solicitors for defendants : *Waddilove & Nutt.*

[5 Probate Division, 229.]

June 17, 1880.

THE CONSETT (1877, R. 376).

Collision—Measure of Damage—Loss of Charterparty—Costs of Reference.

The vessel C., which was proceeding in ballast to Montreal to load a cargo of grain for the United Kingdom pursuant to charterparty, was injured by collision with another vessel, and compelled to put into port to repair. The repairs necessarily occupied so long a time that it was not reasonably possible for the C. to have arrived at Montreal in time to fulfil her charter before the navigation of the St. Lawrence was stopped by ice for the winter. In these circumstances the owners of the C. abandoned the charter, and it was found that they acted prudently in so doing :

Held, that the loss arising from the abandonment of the charter was a loss caused by the collision.

THIS was an action of damage instituted on behalf of the owners, master, and crew of the ship Jessore and the owners 230] of the cargo *of the Jessore, against the steamship Consett for the damages arising out of a collision between the two vessels on the 10th of October, 1877, about 145 miles to the north-westward of Scilly.

The owners of the Consett defended the action, and delivered with their statement of defence a counter-claim, in which they claimed damages arising out of the collision.

On the 25th of January, 1878, the action was heard, and the court pronounced that both vessels were to blame for the collision, and referred the question of damages to the registrar and merchants. The registrar reported that a moiety of the loss or damage sustained by the plaintiffs amounted to the sum of £27,165 12s. 5d., together with interest, and on the 25th of February, 1880, the Court of Appeal ordered that the defendants, the owners of the Consett, should pay the costs of and incident to the reference of the claim of the owners of the cargo ('). The counter-claim of the owners of the Consett, amounting to £2,523 8s. 9d., was filed in the registry, and on the 15th of January in this year, the registrar, after hearing evidence, made a report, reporting that a moiety of the loss of damage sustained by the defendants, the owners of the Consett, in consequence of the collision, amounted to the sum of £1,493 4s., together with interest thereon. The following is a copy of the material portions of such report :

I find that a moiety of the loss or damage sustained by the defendants amounts to the sum of £1,493 4s., together with interest thereon as stated in the schedule hereto annexed.

The principal question disputed in this case was whether the claimants were

(¹) See 5 P. D., 52, 77.

entitled to claim for loss of a beneficial charter or only for demurrage, at the ordinary rate during the detention of the ship consequent on the collision, and on this point I have been asked by the counsel for the plaintiffs to make a special report.

In this suit, which arose out of a collision on the 10th of October, 1877, between the sailing ship Jessore and the screw steamer Consett, both vessels were found to blame. The plaintiffs' vessel Jessore was sunk, and the damages sustained by them in consequence have been previously assessed. The claim now investigated is on behalf of the defendants' steamship Consett of 1,727 tons gross and 1,105 tons net register, and 170 horse power, which sustained certain damages and put into Queenstown for repairs. At the time of the collision the Consett was proceeding in ballast on a voyage from Antwerp to Montreal to load *a cargo of grain for the United Kingdom under a charter dated the 27th   [231 of September, 1877, negotiated by Messrs. Hamilton, Fraser & Co., brokers, on behalf of Messrs. Ross, Smith & Co., of Liverpool. The freight was to be at the rate of 8s. 9d. per quarter if the ship had to call for orders on the homeward voyage at either Queenstown, Falmouth, or Plymouth, and at the rate of 8s. 3d. per quarter if ordered from the port of loading direct to her port of discharge. She had left Antwerp on the 8th of October, and between 3 and '4 A.M. of the 10th came into collision with the Jessore, after which she made for Queenstown, which port she reached in the morning of the 11th, and was hauled into dry dock for survey and repairs in the afternoon of the same day. On hearing by telegram of the accident the owners forthwith sent their marine superintendent Captain McNabb to Queenstown with instructions to superintend the repairs and to urge their completion with the greatest possible despatch, and we are satisfied that every exertion was used by Captain McNabb as well as by the vessel's agent at Queenstown (Messrs. Harvey & Co.) to attain that end, and we are satisfied that as much expedition as could be expected at Queenstown was used, and that no unreasonable delay took place.

It had been anticipated at first that the repairs might be completed in a much shorter time than they ultimately occupied, but at the end of a fortnight it appeared that the ship could not be ready to proceed on her voyage on any day in the month of October.

From the first the charterers on hearing of the collision were very desirous that the charter should be abandoned, on the ground that the ship could not be repaired in time to make the chartered voyage that autumn, as the river St. Lawrence is rendered unnavigable by ice every winter for some months, and they constantly and strongly represented to Messrs. Watts, Milburn & Co., the owners of the Consett, how unjust and injurious it would be to them, the charterers, if from failure of the Consett to arrive in time it should become necessary to warehouse through the winter the cargo destined for her. On the other hand, Messrs. Watts, Milburn & Co. were very anxious to fulfil the charter, as it promised to be a very profitable one, and they only and very reluctantly ultimately acquiesced in its abandonment when it became apparent that the ship could not resume her voyage before the 1st of November. It appears that the usual time up to which ships can leave Montreal is the 25th of November, but in some seasons the winter sets in earlier, and only two years previously, in 1875, Messrs. Watts, Milburn & Co. had had painful experience of that fact by two of their ships being caught by the ice on their homeward voyage from Montreal on or before the 23d of November and being frozen up until the spring. An average passage for such a steamship as the Consett from Queenstown to Montreal would have been fifteen or sixteen days : and as fourteen running days, Sundays excepted [virtually, therefore sixteen days], were allowed by the charter to the charterers for loading and unloading, the risk of the Consett being unable to reach Montreal and load her cargo and get clear of the St. Lawrence before it should be rendered unnavigable by ice was, in our opinion, very considerable, and one which it was right and prudent not to incur. Under all the circumstances we come to the conclusion that the owners acted prudently, and were

justified in acquiescing in the abandonment of the Montreal charter and in avoiding the risk of sending his ship to the port so late in the season.   A further
232]   question then arises whether *the loss occasioned by the abandonment of the beneficial charter to Montreal, and the substituted employment of the ship in a less profitable manner, is one for which the owners of the Consett can recover ; and it was strongly contended by counsel for the plaintiffs that it is • not, and that in fact such damage is too remote even on the assumption that the owner acted with proper prudence in not persisting in the voyage.   It has appeared to me, however, that the case comes within the principle laid down by this court in *The Star of India* (¹), and that such loss must be allowed as damages.   We have therefore proceeded to estimate as accurately as we could what that loss amounted to.   In the first place we have calculated that if the voyage from Antwerp to Montreal and back to the United Kingdom had been prosecuted without interruption or hindrance it might have been performed in fifty days, and that the total gross freight under the Montreal charter at 8s. 3d. per quarter on 10,500 quarters would amount to £4,331 5s., but from that freight deductions should be mode for further expenses beyond those actually incurred which would have been incurred in earning it, including an allowance for wear and tear.   These expenses would have been in respect of coals and engine stores that would have been consumed, insurances, commission on freight, disbursements both at Montreal and the port of discharge, wages and provisions of master and crew, besides other minor charges, the total amounting to £2,110, which deducted from £4,331 5s., would have left a net freight earned in fifty days of £2,221 5s.

As already stated, the collision occurred early in the morning of the 10th of October.   The ship did not come out of dock after repairs until the 1st of November, and was then detained until the following day for the purpose of taking in some extra coals required for the longer voyage on which she was then about to proceed.   The total detention was therefore about twenty-one days, at the end of which period the ship was at the disposal of the owners to employ as they thought fit.   And we consider, in order to fix the amount of loss sustained by the abandonment of the Montreal charter and the subsequent employment of the ship in a less profitable manner, we should allow the net earnings under that charter ascertained as above, and then deduct from that sum the net rate of earnings which we assume such a ship would ordinarily secure to her owner during the remaining twenty-six days when she was restored to their control.   This we take at £25 a day, which is equal to about 3½d. per ton on her gross tonnage, and gives for twenty-six days £650, which deducted from £2,221 5s., leaves £1,571 5s. as the measure of loss arising from frustration of her intended voyage to Montreal.   The claimants have suggested that the comparison should be made with the result of the actual employment of the ship on the substituted voyage to New Orleans.   I am of opinion, however, that the measure we have adopted is a better and more correct one.   If the comparison were made with the result of the particular voyage which the owners may choose to select, the necessity would be imposed upon us of inquiring into the prudence and propriety of the selection, and of investigating the accounts of a voyage which might, as in this instance, occupy a much longer time than the voyage which has been abandoned, and might be greatly affected by the occurrence of special perils of the sea, possibly leaving no net earnings at all.

233]   *The following is a copy of the schedule referred to in the above report:

(¹) 1 P. D., 466.

The Consett.　　　　　　　　　　1880

	CLAIMED.			ALLOWED.		
	£	s.	d.	£	s.	d.
1. Pilotage of the steamship Consett into Cork and out to sea	10	15	5	10	15	5
2. Pilot, shifting and docking steamer ..	1	0	0	1	0	0
3. Towage from sea to passage and docking..	9	10	0	9	10	0
4. Sundry attendances on steamer, running lines to dockyard, &c.	1	13	6	1	13	6
5. Telegrams	2	6	8	●		
6. G. N. Harvey & Sons, as per their account	7	9	0	4	15	4
7. Photographs	7	1	6			
8. Shipping office fees .. ..:	3	5	0			
9. Water	3	10	0			
10. G. B. Dawson, as per his account ..	4	8	6			
11. Messrs. Norton & Wright, surveyors ..	4	4	0	4	4	0
12. United States Consulate fees	1	7	0	1	7	0
13. Copy depositions	0	15	0			
14. Survey fees	12	12	0	12	12	0
15. T. Miller, for rope, &c.	13	0	7	4	8	9
16. New ends to windlass	15	0	0	15	0	0
17. Expenses of agent and Captain McNabb ..	6	11	6 }			
18. Captain McNabb, for expenses and services	49	13	3 }	40	0	0
19. Telegrams, postages, &c.	10	0	0	8	8	0
20. Agency commission, &c.	85	18	11	15	15	0
21. The Cork Harbor Dock and Warehouse Company, for repairs, &c.	1,425	0	0	1,285	19	0
22. Demurrage of the steamship Consett, of 1727 12-100 tons gross, from 10th October to 3d November, 1877, 25 days at 6d. per ton per day	1,079	9	1 }			
23. Loss through change of voyage of the Consett, necessitated by the collision ..	2,293	7	1 }	1,571	5	0
Half	£5,046	17	7	£2,986	8	0
	£2,523	8	9	£1,493	4	0

With interest at four per cent. per annum from the 1st of December, 1877, until paid.

From so much of the report as related to the allowance by the registrar of loss sustained by the owners of the Consett by reason of the cancellation of the charterparty of the 27th of September, 1877, the plaintiffs appealed to the court. They brought in a petition in objection, the material part of which was as follows :

1. The plaintiffs object to the said report in so far as the same allows the claim of the defendants under their counterclaim in respect of alleged loss to the *defendants by [234 reason of their cancellation by agreement of the charterparty of the Consett, dated Liverpool, the 27th of September, 1877, and the procurement in substitution for the same of another charterparty to New Orleans, dated the 29th of October, 1877.

2. The collision in question between the Jessore and the

Consett in respect of which both vessels have been found to
blame, took place on the 10th of October, 1877, about 145
miles to the north-westward of Scilly.

3. The Consett, after the said collision, put into Queenstown where she was repaired, and the said cancellation of
her charterparty took place on the 26th day of October,
187, while she was at Queenstown for the purpose of such
repairs.

4. The learned registrar has found in his report, that it
was reasonable under the circumstances, for the defendants
the owners of the Consett, to effect the said cancellation of
the Consett's charterparty and to procure the said other charterparty in substitution, and has allowed as damages the
net profits which the Consett would have earned on the Montreal voyage, subject to a deduction of £650, being the computed net rate of earnings of the Consett during twenty-six
days when the vessel was under the control of the owners.

5. The plaintiffs object to the said finding in the said report, on grounds partly of fact and partly of law. As
regards matters of fact they submit as follows:

[The objections as regards matters of fact it is not necessary to set out.]

As regards law the plaintiffs submit as follows:

14. The registrar was wrong in taking into consideration
the fact *that there were sixteen lay days stipulated in the
charterparty* and that the Consett might have been detained
at Montreal during that period, as it was proved that the
cargo was ready for loading and the charterers were desirous
of cancelling the charter and chartering another vessel, because their cargo was waiting at Montreal for shipment.

15. The registrar was wrong in awarding damages consequent on the loss sustained by reason of the cancellation of
the charterparty, which cancellation was the voluntary act
of the defendants and the charterers, and the event proved
that the vessel might have performed the charterparty without any danger or risk of injury to herself or her cargo, and
might and would have earned the chartered freight.

16. The circumstance that the shipowners and the charterers were influenced by prudential motives in cancelling
the charterparty does not throw upon the plaintiffs the loss
sustained by the owners of the Consett, by reason of such
cancellation.

17. The damages allowed by the registrar as consequent
on the cancellation of the Consett's charterparty, were not

the proximate and natural result of the collision, and are too remote, and are not recoverable from the plaintiffs.

18. The registrar was wrong in holding that the case comes within the principle of the *Star of India* ('). In that case the charterers cancelled the charterparty in accordance with the stipulation giving them the power to do so.

*June 7. The petition on objection was heard.   [235
Butt, Q.C., and *Myburgh*, for the plaintiffs, in support of the petition.

Cohen, Q.C., and *Phillimore*, on behalf of the defendants, contrà.

SIR ROBERT PHILLIMORE: This is an appeal from the registrar assisted by merchants. The whole history of the case is very clearly set forth in the report. The appeal is not made upon the report generally, but only on one portion of it; and the question before me is, whether the loss of a beneficial charter is to be considered in estimating the damages which the counter-claimants sustained in this case. The collision took place on the 10th of October, 1877, and the Jessore sank. The Consett, at the time of the collision, was under charterparty, whereby she was to proceed in ballast to Montreal to load a cargo of grain, and the freight was to be at the rate of 8*s*. 9*d*. per quarter if the ship had to call for orders on the homeward voyage at either Queenstown, Falmouth, or Plymouth ; and at the rate of 8*s*. 3*d*. per quarter if ordered direct from her port of loading to her port of discharge. The vessel left Antwerp on the 8th of October between 3 and 4 o'clock in the morning, and came into collision with the Jessore ; on the 11th she came to Queenstown, where she remained. Great hopes were entertained that she would be able to proceed on her voyage in the middle of October, but as the repairs were going on it was found that she could not be got ready until the end of a fortnight, and that she would not be able to proceed before the 1st of November. It was calculated that she would not be able to arrive at Montreal, and be able to take a fresh cargo before the 25th of November. And it appears from the evidence before the registrar, which it is not necessary to go into at length, as it has been fully discussed by counsel on both sides, that owing to the ice in the St. Lawrence, the usual time in the autumn up to which ships can leave Montreal, is the 25th of November, but that there is a risk that ships leaving even on that date will be stopped by the ice. The owners of the Consett found themselves, they contend, in

(') 1 P. D., 466.

this position, that they were obliged to give up and abandon
the charter.   It was admitted that it was a profitable char-
236]   ter *to them.   It is not disputed by the appellants
in this case that demurrage or damages for detention, might
be awarded for the whole time the repairs were being done;
but it has been said that the loss of a beneficial charter in
this case, is not a claim that can be dealt with under the
head of damages; and it has been very fairly admitted that
if the damage claimed under this head or a legitimate portion of such damages can be recovered, then the figures mentioned in the report are correct.   The questions then arise
was it reasonably possible for the Consett to have performed
her outward voyage under the charter? and if it was reasonably possible for her to have performed such voyage,
had she any right to abandon her charter and oblige the appellants to pay the loss sustained?   It is not contended
that if it was reasonably possible for her to have performed
her charter, the damages for the loss of the charter could
rightly be claimed.

Now, the registrar and merchants have come to the conclusion that the risk of the Consett being unable to reach
Montreal so as to sail on her homeward voyage before the
St. Lawrence had been rendered unnavigable by ice, was
such as it was not prudent to incur, and that the profit of a
beneficial charterparty being lost was damage for which the
appellants were liable.   It is really a question of evidence
whether it has been on the whole established that it was reasonably possible for the Consett to have performed the charter.   I am of opinion that the evidence has established that
it was not reasonably possible for her to do so; and if this
proposition is established, the consequence must follow that
the loss which the defendants have sustained by reason of
the loss of a beneficial charter in this case must be included
in the category of damages.   I must, therefore, confirm the
report and dismiss the appeal with costs.

June 17.   *Phillimore*, for the defendants, moved the
judge in court, to condemn the plaintiffs in the costs of and
incident to the reference of the defendant's counter-claim to
the registrar and merchants.   Most of the witnesses at the
reference, were called for the purpose of giving evidence as
to the consequential damage sustained by the owners of the
Consett, and the defendants succeeded on the legal question
237]   which arose in consequence *of the evidence of these
witnesses not only both before the registrar but on appeal to
this court.   This is not a case in which the ordinary rule of

condemning in costs claimants who have had a third of their claim struck off is applicable. *The Elina* (¹).

Myburgh, for the plaintiffs: Nearly one half the amount of the defendants' claim in this case was disallowed by the registrar; and it is clearly in accordance with the ordinary rule that the defendants should be condemned in the costs of the reference. The rule is not the less applicable because questions of law have been raised and decided at the reference: *The Empress Eugenie* (²).

SIR ROBERT PHILLIMORE: I am of opinion that the proper order to make in this case is, that the defendants, the owners of the Consett, shall have the costs of proving those items of their claim which are marked 1 to 21 in the schedule appended to the report of the registrar, and that each party shall pay a moiety of the reference fees. As to the residue of the costs of the reference and the costs in the action each party must bear the share of such costs incurred by him. I make this decision in the peculiar circumstances of this case.

Solicitors for plaintiffs: *Gregory, Rowcliffes & Rawle.*
Solicitors for defendants: *T. Cooper & Co.*

(¹) THE ELINA (1877, H. 164). April 13, 1880.

This was a case of damage to a cargo of maize, caused by the heating of a portion of the cargo consequent upon delay arising from the master of the Elina remaining at Queenstown, his port of call, for some days after he had received orders to sail for Newcastle-upon-Tyne. A portion of the cargo it was admitted had been damaged by the perils of the seas, and it was matter of impossibility to ascertain with accuracy what extent of

damage was caused by the delay at Queenstown.

The amount of damage claimed was £1,056 16s. 6d., and the amount allowed by the registrar and merchants on the reference was £600. The court gave the plaintiffs the costs of the reference.

Butt, Q.C., and *G. Bruce*, for the plaintiffs.

Milward, Q.C., and *E. C. Clarkson*, for the defendants.

Solicitor for plaintiffs: *S. R. Hoyle.*
Solicitor for defendants: *T. Cooper.*

(²) Lush., 188.

[5 Probate Division, 241.]

July 19, 1880.

*THE SINQUASI (1879, C. 315).   [241

Collision—Compulsory pilotage—Duty of Pilot on board of Ship in tow.

Where a ship in charge of a pilot whose employment is compulsory is being towed by a steamtug and the steamtug without waiting for orders from the pilot suddenly adopts a wrong manœuvre, and so causes the ship to come into collision, the owners of the ship are responsible.

Semble, where a pilot is in charge of a ship in tow in a crowded river, it is not necessarily incumbent upon him to direct every movement of the tug.

THIS was an action of damage brought by the Company of Proprietors of the Regent's Canal against the bark Sinquasi and her owners.

The statement of claim alleged that in the afternoon on the 4th day of October, 1879, the bark Sinquasi, which was 242] going *up the river Thames in tow of a steamtug, ran against and struck the pier of the plaintiffs and did it considerable damage, and that the collision and damage were occasioned by the negligence of the defendents, the owners of the Sinquasi, or by the negligence and improper navigation of the Sinquasi and her tug or of one of them, and by the neglect of those on board the Sinquasi and her tug or one of them, to take proper measures for keeping the Sinquasi from running against and damaging the said pier.

The statement of defence alleged in substance as follows:

1. The Sinquasi was proceeding up Limehouse Reach in the river Thames in tow of the steamtug Warrior, and in charge of a duly licensed Trinity pilot, whose employment at the time and place was compulsory by law.

2. The Sinquasi had all her sails stowed and the jibboom rigged in.

3. Under these circumstances, whilst the Sinquasi and her tug were manœuvring to clear some craft which were in the river nearly opposite the Regent's Canal Pier, the Sinquasi came into collision with the said pier head and did some damage.

4. The said collision and the damage consequent thereon were caused solely and exclusively by some neglect or default on the part of the said pilot who was in charge of the Sinquasi and her tug at the time of the said collision, and not otherwise.

The pilot who was in charge of the Sinquasi was called as a witness on behalf of the plaintiffs. He stated that he was taken on board the Sinquasi at Gravesend, and he gave such orders to the tug during the passage up the river as he considered necessary, but he left the tug to alter her course to clear craft so long as she was going right. When the Sinquasi was in Limehouse Reach the navigation was intricate. When approaching the Regent's Canal the tug, without any order from him, suddenly ported to pass to the north of a dumb barge and two sailing barges, and pulled the Sinquasi in the direction of the pier. The pilot was then obliged to port the helm of the Sinquasi to clear the dumb barge, but as soon as he had cleared her he put the helm of the Sinquasi to starboard to try and keep her off the pier, but the bark did not answer her starboard helm quickly enough to clear the pier. The pilot stated that if the tug had not ported the tug *and the Sinquasi would have gone [243 clear of the barges, and the accident would not have happened. The rest of the evidence, so far as material, appears from the judgment.

Butt, Q.C., and *E. C. Clarkson*, for the plaintiffs: It is clear that the mistake arose from the act of the tug-master. He was the servant of the owners of the bark, and the manœuvre which caused the damage was not done under orders from the pilot, and the pilot had not time to counteract the wrong manœuvre.

Myburgh, and *Wood Hill*, for the defendants: It was the duty of the pilot in the intricate navigation of Limehouse Reach to give orders to the tug; he ought not to have left the tug-master to take his own course to clear the craft in the river. In point of fact the pilot delegated his authority to the tug-master, and the tug-master must be taken to have acted with the sanction of the pilot. At all events the pilot should at once have countermanded the manœuvre of the tug: *The Duke of Sussex* (¹).

E. C. Clarkson, in reply.

Sir Robert Phillimore: This is a case arising out of a collision which took place between 12 and 1 o'clock in the afternoon on the 4th of October, 1879. The bark Sinquasi, the vessel proceeded against in this action, was going up the river Thames in tow of a steamtug called the Warrior, and struck the jetty or pier of the plaintiffs, and did considerable damage. The owners of the Sinquasi admit that that vessel came into collision with the pier head of the plaintiffs and did the damage complained of, but they contend that the Sinquasi did the damage through the negligence of a Trinity House pilot, whose employment was compulsory by law, and that therefore such pilot was alone to blame for the collision. Now the question mainly turns upon the conduct of the tug towing the Sinquasi in porting her helm and going to the north of the dumb barge and two sailing barges which were going up the river. A great deal of argument has been expended upon the fact of whether there was room sufficient for the tug and the Sinquasi to have gone between the dumb barge and the sailing barges. It is admitted that if there *was sufficient room to pass between the two [244 barges it was the duty of the tug to tow between them; and we are of opinion that there was sufficient room. Upon this point the evidence of Allen, the pilot, was material. He was rowing across the river from north to south, and had a

(¹) 1 No. Ca., 161.

full opportunity of seeing what passed, and he swore positively that there was plenty of room between the barges.

This statement is confirmed by the persons who were on
the pier head.   It is denied by the witnesses for the defendants, but we have more confidence in the witnesses produced
by the plaintiffs.   It was therefore a wrong manœuvre on
the part of the tug to port; and this was primarily the
cause of the collision.   It has been said that the pilot delegated his authority not in terms but in conduct to the master of the tug.   We are not of that opinion.   It is not
necessary, in our judgment, that the pilot should be giving
orders perpetually for every movement of the helm of the
tug.   When the tug suddenly ported without the order of
the pilot the Sinquasi had no option but to follow him.
The tug was the servant of the Sinquasi, and the Sinquasi is responsible for what the tug did.   We believe the
pilot starboarded as soon as he could after clearing the
dumb barge.   The Sinquasi, having regard to her length,
could not recover herself in time to prevent the collision.
In the opinion of the court the Sinquasi is to blame for the
collision, which was not caused by any default of the pilot.

Solicitors for plaintiffs : *Jenkinson & Olivers.*
Solicitors for defendants : *T. Cooper & Co.*

[5 Probate Division, 245.]

July 29, 1880.

245]   *THE ROSALIE (1880, S. 0663).

*Collision—Regulations for Preventing Collisions at Sea—Arts. 12, 18—Sailing
Vessel hove to on Port Tack.*

A sailing vessel hove to on the port tack is bound to keep out of the way of a
crossing vessel under sail close-hauled on the starboard tack.

THIS was a case of collision brought by the owners of
the fishing dandy Young Alonzo against the three-masted
schooner Rosalie.   The collision took place at 11 A.M. in
fine clear weather off Plymouth, the wind at the time being
from the east a fresh breeze.   The Young Alonzo was lying
hove to on the port tack with her foresail sheet to windward
and her tiller about three parts down, and heading about
southeast, and she so remained until the collision; and
hailed to the Rosalie to keep out of her way.

    The Rosalie was a three-masted schooner, and she was
coming up channel close-hauled on the starboard tack and
heading about N.N.E.   She sighted the Young Alonzo

about a mile off bearing about three points on the port bow. The Rosalie kept her course until there was immediate danger of collision, when her helm was put hard down and she came into collision with the starboard side of the Young Alonzo.

J. P. Aspinall, and *F. W. Raikes*, for the plaintiffs: The Rosalie could easily have kept clear of the Young Alonzo; she must have seen that the Young Alonzo was hove to, and according to the ordinary practice of navigation, a ship under way should keep clear of a vessel hove to: *The Lake St Clair* (').

E. C. Clarkson, and *Myburgh*, for the defendants: Art. 12 of the Regulations for Preventing Collisions at Sea applies. The Young Alonzo had the wind on the port side, and if she had put up her helm and let her foresail draw she could have got out of the way of the Rosalie. The Rosalie was entitled up to the last moment to suppose that the Young Alonzo would have obeyed the regulations, and the Rosalie was bound to keep her course: Art. 18; *The James* (*); *The London* (').

*SIR ROBERT PHILLIMORE: I am of opinion that [246 the 12th article of the Regulations for Preventing Collisions at Sea applies to this case. That article is in terms as follows: "When two sailing ships are crossing so as to involve risk of collision, then if they have the wind on different sides, the ship with the wind on the port side shall keep out of the way of the ship with the wind on the starboard side, except in the case in which the ship with the wind on the port side is close hauled and the other ship free, in which case the latter ship shall keep out of the way; but if they have the wind on the same side, or if one of them has the wind aft, the ship which is to windward shall keep out of the way of the ship which is to leeward." The Young Alonzo had the wind on her port side, and the Rosalie had the wind on her starboard side. The Young Alonzo ought to have released her tiller. I am of opinion that the Young Alonzo is to blame. Then there is the question whether the Rosalie is not also to blame. She might have done something in the circumstances to avoid the collision, and ought to have seen the Young Alonzo in time. She did nothing. She ought to have starboarded and passed astern of the Young Alonzo, whereas she ran on to the starboard side of the Young Alonzo. I pronounce both vessels to blame.

Solicitor for plaintiffs: *H. C. Coote.*
Solicitors for defendants: *Ingledew & Ince.*

(') Nomine *Wilson v. The Canada Shipping Co.*, 2 Ap. Cas., 389; 19 Eng. R., 172.   (*) Swa., 60.
      (*) 6 No. Ca., 29.

[5 Probate Division, 250.]

May 11, 1880.

250]   *THE ST. LAWRENCE (1880, M. 18, Liv.).

*Necessaries—Money advanced to pay Dock Dues—Priority over Claim of Bot-
tomry Bondholder.*

The plaintiffs, in an action of necessaries against a foreign ship, having at the
request of the master advanced money to pay dock dues for the ship at the port of
discharge, were held to be entitled to have the amount they had so advanced paid
out of the proceeds of the ship in priority to the claim of a bottomry bondholder
who had advanced money on bottomry at the port of loading.

THIS was an action of necessaries instituted on behalf of
Messrs. Moos & Co., shipbrokers of Liverpool, against the
Norwegian bark St. Lawrence, and her freight, to recover
certain sums of money advanced to pay for necessaries supplied to the St. Lawrence on her arrival at Liverpool in
February last on a voyage from Baltimore. At the time
of the institution of the suit, the St. Lawrence was already
under the arrest of the court, in two actions of bottomry
instituted on behalf of the holders of two bottomry bonds
on ship, cargo, and freight, which had been given for securing the principal sums of £1,521 5s. 7d., and £57 6s. 1d.,
advanced in Baltimore previously to the commencement of
the voyage, and in an action of wages instituted on behalf
of her master and certain of her crew. No appearance
having been entered for her owners, the proceedings against
her in all three actions were carried on by default.

On the 7th of April last a statement of claim, which contained, *inter alia*, the following allegations, was delivered
in the present action:

The St. Lawrence arrived in Liverpool from Baltimore in
February last.

Upon the arrival of the said vessel at Liverpool her crew
became and were entitled to be paid their wages, and to receive their discharge, and there was a sum of money due to
them for wages.

The master of the said vessel had no moneys wherewith to
pay the said wages, and being unable to obtain any, and
being apprehensive that the said vessel would be arrested,
applied to the plaintiffs to advance the necessary sums to
pay the crew their wages, in order to avoid legal proceedings being taken against the said vessel, and the plaintiffs
therefore advanced to the master of the said vessel the sum

of £19, for the purpose of its being paid, and the same was paid to the crew of the said vessel for their wages, which sum is still due and unpaid to the plaintiffs.

*Under the circumstances aforesaid the plaintiffs [251 also, at the request and by the direction of the master of the said vessel, paid the sum of £7 13s. in respect of the charge for pilotage of the said vessel into Liverpool, and the sum of £10 in respect of the charge for a steamer which towed her into Liverpool.

The plaintiffs also under the circumstances aforesaid, and at the request, and by the like direction of the said master, paid the sum of £43 0s. 9d. in respect of the charge for dock dues, the sum of £6 10s. 11d. in respect of the charge for light dues for and on account of the said vessel at Liverpool, and the sum of £2 in respect of the charge for watermen and a boat engaged in docking the said vessel.

The master of the said vessel thereupon requested the plaintiffs to pay, and they therefore paid the sum of £3 3s. for reporting the said vessel at the custom house at Liverpool, and the plaintiffs also, at the request and by the direction of the said master, disbursed various sums of money for and on account of the said vessel in respect of telegrams and postages, &c., amounting to £2 6s. 6d.

The said sums before mentioned were all advanced and paid in the necessary service of the said vessel, and for necessary expenses of the said port, and are still due and unpaid to the plaintiffs.

The said sums were paid, and the said sums advanced by the plaintiffs upon the credit of the said vessel, and not merely on the personal credit of the said master.

On the 27th of April last the present action came on for hearing, and the judge pronounced for the claim of the plaintiffs together with interest and costs, but without prejudice to any other claims against the vessel, or to any question as to priority of payment.

Previously to the hearing of the action the St. Lawrence had been sold under an order of court obtained in one of the actions of bottomry against her, and had realized the sum of £1,000, without deducting the expenses of sale, and the sum of £962 4s. 6d., representing the freight earned by her on the voyage from Baltimore to Liverpool, had been paid into the registry. In these circumstances the owners of the cargo of the St. Lawrence apprehended that if the claims of Messrs. Moos & Co. were paid out of the proceeds of the St. Lawrence and her freight in priority to the claims of the bottomry bondholders, such proceeds would, after payment of the claims of the crew for the balance of their wages, be insufficient to satisfy the bonds, together with interest and costs, and that the bondholders would in such case resort to the cargo of the St. Lawrence, and entered an appearance in the present action as interveners.

Myburgh, on behalf of the plaintiffs, moved the judge in 252] court *to order payment of the amount of the plaintiffs' claim to be paid to them out of the fund in court. The plaintiffs have the same rights as the seamen and the persons by whom the pilotage and towage services have actually been performed, and are in the same position as such seamen and other persons would have been in if their claims had remained undischarged: *The William F. Safford* ('). Similarly the plaintiffs are entitled to the same priority in respect of the sums they paid in discharge of the light dues due from the St. Lawrence, for if the light dues had not been paid payment of them might have been enforced by distress and the ship could not have been cleared (17 & 18 Vict. c. 104, ss. 400, 401). The item claimed in respect of the dock dues of the St. Lawrence at Liverpool must also rank above the bottomry claims in this case. Without adverting to the statutory powers which the dock companies at Liverpool possess to enable them to enforce payment of their dues ('), it is sufficient to point out that the docking of the St. Lawrence was necessary in order to enable her to earn the freight now in court.

W. G. F. Phillimore, for the interveners: The owners of cargo admit that the plaintiffs are right in their contention, that the sums advanced by them for wages, pilotage, watermen, and light dues, ought to be paid out to them in priority to the claims of the bondholders, but they contend that the payment of the amounts advanced for dock dues and reporting the St. Lawrence, and for postages and telegrams, ought to be postponed to the bonds. The rights of a bottomry bondholder have always been considered to be greater than the rights of a material man, and if the security of the bondholder can be lessened by the amount of whatever sums may afterwards be expended for necessaries, the difficulty of raising money on bottomry will be much increased.

Sir Robert Phillimore: It is admitted that the items of the claim, which consists of money advanced to pay the wages, pilotage, towage, watermen, and light dues, men-

(') Lush., 69.   tion Act, 1859 (21 & 22 Vict. c. xcii),
(') See the Mersey Docks Consolida-   ss. 253, 254.

tioned in the statement of claim, ought to be paid out to the plaintiffs, in priority to the claims of the bondholders. The only question, therefore, *which I have to decide is, [253 as to the amounts advanced by the plaintiffs in respect of dock dues, reporting the St. Lawrence, and the sum expended in disbursements, such as telegrams and postages. Now I am of opinion that the amount paid by the plaintiffs in respect of dock dues is in the same category as the amounts paid by them in respect of towage and pilotage, claims which it has been admitted take precedence of the amounts secured on the bottomry bonds executed previously to the time when the St. Lawrence arrived at Liverpool. It is true that pilotage and towage claims are not mentioned by Dr. Lushington in the case of *The William F. Safford* (') as claims which, if paid by a third party, confer any priority on the person so paying them, but the reason of that decision applies to such claims, and indeed I do not understand it to be disputed that a person who discharges claims of that character has the same rights and remedies for their recovery as the person to whom the money has been paid. I consider, therefore, that the sum advanced by the plaintiffs to pay these dock dues must be paid out to them at once. The reasons which apply to the dock dues in this case can have no application to the items which consist of sums advanced for reporting the St. Lawrence or for despatching telegrams or for postages. I must therefore reject the motion as regards these two last items. The motion will be granted as to all the other items of the plaintiffs' claim.

Solicitors for plaintiffs : *Stone & Fletcher.*
Solicitors for interveners : *Simpson & North.*

(¹) Lush., 69.

[5 Probate Division, 254.]

Aug. 3, 1880.

*THE MACLEOD (1880, W. 01284). [254

Wages and Disbursements—Habitual Drunkenness of Master.

A shipmaster who has been habitually drunk during his employment cannot maintain an action for his wages.

THIS was an action by the late master of the ship Macleod for wages and disbursements. The statement of claim alleged in substance that the plaintiff served on board the Macleod as her master from the 1st of June, 1879, until the

18th of June, 1880, when he was discharged, at wages after the rate of £250 per annum agreed by the owners of the said vessel to be paid to the plaintiff for his said services. Whilst so serving as master of the Macleod he performed his duty as master and earned his wages, and he also whilst serving as such master made divers disbursements on account of the said ship.

The plaintiff claimed the sum of £307 9s. 4d., the balance alleged to be due to him, together with ten days' double pay, according to the provisions of the Merchant Shipping Act, 1854.

The statement of defence denied that the plaintiff had performed his duty as master or earned his wages, and alleged that he had forfeited all claims to wages by reason of gross and frequent drunkenness on ship and on shore while he was in command, and by reason of neglect of duty and carelessness of navigation owing to such drunkenness; that he had made certain disbursements on account of the ship, but that such disbursements were in many respects incorrectly stated by him; that he had received, or ought, but for his wilful neglect, to have received sums for which he had not given credit; and that on the balance of the plaintiff's accounts nothing was due from the defendants to the plaintiff.

By way of counter-claim the defendants alleged, *inter alia*, that whilst the plaintiff was in command of the ship he negligently chartered the Macleod at an improvidently low rate of freight without due inquiry or notice to the defendants, whereby the defendants suffered loss and damage.

Aug. 3.   The action was heard before the judge in court. 255]   *Witnesses for the plaintiff and a witness for the defendants were examined.   The result of their evidence is stated in the judgment.

It was agreed with the consent of the court that the questions of damage arising out of the portion of the counter-claim above set out should, with all questions as to the amount of disbursements claimed, be referred to the registrar and merchants.

Butt, Q.C., and *E. C. Clarkson*, for the plaintiff.

Cohen, Q.C., and *Myburgh*, for the defendants.

SIR ROBERT PHILLIMORE: In this case the master is suing for his wages, and he is proved to have been guilty of not occasional, but habitual intoxication. In the case of *The Roebuck* (¹) I had occasion to consider the law very

(¹) 2 Asp. Mar. Law Cas. (N.S.), 387.

fully, and it may be desirable, as I am obliged to come to a decision adverse to the suitor in this case, that I should state my view of the law. I cannot do better than read the following passage from the judgment of Lord Stowell in the case of *The Exeter* (').

Upon the matter of drunkenness, the court will be no apologist for that; it is an offence peculiarly noxious on board a ship, where the sober and vigilant attention of every man, and particularly of officers, is required. At the same time the court cannot entirely forget, that in a mode of life particularly exposed to severe peril and exertion, and, therefore, admitting in seasons of repose something of indulgence and refreshment; that indulgence and refreshment is naturally enough sought by such persons in grosser pleasures of that kind; and, , therefore, that the proof of a single act of intemperance, committed in port, is no conclusive proof of disability for general maritime employment.

And in the case of *The Lady Campbell* ('), which was a cause of wages instituted on behalf of a ship's steward, the same learned judge, alluding to the plaintiff, said,

I learn from one of his two witnesses that he had been drunk once or twice on the whole of the outward voyage, which lasted nine months. Now, though this court does not mean to countenance any criminal excess of that kind, yet it cannot so far blind itself to the ordinary habits of men living for such a length of time in a frequent condition of extreme peril and fatigue, as to feel much surprise that a seaman, having the command, as this man from his station had of strong liquors, should have been betrayed into two acts of indulgence of that nature, nor can it consider them as sinking him below the common average of a seaman's morality.

*In the case of *The Thomas Worthington* ('), my [256 learned predecessor said:

Cases, indeed, may occur, even in this court, where the misconduct may be of so gross a description that, independent of any actual loss sustained by the owners, the entire forfeiture of wages would ensue; as for instance, if a master had attempted to commit barratry; or if throughout a voyage he had shown gross incapacity, or had been constantly drunk. In either of these cases, would this court be justified in pronouncing for any part of his wages under the contract? Unquestionably not; and if any such case came before me I should not hesitate for a single moment in rejecting his claim *in toto*.

I regret to say the evidence in this case is such that I must pronounce that the plaintiff has forfeited his wages.

Solicitors for plaintiff: *Hollams, Son & Coward*.
Solicitor for defendants: *J. McDiarmid*.

(') 2 Rob., 261.   (') 2 Hagg., 5.   (') 3 W. Rob., 128, at p. 133.

1]   *GOULD v. LAKES.

Will—Contents—Parol Evidence of Intention.

Statements of a testatrix, whether made before or after the execution of the will, are admissible to show what papers constitute the will.

THE plaintiff, Robert John Gould, propounded the last will, dated the 1st day of August, 1872, of Dame Martha Rashleigh, of Prideaux, in the parish of Luxulian, Cornwall, widow, who died at Exmouth on the 9th of June, 1879, and he also alleged that the deceased in the will appointed him one of her executors and named him residuary legatee, and that such appointment and nomination were contained in the first sheet of the will and formed part of it. The defendant denied that the plaintiff was appointed executor, or named residuary legatee, or that the words upon the first sheet of the paper formed part of the will, and he alleged that they were written after the execution of it.

2]   *On the death of the deceased, her will was found in her writing desk in an envelope, which had been apparently thrice opened and re-sealed. With the exception of the attesting clause, it was all in her own handwriting, and contained in two sheets of old fashioned note-paper, one within the other, and stitched together bookwise. Upon the first page of the outer sheet were the words "I appoint my two nephews, Robert John Gould and Robert Gould Lakes to be my joint executors, to carry my will into effect. I appoint my nephew Robert John Gould to be my executor and sole residuary legatee.   Martha Rashleigh, and placed with my will the 1st day of August, 1872.

"Stanley Lodge, Exmouth."

The second side was blank, and the next four pages after the blank page, viz., the whole of the inner sheets, were paged 1, 2, 3, and 4. Page 1 was as follows:

"The last will and testament of me, Martha Rashleigh, widow of Sir John Colman Rashleigh, Baronet, of Prideaux, in the parish of Luxulian, Cornwall.

"I bequeath to my nephew John Nutcombe Gould, and to Catherine his wife, the income for their lives of the sum of £5,000, at their death the aforesaid £5,000 to be equally divided and given to their children. I bequeath each of their children, at my death, the sum of £100, free of legacy duty. I appoint Robert John Gould, and Robert Gould Lakes as trustees to the above legacy.

"M. R.
"H. H. T.
"W. P. H."

"I bequeath to my niece, Frances Gould, the sum of £100. "I bequeath to my niece, Charlotte Elliott, widow, the sum of £100. "I bequeath to my niece, Hannah Nutcombe Gould, the sum of £100.

"Martha Rashleigh."

Pages 2 and 3 were filled with specific legacies, and page 4 was as follows :

"I bequeath to my stepson, Sir Colman Rashleigh, Baronet, of Prideaux, Luxulian, Cornwall, the sum of £5,000. *"I declare this to be my last will and testament, [3 and in witness hereof I hereunto set my hand and seal this 1st day August, in the year of our Lord 1872.

"Martha Rashleigh.

"Signed, sealed, and declared to be her last will and testament, by the said Martha Rashleigh, the testatrix, in our presence, who in her presence, and in the presence of each other at the same time, subscribe our names as witnesses :

"Henry H. Tremayne, Manager of the West of England Bank, Exeter ; and
"William P. Hart, Accountant, West of England Bank, Exmouth."

The next page of the document, i.e., the inner side of the outer sheet, was a blank, and the outer side of all contained the indorsement :

"The will of Martha Rashleigh.   August 1st, 1872."

The issues raised on the pleadings were tried by a special jury, before the President, on the 6th of June, 1880. Neither of the attesting witnesses was able to say whether the will was contained in one or two sheets of paper, or to recollect anything, except that it was duly executed in their presence.   Mr. Tremayne who had read the will before its execution, and who had filled up the attestation clause at the request of the executrix, had no recollection whatever of its contents.   It appeared, however, that before the execution of the will, the testatrix repeatedly expressed orally and in letters her intention of making her nephew, Robert John Gould, her executor and residuary legatee ; and it further appeared from declarations of the testatrix, contained

in letters written after the execution of the will, and in
declarations repeated by her shortly before her death, that
she believed she had given effect to this intention in her will.

Sir J. Holker Q.C. (*Bayford*, with him), for the plaintiff,
tendered the declarations made both before as well as after
the execution of the will, as evidence of what were the contents of the will at the time of execution: *Sugden* v. *St.
Leonards* (').

4] **Inderwick* (*Searle*, with him), for the defendant,
objected to both classes of declarations: The will is in
existence, and before the court, and the case of *Sugden* v. *St.
Leonards* (') does not apply. It is a question of due execution, and no declarations by the testatrix are admissible.

The President ruled that the declarations were admissible
for the purpose for which they were tendered.

The jury found their verdict in favor of the plaintiff.

The Court pronounced for the will as contained in the two
sheets of paper, and allowed the defendant costs out of the
estate, the litigation having arisen from the state in which
the testatrix had left her papers.

June 22. *Inderwick* (*Searle*, with him), moved the court
on behalf of the defendant for a rule *nisi* for a new trial, on
the ground of the reception of inadmissible evidence and of
misdirection: The question in the case is simply the due
execution of the paper, and for that purpose evidence of the
intention is inadmissible. Proof of due execution of the
will cannot be made by any statement which the testator
herself might make. The inference to be drawn from the
language of the paper was that the first sheet was written
after the rest of the will, and there is no evidence but declarations to show that it was in existence and formed part of the
will when the document was signed by the testatrix and
attested by the witnesses. *Sugden* v. *St. Leonards* (') does not
apply. There the question was as to the contents of a lost
will; here the documents are in existence, and the court
cannot go beyond the proof which they themselves furnish.

THE PRESIDENT: I am of opinion that there are no statements in the letters written by the testatrix subsequent to
the execution of the will which had any tendency to mislead
the jury upon the only issue raised for their determination.
Her intentions were clear, for it was proved in the letters
written both before and after the will that she intended to
5] constitute her nephew residuary *legatee, and the question for the jury was whether she had done so by bringing
into connection with one another these two sheets of paper

(') Law Rep., 1 P. D., 154; 17 Eng. R., 453.

before she put her hand to the will.   If that be so, how can it be said that any substantial wrong or miscarriage resulted from the admission in evidence of letters in which she shows that her mind continued after the making of the will in the same state in which it was before, namely, that she desired her nephew should be residuary legatee?

On that ground, therefore, I should refuse the rule.

But I am also of opinion that statements made by a testator after the making of the will, not merely with reference to the contents of the lost instrument, but with reference to the constituent parts of it, are admissible.   That has been decided by the Court of Appeal in *Sugden* v. *St. Leonards* ('), and there is no distinction between this case, where the question is what formed part of the will, and the case where the whole will is lost.   In considering whether or no several pieces of paper constitute the will, evidence would be admissible to show that it was the intention of the testator to make dispositions in conformity with those which are found upon the several sheets of paper.

The present question is whether these two papers were joined together, or were before the testatrix at the time she signed.   But the question of law would not be different if the suggestion were that the first sheet was a forgery or an interpolation by somebody after the event.   In such a case could it be said that in order to establish that this sheet was a genuine part of the will, evidence could not be given of a statement of the testatrix before she made the will that she was going to dispose of her property in the manner in which it appears to be left in the paper alleged to have been interpolated? And in my opinion it is also the law that statements to the same effect subsequent to the making of the will would also be admissible to show what was the state of the testatrix's mind and intentions, just as it would be an ingredient in the consideration whether or no a supposed interpolated sheet were a part of the will at the time of the execution.

I think that the case is governed by the decision of the Court of Appeal in the case of *Sugden* v. *St. Leonards* ('), and that any *statements of the testatrix whether made [6 before or after the execution of the will—for I see no distinction between them—are admissible in evidence with a view of showing what were the constituent parts of the will. I therefore refuse the application.

Solicitors for plaintiff : *Geare & Son.*

Solicitors for defendant : *Bell & Stewart.*

(') Law Rep., 1 P. D., 154 ; 17 Eng. R., 453.

[6 Probate Division, 6.]

June 1, 1880.

In the Goods of DOST ALY KHAN, Deceased.

Will abroad of a Foreigner—Property in this Country—Letters of Administration founded on a Foreign Decree—Proof of Persian Law.

D. M. K., a Persian subject, was by a decree of a Persian court declared entitled to certain property in this country. The decree though founded partly upon a will made no mention of it, and the court which had custody of the will refused to give a copy of it.

The Court of Probate granted letters of administration limited to the property mentioned in a duly authenticated copy of the decree.

The court allowed the law applicable to the case to be proved by a Persian ambassador.

DOST ALY KHAN, late minister of finance to his Imperial Majesty the Shah of Persia, died on the 29th of March, 1873, at Teheran in Persia, having previously executed a will valid according to Persian law. He left three children, of whom Dost Mahommed Khan was one.

The will as well as all the property of the deceased was, in accordance with the Persian law called the "Sharâ," taken possession of by the court having exclusive jurisdiction in matters of wills, inheritance and succession. This court is presided over by a class of learned ecclesiastics, called Moojateheds, of whom one is the "Superior Religious Head and the Highest Authority" in all Persia in respect of the said matters, and whose decrees are absolutely irrevocable.

The said "Superior Religious Head" had divided all the property of deceased in the presence of his legatees and heirs, and had in conformity with the "Sharâ" given a document under his hand and seal to each of the persons so interested, specifying the particular part of the property of 7] the deceased apportioned to *such person, and had appointed to the said Dost Mahommed Khan certain property of the deceased (funds standing in the deceased's name in the books of the Bank of England), which was at his death in England, and had given a document marked "A" under his hand and seal.

According to the "Sharâ" neither the original nor any copy of the will is allowed to go out of the possession of the court, nor are the contents of such will published by the court except to and in the presence of the legatees and heirs. There is nothing analogous to probate or administration known in Persia, except the documents so given to each of the legatees and heirs by the Moojatehed under his hand and seal specifying as above mentioned. Such document is the only evidence which is required in Persia, and is sufficient to entitle the person to whom it is given to take all proceedings necessary to get possession of all property therein mentioned.

The document "A" was under the hand and seal of the said superior religious head, and duly verified by the minister for foreign affairs to his Majesty the Shah, and the British minister at the court of Teheran. There was also a translation of the document marked "B," and duly authenticated, the material parts of which were as follows:

"Let it be known that the whole and entire amount of the money which the late Dost Aly Khan Nizamed Dolé deposited in the bank, whatever sum it may be, both capital and interest, is the undoubted right and real and special property of and belongs solely and entirely to his Excellency Dost Mahommed Khan Moayeral Menalik, and no one else of the heirs has any right whatever thereto."

The facts were proved by, amongst other things, the affidavit of Mirza Aly, also a Persian by birth, and a Mussulman, second secretary to the Persian embassy at the court of St. James, and of his excellency General Neriman Khan, a Persian by birth and minister of his Imperial Majesty the Shah of Persia at the court of Vienna, who stated that in Persia there are no professional lawyers, and that the administration of the law is left entirely to the ecclesiastics, who pronounce and perform all judicial acts and decrees, *but that all persons in the diplomatic service of Persia [8 are required to be thoroughly versed in the law, and that therefore he had studied and become acquainted with it.

Dr. Deane (*Gazdar*, with him), moved the court to decree letters of administration of the personal estate and effects of the deceased mentioned in the decree of the Persian court (with or without the document "A" annexed), to the duly constituted attorney for the purpose of Dost Mahommed Khan. *In the Goods of Sidy Hamet Benamor Beggia* (').

THE PRESIDENT (Sir James Hannen): In this case the affidavit of General Neriman satisfies me that the gentleman who deposed to the Persian law was, and is, from the position he has occupied, competent to give evidence to the court upon that subject.

I therefore accept his statement of the law, and the resul' seems to be this. By the law of Persia representation of the estate of a deceased person is not recognized, but the

(') 1 Add., 840.

person entitled beneficially to the property of the deceased takes directly from him, though by the decree of the competent court. In this particular instance the competent court has declared that the present applicant is entitled to certain funds which are deposited in the Bank of England. The mode in which I shall carry out that which is necessary according to the English law with reference to the Persian law will be by directing that administration be granted to the applicant, limited to the property which is referred to in document "B."

Solicitors: *Freshfields & Williams.*

See 16 Eng. Rep., 591 note; Id., 602 note, 25 Am. Dec., 539 note; 11 Am. Dec., 782 note; 25 Eng. Rep., 119 note; 30 id., 284–5 note; Abbott's Trial Evidence, 85.

The unwritten or common law of another State may be proved by the testimony of competent witnesses instructed in its laws; Milwaukee, etc., *v.* Smith, 74 Ills., 197, 199.

As to a certificate of protest in another State—Pennsylvania—not made evidence by the statute of that State: Lawson *v.* Pinckney, 40 N. Y. Superior Ct. R., 188, 196–203.

Where there is no evidence to the contrary, it will be presumed that the *common law* is in force in each of the other States (except Louisiana). If it has been abrogated, changed or modified by a statute of another State, it must be proved either in the way provided by the acts of Congress, or by that contained in section 426 of the Code (sec. 942 of Code Civil Proc.): White *v.* Knapp, 47 Barb., 549; First Nat. Bank *v.* Fourth Nat. Bank, 77 N. Y., 320; Throop *v.* Hatch, 3 Abb. Pr., 23; Hyduck *v.* Burke, 30 Ark., 124; Bliss on Code Pleading, § 180.

Paine *v.* Noclke, 43 N. Y. Superior Ct. R., 176, is clearly not good law.

The presumption in the absence of proof to the contrary, that the law of a foreign state is the same as that of the forum, does not include penal statutes: People *v.* Chase, 16 N. Y. Week. Dig., 143.

There is no presumption that the *common law* is in force in *Russia.* Such presumption applies only to England and the States which have taken the common law from England. In the absence of proof as to the laws of other foreign countries, our own law must

furnish the rule for deciding the rights of parties litigating in this State: Savage *v.* O'Neil, 44 N. Y., 298.

Courts are not at liberty to indulge in any presumption as to what the legislation of another state or country has been, or what statutes it may have enacted. They will not presume that the statute law of another State is the same as that of their own: White *v.* Knapp, 47 Barb., 549.

Courts do not take judicial notice of the laws of a foreign country, but they must be proved as facts. The unwritten law of a foreign country must be shown by the oral testimony of witnesses skilled therein, and the published reports of the decisions of such country, and not by historical works, as provided for in section 748 of the Code: State *v.* Moy Looke, 7 Oregon, 54.

In an action for rent of premises situated in another State, the facts that the demised premises became untenantable and were for that reason abandoned by the lessee, are not available as a defence merely because the statutes of this State relieve tenants, under such circumstances, from liability for rent.

Such a defence would have been of no avail at common law, which, until the contrary is shown, is presumed to prevail in every State of the Union: Graves *v.* Cameron, 9 Daly, 152.

Where defendant in such an action neglects to plead the existence of a statute of the State where the demised premises are situated, making such facts a defence, he will not be permitted to amend his answer by interposing such statute as a defence at the trial: Graves *v.* Cameron, 9 Daly, 152.

A book in two volumes, published in

Stockil v. Punshon.   1880

1860, entitled "The Revised Statutes of the State of Ohio," of a general nature, in force August 1st, 1860, and upon the title page of which appeared the following words in printing : "Published for the State of Ohio, and distributed to its officers under the Act of the General Assembly passed March 16th, 1860," is strictly within the meaning of sec. 47 of article 37 of the Maryland Code, which provides "that public or private statutes of any State may be read in evidence from any printed volume purporting to contain the statutes of the said State," and is therefore admissible in evidence to show the statute law of the State of Ohio : Harryman *v.* Roberts, 52 Md., 64.

To prove the constitution of California, plaintiff produced a book purporting to be the statutes of that State, published by the State · printer. A member of the bar of California testified that the person named was the State printer ; that the volume was the received official publication of the statutes and the constitution ; that it was recognized by the bar and was the only record the court had.

Held, that the book was sufficiently proved to authorize its reception as evidence: Pacific, etc., *v.* Wheelock, 80 N. Y., 278, affirming 44 N. Y. Super. Ct. R., 566.

The Confederate Congress was the legislative department of a *de facto* government, recognized by all the courts of Georgia while it lasted ; and acts published by authority of that government, while in dominion of the territory of this State, will be recognized by its courts whenever they are necessary to throw light upon any litigation therein. The government being overthrown and there being no records by which to establish such acts, parol testimony of a witness that he was a member of the Confederate Congress, that as such he became possessed of certain pamphlets which contained the acts of that body, and that they are genuine, was sufficient to admit the printed acts in evidence : Commissioners *v.* Newell, 64 Geo., 699.

[6 Probate Division, 9.]

Nov. 13, 1880.

**Stockil and Others v. Punshon and Others.   [9

Codicil—Incorporation.

Semble, a document containing the words, "This is a third codicil to my will," is not incorporated in a codicil of subsequent date by the words, "This is a fourth codicil to my will."

Sir Isaac Morley, late of Beechfield, in the county of York, Knight, died on the 1st of December, 1879. On the 31st of August, 1872, he made a codicil· to his will, and thereby bequeathed a sum of £2,000 to the trustees of the Doncaster Grammar School for the purpose of founding a scholarship to be called the "Morley Scholarship." On the 11th of December, 1876, he made another will revoking the previous will and codicil, and on the same day he also made a temporary codicil by which he provided that the codicil for founding the Morley Scholarship should remain in force until he executed another codicil for the same purpose. He subsequently signed six other codicils, the third of which provided for the Morley Scholarship, but this codicil was by inadvertence not signed by one of the attesting witnesses. Each codicil commenced with the words, "This is a first codicil;" "this is a second codicil," and so on throughout the six codicils.

The executors propounded the documents, and asked for probate either of the third codicil as incorporated in or confirmed by the subsequent codicils or of the temporary codicil of the 11th of December, 1876, and the codicil of the 31st of August, 1872, as incorporated and confirmed by it. All the residuary legatees had been made parties to the action, but had not appeared.

Dr. Tristram, for the plaintiffs, the executors: It is true that the only words in the subsequent codicils that would incorporate the third codicil are contained in the commencement of those codicils, i.e., "This is a fourth," "This is a fifth," "This is a sixth codicil," but these are sufficient: *Ingoldby* v. *Ingoldby* (¹); *Burton* v. *Newbery* (²). It is however immaterial to the parties whether this codicil is pronounced for, as the temporary codicil reviving the earlier one is to the same effect.

10] *THE PRESIDENT: As there is no opposition, and it makes no difference whether the so-called third codicil is pronounced valid or invalid, I shall act upon the impression which I have formed, that the mere enumeration of the fourth, fifth, and sixth codicils is not sufficient to incorporate that document, and I shall decree probate of the temporary codicil of the 11th of December, 1876, and the document of the 31st of August, 1872, which is incorporated and confirmed by it.

Solicitors for plaintiffs: *Van Sandau & Cumming*.

(¹) 4 Notes of Cases, 493.   (²) 1 Ch. D., 234; 15 Eng. R., 713.

[6 Probate Division, 11.]

June 8, 1880.

11]   *WICKHAM v. WICKHAM.

Decree Nisi—Re-marriage before Decree absolute.

A. R. W. obtained in 1868 a decree *nisi* for dissolution of her marriage, and in 1871, believing that the decree had been made absolute, she married again.

The court, the Queen's Proctor not opposing, made the decree absolute.

ALICE RUTH WICKHAM obtained a decree *nisi* on the 17th of June, 1868, by reason of her husband's cruelty and adultery. Her solicitor (since deceased) told her on the day the decree *nisi* was pronounced that her attendance would not again be required; that the making of the decree *nisi* absolute was a matter of form, and he would attend to it. On the belief that all things necessary had been done, and that the decree *nisi* had been made *absolute, the peti- [12 tioner on the 17th of September, 1871, went through a cere- mony of marriage with another man.   She did not become aware until the 8th of May, 1880, that the decree *nisi* had not been made absolute, and that her second marriage con- sequently was invalid.

Searle, for the petitioner, moved the court to make the decree *nisi* absolute.

Gorst, for the Queen's Proctor, did not oppose.

THE COURT made the decree absolute.

Solicitor: *The Queen's Proctor.*
Solicitor for petitioner: *H. C. Coote.*

[6 Probate Division, 12.]

June 22, 1880.

BAKER V. BAKER.

Dissolution of Marriage—Lunatic Petitioner—Committee.

The lunacy of a husband or wife is not a bar to a suit by the committee for the dissolution of the lunatic's marriage.

Such a suit may be instituted by the committee of the lunatic.

THIS was an appeal to the full court, consisting of Lord Coleridge, the President, and Sir R. J. Phillimore, from a judgment of the Right Hon. the President, overruling a de- murrer to a petition presented by the committee of the es- tate of a lunatic for a dissolution of the lunatic's marriage.

The facts and arguments are reported, *ante,* p. 364.

The same counsel appeared as in the court below.

Their Lordships affirmed the judgment, and for the same reasons.

Solicitors for petitioner: *Thomas White & Sons.*
Solicitors for respondent: *Surr, Gribble & Bunton.*

[6 Probate Division, 13.]

March 1, 1881.

13] *HALFEN, otherwise BODDINGTON, v. BODDINGTON.

Nullity—Application by Respondent to make Decree absolute.

The court will not upon the application of the respondent make a decree *nisi* absolute for nullity of marriage by reason of the impotence of the respondent.

ON the 10th of March, 1880, the petitioner, then calling herself Emily Caroline Boddington, filed a petition alleging that she was on the 23d of October, 1879, lawfully married to Thomas Boddington, and praying for a restitution of conjugal rights.

The respondent filed an answer alleging divers acts of violence on the part of the petitioner, and praying for a judicial separation. The cause was set down for trial, but before the hearing the petitioner agreed to substitute for her previous petition a petition for nullity of marriage by reason of the respondent's impotence. This was accordingly done, and on the 4th of August, 1880, the petition for nullity was heard in camera and a decree *nisi* of nullity pronounced. Subsequently the petitioner refused to make the decree absolute, and on the 8th of February, 1881, applied that her petition might be dismissed or that the decree should not be made absolute. This was opposed on behalf of the respondent, and leave was given for him to apply to make the decree absolute, but the court directed that the Queen's Proctor should have notice of the application. The Attorney-General declined to direct an intervention, and no one else having appeared to show cause to the contrary, on the 1st of March,

Inderwick, Q.C., and *Pritchard*, moved the court on behalf of the respondent to make the decree absolute: *Ousey* v. *Ousey* ([1]) does not apply. There the court refused to make at the request of the respondent a decree *nisi* for dissolution of marriage absolute, but the court's jurisdiction in such cases is defined by the statute, which in terms gives the power only to grant the relief at the prayer of the innocent party. Here the authority is that which was inherent in the ecclesiastical courts. In *Norton* v. *Seton* ([2]), though the court refused to decree a nullity of marriage at the suit 14] *of the impotent person, it refused upon other grounds than that he was the complainant. In cases of consanguin-

([1]) 1 P. D., 56.   ([2]) 3 Phillim., 147.

ity, affinity, or bigamy, though the wrongdoer seeks the aid of the court and great hardship is often inflicted, the court nevertheless annuls the marriage : *Miles* v. *Chilton* (').

Bayford, contrà : The language of the statute, 36 Vict. c. 31, puts decrees *nisi* for dissolution of marriage and decrees *nisi* for nullity of marriage upon the same footing, and therefore *Ousey* v. *Ousey* (') is directly applicable. The distinction between void and voidable marriages is clearly explained by Lord Penzance in *A.* v. *B.* ('), and governs this case.

Inderwick, Q.C., in reply.

THE PRESIDENT : It is not necessary for me now to express an opinion upon the very difficult question, whether or no a suit can be instituted for a decree of nullity of marriage by the husband in whom the defect is alleged to exist. That may be properly raised before me in a suit for that purpose, but in the present state of things I am of opinion that the respondent is not entitled to have the decree made absolute. His wife, who was the complaining party, obtained a decision in her favor ; but before the operative decree of the court had been pronounced she desired to discontinue further proceedings in the case, and the respondent, who has up to this time always resisted her claim, now comes forward and asks the court not to grant her prayer, but to make the order which she originally asked for, but which she now withdraws from asking. This is contrary to all precedent. I am not aware of any case in which the defendant in a suit has been allowed, because it suited his purpose, to ask that a decree should be made against him.

I have already stated, in the case of *Ousey* v. *Ousey* ('), the reasons which led my mind to the conclusion that in ordinary suits for dissolution of marriage the respondent cannot call upon the court to pronounce a decree upon the petitioner ceasing to desire it, and I am of opinion that the principle of that case governs the present. The decree *nisi* in suits for nullity has been *interposed between the [15 hearing of the cause and the final decree, in precisely the same manner as it exists in suits for dissolution, and the pronouncing of the decree absolute is as much a final step in the one case as in the other, and it is, therefore, competent for the petitioner before that final step in the cause has been taken to withdraw from the suit, and say "I no longer require that the court shall give me the relief for which I formerly asked." It works no injustice, as it enables the respondent to have all the advantage which he could have

(') 1 Robertson, 684.　　　(') 1 P. D., 56.　　　(') Law Rep., 1 P. & D., 559.

had in the suit.   He is entitled to have the petition dismissed
for want of prosecution ; he is entitled to put an end to any
obligation imposed upon him in the course of the suit, as,
e.g., an order for alimony, and, of course, he will be entitled
to make any application which he may be advised to make
on the subject of costs.   In all this he is in no way damni-
fied by being limited to asking that the petition be dismissed,
while at the same time it leaves it open to him, if he should
be so advised, to institute a separate suit for a decree of
nullity of marriage upon the grounds which have been
brought forward in the case.

The application on the part of the respondent that the decree *nisi* be made absolute must therefore be dismissed.

Solicitors for petitioner : *Lewis & Lewis.*
Solicitors for respondent : *Sandilands, Humphry & Armstrong.*

NOTE.—In this case the petitioner afterwards again changed her mind, and
asked that the decree might be made absolute, and this was accordingly done.

[6 Probate Division, 17.]

Dec. 14, 1880.

17]   *In the Goods of* MAYD.

Will—Conditional.

A testator being about to travel, made his will, which contained the following
words: "On leaving this station for T. and M., in case of my death on the way,
know all men this is a memorandum of my last will and testament:"
Held, that the will was not contingent upon his death before arriving at T. or M.
Will admitted to probate.

JOHN GEORGE SUFFIELD MAYD, late of Cooper's Creek;
Queensland, Australia, deceased, died on the 4th of May,
1879, at St. Kilda in Victoria.
Among his papers after his death was found the following :

"Canada Five per Cent.	£1,400
New Zealand	500
West Hartlepool Railway	900
India Four per Cent.	1,000
New Three per Cent. Consols	85
Great Eastern Railway	735
Mrs. May's Bank, Victoria	400
	£5,020

"Eulbertie Station, Cooper's Creek, Queensland.
                              "23d August, 1878."

"On leaving this station for Thargomindah and Melbourne, in case of my death on the way, know all men this is a memorandum of my last will and testament.

"I leave my wife, Robina Mayd, and my brother, William Mayd, barrister of the Inner Temple, London, and now recorder of Bury St. Edmunds, in the county of Suffolk, England, my sole executors of said will. As long as my wife Robina Mayd remains unmarried, and no longer, said Robina Mayd is to have the control of the interest of the above five thousand and twenty pounds invested as above, to be applied for the maintenance and benefit of herself and children—Emily Elizabeth, my daughter, John Herbert Mayd, my second and youngest son, and, if it be required, my eldest son, Jeffray May, with the advice of the said William Mayd, barrister.

*"It is to be clearly understood that I wish my prop- [18 erty to be for the benefit of my wife and children, and on my wife's death, the capital to be divided into four parts, namely, one-quarter to William Jeffray Mayd, one-quarter to John Herbert Mayd, one-half to Emily Elizabeth Mayd, &c., &c.

"Signed this 23d day of August, 1878, &c., &c."

The document was duly executed as a will.

The deceased was entitled to the interest for life of a sum of £5,000 with a power of appointing the same amongst his children.

The deceased joined his wife in Melbourne having completed the journey mentioned, and the will was sent to him from Cooper's Creek by the friend with whom he had deposited it. He kept it in his desk, and on several occasions subsequently spoke to his wife about the contents. He never made any other will or otherwise exercised the power of appointment.

Inderwick, Q.C., moved for probate: The words used are certainly equivocal, but are not such as to make the will conditional: *In the Goods of Dobson* (¹); *In the Goods of Porter* (²).

THE PRESIDENT: I am of opinion that I ought to grant probate of this will. The meaning of general phrases of this kind is, "knowing the uncertainty of human life, and being about to enter on something particulary dangerous, I make this my will," and the court ought not to scrutinize such expressions with too great nicety. *In the Goods of Porter* (²) the words were: "Being obliged to leave Eng-

(¹) Law Rep., 1 P. & D., 88.   (²) Law Rep., 2 P. & D., 22.

land to join my regiment in China, and not having time to make a will, I leave this paper containing my wishes and desires. Should anything unfortunately happen to me while abroad, I wish everything that I may be in possession of at that time, or anything appertaining to me hereafter, whether in lands, goods, clothes, chattels or money, to be equally divided." Lord Penzance says that if the will had stopped at the end of the first sentence it would have fallen within the first class of cases to which he referred, and that is where it does stop in this case, i.e., at the end of the following sentence: "On leaving this station for Thargomindah and 19] Melbourne, in case of my *death on the way, know all men this is a memorandum of my last will and testament." In this case there are no such words as those relied on by Lord Penzance, as leading to a different conclusion, namely, those in which the testator said, "I wish everything that I may be in possession of at that time," i.e., at the time of his death abroad, to be divided; I therefore admit the will to probate.

Solicitors: *Young, Jones, Roberts & Hale.*

See note 2 Jarm. on Wills (Randolph & Talcott's ed.), 509 ; 1d. (Bigelow's ed.), 2 ; 1 Redf. on Wills (4th ed.), 178.

If a will is clearly conditional and contingent, and the contingency contemplated by the will did not happen within the time specified, the recognition of the will by the testator after the failure of the contingency, by mere verbal declarations, does not revive or continue the will as an absolute, valid will: French *v.* French, 14 W. Va., 459, 486–503, and cases cited of wills held conditional and those held not to be.

Testator made his will in writing, and afterwards partly erased and corrected it in lead pencil, in the presence of his brother, saying that "It would be a good will anyhow, if he did not prepare another one before he died." This will was found in his safe at his death. Held, that the will as corrected in lead pencil was properly admitted to probate: Fuguet's Will, 11 Phila. R., 75.

[6 Probate Division, 19.]

Jan. 25, 1881.

In the Goods of WILLIAM EWING, Deceased.

Assets in Scotland and England—Will proved in Scotland only—Right of Legatee to insist upon proof in England.

W. E. died possessed of property of small value in this country, and entitled under the will of J. O. E. to large assets in Scotland, which were being duly administered there. The executors of W. E. proved his will in Scotland only. G. W. H., a legatee under W. E.'s will, applied for a grant of administration of the estate of W. E. in this country, which application was opposed by the executors :

Held, that the court is not bound to make such a grant but that its power is discretionary :

Held, also, that it not having been shown that the executors were not doing their duty there was no necessity for any grant in this country. Application refused.

A similar application was made by another legatee upon the ground also that such a grant was necessary to substantiate proceedings in chancery.

Application refused, on its being proved that the grant was not necessary for the suit in chancery.

WILLIAM EWING, late of Calcutta, in India, merchant, deceased, died on the 26th day of December, 1878, at Umballa, a bachelor.

The deceased made his will on the previous 23d day of December, and therein named his uncles, Archibald Orr Ewing and William Ewing, his executors, and bequeathed the sum of £10,000 (part of his share of the residuary estate of his uncle, John Orr Ewing) to his friend George Wellesley Hope, and the sum of £30,000 (another part of such share) to his stepmother, Sarah Jane Ewing. The residue of his estate was not disposed of.

The property of the deceased consisted of a few articles of *trifling value in India, some books in England, [20 valued at £15 16s., and a reversionary interest in a silver tea-service in England, valued at £13 2s. He was also entitled under the will of his uncle, John Orr Ewing (who died in April, 1878), to one-sixth part of £60,000, and one-sixth also of the residue of John Orr Ewing's estate.

John Orr Ewing by his will gave certain annuities which took precedence of the legacy of £60,000, and there were also other legacies amounting to £14,500 to be provided for before the residue could be divided. The estate of John Orr Ewing amounted altogether to about £400,000, being his share of a partnership in the firm of John Ewing and Co., carrying on business at Glasglow, which share was to be paid by ten annual instalments. The will of John Orr Ewing was proved in Scotland by the executors, and a Scotch confirmation produced and sealed with the seal of this court.

The will of William Ewing was proved in Scotland only, whereupon Mr Hope instituted proceedings in the Court of Chancery to obtain payment of his legacy, and having failed issued a citation from this court to the executors of William Ewing's will to accept or refuse probate, and to James Ewing, his father, to accept or refuse letters of administration *de bonis non* of the estate, or to show cause why the same should not be granted to him (Mr. Hope) as a legatee.

Mrs. Jane Ewing also made a similar application, on her own behalf, in chambers.

The executors of William Ewing's will, together with Mr. James Ewing, the father, opposed the application, and filed affidavits stating the particulars with regard to the property of John Orr Ewing, and that there were ample funds to satisfy the legacy of £60,000, and that the deceased William Ewing's share of the estate would amount to more than £50,000, which would be duly paid, but that at present the amount in the hands of J. O. Ewing's executors was about £1,050 only. They also contended that the estate was being properly administered, that there was no property in this country upon which a grant could operate, and that it would therefore cause the estate unnecessary expense.

21] *Inderwick*, Q.C., and *Bayford*, for Mr. Hope, in support of the motion for the grant.

Dr. Deane, Q.C., and *Dr. Tristram*, contrá.

Searle, for Mrs. Jane Ewing.

Cur. adv. vult.

Jan. 25. THE PRESIDENT: This is a proceeding by citation issued by George Wellesley Hope, a legatee named in the will of William Ewing, deceased, against Archibald Orr Ewing and William Ewing, to accept or refuse probate of the said will as executors named therein, and against James Ewing, to accept or refuse letters of administration (with the will annexed) as the natural and lawful father of the deceased, or, that they should show cause why administration, with the will annexed, should not be granted to G. W. Hope as legatee.

The parties cited have appeared, but show for cause against administration being granted to the applicant that they are not bound to accept or refuse probate or administration, inasmuch as the executors have already proved the will in Scotland where alone there were any assets.

The deceased, W. Ewing, died in India on the 26th day of December, 1878, having, by his will, dated the 23d of December, made the following bequests:

To Sarah Jane Ewing (his stepmother), "£30,000, to be realized and paid out of my share in the will of my late uncle, John Orr Ewing, who died last year."

"And out of the said share in the said will I also bequeath £10,000 to my friend George Hope."

"The remainder of my share from the said will to be divided equally amongst my brothers."

The said will contained no disposition of the general residue, to which therefore the father of the deceased would be entitled as next of kin.

The personal estate and effects, which it is alleged by the applicant were left by the testator within the jurisdiction of this court, are thus described.

"1. One-sixth part of a legacy of £60,000, and one-sixth of the residue of the estate of the late John Orr Ewing, which estate consists of property partly in England and partly in Scotland.

*"2. A library of books.   [22

"3. A silver tea kettle and silver tea set."

The second and third items are valued respectively at £15 16s. and £13 2s.

William Ewing and Archibald Ewing, the persons named in the will of the deceased as executors, are also with four others the executors of the final disposition and settlement of the late John Orr Ewing, and these six persons are now adminstering the estate of the said John Orr Ewing, deceased, in accordance with the law of Scotland, in Scotland, the country of his domicile.

It is sworn, and not denied, that "the share of the deceased, W. Ewing, in the estate of the said John Orr Ewing cannot at present be realized and paid over to the executors of the will of the said W. Ewing, inasmuch as there are annuities given by the will of the said John Orr Ewing which have to be provided for and take precedence over the said legacy of £60,000, and after the payment of the said legacy of £60,000 there are legacies to the amount of £14,500, which under the will of the said J. O. Ewing must be provided for before the residue can be divided. The greater part of the assets of the said J. O. Ewing consists of capital in a firm carrying on business in Glasgow, of which he was a member, and which, according to the articles of partnership, can only be drawn out by instalments spread over several years, and the said executors of J. O. Ewing have now a balance in hand of between £1,030 and £1,050 in Scotland payable to the estate of the said W. Ewing, but no more."

Upon these facts several questions have been suggested, but I do not think it necessary to express a definite opinion upon all of them. The main ground on which this application has been based is that the claim of the estate of William Ewing on the estate of his uncle John Orr Ewing is an asset of W. Ewing's estate in England, by reason of some of the assets of the uncle's estate having been in England at the time of the death of W. Ewing, and therefore that the executors of W. Ewing's will ought to take probate in respect of these assets here.

It is not disputed that the deceased, J. O. Ewing, was a domiciled Scotchman, and that his will was properly proved in Scotland, and is being administered there in accordance with *Scotch laws. The claim of the executors of W. [23

Ewing in respect of the interest of their testator under his uncle's will, is a claim on the executors of the uncle duly to administer his estate and to pay the legacy to W. Ewing out of the funds which may be applicable to that purpose. It cannot be disputed that this claim or interest in the estate of the uncle constitutes an asset of the estate of the deceased W. Ewing, because it is recoverable by the executors of W. Ewing *virtute officii*, but it appears to me that it is an asset in Scotland and not in England : *Executors of Perry* v. *The Queen* (') ; *Forbes* v. *Steven* (').

The executors of J. O. Ewing have availed themselves of the provisions of 21 & 22 Vict. c. 56, which enables the executors of a person who dies domiciled in Scotland to include in the inventory of his effects all his property wherever situate within the United Kingdom, and they have paid or become liable to pay in Scotland probate duty on the property of the testator situate in England, and the Scotch confirmation has been duly produced in the principal registry here and has been sealed with the seal of this court, so that it now has the like effect as if probate had been granted here, but the place where the business of administering and winding up the estate of J. O. Ewing is being carried on is Scotland, and any acts done in England by the executors of J. O. Ewing are only ancillary to the administration which is taking place in Scotland.

I am not aware that the point has been the subject of judicial determination, but all analogies seem to lead to the conclusion that Scotland is the local situation of this asset of W. Ewing. Thus the share of a deceased partner in a partnership asset is situate where the business is carried on, Hanson on Probate Acts, &c., p. 161, and shares in a company are locally situate where the head office is : *Attorney-General* v. *Higgins* ('). And the fact that some of the assets of J. O. Ewing were situate in England does not appear to make any difference. If I were to constitute the applicant administrator with the will annexed of W. Ewing he could not in that character take possession of or recover the outstanding assets of the uncle's estate, he could not claim 24] *those assets themselves *virtute officii*, his only remedy would still be through and by means of his claim upon the executors of the uncle to have his estate duly administered. It is indeed possible that a court exercising equity jurisdiction here could interfere, at the instance of the representative of W. Ewing's estate, to prevent the assets of J. O. Ewing's estate in England being wasted or applied

('') Law Rep., 4 Ex., 27.   ('') Law Rep., 10 Eq., 178.   ('') 2 H. & N., 339.

iu a manner inconsistent with the rights of persons in this
country interested in W. Ewing's estate : *Pardo* v. *Bing-
ham* (¹).   But this is on the supposition that the executors
of J. O. Ewing have done or are about to do something
inconsistent with their duty to the estate of W. Ewing.
No suggestion of this kind is made in the affidavits on
which this application is founded, and I have therefore
nothing before me to show that there is anything which
makes it the duty of the executors of W. Ewing to take
any proceedings against the executors of J. O. Ewing in
England, and so no necessity appears for substituting any
one in the place of the executors of W. Ewing to discharge
a duty neglected by them.

If the applicant should be advised that any such necessity can be established, the facts relied on must be shown
by affidavit ; but I must add that if, as is alleged, the English assets of J. O. Ewing have in the course of administering his estate been removed to Scotland, I doubt whether
a court of equity would now interfere with their being
dealt with in accordance with Scotch law.

But it was further contended that the legacy to Mr. Hope
is a demonstrative legacy, and that he therefore has a claim
on the general estate of the deceased W. Ewing, and that
some of the assets of that estate, namely the books and
plate, were in England at the time of W. Ewing's death.

It is not necessary for me to determine whether this
legacy is demonstrative ; because, assuming that it is, I do
not consider that in the existing state of facts I ought to
grant the administration asked for to the applicant.

This is not, as now presented to the court, a matter of
legal right.   It is an application to the discretionary power
of the court on the non-contentious side of its jurisdiction.
The court is not bound to grant administration to a legatee as
it is to the *next of kin, whose rights are derived from   [25
statute : *Rex* v. *Bettesworth* (²).   And in those cases which
are not within the statute of administration the court is left
to the exercise of its discretion in the choice of an administrator, and no person has such a legal right to preference as
can be enforced at law : Williams on Executors, 444, p. 472,
pt. i, bk. v, ch. iii, § 1, 8th ed.

What case is then made out for the exercise of the discretion of the court in favor of the applicant?   It cannot be
supposed that these proceedings are really taken to enable
the applicant, in the apparently improbable event of W.
Ewing's estate proving insufficient to pay the legacy of

(¹) Law Rep., 6 Eq., 485.   (²) 2 Str., 956.

£10,000, to have recourse to the assets of W. Ewing in England valued at £28 18s.

There is nothing to contradict the statement of the executors of W. Ewing that there are, or will be, ample assets in Scotland of J. O. Ewing's estate to pay the legacy to the nephew, with which to satisfy the bequests of his will.

This being so, it does not appear to me to be the duty of the executors of W. Ewing to take any proceedings to recover from James Ewing, the father of W. Ewing, the books and plate which were in his possession at the time of his son's death, and to which he is entitled as next of kin, unless the share of the estate of the uncle should prove insufficient to meet the legacies left by W. Ewing. Should the time arrive when it shall appear that recourse is necessary in England to the £28 worth of books and plate to make up the applicant's legacy, I shall be willing to consider whether and to whom, in the exercise of my discretion, I should grant administration with respect to those articles. The administration would in that case be limited to the property not disposed of by the will. In the meantime the applicant is not precluded from taking proceedings for the recovery of his legacy in Scotland, where the executors of W. Ewing will be liable as for a devastavit if they neglect at the proper time to collect any assets legally applicable to the payment of legacies.

One or two other points were adverted to at the hearing, but not argued. One was as to the domicile of W. Ewing at the time of his decease. It is unnecessary to pursue this 26] inquiry, *as I hold that W. Ewing had substantial assets in Scotland in respect of which it was proper and necessary that probate should be taken in that country.

Another point adverted to was that either the executors of W. Ewing, or James Ewing his father, may be liable to penalties for dealing with the books and plate without proving the will or taking administration here. But this is not the question I have to determine. It is for the revenue authorities to judge whether this is a proper case in which to take proceedings for such penalties.   ·

On the whole I feel bound to reject the application, on the ground that no necessity or duty towards the applicant or the estate of the deceased at present appears for the executors to take probate in England, and that until such necessity or duty arises I am not called upon to decide, in default of their doing so, to whom administration should be granted.

A similar application was made in chambers on behalf of

Mrs. Sarah Jane Ewing, with this additional circumstance, that it was stated that a representative of the estate of W. Ewing was necessary for the purposes of a suit now pending before the Master of the Rolls between Mrs. Ewing and her husband James Ewing.

The executors of W. Ewing deny that it is necessary for the purposes of the said suit that probate of his will should be obtained in England. In this state of things I thought it expedient to inquire of the Master of the Rolls whether the suit was properly constituted without the executors of W. Ewing being made parties in their representative capacity, and he informs me that he considers that it is.

I therefore refuse Mrs. Ewing's application, as well as that of Mr. Hope.

Solicitors for Mr. Hope: *Stibbard, Gibson & Co.*
Solicitors for parties interested: *Johnson, Upton & Co.*
Solicitors for Mrs. Ewing: *Lattey & Hart.*

[6 Probate Division, 27.]

Jan. 26, 1881.

*WILKINSON v. CORFIELD.   [27

Codicil proved by Legatee—Costs as of Executor proving.

A legatee who has propounded a codicil and succeeded is entitled to the same costs as an executor under similar circumstances.

The defendant, the executor of the will of R. C., had proved the will only. The plaintiffs propounded a codicil. The court having pronounced for the codicil, condemned the defendant in costs, and gave the plaintiffs also out of the estate such sum *nomine expensarum* as would cover the additional expenses.

RICHARD CORFIELD, late of Bradney, in Worfield, in the county of Salop, farmer, deceased, died on the 1st of May, 1879, having made a will dated the 22d of November, 1873, and a codicil dated the 27th of April, 1879.

By the will the testator gave all his property to his brother, the defendant, Thomas Corfield, and his sister Eliza Corfield absolutely, subject to an annuity of £15, and appointed them executor and executrix. By the codicil the testator gave the plaintiff, Mary Wilkinson, wife of the other plaintiff, an annuity of £20 charged upon his property generally. The testator's sister died in his lifetime, and the defendant proved the will only. The plaintiffs thereupon propounded the codicil, to which the defendant pleaded that it was not duly executed, that the deceased did not know and approve of the contents thereof, and that it was revoked by the deceased by having been torn by him and the pieces burnt by the defendant by the direction of the deceased. At the hearing, before the court alone, it was proved that the codicil was duly executed by the testator, who thoroughly approved of it, and that it was given by him to one of the attesting witnesses, who subsequently sent it back to the defendant. The defendant alleged that on the 30th of April he gave the codicil to the testator who tore it into three pieces, and told him to put them on the fire, which he accordingly did. The court nevertheless found that the codicil had not been revoked, and condemned the defendant in costs.

Jan. 12. *Inderwick*, Q.C. (*Bayford*, with him), applied for an order that the plaintiff's extra costs should be paid out of the estate.

28] *A. Staveley Hill*, Q.C., and *Searle*, were for the defendant.

Cur. adv. vult.

Jan. 26. THE PRESIDENT: In this case a legatee having propounded a codicil made in her favor and succeeded, an application was made to me for her costs upon the ground that in propounding the codicil she ought to be allowed those costs, which, if the executor had done his duty, he would have been able to take for himself out of the estate, and I am of opinion that that is a reasonable application. That a legatee is entitled to have his expenses paid when he establishes a testamentary paper is laid down in *Sutton v. Drax*(') in these terms: "Where a legatee propounds a paper and establishes it, thereby fulfilling the duty of the executor, the legatee is entitled to have his expenses paid out of the estate of the deceased. This is the rule of the court." If in this case I gave no more than the ordinary costs, the legatee would have no benefit for a considerable time from her small annuity of £20, and I therefore think I ought to allow her costs on the same scale practically as the executor would himself have been entitled to have received. I shall therefore make the order in the form which I find has been used in the analogous case of *Bremer v. Freeman and Bremer*('), in which a sum was allowed *nomine expensarum*.

The order I shall make will be in these terms: "I further give to the plaintiff *nomine expensarum* such sum as shall be considered by the registrar sufficient to cover the additional expenses of the plaintiff of and incidental to these proceedings, to be paid out of the estate of the deceased."

Solicitors for plaintiff: *Prior & Co.*
Solicitors for defendant: *Truefitt & Gane.*

(') 2 Phillim., 323.   (') Dea. & Sw., 258.

[6 Probate Division, 29.]

Feb. 8, 1881.

*TAYLOR V. TAYLOR.   [29

Administrator pending Suit—Receiver pending Suit—Termination—Costs.

The duties of an administrator and receiver pending suit commence from the date of the order of appointment, and if the decree in the action is appealed from, do not cease until the appeal has been disposed of.

Costs of the administrator and receiver pending suit and of his solicitor allowed from the date of the appointment until the dismissal of the appeal.

THIS was a summons in objection to a taxation of costs.

The plaintiffs, as executors, propounded the will of Henry Taylor, deceased, which was opposed by the defendant, the daughter and heiress-at-law.

The following are the material dates:

1878. Dec. 24th.   Action commenced.
1879. Feb. 25th.   Order appointing Mr. Ward adminis-
                   trator and receiver pending suit.
  "   March 21st. Order for receiver pending suit sealed.
  "   April 5th. Letters of administration pending suit
                   issued.
  "   May 3d and 6th. Action heard. Verdict, and sen-
                   tence pronouncing against the will
                   and condemning the plaintiff in costs.
  "   May 21st.   Rule *nisi* for new trial.
  "   July 1st.   Rule discharged.
1880. March 9th.   Order authorizing Mr. Ward as admin-
                   istrator and receiver pending suit to
                   sell farming stock, &c.
  "   March 23d. Similar order authorizing him to give a
                   tenant notice to quit.
  "   April 20th and 23d. Appeal from order discharging
                   the rule *nisi* heard and appeal dis-
                   missed.
  "   May 10th.   Letters of administration granted to
                   the widow of the deceased.

On the taxation the registrar disallowed all the costs of Mr. Ward and his solicitor between the 25th of February, 1879, and the dates when the letters of administration issued, and the order *for receiver was sealed, on the ground [30 that Mr. Ward had no power to act till then.

The registrar also disallowed Mr. Ward's and his solici-tor's costs from the 6th of May, 1879, on the ground that the final decree was made on that day, and that the defendant might at once have taken out a grant of letters of administration, notwithstanding the appeal, or might have obtained fresh appointments as administrator and receiver pending suit: *Charlton* v. *Hindmarsh* (¹).

Bayford, in objection to the taxation: *Fisher* v. *Joy* (²); *Wells* v. *Wells and Hudson* (³); *Jones* v. *Jones* (⁴).

Jeune, in support of the taxation.

THE PRESIDENT considered that the appeal operated as an extention of the suit, and also that the plaintiffs, by their conduct in the case, and especially by being parties to the orders of the 9th and 23d of March, 1880, were estopped from objecting. He, therefore, allowed all the costs from the date of the order appointing the administrator and receiver.

Solicitors for plaintiffs: *White & Sons*.
Solicitors for defendant: *Chorley, Crawford & Chester*.

(¹) 1 S. & T., 519.   (³) 3 S. & T., 542.
(²) 4 P. & D., 231.   (⁴) 2 P. & D., 333.

[6 Probate Division, 30.]

Feb. 15, 1881.

In the Goods of S. M. HEATHCOTE.

Will—Incorporation.

S. M. H., while a married woman, made a will which was invalid. Afterwards when a widow, she executed a document beginning with the words "this is a codicil to the last will and testament of me." The codicil was written on the same paper as the will and immediately after it, and it was proved that she had made no other will:

Held, that the will was incorporated in the codicil. Probate granted of both documents.

SOPHIA MATILDA HEATHCOTE, late of North Luffenham Hall, in the county of Rutland, widow, died on the 20th of November, 1880.

The deceased had under her marriage settlement an abso-
31] lute *power in the event of her husband surviving her of disposing by will of their settled property, and on the 17th of November, 1874, she made, in the lifetime of her husband, a will bequeathing that property. She survived her husband, and therefore the power never took effect, and the will was invalid. On the 1st of November, 1880, she, being then a widow, made a codicil to the will. This as well as the will was in her own handwriting, and was written upon the same piece of paper as the will immediately after it. It began with the words "this is a codicil to the last

will and testament of me, etc.,'' but contained no other reference to the will. It was, however, agreed by all parties
that no later will than the will of the 17th of November,
1874, had been made by the deceased, and that an affidavit
to that effect could be supplied.

Inderwick, Q.C., and *Searle*, moved for probate of both
documents: Though the will by itself was inoperative in
the events which have happened, *Price* v. *Parker* ('); *Noble* v. *Willock* ('), the codicil with the surrounding circumstances sufficiently identify the will, so as to incorporate it:
Allen v. *Maddock* ('); *In the Goods of Smith* (').

Bayford, for other parties interested, supported the application.

Dr. Tristram, and *Pritchard*, contrà, for parties whose
interests would be prejudiced by probate of both documents.
The will must be identified as then existing by the codicil,
and the surrounding circumstances only: *In the Goods of
Sunderland* ('). Evidence of intention is not admissible:
In the Goods of Almosnino ('). The fact that the codicil is
on the same paper is not of itself sufficient to incorporate it:
In the Goods of John Brewis ('); *In the Goods of Wat-
kins* ('). Nor are the words ''this is a codicil, &c.'' sufficient:
In the Goods of Stockil and others v. *Punshon* (').

THE PRESIDENT: The only question raised for my determination is whether I am satisfied that the will of 1874 is
sufficiently *identified as the last will and testament [32
which is referred to in the codicil.

The case is governed by the passage in *Allen* v. *Maddock* (''), and on the present occasion the Court of Probate is
to a certain extent a court of construction; for it has to determine what is the meaning of the reference made by the
testatrix in her codicil to her last will and testament, and
whether any, and if any, what instrument found at her death
is thereby referred to.

This question is one of fact, and can only be explained by
parol evidence, which must necessarily be received to prove
whether there is or is not in existence at the testatrix's death
any such instrument as is referred to by the codicil. For
this purpose, it must be shown what papers there were at
the date of the codicil which could answer the description
contained in that document, and the court having by these

(') 16 Simon, 198.

(') Law Rep., 7 H. L. C., 580; 7 Eng.
R., 372.

(') 11 Moo. P. C., 427.

(') 2 Curt., 796.

(') Law Rep., 1 P. & D., 198.

(') 1 Sw. & Tr., 510.

(') 3 Sw. & Tr., 473.

(') Law Rep., 1 P. & D., 19.

(') 6 P. D., 9.

(') 11 Moo. P. C., 426, at p. 441.

means placed itself in the situation of the testatrix, and acquired as far as possible all the knowledge which she possessed, must say, upon a consideration of those extrinsic circumstances whether the paper is identified or not.

In the case of *Stockil and others* v. *Punshon and others* (¹) it was of no importance which way the court decided. I therefore did not consider the question of what extraneous evidence would be sufficient to connect the one document with the other, but I acted on the impression that the bare fact of enumeration was not sufficient to incorporate the second paper. But in this case it is to be taken by admission that there is no other known instrument to which this reference made in the codicil could apply, and it is upon that assumption that I decide that this will so referred to in the codicil must be admitted to probate.

An affidavit of the character mentioned by Mr. Inderwick must, however, be supplied.

Solicitor for executors : *M. Jameson.*

Solicitors for the other persons interested : *Cree & Son;* *M. Jameson.*

(¹) 6 P. D., 9; *ante*, p. 469.

[6 Probate Division, 34.]

March 1, 1881.

34] **In the Goods of* SARAH ANN COOPER, Deceased.

Will of Married Woman—Husband's Assent to Probate.

A will was made by a married woman who appointed her husband one of the executors. He assented to the making of the will, and after her death expressed his intention to take probate, but died before doing so :

Held, that he had assented to the probate.

SARAH ANN COOPER, who died on the 19th of September, 1880, made her will, bearing date the 23d of August of that year. The will was made with her husband's consent, and appointed him and her brother executors. Immediately after the execution of the will the husband signed the following memorandum :

"I, James Cooper, of Hagley, in the county of Worcester, builder, hereby acknowledge that the sums of £400 and £200, now in the possession of Mr. L. D. Broughton, are the separate estate of my wife, Sarah Ann Cooper, to will and dispose of as she may think proper."

The will disposed of these sums. After the death of the testatrix the husband expressed, on several occasions, to his co-executor his wish to prove the will, but was too ill to do so. He never recovered from his illness, and died before the will was proved.

Feb. 22. *Pritchard*, for the surviving executor, moved the court for probate. The husband's consent is to be implied from the circumstances, *Brook* v. *Turner* (');   and consent once given cannot be withdrawn : *Maas* v. *Sheffield* (²). Where the husband has consented to the making of the will slight proof will be sufficient to make out the continuance of the husband's consent after death : Fraser's note to *Forse & Hembling's Case* (³).

Cur. adv. vult.

March 1. THE PRESIDENT: In this case the testatrix, a married woman, died in September, 1880, having made her will on the 23d of August in the same year. The will was made with the consent *of her husband, and he signed [35 a memorandum to that effect. After her death it was intended that the will should be proved by her husband and the other executor appointed by it ; but this could not be done in consequence of the husband's illness, and down to his death he never in any way withdrew his consent. In these circumstances, I think the will is entitled to probate.

Order accordingly.

Solicitors : *Kennedy, Hughes & Kennedy.*

(¹) 2 Mod., 172.   (²) 1 Rob., 364 ; 4 Notes of Cases, 350.
                    (³) 4 Co. Litt., 61 b.

[6 Probate Division, 85.]

Dec. 20, 1880.

[IN THE COURT OF APPEAL.]

HARVEY, Otherwise FARNIE, v. FARNIE.

Marriage in England between domiciled Scotchman and English woman—Divorce in Scotland by reason of Husband's Adultery only—Validity.

The English Divorce Court will recognize as valid the decree of a Scotch court dissolving the marriage of a domiciled Scotchman and an English woman, although the marriage was solemnized in England, and the marriage was dissolved upon a ground for which by English law no divorce could have been granted.

The question of divorce is not an incident of the marriage contract to be governed by the *lex loci contractus*, but is an incident of status to be disposed of by the law of the domicile of the parties—that is, of the husband's.

Lolley's Case (Russ & Ry., 287 ; 2 Cl. & F., 567) distinguished.

M'Carthy v. *De Caix* (2 Russ. & My., 614 ; 2 Cl. & F., 568) examined and explained.

APPEAL from an order of the President of the Probate Division, dismissing a petition for declaration of nullity of marriage (¹).

The respondent Henry Brougham Farnie, a domiciled Scotchman, married on the 13th of August, 1861, in England, an English woman. After the marriage they went to Scotland and resided there until 1863, when the wife obtained a decree from a Scotch court for dissolution of the marriage by reason of her husband's adultery only. On the 31st of May, his former wife being still alive, he married the petitioner at All Souls Church, Marylebone.

The president dismissed the petition.

The petitioner appealed.

36]   *Dec. 14.   *Fooks*, Q.C., *Benjamin*, Q.C. (with them, *Horace Davey*, Q.C., and *W. Fooks*), for the appellant: The points relied on by the appellant are, 1, that a marriage solemnized in England between an English subject of the Queen, domiciled in England, and a Scotch subject domiciled in Scotland is an "English marriage;" 2, that the Scotch courts have no jurisdiction to pronounce a decree of divorce between the parties to such a marriage, even when both are domiciled in Scotland, on grounds which by English law are insufficient to justify such a decree ; 3, that such decree, even if valid within the territorial jurisdiction of the Scotch courts, has no extra-territorial effect, and is invalid in England as contrary to the policy which governs the matrimonial and family relations here ; 4, that as an almost universal rule, status, so far as relates to the marriage contract, is governed, not by the law of the domicile, but of the place where the marriage is contracted.

The marriage here was an "English marriage," that is a "marriage solemnized in England" according to the forms and ceremonies required by the English law to make it a valid and binding marriage. The expressions are convertible terms: see *M'Carthy* v. *De Caix*(²), where Lord Brougham so translates the expression "English marriage" used by the judges in *Lolley's Case*(³), and *Tovey* v. *Lindsay*(⁴). And the fact that the husband was a domiciled Scotchman makes no difference, *Shaw* v. *Gould*(⁵), where Lord Colonsay calls the marriage in *Warrender* v. *Warrender* (⁶), i.e.,

(¹) 5 P. D., 153 ; *ante*, p. 374.

(²) 2 Russ & My., 614. The record in this case was brought into court, and on examination of such record the judges were of opinion that the question of divorce was not really raised. See, too, the observations of Lord St. Leonards in *Geils* v. *Geils*, 1 Macq., 255.

(³) Russ. & Ry., 237; 2 Cl. & F., 567.

(⁴) 1 Dow., 117, 124.

(⁵) Law Rep., 3 H. L., 55, 94.

(⁶) 2 Cl. & F., 488; 9 Bl. (N.S.), 89.

a marriage between a domiciled Scotchman and an English lady, an "English marriage," and see also the observations of Lord Westbury at pp. 86, 87 of the same case.

This, then, being an English marriage, *Lolley's Case* (') supports the second proposition, whether the resolution in that case be taken in its wider or more restricted form, that is, whether it be taken as holding that no foreign court can dissolve an English marriage, or that no foreign court can dissolve an English *marriage except for causes which [37 by the English law would justify such a decree. *Lolley's Case* ('), though often attacked· and disparaged, especially by Lord Brougham, is still law, and has been recognized as binding in *M'Carthy* v. *De Caix* (') ; *Dolphin* v. *Robins* ('); *Tovey* v. *Lindsay* (') ; *Shaw* v. *Attorney-General* (').

M'Carthy v. *De Caix* (') is a direct authority in favor of the appellant. A Dane came over to England and married an English lady here, returned to Denmark, retaining his Danish domicile, and finally obtained a divorce there. Lord Brougham there held, upon the authority of *Lolley's Case* ('), that the divorce, though valid as far as the court of Denmark could make it, had by the English law no effect whatever. It is endeavored to get rid of that case as an authority by some observations of Lord St. Leonards in *Geils* v. *Geils* ('), in which he says that the effect of the divorce was not argued in that case ; but it appears from the judgment of Lord Brougham in that case that there had been an elaborate argument with reference to *Lolley's Case* (') before his predecessor Lord Eldon, all of whose notes were before Lord Brougham. No doubt the point was not argued before Lord Brougham, but that was because he did not require argument, as he was satisfied as to the application of *Lolley's Case* ('). And he says there was a valid decree of divorce, and his judgment in the case must be taken as based upon that assumption, and is an equally authoritative exposition of the law, even though the actual point may not necessarily have arisen for decision. The resolution in *Lolley's Case* ('), as representing the unanimous opinion of the twelve judges who were summoned to advise upon the question, must be treated in the same way as the reports in Lord Coke's time—that is, as laying down the general rule of law upon the subject before them of universal application, not controlled by the particular circumstances of the case.

(¹) Russ. & Ry., 237; 2 Cl. & F., 567.   (⁴) 1 Dow., 117, 124.
(⁷) 2 Russ. & My., 614.   (⁵) Law Rep., 2 P. & D., 156.
(³) 7 H. L. C., 390.   (⁶) 1 Macq., 255.

The result then in support of the third proposition is, that although a court may have jurisdiction to carry out the laws of the country which govern the matrimonial relations, it cannot pronounce a decree according to its own laws dis-38] solving an *English marriage between English subjects, but as it must be admitted that the wife acquires the domicile of her husband, it is subject to this modification, that if the courts of the domicile decree a divorce upon grounds which the English courts would recognize as justifying divorce, then that divorce would be good here.   So if here the wife had obtained a divorce on the grounds of her husband's adultery, coupled with cruelty, both parties being domiciled in Scotland, the Scotch court would, in decreeing a divorce, have been enforcing the law of England, that is the *lex loci contractus*, and the English courts, by a like comity, have held marriages void which, by reason of the law of the domicile of both the parties, were incestuous, although not so here: *Brook* v. *Brook* (¹); *Sottomayor* v. *De Barros* (²).   *Warrender* v. *Warrender* (³) is not against the appellant.   The decision there only went to this, that a dissolution, by a decree of divorce by a Scotch court of a marriage between a domiciled Scotchman and an English lady, was of binding effect in Scotland, that is that the Scotch courts had a territorial jurisdiction, which is not disputed. The Lords, in giving their opinions, seem to have carefully so limited the decision.   They say that they were sitting as a Scotch Court of Appeal upon a Scotch question.   That case was followed by *Geils* v. *Geils* (⁴), which is similar, the court holding that the marriage being a "Scotch marriage," the courts of Scotland had jurisdiction in Scotland for Scotch purposes, but what the effect would be in England was another question left undecided.   The case of *Maghee* v. *M'Allister* (⁵), on which the president relied, will be cited against the appellant.   But it is worth noticing that that case, which was decided in 1853, was not referred to in any of the subsequent cases of *Dolphin* v. *Robins* (⁶), *Pitt* v. *Pitt* (⁷), or *Shaw* v. *Gould* (⁸) in the House of Lords, or in the case of *Shaw* v. *Attorney-General* (⁹).   It depends on *Warrender* v. *Warrender* (³) and *Geils* v. *Geils* (⁴), and proceeds on a mistake, for the Lord Chancellor Blackburne says that he was bound by the observations of Lord Lynd-

(¹) 7 H. L. C., 390.
(²) 3 P. D., 1; *ante*, p. 1.
(³) 2 Cl. & F., 488; 9 Bl. (N.S.), 89.
(⁴) 1 Macq., 255.

(⁵) 3 Ir. Ch., 604.
(⁶) 3 H. L. C., 590.
(⁷) 4 Macq., 657.
(⁸) Law Rep., 3 H. L., 55.

(⁹) Law Rep., 2 P. & D., 156.

hurst and Lord Brougham in those *cases, and by the [39 judgment of Dr. Lushington in *Conway* v. *Beasley* (') and the case of *Munro* v. *Munro* ('), to treat the marriage there, i.e., between a domiciled Scotchman and an Irish woman, as a Scotch marriage. But the cases do not warrant that conclusion. *Munro* v. *Munro* (') only decides that by the law of Scotland the subsequent marriage of parents legitimizes their offspring born before marriage, and that such marriage, although it takes place in England, whose law does not recognize subsequent legitimation, has the effect of legitimizing children for the purpose of inheriting Scotch entailed estates, and Lord Cottenham (') gives his view of *Warrender* v. *Warrender* (') that for civil purposes in Scotland a marriage in England of a domiciled Scotchman was to be considered a Scotch marriage. So in *Birtwhistle* v. *Vardill* (') legitimation in Scotland by a subsequent marriage did not entitle the heir to estates in England.

[COTTON, L.J.: That case turned on the Statute of Merton, under which the heir to land in England must be born in wedlock.]

The question is one of status. The law of England, where the marriage was contracted, established the status of the parties. The law of England establishes the status of an English woman who marries in England, whether a foreigner or not; that is, the status of a wife—a status not dissoluble except for special reasons. That status is fixed by the *lex loci contractus :* the wife here, though she acquired a Scotch domicile after the marriage, had an English one when she contracted the marriage, and must be taken to have contracted the marriage on the faith of its being governed by the law of England. The foreigner who comes to England and marries under its laws an English wife, assents as far as he can to her status being that of an English wife, and while he is here the status of the wife is fixed. That status cannot be changed to the prejudice of the policy of English law, and the husband cannot, by taking her away, choose a domicile for her which would enable him to alter that status : see observations of Lord Redesdale in *Tovey* v. *Lindsay* (') and of James, L.J., in *Niboyet* *v. *Niboyet* (') ; [40 Story on Conflict of Laws, s. 88. So, too, in *Shaw* v. *Gould* (') Lord Cranworth says that English courts are not bound by the comity of nations to hold that the Scotch law changed

(') 3 Hagg. Eccl., 639.

(') 7 Cl. & F., 842.

(') 7 Cl. & F., 842, at p. 875.

(') 2 Cl. & F., 488 ; 9 Bl. (N.S.), 89.

(') 2 Cl. & F., 571 ; 7 Cl. & F., 875.

(') 1 Dow., 117, at p. 139.

(') 4 P. D., 1.

(') Law Rep., 3 H. L., 55, at p. 82.

the status of the English wife, that change being to the prejudice of English policy: and see also the observations of
Lord Westbury on that case (') and Huber (').

[LUSH, L.J., referred to the Naturalization Act, 1870.]
That is an enactment governing the relations between
different governments, and was passed exclusively for political purposes. It was a special act, relating not to the
domicile of a wife but to her nationality, and provides that
an English woman marrying a foreigner or becoming naturalized loses her British nationality, and is no longer bound
to the sovereign of this country. It is to meet the old saying, "Nemo potest exuere patriam." If the woman was to go
to Scotland to be married there, then she would be submitting to the Scotch law, and if the Scotchman comes to England
his marriage is under the English law. See Rodenburg (').
In *Niboyet* v. *Niboyet* (') it was held that domicile was not
to be taken as the test of jurisdiction. It cannot be that the
relations between husband and wife are to be subject to
foreign jurisdiction, and to be at the mercy of the husband.
This, as James, L.J., said in *Niboyet* v. *Niboyet* (') would be
"a violation of every principle to make the dissolubility of
a marriage depend on the mere will and pleasure of the
husband, and domicile is entirely a matter of his will and
pleasure." If the law of the domicile is to regulate the question, it must also apply to the case of a Turk, or the subject
of some country which recognizes polygamy, coming over
here and contracting marriage. For these reasons, domicile
cannot settle the question. Where a foreigner comes here
and contracts a marriage which is indissoluble except for
41]   certain specific causes, *how can the courts of England
recognize a foreign decision dissolving the marriage, if,
assuming the action to have been brought before the English
court, that court would have refused to grant relief? The
second marriage is therefore null and void, and the appellant
is entitled to have it so declared.

Dec. 17.   *Dr. Deane*, Q.C., and *Winch*, for the respondent: The cases which have been cited resolve themselves
into two classes—one extensive, commencing with *Lolley's
Case* ('), the other a small class, commencing with *Warrender*

(') Law Rep., 3 H. L., 55, at p. 81.
(') De Conf. Leg., bk. i, tit. 3, s. 2:
"Rectores imperiorum id comiter agunt,
ut jura cujusque populi intra terminos
ejus exercita teneant ubique suam vim,
quatenus nihil potestati aut juri alterius
imperantis ejusque civium præjudicetur."

(') "De jure quod oritur ex diversitate
statutorum." It is appended to Boullenois de la Personnalité, last section of
book.
(') 4 P. D., 1, at p. 8.
(') Russ. & Ry., 237; 2 Cl. & F., 567.

v. *Warrender* (¹). The former class is one in which parties
really domiciled in England, and married in England, go to
Scotland for the express purpose of evading the law of England, and by means of a temporary and fictitious domicile
in Scotland obtaining a benefit which the law of England
would not give them. The domicile in *Lolley's Case* (²) was
fictitious, as was pointed out by Lord Brougham in *Warrender* v. *Warrender* (³) and by Dr. Lushington in *Conway*
v. *Beasley* (⁴), and so it was in the cases of *Shaw* v. *Attorney-General* (⁵); *Dolphin* v. *Robins* (⁶); and *Pitt* v. *Pitt* (⁷).
This case is really disposed of by the other class of cases,
viz., *Warrender* v. *Warrender* (¹) and *Geils* v. *Geils* (⁸). No
doubt both came on appeal from Scotland, but the decisions
are good on general principles, and if the *lex loci contractus*
is but an incident, and all the rights, duties, and obligations
flowing from the contract are to be governed by the law of
the *bona fide* domicile, then these cases will apply to the
present. The domicile here of the husband was clearly
Scotch, and that being so, the wife's domicile became Scotch,
and the marriage here was, in the words of Lord Brougham
in *Warrender* v. *Warrender* (¹), "a marriage had in England
between a Scotchman and an English woman, the residence
or domicile of the husband being *bona fide* Scotch," and, as
he further remarks, the determination upon the question of
domicile makes the *forum originis* of the wife quite immaterial. This displaces a great part of the arguments as to
the lady being originally an English woman, and the judge
in that case shows *that by the marriage with a *bona*   [42
fide domiciled Scotchman, the woman becomes a Scotch
wife, and therefore subject to Scotch law. The case of
Munro v. *Munro* (⁹) shows too that the question of domicile
is the real point to be considered, and the reference to domicile really frees the question of all difficulty. That is what
distinguishes it from the case of *Rose* v. *Ross* (¹⁰), in the latter case the domicile of the husband was English, and Lord
Lyndhurst stated as the ground of his opinion that, although
the marriage was in Scotland, it was the marriage of persons having an English domicile and coming into Scotland
for the purpose of the marriage only, and that being so, the
Scotch law did not apply, and the reason why Lord Eldon
remitted the case of *Tovey* v. *Lindsay* (¹¹) was that he was of

(¹) 2 Cl. & F., 488; 9 Bl. (N.S.), 89.   (⁶) 7 H. L. C., 390.
(²) 2 Russ. & Ry., 237; 2 Cl. & F., 567.   (⁷) 4 Macq., 657.
(³) 2 Cl. & F., 481, at p. 541; 9 Bl.   (⁸) 1 Macq., 255.
(N.S.), 89.   (⁹) 7 Cl. & F., 842.
(⁴) 3 Hagg. Eccl., 639.   (¹⁰) 4 Wil. & Shaw, 289.
(⁵) Law Rep., 2 P. & D., 156.   (¹¹) 1 Dow, 117.

1880   Harvey v. Farnie.

opinion that the husband's domicile was English. Lord Cottenham in *Munro* v. *Munro* (¹) says that in *Warrender* v. *Warrender* (²), it was correctly assumed that for civil purposes in Scotland a marriage in England of a domiciled Scotchman was to be considered a Scotch marriage. It has been decided that divorce is a civil proceeding.

The domicile of the husband, not necessarily at the time of the marriage, but at the time of the action, is the ground on which the jurisdiction of the Scotch court is based. That domicile attracts the wife's domicile, and brings her constructively within the jurisdiction, per Lord Chelmsford in *Shaw* v. *Gould* (³), and the wife having once acquired a Scotch domicile becomes to all intents and purposes subject to and entitled to the benefit of the laws and institutions of Scotland. It is not the law of the country where the contract is entered into, but of that where it is to be enforced that regulates its enforcement, *Don* v. *Lippman* (⁴), and here the contract was to be enforced in Scotland. Huber, De Confl. Leg., sect. 10 ; *Robinson* v. *Bland* (⁵); *Ilderton* v. *Ilderton* (⁶). But the case of *Maghee* v. *M'Allister* (⁷) is on all fours with the present and is conclusive in the respondent's favor, and the observations of Brett, L. J., in *Niboyet* 43] v. *Niboyet* (⁸) show that the *domicile of the husband at the institution of the suit is the fact which gives jurisdiction to decree the divorce.

[They also referred to *Mettee* v. *Mettee* (⁹) ; *Manning* v. *Manning* (¹⁰); *Shedden* v. *Patrick* (¹¹); *Mordaunt* v. *Moncreiffe* (¹²); *Yelverton* v. *Yelverton* (¹³).]

Fooks, Q.C., in reply, referred to *Sottomayor* v. *De Barros* (¹⁴) and *Simonin* v. *Mallac* (¹⁵) as authorities that marriages contracted in this country between persons *bona fide* domiciled in foreign countries had been held subject to the jurisdiction of the courts of this country, and that the *lex loci contractus* and not *lex domicilii* was the governing law. He referred also to *Colliss* v. *Hector* (¹⁶) and *In re Goodman's Trusts* (¹⁷).

Cur. adv. vult.

(¹) 7 Cl. & F., 842, at p. 875.
(²) 2 Cl. & F., 488; 9 Bl. (N.S.), 89.
(³) Law Rep., 3 H. L., 55, at p. 76.
(⁴) 5 Cl. & F., 1.
(⁵) 1 W. Bl., 258.
(⁶) 2 H. Bl., 145.
(⁷) 3 Ir. Ch., 604.
(⁸) 4 P. D., 1, at pp. 12, 19.
(⁹) 1 Sw. & Tr., 416; 28 L. J. (P. M. & A.), 117.

(¹⁰) Law Rep., 2 P. & D., 223.
(¹¹) 2 Sw. & Tr., 170.
(¹²) Law Rep., 2 H. L., Sc., 374.
(¹³) 1 Sw. & Tr., 574.
(¹⁴) 4 P. D., 1.
(¹⁵) 2 Sw. & Tr., 67; 29 L. J. (P. M. & A.), 97.
(¹⁶) Law Rep., 19 Eq., 334; 11 Eng. R., 866.
(¹⁷) 14 Ch. D., 619, under appeal.

Dec. 20.   JAMES, L.J.: In this case I am myself unable to entertain any doubt whatever as to the correctness of the decision of the learned President of the Probate Division.

The question is whether a decree by a Scotch court between Scotch parties has the effect of dissolving a marriage which has been contracted between these parties.

It is said that the decree has no operation, and ought not to be recognized in England, because the marriage was solemnized in England, and because in *Lolley's Case* (') it was held according to one report that an English marriage could not be dissolved by a Scotch court, or any foreign court, except for reasons for which it would have been capable of being dissolved in England ; and according to another report that the words "English marriage" have been construed by somebody, nobody knows when or how, to be a "marriage solemnized in England." Now we know very little of *Lolley's Case* ('), except the facts which the reporter states in Russell and Ryan, and the decision. Of course every judgment of any court must be construed with reference to the facts that were before the court for determination. At the time when the judgment in *Lolley's Case* (') was given by the learned *judges, who were consulted rather than [44 sitting as a tribunal of appeal—whatever may have been the habit of the judges in the time of Lord Coke of laying down abstract general propositions, going far beyond the necessities of the particular case or cases before them—it certainly was not the habit of judges then, any more than it is their habit at this day, to express general propositions or articles of a code, beyond what was required by the particular circumstances of the case.

The particular circumstances of that case were, a marriage between English persons, that is to say, a marriage in England between persons domiciled in England ; and an appeal to a Scotch court by one of those persons as against the other, during a temporary residence in Scotland, it being beyond all question that they were neither of them domiciled in Scotland at the time. And it was held in that case that the decision of a Scotch court affecting the status of English domiciled persons, domiciled in England at the time when the status was originally constituted, and domiciled in England at the time when the status was sought to be removed, was invalid ; that according to English notions of law, the Scotch court ought not to entertain a suit affecting the status of English people. That clearly was the whole of the decision. That decision has to that extent been ad-

(') Russ. & Ry., 237 ; 2 Cl. & F., 567.

mitted to be good law. I do not think it has ever been questioned, nor do I feel myself disposed to say that that case is now capable of being questioned. But the application of that case to the circumstances of the present has certainly been very much questioned, and questioned by the very highest authorities. It is impossible to read the judgment of Dr. Lushington in the case of *Conway* v. *Beasley* (') without seeing that he did not consider that that case established any such universal rule, that he did not consider it was binding upon him or upon any court in this country beyond the actual facts of that case, that is to say, that it was to be confined to a case where there was a fictitious domicile, as Dr. Deane called it, or a domicile where there was no domicile really attached to it, where there was merely a temporary residence in the country the courts of which were appealed to. But more than that, we have the expressions of many learned lords evidently expressing 45] exactly the same view *of that case, that it was only to be considered as applying to the circumstances of that case. And then we have the express authority of the Lord Chancellor of Ireland, Lord Blackburne, in a case exactly applicable to the facts before the court, the very point being raised, with the sole distinction that you must substitute England for Ireland, and substitute the Irish court for the English court, as the place in which the question came to be decided.

Under those circumstances there is no authority, although at first I was pressed with this, that there was an English authority following *Lolley's Case* ('), viz., the case of *M'Carthy* v. *De Caix* ('). That is the case of Lord Brougham's, and we are driven to consider to what extent we are bound by the decision of the Lord Chancellor sitting in a Court of Equity upon a question of law in the Probate and Divorce Court, whether that would be a binding authority. But upon a careful investigation of the facts of that case, however the point arose in Lord Brougham's mind and found its way into his judgment, that case was really not, and could not have been, any authority upon the question before us, because the point was neither raised in the pleadings, nor was it sustained by evidence capable of being made the subject of available argument for that purpose. He seems to have taken the point himself, and evolved the whole thing from some passages in a letter as to the man being a naturalized Dane. But independently of that, the fact upon which so much reliance was placed, namely, that he applied *Lol*

(') 8 Hagg. Eccl., 639.   (') Russ. & Ry., 237; 2 Cl. & F., 567.
        (') 2 Russ. & My., 614; 2 Cl. & F., 568.

ley's Case (¹) to the case of a marriage by a domiciled Dane
in England, who was also a domiciled Dane at the time
of the proceedings for divorce in Denmark, the facts which
gave rise to that litigation never had appeared in any way
in which the court could take judicial notice of it. The
only question in that case was whether the husband, who
had taken out administration to his wife as surviving husband, who had an apparent interest in a gift as surviving
husband, had, by certain letters which are set out in the
proceedings, under the circumstances of the case conclusively bound himself to the gift of that which was supposed
to be his own, and his right to which as the surviving
*husband was not really in question. There was this   [46
further to be observed, that if the facts were as they seem
to have been assumed in the note to the case furnished by
Lord Brougham, to which I shall afterwards refer, that
there had been a marriage in England by a domiciled Dane
with an English lady, and that there had been a dissolution
of that marriage in Denmark, the plaintiff the husband being still a domiciled Dane, and that that dissolution was not
recognized by the English law as being of any validity, the
result would have been, not that the property would have
been distributed according to the English law, but that it
would have been dealt with according to the Danish law;
and the Danish law of course in the distribution of the assets
of a Danish wife would have recognized its own divorce, and
would not have been bound by any decision of this court in
Lolley's Case (¹).

Therefore, really the point could not have been properly
before the court, or determined by the court, and therefore
fully warranted what was said of it in the case of *Geils* v.
Geils (²) as something which fell from the learned judge *per
incuriam.* The whole thing probably emanated from the application of *Lolley's Case* (¹) to the case before him.

Well, that disposes of the only authority at all that in any
way conflicts with the decision of the learned Lord President. And, upon principle, I cannot bring myself to doubt
that what the Lord President has said is right, that if a
domiciled foreigner comes here for the purpose of taking a
wife from this country, the moment the marriage is contracted, the moment the *vinculum* exists, then the lady becomes to all intents and purposes of the same domicile as
the husband, and all the rights and consequences arising
from the marriage are to be determined by the law of that
which by the actual contract of marriage becomes the domi-

(¹) Russ. & Ry., 237 ; 2 Cl. & F., 567.   (²) 1 Macq., 255.

cile of both parties, exactly to the same extent as if they had both been originally of the foreign country. It seems to me that there is no qualification of that rule. A wife's home is her husband's home; a wife's country is her husband's country; a wife's domicile is her husband's domicile; and any question arising with reference to the status of those persons is, according to my view, to be determined 47] by the law of the domicile of those *persons; assuming always that the domicile is a *bona fide* one, not a domicile either fictitious or resorted to for the sole purpose of altering the status. I am not however prepared to say that an English husband could, by going to a foreign country for the sole purpose of domiciling himself in a place where a marriage could be dissolved at pleasure, be enabled to obtain a valid and binding dissolution of his own marriage. That point it is not necessary for us to decide. But where the domicile is the real *bona fide* domicile of the husband, and consequently of the wife, the court, the forum of the country of that domicile, is the forum which has to determine the status; and has to determine whether the status was originally well created, and whether any circumstances have occurred which justify that forum in deciding that the status has come to an end.

I do not think it necessary myself to go further into the cases which have been cited, but I conceive that the principle which is laid down by the learned President is a sound principle and not capable of being questioned; and, that being so, there being in this case originally a marriage, where the marriage home was intended to be Scotch, the marriage became in that sense a Scotch marriage; that is to say, the union became a Scotch union, from the moment of the marriage: and there being further the fact that the parties in this case were domiciled in Scotland at the time the sentence of dissolution was pronounced, I think that that sentence of dissolution ought to be recognized in this country and by all other countries in the world.

COTTON, L.J.: I am of the same opinion. I think a great deal of the difficulty in this case has arisen from the ambiguous use of the words "English marriage." We have been told the marriage in this case is an English marriage, and that therefore, according to *Lolley's Case* ('), and to what was said by the judges in that case, it is indissoluble.

The fallacy lies in this: the word "marriage" is used in two senses. It may mean the solemnity by which two persons are joined together in wedlock, or it may mean their

(') Russ. & Ry., 237; 2 Cl. & F., 567.

status when they have been so joined. The solemnity by which they are *united in marriage, that is to say, the [48 mode in which the marriage is solemnized, and the forms to be followed, must depend upon the law of the country where that solemnity takes place. When the marriage takes place in a country which is not the country of the domicile, the country of the domicile will hold the persons as duly married if they have followed the forms and ceremonies required by the country in which it was solemnized. Of course I am speaking only of Christian countries, and that gets rid of what was put to us by Mr. Fooks, that we have here to consider what would be the consequences of dealing with the law of the domicile supposing it were Turkish. The rule I apprehend prevails universally that where a marriage has been solemnized according to the form and in the manner required by the place where it is celebrated, it will be recognized in the country of the domicile, and being recognized in the country of the domicile the persons will be recognized as married. That is their status. But there arises the question what are the incidents and liabilities of the status, and I take and adopt entirely what was said by Lord West-bury in the case of *Shaw* v. *Gould* ('). "But this right to reject a foreign sentence of divorce cannot rest on the prin-·ciple stated by the Vice-Chancellor in his judgment, namely, that where by the *lex loci contractus* the marriage is indissoluble, it cannot be dissolved by the sentence of any tribunal. Such a principle is at variance with the best established rules of universal jurisprudence, that is to say, with those rules which for the sake of general convenience and by tacit consent are received by Christian nations and observed in their tribunals. One of these rules certainly is, that questions of personal status depend on the law of the actual domicile."

What was the actual domicile here? The husband was, at the time of the solemnization of the marriage in England, Scotch, and always so remained down to the time of the divorce; so that the domicile of the wife after she had been united in marriage to her husband, became Scotch, and throughout the case of *Warrender* v. *Warrender* (') not a doubt was expressed as to the law which decided that case, that when a woman domiciled in one country marries in that country a man domiciled in another country, her domicile at once becomes that of her husband. That, *I think, [49 cannot be disputed or doubted. I know of no case which throws a doubt upon it. Of course that is entirely different

(') Law Rep., 3 H. L., 55, 94.   (') 2 Cl. & F., 488; 9 Bl. (N.S.), 89.

from the question whether a husband and wife can be held
to be domiciled in a country in which greater facilities are
granted for divorce to which the husband has taken his wife
in order to make her subject to the tribunals of that country,
and to the consequences of her being brought within that
jurisdiction. That is an entirely different question. But
here, when the lady married a Scotchman, she consented and
agreed that her domicile from that time forth should be that
of her husband.

Then, we have to consider this question : Is this divorce
an incident of the contract, and in any way to be governed
by the law of the country where the solemnity took place,
or is it a question of status? In my opinion, it is not a
question in any way depending upon the rule that the *lex
loci contractus* governs. That applies, as I have already
stated, to the forms and solemnities by which the marriage
is celebrated. When parties unite themselves in marriage,
it is not part of their contract that according to the laws of
the country where that marriage takes place they shall have
the power or not to dissolve the marriage.

Any act done in violation of the duties incident to the
status is a matter which concerns the country of the domicile,
and, in my opinion, the question of divorce is not in any
way an incident of the contract so as to be governed by the
law of the country where that takes place ; but an incident
of the status to be disposed of by the law of the domicile of
the parties if they are subject to the tribunals of that country. Here we have a real domicile throughout in Scotland,
and in my opinion, the courts of that country, not only for
the purpose of status in that country, but for the purpose
of status everywhere, have the power to entertain this question, and if they think fit to decree a divorce.

Is there any authority contrary to that? It is said that
Lolley's Case (¹) is against it. We have not any report
which purports to give the exact words of the opinion given
by the judges, but no doubt we have an "English marriage"
spoken of, and that is translated in one report as a "marriage in England." But we must remember, that, in that
50] case (and we must regard what *was said by the judges
in reference to the case before them), the marriage was in
both senses an English one, because it was solemnized in
England and the parties to the marriage were English people ; their status was English and the marriage was solemnized in England ; and we must, in my opinion, notwithstanding the expressions which were used and the ambiguity

(¹) Russ. & Ry., 237; 2 Cl. & F., 567.

of the expression "English marriage," look at the facts of
the case for the purpose of seeing what was intended to be
there decided by the judges. In my opinion, that decision
does not at all stand in our way in deciding this case, nor
ought we to be deterred from giving a judgment in accordance
with our opinions by anything that was said in *Lolley's
Case* ('). Now as to the case of *M'Carthy* v. *De Caix* ('), I
will add nothing to what was said by James, L.J. I quite
agree with what he has said, and it is remarkable that in the
case of *Shaw* v. *Gould* Lord Westbury (') says: "The position that the tribunal of a foreign country, having jurisdiction to dissolve the marriages of its own subjects, is competent
to pronounce a similar decree between English subjects who
were married in England, but who before and at the time of
the suit are permanently domiciled within the jurisdiction
of such foreign tribunal, such decree being made in a *bona
fide* suit without collusion or concert, is a position consistent
with all the English decisions, although it may not be consistent with the resolution commonly cited as the resolution of
the judges in *Lolley's Case*"('). He mentions *M'Carthy* v. *De
Caix* ('), but he does not consider that that was a decision
which prevented him from laying down that as a principle
independently of *Lolley's Case* ('). Therefore, I think that
that strengthens what has already been said by the Lord
Justice James as to that case in reference to the present case.

Now we ought to notice what has been said as to *Niboyet* v. *Niboyet* ('). It may be said that our decision there
was in some way at variance with what we are laying down
in this case. What was said by Brett, L.J., was in favor
of the respondent to this appeal, and he was in a minority, but the decision of the other *members of the [51
court turned entirely upon the construction of an English
act of Parliament, and they said, whatever might have been
the consequences independently of those words, this act of
Parliament gives to us, an English court; jurisdiction in the
matter, and says what is to be the consequence if certain
facts are proved in a suit and brought before us under the
act. That was the *ratio decidendi* in that case. As to *Warrender* v. *Warrender* ('), I may say I cannot look upon it
as decisive of the present question, because, although there
are principles laid down consistent with and leading to our
decision, yet, in my opinion, the House of Lords carefully
guarded themselves by saying that they were deciding the

(¹) Russ. & Ry., 237; 2 Cl. & F., 567.   (³) Law Rep., 3 H. L., 55, at p. 85.
(²) 2 Russ. & My., 614; 2 Cl. & F., 568.   (⁴) 4 P. D., 1.
            (⁵) 2 Cl. & F., 488; 9 Bl. (N.S.), 89.

matter as a Scotch Court of Appeal, and not dealing with it as an English court, or saying what the effect might have been in England. If we could have relied on that case as decisive, of course there would have been an end of the matter, but I cannot look upon *Warrender* v. *Warrender* (¹) as decisive of the case before us.

Lush, L.J.: I am of the same opinion. It is obvious to me that the whole difficulty in this case arises from a mistaken use of a phrase in *Lolley's Case* (²), in which the marriage there in question is called an "English marriage." Now the phrase "an English marriage," may refer to the place where the marriage was solemnized, or it may refer to the nationality and domicile of the parties between whom it was solemnized, the place where the union so created was to have been enjoyed.

Now in *Lolley's Case* (²) the phrase embraced both meanings. The parties there were English subjects domiciled in England, married in England, and they went to Scotland for a temporary purpose ; and while there the one party sued the other for a divorce and obtained it. In the present case the words must be taken in reference only to one of those meanings, namely, the place where the marriage was solemnized, because this was a marriage solemnized in England, between a Scotchman domiciled in Scotland and an English lady whose domicile immediately the marriage was solemnized became his domicile. That being so, it strikes me I own that the conclusion at which we have arrived is a
52] logical *sequence from the decision in the House of Lords in *Warrender* v. *Warrender* (¹) ;—not the actual point decided there, because it was not before the court,—but it seems to me, having regard to general convenience and propriety, that it follows naturally from the decision of *Warrender* v. *Warrender* (¹), because what the court decided there was, that in a case like this, where a domiciled Scotchman was married in England to an English lady, but whose domicile remained in Scotland, and the domicile of whose wife was therefore Scotch, he might sue for a divorce in the Court of Sessions of Scotland lawfully. They held therefore that a Scotch court could dissolve in Scotland a marriage which had been created in England. Now to hold that the consequence of that is confined to Scotland, and to hold that a Scotchman, who was released by the law of his own country from the marriage tie in the country where his home was, should, as soon as ever he came over the border into England, be liable to be indicted for bigamy, is something

(¹) 2 Cl. & F., 488; 9 Bl. (N.S.), 89.   (²) Russ. & Ry., 237; 2 Cl. & F., 567.

that shocks all one's notions of morality and public convenience. No doubt, that consequence follows in a case exactly like *Lolley's Case* (') so long as that decision stands; but we are asked to extend it very considerably, and whatever we may think of *Lolley's Case* ('), I think we shall be agreed in this, that it is not one that ought to be extended. There are anomalies enough already arising out of the marriage laws, and we ought to be very careful not to create another, and in this case we should be creating another of a very serious kind, if we were to hold that a man may be free in Scotland by the law of his own country, of his own home, to marry a woman there, and yet to be liable to be indicted for that very act as a bigamous act if he came over the border into this country. That is what we are asked to do. I confess there is something about that which shocks all one's notions of what is right and just and convenient; and if there were no other authority, I should have no hesitation myself in saying that *Warrender* v. *Warrender* (') virtually decides it, because I hold it to be a logical and natural inference from the decision in that case that the union though it was created in England could be dissolved by the Scotch court; and being dissolved, can no longer *exist anywhere; and wherever the parties may hap- [53 pen to be the status is permanently altered.

Now as Mr. Fooks has referred to what is called "marriage" in a country where polygamy is the law, I must take the opportunity also of saying, in accordance with what has fallen from Lord Justice Cotton, that there is no analogy whatever between the union of a man and a woman in a country where polygamy is allowed, and the union of a man and a woman in a Christian country. Marriage in the contemplation of every Christian community is the union of one man and one woman to the exclusion of all others. No such provision is made, no such relation is created, in a country where polygamy is allowed, and if one of the numerous wives of a Mohammedan was to come to this country, and marry in this country, she could not be indicted for bigamy, because our laws do not recognize a marriage solemnized in that country, a union falsely called marriage, as a marriage to be recognized in our Christian country.

As I said before, if there were no decision on the point, and no authority on the subject, speaking for myself, I should conclude, from *Warrender* v. *Warrender* ('), that our decision should be in favor of the validity of the divorce. But then we have authority. We have two, but unfortu-

(') Russ. & Ry., 237; 2 Cl. & F., 567.   (') 2 Cl. & F., 488; 9 Bl. (N.S.),89.

nately we have one on each side, because Lord Brougham's decision in *M'Carthy* v. *De Caix* (¹) decides that in such a case as this the effect of it is confined to the country. Now observations have been already made upon that case, and I need not repeat them to show that it is not really an authority at all. The point which the learned lord undertook to decide did not arise in the case. What he said upon it was only an *obiter dictum*, and contrary, I think, to all principle. We have another case decided some years afterwards by the Lord Chancellor of Ireland, Lord Blackburne, in which the facts were exactly similar, and, notwithstanding the case before Lord Brougham, that learned judge took an entirely different view, and that is an authority which commends itself to my judgment and one which I am very glad to be able to follow.

Therefore, viewing it on every side, however it may be, 54] whether *upon principle or whether upon reliable authority, I come without hesitation to the conclusion that the judgment of the learned President was entirely right, and that this appeal ought to be dismissed.

Appeal dismissed.

Solicitor for appellant : *S. A. Tucker.*
Solicitor for respondent : *T. S. Ward.*

(¹) 2 Russ. & My., 614 ; 2 Cl. & F., 568.

[6 Probate Division, 60.]
Feb. 17, 1881.

60]   *THE LONGFORD (1880, T. 592 ; 1880, O. 593 ; 1880, O. 842).

Salvage—Bullion liable to contribute in the same proportion as other Property.

Where steamtugs rendered salvage service by towing a sinking vessel with passengers, cargo, and bullion on board into safety, it was held, that the bullion was liable to contribute to the salvage reward in proportion to its value ratably with the other property salved.

THERE were three consolidated actions of salvage instituted on behalf of the owners, masters, and crews of four steamtugs, the Rover, the Mersey King, the Knight of Malta, and the Royal Alfred, against the steamship Longford, her cargo and freight.

The Longford, on the 17th of August, 1880, was proceeding up the Mersey from sea with passengers, cattle, and other cargo, and a sum of £50,000 in specie on board, when she came into collision with a steamship anchored in mid-river and received serious damage. The services rendered by the plaintiffs mainly consisted in attending the Longford and taking off a number of the passengers on board her whilst she was crossing to the Liverpool landing stage after the collision, and in towing her from the landing stage into shallow water alongside the wall of the Prince's Dock. The Longford, and the cargo on board her, except the specie, having been arrested in the consolidated actions, her owners and the owners of all the property arrested appeared as defendants, and undertook to put in bail.

On the 24th of November the district registrar at Liverpool ordered that the solicitors for the owners, masters, and crews of the Mersey King and the Knight of Malta, the plaintiffs in action 593, should have the general conduct of the consolidated actions, but that the owners, masters, and crew of the Rover, the plaintiffs in action 592, and the owners, master, and crew of the Royal Alfred, the plaintiffs in action 842, respectively, should be at liberty, if so advised, to deliver separate statements of claim, and to appear at the hearing by one counsel. A statement of claim was then delivered on behalf of the owners, masters, and crews of the Mersey King and the Knight of Malta, another on behalf of the owners, master, and crew of the Rover, and a third on behalf of the owners, master, and crew of the Royal Alfred; and on the *5th of January the solicitors for the own-　[61 ers of the Longford, and the owners of her cargo, other than the specie, delivered a statement of defence, containing, *inter alia*, the following allegations :

1. The Longford is a paddle steamer of 476 tons register, with engines of 300 horse-power nominal, and at the time of the occurrences hereinafter mentioned she was bound on a voyage from Dublin to Liverpool, laden with a cargo of general goods and live stock, and manned by a crew of twenty-six hands. She had 136 passengers on board.

2. About 7.35 A.M. on the 17th of August, 1880, the tide being flood, the weather clear and fine, and the wind light from the S.E., the Longford was in the river Mersey making for her berth at the north end of the Liverpool landing stage, when she struck the stem of the steamship Baltic, which was lying at anchor, with the after end of her starboard sponson, and continued grazing her starboard side till she got clear of the Baltic, when she continued her course towards the stage.

3. Whilst so proceeding the tugs Mersey King, Knight of Malta, Rover, and Royal Alfred, put off from the Prince's landing stage and approached the Longford, hampered her movements, and finally one of them, the Mersey King, im-

They also say that it never was in any danger of damage.

They deny the rendering of any services of any kind to or the acceptance hereof by them or to or by any person or persons on their behalf.

63] *Alternatively, these defendants say that if any services were rendered by the said tugs to the Longford, her cargo and freight (which as aforesaid they deny) such were not nor were any of them salvage services in fact, and also that they were not nor were any of them efficacious as such, because these defendants say that if the alleged services had not been rendered no other or further or more serious consequences or damage could or would have ensued than did in fact ensue after and notwithstanding the rendering (if any, which is denied) of the alleged services.

Feb. 16, 17. The action was heard before the judge, assisted by two Elder Brethren of the Trinity House. Witnesses on behalf of the respective plaintiffs were examined orally in court. No witnesses were called for the defendants. The result of the evidence appears from the judgment. It was admitted that the value of the property, proceeded against other than the specie, amounted to £3,200. It was also admitted that the specie was not taken on board any of the steamtugs, and that the clerk in charge of it had landed from off the Longford, and removed the specie without any assistance from the salvors.

Butt, Q.C., and *W. R. Kennedy*, for the owners, masters, and crews of the Rover, the Knight of Malta, and the Mersey King. It was owing to the exertions of the plaintiffs that the Longford did not sink in deep water. The time occupied in rendering the services was very short, but that circumstance by no means renders the services less meritorious.

E. C. Clarkson, for the owners, master, and crew of the Royal Alfred.

The Admiralty Advocate (*Dr. Deane*, Q.C.), and *G. Bruce*, for the owners of the Longford, and the rest of the property proceeded against, other than the specie.

Cohen, Q.C., and *Pollard*, for the owners and underwriters of the specie, admitted that the specie was liable in respect of life salvage if the court should find that the services rendered entitled the plaintiffs to claim in respect of life salvage: *The Cargo ex Schiller* (') ; *The Cargo ex Sarpedon* (').
The material services in this case consisted in towing the Longford into shallow water. The specie derived little or

(') 2 P. D., 145.   (') 3 P. D., 28; *ante*, p. 25.

no benefit from the assistance of the salvors. The court in awarding salvage *remuneration in cases where a per- [64 ishable cargo is salved has always treated the services rendered as more meritorious, and to be more highly rewarded than where services are rendered to specie or bullion, which, on account of its small bulk, can easily be removed to a position of safety, and in most cases, at the worst, is merely exposed to the danger of sinking, together with the ship on which it is carried, when, as would have been the case here, it can easily be recovered by divers. If then the specie here had been salved at a different time from the other property in this case, the owners of the specie, according to this principle, would have had to pay in proportion a much less salvage reward than the remaining defendants would have had to pay for the salvage services rendered to their property. The same consequences ought to follow where, as in the present case, the specie and the other property proceeded against have been salved on one and the same occasion. The policy of the general rule that all property salved should contribute ratably to salvage reward is undoubted; but it has been recognized that this general rule does not apply to silver or bullion, *The Emma* ('), and consequently in the present case the owners of the specie ought only to contribute in proportion to the benefits they have received.

Butt, Q.C., in reply : No distinction is made in practice, or ought to be made, between the contribution to salvage awards by silver or bullion, and other salved goods. One general rule is applicable in all cases. Indeed, in the case of *The Jonge Bastiaan* ('), where, as in this case, a quantity of specie was taken from a salved vessel before the salvage service terminated, Lord Stowell expressly refused to uphold a similar contention to that now raised by the owners of the specie : *The Vesta* (').

SIR ROBERT PHILLIMORE : This is a case of salvage service rendered in August last, in the river Mersey, to the steamship Longford, of 1,000 tons gross, and 476 net register tonnage. The Longford was on a voyage from Dublin to Liverpool laden with a general cargo, passengers, and live stock. It appears that at the time at which the salvage service in the case was rendered, *the Longford had, by [65 careless and bad navigation, impaled herself on the stem of the screw steamship Baltic. In consequence of so doing the Longford received a wound of a very serious character in her side, and was most seriously injured. Perhaps the best course for the court to adopt in this part of its judgment

(') 2 W. Rob., 315; 3 N. of C., 114. (') 5 Rob., 324. (') 2 Hagg., 189.

will be to refer to the log of the Longford, which contains this entry :

"On the 16th of August sailed with passengers, cargo, and cattle, wind east, fresh breeze ; passed the Collingwood Dock at 7.20 A.M. On the 17th proceeded to landing stage, weather hazy, and while swinging to the tide, passing between two large steamers, our ship did not come round as quickly as I expected, when we fouled the White Star steamer Baltic, at anchor in mid-river, her stem damaging our plates on the starboard side ; ship commenced to fill with water ; kept the engines at full speed to reach the dock wall. The tug Mersey King took our rope and towed us to the wall of the Princess Dock, steamer Rover taking passengers and luggage : Mersey King, Rover, and Royal Alfred taking cattle. About this time passengers commenced to jump on board the tugs."

There is no doubt, therefore, that this vessel, the Longford, was in the most imminent danger of sinking. She steamed across the river to the Prince's landing stage, and she was attended by four tugs, all of about the same size—the Rover, the Mersey King, the Knight of Malta, and the Royal Alfred. When the Longford got over to the other side of the river at the north end of the landing stage, she was taken in tow by the Mersey King, which had stationed herself ahead, and was towed to the dock wall, where she was beached and sank.

Now the merit of the service thus rendered consisted in its promptitude, and not in the length of its duration. It is said that more steamtugs were employed than were needed ; but it must be remembered that in these cases it may be more easy to say this after the danger is over than at the time of its occurrence, when any such calculation as to the degree of danger cannot be made with nicety. It appears to us that these steamtugs are entitled to take equal shares in whatever award the court may make. There were 162 persons on board the salved vessel, 182 cattle, and specie to the amount of £50,000, and the value of the whole property proceeded against amounts to £72,000. There was undoubtedly in this case a salvage service rendered both to life and to property. The defences set up on behalf of the defendants originally were, firstly, that the tugs, instead of assisting, hampered the Longford ; and the second, that the 66] Mersey King improperly threw herself *across the bows of the Longford. Neither of these charges are proved. The court, therefore, has to consider what is the proper

amount of salvage remuneration to be awarded. Much discussion has taken place upon the question as to the extent
to which certain bullion which was on board the Longford
ought to contribute to the payment of salvage of property
in this case. It appears that the specie being in bags and
otherwise protected from loss, was not exposed to the same
peril of being entirely lost as it would have been if the circumstances had been different. Among the authorities
cited as to the proportion in which bullion ought to contribute to the award was a dictum of Dr. Lushington in the
case of *The Emma* (¹). In that case, salvage services had
been rendered to a ship and her cargo; but as regards the
ship, the salvage had been settled out of court, and the only
property proceeded against was the cargo, and in the judgment of Dr. Lushington, as reported in the second volume of
William Robinson's Reports, there is the following passage:

Now in this class of cases the ordinary usage of the court, which is well
known to every person who has practised in it, is to take the whole value of the
ship and cargo and assess the amount of remuneration upon the whole, each
paying his due proportion. I am not aware, excepting in the instance of silver
or bullion, that any distinction has ever been taken, or that parties have been
admitted to aver that the services were of greater importance to the ship than
they were to the cargo, and therefore that the ship should bear the lesser burden, or *vice versa*. Such a distinction, if acknowledged, would in many cases
lead to intricate litigation and questions of great nicety, which it would be exceedingly difficult for the court to adjust. With respect to silver and bullion,
it is true that a distinction is wisely and properly admitted, and this upon the
consideration that it is more easily rescued and preserved than more bulky articles of merchandise.

The case of *The Emma* (¹) is not, however, the only authority on the question, for during the argument the attention of the court has been drawn to other cases material to
the point, and especially to the case of *The Jonge Bastiaan* (²), decided by Lord Stowell in 1804, where salvage services had been rendered to a derelict vessel, a portion of the
cargo of which had been composed of bullion, and the very
same contention as in the present case was raised, but was
not sustained by the court. And from a consideration of
these cases it is clear to me that if in the case of *silver [67
or bullion any such exception as that referred to in the case
of *The Emma* (¹) existed in practice, some mention would
have been made in the report of the case of *The Jonge Bastiaan* (²), either of such exception or of some authorities
tending to support it, but the case as reported contains
nothing to lead to the conclusion that specie salved is not in
the same position as any other salved cargo. It appears to
me that the court would be involved in great difficulty if it
admitted any other principle in salvage cases than that every

(¹) 2 W. Rob., 315; 3 N. of C., 114.   (²) 5 Rob., 124.

description of property salved must, whatever be its nature, contribute equally in proportion to its value towards payment of the amount of salvage remuneration awarded. It must be understood that I found my judgment in this case on that principle, and the defendants must contribute to the award I am about to make in proportion to the value of the salved property belonging to them respectively. I shall award £1,200 as the entire amount of salvage remuneration, to be equally divided among the four steamtugs. In other words, the owners, master, and crew of each steamtug will be entitled to £300.

The plaintiffs, other than the owners, master, and crew of the Royal Alfred will have their costs. With regard to the costs incurred by the owners, master, and crew of the Royal Alfred, I think the justice of the case will be met by their being allowed such costs as they would have been allowed if they had not appeared separately by counsel and had been held entitled to costs. My attention has been drawn to the fact that the district registrar at Liverpool gave leave to the owners, master, and crew of the Royal Alfred to appear at the hearing by one counsel. I wish it to be understood that in all cases where any order is made for a party to be at liberty to appear separately by counsel, it must be considered to be one of the terms of such order that it is granted subject to the disallowance of costs at the hearing.

Solicitors for owners, master, and crew of the Rover, the Mersey King, and the Knight of Malta: *Bateson & Co.*

Solicitors for owners, master, and crew of the Royal Alfred: *Hill & Dickinson.*

Solicitors for defendants: *Simpson & North.*

[6 Probate Division, 68.]

March 22, 1881.

[IN THE COURT OF APPEAL.]

68]   *THE ALHAMBRA (1880, E. 45).

Charterparty—Meaning of words " Safe Port, or as near thereunto as she can safely get, and always lay and discharge afloat "—Rights of Parties when Ship is unable to lie afloat in Port of discharge without being lightened—Evidence of custom of Port.

Where a vessel is chartered to proceed with cargo to a "safe port .... as ordered, or as near thereunto as she can safely get, and always lay and discharge afloat," the master is not bound to discharge at a port where she cannot, by reason of her draught of water, "always lie and discharge afloat" without being lightened, even if she can be lightened with reasonable despatch and safety in the immediate vicinity of the port or in the port itself.

A vessel was chartered to proceed with a cargo of grain from Baltimore to Falmouth for orders, "thence to a safe port in the United Kingdom as ordered, or as near thereunto as she could safely get, and always lay and discharge afloat." The vessel was ordered to Lowestoft. Her draught of water when loaded was such that she could not lie afloat in Lowestoft Harbor without discharging a portion of her cargo, but the discharge of cargo might have been carried on with reasonable safety in Lowestoft Roads. The consignee offered at his own expense to lighten the vessel in the roads, but the master refused to proceed to Lowestoft to discharge, and went to Harwich as the nearest safe port, and there discharged the cargo:

Held, reversing the decision of Sir R. Phillimore, that the consignee could not recover damages against the shipowner for the refusal of the master to discharge a Lowestoft.

Held, also, that evidence that it was the custom of the port of Lowestoft for vessels to be lightened in the roads before proceeding into the harbor was not admissible.

THIS was an appeal from the decision of Sir R. Phillimore (').

On the 8th of November, 1879, the Alhambra was chartered "for a voyage from Baltimore to Queenstown or Falmouth (master's option) for orders, thence to safe port in the United Kingdom, . . . or as near thereunto as she could safely get, and always lay and discharge afloat . . . lighterage (if any) always at the risk and expense of the cargo."

On the 5th of January, 1880, the ship having arrived at Falmouth, the master received orders from Everett & Co., who had become the purchasers of the cargo, to proceed to Lowestoft and there discharge the cargo.

*The Alhambra's draught of water when loaded was [69 16 ft. 6 in. The average high water in Lowestoft Harbor was about sixteen feet, and the average low water about eleven feet.

The master objecting to discharge in Lowestoft, Everett & Co. gave him notice that they were prepared, at their own expense, to lighten the vessel in Lowestoft Roads sufficiently to enable her to lie always afloat in Lowestoft Harbor, if necessary, should her draught of water so require. The master nevertheless went on to Harwich, as the nearest safe port, and there discharged the cargo which Everett & Co. received under protest, and then brought the action against the owners of the ship, claiming damages for breach of the contract.

In the court below evidence was adduced that it was the custom for vessels, which were too deep to enter the port of Lowestoft, to discharge a portion of their cargo in the roads outside, and that it could be done with reasonable safety.

Sir R. Phillimore held that the plaintiffs were entitled to damages for breach of contract.

The defendants appealed.

(') 5 P. D., 256,

Butt, Q.C., and *Clarkson*, Q.C., for the defendants: The master was not bound by the charterparty to go to Lowestoft but to a "safe port."

[BRETT, L.J., referred to *Shield* v. *Wilkins* (') as to what is the meaning of the words "safe port."]

A "safe port" within the meaning of this charterparty means a port safe for a vessel of the class of the Alhambra to go into, loaded to her draught of water, and where she could always lie and discharge afloat. The Alhambra's draught of water when loaded was 16 ft. 6 in., and it is proved in evidence that the low water in Lowestoft Harbor never exceeded 13 feet, and averaged 11 ft. 6 in. Lowestoft, therefore, was not a safe port for the Alhambra, and he was not bound to go there; nor was he bound to lighten her in Lowestoft Roads even if it could have been done with reasonable safety. In the court below objection was taken to the reception of the evidence as to the custom of lightening ships in Lowestoft Roads, and it is not admissible.

70] *In all the cases cited in the judgment below, either the port was named in the charterparty or the master had accepted orders as if the port was named in the charterparty, and in such cases the charterparty is always read as if the name of the port had been inserted in it. Here the port was not named, nor had the master accepted orders for a named port. Even if the principle of *Hillstrom* v. *Gibson* (') governs this case the defendants are not within it, because the amount of lightening the Alhambra would have required would have been unreasonable and excessive. In *Capper* v. *Wallace* (') it was held that one-third was a reasonable amount of lightening. Here the evidence shows that at least two-thirds of the cargo must have been taken out before she could have entered Lowestoft Harbor, and always laid and discharged afloat.

Milward, Q.C., and *Aspinall*, for the plaintiffs: The real question is, what is the custom of the particular port to which the ship was ordered.

[JAMES, L.J.: How can evidence of that be admissible to construe a charterparty? Here it is really a question of the construction of the charterparty.]

When a ship is ordered to a named port, the master, when he gets there, should conform to the custom of that port as to the manner in which cargo is discharged. For this purpose, the evidence is admissible: *Postlethwaite* v. *Freeland* (').

(¹) 5 Ex., 304.   (³) 5 Q. B. D., 163; 29 Eng. R., 246
(²) 8 Sess. Cas., 3d Ser., 463; 8 Mar. L. C., 362.   (⁴) 4 Mar. L. C., 303.

The evidence shows that Lowestoft Roads are large—sufficient for 200 sail—and that the custom is to lighten ships of the tonnage of the Alhambra before they go into the harbor. She could have been lightened in Lowestoft Roads whenever she pleased and with reasonable safety. Lightening a ship anticipatory to her entering harbor or port of discharge is not unreasonable : *Hillstrom* v. *Gibson* (¹). Lowestoft, therefore, according to the custom, was a safe port within the terms of the charterparty for the Alhambra. The order to go to Lowestoft meant "go to Lowestoft Roads and do what is usual there to lighten the ship sufficiently to enable her to proceed into Lowestoft Harbor." Lowestoft Roads are a part of the port of Lowestoft in ordinary and seafaring language.

*JAMES, L.J.: I am of opinion that the question in [71] this case depends really upon the construction of the words used in the charterparty. The owner of the freight, that is the person chartering the ship, had a right to order the ship to proceed to any safe port to deliver there, or to go as near thereto as the ship could safely get, and there to "always lay and discharge afloat."

Upon the construction of the charterparty, independent of the evidence that the experts gave as to what is meant by a safe port, I am of opinion that the plain meaning of the expression a safe port is a port in which the condition of safety was to be got which is referred to afterwards, that is to say, a port into which she could "safely get and always lay and discharge afloat."

That is the place to which she has contracted to go. She has not contracted to go somewhere something like it, or with a little variation from it, or a little change from it which the party ordering her to go may require. The master says "No, you must name me a port and I will go to that port if I can get there, and if from any accident afterwards, or from any cause not my own fault I cannot get there, I will get as near thereto as I can safely get still complying with the conditions given me at first, that is to say, to go to a port where I can get and safely lay and discharge afloat."

Then the question is whether Lowestoft is a port of that kind.

Now it is conceded that Lowestoft is not a port in which a ship of the size and burden of this ship could safely lay,—there is no peculiarity in the ship, she did not differ from any ordinary ship, she was as far as we can see an ordinary ship

(¹) 8 Sess. Cas., 3d Series, 463; 3 Mar. L. C., 362.

of ordinary build and ordinary construction,—nor a port in which there is a sufficient draft of water for a ship drawing sixteen feet when she is loaded.

It is also admitted that at low water there is ordinarily not more than eleven feet of water in the harbor. In my opinion, therefore, that was not a safe port. It appears to me that it is not made a safe port—it is not made a port in which the ship can lay with safety and discharge afloat—by reason of this, that there is something outside, some little distance 72] from the port, a place in *which the ship can lay afloat, and within which place she can discharge part of her cargo, and then when she has discharged a sufficient part of her cargo she can get into the port which is named. That may be all very well, it may be an unreasonable thing or a reasonable thing, but that is not the bargain the parties have entered into. They never entered into a contract to go somewhere not a safe port, to go to a port which would be safe if they stopped at some other place near it and with a little manipulation of the cargo made the ship fit to go into that port. That was not the bargain. The bargain was a plain bargain in plain English, that she should go to a port, provided the other party named a port, which in itself and by itself was a port safe for a ship of such a burden, and complied generally with the other requisites mentioned in the charterparty.

I am of opinion under the circumstances that Lowestoft was not such a port, and that therefore the defendants are entitled to the judgment of the court.

BRETT, L.J.: The question here is what was the sort of port to which, when the ship arrived at Falmouth or Queenstown for orders, the charterers or the person representing the charterer had a right to order the ship to go.

It seems to me that the first necessity was that they should order her to go to a port, to something which is known in seafaring language as a port. Secondly, it should be a port in which she might always lay and discharge afloat, and, according to my view, the meaning of that is that it should be a port in which from the moment she went into it, in the condition in which she was entitled to go into it, she should be able to lay afloat, and that she should be able to lay afloat until the time when she was fairly discharged.

The condition in which she was entitled to go into this port was as fully loaded, and she was not bound to unload before she got into that port. Therefore the meaning of it is that she was entitled to be ordered to a port in which when she was fully loaded she would be able to lay afloat, and a port which would remain in such a condition that she would be able to lay afloat from that moment until she was discharged in a reasonable way.

*But there is something more than that. It must [73 not only be that, but it must be safe. Therefore, if she was ordered to a port in which she could lay afloat from the beginning to the end, but in which she would not be safe laying afloat (there may be such ports), she was not bound to go to that port.

The question is whether Lowestoft was a port into which, taking that construction, these consignees of the cargo were entitled to order her to go. They ordered her to go to Lowestoft.

The meaning of that to my mind, considering what Lowestoft is shown to be, is not to go to Lowestoft Roads but to go to Lowestoft Harbor. Therefore the question must be whether Lowestoft Harbor was a place into which she could go fully loaded, and lay afloat from the moment she went into it, so fully loaded, until she was discharged. In my opinion it was not.

But then it is said she could have done that if she partially unloaded in Lowestoft Roads, and the custom is vouched. It seems to me that that custom is inadmissible, because it is a custom to apply to a contract where she is only bound to go into Lowestoft, something to be done before she gets to Lowestoft. The evidence to my mind was inadmissible. Therefore, it seems clear to me that Lowestoft was a port to which they were not authorized to order her.

The case of *Shield* v. *Wilkins* (¹) seems to me to be authority precisely in point as to the principles of this decision. I will say nothing about *Hillstrom* v. *Gibson* (²). I will reserve my view of how far one is bound to follow that case, until the point which was decided in it arises. It does not seem to be applicable to the present case.

COTTON, L. J.: I am of the same opinion. What we have to consider is this, whether the charterer had a right to order the captain of the vessel to proceed to Lowestoft.

That depends upon the construction of the charterparty. The place to be named is to be a safe port within certain limits; and there is this also in the charterparty—although not immediately following—"where she can always lay and discharge afloat."

In my opinion, simply taking the construction of this charter *(for I think the evidence as to what is meant [74 by a "safe port" could not be safely admitted. A safe port

(¹) 5 Ex., 304.   (²) 5 P. D., 256.

here means a port safe for this vessel loaded, that is to say,
one into which such a vessel loaded can safely get. And in
that construction I am supported very much by what was
said by Lord Cranworth in his judgment in the case of
Shield v. *Wilkins* ([1]).

But there is something more here. We have in this charterparty an explanation of this word "safe," for though
there may be a doubt whether those words, "and always
lay and discharge afloat" apply primarily to the port of
discharge, yet in my opinion it does show what in this charterparty is meant by a safe port, i.e., one into which the vessel in its loaded state can safely get, and in which it can
"always lay and discharge afloat."

The only question we have to consider is this, whether on
the evidence Lowestoft was such a place, or whether there
was anything as regards the custom which, notwithstanding
it was not, can justify the charterers in ordering the ship
there. Whether Lowestoft was such a place must depend
upon this, whether the roads were Lowestoft. The roads
were not the port. The roads were not a part of the port of
Lowestoft, and when the charterer ordered the ship to go to
Lowestoft, the charterparty only authorizing the ship to be
sent to a port, he must have meant to the port of Lowestoft,
and not to Lowestoft Roads. Therefore, in my opinion,
though the ship might have safely unloaded whilst laying
afloat in the roads, that will not save the charterer and
enable him to say he had a right to require the ship to go to
Lowestoft.

It is said there is a custom of this port, and that that
makes a difference. It is perfectly true that when a ship
has to go to a port, and there are stipulations as to the time
of unloading, the unloading must be according to the custom
of the port to which she is bound to go ; that is to say, if
the custom in the port is that the ship is bound to go to
unload part of her cargo at a particular place, and then to
go up to the wharf and unload the remainder, that construes, if there is nothing expressly in the contract to the
contrary, the obligations of the parties under the charterparty. But it is said here, where the construction of the
75] *contract is that the port mentioned is to be one into
which the ship loaded can safely go and lay afloat and discharge, that is to be varied by this fact, that at this particular port ships never do go loaded into port, but stay outside
the port and there take out part of their cargo before they go
in. But, in my opinion, that custom, if it is proved is in nc

([1]) 5 Ex., 304.

way admissible to control what is the true construction of the charterparty, independently of any such custom proved. When the port is named, then the custom of the port may regulate certain things not expressly provided for in the charterparty. But in my opinion, the custom of the port as to the way in which ships are dealt with before they go into the port, cannot show that the port is one to which the charterer had a right under this charterparty to order the ship to go, if without any such custom it would not have been such a port.

JAMES, L.J.: I did not say anything about the custom, but I will sum up in a few words my view of it.

The custom alleged here is that Lowestoft does not mean Lowestoft, but means something else.

Appeal accordingly allowed with costs.

Solicitors for plaintiff: *Hughes, Hooker, Buttanshaw & Thunder*.

. Solicitor for defendant: *H. C. Coote*.

[6 Probate Division 76.]

March 23, 1881.

[IN THE COURT OF APPEAL.]

*THE MARGARET (1879, H. 310).   [76

Collision—Contributory Negligence—Damages—Infringement of Thames By-laws —Cause of Action.

A dumb barge, by the negligent navigation of those in charge of her, was suffered to come into contact with a schooner moored to a mooring buoy in the river Thames. The schooner had her anchor hanging over her bow with the stock above water, contrary to the Thames by-laws. The anchor made a hole in the barge and caused damage to her cargo. But for the improper position of the anchor neither the barge nor her cargo would have received any damage. In an action of damage by the owners of the barge against the schooner:

Held, reversing the decision of the Admiralty Court, that both vessels were to blame, and that therefore the owners of the barge were entitled to half the damage sustained.

THIS was an appeal from the decision of Sir R. Phillimore ([1]).

The action was instituted by the owners of the dumb barge E Wo against the schooner Margaret, for damage caused to the cargo on board the E Wo under these circumstances:

The Margaret was anchored at a proper place in the river Thames, but having her anchor swinging by the cable perpendicularly from the hawse, with the stock of the anchor

([1]) 5 P. D., 238.

not awash, which was contrary to the 20th rule of the rules and by-laws for the navigation of the river Thames.

The E Wo was proceeding up Blackwall Reach with a cargo of tea, and was being navigated by two men who were rowing her, and by reason of their negligence she came into contact with the Margaret and the fluke of the Margaret's anchor penetrated the side of the barge, making a hole through which the water entered and damaged the cargo of tea.

SIR R. PHILLIMORE held the E Wo alone to blame, and dismissed the action with costs.

The plaintiffs appealed from the decision.

Butt, Q.C., and *Raikes*, for the plaintiffs : The schooner sustained no damage at all. The only damage to the barge 77] was *caused by the fluke of the anchor penetrating her side. It is proved by the evidence that if the stock of the anchor had been awash, the fluke of the anchor would not have touched the barge but would have gone under it. Therefore it was the schooner's negligence which caused the collision and the whole of the injury, and therefore she is liable in damages for that injury. The penalty imposed by the Thames Conservancy Rules for an infringement of those rules is no bar to an action of damage where damage has arisen from such infringement. There was no doubt some contributory negligence on the part of the plaintiffs to the collision, but still there would have been no damage at all if the anchor had been properly hung. A man may be a trespasser on the land of another and yet may bring an action for damage arising to him there, if the cause of the damage is improperly there : *Barnes* v. *Ward* ('). Admitting the barge was unlawfully where she was at the time of the collision, *quâ* trespasser, yet the anchor was also unlawfully there and caused the injury. The cases of *The Gipsey King* (') and *Sills* v. *Brown* (') really do not throw any light on this case. The judge founded his decision on the question, who was liable for the collision? But the true test is, Who first contributed to the cause of action ? At any rate, if there has been contributory negligence on the part of the plaintiffs, they are entitled to half the damage sustained.

Milward, Q.C., and *Clarkson*, Q.C., for the defendants.

[JAMES, L.J.: We have no doubt that the barge was negligently navigated.]

Then that was the cause of the collision and the defendants are not liable. The whole real *causa causans* was the negligence of the barge.

(¹) 9 C. B., 392.   (²) 2 Wm. Rob., 537.   (³) 9 C. & P., 601.

[JAMES, L.J.: Suppose the anchor had been properly hung, would there have been a cause of action?]

Probably not, but, *non constat*, there might have been some damage. The first contact was complete in itself and was caused by their action. Therefore it was their clear neglect of duty which contributed to the collision, and they were the parties who *caused the collision. That being [78 so, the defendants are not liable for the injury resulting from that collision. The negligence which caused the collision was also the cause of the damage. The plaintiffs therefore substantially contributed to the occurrence of the injury. The Gypsey King (') is really an authority in favor of the defendants.

Butt, Q.C., in reply.

JAMES, L.J.: In this case we have no doubt that the barge was negligently navigated, but it appears to me that we must consider what the form of the action is, and how the damage was caused. The action is by the owner of the barge who says, "Your anchor was in an improper place, and by its being so improperly placed my barge came into contact with it. It made a hole in my barge, and did a great deal of damage." That is the cause of action. The damage was done immediately by the contact of the improperly placed anchor with the barge. It is a conclusive answer to say, "True it is I had my anchor improperly placed; true it is it came into contact with your barge; and true it is that if the anchor had not been there no damage would have been done. But you are the person who led to the wrong, because if your barge had not been improperly navigated, the collision would not have happened, and the damage would not have occurred; and therefore it was you who caused the damage." It appears to me that that plea cannot be sustained. The true plea would be to say, "True, it is my negligence caused your damage, but without your negligence my negligence would have caused you no damage." There is no contributory negligence unless it leads substantially to the cause of action. This is simply a case in which both parties are equally to blame, because both parties through their own fault caused the damage. Therefore, according to the admiralty rule, the damage is equally divided between them.

BRETT, L.J.: It seems to me that in deciding this case the court must determine what is the legal liability of the parties, and in order to do that the court must deal with the

(') 2 Wm. Rob., 537.

79] cause of *action, and must determine whether there is any liability on the part of the defendants with regard to the cause of action, and, if so, what the legal character of that liability is. Now the cause of action in collision cases is not merely the fact of the ships having come into impact with one another, for that by itself is no cause of action, but that damage in the sense of injury was caused to the property of the plaintiffs by reason of that collision. Therefore, even in a case in which there is no contributory negligence charged against the plaintiffs, it is not sufficient for the court to find that there was a collision in point of fact, and that the collision was caused by the negligence of the defendant. There is no cause of action established by that, although in 999 cases out of 1,000 that is sufficient, because there has been some damage done. But in order to establish a cause of action, the court must find not only that there was a collision, and that it was the result of the negligence of the defendants, but that some damage was done, these being found the liability is made out and the cause of action is established. But if it be asserted that the plaintiff was guilty of contributory negligence: Then the question is, what is contributory negligence? To my mind, strictly stated, it is whether the plaintiff has by negligence of his own contributed to that which is the cause of action, and not merely to the collision. Here you have the fact that the collision is caused by the negligence of the barge, and I cannot see myself that the fact of the impact was assisted by anything done on the part of the schooner. But there would have been no damage at all, and no cause of action at all, but for the fact of the anchor being improperly placed, which was a wrongful act. The schooner was therefore to blame, and, had not the barge been at all to blame, the schooner would have been liable to the whole of the damage. But the barge was to blame so as to contribute to the cause of action, and by reason of this bit of negligence on her part, she came into contact with the anchor. The barge and the schooner both were wrong, and therefore according to the rules of Court of Admiralty the damages ought to be divided.

COTTON, L.J.: I have come to the same conclusion. The question is, have the plaintiffs a right to recover on account 80] of *the damages caused by the improper manner in which the defendants' anchor was hung? The ground of the plaintiffs' claim is, that the anchor of the schooner was improperly hung; but the plaintiffs themselves were in fault in navigating their barge negligently. The result is that the ordinary admiralty rule applies, and the damage ought to be divided between the parties.

Appeal allowed ; no costs of appeal or of court below to either party.

Solicitors for plaintiffs : *Cattarns, Jehu & Hughes.*
Solicitor for defendants: *J. T. Davies.*

[6 Probate Division, 90.]

March 4, 1881.

THE LOVE BIRD (1880, S. No. 4253). .

Damage—Merchant Shipping Act, 1873 (36 & 37 *Vict. c.* 85), *s.* 17—*Regulations for Preventing Collisions at Sea, Articles* 12, 13, 18—*Infringement of Regulations.*

A bark, provided only with a fog-horn, sounded by means of the breath, came into collision, during a fog, with a steamship. The fog-horn was duly sounded before the collision, and was heard by those on board the steamship, and those on board the steamship neglected, for some time after they heard the fog-horn, to stop or reverse the engines. The steamship was held to blame. The bark was held to be deemed in fault for not using a fog-horn, to be sounded by mechanical means, as required by article 12 of the Regulations for Preventing Collisions at Sea, 1879.

The circumstance that the bark left port a few days before the regulations came into force was held not to afford any valid excuse for the neglect of those in charge of her to furnish her with a fog-horn, to be sounded by mechanical means, they well knowing, before she left port, that the regulations would come into force in a few days, and there being no evidence to show that they could not have obtained a fog-horn, according to the regulations, before she left port.

THIS was an action of damage brought on behalf of the owners of the bark Pansewitz against the steamship Love Bird. The collision took place at the entrance to the Skager Rack during a thick fog on the morning of the 4th of September, 1880. The Pansewitz, which was on a voyage from Dieppe to the Baltic, had the wind abaft her beam ; she was provided with a fog-horn, sounded by means of the breath. This fog-horn was, before the *collision, sounded at [81 intervals of less than two minutes three blasts in succession. The bark was not provided with a fog-horn sounded by mechanical means. She had left the port of Dieppe some days before the 1st of September, 1880. The Regulations for Preventing Collisions at Sea, 1879, came into force on the 1st of September, 1880. Before the collision those on board the bark heard the whistle of the Love Bird, and the bark was kept on her course. The Love Bird was proceeding under steam at the rate of about three knots an hour, and those on board of her, before the collision, heard the blasts from the fog-horn of the Pansewitz, which they judged proceeded from a vessel right ahead; the engines of the Love

Bird were kept going ahead, and the helm of the Love Bird
was first ported and then starboarded. The Pansewitz was
then seen about a ship's length off the Love Bird, crossing
her bows from port to starboard, and the engines of the
Love Bird were then reversed full speed, and her helm kept
a starboard.

    Butt, Q.C., and *Myburgh*, for the plaintiffs: The Love
Bird is to blame for neglecting to stop and reverse when she
heard the fog-horn of the Pansewitz: *The Frankland* (').
No blame attaches to the Pansewitz. She duly sounded her
fog-horn which although it was not sounded by mechanical
means was yet of sufficient power to be heard by the Love
Bird, in time to enable the Love Bird to have avoided
the collision. Moreover the Love Bird sailed before the
regulations came into force ; she was properly equipped for
her voyage according to law at the time she sailed, and she
had not afterwards any opportunity of obtaining a mechanical fog-horn.

    E. C. Clarkson, and *W. G. F. Phillimore*, for the de-
fendants: The absence of a proper fog-horn, if it did not
actually contribute to the collision, might possibly have
done so: *The Fanny M. Carvill* ('). The range of a fog-
horn sounded by mechanical means is greater than that of
a fog-horn sounded by means of the breath. Before the
bark left Dieppe it was well known that the regulations
82] were about to come into force, and the owners of *the
bark ought to have equipped her in accordance with those
regulations.

    Butt, Q.C., in reply.   •

    SIR ROBERT PHILLIMORE: In this case I have consulted
with the Elder Brethren, and we have no doubt whatever
that the steamer is to blame for this collision. There was a
thick fog, and those on board the steamer heard the fog-
horn of the sailing vessel according to the evidence nearly
ahead, and the steamer proceeded on her course, neither
stopping nor reversing her engines, which it was clearly the
duty of those on board her in the circumstances to have
done. She is therefore to blame for this collision.

    But it remains to consider whether the sailing vessel is
not also to blame. Now the Regulations for Preventing
Collisions at Sea, which contain the regulations applicable
to this case, came into operation on the 1st of September
last, and the 12th article of these regulations is to this effect :
"A steamship shall be provided with a steam whistle, or

                  (') Law Rep., 4 P. C., 529.
    (') Law Rep., 4 A. & E., 417, 14 Eng. R., 670; 44 L. J. (Ad.), 34.

other efficient sound signal, and an efficient fog-horn, to be sounded by a bellows or other mechanical means, and a sailing ship shall be provided with a similar fog-horn or bell." There is no dispute that the sailing vessel in this case was not provided with a fog-horn to be sounded by mechanical means. The evidence is that she left Dieppe about the 20th of August, 1880, when the Regulations for Preventing Collisions at Sea of 1879 had not yet come into operation, but that those on board her were perfectly aware that they would come into operation after she left Dieppe. It also appears that there was a copy of the regulations on board her the last day she was at Dieppe. The defence raised in her behalf is that the regulations did not come into force until after she had sailed from Dieppe, but there is no evidence to show that a mechanical fog-horn could not have been got at Dieppe before she sailed, and in the judgment of the court the fact of a vessel not having on board an efficient fog-horn to be sounded by mechanical means would be no excuse when those on board the vessel unprovided with such a fog-horn knew, as was the case here, that the regulations would come into force whilst the vessel was at sea. I am therefore very sorry to say *that, though [83 the decision I have come to operates severely upon the sailing vessel, I cannot decide that the present case is one that can be excluded from the operation of the 17th section of the Merchant Shipping Act, 1873, on the ground that the circumstances of the case made a departure from the 12th Regulation necessary. The section I have referred to enacts as follows: "If in any case of collision it is proved to the court before which the case is tried, that any of the Regulations for Preventing Collisions at Sea contained in or made under the Merchant Shipping Acts has been infringed, the ship by which such regulation has been infringed shall be deemed to be in fault unless it is shown to the satisfaction of the court that the circumstances of the case made departure from the regulation necessary." There are several judicial decisions on the construction of this section, and they have decided that, if by any possibility a non-compliance with the regulations referred to could have contributed to the collision, the ship by which the regulations have been infringed is to blame for the collision. I think that in this case the sailing vessel must be deemed in fault under the section. I am sorry I cannot come to the conclusion, nor can the Elder Brethren of the Trinity House come to the conclusion, that by no possibility could the sounding of a mechanical fog-horn, according to the 13th article of the

Regulations, have prevented the collision, or that it would not possibly have given more warning to the other vessel. Therefore I am bound to say that the steamer is to blame, and that the other vessel is equally in fault. There will be no costs on either side.

Solicitors for plaintiffs : *Thomas Cooper & Co.*
Solicitors for defendants : *J. A. & F. K. Farnfield.*

[6 Probate Division, 98.]

March 8, 1881.

98]   *MORRALL V. MORRALL.

Deed of Separation—Maintenance—Subsequent Adultery—Further Maintenance.

A wife, by a deed of separation, agreed to accept certain sums as a provision for her support, and not to sue her husband for any further maintenance. Subsequently having discovered that he had been guilty of incestuous adultery, she obtained a decree for dissolution of the marriage:

Held, that notwithstanding the deed, she was entitled to the usual order for permanent maintenance.

THIS was an application for a further and fuller answer to a petition for permanent maintenance.

The petition alleged that a decree *nisi* had been pronounced for dissolution of the marriage, by reason of incestuous adultery, that the respondent derives an income of about £500 a year from his business of a needle reducer, and that he is possessed of realized property, money at his bankers, and other sources of income.

99]   *The respondent, in his affidavit, stated that he and the petitioner had been living apart since August, 1879, and that on that day a deed of separation had been executed by which he had agreed to secure to her the sum of £30 a year, and to assign to her a sum of £130, besides certain goods and chattels, and that the deed contained, amongst other covenants, the following, viz., "That the said Sarah Morrall, or any person on her behalf, shall not, nor will at any time hereafter, commence or prosecute any suit or other proceeding for compelling the said Edward Morrall to allow her any support, maintenance, or alimony whatsoever, except the yearly sum hereinbefore covenanted to be paid to her . . . and the production of these presents shall be a bar to any action or suit, or other proceeding in respect thereof."

The affidavit of the petitioner stated (amongst other things) that the income of the respondent had considerably increased since their separation, and that the incestuous adultery, by reason of which the decree *nisi* had been made, was not discovered by her until the 31st of January, 1880, i.e.. after the execution of the deed.

Middleton, for the petitioner, in support of the application: The extent to which a wife is bound by such a deed is explained in *Williams* v. *Baily* (1), in which case the court refused to restrain her. In *Powell* v. *Powell and Jones* (2) the wife was the guilty party. *Benyon* v. *Benyon* (3) is a direct authority for the application. *Marshall* v. *Marshall* (4) was a suit for restitution of conjugal rights. [He also cited *Besant* v. *Wood* (5) and *Brown* v. *Brown and Shelton* (6).]

Bayford, contrà. The allowance under the deed was agreed to by the wife after considering what was necessary for her support, and the suit does not alter that state of things: *George* v. *George* (7) and *Weber* v. *Weber and Pyne* (8). In *Williams* v. *Baily* (1) the wife had not accepted the deed, if she had she would have been restrained.

*THE PRESIDENT: In this case a state of facts [100 is proved to exist which was not in the contemplation of the parties when the agreement was executed. By that agreement the wife was to live separate from her husband by reason of differences having existed between them. It was not a license to the husband to commit adultery, incestuous or otherwise, but merely an arrangement for living apart, and while it continued she was entitled to no more than what was stipulated for in the deed. But when she has established that her husband has been guilty of incestuous adultery, a state of things arises not in contemplation when the deed was executed, and the wife is not restrained by the deed. Circumstances now justify her in bringing a suit for dissolution of marriage, and she is entitled to all the incidents of that suit, and amongst them to an allowance based upon her husband's actual income.

I therefore order that the respondent file a fuller and further answer.

Solicitors for petitioner : *Surr, Gribble & Bunton.*
Solicitor for respondent : *Rixons.*

(1) Law Rep., 2 Eq., 731.
(2) Law Rep., 8 P. & D., 55; 10 Eng. Rep., 535.
(3) Law Rep., 1 P. & D., 447.
(4) Law Rep., 5 P. D., 19.
(5) Law Rep., 12 Ch. D., 605.
(6) Law Rep., 8 P. & D., 202; 11 Eng. Rep., 387.
(7) Law Rep., 1 P. & M , 554.
(8) 1 Sw. & Tr., 219.

See 16 Eng. Rep., 771 note ; 2 Bish. Mar. and Div. (6th ed.), § 501.
    The Court of Chancery, upon a de- cree for a divorce or separation, may allow alimony to the wife to continue during her life, although she should

outlive her husband ; and may decree that the allowance for her alimony shall belong to her as her separate estate, without the right to appoint or dispose of such part thereof as may not be used by her in her lifetime, in case her husband should survive her, by an instrument in the ·nature of a will : Burr *v.* Burr, 10 Paige, 20, affirmed 7 Hill, 207.

Where, upon a divorce obtained by the wife on the ground of the husband's adultery, the decree requires him to pay her a certain sum of money annually for her support, this allowance is not affected by her subsequent re-marriage, nor should it be reduced on that account : Shepherd *v.* Shepherd, 1 Hun, 240, 3 Thomp. & Cook, 715, 58 N. Y., 644 ; King *v.* King, 27 Alb. L. J., 177, Ohio Sup. Ct.

In Illinois, it is held that, under such circumstances, the court had power to reduce such alimony : Stillman *v.* Stillman, 99 Ills., 196, 203, 15 West. Jur., 566, 13 Chic. Leg. News, 307,20 Amer. Law Reg. (N.S.), 667, 673 note, reversing 7 Bradwell, 524.

A decree of divorce awarded alimony to the wife, "to be paid" by .the husband "out of his real and personal estate." Held, that these words did not create a *charge* upon the husband's real estate. Held, further, that after the husband's death, the wife's only claim under the decree was that of a judgment creditor of his estate : Lawton *v.* Taylor, 12 R. I., 210 ; Howard *v.* Howard, 15 Mass., 96 ; Appeal of Guenther, 40 Wisc., 115.

In May, 1869, plaintiff was, at her suit, divorced from her husband, who was required to pay her alimony while she remained unmarried. She never married. In 1871 defendant was discharged in bankruptcy from all debts existing against him in May, 1870. He died in 1880, having paid the alimony up to the time of his death. On a claim by plaintiff against her husband's estate for alimony accruing since his death ; held, that after his death there remained nothing but a debt which was discharged by the proceedings in bankruptcy : Beach *v.* Beach, 16 N. Y. Weekly Dig., 169.

A surety on the judgment debtor's bond can be compelled to pay arrears of alimony only by an *action on the*
bond, and not by an order of the court in the divorce suit or other summary proceeding : Appeal of Guenther, 40 Wisc., 115.

Where, by the terms of an antenuptial contract, the intended wife, in case the marriage is consummated and she survives her husband, is to receive a certain sum of money out of his personal estate in lieu of dower, distributive share and allowances of all kinds out of his estate, such provision is a substitute or equivalent for dower, which can only be claimed by her in case she becomes his widow : Jordan *v.* Clark, 81 Ills., 465.

Where, by the terms of an antenuptial contract, a certain sum is provided for the wife to be paid out of the personal estate of the husband as a substitute or equivalent for dower, in case she survives him, a divorce granted to the husband for the fault or misconduct of the wife will bar any claim against his estate under such contract : Jordan *v.* Clark, 81 Ills., 465.

The sum awarded to a wife after divorce for alimony becomes a debt from the former husband to her, and upon her death before payment the husband is not discharged, but the sum due passes to her personal representative precisely as any other money decree, and he may proceed and collect the same : Dinet *v.* Eigenmaun, 80 Ills., 274 ; Thorp *v.* McDonald, *ante,* p. 51.

See, however, Bruslough *v.* Bruslough, 68 Penn. St. R., 495.

An assignment by a husband of his property, with intent to defeat a wife of her claim for alimony, is void: Bruslough *v.* Bruslough, 68 Penn. St. R., 495 ; Chase *v.* Chase, 105 Mass., 385.

An order for alimony *pendente lite* will be vacated, where it is clearly shown that the wife is living in a state of adultery, and where the husband himself is not in default. But where it appeared that the order for alimony had been made for more than two years, and during all that time had been disregarded by the husband, who had paid nothing for the support of the wife, the court refused to vacate the order : Stock *v.* Stock, 11 Phila., 324.

[6 Probate Division, 100.]

March 15, 1881.   .

In the Goods of WILKINSON.

Will—Alterations—Execution.

· The clause appointing executors was written partly on the second and partly on the third side of a will. Subsequently the testator altered the clause, but his signature and those of the attesting witnesses appeared opposite only to the alterations, which were made on the second side. The court granted probate of all the alterations.

JOHN WILKINSON, late of Worksop, in the county of Nottingham, builder and farmer, deceased, made his will dated the 12th of June, 1871.

The will was written upon three sides of a sheet of paper, and the clause appointing executors was commenced in the last line of the second side, and was continued on the top of the third side. The testator subsequently altered this clause, but the alterations on the second side only were signed and attested thus :—

101]

*TOP OF THIRD SIDE.

William Alletson
and John Torr & of Worksop,
in the county of Nottingham,
to be executors of this my will.

. . . .

. . . .

. . . .

. . . .

. . . .

SECOND SIDE.

. . . .

. . . .

. . . .

. . . .

. . . .

. . . .

. . . .

. . . .

I nominate and appoint ~~Chas. Marsh~~ Thos. Mallender,

Wm. Wilkinson.

Witnesses :—

Thos. Newton.
Joseph Barlow.

*It appeared from the affidavit of one of the attest- [102 ing witnesses, that in 1874 the testator produced to the attesting witnesses his will with the obliteration and inter- lineation already made; and said that he had made them him- self and wished to substitute William Alletson as an exec- utor in the place of Charles Marsh. He then signed his name in the margin of the second side, and the attesting witnesses added their names.

Searle, applied for probate to William Alletson, as well as Thomas Mallender and John Torr: By the 21st section of 1 Vict. c. 26, the alteration "shall be deemed to be duly executed if the signature of the testator and the subscrip- tion of the witnesses be made in the margin, or on some other part of the will opposite or near to such alteration or at the foot or end of or opposite to a memorandum referring to such alteration, and written at the end or some other part of the will," and those words include this case—so long as the court is satisfied that the attestation refers to the alteration. And for this purpose parol evidence is admissible, just as it would be to show whether the alterations were made before or after the execution. The court will look to the obvious se- quence and context. The obliteration which is unattested, forms part of the same sentence in which the attested alter- ations occur: *In the Goods of Kimpton* (¹).

Cur. adv. vult.

THE PREIDENT: These alterations are made in a partic- ular sentence, and the execution and the attestation by the witnesses are opposite to that sentence. The alterations in the sentence having been thus authenticated, I am of opinion that I may give effect to them, and I, therefore, grant pro- bate accordingly.

Solicitors: *Williamson, Hill & Co.*

(¹) 3 Sw. & Tr., 427.

[6 Probate Division, 103.]

March 22, 1881.

*CLERKE v. CLERKE.   [103

Will—Feme Covert Executrix—Husband's assent to Probate—20 & 21 Vict. c. 77, s. 78.

A married woman having been appointed sole executrix of a will and universal legatee, her husband objected to her taking probate. The court under s. 73 of 20 & 21 Vict. c. 77, made the grant to her attorney:

Quære, whether a husband has an absolute right to object to his wife's taking probate of a will of which she is executrix.

HANNAH NOBLE WALDEN, late of Newington, in the county of Surrey, widow, deceased, died on the 29th day of May, 1880.

The deceased made her will, dated the 20th day of May, 1880, and therein named the plaintiff, Mary Ann Clerke, universal legatee to her separate use, and appointed her sole executrix. The value of the deceased's estate was about £49, and her debts amounted to about £46.

The defendant, Charles Frederick Clerke, as husband of the plaintiff, entered a caveat against proof of the will.

Powles, for the plaintiff, moved the court to order the contentious proceedings to be discontinued, and that probate of the will might be granted notwithstanding the dissent of the husband. The parties have lived apart for seventeen years, and the husband has no interest in the property.

Searle, for the defendant: The husband fears that the plaintiff will take possession of the property and leave him to pay the debts. He insists upon his right, viz., that a wife cannot take probate against her husband's consent.

[THE PRESIDENT: It has not been the practice in the registry to require proof of the husband's consent.]

The law is clearly in favor of the husband's right to pre-vent her from taking the grant: *Pemberton* v. *McGill*, cited in Cootes' Practice (8th ed.), p. 51 ; Williams on Executors (8th ed.), pp. 236, 456, 967 ; *Bubbers* v. *Harby* ([1]). He would be liable for her devastavit: Williams on Executors (8th ed.), 1844. [The case of *Pemberton* v. *Chapman* ([2]) was also cited.]

104]   *THE PRESIDENT: But suppose the estate were large and the husband's conduct merely vexatious, could he by his refusal deprive her of the benefits given her by the will?]

The grant might go to her nominee, who would have to give security for the due performance of his duties.

Powles, thereupon asked for the grant to her attorney under s. 73 of 20 & 21 Vict. c. 77.

THE PRESIDENT: I think that is the best solution of the difficulty. The grant may be made to the attorney of the plaintiff. She being "willing but not competent to take probate."

Solicitor for plaintiff: *H. W. Cattlin*.
Solicitors for defendant: *H. F. & E. Chester*.

([1]) 3 Curt., 50.   ([2]) 7 E. & B., 210; S. C., Ex. Ch., E. B. & E., 1056.

[6 Probate Division, 104.]

March 22, 1881.

In the Goods of WILLIAM HAMMOND, Deceased.

Administration—38 *Geo.* 3, *c.* 87, *s.* 1; 21 *& 22 Vict. c.* 95, *s.* 18—*Creditor—Administrator out of the Jurisdiction.*

An assignee in bankruptcy of an administrator who is out of the jurisdiction is a creditor within the meaning of 38 Geo. 3, c. 87, s. 1, and 21 & 22 Vict. c. 95, s. 18, and as such may obtain administration *de bonis non* of the intestate limited to the fund to which the assignee is entitled.

WILLIAM HAMMOND, formerly of Scott's Yard, Bush Lane, in the city of London, Esquire, deceased, died on the 2d day of June, 1857, intestate, and a widower.

Letters of administration of his personal estate were, on the 18th day of September, 1857, granted to his son, William Parker Hammond, as his only child, sole next of kin, and only person entitled in distribution to such estate.

William P. Hammond had previously, viz., on the 9th of March, 1855, been adjudicated a bankrupt, and was at the time of his father's death indebted to his father's estate in the sum of £2,250, and after having obtained the letters of administration to his father's estate, he was admitted (as such administrator) as a creditor of his own estate under the bankruptcy.

William P. Hammond, before his father's death, obtained his certificate of discharge under this first bankruptcy, and was again, *on the 12th day of October, 1867, adju- [105 dicated a bankrupt, and Mr Thomas Brooke was appointed creditor's assignee.

In the month of November, 1867, William P. Hammond absconded, and though numerous inquiries were instituted he has never since been heard of.

A sum of £506 5s. was now due to the estate of William Hammond, being a dividend payable to that estate under the second bankruptcy of William P. Hammond.

Searle, for Mr. Thomas Brooke, the assignee, moved the court for grant of letters of administration *de bonis non* of William Hammond. By the statute 38 Geo. 3, c. 87, if an executor, to whom probate has been granted, is resident out of the jurisdiction, the court may grant administration to a creditor, next of kin, or legatee, for the purpose of proceedings in chancery, and by the statute 21 & 22 Vict. c. 95, s. 18, the provisions of the former act are extended to all executors and administrators, whether proceedings in chancery are intended or not. Under these acts a grant has been made to the representative of a legatee, *In the Goods of Collier* ('); and to a trustee substituted by the Court of Chancery for an executor who had gone abroad, *In the Goods of Hampson* ('); and to a residuary legatee, *In the Goods of Ruddy* ('); and to a creditor where an executor of the executor is abroad, *In the Goods of Grant* (').

THE PRESIDENT. I am of opinion that a grant to the estate of William Hammond, deceased, limited to the fund in question may be made to Mr. Brooke, as a creditor in equity of the estate of the deceased.

Order accordingly.

Solicitors: *Linklater, Hackwood, Addison & Brown.*

(¹) 2 Sw. & Tr., 444.　　　　　(³) Law Rep., 2 P. & D., 330.
(²) Law Rep., 1 P. & M., 1.　　(⁴) Law Rep., 1 P. D., 435.

[6 Probate Division, 106.]

May 4, 1881.

[IN THE COURT OF APPEAL.]

106]　　*THE CITY OF MECCA (1879, C. 275).

Ship—Maritime Lien—Jurisdiction—Action in rem to enforce Judgment of Foreign Tribunal of Commerce.

The plaintiffs brought an action and obtained judgment in the Tribunal of Commerce at Lisbon against the captain and owners of a British ship for damages for injury caused by a collision with the plaintiffs' ship. The Portuguese courts recognize no distinction between actions *in personam* and actions *in rem*. The defendants' ship having come into a British court the plaintiffs commenced an action *in rem* against the ship, claiming to enforce the judgment of the Portuguese court against it, and arrested the ship:

Held, reversing the decision of Sir R. Phillimore, that the action in the Portuguese court was a personal action, and that the writ in the present action and all proceedings under it must be set aside, the court having no jurisdiction to enforce a judgment in a personal action by proceedings *in rem*.

All civilized nations recognize the validity of maritime lien, and will enforce it when it has been declared by a foreign court; but it is essential that it should appear from the proceedings of the foreign court that the object of the suit was the sale of the ship, and not a personal remedy against the captain or owners.

The Bold Buccleugh (7 Moo. P. C., 267) considered.

THIS was an appeal from a decree of Sir R. Phillimore, the judge of the Admiralty Court (').

The action was an action *in rem*, instituted on behalf of W. Cotesworth and others, of Lloyd's, underwriters, and Besande & Co., of Lisbon, representatives of the ship Insulano, against the steamship City of Mecca. The indorsement of the writ was in the following terms:

(¹) 5 P. D., 28.

"The plaintiffs' claim is upon a judgment of the Tribunal
of Commerce of Lisbon, by which the court determined that
the City of Meca was alone to blame for a collision, and
ordered the defendants to pay to the plaintiffs the loss sustained by them by reason of the said collision, and the plaintiffs claim £25,000."

The writ having issued, the solicitors of the plaintiffs applied in the registry for a warrant to arrest the City of Mecca.
The affidavit to lead the warrant, which is set out 5 P. D.,
at p. 28, stated, among other things, that "the City of Mecca
went into *Lisbon, and proceedings were there insti- [107
tuted against the said steamship, which subsequently left
Lisbon without giving security in the said proceedings."

It then stated that the owners of the City of Mecca appeared and that the court determined that the City of
Mecca was alone to blame, and ordered the defendants the
owners of the ship to pay to the plaintiffs the loss sustained
by reason of the collision.

The City of Mecca was arrested in the present action, and
the defendants appeared under protest and gave bail to answer judgment.

The defendants then moved to set aside the writ, and all
subsequent proceedings on the ground that the writ had
been improperly issued. The judge having refused the application, the defendants appealed.

On the appeal further affidavits were filed, explaining
more fully the nature and course of the action in Lisbon,
and copies of the record of the proceedings were produced.

It appeared from them that in February, 1875, Besande
& Co., agents for the owners of the Insulano, applied to the
court of first instance at Lisbon, stating that they proposed
to institute proceedings against the captain and owners of
the City of Mecca, and praying for an "embargo" on the
ship, which was then in the port of Lisbon. The court
granted the embargo, the plaintiffs being put under terms to
commence their action within thirty days. The ship was
accordingly arrested, but the owners appealed to the Supreme Court, and the court reversed the order on the ground
that "the certainty of the debt should be proved according
to the requirements of Art. 298 of the Novissima Reforma
Judicial, which certainty it could not possess without its
being verified by competent experts that the ship run into
was unable to avoid the collision; and, moreover, because
assuming the hypothesis that the vessel that ran foul of the
other should be declared liable to make good the damages
caused by the collision, such debt cannot be deemed to be

privileged with a view to laying on the embargo provided in Art. 1311 of the said Commercial Code." The ship was accordingly released, and soon after left Lisbon.

The action was brought by the owners and underwriters 108] of the *Insulano before the Tribunal of Commerce at Lisbon against the captain, owners and consignees of the City of Mecca, and they claimed that the defendants, the captain and owners of the City of Mecca, might be jointly and severally condemned together with the defendants the consignees in their said capacity, to pay to the plaintiffs 31 contos, 500 milreis, with interest.

The defendants appeared and defended the action, and brought countercharges of negligence against the plaintiffs. Eventually, on the 17th of December, 1876, the judge of the Tribunal of Commerce of Lisbon gave judgment, whereby he declared "that the disposition of Article 1567 of the Commercial Code, which ordains that in the event of a collision through the fault of the captain or crew, the entire damage must be borne by the captain of the ship causing such damage, is entirely applicable, and the defendant, D. Anderson, captain of the City of Mecca, and the defendants, the owners of the City of Mecca, are bound collectively according to what is laid down in Art. 1339 of the said Code." And he therefore adjudged the action to be well founded and proved, the countercharges unfounded and not proved, and in conformity therewith he condemned the captain and owners jointly and severally to pay the amount claimed with interest, and to pay the legal penalty both in respect of the petition in the libel and the petition in the counter-charges; the consignees to pay one-twentieth of the costs and the other parties the remainder.

The defendants produced affidavits by two Portuguese advocates. In the affidavit sworn by Manuel Maria da Silva Beirao, president of the Association of Advocates, he stated the effect of the Portuguese law to be as follows: "Modern Portuguese law does not accept in terms the distinction of actions *in rem* and *in personam*, because Portuguese laws deal little in doctrine. In actions for damage the following persons are answerable if the collision was originated by culpability. First, the ship herself; second, the captain of the ship; third, the owners. The ship is the special hypothec of maritime debts of collision; the Portuguese Commercial Code expressly declares it in Article 1567 and following, where the expressions are frequently found: 'The ship is responsible for all the damage occasioned.' 109] 'The ship is under *obligation to indemnify the losses.' In this way an action in respect of damage caused by collision may be said to be *in rem* against the ship as to the ship causing the collision, and also *in personam* against the captain and owners. In actions for damage caused by collision there may be, or may not be, by Portuguese procedure, an arrest. It must, however, be noted that in every case the arrest is dependent on the proof which may be given of the facts, and if sufficient proof shall not have been given, the action is not on this account prevented. It may be prosecuted in the same way with or without arrest. The ship causing the collision is always answerable whether she be arrested or not. Where a ship is sold after the collision, it being a guarantee or special hypothec for the damage occasioned, the new owners acquire only a vessel charged with the burden of being responsible for the damage caused."

Benjamin, Q.C., and *E. S. Roscoe* (*Butt*, Q.C., and *E. C. Clarkson*, Q.C., with them), for the appellants: The judge in the court below proceeded on the supposition that the proceedings in the Portuguese court were proceedings *in rem*, being deceived by the terms of the affidavit on which the warrant was issued. But now that the facts are fully before the court it is clear that, according to the practice of the Portuguese courts, there is no such method of procedure as a proceeding *in rem*. The action is a purely personal one, although the plaintiffs have a right to take a separate proceeding for an embargo on the ship if they can make a case for so doing. But this the plaintiffs failed to do, and they have only their personal judgment against the owners.

But even if the judgment in the Portuguese court was a judgment *in rem*, still the plaintiffs cannot enforce that judgment by proceedings *in rem* in the courts of this country. If they wish to proceed *in rem* in the English court they must found their proceedings on the original cause of action, not on the foreign judgment.

Webster, Q.C., and *Gainsford Bruce* (*W. G. F. Phillimore*, with them), for the respondents: Proceedings *in rem* are the proper course for enforcing a maritime lien. A collision between two ships creates a maritime lien by international law on the ship that *is in fault. It does not [110 arise from the decree, although in the Portuguese court it cannot be enforced before the decree. But as soon as the plaintiff has obtained a decree the lien becomes indelible, and it can be enforced in any court by international law. The purchaser of the ship takes it subject to the lien, and it can be arrested wherever and in whosesoever hands it may be :

The Bold Buccleugh (¹).   The form of the action in the foreign court can make no difference.   The modern Portuguese law does not adopt the distinction between actions *in personam* and actions *in rem;* but if the object of the action is to attach the ship it is in fact an action *in rem*, although it may not be called so: *Castrique* v. *Imrie* (²) ; *The Europa* (³).

JESSEL, M.R.: This is in form an appeal from a decision of Sir Robert Phillimore ; but it is not so in fact, because the facts that are before us are totally different from the facts which were before him.   He decided that there had been a judgment *in rem* by the Portuguese court having jurisdiction in admiralty ; that an action brought on that judgment in the High Court might be brought as an action *in rem*, that is, as an action against the ship, and might be enforced in the way in which process in this action was enforced—by an arrest of the vessel.   The owners have appeared under protest and asked to set aside all those proceedings, and he decided against them on that ground.   It is hardly necessary to read his judgment, but I think it is only fair, arriving as I do at a different conclusion on the present facts, to read this to show that that is what he really said.   He said, "The court is now called upon to be an aidant to the enforcement of a judgment *in rem*, given by the Portuguese court," and then he said that although there is no direct precedent on the point, "it is clearly for the interests of justice that this court should exercise the jurisdiction as prayed, and having its hand upon the *res* should not take it off until the sentence be executed."   That is the foundation of his judgment.   It appears that the real facts of the case were not before him at all.   There was an important affidavit by a clerk to the solicitors.   I am far from 111]   saying that it *was purposely erroneous, but it did lead to an erroneous conclusion in the mind of the learned judge, and it probably would have led to an erroneous conclusion every one else.

It now appears that by the law of Portugal there is no such thing as an action *in rem*—it does not exist at all.   What the reason may be is immaterial to inquire, and the reason given is certainly a very odd one, but the fact is quite plain.   This is what is said by a gentleman of great eminence in Portugal —a Portuguese advocate and president of the Association of Advocates in Lisbon, and he has practised as an advocate since 1840, and he says, "That modern Portuguese law does

(¹) 7 Moo. P. C. C., 267.   (²) Law Rep., 4 H. L., 414, 447.
                    (³) Br. & Lush., 89.

not accept in terms the distinction of actions *in rem* and *in personam*, because Portuguese laws deal little in doctrine." Whether that reason is satisfactory to his mind or not, I do not know. I am afraid it is not satisfactory to mine. That being so, the course of procedure seems to be this: They bring a personal action against the owners and the captain who are liable for the collision, and when they have got judgment in that action, if the owners and captain do not pay, and if the vessel after the judgment comes within the jurisdiction of the Portuguese court, they enforce their personal judgment as against the vessel under the doctrine of the law of nations, which is stated by the two advocates who have made affidavits to be part of the law of Portugal, that damage arising from collision gives a maritime lien on the vessel which is in fault, and that the lien dates from the time of collision, and of course is not created by the judgment, which merely ascertains the amount of the damage and also decides, if that is disputed, whether there is any lien at all, whether there is any fault or liability on the part of the vessel. That being so, the judgment in this case was given actually against the captain and owners by name and there is no other judgment, and the present action is brought on that judgment and on that judgment only. There was in reality in Portugal an attempt to seize the vessel by arrest, which attempt failed, because, as I have already said, the Portuguese law does not allow the arrest of a vessel before the damage is ascertained, and therefore the embargo, as it is called, was discharged and there was no arrest of the vessel, nor does it appear that it has since come within the jurisdiction of the court *of Portugal, nor is there any mari-   [112 time lien or order directing a charge on the vessel or directing the sale of the vessel.

It appears to us clear that this judgment is a personal judgment in a personal action. Then it may be said what is there to argue? The argument presented to us by the respondents is this—First of all it is alleged that the action in Portugal was an action for enforcing a maritime lien; secondly, that whatever the terms of the judgment might be, it was a judgment for enforcing a maritime lien and a judgment *in rem*, and that being so, it was a judgment binding the vessel in the courts of every civilized country under the international law. But I find the simple answer is that it is not an action or proceeding to enforce a maritime lien—nothing of the kind appears on the proceedings. There is no suggestion from beginning to end that the ship is liable; there is no declaration that the ship is liable, and it does not appear on the proceedings that the ship was even within the jurisdiction at the time the action was commenced against the owners. And action for enforcing a maritime lien may no doubt be commenced without an actual arrest of the ship, but there is no suggestion that they intended anything of the kind, and, in fact, the law does not allow it. An action against a ship, as it is called, is not allowed by the law of Portugal. You may in England and in most countries proceed against the ship. The writ may be issued against the owner of such a ship, and the owner may never appear, and you get your judgment against the ship without a single person being named from beginning to end. That is an action *in rem*, and it is perfectly well understood that the judgment is against the ship. In the present case the judgment does not affect the ship at all, unless the ship should afterwards come within the jurisdiction of the Portuguese court, and then it can be made a proceeding by which you can afterwards arrest the ship and get it condemned. Therefore, it seems to me to be plain that this is a personal action as distinguished from an action *in rem*, and it is nothing more or less; and any attempt to make it out something else (because the law of Portugal does not allow actions *in rem*) is really to change the real nature of the action to meet the exigencies of those who want to make the judgment of the court of Portugal go 113] further than it really does. *It appears to me, therefore, we have not now the same state of circumstances as that on which the judge in the court below decided, for there was no action *in rem*, or judgment *in rem*, either in form or substance.

Reference has been made to the case of *The Bold Buccleugh* (¹), from which I will read a few words of the judgment delivered by Sir John Jervis. At page 284 he says: "Having its origin in this rule of the civil law a maritime lien is well defined by Lord Tenterden to mean a claim or privilege upon a thing to be carried into effect by legal process, and Mr. Justice Story (²) explains that process to be a proceeding *in rem*, and adds that wherever a lien or claim is given upon the thing, then the admiralty enforces it by a proceeding *in rem*, and indeed is the only competent court to enforce it. A maritime lien is the foundation of the proceeding *in rem*, a process to make perfect a right inchoate from the moment the lien attaches, and whilst it must be admitted that where such a lien exists a proceeding *in rem* may be had, it will be found to be equally true that in all cases where a proceeding *in rem* is the proper course, there

(¹) 7 Moo. P. C. C., 269.   (²) 1 Sumner, 78.

a maritime lien exists which gives a privilege or claim upon the thing to be carried into effect by legal process."

Then he refers to what occurred in that case, and adds that an action was brought in Scotland against the owners by name—very much like the action in the foreign court below here ; but there is something in addition, because when it comes within the jurisdiction they arrest the vessel to secure the debt, and then this applies exactly to this case, "the arrest by the steamer was only collateral to secure the debt." They did not get so far in Portugal. They tried but failed. Then he says : "We have already explained that in our judgment a proceeding *in rem* differs from one *in personam*, and it follows that the two suits being in their nature different, the pendency of the one cannot be pleaded in suspension of the other." That is, the formal proceedings in Scotland were against the person, although the vessel was arrested as security for the debt. It is really the form of the proceedings which must be looked at to ascertain whether it is a proceeding *in rem* or *personam*, and it lends much greater force *in the case before us when the attempt to arrest [114 the vessel failed altogether. For this reason it seems to me we should go further than we should be warranted by any principle in going if we said that .the judgment was not a personal judgment, and that the court was entitled to order the arrest of the vessel as if it were an action *in rem* and a judgment *in rem*. Therefore I consider this appeal ought to be allowed.

BAGGALLAY, L.J.: I am of the same opinion. In the early part of January, 1875, a collision took place off the Portuguese coast between the British ship City of Mecca and a Portuguese ship called the Insulano, on which an action was brought in the Portuguese court. Subsequently, in the year 1879, an action was brought in the Admiralty Court in England, on which this present appeal has been commenced, and when the writ was issued it was indorsed as a claim upon a judgment of the Tribunal of Commerce of Lisbon, and the plaintiffs claimed £25,000. That judgment of the Tribunal of Commerce at Lisbon was a judgment pronounced on the 17th of December, 1876, which condemned the defendants the owners of the City of Mecca jointly and severally to pay the plaintiffs the amount claimed with interest. It was an action brought by the owners of the Insulano and also by the underwriters who paid certain claims under policies upon the ship, therefore it seems to me impossible to say, looking at the form of the judgment itself, that it was any more than a personal action—a judgment against the defendants per-

sonally for the payment of a specific sum of money. But
before this writ was issued, an application was made to the
judge of the Probate Division for liberty to issue the writ
and to proceed to arrest the ship, and an affidavit was then
made which I am willing to accept was made in ignorance
of the true state of the case, alleging that the action commenced in the Portuguese courts had been proceedings *in
rem* as far as regards the ship. The defendants never seemed
to be aware that this was not the case until after the matter
had been disposed of by the judge of the Probate Division,
when an application was made to him to set aside the writ.
He proceeded, as I read his judgment—entirely on the footing that the proceedings in Portugal had been proceedings
in rem.

115] *For reasons that have been assigned by the Master of the Rolls, which it is unnecessary for me to repeat, it
appears to me that there is no question but that the proceedings in the Tribunal of Commerce in Portugal were entirely personal proceedings—proceedings *in personam*. No
doubt proceedings of a different character were commenced
in the Civil Tribunal of Portugal—those proceedings preceded in the judgment of the Tribunal of Commerce. In
the first instance in the Civil Tribunal an embargo was obtained by the plaintiffs in the present action to arrest the
ship, and the ship was only released by giving security.
But those proceedings were made the subject of an appeal
in the Supreme Court of Lisbon, and ultimately the decision
of the court of first instance was reversed, and on the two
grounds to which reference has already been made, the one
that it was not within the ordinary jurisdiction of the Tribunal of Commerce to grant an embargo, unless it were established that the ship was to blame, so far differing from
proceedings in the English Court of Admiralty, in which,
where the matter is in doubt, the ship may be arrested and
security given if it is allowed to go, but in Portugal it is not
the law while there is a doubt. That was one ground. The
second ground for discharging the embargo, I must confess,
appears to be one more difficult to understand. Whatever
might be the effect of that particular reason which can be
only well understood by an examination of the particular
article of the code to which reference has been made; one
thing is clear, that there were proceedings that could have
been taken in the Civil Tribunal in Lisbon, by which the ar
rest of the ship could be obtained, and this would be a proceeding *in rem* according to my view. The attempt was
made but failed, as it could not be done except after proof

that the City of Mecca was alone to blame, and it was not renewed probably for the good reason that the ship was no longer within the jurisdiction, and it would therefore have been useless. I am at a loss to understand on what grounds, now that we have got these facts which were not before Sir Robert Phillimore, it could be held otherwise than that the proceeding was *in personam* and was not a proceeding *in rem.*

One argument I do not desire to pass over which was addressed to us by Mr. Gainsford Bruce—it was a bold one. It was this—*that on an action on a foreign judgment [116 the English Court of Admiralty will proceed *in rem* whenever the foreign tribunal has established a maritime lien. Mr. Bruce was unable to produce any authority, nor do I think any can be found for the proposition he advanced.

It appears to me that the present proceedings were initiated under a mistake, and that the appeal should be allowed.

Lush, J: The question which we have to decide apart from all technicality is whether the arrest of the vessel in the proceedings out of the Court of Admiralty was a wrongful arrest. That depends, I think, on whether the proceedings in the court of Portugal were proceedings *in rem.* It is part of the law of nations that Courts of Admiralty in different countries have the power to condemn vessels and order them to be sold for the satisfaction of a maritime lien. Maritime liens are recognized by all civilized nations, and damage by collision is classed among those things which create a maritime lien ; and had this been a judgment *in rem,* that is to say, a judgment condemning the ship and ordering the ship to be sold in order to satisfy the maritime lien, that judgment would have been recognized in this country and every other civilized country. But it is most important that proceedings under which the sale of another vessel takes place should show on the face of them the authority why that property is to be diverted from the owner ; because the purchaser's title is recognized by all nations, and the title depends on the circumstances under which the sale takes place. Therefore it is important that the judgment should show on the face of it that the proceedings against the vessel are not merely against the owners as such, or the captain, but that the proceedings had in contemplation the ultimate sale of the ship and a judgment ordering the ship to be sold ; and if this does not appear on the face of the proceedings then the title of the purchaser has nothing to support it. It is not a mere matter of form, but a matter of substance that the decree under which the sale is attempted to be justified should be shown on the face of the proceedings.

Now, upon the face of this judgment, there is not a word about a claim against the ship from beginning to end. It is 117] well known *that the owner of a vessel that has suffered by collision with another has two remedies. He may bring an action against the captain or owner of the other vessel and recover damages, or he may sue in the Court of Admiralty and make the ship pay. It has been stated before us that the Court of Admiralty has been abolished in Portugal and the jurisdiction is transferred to a Court of Commerce, and that there is no power now in that country to institute what are called actions *in rem.* That is what I collect from these proceedings. Whether there is or is not, seems to me immaterial. There certainly is a proceeding by which a vessel can be laid under embargo, that is, arrested, if an action is brought against the captain, in order to secure payment, by lien perhaps, of ultimate damages; but whether that can be carried out to proceedings *in rem* I do not know, nor does it strike me to be material. But what is material in considering an action of the nature claiming damages alone is that there is nothing about the ship from the beginning to the end, as I have said. According to the practice in continental courts in judgments the article of the code upon which the court founds its judgment is there set out, and this article, which is a prominent one, on which the judgment of the court is based, says: it is article of Commercial Code, 1567, "In the event of a vessel being run into by another through the fault of the captain or of the men composing his crew, the entire damage occasioned to the collided vessel and her cargo must be borne by the captain of the ship which causes it," and further on the court says, "consequently the disposition of Art. 1567 of the Commercial Code, which ordains that in the event of a collision through the fault of the captain or crew the entire damage must be borne by the captain of the ship causing such damage," is entirely applicable, and the defendant David Anderson, the captain of the City of Mecca, as the defendants, the owners of the City of Mecca, are bound collectively according to what is laid down in Art. 1339 of the said code." The action being brought against the captain and owners it is also brought against the consignees, and the court gives some special judgment in reference to the consignees which I need not read, and they quote the two articles giving judgment against the captain and giving judgment against the 118] owners of *the vessel. Then the judgment proceeds, and the judge says: "I adjudge the said action to be well-founded and proved, the countercharges unfounded and not proved, and in conformity thereunto I condemn the defendant, David Anderson, and George Smith, and owners, jointly and severally to pay to the plaintiffs the amount claimed with interest, and I do also condemn them to pay the legal penalty both in respect of the petition in the libel and of the petition in the countercharges," and so on. There is not a word about condemning the ship, nor do I see how they could condemn the ship. The ship had been improperly arrested in the first instance, because it was found by the Supreme Court that the plaintiff in the action had not performed the conditions by which alone an embargo could be laid on the vessel, that is to say, it was not proved to the satisfaction of the court that the fault of the collision was entirely due to the City of Mecca, and therefore the court discharged the vessel from the arrest, and the vessel went away. I do not see how it was possible for them to carry and execute a maritime lien when they had not possession of the thing. The vessel was out of their jurisdiction, it was an English vessel, and it naturally left the Portuguese coast; and under the decree of that court, if a purchaser had to prove his title he could not quote a single word of this judgment or any judgment at all that would justify a sale of that ship. It is a judgment purporting to be a judgment against the persons of the captain and owners, and if they ever find them within their jurisdiction they may execute according to the process they have at their command the judgment against them individually. But as to any judgment against the ship, I doubt if the ship were found there now that they could seize it. But even if they found the ship there, and they could without further process seize the ship and sell it in satisfaction, that would not make this a judgment *in rem* which any court in this country could be called on to execute.

For these reasons, therefore, I am of opinion that the action is entirely unjustified, and inasmuch as it is not merely a question of the issuing of the writ, but the vessel has been arrested, and therefore the owners of the vessel were deprived by it of the right of having full command of the vessel, I think we are well *warranted in coming to the [119 unanimous conclusion that the proceedings must be set aside, and in not waiting for the further development of the matter by fresh litigation.

BAGGALLAY, L.J.: I think I ought to express my entire adoption of the definition of proceedings *in rem* and *in per-*

sonam, as quoted by the Master of the Rolls in the case of *The Bold Buccleugh* ('), but I think there is one additional passage that should be read, viz., "This claim or privilege travels with the thing into whosesoever possession it may come. It is inchoate from the moment the claim or privilege attaches, and when carried into effect by legal process by a proceeding *in rem*, relates back to the period when it first attached."

Appeal allowed.

Solicitors for appellants : *Gellatly, Son & Warton.*
Solicitors for respondents : *Pritchard & Sons.*

(') 7 Moo. P. C., 267, 284.

M. W.

[6 Probate Division, 127.]

July 20, 1881.

[IN THE COURT OF APPEAL.]

127]   *PREHN v. BAILEY.

THE ETTRICK (1880, E. 0186).

Limitation of Liability—Shipowner—Wrongdoer—Salvage—Cargo—Thames Conservancy—Powers under Two Acts of Parliament.

The payment into court of £8 a ton under 25 & 26 Vict. c. 63, s. 54, does not place the shipowner in the position of a person who has not done wrong.

The owner of a ship sunk by a collision in the Thames admitted it to be his fault, and paid into court £8 a ton in a suit to limit his liability. The Thames Conservators, having powers under the Removal of Wrecks Act, 1877, and the Thames Conservancy Acts, raised the ship and delivered the ship and cargo to the owner, he undertaking to pay the expenses of raising. Part of the cargo was some wool, which was damaged by being sunk:

Held, that the shipowner was bound to deliver the wool to the owner of the wool without claiming from him, by way of contribution to salvage, any part of the expenses of raising the ship and cargo.

Where a public body has powers under two acts, it must be taken to have proceeded under that which gave it most advantages.

SPECIAL CASE. W. Prehn, the plaintiff, was owner of the steamship Ettrick, on board of which were 293 bales of wool belonging to one Dr. Wendt, put on board by him in London, for delivery at Gravelines. A collision took place in Gravesend Reach, between the Ettrick and another ship, by which the Ettrick was sunk. In May, 1880, the plaintiff commenced an action to limit his liability, in which action he admitted that the collision was caused by the bad navigation of the Ettrick. The usual judgment was pronounced, and the plaintiff paid into court the sum of £1,972 as £8 a ton. Inquiries were directed to ascertain the persons entitled to claim upon that sum, and Dr. Wendt claimed in respect of the 293 bales of wool. In March, 1880, the Conservators of the Thames, acting under the powers vested in them by statute, had raised the Ettrick, with her cargo. The expense of raising was £400, and the value of the Ettrick when raised was £1,100. The expenses of raising were not enhanced by any expenses specially incurred for raising the bales of wool. Upon an undertaking given by the plaintiff to pay the costs of raising, the Ettrick and her cargo were handed *over to him. Dr. Wendt then applied [128 to the plaintiff for the bales of wool, which were given up to him, he by letter dated 27th March, 1880, undertaking to pay the freight as if the cargo had been delivered at Gravelines, and all general average or other charges that might legally fall on the wool. The plaintiff then claimed from Dr. Wendt £124 15s. 2d., as due for general average, salvage, or otherwise ; or to fall on the said wool. A special case was thereupon stated for the opinion of the court, the material contents of which are above given ; the first question being ''Whether under the circumstances above set forth the plaintiff is entitled to the said sum of £124 15s. 2d., or to any and what sum by way of general average, contribution, salvage, or otherwise. 2. Whether the plaintiff is entitled to prove against the said fund in court, as aforesaid, in respect of such sum, or any part thereof, or otherwise, in respect of the matters aforesaid. 3. Whether the plaintiff is entitled to be paid the said sum, or any and what sum, by the said Dr. Wendt personally.''

The case was argued before Sir R. J. Phillimore, judge of the Admiralty Court, on the 30th March, 1881.

Phillimore, for the plaintiff, abandoned the claim on the fund in court, and claimed only against Dr. Wendt and the wool. The arguments so far as relate to the points reported were the same as those used in the Court of Appeal.

Myburgh, for Dr. Wendt.

April 5, 1881. SIR R. J. PHILLIMORE, after stating the facts of the case :—It was contended, on behalf of the owner of the Ettrick, first, that although, apart from the statutory limitation of his liability, he would have been liable to pay this £124 15s. 2d., yet having paid once into court this £8 per ton he is entirely purged of his liability as a wrongdoer and stands in the position of an innocent party, and that to hold him now liable for this £124 15s. 2d. would be to make him liable by that sum in excess of the statutory limitation. In support of this position the case of *Chap-*

man v. *Royal Netherlands Steam Navigation Co.* (') was cited. It was contended, in the second place, that the owner 129] *of the Ettrick, having a right to be treated as an innocent party, was entitled to claim from Dr. Wendt the sum in dispute as a general average contribution, to defray the expenses of salvage service rendered by a third person, that is to say, by the Thames Conservancy. On behalf of Dr. Wendt it was contended that the case did not turn upon the effect of the statutory limitation of liability. The owner of the Ettrick contracted to take the wool to Gravelines, but by the fault of his servants, it was sent with the ship to the bottom of Gravesend Reach, and it became the duty of the owner to raise the vessel, the expenses of doing which, it is admitted, were not enhanced by raising also the bales of wool. This duty was imposed upon the owner either by the Thames Conservancy Act, 1857 (20 & 21 Vict. c. cxlvii), or by the Removal of Wrecks Act, 1877 (40 & 41 Vict. c. 16), or by both. It was contended that if the conservancy authorities had, as it was competent for them to have done, sold the ship, it would have produced ample funds to defray the cost of raising, and there would have been no charge on Dr. Wendt's cargo. I must here observe that the 6th section of the Removal of Wrecks Act seems to prescribe that the proceeds of sale arising from ship and cargo shall be regarded as common fund. As a matter of fact, however, the ship and cargo having been delivered up by the Thames Conservancy to the plaintiff, the 6th section never came into operation. The cargo was given up by the plaintiff to Dr. Wendt in order to get the freight, and an undertaking to pay the freight was given. It was also contended on behalf of Dr. Wendt, that if the owner of the Ettrick had himself salved the property he could not have claimed salvage, and that he could not do so now that some one else had salved it. In support of this three cases were cited, *Schloss* v. *Heriot* ('), where the plaintiff was a shipowner, and his actionable negligence was held to be a bar to claims for general average to contribute to losses caused by such negligence. The *Cargo ex Capella* ('), in which Dr. Lushington says :

The question for me to determine is whether when a collision has taken place between two vessels and both vessels are held to blame, one of them can sue for 130] *salvage for having saved the cargo of the other from the perils consequent on the collision. I do not seek for authorities, but I look to the principle which ought to govern the case. In my mind the principle is this, that no man can profit by his own wrong. This is a rule founded in justice and equity, and

---

(') 4 P. D., 157.   (') 14 C. B. (N.S.), 59.   (') Law Rep., 1 A. & E., 356.

carried out in various ways by the tribunals of this country, and never, so far as I am aware, departed from by any English court. The application of this rule to the present case is obvious. The asserted salvors were the original wrong-doers ; it was by their fault that the property was placed in jeopardy. The rule would bar any claim by them for services rendered to the other ship which was a co-delinquent in the collision. But the present claim, it is to be observed, is a demand for salvage against the cargo, the owners of which were perfectly innocent.

The *Norway* (¹) was also cited, but in that case the facts were very complicated, and portions of the judgment of the Admiralty Court were reversed on appeal (at p. 404), and although I see no reason to. question the soundness of the principles of law laid down by Dr. Lushington (at p. 393) with respect to the responsibility of a shipowner for cargo jettisoned in consequence of the negligence of his servants, I do not rely upon that case. It was further strenuously denied that there was really any salvage properl so called, but simply the performance of a duty under one or both of the two statutes before mentioned, and if there was no salvage there could be no general average, and if no general average, then no lien attached to the wool, and the case of *Schuster* v. *Fletcher* (²) was relied on. In that case it was said that—

The shipowner had an interest in getting the ship off and bringing the cargo into port, in order that he might earn his freight . . . . A great deal of what he has done was in the performance of his own contract ; he was bound to use every effort to convey the cargo safely to its destination, and could only give up the task when it was hopeless.

These observations appear to me applicable to the present case. If the contention of the owner of the Ettrick were well founded, the result substantially would be that he, having broken his contract by damaging the cargo and not bringing it to the port of destination, and having limited his liability for this wrong, would be entitled nevertheless to a pecuniary contribution from the cargo towards defraying the expenses incident to raising the ship in which the cargo was. Thus, the cargo owner would suffer a double injury : first, by limitation of the wrongdoer's liability which debars *him from a *restitutio in integrum;* and, [131] secondly, by compelling him to pay a portion of the cost of repairing the mischief caused by the wrong. At this manifestly inequitable conclusion the court would arrive with great reluctance. In my judgment, however, there was no salvage service properly so called, but a simple performance of a prescribed duty, and if there were a salvage service the limitation of the owner's liability would not entitle him to demand from Dr. Wendt any contribution to it.

(¹) Br. & L., 377, 404.   (²) 3 Q. B. D., 418; 28 Eng. R., 349.

Upon the whole, and after careful consideration of the arguments and the cases relied on, I am of the opinion that the owner of the Ettrick is not entitled to the sum of £124 15s. 2d., or to any sum by way of general average, and that he is not entitled to be paid this or any other sum by Dr. Wendt personally.

Judgment for Dr. Wendt.

The plaintiff appealed.

Millar, Q.C., and *Phillimore*, for the plaintiff: The owner has, by paying the £8 a ton, been released from all further liability in respect of the collision. If the wool had been left at the bottom of the sea Dr. Wendt would have lost it, and could only come upon the money paid into court, and he has done so. As it is, the owner has paid the expenses of raising, and has the same rights as any other salvor. The ship was raised under the Removal of Wrecks Act (40 & 41 Vict. c. 16), the 6th section of which makes the ship and cargo a common fund to defray the cost. No doubt there is the Thames Conservancy Act (20 & 21 Vict. cxlvii, s. 86), but that is merely a private act, and the general act must be taken to apply first. Dr. Wendt has no claim against the owner, who is no longer a wrongdoer: *Chapman* v. *Royal Netherlands Steam Navigation Co.* ('). This is outside the negligence: *The Northumbria* ('). If the ship had been sunk by accident the Conservancy would have raised it, and the costs would then have been borne ratably by ship and cargo; and as far as the owner is concerned that must be taken to be the case now. The acts of the Conservancy cannot alter the rights of other parties. They had possession of ship and 132] cargo, and were bound to hand them *back to the owner, who cannot have any part taken away from him except on payment of whatever claim he may have.

Myburgh and *Stubbs*, for Dr. Wendt, were not called upon.

JESSEL, M.R. (after stating the fact of the case): First of all what is the position of the owner. This is not a case in which it is pretended that £8 per ton would in any way pay the owner of the wool. The wool has been delivered to him in a damaged state, and it is not alleged (which might make the difference) that he has been or will be paid for it. Of course if the £8 had been the value of the wool—if there had been some of the cargo that was not worth £8 per ton, he could not receive the money and get the cargo; but it has been admitted that that is not so, and that the payment of £8 per ton, whatever legal effect it may have under the

(') 4 P. D., 157.   (') Law Rep., 3 A. & E., 6, 24.

statute, as regards the limit of liability, would, irrespective
of that statute, not at all have affected the rights of the parties, the wool having been, as I understand, damaged to a
greater extent. That being so, the statute which limits the
liability of the owner says nothing about the rights of the
ship and cargo, but leaves that to be dealt with by general
law. All it says is, in the 54th section of the Merchant Shipping Act (25 & 26 Vict. c. 63), that the owners of any ship
in certain events, shall not be answerable for damages in respect of the loss to ships or goods to a greater amount than
the sum of £8 for each ton of the ship's tonnage. That is
merely the limit of the liability for damages. It does not in
any way alter the property, though that would be a consequence if it turned out there was a limited liability on account
of the goods. Now, the property not being altered, the
ground upon which the shipowner puts his claim is this: He
says that the payment of £8 per ton not only prevents his being answerable in damages for any more, but is equivalent to
saying that he shall be in exactly the same position as if no
negligence had been committed, and nothing had been done
by him or by his agents that would give rise to any liability.
But I cannot read the act so. All that it says is that he
shall not be answerable in damages for any greater amount.
It does not make his acts right if they were previously wrong.
It does not give him any new rights as far as I can see, and
it appears to me that *if the owner of a vessel and [133
cargo, which by the default of him or his agent had been sunk
in collision, after paying £8, had raised the vessel and cargo
(and it was not a case where £8 a ton was more than the
damage done to the cargo), he would not have any right to
the whole of the cargo, or that having raised the vessel for
his own benefit, if he or his agent had been the cause of sink-.
ing the vessel, he would thereby be entitled to salvage on
the cargo, or to general average, or to anything in the nature
of general average. It seems to me he would have no such
right, for the statute does not destroy the effect of all that
had been done, as it simply diminishes or limits the liability
in damages. If that is so, of course there is an end of the
case. But it seems to me that there is another answer. It
is assumed on the part of the appellant that the ship was
not liable in the first instance to these charges, but that the
ship and cargo were ratably liable under the Thames Conservancy Act; but as I read the Thames Conservancy Act
that is not so. The ship was raised under the powers of
the 86th section, and that section is: that if the Thames
Conservancy think that it is a proper case for raising they

may raise, and then they are required "in case such vessel
shall be weighed and raised, to cause the same, and the furniture, tackle, and apparal thereon, or of any part thereof
respectively, and also all or any part of the goods, wares,
merchandise, chattels, and effects, which may be found on
board the same, to be sold by public auction or otherwise,"
and they are to apply the proceeds of the sale to pay the
charges and expenses of weighing and raising such vessel.
Therefore these three things appear.   First of all injury to
the navigation is caused by the vessel.   Secondly, the Conservators are compelled to sell the vessel.   They are not
compellable to sell the furniture or the goods, or any part of
the furniture, or any part of the goods, but they are compella-
able to sell the vessel, and they have an option of sale as
regards the rest.   It is obvious that the first moneys to be
applied are the proceeds of that which they are compelled
to sell, and that answers the first part of the case.   That
construction is further confirmed by this, that the object of
selling the furniture and the cargo is, no doubt, to defray the
charges which the vessel by its sale will not defray, and no
doubt in that respect it diminishes the deficiency which the
134]   owner has to pay, *although as owner he is the person
who is ultimately liable.   The whole section points to this,
that though the Conservators have a security both on the vessel and cargo, the vessel is primarily responsible, if I may use
the term, and the cargo is secondarily responsible.   I have
been careful to consider in this case that as the value of the
vessel is £1,100, and the charges of raising are only £400, there
would be no charge even as between the Conservators and the
owners of the cargo.   Then, failing that, the appellant says
that the Conservators did not proceed under that act, but
under the general act.   The answer is that the powers given
by the Thames Conservancy Act are so much more advantageous to them that of course they were acting under those
powers, and not under the powers of the general act.   Under
the general act they had no powers against the owner, although they had under the special act.   That being so, it
seems to me, quite independent of the first construction,
that there would be no right to contribution, or anything in
the nature of contribution against the cargo, or even as
against the owner of the cargo.   On this ground also the
appeal must fail.

BRETT, L.J.:   In this case there was a collision, by reason
of which this ship and the cargo were sunk.   That collision
was caused solely by the default of the shipowner, who is the
present plaintiff.   Thereupon he desires to limit his liabil-

ity according to the act of Parliament, and he calls upon everybody who would have a claim against him to come in. Whether they come in or not is immaterial, as he gets a declaration, that in respect of all claims from the owners of the cargoes of the other ship or his own, he shall not be liable to a greater amount than £8 per ton. That £8 per ton will be distributed amongst the claimants, and they can make no further claim against him in respect of the collision. If the matter had ended there, that act of Parliament was done with. But something else happened afterwards—a new series of events, with which to my mind that act of Parliament has nothing whatever to do. The ship and cargo being in the way of the navigation, the Thames Conservancy by virtue of authority given to them, do a thing which they often have done under the circumstances without any such authority, for *supposing there had been no Conservancy Act [135 the Thames Conservancy might have raised the ship as salvors only. However, they raised the ship and the cargo, and in respect to that they have rights. They would have had rights as salvors as it seems to me, but they have other rights, and having done this thing they have under their act a power of sale if they are not paid otherwise. But that power of sale does not prevent them, if the person who is liable to them desires to pay the charges, from receiving payment, and they do so accordingly. The shipowner having paid the money for raising the ship, and possibly for raising the cargo, now says to the owner of the cargo, "I have paid this money. I admit I had not express authority to pay it for you, but I say nevertheless that you are bound to pay me part of what I have paid." As I understand him, he says first of all, "you are bound to pay me because you promised to pay me for a good consideration, and I have a lien upon this cargo; I gave that up to you in consideration of your promise to pay me what I have paid in raising the cargo in the nature of a general average or salvage." The answer to that is, that that is not a promise. It is not an absolute promise, but only a promise to pay him what he has paid in the nature of general average. If that was a promise or a contract, he would have been liable to pay. That is the whole of it. Therefore we are driven to see whether the defendant would have been liable to pay to the plaintiff this contribution in respect of money paid by the plaintiff, if there had been any such made. Now, first of all, could he claim that as a general average contribution? A general average contribution is a contribution in money paid to a person who has been obliged to pay for a general average

loss. If the plaintiff had not been in any fault, I am inclined
at present to think that he would have been entitled to claim
from the defendant if it was a general average contribution.
But he has been in fault, and the authorities are decisive
that if the general average contribution which he claims is a
general average contribution, which arose by reason of a default of his, he cannot claim anything. Therefore, taking
it to be a claim for a general average contribution, he is
ousted by the authorities, because the loss was a loss occasioned by his own default.

136]   *But then, as I understand it, he claims by virtue
of the Conservancy Statutes, which, as he says, enable the
Thames Conservancy to raise the ship and the cargo, and
then to charge ratably in respect of the ship and the cargo;
but to obtain it in the first place from the shipowner, who
therefore was bound to pay in respect of the ship and in respect of the cargo, that being a payment on behalf of the defendant. Now, in the first place, that construction put upon
the statute is wrong. All that the Thames Conservancy are
anxious to do is to obtain payment, and if the ship is not
sufficient they obtain it from the cargo. But even if it were
the true construction, it seems to me the plaintiff would be
met precisely in the same way, because what he would be
claiming, although not strictly speaking a general average
contribution, would be a contribution in the nature of general
average, and then the same principle, which would prevent
him from recovering from the defendant a simple general
average contribution, would equally prevent him from recovering that which is in the nature of a general average contribution. In that case again, what the Thames Conservancy would
be entitled to claim in respect of the cargo would be in respect
of a loss of cargo caused by the plaintiff himself, and therefore, even though he would have been obliged to pay in the
first place for the recovery of cargo, he could not have recovered that payment from the defendant, because the loss
in respect of which the defendant's goods would be liable
was a loss caused by the plaintiff.

But then it is said that the statute which limits the liability to £8 purges the negligence and the default, and puts the
plaintiff, on payment of the £8, into the position of a perfectly
innocent person. Now that act of Parliament is sufficiently
tyrannical as it is, but conceive what it would be upon this
interpretation of it. The adverse ship is lost, and all the
cargo of the adverse ship is lost. The £8 per ton may not,
and very likely will not, pay 10 per cent. of each person's
actual loss, and yet is it to be supposed that the Legislature

have said to the person who occasioned the loss, "You are
an innocent person, you are purged, and you have all the
rights of an innocent person, with regard to people to whom
you have paid less·than 10 per cent. of the loss occasioned
by your default."   Such a construction of the act of Parliament makes *the Legislature say something which it   [137
is ·impossible to conceive that any rational Legislature
would say.

COTTON, L. J.:   I am of the same opinion.   The first question is whether there is a special contract between these parties that the sum claimed shall be paid.   Now, in my opinion,
there is no such contract.   [His Lordship then gave his reason for coming to this conclusion on the construction of the
letter of the 27th of March, 1880.]

Then, independently of the contract, what are the rights
of the parties?   I take it, first of all, without reference to
the Thames Conservancy Act, but treating this as in the nature of a general average contribution, that the claim is one
founded on equity, namely, that where a person has incurred
expense for the general benefit of the whole adventure he
shall claim contribution from all those who are interested.
But it would be against equity to say that the person who
himself has done the wrongful act which caused the expenditure shall claim thereupon from anybody else, and the
cases have decided accordingly that where the expense has
been incurred in consequence of the wrongful act of the person who incurred it, he cannot claim contribution in the way
of general average.   Then it is said that the Merchant Shipping Act makes a difference ; that the result of those sections
in the act which enable a shipowner to limit his liability, is
to purge his wrongful act, and entitle him to say—not while
he is being sued for damages, but while claiming a sum to be
paid to him—that he is not a wrongdoer, and that the expense cannot be considered as having been incurred in consequence of a wrongful act of his.   But these are not the words
of the statute, it only says that he shall not be answerable in
damages with respect to certain loss beyond £8 per ton.
Here there is no claim, as it seems to me, for damages in consequence of the result of the shipowner's wrongful act, but
he is seeking to retain the goods of another person till a payment has been made to him for expenses, simply caused by
his own wrongful act.   Then it is said further that the judgment of this court in *Chapman* v. *Royal Netherlands Steam
Navigation Co.* (¹) supports the plaintiff's contention.   But
the *whole question there was whether there being   [138

(¹) 4 P. D., 157.

actions by both ships, the damages being divided, and each being entitled only to a half, the judgments were to be considered as two judgments, or one judgment only for one damage, and the court held that there were two judgments for two acts of damage.

As to the questions raised under the Thames Conservancy Act, whether that act does or does not require the ship first to be sold, I should be of opinion that it was in no way intended to alter what, irrespective of the act, would have been the rights as between themselves and owners of the ship and the owners of the cargo. It was simply intended to give the conservators power to remove obstructions and to reimburse themselves out of the proceeds of that which they had raised, and in my opinion it could not properly be held, in the absence of express terms, to alter the rights of the shipowner and the owners of the cargo as between themselves. But we have an indication of an intention that the owner of the ship is to be primarily liable, because the right is given to the Conservators to claim from him any deficiency in the amount of expense beyond that which was provided for by the sale of that which they have sold. I think the proper course would be first to sell the ship and that which belongs to the shipowner, and then to proceed if necessary to sell the goods. · But what I principally rely on is the provision that the shipowner is to be liable and capable of being sued by the Conservators, showing that it is meant to give a primary remedy against the shipowner. In my opinion the appeal fails.   *Judgment affirmed.*

Solicitors for plaintiff : *Ingledew & Ince.*
Solicitors for defendant: *Walters & Co.*

                                                        C. M.

See 16 Eng. Rep., 264 note ; 22 Alb. L. J., 165, 185 ; Lord *v.* Steamship Co., 102 U. S. R., 541 ; Steamship Co. *v.* Mount, 103 id., 239 ; The Scotland, 105 id., 24 ; Ex parte Slayton. Id., 451 ; The Wanaba, 95 id., 600 ; The Whistler, 2 Sawyer, 348 ; Matter of New York, etc., 9 Ben., 44 ; Thomassen *v.* Whitwell, Id., 403 ; Id., 458 ; Churchill *v.* The British America, Id., 516 ; Sevenson *v.* Ocean, 17 Alb. L. J., 285, Shipman, J.; King *v.* American, etc., 1 Flippen, 1 ; Haige *v.* New York, etc., 54 How. Pr., 145 ; Checkley *v.* Providence, etc., 60 id., 510 ; Arctic, etc., *v.* Austen, 69 N. Y., 470 ; Bartlett *v.* Spicer, 75 id., 528 ; Hill, etc., *v.* Providence, etc., 125 Mass., 292 ; Georgian Bay, etc., *v.* Fisher, 5 U. C. App. R., 883, reversing 27 Grant, 846.

The United States Supreme Court holds that the owner may avail himself of the provisions of the statute, though he deny all liability : Steamship Co. *v.* Mount, 103 U. S. R., 239.

The Court of Appeals of Ontario holds the contrary, under the English statute : Georgian Bay, etc., *v.* Fisher, 5 Ont. App., 883, reversing 27 Grant (Chy.), 346.

This statute exempts the owners of vessels, in cases of loss, from liability for the negligence of their officers or agents, in which the owners have not directly participated : Walker *v.* Transportation Co., 8 Wall., 150.

This liability of the shipowners may be discharged by their surrendering and assigning to a trustee, for the benefit of the parties injured, in pursuance of the 4th section of the act, the vessel and freight, although these may have been diminished in value by the collision or other casualty during the voyage; and it *seems*, that if they are totally lost, the owners will be entirely discharged. In this respect the act has adopted the rule of the maritime law, as contra-distinguished from that of the English statutes on the same subject : Norwich Company *v.* Wright, 13 Wall., 104.

The act of Congress of 1851, limiting the liability of shipowners, includes collisions, as well as injuries to cargo; so that if a collision happens between two vessels at sea, and one of them is in fault without the privity or knowledge of her owners, the latter will only be liable for the amount of their interest in the vessel and her freight then pending; and that amount being paid into court, if sufficient to pay all the damages

caused, will be apportioned *pro rata* among the owners of the injured vessel, and of the cargoes of both vessels, in proportion to their respective losses: Norwich Company *v.* Wright, 13 Wall., 104.

The proviso to the act of 1851, allowing parties to make their own contracts in regard to the liabilities of the owners, refers to express contracts : Walker *v.* Transportation Co., 8 Wall., 150.

A local custom that shipowners shall be liable in such cases for the negligence of their agents, is not a good custom, being directly opposed to the statute : Walker *v.* Transportation Co., 8 Wall., 150.

The district court, sitting as a court of admiralty, has jurisdiction of cases arising under the act, and may administer the law as provided in the 4th section. The proper course of proceeding in such a case pointed out : Norwich Company *v.* Wright, 13 Wall., 104.

[6 Probate Division, 139.]

July 19, 1881.

[IN THE COURT OF APPEAL.]

*THE LIBRA (1880, J. 1181).   [139

Thames—Rules for the Navigation of the Thames—Rules 22 and 23—Coming to Points—Porting.

The 22d and 23d rules for the navigation of the Thames are not inconsistent, and the intention is that when the 23d rule (as to passing a point) applies, the case for the 22d (as to porting) shall not arise, but if the case does arise the rule will apply.

A steam vessel coming down the Thames against tide to a point on the north shore, and being nearer to mid-channel than to the north shore, eased and, then seeing danger of collision with a vessel coming up with tide, starboarded and reversed. The other vessel was coming up with the tide also near the north shore and rounded the point under a port helm; seeing the other vessel, she ported hard, and stopped, but a collision occurred:

Held, that under the circumstances the 22d rule applied, and that the vessel which had starboarded was to blame.

By Jessel, M.R., and Brett, L.J. (Cotton, L.J., doubting), that under the 23d rule the vessel navigating against tide is to wait until she has been passed by the other vessel, and not merely until the other vessel has passed the point.

ACTION and counter-claim for damages by collision. ·

The Joseph Ricketts was a steamship of 449 tons, and was, on the 11th of November, 1880, coming up the Thames on the north shore towards Tilburyness with a cargo of coal. The Libra was a steamship of 617 tons going down North-

fleet Hope, and according to her account she was on the
north shore, the tide being first-quarter flood. The conclusions of the court as to the distance of the Libra from the
north shore will be seen in the judgments below. The
Joseph Ricketts saw the lights of the Libra over the point
and ported her helm, intending to pass port side to port
side, when she saw the green light of the Libra, whereupon
her helm was put hard a-port and her engines were stopped
and reversed, but she came into collision with the Libra and
suffered damage. The Libra had seen the masthead light
of the Joseph Ricketts and therefore eased and kept her
course, meaning to pass starboard side to starboard side,
but afterwards seeing the red light of the Joseph Ricketts
and that there was danger of collision, her helm was put
hard a starboard and her engines were reversed. A claim
for damages was brought by the owners of the Joseph Rick-
140] etts, *and a counter-claim by the owners of the Libra.
The action was tried in the Admiralty Division before Sir J.
Phillimore and two Nautical Assessors on the 28th of January, 1881. Witnesses were examined on both sides.

Myburgh, and *Phillimore*, for the Joseph Ricketts.

Butt, Q.C., and *Clarkson*, for the Libra.

SIR R. J. PHILLIMORE: This is a case of collision of some
importance, because it calls upon the court for the first time
to put a construction upon the new steering and sailing rules
for the river Thames. The collision took place in Northfleet
Hope, between five and six o'clock on the evening of the
11th of November last year. The weather appears to have
been fine and clear, and the tide was first-quarter flood, running about two knots an hour. The vessels which came
into collision were the Joseph Ricketts and the Libra. The
blow was dealt on the starboard side of the Libra, in front
of the bridge, by the stem of the Joseph Ricketts. The
Joseph Ricketts was a steamship of 449 tons, she was proceeding up the river Thames with a cargo of coal. The Libra was a steamship of 617 tons register, and was going from
London to Hamburg, in ballast, in charge of a duly licensed
pilot. The collision took place about 250 yards above Tilburyness. Those on board the Joseph Ricketts observed
the masthead and red lights of the Libra, about three-quarters of a mile off, and about two points on their port bow,
coming down the reach. The Joseph Ricketts ported and
then steadied, and was proceeding as she says to pass the
Libra port side to port side when the Libra opened her green
light ; the helm of the Joseph Ricketts was put hard a-port,
and her engines were stopped and reversed, but the Libra shut

in her red light and struck the Joseph Ricketts with her starboard side forward of her midships. The Libra says that she was proceeding down Northfleet Hope, and that she saw the masthead light of a steamship, which proved to be the Joseph Ricketts, over Tilburyness, from half to three-quarters of a mile off, and bearing on the port bow of the Libra. The statement of these facts introduces the consideration of the rules which apply to the case, and in my judgment both the 22d *and the 23d of the rules for the navigation of the [141] river Thames apply. [His Lordship then read the rules (').] The object of these rules appears to the court to be to get rid of the many former difficulties with respect to vessels rounding these points, and also as to vessels meeting each other so as to involve risk of collision. In our judgment the Libra did ease her engines, but did not wait as required by the 23d rule. She herself pleads that she was kept on her course, and that when she. saw the red light of the Joseph Ricketts, her helm was put, when about 300 or 400 yards off, hard a-starboard, and her engines reversed full speed astern. This appears to have been half a minute before the collision, and she had at that time way enough on her, it is to be observed, to run on shore. By the manoeuvre of starboarding the Libra ran across the bows of the Joseph Ricketts, and thereby, in our judgment, occasioned the collision. It is complained on behalf of the defendant that the Joseph Ricketts ported too much and ran into the slack tide, but in our opinion the Libra was not justified in attempting to cut in between the Joseph Ricketts and the shore. It appears by the evidence that the Libra had gone off two points under her starboard helm at the time of the collision. Now had she put her helm a-port when she saw the red light of the Joseph Ricketts she would have gone off two points to starboard, and the collision would, in all probability, have been avoided. It appears also from the evidence, that the Libra well knew all along that the Joseph Ricketts was rounding the point under a port helm. The Libra's pilot says that when the Joseph Ricketts got two and a-half points on the Libra's starboard bow he saw all three lights of the Joseph Ricketts, showing that the Joseph

(') Rules and by-laws for the navigation of the river Thames, issued by the Conservators; allowed by Her Majesty in Council, on the 17th of May, 1880.

" 22. When two steam vessels proceeding in opposite directions, the one up and the other down the river, are approaching one another so as to involve risk of collision, they shall pass one another port side to port side.

" 23. Steam vessels navigating against the tide shall, before rounding the following points . . . . Coalhouse Point, Tilburyness, ... ease their engines and wait until any other vessels rounding the point with the tide have passed clear."

Ricketts was under a port helm, and it is apparent that
142]   when the Joseph Ricketts had passed the point *she
was still continuing under a port helm.   In pursuing that
course she, the Joseph Ricketts, obeyed, in our judgment,
the 22d rule, and intended to pass port side to port side,
which she would have done but for the Libra starboarding.
I pronounce the Libra alone to blame.

Judgment for the plaintiffs.

The owners of the Libra appealed.   The only questions
argued on the appeal were as to the construction of the
navigation rules and the conduct of the vessels with reference to those rules.

Butt, Q.C., and *Clarkson*, Q.C., for the Libra: The 22d
rule does not apply to a case like this.   The Libra was coming down under the shore against tide as is usual, and the
Joseph Ricketts was coming up with the tide and would
keep to the south, so that in such a case the 22d rule cannot
apply.   Both rules cannot apply at the same time, and the
Libra properly eased and followed the 23d.   No sailor
would have expected a ship coming up with tide to turn
and go over to the north shore out of the tide.   If the Libra
had ported she would have been carried by the tide right
across the river.   Her proper course was on the north shore
out of the tide, and the proper course of the Joseph Ricketts was well out in the tide.

R. E. Webster, Q.C., and *Myburgh*, for the Joseph Rick-
etts: There may be a difficulty as to the two rules, but the
Libra obeyed neither.   She neither waited nor ported.
(They were stopped by the court.)

Jessel, M.R.:   This is an appeal from a decision of the
judge of the Court of Admiralty, and it raises a point of
construction of the rules for the navigation of the river
Thames, and it also raises a secondary point as to the conduct of the respondent's vessel.   The point of construction
is this, putting it shortly.   It has been argued that wherever the 23d rule applies the 22d does not; and the first
thing to be decided is whether that is a correct mode of construing the rules.   Now, in the first place, it must be remembered what these rules are.   They are issued for the
guidance of masters of vessels, and therefore the proper
mode of construing them is to read them literally.   I do not
143]   say that the *same rule of construction does not apply to other written instruments, except when it will lead
to some inconsistency or absurdity, which must render it
necessary at some inconvenience to give up the literal mean-

ing: but certainly rules issued as these are should be construed literally if they can be construed at all. Now the
rules themselves are not in form inconsistent. [His Lordship read them.]

I think that the 23d rule means that the vessel must wait
until vessels rounding the point have passed clear of the
waiting vessel. It is not "have passed the point" but
"have passed clear." Now, waiting and easing the engines
may possibly, in the case put by Mr. Butt in his argument,
mean when they are in the slack water near the shore, quite
out of the way of the vessel coming with the tide. In this
case it may very well be that the 22d rule may not apply,
because the event contemplated by the rule has not happened, as the vessels are not then approaching each other so
as to involve risk of collision. One is in slack water near
the shore and the other is coming up with the tide driving
her over towards the other shore. Therefore there is no inconsistency in saying that rule 22 does not apply, because,
as I said before, there is nothing for it to apply to. But if,
instead of being close to the shore, the vessel which is coming down is in mid-channel, or near mid-channel, then I can
quite understand that the rule must apply, because then the
vessel that is coming up with tide may be approaching
so as to involve risk of collision. And it appears to me, if it
is so in fact, that there is no reason why the rule should not
apply. In this case the vessel is going at half speed or
slackened speed, but is still going on and may very well port
her helm at that time, so as to pass the other vessel port side
to port side. I can see no inconsistency and no difficulty in
applying the rules. As I understand the facts in this case
found by the learned judge, and not disputed on appeal (because he having found one way it is useless to address the
Appeal Court on the facts), he did find that the Libra was
nearer mid-channel than to the north shore, and that she
starboarded her helm and by doing that caused the collision. If that was so, it was the Libra's conduct that was
the cause of the collision, and it was found by the learned
judge that she was to blame. I now revert to the second
point. The second *point was this; it is said under [144
rule 14, "every steam vessel when approaching another
vessel so as to involve risk of collision shall slacken her
speed, and shall stop and reverse if necessary." Now the
question is whether the Joseph Ricketts (which was the
"other vessel") came under this rule at any time before the
Libra starboarded her helm. As I understand the evidence
she did not, and there was no danger of collision until the

Libra starboarded her helm; and the moment that happened we find from the evidence that the engines of the Joseph Ricketts were stopped and reversed, so that it does not appear to me that the 14th rule does apply so as to involve the Joseph Ricketts in any blame and make her jointly liable with the Libra for the collision. Under these circumstances it appears to me the judgment ought to be affirmed.

, Brett, L.J.:   I think that the facts to be taken in this case are that the two vessels sighted each other when they were the one above and the other below the point, and that they were so near to the point that the 23d rule applied to them, and I think that the Libra was not close in to the north shore and under the point and in the slack water, and that the evidence is, and that the fact must be taken according to the finding of the learned judge, that she was so far out that if she had done nothing there was room for the Joseph Ricketts to have passed to the north side of her, that is, port side to port side.   I think that when the Joseph Ricketts had first come round the point under a port helm, she found the Libra so far out from the north shore that if the Joseph Ricketts had not then been under a port helm for the purpose of passing round the point, they were so near to each other that it would have been right for the Joseph Ricketts to stop and reverse.   There would then have been danger of a collision, but the peculiarity of this case is that the Joseph Ricketts was coming round under a port helm, and that those on board the Libra could see it, and that there was no danger of a collision if the vessels had remained as they were, and it was not until the Libra starboarded that there became danger of collision, and then it is found that the Joseph Ricketts immediately stopped and reversed.   Under these circumstances it is argued that the Libra did nothing wrong, that 145]   she *obeyed the 23d rule, and that the 22d rule did not and could not apply.   In other words it is argued that the rules are so inconsistent that whenever the 23d applies the 22d cannot.   I do not think that that is the right construction of the rules.   I think that the intention of the 23d rule is that when vessels are approaching the point named, the state of things should not arise which would make the 22d rule applicable; but nevertheless if that state of things does arise, there is nothing in the 23d rule which prevents the 22d rule under the circumstances from applying.

Mr. Butt argued that the 22d rule could never apply when the 23d rule applied, because he said that when the 23d rule was obeyed, the vessel going against the stream must always be in the slack water close in under the point.   I do not see that. I do not see that the 23d rule cannot be obeyed without that fact existing. All that the 23d rule says is, that when it is likely that they may meet on the point, the vessel which is going against the tide shall wait. I think the meaning of that is that she shall so far check her speed as to prevent her coming up to the point at the same time when the other vessel would come there. The vessel going against tide is not only to wait until the other has passed the point, but to wait until the other has passed her. That is to say she is not to go up to the point till the other vessel has passed her, and if she was close in and in the slack when the other vessel came round this point, it is obvious that her green light will be to the southward, and the other vessel coming round will come round outside her, and that when she could see the side lights they would be green light to green light, the one outside, and the other close in shore. It seems clear to me that under those circumstances the 23d rule would have been obeyed, and the 22d rule would not be applicable, and therefore there would be nothing for the vessel coming with the tide to do but to keep out. But if the vessel that is coming down the river in such a case as this against the tide is not close in, and is so far out that there is room for the other vessel to pass inside her, they are to pass port side to port side, and then the vessel coming against the tide would have obeyed the 23d rule in this, that she may have waited so as not to come to the point at the same time *as the [146 other, but here she was waiting so far out in the river that there was room for the other to pass port side to port side, and if that be true, although the 23d rule has been obeyed by her waiting, the 22d may be applicable. They may be approaching so as to run the risk of collision, and then their duty is to pass port side to port side, therefore it is not true that, whenever the 23d rule applies, the 22d does not. Neither is the converse true. The truth is that they are independent rules, and that it depends on circumstances whether the 22d rule applies after the 23d rule has been obeyed, or not. In this case it seems to me that the 22d did apply, and that these vessels ought to have passed port side to port side. As far as my view goes the Libra did in this case obey the 23d rule, but did not content herself with that, but being in a position where she ought to have obeyed also the 22d rule, she broke the 22d rule, and broke it not merely passively but actively by starboarding and so preventing the other from going port side to port side, which was the natural and proper course to take. It has been urged upon us that under certain circumstances in obeying the 23d rule, a

1881 The Libra.

vessel might put herself into a position that she could not obey the 22d, that is, if she was brought to a complete stand-still in order to obey the 23d, she could not obey the 22d, because whether she ported or starboarded her helm it would have no effect on her as she had no motion in the water. To my mind it is not necessary in this case to decide that question. A vessel is not to be expected to do the impossible, and she should not be found to blame for not doing what she could not do.

COTTON, L.J.: The most important question is whether rules 22 and 23 both apply in the present case. Now the two rules are not inconsistent. There is nothing in the mere terms of the rules which make them inconsistent, and the utmost that can be urged against them is that under certain circumstances they may produce a result of some difficuly. As I understand rules 22 and 23 they may well apply, and in my opinion they do apply to the the Libra in the present case. Rule 23 has this effect, as I understand. It is intended to prevent the vessel which is coming against the stream from rounding the point at the same time as the 147] vessel *going with the stream. Of course, if the two vessels were rounding the point at the same time there would probably be a collision, and therefore it is intended to prevent, as far as possible, such an occurrence when the vessels are both rounding the point, the one in one and the other in the other direction. I very much doubt whether the vessel which is coming against the tide to these points is bound to wait till the other vessel which is coming up with the tide should pass her. I rather think that the rule means to pass the point, but it is not necessary to decide that question. The 23d rule is to prevent vessels from approaching one another with a chance of collision, but if it had not this effect, and they are approaching one another under circumstances which would involve risk of collision, then rule 22 applies, and then, when they come in a position which involves risk of collision, that not having been prevented by the operation of rule 23, rule 22 comes into operation, and then, in my opinon, that rule is to be obeyed, although rule 23 may have applied already to these steamers, and might under ordinary circumstances have prevented them from coming into the position of vessels approaching with risk of collision, and that is the material point in the case. On the other part of the case, I think it unnecessary to add anything to what has already been said. *Appeal dismissed.*

Solicitors for the Joseph Ricketts: *T. Cooper & Co.*
Solicitor for the Libra: *W. Batham.*

C. M.

[6 Probate Division, 148.]

June 23, 1881.

*THE LEON (1881, P. 76, Folio 6).   [148

Damage—Law applicable in Case of Collision between British and Foreign Vessel.

In an action *in personam*, brought by the owners of a British vessel against the owners of a Spanish vessel to recover damages caused to the British vessel by collision with the Spanish vessel on the high seas, the defendants pleaded that they were Spanish subjects, and that if there was any negligence on the part of those in charge of the Spanish vessel it was negligence for which the master and crew alone, and not the defendants, were liable according to the law of Spain:

Held, bad on demurrer.

THIS was an action of damage, *in personam*, brought by the owners of the British vessel Harelda against the owners of the Spanish vessel Leon, resident in this country, to recover damages for a collision between the two vessels on the high seas.

The 10th paragraph of the statement of defence was as follows :

The defendants further say that, before and at the time of the said collision, the Leon was a Spanish ship sailing under the Spanish flag, and wholly owned by subjects of the King of Spain, and that if the said collision was occasioned by any improper or negligent navigation of the Leon, which the defendants deny, it was wholly occasioned by the negligence of the master or mariners of the Leon, and not by such owners or the defendants, or any of them, and that by the law of Spain in force at the time of the happening of the said collision and now, the master and mariners of the ship, and not the owners, are liable in damages in respect of a collision occasioned as in the statement of claim alleged, and by such law the defendants are not liable in respect of the damage proceeded for in the action.

To this paragraph the plaintiffs demurred.

Benjamin, Q.C., and *Myburgh,* for the plaintiffs, in support of the demurrer: There is no case in the books where a foreign municipal law, differing from the general maritime law as administered in this country, has been held applicable where a collision has taken place on the high seas. The general maritime law as administered by the courts of this country has always been held to govern in cases such as the present : *The Johann Friederich* ('); *The Dundee* (');

(¹) 1 W. Rob., 35.   (²) 1 Hagg., 120.

149] *The Zollverein* ('); *The* * *Wild Ranger* ('); *The Mary Moxham* ('); *The Druid* ('); *The Volant* (').

Webster, Q.C., and *Clarkson*, Q.C., for the defendants, contrà: It may be admitted that if the Leon had not sunk, and had been arrested here in an action *in rem*, the defendants might have been liable for the damage proceeded for, but this is an action *in personam*, and the same consequences by no means follow. In *General Steam Navigation Co.* v. *Guillou* ('), the collision was on the high seas, and the defendant was allowed to plead the law of France. If he could do so for one purpose, why could he not have done so for all purposes? At the present day there is no such thing as a general maritime law in universal use amongst all nations. Each nation has adopted whatever portions of what was formerly known as the general maritime law as was thought desirable, and at the present day the laws in force in the different maritime courts of Europe differ widely: Marsden on Collision, p. 49. The question, therefore, comes to this, there being no general maritime law in existence, ought the decision in this case to be governed by English or Spanish law? Spanish law ought to be applied, because not only are the owners, whom it is sought to render liable, Spanish subjects, but the act, for the consequences of which it is sought to render them liable, was done on board a Spanish ship: *Lloyd* v. *Guibert* (').

SIR ROBERT PHILLIMORE: This is a case in which it appears that an English vessel, the Harelda, was run down by a Spanish vessel called the Leon on the high seas and was sunk. The owners of the English vessel brought an action of damage *in personam* against some of the owners of the Spanish vessel resident in this country, and the defence they set up in the 10th paragraph of their statement of defence is: [His Lordship here read the 10th paragraph of the statement of defence as above set out.] This paragraph is demurred to, and the question now before me is whether the demurrer can be sustained or not. A great deal has been said upon the question of what law is applicable to this case, 150] *and I agree with the observation that has been made that from ancient times the law administered in the Court of Admiralty was the general maritime law, and that that law is still to be followed in this court. It is not necessary for me to go very abstrusely into the subject of what law

(') Sw., 96.
(') Lush., 553.
(') 1 P. D., 107.
(') Law Rep., 1 Q. B., 115.
(') 1 W. Rob., 391.
(') 1 W. Rob., 383 ; 1 No. Ca., 503.
(') 11 M. & W., 877.

must govern in the present case, because two cases of recent date to which I have been referred, *The Wild Ranger* (¹) and *The Zollverein* (²), seem to have disposed of the question. In the first place, however, I must observe that it has been admitted that if the Leon had been arrested in this case in an action *in rem* the liability of the defendants to be condemned in damages, if the collision should be shown to have been caused or contributed to by the negligence of the master and crew of the Leon, could not have been disputed. Now in the case of *The Druid* (³) that learned judge Dr. Lushington said: "The liability of the ship and the responsibility of the owners in such cases are convertible terms; the ship is not liable if the owners are not responsible and *vice versa*, no responsibility can attach upon the owners if the ship is exempt, and not liable to be proceeded against." In the case of *The Volant* (⁴), reported in the same volume and perhaps more accurately in the 1st volume of the Notes of Cases, the same learned judge said:

By the ancient maritime law, the owners of the vessel doing the damage were bound to make it good, though the amount of that damage might infinitively exceed the value of their own vessel and her freight. The owners of the vessel damaged might resort to a court of common law or to the Court of Admiralty, if they preferred coming to the Court of Admiralty they had their choice of three modes of proceeding, either against the owner, or the master personally, or against the ship itself. The court has jurisdiction over the whole subject-matter of damages on the high seas, and the arrest of the vessel is only one mode of proceeding.

Moreover, in the case of *The Johann Friederich* (⁵) Dr. Lushington said, "All questions of collision are questions *communis juris*." But as I have before observed, the question appears to be disposed of by the decisions come to in the recent cases of *The Wild Ranger* (¹) and *The Zollverein* (²). In the former of these cases, which was decided before the passing of the Merchant Shipping Act, 1862, and therefore before the Legislature had expressly *provided that [151 foreign shipowners should be entitled to limit their liability for damage in respect of collision, Dr. Lushington said:

The court has found that the Wild Ranger, an American vessel, by improper navigation, came into collision on the high seas with a British ship; and the ordinary decree has passed condemning the owners of the American vessel in the damages. Under such circumstances, according to the ancient law, as stated by Lord Stowell in the case of *The Dundee* (⁶), the owners of the wrongdoing ship are responsible for all the damage occasioned.

In the latter of those cases (*The Zollverein*) the following passage occurs in the judgment of Dr. Lushington:

(¹) Lush., 553.
(²) Swa., 96.
(³) 1 Rob., 391.

(⁴) 1 W. Rob., 383; 1 No. Ca., 508.
(⁵) 1 W. Rob., 87.
(⁶) 1 Hagg., 120.

Generally when a collision takes place between a British and a foreign vessel on the high seas, what law shall a Court of Admiralty follow? As regards the foreign ship, for her owners cannot be supposed to know or to be bound by the municipal law of this country, the case must be decided by the law maritime, by those rules of navigation which usually prevail among nations navigating the seas where the collision takes place; if the foreigner comes before the tribunals of this country the remedy and form of proceeding must be according to the *lex fori.*

I am of opinion, without going further into the erudition connected with the question, that these authorities, independently of others that might be cited, are sufficient to enable the court to decide that the law, which is applicable here and governs the liability of the defendants in the case, is the general maritime law as administered in this country, and consequently to pronounce that the demurrer must be sustained, and with costs.

June 2. The action was heard before the judge, assisted by two of the Elder Brethren of the Trinity House. After hearing evidence on behalf of the plaintiffs and the defendants, the judge pronounced that both vessels were to blame for the collision, and condemned the defendants in a moiety of the damage proceeded for.

June 23. *Clarkson*, Q.C., on behalf of the defendants, moved the judge in court that the defendants might be at liberty to amend their statement of defence by adding a counter-claim, and that a clause containing directions to that effect might be added to the order made by the court on the trial of the action as above stated. The motion is 152] made for the purpose of saving the expense *of a cross-action. It is clear that on instituting a cross-action the defendants will be entitled to a moiety of the damage they have sustained in the collision.

F. W. Raikes, for the plaintiffs, opposed the motion: No sufficient reason has been shown for the court interfering at this stage of the suit. The proper course is for the defendants to institute a cross-action.

HIS LORDSHIP refused the motion with costs.

Solicitors for plaintiffs: *Stokes, Saunders & Stokes.*
Solicitors for defendants: *Wynne & Sons.*

G. B.

[6 Probate Division, 152.]

March 24, 1881.

THE BUCKHURST (1881, S. 328).

Damage—Inevitable Accident—Costs—Infringement of Regulations for Preventing Collisions at Sea—Arts. 5, 6—The Merchant Shipping Act, 1873 (36 & 87 Vict. c. 85), s. 17.

A sailing ship in a gale drove from her anchors across a sand, and her rudder was so damaged as to render the ship unmanageable; in this condition she came into collision after sunset with a brig at anchor. At the time of the collision the ship had her anchor light exhibited and no other light. In an action of damage by the owners of the brig against the ship it was held that the collision was occasioned by inevitable accident, and that the ship in the circumstances of the case was not to be deemed in fault for not carrying side lights or the three red lights prescribed by Article 5 of the Regulations for Preventing Collisions at Sea, and that the suit ought to be dismissed without costs.

THIS was an action of damage instituted on behalf of the owners of the brig Creole against the ship Buckhurst and her freight. The action was brought to recover the damages sustained in a collision between the two vessels on the evening of the 18th of January, 1881, when the Creole at anchor in Penarth Roads, with a proper anchor light exhibited, was run into and damaged by the Buckhurst. The plaintiffs in their statement of claim alleged that the Buckhurst at the time of collision was under sail but carried no lights, and charged, *inter alia*, that those on board her had neglected to comply with Art. 6 of the Regulations for Preventing Collisions at Sea.

*The statement of defence alleged in substance as [153 follows :

1. The Buckhurst was riding to her port anchor with ninety fathoms of cable out and to her starboard anchor with sixty fathoms out with her riding light duly exhibited and burning brightly and an anchor watch set and kept. The wind at such time was blowing a gale from the E.N.E. varying, and with hurricane force accompanied by thick blinding snow and the tide was about high water.

3. About 6.30 P.M. during a heavy squall the port cable parted and shortly afterwards the starboard cable also parted. Efforts were at once made to wear ship and to get out to sea, and at about 7 P.M. the weather having become worse, and there being a very heavy sea running, the Buckhurst struck heavily on Cardiff Sands, and whilst working over the sands received injuries which caused her to make a great

deal of water and damaged her rudder, thereby rendering
her helpless and unmanageable.

4. In this helpless condition the Buckhurst, from which a
good look-out was being kept, was drifting towards Penarth
Beach, the hurricane and blinding snow still continuing,
when about 8 P.M. the Creole was observed at anchor at a
distance of about 100 yards, a little on the port bow of the
Buckhurst. The helm of the Buckhurst was put to starboard as far as its damaged condition would permit, the
mizen staysail was hauled down and main and cross-jack
yards squared in to try and pay the ship off, but notwithstanding, the Buckhurst came into collision with the Creole,
her jib-boom and headgear crossing the deck of the Creole,
and carrying away her masts.

6. The said collision was not occasioned by any neglect or
default on the part of those on board the Buckhurst, and
the said collision, so far as the Buckhurst was concerned,
was the result of an inevitable accident.

On behalf of the plaintiffs, a reply was delivered wherein
they denied that the Buckhurst was in a helpless and unmanageable condition, as alleged in the statement of defence, and further alleged that if the Buckhurst was in such
helpless and unmanageable condition, then those on board
her neglected to comply with Article 5 of the Regulations
for Preventing Collisions at Sea.

The action was heard before the judge, assisted by two of
the Elder Brethren of the Trinity House. The result of the
evidence appears from the judgment.

Butt, Q.C., and *Nelson*, for the plaintiffs: The Buckhurst infringed the Regulations for Preventing Collisions at
Sea, and must be deemed in fault for the collision under the
provisions of the 17th section of the Merchant Shipping Act,
1873. If she was not unmanageble she ought to have taken
down her anchor light and exhibited her side lights; and if
154] · she was *unmanageable it was her duty to have exhibited the three red lights required by Art. 5 to be shown
by vessels not under command. If the Buckhurst had exhibited the lights required by either of these two articles, those
on board the Creole would have had warning, and might
· have been able to take some measures which would have
had the effect of avoiding the collision. In these circumstances the court ought not to hold that the neglect of the
Buckhurst to obey the regulations could by no possibility
have contributed to the collision.

E. C. Clarkson, and *Myburgh*, for the defendants: The

collision was clearly the result of inevitable accident. The neglect of the Buckhurst to carry the lights ordinarily required for a vessel in motion could not possibly have contributed to the collision. Moreover, the special circumstances of the case were such as to render it unnecessary for the Buckhurst to exhibit either her side lights or three red lights; she had been driven across the sands where no person would expect a vessel to be navigated. Indeed to have shown either side lights under Art. 6, or three red lights under Art. 5, would have been misleading to other vessels.

Butt, Q.C., in reply.

SIR ROBERT PHILLIMORE: This is a case of collision which happened between eight and nine o'clock on the evening of the 18th of January last in the Penarth Roads. The vessels which came into contact were the brig Creole, a small vessel of 275 tons register, lying at anchor in these roads, and the Buckhurst, a vessel of 1,877 tons register, manned with a crew of thirty-five hands, and laden with a cargo of coals. The Buckhurst was at anchor in these roads with her riding light exhibited and burning brightly. According to the evidence, at about six o'clock in the evening, the port cable of the Buckhurst parted and afterwards her starboard cable, and she struck heavily on the Cardiff Sands, and whilst working over the sands received some injuries which made her unmanageable. In the opinion of the Elder Brethren it is unquestionable that no blame attaches to the Creole. The state of the weather was of the worst possible description, and they think that the accident was inevitable.

*But the Buckhurst did not carry any light other [155 than her anchor light,·and it is contended that therefore, though the accident might otherwise have been inevitable, she is to blame for the collision, notwithstanding the state of the weather and the other circumstances of the case. The rule is laid down, and cannot be altered, that where by possibility a non-compliance with any of the Regulations for Preventing Collisions at Sea might have contributed to the collision, the vessel not complying with the regulations is to blame. Now the Buckhurst was on the sands about twenty minutes up to the time of the collision; and I have asked the Elder Brethren whether during that time it was her duty to put up her side lights, and they are of opinion that it was not, and that it would have misled other vessels if she had done so. The 17th section of the Merchants Shipping Act, 1873, provides that the ship by which the regulations have been infringed shall be deemed to be in fault, unless the circumstances of the case show a departure from the regulations to have been necessary; and so far as concerns the time referred to when this vessel was on the sands, having regard to the opinion of the Elder Brethren that she ought not to have put up her side lights, and that if she had done so she might have misled the other vessel, it appears to me that the circumstances of the case did make a departure from the regulations necessary. Moreover, in our opinion, the non-carrying of the side lights or three red lights did not by any possibility contribute to the collision. The Elder Brethren are of opinion that the collision could not have been avoided in the dreadful state of the weather. I must therefore dismiss the suit.

Nelson applied that the action should be dismissed without costs: The practice of the Admiralty Court, which had been followed in this court since the Judicature Act, is that in cases where a collision is the result of inevitable accident no costs are given, unless it was clear to the court that the action ought not to have been brought: *The London* (');
The Thornley ('). In the present case the plaintiffs were
156] justified in bringing *the action, having regard to the fact that the Buckhurst had apparently infringed the Regulations for Preventing Collisions at Sea.

E. C. Clarkson, for the defendants: The plaintiffs came here to prove that the collision occurred by the default or neglect of those on board the Buckhurst. This they have failed to do, and in consequence, according to the practice of all the other Divisions of the High Court, to which the practice of this Division ought to be assimilated, they would be condemned in costs: *The Swansea* ('). Moreover, even if the practice of the Admiralty Court as to costs in cases of inevitable accident is to be followed in this case, the plaintiffs ought still to be condemned in costs, inasmuch as they ought reasonably to have known that the collision in this case was an unavoidable accident, and that the action ought never to have been brought.

Nelson, in reply, was stopped by the court.

SIR ROBERT PHILLIMORE: Having regard to the special circumstances of the case, and that the only light exhibited on board the Buckhurst was her anchor light, I do not think it can be said that the action ought not to have been brought. I think this is a case in which there ought to be no costs.

Solicitors for plaintiffs: *Lowless, Nelson & Co.*
Solicitors for defendants: *Parker & Co.*

G. B.

('} Br. & L., 82.   ('} 7 Jurist, 660.   ('} 4 P. D., 115.

[6 Probate Division, 178.]

April 9, 11, 1881.

*The Maid of Kent (1880, H. 770, fo. 80). [178

Damage—Practice—Tribunal to decide Questions of Consequential Damage.

Although it is the usual practice of the court in collision cases to refer all questions involving the amount of damages to the registrar assisted by merchants, yet, when consequential damages are claimed, it is in the discretion of the court to deal, at the hearing of the action, with the question whether such damages are recoverable.

This was an action of damage brought by the owners of the bark Kate Covert against the paddle steamship Maid of Kent.

The statement of claim alleged, *inter alia*, that on the evening of the 7th of February the bark was lying anchored in Dover Bay with a proper riding light exhibited and a proper watch kept, and that the Maid of Kent ran against and with her mainmast fouled the jib-boom of the bark, and caused the bark to drag her anchors and go upon the Mole Rocks, and thereby damage was done to the bark and she was compelled to take assistance, and great losses and expenses were incurred by the plaintiffs.

The 4th and 7th paragraphs of the statement of defence were, so far as material, in terms as follows :

4. For and by reason of this collision the Kate Covert sustained no other damage save the loss of her jib-boom and some other slight damage to her upper works. It is not true that the Maid of Kent in colliding with her caused the Kate Covert to drag her anchors, or to go on the Mole Rocks, or to receive the damage thereby alleged to have been sustained, or to take the assistance mentioned in the statement of claim.

7. The defendants say that the collision was an inevitable accident, and was not caused or contributed to by any negligence of the defendants or those on board the Maid of Kent. They further say that in any event they would be liable only for the aforesaid damage to the jib-boom and upper works.

April 9.   The action came on to be heard before the judge, assisted by two Elder Brethren of the Trinity House.

The master of the bark was called and examined as a witness on behalf of the plaintiffs, and in cross-examination was asked by the defendants' counsel the following question: Would not the Kate Covert have taken the ground where she was if there had been no collision? This question was objected to on the ground *that it was irrelevant to   [179 the issues which the court had to try, as it could only be relevant to the question of damage, which was a matter to be inquired into by the registrar and merchants and not by the court.

Butt, Q.C., and *Clarkson*, Q.C., for the plaintiffs, in support of the objection: It is clearly in accordance with the practice of the court that questions of damage should be referred to the registrar and merchants. Indeed, if the plaintiffs succeed in proving that they had sustained any damage, however small, they are entitled by the practice of this court to a reference to the registrar and merchants, and it is immaterial that the matter of damage is referred to in the pleadings before the court: *The Thuringia* ('): *The Flying Fish* ('). Moreover, relying on the practice as above stated being adhered to, the plaintiffs are not prepared with evidence as to the consequential damage sustained by the Kate Covert, and, indeed, if the present practice of going before the registrar and merchants in cases of consequential damage is not upheld, and witnesses as to matters respecting damages are examined in court, the expenses at the hearing will in all cases be greatly increased.

Webster, Q.C., and *W. G. F. Phillimore*, for the defendants, the owners of the Maid of Kent, contrà: There is no invariable rule of practice in this court requiring that damage should be referred to the registrar and merchants. Where, as in the present case, matters of nautical skill and knowledge are involved in the claim for damage, the court, having the assistance of the Trinity Masters, is the proper tribunal to entertain the question of damage: *The Mellona* (') ; *The Linda* ('). There is no ground for holding that the plaintiffs have been taken by surprise, as the question of damage is distinctly raised on the pleadings, but if necessary the court would no doubt adjourn the hearing of the case for the production of further evidence.

Butt, Q.C., in reply.

                                            Cur. adv. vult.

    April 11. Sir Robert Phillimore: In this case a 180] question *has arisen as to the practice of the court in cases of consequential damage, and the question was argued on Saturday last, when a good many cases were referred to upon the point, and the court reserved its judgment, which it will now deliver. The question which the court really has to determine is whether it is obligatory for the court in

(¹) 1 Asp. Mar. Law Cases, 283.   (³) 3 W. Rob., 7.
(²) Br. & L., 436.   (⁴) Swa., 306.

every case of this kind to send the matter to the registrar
and merchants. The general competency of the court to
hear and decide upon questions of this description is not
denied, but the point raised is whether in all cases and all
circumstances it is the practice of the court to send a matter
of consequential damage to be tried by the registrar and
merchants. This point has not been expressly decided, and
it may very well be that in some cases such a question should
be referred to the registrar and merchants : but that in other
cases it should not be. In some cases, from motives of
economy, or where questions of nautical skill are involved,
it is very desirable that the matters should be decided by
the judge of the court with the assistance of the Elder Brethren of the Trinity House. Now the cases cited for the plaintiffs I need not go into, because they do not prove more than
that in the special circumstances the questions of consequential damage were considered questions to be referred to the
registrar and merchants. But the cases referred to by the
defendants fully establish the proposition that the court has
full power to deal with questions of this description with
the assistance of the Elder Brethren of the Trinity House.
The cases of *The Mellona* (') and *The Linda* (') and many
more cases were cited, but it is not necessary to refer to them
all. In the case of *The Aline* (') the plaintiffs, whose vessel
was damaged by a collision on a voyage to St. Petersburg,
at the hearing claimed consequential damages caused, as
they alleged, by their vessel being detained for repairs in
this country beyond the Baltic season, and Dr. Lushington
said that he would require it to be satisfactorily proved
that every possible exertion had been made to get the cargo
to St. Petersburg and to come back again before the close
of the season, and not having sufficient evidence before him,
he referred the question of damage generally to the registrar
*and merchants. That was all that was decided in [181
that case. In the earlier case of *The Eolides* (') Sir John
Nicholl came to the conclusion that a claim for consequential
damage could not be sustained. In the subsequent case of
The Linda (') Dr. Lushington came to a similar conclusion.
In the last case I have mentioned, the court itself dealt with
the question whether there was on the facts before it any
claim for consequential damage which could be sustained.
In the present case the statement of claim contains the allegation that damage was done to the Kate Covert and she
was compelled to take salvage assistance, and great losses

(¹) 3 W. Rob., 7, 13.   (³) 5 Monthly Law Mag., 202.
(²) Swa., 306.   (⁴) 3 Hagg., 367.

and expenses were incurred by the plaintiffs.   The allegation
is met by the following averment in the statement of defence.
[His Lordship here read the 4th paragraph of the statement
of defence as above set out.]   And in the last paragraph of
the statement of defence the defendants say, "That the collision was an inevitable accident, and was not caused or
contributed to by any negligence of the defendants or those
on board the Maid of Kent," and they further say, "that in
any event they would be liable only for the aforesaid damage to the jib-boom and upper works," that is to say, that
they are not liable for the consequential damage in this case.
I am of opinion that it is proper that the court should entertain and decide these issues with the advantage of the
advice of the Elder Brethen of the Trinity House.   Indeed,
it was not denied that the court, assisted by the Elder
Brethen, would be a better tribunal to decide the question
of consequential damage in the present case than the registrar and merchants, as the Elder Brethren would bring to
bear on the question that nautical knowledge which they
undoubtedly possess, but which may or may not be possessed by the registrar and merchants.   I am of opinion in
the result that the court itself can and ought to go into the
questions of consequential damage in this case at the present
stage of the proceedings, and that the practice of the court
will not be interfered with by this being done, and I shall
therefore rule accordingly, and allow the question objected
to on the part of the plaintiffs to be put.

The examination of the plaintiffs' witnesses was then pro-
182]   ceeded *with, but before the close of the plaintiffs'
case a settlement of the action was arrived at, and the court,
with the consent of all parties, pronounced that the Maid of
Kent was alone to blame for the collision and assessed the
damages proceeded for at £60.

Solicitors for plaintiffs : *Wynne & Sons.*
Solicitors for defendants : *Clarkson, Greenwell & Wyles.*

G. B.

[6 Probate Division, 182.]

June 27, 1881.

THE KESTREL (1024).

Shipping Casualty Appeal—Shipping Casualty Investigations Act, 1879 (42 & 43 Vict. c. 72,) s. 2—Materials on which Appeal heard—Practice—Evidence of Experts not admissible on Questions of Nautical Skill and Knowledge—Costs.

Although the Wreck Commissioner, or other authority, holding a formal investi-·gation into a shipping casualty under the Merchant Shipping Acts, must, if he deals with the certificate of a master or certificated officer, give his decision in open court, yet he may, subsequently in his report to the Board of Trade, state reasons for his decision not mentioned by him at the time when the judgment was delivered.

In appeals under the Shipping Casualties Investigations Act, 1879, the Court of Appeal will not permit witnesses to be called to give evidence on questions of nautical knowledge and skill.

Where, on an appeal under the Shipping Casualties Investigations Act, 1879, the decision of the Wreck Commissioner, suspending the certificate of a master, was affirmed, but the Court of Appeal recommended that the Board of Trade should shorten the time for which the certificate had been suspended, the parties to the appeal were left to bear their own costs of the appeal.

[6 Probate Division, 198.]

March 9, 1881.

*THE KILLEENA (1880, B. 4456, Fo. 351; 1880, N. [193 948, Fo. 353; 1880, A. 902, Fo. 394).

Salvage—Abandonment of Derelict by Salvors—Waiver of Salvage—Remuneration—Amount of Award.

The bark N. fell in with the K., a derelict bark, in the Atlantic, and put five hands on board of her who navigated her for three days. The K. then fell in with the bark B., and the five hands on board of the K. were, at their own request, taken on board the B. The B. then sent some of her own crew on board the K., and took her in tow, and towed her until the tow-rope broke, when the vessels parted company, and the hands on board the K., with the assistance of the L., a steamship which they afterwards fell in with, brought the K. into Falmouth. In suits instituted on behalf of the master, owners, and crews of the N., the B., and the L., the court held, that the masters, owners, and crew of the N. were not entitled to salvage reward, but awarded salvage to the remaining plaintiffs.

THERE were three consolidated actions of salvage instituted, one on behalf of the owners, master, and crew of the bark Beatrice; the second on behalf of the owners, master, and crew of the Norwegian bark Nora; and the third on behalf of the owners, master, and crew of the German screw steamship Leipzig; against the owners of the bark Killeena, her cargo, and freight. Two statements of claim were delivered in the consolidated actions, one on behalf of the owners, master, and crew of the Leipzig, and the other on behalf of the owners, masters, and crews of the Beatrice and the Nora. The first five paragraphs of this latter statement of claim were, so far as material, as follows :

1. The Beatrice is of 521 tons register, and at the time of rendering the services hereinafter mentioned, was on a voyage from North Shields to Philadelphia, laden with a general cargo and manned by a crew of eleven hands.

2. At about 11 A.M. on the 15th of October, 1880, the Beatrice was in about latitude 48° 6′ N. and longitude 12° 16′ W. The wind at such time was about east, blowing a moderate breeze, and the weather was fine.

3. At such time, a vessel, which proved to be the bark Killeena, the vessel proceeded against in this action, was seen from the Beatrice at the distance of about four miles, with her ensign flying at her gaff, with union down.

4. The Beatrice thereupon bore down upon her and was steered to pass close to the Killeena, and on so passing the vessel was hailed, and asked if she wanted assistance, and the reply was, " We want to be taken off."

5. The Beatrice was immediately hove-to, and her boat, in charge of Martin Cunningham her boatswain, and manned 194] by the plaintiff Damble, A.B., and two *other seamen of the Beatrice, was lowered and sent alongside the Killeena. When the boat of the Beatrice arrived alongside the Killeena, the plaintiffs Cunningham and Damble, boarded her, and found five Norwegians on board her. The Norwegians were part of the crew of a Norwegian bark called the Nòra, a vessel of 783 tons register. On the 12th of the said month of October, the Nora, which was proceeding from Quebec to Barrow, with a cargo of deals and had a crew of sixteen hands, all told, had fallen in with the Killeena, which had then been abandoned by her master and crew, and had put the said five of her men on board the Killeena. The said five men had rigged up a jury-mast and had got sail on the Killeena, and had used their best endeavors to save the Killeena, and had suffered considerable hardships whilst so doing. The Nora, after keeping in company with the Killeena for some hours, had proceeded on her voyage. The Norwegians requested to be taken off the Killeena, and refused to remain on board her, and they and their effects were transferred to the Beatrice by her boat. The plaintiffs Cunningham and Damble remained on board the Killeena. The Nora, when, as aforesaid, her second mate, carpenter, and three others of her crew were put on board the Killeena, was in a damaged condition and exposed to great peril in

consequence of the wind and sea. Her rudder had been broken, and was only roughly repaired, and she was therefore steering badly. The Nora also had such a serious list that the men who went on board the Killeena were able to step down from the Nora's bulwarks into their boat. By thus parting with five hands out of an available crew of sixteen, the safety of the Nora in damaged condition was seriously threatened, and her master took upon himself a heavy responsibility in so parting with his hands, and the labor of such of the crew of the Nora as remained on board their vessel was very materially increased, and they suffered great hardship by reason thereof. The master of the Nora gave to those men who boarded the Killeena every information as to their position and also provided them with a sextant and a pair of side lights, only reserving for himself one set of side lights, the glass of one of these being broken and the efficacy of the light greatly impaired thereby. The carpenter was also allowed to take with him his tools, and by parting with the carpenter the Nora in her disabled condition, was liable to be subjected to still greater peril. Those of the Nora's crew who went on board the Killeena did their utmost to get the vessel under command, and by assuming charge of her removed a great danger to the general navigation.

The statement of claim delivered on behalf of the owners, masters, and crews of the Beatrice and the Nora, further alleged that after two more of the crew of the Beatrice had gone on board the Killeena to assist the boatswain and the able seamen from the Beatrice already on board her, the Beatrice succeeded in taking the Killeena in tow and towed in the direction of Queenstown until the evening of the 19th of October, when the tow-rope parted ; that the two vessels remained in company until the 27th of October, and that from that date the four hands on board the Killeena were left to their own resources and worked the vessel successfully *and without assistance until the 9th of November, [195 when the Leipzig fell in with her and took her in tow.

The statement of claim delivered on behalf of the owners, master, and crew of the Leipzig alleged, *inter alia*, that the Leipzig, belonging to the North German Lloyd's, on a voyage from Baltimore to Bremen, with a crew of sixty-seven hands, twenty-four passengers, the mails, and a valuable cargo, fell in with the Killeena in latitude 49° 23′ N. and longitude 14° 15′ W., and at the request of those in charge of her took her in tow and towed her to the entrance of Fal-

mouth harbor, the two vessels arriving off that port on the
evening of the 12th of November, and that during the
service the hawsers and boats of the Leipzig were damaged
to the extent of £70, and the owners of the Leipzig incurred, by reason of the service and the detention of the Leipzig at Falmouth, certain other expenses amounting to
about £200.

The defendants, the owners of the Killeena, and the owners of her cargo, delivered one statement of defence in the
consolidated actions. The first six paragraphs of this statement of defence contained the following allegations :

1. The Killeena, a bark of 795 tons register, and built of
iron, left New York on the 26th of August, 1880, bound for
Liverpool, laden with a cargo of 1,160 tons of Indian corn
and 389 bales of cotton, and manned by a crew of eighteen
hands, all told.

2. On the 6th of October, whilst the Killeena was on the
said voyage, she encountered a heavy gale of wind, and took
so heavy a list to port, that the master caused the mainmast, and subsequently the foremast, to be cut away in
order, if possible, to right the ship, the mizen topmast was
also carried away. Although the Killeena righted somewhat when relieved of her masts, and notwithstanding that
the weather having moderated, steps were taken by the master and crew to trim the cargo, the ship still continued to
have a heavy list to port.

3. Finding that the ship was unmanageable, and could
not be navigated into port without steam assistance, which
was not forthcoming, and fearing the effect of another gale,
which was threatening, the master and crew on the 9th of
October abandoned the bark. The Killeena at the time of
the abandonment was in latitude 48° 10′ N. and longitude
15° 54′ W. The hull of the Killeena was not damaged below the deck, and she was making no water except some
small quantities which got down from slight damage to the
mast holes, which the master had repaired as far as was
possible.

4. On the 12th of October the Killeena was sighted by the
Norwegian ship Nora, who put a crew of five hands on board
196]   the Killeena, and the two vessels *parted company.
The defendants admit that the men from the Nora rigged a
small jury-mast and made attempts to get sail on the ship
to get her under command, which were unsuccessful.

5. On the 15th of October the said attempted salvors from
the Nora finding that their efforts to salve the Killeena and

her cargo were perfectly futile, hoisted an ensign, union
down, to attract passing vessels, in order that they might
be taken off the Killeena and abandon any further attempt
to bring her into safety.

6. The bark Beatrice bore down upon the Killeena in answer to the said signals, and at their request took off the
said Norwegian salvage crew, who thereupon abandoned
their attempts to salve the said bark and her cargo.

The consolidated actions were heard before the judge, assisted by two of the Elder Brethren of the Trinity House.
Witnesses on behalf of the plaintiffs were examined orally
in court.   The result of their evidence, so far as is material,
is stated in the judgment.   No witnesses were called for the
defendants, but it was admitted that the total value of the
property salved amounted to £12,663.

Webster, Q.C., and *W. G. F. Phillimore*, for the owners,
master, and crew of the Leipzig.

E. C. Clarkson, and *McLeod*, for the owners, master, and
crew of the Beatrice.

J. P. Aspinall, for the owners, master, and crew of the
Nora: The owners, master, and crew of the Nora are entitled to participate as salvors in whatever salvage award
the court may make in this case.   The master of the Nora
incurred great responsibility in sending so many of his crew
on board the Killeena, and the services of the men sent on
board in navigating the Killeena until she fell in with the
Beatrice, materially contributed to the ultimate preservation
of the vessel and her cargo: *The Undaunted* (').

[Sir Robert Phillimore: Assume that the services of
the men from the Nora contributed to some extent to the
saving of the Killeena, the question still remains whether,
having quitted the Killeena *sine animo revertendi*, they are
not to be considered in the circumstances as having abandoned any rights to salvage reward that they might otherwise have successfully asserted here.]

Cohen, Q.C., and *Myburgh*, for the defendants: The
action *brought by the owners, master, and crew of   [197
the Nora ought to be dismissed with costs.   The men put
on board the Killeena from the Nora not only deserted the
Killeena *sine animo revertendi*, thus voluntarily giving up
all their interest in her, together with any rights to salvage
reward to which they might otherwise have become entitled,
but at the time they abandoned the vessel they did not even
know that any attempt to salve her would be made on be-

(') Lush., 90.

half of the Beatrice. The case therefore must be treated
exactly as if the Killeena had been still a derelict at the time
when the men from the Beatrice boarded her. [They referred to *The Yonge Bastiaan* (¹).]

SIR ROBERT PHILLIMORE: This is a case of salvage service rendered to a vessel which was abandoned by her master and crew. The Killeena was a bark of 795 tons, and left
New York on the 26th of August last year, bound to Liverpool with a cargo of Indian corn and cotton. On the 6th of
October she encountered a heavy gale, and took so heavy a
list to port that her master caused the mainmast and the
foremast to be cut away, and finding that she became unmanageable and could not be navigated, her master and
those on board left her, and on the 9th of October she was
abandoned. She drifted about in the Atlantic Ocean until
the 12th of that month, when she was sighted by a Norwegian
ship called the Nora, from which a crew of five hands was
put on board her. On the 15th of October the men who
went on board from the Nora became frightened, and determined to abandon the vessel, and they hoisted an ensign,
union down, and that attracted the attention of those on
board the Beatrice. Here a most important question arises,
whether the owners, master, and crew of the Nora are entitled to anything for their services. Now the principles of
law applicable to the question are laid down in the case of
of *The Undaunted* (²), where is to be found the following
passage:

> Salvors who volunteer, go out at their own risk for the chance of earning re-
> ward, and if they labor unsuccessfully, are entitled to nothing. The effectual
> 198] *performance of salvage service is that which gives them a title to sal-
> vage remuneration. But if men are engaged by a ship in distress, whether gen-
> erally or particularly, they are to be paid according to their efforts made, even
> though the labor and service may not prove beneficial to the vessel.

Now, there is no doubt that where a set of salvors have
done some acts which tend to the ultimate salvage of a vessel they are usually entitled to some remuneration, but there
is a circumstance in this case most material to consider.
The four men and the boy who were put on board from the
Nora deliberately, according to the evidence, when the Beatrice had answered their signal, abandoned and deserted the
Killeena. It appears to me, therefore, that the Killeena was
again a derelict vessel. As the men on board her deliberately determined to leave her, four men were found with
better heart and courage to take the places of these men, and
to do what was necessary for the preservation of the Kil-

(¹) 5 C. Rob., 323.   (²) Lush., 90.

leena. It seems to me that the words of Lord Stowell, in *The Yonge Bastiaan*('), are material to this case. That was a case of salvage, and Lord Stowell in delivering judgment said :

> It appears that the vessel was stuck fast upon a rock, with her bottom beaten in and her rudder lost, when the first salvors went to her assistance, in a very heavy sea, and succeeded in warping her off. She sank afterwards it was true ; but it is not on that account to be said that the first salvors had lost her again, or that they had abandoned their interest in her. They did not stay by the vessel ; but it cannot be supposed that having risked so much for her recovery they meant to desert her, whilst others were employed in their sight in weighing her up, and in saving the cargo.

Now that was the reverse of this case. Here the men from the Nora did not stay by the vessel, and they had not the slightest intention of assisting her. It appears to me that it would be contrary to the principles upon which salvage remuneration is awarded, to allow the Nora's people to appear as salvors in this case, inasmuch as they were, according to the evidence, turning their backs and running away from the danger to which the vessel was exposed. The men from on board the Beatrice had as much reason to be alarmed, but they persevered, and their courage deserves to be rewarded. I am clearly of opinion that the owners, master, and crew of the Nora, are not entitled to claim salvage *remuneration in this case. There are two other [199 vessels—the Beatrice and the Leipzig—whose services have to be considered. The Beatrice towed the Killeena from the 15th to the 19th of October, and then stood by her until the 26th of October, but lost sight of her upon the 27th of October. The Leipzig on the 9th of November spoke the Killeena and offered her services, which were accepted, and after a towage of two days and six hours the Killeena was brought safely into harbor, and thereby very valuable assistance was rendered. The first thing the court has to consider is, what is the total value out of which these services are to be awarded to the salvors. The value of the property salved is £12,663, and out of that I shall make a total award of £4,200. The Beatrice ran great risk in order to save this vessel, and deviated from her course, being thus delayed in the performance of her voyage. Out of this award I shall apportion to the owners, master, and crew of the Leipzig £1,200, and the remaining £3,000 to the Beatrice, to be distributed as follows : £300 to the master of the Beatrice, £1,200 among the four men placed on board the Killeena, of whom the plaintiff Cunningham is to have a

(') 5 C. Rob., 324.

double share, £200 to the rest of the crew of the Beatrice, and £1,300 to the owners of the Beatrice.

Solicitors for owners, master, and crew of the Leipzig: *Clarkson & Co.*

Solicitors for remaining plaintiffs: *Stokes, Saunders & Stokes.*

Solicitors for defendants: *Cooper & Co.*

G. B.

[6 Probate Division, 200.]

July 19, 1881.

200] *THE JOHN McINTYRE (1881, J. No. 917, fo. 238).

Limitation of Liability—Merchant Shipping Act, 1862 (25 & 26 Vict. c. 63), *s.* 54—*Limit of Liability dependent upon Tonnage of Ship at time of Collision.*

In a suit of limitation of liability in respect of damage arising from a collision, the shipowners claimed deductions on account of crew space which appeared on the register of their vessel at the time of their application for a decree :

Held, that they were not entitled to the benefit of any deductions not appearing on the register in force at the time of the collision.

THIS was an action of limitation of liability instituted on the 3d of June, 1881, on behalf of the owners of the British steamship John McIntyre, for the purpose of limiting their liability in respect of the damage arising out of a collision which occurred without the actual fault or privity of the plaintiffs, but owing to the negligence of their servants, between the John McIntyre and the steamship John Ormston, on the 11th of February, 1881.

No loss of life or personal injury was caused by the collision.

The plaintiffs, in their statement of claim, after alleging that the gross tonnage of the John McIntyre, without deduction on account of engine room, was 946.61 tons, claimed, *inter alia*, a declaration that they were not answerable in respect of loss or damage caused by the John McIntyre, to an aggregate amount exceeding £8 for each ton of the gross tonnage of the John McIntyre, without deduction on account of engine room.

The owners of the John Ormston, and the owners of her cargo, having appeared in the action as defendants, required proof of the gross tonnage of the John McIntyre.

In support of the allegations in the statement of claim, the solicitors for the plaintiffs brought in an affidavit, to which there was annexed as an exhibit, a copy of the register of the John McIntyre.

From such copy register it appeared that the John McIntyre had been built in 1863, and had been first registered on
the 15th of September in that year; that at that time the
details of her tonnage were:—Tonnage under tonnage deck
925.11, break *59.64, deductions allowed for propel- [201
ling power 187.14, registered tonnage 797.61 ; that in accordance with a certificate of survey dated 14th of July, 1875,
her gross tonnage had been altered to 984.75, and her registered tonnage (in consequence of an increased allowance in
respect of space for propelling. power) to 315.12. It further
appeared from such copy register that on an allowance for
crew space per Board of Trade survey dated the 27th of
June, 1881, the tonnage of the John McIntyre had been
again altered, and that the details of her tonnage as so
altered were as follows:

		No. of tons
Gross tonnage :		
Under tonnage deck		925.11
Closed in space above the tonnage deck (if any)		
Round house		6.12
Break		59.64
Gross tonnage		990.87
Deductions :		
On account of space for propelling power	317.18	
On account of spaces occupied by seamen. Berthing of officers and crew on deck house and below .	44.26	
Total deduction . . .		361.34
Registered tonnage . . .		629.53

It appeared that no structural alterations had been made
in the ship since the date of the collision, although some
additional provisions had been made for the ventilation of
the crew space.

July 19.   The action was heard before the judge in court.
G. Bruce, for the plaintiffs :   The tonnage which regulates
the liability of the shipowner in an action for limitation of
liability, is the tonnage of the ship according to the register
in force at the date of the application for the decree.   If the
tonnage of the ship had been increased between the date of
the collision and the *present time, can it be said that [202
the owners would not have been liable to the extent of the
increased tonnage? The same principle must be applied

whether the tonnage be increased or diminished, and in the present case there is nothing unreasonable in the contention of the plaintiffs, because no structural alteration has taken place in the ship, and the right to claim the deduction on account of crew space depended simply upon the observance of formal requirements which in no way affected the value of the ship.

W. G. F. Phillimore, for the defendants : If the plaintiffs are right and the "tonnage" referred to in the 54th section of the Merchant Shipping Act, 1862, is the "tonnage" at the date of the application for the order limiting the plaintiffs' liability, the result would be that in cases like the present it would be in the power of a plaintiff by delaying to proceed with his action to diminish the amount of damages recoverable by the defendants. The right of the defendants to recover the damage attached at the time of the collision, and it is from the date of the collision that interest on the sum recovered is due : *The Northumbria* ('). It must follow that the tonnage, by calculation from which the amount recoverable is to be ascertained,. is the tonnage of the wrong-doing vessel at the time of the collision, and if so, the only proper evidence of what that tonnage was is, in the case of a British registered ship, the certificate of registry under which she was sailing when the collision occurred.

G. Bruce, in reply.

SIR ROBERT PHILLIMORE: The only question the court has to decide is whether the tonnage of the John McIntyre at the time of the collision or her tonnage at any subsequent date, is to be taken as affording the basis for computing the limit of the liability of her owners in this action. Now the plaintiffs were wrongdoers from the moment of the collision, and their liability must depend on the state of things then existing. I think that the tonnage on which the limit of the plaintiffs' liability is to be calculated is the "tonnage," that is the gross tonnage without deduction of engine room, 203] taken from the certificate of registry *which states what was the registered tonnage of the John McIntyre at the time when the collision occurred.

Solicitors for plaintiffs : *Gellatly, Son & Co.*
Solicitors for defendants : *Cooper & Co.*

(') Law Rep., 3 A. & E., 6.

G. B.

[6 Probate Division, 203.]

April 27, 1881.

In the Goods of PERCY ALFRED ECCLES ASTON.

Will—Gift of Residue—"Money, Stocks, Funds, or other Securities."

A gift of " such money, stocks, funds, or other securities, not hereafter specially devised, as I may die possessed of," does not constitute a gift of residue.

PERCY ALFRED ECCLES ASTON, late of No. 3 Dean's Yard, Westminster, stock jobber, deceased, died on the 23d of February, 1881.

By his will, dated the 17th day of January, 1880, he appointed executors, but named no residuary legatee unless in the following words, viz.:

"Also to my father, Joseph Keech Aston, a life interest, or until he marry again, of one-third of such money, stocks, funds, or other securities, not hereafter specially devised, as I may die possessed of, such portion of my capital to be invested .... The other two-thirds of my capital, not otherwise hereafter specially devised, I give to such of my brothers and sisters as shall attain twenty-one years .... and on the death of my father, or his second marriage, the one-third .... and also my share of the money of my late mother which then comes to me to be divided amongst my brothers and sisters."

The executors renounced probate of the will, and

E. Thurston Holland asked that a grant of letters of administration with the will annexed might be made to the father as next of kin.

The words are not sufficient to constitute a gift of residue : Jarman on Wills (3d ed.), 730 note ; *Lowe* v. *Thomas* (¹) ; *Williams* v. *Williams* (²) ; *Byrom* v. *Brandreth* (³) ; *Hopkins* v. *Abbott* (⁴).

*THE PRESIDENT :   The grant may be made to the [204 next of kin with a memorandum (which I am informed is according to the usual practice) that the grant is so made as there is no clear disposition of the residue.

Solicitors : *Withall & Compton.*

(¹) 5 D. M. & G., 315.   (³) Law Rep., 16 Eq., 475 ; 6 Eng. R., 818.
(²) 8 Ch. D., 789 ; 25 Eng. R., 686.   (⁴) Law Rep., 19 Eq., 222 ; 11 Eng. R., 807.

R. A. P.

[6 Probate Division, 204.]

May 3, 1881.

In the Goods of J. HATTON.

Will—Mistake—Duplicate—Execution.

An intended will was written in duplicate, one copy of which was signed only by the deceased and the other only by the attesting witnesses:
Held, that neither paper was entitled to probate.

JOHN HATTON, late of Ibstock, in the county of Leicester, tailor, died on the 29th of November, 1876.

On the 24th of February, 1876, the deceased called in two neighbors, viz., William Evitt and John William Hopkins, in order that he might make his will in their . presence. William Evitt, upon the deceased's directions, wrote out a short will, leaving all the property to the deceased's wife and appointing her sole executrix. After this had been done, J. William Hopkins, thinking the language of the will might be improved, wrote out another will in other words, but to the same effect. The deceased then signed the first paper, but the witnesses signed the second paper.

Searle moved the court for probate of both papers : *In the Goods of Braddock* (¹).

THE PRESIDENT : A will may be composed of numerous papers, which together make but one instrument ; but these are separate and independent documents. I am always desirous of correcting error if possible so as to carry out the intentions of a testator, but in this case the names of the testator and the witnesses are on separate papers, and the requirements of the law have not been fulfilled. I must therefore refuse probate.

Solicitors : *F. J. & G. J. Braikenridge.*

(¹) Law Rep., 1 P. D., 438 ; 18 Eng. R., 463.

R. A. P.

Vol. VI.]   PROBATE DIVISION.   591

In the Goods of Stedham.   In the Goods of Dyke.   1881

[6 Probate Division, 205.]

May 10, 1881.

*In the Goods of STEDHAM.   [205
In the Goods of DYKE.

Will—Mistake—Revival—Revocation.

A testator made a will, and afterwards another, which by implication revoked the former will. Subsequently, by the terms of a duly executed codicil, he by mistake, referred to the former instead of the later will:

Held, that the codicil by its language, revived the former will, and that as the later will was not revoked by the codicil all three documents must be admitted to probate.

JOHN STEDHAM, late of Axminster, in the county of Devon, builder, deceased, died on the 23d day of January, 1881.

The deceased had made two wills, one dated the 21st day of May, 1877, and the other the 13th of February, 1878. Each will was made by the same solicitor, who kept them in his safe. On the 24th day of January, 1880, the solicitor prepared a codicil for the deceased, which by mistake commenced with the words "This is a codicil to my will, which bears date the 21st day of May, 1877," thereby referring to the former instead of the later will. The mistake was not noticed at the time, and the codicil was duly executed and attested.

April 27. · *Bayford*, for the executors, asked for probate of the will of the 13th of February, 1878, and codicil: *In the Goods of Steele*(¹), *In the Goods of Ince*(²).

Cur. adv. vult.

May 10. THE PRESIDENT: In this case the testator made a will on the 21st of May, 1877, by which, after making certain specific gifts to each of his six children, he directed that the residue of his real and personal estate should be sold and divided equally amongst his six children. By a subsequent will of the 13th of February, 1878, he directed that all his property, real and personal, should be disposed of and divided equally amongst his six children, but with a direction that as to two of them certain arrears of rent that had accrued to him from them should be *deducted [206 from their shares. In January, 1880, he proposed to make a codicil, the effect of which was to deprive those two children who were in arrear of rent, as appeared from the previous will, of all share in his property, and to direct that

(¹) Law Rep., 1 P. & D., 575.   (²) 2 P. D., 111; 20 Eng. R., 633.

the whole should be divided into four shares instead of six. The solicitor who was instructed to prepare this codicil, instead of making a codicil to the will of 1878, made a codicil to the will of the 21st of May, 1877, and I was asked to treat it as a mere mistake as to the date and to allow probate of the codicil together with the last will of February, 1878. I am unable to do so, for this reason ; that it was not a mere mistake as to the date of the will to which it was intended to append the codicil, but the mind of the solicitor, which must be treated as that of the testator, was actually applied to the provisions of the will of 1877, and he employed the terms and language of that will of 1877 so as to mould it into an expression of what the testator's intention and wishes were at the time of the making of the codicil, and if I were to allow probate of the codicil together with the will of 1878, it would be introducing nonsense into the two instruments, for it would make the codicil refer to provisions in a will, which, when the will is looked at, would not be found in it.

It is always extremely difficult to apply any principles of law to a gross blunder, but having given the case the best consideration I can, I have come to this conclusion, that the codicil thus referring to the will of 1877, so far confirms, and brings that will into existence, that it must form part of the probate in order that the codicil may have an interpretation put upon it; and that as the will of 1878 does contain also the most important of the testamentary dispositions which the testator has made and which have never been revoked, the will of 1878 must also be admitted to probate.

The three documents, therefore, the will of 1877, and the will of 1878, and the codicil, must all in their order of date be admitted to probate, and the general intent to be collected from the three instruments will then become the subject of consideration, if necessary, for a court of construction ; but in order to prevent litigation, I may say that the interpretation I should put upon these three instruments is that the 207] two children have been entirely *excluded from the testamentary dispositions of the testator, and the whole of the property is to be divided amongst the other four children (').

Solicitor : *Edward F. Sealy.*

(') See case on next page.

R. A. P.

In the Goods of DYKE.

FRANCIS DYKE, late of Ballingham, in the county of Hereford, farmer, deceased, died on the 30th day of June, 1880.

He had made a will dated the 29th day of October, 1878, which he revoked by a will dated the 9th day of November, 1878.

By the will of the 29th of October, 1878, he gave (amongst other bequests) the interest of £300 to his daughter Elizabeth Cooke for life, and after her death amongst her children, and he also gave her £100 absolutely, and appointed William Davies and Edwin Corfield, executors.

By the will of the 9th of November, 1878, he gave (amongst other bequests) after the death of his wife, £400 in trust for the children of his daughter Elizabeth Cooke, and appointed the same executors, and revoked all previous wills.

The first will was, about nine months before his death, given by the deceased to Richard Owens, a neighbor, to take care of. The second remained in the custody of the solicitor who prepared it.

On the 9th day of June, 1880, the deceased, being desirous of making some alteration in his will, sent his son to Richard Owens for the first will, and a Mr. Henry Cooke, from instructions given to him verbally by the deceased, drew a codicil to the first will, which was produced to him for the purpose, and the codicil was then executed.

In the codicil, which professed in its terms to be a codicil to the first will and referred to it by its date, the legacies of £100 and of the interest of £300 to his daughter Elizabeth Cooke were recited and revoked, and in lieu thereof, the deceased gave her children £100. He also revoked the appointment of Edwin Corfield as executor, and instead appointed his son executor *jointly with William [208 Davies, and in all other respects confirmed his said will. No mention either before or after the execution of the codicil was made of the second will.

All the parties who were *sui juris* and the parents of the minors had notice of the motion.

Bayford, for the executors, applied for probate of one or other of the wills together with the codicil.

THE PRESIDENT: Where a simple mistake has been made as to the date of an instrument, the mistake can be set right: but in a case like this where the mind of the draftsman, whether the testator himself, or some one employed by him, has been really applied to the words of a particular instrument, it is impossible for me to say that it was by mistake that that instrument was referred to instead of another.   It is plain that that was the actual instrument which the then draftsman had in his mind, and it is not possible to avoid the conclusion that the codicil which purports to be a codicil to the will of the 29th of October, 1878, and which, after making certain alterations, confirms that will in all respects does revive that will.   But has it by implication revoked the intermediate instrument of the 9th of November, 1878?   It does not do so in terms, or except where it deals with the same subject-matter.   The result, therefore, seems to be that in consequence of the unfortunate error which has been fallen into, I must grant probate of all three instruments, and leave it to a court of construction to interpret them together.

Solicitors : *Jones & Starling*.

R. A. P.

[6 Probate Division, 209.]

May 24, 1881.

209]   *In the Goods of* ELIZABETH TOMLINSON.

Married Woman— Will of Realty—Appointment of Executors—Probate—Jurisdiction—Judicature Acts.

A will of a married woman made during coverture, under a power and disposing of real property only, is not entitled to probate, though there is an appointment of executors.

The Judicature Acts do not alter the jurisdiction of the Court of Probate in non-contentious matters.

ELIZABETH TOMLINSON, wife of Edward Tomlinson, died on the 14th day of December, 1872.

By an ante-nuptial settlement, dated the 17th of September, 1850, certain real estate was conveyed to trustees upon trust to pay the annual proceeds to the deceased for life, and if there should be no child of the marriage, then upon such trusts as she should by her last will or codicil appoint. The deceased during the lifetime of her husband, made her will, dated the 13th day of May, 1868, and a codicil, dated the 20th day of July, 1871, and thereby appointed executors and directed the trustees to sell the real estate and stand possessed of the proceeds in trust for her husband for life, and after his death to pay certain legacies and divide the residue.

There were no children of the marriage, and Edward Tomlinson, the husband, died on the 21st day of November, 1880.

Asheton Cross, for the executors, moved for probate of the will.

Cur. adv. vult.

THE PRESIDENT, after stating the facts, said: It was argued before me that as this will appointed executors it was entitled to probate in any case; and it was further argued that as the will by implication directed the sale of the real estate, it was therefore to be treated as personalty. I expressed an 'opinion at the time, and still think that it might perhaps be convenient if all instruments purporting to be testamentary should be admitted to probate, but I am not entitled upon any ground of convenience to assume a jurisdiction which does not belong to me, and I am of opinion that I have no jurisdiction to admit this instrument to probate.

*Where the will is of a man or a feme sole, the ap- [210 pointment of an executor has been held sufficient to entitle the will to proof; but where it is the case of a married woman executing a power by will, different considerations arise. Though it is in the form of a will as required by the instrument giving the power, it is in fact a conveyance by means of the appointment exercised, and although an executor is appointed the executor takes nothing in his character of personal representative. It was upon that ground that Sir Cresswell Cresswell, in an exactly similar case—*O'Dwyer* v. *Geare* (')—refused to admit to probate the will of a married woman in execution of a power which related only to real estate, and the same question was before Lord Penzance in the case of the *Goods of Jane Barden* ('). It was suggested that a subsequent decision of Lord Penzance in the case of the *Goods of Elizabeth Jordan* ('), was inconsistent with his previous decision; but that was not the appointment of a married woman, but the case of a feme sole making her will, in which case 'of course the rule applicable to wills in general would be put in force, namely, that the appointment of an executor *prima facie* entitles a will to be admitted to proof. The case of the *Goods of Tharp* (') was also referred to, but that was a case of personalty, and therefore the considerations are totally different.

It was also urged that some difference might arise in the practice of the court since the Judicature Act, which undoubtedly gives larger powers, but it is to be observed that the Judicature Act has no effect whatever upon the non-con-

(') 1 Sw. & Tr., 465.   (') Law Rep., 1 P. & D., 555.
(') Law Rep., 1 P. & D., 325.   (') 3 P. D., 76; *ante*, 51.

tentious branch of the jurisdiction of this court, and no question of the enlargement of the jurisdiction existing in the
court can arise in the non-contentious business.   It can only
be when a suit has been instituted that any such question
can arise.   I must, therefore, reject the application.

Solicitor: *Richard White.*

[6 Probate Division, 211.]

August 3, 1881.

211]   *In the Goods of the* BARONESS VON BUSECK.

*Will—Foreigner—English Form—Execution—24 & 25 Vict. c. 114—
Naturalization Act*, 1870.

A will of a foreigner executed abroad according to the formalities required by the
English law is invalid, notwithstanding the provisions of 24 & 25 Vict. c. 114, and
the Naturalization Act, 1870.

THE Baroness Caroline Von Buseck Von Altenbuseck,
late of Homburg in Germany, widow, died having executed
(amongst others) a will bearing date the 5th of September,
1876, and two codicils.   The will was executed in accordance
with the English law, and the codicils according to German
law, and all three documents were executed in Germany.
The deceased was born in England of English parents, but
by her marriage had become German.

July 26. *Jeune*, for the executors, asked for probate of
the will and codicils: The will though executed in Germany
according to the English form, is valid either under the
provisions of 24 & 25 Vict. c. 114 ('), as the will of a natural
born British subject, for the deceased was by birth an English woman, and has made the will according to the law of
her domicile of origin, or under the 2d section of the Naturalization Act, 1870 ('), which together with 24 & 25 Vict. c. 114,
gives an alien the power to dispose of property in the same
manner as a British subject.   The codicils are valid as having been executed according to the law of the domicile of the
deceased.   *Cur. adv. vult.*

Aug. 3. THE PRESIDENT, after ·stating the facts, said:
The question turns upon two enactments; the first is that
commonly known as Lord Kingsdown's Act, 24 & 25 Vict.
c. 114, and I should observe its title is "An act to amend
the law with respect to wills of personal estate made by

(') The material sections are set forth   (') This section is set forth in the judg-
in the judgment.   ment.

British subjects," the first *section of which enacts [212 that "every will and other testamentary instrument made out of the United Kingdom by a British subject (whatever may be the domicile of such person at the time of making the same or at the time of his or her death), shall as regards personal estate be held to be well executed for the purpose of being admitted in England and Ireland to probate, and in Scotland to confirmation, if the same be made according to the forms required either by the law of the place where the same was made, or by the law of the place where such person was domiciled when the same was made, or by the laws then in force in that part of Her Majesty's dominions, where he had his domicile of origin."

It can, I think, scarcely be contended, that this act is applicable to the case, because it is limited in the most careful manner to the wills of British subjects, and whatever question may arise in the case of a man, as to whether or not he has changed his nationality, there is no such question in the case of a woman who marries a foreigner; she thereby puts off her own original nationality, and takes that of her husband, and from thenceforth ceases to be in every sense of the word a British subject. But it was contended that the case is within this enactment by virtue of a statute which was passed as I conceive for totally different objects, the Naturalization Act, 1870, by the second section of which it is enacted that, "Real and personal property of every description may be taken, acquired, held and disposed of by an alien in the same manner in all respects as by a natural born British subject, and a title to real and personal property of every description may be derived through, from, or in succession to an alien, in the same manner in all respects as through, from, or in succession to a natural born British subject."

It was contended that although this lady was an alien, she had the same right as a natural born British subject would have had, namely, to make a will according to the forms in force in that part of Her Majesty's dominions, where she had her domicile of origin. But such an interpretation must, I think, be rejected, unless it were made quite plain that the English Legislature intended, with reference to personal property, that an alien should be able to make a will, in a form which is not in conformity with *the law of his own country. Of course an English [213 court might be compelled by plain language to give such a construction to an enactment, but it is not to be presumed that anything, which is so contrary to the comity of nations, has been intended by the English Legislature, and therefore, I reject that as not being the meaning of this section.

On the other hand there is a very plain and intelligible meaning to be given to this act, viz., that while it gives to aliens the same power to take, acquire, hold, and dispose of all real and personal property, in the same manner in all respects, as natural born British subjects, it does not deal with the question of what is to be the form of the will; which must depend upon other considerations. It leaves to be determined in each particular case, what is the form in which according to the law of the alien's country the testamentary disposition shall be carried out, and it gives an alien power to dispose in England of personalty by will, subject to the laws of his own country as to the form in which he shall make that will. This appears to me to be the plain and intelligible construction to be put upon this section, and I must therefore reject the application.

Solicitors : *Paterson, Snow & Bloxam.*

R. A. P.

[6 Probate Division, 213.]

May 24, 1881.

[IN THE FULL COURT.]

JARDINE V. JARDINE.

Divorce—Permanent Maintenance— Weekly or Monthly Payments— Variation— 29 Vict. c. 32.

The provisions of 29 Vict. c. 32, do not apply exclusively to the case of a poor man, and the court may order sums of considerable amount to be paid weekly or monthly as permanent maintenance, and may from time to time modify the order.

THIS was an appeal from an order made by the President for permanent maintenance, after a decree for dissolution of marriage, by reason of the adultery and cruelty of the husband.

214] *Mr. Jardine was a diamond and jewel merchant and broker, and it appeared from the report of the registrar that he derived from other sources an income of about £422 a year. As to his business the report stated that though very large profits had been made in former years—in one year as much as £18,000—there had been no profits for the last few years, and Mr. Jardine's capital now amounted to about £60,000, subject to realization, which it was estimated would produce between £20,000 and £30,000. The report therefore submitted that the case should be dealt with as if Mr. Jardine had an income of £1,600 or £1,700 a year, and

that £450 a year, payable quarterly, should be allowed for
the maintenance and education of the four youngest children
of the marriage, and £400 a year pa a le quarterly for the
maintenance of Mrs. Jardine. His Lordship by his order
increased the amount payable to Mrs. Jardine to £500 a
year, and in other respects confirmed the report. Mr. Jardine appealed against the order, so far as regarded the annuity to Mrs. Jardine, and asked that it should be reduced
to £250 a year.

Dr. Deane, Q.C., and *Dr. Tristram*, for the appellant:
The amount is excessive, inasmuch as the court has no
power to diminish or alter it, for the order is made under
the 32d section of 20 & 21 Vict. c. 85, and can only be made
under that section, as the 1st section of 29 Vict. c. 32 (¹) is
not applicable to the present case.

Inderwick, Q.C., and *Pritchard*, for the re-   [215
spondent.

LORD COLERIDGE, C.J.: In this case it is clear that if Sir
James Hannen had been asked in the first instance to act
under the second act of Parliament instead of under the
first, he would have done so, and made this order an order
for monthly payments. For myself it seems that where the
marriage has been dissolved, it is difficult to make under the
first act an order that could be variable from time to time,
and it was probably for that reason, and for the very purpose of providing for cases in which it was manifestly just
and necessary to vary the order according to the altered
circumstances of the husband, that the second act was
passed. It may be, that it was passed only for a poor man ;

(¹) The following are the material parts of the sections referred to:
"The court may . . . order that the husband shall to the satisfaction of the court secure to the wife such gross sum of money or such annual sum of money for any term not exceeding her own life as having regard to her fortune (if any), to the ability of the husband, and to the conduct of the parties it shall deem reasonable, and for that purpose may refer it to any one of the convey-ancing counsel of the Court of Chan-cery to settle and approve of a proper deed or instrument, to be executed by all necessary parties :" 20 & 21 Vict. c. 85, s. 32.

"Whereas it sometimes happens that a decree for a dissolution of mar-riage is obtained against a husband who has no property on which the pay-ment of any such gross or annual sum can be secured, but nevertheless he would be able to make a monthly or weekly payment to the wife during their joint lives.

"In every such case it shall be law-ful for the court to make an order on the husband for payment to the wife during their joint lives of such monthly or weekly sums for her maintenance and support as the court may think reasonable: Provided always, that if the husband shall afterwards from any cause become unable to make such payments it shall be lawful for the court to discharge or modify the order, or temporarily to suspend the same as to the whole or any part of the money so ordered to be paid, and again to re-vive the same order wholly or in part as to the court may seem fit :" 29 Vict. c. 32, s. 1.

but whether it was so or not, the words are abundantly sufficient to include the case of a person like the appellant,
who has a large capital fairly and reasonably locked up in
trade, so that it is not easy to secure upon it a fixed sum
without doing that which of course it is most desirable not
to do, namely, destroy the very means by which the trade is
carried on. I should therefore have said that this was a
case in which the very words of the second act are clearly
applicable, and the order will be made under that act. As
to the amount awarded by the President, all the evidence I
have heard fails to raise any doubt in my mind that *rebus
sic stantibus* this order is in any way wrong. It may be
that with a variation in trade it may hereafter become
wrong, and if so, being made, as it now will be under the
second act of Parliament, there is under that act—if it is
not given by the order itself—power to come from time to
time to the court to have the order varied according to the
means of the husband. With that variation, I think the
order should be affirmed.

216] *Sir Robert Phillimore: I concur, and for the
same reasons think it ought to be affirmed.

The President: I have the opinion of my Lord and
my brother judge that upon this evidence the amount that
has been arrived at by me is correct; and my only reason
for calling particular attention to it is this: that although
the order is varied it must not be considered that *rebus sic
stantibus* the husband is to come next month and ask that
it be diminished. The view which I took of it at the time
was this: this was a business of which it was impossible to
estimate the profits, as most business are, annually; but it
was necessary to ascertain them on a series of years. If
that is the correct view, it will follow that this gentleman
must not assume that he is entitled to come after only a
short interval and apply that the amount may be reduced.
I will not attempt to define what is a reasonable time, that
will depend upon the circumstances, but a reasonable time
must elapse before he can ask for a diminution of the allowance to the wife.

> *Order accordingly.   The word "monthly" payments
> being substituted for "quarterly" payments.
> Petitioners' costs of appeal allowed.*

Solicitor for appellant: *Sidney.*
Solicitor for respondent: *H. C. Coote.*

R. A. P.

[6 Probate Division, 227.]
April 5, 1881.

*In the Goods of BRAKE.   [217

Will—Misdescription—Extrinsic Evidence.

A testator appointed William McC. of Canonbury, an executor. The only persons at all answering the description were Thomas McC. and William Abraham McC.:

Held, that parol evidence was admissible to prove which person was intended by the testator. Probate granted to Thomas McC.

THOMAS CURTIS BRAKE, late of No. 107 Petherton Road, Highbury, in the county of Middlesex, Congregational minister, died on the 30th day of December, 1880.

The deceased made his will bearing date the 15th day of July, 1879, and therein appointed Henry Simmons, of Quadrant Road, Canonbury, and William McCormack · of Canonbury, executors.

Henry Ratliff Simmons and Thomas McCormack applied for probate.

It appeared from the affidavits that the deceased told a Mr. Maidment, one of the attesting witnesses, that he wished Mr. Simmons and Mr. McCormack, two of the deacons of his chapel, to be his executors, and Mr. Maidment being under the impression that Mr. McCormack's Christian name was William, inserted it accordingly, that there never had been a deacon of the chapel of the name of William McCormack, but the only deacon of any similar name was Thomas McCormack, who had been one of the deacons for ten years. That Mr. McCormack had a son named William Abraham McCormack; but it did not appear that the deceased was acquainted with him.

Agabeg, in support of the motion, cited *In the Goods of Peel* (').

                                         Cur. adv. vult.

HANNEN, J.: In this case the testator appointed two persons *his executors, describing one of them as Wil- [218 liam McCormack, of Canonbury. There was not, in fact, any person of that name, but there was a person named William Abraham McCormack, and the question is, whether extraneous evidence is admissible to show who was intended by the testator. I am of opinion that it is under proposition V, of Sir James Wigram's Treatise, and in accordance with what is said by Cairns, L.C., in *Charter v. Charter* (') :

(') Law Rep., P. & D., 46.   (*) Law Rep., 7 E. & Ir. App., 364, at p. 377.

"The court has a right to ascertain all the facts which were known to the testator at the time he made his will, and thus to place itself in the testator's position, in order to ascertain the bearing and application of the language which he uses, and in order to ascertain whether there exists any person or thing to which the whole description given in the will can be reasonably, and with sufficient certainty, applied."

The extraneous evidence shows that the only person of the name of McCormack of Canonbury, with whom the testator was acquainted, was Thomas McCormack. He is thus identified as the person intended by the testator. I therefore direct that probate be issued to him and Mr. Simmons as executors.

Solicitors : *W. J. Child & Son.*

R. A. P.

See 23 Eng. R., 511 note ; Mr. Stewart's elaborate note to Lanning *v.* Sisters, etc., 35 N. J. Eq., 392.

The intention of a testator must be gathered from the will itself, and its legal meaning and effect cannot be varied by parol evidence : Judy *v.* Gilbert, 77 Ind., 96.

Oral testimony, or writings of the testator not attested as a will, showing an intent contrary to the will, and being in direct contradiction of the plain terms of the will, are incompetent as evidence and ineffectual to change those terms : Williams *v.* Freeman, 83 N. Y., 562.

Mistakes in a will cannot be corrected by courts, except in cases where the mistake is apparent on the face of the will. It cannot be done by extrinsic evidence : Judy *v.* Gilbert, 77 Ind., 96.

Where a will has been read over to and executed by a competent testator, evidence cannot be admitted to prove that certain words were inserted in the will, contrary to the instructions of the testator, by a mistake of his solicitor, unless fraud is proved, or the party who prepared the will himself takes an interest under it : Rhodes *v.* Rhodes, 1 Olliv., Bell & Fitz G., N. Z. Sup. Ct. R., 100, distinguishing Guardhouse *v.* Blackburn, L. R., 1 Prob. Div., 109, and Fulton *v.* Andrew, L. R., 7 H. L., 448, 12 Eng. R., 76.

The declarations of a testator cannot be resorted to, to contradict or explain the intentions expressed in a will : Williams *v.* Freeman, 83 N. Y., 562.

In an action to recover for services rendered to defendants' testator by the wife of plaintiff, who was the adopted daughter of the testator, the defence was that the services were rendered under an agreement that they were to be compensated for by gifts to plaintiff and wife from the testator in his lifetime, and by legacies in his will ; after providing for the payment of debts, a legacy was given to the wife by the will, and one to her daughter, but of less amount than the debt. Defendants offered to prove declarations of the testator, made at the time and to the person who drew the will, that he had made such an agreement, and that said legacies were intended as a payment for the services. Held, that the evidence was properly excluded, that a legacy implies a bounty, not a payment, and to permit extrinsic evidence of the declarations of the testator thus to change the import of the donative words would be to contradict by oral evidence the legal effect of the instrument, and would violate the policy of the statute of *wills* ; that the *legal* presumption that a *legacy from* a debtor to a creditor of a sum as great or greater than the amount of the debt was intended as a satisfaction, did not apply ; first, as the legacies are given "after payment of the debts ;" second, they were of less amount than the debt ; third, the debt was unliquidated; fourth, the legacies are not given to the creditor but to third persons.

Parol evidence of the intention of a testator is not admissible to fortify a legal presumption raised against the apparent intention, or to create a presumption contrary to the apparent intention, where no such presumption is raised by law: Reynolds v. Robinson, 82 N. Y., 103.

A., desiring to buy the "northeast quarter of the southeast quarter" of a certain section of land, borrowed from his wife money to pay therefor, agreeing that if she would loan it to him, he would devise the land to her for life, with remainder to her children, and in pursuance thereof made his will intending to devise such land to her, but, by mistake, the land was described in the will as the "northeast quarter of the southwest quarter" of the same tract, which tract testator never owned.

Held, that there was no mistake apparent on the face of the will, and that parol evidence is inadmissible to show that the testator intended to describe a different tract from that named in the will: Judy v. Gilbert, 77 Ind., 96.

A testator devised lot 6 in square 403. He did not own lot 6 in square 403, with improvements, but was the owner of lot 3 in said square. As correcting the misdescription in the will, evidence was offered to show that the testator intended to leave everything to his brothers and sisters; that he did own lot 3 in the same general system of lots and squares; that lot 6 had no improvements but lot 3 had, and that since his decease the widow and heirs had received the rents of lot 3, and that all the beneficiaries in the will had acquiesced in this. Held, inadmissible: Bach v. White, 14 Chicago Leg. News, 409, Supreme Court, Dist. Col.

A testator devised property to his nephew A. B., and died leaving two nephews of that name, one legitimate, the other illegitimate. Held, that parol evidence was inadmissible to show that the testator intended his illegitimate and not his legitimate nephew to be the object of his bounty: Appel v. Byers, 98 Penn. St. R., 479.

The testatrix, who left a niece Fanny R. Gibson, and a grandniece Fanny Gibson, mother and daughter, gave $1,000 "unto my grandniece Fanny R. Gibson." Held, that this constituted a case of latent ambiguity or equivocation, as to which extrinsic evidence was admissible to prove which of the persons were intended by the testatrix; and as the mother was the nearest of kin to the testatrix, a presumption arises that she was intended: Gallup v. Wright, 61 How. Pr., 286.

The testator appointed as one of his executors his brother-in-law, Edmund O'Kelly. He had no brother-in-law of that name, but he had a brother-in-law named Edward O'Kelly. Held, that evidence of the circumstances, habits, and position of the testator's family was admissible to prove that Edward O'Kelly was the only person to whom the name and description in the will could be applied; and such evidence being satisfactory, it was ordered that probate should be granted to him and the other executors named in the will. Held also, that parol evidence of declarations of intention by the testator could not be admitted: In re Twohill, L. R., 3 Ir., 21.

A testator devised "all the interest in the following described real estate to W.:

"Sixty acres, Se. 25, town. 7)
"Forty acres, Se. 24, town. 6 \
Jasper County, State of Iowa."

Held, that it was competent for the purpose of applying the devise to its subject-matter, to prove by parol testimony in what township and range in Jasper county the testator owned 60 acres of land in section 25, and in what township and range he owned 40 acres in section 24, and that he owned no other land in Jasper county, thus rendering the description of the land devised certain, and the will operative thereon: Chambers v. Watson, 14 N. W. Repr., 336, Sup. Ct., Iowa.

A gift was to "Joseph C. Link's children, Mary and Sethe Link." Joseph C. Link had only two children, Mary and Sarah, who was called in the family Sadie. The will was drawn by a German. Held, that Sarah was intended by the name "Sethe :" Lanning v. Sisters, etc., 35 N. J. Eq., 392.

A testator, by his will, bequeathed "the sum of $500 to each of the four children of my brother G. R., on their attaining their twenty-first year." At the date of this will G. R. had five children—one son and four daughters —which fact was known to the testator, who had been heard to say that he would provide for the daughters, but that G. himself must provide for the son. By a previous will, the testator had bequeathed the sum of $500 to each of the four "daughters" of his brother G. R., and the person who drew the will proved that the testator, in giving him instructions therefor, said that "he wished to leave $500 to each of G.'s four children, the same as in the old will."

Held (1), that evidence of the instructions so given was properly admissible for the purpose of rebutting any presumption of any change of mind of the testator, and thus showing which four of G. R.'s children were intended to be benefited by the bequest; and (2), that the bequest was contingent upon the legatees respectively attaining their majority: Ruthven v. Ruthven, 25 Grant's Chy., 584.

A testator, by his will, provided as follows: "I give, devise, and dispose of all my estate, real and personal, together with any and all estate, right or interest in lands which I may acquire after the date of this will, in the following manner;" and after authorizing his executor to sell any of his real estate "not herein specifically bequeathed or appropriated," he devised his mansion house and the other buildings thereon, and the privileges thereto belonging, "to A. for life, and upon his death to B." After the date of his will, the testator purchased an estate adjoining his mansion house estate, removed the building standing thereon, tore down the fences and made one garden with walks running through both estates, and erected a greenhouse on the purchased estate, which was used in connection with the mansion house, and the whole was thus used and occupied at the time of his death. Held, that the purchased estate passed by the specific devise of the mansion house estate: Kimball v. Ellison, 128 Mass., 41.

[6 Probate Division, 219.]
Nov. 30, 1880.

219]   *NORMAN V. STRAINS.

Will—Compromise—Married Women or Infants.

Semble. In an action as to the validity of a will when terms of compromise are agreed to by the parties who are *sui juris*, the Court of Probate will not make an order binding married women or infants to the terms of a compromise.

ELIZABETH ATKINSON STRAINS, wife of Werter Strains, died on the 2d of March, 1880, having made a will whereby she appointed Edwin Norman, executor, and devised and bequeathed all her separate estate upon certain trusts for her husband Werter Strains for life, with remainder to her cousin Edwin James Denton and his wife, for life, with remainder to their children absolutely. A caveat on behalf of Mr. Werter Strains, was entered against proof of the will, and this caveat had been duly warned and an appearance entered. Subsequently he and Mr. and Mrs. Denton executed an agreement as to terms of compromise.

Nov. 16. *Frank Safford,* on behalf of all the parties to the agreement and the infants, moved the court to sanction the compromise and to order the terms to be filed. 20 & 21 Vict. c. 77, s. 25.

A. D. Tyssen, for the trustees.   *Cur. adv. vult.*

Nov. 30. THE PRESIDENT: In this case I was asked to confirm an arrangement which has been entered into between the parties, so as to bind a married woman and certain infants.

It has been assumed by those who made the application, probably from some analogy to proceedings in the Chancery Division, that this division was possessed of this case in the same manner. But that is not so. There has been no action commenced in this division, for by the Judicature Act an action can only be commenced by issuing a writ, and no writ has been issued and therefore there is no litigation, and nothing upon which this court could proceed. There has been a proceeding by caveat and warning, but they precede the writ.

*I am extremely unwilling, without knowing the [220 circumstances, to bind infants to the consequences of a compromise which is entered into by the parties to a probate cause before me. I have really no means of forming any judgment upon the wisdom or prudence of the compromise. My duty is to determine whether or no a particular will is the will of the deceased person ; but to enable me to say whether there were good grounds upon which counsel came to the conclusion that it would be prudent to make a compromise, it would be necessary that I should be informed of the facts of the case. I am always willing to give my assistance to counsel when I am consulted as to whether or no a particular arrangment should be carried out, but I always do so with this reservation that upon their statement, as far as I can judge, it seems to be expedient ; and I do not thereby intend to bind infants or any persons other than those who are parties to the compromise. I have made these observations as a guide in future cases, but, for the present, it is sufficient to say I am asked to sanction an arrangement in a cause which does not even exist.

Solicitors for plaintiff : *Brighten, Parker & Norman.*
Solicitor for trustees : *T. W. Rogers.*

R. A. P.

[7 Probate Division, 5.]

Dec. 1, 1881.

[IN THE COURT OF APPEAL.]

5]   *THE CITO.

Derelict—Right to Freight after abandonment of Ship.

By the abandonment of a ship by its crew during a voyage, without any intention to retake possession, a right is given to the owner of cargo on board to treat the contract of affreightment as at an end.

A ship with a cargo of resin in barrels, on a voyage from America to Rotterdam, was, owing to the perils of the sea, abandoned by her crew off the American coast. She was afterwards saved by another vessel, and brought with her cargo by the salvors into a port in England, and there arrested in an action for salvage by her salvors. Before the shipowner had released the ship or cargo, the owners of the cargo applied for and obtained from the Admiralty Court an order for the release of the cargo to them without payment of any freight, upon their giving bail to the salvors:

Held, that the cargo owners were entitled to treat the contract of affreightment as at an end, and that therefore the order of the Admiralty Court was rightly made.

APPEAL from an order of Sir Robert Phillimore, the judge of the Admiralty Division, made in an action for salvage on 6] behalf *of the owners of the Norwegian bark Colonist against the Norwegian bark Cito.

The Cito, when on a voyage from Wilmington, U.S., to Rotterdam, with a cargo of resin in barrels, was, owing to the perils of the sea, abandoned by her crew off the American coast. Some time afterwards she was fallen in with by the Colonist, which navigated her to Plymouth, where on her arrival she was arrested with her cargo and freight in an action for salvage by the owners and crew of the Colonist. An appearance in the action was entered on behalf of the owners of the Cito, and afterwards on behalf of the owners of the cargo, who then, and before the owners of the Cito had obtained a release of that ship, moved the Admiralty Court for an order that upon their giving bail to the salvors the cargo should be released to them without payment of any freight. This motion was opposed by the owners of the Cito, on the ground that it was an attempt to defeat their right to freight, and they offered bail for salvage of the cargo. The cargo had been shipped at Wilmington under a bill of lading, by which the cargo was to be delivered at the port of Rotterdam to the order of the shippers or their assigns, they paying freight at a specified rate.

Sir Robert Phillimore considered that he was bound by

the case of *The Kathleen* ('), and he accordingly made the
order applied for the owners of the cargo. The owners
of the Cito appeal'd.

Stubbs (*Butt*, Q.C., with him), for the appellants: The
case of *The Kathleen* (') is distinguishable, as in that case
the cargo was a perishable one, and had it been carried on
to the port of destination, the owner of it could not have
received it in that state in which he had a right to have it.
Here it was different; the cargo, which had neither been
discharged nor sold, could have been taken on in the Cito
to Rotterdam, and so the appellants could have earned
their freight. If not distinguishable, *The Kathleen* (') was
wrongly decided. It is not a decision binding on this court.
When a ship, which by any accident from the perils of the
sea has been abandoned during the voyage, has been afterwards *brought with its cargo into a port of refuge, [7
whether by its own crew with or without assistance, or by salvors as a derelict, if its cargo is not perishable, the shipowner
has a right to carry the cargo on to its port of destination in
that or any other ship, and so earn the freight. Should,
however, the cargo owner desire to receive it at such port of
refuge he is at liberty to have it, but only on payment of
the full freight. The contract of affreightment is not destroyed by the abandonment of the ship: *The Cargo ex
Galam* ('). The shipowners have never refused to perform
their contract, and notwithstanding the abandonment, their
right to the possession of the ship has always continued in
them, subject only to the right of the salvors. The Merchant Shipping Act, 1854, s. 468, shows that the property of
a derelict still remains in the owner. In the present case the
cargo has been improved in value by being brought to this
country, and its owners have got all they practically wanted,
and therefore they should pay freight, if not the entire
freight, at least *pro rata: The Soblomsten* (') and *The Teutonia* ('). Both parties here are foreigners, and the contract
was to be performed by bringing the cargo to a foreign port;
therefore the cargo owners should show that by the law of
that port an abandonment of the ship has destroyed the
contract and entitled them to the cargo at a port of refuge
without payment of any freight. The presumption, in the
absence of anything to the contrary, is that by the cargo
owners claiming the cargo at such port, they have agreed
to pay freight *pro rata*, and the case of *The Cargo ex*

Galam (') shows that the act of the Admiralty Court when moved by the cargo owner is to be treated as the act of the cargo owner.

Myburgh (*F. W. Raikes*, with him), for the respondents: The present case is undistinguishable from *The Kathleen* ('), and that case was rightly decided. There is no question here about liability for *pro rata* freight, for the vessel was abandoned so shortly after she had commenced her voyage, that it is really a liability to pay the whole freight or nothing. In the case of an abandonment the property in the derelict is gone from the owner, and at common law the 8] derelict becomes the property of the *Crown; at all events it belongs to the Crown when it is brought by the salvors into an English port: *Rex* v. *Property Derelict* ('); *The Dantzic Packet* (').

However it is unnecessary to contend for that here, as by the abandonment of the ship and cargo the contract of affreightment was gone. There was by the abandonment a deliberate intention by the shipowners not to perform their contract, and having parted with the possession of the ship and cargo they became unable to carry out the contract of affreightment, and before they had recovered possession, the ship and cargo had been taken and claimed by the salvors. The cargo owners can only now get their cargo by paying for its conveyance to this country by the salvors, and it would be inequitable to ask them to pay again for this in the form of freight.

Stubbs replied.

BRETT, L.J.: I am of opinion that the decision appealed from should be affirmed. Many interesting points have been discussed in this case about which it is not necessary to give any decided opinion. It has been said that such an abandonment of a ship as to make it a derelict together with a subsequent seizure by any one who finds it, makes such seizure the seizure of a droit of the admiralty, and alters the property in the ship. If that were made out it would strongly support the case for the respondents; but I am not, however, prepared to say that such a proceeding would take the property in the ship out of the owner; and for the present purpose I will assume that it does not. It has been also urged that the abandonment of a ship puts an end to the contract of affreightment. I am not prepared to say it does. Suppose a wrongful abandonment, without its being occasioned by the perils of the sea, it is clear that in that

(') Br. & L., 167.   (') 1 Hagg. Adm. Rep., 383.
(') Law Rep., 4 A. & E., 269; 12 Eng. R., 645.   (') 3 Hagg. Adm. Rep., 383.

case the owner of the cargo might sue the shipowner for his breach of contract, so it cannot be said that it puts an end to the contract of affreightment.

It is sufficient, I think, for the determination of the present case, to say that by an abandonment of a ship without any intention to retake possession of it, the shipowner has, so far as he can, abandoned the contract, so as to allow the other party to it, *the cargo owner, to treat it as aban- [9 doned. Then, under these circumstances, the vessel having been abandoned was brought into the port of Plymouth and arrested there by her salvors in the Admiralty Court. Whilst the vessel was in that position, so that her owners could not enforce the contract of affreightment against the cargo owners, the latter went to the Court of Admiralty and claimed to have the cargo released and given to them without payment of any freight, upon their giving bail to the salvors ; and thus the cargo owners thereby sought to exercise their right to elect to treat the contract at an end. The shipowners, however, by a counter motion to the court, endeavored to prevent the cargo owners from exercising this right and asked to have the cargo delivered to them (they being ready to give bail for the same) in order that they might carry it to the port of destination and so earn the freight. Now it seems to me that the Court of Admiralty would have been wrong if it had deprived the cargo owners of their right to treat what the shipowners had done as au abandonment of the contract of affreightment, and therefore that the order which the court made was a right one. We do not decide what would have been the result if after the ship had been brought in as it was by the salvors, and before the cargo owners had come in and exercised their right to the cargo, the shipowners had given bail for the ship and cargo and had carried the cargo on. It is not necessary to do so, and it is sufficient to place our decision on the other ground in order to determine this case and to support the order appealed from and the case of *The Kathleen* ('). It follows from our decision that the cargo owners not having done any wrongful act are not liable for freight either *pro rata* or at all.

Cotton, L.J.: I am of the same opinion. Before the shipowners sought to get possession of the cargo after the arrest by the salvors, the cargo owners had intervened and applied for the cargo, and under those circumstances the Court of Admiralty was right I think in making the order which it made. It is true that the shipowners could not by

('). Law Rep., 4 A. & E., 269; 12 Eng. R., 645.

their own act put an end to the contract of affreightment,
10]   but by their abandonment they gave a right to *the
cargo owners to elect to treat the contract at an end, and the
shipowners could not, in my opinion, after their abandonment have objected, if the cargo owners had found another
vessel and taken the cargo on in it to the port of destination.

LINDLEY, L.J., concurred.   *Appeal dismissed.*

Solicitors for appellants: *Cooper & Co.*
Solicitors for respondents: *Pritchard & Sons.*

W. P.

[7 Probate Division, 10.]

Dec. 20, 1881.

WATSON v. WATSON and Others.

Will—Construction—Residue.

The will of S. C. after bequeathing her property to A. C. and J. C., continued
thus, "in case of the demise of either the said A. C. or J. C., I do hereby bequeath
the same . . . . to the survivor for her sole use and benefit during her or their natural lifetime:"

Held, that the residue was not disposed of, and that A. C. and J. C. took only as
tenants for life.

SARAH CLARKE, of the parish of St. Peter at Gowts, Lincoln, made her will on the 15th day of March, 1851, in her
own handwriting, and in the following words:

"Through the goodness of God, I, Sarah Clarke, of the
parish of St. Peters at Gowts, Lincoln, having become possessed of property in the present possession of several different persons, do hereby bequeath the same all and every of
it to my dearly beloved sisters, Ann Clarke, spinster, of the
parish of St. Peter at Gowts, and Jane Clarke, spinster, of
the said parish of St. Peter at Gowts, and in case of the demise of either the said Ann Clarke or the said Jane Clarke,
I do hereby bequeath the same all and every portion of the
same property to the survivor for her sole use and benefit
during her or their natural lifetime.   This the last will and
testament of me, Sarah Clarke, signed this fifteenth day of
March, in the year of our Lord, 1851.

"Witnesses: Harriet Sharpe; Elizabeth Armstrong."

The testatrix died on the 7th day of August, 1869, and,
11]   there *being no executor named in the will, letters of
administration were granted on the 30th day of June, 1870,
to Ann Clarke, as one of the sisters and next of kin of the
deceased.

Ann Clarke survived her sister Jane Clarke, and died on the 27th day of November, 1880.

Ann Clarke and Jane Clarke had each made wills, and appointed Henry Watson sole executor.

Dec. 7. *Inderwick*, Q.C., and *Pritchard*, on behalf of Henry Watson, moved the court that letters of administration of the estate and effects of Sarah Clarke be granted to Henry Watson as representative of the residuary legatees. The sisters were not merely tenants for life as upon the true construction of the will the residue is bequeathed to them. In the events which have happened the will contains an absolute gift of the residue, the legatees not having died in the lifetime of the testatrix.

The testatrix by the first part of the will gives the property absolutely, and the words "in case of the demise of either," mean in the case of death in the lifetime of the testatrix: Jarman on Wills, 4th ed., vol. ii, p. 752; *Howard* v. *Howard* ('); *Schenk* v. *Agnew* ('); *Clark* v. *Lubbock* ('); *Slade* v. *Milner* ('); *Home* v. *Pillans* ('); *Cambridge* v. *Rous* ('); *Ommaney* v. *Bevan* ('). Either the will constituted an absolute gift if neither died in the lifetime of the testatrix, or she intended that if one of her sisters died in her lifetime the share of the other sister should be limited to that sister's life to her separate use. The words "sole use" are equivalent to "separate use." Hawkins on the Construction of Wills, pp. 116, 117; *Adamson* v. *Armitage* ('); *Ex parte Killick* (').

Searle, for the next of kin: The residue is not disposed of. The ordinary meaning of the words will not admit of any other construction.

Bayford, for other parties interested.

Cur. adv. vult.

*Dec. 20. THE PRESIDENT: I have referred to the [12 cases cited in argument and have found some difficulty in construing this will, as it is a will drawn by a testatrix who was probably, almost certainly, ignorant of the exact meaning of the technical language which she used.

The testatrix leaves her property to her sisters Ann Clarke and Jane Clarke, and she says in "case of the demise of either I hereby bequeath all and every portion of the said property to the survivor for her sole use and benefit during her or their natural lifetime." Several cases have been

(') 21 Beav., 550.
(') 4 K. & J., 405.
(') 1 Y. & C., 492.
(') 4 Madd., 144.
(') 2 My. & K., 15.
(') 8 Ves., 12.
(') 18 Ves., 291.
(') 19 Ves., 416.
(') 3 M. D. & D., 480.

cited, but it is not necessary to go through them *seriatim*, because they only establish the now accepted general rule which is expressed in the 48th chapter of Jarman on Wills so clearly that I think it will be better for me to read the passage than to give it in words of my own. He says (¹) "where a bequest is made to a person with a gift over in case of his death a question arises whether the testator uses the words 'in case of' in the sense of 'at' or 'from,' and thereby as restrictive of the prior bequest to a life interest, i.e., as introducing a gift to take effect on the decease of the prior legatee under all circumstances, or with a view to create a bequest in defeasance of or in substitution for the prior one in the event of the death of the legatee on some contingency. The difficulty in such cases arises from the testator having applied terms of contingency to an event of all others the most certain and inevitable, and to satisfy which terms it is necessary to connect with death some circumstance in association with which it is contingent; that circumstance naturally is the time of its happening; and such time where the bequest is immediate (i.e., in possession) necessarily is the death of the testator, there being no other period to which the words can refer." The cases cited only go to establish that rule, but do not solve the difficulty which arises in this case from the use of the concluding words of the will "during her or their natural lifetime." Some other cases were cited, the effect of which was to show that the words were to be considered to mean for her separate use, but they also give no assistance in determining the meaning of those concluding words. The words "during 13] her or their lifetime" cannot be *rejected, nor can they by any reasonable transposition, if that were allowable, be limited in their effect, and I have therefore come to the conclusion that as they cannot be rejected they have the effect, though they are not strictly grammatical, of indicating that the estate must be taken by these persons for life only, and that there is an intestacy as to the reversion.

Administration granted to the next of kin with the will annexed. Costs of all parties out of the estate.

Solicitors for plaintiffs: *Helder, Roberts & Gillett.*
Solicitors for defendants: *Taylor, Hoare & Taylor.*

(¹) 1 Jarman, 4th ed., vol. ii, p. 732.

[7 Probate Division, 13.]

Jan. 24, 1882.

In the Goods of ELIZABETH WENSLEY, Deceased.

Administration—Insolvency of the Estate—Special Circumstances—20 & 21 Vict. c. 77, s. 73.

J. W., entitled to the property of his wife, E. W., who predeceased him, became indebted to the estate of J. P. The estate of E. W. afterwards became entitled to a share in the residuary estate of J. P.

The executrix of J. W. refused to take out letters of administration to E. W.'s estate, and a grant was necessary to enable the creditors of J. W. to obtain E. W.'s share of the residuary estate in satisfaction of their debt:

The court granted (under s. 73 of 20 & 21 Vict. c. 77) administration of the estate of E. W. to a creditor of J. W.

[7 Probate Division, 15.]

Dec. 20, 1881.

*WHITTAKER v. WHITTAKER.   [15

Attachment of Debt—Judicature Act, 1873, s. 25, subs. 8.

Under subs. 8 of s. 25 of the Judicature Act, 1873, the Court of Divorce has power to attach a debt due to a respondent in order to compel obedience to an order of that court for payments of costs.

[7 Probate Division, 16.]

Jan. 18, 1882.

*L. v. L., Falsely called W.   [16

Nullity—Impotence—Possible cure.

After a partial cohabitation of two years and eight months it appeared that the woman was impotent, but that she might probably be cured if she would submit to an operation involving no great risk of life. This she refused to do. The court made a decree *nisi* of nullity of marriage.

THIS was a petition for nullity of marriage at the suit of the man. The respondent did not appear.

A ceremony of marriage was performed between the parties on the 29th of August, 1876, the man being then twenty-seven and the woman twenty-three years of age. After the ceremony she refused to accompany him home, but a week afterwards they slept together at her father's house for three or four nights, when she objected altogether to any attempt to consummate the marriage, and on one occasion threatened to leave the house. They then lived in separate lodgings, he visiting and sleeping with her about once a fortnight, but making no further effort to have connection with her. She told him that she was not fitted for it, and had no sexual desire. This state of things continued for two years and eight months, when they finally separated. In February, 1879, she was examined by a medical man, who gave evidence that she was suffering from vaginismus, that there was a spasmodic affection of the parts which were extremely painful to touch, and that connexion was then impossible, but that a cure might be effected with no great risk to life. The respondent was informed of this, and was requested to submit to the operation, but refused. The petitioner was inspected under the order of the court, and the inspectors stated that his condition was normal. The respondent refused to obey the order of the court and undergo further inspection.

Dr. Tristram and *Currie*, for the petitioner, cited *D. E. v. A. G.*(¹); *W. v. H.*(²); *G. v. G.*(³).

THE PRESIDENT: In this case the man is capable, and it
17]   is *proved to my satisfaction by the conduct of the parties during the last five years, and the medical testimony, that the woman is incapable. The ends of marriage have not been attained, and it is therefore desirable that the tie between the parties should be put an end to. The difficulty might perhaps be overcome if the lady would undergo an operation, which would probably be successful. But the court cannot compel her to submit, and the man can only be expected to take all reasonable means to persuade her. This he has done, and she has distinctly refused. I therefore make a decree *nisi* for nullity of the marriage.

Solicitors: *Burton & Co.*

(¹) 1 Robert., 279.   (²) 2 S. & T., 240.   (³) Law Rep., 2 P. & D., 287.

R. A. P.

[7 Probate Division 17.] ·
Jan. 19, 1882.

DAGG v. DAGG and SPEAKE.

Dissolution of Marriage—Desertion by Petitioner.

A husband, without reasonable excuse, obtained from his wife an agreement that they should live apart from each other, which they accordingly did, and she subsequently committed adultery:

Held, that under the circumstances he had deserted her, and that a petition by him for dissolution of the marriage must be dismissed.

THIS was a petition by William Pritchard Dagg, a pianoforte tuner, for dissolution of his marriage by reason of his wife's adultery.   Neither the respondent nor co-respondent appeared.

In 1867, the petitioner was a porter, and the respondent cook at a hydropathic hospital, and, she being with child by him, they agreed to be married.   Before the marriage, the following document in the handwriting of the petitioner, was signed by the parties, viz.:

"This is to certify that whereas the undersigned parties do agree that they will marry, and that only to save the female of us from shaming her friends or telling a lie, and that the said marriage shall be no more thought of, except to tell her friends that she is married (unless she should arrive at the following accomplishments—viz., piano, singing, reading, writing, speaking, and deportment) ; and whereas these said accomplishments have in no way been sought after, much less mastered, therefore the aforesaid marriage shall be and is null and void ; and whereas we *agree that   [18 the male of us shall keep his harmonium in the aforesaid female's sitting room, we agree that it shall be there no more than four months, and that from that time the aforesaid and undersigned shall be free in every respect whatsoever of the aforesaid and undersigned female, as witness our hands this 1st of ——, 1867.

"Catherine L. H. Jeffries.
" William Pritchard Dagg."

A month after the marriage the respondent was delivered of a child, at a lodging taken for her by the petitioner ; but he had had no further intercourse with her.   He paid her 2s. 6d. a week until recently, when he discovered that she had been for some years living in adultery with another man.

Searle, appeared for the petitioner.

THE PRESIDENT :   I am of opinion that this petition must be dismissed.   The agreement has been obtained by the husband without the real concurrence of his wife and without justification.   Knowing her frailty it was his duty, when he became her husband, not to have left her to those chances of falling, to which, abandoned as she was by him, she must have been exposed.

It is true that from the birth of the child he allowed her 2s. 6d. a week, but that was not more than the parish authorities could have compelled him to contribute for the maintenance of his child, and when, in order to receive that sum weekly, she came to the hospital in which he was employed, he refused to speak to her.   He withdrew from her that protection to which, as his wife, she was entitled, and it was not to be wondered at that she fell with another man. Though the petitioner made the respondent a small allowance up to March last, he deserted her from the time of the birth of the child, and his desertion of her has probably been the cause of the life she is now leading. I therefore reject the application of the petitioner, and dismiss his petition.

Solicitors: *Newman, Stretton, Hilliard & Willins.*

R. A. P.

[7 Probate Division, 19.]

Jan. 24, 1882.

19]   *PENTY v. PENTY, JOHNSON and SABINGIE.

Divorce—Petition—Co-respondents.

If a petition alleges adultery with persons unknown, the order of the court must be obtained dispensing with making them co-respondents, notwithstanding that there are already other co-respondents who have been served with process.

THIS was a petition for dissolution of marriage by reason of the alleged adultery of the wife.

The petition alleged divers acts of adultery by the respondent with each of the co-respondents, and in a subsequent paragraph it was stated that the respondent had committed adultery on divers occasions with persons unknown to the petitioner. Directions as to the mode of trial were refused at the registry until the order of the court had been obtained dispensing with making the persons mentioned in the last paragraph co-respondents.

Middleton, for the petitioner, moved the court either for directions as to the mode of trial, or for an order dispensing with other co-respondents. It has been the practice not to require further co-respondents as to persons unknown when there is already a co-respondent on the record.

THE PRESIDENT: If adultery is to be relied upon with a person unknown, I do not think it makes any difference that another person has been also charged and served with citation and copy petition. In this case, as the affidavits show that the petitioner cannot ascertain the names of the other persons, I dispense with further co-respondents.

Solicitors: *Chester, Mayhew, Broome & Griffithes.*

R. A. P.

[7 Probate Division, 20.]

Jan. 31, 1882.

*ROSS v. ROSS.   [20

Divorce—Variation of Settlements—Petition—Signature—Practice.

A petition for variation of settlements must usually be signed by the petitioner, but the court will, under special circumstances, allow his solicitor to sign it on his behalf.

THIS was a petition to vary the trusts of a marriage settlement.

The petitioner had obtained a decree *nisi* for dissolution of his marriage by reason of the respondent's adultery with a person unknown, and that decree was made absolute on the 8th of November, 1881. The solicitors for the petitioner then wrote to him and received instructions to file a petition for variation of the marriage settlement, but it appeared by their affidavit that he was in India, and that if the petition was sent to him for signature there would be considerable delay.

Bayford, for the petitioner, moved the court either to dispense with the petitioner's signature to the petition, or to allow his solicitor to sign it on his behalf.

THE PRESIDENT: I think the practice of requiring the petitioner's signature is reasonable as showing that the petition is his act. In this case that is sufficiently shown by the affidavit, and therefore I will allow the petition to be signed by his solicitor on his behalf.

Solicitors: *Lawrence, Graham & Long.*

R. A. P.

[7 Probate Division, 42.]

Nov. 23, 1881.

*THE VANDYCK (1881, S. 234).   [42

Salvage—Constructive Acceptance of Salvage Service—Service rendered to Two Vessels in Collision with each other.

Where two vessels are in collision and are entangled together in a position dangerous to both, salvors who, by towing one of the vessels clear, free both vessels from danger, are entitled to recover salvage reward from the owners of both vessels.

A screw steamship drifted, during a gale of wind, across the bows of a ship at anchor in the Mersey, and with her propeller caught the anchor chains of the ship, and the two vessels were held together in a position dangerous to both. A steamtug went to the assistance of the ship, and held her whilst her chains were slipped and towed her clear of the steamship:

Held, that the owners, master, and crew of the tug were entitled to recover salvage reward from the owners of the steamship.

THIS was an action of salvage instituted on behalf of the
owners, master, and crew of the steamtug Stormcock, against
the steamship Vandyck and her cargo.

The statement of claim alleged in substance as follows:

1. The Stormcock is a twin screw steamtug belonging to
the port of Liverpool, of the burthen of about 465 tons.

2. The Vandyck is a screw steamship of the burthen of
about 1,098 tons registered tonnage.

3. On the 14th day of October, 1881, at about 4.15 P.M.,
the Stormcock was at the Liverpool landing stage, in the
river Mersey. There was a tremendous hurricane blowing
at the time, with a very heavy sea running. The tide was
then about three-quarters of an hour ebb.

4. Those on board the Stormcock saw the Vandyck on
the Cheshire side of the Mersey, opposite the Alfred Dock,
in collision with a large ship, which proved to be the Queen
of Scots, and the Stormcock at once went to the assistance
of both the said vessels.

5. The Stormcock on reaching the said vessels found that
the Vandyck had drifted right across the bows of the Queen
of Scots, striking her with her starboard quarter, and carrying away the jib-boom and other head gear of the Queen of
Scots. The two vessels were grinding against each other
43] heavily, and a large hole *had been knocked in the
after part of the starboard side of the Vandyck. The Queen
of Scots had both her anchors down, and the propeller of
the Vandyck had got between the anchor chains of the
Queen of Scots, thus rendering it impossible for the Vandyck to use her propeller to get away from the Queen of
Scots. A vessel called the Duchess of Argyle was lying
about two cables' length astern of the Vandyck.

6. The Vandyck and those on board her were then in a
position of great danger from the said collision, and in order
to free the said vessels from one another it was necessary
that the Queen of Scots should be towed ahead and that her
anchor chains should be slipped.

7. It was also necessary that the Queen of Scots should be
towed away before her chains were slipped in order that the
Vandyck when set free might be better enabled to clear the
Duchess of Argyle.

8. The Stormcock then gave the Queen of Scots a hawser,
which was made fast, and the Stormcock went on ahead
until the Queen of Scots was enabled to slip her anchor

chains, and the two vessels were thus set free from one another.

9. But for the services rendered by the Stormcock, as aforesaid, the Vandyck would in all probability have sustained considerable further damage, and have sunk, together with her cargo.

10. In the performance of the said services the Stormcock was in considerable danger, and ran great risk.

The defendants the owners of the Vandyck, and the owners of her cargo, on the 15th of November last, delivered a statement of defence, admitting the 1st and 2d paragraphs of the statement of claim, and containing, *inter alia*, the following allegations:

A little after 4 P.M. on the 14th day of October, 1881, whilst the wind was blowing a gale from the N.W., and the tide was first quarter ebb, the steamship Vandyck and the ship Queen of Scots, both of which were at anchor in the river Mersey, fouled one another, the port bow of the Queen of Scots coming in contact with the starboard quarter of the Vandyck. The Vandyck was riding to her starboard anchor, and had her steam up; the Queen of Scots had her port and starboard anchors down. The Queen of *Scots struck the [44 starboard quarter of the Vandyck with her port bow, and the Vandyck fell away to the westward across the bows of the Queen of Scots, and the propeller of the Vandyck was fouled by the starboard anchor chain of the Queen of Scots, and in consequence thereof, the Vandyck was unable to use her propeller and the vessels fell alongside each other, the bows of the Queen of Scots to the stern of the Vandyck. The Vandyck had two tugs, the Merry Andrew and the Victory, in attendance upon her, and they made fast to a line carried from the port quarter of the Vandyck, and held the Vandyck; and the Queen of Scots then slipped her starboard chain, and the Vandyck at once came clear. The Vandyck then cast off the tow-rope, and her head fell round to the tide. The chain of the Vandyck parted with the strain upon it, and the Vandyck then steamed ahead across the river, and afterwards proceeded without assistance to the south of the Woodside landing stage.

The defendants admit that the Queen of Scots cut into the after part of the starboard side of the main deck of the Vandyck, but they say that the Vandyck was not damaged below the water line, and that she made no water, and that as soon as the propeller was clear of the starboard chain of the Queen of Scots, there was nothing to prevent the engines of the Vandyck being used.

The defendants deny that the Stormcock went to the
assistance of the Vandyck or rendered assistance to her.
The defendants deny that the Vandyck was in a position of
great danger as alleged; the two tugs before mentioned were
sufficient to render, and they did render, to the Vandyck all
necessary assistance.

The defendants deny the 7th paragraph of the statement
of claim, and they deny that the Stormcock had begun to tow
the Queen of Scots before her starboard chain was slipped.

The defendants admit that the Stormcock gave the Queen
of Scots a hawser, which was made fast as alleged in the 8th
paragraph of the statement of claim, but they do not admit
the residue of the said paragraph, and they say that any
services rendered by the Stormcock were rendered to the
Queen of Scots, and not to the Vandyck.

As to the 9th and 10th paragraphs of the statement of
claim, the defendants deny, that but for the services ren-
45]   dered by the *Stormcock, the Vandyck would have
sustained further damages, and they do not admit that in
the performance of the alleged services the Stormcock was
in danger, or ran great risk.

Nov. 23.   The action was heard before the judge, assisted
by two of the Elder Brethren of the Trinity House.

Witnesses were examined orally in court on behalf of the
plaintiffs and the defendants.   Amongst the witnesses so
examined was the pilot in charge of the Queen of Scots at
the time of the collision.   He stated, in effect, that the
Stormcock came up to the Queen of Scots about five minutes
after the collision, that at that time the starboard quarter of
the Vandyke was lying across the bows of the Queen of
Scots, and that every time the vessels fell together with the
heaving of the sea the Queen of Scots cut into the Vandyck
nearer the water every time.   He further stated, in cross-
examination, that if the Queen of Scots had slipped her
chains before she had been held up in position, she would
have fouled the Duchess of Argyle.   It appeared from the
evidence of other witnesses called on behalf of the plaintiffs,
that if the Vandyck had remained where she was, the Vandyck, and possibly the Queen of Scots also, would have
sunk.

The witnesses for the defendants proved that when the
Stormcock was holding up the Queen of Scots the steamtug
Merry Andrew was fast to the port quarter of the Van-
dyck, and the steamtug Victory was fast ahead of the Merry
Andrew.

The total value of the property proceeded against was admitted to be £83,500. The result of the remainder of the evidence is stated in the judgment.

An action was brought by the owners of the Stormcock and the owners of two tugs against the Queen of Scots to recover salvage for the services rendered on the same occasion to the Queen of Scots. That action was heard immediately before the present action, and the judge in that action awarded £400 to the Stormcock. It was agreed by the parties to the present action that the evidence in that action should be taken as given in the present action.

Myburgh, and *J. Walton*, for the plaintiffs: The assistance of the Stormcock was directly instrumental in saving the Vandyck *from sinking, and it is immaterial that [46 such assistance was rendered after an express request from the Queen of Scots: *The Annapolis* and *The Golden Light* (');
The Woburn Abbey ('). The services rendered to the Vandyck were services such as no prudent man would have refused to accept.

Butt, Q.C., and *G. Bruce*, for the defendants: The services in this case were services rendered at the express request and directly for the benefit of the Queen of Scots. There was nothing to prevent the Queen of Scots slipping her anchors except the danger of her drifting down upon the Duchess of Argyle, and that was a contingency which in no way concerned the Vandyck. All the assistance the Vandyck required could have been rendered by the Merry Andrew and the Victory, the two steamtugs which were in attendance on her at her request.

Sir ROBERT PHILLIMORE: In this case the steamtug Stormcock brings her action of salvage against the steamship Vandyck, which at the time the services were rendered was in collision with the ship Queen of Scots. Now the first question the court has to decide is, was there any salvage service in its legal sense rendered by the plaintiffs to the Vandyck, inasmuch as there was no request made to the Stormcock to act on behalf of the Vandyck, and several cases were cited to the court to show that the owners of the Vandyck were under no liability to pay salvage remuneration. But I am of opinion that in the circumstances of this case the evidence shows that the services of the Stormcock were accepted by the Vandyck. The next question is, what was the value of the services so rendered to the Vandyck, and looking to the evidence, and after conferring with the Elder Brethren of the Trinity House, I am of opinion that a

(') Lush., 355.   (') 3 Mar. Law Cas., 310.

valuable salvage service was rendered to the Vandyck, though it was one of very short duration, lasting only twenty minutes, and though it is possible the Vandyck might have received great assistance from other tugs that were there. But looking to the evidence, especially to that of the pilot of the Queen of Scots, who described the injury which the Vandyck had sustained from the Queen of Scots, and to all the 47] circumstances of the case, I am of opinion *that a very valuable salvage service was rendered to the Vandyck, and I shall award £300.

Solicitor for plaintiffs : *H. Thompson.*
Solicitors for defendants: *Thornely & Dismore.*

          *   G. B.

[7 Probate Division, 47.]

Feb. 17, 1882.

THE KENMURE CASTLE.

(1882, J. No. 5.   1882, P. No. 52.   1882, Q. No. 11.)

Salvage—Award—Apportionment.

In a suit instituted to recover salvage reward in respect of services rendered in towing a disabled vessel into safety, the court awarded a total sum of £4,000, of which £3,000 was apportioned to the owners.

THIS was an action of salvage brought by the owners, master, and crew of the Belgian steamship John David, against the British steamship Kenmure Castle, her cargo and freight.

The following facts appeared from the pleadings and evidence:

In the early morning of the 15th of November, 1881, the John David proceeding up the Red Sea bound to London, came up with the Kenmure Castle which had broken her crank shaft, and was in other respects damaged in her machinery. After negotiations between the masters of the two vessels, a memorandum in writing was drawn up and signed by the two masters. It stated that the master of the Kenmure Castle had requested that the Kenmure Castle should be towed to Suez to effect repairs, and that it was agreed that the remuneration for the services rendered should be settled by arbitration in London, and that any coals required by the John David should be supplied by the Kenmure Castle at the current rate at Suez. The John David was then lashed alongside the Kenmure Castle for the greater convenience of coaling, and was towed in this position for

some hours when the John David cast off, and towed ahead
of the Kenmure Castle.   The John David continued towing
ahead until the morning of the 19th of November, when the
two vessels were again made fast alongside each other, and
about fifty tons of coal were worked from the Kenmure
Castle on to the John David; when this had *been [48
completed, the towing hawsers were again made fast, and
the John David continued towing ahead until the evening
of the 25th of November, when the vessels arrived in Suez
Roads and came to anchor.   Whilst the Kenmure Castle
was fastened alongside the John David, some damage was
done to the Kenmure Castle in consequence of the vessels
bumping against each other.

The value of the John David was admitted to be £75,000,
and for the purpose of the action the value of the Kenmure Castle, her cargo and freight was taken at the total
value of £75,140.

Feb. 17.   The action was heard before the judge, assisted
by two of the Elder Brethren of the Trinity House.

Butt, Q.C., and *W. G. F. Phillimore*, for the owners and
master of the John David.

Nelson, for part of the crew of the John David.

Morice, for the remainder of the crew of the John David.

Myburgh, Q.C., and *Baden Powell*, for the defendants,
the owners of the Kenmure Castle and the owners of her
cargo.

SIR ROBERT PHILLIMORE: This is a salvage service rendered by one large screw steamer to another in the Red Sea,
beginning on the 15th of November and lasting till the 25th
of that month.   The vessel to which the services were rendered was the Kenmure Castle, a screw steamer of 1,268 tons
register, and 180 horse power nominal, and she was on a
voyage from China to London with a cargo of tea, and was
manned with a crew of twenty-seven hands.   On the 14th of
November, as she was prosecuting her voyage up the Red
Sea, when twenty miles N.W. of the Island of Jebel Zuker,
it was found that her crank shaft was broken.   She was from
that moment a log upon the water, perfectly unable to do
anything for herself, and requiring steam power assistance.
The vessel that rendered the salvage services in this case
was the John David, belonging to the port of Antwerp.   She
was a screw steamship of 1,807 tons gross register, and was
prosecuting a voyage from Bombay to London with a full
cargo of cotton and wheat.   It is a curious incident that the
John David and the Kenmure Castle with her cargo were of

nearly equal value. Now, the towage in this case was an
49] easy one in *one sense. The weather was fine, and
the vessels met with no accident in the whole course of the
towage, but at the same time the court takes into consideration what would have happened if bad weather had set in.
The salved vessel was in a state in which salvage assistance
was necessary. If the weather had become rough, she might
have drifted on the coral reefs, of which there are so many
in the Red Sea. It must be remembered that the salving
vessel was bound in the same direction as the vessel salved,
and that there was no danger to the salvors personally.
Bearing all these matters in mind, I have come to the conclusion, after consulting with the Elder Brethren, that the

With regard to the services of the owners of the John David,
I
v   ent
one set of costs only.

Solicitors for plaintiffs: *Pritchard & Sons.*
Solicitors for defendants: *Cooper & Co.*

G. B.

[7 Probate Division, 49.]

Feb. 8, 1882.

THE R. L. ALSTON (1881, L. No. 3208, fo. 407).

Damage—Construction of Tees Conservancy Regulations—"Maximum speed of
Six Miles per Hour."

The 22d clause of the by-laws of the river Tees, which provides that no steamship
shall be navigated on any part of the river Tees at a higher rate of speed than six
miles per hour, is to be construed as prohibiting a steamship proceeding against the
tide being navigated at a greater speed than six miles per hour through the water.

THIS was an action of damage instituted on behalf of the
owners of the steamship Lady Mostyn and the owners of her
cargo against the steamship R. L. Alston, to recover for the
damage arising out of a collision between the two vessels in
the river Tees on the 6th of November last.

The action was heard before the judge, assisted by two of
the Elder Brethren of the Trinity House.

50] *Witnesses were examined on behalf of the plaintiffs.

It appeared from admissions in the pleadings, and from
the evidence of these witnesses, that the Lady Mostyn was,
on the 6th of November, proceeding down the river Tees on

her way to sea, and making about five knots over the ground; that the tide was then about the last quarter flood, and of about the force of three knots; that at such time she came into collision with the R. L. Alston, which was coming up the river.

It was admitted that by-laws for regulating the navigation of the river Tees were in force at the time of the collision, and that the 22d and 23d clauses of such by-laws were in the following terms:

Clause 22. No steamship shall at any time be navigated in any part of the river at a higher rate of speed than a maximum rate of six miles per hour.

Clause 23. Whenever there is a fog no steamship shall be navigated in any part of the river at a higher rate of speed than three miles per hour.

After the plaintiffs' case had been closed it was agreed between counsel, with the consent of the court, that the question whether, on the facts then before the court, the Lady Mostyn was to blame for the collision should be argued before any evidence had been called on behalf of the defendants.

Butt, Q.C., and *Myburgh*, Q.C.: If the Lady Mostyn was to blame it can only be on the ground that she was proceeding down the river at a greater speed than is permitted under the 22d clause of the by-laws. The maximum rate of six miles per hour mentioned in that clause must refer to the speed of a vessel over the ground. The Lady Mostyn was only going at a rate of five miles over the ground, and she therefore in nowise infringed the clause in question.

Webster, Q.C., and *W. G. F. Phillimore*, for the defendants, the owners of the R. L. Alston, and the owners of her cargo: The rate of speed referred to in the 22d clause of the by-laws is the rate of six miles per hour through the water, and accordingly the Lady Mostyn is to blame for proceeding at the rate of about eight knots through the water.

*SIR ROBERT PHILLIMORE: In this case the Lady [51 Mostyn was admittedly proceeding down the river Tees with a speed of five knots over the ground a few seconds before the collision, and as she had a tide of about three knots against her she was then going at the rate of about eight miles an hour through the water. Now the 22d clause of the regulations for the navigation of the river Tees, in which river this collision took place, provides that "no steamship shall at any time be navigated in any part of the river at a higher rate of speed than a maximum rate of six miles per hour." I am of opinion that I must put a natural construction upon the words of this rule, and this leads me to the conclusion that the framers of the regulations meant to prohibit vessels proceeding against the tide going at a speed of more than six miles through the water. These regulations are framed with regard to the circumstances of all the cases to which they are to be applied, and I must pronounce in this case that the Lady Mostyn, by proceeding at a speed of more than six miles through the water, was guilty of negligence contributing to the collision.

Webster, Q.C.: As the court is of that opinion no evidence will be offered for the defendants, and the counter-claim will be withdrawn.

SIR ROBERT PHILLIMORE: I pronounce both vessels to blame.

Solicitors for plaintiffs: *Gregory, Rowcliffe & Co.*
Solicitors for defendants: *Pritchard & Sons.*

[7 Probate Division, 61.]

Feb. 28, 1882.

61]   *BROWNRIGG v. PIKE and Another.

Will of Realty—Appointment of Executor—Married Woman—Arrears of Rent personalty—Right to Probate.

A married woman having a power of appointment over real property executed the power in favor of herself. She afterwards made her will, by which she directed (amongst other things) that a portion of the property should be sold to pay legacies and to erect a memorial window. She also appointed an executor. There were arrears of rent due at the time of her death and subsequently:

Held, that as she possessed the property as separate estate, and had appointed an executor and directed him to pay the legacies, &c., and as the arrears of rent were part of her personal estate, the will was entitled to probate.

THIS was a demurrer to a statement of claim propounding the will, dated the 28th of January, 1881, of Elizabeth Pike, late of Newport Pagnel, in the county of Buckingham, wife of the defendant Thomas Henson Pike.

By the will the deceased gave "all my real estate which I have power to dispose of" to her husband for life, and directed (amongst other things) that after his death certain portions of the estate should be sold to pay certain legacies and the cost of a memorial window, and the will appointed the plaintiff, John Studholme Brownrigg, executor. To this the defendants demurred, "on the ground (amongst others) that it does not show that the will in question is entitled to probate."

Feb. 24. *Inderwick*, Q.C., and *Bayford*, for the demurrer: The will disposes of real estate only, for though the deceased may have had personal property she has by the terms of the will only disposed of realty, and the executor can only deal with what she has disposed of. The deceased was entitled to the property by virtue of a power, and in such a case the mere appointment of an executor is not sufficient: *In the Goods of Tomlinson* (') ; *Tugman* v. *Hopkins* (').

Patchett, Q.C., *Anderson*, and *Witworth*, in support of the statement of claim : The deceased became entitled to the property under her father's will, which gave her power to vest it *as she thought proper. That power she executed [62 by a previous document and thereby vested it in herself, and the property then became her separate estate. She therefore by the will dealt with the property as separate estate, as to which she had the same powers as a feme sole. The arrears of rent also are personal property: *Vaughan* v. *Vanderstegen* (') ; *Fettiplace* v. *Gorges* (') ; *Taylor* v. *Meads* (') ; *Johnson* v. *Gallagher* (') : *In the Goods of Jordan* (') ; Williams on Executors, 8th ed., p. 231.

Inderwick, Q.C., in reply.

Cur. adv. vult.

Feb. 28. THE PRESIDENT: This was a demurrer to a statement of claim by the executors of the will of a married woman. The statement of claim set out the circumstances in which this will was made. It appears that real property was settled or devised—devised to trustees upon trust for such intents and purposes and in such manner and form as the deceased by an   deed or deeds by her duly executed or by her last will and testament should appoint, whether covert or sole.

The testatrix executed the power so conferred upon her by a deed of the 18th of April, 1878, and conveyed this property to trustees upon trust for herself, her heirs and assigns, for her sole and separate use. Then follow some words which, it appears to me, do not affect her powers of disposition in any way, though their exact meaning is not very clear, to the intent that the said real estate might not be sold, but remain and be dealt with and descend as real estate. After having executed that deed she made her will, which, was the subject of this litigation, and by that she gave and

(') 6 P. D., 209.   (') 1 Ves., 46.
(') 4 M. & Gr., 389.   (') 34 L. J. (Ch.), 203.
(') 2 Drew., 165.   (') 8 De G. F. & J., 494, 509.
                (') Law Rep., 1 P. & D., 555.

The defendants deny that the Stormcock went to the
assistance of the Vandyck or rendered assistance to her.
The defendants deny that the Vandyck was in a position of
great danger as alleged ; the two tugs before mentioned were
sufficient to render, and they did render, to the Vandyck all
necessary assistance.

The defendants deny the 7th paragraph of the statement
of claim, and they deny that the Stormcock had begun to tow
the Queen of Scots before her starboard chain was slipped.

The defendants admit that the Stormcock gave the Queen
of Scots a hawser, which was made fast as alleged in the 8th
paragraph of the statement of claim, but they do not admit
the residue of the said paragraph, and they say that any
services rendered by the Stormcock were rendered to the
Queen of Scots, and not to the Vandyck.

As to the 9th and 10th paragraphs of the statement of
claim, the defendants deny, that but for the services ren-
45] dered by the *Stormcock, the Vandyck would have
sustained further damages, and they do not admit that in
the performance of the alleged services the Stormcock was
in danger, or ran great risk.

Nov. 23.   The action was heard before the judge, assisted
by two of the Elder Brethren of the Trinity House.

Witnesses were examined orally in court on behalf of the
plaintiffs and the defendants.   Amongst the witnesses so
examined was the pilot in charge of the Queen of Scots at
the time of the collision.   He stated, in effect, that the
Stormcock came up to the Queen of Scots about five minutes
after the collision, that at that time the starboard quarter of
the Vandyke was lying across the bows of the Queen of
Scots, and that every time the vessels fell together with the
heaving of the sea the Queen of Scots cut into the Vandyck
nearer the water every time.   He further stated, in cross-
examination, that if the Queen of Scots had slipped her
chains before she had been held up in position, she would
have fouled the Duchess of Argyle.   It appeared from the
evidence of other witnesses called on behalf of the plaintiffs,
that if the Vandyck had remained where she was, the Vandyck, and possibly the Queen of Scots also, would have
sunk.

The witnesses for the defendants proved that when the
Stormcock was holding up the Queen of Scots the steamtug
Merry Andrew was fast to the port quarter of the Van-
dyck, and the steamtug Victory was fast ahead of the Merry
Andrew.

The total value of the property proceeded against was admitted to be £83,500. The result of the remainder of the
evidence is stated in the judgment.

An action was brought by the owners of the Stormcock
and the owners of two tugs against the Queen of Scots
to recover salvage for the services rendered on the same occasion to the Queen of Scots. That action was heard immediately before the present action, and the judge in that action
awarded £400 to the Stormcock. It was agreed by the parties
to the present action that the evidence in that action should
be taken as given in the present action.

Myburgh, and *J. Walton*, for the plaintiffs: The assistance of the Stormcock was directly instrumental in saving
the Vandyck *from sinking, and it is immaterial that [46
such assistance was rendered after an express request from the
Queen of Scots: *The Annapolis* and *The Golden Light* (');
The Woburn Abbey ('). The services rendered to the Vandyck were services such as no prudent man would have
refused to accept.

Butt, Q.C., and *G. Bruce*, for the defendants: The services in this case were services rendered at the express re
quest and directly for the benefit of the Queen of Scots.
There was nothing to prevent the Queen of Scots slipping
her anchors except the danger of her drifting down upon the
Duchess of Argyle, and that was a contingency which in no
way concerned the Vandyck. All the assistance the Vandyck required could have been rendered by the Merry
Andrew and the Victory, the two steamtugs which were in
attendance on her at her request.

SIR ROBERT PHILLIMORE: In this case the steamtug
Stormcock brings her action of salvage against the steamship
Vandyck, which at the time the services were rendered was
in collision with the ship Queen of Scots. Now the first
question the court has to decide is, was there any salvage
service in its legal sense rendered by the plaintiffs to the
Vandyck, inasmuch as there was no request made to the
Stormcock to act on behalf of the Vandyck, and several
cases were cited to the court to show that the owners of the
Vandyck were under no liability to pay salvage remuneration. But I am of opinion that in the circumstances of this
case the evidence shows that the services of the Stormcock
were accepted by the Vandyck. The next question is, what
was the value of the services so rendered to the Vandyck,
and looking to the evidence, and after conferring with the
Elder Brethren of the Trinity House, I am of opinion that a

(') Lush., 855.   (') 3 Mar. Law Cas., 310.

vested the money in them.   But the authority of these executors is only coextensive with the power given by the will,
for the executors here do not take *jure representationis*,
but under the power which the wife was authorized to exercise by making a will as to this particular property."
   But I have shown that in this case the will is not made
under the power but by virtue of the right which a married
woman has to make a will in respect of her separate property.   By appointing an executor her separate personal estate vests in him to be got in by him, and applied either
according to the provisions of the will or as the law directs.
For these reasons I hold that this will is entitled to be admitted to probate, and I overrule the demurrer, and direct
that the trial of the issues of fact be proceeded with.

   Solicitors for plaintiff: *Pattison, Wigg & Co.*
   Solicitor for defendants: *G. P. Rogers.*

                                                    R. A. P.

[7 Probate Division 65.]

March 8, 1882.

In the Goods of FRANK LEYLAND WHITE.

Will—Construction—"Money"—Residue.

A testator bequeathed "the whole residue of money" to A. H. W., "excepting
such things as the under-mentioned," &c. :
Held, that the words were sufficient to pass the residue.

FRANK LEYLAND WHITE, late of Melville Place, in the
city of Liverpool, book-keeper, deceased, died on the 15th
of September, 1881.
   The deceased made his will on the 11th of September,
1881, in the following words:

   "There is a statement of accounts owing by me to different tradespeople and friends.   After these are paid the
whole residue of money to be handed to my sister, Ann
Harnett White, excepting such things as the under-mentioned specified to certain individuals.
66] *"Black portmanteau all clothes to James Blythe
Page, 'brigand and apothecary' to Hanna Monck, unframed
picture of horse to Jane Page."

   The will was signed and attested, and then followed the
statement of accounts referred to.
   No executor was appointed by the will, and the testator's
sister mentioned in the will was a minor.
   Pritchard moved for grant of letters of administration to

J. C. White as guardian of the sister: She is, under the terms of the will, residuary legatee: *Re Bassett* ('); *Wiggins* v. *Wiggins* ('); *Leighton* v. *Bailie* ('); *In the Goods of Cadge* ('); *In the Goods of Bloomfield* (').

THE PRESIDENT: I think the word "money" in this will is, when taken with the context, used in a general sense, and is sufficient to pass the residue. The grant may therefore be made as asked for.

Solicitors: *C. P. Pritchard & Marshall.*

(') Law Rep., 14 Eq., 54; 2 Eng. R., 417.
(') 2 Sim. (N.S.), 226.
(') 3 My. & C., 267.
(') Law Rep., 1 P. & D., 543.
(') 31 L. J. (P. & M.), 119.

R. A. P.

Government obligations or securities do not usually pass under a bequest of "moneys or cash." They are securities: Hertford *v.* Lowther, 7 Beavan, 1, 1 Jarman on Wills (Bigelow's ed.), 769 note 1 ; Glendenning *v.* Glendenning, 9 Beav., 324 ; Beck *v.* McGillis, 9 Barb., 35 ; Mann *v.* Mann, 1 Johns. Chy., 231, 14 Johns., 1 ; Bevan *v.* Bevan, L. R., 5 Ir., 57, 62–4, 65–7, 68–71 ; Stein *v.* Retherdon, 3 Weekly Notes, 65, 19 L. T. (N.S.), 184, 37 L. J., etc., 369 ; Tallent *v.* Scott, 3 Weekly Notes, 236 ; Smith *v.* Burch, 16 N. Y. Weekly Dig., 26.

Though other parts of the will may show an intention that they should pass under the term : 1 Jarm. on Wills (Bigelow's ed.), 769, note 1 ; Matter of Miller's Estate, 48 Cal., 165 ; Dunsmure *v.* Elliot, 17 Scot. L. Repr., 134 ; Easson *v.* Brown, Id., 239 ; Bevan *v.* Bevan, L. R., 5 Ir., 67–8, 68–71.

A bequest of "money and securities for money" does not pass an I. O. U.: Barry *v.* Harding, 1 Jones & Lat., 475. "Choses in action" does not include stocks: Wortham *v.* Tinsley, 1 Quarterly L. Jour., 67.

A mortgage executed by a railroad company upon its then and thereafter to be acquired "property," containing a specific description of the different kinds of such property ; held, that certain municipal bonds, issued to aid in building the road, which are not embraced by such description, did not pass by the use of the general word "property": Smith *v.* McCullough, 104 U. S. R., 25.

"*Ready* money" means money in the house or in bank, in specie or currency ready for use, but does not include money collected on a legacy: Smith *v.* Burch, 16 N. Y. Weekly Dig., 26.

[7 Probate Division, 66.]

March 8, 1882.

JONES V. JONES.

Will affecting Real Estate—Assignee—Leave to cite—20 & 21 Vict. c. 77, s. 61.

In an action as to the validity of a will the court will not order the assignee of the heir-at-law of the testatrix to be cited as a person having or pretending interest in the real estate affected by the will.

THIS was an action for revocation of probate. Hannah Jones, late of Glanrhyd, in the parish of Lanfairnewbwl, in the county of Anglesey, widow, died on the 8th of April, 1876, having, by her will dated the 6th of April,

1876, devised a freehold farm to Owen Jones, who duly obtained probate of the will.

Owen Jones devised the farm to his wife, Elizabeth Jones,
67] and *died on the 14th of July, 1879, and probate of
his will was duly obtained by his widow.

John Jones, heir-at-law and one of the next of kin of
Hannah Jones, brought this action against Elizabeth Jones
for revocation of the will of Hannah Jones; and in his affidavit of documents it appeared that he had assigned to his
brother Robert Jones all his interest as heir-at-law of Hannah Jones.

Searle, for the defendant Elizabeth Jones, moved, under
20 & 21 Vict. c. 77, s. 61 ('), for leave to cite Robert Jones
as interested in the real estate of the deceased Hannah
Jones.   The words of the section are very large, " having or
pretending interest."   If this were a will of personalty,
Robert Jones would, as a matter of course, have a right to
intervene.

Clement Lloyd, contrà :   The interest contemplated by
the words of the statute is an interest by descent, as e.g.,
that of the devisee of a devisee.   The application is too late,
as the action will be heard next week.

THE PRESIDENT: This is a novel application, and one
which the court ought not to grant.   It is also unnecessary,
as the assignee will be bound by the decision in the action
as completely as his assignor.

Application refused.

Solicitors for plaintiff: *Radford & Frankland.*
Solicitors for defendant: *Bloxam & Co.*

(¹) The following are the material parts
of the section :   Where proceedings are
taken for revoking the probate of a will
on the ground of the invalidity thereof
. . . unless . . . the will affects only
personal estate, the heir-at-law, devisees,
and other persons having or pretending
interest in the real estate affected by the
will shall, subject to the provisions of this
act, and to the rules and orders under
this act, be cited to see proceedings.

R. A. P.

[7 Probate Division, 68.]

March 14, 1882.

*MORRELL and Others v. MORRELL and Others. [68

Will—Mistake—Words introduced without the knowledge or approval of the Testator.

A testator, in the instructions for his will, directed that all his B shares should be given to his nephews, but the word "forty," was inserted several times in the will before the word "shares," and the will was executed with that word repeated several times before the word "shares." The jury found that the word "forty" was introduced by mistake, that the clauses including the word were never read over to the testator, and that he only approved of the will upon the supposition that all his B shares were given to his nephews, and thereupon the court ordered the word "forty," wherever it occurred in the will, to be struck out.

IN this case the plaintiffs propounded the will and codicil dated respectively the 19th day of July, 1880, and the 11th day of June, 1881, of John Morrell, late of Mordansweld Road, Birkdale, in the county of Lancaster, gentleman, who died on the 16th day of June, 1881. They also alleged that the will named the plaintiffs legatees of the testator's fully paid-up B shares in John Morrell & Co., Limited, but the word "forty," had been inserted as limiting the number, and that that word wheresoever inserted was inserted by mistake, and the insertion thereof was not known to the testator nor approved by him at the time of execution of either the will or codicil. The defendants, the executors, and also the residuary legatees, denied the allegation that the word "forty" had been inserted by mistake or without the knowledge or approval of the testator.

Inderwick, Q.C., and *C. A. Middleton*, for the plaintiffs.

Sir H. Giffard, Q.C., and *Bayford*, for the defendants.

Dr. Deane, Q.C., and *Bargrave Deane*, for residuary legatees.

The testator, Mr. John Morrell, was a provision merchant in Liverpool, and in May, 1880, converted his business into a limited liability company, under the title of "John Morrell & Co., Limited." The capital of the company was £100,000, divided into 1,000 shares of £100 each, and the testator received £30,000 in money and £40,000 in fully paid-up shares, which were called "B or deferred shares." This amount was in 400 shares of £100 each. In the same month, and before these shares were allotted *to him, he in- [69 structed his solicitor, Mr. Jevons, to draw up his will. Mr. Jevons took the verbal instructions of Mr. Morrell, and reduced them to written memoranda, of which there were sev-

eral successive drafts.   In Mr. Jevons's written "estimate
of value and income of property of John Morrell, Esq."
there appeared among the items "shares in John Morrell &
Co., Limited, £40,000;" but in the memoranda of instructions for the will, Mr. Jevons wrote: "Bequeathed testator's shares in John Morrell & Co., Limited, to his nephews
George Morrell and Thomas Morrell (sons of testator's
brother George), John Morrell the younger (son of testator's brother Robert Morrell), and Thomas Dove Foster (son
of testator's sister Mary Foster, deceased), in equal shares."
The memoranda so worded were sent to a conveyancing
counsel in London, to whom were also forwarded the articles
of association of "John Morrell & Co., Limited," and the
counsel in drawing the will put the bequest of the shares to
the four nephews thus: "In equal shares, the forty fully
paid-up or deferred shares, of the value of £100 each, in
John Morrell & Co., Limited."   In four different passages
of the will the bequest was alluded to in these same terms;
and, in a passage making the bequest free of legacy duty,
Mr. Jevons copied the words used by the conveyancer.
These terms in effect gave only £4,000, instead of £40,000,
among the four nephews, the conveyancer having treated
the shares as if they were only 40 in number, while in reality
they were 400.   It further appeared that, though Mr. Jevons's draft instructions for the will had been more than
once read to the testator, the will, as a whole, never was,
Mr. Morrell himself having said it was unnecessary to read
it to him when, in July, 1880, he was about to execute it,
and the will was executed with the bequest in the terms
drawn by the conveyancer.

   Mr. Jevons gave evidence to the effect that beyond all
doubt Mr. Morrell intended that the whole 400 shares of
£100 each should be divided among his nephews ; and Mr.
Morrell's widow, who had been examined by commission,
deposed to the same effect.   The testator had told her, she
said, of his intention before he made the will, and on various
occasions in a period extending from the time of the execution of the will to the date of his death he spoke to her of his
70]   having left each of his nephews shares of *the value of
£10,000.   Mr. Stead, a friend of the testator, gave corrobora-
tive evidence.

   Feb. 14.   THE PRESIDENT: Gentlemen of the jury—This
case though it may appear simple in itself, is one of very
great importance with reference to other cases hereafter in
which the facts may not be so clear as they appear to be

here. There can be no graver question brought into a court of law than the question, what is a man's last will when he is dead and no longer able to speak for himself, and his property has to be distributed according to the particular words that have been used in a particular instrument. The law has established rigid safeguards in order to have attested evidence of what such intention was ; and no amount of proof that a man intended to give A. or B. the whole or part of his property avails. He must put his intentions in writing, and that writing and his signature to it must be attested by two witnesses. If, therefore, a mistake is made, it matters not how plainly, in leaving out words, however much you may regret their omission, we cannot after his death correct that, because his intention would not have been put into writing and attested as the law requires.

There is a second class of mistake, viz., where words are inserted of which the testator knows nothing. To take a familiar instance, suppose people about the testator at the time of his death take his instructions to leave his property to certain persons and fraudulently introduce into the will their own names instead, and say, "I leave to Tom Smith, £10," &c., and never read that to him. In that case you may strike out the passage, because he did not know it was there or intend that it should be, and therefore it was not his will in any sense of the word.

But there is another case, and this case is somewhat of that kind. It is the case of a man who feels himself unable to express his intentions in a legal and formal manner, and who confides to somebody else the duty of expressing them. I should say that in the majority of cases where a lawyer is employed that is the state of things. The testator prefers to rely on the judgment and skill of a trained mind to express his wishes rather than to run the risk of selecting words himself, and when that is the *case he adopts [71 the words used by that person just as though they were his own. There is no difference between the case of his referring it to a particular person to express his wishes who makes the mistake, and himself, knowing what his own wishes are and setting about to express them, making the mistake. He might foolishly attempt to use technical language ; if, for instance, he had put down heir-at-law when in fact he meant next of kin, he must bear the consequences ; and so if he trusts to anybody else to express his wishes and adopts the words used by that person as his own, then that alone can remain as the evidence of his intention.

You must bear these observations in mind while I comment

on the particular questions, which I trust will lay the foundation for a clear if not perfectly satisfactory conclusion in this case.   I shall take them in order in which I gave them.

As the case is presented on the pleadings, the alleged mistake is that the word "forty" has been introduced throughout the will before the word "shares."   In order to see whether there was the particular mistake of the insertion of the word "forty" before "shares," or whether there was any other mistake in the drawing up of that clause, it is well to look in the first instance to the instructions which were given by the deceased to Mr. Jevons.   In that document there is no mention whatever of the number of shares, but the testator's property, which we now know was of the value of £40,000 in the company, is spoken of simply as his shares. There is no mention of anything but shares, and that continues throughout all the documents down to the time when the draft is sent back by the counsel to Mr. Jevons.   The instructions or directions to counsel to draw the will also only mention "shares" without any reference to number, but from some cause or other which is not explained, the counsel who drew the will inserted into his draft the word "forty" before "shares" wherever it became necessary.

The first question I ask you is, was there a mistake at all in that?   Now, the evidence of Mr. Jevons is quite clear upon the subject, that whenever the matter was discussed the the reference was to the whole number of the shares as being intended for the nephews.   The wife, whose deposition has 72]   been read, is equally *clear that her husband always spoke of the whole of his shares as intended for his nephews; and a friend has been called who speaks to the same effect. I should imagine, therefore, that you would come to the conclusion that there is a mistake in the manner in which that clause is drawn.

But then that leads to the second question, viz., whether the mistake was in putting in the word "forty" at all and in not leaving it as it was in the instructions, "My shares in the company," or does the mistake consist in not having put in the proper number "four hundred" instead of "forty." It is true that if four hundred had been put in it would, we know, have correctly carried out the intention as Mr. Jevons and the testator's wife believe it to have been, but it is not because it would in fact have carried out his intention that therefore that is the way it should have been expressed in his will, and I should say that the more correct way of drawing a will from such instructions as these is not to insert a number which may lead to a mistake, as you see it has done

in this case, but to use the general words which prevent the
possibility of a mistake, namely, by saying "All my shares"
or "the shares" which equally implies it. Did then the
mistake consist in inserting any number, or in not inserting
the proper number?

The third question which I leave to you is, Did he know
of the inserting of the word "forty"? That depends on
Mr. Jevons's evidence, and I am sorry that we should be
left in some uncertainty as to what really took place. Mr.
Jevons went on the 10th of July with the draft which had
been prepared by counsel, and so fully did it to his mind
embody the wishes of the testator that he as a matter of
prudence had it then and there executed, and the question
is, did he read that document over to the testator. I am
sorry to say Mr. Jevons is not able to say whether he did or
not; but you will remember that he himself said that would
be the usual course, but at the present moment he says "my
recollection is indistinct upon the point as to the extent to
which I went into the draft will with the testator;" but he
speaks with confidence as to the following, "I read the passages which made alterations in the draft which he had had
in his possession." I am sorry we have not more distinct
recollection of what took place. I can *only say it [73
seems most unusual not to do one or other of these two
things, viz., either to read over the whole of the document
which the party is about to sign or to go through it passage by
passage, and say there is a clause to this effect and a clause
to that effect and so on. In some states of a testator's health
or in some states of a testator's mind disturbed by pain it
might be expedient to shorten the process, but in some way
or other, so far as my experience goes, I should say it is
the practice of solicitors either to read over the whole instrument or to read and explain clause by clause the effect that
each clause would have. Unfortunately Mr. Jevons does
not enable us to judge by his evidence what course he did
pursue, and you have to draw your inference, but remem-
bering that this was the document which he then got the testator to sign as a valid will, it will be for you to say whether
you do not come to the conclusion that Mr. Jevons did either
by reading the whole or in some way or other call his attention to the several matters of his will. He does say he read
the passages which made alterations in the draft which he
had had in his possession, but then there comes a very important fact. He called his attention to this question of
the legacy duty, and that is repeated twice over in the will.
He had the draft with him, and he says that as to one of

these alterations in which the word "forty" occurs he made
it himself upon the draft; as to the other, he is rather under the impression that he made it at the office for the purpose of making the one part of the draft consistent with the
other.   But with regard to that alteration which he made at
the time you will have to say whether you do or do not believe that he read that passage to him in which the word
"forty" undoubtedly occurs.

Therefore the two questions which you have to consider
as to that are, did he read or bring to the testator's notice
the one particular instance in which at any rate the word
"forty" was inserted before "shares"?

Upon the fourth question, "Did he approve of the words
used as the expression of his wish," I must more fully explain what I have already suggested.   When you employ a
lawyer either to draw a will or a deed which requires skill you
74]   rely on his skill *and, of course, you rely on his integ-
rity, and when he tells you "I have drawn this will according to your instructions," and he puts it before you to sign,
do not you adopt his words as expressing your wish? I do
not desire, as far as this is a question of fact, to take it out
of your hands, but, speaking for myself, it appears to me
the man does approve of the words which his solicitor puts
in for him.   And this seems to divide itself again into two
parts, did he approve of the particular words being used as
the expression of his will, that is, did he approve of such
passages as his attention was particularly directed to, or
generally did he approve the whole will as expressing his
wishes?   When a man leaves his solicitor to draw a will
does he not say in effect, I do not know how to do it; I rely
on you and I accept your words as though I had the power
to do it.

The next question is, did he understand the effect of the
words?   He was a man in failing health and nervous, and
business had become so distasteful to him that he did not
open his letters.   Mr. Jevons himself, also in two instances,
wrote the word "forty" in with his own hand, and did not
understand or notice what the effect was.   You probablly
therefore, would come to the conclusion that the testater
was equally wanting in observation as Mr. Jevons, and did
not understand the meaning of the words.   Lastly, did he
intend his nephews to have all or only the forty shares!
That is a question upon which probably you will have no
difference of opinion, but I have put the question in order
that we may have, as far as counsel and myself can foresee,

everything that may be necessary for determining the law of the case after you have decided the facts.

The jury, after deliberating for a short time, found as follows: 1. That the words were inserted by mistake; 2. That the particular mistake was in inserting the word "forty"; 3. That the testator did not know of the insertion of the word; that it was not read over to him; 4. That he did not approve of the word being used, i.e., that he instructed his solicitor as to the whole of the shares, and only approved of the draft upon the supposition that the solicitor had carried out his wishes; 5. That he did not *understand the [75 effect of the words used; 6. That he intended the nephews to have all the shares.

Cur. adv. vult (¹).

March 14. THE PRESIDENT: The findings of the jury have disposed of the whole matter. It appears that the testator intended to leave all his shares in a particular company to his nephews, and gave instructions to that effect to his solicitor, who embodied them in writing and sent them to a conveyancing counsel in London to draw the will. In those instructions the solicitor spoke, as he had been directed by the testator to speak, of "all" the testator's shares; but, by some accident not accounted for, counsel introduced into the draft will the word "forty" before "shares." Though the solicitor saw this, it never attracted his attention, and he never realized the effect the word "forty" would have on the disposition of the shares made by the testator. The jury have arrived at the conclusion that what the solicitor said on this subject was correct—that he never informed the testator in any way that the word "forty" had been introduced; and it was proved, by other evidence than that of the solicitor himself, that the actual will as executed was not read over to the testator. The jury found that the testator never authorized the introduction of the word "forty" in the will, and never heard that it had been introduced, and that he executed the will in the belief that it carried out his instructions. In the case of *Harter* v. *Harter* (²) I held that the language of a will could not be changed where the testator had seen the words and adopted them; but in *Fulton* v. *Andrew* (³), where a residuary bequest was introduced into a will without the knowledge and authority of the tes-

---

(¹) His Lordship postponed judgment in the belief that the same questions were about to be decided in a case then standing for judgment in the Privy Council. This, however, turned out to be erroneous.

(²) Law Rep., 3 P. & M., 11, 22.

(³) Law Rep., 7 H. L., 448; 12 Eng. R., 76.

tator, the clause containing that bequest was rejected. If so, the same principle may be applied to a single word, and therefore, on the ruling of the House of Lords, in *Fulton* v. *Andrew* ([1]), I hold that the words may be struck out which had been introduced without the authority of the testator.

The court directed that the word "forty" be struck out 76] of the *four places in which it occurred in the will, and, by consent of the parties, directed that the costs be paid by the plaintiffs.

Solicitors for plaintiffs : *Field, Roscoe & Co.*
Solicitors for defendants : *Sharpe, Parkers & Co.; Walker, Son & Field.*

([1]) Law Rep., 7 H. L., 448 ; 12 Eng. R., 76.

R. A. P.

[7 Probate Division, 76.]

Feb. 21, 1882.

WILLIAMSON v. WILLIAMSON and BATES.

Divorce—Wilful Neglect—Imprisonment for Criminal Offence.

Semble, that the conviction of a wife for an offence against the criminal law is no justification for refusing further cohabitation with her, and that, if such refusal conduces to her adultery, the court will not grant her husband a dissolution of his marriage.

THIS was a petition for dissolution of marriage.

The petitioner, James Williamson, a carter, was married in January, 1879, to the respondent, a domestic servant, and a fortnight afterwards she was apprehended and subsequently convicted of theft and sentenced to six months' imprisonment. On her discharge from prison she did not return to cohabitation with her husband but again went into domestic service. While there, and in October, 1879, she asked her husband to live with her again, but he refused owing to her misconduct. He then lost sight of her until November, 1881, when he discovered that she had been living with the co-respondent ever since May, 1880.

Neither the respondent nor co-respondent appeared in the suit.

Searle appeared for the petitioner.

THE PRESIDENT: The conviction and imprisonment of a husband or wife for an offence against the criminal law is no justification to the other party for refusing to live with him or her. However painful it may be for a respectable man to have a wife who has been convicted of felony, such conviction does not in this court justify him in deserting her.

It sometimes happens that wives have husbands who have been convicted of *infamous crimes, and yet those [77 husbands are legally entitled to cohabitation with them. ·

In this case I have to consider not only whether there was desertion by the husband without legal excuse, but also whether that desertion has tended to bring about her adultery. It appears that after coming out of prison she did not go to her husband, but returned, to service, and got a living in the manner she had done before her marriage, and that after his refusal to receive her she again returned to service. I do not think, therefore, that the refusal of the husband to resume cohabitation with the respondent at the time she presented herself to him in October, 1879, can be said to have conduced to her adultery, and therefore I pronounce a decree *nisi*, with costs.

Solicitors: *Botterell & Co.*

R. A. P.

[7 Probate Division, 84.]

April 26, 1882.

*SMITH v. SMITH, MAJOR, CHILD and RABETT. [84

Divorce—Respondent's Costs—Full Costs.

In a divorce suit the usual order had been obtained for securing the wife's costs of the hearing, and there had been no appeal from that order and no further costs were asked for at the hearing. Subsequently the case of *Robertson* v. *Robertson* (6 P. D., 119) was decided in the Court of Appeal, and the Divorce Court was thereupon asked to order payment of the wife's full costs. Application refused.

In future, if in a divorce suit in which a wife is found guilty the court is asked to order payment of her full costs, the court will postpone its decision until after her bill of costs has been taxed.

The case of *Robertson* v. *Robertson* (6 P. D., 119) referred to.

THIS was a husband's petition for dissolution of marriage, by reason of his wife's adultery with the co-respondents. The respondent in her answer denied the adultery, and made countercharges of cruelty, adultery, and connivance.

The cause was heard in the first instance against the respondent and the co-respondent Child before the court and a special jury, when the jury after a two days' trial found, on the 3d of March, 1881, that the petitioner was not guilty of any of the countercharges, but they were unable to agree as to the charge against the respondent and co-respondent.

The cause was again heard on the 5th and 6th of July following, when evidence was given against all the co-respondents, and the jury found that the respondent had committed adultery with each of them, and the court pronounced a

32 ENG. REP.　　　41

85] decree *nisi* with costs *against the co-respondents, and made the usual order for the wife's costs.

March 28. *Dr. Swabey*, for the respondent, applied for an order for payment of the respondent's full costs: In *Robertson* v. *Robertson* (¹) the Court of Appeal has decided that, unless the solicitor has improperly conducted the action, the wife's costs are to be taxed and paid without reference to the sum paid into court or secured. The jury in this case were discharged on the first trial and therefore there can be no doubt that the solicitor was right in defending the wife upon the second hearing. The wife had to be defended against charges of adultery with three co-respondents, but the registrar had only ordered the sum of £40 to be paid in to meet her costs.

Searle, for the petitioner: This case was decided before *Robertson* v. *Robertson* (¹). That was heard on the 19th of July and is not retrospective. Besides, the application is too late. It ought to have been made when all the facts were fresh in the recollection of the court: *Wait* v. *Wait and Flower* (²). Even if the court has now a discretion in the matter the application ought not to be granted, as the respondent greatly increased the costs of the suit by making countercharges for which there was no foundation.

Dr. Swabey, in reply.   *Cur. adv. vult.*

April 26. THE PRESIDENT: This is the first occasion since the case of *Robertson* v. *Robertson* (¹) was decided by the Lords Justices of Appeal on which I have been called upon to consider the effect of their judgment on the practice of this court. The question involved is one of considerable importance, as it affects the exercise of my discretion as to costs in a very large number of the matrimonial causes which are tried before me. In *Robertson* v. *Robertson* (¹) I refused to allow the wife, who was found guilty of adultery and failed to prove any charge against her husband, more than £370 for her costs, for which amount security had been given. The Court of Appeal held that I ought to have al-
86] lowed *her her full costs whatever they might on taxation be found to be. My power as to the costs is conferred by the 51st section of 20 & 21 Vict. c. 85, which enacts that "the court may make such order as to costs as to such court may seem just." I am, of course, aware that this discretionary power must be exercised, not arbitrarily or capriciously, but judicially. If the Court of Appeal had felt itself in a position to overrule the exercise of my dis-

(¹) 6 P. D., 119.   (²) Law Rep., 2 P. & D., 228.

cretion in the particular case, I should have accepted its correction without observation, but the Master of the Rolls says (p. 123): "The learned judge did not exercise any discretion at all ; he simply made the usual order as to costs —an order which had. become usual in the way I have mentioned. Therefore, it is not a case where the appeal is as to the exercise of discretion, but a case where the judge, conceiving himself bound by a rule of practice, which we think erroneous, simply followed that rule." I assume from these observations that the learned judge was not in possession of the facts of the case. I certainly did not conceive myself to be fettered by the practice in the exercise of my discretion, and I was under the impression that I had exercised it. If I had thought it just that the wife should have more than £370 for her costs, there was nothing in the practice to prevent my giving more to her. The facts as they appear on the minutes of the court were these : Security was originally given by the husband for £150. Ten days before the trial application was made by the wife to increase this sum, on account of the expense of bringing witnesses from Italy, and the amount was accordingly increased to £370. The trial took place on three days ; on the second of these days a summons was taken out to further increase the amount. This summons was brought on for hearing in open court. I find on reference to the shorthand writer's notes that I said : "I must have some further explanation. We are now in the middle of the case. It was always known that the adultery was charged to have been committed in Italy ; and it appears from the evidence given to-day that it was known that there was a charge with reference to Bergamo. I must, therefore, see how anything in the course of the case has made it necessary to call further witnesses from Italy. It was always known that Favogrossa was charged as co-respondent. It must, therefore, have been *taken into account when the costs were estimated." [87 I accordingly reserved the question till after the hearing, and subsequently heard the summons in chambers and refused the application, on special grounds affecting the solicitor as well as the respondent. I do not now enter into my reasons, as they would be irrelevant on this occasion ; and my object is not to justify the exercise of my discretion, but to show that I did in fact exercise it in the fullest way in which that duty can be discharged by a judge.

I now proceed to trace the origin and growth of the practice of the Divorce Court as to a wife's costs. I do not think it necessary to say much as to what the Master of the Rolls

terms "the nobler view" which prevailed in the practice of
the House of Lords on bills for divorce. It is matter of legal
history that the expenses of proceedings before that tribunal
were so large that they amounted to a denial of justice to all
but the very wealthy, and it was to remedy this evil that the
Divorce Court was established. In the Ecclesiastical Courts
the wife was entitled to have her costs taxed *de die in diem*,
so as to enable her to defend herself; but if her proctor
neglected to take this precaution it was the invariable practice of the court not to make any order for costs in favor of
a wife who had brought her case to a hearing and had failed.
This question was in 1858 brought to the consideration of
the full court, the then Court of Appeal, consisting of Lord
Chelmsford, Wightman, J., and Sir C. Cresswell, in *Keats*
v. *Keats and Montezuma* (¹). On an application for the
wife's costs, the court said, "You are too late for that now.
Your application should have been made before the cause
was heard. The foundation of the rule of the Ecclesiastical
Court was that the wife should be enabled to bring her case
to a hearing and defend herself, and so up to any time previous to the hearing the husband was generally liable to
have the wife's costs taxed against him, and the court has
so far followed the rule, as in *Evans* v. *Evans and Robinson* (²), *but if the wife has brought her case to a hearing,
howsoever, and fails, the husband has never then been made
liable for her costs.*" Sir C. Cresswell had at the time of
88]   the case referred *to of *Evans* v. *Evans*, established the
practice of directing security to be given for the wife's costs,
out of which her solicitor was entitled, if the court so ordered,
to have his costs. And this was the practice while Sir C.
Cresswell presided over this court. The Master of the Rolls
says (³): "I must say, in fairness to Sir James Hannen,
that this practice did not begin with him, and that he merely
followed the practice of his immediate predecessor, who followed the practice of Sir C. Cresswell." It has been seen
that the practice of the Ecclesiastical Court as adapted by
Sir C. Cresswell to the Divorce Court was expressly sanctioned
by the full court; but Lord Penzance did not merely adopt
the practice established by Sir C. Cresswell, he modified and
embodied it in a rule of court made under the authority of
the act of Parliament. The rule is as follows: (Rules and
Orders, Dec. 26, 1865, No. 159). "When on the hearing or
trial of a cause the decision of the Judge Ordinary or the
verdict of the jury is against the wife, no costs of the wife
of and incidental to such hearing or trial shall be allowed

(¹) 1 Sw. & Tr., 358.   (²) 1 Sw. & Tr., 328.   (³) At p. 121.

as against the husband, except such as shall be applied for
and ordered to be allowed by the Judge Ordinary at the
time of such hearing or trial." I had power, if I had thought
fit, to alter this rule; but so far from my experience of its
working leading me to think it objectionable, I, so to speak,
re-enacted it by the amended rules of the 14th of July, 1875.
Before examining what interpretation the Lords Justices
have put upon the 159th rule, I wish to state what the operation of that rule has been. In a vast majority of divorce
cases the parties are poor. It is, of course, essential to justice that the wife should be provided with the means of
having the charge against her fully investigated, whether
she be guilty or not; but it is of scarcely less importance
that the husband should not be called upon to pay or secure
more costs than are really necessary for this purpose. It
frequently happens that the proceedings are stayed because
the husband cannot pay or secure the required amount, and
by this and other means the proceedings are delayed as much
as possible with the result, if not with the object, that the
husband has to pay alimony to his wife for as long a
period *as practicable. When at length he is able to [89
bring the case to trial it is a common occurrence for the
counsel who represents the wife candidly to say that, as he
is not in a position to call his client to deny the charge, he
will not take up time by contesting the case. It is obvious
that in such cases the respondent has known from the beginning that she had no defence, yet she has put her husband
to great and unjustifiable costs and expenses. That she has
had sufficient means to bring her case to that stage is plain,
res ipsa loquitur. Is it unreasonable to say that she shall
have no more unless she satisfies the judge at the trial that
more was necessary? I am aware that this question is not
one solely between husband and wife, but involves also the
interests of her solicitor; and I have expressed in *Flower* v.
Flower (¹) as strongly as I could my opinion of the necessity
of making sufficient provision for his remuneration. It
would be impossible to ascertain in what cases the solicitor
has become aware that his client was guilty; or at what stage
of the proceedings he may have acquired that knowledge.
Nor do I think that a solicitor, as soon as he discovers that
the wife cannot deny the charge made against her, is bound
to abandon her. If he did so, it would cause her to seek the
assistance of some less scrupulous adviser. There is an
honorable way of defending the worst of cases. But all inducement to economy in the conducting of the wife's defence

(¹) 3 P. D., 134.

will be removed, if the costs of the wife are to be allowed in
every case in precisely the same way, whether she be guilty
or not, without any limitation beyond ordinary taxation for
the protection of the husband.   The limitation afforded by
the 159th rule and the practice as to giving security is intended to strike a fair balance between the interests of the
husband and the wife's solicitor, and it operates in this
manner.   The solicitor gets actual payment of all costs until
the directions are given as to the mode of hearing or trial.
He then states to the registrar what witnesses he proposes
to summon, and all the circumstances which may enable the
registrar to fix the amount of costs required for the hearing.
If the solicitor is dissatisfied with the registrar's order he may
appeal to the judge.   If the circumstances of the case make
90]   it *reasonable, I frequently allow the case to proceed,
reserving to the wife's solicitor the right to have his costs
taxed, and to apply for an order for their allowance at or after
the trial as though security had been given.   If unexpected
incidents are alleged to have arisen, application may be made
to increase the amount to be secured, as was done in *Robertson* v. *Robertson*, and at the trial the solicitor has the opportunity under rule 159 to show cause why costs beyond the
sum secured should be allowed.   Nor do the safeguards for
the solicitor end here, for Lord Penzance held in *Somerville* v.
Somerville (¹) that even after the trial an application on
special grounds with reference to the wife's costs may be
entertained.   Can it be said that the protection of the solicitor is not thus amply provided for?   He is, in fact, the
most favored of practitioners, for he can, whatever the merits
of his case be, stay his adversary's proceedings until all the
costs which he may show can be reasonably anticipated have
been paid or secured.   If the solicitor does not take the
necessary steps to obtain sufficient security or an order of
the court for his costs it is his own fault.   Numerous instances might be cited in the practice of all courts where
costs are lost if not asked for at the proper time.   If, on the
other hand, a general order for all the solicitor's costs is in
every case to be made, the costs of witnesses may have to be
allowed who were not mentioned when the security was fixed,
and who were not called at the trial.   It may be impossible
for the taxing officer to say that their evidence was irrelevant.
It would not be expedient or possible to make the costs of
witnesses depend on whether they or the respondent were
put into the witness-box.   Such a course would tend to dis-
courage that honorable candor of counsel to which I have

(¹) 36 L. J. (P. & M.), 87.   .

referred, and would supply a motive for perjury and the prolongation of hopeless defences. Further, it is impossible for the registrar, who has not heard the case, to know to what extent unnecessary costs have been incurred. It is only the judge, who has heard the witnesses and seen the course the trial has taken, who can form an opinion on this subject; and the 159th rule only aims at this—that the wife's solicitor shall at the *trial, while the circumstances [91 are fresh in the recollection of the judge, show the facts which he alleges justified him in exceeding the costs already provided for.

I assume that, when the Lords Justices say that they have power to overrule the practice of the Divorce Court, they mean, not that they have power to abrogate a rule made under the authority of an act of Parliament, but that they put a particular interpretation upon it; and I now proceed to ascertain what interpretation they have put on the 159th rule. The Master of the Rolls says: "The 159th rule is plain. 'No costs shall be allowed except such as shall be applied for and ordered by the judge at the time of the hearing.' That, of course, means ordered to be allowed in the exercise of a judicial discretion, and it appears to me that there not being a suggestion that the solicitor of the wife has conducted himself otherwise than properly, or that he had not fair grounds for believing that the wife had a defence against the charge of adultery, he ought to be allowed the usual costs." It is to be observed that the Master of the Rolls did not apply this principle to the costs of the appeal either in *Robertson* v. *Robertson* (¹), or *McAlpin* v. *McAlpin* (²). In each of these cases the wife's appeal was partially successful. It cannot, therefore, be said that the solicitors in these cases acted otherwise than properly, or that they had not fair ground for bringing the appeal; yet the wife's costs of the appeal were in both cases refused. Brett, L.J., says (p. 125), "If the solicitor who appears for the wife either knowingly promotes a case which it must be clear to anybody has no foundation at all, so that he is countenancing improper litigation, or if he takes steps which are merely oppressive or obviously unnecessary, or if he crowds a case with absurd evidence, all these are reasons why, if he so misconducts himself, the costs of the wife should be disallowed either in whole or in part." Cotton, L.J., says (p. 126) the 159th rule "gives a discretion to the judge in this way—that where there are certain steps taken improperly by those who are acting for the wife, witnesses called

(¹) 6 P. D., 119.   (²) Not reported.

who ought not to have been called, and so on, those are costs which in his discretion he may disallow."

92] *The result of these passages seems to be that the Lords Justices consider that, on the true construction of rule 159, the wife is not bound at the trial to show why she should be allowed more than the sum which on her own solicitor's statement of the facts the registrar deemed sufficient, but the husband is to show cause why she should not be allowed all that she may claim. This cannot be done at the trial, for the husband does not then know what the wife's claim will be, nor can it be effectually done before the registrar, for he does now know the judge's view of the necessity for the additional costs claimed. The judge himself must, therefore, if required to do so, consider the propriety of the wife's bill of costs when brought in. This is the course which I have proposed to take in every case which has arisen since the decision of the Court of Appeal in *Robertson* v. *Robertson* ('). Thus the consideration of the justice of the wife's claim to increased costs is unavoidably postponed from the trial till some time after. It must be left for future experience to determine whether this will render necessary some change in the rules.

In the present case, however, I do not see how the respondent can invoke the aid of the decision of the Court of Appeal in *Robertson* v. *Robertson* ('). That case had not been decided when I made the order now complained of. I was not asked at the hearing for an order for any costs beyond the amount for which security had been given. There had been no appeal from the registrar's order and no application to increase the amount to be secured. Had I been asked at the trial to give her a larger amount, I should have considered the application, having regard to all the circumstances of the case. Even after the hearing I should, in conformity with the decision of Lord Penzance in *Somerville* v. *Somerville and Webb* ('), have entertained any application on special grounds for an order to increase the wife's costs. But eight months were allowed to pass, and in the meantime the decree *nisi* has been made absolute. I consider that I have now no more power to alter my order in this case than to do so in every one of the very numerous cases in which I have made similar orders during the last ten years. The court has not authority, after a case is concluded, to recall 93] an order, however erroneous, which *correctly ex· pressed the judge's meaning at the time: *In re St. Nazaire* ('). I must therefore refuse this application. I was

(') 6 P. D., 119.   (') 36 L. J. (P. & M.), 87.   (') 12 Ch. D., 88.

asked, in the event of my decision being as it is, to give leave
to appeal, but it would seem that the respondent does not
need my leave.   I was not asked to give leave to appeal in
Robertson v. *Robertson* (¹) or in *M'Alpin* v. *M'Alpin* (²)
another case in which for special reasons I refused on summons heard after the trial to allow the wife's costs beyond
the amount secured; and in so far as this is a question of
costs only I doubt whether I have the power to give leave to
appeal.   By the Matrimonial Causes Act no appeal is allowed
on the subject of costs only, and although the appellate
tribunal is now changed, the law relating to the Divorce
Court remains unaltered.   The rules made under the Judicature Acts do not affect the practice or procedure in matrimonial causes.   However, as I do not desire to throw any
obstacle in the way of an appeal, I will say, if it be necessary, and so far as I have power to do so, I grant leave to
appeal.

Solicitor for petitioner: *T. E. Watkin.*
Solicitors for respondent: *C. O. Humphreys & Sons.*

(¹) 6 P. D., 119.   (²) Not reported.

R. A. P.

[7 Probate Division, 102.]

Feb. 14, 1882.

*In re Goods of MARY GUNSTAN.   [102

BLAKE v. BLAKE.

[1881 G. 1005.]

*Will—Acknowledgment of Signature—Testator's Signature not seen by Attesting
Witnesses— Wills Act, 1837 (1 Vict. c. 26), s. 9.*

To constitute a sufficient acknowledgment, within s. 9 of the Wills Act, the witnesses must at the time of the acknowledgment see, or have the opportunity of seeing, the signature of the testator, and if such be not the case it is immaterial whether
the signature be, in fact, there at the time of attestation, or whether the testator say
that the paper to be attested is his will, or that his signature is inside the paper.

Hudson v. *Parker* (1 Robert., 14) followed.

Gwillim v. *Gwillim* (3 Sw. & Tr., 200) and *Beckett* v. *Howe* (Law Rep., 2 P. D., 1)
disapproved.

THIS was an action commenced in the Probate Division by
Henry Blake, claiming probate in solemn form of a document *alleged to be the last will of Mary Gunstan,   [103
deceased, dated the 12th of August, 1880, whereof he had
been appointed executor.   Mary Gunstan died on the 14th
of March, 1881.

The document propounded as a will by the plaintiff was executed and attested as follows:

"Signed by me in the presence of the
undersigned, who in my presence and in
presence of each other, at same time,
signed their names as witnesses.

"Mary Gunstan,
"Holdernesse House, Brixton Road.
"Ann Harradine,
"Holdernesse House, Brixton Road.
"Susan Harradine,
"Arrington, Cambridgeshire."

On being taken to the Probate Office certain erasures were observed, and the attesting witnesses being required by the registrar to make an affidavit as to the time such erasures were made they were unable to do so, or to say whether they had in fact seen the testatrix sign. The registrar thereupon refused probate in common form, and the present action was in consequence instituted.

It appears from the evidence on the trial before the president that the testatrix, who was a widow lady of admitted capacity, had consulted a friend, formerly a clerk in the Probate Office, as to making her will, and that he had given her written directions as to the form in which a will should be drawn and executed—he had also sketched out the form of attestation clause which she had copied out at the foot of her will.

It appeared from the evidence of Ann Harradine (servant of the testatrix) given at the trial, and from the deposition of Susan Harradine (aunt of Ann Harradine), which was read at the trial, that neither of the witnesses saw the testatrix sign her name—that on their entering the room whither they had been summoned by the testatrix she was laying down her pen—that neither of them knew what they were wanted for, or that the document on which they were writing their names was a will, Ann Harradine remarking that "if she had known she would have taken more notice." 104] *According to Ann Harradine, the testatrix said: "This is a little whim of mine." According to Susan Harradine, she said; "We have all our little wishes, and this is one of mine," and further that she was going out of town, and "when we go from home we never know what may happen."

It further appeared that neither of them could see the signature of the testatrix, there being a piece of blotting-paper

covering about one-third of the sheet on which they wrote
terminating at the lowest crease, which brought it down to
close above the signature of Ann Harradine, the first attesting witness.

In cross-examination Ann Harradine at first adhered to
her statement that she could not see Mrs. Gunstan's signature, adding however, "Sometimes I have thought I did,
but I could not say whether I did or not."

The defendants, by their statement of defence, denied that
the will was duly executed, and claimed that the court
should pronounce against the will propounded by the
plaintiff.

William Willoughby Gunstan, a legatee under the will
for £1,000, obtained leave to intervene.

Bayford, appeared for the plaintiff.
Inderwick, Q.C., and *Middleton*, for the defendants.
H. F. Dickens, for W. W. Gunstan, intervener.

Dec. 9, 1881. SIR J. HANNEN, President: I am extremely
sorry that in this case I should be obliged to find against
an instrument of this kind, which there can be no doubt
does carry out the lady's wishes, and which she supposed
to be a will. But, unfortunately, she has not followed the
excellent advice which was given to her of employing a professional man who would have seen everything done properly. And I therefore have to deal with the question upon
the evidence of two persons whose intention to tell the
truth I do not for a moment doubt, but who, from their
want of experience in such matters, have not been able to
apply their minds to the subject, as it was desirable the
minds of witnesses should be applied when a will is executed, and I have with great difficulty to pick out from their
somewhat differing (without saying conflicting) statements
what really happened. That this lady knew from the information that had been given *her, what was wanted, [105
I cannot doubt. She has written out the attestation clause
herself, and had it explained to her by a competent person.

Now I am afraid it results from the evidence of the two
witnesses that certainly neither of them saw the testatrix
sign the will. They differ as to their account of the incidents, but they both of them agree in that.

The aunt says that Mrs. Gunstan was laying down the
pen and putting the blotting-paper on the writing when she
went in. The niece says she had got the pen in her hand,
and the first thing she did was to ask her to sign, but, as I
say, they neither of them allege, and from the course of

events I cannot see any ground on which I can come to the conclusion, that she did in fact sign in their presence. And it therefore comes to the question whether or not she acknowledged it in their presence.

Now that she did not use any expression with reference to her signature seems to be agreed upon by both of them. Neither of them use any language which leads to the conclusion that she in any way said "This is my signature." They both of them agree that they did not see her signature, and it seems rather to depend upon whether or not she said it was her will, but neither of them says she used that expression. Without entering into the question whether a mere statement to that effect would be sufficient, at any rate when there is an absence of acknowledgment that the instrument is the will of the testatrix, and an absence of acknowledgment of the handwriting, the statute is not complied with.

As I have already said, I greatly regret that I should be obliged to come to the conclusion, but I cannot say that my mind is satisfied that this lady did either sign the will in the presence of the two witnesses or acknowledge it in their presence, and, therefore, with the reluctance which I have more than once expressed, I am compelled to say that there is no proof that the will was duly executed. But as it fails entirely by reason of the action of the testatrix, while rejecting proof of the will I allow the costs of both parties out of the estate.

The costs of W. W. Gunstan, the first intervener, were also allowed out of the estate.

106] *From this decision W. W. Gunstan appealed. The appeal came on to be heard on the 13th of February, 1882.

Dr. Deane and *Dickens*, for the appellant: The attestation clause supplies the deficiency in the parol evidence of the witnesses. It is not contended that the will was signed in the presence of the witnesses, but that it was acknowledged in their presence.

[JESSEL, M.R.: The attestation clause only refers to signature; how can it help you if you admit that the will was not signed in the presence of witnesses?]

If the court is satisfied that the signature is there, and the testator acknowledges the will, that is enough: *Vinnicombe* v. *Butler* (') ; *Gwillim* v. *Gwillim* (') ; *Beckett* v. *Howe* (').

The rule "Omnia præsumuntur ritè esse acta" applies •

(') 3 Sw. & Tr., 580.   (²) 3 Sw. & Tr., 200.   (³) Law Rep., 2 P. & D., 1.

even where the attestation clause is incomplete: *Vinnicombe* v. *Butler* (').

[JESSEL, M.R.: I think the question ought to be argued whether the will must not be taken to have been signed in the presence of the witnesses.]

The testatrix had been distinctly informed that the will must be signed in the presence of witnesses, and an attestation clause was made out on that footing. In such a case the presumption arising from the attestation clause is greatly strengthened, *In re Huckvale* ('), and can only be rebutted by most distinct evidence that the will was not signed in the presence of the witnesses.

Inderwick, Q.C., *C. A. Middleton*, and *T. Lee Roberts*, contrà: The witnesses agree in saying that all that was done to the will was complete before they came in.

[JESSEL, M.R.: *Lloyd* v. *Roberts* (') is in your way.]

Both witnesses speak positively to the fact of the blotting-paper being over the sheet so that they could not see any signature. In *Ilott* v. *Genge* (') a distinction is drawn between *signature under the Statute of Frauds and [107 signature under the Wills Act, and a mere calling in witnesses to sign a paper without their being able to see whether there was a signature was held insufficient: *Ilott* v. *Genge* ('), *Doe* v. *Jackson* ('), there referred to, and *Hudson* v. *Parker* ('), are against the sufficiency of the acknowledgment. *In re Swinford* (') ; *Beckett* v. *Howe* (') ; *Pearson* v. *Pearson* ('°) are in our favor. The witnesses have not simply forgotten the transaction, they remember a great deal, and everything they remember is against the appellant. Signature in the presence of the witnesses is decidedly disproved.

[*Smith* v. *Smith* ('') and *Cooper* v. *Bockett* ('') were also referred to.]

Dr. Deane, in reply: It does not appear that there was any attestation clause either in *Ilott* v. *Genge* (') or in *Hudson* v. *Parker* ('').

Feb. 14. JESSEL, M.R.: I regret that I am unable to come to the conclusion that this will was properly executed. I say I regret, because from a mere accident, a want of form, that which was clearly the last will of this lady must fail

(') 3 Sw. & Tr., 580.
(') Law Rep., 1 P. & D., 375.
(') 12 Moo. P. C., 158.
(') 4 Moo. P. C., 265.
(') 3 Curt., 160.
(') 3 Curt., 181.
(') 1 Rob., 14, 25.
(') Law Rep., 1 P. & D., 680.
(') Law Rep., 2 P. & D., 1.
('°) Law Rep., 1 P. & D., 451.
('') Law Rep., 1 P. & D., 143.
('') 4 Moo. P. C., 419.
('') 1 Rob , 14.

of effect, and the persons interested under it be disappointed.

The real question is, what the law requires to be proved in order to support a will so that it shall be validly executed.

In this case it does not appear that the testatrix signed her name to this document in the presence of the witnesses. I invited the counsel for the appellant to argue the question upon the basis of these witnesses having seen the lady sign her name, but I agree that Dr. Deane knew more of the case than I did, and was wise in declining to argue it on that footing, for on careful examination of the evidence in this case I think it is clear that this will was not signed in the presence of either witness; it is evident that the signature took place before they came into the room. The question, then, arises whether the testatrix acknowledged her signa-
108] ture before the witnesses. What is in *law a sufficient acknowledgment under the statute? What I take to be the law is correctly laid down in Jarman on Wills, 4th ed., p. 108, in the following terms: "There is no sufficient acknowledgment unless the witnesses either saw or might have seen the signature, not even though the testator should expressly declare that the paper to be attested by them is his will;" and I may add, in my opinion, it is not sufficient even if the testator were to say, "My signature is inside the paper," unless the witnesses were able to see the signature. There is a great deal of authority on this point, several cases are referred to in the note to the passage which I have read, but I think it is sufficient to mention three cases only. The first is *Hudson* v. *Parker* ('), where (') the matter is most elaborately discussed by Dr. Lushington. He tells us what in his view is the plain meaning of acknowledging a signature in the presence of witnesses; he says, "What do the words import but this? 'Here is my name written, I acknowledge that name so written to have been written by me; bear witness.' How is it possible that the witnesses should swear that any signature was acknowledged unless they saw it? They might swear that the testator said he acknowledged a signature, but they could not depose to the fact that there was an existing signature to be acknowledged. It is quite true that acknowledgment may be expressed in any words which will adequately convey that idea, if the signature be proved to have been then existent; no particular form of expression is required either by the word 'acknowledge' or by the exigency of the act to be done. It would

(') 1 Rob., 14.   (') 1 Rob., at p. 25.

be quite sufficient to say 'that is my will,' the signature
being there *and seen* at the time; for such words do import
an owning thereof; indeed, it may be done by any other
words which naturally include within their true meaning,
acknowledgment, and approbation."

Now I have to consider the case of *Beckett* v. *Howe* ('),
where a different rule was laid down by Lord Penzance.
At page 5 he says, "The doctrine of *Gwillim* v. *Gwillim* (')
is this, that if the testator produces a paper and gives the
witnesses to understand it is his will, and gets them to sign
their names, that amounts to an *acknowledgment [109
of his signature, if the court is satisfied that the signature
of the testator was on the will at the time. Whether that
decision was right or wrong I have not to determine. It
was founded on other cases. Provided the testator acknowledges the paper to be his will and his signature is there
at the time, it is sufficient." I dissent from the prop s t on
of Lord Penzance, and agree with the ruling of Dr.oLinsh-
ington, and therefore I hold that it is not sufficient to say
"This is my will." The argument that that will do is
founded on the notion that the statement by the testator
"This is my will" implies that his signature is affixed to it;
but that is not so, a will ·is not a valid will until it is attested, and there is no necessary implication that it already
bears the testator's signature. It may be that the testator
has not yet signed it, but may intend to do it, and it is quite
possible that he may in that sense call it a will, inasmuch as
it will, when executed, be a will. But I say that if he had
distinctly said that he had signed the will, but yet the witnesses would not be able to see his signature, that is not a
sufficient acknowledgment. Is there any doctrine to the
contrary? Lord Penzance does not, to my mind, lay down
any new doctrine, he thought himself bound by the decision
of Sir Cresswell Cresswell in *Gwillim* v. *Gwillim* ('). I will
now turn to that case, and with great deference to Lord
Penzance, I do not think Sir C. Cresswell laid down such a
doctrine. I agree people may, in reading the decision, as I
am bound so to say considering that Lord Penzance so read
it, come to the same conclusion as he did, but I think that
Sir C. Cresswell did not decide or intend to decide anything
of the kind. In *Gwillim* v. *Gwillim* (') the signature of the
testator (as printed in the report) is placed immediately
above the signature of the witnesses. If nothing was put
upon the signature it was impossible for the witnesses to
sign their names without seeing the signature if it was there,

(°) Law Rep., 2 P. & D., 1.   (°) 3 Sw. & Tr., 200; 29 L. J. (Pro.), 31.

and the argument therefore turned upon the question whether the signature was there or not. The present question was not under discussion. The material part of the judgment is on p. 205, "I am therefore at liberty to judge, from the circumstances of this case, whether the name of the testator was on the will at the time of the attestation or not. 110] It is hardly likely that this testator, *who knew that there must be two witnesses to the will, did not also know that he must sign it before they did, and either sign it or acknowledge it in their presence. Then if I look at the position of the words, I find at the top of the third page, 'My will and testament, 1856, March 31st.' Under that comes 'Brange, Mar. 31, 1856,' that being the time and place at which the old ladies say they were asked to sign the will. Under that comes 'John Gwillim,' and then the word 'witness' a little below on the left hand side where one would expect to find it. I cannot, therefore, but think that the name of the testator was written at that time, and that by asking these old ladies to witness his will he did acknowledge his signature."

Now that I say is *Hudson* v. *Parker* ([1]). The witnesses were taken to have seen the signature and the testator having then asked them to witness his will, he was held to have acknowledged his signature. I cannot find one word in the judgment to show that Sir C. Cresswell was of opinion that if the witnesses were unable to see the signature, the testator saying he had signed would be sufficient. I do not think the decision bears out the interpretation put upon it by Lord Penzance, namely, that there was any new doctrine laid down in that case different from the doctrine of *Hudson* v. *Parker* ([1]). The existence of any such doctrine rests entirely on the statement of Lord Penzance in *Beckett* v. *Howe* ([2]); and as I think there was no sufficient ground for that statement, I am of opinion that the case of *Beckett* v. *Howe* ([2]) is no authority.

If that is so, there is only one other point, and that is, did the witnesses see the signature? I am of opinion upon the evidence that they did not. Susan Harradine says in express terms that she did not; that there was a piece of blotting-paper over the signature. I have looked carefully at the original writing, and the appearance of the document strongly confirms the statement of this witness. The words, including the signature of the testatrix, are dull and blurred as if they had been blotted, and it would appear as if the blotting-paper reached down below the signature of the tes-

([1]) 1 Rob., 14.   ([2]) Law Rep., 2 P. & D., 1.

tatrix. The other witness says the same thing in the first instance, and then subsequently that she sometimes thought *that she did see the signature, but she could not say [111 whether she did or not. I must upon this evidence come to the conclusion that it is most satisfactorily, or rather most unsatisfactorily, proved that these witnesses did not see the signature.

I refrain from going into the next question whether sufficient expressions were used by the testatrix as to the document being her will. If it were necessary I should take more pains to consider the meaning of the words used; but I think it is unnecessary to do so on the present occasion, having regard to the conclusion of fact that the witnesses did not see the signature of the lady, and the decision of the learned President pronouncing against the will must be affirmed.

Brett, L.J.: In this case we have a document which is in form a will, leaving a large amount of property, and it is undoubted that the testatrix meant thereby to deal with her property in the manner therein pointed out, and it is equally clear that she signed the document meaning it to be her will, and equally clear that she thought she was complying with the requirements of the statute, and that this document represents her last and final intentions as to the disposition of her property.

That being so, no one can be astonished if the court should have made every endeavor to uphold it so far as it could in accordance with law, for one must feel distressed at the result that the disposition of her property which this lady intended to make must depend upon the accident of putting a piece of blotting-paper a quarter of an inch higher or lower. But we have to consider here an enactment of a statute, in which there is no elasticity, we are bound to say whether this particular will complied with the requirements of the statute.

I think it did not, and our decision must be attended with the unhappy consequence that the clearly known and expressed intention of this lady with regard to her property must be set aside, and persons whom she clearly meant to benefit be deprived of all benefits under it.

The first point is what are we now, as a Court of Appeal, to assume to be the real facts of the case as shown by the evidence in the court below. If the learned president of the Probate *Division had come to the conclusion from [112 the evidence before him, and on seeing the witnesses, even if they had used the expressions which are now before us on

paper, that in fact this lady did sign in the presence of these
witnesses, I should not be inclined to disagree with his conclusion ; or if he had found or collected from what the witnesses said, that they could not say whether the signature
was or was not under the blotting-paper, and he had come
to the conclusion that the signature was visible, and that
what the lady said was "This is my will," I should have
agreed. But I think that he must be taken to have come to
the conclusion from the evidence, and the conclusion seems
borne out by the appearance of the document itself, that
the blotting-paper was so placed that the witnesses not only
did not but could not see the signature. If then they did
not and could not see the signature, did this lady say "This
is my whim," or " This is my will." I shall assume, as being against rank absurdity, that she said " this is my will."
The question then raised is whether it is a compliance with
the statute, if a testatrix, when two witnesses are present
for the purpose of attesting a document, should say in their
presence "this document is my will," whether that is a
sufficient acknowledgment if at the time the witnesses did
not and could not see the signature. That is a point of
law, and on this point we must give our judgment. It is a
point which must be decided upon the statute itself, and
even if twenty cases decided that it would be a sufficient
acknowledgment, if we were clearly of opinion that according to the true construction of the statute it would not do,
we should not be bound by those cases. Where there have
been several decisions or a series of decisions upon any statute, I should dread to overrule those decisions or that series
of decisions, but still we should be compelled so to do if we
thought that those decisions were not in accordance with the
statute. But in this case we have no long line of decisions
one way; there seem to be conflicting decisions, and we
must accordingly exercise our own judgment on the question independently almost, if not quite, of every former decision.

It is clear that *Hudson* v. *Parker* (¹) dealt exhaustively
with the very point, and the opinion of Dr. Lushington was
113]   that, whatever *might be the case under the older
statute, on the statute then before him, and which is now
before us, where a will has not been signed by the testatrix
in the presence of two witnesses, and where it is necessary
therefore to rely on an acknowledgment under the statute,
then even though the signature be there, and whatever is
done be done in the presence of two witnesses together at the

(¹) 1 Rob., 14.

same time, if they do not see or do not have the opportunity
of seeing the signature, whatever the testator may say there
is not an acknowledgment in the meaning of the words of the
statute.　To make it such an acknowledgment they must see
or have the opportunity of seeing the signature.　That is the
interpretation put by Dr. Lushington on the statute, and by
the course of reasoning with which I wish respectfully to express my full agreement, it seems obvious that where an
acknowledgment has to be relied upon, the witnesses must
see or have the opportunity of seeing the signature.　When
they are required to attest the signature, they must see or
have the opportunity of seeing the person signing the document.　The doctrine is the same where the testator has to
acknowledge his signature.　I must say that looking at
the statue alone, you can only get at this necessity from the
meaning of "acknowledgment," not from the words "the
witnesses shall attest," because it is not the signature they
are to attest, but the will.　The question turns on what is
meant by acknowledgment.

When you find that in order to make the signature sufficient the witness must see the person sign, so when a signature is to be acknowledged they must see that there is a
signature, and the testator must then in their presence say
something equivalent to "That is my signature;" so that if
they do not have the opportunity of seeing the signature,
even if he say before them, "My signature is in this instrument," that will not do.　That I take to be the decision of
Hudson v. *Parker* (¹).

It is said that the case of *Gwillim* v. *Gwillim* (²) before
Sir C. Cresswell, and the case of *Beckett* v. *Howe* (³) before
Lord Penzance are to the contrary.　As to the latter case
there is no doubt that it is—and so it has been held.　It is
said that Lord *Penzance decided it on the authority of　[114
Gwillim v. *Gwillim* (²), and that that case does not decide
what his Lordship thought it did.　As regards this proposition I feel very great difficulty.　There has never been, certainly not in our time, so great a master of what I would
call transparently lucid exposition as Sir C. Cresswell, and
therefore when I find that learned judge saying this, "I am
therefore at liberty to judge from the circumstances of this
case, whether the name of the testator was on the will at the
time of the attestation or not," I cannot bring my mind to
think that the proposition which he thought he had to solve
was not this, and this only, whether the signature was or not
on the will at the time of the attestation.　Moreover, if there

(¹) 1 Rob., 14.　　　　(²) 3 Sw. & Tr., 200.　　　　(³) Law Rep., 2 P. & D., 1.

is a judge who is less likely to make a mistake as to what another judge has said, that judge is Lord Penzance, a clearer mind does not exist : and, therefore, when he comes to the conclusion that Sir C. Cresswell meant what he says he meant, it strengthens my view as to the meaning of Sir C. Cresswell in that case. Therefore we are reduced to this misfortune in arriving at the conclusion we have come to, that we are differing from both those judges. It may be said that in *Gwillim* v. *Gwillim* (¹) the point was not raised or was not argued, and the case of *Hudson* v. *Parker* (²) was not even cited—the argument went on another line—but I do think that Sir C. Cresswell did intend to lay down the proposition of law which Lord Penzance understood him to lay down.

But on mature consideration, all I can say is that I differ on this question from those judges, and I feel bound to say that when I do differ from two such judges, I entertain much more doubt as to the propriety of my decision than of theirs. But still it is our duty to decide to the best of our powers, and I am of opinion that, according to the true construction of this statute, witnesses must see or have the opportunity of seeing the signature. It has been brought to this, where the witnesses cannot see, have no opportunity of seeing, the signature, it is immaterial what the testator says, there cannot be an acknowledgment; but that when the signature is there and they see or have the opportunity of seeing it, then 115] if the testator says this is my will or *words to that effect, that is sufficient acknowledgment, although he does not say this is my signature. I therefore think that this will cannot stand.

HOLKER, L.J.: I also regret that the court is constrained to come to a conclusion which will invalidate the will, but the court must be relentless and must judge according to law and fact without regarding the possible consequences of the decision it feels bound to give.

The appeal has been argued on two grounds, first that the evidence was not enough to show that the testatrix did not sign her will in the presence of two witnesses ; and, secondly, that if she did not she acknowledged her signature before other witnesses.

The first ground was put forward by Dr. Deane rather on the suggestion of the court. The will is, upon the face of it, in due form ; the lady who made the will was properly instructed as to what she had to do ; she knew that it was necessary to sign it before the witnesses, and that they

(¹) 3 Sw. & Tr., 200.   (²) 1 Rob., 14.

should sign in her presence. The attesting clause was in proper form; it is said that all these matters being strictly correct, the maxim of law, "*Omnia præsumuntur rite esse acta*," must apply. It is further said that the result should be the same, even though this finding would not be quite in accordance with the testimony of the witnesses. That might be the case if the witnesses who came forward to prove the will had been in doubt or could not remember whether they did or did not see the testatrix sign. The fact that everything appears to have been rightly done would entitle the court to come to the conclusion that they did in fact see her sign. But when you have to prove a will strictly, and if they both say, or one of them says, they did not see her sign, it is impossible to say that there is proof of due execution. Therefore, where as here one positively says that she did not see her sign, and the other doubts, it is clear that that kind of testimony is not sufficient to establish the validity of the will.

The other ground on which Dr. Deane relied was that there was here a sufficient acknowledgment of the signature of the testatrix to her will made to the two witnesses. Now we come upon the second ground, as to what the cases have decided. What *sort of acknowledgment is enough? [116 According to the statute the signature is to be made before two witnesses, or the signature is to be acknowledged before two witnesses. For what purpose? To enable them to testify to the signature or to the acknowledgment of the signature.

It is clear that good sense requires that the acknowledgment to which the witnesses are to bear testimony should be an acknowledgment of the signature seen or capable of being seen by the witnesses. Although the words of the statute are, "such witnesses shall attest the will" and not "the signature," it seems to me that it comes to the same thing, for when the document is properly signed or acknowledged in the presence of the witnesses, it becomes a will. So to my mind, to bear testimony to a will is the same thing as to bear testimony to the signature.

That being so, it was decided in *Hudson* v. *Parker* (¹) that the true view of the section was that, to constitute an acknowledgment sufficient within the statute, the witnesses must see, or be able to see, the signature of the testator, and if so, there is no such acknowledgment in the present case, because, as far as the evidence goes, the signature of this testatrix was carefully concealed. Certainly both witnesses

(¹) 1 Rob., 14.

did not see the signature. But putting that difficulty out of the way, I should think it was not enough to prove that the witnesses saw the signature, but they should also know what this document which is signed really is. But the evidence goes to this, that this lady never said, "This is my will." According to Susan Harradine she said, "We have all our little wishes and this is one of mine." According to Ann Harradine she said, "It is a little whim of mine." To my mind it is not very extraordinary that this lady getting these two servants to attest should not care particularly for them to know that this was her will, she might be afraid of exciting curiosity; and at any rate Ann says in her evidence that if she had said that it was her will, she would have taken more notice.

The testatrix does not say, so far as the evidence goes, that it is her will, she does not say even that her signature is under the blotting-paper, therefore even if *Hudson* v. *Parker* ([1]) were out of the way, it would be a difficult thing 117] to say that this signature *was acknowledged in the presence of two witnesses. I am therefore of opinion that this decision of the president is right and must be affirmed.

> *Appeal dismissed, but under the circumstances costs of all parties ordered to be paid out of the estate.*

Solicitor for appellant: *W. H. Orchard.*
Solicitors for respondents: *Lucas & Son; Bell, Brodrick & Grey; Cooper & Walker.*

([1]) 1 Rob., 14.　　　　　　　　　　　　See *ante*, p. 356 note.

M. W.

[7 Probate Division, 117.]

April 4, 1882.

[IN THE COURT OF APPEAL.]

THE RORY.

Damage to Cargo—Practice—Particulars.

The rule as to giving the opposite party particulars of any general allegation in pleadings ought to be the same in the Admiralty as in the Queen's Bench Division. Where, therefore, in an action in the Admiralty Division by cargo owners against shipowners for delivery of cargo in a damaged condition, the statement of claim alleged that the damage was not occasioned by any of the excepted perils mentioned in the bill of lading under which the cargo has been shipped, but was occasioned by the defective condition of the vessel or by the negligence or breach of duty of the defendants or their servants, it was *held* by the Court of Appeal (Lord Coleridge, C.J., and Brett and Holker, L.JJ.), reversing the decision of Sir Robert Phillimore, that the defendants were entitled to particulars of the defects rendering the vessel not fit to carry the cargo.

THIS was an action under the 3d section of the County
Courts Admiralty Jurisdiction Act, 1869,(32 & 33 Vict. c. 51),
instituted in the City of London Court on behalf of the as-
signees and indorsees of bills of lading of a cargo of pease
laden on board the steamship Rory against the steamship
Rory, and transferred to the Admiralty Division of the High
Court under the provisions of the same act and the County
Courts Admiralty Jurisdiction Act, 1868 (31 & 32 Vict. c. 71).

The statement of claim alleged in the first five paragraphs
thereof that the cargo of pease had been shipped on board
the Rory at Montreal in good order and condition, and by
the terms of such bills of lading was to have been delivered
at the port of London in the like good order and condition,
certain perils and *casualties therein mentioned only   [118
excepted; that the Rory sailed on her voyage and arrived
in London, and that the cargo had been then delivered to
the plaintiffs, but not in as good order or condition as when
shipped at Montreal, and, as to a large portion thereof, in a
damaged condition. The 7th and 8th paragraphs of the
statement of claim were in terms as follows:

7. The damage and deterioration of the said cargo were
not occasioned by any of the perils, casualties, and causes in
the said bills of lading excepted.

8. The said damage and deterioration were occasioned
by the defective condition of the said vessel by reason that
the said vessel was not reasonably fit to carry the said cargo
on the said voyage, or by the negligence or breach of duty
or contract on the part of the defendants, their servants or
agents.

On the 21st of February the solicitor for the defendants,
the owners of the Rory, took out a summons calling upon
the plaintiffs to show cause before the registrar why the
plaintiffs should not deliver particulars of the defects, negligence, and breaches of duty or contract alleged in the 8th
paragraph of the statement of claim.

The summons was heard before the registrar on the 25th
of February, and the registrar ordered that the plaintiffs
should deliver to the defendants particulars of the defects
rendering the Rory not reasonably fit to carry her cargo, as
alleged in the 8th paragraph of the statement of claim.

Feb. 28. *Butt*, Q.C., for the plaintiffs, moved the judge
in court to rescind the above mentioned order of the registrar
of the 25th of February. The particulars asked for by the
defendants cannot be presumed to be within the knowledge
of the plaintiffs or their agents, and therefore it would be

contrary to the practice of the High Court of Admiralty to
order the plaintiffs to deliver them : *The Freedom* (').   The
plaintiffs are entitled to rely upon proving by cross-examination of the defendants' witnesses at the trial that defects
as to which they cannot now furnish specific information
existed in the Rory.   Moreover, independently of the charges
contained in the 8th paragraph of the claim, the defendants,
119]   *in order to successfully defend the action, must at
the trial account for the damage to the goods and show that
it was occasioned by the excepted perils, and thus incidentally they must prove the seaworthiness of their ship.   The
8th paragraph therefore does not substantially impose any
additional onus of proof upon the defendants.

G. Bruce, for the defendants :   The plaintiffs have chosen
to allege that the ship was in a defective condition, and
the defendants at the trial must be prepared to meet that
charge, and they cannot do so unless they have some information by way of particulars of the nature of the defects
alleged.   In the Queen's Bench Division such particulars
would be ordered as of course, and since the Judicature
Acts the practice in this division as to particulars ought to
be the same as the practice in the other divisions of the
High Court.

An order for particulars similar to that made by the registrar in this case was recently made by the judge in chambers in the case of *The Signet* (').

· SIR ROBERT PHILLIMORE :   I am of opinion that the order
of the registrar must be rescinded as asked for by the motion.   I do not consider that the defendants are entitled to
obtain from the plaintiffs particulars of the defective condition of their ship.   The motion will be granted with costs.

                                                        G. B.
The defendants appealed.

                        ————

April 4.   *Cohen*, Q.C. (*G. Bruce*, with him), for the defendants.

Gray (*Butt*, Q.C., with him), for the plaintiffs.

LORD COLERIDGE, C.J.:   I am of opinion that this appeal
should be allowed.   The action is in the Admiralty Division,
120]   and *is brought by the indorsees of bills of lading of

---

(¹) Law Rep., 2 A. & E., 346.
(²) [1881 R. No. 767.]   This case is not
reported.   It was a case of damage to
cargo in which the statement of claim
was similar to the statement of claim in
the above case of the Rory, and on the
10th of November, 1881, an order was

made by the judge in chambers that the
plaintiffs should deliver particulars of the
alleged unseaworthiness of the ship.   The
plaintiffs' counsel did not oppose the making the order.   Solicitors for plaintiffs :
T. W. Rossiter.   Solicitors for defendants : *Gregory, Rowcliffes & Co.*

cargo shipped on board a steamship against the shipowners, for the delivery of such cargo in a damaged condition, such damage being alleged in the statement of claim not to have been accasioned by any of the excepted perils in the bills of lading, but by reason of the vessel not being reasonably fit to carry the said cargo, or by the negligence of the defendants or their servants. I think that such a mode of pleading as this general allegation in the plaintiffs' statement of claim may be allowed in order to avoid prolixity, but then to prevent the defendants from being taken by surprise, this should be supplemented by particulars, and if the defendants ask for them the plaintiffs should be required to say on what defects in the vessel they rely as making it unfit for the carriage of the cargo. If it be only an inference they draw from the state in which the cargo was when it arrived let them say so, but they are bound to communicate what they know, and if at any other time before the trial they should obtain any other knowledge of any matter occasioning the damage on which they should wish to rely they should give it to the defendants, by amending the particulars, which they might do from time to time as they should obtain fresh information on the subject. I do not think that the general principles laid down by Sir R. Phillimore in *The Freedom* (¹) conflict with this. The object of the rules of pleading is, he says, to prevent either party being taken by surprise at the hearing, and if during the trial it should appear that one of them relied on any act of which he had knowledge which took the other by surprise, Sir R. Phillimore would probably adjourn the trial in order to enable such other to produce evidence in contradiction. That may be very proper in the Admiralty Division, but it would not do to pursue that course in the Queen's Bench Division. In this case I think that the particulars asked for should be given.

BRETT, L.J.: It would be strange if a different rule as to giving particulars to the opposite party should prevail in the Admiralty Division from that which prevails in the Queen's Bench Division, for this is really a common law action which might have been brought in the Queen's Bench Division, but which has been given *to the Admi- [121 ralty Division in order to enable the plaintiffs to enforce their claim against the ship. The rule, however, as to the delivery of particulars is founded on considerations which are applicable to all courts. In order to prevent the necessity of a minute statement of all the facts in pleading a general

(¹) Law Rep., 2 A. & E., 846.

allegation is often allowed, as, for instance, in the case of fraud, but then in order to have a fair trial the party who makes such general allegation is always bound to give particulars of it to the opposite party, so that he shall not be taken by surprise, and shall also be able to defend himself against that with which he is charged. Now how are the defendants to meet the case contained in the 8th paragraph of the statement of claim ? Do the plaintiffs mean by what is there stated that there was a defect in the construction of the ship, or that there was not a proper crew, or that the master was drunk, or that he did not put the hatches down when there was a storm. If the plaintiffs were to state in their particulars that they rely on one only of these matters, then there would be no necessity for the defendants to send all over the world to meet a case founded on the others, as they might otherwise have to do. I can see no reason why the procedure in this respect should be different in the Admiralty Division from what it is in the Queen's Bench Division. In *The Freedom*(') the reason given by Sir Robert Phillimore for not allowing particulars in the Admiralty Division is that if the parties are taken by surprise the Admiralty Court can postpone the inquiry. That is not a reason to be adopted ; in such a case as the present the trial might have to be postponed until a commission had been sent to the other side of the world, and I cannot agree to there being a different proceeding in such a matter as the present between the Admiralty and the other Divisions of the High Court.

HOLKER, L. J., concurred.

Appeal allowed.

Solicitors for plaintiffs : *J. Cooper & Co.*
Solicitor for defendants : *James Neal.*

(') Law Rep., 2 A. & E., 346.

W. P.

See 31 Eng. R., 276 note.

Where, in an action for slander, the answer sets up matters in justification, but does not state when or where the crimes charged were committed, the court has the power to, and should grant a motion for a bill of the particulars thereof : Daniel v. Daniel, 2 Civ. Proc. Rep., 238.

The complaint alleged that defendant uttered certain defamatory words "on or about certain days of the years 1880 and 1881, at Russell, in the presence of divers good and worthy citizens." Defendant made affidavit that he had no knowledge, information or belief as to the times or places, or in whose presence plaintiff expected to prove that the words were spoken.

Held, a proper case for a bill of particulars : Gardinier *v.* Knox, 15 N. Y. Weekly Dig., 222.

In an action for criminal conversation, the defendant, immediately after the action was commenced, demanded a bill of particulars which plaintiff did not furnish. One year elapsed ; the case appeared on the day calendar ; defendant moved for a bill of particulars, and plaintiff set up laches in opposition to the motion. Held, that defendant was diligent in making the demand, and the question of laches could not be successfully urged against him. It was the duty of the plaintiff to have complied with that demand, and not to have driven defendant to compulsory measures. A bill of particulars is proper in such a case : Shaffer v. Holm, 16 N. Y. Weekly Dig., 127, Sup. Ct., 1st Dept.

Where it appears that the plaintiff has not the information that would enable him to prepare and serve the bill of particulars, but that the facts are all in the possession of defendant, the plaintiff should not be required to furnish the particulars on which he relies : Powers v. Snedeker, 5 Monthly Law Bull., 22.

Under the Code of Civil Procedure (§§ 531, 822), the court has power to strike out the complaint in an action, as a penalty for disobedience of an order requiring the plaintiff to serve a bill of particulars : Gross v. Clark, 87 N. Y., 272.

[7 Probate Division, 122.]

June 6, 1882.

[IN THE COURT OF APPEAL.]   ·

*MEDLEY v. MEDLEY.   [122

Practice—Divorce Court—Alimony—Permanent Maintenance—20 & 21 Vict. c. 85, s. 32 [Revised Ed. Statutes, vol. xiii, p. 256]—29 & 30 Vict. c. 32, s. 1 [Revised Ed. Statutes, vol. xv, p. 36]—Husband's Property Abroad.

The provisions of 20 & 21 Vict. c. 85, s. 32, respecting permanent maintenance empower the court to order a gross or annual sum to be secured for the benefit of the wife, but not to make a direct order on the husband to pay a gross or annual or other periodical sum to the wife.

The qualification that the maintenance is to be for the wife "dum sola et casta vixerit" is not usually inserted in the order but in the deed of security.

The provisions of 29 & 30 Vict. c. 32, respecting the payment of monthly or weekly sums to the wife do not apply to the case of a husband who has property abroad sufficient and available for a security.

Per Jessel, M.R., an order for maintenance cannot be made in the alternative for securing a gross or annual sum of money, or else for the payment of monthly or weekly sums by the husband.

IN this case a petition was presented in the Probate Division in April, 1880, by Mrs. Medley, for a dissolution of marriage on the ground of her husband's bigamy and adultery. The marriage took place in November, 1877, and the parties after living for a short time together separated, when Mr. Medley agreed to make an allowance to his wife of £500 a year.

On the 28th of July, 1881, a decree *nisi* for the dissolution of the marriage was made, which in due course was made absolute.

On the 5th of November, 1881, Mrs. Medley presented a petition for permanent maintenance. A reference having been directed as to her husband's property, it appeared that it consisted almost exclusively of shares and mortgages in foreign countries, and that he resided in Paris, where he rented an expensive house and lived in considerable style. The registrar estimated his income at £1,660.

On the 29th of April, 1882, the President (Sir J. Hannen) made an order in the following terms: That T. P. Medley do to the satisfaction of the court secure to the petitioner the gross sum of £7,500 within one month from this date, or that within the same time he do secure to the petitioner the sum of £500 per annum for her life; and in the event of his 123] not doing so then that *he pay to the petitioner the sum of £500 per annum, by equal monthly payments of £41 13s. 4d., the first payment to be made on the 29th of June next, and the succeeding payments to be made respectively on the 29th day of each following month.

From this order the respondent appealed.

Searle (*McIntyre*, Q.C., with him), for the respondent: The order is irregular in two respects; first, the allowance is made to the petitioner absolutely, whereas it ought to have been *dum sola et casta vixerit*. It is the usual course to introduce this qualification, except under special circumstances: *Fisher* v. *Fisher* ([1]); *Sidney* v. *Sidney* ([2]). Secondly, the order is made in the alternative either for a gross sum or an annuity to be secured, which is done under the provisions of the 20 & 21 Vict. c. 32, or else for a monthly payment to be made by the husband, which is done under the 29 & 30 Vict. c. 32, s. 1. But these acts apply to different cases, the first act being applicable where the husband has available property, and the second where he has none. In the present case the husband has sufficient available property, and the act of 1866 is not applicable. Consequently, the second part of the order ought to be struck out. Moreover, the amount ordered to be secured for the wife is unreasonable, and is not justified by the evidence of the amount of the husband's property.

Inderwick, Q.C., and *Bayford*, for the petitioner: Sir J. Hannen declined to insert the words "dum sola et casta vixerit" in the order, because it is unusual to do so. If they are inserted at all this will be done in the deed, which will have to be settled by the conveyancing counsel of the court. With respect to the second point, the act of 1866 is applicable, because, although the husband has considerable property, it is none of it in this country, and is not available as a security for the sum ordered to be secured. There is nothing unreasonable in making an alternative order in this form, for it may be found impossible to obtain the security ordered.

([1]) 2 Sw. & Tr., 410.   ([2]) 4 Sw. & Tr., 178, 182.

JESSEL, M.R.: In the first place, as to the substance of this *order, namely, the amount of the allowance ordered,   [124 I am clearly of opinion that this court ought not to interfere with the discretion exercised by the judge, more especially as upon the motion before us, the sum awarded does not appear too large, and the husband, who has declined to attend to give evidence as to his property, had on the occasion of his separation from the petitioner in 1878, agreed to make her an annual allowance of £500.

As to the second point—the insertion of the proviso "dum sola et casta vixerit," it appears from the note of what took place before the learned judge that he did not decide adversely to the appellant, but left the question to be determined when the deed by which the allowance was to be secured came to be settled. Therefore the appellant has nothing to complain of on that point.

The further point was, however, one of more difficulty, as to the form of the order by which the appellant was ordered in the alternative to pay the petitioner the annual sum of £500 by monthly payments. Now, when we look at the 32d section of the 20 & 21 Vict. c. 85, the word "secure" appears to be used in a particular way. It is contrasted with payment. The words are, "that the court may order that the husband shall to the satisfaction of the court secure to the wife such gross sum of money or such annual sum of money for any term not exceeding her own life as having regard to her fortune, &c., it shall deem reasonable;" and then at the end of the section it provides that "upon any petition for the dissolution of marriage the court shall have the same power to make interim orders for payment of money by way of alimony or allowance to his wife as it would in a suit instituted for ju c al separation." Therefore I think that the intention of the Legislature was that the gross or annual sum should not be ordered at once to be paid over to the wife but should be secured, and being secured should be paid to her from time to time; that would give a meaning to the word "secure" as contrasted with "pay." What confirms me in this construction is the passing of the Amendment Act, 29 & 30 Vict. c. 32. If "securing" in the first act included payment, the second act would have been useless. That act, after enacting that *it sometimes hap-   [125 pened that a decree for dissolution was obtained against a husband who had no property on which the payment of a gross or annual sum could be secured, provided that the court might order monthly or weekly payments to be made by the husband to the wife. This act could not have been passed to meet any supposed difficulty that an "annual sum" could only be paid once a year, and to enable the sum secured to be paid by monthly or weekly instalments. The recital shows this. It refers expressly to husbands "who have no property on which the payment of any such gross or annual sum can be secured." And that expression is an answer to the argument that it is applicable to a case like the present, in which the husband has property abroad but not in this country. If he has property abroad then he has property on which the payment of the alimony can be secured, and he can be attached if he fails to comply with the order.

Therefore it appears to me that it was not intended by the first act that an order should be made for payment of the allowance directly by the husband to the wife. And I also think that the second act is not applicable, because the husband has property on which the allowance can be secured. Besides, I do not think that you can make an alternative order of this kind. You must proceed under one act or the other. The result is that the alternative part of the order must be discharged.

LINDLEY, L.J.: I am of the same opinion. The first question is, what is the true construction of the 32d section of the 20 & 21 Vict. c. 85? At first sight it might appear as if the term "secure" would include payment, but when looked at more closely, and when the second act is taken into consideration, I think it is clear that it does not include payment, but that the sum gross or annual was to be secured so as to provide a fund for the wife. Therefore the alternative part of the order cannot be sustained under the 32d section of the first act.

Then the second act (29 & 30 Vict. c. 32) only authorizes monthly or weekly payments to be ordered when the husband has no property upon which such sum can be secured, and does not apply to a case like the present in which the husband has property which is abundantly sufficient for a 126] security although it *is situate abroad. Therefore neither on the first nor second act can the alternative part of the order be sustained.

As to the amount of the sum ordered to be secured, I agree with the Master of the Rolls that there is no cause for reducing it. With respect to the clause "dum sola et casta vixerit," the matter stands in this way. The act says nothing about it, and the only question is whether the order should be qualified by the insertion of such a clause, or whether it should be left to be decided when the deed of security is settled. The latter appears to be the ordinary course, and I see no reason for departing from it.

The respondent having failed in the material part of his appeal, must pay the costs of the appeal.

BOWEN, L.J., concurred.

Judgment accordingly.

Solicitors for petitioner: *Harwood & Stephenson.*
Solicitors for respondent: *Eardley, Holl & Richardson.*

M. W.

[7 Probate Division, 126.]

July 3, 1882.

[IN THE COURT OF APPEAL.]

THE MAC.

Salvage—Appeal from Justices—Jurisdiction—Merchant Shipping Act, 1854 (17 & 18 *Vict. c.* 104), *ss.* 2, 458, 460—*Meaning of " Ship or Boat stranded or otherwise in distress on the shore of any Sea or Tidal Water."*

Justices awarded salvage in respect of services rendered to a hopper-barge, which had been found adrift without any person on board of her in the Wash about three miles from Boston. The barge was not furnished with any means by which she could be propelled, and was used for dredging purposes:

Held, that the barge was a "ship in distress on the shore of a sea or tidal water" within the meaning of the Merchant Shipping Act, 1854, s. 458, and that the justices had no jurisdiction to award salvage.

The Leda (Sw., 40) followed.

APPEAL by the owners of the Saucy Polly from the judgment of Sir R. Phillimore in favor of the owner of the Mac.

*The facts of the case are fully stated in the report [127 of the proceedings in the Admiralty Division (').

June 30, July 3. *Bucknill,* for the owners of the Saucy Polly: It is submitted that the Mac was a "ship," as that word is defined by the Merchant Shipping Act, 1854, s. 2. It is true that she could not propel herself; but no case appears to exist in which it has been held that a vessel which does not propel herself is not a "ship" within the meaning of that enactment. The Mac had a mast, she was capable of being towed, and the facts proved at the hearing before the justices established that she had been towed from Holland. She was found at sea. These circumstances show that she was a "ship." In *Ex parte Ferguson* (') it was held by Blackburn, J., that if a vessel is capable of going to sea she must be considered to be a "ship." In *The An-*

(') 7 P. D., 38.   (') Law Rep., 6 Q. B., 280, at p. 291.

dalusian (') it appears to have been held by Sir R. Phillimore that an unfinished vessel which is being launched is a "ship."

W. G. F. Phillimore, for the owner of the Mac: The decision in *The Andalusian* (') is not in point. No vessel which is incapable of moving herself can be considered a "ship." The Mac did not go to sea ; she was used merely for dredging purposes ; therefore she cannot be a "ship:" *The C. S. Butler* ('). The jurisdiction of the justices must be construed strictly. Originally the Court of Admiralty had no jurisdiction over salvage arising within the body of a county. By 3 & 4 Vict. c. 65, s. 6, jurisdiction over claims of that description was conferred, but it extended only to ships or sea-going vessels: *The Raft of Timber* ('). This enactment was enlarged by 9 & 10 Vict. c. 99, s. 40. By the Merchant Shipping Act, 1854 (17 & 18 Vict. c. 104), ss. 458, 460, jurisdiction is given to justices in respect of a ship, boat, cargo, apparel, or wreck ; but it does not extend further. Timber found floating without an apparent owner at sea, having drifted from the place where it was moored in a river, is not "wreck" within the meaning of that statute: *Palmer* v. *Rouse* ('). The owner of the Mac can accept the definition 128] of a "ship" given by Blackburn, J., *in *Ex parte Ferguson* ('), for, as she was used only for dredging purposes, she must remain in shallow water, and could not be a sea-going vessel.

But, further, the Mac at the time when she was rescued was not "stranded or otherwise in distress on the shore of any sea or tidal water situate within the limits of the United Kingdom" within the meaning of the Merchant Shipping Act, 1854, s. 458.

[*Bucknill*, for the owners of the Saucy Polly, objected that this question could not be raised, as the owner of the Mac had not given any notice of a cross-appeal.

PER CURIAM: We think that this point can be entertained ; the judgment of the Admiralty Division was wholly in favor of the owner of the Mac, he could not appeal from the reasons given by the judge.]

The phrase "on the shore" means "touching the ground"; the word "stranding" must be confined to cases where the vessel takes the ground in the course of navigation. If the Legislature had intended to include cases in which the ves-

(') 3 P. D., 182, at p. 189 ; *Ante*, p. 110.   (⁴) 2 Wm. Rob., 251.
(²) 3 P. D., 182; *Ante*, p. 108.   (⁵) 3 H. & N., 505.
(³) Law Rep., 4 A. & E., 238 ; 11 Eng.   (⁶) Law Rep., 6 Q. B., 280, at p. 291.
R., 406.

sel is not touching the 'ground, it would have used the phrase "on or off the shore of any sea or tidal water."

Bucknill was not called upon to reply.

LORD COLERIDGE, C.J.: Two points have been argued in this case: the one as to the ground upon which the judgment is founded, and the other as to a matter in which the judge of the court below took a view in favor of the salvors.

As to the first point, I am of opinion that the judgment of the court below cannot be supported. I think it immaterial to consider whether the hopper-barge was "used in navigation" within the meaning of the Merchant Shipping Act, 1854, s. 2, because that enactment directs that the word "ship" shall "include every description of vessel used in navigation not propelled by oars." It does not exclude other meanings of the word. I agree that to hold that a mud-barge is a ship may seem to go very far in the way of interpretation; but we must not overlook the consequences of holding that the hopper-barge is not a "ship." She could take men on board. She falls within the definition cited in Todd's *Johnson's Dictionary of the word [129 "ship" from Horne Tooke, namely, "formatum aliquid, in contradistinction from a raft for the purpose of conveying merchandise, &c., by water, protected from the water and the weather." Although this may not be the definition of Johnson, it is the definition of a great master of language; and I think that it applies to the present case. The learned judge in the court below seems to have decided upon the ground that the interpretation clause (s. 2) of the Merchant Shipping Act, 1854, excluded every meaning besides the definition therein stated; he fails to deal with the question whether the hopper-barge may not be considered a "ship" in the ordinary and popular sense of the word. I decide that she is a ship in the common meaning of that term.

The second point was whether at the time when the salvage services were rendered, the hopper-barge conld be considered "to be stranded or otherwise in distress on the shore of any sea or tidal water." I think that the counsel for the owner of the Mac was entitled to raise this point. It has been argued that as the hopper-barge was not stranded, the justices had no jurisdiction to award salvage. The learned judge in the court below appears to have thought himself bound by the decision in *The Leda* ('), and undoubtedly he was bound by it. As this is a Court of Appeal, we are at liberty to consider the question apart from authority. Now the hopper-barge was not literally "on the shore." But

(') Sw., 40.

the statute contains the words "otherwise in distress;" this phrase plainly contemplates some misadventure other than stranding; and it shows that "on the shore" does not mean that the vessel must be actually touching the ground. The jurisdiction of justices under sections 458 and 460 of the Merchant Shipping Act, 1854, can only arise when the services are rendered upon the very shore itself or within three miles thereof; here the hopper-barge at the time when she was rescued, was from two to three miles distant from the land. I think that the judgment of Dr. Lushington in *The Leda* (¹) was right, and that the learned judge in the court below was right; "on the shore" means "near the shore." The contention for the owner of the Mac as to this latter point wholly fails.

130] *BRETT, L.J.: This case comes within the words of s. 458 of the Merchant Shipping Act, 1854, if they are read in their ordinary sense and without the assistance of the interpretation clause; but, as it seems to me, it falls also within that clause. In s. 458, the words "ship" and "boat" are used; but it seems plain to me that the word "ship" is not used in the technical sense as denoting a vessel of a particular rig. In popular language, ships are of different kinds; barks, brigs, schooners, sloops, cutters. The word includes anything floating in or upon the water built in a particular form and used for a particular purpose. In this case the vessel, if she may be so called, was built for a particular purpose, she was built as a hopper-barge; she has no motive power, no means of progression within herself. Towing alone will not conduct her, she must have a rudder, and therefore she must have men on board to steer her. Barges are vessels in a certain sense; and as the word "ship" is not used in a strictly nautical meaning, but is used in a popular meaning, I think that this hopper-barge is a "ship." She is not propelled by oars. The interpretation clause of the Merchant Shipping Act, 1854 (s. 2), does not limit the meaning, it enlarges it. This hopper-barge is used for carrying men and mud; she is used in navigation; for to dredge up and carry away mud and gravel is an act done for the purposes of navigation. Suppose that a saloon barge capable of carrying 200 persons, is towed down the river Mersey in order to put passengers on board vessels lying at the mouth; she would be used for the purposes of navigation, and I think it equally true that the hopper-barge was used in navigation.

With regard to the second point, I am prepared to adopt

(¹) Sw. 40.

the view of Dr. Lushington in *The Leda* (').   The expression
"on the shore," is a nautical phrase, and is used in an extended meaning; it is so used in acts of Parliament. I do
not think that the Legislature intended that the phrase
should be used in a literal sense.

COTTON, L.J.: This appeal is brought on the ground that
the justices had no jurisdiction to award salvage.

The first point is that the hopper-barge is not a "ship."
The *interpretation clause does not confine the mean-   [131
ing of the word, it does not confine it simply to what is used
in navigation. I think that the hopper-barge is a "ship,"
both within and without the interpretation clause. "Ship"
is a general term for artificial structures floating on the
water; this is plain upon looking at the meanings given in
Johnson's Dictionary; and it is to be observed that one of
the meanings of "boat" is therein stated to be "a ship of a
small size." I think that the proper meaning is "something
hollowed out." Some expressions of Blackburn, J., in *Ex
parte Ferguson* ('), may appear to support a different view;
that learned judge seems at first sight to have been of opinion that a "ship" meant a sea-going vessel; but I think
that the remarks which he made must be read with reference
to the subject-matter before him, and that he was merely
explaining that the vessel in question was a "ship." It is
plain to my mind, that in order to be a "ship" within the
Merchants Shipping Act, 1854, a vessel need not be sea-going: it is only necessary to refer to s. 19 of that statute
which provides that British ships must be registered, except
"ships not exceeding fifteen tons burden employed solely in
navigation on the rivers or coasts of the United Kingdom, or
on the rivers or coasts of some British possession within which
the managing owners of such ships are resident." I think
that this shows that the hopper-barge was a "ship" within
the act. The question cannot depend on the circumstance
whether she carries a cargo from port to port. She was
propelled by towing, and she carried mud with a crew on
board.

As to the second point, I think that the counsel for the
owner of the Mac was justified in raising it; he was satisfied
with the judgment which he had obtained in the Admiralty
Division, and he could not appeal against the reasons assigned by the judge; but as to the merits he cannot succeed
upon this point. I think that *The Leda* (') was rightly decided. The 458th section of the Merchant Shipping Act,
1854, uses the words "stranded or otherwise in distress;"

(¹) Sw., 40.   (²) Law Rep., 6 Q. B., 280, at p. 291.

and this shows that the ship need not be touching the ground.
132] In this case, the hopper-barge was within *three miles
of the shore and was therefore near to it. The justices,
therefore, had jurisdiction.

Appeal allowed.

Solicitors for owner of the Mac: *Thompson & Co.*
Solicitors for owners of the Saucy Polly: *Whyte, Colli-
son & Pritchard.*

J. E. H.

[7 Probate Division, 132.]

July 4, 1882.

[IN THE COURT OF APPEAL.]

THE GUY MANNERING.

*Damage—Pilot compulsorily taken on Board but not compulsorily in Charge—
Liability of Shipowner for Collision in Suez Canal solely caused by Negligence of
Suez Canal Company's Pilot.* ··

Where a collision in the Suez Canal has been caused by the negligence of a Suez
Canal Company's pilot compulsorily taken on board the wrongdoing ship, the owner
of such ship is not exempt from liability for the damage arising out of the collision.

The effect of the Regulations for the Navigation of the Suez Canal is to constitute
a pilot taken on board a ship traversing the canal the adviser of the master, and to
leave the control of the navigation of the ship solely with the master.

APPEAL by the defendants from the judgement of Sir R.
Phillimore upon a special case.

The facts of the case are fully stated in the report of the
proceedings in the Admiralty Division (¹).

Butt, Q.C. (*Nelson,* with him), for the defendants: The
injury to the plaintiffs' ship was caused solely by the negligence of those on board the defendants' ship. The defendants were compelled by the Regulations for the Navigation
of the Canal to employ a pilot, and he was *de facto* acting
in charge of the ship. Under these circumstances the defendants are not liable. It is true that s. 388 of the Merchant
Shipping Act, 1854, may not apply out of the United Kingdom; but it is only declaratory of the general law, and the
defendants can rely upon the general principle that an employer is not liable for the acts of a subordinate whom he
133] *is forced to take into his service. The relation of
masters and servant did not exist between the defendants
and the pilot. The Regulations for the Navigation of the
Suez Maritime Canal are in many respects *ultra vires:* they
cannot alter the general rules of law. The authorities simi-

(¹) 7 P. D., p. 52.

lar to the present case support the argument for the defendants. In *Lucey* v. *Ingram* (') it was held that as a licensed pilot was on board, the owner was not liable for his negligence, although pilotage was not compulsory. A decision to the same effect may be found in *General Steam Navigation Co.* v. *British and Colonial Steam Navigation Co* ('). The law of a foreign country as to a tort is not recognized in the courts of this country if it is contrary to English law: *The Halley* ('). It is the licensed pilot, and not the owner of the ship, who is liable for the pilot's negligence: *M'Intosh* v. *Slade* ('). The defendants contracted with the pilot to navigate their steamship through the canal: that pilot exercised an independent employment, and they are not responsible for the consequences of his negligence: *Milligan* v. *Wedge* (').

W. G. F. Phillimore (*Cohen*, Q.C., with. him), for the plaintiffs: The fallacy of the argument for the defendants lies in their interpretation of the word "pilot" as used in the Regulations of the Suez Canal; it there means only a guide and not a "pilot" in the ordinary sense of the word. The doctrine as to compulsory pilotage was discussed in *The Maria* (') by Dr. Lushington; but it is plain that where the so-called "pilot" does not take upon himself the navigation of the vessel, but is a mere adviser of the captain, the owners are responsible if any injury is done by unskilful management.

Butt, Q.C., did not reply.

LORD COLERIDGE, C.J.: This case has been well argued by the counsel for the defendants. Nevertheless, I am of opinion that the judgment of the court below is correct, and need only say that I agree with the reasons on which that judgment is founded.

*BRETT, L.J.: I am of the same opinion, and I also [134 agree with the reasons assigned by the judge in the court below. It is said by the defendants' counsel that as the captain allowed the pilot to act, the owners of the Guy Mannering are not liable, and, further, that the limitation of the pilot's authority is *ultra vires*. I see no reason for upholding the argument as to the latter point. The regulations for the navigation of the Suez Canal must be taken to be a part of the law of the country ; and no facts are stated by which they can be impeached. It is said that the pilot-

(') 6 M. & W., 302.   (³) Law Rep., 2 P. C., 193.
(⁷) Law Rep., 3 Ex., 330; in Ex. Ch., (⁴) 6 B. & C., 657.
4 Ex., 238.   (⁵) 12 A. & E., 737.
                    (⁶) 1 Wm. Rob., 95.

age is compulsory, and that a shipowner is not liable for the acts of the pilot, whom he is compelled to employ. In England the shipowner is not liable for the acts of the pilot, where pilotage is compulsory: the statutes as to merchant shipping do not accurately define the duty of a pilot; but it is plain that he is to conduct the navigation. On the one hand he has no power to place the crew at particular posts in the ship or to regulate the discipline : on the other hand he is to regulate the course of the ship through the water; he is taken on board in order to control the management of her for this purpose : a sailing vessel cannot be steered unless her sails are regulated in a particular manner ; and therefore he has power to regulate the management of the sails. The owner of the ship is not liable for the consequences of the wrongful or negligent acts committed by the pilot, whom he is compelled to employ. But if the ship goes wrong in consequence of a failure of duty by the look-out man, it is not the fault of the pilot and the owner is responsible. If the pilot's orders as to steering the ship are not obeyed, and if mischief in consequence ensues, the owner cannot escape from liability. It may be that when the owner of the ship is compelled to take a pilot on board, and is compelled to pay him fees for the whole of a certain distance, he is protected from all the consequences of the pilot's negligence wherever they may happen, although during part of the distance pilotage is not compulsory ; in fact, obligatory payment to a pilot may be deemed to stand on the same footing as the compulsion to take him on board ; and this doctrine explains one of the grounds upon which *General Steam Navigation Co.* v. *British and Colonial Steam Navigation* 135] *Co.* (¹) was *decided ; it was there held, that as a pilot taken on board for the distance between Dungeness and London could claim payment for his services as far as Gravesend, the owner was not liable for his negligent acts even after the ship had entered the limits of the port of London, to which she belonged, and in which the employment of a pilot was not in her case compulsory. *Lucey* v. *Ingram* (²) always seems at first sight a stumbling-block, but it was decided on the ground that the Legislature had intended under the circumstances of that case to exempt the owner from liability. It has been argued that the relation of masters and servant did not exist between the owners of the Guy Mannering and the pilot, and that the doctrine as to the exemption of owners where pilotage is compulsory, must be always upheld in English courts ; but all theory fails to

(¹) Law Rep., 3 Ex., 330 ; in Ex. Ch., 4 Ex., 238.   (²) 6 M. & W., 302.

assist the defendants, because the duties performed by a
pilot of the Seuz Canal Company are not the same as those
of an English pilot. He does not take the control of the
course of the ship : he is not bound to direct how she is to be
navigated. In the words of Article 4 of the Regulations for
the Navigation, "pilots place at the disposal of captains of
vessels their experience and practical knowledge of the
canal ;" that is to say, a pilot is to tell a captain of the condition, the formation, and the depth of the canal ; he is in
fact to be a kind of living chart. But a pilot is not to go
beyond this : the captain must direct how the ship is to be
steered and the whole duty of managing her devolves upon
him. In the words of Article 4, "the captain is held responsible for all groundings and accidents of whatsoever kind resulting from the management and manœuvring of his ship."
The captain of the Guy Mannering was in fault, for he mis-
construed his own powers. He thought that he was in the
same position with regard to the pilot as an English captain
is when he is compelled by English law to employ a pilot.

COTTON, L.J.: The ground of the present appeal is that
at the time of the accident the employment of a pilot was
compulsory. By the English law, the owner of a ship is not
liable for the negligence of a pilot whom he is compelled to
employ ; and the *reason is that the pilot is not the   [136
servant of the owner. In some of the sections of part 5 of
the Merchant Shipping Act, 1854, such as ss. 359, 362, 388, a
pilot is said to "have charge" or to "take charge," or to be
"acting in charge ;" this language seems to show that in the
opinion of the Legislature, when a pilot comes on board, he
takes the management of the vessel ; in fact, the management of the vessel passes out of the hands of the captain ; and
therefore it is only reasonable that when pilotage is compulsory, the owner should not be liable for the negligence of the
pilot. But how does that principle apply here ? The duties
of a pilot on the Suez Canal are prescribed by the regulations of the company, and these declare that when an
accident of whatsoever kind happens, the captain is to be responsible. The reason, as stated in Article 4 of the Regulations, is as follows : "Pilots place at the disposal of captains
of vessels their experience and practical knowledge of the
canal ; but as they cannot be especially acquainted with the
defects or peculiarities of each steamer and her machinery
in stopping, steering, &c., the responsibility as regards the
management of the ship devolves solely upon the captain."
It is not a part of the pilot's duty to direct the management
of the ship whilst passing along the canal ; if any accident

happens through a mistake of the pilot, it cannot be said to occur through the default of the person in charge : the pilot has not the control of the vessel : the captain has the control, and is the person in charge. I cannot think that the rules of the company are *ultra vires ;* upon the facts before us, we must assume that they have been made pursuant to a competent authority.

Appeal dismissed.

Solicitors for plaintiffs : *Pritchard & Sons.*
Solicitors for defendants: *Lowless & Co.*

J. E. H.

[7 Probate Division, 187.]

· May 26, 1882.

[IN THE COURT OF APPEAL.]

137]   *THE GAETANO AND MARIA.

Bottomry—Foreign Ship—Law of the Flag.

The owner of cargo who ships it on board a foreign vessel, ships it to be dealt with by the master according to the law of the flag, that is, the law of the country to which the vessel belongs, unless that authority be limited by express stipulation at the time of the shipment. Therefore a bond made by the master of a foreign ship hypothecating cargo laden on board such ship, if valid according to the law of the flag of the ship, will be enforced by the English Admiralty Court, on the arrest of the ship and cargo at the port of London (the port of discharge within the meaning of the bond), although the conditions imposed by English law as essential to the validity of such bond have not been complied with.

APPEAL by the plaintiffs the indorsees of a bottomry bond, from the judgment of Sir Robert Phillimore, the judge of the Admiralty Division, on a demurrer by the defendants to the 4th and 5th paragraphs of the plaintiff's reply (¹).

By the statement of claim the plaintiffs alleged that in the month of April, 1881, the Italian vessel Gaetano and Maria was at the Island of Fayal, in the Azores, in distress laden with cargo bound on a voyage to London, and her master, Giovanni Frugoni, being without funds or credit at Fayal, was compelled to borrow on bottomry of the said ship, her cargo and freight the sum of £2,330 2s. 7d. for the necessary disbursements and expenses of the said ship and cargo to enable her to proceed on her said voyage.

That on the 22d of April, 1881, the said master (who was a part owner of the Gaetano and Maria) by a bottomry bond dated on that day, and by him duly executed in consideration of the sum of £2,330 2s. 7d. lent to him by An-

(¹) 7 P. D., p. 1.

tonio Silveira d'Avila Coeltro bound himself and the said ship, her tackle apparel and furniture, her cargo, and the freight to be earned by her on her said voyage, to pay to the said Antonio Silveira d'Avila Coeltro or his order the said sum of £2,330 2s. 7d. sterling, together with the maritime premium thereon upon the safe arrival of the said ship at *her port of discharge with a proviso that the bond   [138 was not to be enforced till three days after arrival.

That the said bottomry bond was indorsed by the said Antonio Silveira d'Avila Coeltro to the plaintiffs, who were the lawful owners thereof.

That the Gaetano and Maria subsequently proceeded on her said voyage, and on the 15th of May, 1881, arrived with her cargo on board at the port of London, which was her port of discharge within the meaning of the said bond.

The owners of the cargo appeared as defendants in the action, and delivered a statement of defence, in which, after stating that they were domiciled in England, and after denying the power or authority of the master of the said vessel to bind them by any such bottomry bond, they alleged in the 6th paragraph as follows :

6. These defendants further in the alternative say that the said master of the said vessel at the time of his arrival at Fayal was aware that the said cargo was shipped by Messrs. William H. Power & Co., of New York, and that the ship was chartered for the said voyage by Messrs. Rodocanachi, Sons & Co., of London. There was postal and telegraphic communication with England and the United States of America, and the said master did not communicate to the owner of the said bark or to the said shippers or to the said charterers of the said vessel, as he might and could have done, his intention to hypothecate the said cargo or the circumstances which might render such hypothecation advisable or necessary, or take any steps to ascertain who were the actual owners of the said cargo, but on the contrary, without reasonable cause or excuse, abstained from so doing when communication should have been made, and these defendants further say that the said shippers did not know, nor did they the said defendants know of the said bond till the arrival of the said vessel at Falmouth, and that the said bond is bad and invalid against the said cargo.

The 4th and 5th paragraphs of the plaintiffs' reply were as follows : .

4. And by way of further reply to the several allegations in the said 6th paragraph of the statement of defence, the 139] plaintiffs say *that by the law of Italy to which country the Gaetano and Maria belonged at the time that the bottomry bond in question was executed, and at the time when it became due, the bottomry contract had to be entered into, and the said bottomry bond had to be executed as they, in fact, were in the presence and with the intervention and sanction of the Italian consul or consular agent at the port of Fayal, and that upon their being so entered into and executed, they became and were valid and effectual to bind both ship and cargo without any previous communication being made by the master to the owners of the ship or to the owners of the said cargo.

5. In the alternative the plaintiffs say in answer to the allegations in the same paragraph that, by the law of Italy to which country the Gaetano and Maria belonged at the times aforesaid, a bottomry contract can be lawfully made, and a valid bottomry bond can be executed without any previous communication with the owners of the ship or the owners of cargo, and that all the formalities and conditions required by the Italian law in order to make a good and valid bottomry bond were complied with and satisfied before the said bottomry bond was executed.

The defendants demurred to the said 4th and 5th paragraphs of the reply.

SIR ROBERT PHILLIMORE being of opinion that the case was governed by that of *The Hamburgh* ('), and that the validity of the bottomry bond was not to be determined by the law of the ship's flag, gave judgment on the demurrer for the defendants.

The plaintiffs appealed.

May 11. *C. Hall*, Q.C., and *W. G. F. Phillimore*, for the plaintiffs: It must be admitted that according to the law of England the master would have had no authority to hypothecate the cargo, if he had the means at the foreign port of first communicating with the cargo owners and neglected to avail himself of such means; but the question here is whether the cargo having been shipped on a foreign ship, the law of the country of that ship is not to prevail rather than the law of England in determining the validity of the 140] *bottomry bond. That question was really not considered by Dr. Lushington in *The Hamburgh* ('), as there was no sufficient evidence there to raise it. " I am well

(') Br. & Lush., 253.

aware," says Dr. Lushington in that case, "that much has
been said upon this subject, and that many questions have
been discussed, whether the law of the country of the vessel
ought or ought not to prevail, and also whether the *lex loci
contractus* ought not to be the governing principle. I abstain, however, from going into these questions, and for the
following reasons. In the case of *The Gratitudine* ('), an
imperial vessel, in that celebrated judgment where Lord
Stowell exhausted all the authorities, not a word is said nor
any authority cited to show that any law should be applied
to the case save the ordinary maritime law. There is nothing mentioned of the *lex loci contractus*, nor of the law of
the country to which the ship belonged. The same observation applies to the case of *The Bonaparte* ('), a Swedish
vessel, and to many other cases. In this case, therefore,
and for the present, I must take as my guide the ordinary
maritime law. The state of the pleading also is so vague,
and the evidence so loose and unsatisfactory, that I can take
no other course. Whenever any specific law is averred to
be the governing law, with sufficient distinctness and proper
evidence produced, I shall be ready to consider the question." The Privy Council on appeal in that case simply
agreed with Dr. Lushington as to this. Now on the demurrer in the present case the law of Italy, the country to which
the vessel belonged, is clearly stated, so that the point is
raised here. *Lloyd* v. *Guibert* (') is a strong authority in
favor of the plaintiffs, as showing that the law of the flag
must govern the rights of the parties. It is true that that
was with reference to the contract of affreightment, but the
principle is the same as that by which authority is given by
a cargo owner to the master of the vessel to bind the cargo
by a bottomry bond. The case of *The Karnak* (') also decides that the extent of the authority conferred on the master of a vessel to bind the owners either of the ship or cargo,
is derived from and governed by the law of the flag. To
the same effect is *Pope* v. *Nickerson* ('). *The case [141]
of *Kleinwort, Cohen & Co.* v. *The Cassa Marittima of Genoa* ('), which was relied on in support of the demurrer,
never raised the question whether the law of the flag should
prevail, but only decided what is not disputed to be the
English law, that the master cannot hypothecate the cargo
without communicating with the owner of it if such communication be practicable. The question, by what law the

(') 3 Ch. Rob., 240.   (⁴) Law Rep., 2 P. C., 505.
(²) 8 Moo. P. C., 459.   (⁵) 3 Story, 465.
(³) Law Rep., 1 Q. B., 115.   (⁶) 2 App. Cas., 156–7 ; 19 Eng. R., 10.

master had authority to sell the vessel at a foreign port, was considered by Dr. Lushington in *The Eliza Cornish*(').

Butt, Q.C., and *Myburgh*, Q.C., for the defendants, the owners of the cargo: "In no instance has a bottomry instrument been held valid by a court of this country, except where the requirements of the law of the tribunal have been complied with:" 1 Maude & Pollock's Law of Merchant Shipping, 4th ed., p. 570. The proposition on the part of the plaintiffs is not to construe a contract by the Italian law, nor to apply that law to an existing contract, but to make a contract by virtue of that law, where the parties are English and where the court to give force to it is an English court. By the English law the master would not be the agent of the defendants and authorized by them to enter into this bottomry bond except by necessity; and where there was power within a reasonable time for the master to communicate with the cargo owners there would be no such necessity, and consequently no authority to act as agent for the cargo owners.

[LORD COLERIDGE, C.J.: Lord Stowell in *The Gratitudine* (') points out the difficulty of the master getting the directions of the cargo owners in the case of a general ship, where the cargo may be owned by different persons.

COTTON, L.J.: Do you say that the right to bind the cargo owner by a bottomry bond must depend on the law of the country of such owner?]

No. The law of the port of discharge where the bond is payable is the law to govern the rights of the parties, and that here was the English maritime law. The power to make the contract to bind the cargo owner must depend on the fact of necessity which must be proved, and that is a matter 142] of evidence and must *therefore be according to the *lex fori*: *The Halley* ('). So according to Story's Conflict of Laws, sec. 242, the law of the place of performance is to govern. Moreover, where the English Admiralty Court is applied to in order to enforce a lien, it may well refuse to lend its aid for that purpose, except to enforce it according to the English law. Here the charterparty was made in London.

[COTTON, L.J.: That does not appear on the pleadings, and one cannot look to anything which is not stated there.]

[*W. G. F. Phillimore:* There is no objection to the pleadings being mended in this respect (').]

(') 1 Spink's Ec. & Ad., 36.
(') 3 W. Rob., 240, at p. 262.
(') Law Rep., 2 P. C., 193.
(') By consent the pleadings were to be taken as amended by a statement in them that the charterparty was made in London.

Then as there is here a contract of affreightment made in London where the cargo is to be delivered, surely the validity of the bottomry bond must be determined by the law of the port of London, which is the port of discharge where the bond is to be enforced.

W. G. F. Phillimore replied.

Cur. adv. vult.

May 26.   BRETT, L.J.:   This is a case which I regret to say arises on demurrer, for I would much rather that it had arisen on the facts as proved.   I think, however, that we must take the facts to be that goods were shipped by the defendants, who whether British subjects or not are domiciled in England, and that such goods were shipped abroad on board an Italian ship in fulfilment of a charterparty which was made in London, and for the purpose of being carried to England ; that the ship met with misfortune and was taken into Fayal, a Portuguese port, and whilst in such Portuguese port the master entered into a contract of bottomry by which he hypothecated the ship and the cargo ; that the vessel and the cargo afterwards arrived in England, and that the ship and cargo were arrested in the English Admiralty Court.   It was asserted in the statement of defence that there were means of communication between Fayal and England of such a kind that the master might, if he had so pleased, have communicated with the owners of the cargo before he thus hypothecated their cargo, *and this,   [143 by the pleadings in reply, is not denied.   But it is stated that according to Italian law, even though he could have thus communicated, yet was entitled under the circumstances to hypothecate the cargo or to cover it by a bottomry bond, if he did so before the consul, which he did do in this case.   And it is in effect further stated that although there were these means of communication, yet, that by the Italian law the master of a vessel may cover the cargo by a bottomry bond without communicating with the owner under certain conditions, all of which conditions were fulfilled in this case.

The demurrer therefore raises this question, whether although there were the means of communication before the bottomry bond was executed, yet nevertheless the defendant's goods are bound in the English Admiralty Court by that bottomry bond so entered into by the master.

Now the first question raised on the argument before us was what is the law which is administered in an English Court of Admiralty, whether it is English law, or whether

it is that which is called the common maritime law, which is
not the law of England alone, but the law of all maritime
countries. About that question I have not the smallest
doubt. Every Court of Admiralty is a court of the country
in which it sits and to which it belongs. The law which is
administered in the Admiralty Court of England is the English maritime law. It is not the ordinary municipal law
of the country, but it is the law which the English Court of
Admiralty either by act of Parliament or by reiterated
decisions and traditions and principles has adopted as the
English maritime law ; and about that I cannot conceive
that there is any doubt. It seems to me that this is what
every judge in the Admiralty Court of England has promulgated (Lord Stowell and those before him, and Dr. Lushington after him), and I do not understand that the present
learned judge of the Admiralty Court differs in the least
from them. He says that this case must be determined by
the general maritime law as administered in England—that
is in other words by the English maritime law.

Now if this ship had been an English ship, if the captain
had been an English master, and if the owners of the cargo
144]   had been *English subjects, there is no doubt that the
master would have had no authority to bind the owners of
the cargo unless certain necessities had arisen. The ship
must have been in a state of distress, and in a port of distress where the owner of her had no means or credit by
which to find the money required for doing the necessary
repairs, and besides this in order to require the hypothecation by bottomry of the cargo, the value of the ship must
not of itself be large enough. Moreover, if this had been an
English ship, and an English captain, even though all these
necessities had existed, yet the master would not be authorized to charge the cargo if before doing so he had the means
of communicating with the owner of the cargo within a reasonable time, so that on receiving notice the owner of the
cargo might determine whether he would allow the cargo to
to be bottomried or whether he would take other means for
the disposal of the cargo.

Therefore if this had been an English ship, there can be
no doubt but that the cargo of the defendants would not on
the facts pleaded in this case have been liable ; because it is
admitted that before hypothecating the cargo a communication might have been made by the captain to the cargo
owners.

Now it is alleged that this rule must bind the plaintiffs,
although the ship is an Italian ship, because it was said that

the matter to be proved was, whether there was a necessity which gave the captain a right to hypothecate the cargo in this way, and that inasmuch as that is a matter of procedure it is to be governed according to the law of the forum. That raises the question whether this is a matter of procedure. It is said it is, because it is a matter of evidence. Now the manner of proving the facts is matter of evidence, and, to my mind, is matter of procedure, but the facts, to be proved are not matters of procedure; they are the matters with which the procedure has to deal. Here the facts, which are to be proved in order to give the captain the authority, are not the evidence of those facts. The thing to be proved cannot be evidence of the thing which is to be proved, and therefore it seems to me that this is not a matter of procedure to be governed by the law of the forum.

Then arises this consideration. What is the nature of that which has to be proved? It is the authority of the master. *There is no contract between the master [145 and the owner of the cargo which enables the master to deal with the cargo; but there is a contract between the owner of the ship and the owner of the cargo with which I will presently deal.

I doubt myself (but it is not necessary to decide it in this case) whether the master is ever the agent of the owner of the cargo. The master is the agent of the owner of the ship, and it may be that the master, as agent of the owner of the ship, has certain rights with regard to the cargo. But suppose that the master can be under circumstances of neccessity the agent of the owner of the cargo, out of what does the authority of the master arise? Now this authority of the master of the ship to hypothecate the ship or cargo is peculiar. It does not arise merely out of a contract of bailment, for that contract gives no such right. It does not arise even out of a contract of carriage on land. I doubt whether it arises on a contract of sea carriage, where it is all within the realm, but it is not necessary that this should be now decided. It does arise where goods are shipped on board a ship to be carried from one country to another. That is acknowleged by the maritime law of England, and, as far as I know, is equally acknowledged in every maritime country. It arises from the necessity of things; it arises from the obligation of the shipowner and the master to carry the goods from one country to another, and from it being inevitable from the nature of things that the ship and cargo may at some time or other be in a strange port where the captain may be without means, and where the shipowner may have

no credit because he is not known there, that for the safety
of all concerned and for the carrying out of the ultimate object of the whole adventure, there must be a power in the
master not only to hypothecate the ship but the cargo. That
power of the master does not arise out of the bill of lading
nor out of the charterparty, because it may exist where
there is neither bill of lading nor charterparty. It arises out
of the contract of maritime carriage, by the shipment of
goods on board a ship for the purpose of being carried from
one country to another, and it exists the moment the goods
are put on board for such a purpose. It is regulated, and
often limited, by terms in the bill of lading or by terms in
146] the charterparty; but unless such terms *specifically
do away with this authority of the master, the authority of
the master exists by virtue of the contract which arises between the shipowner and the cargo owner by the shipment of
the goods. It is not necessary to decide whether this authority is given to the master by way of contract or by means
of the law.

Then what is the principle which ought to govern this
case? The goods are put on board an Italian ship, and the
person to exercise authority is an Italian master. Is the authority of the Italian master to depend upon the law of the
country of the shipper, when that law is contrary to the law
of his own country? Why should it? Is the master of a
ship to be taken to know the law of the country of each shipper of the goods which are put on board his ship? It would
be strange if that were so. If a merchant puts his goods into
the power of an Italian master on board an Italian owner's
ship, what is the meaning of the transaction, but that he is
to deal with the goods as an Italian master is to be taken to
deal with goods on board his ship, unless he is bound to
another mode? Upon principle it seems to me that he who
ships goods on board a foreign ship, ships them to be dealt
with by the master of that ship according to the law of the
country of that ship, unless there is a stipulation to the contrary. Therefore, when these goods were shipped on board
an Italian ship, it seems to me that by the contract of the
parties arising out of that shipment it must be taken that the
goods were to be dealt with under circumstances which might
arise and which are generally considered likely to arise by
all maritime countries, in the way in which that master would
deal with the goods according to the law of Italy, unless
there was some stipulation to the contrary. Now that is
how it stands on principle. How are the authorities? The

case of *Lloyd* v. *Guibert* (') does not seem to me to govern
this case absolutely, because the question there was whether
or not a certain stipulation was implied in a contract. The
contract was a contract of affreightment and the question
was whether there was to be implied into that contract a
stipulation that if certain circumstances arose, and the master delivered up his ship and freight, the shipowner should
not be made liable beyond the amount specified. The owner
of the ship could only *be relieved if there was such   [147
a stipulation in the contract of affreightment. There would
have been no such stipulation if it was to be judged according to the law of the forum, that is, the law of the English
court. But there would be such a stipulation if the contract of affreightment was to be construed according to the
law of the ship. It was there held that inasmuch as the
contract of affreightment was made with the master or owner
of a foreign ship abroad, the contract was the contract of the
country of the ship; in other words, that it was governed by
the law of the " Flag" of the ship, and inasmuch as in the
country of that flag such a contract of affreightment would
have had such a stipulation in it, then the English court
would hold that it had this stipulation in it. That is not
this case, because the matter here is not the question of the
construction of a contract, but of what authority arises out
of the fact of a contract having been entered into.' Still, if
the contract was held there to be a foreign contract, because
it was made with regard to the shipment of goods on board a
foreign ship, the principle governs this case, and would
authorize our saying that the authority which arises out of
the contract of shipment is the authority which the law of
the country of the ship would give to the master; and in
accordance with that principle I think this case ought to be
decided. The learned judge of the Admiralty Court considered that this case was governed by *The Hamburgh* ('), but
with great deference I do not think that that case ought to
govern the present one at all. There, Dr. Lushington treated
the ship as an English ship, and said that he was administering the maritime law of England. It was urged upon him
that he ought to administer some other maritime law, but his
answer was, "I do not judge what it should be, if there had
been any evidence before me that the maritime law of some
other country was different from the law of England, but no
such evidence has been given before me in this case." This
point, therefore, did not arise there, and neither Dr. Lushington nor the Privy Council on appeal, decided if the law

(') Law Rep., 1 Q. B., 115.   (') Br. & Lush., 253.

of the countries had been different in the case of *The Hamburgh* ('), which law would have been administered. I cannot therefore think that the case of *The Hamburgh* (') is in 148] conflict with the *decision to which I have come in the present case, nor in conflict with the case of *Lloyd* v. *Guibert* (²). Therefore, acting upon the principle of *Lloyd* v. *Guibert* (²), and upon the principle which arises from the mercantile transaction itself, it seems to me that whoever puts his goods on board a foreign ship puts them on board subject to be dealt with by the master according to the law of the country to which the ship belongs, unless that authority is limited by express stipulation between the parties at the time of the shipment.

There was another and a minor point taken which was that if that be the law yet it was not the law to be administered in this case, because the contract of affreightment here was actually made in England. But that makes no difference in my view of the case; the right arises out of the contract which is instituted by the shipment, and which is not controlled in this respect by any stipulation in the bill of lading or in the charterparty. I am therefore of ·opinion that the demurrer in this case ought not to have been allowed, and that the rights of the parties ought to be decided according to the law of the flag.

COTTON, L.J.: The question in this case is as to the validity of the bottomry bond against the owners of the cargo in the ship. According to the English law with reference to the facts of this case notice ought to have been given to the cargo owners, but there is a statement in the reply that, according to Italian law, it was not necessary that such notice should be given in order to make the bond valid, and that the ship was an Italian ship.

The question therefore which we have to consider is whether the English law or the Italian law is to determine the validity of the bond ?

The point turns not on the express terms of any contract, but, in my opinion, on an implied authority arising out of the contract between the owners of the cargo and the owner of the ship when the goods were put on board for the purpose of being carried ; and, like all other implied terms, it must be governed by the law applicable to the country in which it is implied. It was said that necessity gives the authority to hypothecate. In my opinion *that is putting it wrongly. Necessity is the condition of the exercise of the authority; but, in my opinion, the implied authority

arises out of the contract and is not properly given by necessity. Now what law must govern it? It was said that it
must here depend upon the *lex fori*, and that as I understand for two reasons. First, it was said that the remedy to
be given depends upon the *lex fori*. Undoubtedly it does.
But we are not considering here what is the proper remedy,
but whether the bottomry bond is valid or not? Secondly,
as pointed out by Lord Justice Brett, it cannot be considered
to depend upon the *lex fori*, because the proof of the necessity, which is the condition precedent to the exercise of the
authority, is a matter of procedure. The mode of proving
the facts to show the existence of the necessity is part of the
lex fori, and depends upon the *lex fori*, but the facts necessary to establish the right of the party are not the evidence
to prove such facts, and the facts as distinguished from the
way in which they are to be proved, are not part of the *lex
fori*. Next it was said that the authority to hypothecate
must depend upon the place where the contract was made,
and it was put in two ways. It was said that as a rule the
law of the place where the contract is made was to be implied as to all those matters which are not in express terms
in the contract, subject to this, that where the contract is
made in one place to be performed in another, the law of
the place of performance was to govern. Here the place of
performance was said to be England, because the goods were
to be carried there. But this really is a fallacy. The performance of the contract is not merely the landing of the
goods in England. They are taken on board to be ultimately landed no doubt in England; but what law of the
numerous countries to which the goods may be taken during their carriage to England is to be implied? In my opinion the rule stated by Lord Justice Brett, in the absence of
authority, would be the right one,—that when the owner of
goods puts them on board a vessel he must authorize the
owner of that vessel, and his agent the captain, to deal with
those goods according to the law of the country to which
that vessel belongs, and therefore if, as it was here, an Italian ship, according to the law of Italy. The rule is applicable because no one who ships goods on board a vessel can
*be ignorant of the flag, that is, of the country to [150
which the ship belongs, whilst the master would be in a very
difficult position if he had to inquire what was the law o
the country of the goods, if, as regards one portion of the
cargo, he had the power to deal with it when the necessity
arose, in one way, and as regards another portion of the
cargo, in another way.

In my opinion the rule stated by Lord Justice Brett, to which I have referred, is a sensible rule and one that should be adopted if there were no authority upon the subject, but I think there is authority given by express decision; be-
) leads to the conclusion
and in which I concur.
of *The*
under-
he does
is this:
ence so
no other course.
be the governing

was not consider-
ing
con
I may say that the Lord Chief Justice has told us that he concurs in our decision.

Appeal allowed.

Solicitors for plaintiffs : *Lowless & Co.*
Solicitors for defendants : *Thomas Cooper & Co.*

(¹) Law Rep., 1 Q. B., 115.   (²) Br. & Lush., 253.

W. P.

[7 Probate Division, 151.]

June 21, 1882.

[IN THE COURT OF APPEAL.]

151]   *THE DOUGLAS.

*Damage—Collision caused by Vessel approaching the spot where
River rendered Dangerous by sunken Vessel—Vessel*

The D. in consequence of the sole default of her master and crew had sunk in the Thames, and had become a wreck obstructing the navigation of the river.   Her mate

ing been instituted on behalf of the owner
of the D., the judge at the trial refused to
of the D. had sent a message to the harbo
to light the wreck:

The Douglas.   1882

Held, that the evidence was wrongly rejected, that the collision had not been caused by the negligence of the owners of the wreck, and that they were not liable for the damage done.

THIS was an action of damage brought by the owner of the steamship Mary Nixon against the steamship Douglas and her freight.

The statement of claim alleged that shortly after midnight on the 27th of October, 1881, the Mary Nixon was proceeding up the river Thames about mid-channel in Gravesend Reach with her regulation lights exhibited and a proper look-out, when she struck against one of the masts of the Douglas as that vessel was lying a sunken wreck in a position obstructing the navigation of the river, and thereby suffered considerable damage; that the collision was not contributed to by any negligence on the part of those in charge of the Mary Nixon, whilst no lights or warning of any sort were exhibited on or near the wreck of the Douglas, and there was nothing to warn those on board the Mary Nixon of the wreck. The statement of claim further alleged that it was by reason of the negligence of those in charge of the Douglas in coming into collision with two vessels called respectively the Duke of Buckingham and the Orion, that the Douglas sank in the position she lay *in when [152 the Mary Nixon came into collision with her, and attributed negligence to the defendants, the owners of the Douglas, for not taking means to warn approaching vessels of the position of the wreck.

The defendants delivered a statement of defence, and therein, after admitting that the Douglas had sunk in consequence of a collision with the Duke of Buckingham, and that that collision had been caused by the negligent navigation of the Douglas, but alleging that afterwards a white light had been placed in the main rigging of the Douglas and remained there until the Douglas sank, raised the defence that after the Douglas sank and before the Mary Nixon struck upon the wreck a reasonable time to exhibit lights as a warning in or near the wreck had not elapsed, that the Mary Nixon had been sufficiently warned of the position of the wreck by hailing; and in the alternative that "at the time when the Mary Nixon struck the Douglas, the Douglas was a wreck lying sunk on the bed of the river Thames, and that before and at the time when the Mary Nixon struck the Douglas, the defendants had wholly ceased to have the possession, management, or control of the same."

April 18. The action was heard before the judge of the

PROBATE DIVISION.

Admiralty Division, assisted by two of the Elder Brethren of the Trinity House.

Witnesses were examined on behalf of the plaintiff and of the defendants. From the evidence of the witnesses it appeared that the Mary Nixon had struck the wreck of the Douglas about six hours after the Douglas had sunk, and that at the time the officers of the Thames Conservancy had not taken possession of her.

It was proposed to be proved on behalf of the defendants by the evidence of the captain of a tug called the Endeavour, that warning was given to the harbor-master at Gravesend, and that the harbor-master said that the proper wreck-lights would be immediately sent to the Douglas, and that the statement of the harbor-master was reported to one of the officers of the Douglas. This evidence was objected to by the plaintiff on two grounds: first, that it was hearsay evi-
153] dence; and secondly, that it was *immaterial, inasmuch as the defendants could not delegate the duty of guarding the wreck to the harbor-master. The court rejected the evidence on its being tendered. It appeared, however, from the examination in writing of Griffith Williams, the mate of the Douglas, that he instructed the master of the tug called the Endeavour to report the sinking of the Douglas to the harbor-master, and that shortly afterwards the captain of the Endeavour reported to him that the harbor-master had said that he would send down something in the course of an hour. It further appeared from the defendants' answers to interrogatories, that they had never abandoned their interest or ownership in the Douglas, and that they still claimed to be her owners. The other facts are sufficiently noticed in the judgments hereafter set out.

Butt, Q.C., and *G. Bruce*, for the plaintiff: The Mary Nixon would never have struck the wreck, if the Mary Nixon had been warned of the position of the wreck in sufficient time for her to avoid running into it; the duty of warning the Mary Nixon clearly lay on the defendants, as the sinking of the Douglas was brought about solely by the negligence of their own servants: *Brown* v. *Mallett* ('); *White* v. *Crisp* ('); *Harmond* v. *Pearson* ('). In these circumstances the defendants must be held to be alone to blame for the damage done to the Mary Nixon. At the time the damage was done they had not abandoned the possession or management of the wreck, and it was incumbent on them after the Douglas had sunk "to use reasonable skill and care to prevent mischief to others," just as much as it was their duty to do so

---

(') 5 C. B., 599.   (²) 10 Ex., 312.   (³) 1 Campb., 515.

when this vessel was afloat. It is not as if it had been impracticable for the defendants to place a light near the wreck,
or otherwise to warn the Mary Nixon of her danger.

Myburgh, Q.C., and *Bucknill*, for the defendants: At
the time of the accident to the Mary Nixon the defendants
had not the power of exercising and were not in fact exercising any possession, management, or control over the wreck
of the Douglas, and if any duty then existed under which a
light ought to have been placed to mark the position of the
wreck, it was a duty to be performed *at the discre- [154
tion of the Thames Conservancy, and for the non-performance of which the defendants ought not to be held liable.

Butt, Q.C., in reply.

                                                    Cur. adv. vult.

April 25. SIR ROBERT PHILLIMORE : This is an action
for damages in consequence of a collision between the screw
steamship Mary Nixon and another screw steamship called
the Douglas. It occurred in Gravesend Reach at midnight
on the 27th of October, 1881. The Douglas had previously
come into collision with the steamship the Duke of Buckingham, and had in consequence sunk. It is admitted that
the collision with the Duke of Buckingham was due to the
negligent navigation of the Douglas. At the time of the
collision between the Mary Nixon and the Douglas, the
Douglas was lying sunk in the river about mid-channel with
one of her masts above the water. The contention of the
Mary Nixon was that it was the duty of the Douglas to
warn approaching vessels of the wreck, and that no such
warning was given, and therefore that she was responsible
for the damage. The defence of the Douglas is that a white
light was placed in her main rigging within a reasonable
time ; that the Mary Nixon was warned by hailing from another vessel in sufficient time to enable her to avoid the
Douglas, and, as an alternative defence, that the defendants
had wholly ceased to have possession, management, or control of the Douglas, and therefore were not responsible.

To deal first with the facts, I am of opinion that no hailing
on the part of the Douglas is proved. I have consulted the
Trinity Masters, and I agree with them that a reasonable
time had elapsed between the collision with the Duke of
Buckingham and the collision with the Mary Nixon for giving some warning to approaching vessels of the position of the
Douglas, and that the means of such warning could have
been obtained without difficulty. It appears that a light
was put up in the main rigging of the Douglas after the col-

lision with the Duke of Buckingham, which light remained till the Douglas sank; but at the time of the collision with the Mary Nixon no light appears to have been exhibited and no kind of warning given. I have now to deal with the question of law arising on these facts. The plaintiff contends 155] that the Douglas *having had her lights knocked out by the previous collision, was bound to adopt some measures of warning, by lights or otherwise, to approaching vessels. The defendants say that no persons being left on board the Douglas, it was not the duty of any private person to give such warning, but that it became a matter for the intervention of public authority; that during the period between the crew leaving the ship and the intervention of the public authority the risk, however great, must be borne by the public; that in this case, although there was an *animus revertendi*, still the control and possession of the ship had been given up. I confess I listened to this argument with great alarm. The consequences of such a doctrine are fraught with danger to the interests of navigation and also to human life. It is, however, not necessary, in the view which I take of this case, to decide the exact point when the private obligation ends and that of the public authority begins. Two cases were relied upon: *Brown* v. *Mallett*, decided in 1848 ('), and *White* v. *Crisp*, decided in 1854 (²). The principle of law applicable to cases of this description appears to me to be contained in the judgment of Alderson, B., in *White* v. *Crisp* (²), citing the opinion of Maule, J., in *Brown* v. *Mallett* ('), in which it is laid down that "it is the duty of a person using a navigable river with a vessel of which he is possessed and has the control and management, to use reasonable skill and care to prevent mischief to others." And he adds that this liability "is the same whether his vessel be in motion or stationary, floating or aground, under water or above it." Now in my opinion it has been proved that the possession, management, and control of the Douglas was not abandoned by her master and crew, and, consequently, that the duty, which Alderson, B., referred to in the passage that I have quoted, continued a duty on their part up to the time of the collision with the Mary Nixon. I must therefore pronounce that the Douglas is alone to blame for the collision with the *Mary Nixon* (³)

G. B.

(¹) 5 C. B., 599.
(²) 10 Ex., 312.
(³) The 9th Article of the by-laws for the Regulation of the Navigation of the River Thames, approved by Order in Council of the 18th of March, 1880, and published in the *London Gazette*, Friday, 19th March, 1880, p. 2135, provides "that all vessels when employed to mark the positions of wrecks or other obstruc-

The defendants appealed.

Bucknill, for the defendants: The evidence as [156 to the message sent by the mate of the Douglas to the harbor-master at Gravesend was wrongly rejected: it was admissible as tending to disprove negligence on the part of those representing the defendants.

Butt, Q.C., and *G. Bruce*, for the plaintiff: The conversation between the harbor-master and the captain of the tug Endeavour was not admissible: it was merely hearsay evidence. And, further, it was immaterial. The captain and the mate of the Douglas could not delegate their duty to take proper care of the wreck to the harbor-master; they did not on behalf of the defendants abandon it. It is not the harbor-master's duty to take possession of the wreck; he is merely authorized to remove it. The defendants were as much bound to light the wreck as if they had contracted to do so: a legal duty was imposed upon them. They were guilty of causing an obstruction in a navigable river by leaving the wreck in it, and it does not appear that the harbor-master affixed lights to the wreck. The defendants certainly gave no notice to the plaintiff's vessel where the wreck was lying. It is true that by the Thames Conservancy Act, 1857 (20 & 21 Vict. c. cxlvii), ss. 86, 87, power was given to the conservators to remove vessels obstructing the navigation of the river, and by the Removal of Wrecks Act, 1877 (40 & 41 Vict. c. 16), s. 4, a conservancy authority "may" remove any vessel that is sunk, stranded, or abandoned, and "may" light or buoy her until removal; but the powers conferred by the latter act are merely permissory, and not obligatory, and some delay must take place even if the conservancy acted under the power of this statute. It is no defence that the harbor-master was asked to put up a light on the wreck.

[BRETT, L.J.: The Removal of Wrecks Act, 1877, relates to the performance of a public duty. Is not the word "may" in s. 4 to be read "must?"]

It follows from the reasoning of the Court of Common Pleas in *Brown* v. *Mallett* (¹) and of the Court of Exchequer in *White* v. *Crisp* (²) that the defendants are liable [157 for leaving the wreck of the Douglas sunk in the Thames without giving any warning to approaching vessels. It is unnecessary to say that any one of the crew was guilty of negligence in not affixing a light after the vessel had sunk;

tions, shall exhibit two bright lights   (¹) 5 C. B., 599:
placed horizontally not less than six nor   (²) 10 Ex., 312.
more than twelve feet apart."

but the mate might have done so. It was an act of negligence to leave the wreck of the Douglas without a light; the act of lighting the wreck was merely discretionary on the part of the Thames Conservancy, *Forbes* v. *Lee Conservancy Board*(¹); *The Ettrick*(²), and the mate of the Douglas was not justified in assuming that the Thames Conservators would by the harbor-master perform it. The mate might have obtained a boat and himself might have affixed a light to the wreck.

Bucknill was not called upon to reply.

LORD COLERIDGE, C.J.: It seems plain to me that the judgment of the Admiralty Division cannot be supported. Two courses are open to us: we can either send the case back for a new trial, or pronounce judgment upon the materials before us. As the evidence was not given, and it is not certain what it would turn out to be, we could only grant a new hearing if the rejection of the evidence tendered were the only matter which we had to determine; but upon the facts before us we can reverse the judgment of the Admiralty Division, and enter judgment for the defendants.

The only question upon the evidence before us is whether the defendants were guilty of negligence; of course I am not speaking of the original negligence conducing to the original collision. It appears from all the facts that there was no negligence of which the plaintiff can take advantage. There was a collision between the Douglas, the Duke of Buckingham, and the Orion, and afterwards between the Douglas and the Mary Nixon. After the Douglas had been sunk, a light was fixed in her rigging. The master of the Douglas having been thrown into the water was taken in a boat to near Gravesend. Then the tug called the Endeavour went to Gravesend: there the mate instructed the captain to go to the harbor-master and to request him to take care of the 158] wreck. The defendants caused the captain of *the Endeavour to be called as a witness. The counsel for the plaintiff objected that the conversation between the harbor-master and the captain of the Endeavour took place behind the back of the plaintiff, and therefore could not be received in evidence. The judge of the Admiralty Division excluded it. The objection has not been seriously supported to-day; for the evidence was tendered as relating to an act done and tending to disprove negligence, a competent person having been sent to inform the harbor-master. It was urged that the evidence was immaterial, because the master and the mate of the Douglas had no right to delegate their duty to

(¹) 4 Ex. D., 116; 81 Eng. R., 403.   (²) 6 P. D., 127.

take due and proper care of the wreck to the harbor-master; for it appears clear that the defendants still claimed to be owners of it. The evidence was not immaterial. I think that it was wrongly rejected. But it was stated to the mate of the Douglas that the harbor-master had undertaken to light the wreck; there was therefore evidence that the mate who represented the defendants thought that the harbor-master had undertaken to light the wreck. The harbor-master *may* exercise the powers of the Removal of Wrecks Act, 1877, and it is unnecessary to give any opinion as to the construction of the act, and to determine whether he *must;* for having the power he appears to have undertaken to do the duty. It is to go too far to say that the captain and the mate of the Douglas were guilty of negligence; for even upon the present facts it must be inferred that the mate asked the official to do that which he had the power by statute to perform. It has been argued that an action is maintainable, because it does not appear that the harbor-master performed the duty : but it must be inferred upon these facts that he undertook to do the duty, and at least the mate of the Douglas had fair ground for supposing that he would perform it. The master and the mate of the Douglas had no power to retain the Endeavour to light the wreck. No act has been pointed out which they might be fairly expected to do. The evidence was improperly rejected, but sufficient evidence is before us to show that all things reasonable were done; there is no ground for finding that the master and the mate of the Douglas were guilty of actionable negligence.

I think it unnecessary to discuss the two cases which have been *mentioned, *Brown* v. *Mallett* (') and *White* v. [159 *Crisp* ('). I entertain a great respect for the learned judges who decided them ; but I do not think that they trench upon our decision, for they assume that the possession and the control over the sunken ship must remain in the owners in order to render them liable ; these cases may be good in law, for in *Brown* v. *Mallett* (') it was held that the owner of the barge was exempt from liability on the ground that the declaration did not show him to be in possession at the time of the damage to the plaintiffs' steamship, and in *White* v. *Crisp* (') the action was founded on the circumstances that the defendants had the possession and the control of the wreck.

Upon the grounds that I have stated, I am of opinion that the materials before us show that the judgement of the Admiralty Division must be reversed.

(¹) 5 C. B., 599.   (²) 10 Ex., 312.

BRETT, L.J.:   This is an action to recover damages for
the injury occasioned to the plaintiff's steamship the Mary
Nixon by the negligence of those in charge of the defendants'
steamship, the Douglas.   The facts may be shortly stated
as follows: the Douglas whilst going up the Thames came
into collision with another vessel, the Duke of Buckingham,
and sank; the collision was due to the negligence of those
on board the Douglas; a light was fixed in her rigging, but
it was extinguished upon her sinking.   The mate of the
Douglas went up to Gravesend and requested the captain of
the tug called the Endeavour to ask the harbor-master to
fix some lights on the wreck; the harbor-master said that
he would do this, and his answer was reported to the mate
of the Douglas.   Before any lights were fixed to the wreck,
the plaintiff's steamship in passing up the river struck
against the sunken wreck of the Douglas and sustained the
injury in respect of which this action is brought.   The liability of the defendants was alleged to exist upon three
grounds.   First, it was said by the plaintiff's counsel that
a duty was imposed upon the defendants to light the wreck,
that the duty was of the same nature as if the defendants
had contracted with the plaintiff to light it, and that they are
absolutely liable for the breach of it; this really seems to me
to be almost the same as to argue that there was a contract:
160]   *the contention is quite unsustainable, no duty at
least of that description can exist.   Secondly, it was assumed
in the argument that the defendants had committed an indictable offence in the channel of a navigable river; that
was the effect of the argument addressed to us, although this
contention was not put forward in direct terms.   To wilfully
scuttle a ship in a tide-way so as to cause an obstruction
may possibly be an indictable offence.   But what the defendants did was no indictable offence.   Their own ship sank.
It seems to me clear that no greater liability can exist against
the defendants than if their steamship had sunk without
negligence.   What is the liability of the owners of a sunken
ship which is lying in a tide-way? if they keep possession
of her, they must give notice where she has gone down.
This is all their liability.   Thirdly, it was said that the defendants did not take care to give notice where the wreck
of the Douglas was lying.   I incline to agree that if the
owners of a wreck abandon it their liability ceases.   But
here the defendants claim the ownership of the wreck.   It
may be that the defendants did not hear of the accident for
some time; as to those employed by them, the captain is

prima facie to act; it is for the plaintiff to prove that there was negligence. The captain appears to have gone ashore after the Douglas sank: what was he to do? he was not guilty of negligence. As to the mate, he gave instructions to the captain of the tug Endeavour to inform the harbor-master. The latter evidently took it as a piece of information upon which he was to act, for he in effect promised to send lights within an hour. The mate of the Douglas had a right to assume that the harbor-master would do what he promised. Upon the evidence before us there was no negligence and no liability upon the defendants. The judgment of the Admiralty Division cannot be supported. I say nothing as to *Brown* v. *Mallett* (¹) and *White* v. *Crisp* (²) except that they were decided on demurrer.

COTTON, L.J.: I think that the evidence was improperly rejected. Under the Removal of Wrecks Act, 1877, s. 4, the harbor-master had power to put up lights, and I think it became his duty to remove a dangerous obstruction. In my opinion the *evidence if it had been received [161 would have shown that the defendants had for the time abandoned the control of the wreck. There was therefore a wrongful rejection of evidence; but I agree that there ought not to be a new trial, for it is proved by the deposition of the mate of the Douglas that the collision was reported to the harbor-master, and that the mate did receive a communication from the harbor-master. This circumstance exonerates the defendants from the charge of negligence, for it gave the harbor-master notice to perform the duty. The plaintiff cannot say that the injury to his steamship, the Mary Nixon, was occasioned by the defendants' wrongful act; his loss did not happen through their negligence.

Judgment reversed.

Solicitors for plaintiff: *Gellatly, Son & Warten.*
Solicitors for defendants: *William A. Crump & Son.*

(¹) 5 C. B., 599.   (²) 10 Ex., 312.

J. E. H.

<hr>

When a vessel sinks in a navigable river, the owner, so long as he retains the possession and control of it, is bound to take due precautions to prevent injury to other vessels by their running against it: White v. Crisp, 10 Exch., 312.

Otherwise if he have abandoned it entirely: King v. Watts, 2 Esp., 675; Brown v. Mallett, 5 C. B., 619, 57 Eng. C. L.; White v. Crisp, 10 Exch., 322;

Buffalo v. Yattan, 1 Buff. Super. Ct. R., 486–7.

See Taylor v. Atlantic, etc., 9 Bosw., 369, 37 N. Y., 275, 284; Hancock v. York, etc., 10 C. B., 348, 70 Eng. C. L.

Section 2 of the act of Congress of July 25, 1866, authorizing the construction of bridges across the Mississippi river, and across the Missouri river at Kansas City, construed as requiring that the passageway for vessels between the piers of any drawbridge built under said act shall be 160 feet wide in the clear, measuring by a line running directly across the channel, and at right angles with the piers of the bridge. Where a bridge is built diagonally across the river, a measurement along the line of the bridge is not the proper measurement.

The fact that a bridge has been constructed under said act of Congress does not render it a legal structure, except in so far as it conforms to the terms and limitations of the act. If the powers granted by the act were exceeded, or were exercised in a manner different, from that provided in the grant of authority, the grant will be no protection.

Although the width between the piers of such a bridge may be less than the act of Congress requires, yet this will not render the owner of the bridge liable for damages to a passing vessel, unless the unlawful structure caused or contributed to the injury. Where it is alleged that a sunken pontoon, placed and kept in the channel by the defendant, had caused a change in the current of the river which had thrown plaintiff's vessel over against a pier of defendant's bridge, and that the accident was the result of two causes combined, to wit, the presence in the channel of the pontoons and of the bridge pier, both unlawful structures, held, that these facts being established plaintiff could recover. Those navigating the river are under no obligation to remove wrecks which may be made in the ordinary and proper course of navigation, but he who, for his own benefit, uses any part of a navigable river, is liable in damages to any party injured, if such use causes a change in the ordinary course of the channel. If defendant had a right to keep the pontoon in the river in connection with the bridge, and it was sunk by unavoidable accident, defendant was entitled to a reasonable time in which to raise and remove it, but was not at liberty to leave it in the channel for an indefinite period.

A person who places an obstruction in the navigable channel of a river is not entitled to notice to remove the same, or to abate the nuisance caused thereby.

The true rule of damages in suit for injuries done to a vessel by collision is that the plaintiff shall recover the loss necessarily incurred in repairing the injured vessel, and also for the use of the boat during the time necessary to make the repairs and fit her for business : Missouri, etc., v. Hannibal, etc., 1 McCrary, 281.

The defendants were held not liable for an injury to plaintiff's vessel caused by running against an old sunken pier : Distinguishing Mersey, etc., v. Gibbs, L. R., 1 H. L., 93 ; Winch v. Conservators, etc., L. R., 7 C. P., 458, 3 Eng. R., 344, 9 id., 378, 10 id., 213 ; Parnaby v. Lancaster, etc., 11 Ad. & E., 223, on the ground that in this case the harbor was a natural one, open to the public as of right, not an artificial work erected by the defendants, and which they invited the public to use on the payment of tolls.

That under the statute there was no duty imposed upon defendants to employ the funds placed under their control, and the tolls which they were authorized to impose in removing the obstruction complained of, which existed before their incorporation, but that a discretion was vested in them not to be controlled by a jury : Hood v. Commissioners, etc., 37 C. C. Q. B. R., 72, affirming 34 id., 87.

According to the principles of the common law, the owner of a wharf who receives or is entitled to receive wharfage for vessels moored to said wharf, is bound to use at least ordinary care and diligence in keeping the water adjacent to such wharf in which vessels lie while moored thereto free from obstructions, and is liable for any damage done to any such vessel by reason of the neglect of such duty ; and the same principles apply, whether such owner be an individual or a corporation, whether such corporation be private or municipal.

The city of Petersburg owns a wharf in the Appomattax river, for the use of which the city is authorized to charge, and does charge wharfage. In October, 1872, the vessel of A. not being able to get to the wharf at which she was to deliver her load, on account of an obstruction in the stream by another vessel, drew up to the city wharf and moored to it, and whilst waiting there she sunk on the next low water, from a pile going through her bottom. This pile was oak, being about two feet from the wharf, in the stream where a vessel at the wharf would probably lie, and was not visible at low water, though it was some two feet or more above the bed of the river, and was firmly fixed there.

Held, 1. The allowing such an obstruction in the place where it was, was negligence ; and the city of Petersburg, being the owner of the wharf, is liable for the damages occasioned by it.

2. The fact that the city had appointed a port warden, whose duty it was to attend to the removal of obstructions in the stream, and to attend to the duties of the city in regard to the city wharf, does not exempt the city from liability for the damages. The port warden in this matter is but the agent of the city, and the principal is always bound for the acts and neglects of his agents.

The same rule which applies to a private principal, applies to a corporation, whether ordinary or municipal, and a fortiori to a corporation which can only act by an agent. The fact that it has been made by statute the duty of the Lower Appomattax Company to dredge and remove obstructions from the river at and below Petersburg, cannot relieve the city from her liability. The city is in fact the company owning all the stock and appointing the officers of the company. But even if it was an independent organization, its obligation to perform a duty which the city is also bound to perform on common law principles, would not relieve the city from its common law liability for the non-performance of such a duty, nor can it make any difference that the United States have made appropriations to the improvement of the navigation of the river, and have occasionally dredged it. This does not relieve the city from its common law liability in regard to the city wharf. Nor does it make any difference that in this case no wharfage was actually received by the city, and that it does not usually charge wharfage in cases where the vessel mooring

at her wharf is not to be unloaded there. It is sufficient that the city was entitled to charge wharfage : Petersburg v. Applegarth, etc., 28 Grattan (Va.), 321.

A canal boat loaded with stone was accidentally sunk in the harbor of Buffalo, and then deserted by her master and crew, who made no effort to raise or care for her, and the wreck formed a serious obstruction and hindrance to commerce and navigation. The common council of the city, in pursuance of the powers conferred by the charter, after waiting a reasonable time for the owner so to do, ordered the boat and cargo to be removed without delay, and if not done in three days, the harbor master was directed to remove the same at the expense of the boat and cargo. Nothing being done to effect such removal, the harbor master caused the boat to be raised and protected, and the cargo to be saved at a large expense. Held, that the city had acquired a lien upon the boat and cargo for the amount of the expenses which could be established and enforced.

The Legislature having conferred the power upon the city, to regulate and control the use of the harbor, and preserve and protect it from encroachments and obstructions, and to remove and abate them when they occurred, the duty of exercising the power devolved upon the city.

In an action to establish and enforce the lien, it is proper to implead the owner and all others having claims upon the boat, in order that their rights might be foreclosed and extinguished.

The owner having the right to abandon the boat after the accident, a personal judgment for a deficiency cannot be ordered against him : Buffalo v. Yattan, 1 Buffalo Super. Ct. R., 483.

See to same effect, Janvrin v. Exeter, 48 N. H., 84 ; Hersen v. Pike, 16 Ind., 140 ; Moak's Van Santvoord's Pl., 422.

One who raises or destroys a sunken vessel has no lien upon the cargo if it do not belong to the owner of the vessel, for the expenses of so doing : Vivian v. Mersey Docks, etc., L. R. 5 C. Pl., 19.

[7 Probate Division, 168.]

April 18, 1882.

[IN THE COURT OF APPEAL.]

168]   *GANDY v. GANDY.

Separation Deed—Covenant not to sue for greater Allowance—Subsequent Adultery—Permanent Alimony.

A husband having committed adultery, disputes arose between him and his wife which led to his committing acts of legal cruelty. A separation deed was then executed, by which he agreed to allow her £250 a year, and to maintain the two youngest children, who were not to be in her custody; and she covenanted not to take any proceedings to compel the husband to allow her a larger amount alimony. Subsequently the husband committed adultery, and the wife obtained a decree for judicial separation and an order that she should have the custody of the two youngest children. The husband had since the date of the separation deed become wealthy, and the wife applied for an inquiry as to his means with a view to obtaining increased alimony:

Held, reversing the decision of the president, that increased alimony could not be ordered, for that as the court had not, as it would have had in the case of a decree for dissolution, power to alter the separation deed, the covenant by the wife not to sue for increased alimony was binding on her, and must have effect given to it, the husband not having, in the opinion of the court, been guilty of such misconduct as under the circumstances of the case would disentitle him to claim the benefit of the deed.

THIS was an appeal by Maurice Gandy, the husband, from a decision of the President of the Divorce Court (¹). The facts appear from the judgments of the President and of the Master of the Rolls.

Robinson, Q.C., and *Middleton*, for the appellant: The separation deed bars all right to increased alimony. The decision below was that a separation deed is binding only so long as the party claiming the benefit of it lives in chastity. But it has been repeatedly decided that in the absence of express stipulation, unchastity does not affect the operation of a separation deed. *Evans* v. *Carrington* (²) proceeds on that principle, and the cases at law are clear: *Jee* v. *Thurlow* (³).

[JESSEL, M.R.: You need hardly cite cases to show that it is so at law. The question is, whether a court of equity would have restrained proceedings for further alimony?]

169]   *In *Williams* v. *Baily* (⁴) there was no sufficient proof of an unqualified acceptance by the wife of the provisions of the separation deed, and an injunction was refused; but the observations of the Vice-Chancellor show that he thought the wife might have been bound by the

(¹) 7 Prob. Div., 77.   (²) 2 B. & C., 547.
(³) 2 D. F. & J., 481.   (⁴) Law Rep., 2 Eq., 731.

provisions of such a deed, so as to be pre lu e from suing
for further alimony, if she had acceded todt. d The judgment
of the President went much on *Morrall* v. *Morrall* (¹) and
other cases decided by himself, in which alimony beyond
what was given by a separation deed was granted; but they
were cases where a dissolution of marriage had been pronounced, so that the powers given by 22 & 23 Vict. c. 61, s. 5
and 41 Vict. c. 19, s, 3, as to altering settlements, gave the
court greater power. *Besant* v. *Wood* (²) shows that the
court will enforce a stipulation in a separation deed not to
sue in the Divorce Court. The statute 20 & 21 Vict. c. 85,
s. 17, enables the court to make such order as to alimony as
shall be just, but assuming that the covenant does not absolutely bar the wife from suing, still what allowance is just
cannot be determined without regard to a contract between
the parties.

Inderwick, Q.C., and *Tatham*, contrà: The statute enables the court in any case of judicial separation to make
any order as to alimony which shall be deemed just.

[JESSEL, M.R.: That means which shall be just; and if a
wife has bound herself to accept a certain amount is it just
to give her more?]

The husband substantially is suing for specific performance of the separation deed, and the question is whether
his conduct has not been such as to entitle the wife to say
that he cannot enforce it.

[JESSEL, M.R.: The president seems hardly to have considered this point, that he was not in a position to give what
alimony he thought just, for if he thought that alimony to a
less amount than what was given by the separation deed was
proper he could not take away what the deed gave.

LINDLEY, L.J.: Was there any object in the suit except
alimony?]

*Yes; the custody of the two younger children, [170
from which she was excluded by the deed, but which she
gained in the suit. The husband's conduct has been such
as to disentitle him to the benefit of the deed. The judge
considered that a woman might agree to take less than the
court would give her in order to settle the matter out of
court and to avoid publicity, but that she ought not to be
bound by it if there was serious misconduct afterwards on
the part of the husband such as to justify her taking proceedings for a separation.

Middleton, in reply.

[LINDLEY, L.J.: Is there any case in which a husband,

(¹) 6 P. D., 98.   (²) 12 Ch. D., 605.

who after a separation deed has grossly misconducted himself, has obtained an injunction?]

Evans v. *Carrington* (¹) is the only case in equity which touches on the point. Somewhat similar questions were raised on equitable plea in *Goslin* v. *Clark* (²) and *Kendall* v. *Webster* (³).

JESSEL, M.R.: This case raises a point which is at once novel and important. There was a separation deed between the husband and wife after the husband had committed adultery to the knowledge of the wife, and had thereby caused quarrels which led to acts of legal cruelty by the husband towards the wife, and ultimately caused the separation. By the separation deed the husband, not then having made so large a fortune as he afterwards made, agreed, after provisions for the maintenance of the children, to allow the wife £250 a year, and she agreed that she should not, nor should any person in her behalf at any time thereafter, commence or prosecute any suit or other proceeding. for compelling the husband to allow her any support, maintenance, or alimony, except as aforesaid, or to cohabit or live with her. At a subsequent period the husband renewed his intercourse with a woman with whom he had previously committed the adultery which led to the separation, and the wife instituted a suit in the Divorce Court for judicial separation, and obtained a decree. She was entitled to institute this suit because, as she said, she was deprived by the deed of the custody of her two younger daughters who were 171] *to be maintained by the husband and kept at school, and she claimed the right to their custody, and succeeded in obtaining it. Probably considering that the two younger children were girls, and that the mother was free from blame, it would have been impossible to interfere so as to prevent her from commencing and continuing her suit to a successful conclusion, having regard to her rights as regards those children, and having regard to the benefit of the children themselves. But the husband remained liable under the deed, and is still liable to the maintenance of those younger children.

It is however very clear to my mind that there was another motive for the institution of these proceedings. The husband, it appears, had made an invention which turned out very successful, and it was stated on one side, and was not denied on the other, that he had thereby made a very considerable fortune. It appears to me obvious that this accession of fortune was also an inducement to the institution of this suit.

(¹) 2 D. F. & J., 481.   (²) 12 C. B. (N.S.), 681.   (³) 1 H. & C., 440.

After arrangements had been made in the suit as to the
custody and maintenance of the children, au application was
made for further alimony on the part of the wife, which
application was granted in substance, though not in form,
by the order appealed from.   I say in substance, because the
case was not argued merely on the question as to whether
the court should be put in possession of the facts as regards
the husband's fortune before coming to a conclusion, but
on the assumption that (as was well known to all parties to
be the fact) the husband's fortune had now become very considerably larger than it was before, and that if the wife succeeded in the application to have an inquiry directed as to
the means of the husband she would succeed in the application for an increase of alimony.   The learned judge of the
court below decided that by. reason of the subsequent adultery of the husband under the circumstances I mentioned,
the wife was entitled to apply for and obtain a larger sum in
the shape of alimony than the £250 allotted to her by the
deed.   The question is whether that was right.

The first point to be considered is that the contract made
by the husband in the deed of separation cannot be affected
by the subsequent adultery of the husband.   He is liable under his covenant whether he commits adultery or not,
and in fact he *would be liable under the covenants, [172
even if the wife had committed adultery.   That is settled
law.   The Legislature has not thought fit in the case of judicial separation to give the same powers to the court that
it has given in the case of dissolution of marriage.   In the
case of dissolution of marriage the court has had conferred
upon it the right to vary not only post-nuptial but ante-nuptial settlements, and to deal with them in any way which
may be thought just and expedient.   But in the case of judicial separation, there being no such power, the deed remains
binding.   The wife is entitled to the annuity secured her by
the deed, the husband is liable to pay the annuity.   It is
impossible, therefore, for the court to allot such alimony as
it may think just, because in the case of its thinking that
the amount of alimony should be less than the annuity secured by the deed, it has no power of setting aside the deed
and no power to stop an action brought under the covenants
of the deed by the trustees against the husband.   It is, therefore, a case where the ordinary powers of the court cannot
be exercised, except in one direction, viz., by increasing the
amount of alimony.   That being so, we must consider
whether in such a case of contract the court can interfere
except when one of the parties to the contract has so acted

as to disentitle him to rely upon the contract at all.   I am
not saying that there may not be such a case; on the contrary, I can quite conceive such a case.   But, unless there
is such a case, why should the court interfere with the contract?   I see that the learned judge put it on the ground of
public policy.   I have explained more than once, and especially in a case which has been referred to by the learned
judge himself of *Besant* v. *Wood* ('), that there is no reason
more dangerous to give, and no reason on which such difference of opinion exists, as public policy.   He has said, "If
you do not allow the wife to ask for increased alimony in
such a case as this you allow the husband to commit adultery with impunity."   I am by no means prepared to say
that this remark is correct.   It is not impunity merely because he is not obliged to pay more money.   I do not
consider that payment of alimony is the only punishment
for adultery if the word "punishment" should be used in
connection with it.   No doubt he may be to some extent
173]   *relieved from that liability, but the contract is one
by which he is compelled to pay an amount having regard
to his then state of fortune which might have been much
larger then than at the date the decree for separation, for his
fortune might have diminished instead of increasing.   It
appears to me a very strong thing to say that by his committing an act which does not affect the wife either directly
or indirectly her rights to participate in his fortune should
be altered.

Now, in the present case, how is the position of the wife
affected by the husband's subsequent conduct?   She was
separated *de facto* and *de jure* before the institution of the
suit.   Her maintenance was the same whether her husband
did or did not live with another woman.   Her rights in
every respect remained unaltered.   It may be said, no doubt,
in one sense, that her position was affected by his conduct,
which made it less probable that he would return to cohabitation.   But people who execute deeds of separation under
such circumstances, are not presumed to suppose or to
assume that the return to cohabitation is very probable.   It
does not appear to me, looking at what occurred before the
separation, and considering what the husband has done
since, that you can say he is in such a position as to have
forfeited all his rights under the deed, leaving him subject
to all his liabilities under it.

It seems to me that, having regard to the relative positions of the husband and wife, there has not been miscon-

('¹) 12 Ch. D., 605.

duct on the part of the husband so affecting the position of
the wife as to entitle her to repudiate the contract she entered into, therefore the contract is still binding and the appeal must be allowed.

COTTON, L. J.:   In this case there has been an application
by the wife, under which she has obtained a reference to
ascertain what is the income of her husband, for the purpose
avowedly of obtaining maintenance to a larger amount than
is given by the deed of separation.   This is clearly contrary
to one of the covenants contained in that deed, and the
question we have to consider may be put in two ways,
whether that covenant can, under the circumstances, be disregarded, or, as was put by the judge in the court below,
whether a court of equity would, under *the circum-   [174
stances, have enforced this covenant against the wife.   I do
not intend to give any opinion on the latter view of the question, because, in my opinion, it is not necessary to decide it,
though I am far from saying that a court of equity would
not in former days have interfered by injunction to restrain
such an application as that now made by the wife.   But the
learned judge seems to have decided the matter on principles that would lead to the conclusion that the deed was bad
altogether at law (which it is not), because he said this deed
must be read as containing an implied condition that it
shall be operative so long as the parties shall live chaste-
ly, and that to hold that the present appellant was right
would be to say that this deed contemplated and allowed
adultery on the part of the husband.   I cannot agree with
such a conclusion.   The question is whether the misconduct
of the husband is such misconduct towards the wife as, having regard to the circumstances known to her at the time
the deed was entered into, entitled her to say this covenant
is not to be regarded upon the application for alimony.   In
my opinion, unless the conduct of the husband has been
such since the deed as entirely to prevent him from relying
on the deed at all, then even if he could not under the old
practice have obtained an injunction to restrain the proceedings of the wife, still the deed must be taken into account in
considering what allowance it is just to make.   It is very
true that the deed did not contemplate or provide for future
adultery, but the conduct of the appellant towards the wife
is of the same character and nature as that of which she was
aware when she entered into the deed.   It is not suggested
that there was any representation made to her which induced her to take this £250 as an allowance.   It is said that
she has to maintain two children whom she had not with her

before. But that is not so. The husband still remains liable under his covenant to provide for the two younger children, and they are still left at the school pointed out by him. All the difference is that she is to have them during the holidays, leaving her husband still liable for their maintenance. In my opinion, the conduct of the husband since the deed is not such, as, having regard to what was known to the wife at the time she entered into the deed, can disentitle him from relying on the deed. I put it that way, because I quite *agree with the Master of the Rolls,
175] that we ought not to say, and I do not entertain the opinion, that there can be no misconduct on the part of a husband such as would disentitle him to set up a deed of separation of this kind when the wife is making an application for an increased allowance. The case of *Morrall* v. *Morrall* ('), one of the cases referred to by the learned judge, as leading to the conclusion at which he arrived, is an instance. There, there was a deed of separation with a provision as to what maintenance the wife was to have. She subsequently ascertained that the husband was living in incestuous adultery. It may well be that such gross misconduct, misconduct of a nature so entirely different from that which the parties were providing for when they entered into the deed of separation, might prevent the husband from in any way relying on that deed, and might render it just that the bargain made by the wife for maintenance should be disregarded on an application to the court for alimony. Here, in my opinion, the circumstances are not such as to entitle the wife to disregard her bargain.

LINDLEY, L.J.: The question we have to consider may be put in this shape, whether there has been any sufficient reason given for holding the wife discharged from her covenant not to sue for further alimony. *Prima facie*, she is bound by that covenant in all the courts, whatever difficulty there may be about specific performance or injunction. It is a perfectly good covenant. The order appealed from is an order which does not give effect to that covenant, but sets it aside, and the question is whether, under the circumstances, that is right? The power of dealing with this question of alimony is given or governed by 20 & 21 Vict. c. 85, s. 17. This being only a suit for judicial separation, the power of the Divorce Court over these deeds is much less than it would be after a decree for dissolution of marriage. It is a much more restricted jurisdiction and power, and it appears to me that the cases, of which *Morrall* v. *Morrall* (')

(') 6 P. D., 98.

is one, where the Divorce Court has dealt with separation deeds after decrees for dissolution of marriage, are rather misleading, when they are applied, or sought to be applied, in a case where the court has no *such extensive juris- [176 diction.   Now, the language of s. 17, as regards alimony, is this: "Where the application is by the wife the court may make any order for alimony which shall be deemed just." That must be taken to mean "just under the circumstances of the particular case," and one of the most important circumstances in any case is the bargain, if any, which has been made between the parties.   If the parties have agreed that a certain sum shall be sufficient, *prima facie* that is just, and *prima facie* the court cannot either increase or diminish it.   Indeed, I doubt very much whether under the powers of this section, the court could under any circumstances, say that less than £250 was just.   I do not think the section goes that length. If that be so, the analogy between the statutory power of dealing with alimony under s. 17, and the statutory powers of dealing with separation deeds, after a decree for dissolution, fails altogether.   If that section is to be read in the way in which it appears to have been read by the president of the court below, the power is limited in one direction but not in the other, which I cannot think correct.

It strikes me, on the whole, the case is reduced simply to this : There has been on the part of the husband no misconduct towards the wife except adultery with another woman, and now that we understand the position of the children, there was no reason that I can see for the wife's seeking judicial separation, except as a means of getting further alimony.   Under those circumstances—is the mere fact of the adultery sufficient to deprive the husband of the benefit of the stipulation as to alimony ?   I do not think that it is, and therefore I agree with the other members of the court, that the order appealed from must be discharged.

Appeal allowed.

Solicitors for appellant: *Gregory, Rowcliffes & Co.*
Solicitors for respondent: *W. & A. Ranken Ford.*

H. C. J.

[7 Probate Division, 177.]

March 15, 1882.

[IN THE COURT OF APPEAL.]

177]   *WIGNEY V. WIGNEY.

Dissolution of Marriage—Variation of Settlements—22 & 23 Vict. c. 61, s. 5—41 Vict. c. 19, s. 3.

The fortune of a wife was settled as to a part producing £950 a year on the husband for life, then on the wife for life ; as to the residue producing £1,200 a year on the wife for life, then on the husband for life; and after the decease of the survivor, in default of children of the marriage, then as to the whole property on such trusts as the wife should by will appoint, and in default of appointment to the husband absolutely. There was no child of the marriage. The wife obtained a decree for dissolution of the marriage on the ground of adultery and cruelty. The husband had mortgaged his life interest for debts incurred in keeping up the joint establishment, and alleged that he had incurred other debts for the same purpose. The President of the Divorce Court, upon the wife's petition, made an order that the trustees of the settlement should stand possessed of all the funds upon the trusts which would be applicable thereto if the husband were dead, and had died in the lifetime of the wife, and free from the ultimate trust in default of appointment, but subject to the wife undertaking to pay the charges made by the husband on the trust funds:

Held, on appeal, that the order must be affirmed, with this variation, that an account should be taken of all debts due from the husband incurred for the purpose of the joint establishment, and that the wife must undertake to pay them.

Though the power given to the court of varying settlements is not given for the purpose of punishing the guilty party, but of making due provision for the parties, their conduct is to be taken into consideration in determining what provisions ought to be made for them respectively.

The judge has an absolute judicial discretion as to the provisions to be made for the parties respectively out of settled property, and the Court of Appeals will not interfere with that discretion, unless there has been a clear miscarriage in its exercise.

By a settlement, dated the 16th of September, 1863, made on the marriage of Captain and Mrs. Wigney, the wife's fortune was settled as follows : As to such part of it as was mentioned in the first schedule upon trust to pay the income to the husband for life, and after his death to the wife for life. As to such part as was mentioned in the second schedule upon trust to pay the income to the wife for life for her separate use, and after her death to the husband for life. After the death of the survivor, all the property was to go 178] to the children of the marriage, and if *none, then to such persons as the wife should by will appoint, and in default of appointment to the husband. There was a covenant to settle after-acquired property of the wife upon the same trusts as the property in the second schedule.

At the time of the marriage the property in the first schedule was worth about £15,000, and that in the second schedule about £6,500, but this latter amount was afterwards increased to about £25,000, by the addition of after-acquired property of the wife. The husband brought nothing into settlement.

On the 2d of July, 1880, the wife obtained a decree for dissolution of the marriage on the ground of adultery and cruelty, which decree was made absolute on the 11th of January, 1881. There was no issue of the marriage.

The wife after the decree had been made absolute, presented her petition asking that the interest, rights, and powers of the respondent under the settlement might be extinguished, and that the property might be held upon the same trusts as if the respondent had died in the petitioner's lifetime, freed and discharged from the ultimate trust in his favor in the event of the petitioner making no appointment by will.

The husband alleged in defence that at the time of this marriage he was a captain in the army holding a staff appointment, and had a professional income of £1,800 a year, that at his wife's request he gave up his appointment and retired from the service, and had now no means but his half-pay of 7s. a day.

He further alleged that he and his wife had lived beyond their income, and that to pay the expenses of their joint establishment he had borrowed on mortgage of his life interest with policies of insurance sums amounting to £4,200, the interest amounting to £210 per annum, and the premiums to £118 18s. 9d. He further alleged that he owed about £2,000 for debts incurred during the cohabitation in keeping up the common household. This, however, was disputed by the petitioner, and it had not been ascertained how the case really stood. He had also mortgaged his life interest to his solicitors for the costs of the divorce suit.

At the time of the dissolution the income payable to the respondent under the settlement was £948 7s. 2d., that payable to the petitioner was £1,165 2s. 5d.

*The matter was referred to the registrar for inves- [179 tigation, and he made a report submitting that it was proper to make an order that the trustees of the settlement should stand possessed of the funds upon the trusts which would be applicable thereto if the respondent were dead, and had died in the lifetime of the petitioner, and free from the ultimate trust in favor of the respondent in default of appointment by the petitioner by her last will.

On the 7th of February, 1882, an order was drawn up, directing that the report should be confirmed subject to the following directions, and that it should be referred back to the registrar to draw up and settle an order of the court to carry the same into effect, and that the same should contain a provision that the petitioner should undertake the payment of all charges by the respondent on the trust funds, all questions as to the charge created by him in favor of his solicitors being reserved, and that upon payment by the petitioner of all the charges, the policies of assurance on the life of the respondent should be handed over to the respondent as soon as he had paid all costs of the suit for which he was liable to the petitioner, and it was ordered that in the meantime the policies should stand charged with the above costs, and that if the respondent should not pay those costs within three calendar months from the time when the charges were paid off, the petitioner should be at liberty to sell the policies, and should pay the balance to the respondent after deducting the costs.

The husband appealed from this order.

Searle and *Farwell*, for the appellant: The object of the enactments 22 & 23 Vict. c. 61, s. 5, and 41 Vict. c. 19, s. 3, is not to punish the guilty party, but to prevent the innocent party from suffering pecuniary loss by the dissolution: *Maudslay* v. *Maudslay* ([1]). It was said in *Fitzgerald* v. *Chapman* ([2]), that the Chancery Division is not a court of criminal jurisdiction, neither is the Probate Division. The husband's income ought to be left to him, subject to the liabilities which he has incurred. The enactments do not con- 180] tain a word about the relative guilt of *the parties, and when the Legislature intended conduct to be inquired into it said so, as is done in various clauses of 20 & 21 Vict. c. 85. The clauses were not intended for the purpose of punishment. The confining the earlier clause to a case where there were children shows the view of the Legislature. The clause would enable the court to make provision for a guilty wife. The object was to enable the court to put the parties in the same pecuniary position as if there had been no dissolution, *Benyon* v. *Benyon* ([3]), and this order places the wife in a better.

Inderwick, Q.C., and *Middleton*, contrà: In *Boynton* v. *Boynton* ([4]), the husband, who was the guilty party, was deprived of his life interest in the wife's property, and this has been followed ever since. In *Maudslay* v. *Maudslay* ([1]), the husband was deprived of all interest in the wife's property, and his own property was to some extent interfered

(¹) 2 P. D., 256; 21 Eng. R., 638.　　　(³) 1 P. D., 447.
(²) 1 Ch. D., 563; 16 Eng. R., 634.　　　(⁴) 2 Sw. & Tr., 275.

with for the wife's benefit. In *Gladstone* v. *Gladstone* ('),
the whole income of the wife's fortune was given to her.

[LINDLEY, L.J.: The income there was a small one.]

The merits of the case are that the husband eighteen
months before the decree eloped with a young woman whom
it is believed that he intends to marry, and he strongly contested the case of cruelty in order that only a decree of
judicial separation might be made, and his rights under the
settlement not be interfered with. The remarks in *Cooke* v.
Cooke (') are strongly in favor of the respondent's contention.

Searle, in reply.

JESSEL, M.R.: This case raises an important point, viz.,
what is the power of the court, under s. 5 of 22 & 23 Vict.
c. 61, as amended, not in the most artistic way, by the subsequent enactment 41 Vict. c. 19, s. 3.   The first enactment
enables the court to apply all or any part of the settled property "either for the benefit of the children of the marriage
or of their respective parents," and the second provides that
the powers of the former may be exercised, notwithstanding
that there are no children of *the marriage.   This is in [181
terms enabling the court to provide for parents who have no
child, but of course it means that the court shall have the same
power of applying the property for the benefit of the divorced
parties or either of them, though there is no child, as it would
under the former enactment have had if there were children.
The first enactment runs thus : "The court after a final decree of nullity of marrige or dissolution of marriage may
inquire into the existence of ante-nuptial or post-nuptial settlements made on the parties whose marriage is the subject
of the decree, and may make such orders with reference to
the application of the whole or a part of the property settled
either for the benefit of the children of the marriage or of
their respective parents as to the court shall seem fit."
There are two possible constructions of this enactment, one
is to read it as saying that the court may make such orders
as it shall think fit with reference to the application of the
property for the benefit of the parties, which leaves the matter in the absolute judicial discretion of the court.   The other
is to read it as authorizing the court to make a reasonable
provision for the parties with a view to their benefit.   My
opinion is that the literal construction of the section is the
right one, and that the court has full discretion as to what
order it will make for the benefit of the parties or either of
them.   It was pressed on us that guilt ought to make no difference, but in my judgment the conduct of the parties is a ma-

(') 1 P. D., 442.   (') 2 Phillim., 40.

terial circumstance, and it is the duty of the court to consider
whose fault it is that the marriage has come to an end, not
with a view of punishing the guilty party, but for the purpose of seeing what provisions it is reasonable to make. It
was the course of the House of Lords in marriage annulling
bills to allow maintenance to a guilty wife, and it would be
reasonable for the court in the same case to exercise its discretion in the same way, but it would not be right to make
the same provision for her if guilty as would be made if she
were innocent. In the case of a husband similar considerations must be entertained. Suppose a guilty husband is
incapacitated by physical infirmity from earning a livelihood,
and has no means of his own, I do not say that no provision
can in any case be made for him out of the wife's property.
That being so, this is a case of judicial discretion, and ac-
182]   cording to the *rules which govern the Court of Appeal on appeals from the discretion of the judge below, in
order to obtain a reversal, a case of miscarriage must be
shown. It is not sufficient for the appellant to convince the
judges of the Court of Appeal that the order is one which
they would not in the first instance have made, but he must
show that the judge has gone wrong in his law or made a
mistake of fact, or ordered something so utterly unreasonable that the Court of Appeal is obliged to say there has not
been a reasonable exercise of his discretion.

In the present case an officer in the army married a lady
twelve years his senior. He had no fortune, but held a staff
appointment. The lady had a fortune of about £2,000 a
year. This fortune was settled so as to give the husband
and wife successive life estates, the husband having the first
life estate in a part now producing about £950 a year, and
the wife the first life estate in the remainder producing
£1,165 a year. After the death of the survivor of the husband and wife, in default of issue of the marriage, the whole
property was to go as the wife should by will appoint, and
in default of appointment, to the husband. After eighteen
years the marriage was dissolved on the ground of the adultery and cruelty of the husband. At the time of the dissolution he had his half-pay of 7s. a day, or about £128 a year
—he was a man in middle life able to do something to add
to his income. Under these circumstances I do not see that
it was obligatory on the court to make further provision for
him. What the court did was to treat the incumbrances
effected by him on his life interest as valid incumbrances,
and subject to those incumbrances which absorbed between
£300 and £400 of the income, the life interest was taken

away from him. Was that unreasonable? Suppose the
second view of the enactment to be taken, then as the wife
gives up between £300 and £400 a year out of the income
of her fortune, can I say that it was unreasonable to give
her all the rest? The marriage having come to an end by
the husband's fault, can he complain that the consideration
having ceased the right of property should cease also? I
cannot say that the judge exercised his discretion unreasonably.

There is, however, another point to be considered. The
husband alleges that when he left his wife he had incurred
debts for the *purposes of the joint establishment. As [183
he was in receipt of about £900 a year from the settled funds
he might expect to be able to pay out of that, and moreover he would naturally look to his wife's income of £1,100.
I think, therefore, that there would be nothing unreasonable
in his incurring debts on account of the joint establishment
to an amount not exceeding £2,000. Is it right that the
tradesmen to whom these debts are owing should remain unpaid because the husband has behaved ill to his wife? I
think not. Is it right as regards the husband that he should
be left to pay these debts out of his own means? He may
say, "I incurred these debts for the joint purposes of myself and my wife while I was giving the marriage consideration, and on the faith of the income of her property. Ought
I not to have them paid out of it?" I think that he is entitled to have them so paid. Some expenses also are stated
to have been incurred for the same purposes since the husband left the wife, and they come within the same principle.
There must be an inquiry what debts there were owing by
the husband for the purposes of the joint establishment at
the time of the desertion, and what debts have since been incurred for the purposes of the joint establishment, and the
wife undertaking to pay what shall be found due on the result of this inquiry, the order appealed from will in all other
respects be affirmed.

COTTON, L.J.: I am of the same opinion. The enactment
22 & 23 Vict. c. 61, s. 5, as amended by 41 Vict. c. 19, s. 3,
does not give the court power to declare a forfeiture, but to
apply the property for the benefit of the husband and wife
and their children, if any. This is a power which may be
exercised so as to make due provision for either party. But
in making that provision the court ought to have regard to
all the circumstances of the case, and cannot leave out of
view the conduct of the parties. Can it be said here that the
judge has exercised his discretion wrongly? If the case had

come before me originally, I should not have made exactly
the order which he has made, but that is not the question—
the question is whether the judge has gone so wrong that it
is the duty of the Court of Appeal to interfere. I cannot
say that it is wrong to give the wife the whole income of
184] *her own property, subject to the incumbrances
created by the husband on his life interest in part of that
property, for she will not get so much as she had originally,
but the allowances must be made which the Master of the
Rolls has mentioned.

As regards the cases, I do not think that they lay down
any rule adverse to my judgment. In *Boynton* v. *Boynton* (¹) it could not be said that the whole income of the
wife's property was too much to give her. In *Gladstone* v.
Gladstone (²) the income was only about £300, and it could
not be said that the whole of that was too much. If *Boynton* v. *Boynton* (¹) had decided that whenever the husband is
the guilty party the wife must have the whole income of her
own property, I should have held myself bound by the
decision, though I should not agree with it, but I do not
think that it did decide that point.

LINDLEY, L.J.: I also agree that the judgment should be
affirmed, except as modified by the inquiry mentioned by
the Master of the Rolls. The question is whether the judge
has gone too far in striking out of the settlement the trusts in
favor of the husband. Taking the two enactments together,
I think that they give the judge a discretion how the settled
property shall be applied for the benefit of the parties or
their children. So long as he confines himself to that purpose he has a discretion, and we cannot, except in a strong
case such as has been mentioned by the Master of the Rolls,
review his decision, and if I were called upon to give an
opinion, I should say that he has, in the present case, exercised his discretion reasonably. Suppose the appellant were
to marry the woman with whom he has eloped, it would be
shocking that any part of the wife's income should go to
maintain him and the woman who is at the bottom of the
mischief. I think that the provision as to the mortgages,
and the inquiry which we now direct, give the husband all
the provision that ought to be made for him.

Solicitors for appellant: *Stokes, Saunders & Stokes.*
Solicitors for respondent: *Ayrton & Briscoe.*

(¹) 2 Sw. & Tr., 275.   (²) 1 P. D., 442.

[7 Probate Division, 185.]

Feb. 7, 1881.

*THE MIRANDA (1881, C. No. 6699 ; 1881, L. No. 3690). [185

Practice—Damage—Refusal to amend Preliminary Act.

The court will refuse to allow a mistake in a preliminary act to be amended, even though the application for an amendment be made before the hearing of the suit and be supported by affidavit.

THIS was a motion to amend the plaintiffs' preliminary act in an action of damage brought by the owners of the steamship Cleanthes against the steamship Miranda. In support of the motion an affidavit was brought in, in which a member of the firm of solicitors having the conduct of the action on behalf of the plaintiffs, stated that he believed that certain clerical mistakes and omissions had been made in the fair copy of the plaintiffs' preliminary act filed in the registry ; that the discovery of the probable existence of the errors and omissions in question had been made by him before the defendants' preliminary act had been opened, and when he was not aware of anything contained in it ; and that the application for amendment was made *bona fide*, and not for the purpose of directly or indirectly prejudicing the case of the other side, or in consequence of anything which had come to the knowledge of the plaintiffs since the preliminary act sought to be amended had been filed. At the time this affidavit was made no pleadings had been delivered in the action.

W. G. F. Phillimore, for the plaintiffs, in support of the motion : The court has the power to order a preliminary act to be amended, and should, in its discretion, allow an amendment, where as in the present case the object of the amendment is to correct a clerical error, and the application to amend is made before the hearing and is supported by affidavit : *The Vortigern* ('). The 12th article of the draft copy of the plaintiffs' preliminary act contains words to the effect that when the collision was seen to be imminent " the engines of the Cleanthes were put full speed about between two and three minutes before the collision," and the principal amendment now asked for is that in this article *the words " full speed " should be struck out [186 of the copy brought into the registry, and the words " full speed astern " be inserted in their place.

Myburgh, Q.C., for the defendants, was not called upon.

(') Sw., 518.

SIR ROBERT PHILLIMORE: I shall adhere to the practice I have always followed with regard to applications for leave to amend preliminary acts, and refuse to allow any such amendments to be made. The parties in an action of damage are not bound in their pleadings to repeat any errors or omissions which may exist in their preliminary acts, and it is open to them in their statement of claim, or statement of defence, to state correctly any facts which may have been omitted or erroneously stated in their preliminary acts, but I am quite sure that it would be improper for the court to allow any alterations to be made in the preliminary acts. I therefore cannot accede to the application in this case, and I must reject the motion with costs.

Solicitors for plaintiffs: *Botterell & Roche.*
Solicitors for defendants: *Cooper & Co.*

G. B.

[7 Probate Division, 186.]

March 7, 1881.

THE BREADALBANE (Q. No. 557, fo. 423).

Damage—Regulations for Preventing Collisions at Sea, Art. 11.

A ship does not, by carrying a fixed white binnacle light in such a position as to be reflected astern, comply with the provisions of the eleventh article of the Regulations for Preventing Collisions at Sea, which provides that a ship which is being overtaken by another shall show from her stern to such last mentioned ship a white light or a flare-up light.

THIS was an action of damage instituted on behalf of the owners of the foreign brig Conrad and the owners of her cargo, against the ship Breadalbane, to recover for the damage arising out of a collision between the two vessels in the English Channel after dark on the 21st of October last.

After a statement of claim had been delivered on behalf of the plaintiffs, stating that the collision had occurred owing to the Breadalbane overtaking the Conrad and not getting out 187] of her *way, and that so much damage had been done in the collision that the Conrad sank with everything on board her, the solicitor for the defendants, the owners of the Breadalbane, delivered a statement of defence and counterclaim, wherein it was alleged by way of defence that immediately before the collision those on board the Breadalbane had seen the green light of the Conrad about a quarter to half-a-mile off, and about five or six points abaft the port beam of the Breadalbane; that therefore the Breadalbane

had been kept on her course, and a bright light had been
shown over the stern of the Breadalbane, but the Conrad
continued to approach and ran into the Breadalbane and
did her much damage.

By way of counter-claim the defendants repeated the allegations in the statement of defence, and claimed judgment
against the plaintiffs and their bail for damage occasioned
to the plaintiffs by reason of the collision.

Dec. 9.   The action came on to be heard before the judge,
assisted by two of the Elder Brethren of the Trinity House.

Charles Russell, Q.C., and *Myburgh*, for the defendants,
applied to the court to direct that all proceedings in the action should be stayed on the ground that the plaintiffs, the
owners of the Conrad, had neither given security for the
costs of the counter-claim nor put in bail to answer judgment on such counter-claim.

Webster, Q.C., and *W. G. F. Phillimore*, for the plaintiffs.

Phillimore admitted that the owners of the Conrad had
not given either bail or security for costs, and asked that
the hearing of the action might be adjourned. . To this application the court acceded.

Dec. 10.   The action was again called on, and bail, or an
undertaking in lieu of bail, not having been given on behalf
of the owners of the Conrad, the court directed that their
names should be struck out of the proceedings, and that the
action should proceed as an action by the owners of the
cargo of the Conrad alone.   Witnesses on behalf of the plaintiffs, the owners of the cargo of the Conrad, and the defendants were then called and examined in support of the
statement of claim and the statement of defence respectively.
It appeared from the evidence of the witnesses called on behalf of the plaintiffs that the steering *compas of the   [188
Conrad was fitted with two binnacle lamps, and was fixed
inside a deck house on the poop of the Conrad, but in such
a position that the steersman could see to steer by it if he
looked through a pane of glass in the after part of the deck
house ; that on the night of the collision one of the binnacle
lamps in question was lighted, and the reflection from the
light given out by it, would pass through the pane in the
after part of the deck house and would be visible astern to
overtaking vessels.   It also appeared in evidence that when
those on board the Conrad had first seen the Breadalbane
before the collision the foretopsail of the Breadalbane had
been set, but that it blew away very shortly before the colli-

sion.   The result of the remainder of the evidence is sufficiently stated in the judgment.

SIR ROBERT PHILLIMORE: This is a case of collision
which took place at 11 o'clock on the 21st of October in this
year, between a Swedish brig and a sailing ship off the
coast of Cornwall, near the Longships lighthouse.   The direction of the wind was about S.E. by S.   The vessels which
came into collision were a brig called the Conrad of 322 tons
register, bound from Cardiff to Stockholm, with a crew of
ten hands and a cargo of coals; and a ship called the
Breadalbane of 1,427 tons register, on a voyage from Hamburgh to Cardiff in ballast.   The Breadalbane ran into the
starboard side of the brig and sank her.   The action in this
case was brought by the owners of the cargo of the Conrad,
who contended that the collision was caused by the Breadalbane neglecting to take proper steps to keep out of the
way of the Conrad; on the other hand the defendants contended that the collision was caused by the Conrad not
keeping out of the way of the Breadalbane.   Now it appears that the Conrad was heading about E. by N., and was
close hauled on the starboard tack, and that the Breadalbane was heading N.E. by E. half E., also close hauled on
the starboard tack.   The speed of the vessels was between
one and two knots an hour.   The case of the plaintiffs is
that those on board the Conrad saw the Breadalbane about
half a mile off, and about four points abaft the starboard
beam, and the defendants say that those on board the Breadalbane saw the Conrad from a quarter to half a mile off,
189]   and about five or six *points abaft the port beam.
The Elder Brethren advise me that if either of these statements be true, considering there was one and a half points
of difference between their courses, they were crossing ships
and not overtaking ships.   But this was not the case set up
in the pleadings nor argued before me.   The contention of
the plaintiffs has been that the Breadalbane was overtaking
the Conrad, and that therefore the Breadalbane as the overtaking ship was bound to keep out of the way.   A careful
consideration of the evidence leads us to the conclusion that
the Breadalbane was, owing to the loss of her foretopsail,
brought into close quarters with the Conrad, and came
bodily down upon her and sank her.   Now Article 11 of the
Regulations for Preventing Collisions at Sea, provides that
"a ship which is being overtaken by another, shall show
from her stern to the last mentioned ship a white light or a
flare-up light," and we are clearly of opinion that the Conrad did not by carrying a fixed binnacle light in the manner

proved in this case comply with the provisions of this article. The article does not provide that the white light mentioned in it is to be a fixed stern light; and the placing of a
binnacle light so as to be visible astern in the manner proved
in this case cannot satisfy the article, because the light itself
could not be seen but only the reflected rays of it. The
Conrad, therefore, has infringed the article in question, and
accordingly must be deemed in fault under the 17th section
of the Merchant Shipping Act, 1873, unless her infringement
of the article could not by possibility have contributed to
the collision. The Elder Brethren, however, are of opinion,
and I agree with them, that the infringement of the article
in this case could not by any possibility have contributed
to the collision. Looking to the whole of the evidence, in
our opinion, that on the part of the Conrad is the most
trustworthy. It only remains for the court to pronounce
which of these two vessels is to blame for the collision. We
think that the Breadalbane is alone to blame for the collision. And I pronounce accordingly.

March 7. *Bucknill*, on behalf of the owners of the Breadalbane, moved the judge in court to postpone the hearing of
the reference in the action until an appeal, brought on behalf of the *owners of the Breadalbane against the [190
above-mentioned judgment of the 13th of December had
been disposed of.

Pyke, for the owners of the cargo of the Conrad opposed
the motion.

THE COURT directed that the hearing of the reference
should be proceeded with without prejudice to the appeal.

Solicitors for owners of the Conrad and owners of her cargo: *Ingledew & Ince.*

Solicitors for owners of the Breadalbane: *Gregory, Rowcliffes & Co.*

                                                    G. B.

[7 Probate Division, 190.]
April 25, 1882.

THE CLAN GORDON.

[1881 N. 267.]

*Damage—Collision with Pier—Non-liability of Shipowners for negligence of Pilot
in charge by compulsion of Law—Harbors, Docks and Piers Clauses Act, 1847
(10 Vict. c. 27), s. 74—The New Brighton Pier Act, 1864 (27 & 28 Vict.
cclxvii), ss. 2, 89—Merchant Shipping Act, 1854 (17 & 18 Vict. c. 104), s. 388.*

The 74th section of the Harbors, Piers and Clauses Act, 1847, which act is incorporated with the New Brighton Pier Act, 1864, save and so far as any of the clauses
and provisions of the two acts are inconsistent, declares that the owner of every ves-

sel shall be answerable to the undertakers of every pier to which the Harbors, Docks
and Piers Clauses Act, 1847, is applied, for any damage done to such pier, but provides that nothing therein contained shall extend to impose any liability for such
damage upon the owner of any vessel where such vessel shall at the time when such
damage is caused be in charge of a duly licensed pilot whom such owner or master
is bound by law to employ. By the 39th section of the New Brighton Pier Act,
1864, it is enacted that if any person having the care of any ship shall wilfully or
carelessly cause, permit, or suffer any damage or injury to be done to the New
Brighton Pier, then and in every such case the owners of every such ship shall be
answerable and liable to make satisfaction to the New Brighton Pier Company for
all such damage or injury. A steamship came into collision with and did damage to
the New Brighton Pier, and to recover for the damage so done the New Brighton
Pier Company brought an action against the steamship. The owners of the steamship alleged in their statement of defence that at the time the damage was done the
steamship was in charge of a pilot employed by compulsion of law; that the collision
was not caused or contributed to by the negligence of the defendants or any other
persons than the pilot of the steamship, and that the damage was not permitted or
191]   suffered by any persons having the care of the steamship within *the meaning of the New Brighton Pier Act, 1864. The plaintiffs demurred to these allegations in the statement of defence:

Held, that the provisions of the New Brighton Pier Act, 1864, did not preclude
the defendants from setting up the defence of compulsory pilotage and that the demurrer must be overruled.

THIS was an action of damage instituted on behalf of the
New Brighton Pier Company against the steamship Clan
Gordon.

The statement of claim alleged in substance that the plaintiffs were incorporated by the New Brighton Pier Act, 1864,
and were the owners of a pier built under the powers conferred by that act; that by s. 39 of the same act, if any person having the care of any ship, boat, or barge, or other
vessel, should wilfully or carelessly cause, permit, or suffer
any damage or injury to be done to the said pier or works
by any such ship, boat, barge, or other vessel, then and in
every such case the owner of every such ship, boat, barge,
or other vessel was made answerable and liable to make
satisfaction to the plaintiffs for all such damage or injury,
and that the Clan Gordon had on the 9th of October last by
the negligence of the person or persons in charge of her come
into collision with the said pier and greatly injured it.

The statement of claim further alleged so far as might be
necessary that the collision and damage were due to negligence on the part of the servants of the owners of the Clan
Gordon.

On behalf of the defendants the owners of the Clan Gordon, a statement of defence was delivered of which the second, third, and fourth paragraphs were in substance as
follows :

2. The defendants deny that the damage proceeded for
was caused by the Clan Gordon within the meaning of the
New Brighton Pier Act, 1864.

3. The defendants also say that before and at the time when the said damage was caused the Clan Gordon was in charge of a duly licensed pilot, whom the owners and master of the Clan Gordon were bound by law to employ and put their vessel in charge of, within the meaning of s. 74, of the Harbors, Docks, and Piers Clauses Act, 1847.

4. The defendants further say that the collision and damage were not caused or contributed to by any negligence of the defendants or of their servants, or of any person other than the duly *licensed pilot, who was as aforesaid [192 by compulsion of law in charge of the Clan Gordon, and who was directing and controlling the management and navigation of the Clan Gordon.

The plaintiffs demurred to the 2d, 3d, and 4th paragraphs of the statement of defence.

April 25. *W. R. Kennedy* (*Webster*, Q.C., with him), for the plaintiffs : The 74th section of the Harbors, Docks, and Piers Clauses Act, 1847, is inapplicable to the New Brighton Pier, for the provisions of that section are inconsistent with the provisions of the 39th section of the New Brighton Pier Act, 1864, and by the 2d section of the New Brighton Pier Act, 1864, the act of 1847, and the New Brighton Pier Act, 1864, are only to be incorporated together where the act of 1847 is not expressly varied or is not inconsistent. The effect of the 39th section of the act of 1864 is to render a shipowner liable if the master of his ship, in whom the care of the ship still remains though a pilot employed by compulsion of law be on board, suffers or permits the pilot to act carelessly so as to cause damage. If this construction of the section is the right one, it is a question of fact, whether the defendants are not liable for the wrongful act of their master in allowing the pilot to damage the plaintiffs' pier. Apart from statutory provision, it is the duty of a master to take the charge of his ship out of the hands of a pilot who is incompetent or misconducts himself : *The Duke of Manchester* (¹).

Butt, Q.C., *MacLeod*, Q.C., and *W. G. F. Phillimore*, for the defendants : The 39th section of the New Brighton Pier Act, 1864, a local act, has not either expressly or by implication repealed either the 74th section of the Harbors, Docks, and Piers Clauses Act, 1847, or the 388th section of the Merchant Shipping Act, 1854, which latter section expressly provides that no owner or master of any ship shall be answerable to any person whatsoever for any loss or dam-

(¹) 4 N. of C., 575.

age occasioned by the fault of any pilot employed by compulsion of law : *The Conservators of the Thames* v. *Hall* (¹). The object of the 39th section of the New Brighton Act was not to alter the law of compulsory pilotage, but to enable the New Brighton Pier Company to recover against the 193] *owner of a vessel for damage wilfully done by the master or other servant of the shipowner, and but for the provisions of the section the plaintiffs in the case of damage wilfully done by a master without the scope of his authority would have no remedy against the shipowner: *The Ida* (²); *The Druid* (³). If this construction be right, it is clear that the 39th section of the act of 1864 is not inconsistent with, but must be read together with, the act of 1847, and that consequently the present case is governed by the 74th section of the latter act which contains an express proviso applicable to cases of compulsory pilotage.

Kennedy, replied.

SIR ROBERT PHILLIMORE : I am of opinion that this demurrer is bad and cannot be allowed. In order to sustain it the counsel, who has argued this case with great ability on behalf of the plaintiffs, was driven to contend that by implication both the 388th section of the Merchant Shipping Act, 1854, and the 74th section of the Harbors, Docks, and Piers Clauses Act, 1847, were repealed. I think that would be a conclusion to which the court would be very loath to come, and would be very anxious to avoid. I am of opinion that the 74th clause of the Harbors, Docks, and Piers Clauses Act, 1847, remains unaffected by the provisions of the local act on which the plaintiffs rely, and that the argument urged by Mr. Butt that the words in the 39th section of the New Brighton Pier Act, 1864, "any person having the care of any ship, boat, barge, or other vessel," are not the proper or necessary description of a pilot taken on board by compulsion of law, and were not intended to apply and do not apply to such a pilot, is a sound argument. In the result I am of opinion that the argument of Mr. Kennedy, which, speaking in general terms, is neither more or less than that the general law upon the question of compulsory pilotage is repealed by implication by the 39th section of the New Brighton Pier Act, 1864, cannot be sustained. I must, therefore, overrule the demurrer with costs.

Solicitors for plaintiffs : *Laces, Bird, Newton & Co.*
Solicitors for defendants : *Bateson, Bright & Warr.*

(¹) Law Rep., 3 C. P., 415.   (²) Lush., 6.   (³) 1 W. Rob., 391.

[7 Probate Division, 194.]

May 15, 1882.

*THE GOLDEN SEA.   . [194

Shipping Casualty Appeal—Shipping Casualties Investigations Act, 1879 (42 &
43 *Vict. c.* 72), *s.* 2.

A shipowner, who has appeared as a party at the hearing of an investigation under the Merchant Shipping Acts into the circumstances attending the loss of a ship
owned by him, has no right of appeal, notwithstanding that the tribunal investigating the case has given a decision suspending the certificate of the master of the
ship, and condemning the shipowner in costs.

The Wreck Commissioner, having been requested to hold an investigation into the
loss and abandonment of a British ship, found that the loss of the ship was due to
certain improper ballast taken on board her at an English port having been converted into mud by mixture with the water made by her during the voyage, and so
choking the pumps that they could not be used, whereby the ship foundered, and
for these wrongful acts and defaults suspended the certificate of the master of the
ship for three months. The master appealed.

The Probate, Divorce, and Admiralty Division being of opinion that the evidence
before the Wreck Commissioner established that the master had authority from his
owner to provide ballast for the vessel without restriction as to price, and had been
aware of the character of the ballast which she had taken on board, and that the
carrying of such ballast contributed to her loss, dismissed the appeal with costs.

On the 20th of October, 1881, the British sailing ship
Golden Sea, whilst on a voyage from Bristol to St. John's,
New Brunswick, was abandoned by her master and crew,
and was totally lost four hours after she had been so abandoned. Afterwards the Board of Trade ordered a formal
investigation under the Merchant Shipping Acts into the
the circumstances attending her abandonment and loss to be
held, and caused notices of investigation under rule 5 of the
Shipping Casualties Rules, 1878, to be served on her master
and on her managing owner.

On the 13th, 14th, and 15th of December, 1881, the formal
investigation was held at Bristol before the Wreck Commissioner (H. C. Rothery, Esq.) and nautical assessors.
Both the master and managing owner appeared at the inquiry
and took part in the proceedings, and at the close of the
case the court suspended the certificate of the master of the
Golden Sea for three months, and ordered the managing
owner of the Golden Sea to pay to the solicitor of the Board
of Trade the sum of £100 on account of the expenses of the
investigation.

*Subsequently the following report of the court [195
was sent to the Board of Trade.

Report of Court.

The court, having carefully inquired into the circumstances of the above mentioned shipping casualty, finds, for
the reasons annexed, that the loss of the said vessel Golden
Sea was due to the improper ballast which she took on
board at Bristol, and which, having become converted into
mud by the water she made, caused the pumps to be choked
and the vessel to founder ; but that the abandonment of the
vessel when it took place was justifiable.

For these wrongful acts and defaults the court suspends
the certificate of Frederick Bowles, the master of the Golden
Sea, for three months from this date, and condemns Richard
George Guy, the managing owner of the said vessel, in the
sum of one hundred pounds (£100) *nomine expensarum.*

Dated this 15th day of December, 1881.

(Signed)   H. C. Rothery,
Wreck Commissioner.

We concur in the above report.

(Signed)   Robert Harland, } Assessors.
R. Methven,

Appended to the report was an "annex" containing a
statement of all the material facts of the case, and the
grounds on which the report proceeded. The substance of
the annex so far as material may be gathered from the judgment of the President set out below.

The master and the managing owner appealed.

April 3, May 8.   The appeals were heard together before
the President and Sir Robert Phillimore, assisted by two of
the Elder Brethren of the Trinity House.

W. G. F. Phillimore, for the managing owner of the
Golden Sea : Objection will be taken by the respondents
that the managing owner has no right of appeal.   The right
of appeal is conferred by the 2d section of the Shipping
Casualties Investigation Act, 1879, and it is submitted that
196]   the words of that *section are wide enough to include
any owner who having been party to the proceedings on a
shipping casualty investigation has been aggrieved by the
decision of the court investigating the case.

Cottingham, for the master, argued that upon the evidence
it did not appear that the loss of the Golden Sea was caused
by the wrongful act or default of the master within the
meaning of the 242d section of the Merchant Shipping Act,
1854.

Norris, Q.C., and *Danckwerts,* for the respondents, the

Board of Trade, objected that the managing owner had no right of appeal, but were not called upon to argue the point. Their arguments were directed to support the finding of the court of investigation with respect to the master.

Cur. adv. vult.

May 15. THE PRESIDENT: This is an appeal from a decision of the Wreck Commissioner, suspending the certificate of Frederick Bowles, the master of the Golden Sea, for three months, and condemning R. G. Guy, the managing owner of that vessel, in the sum of £100, *nomine expensarum.* The learned Wreck Commissioner found that the loss of the Golden Sea was due to the improper ballast which she took on board at Bristol, and which having been converted into mud by the water she made, caused the pumps to be choked and the vessel to founder. We entirely concur in this finding. The ballast was largely composed of dirt, which was liable to be washed away by the water which came into contact with it. The man who supplied it stated that it was not proper ballast for a ship without limbers, and that the common sense of the master would teach him that it was soluble in water. It was contended that this vessel had limbers, and therefore that there was no reason to suppose that water in ordinary circumstances would come in contact with the ballast; but whether there were what might technically be called limbers or not, we are of opinion that there was not sufficient security against the action of the water upon the ballast in the event of such ordinary incidences of the voyage arising as the master was bound to contemplate and guard against. He himself says, in his evidence, that the pumps sucked at fourteen inches, and that on the previous voyage he noticed that when there were sixteen inches of water in the well *he would find water over the [197 skin of the vessel. This would at once bring it in contact with the dirt ballast which was laid upon the skin, and the mud that then formed would be carried by the water into the pump-well and would gradually choke the pumps. The Wreck Commissioner, with the concurrence of the assessors who assisted him, found that this was what, in fact, took place, and that the consequence was that with such ballast with the water that there was in the vessel between the 14th and the 20th of October, when she was abandoned, it was impossible to keep the pumps clear. In this opinion we, together with our assessors, concur. The only point on which our assessors have felt any doubt is whether the gales which the vessel encountered between the 14th and the 19th did not

prevent the master and crew from doing more than was done
to keep the pumps clear, and whether, therefore, the loss of
the vessel must not be attributed to these gales. We, however,
are of opinion, that, as the improper ballast contributed to
the helpless condition in which the ship was on the 19th of
October, the master must be held responsible for that condition. It is possible that if the weather had been less severe,
and the vessel had not sprung a-leak, the pump-well might
have been kept clear; but on the other hand, it is impossible
to say that if the crew had only had to contend with ordinary water instead of water laden with dirt, they would not
have been able to keep the vessel afloat. A master is not
justified in proceeding on a voyoge across the Atlantic with
ballast on board of such a kind and so stowed as to clog the
pumps in the event of bad weather making the safety of the
vessel depend on their proper action. We think that the
event clearly establishes this. The master knew the character of the ballast. He bought it on his own responsibility,
and no restriction was placed upon him by his owner as to
the price he should pay. We have no doubt that he acted
in what he thought was the interest of his owners in obtaining this cheap dirt rather than the better material which
could have been obtained at a higher price, but this cannot
relieve him of the responsibility for the consequence of his
improper selection. We are therefore of opinion that the decision of the Wreck Commissioner as to the master was correct, and we dismiss his appeal.

198]   *With regard to the owner the case is very different.
It has been our duty in the interest of the master carefully
to investigate all the facts, and we feel bound to say that so
far as the case has been presented to us we do not see any
reason to impute blame to the owner. But an objection has
been taken on behalf of the Board of Trade that no appeal
lies from the decision of the Wreck Commissioner condemning the owner. We feel constrained, though with great regret, to give effect to this objection. The appeal to this
division is given by the Shipping Casualty Investigations
Act, 1879. By the 2d section of that act it is enacted, first,
that "where an investigation into the conduct of a master,
mate, or engineer, or into a shipping casualty has been held
. . . . the Board of Trade may in any case, and shall" in
certain cases, order the cause to be reheard; secondly, that
"where in any such investigation a decision has been given
with respect to the cancelling or suspension of the certificate
of a master, mate, or engineer, and an application for a rehearing has not been made, or has been refused, an appeal

shall lie from the decision." We are of opinion that the clear meaning of these words is, that the decision from which an appeal is allowed is a decision with respect to the cancelling or suspension of the certificate, and not any other decision. If the reason of the enactment is considered, it confirms the view we take of the construction of the section. The decision of the Wreck Commissioner may deprive the master of the means of earning his livelihood. It was thought fit, therefore, to give the master a right of appeal. If it had been intended to give the owner a right of appeal we cannot conceive any reason why it should be made to depend on whether the master's certificate had been dealt with, for the injury inflicted on the owner by an erroneous decision is the same, whether the master is found to blame or not. It is possible that no appeal was given to the owner because the Wreck Commissioner has only the power to express an opinion on his conduct, and has not directly the power of punishing him. But it is evident that the reflection on the character of the owner arising from an adverse finding against him is of a very serious nature. He has in fact, though not in form, been found guilty of a misdemeanor in sending a ship to sea in such an unseaworthy *state [199 that lives were likely to be thereby endangered. In addition to this he has in effect been subject to a fine, *nomine expensarum*, of £100. We think that an amendment of the law is called for, and that the right of appeal should be extended to the owner. Entertaining the opinion we have expressed, we are compelled to reject the owner's appeal, but we do so without costs.

Solicitors for appellants: *Fielder & Sumner.*
Solicitor for Board of Trade: *Murton.*

G. B.

[7 Probate Division, 199.]

April 26, 1882.

THE LOTUS (1881, D. No. 431, fo. 92).

Salvage—Practice—Adequate, but illiberal Tender—Costs.

In a case of salvage, in which the defendants pleaded a tender and payment into court of £300, the court pronounced for the tender and condemned the defendants in costs up to the time of payment into court, but made no order as to the costs incurred after that time.

THIS was an action of salvage brought by the owners, master, and crew of the steamship Dora against the steamship Lotus, her cargo and freight. The owners of the Lotus

appeared as defendants in the suit, and delivered a statement
of defence. The defendants by the statement of defence
traversed some of the allegations in the statement of claim,
and alleged in the 12th paragraph in substance as follows:

The defendants tendered to the plaintiffs, and on the 27th
of March, 1882, paid into court the sum of £300 for the services rendered to the Lotus, her cargo and freight, and submit that the same is ample and sufficient.

The plaintiffs in their reply denied that the sum paid into
court, as pleaded in the 12th paragraph of the statement of
defence, was sufficient.

April 26. The action was heard.

The services in respect of which the suit was brought
mainly consisted in towing the Lotus, which had broken
her shaft, and when the Dora fell in with her, was lying at
anchor in twenty-eight fathoms of water off the west coast
of France, about sixteen miles from Point Baleines, a dis-
200]   tance of seventy-five to eighty *miles, into a place of
safety off Pauillac, at the mouth of the Bordeax river, where
the two vessels arrived about sixteen hours after the towage
commenced.

For the purposes of the suit the value of the Dora, her
cargo and freight, was taken to be £25,000, and the value
of the property proceeded against £20,000.

Myburgh, Q.C., and *W. G. F. Phillimore*, for the plaintiffs.

Butt. Q.C., and *Stewart*, for the defendants.

SIR ROBERT PHILLIMORE: Looking to the circumstances
of this case, I am of opinion that the tender is adequate,
though not liberal. There is a question of some importance
as to costs. I find that my predecessor, Dr. Lushington, in
the case of *The William* (¹), upon the subject of costs, said:
"I have considerable difficulty upon the subject of costs.
In ordinary cases, the rule of the Court of Admiralty has
been this: If a tender is made and rejected, which is afterwards pronounced sufficient, it ought to be followed by con-
demnation of the salvors in the costs, and no doubt if I look
to the practice of the other courts—I allude particularly to
the opinion expressed by Lord Cottenham and the Master
of the Rolls—costs are not given with a view of punishment,
but as a matter of justice to the other party. I have considered how far this doctrine is applicable to cases of salvage, and I confess I have great difficulty in applying it with
all its rigidity to such cases, for this reason: in the very

(¹) 5 N. of Cas., 108.

nature of salvage services, there is something so loose and indefinite, and so difficult to be determined by the best constituted minds, when looking at their own case, that I am not inclined to press the doctrine to its full extent.   Where there has been an offer on the face of the proceedings so large that it ought to have been accepted, I must administer justice in conformity to the rule I have mentioned. In the present case, however, whilst I certainly think the tender ought to have been accepted, yet, at the same time, looking at the value of the property and all the circumstances, I do not think that I ought to deprive the salvors of all reward ; nor do I think it would be for the interest of the public if I were to do so ; because it is desirable to hold out *a degree of extra encouragement, if I may say so,   [201 for the preservation of property.   Upon the whole, therefore, in this case, though it is with some doubt, I do not condemn the salvors in costs." Dr. Lushington therefore held, in that case, that in a cause of salvage where the tender was sufficient but not liberal, he had a discretion in the matter of costs.   The exercise of this discretion as to costs is not affected either by the Judicature Acts or the rules of the Supreme Court, and I shall give the salvors in this case their costs up to the time when the money was paid into court, and I shall make no order as to the costs after that time.

Solicitors for plaintiffs : *Waltons, Bubb & Walton.*
Solicitors for defendants : *Walker, Son & Field.*

G. B.

[7 Probate Division, 201.]

May 23, 1882.

THE MARY (1881, G. 673).

Collision—Practice—Both Ships to blame—Costs of Reference.

Where in an action of damage the defendant sets up a counter-claim relating to the collision in respect of which the action is brought, and both ships are held to blame, and a reference is ordered to ascertain the amount of damage sustained by each ship, each party is, as a general rule, entitled to the costs of establishing his claim before the registrar, provided that not more than one-fourth of his claim has been disallowed.

THIS was an action of damage carried on on behalf of the owners of the steamship Violet against the steamship Mary.

The owners of the Mary appeared as defendants in the suit, and delivered a statement of defence and counter-claim, claiming by way of counter-claim the damages occasioned

to them by reason of the collision in respect of which the
action was brought; and on the 3d of May, 1881, the court
pronounced that the collision in question was occasioned by
the default of the master and crew of the Violet, and by the
default of the master and crew of the Mary; condemned the
owners of the Mary and their bail in a moiety of the plaintiff's claim in respect of the damages occasioned by the collision, and the owners of the Violet and their bail in a moiety
of the defendants' counter-claim in respect of the said damages, and referred the said damages to the registrar, assisted
by merchants to assess the amount.

202]   *Subsequently the owners of the Violet brought in
their claim, amounting to £944 15s. 9d., and the owners of
the Mary their counter-claim amounting to £5,711 14s., to
the registry; and on the 14th of April last the registrar reported that the owners of the Violet and the owners of the
Mary had respectively sustained loss or damage by reason
of the collision aforesaid to the extent of £775 13s. 3d. and
£4,672 8s. 5d. respectively.

No recommendation was made by the registrar as to how
the costs of the reference should be borne.

Bucknill, on behalf of the defendants, moved the judge
to order that the plaintiffs do pay the defendants' costs of
the reference so far as regards the defendants' counter-claim,
and to condemn the plaintiffs in the costs of the motion.
Ever since the Court of Appeal decided in the case of *The Consett* (¹) that the costs of and incident to references in damage
suits in this court must be dealt with as the costs of a fresh
litigation and independently of the result of the issues tried
in court, it has been the settled practice in cases similar to
the present, where less than one-fourth the amount of a
plaintiff's and defendant's claim or counter-claim has been
disallowed, that the parties bringing in such claim or counter-claim should have their costs of the reference: *The
Savernake* (²).   In the present case there are no peculiar circumstances, and no sufficient reason can be shown for refusing to grant the motion.   The defendants on their part are
prepared to pay the costs of the reference so far as regards
the claim of the plaintiffs.

W. G. F. Phillimore, for the plaintiffs, opposed the motion: There is no reported decision of this court as to how
the costs of the reference in a damage suit are to be borne in
cases where both vessels have been found to blame, and
both the plaintiffs and defendants have attended the reference and have succeeded in proving that they are entitled

---

(¹) 5 P. D., 77; *ante*, p. 304.   _   (²) 5 P. D., 166; *ante*, p. 86.

to more than three-fourths of the damages respectively claimed by them. In the case of *The Consett* (') nearly half of the defendants' claim was disallowed by the registrar, and this court in making the order as to how the *costs [203 of the reference should be borne expressly refrained from laying down any general rule.

Sir ROBERT PHILLIMORE: In this case I must follow the decision of the Court of Appeal in the case of *The Consett* ('), and applying the principle laid down in that decision, I think that that portion of the motion which asks for payment of the costs of the reference so far as regards the counter-claim is a proper application, and that it ought to be granted. With respect to the remainder of the motion, I think in the circumstances that the plaintiffs and defendants should each bear their own costs on this application before me to-day. There will, therefore, be no order as to the costs of the motion.

W. G. F. Phillimore applied that the costs of the reference so far as regards the plaintiffs' claim should be paid by the defendants.

Sir ROBERT PHILLIMORE: Yes; the plaintiffs ought to have the costs of substantiating their claim.

Solicitors for plaintiffs: *Pritchard & Sons.*
Solicitor for defendants: *W. Batham.*

(') 5 P. D., 229; *ante*, p. 444.   (') 5 P. D., 77; *ante*, p. 305.

G. B.

[7 Probate Division, 203.]

April 20, 1882.

[IN THE COURT OF ADMIRALTY OF THE CINQUE PORTS.]

THE MARIE.

Salvage—Misconduct of Salvors diminishing amount of Reward.

Violent and overbearing conduct on the part of salvors, although it may not amount to such wilful misconduct as to cause an entire forfeiture of salvage reward, will yet operate to induce the court to diminish the amount of the reward.

THIS was a cause of salvage instituted on behalf of the owners, master, and crew of the lugger Lady Compton, and the owners, master, and crew of the steamtug Lord Palmerston, against the French brig Marie, her cargo and freight. The suit was entered in the sum of £800, but an appearance having been entered on behalf of the owners of the Marie, as defendants, on their application the Marie was *released on bail in the sum of £400, and with the [204

consent of all parties the judge directed that for the purpose of saving expense the cause should be heard without
pleadings.

April 19, 20. On these days the cause was heard before
the judge (Arthur Cohen, Esq., Q.C.). Witnesses were examined orally in court on behalf of the plaintiffs and the
defendants.

The substance of the evidence appears from the judgment.

Glyn, for the plaintiffs, cited *The Dosseitei* (¹) ; *Hartford*
v. *Jones* (²) ; *Nicholson* v. *Chapman* (³).

W. G. F. Phillimore, for the defendants, cited *The Lady
Worsley* (⁴) ; *The Martha* (⁵) ; *The Dantzic Packet* (⁶) ; *The
Black Boy* (⁷) ; *The Champion* (⁸).

THE JUDGE : This is an action of salvage brought by the
plaintiffs the owners, master, and crew of the lugger Lady
Compton, and the owners, master, and crew of the tug Palmerston against the owners of the French brig Marie, of 108
tons register, laden with a cargo of stone and with her cargo
and freight of the value of £550. There are many facts in
the case which are not at all in dispute. On the 26th of
March last there was blowing an extremely heavy gale,
and the Marie was in the neighborhood of other vessels in
the Downs. One anchor was slipped to avoid a collision,
and then a second anchor was let go when she began to
drive, and then that was also slipped. Under these circumstances, I think that the vessel was in distress and was in
danger. A signal was hoisted on board the Marie, those
on board the Lady Compton perceived the signal and went
up to the brig, and ten men boarded the brig. The brig
was got before the wind, and when they got round the
South Foreland, a tug, which proved to be the Lord Palmerston, was hailed by the master of the lugger. An arrangement was made that the tug was to tow the brig and
hold her in the roads ; and it was agreed that the Lord Palmerston was to receive a proportion of the salvage remuneration. The tug took hold of the brig at about half-past 10
205] o'clock and towed her *until about a quarter to 12
o'clock, and then held her till the tide suited and ultimately
took her into Dover harbor. As to the facts which I have
just mentioned, the evidence leaves no doubt. I am of opinion that these services rendered by the master of the lugger
and the tug were salvage services, because the brig was in

(¹) 10 Jur., 865.   (⁵) Sw., 489.
(²) 1 Ld. Raym., 393.   (⁶) 3 Hagg., 885.
(³) 2 H. Bl., 254.   (⁷) 3 Hagg., 386 n.
(⁴) 2 Spks., 256.   (⁸) Br. & L., 69.

distress and in danger. But I am also of opinion that the services did not require much skill and labor and involved no risk at all. The services lasted but a very short time. I think that the services of ten men as salvors were by no means required ; and I am of opinion that the master of the Marie when he signalled did not mean to signify more than that he wanted no other service than the services of a man who could pilot his vessel. If he had had a pilot on board all that he desired could have been done. There was no skill involved, and there was no necessity for those ten men to board this small brig ; and I therefore do not think it right to award any larger amount of salvage remuneration than it would have been the duty of the court to award if only three men had boarded the brig. I come now to the services of the tug. The weather was not bad for the tug. She towed the vessel a short distance and held her for about two hours. The brig was not in danger. But then it is said that all salvage remuneration in this case has been forfeited by misconduct, and that the conduct of the salvors was throughout violent, overbearing, and threatening. I believe that the evidence of the master of the brig is substantially true : that what he wanted was the service of some person who could pilot the vessel to Dover Roads, and he did not require the services of ten men to assist in the navigation of his vessel. I am however willing to assume that until Mr. Hodges, the agent, came on board, there was a misunderstanding between the salvors and the master of the brig. It is not quite certain what the master of the Marie intended to do, but I am willing to assume that he intended to go to Dover Roads and remain there until he could get an anchor and chain, and that what was done up to the time when Mr. Hodges came on board was not done contrary to the intentions of the master of the brig; but I am also of opinion that after Mr. Hodges came on board the master and crew of the lugger did act in a violent and overbearing manner towards the master of the brig, and insisted on having their own *way. It appears to me that a court of justice [206 ought to express some kind of censure on ten men who boarded a small French brig, and who undoubtedly intended to have their own way, whatever the captain of that small vessel might do. On the other hand I am also of opinion that that misconduct is not such criminal misconduct as should lead to an entire forfeiture of salvage reward. In the case of *The Atlas* (¹) it was held in substance that wilful or criminal misconduct of salvors may work a forfeiture of sal-

(¹) Lush., 518.

vage, but that mere misconduct other than criminal, even though it occasion loss, will only work a diminution of reward. I cannot say that there was in this case wilful or criminal misconduct within the meaning of the judgment in *The Atlas* ('). I entertain considerable doubt whether the master of the brig has sustained any pecuniary loss at all by what was done by the salvors, and see no reason to believe that the salvors did that which occasioned any extra expenditure. On the whole, taking into consideration the opinion of Dr. Lushington in the case of *The Atlas* ('), it is impossible to hold that what was done by the salvors worked a forfeiture of the whole of their remuneration; but I think that the plaintiffs' improper conduct during part of the time when they were rendering salvage services should lead the court to diminish the amount to which otherwise they would have been entitled, and I therefore award to the plaintiffs £70 and costs.

I observe with regret that no tender has been made in this case, but I do hope that in future tenders will be made in cases where the services are similar to those in the present case. I also think it would be very desirable that in cases where tenders have been made, plaintiffs should consider the advisability of naming a sum which, having regard to the amount of the tender, they would be prepared to receive in discharge of their claim. In this way many of these cases might be settled out of court, and thereby great expense saved to all parties, especially as the court would give costs with reference to the amount so put forward by the respective parties as a proper salvage remuneration.

Solicitors for plaintiffs : *Mowll & Mowll.*
Solicitors for defendants : *Lowless & Co.*

(') Lush., 518.

G. B.

[7 Probate Division, 207.]

May 18, 1882.

207]   *THE FAMENOTH.

Shipping casualty Appeal—The Merchant Shipping Act, 1854 (17 & 18 Vict. c. 104), ss. 242, 432—"*Wrongful act or default*"—*Fresh Evidence on Appeal* —*Costs.*

On a shipping casualty appeal where it is desired to adduce fresh evidence at the hearing of the appeal, application for leave to do so should be made to the Court of Appeal by motion prior to the hearing of the appeal.

An error of judgment on the part of the master of a vessel at a moment of great difficulty and danger does not amount to a wrongful act or default, within the meaning of the 242d section of the Merchant Shipping Act, 1854, so as to justify the suspension or cancellation of the master's certificate.

On a successful appeal the Board of Trade having appeared in support of the decision appealed from were directed to pay the costs of the appeal.

THIS was an appeal under the 2d section of the Shipping Casualties Investigations Act, 1879, against a decision of the Wreck Commissioner (H. C. Rothery, Esq.), and assessors with respect to the suspension for three months of the certificate of the appellant William Cowan Auld, late master of the sailing ship Famenoth. The decision appealed against was given on the conclusion of a final investigation held at Westminster on the 27th and 28th of April into the circumstances attending the stranding of the Famenoth. The Famenoth was stranded on the Pan Sand off Whitstable, on the 27th of March, 1882, and four of her crew and a Trinity House pilot left her in one of her boats to transfer some of her passengers to one of three steamtugs in attendance. After the passengers were safely transferred, the boat went adrift and those in it were drowned.

The report of the Wreck Commissioners made to the Board of Trade was in terms as follows:

"The court, having carefully inquired into the circumstances of the above-mentioned shipping casualty, finds, for the reasons annexed, that the stranding of the said ship was due to her having been kept on a S.S.E. course for too long a time, instead of being laid on an E.S.E. course immediately after passing the West Girdler Buoy, heading for the Prince's Channel; and that the blame for the vessel having gone ashore rests with Edward John Taylor, the pilot, who was in charge of her at the time, but was subsequently drowned.

*"The court is further of opinion that William [208 Cowan Auld, the master of the Famenoth, is to blame for having kept the three steamtugs, the Benachie, Daring, and Victoria, in attendance on the vessel, instead of sending one of them off to the assistance of the five men who had gone adrift in the Famenoth's boat, the vessel herself being in no immediate danger, whereas the five men were in imminent risk of losing their lives.

" For this wrongful act and default the court suspends the certificate of the said William Cowan Auld for three months.

" The court is not asked to make any order as to costs.

"Dated this 28th day of April, 1882. H. C. Rothery, Wreck Commissioner. We concur in the above report.

Benjamin S. Pickard, George William Ward, R. Wilson, Assessors.''

Appended to the report was an annex, signed by the Wreck Commissioner and the assessors, which, after describing the circumstances attending the drifting away of the Famenoth's boat, and discussing the point whether the master of the Famenoth had done or omitted any act which conduced to the loss of the five men in such boat, concluded with the following passage:

"The whole responsibility in our opinion for the loss of the lives of these five men rests with the master of the Famenoth. He had two steamers, the Benachie and the Daring, alongside of him, and the Victoria was fast coming up; all the female passengers and children had been transferred to the Benachie and the Daring; his vessel was in no immediate danger; whereas he must have known, if he had thought of it, that the occupants of the boat would be in very great danger. As soon therefore as the Benachie had got back to him, he ought to have sent her to pick up the boat before it could reach the sands, over which it was no doubt driven, and where these unfortunate men in all probability perished; and for not having so done, we think that he is very greatly to blame.

"I think that I have now answered all the questions which we have been asked . . . and the last point which we have to decide is whether we are to accede to the application . . . that we should deal with this master's certificate. The master stated that it had never occurred to him 209] to send the steamtug after them, but in *the opinion of the assessors it ought to have occurred to him. This is not a mere error of judgment, it is an act of negligence which has resulted in the loss of five valuable lives; and under these circumstances the assessors think that they would not be doing their duty unless they marked their sense of the master's conduct by suspending his certificate, and notwithstanding the very high character which we are told his owners are prepared to give him, and the time during which he is said to have been in their service, we think that we cannot do less than suspend his certificate for three months from this day. The court was not asked to make any order as to costs.''

The notice of appeal served on the Board of Trade alleged in substance that the decision of the Wreck Commissioner and assessors, so far as it found that the appellant had been guilty of negligence in not ordering the Benachie to follow the boat of the Famenoth, and in suspending the certificate of the appellant, was wrong, because the evidence before the court did not justify the finding of any wrongful act or default on the part of the appellant.

May 8. *W. G. F. Phillimore*, on behalf of the appellant, moved the court (the President and Sir Robert Phillimore), for leave to adduce fresh evidence on the hearing of the appeal. The fresh evidence the appellant desires to adduce relates to the issue whether the loss of those on board the boat was caused by the wrongful act or default of the appellant. The appellant was not aware until the case was actually being heard at Bristol that the Board of Trade made any charge against him in respect of his conduct after the Famenoth had stranded.

Israel Davis, on behalf of the Board of Trade, opposed the motion.

THE PRESIDENT: We have decided to give the appellant leave to produce on the hearing of the appeal, the further evidence which he has asked to be allowed to bring before us, but it must be understood that it will be a question for consideration hereafter how the costs should be borne. We think that it is right that the application for leave to give further evidence *should have been made now rather [210 than at the hearing of the appeal.

May 15. The appeal came on for hearing before the court (the President and Sir Robert Phillimore), assisted by two of the Elder Brethren of the Trinity House.

The *Admiralty Advocate* (*Dr. Deane*, Q.C.), and *W. G. F. Phillimore*, for the appellant.

Israel Davis, for the Board of Trade.

In pursuance of the leave given by the court as above stated, two passengers who had been on board the Famenoth on the occasion of her stranding, and had then heard a conversation which had taken place between the master of the Famenoth, and the master of the Benachie were called and examined as witnesses on behalf of the appellant. The result of their evidence and of the evidence taken in the court below is, so far as material, stated in the judgment of this court.

Cur. adv. vult.

May 18. THE PRESIDENT: This is an appeal from a decision of the Wreck Commissioner, by which he found W. Cowan Auld, the master of the Famenoth, to blame for keeping three tugs in attendance on his vessel, instead of

sending one of them to the assistance of five men who had
gone adrift in the Famenoth's boat, "the vessel herself being
in no immediate danger, whereas the five men were in imminent risk of losing their lives." The master's certificate was
suspended for three months. The Famenoth, of the port of
Aberdeen, was, on the 27th of March last, being towed down
the river from the Nore by a tug called the Benachie. She
had a crew of twenty-four hands, all told, and more than
twenty passengers on board. She was in charge of a duly
licensed Trinity pilot named Taylor. A violent gale from
the north-west having come on, the Famenoth was driven
broadside on the Pan Sand. The blame for this has been
found to rest with the pilot who was afterwards drowned.
What occurred after the vessel struck is clearly stated in
the Wreck Commissioner's report in the following passage:

"As soon as it was seen that the vessel was hard and fast,
211] the *captain of the Famenoth began to take measures
to provide for the safety of his passengers, and with this
view orders were given to get out the starboard lifeboat, but
before this could be done a sea struck her and stove her in;
upon which orders were given to get out the gig, which was
done, and the second and third mates, one able and one ordinary seaman, having got in, some six or seven of the
female passengers and children were put into her; Taylor,
the pilot, also got into her, but apparently without any
orders from the captain. The boat then pushed off, and
having got alongside the Benachie, which was lying off at a
short distance to leeward, a rope was thrown to her, and all
the passengers were then transferred to the Benachie. The
master of the Benachie then hailed the men in the boat to
take a turn round one of the thwarts of the boat, saying that
he would tow them back to the ship; and shortly afterwards, thinking that the boat was fast, the master of the
Benachie gave orders to go ahead; unfortunately, however,
the rope in some way or other slipped, and the boat went
adrift, and she began to drift towards the sand. On seeing
which, the master of the Benachie at once backed astern until he was in ten feet of water, when fearing to get his vessel
aground he put her ahead again; but the boat herself, notwithstanding the efforts of her crew to pull her to windward
so as to regain the ship was carried by the force of the wind
and sea over the sand, and when last seen they were on the
other side of the sand, but were still pulling to windward.
The Benachie then returned to the Famenoth, but in the
meantime another steamtug, called the Daring, had come up
and the remainder of the female passengers having been put

into the damaged lifeboat, they were sent off, and taken on board the Daring. When, however, the Benachie came alongside, the captain of the Famenoth told the master of the Benachie to pass his tow rope on board, and a third tug, the Victoria, having also come up, all three passed their tow ropes to the Famenoth and began to tow. Up to this time the vessel was making no water, but they had hardly been towing for more than five minutes, when it was reported that she was filling fast, upon which the captain ordered them to cease, and the tow rope was slipped. The Benachie was then ordered to come alongside to take off the remainder of the passengers and crew; this she *succeeded in do- [212 ing, but not without considerable difficulty, at the same time smashing her sponson; and between 1 and 2 o'clock all hands had left the Famenoth and gone on board the Benachie."

On these facts eighteen questions were put by the Board of Trade. The only one which it is necessary to consider is the fourteenth, whether after the gig left the Benachie the master of the Famenoth did or omitted any act, the doing or omission of which conduced to the loss of the gig and those in her. On this point the Wreck Commissioner's judgment is as follows:

"But then the question arises, ought not some effort to have been made to follow the boat and pick her up? When the Benachie ceased following the boat over the sand she returned to the Famenoth; but in the meantime the Daring had come up, and the master of the Famenoth then desired them to pass their tow ropes on board, which they did, as did also the steamtug Victoria, which came up shortly afterwards, and all these steamtugs then began to tow the vessel, but had to leave off a few minutes afterwards owing to the Famenoth filling with water. During all this time the boat was, no doubt, being driven before the gale, notwithstanding all the efforts of her crew to keep her to windward. Now it certainly does appear to us that either the Benachie or one of the other steamers should have been sent round the sand to look after the boat and pick her up; for at this time all the female passengers and children had been safely transferred, part of them to the Benachie, part to the Daring; the Famenoth had two steamtugs in attendance upon her, and a third was fast coming up, and the vessel herself was in no immediate danger. With the wind and tide as they then were, one of these steamtugs could have run round to the south of the Pan Sand in a few minutes, and without any risk to herself or to those on board her; and had she been sent off at once, she would in all probability have picked up the boat long before it had reached the sands, and have rescued the men in her ; and to us it is inconceivable why this was not done."

The decision of the Wreck Commissioner rests upon these two propositions, that the master of the Famenoth kept the tugs in attendance instead of sending one of them after the 213] boat and that *his vessel was in no immediate danger. It appears from the evidence that when the boat was seen to be adrift the master of the Famenoth signalled to the master of the Benachie to go after her, which he did ; but before he could reach the boat the tug herself touched the ground. The boat continued to drive through the breakers over the sand into the open water beyond. The Benachie finding that she could not follow the gig returned towards the Famenoth to pick up another boat load of passengers who were being embarked in the damaged lifeboat of the Fame- noth ; but as another tug, the Daring, had just arrived, it be- came unnecessary for the Benachie to take any passengers on board. The captain of the Famenoth, who had been en- gaged in getting the rest of the women and children into the lifeboat, while the Benachie was going after the gig, upon the tug returning asked the captain why he had not gone to the gig ? and he stated that he had gone as far as the draught of water would allow him, and this was the fact. This evi- dence of the captain given before the evidence affecting him was put in by the Board of Trade is confirmed by two wit- nesses who have been called before us. They say that the master of the Famenoth said, "Can't you do anything more for that boat ?" The answer was, that he could not go any farther after her. It has been observed that these witnesses fix the time of this incident later by the clock than the return of the Benachie from following the gig, but one of them ex- pressly says that it was at that time, and we have no doubt that this is correct. In any case it confirms the inference we draw from the evidence of the captain of the Benachie that he was not prevented from going round the sand by the orders of the master of the Famenoth, but that it did not occur to him that it might be of use. Up to this point, therefore, no blame attaches either to the captain of the Benachie or of the Famenoth. But it is said that the cap- tain of the Famenoth ought at once to have sent the Bena- chie round the sand, and that instead of doing so he de- tained the tug to attend on him, and the Wreck Commissioner finds that no blame attaches to the captain of the tug be- cause he was bound to obey the orders from the Famenoth.

But the captain of the tug does not excuse himself on this ground. He was asked, "Finding that the boat had driven across the sands ought you not to have run down the channel by *the North Tongue or round the sand a little far-   [214 ther to meet this boat driving down the channel and picked her up?—A. Yes, it might have been done.   Q. If you had gone round you would have caught the gig before she would have been driven on to the Margate Sands, would you not? —A. I do not say that.   Q. Did it not occur to you that it was a proper thing to do?—A. No, or I should certainly have done it.   The mode of getting round the sand by the channel by the North Tongue suggested in this question would have been useless, for it would have taken the tug a course of many miles to get round.   But it has with more reason been argued that the tug might have gone round by the western end of the Pan Sand.   This we are informed by our assessors would have taken the tug a course of about three miles to bring her to the tail of the sand on the track of the gig.   But whatever course it would have been possible to take, the answer of the tug master is distinct that, if it had occurred to him that it was the proper thing to go round the sand, he would certainly have done so.   This clearly shows that he did not feel restrained by any orders of the master of the Famenoth from going after the gig.   But in fact it did not occur to him to suggest to the master of the Famenoth that he could by going round the sand have a chance of overtaking the gig.

The question then arises whether there was culpable negligence on the part of the master of the Famenoth in not ordering the Benachie to go round the sand.   It was clear that when his immediate anxiety as to the gig was relieved by seeing her on the other side of the sand, he turned his attention to saving the rest of the women and children.   It does not appear, and there is no reason to suppose, that he had any special knowledge of the sands and the channels around them.   He had lost the pilot, who was in the gig; and the deep sea pilot who was on board did not suggest that the tug could go round the sand, and, as we have seen, the master of the Benachie did not suggest it.   It is true that by looking at the chart we can now see a course that might have been taken round the sand, but we think that it cannot be imputed to the captain as culpable negligence that he did not see at the time that such a course might have been followed with a chance of success.   We are of opinion that the master *of the Famenoth did not recklessly   [215 detain the tug knowing that it could have usefully followed the gig, but that not knowing that she could do so he employed her with the other two tugs in an endeavor to get his vessel off the sand. It is not disputed that this was a proper course for him to take apart from the question of the propriety of his conduct with reference to the gig. It is unnecessary to refer more in detail to the non-employment of the Daring and the Victoria to look for the gig. If any one of the three tugs ought to have been sent it would have been best to send the Benachie, as the masters of the other tugs did not know that the gig had gone adrift. But further we are of opinion that the Famenoth was, and all on board her were, in immediate danger. That the captain of the Famenoth thought so is shown by his transferring the passengers into the tugs; but it is proved that it was blowing a hurricane at the time, and the vessel was being fast embedded in the sand. We are advised, and without such advice we should have thought it manifest, that the Famenoth and all on board her were in great and immenent peril, and, in fact, within a few minutes after the tugs began to tow, the Famenoth was found to be filling fast. In such circumstances no one could predict what would happen to her. The fact that the Famenoth was afterwards got off can make no difference in our consideration of the position in which her captain was at the time. He could have no assurance that the vessel and all on board her would not be lost if he had not availed himself of the help of the tugs which he had at hand. We ought to add that our assessors are of the opinion, in which we concur, that in the circumstances the utmost that can be said against the behavior of the captain of the Famenoth is that it manifested an error of judgment at a moment of great difficulty and danger, but that it did not amount to any act of culpable negligence. We therefore think that the judgment was erroneous and must be reversed.

The Admiralty Advocate: In accordance with the decision of this court in *The Arizonia* (¹) and other cases, the appellant, it is submitted, is entitled to the costs of the appeal.

Israel Davis: The question as to how the costs inci-
216] dental to *and occasioned by the admission of further evidence on the appeal should be borne has been reserved. It is submitted that at least the court ought not to direct the Board of Trade to pay these costs.

THE PRESIDENT: Undoubtedly the court intimated at the time that, while admitting additional evidence, it would depend upon the effect of that evidence whether or not the costs would be given to either of the parties. That is to say,

(¹) 5 P. D. 123.

if the ultimate decision of the case had turned upon the additional evidence, then undoubtedly it would have been a reason for not allowing the costs although the appeal was successful; but in this case the additional evidence was only relied upon for the purpose of confirming the inference which we draw from the original evidence.

The learned counsel for the Board of Trade has spoken of a direction that the Board of Trade should pay the costs of the appeal as being unfair to the court below, which had not the additional evidence before it. It must be remembered that it is a course which the law allows when, instead of a simple appeal, it permits a rehearing, which is the case here; therefore in no proper sense of the word can it be said to be unfair. The object of all tribunals is to arrive at the truth and justice of the case before them, and that must be in some cases attained by receiving additional evidence. We see no reason for saying that this evidence was kept back. The charge against the captain was only developed when all the evidence had been given. The two witnesses who have been called before us are not shown to have been present at the hearing before the Wreck Commissioner; I do not think there was any suggestion that they were present. They were not seafaring people, but it turns out that they happened to be standing by the captain at the time when the boat drifted away, and they were able to confirm by their evidence the truth of the statement which the captain himself had made.

We therefore think that there is no reason why the usual rule should be departed from in this case.

It has been mentioned that we have not only in the case which immediately preceded this ('), but in other cases, given the Board *of Trade the costs when it has suc- [217 ceeded. We must apply the same rule in favor of the appellant when the Board of Trade is unsuccessful.

Solicitors for appellant: *Lowless & Co.*
Solicitor for Board of Trade: *Murton.*

(') *The Golden Sea*, supra, p. 194.   G. B.

Perfect presence of mind, accurate judgment, and promptitude under all circumstances are not to be expected: Walpole's Rubric of the Common Law, 223; The Bywell Castle, 4 Prob. Div., 219, *ante*, pp. 250, 253, 256, 258.

Fault on the part of a sailing vessel at the moment preceding a collision (assuming fault to have existed), does not absolve a steamer which has suffered herself and a sailing vessel to get into such dangerous proximity as to cause inevitable confusion and collision as a consequence: The Lucille, 15 Wall., 676; Lewis *v*. Baltimore, etc., 38 Md., 588.

One, who through his negligence, places another in peril, cannot complain if the latter does not exercise the best judgment in extricating himself;

all that is required of him is to do the best he can, and if he does this and fails, the party placing him in peril is responsible : 3 Amer. and English R. R. Cas., 364 note.

Alabama : Cook *v.* Central, etc., 67 Ala., 533, 12 Repr., 356.

Illinois : Chicago, etc., *v.* Becker, 76 Ills., 25.

New York : Voak *v.* Northern, etc., 75 N. Y., 320 ; Twomley *v.* C. P., etc., 69 id., 158, 160, 25 Amer. R., 162, 164 note ; Buel *v.* N. Y. Cent., etc., 31 N. Y., 314, 318 ; Dyer *v.* Erie, etc., 71 id., 235–6 ; Coulter *v.* American, etc.,

56 id., 585, 587–8 ; Smith *v.* British, etc., 86 id., 408 ; Cuyler *v.* Decker, 20 Hun, 173.

Ohio : Iron Railroad, etc., *v.* Mowery, 86 Ohio St. R., 418.

Pennsylvania : Wright's Appeal, 89 Penn. St. R., 67.

United States : Haaf *v.* Minneapolis, etc., 14 Fed. Repr., 558, Cir. Ct., Nelson, J.

West Virginia : Fowler *v.* Baltimore, etc., 18 West Va., 580, 14 Repr., 189.

Wisconsin : Schultz *v.* Chicago, etc., 44 Wisc., 638, 644–5.

[7 Probate Division, 217.]

Nov. 5, 1881.

THE CACHAPOOL (1881, G. No. 1923, fo. 295).

Damage—Duty of Vessels anchored in Track of Launch—Compulsory Pilotage— The Mersey Docks Consolidation Act, 1858 (21 & 22 Vict. c. xcii), s. 139— *Meaning of "Proceed to Sea."*

A bark was at anchor in the Mersey in the way of the C., a vessel about to be launched. The launch was delayed as long as was prudent, but the bark not having been got out of the way in time was struck by the C. in coming off the ways and both vessels were damaged. Reasonable notice had been given of the launch, and a steamtug had been sent by those superintending the launch to tow the bark out of danger, and would have done so in time to have prevented the collision but for the obstinacy of those on board the bark :

Held, that the bark was alone to blame for the collision.

The bark had been towed out of dock into the river the previous day in order that she might proceed to sea before daybreak on the morning on which the collision happened. But an accident having happened to the mainyard of the bark she was unable to proceed to sea as intended, and at the time of the collision was waiting in the river to have repairs executed. She had on board of her a duly licensed Mersey pilot :

Held, that she was not at the time of the collision proceeding to sea within the meaning of the Mersey Docks Consolidation Act, 1858, s. 139, and that the pilot on board her was not at the time employed by compulsion of law.

Rodrigues v. *Melhuish* (10 Ex., 110) followed.

THIS was an action of damage instituted on behalf of the owners, master and crew of the bark Gladstone against the vessel Cachapool.

The statement of claim alleged, *inter alia*, substantially as follows :

1. On the 8th of August, 1881, the Gladstone, which was a bark belonging to the port of South Shields, left the Salthouse Dock, Liverpool, manned by a crew of eleven hands, all told, and in charge of a duly licensed pilot for the port of Liverpool. The Gladstone was bound for Viborg in Russia.

*2. Shortly after leaving the said dock, and whilst [218 in the course of proceeding to sea on the said voyage, the said bark was by directions of the said pilot brought to an anchor in the river Mersey about abreast of Tranmere Ferry landing stage.

3. At about 10 A.M. on the 9th of the said month, the weather was fine and clear with a fresh breeze from about north-west by north, and the tide was last quarter flood and of the force of about four knots, and the Gladstone was lying at anchor in the same place, when a tug called the Hercules came to the Gladstone and told those on board her that a launch was going to take place from a building yard on the Cheshire side of the river, and asked the pilot of the Gladstone if the said ship was not in the way. The Gladstone could not then be moved without assistance, and those on board inquired if the Hercules had authority to and would help to move her.

4. The Hercules which was in attendance at the launch and employed by the defendants and their servants who had the conduct thereof declined at that time to render any assistance in moving the Gladstone, and went away.

5. Shortly afterwards the Hercules returned to the Gladstone, and at the request and by the direction of those on the said tug the tow rope of the Gladstone was passed on board the Hercules, which commenced to tow the bark and the helm of the Gladstone was ported to sheer her out into the river, but the Hercules getting out of position slipped the hawser.

6. The hawser was then again passed on board the Hercules, which again began to tow, but before the Hercules had towed the Gladstone ahead of her anchor, the launch, which proved to be the Cachapool belonging to the defendants, left the ways and approached the Gladstone at great speed and caused risk of collision, and notwithstanding orders were given to veer away the Gladstone's chain the Cachapool with her stern struck the Gladstone on the port side doing so much damage that the Gladstone sank almost immediately, and with her cargo and the effects of her master and crew became a total loss.

7. Those in charge of the Cachapool and of the said launching operations improperly neglected to keep a good look-out.

8. The Cachapool was improperly launched, having regard to *the position of the Gladstone, prior to and [219 at the time of the said launch and the state of the wind and tide.

9. Those in charge of the Cachapool and of the said launch-

ing operations, improperly neglected to supply the Cacha-pool with efficient anchors and cables and improperly neglected to take proper measures and precautions for checking, controlling, arresting or directing the course and speed of the Cachapool, and improperly neglected before the collision to bring her up or to keep her clear of the Gladstone.

10. Those in charge of the Cachapool, and of the said launching operations improperly neglected to give due notice of the said launch taking place, and improperly neglected to take due and proper precautions for the safety of vessels lawfully in the neighborhood of the said launch.

11. The said collision, and the damages consequent thereon, were caused by the neglect or default or want of proper care and skill on the part of those having charge of the Cachapool, and of the said operations for launching her, and were not caused or contributed to by those on board the Gladstone.

The defendants, the owners of the Cachapool, delivered a statement of defence and counter-claim, which, after stating that about 9 A.M. on the 9th of August, 1881, the time appointed for the launch, the Hercules had been sent to warn the Gladstone to move out, but that those on the Gladstone had neglected to do anything, alleged in the 3d and subsequent paragraphs as follows :

3. Later on the Hercules returned to the Gladstone and offered to tow her out of danger, and asked for a hawser. After some delay those on board the Gladstone passed a hawser on to the Hercules, which at once began towing her out of the way to the north and east, but in consequence of those on board the Gladstone neglecting to assist by heaving on their anchor, the Hercules got out of position, and had to slip the hawser.

4. The Hercules went back to the Gladstone to get her hawser again, but those on board the Gladstone then for a long time refused to give the Hercules a hawser. When they did give the Hercules a hawser again she at once went ahead, towing to the north and east, and the Gladstone was moved ahead by her.

220] *5. When those in charge of the launch saw the Gladstone being thus towed ahead, it was considerably past the time appointed for the launch, which could not with safety to life and property be further delayed, and the launch was let go from the ways. Very shortly afterwards it appeared that the Gladstone had been brought up by her chain, and that the launch was moving in the direction of the Gladstone. The anchor of the launch was then let go immediately, the Hercules towed away at the Gladstone, and got her ahead of her anchor, and the Gladstone was hailed to pay out chain. Those on board the Gladstone neglected to pay out chain, and the anchor of the launch dragged, and she with her stern struck the port side of the Gladstone about the main rigging, and suffered considerable damage. This was about 10.30 A.M. The Gladstone unfortunately sank in a few minutes.

6. Save, as aforesaid, the defendants deny the several allegations in pars. 1, 2, 3, 4, 5, 6, and 7 of the statement of claim. Those in pars. 8, 9, 10, 11, and 12 they deny altogether.

7. The date of the said launch had been fixed for several days and the defendants had given all the usual and necessary notices of the same. The launch and the Hercules and other vessels in attendance were dressed with flags. Those in charge of the Gladstone knew, or had full notice and means of knowing of the intended launch, and that it could not with safety be postponed, and had ample time to move her or cause or suffer her to be moved out of the way, but they neglected and refused to do so until it was too late.

8. Those on board the Gladstone improperly neglected to move her out of the way, and improperly refused and delayed to take the assistance offered by the Hercules.

9. Those on board the Gladstone neglected to get in chain on her anchor, so as to suffer her to drag her anchor, and when she was being towed, and it was too late to get in chain for this purpose, they neglected to pay out chain and to take any steps so as to enable the Hercules to tow her further ahead of her anchor and into a position of safety.

10. The collision was caused by some or all of the matters and things stated in the 7th, 8th, and 9th paragraphs hereof or otherwise by the negligence of the plaintiffs or of those on board the Gladstone.

*11. The collision was not caused or contributed [221 to by the defendants or by any of those on board the Cachapool.

By way of counter-claim the defendants repeated the allegations made by them by way of defence, and alleged that they had sustained great damage by reason of the collision.

Nov. 4, 5. The action was heard before the judge, assisted by two of the Elder Brethren of the Trinity House.

Witnesses were examined orally in court on behalf of the

plaintiffs and of the defendants.   The pilot of the Gladstone
was examined as a witness on behalf of the plaintiffs, and
stated that he was a duly licensed Liverpool pilot, and took
charge of the Gladstone in dock on the morning of the 8th
of August, 1881, and brought her out into the river and anchored her nearly abreast of Tranmere Ferry stage by her
port anchor and forty-five fathoms of chain: that all the
crew of the Gladstone were on board her by 7 o'clock that
evening, and it was intended that she should go to sea early
the next morning, a tug having been ordered to come to her
for the purpose of taking her in tow at 1 A.M.; but that at
8 P.M. of the 8th of August an accident happened to her
mainyard arm, whereby it was so damaged that it would
take two days to repair; that accordingly when the tug
came to take the Gladstone to sea in the morning as ordered
she was sent away, and the vessel remained at anchor.

The same witness further stated that the weather on the
morning of the 9th of August would not have permitted
the Gladstone going to sea, even if there had been no accident
to her yard-arm; that he had had no notice that any launch
was going to take place until he saw the Cachapool decorated
with flags after 6 A.M. on that day; and that he was in
charge of the Gladstone at the time of the collision, and that
all the orders he gave had been properly obeyed.   The result
of the remainder of the evidence in the case is stated in the
judgment.

Butt, Q.C., and *Myburgh*, for the plaintiffs: Even admitting that sufficient previous notice was given that the
Cachapool was going to be launched yet the defendants are
still to blame in this case.   Sufficient precautions were not
222]   taken to check and guide the *Cachapool after she
had left the ways.   Moreover she was launched at a time
when it was known that the Gladstone was in her track.
The Gladstone would have been towed clear in a very few
minutes, and even if the launch could not have been stopped after the dog shores were knocked away, those in charge
of the launching operations ought not, whilst the Gladstone
remained in the way, to have proceeded so far with them
as to put it out of their power to prevent the collision.
[They referred to *Davies* v. *Mann* (¹).]

If the court should be of opinion on the evidence that the
Gladstone was "proceeding to sea" at the time when the
collision occurred, then the pilot on board her was employed
by the plaintiffs by compulsion of law; The Mersey Docks

(¹) 10 M. & W., 546.

Consolidation Act, 1858, s. 139, *The City of Cambridge* (¹); and the plaintiffs even if the Gladstone should be found to blame, are not liable for the damage proceeded for.

Cohen, Q.C., and *W. G. F. Phillimore*, for the defendants: The pilot and master of the Gladstone had ample notice of the launch being about to take place, and it was their duty to have taken all possible measures to have had the Gladstone towed clear of the track of the launch. Thi duty they neglected to perform, and it was solely by their default in this respect that the collision was occasioned. Those in charge of the launch had a right to assume that the Gladstone would not remain in the way of the launch, and when it was found that this assumption was a mistake it was too late to stop the launch without great danger, even if it had been possible to do so. With respect to the plea of compulsory pilotage it is clear on the authority of *Rodrigues* v. *Melhuish* (²) that as the Gladstone at the time of the collision was not ready to go to sea, owing to the damage done to her main yard on the previous evening, her pilot was not in charge of her by compulsion of law when the collision occurred.

Myburgh, in reply.

SIR ROBERT PHILLIMORE: This is a case of collision which happened in the river Mersey at about twenty-five minutes past ten o'clock on the morning of the 9th of August last, about *abreast of the Tranmere Ferry. The vessels [223 that came into collision were the bark Gladstone and a vessel which was being launched from a building yard on the Cheshire side of the river. The Gladstone was lying at anchor with her head down the river, and was about abreast of the Tranmere Ferry stage. The launch was a vessel named the Cachapool, and with her sternpost she struck the port side of the Gladstone near the main rigging, and the Gladstone was sunk almost immediately after the collision. The law with respect to the notice that must be given by vessels about to be launched has been several times discussed in this court, and for the purpose of stating what that law is, I will only refer to the case of *The Glengarry* (³). In that case, in which I gave judgment, I said: "There is no doubt whatever as to the law which has been laid down for a considerable period and always observed in this court, namely, that it is the duty of those who launch a vessel to do so with the utmost precaution, and to give such notice as is reasonable and sufficient to prevent injury happening from that event,

(¹) Law Rep., 4 A. & E., 161; 8 Eng.   (²) 10 Ex., 110.
R., 640; 5 P. C., 451; 9 Eng, R., 256.   (³) 2 P. D., 235; 21 Eng. R., 619.

and that the burden of proof lies on them. There is no
doubt at all that those who defend the cause of the launch
have the obligation cast upon them of showing that it took
place in such circumstances as ought with reasonable precautions on the other side not to have brought her into collision. What is reasonable notice must of course depend
very much on the facts of each case. To the propositions
of law so laid down I intend to adhere in the judgment I am
about to deliver. The dates in this case are not immaterial.
It is pleaded in the 3d article of the statement of claim "that
the weather was fine and clear at about ten o'clock, and that
the Gladstone was then lying at anchor." That is a misstatement of nearly an hour and a quarter, and the time becomes very material in the history of this case. It appears
that flags were up at 6 o'clock in the morning, and that the
Cachapool was ready to be launched at 9 o'clock ; and it is
alleged, and has been admitted, that notice was given at 7
A.M., the collision not taking place until 10.30 A.M. The
question here is not whether the notice was sufficient, which
it is admitted to have been, but whether there was any mis-
224]   conduct on the part of the launch, *or whether the
Gladstone was to blame. The Elder Brethren say, and I
agree with them, that the conduct of the pilot of the Gladstone appears to have been reprehensible. He appears to
have been quite indifferent as to what was taking place on
the shore. On his own showing he came on deck at 9 o'clock,
and it was his duty to have got clear and to have been towed
over to the north-east, and if necessary to have let his starboard anchor go. The Elder Brethren are of opinion, and I
concur with them, that the launch was delayed as long as it
was prudent do so. It has been contended that it was the
duty of the owners of the Cachapool to have taken such
precautionary measures as would have prevented a collision.
The launch being about to take place at about high water,
which on that day was at ten minutes past ten o'clock, it
appears to us that every reasonable precaution was taken
by those in charge of the Cachapool, not only by the deco-
ration of that vessel, but by sending notice to all steamers
and vessels in the river near the spot that a launch was going
to take place. According to the evidence the Hercules tug
came up between nine and five minutes past, and warned
the Gladstone to get out of the way of the launch, which
was about to take place. The plaintiffs contend that no
offer was made as to the Gladstone being towed away by
the Hercules, and it is admitted that no such offer was then
made. The Hercules, however, went away to look after

some other vessels, and returned in about five minutes, and after her return she offered to take the Gladstone in tow. It appears upon the evidence that when the Hercules on her return would have taken a hawser the pilot of the Gladstone said, "I will not give it you, but the captain may if he likes." In the end, from fifteen to twenty minutes was wasted in arguing about the question of towing the Gladstone out of the way. A question which has been much considered by the court is whether, even after the Gladstone was taken hold of by the tug at half-past nine or a quarter to ten o'clock, those on board the Gladstone did anything which contributed to the collision, or neglected to do anything which would have prevented it. The Elder Brethren are of opinion that if the Hercules in the first instance, instead of giving the warnings she did, had taken the Gladstone in tow, the result would have been different, and also that if those in *charge of the Gladstone had not been [225 obstinate and had allowed the Hercules to take their vessel to the north-east the launch would have gone clear.

In these circumstances the Elder Brethren are of opinion, and I agree with them, that the Gladstone was alone to blame for the collision. With regard to the plea of compulsory pilotage I am of opinion that the Gladstone was not a vessel "proceeding to sea;" that she did not come within the operation of the compulsory clause of the act which has been referred to, and that her owners are not relieved from liability upon that ground.

Solicitors for plaintiffs : *Cooper & Co.*
Solicitors for defendants : *Toller & Sons.*

G. B.

[7 Probate Division, 225.]

May 11, 1882.

ROSE v. ROSE.

Cruelty—Condonation by Deed—Revival.

A husband had been guilty of cruelty and the wife had stipulated in a deed of separation not to take any proceedings against him in respect of that cruelty. He subsequently committed adultery:

Held, following the case of *Gandy* v. *Gandy* (ante, p. 704) that the subsequent adultery did not revive the wife's right to complain of the cruelty.

THIS was a petition for dissolution of marriage by reason of the husband's cruelty and adultery. The husband had been guilty of cruelty, and the parties separated and lived apart under the provisions of a deed, the last clause of which was as follows:

"No proceedings shall be commenced or prosecuted by or on behalf of either party against the other in respect of any cause of complaint which now exists or has arisen before the date of these presents, and every offence (if any) which has been committed or permitted by either party against the other shall be considered as hereby forgiven and condoned, and in case hereafter either shall commence or prosecute any proceedings against the other in respect of any cause of complaint which may hereafter arise, no offence or misconduct which has been committed or permitted before the execution of these presents, and no act, deed, neglect, or default of either party in relation to any such offence or 226] *misconduct shall be pleaded or alleged by either party or be admissible in evidence."

The wife filed a petition in which she alleged adultery and cruelty committed both before and after the execution of the deed. The husband, amongst other things, denied the charge of cruelty since the deed, and alleged that the petitioner had by the deed condoned all the previous acts.

At the hearing the adultery was admitted, and the court found that the respondent had not been guilty of cruelty since the execution of the deed.

Dr. Tristram, Q.C., and *J. Thompson*, for the petitioner.
E. Willis, for the respondent.

THE PRESIDENT: I am of opinion in *Gandy* v. *Gandy*('), having regard to the practice of this court, that adultery committed by a husband after the execution of a deed of separation revived the wife's rights and relieved her from the restraining covenants of the deed, but the Court of Appeal arrived at a different conclusion (').   In that case the restraining covenant was not to sue for alimony; but I do not see any distinction between that and a covenant not to sue in respect of offences committed before the date of the deed.   The Court of Appeal held that the contract made by the deed of separation cannot be affected by the subsequent adultery of the husband.   This court is bound by that decision, and I am therefore unable to pronounce a decree *nisi* for the dissolution of the marriage in the present case. The adultery of the husband, however, having been proved, I pronounce a decree for judicial separation with costs.

Solicitors for petitioner: *Hicklin & Washington.*
Solicitor for respondent: *W. Doveton Smythe.*

('') *Ante*, p. 641.   (') *Ante*, p. 704.

W. P.

[7 Probate Division, 227.]

'June 6, 1882.

*SMITH v. SMITH and PALK.   [227

Costs, Security for.

In a petition for dissolution of marriage, the husband, who was an uncertificated bankrupt, claimed damages. Upon application by the co-respondent:

Held, that unless the claim for damages was withdrawn the petitioner must give security for the costs of the action.

THIS was a summons for security for costs.

The petitioner had filed a petition for dissolution of marriage by reason of his wife's adultery with the co-respondent, and he also claimed £2,000 as damages. The co-respondent filed an answer, denying the charges and alleging counter-charges, and also (amongst other things), that the respondent was, to the knowledge of the petitioner, living a life of prostitution, and that he had received from her moneys that he knew had been obtained by her prostitution.

The co-respondent now filed affidavits showing that the petitioner was an uncertificated bankrupt.

Searle, for the co-respondent, applied for security for costs and a stay of proceedings until the security had been given. The proceedings, so far as damages are claimed, are in the nature of an action for crim. con. to which the practice at common law is applicable.

THE COURT granted the application, unless the petitioner within a week withdrew the claim for damages.

Solicitors for petitioner: *Lewis & Lewis.*

Solicitor for co-respondent: *J. C. Stogdon.*

W. P.

[7 Probate Division, 228.]

June 6, 1882.

*WIGNEY v. WIGNEY.   [228

Variation of Settlements—Lis Pendens—Rights of Third Parties—Charge for Solicitor's Costs.

Upon a petition for variation of settlements, the court has power to make an order in favor of the interests of third parties created before the filing of that petition.

Until a decree has been made for dissolution of a marriage, there is no *lis pendens* with reference to the property included in the marriage settlements.

Before a decree *nisi* was made for dissolution of the marriage, the respondent had charged his interest under the marriage settlement with payment of his solicitor's costs of suit:

Held, that, under the circumstances, the charge was valid and that the respondent's interests could not be extinguished without providing for this charge.

THIS was a petition for variation of settlements, and involved a question as to the validity of a charge affecting a respondent's interests and made before the decree *nisi* in the action.

The parties were married on the 16th of December, 1863. The husband had, at the time of the marriage, an appointment in the Indian Staff Corps, which he then resigned, and retired upon half-pay amounting to £120 a year. This remained his sole income. The wife was possessed of £40,000, which was settled as follows: The income of £15,000, amounting to £948, was given to the respondent for life, and the income of £25,000, amounting to £1,165 to the petitioner for life. The wife had, in the event which had happened, of no issue, the right to appoint the whole fund absolutely; but there was an absolute right in the fund to the husband in default of her appointment. The husband had borrowed the sum of £4,200 on mortgage of his life interest under the settlement and of certain policies of assurance upon his life. The interest on the mortgage amounted to £210 a year, and the premiums on the policies to £120 a year. The whole of the £4,200 had been spent by the husband upon their joint establishment.

The wife subsequently petitioned for a dissolution of marriage by reason of her husband's cruelty and adultery. The petition came on for hearing on the 2d of July, 1880, and on that day and before the action was heard, the respondent had charged his interest under the settlements with pay-
229] ment of his costs of the *action. The court made a decree *nisi* on the 2d of July, which was made absolute on the 11th of January, 1881.

The petitioner petitioned for a variation of the settlements by extinguishing the respondent's interests as if he were then dead, and the court made an order accordingly, but without prejudice to the rights of the mortgagees, and this order was confirmed upon appeal, *ante*, p. 177.

At the time when this order was made, the question now for consideration, viz., as to the charge in favor of the solicitors, was reserved by consent.

Inderwick, Q.C., and *Middleton*, for the petitioner: The solicitors are not entitled to the benefit of this charge. At the time when they took it they were aware that the respondent's interests in the settlement would be entinguished and therefore had notice of the petitioner's rights. Those rights were then in existence, for there was a *lis pendens* as to them, and if so they would be affected by it: Sugden on

Vendors (ed. 1862), p. 758; *Bellamy* v. *Sabine* (').   This is
the proper tribunal to decide the question.   The Judicature
Act, 1873, s. 24, subs. 4 and 7, and the interpretation
clause (').   This is an equitable right (if any), which a court
of the Chancery Division would have recognized if the suit
had been instituted there, and, if so, this court is bound to
consider such equitable claim.

Farwell, for the solicitors: The court's jurisdiction in
this matter is restricted to an order for the benefit of the
children *and parents, 22 & 23 Vict. c. 61, s. 5 ('),   [230
and cannot interfere with any other charge.   The charge
does not arise until after the decree absolute, and the order
cannot be retrospective so as to regard things previously
done: *Paul* v. *Paul & Farquhar* (').   A prisoner may before conviction make a valid assignment of any of his property: *Perkins* v. *Bradley* ('); *Chowne* v. *Baylis* (').   The
lis pendens only referred to the principal matter of the suit,
viz., the right to a dissolution of the marriage.   It cannot
affect the rights of third parties, or at all events, rights acquired prior to the decree.

Cur. adv. vult.

June 6.   THE PRESIDENT: The decree *nisi* pronounced
on the 2d of July, 1880, for the dissolution of the marriage
of these parties by reason of the cruelty and adultery of the
respondent was made absolute on the 11th of July, 1881.
On the 2d of February Mrs. Wigney filed a petition for the
variation of the settlement made on her marriage.

By that settlement (of the 18th of September, 1863) the
petitioner's fortune was settled as to certain property, the
income of which amounted to £948 7s. 2d. to pay upon
trust the same to the respondent and his assignees during

(¹) 1 De G & J., 566.
(²) Sub-section 4: The said courts respectively . . . . shall recognize and take
notice of all equitable . . . . rights . . .
appearing incidentally in the course of
any cause or matter in the same manner
in which the Court of Chancery would
have recognized and taken notice of the
same . . . . before the passing of this
act.
Sub-sect. 7: The High Court of Justice and the Court of Appeal respectively,
in the exercise of the jurisdiction vested
in them by this act, in every cause or
matter pending before them respectively,
shall have power to grant and shall grant,
either absolutely or on such reasonable
terms and conditions as to them shall

seem just, all such remedies whatsoever
as any of the parties thereto may appear
to be entitled to in respect of any and
every legal or equitable claim properly
brought forward by them respectively in
such cause or matter, so that as far as
possible, all matters so in controversy between the said parties respectively, may
be completely and finally determined, and
all multiplicity of legal proceedings concerning any of such matters avoided.
Interpretation clause: Matter shall include every proceeding in the court, not
in a cause.
(³) See *post*, p. 760.
(⁴) Law Rep., 2 P. & D., 96.
(⁵) 1 Hare, 219.
(⁶) 31 Beav., 351.

his life, and after his death to pay the same to the petitioner for her life, and as to certain other property, the income of which amounted to £1,165 2s. 5d. to pay the same to the petitioner for life, and on her death to the respondent and his assigns for life, and after the death of the survivor as to both funds in trust for the children of the marriage, and if none, in trust as the petitioner should by will appoint, and in default of appointment for the respondent absolutely.

The respondent, who brought no property into settlement and is possessed of no income, beyond a pension of £120 as a retired captain in the army, borrowed £4,200 on the security of his life interest. On the day on which the decree *nisi* was pronounced, but before it was pronounced, the respondent executed a further mortgage of his life interest to his solicitors, Messrs. Saunders & Stokes, for £215 and such further sum as they might become entitled to have in respect of the divorce suit.

On the hearing of the petition for variation of the settle-
231] ments I *directed that the interest of the respondent in the settled property should be extinguished, but without prejudice to the mortgagees for £4,200. The question of the rights of the respondent's solicitors under their mortgage was not then before me, but was reserved at the instance of the parties. I have now been called upon by the petitioner to declare that the derivative interest, if any, of Messrs. Saunders & Stokes in the property settled is determined by the extinguishment of the respondent's interest.

The authority under which the court is called upon to act is conferred by the 5th section of 22 & 23 Vict. c. 61, by which it is enacted "that the court after a final decree of nullity or dissolution of marriage may inquire into the existence of ante-nuptial or post-nuptial settlements made on the parties whose marriage is the subject of the decree, and may make such order with reference to the application of the whole or a portion of the property settled either for the benefit of the children of the marriage or of their respective parents as the court shall deem fit." I think that under this enactment the court has the power to make an order which may affect the interests of third parties created before the institution of proceedings for variation of the settlement. For example, I have in a case, which I believe is not reported, made an order in favor of a husband, although it prejudiced the rights acquired by a co-respondent by his marriage with the guilty wife, and other cases of a like kind may be imagined, but as a rule it appears to me that the court is bound to respect the rights of mortgagees cre-

ated before the petition for variation of the settlements is
presented, and I acted on this principle in the present case.
The Court of Appeal went even further, and ordered that
the wife should pay unsecured debts which have been incurred by the husband in keeping up the household while
the parties lived together, a question which had not been
raised before me.

I have then to consider whether I ought to deprive Messrs.
Saunders & Stokes of the security for their costs, which
they obtained from the respondent on the day the decree
nisi was pronounced.   I am asked to declare that the interests of these gentlemen is already determined by the order
extinguishing the husband's interests, but it is clear that I
cannot do this because this question was expressly reserved,
and it must be decided upon *the merits as though   [232
they had been investigated at the time of the original hearing of the petition for variation of the settlements.

It was urged on behalf of the petitioner that there was at
the time of the creation of this charge a *lis pendens* with
reference to the settlements, of which the solicitors of the respondent had express notice, but I think that this argument
fails as there was not and could not be any *lis pendens* as
to the settlements until the dissolution of the marriage.

The question must therefore be considered upon such general principles as may appear applicable to this peculiar
power with which the court is invested.   All the circumstances must be taken into account.   If the life interest of
the respondent had extended to the whole income derived
from the wife's property, and he had attempted to deprive
her of all benefit from that property during his life, I should
have thought myself justified in preferring the interest of
the wife, at least to some extent, to that of the husband's
creditors, but here the petitioner is in possession of a considerable income altogether independent of her husband.
The husband had no means of his own with which to pay
his solicitors' costs.   The case therefore bears some analogy
to that of a wife who is without the means of defending herself in a suit for dissolution of her marriage to this extent
at least, that I do not think I ought to deprive the solicitors
who have not been guilty of misconduct of a security for
their reasonable costs given by the husband in the exercise
of the legal right of which he was possessed at the time.
The charge of cruelty on which the petitioner's success in
the suit depended was not one to which the solicitors could
see there could be no defence.

I think, therefore, that in taking the security offered them

by their client the solicitors cannot be deemed to have done
anything inequitable towards the petitioner, although it is
possible that they may have anticipated that her interests
would be affected by the security they acquired.

I therefore refuse the application.

Solicitors for petitioner: *Ayrton & Biscoe.*
Solicitors for mortgagees: *Stokes, Saunders & Stokes.*

W. P.

[7 Probate Division, 233.]

July 18, 1882.

233]   *MASON v. MASON and McCLUNE.

Dissolution of Marriage—Unreasonable Delay.

A husband in 1878 obtained a judicial separation and £50 damages by reason of
his wife's adultery. The wife continued to cohabit with the adulterer, and the husband in 1882 petitioned for a dissolution of his marriage:
Held, that he had been guilty of unreasonable delay. Petition dismissed.

THIS was a petition for dissolution of marriage by reason
of the adultery of the respondent and co-respondent.

The petitioner and respondent were married in 1871, and
in 1875 the respondent committed adultery with the co-respondent, who was in partnership with the petitioner as a
baker. This the petitioner forgave, but they again committed adultery, and in 1878 the husband filed a petition for
dissolution of marriage and claimed damages. £50 were
awarded as damages but the petitioner at that time asked
only for a judicial separation, which was accordingly decreed. The respondent and co-respondent continued to live
together, and the petitioner now filed another petition, asking for a dissolution of his marriage by reason of the adultery
committed since the last suit. The petitioner explained
that he had not asked for a dissolution of his marriage in
the previous action, because he then hoped that his wife
would return to live with him. It also appeared that if he
had made inquiries at any time after the first suit he might
have ascertained that his wife was cohabiting with the co-
respondent.

C. A. Middleton appeared for the plaintiff.

THE PRESIDENT: The facts of the case raise a novel question, but the objection that has occurred to my mind has
not been displaced. The petitioner in 1878 asked for a decree of judicial separation instead of that to which he would
have been entitled, viz., a decree for dissolution of his mar-

riage, and now in 1882, having taken no steps in the meantime with a view to induce his wife to break off her connection with the co-respondent, he asks for a decree *nisi*. He gives as his reason for not having before sought for such decree that he had hopes of inducing his wife to *come [234 back to him. I cannot regard his reason as one which is to extend for an indefinite time, until he should alter his mind, and having regard to the fact that this is the only ground on which he seeks to excuse his delay, I must dismiss his petition, as in my judgment the circumstances of the case show him to have been guilty of unreasonable delay.

Petition dismissed.

Solicitors for petitioner : *Gregory, Rowcliffes & Co.*, agents for G. E. Pickering, Leeds.

W. P.

[7 Probate Division, 234.]

May 23, 1882.

PERCIVAL v. CROSS and Others.

Probate—Infants—Guardian ad litem.

When a will is disputed by a guardian *ad litem* on behalf of infants, the Court of Probate has power to inquire whether the suit is for their benefit.

THIS was an action for probate of the will, dated the 18th of June, 1880, of Walter Percival, late of Mile End New Town, horsehair manufacturer, deceased.

The deceased left him surviving his widow and three children, two of whom were minors and one an infant; and by the will in question he had given certain legacies to his widow and children, and directed that his business should be carried on for their benefit. Joseph Percival, a paternal uncle, had obtained an appointment of himself as guardian *ad litem* of the infants, and as such had denied the validity of the will, and propounded an earlier will, which, amongst other things, directed that the business should be sold immediately after the death of the testator.

Bayford, for Matilda Percival, the mother, who had obtained an order adding her as a defendant, moved to supersede the order appointing a guardian. The affidavits show that the uncle is not a proper person to be appointed guardian, and that the suit is not for the benefit of the infants. He cited Daniell's Chancery Practice, vol. i, p. 69.

Searle, for defendants, the executors of the later will.

Fillan, for plaintiff.

1882   Bradley v. Bradley.

235]   *THE PRESIDENT ordered that it be referred to one of the registrars to report whether the action is for the benefit of the infants, and if so to appoint another guardian *ad litem.*

Solicitors for plaintiffs: *Hatchett, Jones & Letcher.*
Solicitors for defendants, the executors: *T. Beard & Son.*
Solicitor for Matilda Percival: *W. Playters Moore.*

W. P.

[7 Probate Division, 237.]

June 6, 1882.

237]   *BRADLEY V. BRADLEY.

Dissolution of Marriage—Maintenance—Dum Casta Clause.

A deed had been executed securing a maintenance for the wife after the decree absolute. The deed did not contain a *dum casta* clause:

Held, that the court had no power to set aside the deed by reason that the wife was no longer chaste.

THIS was a motion that a deed providing an annuity to the petitioner on the dissolution of her marriage might be cancelled, by reason that since the execution of the deed she had ceased to be chaste.

On the 30th of November, 1877, the petitioner (the wife) had obtained a decree absolute for dissolution of her marriage, and by order of the court a deed was, on the 29th of July, 1878, executed between the parties and a trustee, whereby the respondent secured to the petitioner an annuity of £100. The deed had been settled by one of the conveyancing counsel of the Chancery Division, and did not contain the *dum casta* clause.

April 20. *Dr. Tristram,* Q.C., for the respondent. moved that the deed be delivered up to be cancelled. The affidavits show that the petitioner has been unchaste, and it was never intended that the respondent should be bound to contribute to her support after she ceased to be chaste: *Fisher* v. *Fisher* (¹); *Chetwynd* v. *Chetwynd* (²).

Dr. Swabey, contrà: The charge of unchastity is denied, but it is not necessary to consider this as the court has no power in the matter. This is not an application to vary an order of the court, but to set aside a deed: *Narracott* v. *Narracott and Heskett* (³); *Gladstone* v. *Gladstone* (⁴).

Dr. Tristram, in reply.

Cur. adv. vult.

(¹) 2 S. & T., 410.   (²) 4 S. & T., 76.
(²) Law Rep., 1 P. & D., 39.   (⁴) 1 P. D., 442.

June 6. SIR J. HANNEN (The President): The marriage between the parties was dissolved on the 20th of November, 1877, on the ground of the husband's cruelty and adultery. The respondent *was afterwards ordered to secure to [238 the petitioner £100 a year for permanent maintenance ; and it was referred to one of the conveyancing counsel of the Court of Chancery to settle and approve a proper deed for the purpose. The deed prepared by counsel did not contain a clause that the provision should be payable only so long as the wife should remain chaste, and I refused to order that such a clause should be inserted. The deed was executed on the 29th of July, 1878. It is now asserted that the petitioner has since the execution of the deed led an immoral life, and I am asked on that ground to cancel the deed.

It was objected on behalf of the petitioner, without admitting the charge of unchastity, that I have not the power to cancel the deed, and I am of opinion that this contention is well founded. The deed was settled in accordance with what I believe to be the practice of conveyancing counsel in such cases, and if I was wrong in refusing to order a *dum casta* clause to be inserted in the deed, that should have been made the subject of appeal at the time. But the deed once executed, in the absence of fraud, it became binding according to its terms. I should add that if any ground for setting aside the deed, on the ground that it did not express the intention of the parties, had been established, this would fall within the description of business assigned to the Chancery, and excluded from the jurisdiction of this, Division.

The application must be rejected, with costs.

Solicitors for petitioner : *Shaen, Roscoe & Massey.*
Solicitors for respondent : *Nash & Field.*

R. A. P.

[7 Probate Division, 239.]

July 27, 1882.

*HOCKLEY and Others v. WYATT.   [239

Will—Proof in solemn Form—Rule 41—*Costs—Residuary Legatee under prior Will.*

The rule and practice by which a party may compel proof of a will in solemn form, without liability for costs, do not extend to a residuary legatee under a prior will.

THIS was an action propounding the will, dated the 24th of December, 1881, of Jane Platt Walton, who died on the 28th of December following.

The plaintiffs were the executors, and probate was opposed by the defendant, who was one of the residuary legatees of a prior will of the deceased. The defendant denied the due execution of the will, and the capacity of the deceased at the time, and alleged that the deceased did not know and approve of the contents of the will, and with his statement of defence he also delivered a notice under Rule 41 of the Rules and Orders of the 20th of July, 1862 (').

At the hearing the court pronounced for the will.

J. G. Witt, for the plaintiffs: The defendant ought to be condemned in costs. The notice is no protection to a legatee under a former will. The practice of the Prerogative Court, to allow a party to put the other side upon proof of a will in solemn form without liability for costs, never extended beyond a next of kin or an executor of a former will who had already proved that will: *Boston* v. *Fox* (') ; *Leeman* v. *George & Rosser* (') ; Williams on Executors, 8th ed. p. 344.

Bayford, for the defendant: The practice does extend to a residuary legatee, but if it does not the circumstances of 240] this *case are such that the court ought not to condemn the defendant in costs.

THE PRESIDENT: This question has been before me on previous occasions, but has not yet been the subject of judicial decision. I have now had my attention directed to the authorities, and it seems to me that, according to the practice of the Prerogative Court by which I am bound, the privilege of putting an executor to proof in solemn form without liability to costs was not extended to a legatee under a previous will. I therefore hold that the notice given by the defendant affords him no protection.

His Lordship thereupon reviewed the facts of the case, and came to the conclusion that each party should pay his own costs.

Solicitors for the plaintiffs: *Sharland & Hatton.*

Solicitor for the defendant: *T. Sismey*, for a Tolhurst, Gravesend.

(') In all cases the party opposing a will may, with his plea, give notice to the party setting up the will that he merely insists upon the will being proved in solemn form of law, and only intends to cross-examine the witnesses produced in support of the will, and he shall thereupon be at liberty to do so, and shall be subject to the same liabilities in respect of costs as he would have been under similar circumstances according to the practice of the Prerogative Court.

(') 29 L. J. (P. & M.), 68.

(') Law Rep., 1 P. & D., 542.

R. A. P.

[7 Probate Division, 240.]

April 25, 1882.

THE VESTA (1881, C. No. 6064, fol. 12).

Damage—Compulsory Pilotage—London Trinity House District—Foreign Vessels carrying Passengers from London to Hamburgh—Pilotage Act, 1825 (6 Geo. 4, c. 125), s. 59—Pilotage Amendment Act, 1853 (16 & 17 Vict. c. 129), s. 21—Order in Council, February 18th, 1854—Merchant Shipping Act, 1854 (17 & 18 Vict. c. 104), ss. 353, 370, 376, 388—Harbors and Passing Tolls Act, 1861 (24 & 25 Vict. c. 47), s. 10.

Sections 353 and 376 of the Merchant Shipping Act, 1854, render foreign vessels trading with cargo and passengers from the port of London to ports between Boulogne and the Baltic subject to compulsory pilotage on their outward passages between London and Gravesend, unless their masters or mates have pilotage certificates from the London Trinity House; and the operation of these sections, so far as such vessels are concerned, is not affected either by the Order in Council of February 18th, 1854, or by the provisions contained in the Harbors and Passing Tolls Act, 1861.

The Hanna (Law Rep., 1 A. & E., 283) followed.

THIS was an action of damage instituted on behalf of the owner, master, and mate of the sailing barge Audacious against the German steamship Vesta. The plaintiffs, in their statement of claim, after alleging that on the 27th of September, 1881, the Vesta coming down the *Thames under steam had run into and damaged [241 the Audacious, and attributing blame for the collision to those on board the Vesta, claimed judgment against the defendants, the owners of the Vesta.

The defendants delivered a statement of defence, of which the 1st, 2d, and 3d paragraphs were, so far as material, as follows:

1. The Vesta, a German screw steamship, 623 tons register, of which the defendants are the owners, left Horselydown, in the river Thames, shortly after noon on the 27th of September, 1881, manned by a crew of twenty-three hands and a pilot, and a general cargo and passengers, bound to Hamburgh.

2. About 1.30 P.M. of the same day, the Vesta, on her way down the river, was in the lower part of Blackwall Reach, a little to the south of midstream, heading straight down the reach, and making from three to four knots an hour through the water under steam alone.

3. About the same time the Audacious was observed half a mile ahead of and a little on the starboard bow of the Vesta, sailing up the river with her sails full. When the Audacious was close to the Vesta she headed across the

act abolishes all differential dues, and that to impose pilotage on foreign vessels where it is not imposed on British vessels would be to impose a differential due.

I will deal first with the contention of the plaintiffs founded upon the act of Geo. 4 and the Order in Council of February, 1854. The 6 Geo. 4, c. 125, s. 59, provides that "the master of any collier, or of any ship or vessel trading to Norway, or to the Cattegat, or Baltic, or round the North 244] Cape, or into the White *Sea, on their inward or outward voyages, or of any constant trader inwards, from the ports between Boulogne inclusive and the Baltic (all such ships and vessels having British registers, and coming up either by the North Channel but not otherwise)"—whatever that may mean—"shall and may lawfully," and without being subject to any of the penalties imposed by that act, "conduct or pilot his own ship or vessel when and so long as he shall conduct or pilot the same without the aid or assistance of any unlicensed pilot or other person or persons than the ordinary crew of the said ship or vessel." The clumsy and careless language of this section leaves two important omissions, viz., no provision is made, first, for vessels trading *outwards* to the ports between Boulogne and the .Baltic ; secondly, for vessels coming inwards by the south channels ; the north being the only channel mentioned. The regulations for the extension of the then existing exemptions from compulsory pilotage annexed to and approved of by the Order in Council of the 18th of February, 1854, are headed : " Regulation for the extension of the exemptions from compulsory pilotage now existing under the provisions of the 59th section of the act 6 Geo. 4, c. 125, submitted by the Corporation of the Trinity House for the consideration of Her Majesty in Council, pursuant to the provision of the 21st section of the act 16 & 17 Vict. c. 129," and provide that, subject to the provisions contained in the 59th section of 6 Geo. 4, c. 125, in respect of the employment of unlicensed persons, exemption from compulsory pilotage shall be allowed to the masters.

> "Of ships and vessels trading to Norway, or to the Cattegat, or Baltic, or round the North Cape, or into the White Sea when coming up by the South Channels :
> "Of ships and vessels trading to ports between Boulogne (inclusive) and the Baltic on their outward passages, and when coming up by the South Channels:
> "Of ships and vessels passing through the limits of

any pilotage district on their voyages from one port to another port, and not being bound to any port or place within such limits nor anchoring therein."

The plaintiffs contended that the words "ships and ves- sels" *mean all ships and vessels foreign as well as [245 British. It is somewhat strange that no judicial decision as to the meaning of these words should have been given, but such I am informed and believe is the case. If the plain- tiffs' construction be right the Order in Council, which was evidently intended to remedy a defect, would have intro- duced a new one, inasmuch as if the exemptions in the Order in Council do apply to vessels not having a British register, the court would be bound to hold that a foreign vessel trading to ports between Boulogne and the Baltic is not under its provisions exempted from compulsory pilotage on her in- ward passage if she comes up the Thames by the North Channel; the exemptions in the Order in Council relating to traders to ports between Boulogne and the Baltic being expressly confined to vessels "on their outward passages and when coming up by the south channels;" and the ex- emption in the 59th section of 6 Geo. 4, c. 125, as to constant traders inwards from ports between Boulogne inclusive and the Baltic, expressly relating only to British ships. In other words, according to the construction put on the Order in Council by the plaintiffs, by the joint operation of the Order in Council and the 59th section of 6 Geo. 4, c. 125, a foreign ship to Hamburgh would be exempted from com- pulsory pilotage in the Thames on her outward passages, but would still be liable to compulsory pilotage on her inward passages when coming up by the North Channel. I am of opinion that this absurdity does not arise, and that the exceptions in this Order in Council do not apply to for- eign vessels, but that the words "ships and vessels," when used in the portion of the Order in Council I have read, must mean British ships and vessels, which alone are dealt with by the material portions of the 59th section of 6 Geo. 4, c. 125, to which section the Order in Council in question, so far as it relates to exemptions, is subsidiary, and of which it is explanatory. I think moreover that this was the opinion to which Dr. Lushington inclined in the cases of *The Earl of Auckland* (¹) and of *The Hanna* (²).

I now come to the second point relied upon by the plain- tiffs, namely, that all differential dues are abolished by the Harbors and Passing Tolls Act, 1861, and that a pilotage

(¹) Lush., 164.   (²) Law Rep., 1 A. & E., 283.

246] due imposed on *a foreign ship which is not imposed on a British ship would be a differential due and therefore has ceased to exist. The sections relied upon are the 2d, 10th, and 11th of the Harbors and Passing Tolls Act, 1861. By the 2d section the term "differential duties" is defined to include any dues, rates, or taxes levied on foreign ships, &c., which are not levied under like circumstances on British ships, and the plaintiffs' counsel contend that that term would include compulsory pilotage. To this argument I cannot accede. In the first place, the act of 1861 clearly did not contemplate the subject of compulsory pilotage at all, and it would be a very forced construction of the statute to hold that any legislation on that subject was indirectly effected by it. In the next place, the subject seems already disposed of by Dr. Lushington's judgment in the case of *The Hanna*([1]) already referred to. In that case reliance was placed on the expression contained in a convention of commerce between this country and Sweden. Dr. Lushington referring to 6 Geo. 4, c. 125, s. 59, as showing that the exemptions under that section could not apply to a vessel not having a British register, said: "But the plaintiffs would escape from this difficulty by invoking a convention of commerce and navigation made between this country and Sweden in March, 1826, that is to say, a few months before the passing of 6 Geo. 4, c. 125. The 2d section of the convention is as follows: 'British vessels entering or departing from the ports of the kingdoms of Sweden and Norway and Swedish and Norwegian vessels entering or departing from the ports of the United Kingdom of Great Britain and Ireland shall not be subject to any other or higher ship duties or charges than are or shall be levied on national vessels entering or departing from such ports respectively.' The plaintiffs contended that compulsory pilotage was a charge within the meaning of the above section of the convention, and, consequently, that notwithstanding anything in the 59th section of 6 Geo. 4, c. 125, Norwegian vessels could not be subjected to compulsory pilotage where British vessels were exempt. This view, however, seems to me untenable; the theory of the Legislature whether right or wrong must be taken to be that compulsory pilotage is not a charge upon 247] vessels, but rather a regulation *instituted for their benefit." With this opinion I entirely agree.

I have considered the argument founded on 59 Geo. 3, c. 54. It seems to me not to affect the question of compulsory pilotage, though it may perhaps refer to pilotage

([1]) Law Rep., 1 A. & E., 283.

dues where the legal necessity to take a pilot does not exist. Upon the whole, I am of opinion that the plaintiffs have failed to establish their position that the Vesta was not under compulsion of law to employ a pilot, and I must therefore order judgment to be entered for the defendants on the question of law.

Solicitors for plaintiffs: *J. A. & E. Farnfield.*
Solicitors for defendants : *Stokes, Saunders & Stokes.*

G. B.

[7 Probate Division, 247.]

May 2, 1882.

THE RONA (1881, C. No. 2117, fo. 243).

County Court—County Courts Admiralty Jurisdiction Act, 1868 (31 & 32 Vict. c. 71), *s.* 3—*County Courts Admiralty Jurisdiction Act Amendment Act,* 1869 (32 & 33 Vict. c. 51), *s.* 2—*Jurisdiction*—"*Claim in relation to the carriage of Goods in any Ship.*"

A court having county court admiralty jurisdiction under the County Courts Admiralty Acts, 1868 and 1869, has jurisdiction to try and determine an action at the suit of the holder of a bill of lading against a British ship to recover for a breach of the contract of carriage in the bill of lading, notwithstanding that it is shown to the court that at the time of the institution of the suit the owner of the ship proceeded against was domiciled in England or Wales.

The Cargo ex Argos (8 Eng. Rep., 103) and *The Alina* (31 Eng. Rep., 652) followed.

THIS was an action commenced in the City of London Court (admiralty jurisdiction) by a summons the material part of which was as follows :

"Whereas an action for damage to cargo has been instituted in this court on behalf of Messrs. Cole & Kirkman, of Liverpool, the legal holders of two bills of lading of cargo lately laden on board the ship Rona, against the owner or owners unknown of the said ship, now lying in the port of London, in the sum of £300 and costs, you are hereby summoned to enter an appearance in the said action within four clear days of the service hereof."

An appearance having been entered for the owners of the Rona *the action came on to be heard before the [248 judge of the City of London Court (Mr. Commissioner Kerr) on the 28th of April, 1881, and witnesses on behalf of the plaintiffs were then examined. From the evidence of these witnesses and from admissions made by the parties to the suit it appeared that the Rona had taken on board at New York a cargo of flour for delivery at the port of London under the terms of bills of lading, signed by the master of the Rona; that the cargo had arrived at the port of London, and had been delivered in a damaged condition, and that the plaintiffs were holders of the bills of lading, and sought to recover the damages they claimed by reason of the cargo having been delivered damaged in breach of the contract contained in the bills of lading. It further appeared to the satisfaction of the judge of the City of London Court that at the time of the institution of the suit a part owner of the Rona was domiciled in England.

After hearing counsel on behalf of the plaintiffs and defendants, the judge of the City of London Court disimissed the suit on the ground that he had no jurisdiction to entertain it.

The plaintiffs appealed.

April 28. The appeal came on to be heard.

For the purpose of the appeal it was taken as admitted that the owners of the Rona were domiciled in England, and that the appellants were holders of the bills of lading and entitled to sue for any breaches of the contract therein contained.

Myburgh, Q.C., and *W. R. Kennedy*, for the plaintiffs.
Bucknill, for the defendants.

The arguments sufficiently appear from the judgment.

Cur. adv. vult.

May 2. SIR ROBERT PHILLIMORE: This is an appeal from a decision of the judge of the City of London Court in an action *in rem* brought in the City of London Court by the holders of a bill of lading against the owners of the ship Rona, for damage to goods on board the Rona, alleged to have been caused by the negligence of the master during a voyage from New York to this country.

At the trial in the City of London Court it was contended 249] by *the defendants that the action was brought under the Admiralty Court Act, 1861, and the County Courts Admiralty Jurisdiction Act, 1868, and that therefore, as an owner of the Rona was domiciled in England, the City of London Court had no jurisdiction. The learned judge, who considered himself bound by the judgment in the recent case of *Allen* v. *Garbutt* ([1]), dismissed the action for want of jurisdiction, and the plaintiffs have appealed to this court.

It has been admitted, at least for the purposes of the appeal, that the owners of the Rona are domiciled in England, and that the jurisdiction of the City of London Court is the only question now to be decided. This question mainly

([1]) 6 Q. B. D., 165; 29 Eng. R., 542.

depends upon the construction to be put on the following sections in three several acts of Parliament. It is enacted by the 6th section of the Admiralty Court Act, 1861, that the High Court of Admiralty shall have jurisdiction over any claim by the owner or consignee or assignee of any bill of lading of any goods carried into any port in England or Wales in any ship, for damage done to the goods or any part thereof by the negligence or misconduct of or for any breach of duty or breach of contract on the part of the owner, mas-ter or crew of the ship, unless it is shown to the satisfaction of the court that at the time of the institution of the cause any owner or part owner of the ship is domiciled in England or Wales."

The 3d section of the County Courts Admiralty Jurisdic-tion Act, 1868, provides that any court having admiralty jurisdiction shall have jurisdiction and all powers and au-thorities relating thereto, to try and determine, subject and according to the provisions of this act, the following causes (in the act referred to as Admiralty causes) . . . "As to any claim for damage to cargo or damage by collision,— Any cause in which the amount claimed does not exceed three hundred pounds." Lastly, the 1st sub-section of the 2d section of the County Courts Admiralty Jurisdiction Act, 1869 (the full title of which act it is important to observe is " An act to amend the County Courts Admiralty Jurisdic-tion Act, 1868, and to give Jurisdiction in certain Maritime Causes") provides that "Any county court appointed or to be appointed to have admiralty jurisdiction shall have juris-diction, and all powers and authorities relating thereto, to try and *determine the following causes. . . . As [250 to any claim arising out of any agreement made in relation to the use or hire of any ship, or in relation to the carriage of goods in any ship, ... provided the amount claimed does not exceed three. hundred pounds. . . . ." The 3d section of the same act, provides that the jurisdiction con-ferred by the two acts of 1868 and 1869, may be exercised, either by proceedings *in rem* or by proceedings *in per-sonam.*

The appellants who were plaintiffs in the court below, contended that the action was brought under subs. 1 of s. 2 of the act of 1869, and that therefore it came within the ad-miralty jurisdiction of a county court, although in conse-quence of the exception in the 6th section of the Admiralty Court Act, 1861 (which I have already read), it would not have come within the jurisdiction of the High Court of Admiralty, unless brought thither by way of transfer, or by way of appeal.

I may say here, that the City of London Court by virtue of an Order in Council possesses the admiralty jurisdiction of a county court, and that all the law relating to the admiralty jurisdiction of county courts applies equally to the City of London Court.

I have been referred to several cases, which I have carefully examined, and which I think it expedient to mention in chronological order: *Everard* v. *Kendall* ('), decided in April, 1870; *The Dowse* ('), decided in June, 1870; *Simpson* v. *Blues* ('), decided in May, 1872, the decision in which it was admitted could now not be relied upon; *The Cargo ex Argos* ('), decided in the Admiralty Court in July, 1872, and on appeal, in February, 1873; *Brown* v. *The Master of the Alina* ('), decided in February, 1880; and, lastly, *Allen* v. *Garbutt* ('), decided in December, 1880.

The appellants supported their contention by citing the case of *The Cargo ex Argos* ('), a case which, like the present, arose on a bill of lading, and is so far directly in point, and *Brown* v. *The Master of the Alina* ('), which was decided in 1880 by the Court of Appeal and expressly approved of the case of *The Cargo ex Argos* ('). On the other **251]** hand the respondents, defendants in the *court below, contended that the action was brought, not under the act of 1869, but under the 3d section of the act of 1868, which section expressly mentions claims for "damage to cargo," and they argued that therefore as the High Court of Admiralty could have had no jurisdiction in such a cause (inasmuch as the owner's domicile was English), so neither can a county court have jurisdiction. They rely upon the authority of the case of *Allen* v. *Garbutt* ('), which, following the earlier cases of *Everard* v. *Kendall* (') and *The Dowse* ('), decided that an action for "necessaries" which had clearly been brought under the act of 1868, did not, where the owners of the ship were domiciled in England, come within the admiralty jurisdiction of a county court. It was alleged on both sides that these decisions in the cases of *Brown* v. *The Master of the Alina* (') and *Allen* v. *Garbutt* ('), are distinguishable, the former dealing with an action under the act of 1869, the latter with one under the act of 1868.

(¹) Law Rep., 5 C. P., 428.
(²) Law Rep., 3 A. & E., 135.
(³) Law Rep., 7 C. P., 290.
(⁴) Law Rep., 3 A. & E., 568; 5 Eng.
R., 552; 5 P. C., 134; 8 Eng. R., 103.

(⁵) 5 Ex. D., 227.
(⁶) 6 Q. B. D., 165.
(⁷) 6 Q. B. D., 165; 29 Eng. R., 542.
(⁸) 5 Ex. D., 227; 31 Eng. R., 652.

It is not necessary to consider whether these cases are reconcilable or not, because in fact, the issue is narrowed to this point :—Was the action against the Rona brought under the act of 1868 alone, or under that of 1869, read and inter-preted as one with the previous act ? It appears to me to follow. from the arguments of the respondents, that the action could not properly have been brought under the act of 1868, and I am of opinion that this is "a claim arising out of an agreement made in relation to the carriage of goods in a ship," and that the action clearly falls within the words of subs. 1 of section 2 of the act of 1869.

I hold, therefore, that the City of London Court has jurisdiction, and that the appeal must be allowed.

Solicitors for plaintiffs ; *Pritchard & Sons.*
Solicitors for defendants : *Toller & Sons.*

CASES

DETERMINED BY THE

CHANCERY DIVISION

OF THE

HIGH COURT OF JUSTICE,

AND BY THE

CHIEF JUDGE IN BANKRUPTCY,

AND BY THE

COURT OF APPEAL

ON APPEAL FROM THE CHANCERY DIVISION AND THE CHIEF JUDGE

AND IN

LUNACY.

———•●•———

[11 Chancery Division, 701.]

V.C.M., March 29; April 5: C.A., Dec. 20, 1878; Jan. 14, 18, 20, 1879.

701]   **In re* GOLD COMPANY.

*Company—Winding-up—Petition by Shareholder for Compulsory Winding-up
after Resolution for Voluntary Winding-up—Companies Act, 1862, s. 145—
Division of unallotted Shares among Shareholders without Consideration—Reduction of Capital—Companies Act, 1867, ss. 9, 25.*

After a resolution has been passed for winding up a company voluntarily a shareholder cannot, as a general rule, obtain a compulsory order for winding up, or an
order for continuing the voluntary winding-up under supervision. The only exceptions to the rule are where the resolution has been passed fraudulently, or where
creditors appear to support the petition.

By the articles of association of a limited company the directors were authorized,
when it should appear to them that the capital for the time being subscribed was
sufficient for the purposes of the company, to allot the remaining unallotted shares
among the shareholders in proportion to the number of shares then held by them,
without receiving any money for them.

·When shares to the amount of one-fourth of the nominal capital had been allotted
and paid up, the directors allotted the remaining three-fourths, as fully paid up
shares, among the existing shareholders without further consideration; and the petitioner became a purchaser of some of these shares in the market. The company

passed a resolution for a voluntary winding-up, and afterwards the petitioner presented a petition for a compulsory winding-up:

Held, that the provision in the articles was highly improper; but that if it amounted to a fraud it was a fraud upon the petitioner in his individual capacity of purchaser of the shares, and was not committed by or upon the company, and, therefore, it was not within the scope of the Winding-up Acts to give relief in respect thereof. The petition for winding up was accordingly dismissed.

The decision of Malins, V.C., reversed.

THE Gold Company, Limited, was incorporated in November, 1873, for working gold mines in Wales, with a nominal capital of £100,000, divided into 100,000 shares of £1 each.

The 7th clause of the articles of association provided for the increase of the capital of the company by the issue of new shares.

The 11th clause was as follows : "The directors may allot and issue shares in the present capital, other than the shares mentioned in clause 7 hereof, to such persons, upon such terms, and at such times as they may think fit. If at any time it shall appear to the directors that the capital of the company for the time being subscribed will be sufficient for purposes of the company, they *may allot any shares [702 which then remain unallotted to and among the then shareholders in proportion to the number of shares respectively held by them, and such shares may be allotted as fully or partially paid-up shares, although no money may be received in respect of such shares from any allottee thereof."

By a contract in writing dated the 31st of December, 1873, and made between the company of the first part, certain persons named in the 1st schedule of the second part, and all the persons who were then shareholders of the company of the third part, it was agreed that certain shares should be allotted as fully paid-up shares to the parties of the second part in consideration of moneys stated to have been advanced by them for the benefit of the company.

This contract was duly registered on the 8th of January, 1874.

At the date of the contract only 2,375 shares had been allotted, and under the provisions of the contract 22,625 more were allotted, making together 25,000 shares.

On the 12th of January, 1874, the directors passed a resolution to the effect that in their opinion sufficient capital had had been subscribed for the purposes of the company, and they proceeded to allot the whole of the remaining 75,000 shares as fully paid-up shares, in pursuance of the 11th clause of the articles of association, to the then existing shareholders of the company in proportion to the number of shares held by them. This allotment was also registered.

Many of these gratuitous shares were sold in the market, and Mr. Carter, the present petitioner, bought 100 of them in March, 1875, at which time they were at a small premium.

The Stock Exchange having refused the company a settling day, and the mine having proved a failure, a resolution was passed on the 9th of May, 1877, to wind up the company voluntarily, and the secretary of the company was appointed liquidator. The meeting was duly advertised, but was attended by seventeen shareholders only out of 384. Of these seventeen, eleven voted for the winding-up, two against it, and four did not vote at all. No poll was demanded, and the chairman accordingly declared the resolution carried.

On the 23d of February, 1878, Mr. Carter presented the 703] *present petition for the compulsory winding-up of the company, which came on to be heard before Vice-Chancellor Malins on the 29th of March, 1878.

Higgins, Q.C., and *Oswald*, appeared for the petitioner.

Glasse, Q.C., and *Buckley*, for shareholders in support of the petition.

J. Pearson, Q.C., and *J. Wilkinson*, for the company.

Bristowe, Q.C., and *Deane*, for the principal part of the creditors and some of the shareholders.

MALINS, V.C.: The transactions of this company have been of a most extraordinary and unusual character. The articles and memorandum of association contain a power in the 11th clause which I have never seen before, and which certainly ought not to be found in any articles of association. I do not express any opinion whether this clause was inserted with a fraudulent intent, but it certainly is a clause which may very well be turned to fraudulent purposes. The course taken was this : According to the statements of the directors 18,775 shares only were taken up. The company was formed in November, and six weeks afterwards, when it was impossible for any one to form an opinion as to what capital would be necessary to work the mine, the directors hold a meeting, and they allot to every man who held shares three shares for every share so held, so that, for instance, Mr. Aspinall, who held 500, received 1,500 more shares. Mr. Attenborough, the chairman of the company, who held 575 shares, received an allotment of 1,725 shares, and so on, all receiving three free shares for every share held. What could have been the object of this transaction?

Is it possible to believe that it was intended to be a straight-forward and honorable dealing ? How did it work ? Every one of these men who had received the allotment was at liberty to go into the market and sell his shares. They even tried to get a settling-day on the Stock Exchange, but the committee of the Stock Exchange discovered the state of affairs and refused the application. However, *the [704 shares were extensively sold, and Mr. Carter, the petitioner, in consequence of the representations made as to the flourishing condition of this company, was induced, in the year 1875, to purchase from Mr. Edward Vickers, one of the gentlemen who signed the memorandum of association, 100 of these worthless shares of £1 each, at a premium of 9d., so that he gave £1 0s. 9d., for what was not worth a farthing. At this time the directors and others who sold the shares, and every one connected with the company must have been perfectly convinced that the thing was an utter failure, and that the company ought at that time to have been wound up. Then, in 1875, it appears by the banking account that the company was in a state of utter exhaustion. The balance against them was £122. In the succeeding year their total receipts were £124, and the balance against them £4 12s. 4d. In the year 1877 they commenced with a balance in hand of £35, and afterwards received £30 more, which was all paid away before the 9th of May, when a resolution was passed for a voluntary winding-up. The meeting for that purpose was composed of seventeen persons, of whom eleven voted in support of the resolution, two voted against it, and four declined to vote at all : still they had the requisite majority of three-fourths, because I must consider those who declined to vote as not being present, but the majority, as I collect, were persons who had been engaged in the original transaction, and who had adopted this most improper course of allotting to themselves three free shares for every one share. What, then, was their object in this transaction ? It must have been to screen themselves, and to blind the public, so far as the public had had dealings with them, and they appoint their own secretary, who has been their servant from the beginning, who had aided and abetted them in all these transactions ; they appoint him liquidator, and no wonder, therefore, they are desirous that the management of the liquidation should remain in his hands, for he will certainly take no step likely to be disagreeable to the directors, nor do anything for the benefit of the creditors.

One of the most extraordinary things in this case is that I have actually had counsel appearing for creditors opposing the petition, which, if acceded to, may give them something 705] and can cost them *nothing, since the creditors are not liable for the expenses of winding up.

The only conclusion I can come to upon this case is, that the directors who have been guilty of these practices are very desirous of keeping the winding-up in the hands of their friend the secretary, and thus to escape all investigation of the transactions which appears to me eminently to call for investigation, and of this I am quite certain, that the present liquidator will never make a proper investigation.

On the other hand, if I appoint a liquidator, he will look into all the transactions, and will see whether all the money stated to have been paid by these persons for their shares has in fact been paid, or whether they are not liable to pay something more for the shares they admit they had, even if the issue of the extra shares is valid.

The petition has been opposed on various grounds, amongst others, that I have no authority to make a compulsory order to wind up after a voluntary winding-up. I confess I am much inclined to look at that meeting which resolved upon the winding-up as a delusive meeting having no good faith in it, held, as it appears to me at present, mainly for the purpose of screening the directors, smothering the transactions of the company, and keeping them from investigation. But, however, it has been argued by Mr. Deane that I cannot do this in the face of the 145th section, which is in these words: "The voluntary winding-up of a company shall not be a bar to the right of any creditor of such company to have the same wound up by the court, if the court is of opinion that the rights of such creditor will be prejudiced by voluntary winding-up." It was very fairly urged that if a voluntary winding-up of a company shall not be a bar to the right of any "creditor" of such company, that means that it is a bar to the right of any person other than a creditor, and therefore that it is a bar to the right of a shareholder. But Mr. Higgins has drawn my attention to the authorities collected upon that section in Mr. Buckley's book (¹), from which it appears, and particularly by *In re Littlehampton, &c., Steam Company* (²), that it has not been the practice of the court to consider that as an absolute bar, 706] but to *look at all the surrounding circumstances, and if it sees that the resolution to wind up voluntarily has been obtained under such circumstances as to require further investigation, the court will make a compulsory order.

Then another point was that it was unnecessary to make

(¹) Page 278.   (²) 2 D. J. & S., 521.

such an order, because the remedy may be obtained under the 138th section, and that whatever they could get under a compulsory winding-up could be obtained under that section, which is, that "Where a company is being wound up voluntarily, the liquidators or any contributory of the company may apply to the court to determine any question arising in the matter of such winding-up, or to exercise, as respects the enforcing of calls, or in respect of any other matter, all or any of the powers which the court might exercise if the company were being wound up by the court; and the court, if satisfied that the determination of such question or the required exercise of power will be just and beneficial, may accede wholly or partially to such application on such terms," and so forth. I am satisfied that practically it will be impossible to have a proper investigation under any application on that section, and it will be utterly impossible, in my opinion, that any proper investigation of the transactions of this company can take place while the friendly liquidator remains in office, the servant of the men who have been guilty of these practices of which so much complaint has been made.

This case illustrates very forcibly the rule which I have, on the suggestion of my my chief clerks, founded on their experience, directed them to adopt, in no case whatever to appoint any official of the company liquidator. They are always under some improper influences, and you cannot get as fair an investigation in an impartial and proper manner from a secretary or even a co-director, as from a person who would be indifferent in the matter. Therefore, my great object in making the compulsory order which I intend to make in this case, is that I may have an impartial and indifferent liquidator, and I shall take care to select some man fully competent to do it, to investigate the affairs of this company, and to see whether the moneys which are alleged to have been paid by these directors have been paid; and to bring before the court in the proper manner the question of the liability on these *transactions, which are, in my opin- [707 ion, of the most blamable character. Whether they have incurred a liability or not, they are proceedings which no court can approve.

They are, in my opinion, so improper from the beginning to the end, that, if they were not fraudulent, they were calculated to be the means of fraud, and I am perfectly clear that they have been the means of fraud, when I find that they were the means of selling these shares at a premium at a time when everybody perfectly well knew that the company was in the last stage of decay and ruin.

On all these grounds, therefore, I make the usual order to wind up compulsorily, with the usual order as to costs.

From this order the company appealed. The appeal came on to be heard on the 20th of December, 1878.

J. Pearson, Q.C., and *J. Wilkinson*, for the appellants, and

Bristowe, Q.C., and *Deane*, for the creditors and shareholders: Our first objection to the petition is that the petitioner is a paid-up shareholder, and therefore cannot have any further liability. He has therefore no *locus standi* to obtain a winding-up order.

[The Court having intimated an opinion that this objection could not be sustained, they continued their argument.]

Another objection is, that a contributory who is not a creditor cannot obtain a compulsory winding-up order after a resolution for voluntary winding-up. The 145th section of the Companies Act, 1862, gives that power only to creditors: *In re Bank of Gibralter and Malta* ('). It is only under very exceptional circumstances that the court will interfere, on the application of a contributory, with a voluntary winding-up; for instance, where there has been fraud in obtaining the resolution, or where it is supported by the creditors, which is not the case here: *In re Beaujolais Wine Company* (*); *In re Imperial Bank of China* (*); *In re London and Mercantile Discount Company* (*); *In re* 708] *London *Flour Company* ('). An attempt has been made to show that the resolution to wind up was not duly passed; but the chairman certified the majority, and if it was disputed it ought to have been challenged at the time.

With respect to the merits of the case, there has been nothing fraudulent in the allotment of shares. Every one who purchased shares or dealt with the company had notice of the 11th clause of the articles, and of the contract of the 31st of December, 1873, which was duly registered. Nothing that was done altered the relations of the shareholders *inter se*.

Higgins, Q.C., and *Oswald*, for the petitioner: There are no negative words in the 145th section of the Companies Act, 1862, to prevent a contributory from obtaining a winding-up order after a resolution to wind up voluntarily; and the cases of *In re Littlehampton, &c., Steam Company* ('),

(') Law Rep., 1 Ch., 69.   (') Law Rep., 1 Eq., 277.
(') Law Rep., 3 Ch., 15.   (') 16 W. R., 474, 552.
(') Law Rep., 1 Ch., 339.   (') 2 D. J. & S., 521.

In re West Surrey Tanning Company ('), *In re Imperial Bank of China* ('), *In re Fire Annihilator Company* ('), and the cases referred to by the appellants, show that a resolution to wind up is not an insuperable bar to a compulsory order, but that the court has power to make such an order if the justice of the case requires it.

But should the court be of opinion that we have no *locus standi* to obtain a winding-up order, we are, at all events, entitled to an order to continue the winding-up under supervision. This is peculiarly a case in which the fullest investigation is necessary, which can never be obtained unless the winding-up is carried on under the control of the court. The insertion of the 11th clause of the articles was itself fraudulent ; it was a contrivance to evade the Companies Act, 1867, by issuing three-fourths of the shares of the company without consideration. Moreover, it was a device for reducing the capital of the company without complying with the provisions of the Companies Acts. It was also a fraud upon the purchasers of shares ; for the effect of the transaction was that none of the allottees paid more than one-fourth of the value of their shares ; in other words, they threw upon the *market, as fully paid-up £1 shares, [709 shares on which in fact only 5s. had been paid. The registration of the contract under the 25th section of the act of 1867 could not make a bad contract good. The whole transaction is tainted with fraud, and is one which the court will not support : *Society of Practical Knowledge v. Abbot* (') ; *New Sombrero Phosphate Company v. Erlanger* (').

In default of all other relief, we ask for permission to use the name of the liquidator in taking proceedings against the directors.

Buckley, for other shareholders, one of whom he stated to be also a creditor.

JAMES, L.J.: The first question raised on this appeal is a very important general question, far beyond the issue involved in the case before us, that is, whether the petitioner, being a shareholder, has a right to a compulsory order for winding up after a resolution for a voluntary winding-up has been passed by the company. If the matter were what we call *res integra*, I myself should have come to the conclusion, upon the construction of the act of Parliament, that the voluntary winding-up is a bar, or, to use Mr. Higgins', expression, an insuperable bar, to the making of a compul-

(¹) Law Rep., 2 Eq., 737.   (⁴) 2 Beav., 559.
(²) Law Rep., 1 Ch., 339.   (⁵) 5 Ch. D., 78 ; 21 Eng. Rep., 798 ;
(³) 32 Beav., 561.   S. C., 3 App. Cas., 1218 ; 24 Eng. R., 774.

sory order for winding-up. There is a clause in the act which provides that a voluntary winding-up shall be no bar to an application by a creditor for a compulsory winding-up, and *expressio unius* generally speaking *est exclusio alterius.* Beyond that, the act appears to contain a great number of provisions intended, and it seems to me calculated, to prevent any mischief which might otherwise arise from any wrong done to a shareholder by the voluntary winding-up. There have been several cases in the courts in which, notwithstanding that language in the act, a contributory has obtained an order for winding up after the commencement of a voluntary winding-up. The leading case, in my view of the subject, and the one which seems to me to establish the principle, is *In re West Surrey Tanning Company* (¹), where the court, in fact, came to the conclusion that the voluntary 710] winding-up, *or the resolution to wind up voluntarily, was, under the circumstances, a sham. There was one man whose conduct was impeached, whose dealings and transactions with the company required investigation, and he himself had a complete majority of votes, so that he could by his own votes have determined that no proceedings should be taken against himself, and that there should be no investigation into his dealings. I can conceive a case in which that might apply to the majority of the shareholders—that is to say, where the majority of the existing shareholders were so mixed up with the matters complained of and the matters requiring investigation, that the resolution of a general meeting would be a decision by an interested judge, if I may use the expression, by persons incompetent to decide by reason of their personal interest in the matter. I am of opinion that, to enable the court to make such an order as the Vice-Chancellor has made, the case must, at all events, be brought up to a case of that kind—that is to say, to a case in which, from the circumstances which have occurred, the court sees that the shareholders cannot be trusted to determine the matter for themselves. But I cannot find anything like that made out or even alleged in the present case; because, although all the shareholders at one time were parties to the transactions complained of, which I shall consider afterwards, the case of the petitioner is that there were dealings in the shares on the Stock Exchange, and there were transfers of shares, the result of which was that there are now several hundreds of shareholders, over 300, holding 40,000 or 50,000 shares in the company, every one of whom is in the

(¹) Law Rep., 2 Eq., 737.

same interest with the petitioner, and acquired his shares in the same manner, and has exactly the same ground of complaint as he has. I cannot find anything in this case to satisfy the court, or to entitle the court to say that it can deprive those shareholders, for they are persons interested, of the right which belongs ordinarily, and except under very exceptional circumstances, to the shareholders of every joint stock company or corporation of this kind, of determining amongst themselves, for themselves, by a majority, according to their view of what is most for their interest, what ought to be done or ought not to be done, either in the disposal of the property of the company, or in making any claims against any supposed *debtors to or persons [711 liable to the company. I am of opinion, therefore, that in this case there was no ground for a compulsory order to wind up.

That, however, does not dispose of the case, because it was suggested, and I think properly suggested, by Mr. Higgins, that although we could not grant, for those reasons, the order for a compulsory winding-up, there might be, and ought to be, some other less order. The petitioner asks, no doubt, for a compulsory winding-up, but he says he is entitled at all events to have what is called a supervision order, that is to say, an order for placing the matter under the supervision of the court, which would enable the court to do justice as between the different classes of shareholders, or some other order that he may use the name of the company in instituting proceedings to obtain relief. Therefore it is necessary to consider whether the petitioner is in this case entitled to any relief.

Now, for the purpose of this petition it seems to me that the material facts are few and undisputed. The deed of settlement certainly contains a most extraordinary provision, a provision which the Vice-Chancellor has denounced in very strong terms, and I am not prepared to differ from him with respect to it. But still it was one of the terms of the constitution of the company, and the petitioner became a shareholder in a company of which that was one of the terms and conditions. First of all it was intended to issue 25,000 shares, and that clause was one enabling the directors, if they thought fit, if they came to the conclusion that they did not want any more money, to issue 75,000 amongst the holders of the 25,000 shares. However, there is that provision, and it was carried into effect by an instrument duly registered within the provisions of the act, so as not to be obnoxious to the special provision, which requires that all shares shall be issued for money, and not otherwise, unless

by an agreement duly registered. By that instrument, all the persons then interested in the company being parties to it, a large number of shares were allotted for that which all the then shareholders considered to be a.sufficient consideration, partly for money, partly for services rendered, partly for debts or sums said to have been advanced to the company. At all events 25,000 shares were allotted to the then
712] *shareholders, and immediately after the execution of the contract the directors, in pursuance of the clause I have mentioned, allotted the remaining 75,000 shares between the holders of the 25,000 shares, that being done with the assent of the holders of the 25,000 shares who accepted the allotment. The fact of that allotment, and the circumstances under which it was made, were also registered so as to escape the provisions of the Companies Act. Whether it complied with the spirit of the act it is not for me to say. However, that was done.

What was the legal result of what was so done? All the persons interested in the company by this transaction in effect divided the property between themselves, in fractions of which the common denominator was 100,000. Of course where the shares are all paid up and nothing remains to be called, all the company has got is its property. Therefore, as I said, they divided the whole property between themselves, in fractions of which the denominator was 100,000. One can see a motive for it, of course, which I shall afterwards mention. Now upon whom was that a fraud, or to whom was it a wrong? It could not be a fraud upon, or a wrong to the existing shareholders, because every one of them was a party to the transaction. It could not be a fraud upon or a wrong to future shareholders—I mean in the sense of the allottees of shares—because the very essence of the transaction was that no more shares were to be or could be issued thereafter. It was no fraud upon or wrong to the existing creditors, if existing creditors there were, because it appears that if there were any existing creditors, they either were satisfied, or paid, or have acquiesced in what has been done, and *volenti non fit injuria.* It was no legal wrong to any future creditors, because by the transaction the most distinct notice was given to any person not a shareholder that he had no uncalled capital to look to, that there were no shares remaining to be issued, that there was to be no money derived either by the issue of shares, or by calls on existing shareholders, and if anybody chose to give credit under the circumstances to such a company, he was giving credit to the property of the company, whatever it was, just in the same way as a person gives credit to the Bank of England when he takes a £5 note, or to any other corporation which has all its capital paid up.

*Then what is the fraud upon or wrong to persons [713 like the petitioner who bought shares in the market? The petitioner got exactly what was offered to him. He got for the £100 which he gave the thousandth part of the mine as it stood. He derived his title in fact from and through the very transactions which are complained of, the shares being paid-up shares, most of which were obtained in that way. He obtained the shares from a person who was a party to the transaction which I have described, and he obtained them with full notice in point of law that every other shareholder in the company was in exactly the same position as himself, that is to say, that no shareholder was to pay anything, and that there were no shares to be issued, and therefore in that sense there was no wrong done to him. And in truth when his case, as alleged and proved by him, comes to be looked at, it is a case, as it seems to me, wholly outside the provisions for winding up companies. His case is, that by this mode of creating shares, by this mode of dealing with the shares, and by subsequent devices and practices—I will not say on the Stock Exchange, because the Stock Exchange refused to allow a settling-day—but by devices and practices in the stock market he was deluded into giving £100 for that which was not worth 100 farthings. The Vice-Chancellor used strong language, but I cannot help thinking that he did not use too strong language in describing what was done as against some of the persons connected with it. I cannot help thinking that it was intended by some persons or other connected with this transaction to call the capital £100,000 with a view of giving it a false reputation in the market, and inducing persons to think they were getting something of value when they were getting in fact that which was utterly valueless. But, then, that is a wrong done to each individual purchaser. Anybody who has been deluded, as this petitioner says he has been, into giving money for that which was an utter sham, or nearly so, has a ground of complaint to himself individually; it is a wrong done to him personally; it was not a wrong done by the company or to the company. It was not a wrong done by persons in a fiduciary character towards the company for whom they were trustees, but a wrong done by the individual, whoever he was, who deluded him into making the purchase, and by those persons who enabled that fraud *to be practised, who assisted in perpetrating the [714 fraud upon him, and against whom, therefore, he may have the relief which the law entitles him to have. But, as I repeat, that has nothing at all to do with winding up the company, either compulsorily or otherwise. It is not the function of a winding-up order to give remedies for wrongs connected with the dealing in shares, to give relief or redress to the man to whom the wrong is done by his being induced to become a shareholder, a wrong not done to him in his character of shareholder, not done to anybody whose shares he takes, but done to him in his character of a purchaser of shares in the market. Now that wrong is one for which, as I have said, he may have redress. There may be circumstances which might possibly have induced the public authorities to intervene in the matter, but it is not, according to my view, within the function of the Winding-up Act, nor within the province of this court to give relief under this act for the purpose of enabling such a complainant to get redress, or for the purpose of enabling him to investigate the books and documents or transactions of the company by way of discovery to assist him in making out his case against the persons against whom he has a case. In my opinion, therefore, this court cannot give him any relief whatever upon those principles.

I say nothing about the neglect, the length of time which elapsed before the petitioner presented his petition, though that would of itself have been a very important matter for consideration. I do not wish to weaken what I have said on the general principle by laying any stress upon the delay, but it would have been, I think, a very serious impediment in the way of his obtaining any relief on this petition that he allowed the voluntary winding-up to go on for nearly a year with full notice of what had been done, and allowed it to be completed before he took the proceedings which he has done. I therefore say that in my opinion the petition has failed, and that the order of the Vice-Chancellor ought to be discharged with costs.

Although all the persons are not before us, I do not feel any hesitation in concurring with the Vice-Chancellor in the hope that such a clause as the 11th clause, to which I have referred, will never again be inserted in articles of association, and that no such *transaction will again be resorted to, because if there was not actual fraud proved—and I do not like to say there was actual fraud in anybody connected with this transaction—if there was not actual fraud proved, the transaction was such as the Vice-Chancellor truly says was very likely to lead to fraud. I agree with

the Vice-Chancellor in expressing my strong disapproba-
tion of such machinery having been resorted to, which, at all
events, might have been the means, and not improbably was
the means, of fraud on those unwary persons who might
have been induced to buy in the market such things as they
did buy in this case for large sums of money.

BAGGALLAY, L.J.: The petitioner in this case is the holder
of 100 shares, all fully paid up, in the company which he
now seeks to have wound up under the order of the court.
There are one or two circumstances in the case which are
not at all in dispute which I will first allude to, because I
think they have a material bearing on the ultimate disposal
of the case. This company was incorporated in November,
1873. In June, 1875, the present petitioner acquired his
shares by purchase, having bought them in March, and
completed the purchase in June, 1875. The resolution for
a voluntary winding-up was passed in May, 1877; and it
was not till some time in the year 1878 that he presented
this petition. Now, whether he had or had not an opportunity of seeing the earlier balance-sheets which were published by the company, he must, at any rate, have had full
opportunity of seeing that which was made in 1876, and was
published and issued prior to the time when the voluntary
winding-up was resolved upon. He now comes before the
court alleging irregularities in the formation of the company, irregularities in the conduct of the business by the
directors, and irregularities as far as regards the obtaining
of the resolution for the voluntary winding-up. He says
that with regard to these allegations he has not sufficient
protection under the provisions of the 138th section of the
Companies Act, 1862, and he asks relief by the terms of his
petition in the form of a compulsory order for winding up;
but at the bar it has been urged upon us that he may be entitled either to a compulsory order, or, if not to a compulsory order, to a continuation of the voluntary winding-up
under *supervision, and, if to neither of those two, [716
that he is entitled to that which was granted in the case of
the *Imperial Bank of China*(') by the Lords Justices,
namely, leave to use the name of the voluntary liquidator,
indemnifying him, for the purpose of prosecuting such proceedings as he may be advised against the directors.

Now the petition was opposed on three grounds—first,
that he is a paid-up shareholder, all the shares he holds having been paid up in full; secondly, that being a contributory
he was not at liberty to present a petition for an order for

(') Law Rep., 1 Ch., 339.

compulsory winding-up, or for the continuation of the winding-up under supervision; and thirdly, on the general mertis of the case. The first ground of opposition, that he wast he holder of fully paid-up shares, was taken as a preliminary objection, and was then disposed of. Though, no doubt, a shareholder who has paid up in full may, under certain circumstances, present a petition, and obtain a winding-up order from the court, there must be very special circumstances shown for that purpose, as, for instance, that by the course which is suggested there may possibly be something to be returned to the shareholder, or to him and to other shareholders. As regards the second ground of objection, namely, that the petitioner being a contributory, and there being a voluntary winding-up, that voluntary winding-up is a bar to his presenting a petition for a compulsory winding-up, I entirely agree with what the Lord Justice has just now said, and if the matter were *res integra*, I should be very much disposed to hold that it was a bar to his presenting a petition for a compulsory winding-up or for a supervision order. But there is authority for saying that it is not a bar. In the case of *In re Bank of Gibraltar and Malta* (¹) Lord Justice Turner expressed a very strong opinion that it was not within the jurisdiction of the court to entertain a petition presented by a contributory after there had been a voluntary winding-up; since that case the question has frequently arisen; every important case on this subject is, I think, referred to in Mr. Buckley's very able and very useful book, of which I am happy to find there is a new edition bringing it down to the present time; and the result of the cases appears to be this, that 717] the court will not entertain a petition *from a contributory after there has been a voluntary winding-up unless it is shown that there has been fraud. There may be special circumstances, perhaps not amounting to fraud in the ordinary and everyday meaning of the word, but which are yet almost equivalent to fraud, and show that there ought to be a compulsory order. There were such circumstances in the case of *In re Fire Annihilator Company* (²). In that case the voluntary winding-up had been going on for five years, and nothing had been done satisfactory under it, and therefore the court treated it as if there had been no voluntary winding-up at all, and made a compulsory order. The case that was relied upon by the Vice-Chancellor as one which supported his decision in granting the winding-up order on the present application was that of *In re Little-*

(¹) Law Rep., 1 Ch., 69.   (²) 32 Beav., 561.

hampton Steam Packet Company (¹), but in that case the petition was presented before even the preliminary steps had been taken for obtaining a voluntary winding-up, though the resolution for the voluntary winding-up was passed before the compulsory order was made.

As regards the case of *In re West Surrey Tanning Company* (²), I have looked into the facts, and I find that a petition for a compulsory winding-up was presented in the interval between the first resolution for a voluntary winding-up and the meeting at which that resolution was confirmed; and therefore the court had obtained jurisdiction over the case before there had been any complete voluntary winding-up. But even in that case there were special circumstances which I think would have justified the interference of the court, namely, that the voluntary winding-up had been obtained, if not by fraudulent means within the ordinary intent and meaning of the word, yet by an overpowering body of shareholders acting under the influence of a single person. But I think the answer to any argument based upon *In re West Surrey Tanning Company* is this, that the court had commenced its jurisdiction in the matter before there had been a complete voluntary winding-up resolution. A suggestion was made by Lord Justice James in the course of the argument, which I think is one of considerable weight, namely, that if you make a compulsory order for winding-up upon the petition of a contributory after a voluntary *winding-up has been resolved upon, you have this [718 difficulty, although no doubt it is a difficulty you might have equally to deal with on a creditor's petition, namely, that you have a different period for the commencement of the winding-up. The voluntary winding-up dates from the time the first resolution is passed, but the compulsory winding-up dates from the time when the petition is presented, which certainly is an inconvenience not unnecessarily to be incurred. Therefore, though I do not think it necessary to express any decided opinion on the present occasion as to whether a contributory, after a voluntary winding-up has been resolved upon, can present a petition for a compulsory winding-up of the company, I still desire to intimate a very strong bias in my own mind at the present time in favor of the view that no such petition can properly be presented. But I think there is quite sufficient to dispose of this case without relying on that objection.

I think, also, that the objections are equally great to a contributory obtaining a supervision order, and this view

(¹) 2 D. J. & S., 521.   (²) Law Rep., 2 Eq., 787.

has been from time to time acted upon. After there has been a resolution for a voluntary winding-up, it has always been held that a contributory must prove some very special circumstances before he can obtain a supervision order.

It has, however, been pressed upon us that cases have occurred in which a petition by a contributory for a compulsory order after a voluntary winding-up has been listened to and acted upon by the court, but it will be found that those have been cases in which creditors have appeared and have supported the petition for the winding-up; and in those cases, possibly for the purpose of saving the necessity of dismissing one petition and causing another to be presented immediately afterwards, the court has more than once made an order for a compulsory winding-up, although the creditor has not actually joined in the petition. In this case Mr. Buckley, suggesting that he appeared for a creditor, asked us to consider that the petition was supported by a creditor, but we can only deal with the order under appeal, and on the face of that order Mr. Buckley is only entered as appearing for shareholders supporting the petition and not on behalf of any creditor.

As regards the general merits of the case, I do not consider it necessary after what has been said by the Lord Justice to go *through the circumstances in detail. I have already pointed out that the petitioner was for three years a shareholder in the company before he thought fit to present the present petition, and that he did not present it until nearly a twelvemonth after the time when the resolution for a voluntary winding-up was passed.

As I have already mentioned, he had the fullest opportunity of knowing the whole of the circumstances of the company. He purchased 100 shares in the company; he did not think it necessary to look at the articles of association for the purpose of seeing what powers the directors had and what they might have done under those powers. I do not think he has pledged his oath to the fact that he did not know of all these facts, but on the assumption that he was ignorant, he was only ignorant by reason of his own carelessness. Then is he the person to come here and complain of what has taken place? I cannot think that he is. Assume that but for his own conduct there was the fullest power and jurisdiction to come here and to ask either for a compulsory order or for a supervision order, it seems to me that he is barred by his own laches and by his own conduct from coming forward to raise these questions, assuming the irregularities charged by him to have been substantiated.

With regard to these irregularities, he says that the resolution for a voluntary winding-up ought not to stand in his way, because it was obtained by fraud. Well, if the resolution for a voluntary winding-up had been obtained by fraud, and if that fraud had been clearly proved, I am by no means certain that this would not be a case in which the court would entertain his petition and grant relief. But what are the facts? He first of all endeavored to establish a technical objection that the requisite majority of three-fourths had not been obtained. He was, however, precluded from taking this objection by the terms of the section of the act of Parliament, which says that where a poll is not demanded, there the decision of the chairman that the resolution has been carried is to be quite sufficient without any proof of the number of voters or the proportion of their votes. Had a poll been demanded, the voting would have been by a numerical calculation of the votes held by the various shareholders. Possibly there was a very sufficient reason why at that meeting no poll was demanded, apart from the question that it *requires five shareholders to demand a poll, [720 and he could not succeed in finding as many as five to support his views.

We must also bear in mind that there were only seventeen shareholders present at this meeting, and there were over 300 shareholders in the company, who for some reason or other did not think it necessary to attend the meeting. They knew what the meeting was summoned for, because the Companies Act, 1862, requires that when a meeting is convened for the purpose of winding up a company, that must be expressly stated in the notice summoning the meeting. I think we may fairly assume that they were indifferent to what was to be done. I think, therefore, that any allegations to the effect that there were irregularities with respect to obtaining the winding-up resolution are entirely displaced by the evidence.

There is one other matter to which I would refer. It was suggested that if the petitioner was not entitled to a compulsory order, or to a winding-up under supervision, he was at least entitled to have leave to prosecute proceedings against the directors, and, upon giving an indemnity, to use the name of the liquidator for the purpose. I think that this court would grant relief of this kind when a proper case was made for it. A proper case was considered to be made for it in the case of *In re Imperial Bank of China* ([1]). But where are the circumstances in this case to authorize any

([1]) Law Rep., 1 Ch., 339.

such proceedings being taken. In all probability it was a suggestion of counsel after the petition was presented, and after it was brought on in court. I do not know that such a course is now open to the petitioner, still, if he is able to satisfy the Vice-Chancellor by an application under the 138th section of the Companies Act, he may possibly obtain leave to do that if any proper case be made for it ; at present there does not appear to me to be any case made for it at all.

I have only to make one observation as far as regards the irregularities alleged to have been committed. As far as regards the formation of this company and the conduct of the directors with reference to it, I do not think it is material to the decision of this question whether those irregularities are established or not. For the reasons already assigned by 721] the Lord Justice, and for those *assigned by myself, I do not think that the present petitioner is the person to complain of them. But I do agree with the observations which were made by the Vice-Chancellor in this case, to the effect that he did not desire to express any opinion whether the 11th clause was inserted in the articles of association with any fraudulent intent, adding, "I do not express any opinion whether this clause was inserted with a fraudulent intent, but it certainly is a clause which may very well be turned to fraudulent purposes." Apart from what the particular object or purpose of the framers of that clause may have been, I must confess that it appears to me to be an attempt to evade the provisions of the Companies Act, 1867, with regard to the reduction of capital. It may have been such an invasion as keeps within the law, but if at any proper time the question had been raised whether that clause was *ultrà vires* or not, it appears to me that there would have been strong reasons for holding that it was.

BRAMWELL, L.J.: I am of the same opinion. I so entirely agree with all that has been said by my Brethren, that I shall say nothing except on one matter which has come before us, as to which I desire to say a few words, because I do not like simply to say that I assent to the blame which has been passed on these people without giving a reason for it. I think that clause 11 of the articles of association was a most improper clause ; and although we ought to speak with hesitation, inasmuch as we have got neither the whole of the facts nor the parties before us to be heard in their defence, it seems to me almost impossible to think that it was not put into the deed for a fraudulent purpose. Let us see what it is: twenty-five thousand pounds are subscribed in one way or another, and then, by virtue of clause

11 and the resolution come to by the directors immediately
after they were appointed and before they could really *bona
fide* have known whether they would want more money or
not, the apparently subscribed capital of the company, although £25,000 only had been subscribed, is made £100,000,
and every man who was formerly a holder of one £1 share
became a holder of four £1 paid-up shares. Well, now, as
far as the company is concerned that did it no injury.
Each man who held a share beforehand held *one- [722
twenty-five-thousandth part of the subscribed capital of the
company, and the effect of what was done was simply to
alter the denominator from £25,000 into £100,000, and to
make each holder of a share the holder of four hundred-
thousandth parts of the capital of the company, which is the
same thing. Therefore, as far as the company was concerned, no harm was done to it at all, although they chose
to call these four £1 paid-up shares, instead of calling them
four 5s. paid-up shares, which would have been the truth.
But the mischief that was done was done, not to the company or to any of their shareholders in the company, for
they were all parties to it, and one got as much benefit as
the others did, which was no benefit at all if they had kept
their shares,—in that case it would have been utterly unimportant,—but the mischief that was done was this, that they
could with these, what I must call preten e shares, go into
the market, and of course any man having a £1 share offered
to him for sale—for although if he had inquired he would,
no doubt, have found out that in reality it was only a 5s.
share, yet it is very well known that people do not do so—
would think it was worth £1, or perhaps £1 with 1s. or 2s.
or perhaps 5s. premium; but if he had been told the truth,
that it represented 5s. only in money paid, it is not to be
conceived that he would have given £1, which would have
been putting it at a premium of 300 per cent. I have not
the slightest doubt that many people were deluded, I will not
say defrauded, because I do not like at the present moment
to say that there was any intention to defraud in the matter
—but many people were deluded into buying these shares
upon the footing that they were buying that which represented a payment or value of £1 having been given by the
original allottee, which is a most mischievous thing. Now,
I am perfectly certain that all the shareholders were not
fraudulent persons, for two reasons, both entirely satisfactory to my mind: one is, that amongst them are the names
of persons who I am certain are incapable of fraud, and
another is, that they did not all sell their shares, but many

of them kept them, and therefore made no profit out of this transaction. But speaking with reserve, I cannot feel any doubt that while there were some persons who, I will not say were perfectly free from blame in the matter, but who had accepted without consideration what was done by others, 723] *there were some also who by this clause, and what was done under it, intended the delusion upon the public which has been practied to the extent of about 50,000 shares in this case. The reason I make this remark is, that I am by no means clear that a remedy might not be had against such persons if any one could prove the case. I suppose there was some public announcement of the company as having a capital of £100,000 paid up, which was untrue. If anybody could prove that he had been deceived by that, he might be able to maintain an action against the fraudulent persons who had deluded him and caused damage to him. Another thing which it may be as well for gentlemen to bear in mind who have such schemes as this in their heads, is, that it is by no means clear that if they were indicted for a conspiracy they could not be very properly convicted and suffer punishment for it, for it is perfectly certain that in this case a false impression must have been created. It is impossible to suppose that these shares would have been sold at the average price at which they were sold, if the truth had been known. I have thought it right to express this opinion with a view to prevent others from repeating practices which are here so objectionable.

The appeal was accordingly allowed and the petition dismissed with costs.

Solicitors: *Stevens & Harries; Wild, Browne & Wild; Morley & Shirreff.*

Vol. XI.]   CHANCERY DIVISION.   799

C.A.   Polini v. Gray.   Sturla v. Freccia.   1879

[11 Chancery Division, 741.]

C.A., April 30, 1879.

*POLINI v. GRAY.   [741

[1873 P. 162.]

STURLA v. FRECCIA.

[1876 S. 353.]

Practice—Appeal—Security for Costs.

It is not the practice of the Court of Appeal when ordering an appellant to give
security for costs to fix a time within which this is to be done. If the order is not
complied with in a reasonable time the respondent may move to dismiss the appeal
for want of prosecution; but what is a reasonable time must depend on the circumstances of each case.

In re Ivory (¹) explained.

THE suit of *Polini* v. *Gray* was instituted to ascertain the
persons entitled to the estate of Mrs. Maria Brown, who died
in the year 1871 possessed of personal property exceeding
£200,000. She was the only daughter of Antonio Mangini,
formerly consul of the Ligurian Republic in London. After
considerable litigation, the court decided that the family of
the Freccias, who were five in number, were entitled in equal
shares to the property, as being the next of kin of Antonio
Mangini. After two of the shares had been paid out of
court, Madame Sturla and others commenced the action of
Sturla v. *Freccia*, claiming the property as nearer of kin
to Mangini than the Freccia family. The case was heard by
Vice-Chancellor Malins in January, 1879, on a summons to
vary the Chief Clerk's certificate, and on the 26th of February his Lordship decided in favor of the Freccia family,
and dismissed the action of *Sturla* v. *Freccia* with costs.
But in order that the unsuccessful parties might have an
opportunity of considering the grounds of his decision, he
continued the injunction which had been granted restraining
the defendants from taking out the fund which was still in
court in *Polini* v. *Gray* till further order.

*The plaintiffs in *Sturla* v. *Freccia* gave notice of   [742
appeal against this decision.

On the 26th of March the defendants applied to the Court
of Appeal that the plaintiffs might give security for costs,
and their Lordships ordered that the sum of £1,500 should
be deposited in court by the plaintiffs.

On the 26th of April, that sum not having been paid into
court, the defendants gave notice of motion that the appeal

(¹) 10 Ch. D., 372; 26 Eng. R., 767.

of the plaintiffs against the order of the 26th of February might be dismissed for want of prosecution, and that the injunction restraining the payment of the fund in court might be dissolved, and the fund in court paid to the defendants ; or that a day might be fixed for payment of the security.

Bagshawe, Q.C., and *Eyre*, for the defendants the Freccia: A reasonable time has passed for the payment of the sum named as security, and the defendants are now entitled to have the appeal dismissed : *In re Ivory* ('). In that case the appeal was dismissed after the appellant had made default for a month. If the court should not think fit to dismiss the appeal at once, we ask that a time may be fixed within which the security shall be paid in.

Higgins, Q.C., and *Everitt*, for other defendants.

J. Pearson, Q.C., and *E. Beaumont*, for the appellants : Since the order for giving security was made the plaintiffs have done their best to raise the money required, and we have reason to believe that it will be paid into court in a few days. It is the practice of the court to allow a much longer time than a month to elapse before making such an order as that now asked for.

Bagshawe, in reply.

JESSEL, M.R.: This is an application to dismiss an appeal for want of prosecution, *on the ground that security for costs has not been given within a reasonable time, or that a day may be fixed for giving such security. The practice is settled that the Court of Appeal does not fix a time for giving security, but if the appellant does not give security within a reasonable time the respondent may move to dismiss the appeal for want of prosecution. In *Vale v. Oppert* (') the time which had elapsed was four months, but the question what is a reasonable time must depend on the circumstances of each case. We cannot lay down what is a reasonable time in all cases.

Therefore the question in the present case is whether a reasonable time has elapsed since the order for giving security was made, which was on the 26th of March. We have been referred to *In re Ivory* ('), in which case the appellant, who was a pauper receiving parish relief, was ordered on the 2d of November to deposit £20 in court ; and it appears by a note at the end of the report that on the 27th of November the appeal was dismissed for want of prosecution. But no particulars are stated from which we may tell why the order to dismiss was made so early. The appellant may

[743]

(') 10 Ch. D., 872; 26 Eng. R., 761.　　　　　(') 5 Ch. D., 633.

not have appeared, or he may have appeared and said that he did not mean to go on with the appeal (¹). It was a peculiar case, and the court probably thought it was merely a speculative appeal.

But here we have to deal with an appeal involving a very large sum of money, and the security to be deposited is £1,500. The order was made on the 26th of March, and there was afterwards some discussion whether the appellant should pay money into court or give security. The time that has elapsed since that day cannot be said to be unreasonable. I think this motion must be refused with costs.

BRETT, L.J.: I am of the same opinion. I only wish to add that it seems to have been thought that there is a difference in the practice in *appeals from the Chancery [744 and Common Law Divisions on this subject. I am not aware of any such difference.

With respect to the case of *In re Ivory* (²) I have no doubt that the court was satisfied that the appellant did not mean to go on with the appeal.

COTTON, L.J., concurred.

Solicitors: *Lowless & Co.; G. L. P. Eyre & Co.; Foster & Spicer.*

(¹) The appellant was served with the notice of motion to dismiss the appeal for want of prosecution, but did not appear.
(²) 10 Ch. D., 372 ; 26 Eng. R., 761.

[11 Chancery Division, 745.]

M.R., April 7, 1879.

*SWEETAPPLE V. HORLOCK.   [745

[1879 S. 164.]

Marriage Settlement—Covenant to settle Wife's Property—Appointment to Wife —Instrument creating Power—Period of Vesting—Acquisition of Interest by Appointee.

Under a marriage settlement real estate stood limited to H., the husband, for life, with remainder to the use of such of the children or issue of the marriage as he should by deed or will appoint; and in default of appointment, to the use of the children of the marriage equally as tenants in common in fee.

There was issue of the marriage two children only, a son and a daughter. The daughter married, and by her marriage settlement she and her intended husband covenanted with the trustees for the conveyance and settlement of all property which she then was "seised of, or interested in, or entitled to," upon the trusts therein mentioned, including in effect reversionary interests.

The daughter survived her husband, and thereupon H. by deed appointed the real estate comprised in the original settlement, subject to his life estate, to his son and daughter equally in fee, the daughter thus taking the same share as she would have taken in default of appointment;

Held, that inasmuch as the reversionary moiety appointed to the daughter constituted a new interest acquired by her subsequently to the date of her settlement, such moiety was not bound by the covenant in her marriage settlement.

In re Frowd's Settlement ([1]), *In re Vizard's Trusts* ([2]), and *De Serre* v. *Clarke* ([3]) discussed.

BY the settlement, dated the 1st of October, 1832, made on the marriage of Dr. and Mrs. Horlock, certain real estate of considerable value belonging to Dr. Horlock was settled to the use of Dr. Horlock for life, with remainder to certain uses in favor of Mrs. Horlock—which failed in consequence of her death in her husband's lifetime—with remainder to the use of an only child or of such one or more of all the children or issue of the said marriage living at the decease of Dr. Horlock, or to the use both of all or such one or more of the children or issue of the said marriage living as aforesaid, at such times, for such estates or interests, and in such shares, as Dr. Horlock should by deed, with or without power of revocation, or by will or codicil, appoint; and, in 746]   default *of such appointment, to the use of an only child, or to the use of all the children or issue of the said marriage as Mrs. Horlock, if she should survive her husband, should appoint; and, in default thereof, to the use of the child or children of the said marriage equally as tenants in common, and the heirs and assigns of such child or children respectively.

Mrs. Horlock died in 1858.

There was issue of the said marriage two children only, a son, and a daughter, Elizabeth Horlock, who attained twenty-one and married Thomas Sweetapple.

By the settlement, dated the 11th of February, 1861, made prior to the marriage of Mr. and Mrs. Sweetapple, certain personal estate belonging to the latter was settled upon trusts for the husband and wife and their children. The settlement then contained a covenant by the husband and wife with the trustees as follows: "In case the said Elizabeth Horlock now is, or if at any time during the continuance of her said intended coverture, she the said Elizabeth Horlock, or the said Thomas Sweetapple in her right, shall, by transmission, devise, bequest, gift, conveyance, donation, representation, inheritance, or otherwise, become beneficially seised of, or interested in, or entitled to, any real or personal property, estate or effects whatsoever, not being the premises hereinbefore settled by her the said Elizabeth Horlock, or intended so to be, of the value or to the amount of £100 at any one time, for any estate or interest whatsover (other

([1]) 10 L. T. (N.S.), 367; 4 N. R., 54.   ([3]) Law Rep., 18 Eq., 587; 11 Eng.
([2]) Law Rep., 1 Ch., 588,   R., 554.

than and except interests which shall be effectually settled
to the separate use and benefit of her the said Elizabeth
Horlock, and other than and except jewels, &c.), then and
in such case " the husband and wife would at the cost of the
trust estate convey and assure all such real and personal estate to the trustees upon trust, as to the real estate and as
to such part of the personal estate as should not consist of
money, "with all convenient speed, after such interest of
the said Elizabeth Horlock or of the said Thomas Sweetapple in her right shall fall into possession, to sell, dispose
of, and convert into money the same," and to hold the proceeds upon the trusts declared concerning the wife's property thereinbefore settled.

There was issue of the marriage of Mr. and Mrs. Sweetapple one child only, now an infant.

*Mr. Sweetapple died in 1867.   [747

By a deed-poll, dated the 26th of June, 1873, Dr. Horlock, in exercise of the power given him by his marriage
settlement, irrevocably appointed the whole of the real estate thereby settled, after his decease, to the use of his son
and daughter, their heirs and assigns, as tenants in common.

Dr. Horlock was still living.

The question was whether the undivided moiety appointed to Mrs. Sweetapple by her father was bound by the
above mentioned covenant contained in her marriage settlement.

The question was raised by an action by Mrs. Sweetapple
against her trustees and infant child, to have it declared that
her moiety was not so bound.

Ince, Q.C., and *Shebbeare*, for the plaintiff: The only
authority directly against our view is *In re Frowd's Settlement*(') before Vice-Chancellor Wood; but that decision is
contrary to *Lee* v. *Olding* ('), and was overruled by the Court
of Appeal in *In re Vizard's Trusts* ('), an authority which
Vice-Chancellor Malins felt himself bound to follow in *De
Serre* v. *Clarke* (').

Dobbs, for the defendants: I rely on *In re Frowd's Settlement*, which I submit was not overruled by *In re Vizard's
Trusts*, for the Lord Justice Turner does not even notice the
case in his judgment, although it was discussed in argument. The actual ground of the Lord Justice's decision
was that the interest of the appointee under the original
settlement was altered by the exercise of the power, which

(¹) 10 L. T. (N.S.), 867; 4 N. R., 54.   (²) Law Rep., 1 Ch., 588.
(³) 25 L. J. (Ch.), 580; 2 Jur. (N.S.),   (⁴) Law Rep., 18 Eq., 587; 11 Eng.
850.   R., 554.

is not the case here; and it is to be noticed that he expressly declines to say that the appointment was sufficient of itself to defeat the original limitations in default of appointment. Moreover, Vice-Chancellor Malins, in *De Serre* v. *Clarke*, expressed his concurrence with Vice-Chancellor Wood's view, though he considered himself bound by *In re Vizard's Trusts.*

The result, therefore, is that the decision in *In re Frowd's* 748] *Settlement* (') *practically remains untouched, and that in the present case, inasmuch as Mrs. Sweetapple had at the date of her marriage, under her father and mother's settlement, an interest actually vested in her, and not really altered by the subsequent appointment that interest is bound by the covenant.

JESSEL, M.R.: I do not feel any doubt as to this case.

I must, first of all, consider the question independently of the authorities, and then see what the authorities compel me to decide. [His Lordship then read Dr. Horlock's settlement as above stated, and continued:]

So that, at the date of the marriage settlement I am going to mention, matters stood thus: Dr. Horlock was tenant for life with a power to appoint among the children or remoter issue of his marriage; in default of appointment, the property—which was real estate—was to go to the children of the marriage—there were two—as tenants in common in fee.

Miss Horlock being thus entitled, in default of appointment by her father, to one-half of the settled property, married Mr. Sweetapple, and being of age she and her intended husband entered into the following covenant with the trustees of their settlement: [His Lordship read the covenant, and continued:] The words are: "Now is . . . interested in or entitled to any real property." She certainly then was interested in or entitled to a contingent reversionary interest in real property under her father and mother's settlement. Moreover, the covenant is to settle upon trusts which show at once the parties contemplated reversionary property, because it directs what is to be done with any interest which shall "fall into possession."

Then Mr. Sweetapple died; and then, after his death, Mr. Horlock, the father, in exercise of his power, appointed by a deed-poll of the 26th of June, 1873, the whole of the real estate comprised in his settlement to his two children equally. So that Mrs. Sweetapple took under the appointment precisely the same estate as she would have taken in default of appointment, that is to say, she took one-half of

(') 10 L. T. (N.S.), 367; 4 N. R., 54.

the property as tenant in fee. Now is that comprised in the covenant or not? The words are: "In case the *said [749 Elizabeth Horlock now is, or if at any time during the continuance of her said intended coverture, she the said Elizabeth Horlock, or the said Thomas Sweetapple in her right, shall . . . become seized of, or interested in, or entitled to any real or personal property," they will by effectual conveyances convey to the trustees. It is clear that that part of the covenant relating to the settlement of property to be acquired during the coverture does not affect the question, as the appointment was executed after the coverture. Therefore if this property is comprised in the covenant at all it is so under the words "Now is."

Now she was at the date of her settlement entitled to this one-half in reversion in default of appointment.' Supposing she had immediately afterwards conveyed this interest, would that conveyance have passed what came to her subsequently by the appointment? I should have thought clearly not—apart from the authorities. A conveyance by a person by an innocent assurance of an interest expressed as being subject to be defeated by the exercise of a power, does not convey an interest which that person might take under the power. This is not like a settlement of all property which might come to the wife in any event, but only of that which was then vested in or belonging to her. Persons claiming under such a settlement cannot be in a better position than if the settlement covenanted to be executed had been executed the day after the marriage.

So it seems apart from the authorities, but as not unfrequently happens, I find myself embarrassed by the state of the authorities.

The first case we have is *In re Frowd's Settlement* ('), decided so long ago that there is great difficulty in dealing with it apart from other authorities.

There by a marriage settlement certain funds were settled upon trust for the children, grandchildren, and issue of the marriage as the survivor of the husband and wife should by will appoint, and in default of appointment, for the children of the marriage in equal shares. There was only one child of the marriage, a daughter, who married. The settlement made upon her marriage contained a covenant very like this, for the settlement of all the property vested in the lady at the date of her marriage, or *to which she [750 or her husband in her right become entitled during the coverture. There was, as I have said, a power in the mar-

(') 10 L. T. (N.S.), 367; 4 N. R., 54.

riage settlement of the lady's father and mother—a power, as here, to appoint by will, so that by an exercise of that power a grandchild could take to the exclusion altogether of the lady herself.

Then by the marriage settlement of the lady she and her husband covenanted with their trustees that they would convey, assign, and assure to the trustees all the real and personal estate "then vested" in the lady, or which should become vested in her husband in her right, and all the real and personal estate which the wife or her husband in her right "during the said coverture might become entitled to under or by virtue of any gift, devise, or bequest, or by succession, or otherwise."

The words are not quite the same as those in the present case. Here the words are, "In case the said Elizabeth Horlock now is," or if at any time during the coverture, she or her husband in her right should become "seised of or interested in or entitled to any real or personal property." There the covenant was to convey all property "then vested." However, I cannot see any real difference: it is substantially the same thing. Then after the marriage there was an appointment to the lady absolutely, for her separate use, and the question was whether or not the appointed property passed by the covenant in the lady's settlement to settle what was "then vested" in her. It was argued that it did not pass because she took as appointee only, and not under the original settlement as one of the children in default of appointment. On the other side it was said that it was an interest under the settlement which created the power, though uncertain in amount until the power was exercised, and that argument was adopted by the Vice-Chancellor, who said that "Mrs. Highett was entitled, in default of appointment, to the whole fund, and that the appointment did not in any respect change her interest." That is rather a play upon words. It did not change her interest in point of amount, no doubt, but it did change her interest as an object of the settlement.

Then the Vice-Chancellor says, "Her share might have been altered in amount, but in fact the whole fund had been given to her. It would be far too great a refinement to say that distinctions, which might hold good in relation to real 751] estate, were *to be introduced in dealing with a sum of money. The limitation to the separate use could make no difference. The covenant, too, was by the wife as well as by the husband. At the date of the settlement of 1851 something was actually vested in Mrs. Highett under the original settlement, though it was liable to be devested by an execution of the power. By the appointment which was made, nothing was taken from her; its only effect was to ascertain the share she took. He must therefore hold that this fund was subject to the covenant in question, and it must be paid to the trustees of the settlement of 1851."

Now one observation to make upon that judgment is that the Vice-Chancellor distinguishes the case before him from one relating to real estate, by saying that there were distinctions which might hold good as to real estate, but that they were not to be introduced in dealing with a sum of money: so that I may avail myself of that decision to say that *In re Frowd's Settlement* (¹) does not bind me upon a question of real estate; and I will say further, that I should hold it not binding upon me upon a question of personal estate either, if I were at liberty to do so.

Then the point came before the Court of Appeal in *In re Vizard's Trusts* (²). There a fund was settled by will upon trust for a person for life, with remainder to all or such one or more of the children or issue of the testator's deceased brother, as the tenant for life should appoint, and in default of appointment to the children of the brother equally. One of the children, a son of the testator's brother, made a general assignment of all his property to a trustee for his creditors, under the Bankruptcy Act. After this the tenant for life appointed the fund by will to the children of the brother equally, the result being that the son took the same share under the appointment as he would have taken in default of appointment. It was held by Lord Justice Turner, affirming the decision of Vice-Chancellor Stuart, that the son's deed of assignment did not pass his after-acquired property: that his interest in default of appointment was defeated by the appointment which gave him an interest determinable by lapse, which did not happen, and that such interest must therefore be considered a new interest, and consequently did not pass to the trustee.

*The Lord Justice says this (³): "It was insisted [752 on the part of the appellant (the trustee) that whatever F. Vizard (the son) took, he took under the will of the testator, and that the appointment did not displace or alter the interest which he took under the will in default of appointment, and which had passed to the appellant by the deed, the power being, as it was said, a power of selection only. I think, however, that the power in this case was something

(¹) 10 L. T. (N.S.), 867; 4 N. R., 54.   (²) Law Rep., 1 Ch., 588.
(³) Law Rep., 1 Ch., 592.

more than a power of selection. It was a power to distribute, no less than to select, and it enabled an appointment to be made in favor of persons who would not take in default of appointment, and, certainly, I am not satisfied that the execution of the power of appointment was not of itself sufficient to defeat the limitations in default of appointment contained in the testator's will, but it is not, in my opinion, necessary to decide this point, for I think that the interest of F. Vizard was altered by the exercise of the power." Then the Lord Justice points out that, in the one case, under the will, the son took a fifth as a vested interest, and in the other case, under the power, he took a fifth contingently on his surviving the testator's widow, the tenant for life. So the Lord Justice clearly decided the question on the ground that the appointed share was different in *quantum* of interest from the contingent share, but he appears to doubt whether an appointment to the son of the same share as he would have taken in default of appointment would not also have given him a new interest. But it is difficult to see why, if the share appointed is something more or less than the share in default of appointment, it will pass as a new interest, whereas if it is the same it will not so pass. It is difficult to see why, if a fourth would pass, a fifth should not pass. With great respect to the learned Lord Justice it is a distinction without a difference.

The Lord Justice then decided, affirming the decision of Vice-Chancellor Stuart, though the Lord Justice Knight Bruce appeared to entertain a different opinion, that the appointed share did not pass by the assignment, inasmuch as the deed of appointment conferred a new interest.

That was also the view taken in *De Serre* v. *Clarke* (¹) by the Vice-Chancellor Malins, who argued *In re Vizard's* 753] *Trusts* (²). Now *I must say I cannot agree with the observations of the learned Vice-Chancellor in *De Serre* v. *Clarke* (¹) any more than with the observations of the Lord Justice Turner in *In re Vizard's Trusts* (²).

In *De Serre* v. *Clarke* the facts were these: A testator gave his residuary estate to trustees upon trust to pay the income to his daughter for life for her separate use, and after her death to pay the fund to the children of the daughter as she should by deed or will appoint, and in default of appointment amongst them equally. The daughter appointed by deed the whole of the fund amongst her children, giving the plaintiff, who was one of them, a specified sum for her separate use absolutely. The plaintiff, after the death

(¹) Law Rep., 18 Eq., 587; 11 Eng. R., 554.   (²) Law Rep., 1 Ch., 588.

of her grandfather, and before the date of the appointment by her mother, married a Frenchman, domiciled in France. He died before the date of the appointment, and there was one child only of the marriage. There having been no settlement on the marriage, the question was whether, under the French law, the appointed fund fell into the community of goods as being property acquired during the marriage. The Vice-Chancellor held that a new title accrued to the plaintiff under the appointment, and to that I entirely assent, but the judgment is, in my opinion, somewhat singular ; because, after deciding in the way I have mentioned and saying that he felt himself bound by the decision of Vice-Chancellor Stuart in *Lee* v. *Olding* ('), which did not decide the exact point, he expresses some dissent from *In re Vizard's Trusts*, where certainly the precise point did arise.

After stating the facts in *Lee* v. *Olding* and *In re Vizard's Trusts* the Vice-Chancellor says : "Then the question is, whether I am at liberty to disregard these authorities, and to say that this lady had at the date of the marriage an interest in the property which she took under the appointment, and that what she so took is subject to the French code. I consider that on these grounds I am bound to come to the conclusion that she took under the appointment and not under the will." Up to that point I entirely assent to the Vice-Chancellor's judgment ; but then he goes on : "Mr. Pearson pressed on me very strongly *In re Frowd's Settlement* ('), and I think there is much to be said in favor of it and *against *In re Vizard's Trusts* ('), and if I were [754 at liberty to treat the question as still open, I am by no means prepared to say what view I should take. *In re Frowd's Settlement* (') was decided before *In re Vizard's Trusts*, and though it does not appear from the report, I have no doubt that that case was commented upon by myself and Mr. Pearson in the arguments. But the facts of the two cases are not quite similar. *In re Frowd's Settlement* was a case of a covenant in a marriage settlement to settle all property then vested in the wife, and at the time of the marriage she was entitled, in default of appointment, to the funds settled by her father's marriage settlement, and those funds were afterwards appointed to her absolutely for her separate use, and the Vice-Chancellor Wood held that the appointment did not divest her interest in the fund, so as to

(') 25 L. J. (Ch.), 580; 2 Jur. (N.S.), 850.　(') 10 L. T. (N.S.), 867; 4 N, R., 54.
(') Law Rep., 1 Ch., 588.

take it out of the operation of the settlement.   I am bound to say that, although my own opinion might coincide with that view, I consider that the law is settled the other way."

The result, therefore, is a most singular state of authority. First, there is a decision of Vice-Chancellor Stuart holding that the interest of the appointee was acquired under the appointment and not under the original settlement.   Then there is a decision of Vice-Chancellor Wood distinctly holding that the appointment did not divest the interest under the settlement.   Then there is a decision of the Court of Appeal, affirming a second decision of Vice-Chancellor Stuart, on the distinct ground that the appointment conferred a new interest.   Then there is a decision of Vice-Chancellor Malins following the two decisions of Vice-Chancellor Stuart, not on principle, but because of the expression of opinion of Lord Justice Turner, though agreeing with the decision of Vice-Chancellor Wood.

It appears to me that, in that state of the authorities, I may say I am not compelled to decide that in the present case this appointed share is bound by the covenant; and apart from authority I am prepared to say I am entitled to come to the decision I do, namely, that the share is not bound by the covenant.

There will therefore be a declaration in the terms of the claim.

Solicitor :   *W. H. Bennett*, agent for E. Newman, Yeovil; E. Newman.

[11 Chancery Division, 772.]

Fry, J., April 25, 1879.

772]   *In re* West of England and South Wales District Bank.

Ex parte Dale & Co.

Agent—Bank—Following Money—Priority.

A banking company were employed as agents to collect money and to remit it to their employers.   The bank received the money in cash, placed it with the other cash of the bank, and informed their employers that the money had been remitted; but before the money was actually remitted the bank went into liquidation:—

Held, that the money was part of the general assets of the bank, and that the employers of the bank were not entitled to be paid in priority to the other creditors.

Pennell v. *Deffell* ([1]) considered.

([1]) 4 D. M. & G., 372.

MESSRS. DALE & Co. were bankers at South Shields. They had no account with the West of England and South Wales District Bank, but were in the habit of employing that bank as special agents to collect money for them. On the 5th of December, 1878, Dale & Co., having eight sums of money to receive at Cardiff on what were called average orders, sent the eight average orders to the Cardiff branch of the West of England Bank, with directions to collect the money and pay it when received to the account of Dale & Co. with Glyn & Co., of London, who were agents for both the banks. The West of England Bank collected the sums due on six of these average orders, amounting to £247 7s. 7d. (which was received by a check on another bank for £172 10s. and by cash £74 17s. 7d.), and on the 7th of December, wrote to Dale & Co. that the amount had been remitted to Glyn & Co. This, however, had not been done, and the West of England Bank ceased to carry on business after the 7th of December. The 8th of December was Sunday, and on the 9th of December the bank went into liquidation. The two uncollected average orders were returned to Dale & Co., and Dale & Co. took out a summons in the liquidation for payment of the £247 17s. 7d. as having been received by the West of England Bank for a specific purpose, and not forming part of the assets of the bank. It *appeared that the check for £172 10s. remained in [773 the bank at the time of the liquidation, and during the argument the liquidators submitted to pay that sum to Dale & Co. The only question, therefore, was as to the £74 17s. 7d. cash, which had been mixed with the general cash of the Cardiff branch of the West of England Bank.

Higgins, Q.C., and *Everitt*, for Dale & Co.: The duty of the bank was to receive this money and at once to send it on to Glyn & Co. for Dale & Co. It ought not to have gone into their general account. Dale & Co. could have followed the clerk who received it and have taken it from him. They had no banking account with the West of England Bank, who were merely employed to collect this money: *Taylor* v. *Plumer* (¹); *Ex parte Cooke* (²). The money was never in the order and disposition of the bank.

[FRY, J., referred to *Whitecomb* v. *Jacob* (³).]

If the bank has improperly mixed this money with other money it can be followed and claimed: *Brown* v. *Adams* (⁴);

(¹) 3 M. & S., 562.   (³) 1 Salk., 161.
(²) 4 Ch. D., 123; 19 Eng. R., 714. (⁴) Law Rep., 4 Ch., 764.

Middleton v. *Pollock* (¹) ; *Birt* v. *Burt* (²) ; *Pennell* v. *Deffell* (³) ; *Frith* v. *Cartland* (⁴).

774]   *Glasse*, Q.C., and *Romer*, for the liquidators: The only question is, whether this money belongs to the general body of creditors or to this particular creditor. Was it the duty of the bank to keep this money separate, or merely to receive it and remit it, perhaps with other money to Glyn & Co., who were agents for both banks? They could not send on the particular coin received, and what were they to do with it? There was no wrongful act in mixing it with their other money. In no case has any one creditor been paid out of the mixed fund unless the mixing was unlawful: *Middleton* v. *Pollock* (⁵). In *Birt* v. *Burt* the money was traced.

Higgins, in reply.

FRY, J., after stating the facts of the case, continued:

It appears to me clear that the bank, in the collection of these average orders, was a special agent of the claimants,

(¹) 4 Ch. D., 49 ; 19 Eng. R., 658.

(²) V. C. M. May 30, 1877.

BIRT *v.* BURT.

The trustees of the will of Lord Southampton had employed one Birt as agent in the sale of Lord Southampton's estates. On some of the sales Birt had received the purchase-moneys, and had paid them to his own account with his bankers, Messrs. Drummonds. Birt was dead, and the whole amount standing to his credit with Messrs. Drummonds had been paid into court in an action for the administration of his estate. The trustees of Lord Southampton's will presented a petition for the transfer of the money in court to a suit which had been instituted for the administration of Lord Southampton's estate.

The petition was heard before Vice-Chancellor Malins on the 13th of April, 1877.

Robinson, Q.C., and *Vaughan Hawkins*, in support of the petition: Birt acted as agent of the trustees in the sale of the estates of Lord Southampton, and the trustees are entitled to follow the sums which he had paid to his own account at his bankers and which ought to have been paid to the account of the trustees.

Higgins, Q.C., and *Bleby*, for Birt's representatives, submitted that there could be no segregation of a banking account; that Birt acted more as a banker than an agent; and that an account be-

tween the parties ought to be taken including matters which had occurred before Lord Southampton's death from which a set-off could be shown.

MALINS, V.C., said that as Birt had acted in the capacity of agent for the trustees in the sale of Lord Southampton's estate, it was his duty to pay the money he received to the account of the trustees, instead of which he had paid it into his own banking account. The sums he had paid in answered in almost every instance to the amount he had received on each particular occasion. He had no right to set off any debt due from Lord Southampton in case there had been any, which was extremely doubtful; and if there was not any debt due from the trustees he had no right to commit a breach of trust in retaining this money. The trustees were entitled to follow the amount, and to have it paid over, as prayed, to the account of the administration suit.

Birt's representatives appealed.

1877. May 30. The Court of Appeal (Jessel, M.R., Coleridge, C.J., and Baggallay, L.J.,) considered the case too clear for argument, and dismissed the appeal with costs.

Solicitors: *Ingle, Cooper & Holmes ; Farrer, Ouvry & Co.*

(³) 4 D. M. & G., 372.

(⁴) 2 H. & M., 417.

(⁵) 4 Ch. D., 49 ; 19 Eng. R., 658.

and stood in what has often been called a fiduciary relation towards them. It appears further clear that if the money which they had so *received under their special [775 agency had been kept separate from all the other moneys in the bank, or if it had been invested rightfully or wrongfully in some property into which the specific money could be traced without any mixture having taken place, then in either of those two cases Messrs. Dale & Co. could follow the money or the property into which the money had gone. In fact it has been very fairly and properly admitted by the learned counsel for the bank that one of those principles does govern the case of the check; that the check was at the time of the liquidation specific property resulting from the special agency, and, as such, belonged to the principals.

The question arises, however, with regard to the money received under the agency and mingled with the money of the agent, that is to say, the £74 17s. 7d. cash. It appears to me that there is a long line of authorities which regulate this case, and to which I must pay the greatest attention. Before referring to them let me observe that, in my opinion, the agent receiving these average orders was bound to convert them, so to speak, into money, that is to say, was bound to receive the money for which the orders were given, and that he might with propriety place the money in his till, provided he directed his agents in London to credit the account of Messrs. Dale & Co. in London with the amount so received.

That being the duty of the agent, I now turn to the authorities, and I find that so long ago as the 9th year of Queen Anne the case of *Whitecomb* v. *Jacob* (¹) was determined in these terms: "If one employs a factor and intrusts him with the disposal of merchandise, and the factor receives the money and dies indebted in debts of a higher nature, and it appears by evidence that this money was vested in other goods and remains unpaid, those goods shall be taken as part of the merchant's estate and not the factor's; but if the factor have the money, it shall be looked upon as the factor's estate, and must first answer the debts of a superior creditor, &c.; for in regard that money has no ear-mark, equity cannot follow that in behalf of him that employed the factor." Now, with the single exception that it appears to have been held subsequently that money may be so far *ear-marked that it may be followed if it has been [776 kept separate, that case appears to have been always held to be an authority. Therefore it comes to this, that if a

(¹) 1 Salk., 161.

factor properly converts goods into money, and that money gets mixed with his own money, that money cannot be followed by the principal.

In the celebrated case of *Ryall* v. *Rolle* (¹) Mr. Justice Burnet, in delivering judgment, says (²): "Suppose goods are consigned to a factor who sells them and breaks, the merchant for the money must come in as a creditor under the commission; but if the money is laid out in other goods these goods will not be subject to the bankruptcy." In another case of *Ex parte Dumas* (³), before Lord Hardwicke, the petitioners were certain persons who had claimed bills arising from the produce of certain goods transmitted to them, and the Lord Chancellor said: "Suppose the petitioners had consigned over goods to Julian as their factor, and he had sold them, and turned them into money, the principal then could only have come in as a general creditor under the commission; but if the goods had continued in specie and had been found in Julian's hands at the time of his bankruptcy, it would have been otherwise, and has been so determined in several cases." That he treats as well ascertained law at that time. Then Mr. Justice Willes, in delivering the considered judgment of the Court of Common Pleas in the case of *Scott* v. *Surman* (⁴), says (⁵): "We are all agreed that if the money for which the tar had been sold had been all paid to the bankrupt before his bankruptcy, and had not been laid out again by him in any specific thing to distinguish it from the rest of his estate, in that case the plaintiffs could not have recovered anything in this action, but must have come in as creditors under the commission, as is laid down in the case of *Whitecomb* v. *Jacob* (⁶) and in many other cases." In the year 1800 the Lord Chancellor, in *Ex parte Sayers* (⁷), adopted the same view. He considered that there were in that case special circumstances which showed that although the money had got into the general fund constituting the estate of the *bankrupt it had got out 777] again, and he said it had acquired an identity and a distinction from the rest of the fund. Still he adopted the general principle that if it had been in the form of money at the time of the bankruptcy the creditor could only rank with the other creditors. Lastly, in the well known case of *Taylor* v. *Plumer* (⁸), Lord Ellenborough adopted the same view. He said: "It makes no difference in reason or law

(¹) 1 Atk., 165.
(²) 1 Atk., 172.
(³) 1 Atk., 232.
(⁴) Willes, 400.

(⁵) Willes, 403.
(⁶) 1 Salk., 161.
(⁷) 5 Ves., 169.
(⁸) 3 M. & S., 562, 575.

into what other form different from the original the change
may have been made, whether it be into that of promissory
notes for the security of the money which was produced by
the sale of the goods of the principal, as in *Scott* v. *Surman* ('), or into other merchandise, as in *Whitecomb* v.
Jacob ('), for the product of or substitute for the original
thing still follows the nature of the thing itself as long as it
can be ascertained to be such, and the right only ceases when
the means of ascertainment fail, which is the case when the
subject is turned into money and mixed and confounded in
a general mass of the same description.   The difficulty which
arises in such a case is a difficulty of fact and not of law,
and the *dictum* that money has no ear-mark must be understood in the same way ; i.e., as predicated only of an undivided and undistinguishable mass of current money."

That decision introduces the distinction from the case of
Whitecomb v. *Jacob* which I referred to, and shows that
money may be treated as ear-marked when it is physically
separated from other moneys.

Those authorities appear to me to prove that the £74 17s.
7d. must be treated as being part of the common property
of the bank, and in respect of that sum the claimants must
come in as creditors.

Before parting with the case I am bound to say that upon
principle I feel the greatest difficulty, because I think that
the principles of equity are very much opposed to that line
of decision.   Let me put the point in this way : If it be a
case of trustee and *cestui que trust*, and the trustee mingles
with his own money the money which he holds in trust, can
he as against the *cestui que trust* say that the money has so
lost its character of trust money that it cannot be followed?
Upon that point the observations of *Lord Justice [778]
Knight Bruce in the case of *Pennell* v. *Deffell* (') appear
most forcible.   He supposed the case of a trust fund kept
separate, and he then refers to the case of a trust fund mingled, and asks whether that can make any difference, and
says, "None, as I apprehend, except (if it is an exception)
that his executors would possibly be entitled to receive
from the contents of the repository an amount equal to the
ascertained amount of the money in every sense his own so
mixed by himself with the other money.   But not in either
case, as I conceive, would the blending together of the trust
moneys, however confusedly, be of any moment as between
the various *cestuis que trustent* on the one hand, and the executors as representing the general creditors on the other."

(') Willes, 400.   (') 1 Salk., 161.   (') 4 D. M. & G., 372, 382.

816   CHANCERY DIVISION.   [Vol. XI.

1879   In re West of England, &c., Bank.   Ex parte Dale & Co.   Fry, J.

That seems a decision that as between *cestui que trust* and trustee the mixing of the fund is immaterial so long as there is a fund on which the *cestui que trust* can lay his hands. Does it make any difference that instead of trustee and *cestui que trust*, it is a case of fiduciary relationship? What is a fiduciary relationship? It is one in respect of which if a wrong arise, the same remedy exists against the wrong-doer on behalf of the principal as would exist against a trustee on behalf of the *cestui que trust*. If that be a just description of the relationship, it would follow that wherever fiduciary relationship exists, and money coming from the trust lies in the hands of persons standing in that relationship, it can be followed and separated from any money of their own. That seems to me to be the logical result of *Pennell* v. *Deffell*: but that result is opposed to the long line of authorities to which I have referred and from which I do not feel myself justified upon any reasoning of my own in departing.

The result is, I hold that the £172 10s. belongs to the claimants, and the £74 17s. 4d. belongs to the general estate. The costs of both parties will come out of the estate.

Solicitors for Dale & Co.: *Clarke, Rawlins & Clarke.*
Solicitors for West of England Bank: *Clarke, Woodcock & Ryland.*

The C. N. Bank having received from a customer of the M. and M. Bank a check upon that bank, sent it to the drawee for payment; the M. and M. Bank charged the check to the drawer, whose account was then good for the amount, and returned the check to the drawer as paid; it sent to the C. N. Bank a draft on a New York bank for the amount of the check; two days after the M. and M. Bank closed its doors, and a receiver of its assets was appointed: the draft was not paid. On application by the C. N. Bank for an order requiring the receiver to pay the amount of the check, upon the ground that the assets came to the hands of the receiver impressed with a trust in favor of the C. N. Bank, held, that the order was properly denied; that in order to authorize the relief prayed for, it was necessary to trace into the hands of the receiver money or property which belonged to the C. N. Bank, or which had, before the receivership, been set apart and appropriated to the payment of the check; that charging said check and returning it to the drawer did not amount to a payment and setting apart of sufficient of the drawee's deposit to cover it, nor did it impress a special trust on any part of the drawee's assets; but by the transaction the drawee simply reduced its indebtedness to its depositor to the amount of the check, and constituted itself a debtor to the holder to a corresponding amount: The People v. Merchants and Mechanics' Bank, 78 N. Y., 269.

Where the clerk of the court, by order of the court, deposits funds belonging to the court with a bank, and the bank afterwards becomes insolvent, the deposit not being a special one, or mere naked bailment, and there is no means of identifying the money deposited, even if the assets of the bank are in the hands of a receiver, it is error to require the receiver to pay such deposit in full; the clerk must share *pro rata* with other depositors and creditors of the bank.

Where moneys deposited in a commercial savings bank were not kept separate from the general funds of the

Vol. XI.]   CHANCERY DIVISION.   817

Fry, J   In re West of England, &c., Bank.   Ex parte Dale & Co..   1879

bank or distinguished therefrom, and the entries of the same upon the bank books and upon the deposit book of the officer making the deposit, were the same as with all other depositors, except that no interest was to be paid thereon, it was held that the deposit, though made under a general order of the court, was not a special one, or a mere bailment, and that the money so deposited became that of the bank, which was liable for its repayment the same as to any other depositor or creditor.

Where the court places the assets of an insolvent bank in the hands of a receiver, it is for the benefit of all the creditors of the corporation, to be administered, distributed and paid according to the equitable claims of all such creditors, and such act cannot affect or change in the slightest degree the rights of a single creditor; and the fact that the court has acquired possession of the assets and funds, confers no legal right to retain it over general deposits in full, where the moneys deposited under its direction with the bank cannot be identified: Otis v. Gross, 96 Ills., 612.

Where one person deposits money with another for investment, with the understanding that the recipient is to pay interest on the amount until invested, the relation established between the parties is that of debtor and creditor, not that of trustee and cestui que trust.

A. sent $1,300 to B. for investment, with the understanding that B. was to pay interest thereon until invested. B. deposited the amount in bank, and afterwards becoming insolvent, absconded. A. demanded payment of the $1,300, which was refused, and on the same day the money was paid by the bank to the sheriff by virtue of a writ of sequestration directed against B. In a suit by A. against the bank to recover the amount of the deposit, held, that the agreement to pay interest on the fund until invested, constituted B. the debtor of A. and not his trustee; that hence the sum deposited in the bank was the money of B., not of A.; and that therefore the plaintiff was not entitled to recover: Pittsburg, etc., v. McMurray, 98 Penn. St. R., 538.

In New York, by statute, savings

banks are entitled, in case of the insolvency of a bank in which its funds are deposited, to a preference in the payment thereof : In the matter of Patterson, 18 Hun, 221, 78 N. Y., 608; Upton v. Erie, etc., 13 Hun, 269.

The act, however, only applies to deposits made in the ordinary course of business, and subject to the drafts of the depositor to an amount not exceeding that authorized by the act. Loans, whether on time or payable on call, are not deposits within the meaning of the act,: Rosenback v. The Manufacturers, etc., 69 N. Y., 358.

September 2, 1873, the Erie Railway declared a dividend of one per cent. upon its stock, and deposited the money to pay the same with Duncan, Sherman & Co. On December 10th, 1874, the money then remaining with the said firm was withdrawn by the company and subsequently passed, with its other property, to a receiver of the road. This application was made by the petitioner, who, at the time the dividend was declared, was and still is a stockholder of the said road, to compel the receiver to pay to him the amount of his dividend.

Held, that the fund deposited with Duncan, Sherman & Co. should be regarded as specifically appropriated for the payment of the dividend, and that the stockholders acquired in equity a lien upon such fund to the extent of the amount to which they were respectively entitled, and that such lien followed the fund in the hands of the receiver.

That a stockholder might apply on petition for such dividend, and was not obliged to bring an action therefor: Matter of Le Blanc, 14 Hun, 8, affirmed 75 N. Y., 598; Fullerton v. National, etc., 63 How. Pr., 5, 12, and cases cited; Douglass v. Martin, 103 Ills., 25.

Where a stockholder receives from a corporation dividends, declared and admitted by it to be due to him on shares of the corporate stock, an action is not maintainable against him in the first instance, at the suit of one claiming to be entitled to share in the dividends, but whose rights had been ignored by the corporation, to recover, as for moneys had and received, the proportions of the dividends so received, which plaintiff would have been entitled to had his shares participated.

It seems, that the remedy of one thus wrongfully excluded from the rights of a stockholder is against the company. He cannot follow the assets of the company in the hands of parties to whom it has paid them, until at least he has established his rights as a creditor of the company, and has exhausted his legal remedies against it: Peckham v. Van Wagenen, 83 N. Y., 40, distinguishing Le Roy v. Globe Ins. Co., 2 Edw. Chy., 657 ; In re Le Blanc, 75 N. Y., 598.

[11 Chancery Division, 779.]

C.A., Feb. 18, 1879.

779]   *TAUNTON V. MORRIS.

[1874 T. 94.]

Husband and Wife—Wife's Equity to a Settlement—Life Interest—Amount to be settled.

A married woman has the same equity to a settlement, as against her husband or his general assignee, out of property in which she has only a life interest, as out of property in which she has an absolute interest; and the court will make no distinction between the two cases as regards the amount to be settled. In every case the court will exercise its judicial discretion as to the amount to be settled, having regard to all the circumstances.

A husband became insolvent in 1861 to a large amount, and his estate paid no dividend. In 1876 his wife became entitled to the income of property amounting to £500 a year.

The Court (affirming the decision of Malins, V.C.), ordered the whole income to be settled on the wife.

THIS was an appeal from a decision of Vice-Chancellor Malins (¹).

Mr. Taunton, the husband of the petitioner, Mrs. Taunton, became insolvent in July, 1861, being indebted to various creditors to the extent of £25,000; no assets of his estate had been discovered, and no dividend had been declared.

The petitioner became entitled in 1876 to an income of about £500 a year, the capital being settled on her children under the will of her father, the testator in the cause. The income was not settled to the separate use of Mrs. Taunton, and no settlement or agreement for a settlement was executed on her marriage.

Mrs. Taunton asked to have the whole income settled on her.

The provisional assignee under Mr. Taunton's insolvency claimed half of the income for the benefit of the creditors.

The Vice-Chancellor directed the whole income to be settled on Mrs. Taunton. The provisional assignee appealed from this decision.

Glasse, Q.C., and *Langley*, for the appellant : We admit

(¹) 8 Ch. D., 453; 25 Eng. R., 423.

that if the property in this case had been capital the court could, in the exercise of its discretion, have settled the whole *of it on the wife and children. But the court has [780 never acted on the same principle with respect to a life interest. The children have no interest in the income, and it is only a question between the wife and the husband or his assignees. The usual rule is to give half to the wife, and there is no reason why that rule should be departed from in the present case: *In re Duffy's Trust* ('); *Tidd* v. *Lister* ('); *Lea* v. *Church* ('); *Vaughan* v. *Buck* (').

J. Pearson, Q.C., and *W. W. Karslake*, for Mrs. Taunton : The court has never recognized a distinction between corpus and income when considering the amount to be settled on a married woman as against the general assignee of the husband. In every case, whether the property be corpus or income, the court will exercise its judicial discretion, having regard to all the circumstances of the case : *Gardner* v. *Marshall* (') ; *Scott* v. *Spashett* (') ; *Squires* v. *Ashford* (') ; *Dunkley* v. *Dunkley* (') ; *Smith* v. *Smith* (').

Glasse, in reply.

JAMES, L.J.: I do not know whether, if this case had come before me in the first instance, I should have made the same order as the Vice-Chancellor has done ; but I cannot say that I differ from him so much that I feel myself constrained by the principles on which this court acts to overrule his decision. One point that was pressed upon us in the argument was that a distinction is made in the authorities between the corpus and income of property in which a married woman claims an equity to a settlement. No doubt there is a distinction where the income has been sold by the husband to a particular assignee, as pointed out in *Tidd* v. *Lister* ('"). The income may have been sold for the benefit of the wife and her family, or it may be a question whether the husband has neglected to support his wife ; but a general assignee *of the husband is in exactly the same [781 position as the husband himself, and as against him there cannot be any distinction between a life interest and corpus.

Then the question is what ought to be done in the present case. The general rule is that it requires special circumstances to induce the court to give more than one-half to the wife. Here the wife's whole interest is £500 a year, which is not much more than in the case before Vice-Chancellor

(¹) 28 Beav., 386.
(²) 10 Hare, 140; 3 D. M. & G., 857.
(³) 3 W. R., 603.
(⁴) 1 Sim. (N.S.), 284.
(⁵) 14 Sim., 575.
(⁶) 3 Mac. & G., 599.
(⁷) 23 Beav., 132.
(⁸) 2 D. M. & G., 390.
(⁹) 3 Giff., 121.
(¹⁰) 3 D. M. & G., 857.

Stuart, *Smith* v. *Smith* (¹).   The Vice-Chancellor has not
considered that too much, and I cannot help thinking that
if you take any of it away from the wife, it will only be
thrown into the ocean of costs.   It will not make a difference of more than twopence or threepence in the pound to
the creditors, many of whom may be now dead.   Therefore,
under all the circumstances, I do not sufficiently differ from
the Vice-Chancellor to induce me to reverse this decision.

BRAMWELL, L.J., concurred.

BRETT, L.J.:   The principle of the courts of equity is one
which we cannot but admire, that a settlement should be
made of the wife's property.   But in the course of time an
artificial rule for carrying it out has been made, under which
a certain proportion only is given to the wife.   In modern
times this artificial rule has fallen through ; several cases
have been cited in which the whole of the wife's property
was settled, no distinction being made in them between corpus and income.   The modern rule seems to be that all the
circumstances of the case should be looked at, and that
the judge should exercise his judicial discretion as to the
amount to be settled.   Such circumstances are the amount
of the property in question, the amount of the husband's
debts, and the length of time since the insolvency.   In the
present case I think the length of time since the insolvency
renders it quite an exceptional case.   If it was not for the
debts being kept alive by the insolvency all the husband's
debts would have been barred by lapse of time ; and doubt-
less, in fact, all have long ago been written off by the creditors as bad debts.

782]   *Another thing to be considered is the amount of
the property in question.   If it had been an income of
£1,000 a year, probably the Vice-Chancellor's decision
might have been different.   Also, the relation of that
amount to the amount of the debts must be taken into account.   Whatever is not settled will certainly be frittered
away in law expenses, and the creditors will get nothing.
All these things must be considered in applying the principle of the courts of equity.   On the whole, I entirely agree
with the Vice-Chancellor's decision.

The appeal must be dismissed.   The costs will be paid out
of the income.

Solicitors: *A. S. Twyford ; J. Crowdy & Son.*

(¹) 8 Giff., 121

[11 Chancery Division, 782.]

C.A., April 28, 29, 1879.

WEST CUMBERLAND IRON AND STEEL COMPANY V. KENYON.

[1876 W. 80.]

Mine—Use of Property—Water discharged into Neighboring Mine—Appropriation of Water.

The defendants, the owners of a mining property, sunk a shaft by which they tapped the water which had formerly found its way into certain old workings on their own ground, and had thence percolated into the plaintiffs' mines. The defendants then made a borehole at the bottom of the shaft. It was admitted that the making it was not in due course of mining, but only for the purpose of getting rid of the water. The effect of the borehole was to let off the water into the above-mentioned old workings on the defendants' ground, whence it percolated into the plaintiffs' works in the same way in which it would have done if neither shaft nor borehole had ever been made:

Held (reversing the decision of Fry, J.), that the defendants had not by making the shaft so appropriated the water as to lay themselves under an obligation to keep it from coming upon the plaintiffs' land, and that, as the effect of the defendants' operations was not to throw upon the plaintiffs' land any burden which it had not borne before, the plaintiffs' case failed.

THIS was an appeal by the defendants from a decision of Mr. Justice Fry (¹)

Herschell, Q.C., *Cookson*, Q.C., and *Plummer*, for [783 the appellants: We do not dispute the finding of facts by the judge, but we deny that there was any cause of action. The borehole was made to get rid of the water. If we had done nothing the water would have come to the plaintiffs' mine just the same. It is not correct to say that we appropriated the water for our own benefit: we only wanted to get rid of it. No one has a right to complain of what I do on my own land, if what I do leaves him in the same condition as if I had done nothing: *Smith* v. *Kenrick* (²); *Smith* v. *Fletcher* (³); *Nichols* v. *Marsland* (⁴). It is for the plaintiffs to show that a larger volume of water comes to them than would have come if there had been no borehole, which they have not done. No damages can be claimed for any injury arising from gravitation and percolation: *Wilson* v. *Waddell* (⁵), Bainbridge on Mines (⁶).

North, Q.C., and *Ingle Joyce*, contrà: The question which the defendants argued below was whether this borehole was made in the legitimate course of mining operations.

(¹) 6 Ch. D., 773; 23 Eng. R., 336.   (⁴) 2 Ex. D., 1.
(²) 7 C. B., 515.   (⁵) 2 App. Cas., 59; 19 Eng. R., 1.
(³) Law Rep., 9 Ex., 64; 8 Eng. R., 510;   (⁶) Page 307.
2 App. Cas., 781; 21 Eng. R., 38.

They denied that it was made for the purpose of getting rid
of the water. This ground they now give up. We do not
dispute that the defendants may allow the water to flow to
our mines in the natural way.

[JAMES, L.J.: What the defendants say is, that they have
a right to do what they please on their own ground provided
they do not by their operations make the water come to your
mines in a different quantity, or by a different channel, or at
a different time.]

We rely on the principle laid down in *Hurdman* v. *North
Eastern Railway Company* ('), that the causing by an artificial work the passage of water into a neighbor's land gives
a right of action. If water which would have reached my
land at one time is made by artificial means adopted for
that purpose to reach it at an earlier time, that is an action-
784]   able wrong. The case of * *Westminster Brymbo Coal
and Coke Company* v. *Clayton* (') is very like the present.

[JAMES, L.J.: In that case the same water would not have
found its way to the plaintiffs' land if the defendants had
done nothing.]

If a man artificially stores up water on his ground he has
appropriated it, and cannot then send it on his neighbor's
ground : *Lomax* v. *Stott* ('). The rule is laid down in our
favor in *Smith* v. *Fletcher* ('), and we contend that the
Exchequer Chamber did not differ from the court below as
to the point of law, though a new trial was granted. The
law is settled by *Baird* v. *Williamson* (') and other cases,
that a mine-owner is not liable for a flow of water owing to
gravitation and percolation, but he must not be an active
agent in sending it on his neighbor's mine. Here the borehole must have accelerated the flow of water into the plaintiffs' land, or it would have been of no use to make it.

Herschell, in reply.

JAMES, L.J.: Upon the question of fact in this case, I
have arrived at the same conclusion as Mr. Justice Fry, and,
as it appears to me, there is no real conflict of evidence.
The evidence shows that the water which was tapped by the
New Banks Shaft, and which was afterwards discharged
through the borehole into the defendants' old workings at
the Limefitts Pit, was water which, following the stratification of the country, had previously found its way into the
same subterraneous hollows from which water was pumped
up by the pumps which at one time were used at the Lime-

(') 3 C. P. D., 168 ; 30 Eng. R., 81.   (') 39 L. J. (Ch.), 834.
(') 36 L. J. (Ch.), 476.   (') Law Rep., 7 Ex., 305 ; 8 Eng R., 510.
                 (') 15 C. B. (N.S.), 376.

fitts Shaft, and that the same water practically and substantially found its way down into those hollows to the same extent as it found its way afterwards through the shaft and the borehole. The evidence upon that is plain. Several witnesses were called, experts who knew the country, who said that they had no doubt that every *particle of   [785 water would have gone down and must have been going down into the Limefitts Shaft when the pumps were going on ; that being the course by which these water-bearing strata discharged their water so as to prevent its rising up above the sixteen fathoms, down to which distance the stratification was quite dry. It seems to me upon all the evidence, that there were these water-bearing strata draining down into the hollows that had been formed by the old workings of the principal vein of the Limefitts property, and thence into the lowest level, and that the defendants made a shaft which did to a certain extent tap that water, but only diverted into that shaft (as I am satisfied) for a time the water, which previous to that diversion, was finding its way down into the lowest level.

Several witnesses, both for the plaintiffs and defendants, give evidence in exactly the same way, and if there was any case intended to be made that what the defendants have done produces an extra substantial burden or change in the position of the defendants by reason of more water being thrown upon them, I should have expected that there would have been some evidence directed to that point, and that there would have been some cross-examination of the defendants' witnesses upon the point which they prove so distinctly, that is to say, that in their judgment and belief, and according to their knowledge, all the water had originally found its way down to the plaintiffs' levels. Then, if that be so, the working of the defendants' shaft and the borehole has not been shown to have thrown any additional water whatever on the plaintiffs. On the other hand, this is to be borne in mind, that the way in which the case is now presented to us on behalf of the defendants is this : "We do not treat it as a mining question, it has nothing to do with the case of *Smith* v. *Kenrick* (¹), or any particular law as applicable to mining, we deal with it exactly as if it were something on the surface. We have made certain things upon our land and we have done that without doing you any mischief whatever. That is to say we have done something on our own land, as we had a right to do ; we had occasion (or not having any occasion we were minded) to sink a shaft in our

(¹) 7 C. B., 515.

own land, and finding that that shaft was getting filled with
786]   water, we made *a drain from the bottom of that shaft
so as to prevent the water accumulating which would have
destroyed it.   But we drained that water into our own land,
we drained it into some old hollows which were there, and
which were calculated to receive the water, and from which
hollows the water no doubt found its way into the plaintiffs'
land, but found its way exactly in the same course as far as
the plaintiffs are concerned as before it left our hollow, in
exactly the same place and in exactly the same way, and to
exactly the same extent as it would have done if we had not
done anything of the kind."

   Now Mr. Justice Fry seems to have thought that if once a
man appropriated water (which does not seem to me to be a
very accurate expression, because the very last thing in the
world the defendants intended to do was the storing water
so as to appropriate it), that the moment he had done something by which the water became collected in his hollow,
then he became bound to discharge that water in such a way
that it would never reach his neighbor's land.   I am not
aware that there is any principle or any authority for that
proposition.   I have always understood that everybody has
a right on his own land to do anything with regard to the
diversion of water, or the storage of water, or with regard
to the usage of water, in any way he chooses, provided
that when he ceases dealing with it on his own land, when
he has made such use of it as he is minded to make, he
is not to allow or cause that water to go upon his neighbor's land so as to affect that neighbor's land in some other
way than the way in which it had been affected before.
That is the common use of water.   A man receives the rain
water from his roof, he does not allow it to settle upon the
surface, but he receives it on his roof, and collects it into
the pipes, and then lets it go down upon his own land, and
from his own land it gets into his neighbor's land.   But unless his neighbor receives that water in some different way
or quantity from what he had done before, there is no legal
right of action.   If a man chooses to make any quantity of
fish ponds, or mill ponds, or artificial lakes, or pleasure
waters, or fountains, or anything of that kind on his own
land, he is at liberty to do so, provided that when he has
finished doing so he does not increase the burden upon his
787]   neighbor.   And if his neighbor complains, he *has a
right to reply, "What is it to you what I have been doing
on my own land? The same quantity of water leaves my
land, and leaves my land through exactly the same aperture,

and gets into your field in exactly the same way as it did before." If there is a lake on my property into which I drain my field, and there is a passage from that lake into my neighbor's land, how can it signify whether I drain my field into the lake by one, two, or three openings, provided the same overflow as before goes through the same outlet into my neighbor's land? If the fact be, as we have found it to be, that the water which was turned by the shaft and borehole into the hollows about the Limefitts Pit was the same water which would have found its way into the same hollows independently of that shaft and borehole, it seems to me that the plaintiffs have nothing whatever of which to complain.

The defendants are no longer justifying themselves by the false issue which was fought in the court below for so many days, namely, whether this was a proper mining operation. That false issue having been abandoned, we have nothing but a common case which may occur to anybody on the surface; that is to say, a man makes a pit on his land, and to prevent it being filled with water he puts a drain at the bottom of it and runs the water off into his own land, whence it finds its way to his neighbor's land in the same way as it had done before. I am of opinion that this is a case in which the defendants have used their own land, and have not been shown to have injured their neighbors in so using it, that the plaintiffs have failed in showing that they have any legal ground of action, and the action ought therefore to have been dismissed.

Brett, L.J.: This action is brought on the ground of an alleged breach of the maxin *sic utere tuo ut alienum non lædas.* The cases have decided that where that maxim is applied to landed property, it is subject to a certain modification, it being necessary for the plaintiff to show not only that he has sustained damage, but that the defendant has caused it by going beyond what is necessary in order to enable him to have the natural use of his own land. If the plaintiff only shows that his own land is damaged by the defendant's using his land in the natural manner, he cannot *succeed. So he must fail if he only proves that the [788 defendant has used his land otherwise than in the natural way, but does not prove damage to himself. Both points are here in issue. For a long time both parties contended about one of these points, and not about the other. The plaintiffs proved that the defendants used their property otherwise than in the natural manner necessary to give them the due enjoyment of their rights of ownership, and otherwise than in the regular course of mining; but they failed to prove that any greater burden was thrown upon their land than it would have had to bear if the defendants had done nothing, and Mr. Justice Fry seems to have been of that opinion.

If water percolates through the defendant's land, and gets into a defined channel, and then goes into the plaintiff's land, and the defendant makes a pond which receives this water, and then makes a cutting which allows the water to go again into the same defined channel, so that the old flow into the plaintiff's land is resumed, is the defendant liable? Mr. Justice Fry says that he is, on the ground that the defendant having collected the water has made it his property, and is bound to control it, and may not restore things to their original condition. With deference to him, I know of no such law. The merely obtaining a temporary control over the water does not impose on the defendant the obligation of keeping it, nor prevent him from restoring it to the strata from which it came, unless he makes it flow differently. Therefore, agreeing with Mr. Justice Fry as to what I believe to have been his findings of facts, and his inferences from those findings, viz., that no larger quantity of water came to the plaintiffs' land than if no shaft had been made, I differ from his view that the defendants having once intercepted the water were not at liberty to let it go again.

COTTON, L.J.: The case launched by the plaintiffs is that by reason of the operations of the defendants, a large quantity of foreign water is thrown upon the plaintiffs' land, and that the defendants have no right to send it there to the damage of the plaintiffs. This is subject to the exception that if the flow of water is only the result of the defendants using their 789] land in the natural way, the *plaintiffs cannot complain; and it is established by the cases that taking out minerals is a natural use of mining property, and that no adjoining proprietor can complain of the result of careful and proper mining operations. To meet this the plaintiffs allege that making the borehole is not a proper mining operation, and this is now admitted.

The question remains whether any substantial quantity of foreign water has been thrown upon the plaintiffs' lands by the operations complained of, and this is a question of fact. Mr. Justice Fry does not appear to have come to a positive conclusion on this point, but he seems to have considered that the water which went through the borehole would have found its way to the plaintiffs' land if the defendants' shaft hand not been made. In this I agree with him.

Now, underneath the defendants' land were old workings reaching up to the Limefitts Shaft. While the pumping was continued there, the water was prevented from finding its way to the plaintiffs' land. The pumps were abandoned, and the water from the old workings penetrated into the plaintiffs' land, and threw additional pumping upon them. The water which passed through the borehole went into these same old workings, and thence percolated into the plaintiffs' land. The plaintiffs say it lies on the defendants to show that the making the borehole threw no additional burden on the plaintiffs' land. Assuming that to be so, the question is whether we ought not on the evidence to say that without the borehole the same water would have found its way to the plaintiffs' works, and that therefore no additional burden is imposed on them. I am of opinion that this is the conclusion to be drawn from the evidence.

We then come to the ground taken by Mr. Justice Fry. He says that the defendants, by making the shaft, appropriated the water, and made themselves masters of it, and so became bound to prevent it from flowing into the plaintiffs' works. This is a fallacy. The action is not for damage done by allowing that water to escape. If a case were made that the water was allowed to escape suddenly, it would be quite a different matter, but nothing of the kind is alleged. The complaint made is that the defendants, by making the borehole, have prevented their shaft *from being a [790 water-containing reservoir. Now, if, in consequence of this, the water had entered the plaintiffs' land by a different course, the plaintiffs would have had quite another case, but all that the defendants have done is to alter the course of the water into a reservoir on their own land. There is an alteration in the way it gets there, but there is no addition to the water thrown into the plaintiffs' lands, nor any variation in the time of its getting there. I am therefore of opinion that the action fails.

Solicitors: *Bischoff, Bompas & Bischoff; Speechly, Mumford & Co.*

See 31 Eng. Rep., 373 note; 2 Am. Law Mag., 43.

A municipal corporation or village is liable for collecting waters of a large acreage and discharging them on plaintiff's lands, though such acts are done in changing the grade of streets under its charter: Baker *v.* Oneonta, 15 N. Y. Weekly Dig., 224; S. C., Mem., 27 Hun, 544.

Plaintiff's premises were damaged by the negligent building of a sewer, by reason of which its contents were discharged so as to create a nuisance. This resulted from a failure of defendants' officers to carry out the plans which had been adopted. Held, such failure was not a mere exercise of discretion which exempted the city from liability, and that the act complained of having been performed in the prosecution of a lawful purpose and in the discharge of a plain duty, it cannot be said that the water board acted outside of the powers conferred by the charter, and that the city is relieved from liability: Hardy *v.* Brooklyn, 15 N. Y. Weekly Dig., 563, Ct. Appeals.

The law regarding surface water is, that no individual or corporation can make any change thereof to the injury of any one, without being responsible in damages for such injury.

If a city constructs a sewer in such a manner that an *additional* flow of surface water in a lot is caused thereby, the owner of such lot may recover such damages as may have been caused by such *increased* flow.

A city, in the progress of constructing its sewerage, is not responsible for any depreciation in the rental value of property caused by the bad smells of a sewer in course of construction, unless it is kept open an unreasonable length of time: Arn *v.* City of Kansas, 14 Fed. Repr., 236.

An action lies for such damages as are caused by snow thrown from one person's premises upon those of another, although the damages may be more consequential than direct.

But damages cannot be recovered on account of water dripping from a house on adjacent premises, without proof that it was caused by some neglect of duty on the part of the house owner: Barry *v.* Peterson, 48 Mich., 263, affirming Underwood *v.* Waldron, 33 id., 239.

The firm of W. & Co., plaintiff's assignors, occupied a store in the city of New York, having a cellar and subcellar, and also a vault under the sidewalk in front. Defendant erected a building on an adjoining lot, and constructed a vault under the sidewalk in front thereof. In so doing, it took up the curb and gutter of the street and excavated a space in the street extending about two feet outside of the curb, and left the space in front of the outer wall of the vault unfilled. It also excavated a space on the lot of W. & Co. between the wall of said vault and the wall of the vault of W. & Co., which did not come quite to the line of the lot. Such excavation extended below the foundation of the latter wall; this space communicated with that left in the street. The grade of the street descended, so that when the premises were in the ordinary condition, the surface water flowed through the gutter in front of the store of W. & Co.

and passed off through the gutter in front of defendant's premises. Defendant constructed a dam from the sidewalk in front of the store of W. & Co., which turned the water across the street into the gutter on the other side, but during a heavy rain the dam gave way and let the water into said excavation; thence it found its way under the foundation of, and into, the vault of W. & Co., and their sub-cellar, damaging goods therein. In an action to recover the damages, held, that defendant was liable, and this without regard to any question of negligence; that it was no defence that the dam was built properly, and due care was taken on its part to protect the premises.

Conceding the rule that, as to the travelling public, an excavation in a street made by consent of the municipal authorities, is not *per se* unlawful, and a nuisance, and that the person making the same is only liable for the omission of proper care; such rule does not apply when the excavation causes injury to adjoining land, by collecting surface water, or diverting it from its proper channel and thus throwing it upon such land.

A municipal corporation cannot delegate power to private individuals, to be exercised for their own private benefit, to do injury to the property of their neighbors, and relieve them from responsibility from the damages, or reduce their liability to such as may result from want of proper care.

Where one, in making improvements upon his own premises, or without lawful right trespasses upon or injures his neighbor's property by casting material thereon, he is liable absolutely for the damage irrespective of any question of care or negligence, and a license from the municipal authorities cannot affect the question of responsibility.

It was claimed by defendants that the water, or a portion thereof, which did the injury, found its way through holes in the sidewall of the store of W. & Co. Held immaterial; that they were under no obligation to make their wall impervious to water wrongfully thrown upon their premises: Mairs *v.* Manhattan Real Estate, etc., 89 N. Y., 498.

In an action against a city to recover for an injury to a building, alleged to have been caused by the wrongful and negligent obstruction of the natural channel and diversion of the course of a stream by the defendant, the failure of plaintiff to use ordinary diligence and effort to prevent damage, and to incur moderate expense, if thereby the injury might have been prevented, would constitute contributory negligence, and entirely bar recovery; and an instruction that in such case he would still be entitled to recover such sum as would have prevented the injury if it had been expended, was erroneous.

An instruction that if the plaintiff erected his house where the creek had flowed for ten years and where, but for the house, it would still have flowed, and the damage was caused thereby, he would still be entitled to recover, unless it had so flowed with his knowledge and consent, was erroneous. In such case he had no right to divert the flow of the creek, whether such flow had been with his knowledge and consent or not.

Where a stream meanders through a city, and lots and streets have been platted without reference to it, nor bounded by it, the doctrine of superior proprietorship is not applicable; and an instruction applying that doctrine to this case was error.

Under the circumstances of this case, an instruction that the adoption in good faith by the defendant, of the plans of skilful and competent engineers and workmen in constructing and repairing bridges and culverts across the creek in question, would not protect the defendant, was erroneous. Where the city acts in good faith and an unexpected damage result, the city is not liable.

Where the evidence showed that if any cause of action existed, it must have arisen within five years before the commencement of the suit, an instruction excluding the question of the statute of limitations from the jury was proper: Hoehl v. City of Muscatine, 57 Iowa, 444; S. P., Fulleam v. Muscatine, Id., 457.

A railroad corporation is not liable for damages to any person from the overflow of the water of a stream, caused by the necessary and proper elevation of its road-bed, not in the channel of the stream but upon its own land.

Plaintiff's complaint alleged that de-

fendant had constructed an embankment on the side of the M. river, thus narrowing its channel, so that in times of floods the water was thrown in unusual quantities upon her land contiguous to the river on the opposite side. On the trial, evidence was offered by plaintiff, showing damage caused by the raising of defendant's road-bed; this was objected to, on the ground that it was not alleged in the complaint, and that no liability accrued in raising the tracks. The objection was overruled and defendant excepted. The referee found that, at a time specified, defendant, to prevent its tracks from being flooded, raised the bed of its road and built an embankment out into the river, causing the current to flow on and over plaintiff's lands, damaging them to an amount specified; that at another time, for the purpose of laying additional tracks, defendant built said embankment further out into the river, causing further injury to an amount specified; that a portion of the damage was caused by raising the road-bed; that the embankments were built in a workmanlike and skilful manner, and, as a conclusion of law, that defendant was liable for such damages. Defendant's counsel excepted in the following form, "separately to each and every of the referee's findings of fact, save as to one that was specified," and also excepted to the conclusion of law.

Held, that although there was no evidence justifying the findings that defendant, at the time first specified, when raising its road-bed, built an embankment into the river, and such finding was therefore error; there was no exception presenting this error; but that the exception to the evidence as to the damages caused by raising the road-bed, and to the conclusion of law that defendant was liable for such damages, presented the question as to its liability, and that such exceptions were well taken: Moyer v. N. Y. Cent., etc., 88 N. Y., 351.

On the 6th of January, 1877, there was a heavy fall of snow, and the Baltimore City Passenger Railway Company, in clearing its track running along the bed of Gay street and across Hoffman street, threw the snow into a mass at the intersection of those streets. Near by on Hoffman street was the house of the plaintiff. On the night of the day mentioned it rained very hard, and the plaintiff's house was flooded with water. He thereupon brought suit against the railway company, alleging that in removing the snow from its track and throwing it into the street it had obstructed the natural flow of water, whereby the plaintiff's house was injured. This was denied by the defendant. The verdict and judgment being for the defendant, the plaintiff appealed. Held,

1. That the defendant had a right to remove the snow from its track, and in clearing its track and in throwing the snow on the bed of the street adjoining thereto, the defendant did not use the bed of the street in an unusual or unreasonable manner.

2. That it had no right to throw the snow in the gutter and thereby obstruct the natural flow of water from the street, because in so doing it would have been guilty of negligence; nor had it a right to bank up the snow on Gay street so as necessarily to obstruct the natural flow of water. On the contrary, it was obliged to exercise ordinary care and prudence, not only in removing the snow from its track, but also in throwing it on the street.

The true test of exemption from liability in actions for injury to another's property, resulting from the exercise of rights incident to the dominion and ownership of property is whether, in the act complained of, the owner has used his property in a reasonable, usual and proper manner, taking care to avoid unnecessary injury to others: Short v. Baltimore City, etc., 50 Iowa, 73.

[11 Chancery Division, 790.]

V.C.H., July 4, 1878: C.A., May 2, 3, 5, 1879.

ALLEN v. SECKHAM.

[1876 A. 146.]

Constructive Notice—Lights—Agreement.

Disputes having arisen between the plaintiff and W. whether a window in the plaintiff's house overlooking W.'s land was an ancient light, an agreement, not under seal, was signed by which W. agreed that the plaintiff should have access of light to the window, and the plaintiff agreed to keep the window opaque and make it open only in such a way that no person could look out of it. W.'s land was afterwards sold to the defendant, who had no actual notice of the agreement, but knew of the existence of the window:

Held, by Hall, V.C., that the defendant, seeing the window when he purchased, was put upon inquiry, and was affected with constructive notice of the agreement, and therefore must be restrained from interfering with the access of light to the window.

Held, on appeal, that the mere fact of there being windows in an adjoining house which overlook a purchased property is not constructive notice of any agreement giving a right to the access of light to them.

The *dicta* of Lord Chelmsford in *Miles* v. *Tobin* ([1]) dissented from.

IN 1867 the plaintiff purchased certain property at Wellingborough upon which was an old building which he pulled down and rebuilt. A question then arose between him and Mrs. Wallis, the owner of the adjoining property, whether a certain window in the new building, which the plaintiff alleged to be substantially identical with an ancient window in the old building, was an *ancient light. Ultimately the dispute was settled by an agreement in writing, not under seal, dated the 6th of March, 1869, by which,

([1]) 16 W. R., 465.

inter alia, it was agreed that the plaintiff should have au indefeasible right to the access of light and air to the window on condition that he should forthwith make the glass of the window opaque, and that he, his heirs and assigns, should keep it opaque, and make it open in such a way as only to admit air without allowing any one to look out.

In May, 1876, the defendant purchased the property of Mrs. Wallis, and it was not disputed that he completed his purchase without any actual notice of the above agreement.

The defendant shortly after his purchase pulled down a wall which stood on his property opposite to the window, and commenced erecting a building of greater height and slightly nearer to the window than the old wall was.

The plaintiff on the 18th of July wrote to the defendant stating that the proposed new building would entirely obstruct his light and air, that he could not allow his right to be infringed, and that if the defendant built according to the plans, he must do so at his own risk. He did not in any way refer to the agreement of 1869. The defendant then negotiated with the plaintiff for the purchase of the plaintiff's property, but the negotiation proved abortive, and the defendant proceeded to build. The building was carried to its full height before the writ in this action was issued.

On the 28th of September, 1876, the plaintiff commenced his action for an injunction to restrain the defendant from building or suffering to remain built on his premises any wall or building so as to darken, injure, or obstruct the access of light and air to the plaintiff's window.

The action came on for trial before Vice-Chancellor Hall on the 4th of July, 1878.

Chester, for the plaintiff.

Dickinson, Q.C., and *Owen*, for the defendant: There is an entire absence of notice of the agreement; there is not any evience that the light is an ancient one, and there is no proof of any substantial injury to make a case for an injunction.

*Hall, V.C.: I do not give any opinion on the [792 question whether the plaintiff has established a right to protection in respect of an ancient light. I determine the case in the plaintiff's favor upon his right founded upon the agreement between himself and Ann Wallis dated the 6th day of March, 1869. That agreement, which was entered into after certain disputes had arisen between the parties, clearly provides for the enjoyment of the light at that time existing. It was submitted that the defendant had not notice of the agreement, and was therefore not bound by it; but he saw the window when he purchased the property, and seeing it, I hold that he was put upon inquiry, and in that respect his rights are no higher than those of Ann Wallis, through whom he claims.   There are, I think, many authorities for that opinion, but I will refer to only one, *Davies* v. *Marshall* (¹).   I think there has been substantial interference with the plaintiff's light.   There has not been anything in the plaintiff's conduct—laches or acquiescence—to deprive him of his right, and therefore I grant a mandatory injunction, which must be so framed as to show the title arising under the agreement of 1869, and define the limits within which the defendant must keep his new building upon the property acquired from Ann Wallis's representatives.   The order must be limited so as to determine in case of a right to obstruct the light arising under the agreement with Ann Wallis, her heirs and assigns.

The defendant appealed.   The appeal came on for hearing on the 2d of May, 1879.

Owen, for the appellant: The defendant had no notice. No case was cited below on the question whether seeing the window was notice, the case of *Davies* v. *Marshall*, referred to by the Vice-Chancellor, turning on an entirely different point.   The only case I find having any bearing on the question is *Hervey* v. *Smith* (²), which is disapproved of by Lord St. Leonards (³) ; and if sound, it does not govern this 793]   case, *for there the party complaining was in actual possession of an erection upon his neighbor's land.   The plaintiff has no legal right apart from notice of the agreement: *Leech* v. *Schweder* (⁴).   Apart from the agreement, this is not on the evidence an ancient light.   The plaintiff is bound by acquiescence, for he did not say anything about the agreement when he complained of the defendant's building.

[JAMES, L.J.:   He insisted that he had a right, so there cannot be acquiescence, though he did not tell you on what his right was founded.]

But supposing the light to be an ancient light, the plaintiff cannot have a mandatory injunction, for my building was carried to its full height before the writ issued.   The court will not in such a case grant a mandatory injunction unless the injury is extreme : *Durell* v. *Pritchard* (⁵), *City of London Brewery* v. *Tennant* (⁶).   In *Krehl* v. *Burrell* (⁷) the building was erected after writ issued.

(¹) 10 C. B. (N.S.), 697.
(²) 1 K. & J., 389; 22 Beav., 299.
(³) Sug. V. & P., 14th ed., p. 765.
(⁴) Law Rep., 9 Ch., 463, 475; 9 Eng. R., 559.

(⁵) Law Rep., 1 Ch., 244.
(⁶) Law Rep., 9 Ch., 212; 8 Eng. R., 827.
(⁷) 7 Ch. D., 551; 23 Eng. R., 703; 11 Ch. D., 146; 27 Eng. R., 404.

Chester, contrà, was desired in the first case to address himself to the question of notice : The existence of a window suggests a right to light, and puts a person who sees it upon inquiry, especially where the height of the buildings opposite is much less than is usual in metropolitan buildings. The case comes within the principle which Mr. *Dart* (¹) deduces from *Morland* v. *Cook* (³), and *Hervey* v. *Smith* (⁴).

[JAMES, L.J.: In the latter case a person was enjoying something in his neighbor's land, and was a trespasser unless there was some agreement.]

In *Davies* v. *Sear* (⁵) the existence of an archway was held to give notice of a right of way under it. In *Miles* v. *Tobin* (⁶) Lord Chelmsford held that the existence of windows was constructive notice of a right of access of light to them.

*JAMES, L.J.: I am of opinion that the decision of [794 the Vice-Chancellor cannot be sustained on the ground on which he put it, and that it would be very dangerous to carry the doctrine of constructive notice to this length. That doctrine, as applied by the Vice-Chancellor, would come to this, that a purchaser is to be held to have constructive notice of every agreement relating to any structure which he sees on the adjoining ground. A man often builds a house with windows overlooking his neighbor's ground, taking his chance of acquiring a right to access of light by twenty years' enjoyment, and to say that a purchaser of the adjoining property is bound to inquire whether he has not acquired that right by agreement, is a strong and dangerous extension of the doctrine of constructive notice. The cases cited are quite different in principle. In *Morland* v. *Cook* (³) the purchaser saw the property protected by a sea-wall, and the court considered that every reasonable man under such circumstances must be taken to have known that the wall existed for the protection of the lands below the level of the sea, and that there must be some provision made for its maintenance and repair, and that therefore he was put upon inquiry. As to *Hervey* v. *Smith* (⁴), which is doubted by Lord St. Leonards, it is not necessary to decide whether it stretched the law beyond proper limits ; it is sufficient for the present purpose to say that it went on a principle not applicable to the present case, for there the purchaser was taken to have seen that the owner of the adjoining house

(¹) Dart, V. & P., vol. i, p. 453.   (³) 1 K. & J., 389 ; 22 Beav., 299.
(²) Law Rep., 6 Eq., 252.   (⁴) Law Rep., 7 Ex., 427.
                        (⁵) 16 W. R., 465.

had the actual possession and use of flues which in the absence of agreement must have been part of the purchased
property. The case of the archway is also quite distinguishable from this. An archway is only left for a purpose,
and its existence suggests an agreement giving a right of
passing under it. How does that apply to the existence
of windows? A man is at liberty to build upon his own
land a house having as many windows as he likes. He is
not by so doing interfering with any rights of his neighbors.
He may acquire a right under the Prescription Act, but
there is nothing in the mere sight of a window to put a person on inquiry what title there is to access of light to it, any
more than to put him on inquiry as to the obligation of the
795]   owner of the *window to keep it opaque, or to make
it open only in a particular way. In *Miles* v. *Tobin* (¹)
Lord Chelmsford used some expressions which are strongly
in the plaintiff's favor, but they were wholly extra-judicial,
for nothing in that case turned on notice. The defendants
knew that the plaintiffs derived title from the same grantors
as themselves, the common grantors being the trustees of a
charity. The court came to the conclusion that the lease
under which the plaintiffs claimed, and which was prior to
the lease to the defendants, bound the plaintiffs to build according to particular plans ; the lease, therefore, if not in
express terms, at all events by necessary implication, gave
the plaintiffs a right to the use of the windows prescribed by
those plans. This was a right granted by deed, which
bound the adjoining lands of the grantors, apart from any
question of notice. Any person who buys land in this
country buys subject to the chance that the vendor may
have granted all manner of rights over it, and against this
chance he guards himself by taking the covenants of the vendor. The case of *Miles* v. *Tobin* was simply one of a grant
by deed made by the person under whom the defendants
derived title, and the remark of Lord Chelmsford, which has
been relied on, was a mere *obiter dictum*, which appears to
have remained in the Weekly Reporter, and not to have
found its way into any other books so as to become part of
our traditional law. We therefore do not consider ourselves bound by it, and we think that such an extension of
the law as to constructive notice would be dangerous and
unwarranted.

BRETT, L.J: The doctrine of constructive notice ought
to be narrowly watched and not enlarged. Indeed, any-

(¹) 16 W R., 465.   (²) Law Rep., 6 Eq., 252.

(³) 1 K. & J., 389; 22 Beav., 299.

thing "constructive" ought to be narrowly watched, because it depends on a fiction. We are, however, bound by the authorities, and I conceive that when a person purchases property where a visible state of things exists which could not legally exist without the property being subject to some burden, he is taken to have notice of the extent and nature of that burden. But it seems that the rule goes further, *and that when a state of circumstances exists which [796 is very unlikely to exist without a burden, he is affected with notice. The case of an existing tenancy is an instance of the first proposition. The tenant cannot legally be in possession without having some rights, and his possession is held to give notice to a purchaser what those rights are. In the case of the chimneys, Lord St. Leonards doubted whether there was notice. If it had been shown that the purchaser knew that there were flues in his house which belonged to fire-places in the other house, then there would have been a visible state of circumstances which could not have legally existed without the owner of the other house having some right. The difficulty is in attributing to the purchaser knowledge of a fact which would be so likely to be overlooked. The case of the sea-wall comes within the principle that a visible state of circumstances exists, such as to make it extremely probable that there is a servitude. So in the case of the archway: a man seeing an archway leading to a neighbor's back land, and apparently forming the only approach to it, would at once infer that the neighbor in all probability had a right of way. The case before Lord Chelmsford did not require the decision of any point as to notice at all, for there was a deed of grant imposing a servitude, and if his Lordship meant to say that the mere fact of the existence of windows puts a purchaser upon inquiry as to the right to use them, which probably is going further than he meant, we must, with all respect, say that such a doctrine is more than reason requires; and as the case did not really involve the point, the remarks are not binding on us. Windows are frequently made in situations where they are liable to be obstructed, the owner being in hopes of coming to some arrangement about lights, or being disposed to take his chance of acquiring a right by lapse of time. This is not, therefore, a case where the visible state of things makes the existence of a servitude extremely probable, and to hold that the purchaser was affected by notice would be to stretch the rule beyond reason.

COTTON, L.J.: In this case there is no covenant running with the land, and the defendant can only be affected by the

797]   agreement in question if *he bought with notice of it.
It is clear that he had no actual notice, and the only circumstance by which he can be affected with constructive notice
is, that he knew of the existence of the window. Now, on
what principle is notice of the agreement to be inferred?
Where a tenant is in possession of the property sold, the
principle is, that his being there is manifestly inconsistent
with the vendor's being absolute owner. The tenant must
have some rights, so the purchaser is bound to inquire what
they are. But this cannot be applied to a window. A man
by opening a window claims no right over his neighbor's
property ; the fact of the window being there raises no presumption of any right. Then as regards the authorities.
Whether the case of the chimney-pots be right or wrong, it
is wholly different from this, for there a person was using a
flue in his neighbor's house ; here the owner of the window
is doing nothing of which anybody could possibly complain.
The case of the sea-wall cannot be treated as analogous.
The Master of the Rolls there came to the conclusion that
the purchaser must have seen that he had the benefit of the
sea-wall, and therefore could not evade the burden. In
Davies v. *Sear* (¹) the purchaser bought a house with an
archway evidently intended as a means of transit to the land
beyond; he let people go on building till it was the only
means of transit to that land, and then wished to close it.
The question in that case really was whether, in the conveyance to him, there was not by implication a reservation of a
right of way, and whether, after lying by as he did, the purchaser could insist on his right if he originally had any.
The only other case is that before Lord Chelmsford, and
everything that fell from him deserves great respect, but we
must look to the facts. That was a case where the defendants had taken a lease of building land, with knowledge
that the same lessees had let other land to the plaintiffs for
building purposes, and that under that lease a building
had been erected with windows overlooking the land
taken by the defendants. A case so circumstanced cannot be cited as an authority for the general proposition
in support of which it is relied on, and the Vice-Chancellor
does not refer to it in his judgment. I agree, therefore, in
798]   considering that the *defendant is not to be taken to
have purchased with notice of the agreement.

The case then proceeded upon the question whether the
light was an ancient light, and the court came to the con-

(¹) Law Rep., 7 Eq., 427.

clusion that it was, and that there had been sufficient diminution of light to give the plaintiff a cause of action, but that as the injury was trifling, and the action had been commenced so late, the case was not one for a mandatory injunction. To avoid the expense of further proceedings, the court assessed the damages at £50, the defendant undertaking to put clear glass into the plaintiff's window.

Solicitors: *J. J. Rae; R. Metcalfe.*

[11 Chancery Division, 798.]

Fry, J., Nov. 28, 29, 1877.

ROBINSON v. DULEEP SINGH.

[1876 R. 78.]

Common Appurtenant—Fold-course—Right of Lord to approve—Digging Gravel Pits—Inclosure round Warren-house—Curtilage—Statute of Merton (20 Hen. 3), c. 4—Statute of Westminster the Second (13 Edw. 1), c. 46—Grant—Construction—"Warren of Conies"—Estoppel—Practice—Verdict on Issues in Suit between Predecessors of Parties.

A fold-course is not a several right to the herbage, but a right of common appurtenant of pasture for sheep.

Lords of manor can by the Statute of Merton approve against common appurtenant of pasture. The proviso in the Statute of Westminster the Second, c. 46, only prevents derogation from an express grant.

A demise of "all that warren of conies in L.:"

Held, by Fry, J., under the circumstances, to pass the soil of the warren and not merely a franchise.

Hall v. *Byron* ([1]) followed.

Observations on *Earl Beauchamp* v. *Winn* ([2]).

The verdict on issues in a suit between predecessors in title does not in itself create an estoppel. The decree and the pleadings must be taken into consideration.

([1]) 20 Eng. R., 826.   ([2]) 6 Eng. R., 37.

[11 Chancery Division, 852.]

M.R., May 31, 1878: C.A., June 13, 14, 16; July 1, 1879.

STURGES v. BRIDGMAN.   [852

[1877 S. 223.]

Easement—Noise—Prescription—Prescription Act (2 & 3 Will. 4, c. 71)—User—Affirmative and Negative Easements.

User which is neither physically capable of prevention by the owner of the servient tenement, nor actionable, cannot support an easement. And this is applicable both to affirmative and negative easements.

On this principle the right to make a noise so as to annoy a neighbor cannot be supported by user unless during the period of user the noise has amounted to an actionable nuisance.

In considering whether any act is a nuisance, regard must be had not only to the thing done, but to the surrounding circumstances. What would be a nuisance in one locality might not be so in another.

A confectioner had for more than twenty years used a pestle and mortar in his back premises, which abutted on the garden of a physician, and the noise and vibration were not felt as a nuisance and were not complained of. But in 1873 the physician erected a consulting-room at the end of his garden, and then the noise and vibration became a nuisance to him. He accordingly brought an action for an injunction :

Held (affirming the decision of Jessel, M.R.), that the defendant had not acquired a right to an easement of making a noise and vibration, and the injunction was granted.

THE plaintiff in this case was a physician. In the year 1865 he purchased the lease of a house in Wimpole Street, London, which he occupied as his professional residence.

Wimpole Street runs north and south, and is crossed at right angles by Wigmore Street. The plaintiff's house was on the west side of Wimpole Street, and was the second 853] house from the north *side of Wigmore Street. Behind the house was a garden, and in 1873 the plaintiff erected a consulting-room at the end of his garden.

The defendant was a confectioner in large business in Wigmore Street. His house was on the north side of Wigmore Street and his kitchen was at the back of his house, and stood on ground which was formerly a garden and abutted on the portion of the plaintiff's garden on which he built the consulting-room. So that there was nothing between the plaintiff's consulting-room and the defendant's kitchen but the party-wall. The defendant had in his kitchen two large marble mortars set in brickwork built up to and against the party-wall which separated his kitchen from the plaintiff's consulting-room, and worked by two large wooden pestles held in an upright position by horizontal bearers fixed into the party-wall. These mortars were used for breaking up and pounding loaf-sugar and other hard substances, and for pounding meat.

The plaintiff alleged that when the defendant's pestles and mortars were being used the noise and vibration thereby caused were very great, and were heard and felt in the plaintiff's consulting-room, and such noise and vibration seriously annoyed and disturbed the plaintiff, and materially interfered with him in the practice of his profession. In particular the plaintiff stated that the noise prevented him from examining his patients by auscultation for diseases of the chest. He also found it impossible to engage with effect in any occupation which required thought and attention.

The use of the pestles and mortars varied with pressure of the defendant's business, but they were generally used between the hours of 10 A.M. and 1 P.M.

The plaintiff made several complaints of the annoyance, and ultimately brought this action, in which he claimed an injunction to restrain the defendant from using the pestles and mortars in such manner as to cause him annoyance.

The defendant stated in his defence that he and his father had used one of the pestles and mortars in the same place and to the same extent as now for more than sixty years, and that he had used the second pestle and mortar in the same place and to the *same extent as now for more [854 than twenty-six years. He alleged that if the plaintiff had built his consulting-room with a separate wall, and not against the wall of the defendant's kitchen, he would not have experienced any noise or vibration; and he denied that the plaintiff suffered any serious annoyance, and pleaded a prescriptive right to use the pestles and mortars under the 2 & 3 Will. 4, c. 71.

Issue was joined, and both parties went into evidence. The result of the evidence was that the existence of the nuisance was, in the opinion of the court, sufficiently proved; and it also appeared that no material inconvenience had been felt by the plaintiff until he built his consulting-room.

The action came on for trial before the Master of the Rolls on the 31st of May, 1878.

Waller, Q.C., and *S. Dickinson*, for the plaintiff, contended that noise should be put in the same category as light and air, and the defendant had not acquired a prescriptive right to interfere with the plaintiff's enjoyment of his own property. They cited *Webb* v. *Bird* (¹); *Angus* v. *Dalton* (²); *Moore* v. *Rawson* (³); *Ball* v. *Ray* (⁴).

Chitty, Q.C., and *Methold*, for the defendant, contended that he had acquired an uninterrupted right to use his mortars as he had done; that the nuisance, if it was in fact a nuisance, had been legalized by prescription; and that, if necessary, a lost grant might be presumed. They cited *Flight* v. *Thomas* (⁵); *Wright* v. *Williams* (⁶); *Elliotson* v. *Feetham* (⁷); *Bliss* v. *Hall* (⁸); *Bealey* v. *Shaw* (⁹); *Baxendale* v. *McMurray* (¹⁰); *Cross* v. *Lewis* (¹¹); *Crump* v. *Lambert* (¹²).

JESSEL, M.R.: I think this is a clear case for the plaintiff. There is really no *dispute as to this being a [855

(¹) 10 C.B. (N.S.), 268; 18 C. B. (N.S.), 841.
(²) 3 Q. B. D., 85; 28 Eng. R., 80.
(³) 3 B. & C., 332.
(⁴) Law Rep., 8 Ch., 467; 6 Eng. R., 435.
(⁵) 11 A. & E., 688; 8 Cl. & F., 231.
(⁶) 1 M. & W., 77.
(⁷) 2 Bing. N. C., 184; 2 Scott, 174.
(⁸) 4 Bing. N. C., 183; 5 Scott, 500.
(⁹) 6 East, 208.
(¹⁰) Law Rep., 2 Ch., 790.
(¹¹) 2 B. & C., 686; 4 D. & R., 234.
(¹²) Law Rep., 3 Eq., 409.

nuisance; in fact, the evidence is all one way, and, as has been often said in these cases, the plaintiff is not bound to go on bringing actions for damages every day, when he is entitled to an injunction.

The only serious point which has been argued for the defendant is that by virtue of the statute, or by prescription, he was entitled as against the plaintiff to make this noise and commit a nuisance. Now the facts seem to be that until a very recent period it was not a nuisance at all. There was an open garden at the back of and attached to the plaintiff's house, and the noise, it seems, if it went anywhere, went over the garden, and, of course, was rapidly dispersed; as far as I can see upon the evidence before me, there was until a recent period no nuisance to anybody—no actionable nuisance at all. The actionable nuisance began when the plaintiff did what he had a right to do, namely, built a consulting-room in his garden, and when, on attempting to use the consulting-room for a proper purpose, he found this noise too great for anything like comfort. That was the time to bring an action for nuisance.

Now, under those circumstances, it appears to me that neither the defence of the statute, nor the defence of the right by prescription, can possibly avail. I pass over technical grounds, for it appears that in fact both the plaintiff and the defendant are lessees under the Duke of Portland, the defendant having a lease in 1845 and the plaintiff in 1854. On what theory of law I am to presume a grant as against the Duke of Portland's lessee I do not know.

I will state the authorities as shortly and in as few words as I can. There are a great many authorities on the subject, but there is one authority which I have been looking at for another purpose, to which I shall refer. That is the case of *Webb* v. *Bird* ([1]), which states the law as explicitly as it possibly can be stated. There Justice Wightman, who delivered the judgment of the court, says ([2]), "We think, in accordance with the Court of Common Pleas, and the judgment of the House of Lords in *Chasemore* v. *Richards* ([3]), 856] that the presumption of a grant from long *continued enjoyment only arises where the person against whom the right is claimed might have interrupted or prevented the exercise of the subject of the supposed grant."

Now in the case before me that was simply impossible. The noise was made on the defendant's own premises—in his kitchen. Of course you could not go into his kitchen without being a trespasser. You could not interrupt it there,

([1]) 13 C. B. (N.S.), 841.   ([2]) 13 C. B. (N.S.), 843.   ([3]) 7 H. L. C., 349.

nor could you interrupt it on your own land, because you had no control over the waves of sound ; nor could you even have interrupted it by an action, because there was originally no actionable nuisance. It did not hurt anybody as long as the plaintiff's premises remained as a garden. It did not hurt anybody until the room was built. Therefore it is quite plain that independent of the technical ground, namely, the fact of there having been two leases, there would have been no ground for presuming a grant. That puts an end to any notion of prescription.

Then the only other question is whether the defendant can claim any defence under the statute. The 2d section of the statute (2 & 3 Will. 4, c. 71) says, "That no claim which may be lawfully made at the common law, by custom, prescription, or grant, to any way or other easement, ... to be enjoyed or derived upon, over, or from any land . . . . when such way or other matter . . . . shall have been actually enjoyed by any person claiming right thereto without interruption for the full period of twenty years, shall be defeated or destroyed by showing only that such way or other matter was first enjoyed at any time prior to such period of twenty years, but nevertheless such claim may be defeated in any other way by which the same is now liable to be defeated."

Now I get rid of this claim at once by saying that, from its nature, I do not presume a lost grant. So that the statute really has no application at all. It seems to me it is quite unnecessary to discuss the question ; but inasmuch as the case may possibly be taken elsewhere, I think it just as well to give my reason for saying why the 2d section of the statute can have no application, and that is this : the easement there referred to is an easement to be enjoyed or derived "upon, over, or from" the land of the servient tenement. That is what it means ; and it is to be *actually enjoyed by [857 a person claiming a right without interruption for the full period of twenty years.

There are really all sorts of difficulties in the defendant's way. In the first place the easement must be an easement "*upon, over*, or *from*." Now the noise in question, in my opinion, is not properly described in that way. No doubt the waves by which the sound is distributed pass over the plaintiff's land ; there is no question about that. But is that an easement enjoyed "*upon, over*, or *from* any land ?" Well, I think it is not. That appears not only from the natural meaning of the words, but from authority.

In the report of *Webb* v. *Bird* (¹), Lord Chief Justice Erle says, "I do not think the passage of air over the land of another was or could have been contemplated by the Legislature when framing that section." Now, what he means by the passage of air is the passage of air in motion, the waves of air; for the ground of action in that case was wind: that is, what was wanted was not the air but the wind, for still air would have been of no use. The plaintiff complained that his windmill would no longer turn, and therefore he claimed a right to the passage of air in motion. Then the Lord Chief Justice proceeds: "They evidently intended it to apply only to the exercise of such rights upon or over the surface of the servient tenement as might be interrupted by the owner if the right were disputed." Then he goes on to say: "I am clearly of opinion that the 2d section of the statute meant to include only such easements upon or over the surface of the servient tenement as are susceptible of interruption by the owners of such servient tenement, so as to prevent the enjoyment on the part of the owner of the dominant tenement from ripening into a right." Then in another passage he says, "The Legislature evidently considered the passage of light—which bears a very close analogy to that of air—to stand upon a different footing from the other easements with which it had been dealing in the preceding section; and, if it had intended to extend the right to the uninterrupted passage of wind and air, it would have done so in express terms."

Now it must be recollected that all the defendant claims 858]   here *is a right to the uninterrupted passage of air or either—nothing else. He claims the right of setting the air or either in motion by something or other that he does upon his own property.

It is exactly, therefore, within the principle as laid down by Chief Justice Erle, as a case to which the act does not apply. But Mr. Justice Willes, in the same case, put it very plainly; and what he says applies both to the act of Parliament and to the presumption of lost grant or prescription. He first of all says (²), "That which is claimed here amounts to neither more nor less than this—that a person having a piece of ground, and building a windmill upon it, acquires by twenty years' enjoyment a right to prevent the proprietors of all the surrounding land from building upon it, if by so doing the free access of the wind from any quarter should be impeded or obstructed." It comes to the same thing here. It prevents a man building upon it so as

(¹) 10 C. B. (N.S.), 268, 282, 283.   (²) 10 C. B. (N.S.), 284.

to enjoy his building. "It is impossible to see how the adjoining owners could prevent the acquisition of such a right except by combining together to build a circular wall round the mill within twenty years. It would be absurd to hold that men's rights are to be made dependent on anything so inconvenient and impracticable." Then he says, as regards light, "All that can be said, however, of these cases, is, that, as compared with the general law, they are anomalous. In general,"—and this applies, as I said, to lost grants—"a man cannot establish a right by lapse of time and acquiescence against his neighbor, unless he shows that the party against whom the right is acquired might have brought an action or done some act to put a stop to the claim without an unreasonable waste of labor and expense."

That puts the thing, if I may so say, on what is really a sensible ground. If a man has a noisy business in the middle of a barren moor which belongs to somebody else to whom the business carried on does no injury, the owner of the moor cannot bring an action, and he cannot interrupt. Take the case of putting a blacksmith's forge in the midde of a moor: you cannot enter the blacksmith's forge, inasmuch as that belongs either to him or to his landlord, and the owner of a moor which has no game upon it has nothing which can be injured by the noise. There is no remedy whatever, *because it is a barren moor. Presently, [859 this which is useless as a barren moor becomes available for building land by reason of the growth of a neighboring town: is it to be said that the owner has lost the right to this barren moor, which has now become worth perhaps hundreds of thousands of pounds, by being unable to build upon it by reason of this noisy business? The answer would be simply, "I could not stop you: I could not interrupt. It is physically impossible, because it would be a trespass; legally impossible, because I had suffered no damage and could not maintain an action. How could you therefore acquire a right to deprive me of the fair and ordinary use of my property?" That seems to me to be an answer to all the cases put. You must have regard to the position of the property and all the surrounding circumstances to see if you can presume any grant. A man cannot presume a grant of that to which, so far as he is concerned, he has no right. You have no occasion to presume a grant. It is not a license to use a thing, because the use does not injure you. When you find a man doing an act which is a manifest injury to another, such as fouling a stream by pouring the refuse of a manufactory into the bright trout stream of his

neighbor, and his neighbor allows that to go on for a great
number of years, it is not unreasonable to presume that he
did it under some right. If he has done it openly and his
neighbor does not complain of that injury, although it is a
very serious injury, it is not unreasonable to suppose that
they did come to terms at some antecedent period for granting a right. But here, in the case I have before me, I cannot see a pretence for it. The fact that the man has made a
noise which has not injured me or interfered with my comfort or enjoyment in any way, cannot deprive me of my
right to the land, or interfere with my right to come to the
court when it does seriously interfere with my comfortable
enjoyment.

It seems to me that, neither on the theory of lost grant
nor on the statute, can the defendant claim to do what he
has done, and therefore the plaintiff is entitled to an injunction ; but as it would be somewhat hard upon a confectioner
to alter his mode of business at the height of the London
season, I will give him a reasonable time, say until the 1st
of August, to alter the position of his mortars.

860]　*From this decision the defendant appealed. The
appeal came on to be heard on the 13th of June, 1879.

Chitty, Q.C., and *Methold*, for the appellant : In the case
of analogous easements it has always been laid down that a
right is acquired by twenty years' user, a grant being presumed : *Baxendale* v. *McMurray* (¹) as to right to pollute
water ; *Crump* v. *Lambert* (²) as to noise and smell ; Gale
on Easements (³) ; *Ball* v. *Ray* (⁴).

The effect of the decision under appeal, if upheld, might
be most disastrous in London. Suppose a printing press
established for more than twenty years, the neighbors not
complaining. Another person purchases one of the adjoining properties and applies it to a new purpose, such that
the noise and vibration of the presses are found a nuisance ;
according to this decision he can stop them.

[THESIGER, L.J.: How can an adjoining owner stop the
noise here complained of, as he had no house on the ground
and suffered no inconvenience ?]

We apprehend that a person might set up a tent close to
the wall, and bring an action on the ground that he could
not sleep in it for the noise. In *Elliotson* v. *Feetham* (⁵)
and *Bliss* v. *Hall* (⁶) it was intimated that twenty years would

(¹) Law Rep., 2 Ch., 790.　　　　　　(⁴) Law Rep., 8 Ch., 467, 471 ; 6 Eng.
(²) Law Rep., 3 Eq., 409, 414.　　　　R., 435.
(³) 4th ed., p. 20.　　　　　　　　　(⁵) 2 Bing. N. C., 134.
　　　　　　　　(⁶) 4 Bing. N. C., 183

give a right. In *Flight* v. *Thomas* (') the case was disposed of on a point of pleading, but it was intimated that twenty years' user would confer a right of sending out bad smells. *Wright* v. *Williams* (') is also a case in our favor. In *Gaunt* v. *Fynney* (') the Lord Chancellor treats noise as standing on the same footing with other nuisances, and as legalized by twenty years; and *St. Helen's Smelting Company* v. *Tipping* (') assumes the law to be so. The cases are discussed in *Angus* v. *Dalton* ('). Twenty years' user gives a right of support to a house, *Partridge* v. *Scott* ('); though there is no right of action in the meantime. If a grant is presumed after *twenty years, how can that [861 presumption be rebutted in the twenty-first by an alteration in the servient tenement? The Master of the Rolls relied on *Webb* v. *Bird* ('); but that was an exceptional case, where an attempt was made to claim an easement of access of wind, a kind of right which had never been heard of before. This is a case in which a grant may fairly be presumed. It is not a question whether such a grant is probable, but whether it is possible: *St. Mary Magdalen College* v. *Attorney-General* ('); *Moore* v. *Rawson* ('). It is not correct to say that the plaintiff might not have interfered before. There was always some noise and vibration which might, if a right were established, become a nuisance, and that was an injury to the property which might have been stopped by an action: *Kidgill* v. *Moor* (''); *Metropolitan Association* v. *Petch* (''); *Chalmer* v. *Bradley* ('').

Waller, Q.C., and *S. Dickinson*, for the plaintiff: The defendant cannot have acquired a right to an easement over the plaintiff's land by prescription; for no grant can be presumed where the owner of the servient tenement had no power to prevent the easement either by physical interference or by an action. In order to acquire a right by prescription the exercise of the right must not be secret, but palpable and adverse to the owner of the servient tenement. In the present case the plaintiff could not have entered the defendant's house to stop the noise and vibration, nor could he have brought an action, because there was nothing that amounted to a nuisance till the consulting-room was built:

(') 11 A. & E., 688.　　　　　(') 3 M. & W., 220.
(') 1 M. & W., 77.　　　　　(') 10 C. B. (N.S.), 268.
(') Law Rep., 8 Ch., 8, 11; 4 Eng. R.,　　(') 3 Jur. (N.S.), 675.
718.　　　　　(') 3 B. & C., 332.
(') 11 H. L. C., 642.　　　　　(') 9 C. B., 364.
(') 3 Q. B. D., 85; 28 Eng. R., 80; 4　　('') 5 C. B. (N.S.), 504.
Q. B. D., 162; 28 Eng. R., 706.　　　('') 1 Jac. & W., 51.

Webb v. *Bird* (¹); *Chasemore* v. *Richards* (²); *Crump* v. *Lambert* (³); *Gaunt* v. *Fynney* (⁴); *Ball* v. *Ray* (⁵); *Elliot-son* v. *Feetham* (⁶); *Flight* v. *Thomas* (⁷); *Anyus* v. *Dal-ton* (⁸); *Bright* v. *Walker* (⁹); *Wilson* v. *Stanley* (¹⁰) If the 862] defendant's *contention is correct, a person who is subject to acts by his neighbor which he fears may grow into a nuisance is in a serious difficulty. If he bring an action at once, he is told there is no nuisance; if he waits till the acts amount to a nuisance, he is told that a title by prescription has been acquired. It is true that the plaintiff experienced no nuisance till he built his consulting-room; but every man has a right to the free use of his property for whatever purpose he pleases, provided he does not annoy his neighbors, and he is entitled to be protected in such use.

Methold, in reply.

1879. July 1. THESIGER, L.J., delivered the judgment of the Court, (James, Baggallay, and Thesiger, L.JJ.,) as follows:

The defendant in this case is the occupier, for the purpose of his business as a confectioner, of a house in Wigmore Street. In the rear of the house is a kitchen, and in that kitchen there are now, and have been for over twenty years, two large mortars in which the meat and other materials of the confectionery are pounded. The plaintiff, who is a physician, is the occupier of a house in Wimpole Street, which until recently had a garden at the rear, the wall of which garden was a party-wall between the plaintiff's and the defendant's premises, and formed the back wall of the defendant's kitchen. The plaintiff has, however, recently built upon the site of the garden a consulting-room, one of the side walls of which is the wall just described. It has been proved that in the case of the mortars, before and at the time of action brought, a noise was caused which seriously inconvenienced the plaintiff in the use of his consulting-room, and which, unless the defendant had acquired a right to impose the inconvenience, would constitute an actionable nuisance. The defendant contends that he had acquired the right, either at common law or under the Prescription Act, by uninterrupted user for more than twenty years.

(¹) 10 C. B. (N.S.), 282; S. C., 18 C. B. (N.S.), 282.
(²) 7 H. L. C., 349.
(³) Law Rep., 3 Eq., 409.
(⁴) Law Rep., 8 Ch., 8.
(⁵) Law Rep., 8 Ch., 467.
(⁶) 2 Bing. N. C., 134.
(⁷) 11 A. & E., 688.
(⁸) 3 Q. B. D., 85; 28 Eng. R., 80; 4 Q. B. D., 162; 28 Eng. R., 706.
(⁹) 4 Tyrw., 502.
(¹⁰) 12 Ir. C. L. Rep., 345

In deciding this question one more fact is necessary to be stated. Prior to the erection of the consulting-room no material annoyance or inconvenience was caused to the plaintiff or to any previous occupier of the plaintiff's house by what the defendant did. It is *true that the defend- [863 ant in the 7th paragraph of his affidavit speaks of an invalid lady who occupied the house upon one occasion, about thirty years before, requested him if possible to discontinue the use of the mortars before eight o'clock in the morning; and it is true also that there is some evidence of the garden wall having been subjected to vibration, but this vibration, even if it existed at all, was so slight, and the complaint, if it could be called a complaint, of the invalid lady, and can be looked upon as evidence, was of so trifling a character, that, upon the maxim *de minimis non curat lex*, we arrive at the conclusion that the defendant's acts would not have given rise to any proceedings either at law or in equity. Here then arises the objection to the acquisition by the defendant of any easement. That which was done by him was in its nature such that it could not be physically interrupted; it could not at the same time be put a stop to by action. Can user which is neither preventible nor actionable found an easement? We think not. The question, so far as regards this particular easement claimed, is the same question whether the defendant endeavors to assert his right by common law or under the Prescription Act. That act fixes periods for the acquisition of easements, but, except in regard to the particular easement of light, or in regard to certain matters which are immaterial to the present inquiry, it does not alter the character of easements, or of the user or enjoyment by which they are acquired. This being so, the laws governing the acquisition of easements by user stands thus: Consent or acquiescence of the owner of the servient tenement lies at the root of prescription, and of the fiction of a lost grant, and hence the acts or user, which go to the proof of either the one or the other, must be, in the language of the civil law, *nec vi nec clam nec precario;* for a man cannot, as a general rule, be said to consent to or acquiesce in the acquisition by his neighbor of an easement through an enjoyment of which he has no knowledge, actual or constructive, or which he contests and endeavors to interrupt, or which he temporarily licenses. It is a mere extension of the same notion, or rather it is a principle into which by strict analysis it may be resolved, to hold, that an enjoyment which a man cannot prevent raises no presumption of consent or acquiescence. *Upon this princi- [864 ple it was decided in *Webb* v. *Bird* (¹) that currents of air blowing from a particular quarter of the compass, and in *Chasemore* v. *Richards* (²) that subterranean water percolating through the strata in no known channels, could not be acquired as an easement by user; and in *Angus* v. *Dalton* (³) a case of lateral support of buildings by adjacent soil, which came on appeal to this court, the principle was in no way impugned, although it was held by the majority of the court not to be applicable so as to prevent the acquisition of that particular easement. It is a principle which must be equally appropriate to the case of affirmative as of negative easements; in other words, it is equally unreasonable to imply your consent to your neighbor enjoying something which passes from your tenement to his, as to his subjecting your tenement to something which comes from his, when in both cases you have no power of prevention. But the affirmative easement differs from the negative easement in this, that the latter can under no circumstances be interrupted except by acts done upon the servient tenement, but the former, constituting, as it does, a direct interference with the enjoyment by the servient owner of his tenement, may be the subject of legal proceedings as well as of physical interruption. To put concrete cases—the passage of light and air to your neighbor's windows may be physically interrupted by you, but gives you no legal grounds of complaint against him. The passage of water from his land on to yours may be physically interrupted, or may be treated as a trespass and made the ground of action for damages, or for an injunction, or both. Noise is similar to currents of air and the flow of subterranean and uncertain streams in its practical incapability of physical interruption, but it differs from them in its capability of grounding an action. *Webb Bird* and *Chasemore* v. *Richards* are not, therefore, direct authorities governing the present case. They are, however, illustrations of the principle which ought to govern it; for until the noise, to take this case, became an actionable nuisance, which it did not at any time before the consulting-room was built, the basis of the presumption of the consent, 865]   *viz., the power of prevention physically or by action, was never present.

It is said that if this principle is applied in cases like the present, and were carried out to its logical consequences, it would result in the most serious practical inconveniences,

(¹) 13 C. B. (N.S.), 841.   (²) 7 H. L. C., 349.
(³) 4 Q. B. D., 162; 28 Eng. R., 706.

for a man might go—say into the midst of the tanneries of Bermondsey, or into any other locality devoted to a particular trade or manufacture of a noisy or unsavory character, and, by building a private residence upon a vacant piece of land, put a stop to such trade or manufacture altogether. The case also is put of a blacksmith's forge built away from all habitations, but to which, in course of time, habitations approach. We do not think that either of these hypothetical cases presents any real difficulty. As regards the first, it may be answered that whether anything is a nuisance or not is a question to be determined, not merely by an abstract consideration of the thing itself, but in reference to its circumstances; what would be a nuisance in Belgrave Square would not necessarily be so in Bermondsey; and where a locality is devoted to a particular trade or manufacture carried on by the traders or manufacturers in a particular and established manner not constituting a public nuisance, judges and juries would be justified in finding, and may be trusted to find, that the trade or manufacture so carried on in that locality is not a private or actionable wrong. As regards the blacksmith's forge, that is really an *idem per idem* case with the present. It would be on the one hand in a very high degree unreasonable and undesirable that there should be a right of action for acts which are not in the present condition of the adjoining land, and possibly never will be any annoyance or inconvenience to either its owner or occupier; and it would be on the other hand in an equally degree unjust, and, from a public point of view, inexpedient that the use and value of the adjoining land should, for all time and under all circumstances, be restricted and diminished by reason of the continuance of acts incapable of physical interruption, and which the law gives no power to prevent. The smith in the case supposed might protect himself by taking a sufficient curtilage to ensure what he does from being at any time an annoyance to his neighbor, but the neighbor himself would be powerless in the matter. Individual cases of hardship *may oc- [866 cur in the strict carrying out of the principle upon which we found our judgment, but the negation of the principle would lead even more to individual hardship, and would at the same time produce a prejudicial effect upon the development of land for residential purposes. The Master of the Rolls in the court below took substantially the same view of the matter as ourselves and granted the relief which the plaintiff prayed for, and we are of opinion that his order is right and should be affirmed, and that this appeal should be dismissed with costs.

Solicitors: *Garrard, James & Wolfe; Clarkson, Son & Greenwell.*

See 31 Eng. Rep., 517 note.

An injunction to restrain an offensive trade will issue when the nuisance renders life uncomfortable, though it may not be injurious to health. Any nauseous pollution of the air, offensive to the delicate and sensitive, though not so to the strong and robust, will be restrained: Roberts *v.* Thomas, 2 Leg. Record Rep., 151.

Where, in an action for damages for the erection and use of gasworks, the jury found the works were of a permanent character, but considered they were incompetent to decide whether such erection and use were a permanent injury to plaintiff's property; held, the jury intended and found thereby that the injury was of a permanent character, and began when the works were erected and used; and that the action was barred in five years after such erection and use: Baldwin *v.* Oskaloosa Gaslight Co., 57 Iowa, 51.

Possession to be adverse must be upon a claim of right or title. If it be taken furtively or secretly, it will not be adverse in law. If acquired openly and publicly by one of two owners of adjoining lands in erecting a building immediately on the verge of his above the surface of the ground, but by digging a cellar and laying the foundation and building one of the walls of it partly within the limits and entirely below the surface of the adjoining lands, the possession will be adverse against such adjoining owner, and if held uninterruptedly under a claim of right, it will after twenty years have ripened into a good title; and the adjoining owner after that, in erecting a house on his land, will have no right to build his cellar wall upon the foundation of it: O'Daniel *v.* The Bakers' Union of Wilmington, 4 Houst. (Del.), 488.

As to the effect of fraudulent use of the lands of another under ground, see Hunter *v.* Gibbons, 1 Hurl. & .Norm., 459.

So in fraudulent tapping gaspipes: Imperial, etc., *v.* London, etc., 10 Excheq., 39, 45 note.

As to what is sufficient to show knowledge by the owner of an adverse user: Ward *v.* Warren, 82 N. Y., 265, affirming 15 Hun, 600; Weisman *v.* Lucksinger, 84 N. Y., 31.

The owner of a lot adjoining a highway has no right to so dig or excavate upon his own land as to render the highway unsafe, or cause the earth thereof to subside or fall down.

The owner of a lot, access and entrance to which is given by the highway, may maintain an action to restrain such unlawful interference therewith: Milburn *v.* Fowler, 27 Hun, 568.

If several persons contribute to the injury, each is liable only for the damages which he himself has caused: Baldwin *v.* Gaslight Co., 57 Iowa, 51, 57.

Where damages are sought for injury from gasworks, no damages should be allowed for the erection of the works themselves, but only for the damages arising from the use thereof—i.e., the offensive odors, etc.: Baldwin *v.* Gaslight Co., 57 Iowa, 55.

·[11 Chancery Division, 866.]

C.A., June 30; July 1, 1879.

RENALS v. COWLISHAW.

[1876 R. 89.]

Restrictive Covenant—Covenantee, Assign of—Right to sue.

The owners in fee of a residential estate and adjoining lands sold part of the adjoining lands to the defendant's predecessors in title, who entered into covenants with the vendors, their heirs and assigns, restricting their right to build on and use the purchased land. The same vendors afterwards sold the residential estate to the plaintiff's predecessors in title. The conveyance contained no reference to the restrictive covenants, nor was there any contract or representation that the purchasers were to have the benefit of them:

Held (affirming the decision of Hall, V.C.), that the plaintiffs were not entitled to restrain the defendants from building in contravention of the restrictive covenants entered into by their predecessors in title.

THIS was an appeal by the plaintiffs from a decision of Vice-Chancellor Hall (').

Hastings, Q.C., and *Renshaw*, for the appellants: We contend that a covenant must be treated in equity as running with the land to assigns of the covenantees if three requisites are satisfied—1, that the covenant must extend to assigns; 2, that the person claiming the benefit of the covenant must be assign of the same estate as the covenantee; and, 3, that there is not anything in the nature of the transaction to show that *it was not the intention of the [867 parties that the covenant should run with the land.

[JAMES, L.J.: With what land do you say that the covenant runs? If the vendors had also had property in Yorkshire, a purchaser of that would have been an assign. Could he enforce the covenant?]

We say it runs with the Mill Hill estate, which is mentioned in the covenant as belonging to the trustees. The covenant cannot have been intended for their personal benefit, but must have been intended to enure for the benefit of the neighboring unsold lands. We are equitable assignees of the covenant: *Western* v. *Macdermott* (').

[JAMES, L.J.: There a particular field was clearly referred to, and it was a case of reciprocal rights.

BAGGALLAY, L.J.: Both parties derived title under a deed embodying a general building scheme.]

The Master of the Rolls puts it on this, that the covenant was a covenant entered into for the benefit of the unsold

(') 9 Ch. D., 125; 25 Eng. R., 827.   (') Law Rep., 1 Eq., 499; Law Rep., 2 Ch., 72.

property, and that the plaintiff, as assign of part of that property, was entitled to the benefit of the covenant. The Vice-Chancellor holds that it is not enough for the subsequent purchaser to be an assign of the land, but that he must show an intention to give him the benefit of the restrictive covenants. This is a novel doctrine, and inconsistent with what was said by Lord Hatherley in *Child* v. *Douglas* (').

[BAGGALLAY, L.J.: Was not the land there laid out according to a building scheme?]

Yes; but we say it is not necessary that there should be any express notice or mention of the restrictive covenant. The purchaser takes the land with the advantages appurtenant to it.

[JAMES, L.J.: Is there any case to show that if the owner of 100 acres sells an acre, taking a restrictive covenant, and sells the remainder in lots of an acre each, every one of the ninety-nine purchasers can enforce the covenant against the purchaser of the first acre?]

868]　*The case does not seem to have occurred at law, but in equity there are *Mann* v. *Stephens* (') and *Eastwood* v. *Lever* ('), where the law is laid down in our favor, though the plaintiff there was held to have lost his right by acquiescence.

[JAMES, L.J.: There was a building scheme, and the covenants were entered into for maintaining the general character of the neighborhood. If the general character of the neighborhood changes the obligation ceases: *Duke of Bedford* v. *Trustees of British Museum* (').]

Child v. *Douglas* (') is an authority that express words are not wanted. Here we have all the elements of that case. In *Eastwood* v. *Lever* no doubt stress is laid on the particular ground mentioned in the judgment, but there is nothing laying down that in the absence of that ground the plaintiff could not have sued. The Vice-Chancellor thought that this case was governed by *Keates* v. *Lyon* ('), but there the covenant did not mention assigns.

[JAMES, L.J.: That is immaterial in equity, though it is important on the question whether a covenant runs with the land at law.]

In *Master* v. *Hansard* (') the plaintiff was not assign of the same estate as the covenantee; he was only another lessee under the covenantee.

(') 2 Jur. (N.S.), 950.　　　　　　(') 2 My. & K., 552,
(') 15 Sim., 377.　　　　　　　　(') Law Rep., 4 Ch., 218.
(') 4 D. J. & S., 114.　　　　　　(') 4 Ch. D., 718; 21 Eng. R., 671.

W. Pearson, Q.C., and *Bury*, for the respondents, were not called upon.

JAMES, L.J.:   I am of opinion that the decision of Vice-Chancellor Hall is correct. It is impossible, as it seems to me, to distinguish this case from the cases to which he has referred. To enable an assign to take the benefit of restrictive covenants there must be something in the deed to define the property for the benefit of which they were entered into. Supposing I were now framing *the deed afresh, I [869 should not have the remotest idea how the covenant ought to be framed, as I cannot tell what the property was which the parties intended to be protected, and within what limits.

I do not think it necessary to add anything more, except that I entirely concur with every word of the judgment of Vice-Chancellor Hall.

BAGGALLAY, L.J.:   I am of the same opinion with the Lord Justice, and I adopt entirely the language of the Vice-Chancellor in his judgment, as reported (¹).

THESIGER, L.J.:   I am of the same opinion.

Solicitors: *Satchell & Chapple; R. Wastell.*

(¹) 9 Ch. D., 125.

See 27 Eng. Rep., 525 note.

Where a penalty or forfeiture is inserted in a contract merely to secure the performance or enjoyment of a collateral object, the latter is considered as the principal intent of the instrument, and the penalty is deemed only as accessory: Klein *v.* Ins. Co., 104 U. S., 88.

The obligor is nevertheless bound to perform, unless it appear from the particular language, construed in the light of the surrounding circumstances, that it was the intention of the parties to make the penalty the price of non-performance, to be accepted by the covenantee in lieu thereof. If the primary intent was that the covenant should be performed, the penalty is regarded merely as a security, not as a substitute therefor : Phœnix, etc., *v.* Continental, etc., 87 N. Y., 400.

In a deed from H. to S., the grantee covenanted for himself, his representatives and assigns, not to erect, or cause to be erected, any building or erection on a certain specified part of the premises conveyed, which adjoined the remaining land of the grantor ; the succeeding clause was as follows: "And

for a violation of the covenant, the said party of the second part, for himself, his administrators and assigns, hereby covenants and agrees to pay the said party of the first part, their heirs, executors, administrators and assigns, the sum of $1,500 liquidated damages."

Upon the remaining lands of H. was a large building, the rear of which abutted upon, and had windows opening on the strip of land as to which the covenant applied, and was dependent thereon for air and light. Defendant succeeded to the title of S., having notice of the covenant when it purchased, and its deed was in express terms made subject to all the restrictions and conditions in the deed from H. to S. Held, that both by the covenant itself and the surrounding circumstances, it was apparent that the primary intent was to have the covenant performed and thus to secure, in permanence, an open space for the benefit of the premises not conveyed, and that the intervention of a court of equity to enforce the covenant was proper.

Also held, that the right to enforce

the covenant passed to plaintiff, as subsequent grantee of H. of the dominant premises, and that as defendant purchased with notice of the covenant, it was binding upon and enforceable against it.

Also held, the fact that the covenant in question followed the *habendum* clause in the deed, while other covenants restraining in other respects the use of the granted premises preceded it, was not material in determining the intent.

It seems, that such a covenant, both in respect to the burden and the benefit, adheres to and follows the respective parcels of land through all devolutions of the title : Phœnix Ins. Co., *v.* Continental Ins. Co., 87 N. Y., 400.

Land was conveyed subject to the "restrictions and conditions" that no building should be erected upon it to be used for certain trades, or within a certain distance of a street. The deed provided further, that any breach of these provisions should not work a forfeiture of the estate, but give a right of entry to remove the building. Held, that they were not conditions but restrictions which, although unlimited in point of time, were valid, and could be enforced in equity.

Restrictions imposed upon a number of parcels of land included in one tract, in pursuance of a general scheme of improvement, may be enforced by a grantee of one parcel against his neighbor.

A restriction that no building shall be placed upon a parcel of land within a certain distance of a street, refers to the street as existing at the time the restriction is imposed, and not to the street as subsequently altered by public authority.

The sale of groceries and provisions is not within a restriction forbidding the use of a building for the trade of a butcher, or for any "nauseous or offensive trade whatsoever," or for a purpose "which shall tend to disturb the quiet or comfort of the neighborhood:" Tobey *v.* Moore, 130 Mass., 448.

The owner of a large tract of land divided it into lots, shown on a plan, and conveyed one lot, rectangular in shape, bounding it, beginning at a certain distance from the westerly corner of a fence around a distant lot, and thence by a line running around the lot conveyed, the courses and distances of which were given. The deed also contained a condition that the front line of the house should be a certain distance from the street on which it bounded ; a condition that the house should occupy the entire width of the lot ; and a recital that the house then on the lot was in compliance with these conditions. An adjoining lot was conveyed to the same person by a deed containing a similar description, and similar conditions and recitals. The grantee then conveyed the first lot, using the same description as in the deed to him. Held, that his grantee had title to the centre of the partition wall between the two estates, even though the effect of measuring from the fence of the distant lot would be to place the whole of the partition wall in the second lot. A lot of land twenty-one feet wide was conveyed subject to the condition that the front line of the building should be fifteen feet from the street on which the land bounded, and the deed recited that the building then on the land conformed to the condition. The front line of the building thus referred to was straight. Subsequently the owner built a rectangular addition to the front, eight or nine feet wide, and projecting three feet and three inches towards the street. This structure began four feet above the ground and extended to the top of the building. Held, that there was a violation of the condition.

A deed of a lot of land bounded on a street, contained a condition that "no dwelling house or other building shall be erected on the rear of said lot." The deed also stated that the building then on the land conformed to the condition. Held, that there was no ambiguity as to what was meant by the rear of the lot, although the same condition had been inserted in an agreement for a deed made when the land was vacant : Sanborn *v.* Rice, 129 Mass., 387.

The superiors in a feu-contract took the vassal bound to erect on the ground feued out to him, and thereafter to maintain two detached villas of a certain size and value, according to plans to be submitted for their approval. Soon after the defender removed the interior stair and built an outside stair at the back of the house to form a communication to the dwelling house above, thus converting the structure into two flats, for the accommodation of two separate families. In an action raised against him to have the house restored to its original condition—held (*rev.* Lord Ordinary), that under the feu-contract the structure was unobjectionable, and that the use proposed to be made of it was no violation of any restriction in the feu-contract : Mair's Trustees *v.* McEwan, 17 Scottish L. Repr., 765.

While a court of equity has jurisdiction to enforce the observance of covenants made by an owner of lands in a city with an adjoining owner, in consideration of similar reciprocal covenants on the part of the latter, restricting the use of the lands to the purposes of private residences, the exercise of this authority is within its discretion ; and where there has been such a change in the character of the neighborhood as to defeat the object and purposes of the agreement, and to render it inequitable to deprive such owner of the privilege of conforming his property to that character, such relief will not be granted.

B., who was the owner of lands at the corner of Fiftieth street and Sixth avenue, in the city of New York, entered into a contract with plaintiff, the owner of adjoining lands on Fiftieth street, wherein, as stated, "to provide for the better improvement of the said lands, and to secure their permanent value," the parties mutually covenanted for themselves, their heirs and assigns, that only dwelling houses should be erected upon their respective premises, and that neither would permit or carry on "any stable, school house, engine house, tenement or community house, or any kind of manufacture, trade or business" on any part of said lands, after the commencement of this action to enforce the performance of the covenant by the successors in title to B., and after a decision therein sustaining the validity of the covenant (70 N. Y., 440), T. purchased with notice, and was brought in as a party defendant : Held, that the binding obligation of the covenants could not be questioned by him. The complaint alleged that a portion of the building on defendant's premises was occupied

in part by "a real estate and insurance agent or broker," and in part by "sign or fresco painters." The court found that, at the time of the trial, T. permitted the building to be used by his tenants for the business of a tailor, milliner, insurance agent, express carriers, and tobacconist. Held that the vocations specified in the complaint were within the prohibitions of the covenant ; also that in such an action the relief given must depend upon the condition of things at the time of the trial, and that the several occupations found by the court were violations, not only of the spirit, but of the letter of the covenant.

It appeared that the general current of business had reached and passed the premises fronting on Sixth avenue, and that during the pendency of the action an elevated railroad was built on Sixth avenue with a station at the intersection of Fiftieth street, in front of the premises in question, which the court found "affect the premises injuriously, and render them less profitable for the purpose of a dwelling house, but do not render their use for business purposes indispensable." The evidence disclosed that the station covered a portion of the street, its platform occupied half the width of the sidewalk in front of defendant's premises, and from it persons could look directly into the windows ; and that this, with the noise of the trains, rendered privacy and quiet impossible ; so that large depreciations in rents and frequent vacancies followed the construction of said road. Held, that a contingency having happened not within the contemplation of the parties, which imposed upon the property a condition frustrating the scheme devised by them, and defeating the object of the covenant so far at least as defendant T. was concerned, thus rendering its enforcement oppressive and inequitable, a court of equity would not decree such enforcement : Trustees, etc., *v.* Thacher, 87 N. Y., 311 ; S. C., 10 Abb. N. C., 235, reversing 46 N. Y. Supr. Ct. R., 305.

Land bounded on one side by a street and on another side by a railroad, was conveyed "subject to the condition that no building shall ever be placed on that part of the same lying within twenty-five feet of said street, and also that the present occupant of a part of the premises near said railroad for a lumber yard shall be allowed the time until the first day of October next after the date hereof to remove his lumber and evacuate the premises, but no longer, without the consent of said grantee." Held, that both clauses of the provision took effect only by way of restriction ; and that the restriction as to building, in the absence of evidence that it was imposed for the benefit of other land, must be construed as a personal covenant merely with the grantor, which his heirs could not enforce after his death : Skinner v. Shepard, 130 Mass., 180.

A deed of land contained restrictions that no building erected on it should be less than a certain height, or have exterior walks of any other than specified material, or be used for certain purposes ; and that no building should be erected within ten feet of the street. Held, that the erection of a brick wall six feet in height with a coping one foot in height, to be used as a fence or wall, on the line of the street, was not a violation of the last named restriction: Newell v. Boston, etc., 130 Mass., 209.

[11 Chancery Division, 869.]

C.J.B., March 24: C.A., July 8, 1879.

Ex parte KIMBER.   In re THRIFT.

Practice— Vacating Appointment of Trustee—Proof improperly rejected.

It is the settled practice of the Court of Bankruptcy not to vacate the appointment of a trustee merely because a proof has been improperly rejected.

In order to induce the court to vacate the appointment, special circumstances—such as that the rejection of the proof has been procured by fraud—must be shown. At any rate an application for such an order must be made very promptly after the rejection of the proof.

Ex parte Crowther (1) not followed.

---

(1) 24 L. T. (N.S.), 330.

●

[11 Chancery Division, 873.]

C.A., April 25, 26, 1879.

873]   *RALPH v. CARRICK.

[1870 R. 157.]

Will—Bequest after Death of Wife—Life Estate by Implication—Descendants taking Parent's Share.

A testator, who died in June, 1837, gave to trustees the whole of his property in trust for the payment of his debts, with full power to sell all or any part of his estates or to demise the same; and directed them out of the moneys produced or out of the rents to pay his testamentary expenses and debts, and then gave certain legacies, and directed that after the death of his wife, and after the payment of all debts and legacies, the whole residue of all his remaining property should be divided into twelve portions, three of which should be given " to the children " of his late aunt, Mrs. W., " equally among them, the descendants, if any, of those who might have died being entitled to the benefit which their deceased parent would have received had he or she been then alive," with similar gifts to the " children and descendants " of his other aunts; "and should there be no children or lawful descendants of any of his aunts remaining at the time the bequests should become payable, then the portions" were to fall into the residuary fund. The testator declared that it should not be incumbent on his executors to pay the legacies sooner than two years after his decease, nor to divide the residue amongst his relatives until two years after the death of his wife, and made provision for payment of an annuity of £700 to which his wife was entitled under her marriage settlement. The wife died in 1876. The testator's co-heirs were certain of the children of the aunts, and his next of kin were certain children of the aunts. The children of the aunts were all dead, but many of them had left children and grandchildren:

Held (affirming the decision of Hall, V.C.), that the widow did not take a life estate by implication.

A life estate in A. B. will not be implied from a gift on the death of A. B., to the testator's heir-at-law or next of kin along with other persons.

Held (reversing the decision of Hall, V.C.), that the substitutionary *gift to [874 "descendants" of children of an aunt was not confined to children of those children.

The word "descendants" is less flexible than "issue," and requires a stronger context to confine it to children.

Held, that if the word used in the present case had been "issue" instead of "descendants," the gift over would have prevented the court from confining the word to children.

Ross v. *Ross* ([1]) approved.

Notice by a respondent under Rules of Court, 1875, Order LVIII, rule 6, to vary the decision of the court was proceeded upon, though the point was one in which the original appellant had no interest.

THIS case came before the court on an appeal by the personal representative of the widow of the testator in the cause from a decision of Vice-Chancellor Hall holding that she did not take a life estate in the testator's property. The case is reported ([']).

W. Pearson, Q.C., and *Byrne*, for the appellant: If a person gives real estate after the death of A. to a person who happens to be his own heir-at-law, A. takes a life estate. So if he gives personalty after the death of A. to his sole next of kin. When the ulterior gift is to other persons along with the heir or next of kin the case is more doubtful. The issue, it must be observed, take only by way of substitution, the children being the primary objects of gift, and we contend that if after the death of A. there is a gift to B., who is the heir-at-law, with a substitutionary gift in the event of B.'s death, the construction is the same as if there was no such gift over. Unless some rule of law interferes, a will ought to be construed as an ordinary intelligent person would construe it; and a gift to the heir-at-law along with somebody else at a future time shows that the heir is not to take at once. Now as to the cases where the heir-at-law or next of kin are some only of the class of ulterior takers, *Hutton* v. *Simpson* (') is in our favor, but as the inaccuracy of that report is shown in *Rex* v. *Inhabitants of Ringstead* (') we cannot rely on it. The cases of *Blackwell*

([1]) 20 Beav., 645.   (") 2 Vern., 722.
(') 5 Ch. D., 984; 22 Eng. R., 589.   (⁴) 9 B. & C., 218.

v. *Bull* ('), *Bird* v. *Hunsdon* ('), and *Cockshott* v. *Cockshott* (')
support our contention.

875] *[COTTON, L.J.: I do not find that in any of the
cases the rule is laid down that a gift to the heir-at-law
along with others, after the death of A. B., raises the implication of a life estate in A. B. They seem to go on the
ground that, taking the whole will together, an intention to
give a life estate was to be discovered.]

In *Blackwell* v. *Bull* (') there was nothing else from which
to raise the implication. *Humphreys* v. *Humphreys* (') is
in our favor, as also *Roe* v. *Summerset* (') there referred to.
In Jarman on Wills (') it is laid down that on a devise to
one of several co-heirs after the death of another the implication does arise, but that on a devise to an heir along with
others it does not. Yet the only case he refers to on the
latter point is *Blackwell* v. *Bull*, which decides the contrary. *Aspinall* v. *Petvin* (') is relied on against us, but
that case went on the ground that the future devise was to
a stranger. *In re Smith's Trusts* (') shows what circumstances the court will take into consideration. *Cock* v.
Cock (') is an instance of implication from a gift to several of
the next of kin after the death of the other of them. The
Vice-Chancellor has not attributed sufficient importance to
the fact that the gift to the issue is merely substitutionary.

Makceson, Q.C., and *W. W. Karslake, Dickinson*, Q.C.,
and *H. A. Giffard, Horne, Bristowe*, Q.C., *J. Gerard Laing*,
and *G. I. F. Cooke*, for the respondents, were not called on.

JAMES, L.J.: I am of opinion that it is impossible for
us to differ from the Vice-Chancellor's conclusion as to the
meaning of this will. Possibly we may say, as was said by
Lord Alvanley in *Upton* v. *Lord Ferrers* (''), that a private
man would undoubtedly say that the testator must have intended his wife to take for her life. Courts of law, however, as his Lordship went on to observe, have always said
that they cannot in such a case as this draw that inference.
876] *Where there is a gift to the heir-at-law after the
death of A. B. that gift is useless except for the purpose of
expressing that the heir-at-law is not to take till after the
death of A. B., and the inference has been drawn from that
that A. B., after and not until whose death he is to get it,
takes it in the meantime. The same principle has been ap-

(') 1 Keen, 176.
(') 2 Sw., 342.
(') 2 Coll., 432.
(') Law Rep., 4 Eq., 475.
(') 5 Burr., 2608.

(') 3d ed., vol. i, p. 497.
(') 1 S. & S., 544.
(') Law Rep., 1 Eq., 79.
(') 21 W. R., 807.
('') 5 Ves., 800.

plied to the case of next of kin. Where the gift is not a gift *simpliciter* to the person who was heir-at-law or next of kin at the date of the will, all the cases except the case before Vice-Chancellor Stuart, which is inconsistent with the current of authority, treat a future gift to persons of whom the heir-at-law is one as insufficient to raise the implication. Here the ultimate gift is to a class of persons to be ascertained at the death of the wife. It is not a gift to a person who is heir-at-law or next of kin, but must be dealt with as a gift to persons who do not stand in either of those positions, and in that case there is no implication in favor of the wife. If we held that there was, we should be deciding that A. B. is to have a life estate merely because the gift of the property is postponed till afer A. B.'s death, which is in contravention of the rule laid down by the authorities. There is nothing in this case except that the gift is not to take place till after the death of A. B., with a direction that the estate shall not be sold for two years, which does not seem to make any difference. It is a mere case of a gift to a class of persons after the death of another person, those persons not being necessarily heirs-at-law or next of kin of the testator. I do not think it necessary to go through the cases which the Vice-Chancellor has gone through, and I need only say that I agree with him, except that I think the cases are rather stronger than he has represented them.

BRETT, L.J.: It sometimes amuses me when we are asked to say what was the actual intention of a foolish, thoughtless, and inaccurate testator. That is not what the court has to determine: all the court can do is to construe, according to settled rules, the terms of a will, just as it construes the terms of any other written document. This is obviously the will of a foolish, thoughtless, and inaccurate man. If he really intended his wife to have an estate for her life, what *was more easy than for him to say so? [877 If he had any such intention in his mind at the time, he must have deliberately refrained from expressing it.

The real question then is, what, according to recognized rules, is the construction of this will? The first argument was, that in order to give an estate for life by implication, it suffices that some one of the persons to whom the property is given after the decease of the person named in the will should be the heir-at-law or next of kin. If that rule were really established as a rule of construction it would be applicable to this will, and we ought to decide according to it; but to my mind, not only is it not made out that that is such a rule, but the contrary is made out. It seems to me that in *Aspinall* v. *Petvin* (¹) and in *Stevens* v. *Hale* (²) the law is laid down directly to the contrary of the rule contended for. It is·true that the rule laid down by Vice-Chancellor Stuart in *Humphreys* v. *Humphreys* (³) would support the appellant's case, and if the authorities had not decided the contrary I should have been happy to hold with him what he was inclined to hold in that case, but I think that the authorities are conclusive against that view. It might have been said that the case of *Hutton* v. *Simpson* (⁴) was an authority in favor of that proposition, but when that case was examined by Mr. Justice Bayley in the case of *Rex* v. *Inhabitants of Ringstead* (⁵), it was found not to be so. The proposition contended for by the appellant is not made out by any case. It has in its support the *dictum* in *Humphreys* v. *Humphreys*, but I am sorry to say I think that *dictum* cannot be supported. Unless, therefore, there are some particular expressions in the will to take it out of the general rule, we must decide against the appellant. I do not see anything in the context of this will to assist his contention, and therefore I am of opinion that the decision of Vice-Chancellor Hall was correct.

COTTON, L.J.: .I am of opinion that upon the point now argued the decision of the Vice-Chancellor was correct; and 878] in consequence of the course *the argument has taken, I think it right to say something as to the general rules that should govern us in deciding on the construction of wills, and as regards the rule applicable to gifts which it is attempted to raise by implication.

As regards our duty when wills come before us for construction, it is obvious to say that it is in each case to consider the words of the will. I say that, for the purpose of calling attention to the argument that in the absence of any rule of law laid down or established by cases, we are at liberty to construe wills as ordinary intelligent persons would do. There is a fallacy in this. We are bound to have regard to any rules of construction which have been established by the courts, and subject to that we are bound to construe the will as trained legal minds would do. Even very intelligent persons whose minds are not so trained are accustomed to jump at a conclusion as to what a person means by considering what they, under similar circumstances, think they would have done. That is conjecture

(¹) 1 S. & S., 544.　　　　　(³) Law Rep., 4 Eq., 475.
(²) 2 Dr. & Sm., 22.　　　　　(⁴) 2 Vern., 722.
(⁵) 9 B. & C., 218.

only, and conjecture on an imperfect knowledge of the circumstances of the case, because the facts known to the testator may not all be before them, and the testator's mind, as regards the attention to be paid to the claims of the different parties dependent upon him, may not have been constituted as their minds are constituted, so that it cannot be concluded that he would have acted in the same way as they. We therefore must construe the will as we should construe any other document, subject to this, that in wills, if the intention is shown, it is not necessary that the technical words which are necessary in some instruments should be used for the purpose of giving effect to it.

Let us see, before we come to this will, whether or no there is any general rule that will help us in interpreting it. As regards the raising gifts for life by implication arising from a gift to some person after the death of the person to whom it is sought to give a life estate by implication, we have two rules. As to real estate, if there is a gift to a testator's heir-at-law after the death of A., that does give by implication a life estate to A. If there is a gift of the testator's real estate to a stranger after the death of A., that does not raise the implication.

Then, for the purpose of seeing whether the principle of one of *those rules or of the other applies to the [1879 present case, we must consider what is the principle of the two rules. As regards an heir-at-law, if the real estate is given to him alone after the death of A. B., there is a gift to him at that time of what, in the absence of any gift, he would take immediately after the death of the testator. To make sense of this you must take it as expressing an intention to exclude the heir-at-law till that time arrives. Now an heir-at-law can only be excluded by giving the property to somebody else, and therefore, when there is a gift to the heir-at-law alone of real estate after the death of A., a gift of a life estate to A. is implied, because in no other way can the heir-at-law be excluded. But if the gift of the estate after the death of A. is to a stranger, that reasoning does not apply, for the stranger takes simply and entirely by the bounty of the testator, and in the absence of any gift, neither after the death of the named person nor at any other time, will he take anything, and it is not necessary to give anything to A. in order to postpone the gift to the stranger, for there is no difficulty in giving an estate to the stranger on the death of A., leaving it in the meantime to go to the heir-at-law.

Is there any rule established by the authorities as applicable to a gift to the heir at-law and another person jointly after the death of A. I am of opinion that none of the cases establish any rule of construction applicable to such a case. Although cases have been cited in which, in a gift to an heir-at-law and others after the death of A., a life estate to A. has been implied, none of the judges have laid down that there is a general rule of construction which, unaided by anything else in the will, will raise the implication from a devise in those terms. In each case the decision has been rested on the particular expressions of the will, and this negatives the existence of any such general rule of construction as has been contended for. I must of course except the case before Vice-Chancellor Stuart, in which he does lay down a general rule applicable to these cases, but in my opinion he went beyond the authorities on which he purported to rely, and laid down a rule which cannot be supported.

That being so, does this case come within the principle of the rule applicable to a gift to the heir-at-law after the death of A., or within the principle of the rule applicable to a gift 880] to a *stranger after the death of A.? In my opinion it comes within the latter, because, although the heir-at-law is one of the persons to whom the gift is made, it is not necessary to give to anybody else in order to postpone the interest he is to take under the will, as he does not under the gift take that which, independently of gift, would come to him. Independently of gift he takes the whole real estate, but under that gift he takes only a share in it. So that, both as regards the interest given to the stranger and as regards the modification of the interest which the heir-at-law takes, it cannot be said that the gift after the death of A. is inoperative, unless you treat it as a postponement of the gift and give a life interest to A.

There being, then, no such canon or rule of construction as the appellant contends for, he must fail unless there be on the face of the will an expressed intention by the testator that the widow shall have a life estate. I can see nothing in this will that can be held to show such an intention, and I should say that there was rather an indication of an intention to the contrary, because the testator refers to the fact that the widow was to have £700 a year, and directs it to be paid out of the income of his estate, and if he intended to give her a life estate it is extraordinary that he should not go on to direct the surplus to be paid to her. Possibly the necessity of providing for his wife's annuity may have been the ground for postponing the division of his estate. That is conjecture, but to give a life interest to his widow would be only a conjecture, and we are not entitled to conjecture what the testator meant to do. We can only look to what on the face of the will he has said is to be done. The order of the Vice-Chancellor on this point must, therefore, be affirmed.

Eddis, Q.C., and *Ford*, for the plaintiff, who had given notice under Order LVIII, rule 6, that he should contend that the decision ought to be varied : We contend that the Vice-Chancellor was wrong in applying the doctrine of *Sibley* v. *Perry* (¹) to this case.

[JAMES, L.J.: Is this case within Order LVIII, rule 6, the point being one in which the appellant is in no way interested ?]

*They referred to *Hunter* v. *Hunter* (before the [881 Court of Appeal, April 7th, 1876), and the case was allowed to proceed.

The question is, whether this case ought to be determined according to *Sibley* v. *Perry* (¹) or *Ross* v. *Ross* (²). The gift being *per stirpes*, the children and parents cannot take concurrently: *Gibson* v. *Fisher* (³). The distinction between *Sibley* v. *Perry* and *Ross* v. *Ross* is in the gift over. The Master of the Rolls observes in the latter case that if the doctrine of *Sibley* v. *Perry* is applied, the gift over is interfered with, and an intestacy may result. Every descendant, however remote, must have a parent; so a direction that issue shall only take their parent's share is perfectly sensible, without confining issue to children of the person first mentioned. In *Pruen* v. *Osborne* (⁴) it is said that the rule in *Sibley* v. *Perry* is to be applied if there is nothing else in the will. Here there is a something else, a gift over couched in unambiguous terms, such that if the children had died, yet if there were grandchildren living, the gift over could not take effect ; so if there is no gift to the grandchildren there must be intestacy. In the gift over the word "descendants" cannot possibly be used as a synonym for "children," so it ought not to be taken to be so used in the previous gift. The word "descendants" is not so readily cut down to mean "children" as the word "issue," which in popular language is only applied to children. *Ross* v. *Ross* was followed by the Master of the Rolls in *Robinson* v. *Sykes* (⁵) and *Smith* v. *Horsfall* (⁶), and is treated by the text-writers

(¹) 7 Ves., 522.   (⁴) 11 Sim., 132.
(²) 20 Beav., 645.   (⁵) 23 Beav., 40.
(³) Law Rep., 5 Eq., 51.   (⁶) 25 Beav., 628.

as establishing a modification of *Sibley* v. *Perry:* Jarman on Wills(¹) ; Hawkins on Wills (¹).

Bristowe, Q.C., and *G. I. Foster Cooke*, contrà : *Sibley* v. *Perry* has always been treated as laying down the general rule that where issue are directed to take their parent's share, "issue" means children. This was recognized in *Pruen* v. *Osborne* and *Heasman* v. *Pearse*(²), and was ad-

882] mitted in *Ross* *v. *Ross* (³). The same rule is affirmed in *Martin* v. *Holgate* (⁴) and *Bryden* v. *Willett* (⁴).

[COTTON, L.J.: In *Sibley* v. *Perry* (¹) Lord Eldon considered that the testator explained "issue" to mean children. Here, in the gift over, the testator does not use "descendants" in the sense of children.

JAMES, L.J.: "Issue" popularly means children, and can hardly be treated as synonymous with descendants.]

Each is *nomen generalissimum*, and it would be difficult to lay down any distinction between them. The gift over must be read with reference to the original gift. In *M'Gregor* v. *M'Gregor* (⁵) there was a gift over as in *Ross* v. *Ross*, but it was not held to alter the construction. *Ross* v. *Ross*, as explained by the Vice-Chancellor in this case, turned upon the special wording of the will.

JAMES, L.J.: In my opinion we cannot agree with the decision of the Vice-Chancellor. It is, I think, much to be regretted that *Sibley* v. *Perry* was ever made a leading case, because, according to the report of what Lord Eldon himself said in that case, it is, to my mind, perfectly clear that he never intended to lay down any general rule or canon of construction, but was dealing only with the peculiar language of the will in that particular case. He found one clause in which he considered that the testator had used the word "issue" to signify children only, and then he said, I give the same meaning to the word "issue" in other parts of the will. It is, however, I think, settled, but rather by the case of *Pruen* v. *Osborne* (²) rather than by *Sibley* v. *Perry*, that as a general rule when you find a gift to a person and then a gift to the issue of that person, such issue to take only the parent's share, the word issue is cut down to mean children. I am not sure that some of the consequences of such a rule have always received the attention they ought to have received. Suppose a man to leave his property to

(¹) 3d ed., vol. ii, p. 92
(²) 1st ed., p. 89.
(³) Law Rep., 7 Ch., 275 ; 8 Eng. R., 557.
(⁴) 20 Beav., 645.

(⁵) Law Rep., 1 H. L., 175.
(⁶) Law Rep., 7 Eq., 472.
(⁷) 7 Ves., 522.
(⁸) 1 D. F. & J., 63.
(⁹) 11 Sim., 132.

*his wife for life, and at her death to all his children [883
then living and the issue of such of them as should be then
dead, equally to be divided between them, the issue of any
of them who might be then dead to take only their parent's
share.   Suppose then his children all to die before the period
of division, having had children who predeceased them leaving families.   The grandchildren might go to the workhouse,
and the family property go to a stranger under the residuary
gift.   That seems a possible result of that rule.

Now the word "issue" is an ambiguous word.   In the
ordinary parlance of laymen it means children, and only
children.   When you talk of what issue a man has, or what
issue there has been of a marriage, you mean children, not
grandchildren or great-grandchildren.   But in the language
of lawyers, and only in that language, it means descendants; and in the case of *Sibley* v. *Perry* (¹) Lord Eldon
found ground for coming to the conclusion that the word
"issue" had, in the will before him, the layman's meaning
of children, and not the lawyer's meaning of descendants.
But in this case there is what appears to me to be a perfectly
unambiguous word—"descendants"—a word which I ven-
ture to say no layman or lawyer would use to designate children only.   Descendants means children and their children
and their children to any degree, and it is difficult to conceive any context by which the word "descendants" could
be limited to mean children only.   I should therefore say
that the case of *Sibley* v. *Perry* has really no application to
this will.

But supposing the word "issue," and not the word "descendants," had been used, it seems to me impossible to distinguish the case from *Ross* v. *Ross* (²), or to say that *Ross*
v. *Ross* was not decided upon very sound principles.   There
it was held that the language of the gift over rendered it
impossible to give the limited meaning of "children" to the
word "issue."   It is one of the most settled, and appears to
me one of the most reasonable rules of construction, that
where there is a gift over on the failure of certain persons
the previous gift must, if the words reasonably admit of it,
be construed as a gift to the same persons.   Here it is beyond all question that the gift over is only to take effect
upon *an absolute failure of the descendants of all [884
the aunts.   There is nothing whatever to limit the words,
and we are bound, unless there is something which absolutely compels us to the contrary, to suppose that the original gift was to the persons on failure of whom the gift over

(¹) 7 Ves., 522.   (²) 20 Beav., 645.

was to take effect. The courts have constantly applied this principle by way of implication. If before the Wills Act an estate was devised to A. for life, and if he should die without issue, then over, as the estate was not to go over until the general failure of issue, an estate tail carrying the property to the issue was implied. So also cross remainders are constantly raised by implication in the same way. Here we have a gift over of all the funds provided for the aunts and their descendants, which gift over is not to take effect except on failure of all the descendants of the aunts; and this appears to me to exclude the limited construction which it is sought to give to the original gift. That was decided in *Ross* v. *Ross* ('), and it seems to me rightly decided. I really cannot bring myself to entertain any doubt that when this testator said descendants he meant descendants, and that the effect of the direction as to their taking their parent's shares is, that they take *per stirpes* not *per capita*, so that children do not take concurrently with their parents. This gives full effect to the words, so that there is no incongruity or inconsistency in the will.

BRETT, L.J.: I think, after the way in which *Sibley* v. *Perry* (') has been spoken of in subsequent decisions, we are not at liberty to say that it does not lay down a general rule. But I think the fate of that general rule will be the fate which usually accompanies a rule which is not liked, namely, that it will.be applied to cases exactly like *Sibley* v. *Perry*, and to no others; or, in other words, it will be no general rule at all, and, after hearing what the effect of such a general rule may be as described by Lord Justice James, I should have no objection to be present at the funeral of *Sibley* v. *Perry*. But assuming *Sibley* v. *Perry* to lay down a general rule, that general rule, as it seems to me, is not applicable to this will. That general rule applies to the collocation in a particular manner of the words " issue " and 885]   " parent," but it seems to me that it does *not apply, neither does the principle of it apply, to any collocation of the words, "descendants" and "parents." In ordinary parlance the *prima facie* meaning of issue is children. In legal documents its *prima facie* meaning is " descendants," that is to say, the word "issue" may mean children only or it may mean descendants. But the *prima facie* meaning of "descendants" in ordinary parlance is all descendants, and not only children, and I know of no authority for saying that the word, merely because it is in collocation with the word "parents," is to have any other than its ordinary

(¹) 20 Beav., 645.   (²) 7 Ves., 522.

meaning. I do not think that it can properly be said that because issue may mean either children or descendants, therefore descendants may mean either children or descendants. It would require to be shown by something much more clear than the mere collocation of the words "parents" and "descendants" that a testator had used the word "descendants" in a way in which no other person would use it so as to bring the case within the rule of *Sibley* v. *Perry* ('). But even if the word "issue" here had been used in the first part of this will, it seems to me nevertheless that the construction of this will would have been in accordance with *Ross* v. *Ross* (').

Now with regard to the case of *Ross* v. *Ross*, I confess that I do not understand the first part of the judgment of the Master of the Rolls. We gain, however, from that case a very distinct ground of decision arising from the gift over. It is an authority for holding that where the word "issue" is used in its more extended meaning in the gift over, that more extended meaning is to be carried back to the former part of the will, though the word is there in collocation with parents, and that the case is thus taken out of the operation of the rule in *Sibley* v. *Perry*.

COTTON, L.J.: I am also of opinion that the decision of the Vice-Chancellor on this point cannot be sustained. It has been very much pressed upon us that there was a general rule laid down by Lord Eldon in *Sibley* v. *Perry*, and that to reverse the decision of the Vice-Chancellor would be to depart from the general rule so laid down. Certainly if Lord Eldon had laid down any general rule of construction *which would apply to the present case I should [886 follow it. But we must remember that general rules of construction are not fetters which prevent the court from giving due weight to any expressions of the testator which tend to take a case out of those rules. As I understand it, a rule of construction comes to this, that certain expressions are to bear a particular meaning, unless there is something in the will to control them. Thus, for instance, if there is a life estate followed by a gift among a number of persons or the survivors of them, the general rule of construction is that the word "survivors" refers to those who survive the tenant for life, and if there is not a life estate, then, *prima facie*, as a general rule, it refers to those who survive the testator, but this rule is liable to be controlled in each particular case by the expressions used by the testator. So that, even if there had been a general rule laid down in *Sibley* v.

(¹) 7 Ves., 522. (²) 20 Beav., 645.

Perry ('), we should have to consider how far the words
used in this particular will do or do not take the case out of
that general rule. It has been argued as if *Sibley* v.
Perry had laid down this general rule, that wherever you find issue
and parent in collocation, issue, although unless restrained
the word is most general in its meaning and includes all descendants, will be cut down to mean children of the persons
described as parents. Now in the first place *Sibley* v.
Perry, as far as decision went, laid down no such general
rule, for Lord Eldon was careful to declare his opinion in
these terms : "I shall express the ground of my opinion in
the declaration. Declare that upon the true construction of
this will and the whole of it taken together, the testator by
the words 'lawful issue' in these clauses meant children,
and the distribution shall be accordingly." He laid down
no general principle except this, that issue included all descendants, but was a word capable of being controlled by
the context, and then says that in the particular will it was
cut down and confined to children. The point most favorable to the respondent's contention on this appeal is that
which arises on the third clause of the will in *Sibley* v.
Perry, which no doubt Lord Eldon did consider to assist
him in arriving at the meaning of the word "issue" in other
clauses.   That third clause was a clause which gave £1,000 to
887]   each of three persons named, and *then it went on :
"And if all or any of them shall die before I do, then I will
that the lawful issue of every one of them so dying before me
shall share and share alike, have and enjoy that £1,000 stock
which their respective parents if living would have had and
enjoyed."   Now no person or parent of anybody could enjoy
£1,000 stock as a whole except the three individuals named,
and Lord Eldon held that parent in that clause must bear
its proper meaning of father or mother as there was nothing
to control it.   A person to whose issue there was a gift was
referred to as the parent of all the issue to whom the gift is
made : therefore issue in that clause must mean children.
That was all that Lord Eldon laid down. He also goes
through the rest of the will most carefully to see whether,
having regard to all the clauses of the will, he could not see
that throughout the will the testator had used the word
"issue" as synonymous with child.

Now, how far does that govern the present case? Here
we have a gift of certain shares of the estate "to the children of my late aunt Mrs. Winegate equally among them,
the descendants (if any) of those who may have died being en-

('') 7 Ves., 522, 533.

titled to the benefit which their deceased parent would have received had he or she been then alive." There is nothing there to show that the person there referred to as parent must of necessity be the child of Mrs. Wingate, and if that be so, the foundation of Lord Eldon's decision upon the third clause of the will in *Sibley* v. *Perry* (¹) has no application. But assume that "descendants" here could be construed to be children of the children of Mrs. Wingate. If Lord Eldon laid down a general principle, it was this, that he considered the word "issue" in the portion of the will under consideration as children, because it was the meaning which the testator showed throughout the will he intended to give to that word. Now, can we say that throughout this will descendants is used as children? It cannot be so used, because there are these words, "and should there be no children or lawful descendants of any of my aunts above named remaining at the time these bequests shall become payable," then their shares are to fall into the residue. Here "descendants" are expressly distinguished from "children." In that last gift over I can see nothing to restrict the meaning of *the word "descendants," and therefore I con- [888 sider that throughout the will the testator has not used the word "descendants" as meaning children only. I think that the share given originally to one of the *stirpes* was only to go over if there was an entire failure of that *stirps*. I think it is a sound principle that when there are ambiguous words in the original gift you should not construe the gift over in a restrictive sense which it does not otherwise bear, but should construe the ambiguous words contained in the previous gift so as to agree with the unambiguous words contained in the gift over. If there were any such general rule as the respondents contend for, this will contains expressions which would control that general rule, and show that the word "descendants" is used in its ordinary unrestricted sense. It is therefore not necessary in this case to consider how far the word "descendants" is liable to be restricted. But I must say that, as a mere matter of ordinary construction, "descendants" is a more difficult word to control than "issue."

Solicitors : *Patrick; Clarke, Woodcock and Ryland; Walter, Moojen & Sons; Nelson, Son & Hastings; Wills & Watts; Phelps, Sidzwick and Biddle.*

(¹) 7 Ves., 522.

[11 Chancery Division, 888.]

C.A., May 3, 1879.

In re HODGSON (a person of Unsound Mind).

LORD KENLIS V. HODGSON.

[1870 K. 10.]

One of several Trustees of Unsound Mind—Irish Railway Stock—Transfer into Court.

One of the trustees of an estate which was being administered by the court having become of unsound mind, an order was made under the Trustee Act, 1850, s. 5, appointing a person to concur with the other trustee in transferring into court certain Irish railway stock standing in the names of the trustees. It being discovered before the order was drawn up that owing to sect. 56 of the act such an order could not be made as to Irish stock, an order was made appointing a person new trustee of the Irish stock in the place of the person of unsound mind, and directing him to concur with the other trustee in transferring the stock into court.

———————

[11 Chancery Division, 891.]

C.A., May 16, 1879.

891]   *GEE V. MAHOOD.

[1871 G. 104.]

Will—Annuity—Corpus or Income—Bequest of Residue—Direction to set apart Investments.

A testator empowered his trustees to make demises of his estate for building purposes, and also at their discretion to sell his real and personal estate, and directed them to invest the proceeds, and the rents, issues, and profits of his estate, and to set apart a sufficient part of such investments to produce an annuity of £1,200, which he bequeathed to his wife for her life, payable on the usual quarter days; and he gave the entire residue of his said trust estate, and also that part thereof set apart for his wife after her death, upon certain trusts for the benefit of his children. The income of the estate was not sufficient to provide for the widow's annuity of £1,200 :

Held (reversing the decision of Hall, V.C.), that the widow was entitled to have the deficiency raised out of the corpus of the trust estate.

Baker v. *Baker* (1) distinguished.

THIS was an appeal from a decision of Vice-Chancellor Hall ('). Robert Gee, by his will made in September, 1868, after appointing his wife and two other persons trustees, and giving his household effects and other things, and a sum of £1,200 Consols to his wife, an annuity of £20 to Mary Drabble, and all his estate situate at Norwood to his wife, gave all other his real estate, and the residue of his personal estate, to the trustees upon trust to receive the rents, issues, and profits thereof upon the trusts thereafter declared. The

(1) 6 H. L. C., 616.   (2) 9 Ch. D., 151; 25 Eng. R., 850.

testator then empowered the trustees to make demises of his estate, or part thereof, for terms of years for building purposes, and also at such times as they should think proper during the widow's life to sell and dispose of his real and personal estate, and directed them to stand possessed of and interested in the money which should arise from the sale or sales of his said estates, and from his personal estates and effects, and the rents, issues, and profits thereof as aforesaid in trust to invest the same in manner therein mentioned. The said will then proceeded as follows: "And upon further trust to set apart a sufficient portion of *such investments as will produce the annuity of [892 £1,200 a year which I bequeath to my wife for her life, payable quarterly on every the 25th day of March, the 24th day of June, the 29th day of September, and the 25th day of December, the first quarterly payment to become due on the first of such days as shall happen after my decease, such annuity, in case of my said wife's second marriage, to be reduced to the annual sum of £150, instead of the said sum of £1,200, such annuity of £150 to be paid on the same days as the £1,200 annuity would otherwise have been payable, the first payment to be made on such of the said days as shall first happen after my said wife's second marriage and the investment so set apart to be reduced accordingly. And subject to such investment in favor of my said wife, in trust to set apart £5,000, other part thereof, for my daughter Zara on her attainment of the age of twenty-one years or marriage, which shall first happen, to be settled upon her, &c. And as to the entire residue of my said trust estate, and also as to that part thereof set apart in favor of my said wife after her death; and as to such part thereof as should be no longer required to be set apart in consequence of her second marriage," upon the trusts in the will declared; which were, as to one ·moiety, for the benefit of the three children of the testator's daughter Jane T. Carmichael in equal shares, with other trusts in case of their dying under the age of twenty-one unmarried; and as to the other moiety, for the benefit of his daughter Zara and his other daughters.

The testator died in July, 1869. The bill was filed in 1871 by Zara, who was the only child of the testator who survived him, for the administration of his estate.

The yearly income of the trust estate did not amount to £1,200, and the principal question in the suit was whether the widow, who had not married again, was entitled to have the deficiency raised out of the corpus of the estate.

The testator's real estate had not been sold, but remained in the state in which it was at the time of his death.

The Vice-Chancellor held that the widow was not entitled to have the deficiency made up out of the corpus of the estate.

An appeal was brought from this decision by an incumbrancer of the widow's interest.

893] *Farwell*, for the appellant: The rule is clearly established that where there is an actual gift of the annuity, the annuitant is entitled to have the deficiency made up out of the corpus; and there is a further rule that where the investment which produces the annuity is treated as part of the residue, the residuary legatee can only take it subject to the payment of all arrears of the annuity, so that in that case also the deficiency is payable out of the corpus: *In re Mason* ('); *Wright v. Callender* ('); *In re Tootal's Estate* ('); *May v. Bennett* ('); *Mills v. Drewitt* ('); *Perkins v. Cooke* ('); *Bright v. Larcher* ('). In the present case we have first, a direct gift of the annuity. Secondly, a direction to pay on certain fixed quarter days, one of which might happen directly after the testator's death and before any investment could have been made. Thirdly, the gift of the £5,000 to Zara Gee made "subject to the investment," which is the annuity. Fourthly, the investment is made part of the residue. Fifthly, there is a blended fund of capital and income, which is to be invested for payment of the annuity. All these circumstances show that the testator intended a gift of an annuity of £1,200, not merely the annual income of a particular fund.

W. Pearson, Q.C. (*V. Hawkins* with him), for the Carmichael family: The principle on which this question may be decided is a simple one. Wherever there is a direct gift of an annuity, and then a gift of residue, whether there be a direction for investment or not, the annuitant is entitled to full payment of the annuity and the residuary legatee can take nothing till he is paid. And on the other hand where there is no direct gift of the annuity, but a sum is directed to be set apart to produce an annual sum, and after the death of the annuitant the corpus is given over, the annuitant is only entitled to the income. In the present case there is no direct gift of the annuity; the words must be taken according-

894] ing to *their grammatical construction. The word

(') 8 Ch. D., 411; 25 Eng. R., 381.   (') 1 Russ., 370.
(') 2 D. M. & G., 652.   (') 20 Beav., 632.
(') 2 Ch. D., 628, 633; 17 Eng. R., 650. (') 2 J. & H., 393.
                (') 3 De G. & J., 148.

" which " does not refer to the annuity, but to the investment set apart to answer it. The fund is given to the widow for her life, and after her death it is given specifically to the Carmichael family and Zara Gee. It is true that it is given to the same persons as those to whom the residue is given, but it is not made part of the residue. In all the cases relied on by the other side there has been not only a direct gift of the annuity but a gift over of the fund as part of the residue. In the present case there is neither : *Baker* v. *Baker* (¹) and *Tarbottom* v. *Earle* (²) are distinctly in point. The whole frame of the will shows that the testator was dealing with the income only and meant the capital to be invested and to remain intact.

Maidlow, for the defendant Mahood.

JAMES, L.J.: With all deference to the Vice-Chancellor's judgment in this case, and with all respect for the argument which Mr. Pearson has addressed to us, I cannot bring myself to doubt that the real meaning of this will is what has been called the grammatical construction of it. The grammatical construction of the will is this : the testator says, " I direct my trustees to invest sufficient of my estate to produce an annuity of £1,200 a year, which I give to my wife." There is no magic in the position of the words, whether he says I give it or direct it to be invested, it is the same thing. With regard to the plain meaning of the words of this will, it appears to me quite clear that the testator did intend to give £1,200 a year to his wife for her life, and then in order to provide for that £1,200 for life, which is a general legacy—it makes no difference that it is called an annuity or annual sum or yearly sum, it is a legacy of £1,200 a year for so many years as she shall live, that is what the testator has given her—in order to provide for the legacy of so many sums of £1,200, he directs his executors and trustees to sell the estate as they shall think fit, and from time to time as they shall think fit to make investments and change those investments ; but in the *meantime he says she is to [895 have the annuity and the annuity is to be paid to her on the first quarter day after his death, and in a particular event that annuity is reduced to another sum which he stills calls an annuity of £150 to be paid to her. There is the actual express gift to her of an annuity of £1,200 a year, and that is what remains now to be paid to her from the first quarter day.

Now, Mr. Pearson's argument is, that we are to say that this does not mean £1,200 a year to be paid quarterly, but

(¹) 6 H. L. C., 616.   (²) 11 W. R., 680.

it means she is to have the income of the investment which
may not be made for years, she is to have nothing but the
income of an investment which is to be made as the trustees
shall find it convenient in the proper and due exercise of
their trust to be obtained by realizing the estate. That is
not construing the words, but it is introducing an entirely
new phrase without any ground for it. He does not say,
"I direct the trustees to make an investment so as to produce
£1,200 a year, and I give her the income of those investments"
—nothing of the kind is said. The question is, are we to
put those words into the will which we do not find? I am
of opinion it is an unreasonable thing to suppose that the
testator intended that his wife should have nothing until the
investment was made, and that if the investment produced
more at some time, she was to have more. It seems to me
on that point, which is the foundation of the argument, Mr.
Pearson's contention fails.

But it is said, that from the language of the gift over you
may see that it was intended she should only have the income. I see nothing in the gift over. It is said that it is a
gift distinct from the residuary gift; but I cannot bring my
mind to doubt it is really, with all deference to the Vice-
Chancellor, an entirely residuary gift. The testator thought
the residue would be payable at different times. First, he
said, "When you invest, invest enough to produce £1,200 a
year, and £5,000 for my daughter. Having done that, there
may then be a residue immediately available, and I give
that surplus to my residuary legatees." It seems to me you
are following the words and not the spirit—that you are
sticking in the bark and not in the tree—if you are to say
the words, "I give that, and all that part of the residue
which is set apart," have a different meaning from those
896] which we *have before us. The residue includes it,
and he says I direct it shall be included.

It seems to me that the real question is, whether upon the
construction of this will, it is a gift of an annuity or yearly
sum of £1,200 out of the estates, or only a gift of the income
of particular investments, or gift of income of this particular investment, to be limited from time to time to £1,200. I
cannot doubt it is a gift, answering the exact description
Mr. Pearson has given, of a pecuniary legacy measured by
the number of years she shall live, multiplied by £1,200.

BRETT, L.J.: The question in this case, it seems to me,
may be thus stated: Is the wife entitled for life to an annuity
of £1,200 to be procured, if possible, out of the whole estate,
or is she entitled for life to the income of an investment

which is directed to be made? When and if that investment is once made Mr. Pearson wishes us to decide, or says we ought to decide, that all that she is entitled to is the income of an investment.

Now, in the first place, the terms which are used in the will are that she is to have an annuity, and the terms are not that she is to have the income of an investment. If you take the simple terms which are used in the will in their ordinary sense it is an annuity, and it is not the income of an investment. Then it is said, if you look at other parts of this will, you must see that what was intended was the income of an investment; but then, when Mr. Pearson was pressed with the result of such a construction, he was obliged to admit that inasmuch as here the trustees are given a discretion as to the time and mode of the investment, if they did not for a considerable time invest, the wife would not be entitled to anything until they did invest. That seemed to me to be a fatal admission, because it is not only an incomprehensible idea on the part of the testator (who certainly was providing for his wife), but it seems to be inconsistent with the terms of the annuity which is granted, as was pointed out by my Lord, at all events for the first quarter, for there is a direction that she is to be paid on the first quarter day after the death of the testator. It would be almost impossible that the investment should be made *by that [897 time. But then Mr. Pearson was obliged further to admit, if his construction be true, and if the trustees were anxious to make an investment, which at the time of the investment produced £1,200, that afterwards, if the income from the investment was to increase, the wife would be entitled to more than £1,200, and to the full income of the investment, whatever in the result it might turn out to be. That seems also to me to be quite an incomprehensible idea on this will. Therefore, Mr. Pearson's interpretation, if carried out in this will, shows two results, both of them, as it seems to me, practically absurd, and one of them inconsistent with the other terms of the will. Those are tests to show that the ordinary language is to be followed, and that this is to be held to be an annuity and not to be the income of an investment.

Now, other tests have been proposed on the one side and on the other, which have been applied in other cases to other wills, or, in other words, authorities have been cited in order to enable us if possible to construe this will. It seems to me they are cited with the usual effect, that is to say, they are inapplicable to this will. This decision will probably go into the reports as another test applied to this will, and it will hereafter be attempted to be applied to other wills with the same effect that those have been attempted to be applied to this ; that is to say, it will afford no help till you find another will practically in the same terms as this.

COTTON, L.J.: It is important, if any general rule of construction has been established, that the court should not depart from such rule, but I can hardly see there is any general rule of construction laid down applicable to the present case, except this, that if there is a direct legacy of an annuity, then *prima facie* the annuitant is entitled to have that made good, not only out of the income, but out of the capital, unless there are words sufficient to cut down the claim of the person to the income only ; to which I may add that the residuary legatee, that is to say, one taking a residuary legacy, cannot take anything until all legacies have been provided for.

What has been argued in the present case by Mr. Pearson is, that the widow stands in the position of tenant for life of 898] a particular *fund set apart out of the estate, and that the fund is given after her death or second marriage as a fund separate from the residue, and not as a part of the residue. The first question we have to consider here is whether originally the gift to the widow is a gift of an annuity to be provided for in a particular way, if that way is sufficient, or whether there is a gift to her of the annual produce of the fund which is directed to be set apart.

I quite agree with Mr. Pearson that in considering a will you ought to deal with it as with every other document ; see what the words are, and, unless there is anything plainly incongruous in so doing, put on the words their fair grammatical construction. Now, what is the will? "On further trust to set apart a sufficient portion of such investments as would produce the annuity of £1,200 a year." That is the direction. Then, what is the gift to the wife? "Which I bequeath to my said wife for her life, payable quarterly" on every quarter day, "the first payment to be made and become due on the first of such days as shall happen after my decease." Now, the words of gift to the wife, if you take them grammatically and strictly, are a short expression for this : "And this annuity of £1,200 a year I bequeath to my said wife." If you take it grammatically, and expand the relative by substituting the antecedent, it is a gift, not of annual income or dividends arising from the fund, for that has never been mentioned, but only of that antecedent which has been mentioned, namely, the annuity of £1,200 a year. If you not only depend on the substitution of the antecedent for the relative, but also look at the rest of the sentence, it all points to the gift of the annuity as such, that is to say, of an annual sum as a legacy, and not to a gift to one as tenant for life of a particular fund, because the testator directs the first payment to be made on the regular quarter day. If you once ascertain that what is given to her is not an annuity, but a tenancy for life of an ascertained investment, no alteration can be produced in the gift to her by any direction made as to the time when it is to be paid to her. But when it is doubtful and ambiguous what the gift to her is, and of what and how she is legatee, then you must look at all parts of that which constituted her legatee. Again, when you come to the subsequent part of the gift to her, where the reduction is made in that which is to be *paid to her, it is treated throughout as an [899 annuity, and not as a payment or gift to her as tenant for life of an ascertained fund. Again, when you come to a gift to the persons who are now contending that they can take something before the annuity is provided for, the question is are they residuary legatees? Do they take as residuary legatees, or do they take what is directed to be set apart for the annuity, as a specific sum to be handed over to them intact? Although there is a gift of an annuity, yet there may be expressions in the will that show that what the testator has provided as a fund for payment of the annuity is to be handed over to those who are to take after the death of the annuitant in the same state as when first set apart. In my opinion all that is given to Mr. Pearson's clients is given to them as residue. It is true there is a reference, and an unnecessary reference, to the fund set apart to provide for the annuity given to the widow, but I agree with Lord Justice James that that is what is often done, namely, a gift immediately of what remains after setting apart what the testator had directed to be and contemplated would be set apart, and then a statement that the residuary legatees must wait for the enjoyment of that which he has directed to be set apart and retained until it can be seen whether or no the £1,200 a year has been provided for, that is, until the death of the widow.

The case depends on the construction of the will itself, and it is unnecessary to refer to authorities, but as the Vice-Chancellor relied on the case of *Baker* v. *Baker* ('), and as Mr. Pearson has much pressed us with that case, I think it right to refer to it. That case, in my opinion, is entirely different. It was the same in principle, because there, on

(') 6 H. L. C., 616.

the construction of the will, the court held that the widow was tenant for life only of a particular fund, and that it was given after her death as a fund intact, so that she could have no claim on the corpus of the fund of which she was tenant for life, and the words of the will in that case bear that interpretation, because there was a direction to set apart such a sum of money as when placed out or invested would realize a clear annual sum of £200, and a direction, without any gift of annuity to the widow, "to permit and 900] suffer my said wife to *receive and take such dividends, interest, or annual income by two equal half-yearly payments for and during the term of her natural life, provided she shall so long continue my widow, but not otherwise. And from and after her decease or second marriage, whichever shall first happen, it is my will and I further declare that in case I shall die without issue the said trustee shall stand possessed of the said principal or trust moneys, and the stocks, funds, and securities in or upon which the same shall be invested upon trust for" certain named persons. Although those afterwards took the residue, this was not given as part of or in conjunction with the residue or under the gift which gave them the residue, but as a separate and distinct fund ; and the direction as to the widow is the ordinary direction to pay her the dividends and income as tenant for life. That is a clear case of a tenant for life of a fund, the amount of which was to be ascertained by the annual income which it would produce, and is not the case of a gift to the widow of an annuity, and of a gift subject to her annuity, or of a gift to persons to take as residuary legatees.

Solicitors: *Stokes, Saunders & Stokes ; Hicks & Co.; Billinghurst & Wood.*

See 31 Eng. Rep., 328 note.

Where the construction of a will involves the question whether income or accretions—such as stock, dividends or shares, in a corporation, belonging to the estate—go to the life tenant or the remainderman, the life tenants are necessary parties to a proceeding awarding payment thereof to the life tenant : Riggs v. Craggs, 89 N. Y., 479, 11 Abb. N C., 401, reversing 26 Hun, 89.

By a decree of the surrogate in 1874, the rest, residue and remainder of a decedent's estate was, in accordance with the directions of his will, set apart to the executors as trustees to apply the income thereof for the benefit of decedent's widow during her life. The widow has since died, and the executors and trustees have presented the account of their transactions preparatory to the distribution of the principal of the trust funds among the parties who have become entitled thereto. Held, that the commissions of the executors and trustees should be paid out of the principal fund, and are not chargeable on the interest of the life beneficiary alone : Matter of Cammann, 5 N. Y. Monthly Law Bull., 24.

Vol. XI.]   CHANCERY DIVISION.   879

C.A.   Ex parte Paterson. In re Throckmorton.   1879

[11 Chancery Division, 900.]

V.C.H., April 8: C.A., May 20, 1879.

In re BENTHAM MILLS SPINNING COMPANY.

Company—Transfer of Shares—Registration—Articles of Association—Companies Act, 1862, Table A, Arts. 10, 13.

The 10th clause of Table *A* of the schedule to the Companies Act, 1862, does not apply to persons claiming shares by transmission under the 13th clause. Therefore, where a company has adopted Table *A* as its articles of association, it cannot refuse to register the name of a trustee in bankruptcy of a shareholder on the ground that the shareholder is indebted to the company.

Decision of Hall, V.C., reversed.

[11 Chancery Division, 908.]

C.A., June 12, 1879.

**Ex parte* PATERSON. *In re* THROCKMORTON. [908

Trustee in Bankruptcy—Disclaimer—Expired Lease—Leave of Court—Bankruptcy Act, 1869 (32 & 33 Vict. c. 71), s. 23—Bankruptcy Rules, 1871, r. 28.

A lease of a house was vested in a bankrupt as assignee. The trustee in the bankruptcy did not disclaim the lease, but he did not take possession of the property or exercise any act of ownership over it. The bankrupt continued to live in the house, his friends paying the rent for him. After the expiration of the term the lessor sued the original lessee on his covenant to repair, claiming £400 damages. The lessee served a third party notice on the trustee, claiming to be indemnified by him, as assignee of the term, against all breaches of the covenant since the date of the bankruptcy and the trustee's appointment. The trustee then applied to the Court of Bankruptcy for leave to execute a disclaimer in respect of the lease. The lessor opposed the application, and the registrar refused it on the ground that the lease had expired. The trustee appealed, giving notice to the lessor, who did not. appear on the hearing of the appeal:

Held, that leave to disclaim might be given, as it could not prejudice the rights of any person who was not before the court.

THIS was an appeal from a decision of Mr. Registrar Hazlitt, acting as Chief Judge in Bankruptcy.

By an indenture dated the 20th of May, 1871, J. G. Scott demised to G. N. Taylor a house and premises, and the fixtures and furniture therein, for the term of seven years from the 15th of July, 1871, at a yearly rent of £249. The lease contained a covenant by Taylor to repair the demised premises. On the 21st of July, 1873, Taylor assigned the premises comprised in the lease to Richard Throckmorton for the remainder of the term, Throckmorton covenanting to perform the covenants contained in the lease, and to indemnify Taylor in respect of any breach thereof. Throckmorton was adjudicated a bankrupt on the 26th of October, 1876. He continued to live in the house, the rent being paid for him by his friends. The lease was mentioned in his statement of affairs, but he said that he did not consider it of any value. The trustee did not take possession of the demised premises, or exercise any act of ownership over them, and no application was made to him by the lessor requiring him to disclaim the lease. On the 17th of December, 1878, Scott 909] commenced an action in the *Queen's Bench Division against Taylor, claiming £400 damages for breach of the covenant to keep the demised premises in repair. On the 27th of February, 1879, Taylor served on the trustee a third party notice, under the provisions of Rules of Court, 1875, Order xvi, rule 17, stating that he claimed to be indemnified by the trustee, as assignee of the term, against all breaches of the covenant in the lease since the date of the bankruptcy and the appointment of the trustee. On the 21st of March, 1879, the trustee applied to the Court of Bankruptcy that he might be at liberty to execute a disclaimer in respect of the lease. The lessor appeared by counsel, and opposed the application, and the registrar refused it, on the ground that a disclaimer could not be executed of a lease which had expired. The trustee appealed. The notice of appeal was served only on the lessor.

Yate Lee (*Jelf* with him), for the appellant : Sect. 23 is wide enough in its terms to authorize a disclaimer in such a case ; the object is to enable the trustee to get rid of every liability resulting from contracts of the bankrupt. Rule 28 of the Bankruptcy Rules, 1871, which requires the leave of the court to be obtained for a disclaimer of a lease, was only intended to protect the lessor. The lessor does not now appear, and it is understood that his claim has been satisfied by his lessee. Suppose a lease expired within a week after the appointment of the trustee, ought he to be personally liable in respect of breaches of covenant because he did not at once disclaim the lease, before he had had an opportunity of learning anything about it?

[JAMES, L.J.: How can you disclaim that which does not exist?]

It is not more impossible than it is to assume, as sect. 23 provides, that a lease which is disclaimed shall be deemed to have been surrendered at a time since which rent may have been paid. Difficulties must arise when an act is to be treated as being in law that which in fact it is not: *Ex parte Brook* ('). A disclaimer can affect the rights of no one but the landlord and the trustee: *Smyth* v. *North* ('). There

('} 10 Ch. D., 100, 110; 26 Eng. R., 543.   (') Law Rep., 7 Ex., 242.

it was held that the disclaimer of a *lease by the [910 trustee of an assignee did not affect the rights and liabilities *inter se* of the lessor and original lessee. If Taylor is injured by the disclaimer, he will have a right of proof in the bankruptcy. The trustee will be personally liable as assignee of the lease by operation of law, unless he is allowed to disclaim. If it can be said that there is now a lease to disclaim, it is a proper case for giving leave to disclaim; if there is nothing in the nature of a leasehold interest to disclaim, the trustee can disclaim without leave.

No one appeared for the lessor.

JAMES, L.J.: So far as the court is concerned you are at liberty to disclaim. We shall not be prejudicing the rights of any persons who are not before us by giving you leave. But we express no opinion as to those rights.

BAGGALLAY, L.J., and THESIGER, L.J., concurred.

The order was drawn up as follows:

This Court doth order that the order made by Mr. Registrar Hazlitt, and dated the 21st day of March, 1879, be discharged. And it is ordered that the trustee have leave to execute a disclaimer so far as the formal leave of the court is required for such purpose, but not so as to prejudice by the expression of any opinion of this court any person other than the respondent as to the effect of such disclaimer.

Solicitors : *Peacock & Goddard.*

See 31 Eng. Rep., 621.

An assignee for the benefit of creditors who, in the conduct of the business of his trust, continues in the possession of premises let to his assignor, does not thereby subject himself to a personal liability for the rent. To create such liability, there must be a special agreement. And when the assignee is sued personally, the fact that he may have assets as assignee will not authorize recovery : White *v.* Thomas, 75 Missouri, 454.

The liability of an assignee of a term is founded upon the privity of the estate, and does not spring from any contract relation between the assignor and lessor : Morgan *v.* Yard, 30 Pittsb. Leg. Jour., (13 N.S.), 138.

882   CHANCERY DIVISION.   [Vol. XI.

1879   Ex parte Bates.   In re Pannell.   C.A.

[11 Chancery Division, 911.]

C.A., June 12, 1879.

911]   *Ex parte CHALMERS.   In re SAWERS.

Practice—Bankruptcy Petition—Representation of Debtor's Estate—Appeal by Receiver before Appointment of Trustee.

After the presentation of a bankruptcy petition and the appointment of a receiver, but before the appointment of a trustee, an order was made that the receiver should deliver up to the applicants some bills of exchange which had come into his hands, on the ground that they did not form part of the debtor's estate. Notice of the application had been addressed to the receiver, the debtors, and the petitioning creditor. Notice of appeal was given in the name of the receiver alone.

Held, that the notice must be amended by naming the debtors and the petitioning creditor also as appellants.

This having been done, the order was affirmed on the merits.

See 26 Eng. R., 430 note ; Ex parte Learoyd, 26 Eng. R., 452.

A co-defendant is not an "opposite" party, so as to render it necessary to serve him with notice of appeal, especially when he has not appeared at the hearing : London, etc., v. Duff, 5 Wy., Webb. & A'B. (Eq.), 19.

On a proceeding to sell real estate of a decedent to pay debts, if a creditor appeal, the heirs at law must be made parties. They cannot be made parties after the time to appeal has expired: Patterson v. Hamilton, 26 Hun, 665.

[11 Chancery Division, 914.]

C.A., July 3, 1879.

914]   *Ex parte BATES.   In re PANNELL.

Proof—Contingent Liability—Covenant to pay Annuity—Valuation—Death of Annuitant after Payment of Dividend—Bankruptcy Act, 1869 (32 & 33 Vict. c. 71), s. 31.

A bankrupt had covenanted to pay a life annuity to trustees for the benefit of his wife. The annuity was valued, and proof was made by the trustees for the amount thus ascertained, and a dividend was paid to them. The wife died, and the dividend which the trustees had received exceeded the amount of the payments of the annuity which the bankrupt would have had to make if he had remained solvent :

Held (reversing the decision of the registrar), that the trustees could not be called upon to refund the excess of the dividend above the payments of the annuity which accrued due during the wife's life.

Ex parte Wardley ([1]) distinguished.

THIS was an appeal from a decision of Mr. Registrar Hazlitt, acting as Chief Judge in Bankruptcy.

In the year 1874 Mrs Pannell, the wife of Mr. Charles Pannell, petitioned the Divorce Court for a judicial separation. On the 7th of July, 1874, certain terms of arrangement were agreed to upon which all further proceedings in the suit

([1]) 6 Ch. D., 790; 23 Eng. R., 356.

were to be stayed, and on the 23d of July, 1874, a deed was
executed to carry out the arrangement. This deed was
made between Pannell of the first part, Mrs. Pannell of the
second part, and Thomas Bates and John Gibbs, as trustees,
of the third part. The deed contained (*inter alia*) a covenant by Pannell that he, his executors, administrators, or
assigns, should, during the life of his wife, pay a yearly sum
of £200 to the trustees, to be held and applied by them on
trust for the wife for her separate use.

On the 18th of September, 1876, Pannell was adjudicated
a bankrupt.

The trustees of the deed tendered a proof for £3,493, the
amount at which the annuity of £200 had been valued by an
actuary as at the date of the adjudication. This proof was
admitted.

The trustees also tendered a proof for £148, arrears of the
annuity due at the date of the adjudication. This proof was
also admitted.

*The trustees in the bankruptcy afterwards paid [915
to the trustees of the deed the sum of £698 12*s*., being a dividend of 4*s*. in the pound in respect of the proof for the value
of the annuity. On the 21st of September, 1878, Mrs. Pannell died. On the 25th of March, 1879, the trustee in the
bankruptcy applied to the court for directions as to dealing
with the proof for £3,493.

The registrar ordered that the trustees of the deed should
repay to the trustee in the bankruptcy the sum of £297,
being the difference between the sum of £698 12*s*. (the dividend received by them in respect of their proof for £3,493)
and the sum of £401 12*s*., the amount of the payments of the
annuity which accrued due to Mrs. Pannell under the covenant, from the date of the order of adjudication to the day
of her death, and that no further dividend should be paid
in respect of this proof.

The executor of Mrs. Pannell's will appealed from the
order.

Lush, for the appellant: The registrar proceeded on the
authority of *Ex parte Wardley* ([1]). In that case a marriage
settlement provided that the trustees should apply the income of a sum of £5,000 in the first instance in paying the
premiums on certain policies on the husband's life, or so
much thereof as the husband should neglect to pay. And
there was a covenant by the husband to pay the premiums.
He paid the premiums for a time, but ultimately he failed
to do so, and filed a liquidation petition ; and after this the

([1]) 6 Ch. D., 790.

trustees paid the premiums.   They proved in the liquidation
for the estimated value of the husband's covenant.   A dividend was declared, but before the trustees had received it on
their proof the husband died.

The Chief Judge held that the trustees were not entitled
to receive the whole dividend (which exceeded the amount
which they had actually paid for premiums), but only the
amount which they had actually paid, together with the
interest which the dividend had been making since its declaration.

In the present case the dividend has been actually paid, so
that there is a distinction between it and *Ex parte Wardley*.
But, if necessary, this court can overrule *Ex parte Wardley*.   Sect. 31 of the Bankruptcy Act, 1869, distinctly provides that a contingent debt or liability of the bankrupt
916] shall be valued, and that "the *amount of such
value when assessed shall be provable as a debt under the
bankruptcy."

[He was stopped by the court.]

F. G. Bagshawe, for the trustees of the deed.

Doria, for the trustee in the bankruptcy :   The proof was
made for the purpose of providing a fund to answer the annuity as it should become payable.   It has been paid in full.
If the whole of the dividend is now to be retained, the trustees of the deed will have received from the husband's insolvent estate more than they could have got from him if he
had remained solvent.   They will get more than 20s. in the
pound, while the other creditors will get less.   This is contrary to the equality which is the principle of the administration in bankruptcy.   The registrar's decision is founded
on *Ex parte Wardley* (¹).

JAMES, L.J.:   I do not think it is necessary for us to decide what ought to be done in the exact state of facts which
arose in *Ex parte Wardley*.   There the Chief Judge appears
to have thought that the case was like that of a debt, for
which the bankrupt and another person were liable, being
paid by that other person.   But the present case is simply
that of an annuity payable by A. to B.   The provision of
the statute is plain.   It says that such future or contingent
debts or liabilities of a bankrupt are to be valued in the best
way possible, and that, when the value has been ascertained,
the sum so assessed is to be provable as a debt in the bankruptcy.   The statute has converted the annuity for the purpose of proof into a gross sum immediately payable, and on
that sum the creditor is entitled to receive dividend ; both

(¹) 6 Ch. D., 790.

parties, the creditor and the trustee, taking the proof for better or for worse.   The order of the registrar seems to me a direct violation of the words of sect. 31, and the case is not governed by *Ex parte Wardley*, where the circumstances were peculiar.

BRETT, L.J.:   It seems to me that the case is governed entirely by the words *of the act.   The liability to pay the [917 annuity was a liability contingent on the life of the annuitant, i.e., contingent on the happening of a future event. It is within the precise words of sect. 31.   The section says that such a contingent liability is to be provable in the bankruptcy, and says how it is to be proved.   An estimate is to be made of the value, and the value so assessed is to be provable in the bankruptcy for all purposes, so long as the bankruptcy lasts.

COTTON, L.J.:   I am of opinion that the appellant is right.   We must look at the act and see what it provides. The liability to pay the annuity is one which could not be said to be a debt at the time of the bankruptcy.   But sect. 31 says that a valuation is to be made of such a liability, and that proof is to be made for the amount so ascertained. The proof must be made for better or for worse.   It might turn out to be very much for the benefit of the person proving, or it might turn out very much the reverse.   In the present case it has turned out that the amount of the proof is greater than that which the bankrupt would have had to pay if he had remained solvent.   But that cannot justify us in now setting aside the proof and disregarding the provisions of the act of Parliament.   It seems to me impossible to treat the proof for the value of the annuity as satisfied by dividends to an amount equal to the payments of the annuity which in fact accrued after the commencement of the bankruptcy.   I suggested during the argument that possibly the trustees of the settlement might hold the surplus, after paying all the arrears of the annuity in full, on a resulting trust for the covenantor.   But we cannot decide that point now. We can only decide that dividends must be paid on this proof, just as on all other proofs.   The case differs entirely from that of a proof on a bill of exchange where funds have been provided from another source to pay it; then, of course, if the amount of the bill had been satisfied, the proof would be ─   ─.

*he appellant: *Truefitt & Gane.*

le trustee in the bankruptcy: *Stones, Morris*

886   CHANCERY DIVISION.   [Vol XL

1878   Emma Silver Mining Company v. Grant.   M.R.

[11 Chancery Division, 918.]

M.R., Nov. 22, 1878: C.A., Feb. 14, 1879: M.R., Feb. 20, 24, 1879.

918] *EMMA SILVER MINING COMPANY V. GRANT.

[1877 E. 103.]

*Order for Trial of Issues—Application by Plaintiffs—Rules of Court, 1875,
Order xxxvi, r. 6—Undertaking by Plaintiff to discontinue Part of Action—
Company—Liability of Promoter—Secret Profit—Allowances for Money bona
fide expended.*

In an action against several defendants involving various issues, the plaintiffs
having applied under Rules of Court, 1875, Order xxxvi, rule 6, for an order for two
simple issues to be tried as between themselves and two of the defendants before the
rest of the action, the court made the order on the plaintiffs' undertaking not to seek
relief against the said two defendants in respect of any cause of action other than
that covered by the issues so to be tried, and also discontinuing such portion of the
action as the court should direct.

By an agreement between the vendors of a mine and G., a financial agent, the vendors agreed to sell the mine to a company to be formed by G. for its purchase at the
price named, and that G. should receive 20 per cent. of the amount of the allotted
capital of the company. By a second agreement between P., the agent of the vendors, and D. (a nominee of G.), described as agent of the intended company, P.
agreed to sell the mine to the company for the price mentioned in the former agreement, but no reference was made to the percentage which G. was to receive. Shortly
afterwards the company was formed; the memorandum of association and prospectus, which were settled by G., stated that its object was to carry-out the second
agreement and for the purchase and working of the mine, but they contained no reference to the first agreement, under which G. received the amount therein agreed
upon. G. secured the services of the first directors, provided their qualifications,
and launched the company. In an action by the company to make him liable for
what he had received without the knowledge of the company :

Held, that G. was liable for the amount of the secret profit which he had made;
also, that in estimating the amount of such profit he was entitled to be allowed all
sums *bona fide* expended in securing the services of the directors and providing their
qualification, and in payments to the brokers and officers of the company and to the
public press in relation to the company.

THIS was an action by the Emma Silver Mining Company,
Limited, against the following defendants: Albert Grant,
Maurice Grant, G. Anderson, J. H. Puleston, T. W. Park,
H. H. Baxter, W. M. Stewart, R. C. Schenck, the Emma
Silver Mining Company (a corporation incorporated accord-
ing to the laws of the State of New York in the United
States of America), and Mr. Lincoln.

The action related to the purchase of a mine in the terri-
919]   tory of *Utah, in the United States, called the
"Emma Mine" in which, at the time of the negotiations
hereafter mentioned, the defendants Park and Baxter, who
then resided in the United States, were interested, and the
mineral property in which had been vested in the defendant
company in America.

In 1871 the defendant Park and the defendant Stewart, who also resided in the United States, acting on behalf of the defendant company, came over to England to negotiate a sale of the said mine, and to promote a company for the purpose of purchasing the same.

On the 2d of November, 1871, an agreement was purported to be entered into between Park and Stewart and the defendants Albert Grant and Maurice Grant, who, as the statement of claim alleged, were then and had since been carrying on business in London as financiers, bankers, and promoters of companies, under the name of Grant & Co., though it appeared that Maurice Grant was not at that time partner in the firm or a party to the agreement which was entered into by Albert Grant alone under the style of Grant & Co.

The agreement, so far as material to be stated, was as follows:

"Memorandum of an agreement made the 2d of November, 1871, between T. W. Park, of Vermont, and W. Stewart, of Nevada, part owners of the Emma Mine, and acting under full authority from all the other owners, hereinafter called the "vendors," of the one part, and Messrs. Grant & Co., bankers, of the other part, whereby it is agreed as follows:

"1. The vendors shall sell the Emma Mine, and all the appurtenances, rights and privileges now held, used, and enjoyed therewith as a mine in operation, together with all the ore in hand and £46,300 in cash, to a joint stock company to be formed by Grant & Co., for the purchase of the property.

"2. The price to be paid for the said purchase shall be the sum of £1,000,000, one half thereof to be paid in cash at the date mentioned in the prospectus for the payment of the instalment, and upon the said mine, property, ore, cash, and appurtenances being duly transferred to and absolutely vested in the said company, and the remaining half to be paid in fully paid-up shares of the said company.

*"3. The share capital of the company shall be [920 offered to the public for subscription to the amount of £500,000, at the expense of Messrs. Grant & Co., and Messrs. Grant & Co. shall be entitled to receive and be paid by the vendors 20 per cent. of the amount of the capital of the company which may be allotted and taken up after deducting the amount of any shares which may have to be and are repurchased."

The said agreement contained other provisions as to the allotment of shares, which were subsequently modified by an agreement of the 5th of December, 1871.

The statement of claim alleged that, upon the said agreement between Grant & Co. and the defendants Park and Stewart having been entered into, Grant & Co., acting as promoters of the company that was afterwards formed (being the plaintiff company), proceeded to organize the company, and to obtain the consent of certain influential persons and firms to act as directors and officers of the same ; and that they obtained the consent of the several persons therein named to become directors.

On the 4th of November, 1871, an agreement was entered into between Park, on behalf of "the vendors," of the one part, and G. H. Dean, a nominee of Albert Grant, described as "acting on behalf of a company then intended to be formed and incorporated under the laws of England by the name of the Emma Silver Mining Company, Limited," of the other part, for the sale of the mine to the intended company. The purchase was to include the mine therein described, with the plant, goods and chattels in and about the same, and all the stocks of ores in the mine, and the sum of £46,300 proceeds of ore sold and then in hand. The agreement stated that the purchase-money was to be the sum of £1,000,000 sterling, of which £500,000 was to be paid in cash and £500,000 in fully paid-up shares of the company. The vendors were to pay all the expenses of and incidental to the formation of the company up to the allotment of shares.

It was alleged that the defendant Park, during his negotiations, prepared a prospectus to be issued by the proposed company, and that the same, as altered by the defendant Albert Grant, was submitted to the persons who had agreed to become directors. The qualifications of the directors were provided by Albert Grant.

921]   *On the 8th of November, 1871, the plaintiff company was formed under the provisions of the Companies Act. By the memorandum of association the objects of the company were stated to be "the carrying out of the agreement of the 4th of November, 1871, the purchase, acquisition, and working of the Emma Mine, the purchase of other lands or mines in the territory of Utah, and such machinery and implements as might be necessary for carrying out the working of the mines," and other objects expressed in the memorandum. The nominal capital of the company was defined at £1,000,000, divided into 50,000 shares of £20 each.

By the articles the contract of the 4th of November, 1871, was expressed to be adopted by the company so far as its provisions were intended to be binding on the company therein contemplated. The articles provided that the defendants Park, Schenck, and Stewart, and three others therein named, should be the first directors of the company.

At the same time that the plaintiff company was incorporated a prospectus prepared by the defendants Park and Albert Grant was issued inviting subscriptions for 25,000 shares of £20 each, described as the unappropriated capital of the company. In this prospectus the defendants Anderson, Schenck, and Puleston were described as trustees of the plaintiff company, and it was stated that they had consented to act as trustees for the shareholders until the property was duly transferred. This prospectus was circulated by and at the expense of Albert Grant, with the approval of Park and Stewart, and was based on the representations made by Park to them and to some of the directors.

Neither the agreement of the 4th of November, 1871, nor the memorandum and articles of association, nor the prospectus, contained any reference to the provision in the agreement of the 2d of November, 1871, as to the payment by the vendors to Grant & Co. of 20 per cent. of the amount of the capital of the company, nor to any profit to be received by Albert Grant as promoter of the company.

Before the 1st of December, 1871, more than £400,000 had been paid to the credit of the said trustees on account of the 25,000 shares in the plaintiff company which had been allotted to applicants according to the terms of the prospectus; but, the *trustees not having received a certificate [922 from the solicitors of the plaintiff company that the transfer of the property had been completed, no part of the purchase-money had then been paid to the vendors.

By an agreement dated the 1st of December, 1871, and made between Park and the said trustees, it was agreed that Park should complete and deliver all transfers and assurances required by the solicitors to the company, and give to the company actual possession of all the property, including the sum of £46,300 cash as past earnings, and that, upon the solicitors receiving notice from their agent at New York that the title was good, the trustees should pay the said sum to Park.

The statement of claim alleged that Grant & Co. advanced to Park the sum of £45,000 upon the security of the first moneys payable to the vendors in respect of the purchase-money to enable him with that and another smaller sum to place £46,300 to the credit of the plaintiff company with their bankers, representing the same to be the produce of the ore derived from working the mine.

By a memorandum of agreement dated the 5th of December, 1871, made between Park and Stewart, described as owners of the Emma Mine of the one part, and Grant & Co. of the other part, it was agreed that certain stipulations in the said agreement of the 2d of November, 1871, as to the allotment of the shares in the plaintiff company should be modified, and it was further agreed, in consideration of the further services of Grant & Co. in carrying out the arrangement for the acquisition of the mine by the company, and the further expenses incurred by Grant & Co. in relation to the company, and in consideration of Grant & Co. agreeing to absolve Park and Stewart from all claim in respect of Grant & Co.'s expenses under the agreement of the 2d of November, 1871, that the vendors of the mine should deposit with a nominee of Park and Grant & Co. all the £500,000 of fully paid-up shares in the company to which the vendors were entitled as part of the purchase-money for twelve months, unless they should be disposed of as thereinafter provided ; also that Grant & Co. might, as long as the said shares remained so deposited, dispose of the said £500,000 of shares, unless Park should elect to take the 923] *same as therein provided, and that upon every sale that might be effected of any of the said shares, Park should pay to Grant & Co. the commission of £1 per share, and should also pay, and Grant & Co. be entitled to retain, one-half of the net proceeds of the sale of the said shares. It was also agreed that Park should be at liberty to withdraw from deposit a certain number of the shares, in which case Grant & Co. were not to be entitled to any remuneration.

This agreement was, it was alleged, concealed from the directors of the plaintiff company, other than Park, Baxter, and Stewart, and from the company.

The statement of claim alleged that on the 5th of December, 1871, the trustees, under Park's direction, paid to Grant & Co. out of the £400,000 then standing to their credit, the sum of £145,000, and paid the balance to Park ; also that the sum paid to Grant & Co. was paid on account of the £45,000 lent to Park as before mentioned, and on account of the £100,000 payable to Grant & Co. under the agreement of the 2d of November, 1871 ; also that the defendants Park, Baxter, Stewart, Albert Grant and Maurice Grant, or some or one of them, with the knowledge of the others, had, before the issuing of the prospectus, agreed to make the various payments or allotments of shares to the several persons in the statement of claim mentioned, out of the moneys and shares which the vendors were to receive from the company, or out of so much thereof as Grant & Co. were to receive as promoters, and that such sums and shares had since been paid or allotted, but concealed from the plaintiff company. These payments included payments to brokers for sustaining the market, a sum of £10,000 paid to another firm of brokers, in lieu of a share of the profits which Albert Grant had agreed to give them for waiving an alleged option to purchase previously given them, and sums paid to the solicitors employed in preparing the memorandum and articles of association, and who became the solicitors of the company, and to the metal brokers and bankers whose names appeared in the prospectus, and to a gentleman who had assisted the defendant Albert Grant in procuring the services of directors.

The statement of claim further alleged that the defendants *Albert Grant and Maurice Grant had sold a large [924 number of shares retained by Park as part of the vendors' shares at prices considerably exceeding their par value, and had received from Park, by way of commission and as their share of net profits under the agreement of the 5th of December, 1871, sums amounting to £32,421, of which £19,600 was received on account of commission on the shares sold by them, including those bought by them for the purpose of keeping up the market, and afterwards resold; and that the last mentioned sums were all paid to them out of the purchase-moneys received by Park from the plaintiff company.

It also alleged that in calculating the said net profits the defendants Albert Grant and Maurice Grant deducted all the sums paid by them to the directors, brokers, solicitors, and other officers of the company, as well as many other payments made by them to members of the newspaper press and others to facilitate the promotion of the company and to enable them to dispose of their shares. The statement of claim contained various charges of misrepresentation with reference to the mine, and of fraudulent concealment.

The plaintiff company claimed a declaration that the acts of the directors of the plaintiff company (being the nominees of and paid by and under the control of the vendors and promoters) in adopting and carrying out the agreement of the 4th of November, 1871, were not binding on the plaintiff company, and that the purchase of the mine by the plaintiff company might be set aside; secondly, that accounts might be taken of the profits derived by the defendants Park, Baxter, Stewart, Albert Grant and Maurice Grant, or any

892   CHANCERY DIVISION.   [Vol. XI

1878   Emma Silver Mining Company v. Grant.   M.R.

of them, on the shares sold by them beyond the par value ;
and that the same defendants and the defendant company
might be jointly and severally liable for the whole purchase-
money of the mine ; also, that, whether the purchase be set
aside or not, the several defendants therein named might be
declared liable to the company in the various amounts mentioned, and that the various defendants might be ordered to
pay to the plaintiff company all sums of money and the
value of all shares which they respectively had obtained,
and all profits which they might have derived as promoters,
directors or trustees of or for the plaintiff company, either
925]   out of the moneys and shares to be paid and *allotted
under the agreement of the 4th of November, 1871, or otherwise.

The defendants Albert Grant and Maurice Grant, by their
respective statements of defence, denied many of the allegations contained in the statement of claim.   The only defendants who had entered appearances were the defendants A.
and M. Grant, Anderson, and Puleston.

In July and August, 1878, Professor Blake, who had
made one of the reports on the mine referred to in the prospectus, being on a visit to this country, was examined before
a special examiner, and cross-examined for many days by
counsel on behalf of the defendant A. Grant, and the defendant A. Grant afterwards applied by summons in chambers
for a commission to take evidence in America, and his application was supported by M. Grant and the defendant
Anderson.

1878. Nov. 22.   A motion was now made on behalf of
the plaintiff company, under Rules of Court, 1875, Order
XXXVI, rule 6 ('), that the following issues of fact might be
tried as against the defendants Albert Grant and Maurice
Grant before the rest of the action as against them and the
other defendants, namely :

First, whether the defendants Albert Grant and Maurice
Grant, or either of them, were or was promoters or a promoter of the plaintiff company.

Secondly, whether any and what sums of money were
received or derived by the defendants Albert Grant and
Maurice Grant, or either of them, without the knowledge of
the plaintiff company under the agreements of the 2d of

(') "The court or a judge may, in any   fact be tried before the others, and may
action at any time or from time to time,   appoint the place or places for such trial
order that different questions of fact aris-   or trials, and in all cases may order that
ing therein be tried by different modes   one or more issues of fact be tried before
of trial, or that one or more questions of   any other or others."

November, 1871, and the 5th of December, 1871, or either of
them, or otherwise, as promoters or a promoter, from the
vendors to the plaintiff company, or out of the purchase-
money payable in cash and shares by the plaintiff company,
or otherwise, for which the said defendants or either of them
were or was accountable.

Davey, Q.C., *C. S. C. Bowen*, and *Grosvenor* [926
Woods, for the plaintiff company, in support of the motion,
submitted that this was a proper case for the order asked
for to be made, especially as the defendants had applied for
a commission to Utah which would delay the trial of the
action.   These issues could be tried on the pleadings and
on such evidence as could be at once obtained consisting almost entirely of the defendants' own books and the admitted
documents.   They offered, if the issues were directed against
the defendants Albert Grant and Maurice Grant, not to seek
any further relief in the action as against those defendants
except that which was included in those issues.

Moulton, for the defendant Albert Grant, and *Romer*, for
the defendant Maurice Grant, opposed the motion.

JESSEL, M.R.:   I do not intend to lay down any general
rule for the proper construction of Order XXXVI, rule 6,
because, first of all, I think one judge has no right to em-
barrass other judges by laying down general rules of construction; and, in the second place, I think it is very
undesirable to limit the operation of a rule expressed in
general terms by stating the circumstances, or all the circumstances under which the judge thinks the discretion
ought to be exercised.   The discretion is general.   Of course
it is a judicial discretion, and there must be sufficient reason
for exercising it; but what I intend to do is to state one or
two cases in which I have been asked to put the rule in force,
and what I have done, and why; and then I shall state
why I think I ought to put the rule in force in the present
instance.

I have been asked to do so in the case of a defendant.
The first case that came before me was a case in which a
lady alleged that she was the legitimate child of somebody,
and that as such she was entitled to take some very long
and expensive and intricate accounts against some trustees.
The trustees showed by affidavit that the lady was born before the marriage of her parents, and that there were very
strong grounds indeed for supposing that she was not a
legitimate child at all.   I thought it a proper case, inasmuch
as the expense of taking the accounts would *have [927
been enormous, and the whole suit would have ended in

nothing but costs if the plaintiff did not establish her legitimacy, for the issue of legitimacy or illegitimacy to be tried first under this rule. I so directed, and, as I am informed, the result was that the lady did not succeed in establishing her legitimacy, and there was an end of the action, which was exactly what I anticipated.

In a case of this kind my opinion is that the judge must have some evidence which will make it at least probable that the issue will put an end to the action. The plaintiff is not to be harassed at the instance of the defendant by a series of trials, each trial taking issue on every link of the plaintiff's case. That is not the meaning of the rule as I understand it, but it may properly be applied in such a case as that I have stated, where the judge has serious reason to believe that the trial of the issue will put an end to the action.

I have had a case in which the plaintiff alleged a very long title to, and claimed an estate. He alleged himself to be the heir-at-law of a person who was entitled to this estate. He wanted a great deal of discovery, and the possession of large property. The defendant said that the plaintiff was a pauper, that it was a mere experimental action, and that there was not a shadow of ground for his claim. In that case I felt no hesitation in directing an issue whether the man was heir-at-law. It turned out that he was not, and I believe the case was abandoned and was never tried at all.

There was a third case I remember before me at chambers —I only give these instances as illustrations—in which a man brought an action on behalf of himself and all other the tenants of a manor to restrain the inclosure of a common. The defendant said, "This will be a very expensive action to try; it will involve the customs of the manor as to rights of common," and that, as usual, they had put up a man, who, although not technically, was really a pauper, to sue on behalf of himself and all others, the only result of which action could be that the defendants, if successful, would have to pay the costs out of their own pockets. They alleged and proved by affidavit that the person who was plaintiff, and who said he was tenant of the manor, was not so, and that his name or the name of his ancestors 928] had never appeared on the court rolls of *the manor. The only answer that I could get from the plaintiff was that he believed he was a tenant, but he could not show how. I thought, before the defendants were put to the enormous expense of a trial of all the issues, it was right to put the plaintiff to the proof that he was a tenant at the time when the action was brought.

But I do not remember before having had an application on the part of the plaintiff, and, as far as I can learn from the inquiries I have made, no one else is aware of any such case.

Now, it appears to me that when the plaintiff makes the application, different considerations arise. The defendant has of course a right to shape his own case, and to say to the plaintiff, "You must prove every part of your case; if I can put my finger on one part of your case and show that there is no foundation for it whatever, it is quite wrong to subject me to the whole expense of a protracted investigation, and especially when you, the plaintiff, cannot pay the costs of it." But when a plaintiff has chosen to frame his case in this way, and has chosen to join several defendants, because they are more or less connected with some part of the subject-matter of the action, although not connected with the whole of it, that is the mode in which he has elected to frame his case for his own convenience, and it does not then at all follow as a matter of course that he is to be at liberty to retire from it as to any portion of the case and say, "I should like to try one part of it only, and to leave the defendant afterwards to be subject to a second or third trial to try the rest of it." I think the defendant has, speaking generally, a right to answer, "You ought to have thought of this before you brought your action or put in your statement of claim ; if you wanted any part of the action to be tried separately you should have brought a separate action." I do not wish to be understood as saying that subsequent events may not have occurred which may justify the plaintiff in making the application, but subject to that it appears to me as a general rule that the plaintiff has no right to make the application if the defendant objects.

But if the plaintiff comes into court and says this, "Since the commencement of my action subsequent events have occurred which convince me that I had much better give up the right of *action as against particular defendants, [929 and limit my action to the trial of certain issues only, and ask the court to try those issues," it does not appear to me the defendants have any right to complain. There will only be one trial, therefore there will be no increased costs ; and, as against those defendants, they get the benefit of the abandonment of the further relief asked against them, because the plaintiff says that he will limit his relief to what will result from the issues which are to be tried. So far as those defendants are concerned it must be a benefit—that is, a benefit in one sense only, a benefit theoretically, because practically it is no benefit—and if they are wrong, the sooner the action is tried against them the worse for them, and the greater the delay the better for them; but I am not now putting it in that way at all. Here the plaintiff company say, in effect, "When we brought the action we intended to try it against all the defendants according to the terms of the agreement; and we have, according to our view, a clear case against the defendants the Grants for a certain cause of action." The other defendants, including the Grants, have chosen, as regards another cause of action, to apply for a commission to Utah in the United States, and the plaintiff company say that if they succeed upon that application, the result will be that the trial of the remaining cause of action will be delayed until an indefinite period, and to avoid that they submit to limit their cause of action against the defendants the Grants to the one cause of action as to which they want the issues stated. It seems to me that in some shape or other that application is reasonable and should be acceded to. It is one that, except as regards delay, cannot injuriously affect the defendants, and it may obviously be very beneficial to the plaintiff company if it avoids the delay of the trial of the action.

I think the case before me comes under the 6th rule of Order XXXVI, the words of which are, "The court or a judge may, in any action at any time or from time to time order that different questions of fact arising therein be tried by different modes of trial, or that one or more questions of fact be tried before the others." Now, if I stayed the action, it might be objected that there were no other issues to try; but there are other issues to try as between the other de-930] fendants, and issues as *to which they may desire the Grants to be present, and therefore I shall only put the plaintiff under terms not to ask relief against the Grants in respect of any other cause of action than that included in the issues.

Then there is one other point which I think I ought to decide. I think the case to be brought within this rule ought to be one of simple issues. I do not think it is convenient to travel through a long record, and to get a number of complicated issues, and except them, so to say, from the pleadings. But in this case it appears to me the issues are simplicity itself. There are two issues in form. In reality they are only one. The real issue to be tried is whether the Grants, as promoters of the company, pocketed £100,000, or thereabouts, out of the purchase-money without the knowledge of the company. That is really the only question I have to try. It appears to me to be a very simple issue, which I can try very well, and therefore I shall make the order in the terms proposed.

I reserve the costs of the motion and the rest of the costs of the action, and I take from the plaintiff company the following undertaking, to be stated in this order:

"The plaintiffs by their counsel undertaking not to seek relief against the defendants Albert Grant and Maurice Grant in respect of any cause of action other than that covered by the issues, and also undertaking to consent to an order to discontinue such portion of the action as and when the court shall direct."

From this order the defendants Albert Grant and Maurice Grant appealed. The appeal came on for hearing on the 14th of February, 1879.

Benjamin, Q.C., and *Pollard*, for the defendant Albert Grant, and

Levett (*Romer* with him), for the defendant Maurice Grant, referred to Order XXIII, and contended that if the said issues were ordered to be tried, the defendants the Grants were entitled to an actual, and not to a future and contingent, discontinuance of the action as to all matters not covered by those issues.

Davey, Q.C., *C. S. C. Bowen*, and *Grosvenor Woods*, for the plaintiff company.

*THE COURT (James, Bramwell, and Brett, L.JJ.) [931 varied the order by substituting for the latter part of the undertaking these words: "The plaintiffs discontinuing such portion of the action as the court shall direct."

1879. Feb. 20, 24. The issues thus directed to be tried now came on for trial. No witnesses were called, and the evidence consisted of the answers to interrogatories and the documents admitted by the defendants' affidavits.

It appeared from these documents and the books of the defendants Grant, which were produced, that the defendant Maurice Grant did not become a partner with his brother until the beginning of 1872, and that in 1871 he was in receipt of a salary with a commission on profits.

The books showed that, after deducting from the £100,000 commission payable under the agreement of the 2d of November, 1871, a rebate of £15,000 and a sum of over £38,000 charged as expenses, and including payments to brokers for purchases of shares in order to sustain the market, a sum of £46,662 5s. 6d. was treated as profit on that account and credited as cash in the commission account under date the 30th of December, 1871. From other accounts in the books it appeared that Albert Grant or the firm had received as profits the sums of £45,421 6s. 4d., £8,414 0s. 6d., £6,190 12s. 6d., and £1,500, on or before the 30th of June, 1872. These sums consisted partly of the £1 per share commission payable under the agreement of the 5th of December, 1871, partly of the share of net proceeds of sale of the shares sold under that agreement, and partly of the profits made by A. Grant or the firm by sale of other shares in the company which he had received from Park under his arrangements with him, and by dealing with which he had kept up the market for the shares.

. In the course of the trial the case against the defendant Maurice Grant was compromised, and an order was made by consent that he should pay to the plaintiff company the sum of £2,250, with interest at £4 per cent. from the 12th of May, 1872, in satisfaction of all claims against him under the said issues or either of them.

932]   *Davey, Q.C., C. S. C. Bowen, Grosvenor Woods, and Foulkes, for the plaintiff company: The defendant Albert Grant, as the promoter of the company, stood towards the company in a fiduciary relation, and was not entitled to receive, under the agreements of the 2d of November, 1871, or the 5th of December, 1871, any part of the purchase-money for the mine, nor any profit or commission on the shares sold by him without disclosing the same to the company: Bagnall v. Carlton ('). In this case the real purchase-money was the nominal amount of the purchase-money less the amount agreed to be returned to the promoter. In estimating the amount of the profit which he is liable to make good, although, according to Bagnall v. Carlton, a promoter is entitled to be allowed his expenses properly incurred, yet he cannot be allowed such expenses as payment to an agent for securing the services of directors, payments to the press for writing up the company, or to brokers for sustaining the market.

The defendant Albert Grant appeared in person, and contended first, that the issues could not be tried at present, as there was a subsisting claim by the plaintiff company against the defendants for a rescission of the contract for the purchase of the mine on the ground of fraud, which was an election by the plaintiff company to disaffirm the contract, and give up all right under it; the plaintiff company were, therefore, precluded from now claiming against himself as

(') 6 Ch. D., 371; 23 Eng. R., 1.

promoter. Further, there was no such fiduciary relation
shown as would entitle the plaintiff company to recover the
amount paid to him as promoter, and even if he was liable, at
any rate he was entitled to be allowed all sums *bona fide*
expended by him in any way in launching the company.

JESSEL, M.R., after stating the issues he had to try, referred to the first objection taken by the defendant Albert
Grant, observing with respect to him:

I must say he has taken every point which I believe he
could have taken, and a good many that I think nobody
could say ought *to have been taken; still he de-   [933
serves the credit of having taken all points possible.

[His Lordship then expressed his opinion on the objection
to the trial of the issues on the ground of the pending action
for the rescission of the contract, and said that it now came
too late, not having been taken either on the motion or before the Court of Appeal, and even if it could be taken now,
it was, in his Lordship's judgment, quite untenable. His
Lordship then continued :]

Assuming the contract to be a valid contract, what have
we here? We have, it appears to me, a case wholly undistinguishable from the case of *Bagnall* v. *Carlton* (¹) on any
principle. The case is a somewhat singular one in one or
two of its features, but I am afraid not singular in all its
general features.

[His Lordship then stated the effect of the two agreements
of the 2d and 4th of November, 1871, and the transactions
connected with the purchase of the mine and the issuing of
the prospectus, and continued :]

That being the position of matters, the first point to be
considered is, whether that was a transaction which on the
face of it amounted in equity to a fraud. Now, a very eminent judge has said that it is not necessary to be a lawyer
in order to be an honest man, and I quite assent to that
proposition; I do not think it is necessary to understand
equity law in order to be convinced that it is a fraud if you
tell the public that a mine is sold by the vendors for a million of money, when in fact it was agreed to be sold for a
million of money less £200,000 to be retained by the real
purchaser, the man who agreed that it should be sold to a
company to be formed by himself, and that he should provide some small expenses. I think that such a representation is one by which the public would be deceived. Of
course, if it were a real sale for a million to a person really
buying, the public would suppose that they had the protec-

(¹) 6 Ch. D., 371 ; 23 Eng. R., 1.

tion of a real purchaser, a person who, therefore, would look to some extent after the value of the thing to be bought; and when they saw a respectable list of directors, in fact something more than respectable, a distinguished list of directors, advertised, who would of course be supposed to look after their own interest in a company in which they 934] *would take a considerable stake in the shape of shares, and in whose management they would take part, and to whose recommendation to the public they lent the sanction of their names and their high social position, they would naturally suppose that they had looked after the thing, and that they had taken care to see that the company about to be formed would have value for its money. All that appears to me untruly represented by this prospectus. It is represented as a *bona fide* purchase for £1,000,000, with the sanction of these eminent gentlemen as directors, when in fact it was in substance, though not exactly, a purchase for £800,000, put off on the company for £1,000,000.

In order to show the view which has been taken by a court of justice of this kind of transaction, I will read a few words from the judgment of Vice-Chancellor Bacon in the case of *Bagnall* v. *Carlton* (¹). He speaks of the prospectus, and the words apply exactly to the prospectus before me with some additions: "It wholly omits the consideration that the employment of the agent was for the purpose of forming a company, and of inducing other persons to subscribe in reliance upon a representation which was untrue; for it was not true that the purchase-money payable to the vendors was the sum mentioned in the prospectus, but it was the purchase-money stated in the ostensible agreement, minus the amount to be paid by the vendors to their agents as a reward for procuring the subscription; and the nominal purchase-money so diminished was the true sum which was to go into the pocket of the vendors." I think that the answer to that, namely, that the amount made no difference, is fallacious. The amount makes all the difference. If you represent that a sum is to be paid, you may honestly, and perhaps fairly, omit a trifling amount of commission, say 2s. 6d. per cent., for the brokerage on the stock, or anything of that kind. The rule is *de minimis non curat lex*, but where you actually take out one-fifth of the purchase-money, of course it is quite clear the amount does make that an untrue representation which might be substantially true if the amount was trifling.

Then it may be said, "But what had Mr. Grant to do with

(¹) 6 Ch. D., 387; 23 Eng. R., 1.

it ?" The answer is that Mr. Grant was not only the promoter, which *he was by forming the company, but [935 he was the person who made the representation. He actually settled and signed the prospectus which was issued; and again I will quote a few words from the same judgment of Vice-Chancellor Bacon('): "But if the case were not supported by authority, I should not hesitate to say that the persons by whom this representation was made did by making it—by inviting and soliciting the confidence of the persons to whom it was addressed—contract fiduciary relations with those persons." That is if he took upon himself to represent to them, not the whole of the facts but a por-. tion of the facts, and to omit what he ought to have known and must be taken by a court of justice to have known was a very material statement. But, as I said before, something must be added to this case. Mr. Grant not only formed the company, but he obtained with one exception the names of the directors, and these directors were known to him not to be independent directors.

[His Lordship then referred to the way in which the directors had been obtained.]

It is again an unfair representation to hold out to the public that this is a sale by the mine owner to the nominee for the company, so to say, approved of and controlled by an eminent and independent body of directors. The whole of it is, in my opinion, an untruthful representation by reason of the suppression and concealment of truth, not untruthful in the sense of direct falsehood, but untruthful because it is intended to convey to the public an impression different from the reality, and because it is known by the person who conveyed it, or ought to be known by him, to be materially different from that which was the real state of the case.

That being so, it appears to me that the promoter who issues such a prospectus as this, and acts in the way I have mentioned, has really nothing to complain of if his conduct is described in the way in which Vice-Chancellor Bacon described it in *Bagnall* v. *Carlton*.

I now come to the next question. For what sum ought Mr. Grant to be made liable? And that depends upon what the principle is on which the court decides these questions. Mr. Grant becomes, as I understand it under the authorities, a *trustee, agent, or person in a fiduciary posi- [936 tion as regards the company, one who has undertaken a duty towards the company of such a character as incapaci-

(') 6 Ch. D., 386; 23 Eng. R., 1.

902   CHANCERY DIVISION.   [Vol. XI.

1879   Emma Silver Mining Company v. Grant.   M.R.

tates him from making a secret profit at the expense of the company.

That he has undertaken that duty in this case I think is very plain indeed, because he not only was the person who was to form the company, but he himself bought on behalf of the company by the very first contract. The second contract again is by a nominee of his on behalf of the company, and he himself—whether he actually drafted or whether he settled and approved the memorandum and the articles of association is quite immaterial—was the person who was the author of those intruments, adopted the contract on behalf of the company, and acted from beginning to end for the company, formed it, provided it with directors, made a contract for it, and adopted that contract for it.

Now, it has been decided by a very great number of cases that a person in that position is in a fiduciary position, he is a pomoter. It is not necessary that he should have done all these things to make him a promoter, even some of them would be sufficient, but he is undoubtedly a promoter, and, as a promoter, as the man who has formed the company, he cannot take a secret profit; he must let his company know what profit he has taken, and deal with them, so to say, at arm's length.

In a well-known case, the *New Sombrero Phosphate Company* v. *Erlanger* ('), Lord Justice James says this (') : "A promoter is, according to my view of the case, in a fiduciary relation to the company which he promotes or causes to come into existence. If that promoter has a property which he desires to sell to the company, it is quite open to him to do so; but upon him, as upon any other person in a fiduciary position, it is incumbent to make full and fair disclosure of his interest and position with respect to that property. I can see no difference in this respect between a promoter and a trustee, steward or agent."

Let us see what the position of Mr. Grant was. He had a contract with Park and Stewart to buy the mine of them, and that they should sell it to a company of his nomination, and· he formed the company to buy. Can he say after that, that he is not in a fiduciary position within the authorities 937] towards that company? *It is clear that he cannot. Therefore, the only question is, whether he can make any profit at all and not disclose it? Upon that the authorities are quite plain. The moment a man is in a fiduciary position, however that fiduciary position may arise, before he can retain a profit to himself he must deal with his princi-

(') 5 Ch. D., 73; 21 Eng. R., 798.   (') 5 Ch. D., 118; 21 Eng. R., 838.

pal on the footing of making a full and fair disclosure of everything material in relation to the dealing or transaction in which he acts in the fiduciary capacity.

The case of the *Liquidators of the Imperial Mercantile Credit Association* v. *Coleman* (¹) is a very good illustration of that. There Coleman was a stockbroker, and he told his fellow directors that he had an interest in the transaction. He did not tell them the extent of his interest, and it was decided that, inasmuch as his fellow directors might have been under the impression that he merely took his ordinary commission as a stockbroker, and thereupon confirmed the transaction, he was liable to refund all his profits, because it turned out that he had made a large and extraordinary profit beyond the usual commission of a stockbroker, and it was decided that he was compellable to state not only that he had an interest, but what interest it was before he could sustain the transaction.

The case of *Bagnall* v. *Carlton* (²) is so like the present case—in fact one of the defendants there was Albert Grant himself—that it is hardly possible, I think, to suggest any distinction at all in favor of the defendant in this case.

But then the question arises, what is he liable to pay? Now, as I understand it, he is liable to pay the amount of the profit he has made. It has been argued that, though in a sense he gets part of the purchase-money, he is liable on the ground of his paying back the difference of the purchase-money. That cannot be, as it appears to me, the true ground. No doubt in substance the representation that the contract is a contract for the purchase for £1,000,000, when £200,000 is to be deducted as a commission, is substantially a misrepresentation by over-stating the purchase-money, but it does not make·that commission part of the purchase-money in that sense. In other words,. suppose the purchaser agrees with the vendor to confirm the contract, and takes a larger sum from him than the commission, that would not, as was *decided in the case of *Bagnall* v. *Carl-* [938 *ton* (²), affect the position of the agent who had negotiated the contract.

If it could be proved, for instance, that the original purchase-money was, we will say, £100,000, that the vendors agreed to take £90,000, and paid £10,000 as commission to the agent, and that they had refused an offer of £89,000, and if after the matter was discovered, rather than submit to exposure, or for other reasons, they agreed to a confirmation of the contract and to accept £80,000, so that the pur-

(¹) Law Rep., 6 H. L., 189; 6 Eng. R., 18.　　　(²) 6 Ch. D., 371; 23 Eng. R., 1.

chaser had never paid more than £80,000, the purchaser would not be the less entitled to recover £10,000 from his agent. The purchase-money is now reduced to £80,000, but he would have the right to say to his agent, "You made a profit by that position of trust and confidence which was reposed in you as agent, you cannot hold that profit as against me. Although the result of your misconduct was really to entitle me to obtain the property, and enabled me to obtain the property at a less price than I could have obtained it if you had not been guilty of misconduct, yet that advantage to me will not enure to your advantage, and cannot entitle you to retain one single shilling of the improper profit you made." It appears to me that is the true view of the case, that the person in the fiduciary position cannot keep the secret profit, and that the fact that the relations of the profit to the purchase-money originally are altered can make no difference. Indeed, we might have it the other way. The purchaser might like his bargain, and might say, "Though I have given £100,000 for this which I might possibly have bought at £90,000, I will not give it up, I will affirm the contract, I think it is worth more." He might have sold it for more a week afterwards, and yet he would be entitled to take from his own agent the commission improperly received by the agent from the vendor.

If that be the true principle, it remains to consider what is the amount of profit derived by the agent in this transaction. The broad view of the case is to take the whole transaction together, and see how much more money he has got than he would have had if he never entered into it at all.

As I read *Bagnall* v. *Carlton* ('), although the point did not arise there exactly as it arises here, I think that was the view of the Court of Appeal.

939] *Lord Justice James says this with regard to the costs, charges, and expenses incurred by the defendants ('): "The costs, charges, and expenses, I think they had a right, independently of the offer in the bill, to deduct, because what they were liable to pay the company was the profits which they had made in a fiduciary character, that is to say, the net profits which they had made, and I think that costs, charges, and expenses might properly be deducted in ascertaining the net profits, and to that extent, therefore, they were, I think, entitled, independently of the offer in the bill." Lord Justice Baggallay concurs.

(') 6 Ch. D., 371; 23 Eng. R., 1.　　　(') 6 Ch. D., 400; 23 Eng. R., 27.

Lord Justice Cotton says this (¹): "That being so"—that is, as to the fiduciary relation—"the principle of equity clearly applies. Carlton and Grant are trustees for the company. They cannot, by any possibility, secretly make to themselves a profit in the transaction in which they were trustees." Then he says this (²): "I think I need add nothing to what has been said by the Lord Justice as regards the charges and expenses. The principle on which I decide this case is, that the trustee cannot make for himself a secret profit; and the profit is the net balance of the £85,000, after deducting any charges and expenses properly incurred in the formation of the company." He uses these words "properly incurred" because there was no contest in that case as to whether they were properly incurred or not. He defines it at the beginning as a "secret profit."   .

That being so, what is the amount of Mr. Grant's profit? If he believed that, as I am satisfied from his own statement he did believe—however he managed to convince himself of it—that he was the owner of this large sum of money, and was legally and morally entitled to retain it, how did he deal with it? He dealt with it in forming the company, and he dealt with it by paying the ordinary expenses of forming the company, and by making divers large payments which have been challenged as improperly made.

Assuming that what was alleged was all proved (though I do not say it was all proved, because a great deal of it was inference from entries in the books), the result is this: First, he paid a sum of money to the gentleman by whom the directors were introduced. *In the next place he [940 furnished shares to the directors who were introduced. In the next place he paid very large sums in various ways to brokers for sustaining the market. In the next place he paid £10,000 to a firm of brokers for a share of the profits which he agreed to give them for waiving and giving up a kind of option to purchase which they possessed previously; and lastly, he paid considerable sums of money to persons connected with the press, either as writers in it or otherwise, for puffing or laudatory statements respecting the company or mine; and it is said that all those payments were immoral and improperly made, and ought to be disallowed.

Now I am not trying that question. It does not appear to me that the amount of profit can be decided by the fact of some of the payments being such payments as will not obtain for them the commendation of the court. That is

(¹) 6 Ch. D., 407; 23 Eng. R., 34.   (²) 6 Ch. D., 408; 23 Eng. R., 35.

not the question. They were *bona fide* made by Mr. Grant
at the time when he believed this money was his own. They
were not payments for nothing. Mr. Grant is a man of
business, and he only paid for value received. He assumed, and I dare say correctly assumed, that the services
for which he paid were worth the money he paid for them ;
and that being so, can I say that the expenses he so incurred
are not to be deducted from the amount he received in estimating his secret profit? You have a right to take from
him that which he improperly acquired by means of his being concerned in this illegal transaction ; and it is no answer
to say that one part of his receipts were illegally obtained,
and another part of his expenses were illegally and improperly made in ascertaining what that profit was. These are
expenses connected with and forming part of the entire
transaction ; and it seems to me that in estimating his profit
I ought to find out his real profit, that is, the net result of
the transaction which was left to him ; but whether I approve or disapprove of the mode in which he carried out the
transactions, or the items of expenditure which he made,
the result in ascertaining the net profit cannot be affected
by the moral nature or propriety of that expenditure. I
think, therefore, we ought to ascertain the net profits simply
on the principle of deducting from all the receipts all the
payments.

Now I come to the items. The first item is the receipt of
941]   *£100,000 in money. He must be charged with that.
The second item of receipt is a sum of £45,000, or thereabouts, which was the net result of the sale of shares, and
which came in lieu of the £100,000 worth of shares which he
was to have by the first agreement. Of course those are
sums received. Then there were two small sums which he
received for sustaining the market, for the result, as appears
by the books (which appear to me to be admirably kept),
of sustaining the market was in this case a profit. That sum
again he received for sustaining the market by dealing with
those shares in the way I have mentioned. Then there is a
small sum of £1,500, or thereabouts, which really falls into
the same category as the £45,000. It is a portion of the
shares which it was said he was entitled to take and sell for
his own benefit. That is the amount of profit derived by
those sums. I think they are chargeable and should be
charged against him.

I then deduct all sums actually paid by him, whether to
brokers for getting rid of the option, or to brokers for getting
rid of the shares, or for sustaining the market, or to the di-

rectors, or to the agent who procured the directors, or to the gentlemen connected with the press for the part they took in the transaction. It seems to me all those sums ought to be allowed to him. Taking the books to be correct, and they are not challenged, and I see no reason for challenging them, those sums will be deducted from the sums he is charged with. I find as a verdict that he is liable, as promoter, for the balance together with interest at 4 per cent. from the date which has been mentioned.

Order:—That this court doth as to the first issue find that the defendant Albert Grant was a promoter of the company, and as to the second issue that the defendant Albert Grant received as profit under the agreements of the 2d of November, 1871, and the 5th of December, 1871, or one of them, the sum of £108,188 6s. 11d. as a promoter of the company without the knowledge of the company, and was accountable to the company for the same, less the sum of £2,250 ordered by consent to be paid by the defendant Maurice Grant to the company, with interest at the rate of 4 per cent. per annum on £46,662 5s. 6d. from 31st of December, 1871, and on the balance from the 30th of June, 1872.

Solicitors for plaintiff company: *Snell & Greenip.*
Solicitors for defendants: *J. J. Ridley ; Lewis & Lewis.*

See 30 Eng. Rep., 631 note.

A director of a corporation occupies a position of trust towards the ·corporation and its stockholders, and can neither do nor take part as a necessary quorum in an act as between himself and his corporation: Hudson River, etc., v. White, 5 N. Y. Monthly Law Bull., 18.

Advances by a director, made to pay the debts of a company, and secured by a mortgage upon the land so discharged, will be protected: Alexander v. Berney, 28 N. J. Eq., 90.

See Roberts v. Page, 17 Eng. R., 138, 143 note.

A director of a corporation may become its creditor, and take and enforce a mortgage on its property, but he is not thereby divested of his responsibility as a director nor the duties which as such he owes to the corporation, and he is bound to act in the utmost good faith throughout the transaction ; if he do not, a sale under a mortgage held by him will be set aside: Hallam v. The Indianola, etc., 56 Iowa, 178, 21 Amer. Law Reg. (N.S.), 443, 446 ; Alexander v. Berney, 28 N. J. Eq., 90.

As to dealings between directors and their corporations, see 21 Amer. Law Reg. (N.S.), 446 et seq.

Where trustees holding the title to lands for the benefit of a railroad company, conveyed certain of the same for their own personal benefit in payment for their services as such trustees, under authority from the board of directors of the railroad company, it was held that the validity of such conveyance could not be attacked by one claiming the land through a title adverse to that by which it was held by the railroad company: Miller v. Iowa, etc., 56 Iowa, 374.

A purchase by an attorney from or of the property of his client, is voidable and not void. If not repudiated by the client within a reasonable time, under all the circumstances, after knowledge of the facts, it will be allowed to stand: Wills v. Wood, 28 Kans., 400.

A creditor, who is also a member of a corporation, cannot maintain a bill in equity to enforce the personal liability of the stockholders, under the statute of 1862, chap. 218 ; and a person to whom a stockholder has transferred a promissory note of the corporation for the sole purpose of enabling him to obtain judgment upon it in his own name, and to bring a bill in equity to enforce the personal liability of the stockholders, stands in no better position than his assignor : Potter v. Stevens, etc., 127 Mass., 592.

Upon a breach of trust and a misuse of trust funds, when the identical fund is traced, a prior equity exists in favor of the *cestui que trust* as against creditors of the wrongdoer; and in an action to enforce such equity, such creditors are not necessary parties: Cooley *v.* Gieve, 9 Daly, 104, 82 N. Y., 625.

The managing officer of the bank of Statesville became indebted to the bank in a large sum of money, which he used in the purchase of land, and died leaving a will devising it to his wife: Held, that the fund used in the purchase being the property of the bank, the land should be charged with its payment: Bank *v.* Simonton, 86 N. C., 187.

Although the relation between a bank and its depositor is that merely of debtor and creditor, the money which he deposits, if held by him in a fiduciary capacity, does not change its character by being placed to his credit in his bank account. The bank contracts that it will pay the money on his checks, and, when they are drawn in proper form, it is bound to presume, in case the account is kept with him as a trustee or as acting in some other fiduciary character, that he is in the course of lawfully performing his duty, and to honor them accordingly; but when against such an account it seeks to assert its lien for an obligation which it knows was incurred for his private benefit, it must be held as having notice that the fund is not his individual property, if it is shown to consist in whole or in part of money which he held in a trust relation.

As long as trust property can be traced and followed, the property into which it has been converted remains subject to the trust; and if a man mixes trust funds with his, the whole will be treated as trust property, except so far as he may be able to distinguish what is his. This doctrine applies in every case of a trust relation, and as well to moneys deposited in bank and to the debt thereby created, as to every other description of property.

A banker's lien on the securities and money deposited in the usual course of business, for advances which are supposed to be made upon their credit, ordinarily attaches not only against the customer but against the unknown equities of all others in interest, unless it be modified or waived by some agreement express or implied, or by conduct inconsistent with its assertion; but it cannot prevail against the equity of the beneficial owner, of which the banker has either actual or constructive notice.

Where a bank account was opened in the name of a depositor as general agent, and it was known to the bank that he was the agent of an insurance company,—that conducting its agency was his chief business, that the account was opened to facilitate that business, and used as a means of accumulating the premiums on policies collected by him for the company and of making payment to it by checks,—the bank is chargeable with notice of the equitable rights of the company, although he deposited other money in the same account, and drew checks upon it for his private use. The company may enforce by bill in equity its beneficial ownership therein, against the bank claiming a lien thereon for debts due to it which he contracted for his individual use: Bank *v.* Insurance, etc., 104 U. S., 54.

One who claims as a *bona fide* holder or purchaser of negotiable paper fraudulently procured or misapplied, must plead the facts showing and prove that he is such: Totten *v.* Buey, 57 Md.. 446, 453 and numerous authorities cited; Lord Drogheda *v.* Malone, Finlay's (Irish) Digest, 449 note, not elsewhere reported.

Vol. XI.]   CHANCERY DIVISION.   909

M.R.   Hamer v. Giles.   Giles v. Hamer.   1879

[11 Chancery Division, 942.]

M.R., April 7, 1879.

*HAMER V. GILES.   [942

[1876 H. 140.]

GILES V. HAMER.

[1876 G. 69.]

Practice—Partnership Action, Costs of—Misconduct of Partner—" Partnership Assets "—Solicitor—Costs—Charging Order—Proceeding by Summons or Petition—Title of Proceeding—Garnishee Order Nisi—Service—Priority—Attorneys and Solicitors Act, 1860, s. 28—Rules of Court, 1875, Order XLV, rr. 2, 3, 6.

The rule as to costs in a partnership action is the same as in any other administration action, that is, they are payable out of the assets; "partnership assets" meaning the assets remaining after payment of all the partnership debts, including balances due to any of the partners. If the assets are insufficient for payment of the costs of the action, then such costs must be borne by the partners in proportion to their shares in the profits.

Where, however, a partnership action has been rendered necessary by the *negligence or other misconduct of a partner, the court will order that part- [943 ner to pay the costs of the action so far as they have been occasioned by his misconduct, including the costs up to the trial.

An order giving a solicitor a charge under sect. 28 of the Attorneys and Solicitors Act, 1860, for his costs as between solicitor and client, on property recovered by him for his client in an action, is sufficient if intituled in the action: it may be obtained either on summons or petition, and need not be intituled either in the matter of the act or of the solicitor.

A garnishee in order *nisi* does not create a charge until service of it on the garnishee.

A judgment creditor of the defendant in a partnership action obtained a garnishee order *nisi* to attach all moneys in the hands of the receiver in the action appearing to be due to the defendant on taking the accounts. On the following day, and before service of the order *nisi*, the defendant's solicitors obtained, on a summons served on the receiver, a charging order intituled in the action, declaring that they were entitled to a charge for their costs upon all moneys coming to the defendant under the action. On the next day the garnishee order *nisi* was served on the receiver, and was subsequently made absolute:

Held, that the solicitors were entitled to their costs in priority to the claim of the creditor under the garnishee order both under the act and independently of it.

[11 Chancery Division, 949.]

V.C. H., Feb. 4, 5, 1879.

949]   *CHAMPNEY v. DAVY.

[1874 C. 287.]

Will—Charitable Legacy—Pure and Impure Personalty—Mortmain Act (43 Geo. 3, c. 108)—Particular Residue—General Residue—Lapse or Invalidity.

A testatrix bequeathed certain specific portions of her personal estate to trustees upon trust for sale and conversion, payment of debts and legacies, investment and payment of the income to her mother for life, and, after her death, as to £2,000, part of the fund, to pay the same to the vicar of M. to be disposed of at his discretion " in or about restoring, altering, and enlarging and improving the church, parsonage house, and school " of M.; " and as to the residue thereof," upon the trusts thereinafter declared concerning the moneys to arise from the sale of her real estate. The testatrix then gave " all the rest, residue, and remainder of her personal estate" to her mother absolutely, and devised her real estate to the same trustees in trust for sale, and directed them to hold the sale moneys and the residue of the said trust moneys, stocks, funds, shares, and securities in trust for the children of C. absolutely.

Part of the property comprised in the bequest to the trustees consisted of impure personalty:

Held, first, that, the church being situate on land already in mortmain, there must be an inquiry to ascertain whether the parsonage house and school, or which of them were or was also so situate, and what sums of money would be required to be laid out in restoring, altering, and enlarging and improving such of the said three objects of the legacy as were or was so situate, and that the legacy was valid, so far as the objects were concerned, to the extent of the money so ascertained to be required:

Secondly, that (following *Sinnett* v. *Herbert* (1)) the amount of the legacy required for the objects already in mortmain must be apportioned between the pure and impure personalty, and be paid out of the pure personalty to the extent of its proportion, and, under 43 Geo. 3, c. 108, out of the impure personalty to the full extent of £500:

Held, also, that so much of the £2,000-as failed passed to the legatees of the particular residue of the fund out of which it was given, and not under the general gift of residuary personal estate.

The construction of a particular residuary gift is not affected by the presence or absence of a general residuary gift, nor is there any sound distinction between lapsed and invalid dispositions, whether under a power of appointment or in exercise of ownership.

FURTHER consideration of an administration suit. The testatrix in this suit, who died in 1874, by her will 950] dated *in 1872, after giving certain pecuniary legacies, bequeathed to trustees, their executors, administrators, and assigns, "all her moneys, securities for money, money secured on mortgages, railway stocks and shares, moneys to be produced from the sale of any property at Scarborough or Peterborough to which she was entitled, all moneys to which she was or might be entitled under the will of her late grandfather Thomas Phillips, and also all her moneys invested upon any securities in any way or manner howso-

(1) Law Rep., 7 Ch., 232.

ever," upon trusts for sale and conversion into money; and
out of the moneys arising therefrom to pay her debts, funeral
and testamentary expenses, and the legacies given by her
will; and directed the trustees to stand possessed of the
residue thereof upon trust to invest the same upon certain
stocks, funds, or securities therein mentioned, and to stand
possessed of the said trust moneys, stocks, funds, and securities, and the income thereof, upon trust to pay the income
to her mother Hannah West (since deceased) during her life,
and after her mother's decease, upon trust to stand possessed of the said trust moneys, stocks, funds, and securities,
and the interest, dividends, and annual produce thereof,
upon trust as to £2,000, part thereof, to pay the same to the
vicar for the time being of Muston, to be by him applied
and disposed of in such manner as he in his absolute discretion should think proper in or about restoring, altering,
and enlarging and improving the church, parsonage house,
and school attached thereto, whose receipt for the said sum
of £2,000 should be a sufficient discharge to her said executors; and as to the residue thereof, upon the trusts thereinafter expressed and declared of and concerning the moneys
to arise and be produced from the sale of her real estate as
thereinafter mentioned.   And the said testatrix gave and
bequeathed unto her said mother all the rest, residue, and
remainder of her personal estate and effects, whatsoever and
wheresoever, for her own absolute use and benefit.   And the
testatrix thereby devised all her real estate to the same trustees, their heirs and assigns, on trust for sale, and declared
that her trustees should stand possessed of the money to
arise from the sale of her real estates, "and the residue of
the said trust moneys, stocks, funds, and securities,".and
the rents, ·interest, and annual produce thereof, in trust for
all and every the children of Elizabeth Curtis Davy, in equal
shares absolutely.   The testatrix *thereby also de-   [951
clared that all income directed to be paid to her mother
should be paid for her separate use, and that any disposition by way of anticipatition of such income should be
void, and that immediately thereupon such income should
become forfeited.

Part of the property comprised in the bequest to the trustees consisted of impure personalty, and in particular the
property at Scarborough and Peterborough was of leasehold
tenure, and the mother of the testatrix having died, three
questions were now argued.   First, to what extent the legacy
of £2,000 to the vicar of Muston failed under the general
provisions of the Mortmain Acts as being a bequest of money

to be laid out on land not already in mortmain. Secondly, to what extent the same legacy was payable out of the impure personalty under the statute 43 Geo. 3, c. 108 ([1]): and, thirdly, whether the residue of the fund out of which the £2,000 legacy was given passed as particular residue upon the trusts declared of the sale moneys of the real estate in favor of the children of Elizabeth Curtis Davy, or was included in the general residuary gift of personal estate to the mother of the testatrix.

The two questions arising as to the legacy of £2,000 were argued first.

Hastings, Q.C., and *Nalder*, for the trustees of the will.

Robinson, Q.C., and *Sutton*, for the Vicar of Muston: The objects for which this legacy of £2,000 is given being within the statute 43 Geo. 3, c. 108, the legacy must be apportioned between the pure and the impure personal estate 952] comprised *in the bequest of the property out of which it is payable ; and after the amount apportioned in respect of the pure personalty has been satisfied thereout, the legatee will be entitled under the statue to have the legacy further satisfied to the full extent of £500 out of the impure personalty comprised in the bequest: *Sinnett* v. *Herbert* ([2]).

W. Pearson, Q.C., and *Speed*, for the defendants, the children of Elizabeth Curtis Davy : The legacy of £2,000 is altogether void, for it might be applied for objects rendered illegal by the Statute of Mortmain : *Pratt* v. *Harvey* ([3]) ; *In re Watmough's Trusts* ([4]).

It is given for four purposes applicable to three objects, i.e., for "restoring, altering and enlarging and improving the church, parsonage house, and school." All those purposes, and also all those objects, are coupled together, and it is impossible to separate or split them up, or to say how much should be apportioned to any particular purpose or object. The "enlarging" contemplates expressly the bring-

---

([1]) The statute 43 Geo. 3, c. 108, enacts (sect. 1) that every person having in his own right any estate or interest in any lands or tenements, or any property in any goods or chattels, shall have power by deed inrolled or by will, such deed or will being duly executed three calendar months at least before the death of the grantor or testator, to give to and vest in any person or body polilitick or corporate, and their heirs and successors, all his estate or property in such lands or tenements not exceeding five acres, or goods or chattels not exceeding in value

£500, for or towards the erecting, rebuilding, repairing, purchasing, or providing any church or chapel where the liturgy and rites of the said United Church are or shall be used or observed, or any mansion house for the residence of any minister of the said United Church officiating or to officiate in any such church or chapel, or any outbuildings, offices, churchyard, or glebe for the same respectively.

([2]) Law Rep., 7 Ch., 232.
([3]) Law Rep., 12 Eq , 544.
([4]) Law Rep., 8 Eq., 272.

ing of land into mortmain, and renders the whole gift void. The parsonage house and school, or one of them, may not be on land already in mortmain, so that the legacy may at all events be void as to part, and as it cannot be ascertained as to what part, it must altogether fail : *Hoare* v. *Osborne* (') ; *In re Rigley's Trust* (').

Again, the legacy is not within the statute 43 Geo. 3, c. 108, first, because the proceeds of the sale of lands of any tenure are not within the scope of that act, and secondly, because "enlarging" is not one of the purposes, nor is a "school" one of the objects for which it permits lands or money to be given : *Sinnett* v. *Herbert* is not applicable to the present case. There the gift was in the alternative, for "erecting or endowing." And one purpose, the erecting, being authorized by the statute of Geo. 3, and separable from the other purpose "endowing," which was not so authorized, the whole gift was applicable to the alternative legal purpose, and was good. But that is not so here. This case *is more like the *Incorporated Church* [953 *Building Society* v. *Coles* ('), and the legacy is bad altogether.

Dickinson, Q.C., and *Ingle Joyce*, for the executor of Hannah West, the mother of the testatrix : We adopt the same arguments. The legacy must, under any circumstances, be cut down to £500 ; and if it is so cut down, what is the legatee to do with it ? He cannot apply any part of it towards the school, for that is not one of the objects rendered legal by the act of Geo. 3, whilst if he does not so apply it, he will not be acting in accordance with the will ; and the result is that there is a gift applicable for purposes contrary to the Statute of Mortmain, and the legacy fails.

Robinson, in reply : If the church, parsonage house, and school are situated on land already in mortmain, all the objects and purposes of this gift are legal, and *Sinnett* v. *Herbert* (') shows that so far as the objects are legal the court will carry them out. The *Incorporated Church Society* v. *Coles* only decides that a testator does not bring himself within the act by devising land in trust for sale. [He distinguished the other cases cited on the other side, and referred to Theobald on Wills ('), and the cases there cited].

HALL, V.C.: I have now to dispose of the questions which have been discussed as to the validity of this legacy

(') Law Rep., 1 Eq., 585.   (') 1 K. & J., 145, 155 ; 5 D. M. & G., 324.
(') 36 L. J. (Ch.), 147.   (') Law Rep., 7 Ch., 232.
                         (') Page 196.

of £2,000, and I shall first deal with the distinction between the pure and impure personal estate with reference to this disposition. As regards the pure personal estate there is no possible objection to this legacy so far as there is pure personal estate to answer the gift; except in so far as that pure personal estate has been directed, if at all, to be laid out for purposes which are prohibited by the Statute of Mortmain. Now, the fund is to be applied "in or about restoring, altering, and enlarging and improving the church, parsonage house, and school attached thereto;" and it may be that the 954] *parsonage house and school are not in mortmain, in which case this would practically be a legacy of money to be applied in or towards acquiring or purchasing land not already in mortmain. As to that, therefore, if it be desired, I must direct an inquiry to ascertain whether the site of the parsonage house and the school are in mortmain, and to the extent to which such sites are not in mortmain the gift must fail. Subject to that, it appears to me that the gift is perfectly good. I say to that extent, and it is an observation which applies both to pure and impure personal estate. I do not think that the circumstance of there being three subject matters upon which the money might be laid out gives rise to any real difficulty. No doubt there was an observation of Vice-Chancellor Wood in *Sinnett* v. *Herbert* (¹), and there are observations in other authorities, that where there are several objects of a charity, one of which is illegal, the whole gift must fail, there being no means of determining the amount to be devoted to each object. But I do not take that to be the law in a case where you can ascertain how much ought to go to each object. In fact, in *Hoare* v. *Osborne* (²), and *In re Rigley's Trust* (³), it was only because the Vice-Chancellor Kindersley considered that from the nature of the subject-matter it could not be ascertained what amount ought to be set apart for each object, that he adopted the rule, not of the invalidity of the entire gift, but of the division of the fund according to the number of the objects specified.

The same question came under the consideration of Vice-Chancellor Wood in *Fisk* v. *Attorney-General* (⁴). In that case there was a gift by will of £1,000 consols to the rector and churchwardens of a parish and their successors upon trust to apply such dividends thereof as should from time to time be necessary or required, in keeping in repair a family grave, and to pay and divide the residue of the said div-

(¹) Law Rep., 7 Ch., 232.   (²) 36 L. J. (Ch.), 147.
(²) Law Rep., 1 Eq., 585.   (⁴) Law Rep., 4 Eq., 521.

idends, at Christmas every year forever, amongst the aged poor of the parish; and it was held, that though the amount of the gift for the repair of the grave was not specified, the court could, if necessary, have estimated the amount "necessary and required" for the purpose, and so have prevented the gift of the residue from being void for uncertainty. *The Vice-Chancellor came to that conclusion after [955 observing upon the case of *Chapman* v. *Brown* ([1]), which has always been considered as being a case looking the other way.

Therefore, I hold that for the purpose of ascertaining the *quantum* and validity of this legacy, supposing it should turn out that the parsonage house or school are not on land already in mortmain, there must be an inquiry to ascertain whether the church, parsonage house, and school of Muston, or which of them were or was situated upon lands already in mortmain, and what sums of money will be required to be laid out in restoring, altering, and enlarging and improving such of them as are already in mortmain; and the gift will prevail to the extent to which it may be ascertained that the money will be required for the objects already in mortmain, and it will fail as to the rest.

Then as to the extent to which the legacy is to come out of the impure personal estate, it appears to me that, having regard to the 1st and 2d sections of the statute of 43 Geo. 3, c. 108, I must give effect to the gift to the extent to which the law will allow it to take effect out of the impure personal estate. In that respect I follow *Sinnett* v. *Herbert* ([2]); and the result is that the amount of the legacy required for the objects already in mortmain must be apportioned as between the pure and impure personalty comprised in the bequest, and must be paid out of the pure personalty to the extent of its proportion, and out of the impure personalty to the full extent of £500.

The third question was then argued, viz., whether the part of the £2,000 legacy which failed passed under the gift of the residue of the particular fund out of which that legacy was given, or under the general gift of residuary personal estate to the mother of the testatrix.

W. Pearson, Q.C., and *Speed*, for the defendants, the children of Elizabeth Curtis Davy, in trust for whom the particular residue was given: The manifest intention of the testatrix was by this request to dispose of everything comprised therein in favor of these *defendants, [956 subject only to the payment of the debts and legacies payable

(¹) 6 Ves., 404.   ·(²) Law Rep., 7 Ch., 232.

thereout and of the £2,000 legacy; and everything comprised in the bequest and not effectually disposed of passes to the defendants under the gift of the particular residue: *Carter* v. *Taggart* ('); *De Trafford* v. *Tempest* (*); *In re Harries' Trusts* ('). There is no intention whatever that the general residuary legatee should take absolutely any part of the particular fund. On the contrary, she is herself the tenant for life of that very fund.

[They also referred to Theobald on Wills (').]

Dickinson, Q.C., and *Ingle Joyce*, for the executor of the mother of the testatrix: The question in all these cases is whether the legacy which has failed was given by way of a charge upon the particular fund or by way of an exception of an aliquot part out of it. In the first case the legatee of the particular residue satisfies it; in the second case he does not, and it lapses to the legatee of the general residue; for the particular legatee has no right to anything that is not actually given to him; and where, as here, the legacy is illegal, the construction in favor of its passing under the gift of general residue applies with greater force: *In re Jeaffreson's Trusts* (*); *Easum* v. *Appleford* (*); *Oke* v. *Heath* ('); *Falkner* v. *Butler* (*); *Bernard* v. *Minshull* ('); *Skrymsher* v. *Northcote* (''); *Lloyd* v. *Lloyd* (''). The contention of the other side is that although the testatrix has given the £2,000 to the Vicar of Muston, she intended so much of it as failed to go to the particular legatee away from whose fund this aliquot part was taken, and to whom it was never given. This cannot be the intention, and the general legatee is entitled.

W. Pearson, in reply: The cases cited are all cases of a gift of a specific portion of a fund to A., and of the ascer-
957] tainable residue to B.; but here the *debts and funeral expenses are to be paid out of the bequeathed property as well as the legacy of £2,000, so that there are charges of uncertain amount, a circumstance which is strongly in favor of the particular legatee. Moreover, as the life interest is subject to forfeiture, the mother of the testatrix had, according to the contention of the other side, only to forfeit the income and she would immediately come into the capital of the legacy.

(¹) 16 Sim., 423.
(²) 21 Beav., 564.
(³) Joh., 199.
(⁴) Pages 93, 94.
(⁵) Law Rep., 2 Eq., 276, 283.
(⁶) 5 My. & Cr., 56.
(⁷) 1 Ves. Sen., 135.
(⁸) Amb., 514.
(⁹) Joh., 276.
(¹⁰) 1 Sw., 566.
(¹¹) Beav., 231.

[He referred to *Wollaston* v. *King* (').]

HALL, V.C.:   I will dispose of this question to-morrow.

Feb. 5.   HALL, V.C.:   In *Falkner* v. *Butler* ('), under a limited power of appointment, the donee appointed a sum to persons not objects of the power, and this sum was held to pass under the appointment of the residue, i.e., it fell into the residue.   So in *Wollaston* v. *King* it was held, there being an invalid appointment of part of a trust fund, that that part of the fund passed under an appointment "subject to the appointment thereinbefore contained .of all the trust moneys subject to the trusts of the settlement." In *Carter* v. *Taggart* ('), the testatrix, exercising a power over a specified sum, gave part of it to a person who died before her, and gave all the rest and residue of the sum "after deducting therefrom the legacies above mentioned." The part which lapsed was held to fall into the residue. This decision, I think, turned upon the particular will, indicating (particularly by a life estate being given in part with a direction that that part should fall into the residue) an intention that all should pass, subject only to the charge. In *De Trafford* v. *Tempest* (') a lapsed gift of particular furniture was held to fall into a gift of furniture not thereinbefore otherwise disposed of, and not to pass under a general residuary gift.   In *Easum* v. *Appleford* ('), which was a case of an appointment under a power, Lord Cottenham considered that the fund was a definite *one, that the   [958 last disposition, though of "residue," was in substance to be read as if the amount had been inserted in the disposition.   In *In re Harries' Trusts* ('), Vice-Chancellor Wood held, upon the whole instrument, that a lapsed share of a definite sum passed under an appointment of the residue of the moneys after deducting certain specified sums.   He considered *Carter* v. *Taggart* (') and *Falkner* v. *Butler* (') to apply, rather than *Easum* v. *Appleford* (').   In *In re Jeaffreson's Trusts* ('), which was a case of the execution of a power, the donee appointed £100, part of the fund, to a person not an object of the power, and appointed the balance of the fund, after payment of certain other sums well appointed, which sums he described as £260, to pay her own debts (which was an invalid direction), and "should any surplus remain" he gave it to an object of the power.   Here

(¹) Law Rep., 8 Eq., 165.   (⁴) 21 Beav., 564.
(²) Amb., 514.   (⁵) 5 My. & Cr., 56.
(³) 16 Sim., 423.   (⁶) Joh., 199.
                    (⁷) Law Rep., 2 Eq., 276.

there were two invalid gifts ; the latter was held to fall into the ultimate surplus, the former was held to pass as unappointed. That decision as regards the £100 followed *Easum* v. *Appleford*, the £100 not becoming part of and passing with the balance, because that was defined as £260. That case, therefore, is not an authority in favor of the general residuary legatee in the present case ; and, construing the whole will, and having regard to the authorities, I hold that the particular residuary legatees are entitled to so much of the £2,000 legacy as is not well disposed of.

I do not think there is any sound distinction between cases of lapsed and cases of invalid disposition, whether the disposition be under a power of appointment, special or general, or in exercise of ownership ; nor do I think that the construction of a particular residuary gift is affected by the presence or absence of a general residuary gift.

Solicitors : *Collyer-Bristow, Withers & Russell ; Richard Smith & Wilmer*, agents for Ford & Warren, Leeds ; *J. & F. Needham*.

[11 Chancery Division, 959.]

V.C.H., March 19, 1879.

959]   *HODGSON V. HALFORD.

[1878 H. 143.]

Power of Appointment—Exclusive—Exercise of—Forfeiture Clause—Change of Religion by Appointee—Cesser of Life Interest—Remoteness—Public Policy.

A testatrix, by will, dated in 1845, limited to a daughter an exclusive power of appointment by will amongst her children. The daughter, by her will, dated in 1874, in exercise of the power, appointed the fund amongst the objects of the power in certain shares, giving to two of her daughters life interests only, and declared that if either during her life or after her death any son or daughter of hers should marry a person who did not profess the Jewish religion, or was not born a Jew though converted to Judaism, or should forsake the Jewish and adopt the Christian or any other religion, then such son or daughter should forfeit all share in the fund, and in case of forfeiture the forfeited share was to accrue and go over to the other or others of the children living at the time of the forfeiture.

Julius, a son of the appointor, married a Christian in his mother's lifetime, but without her consent. The plaintiff, one of the two daughters of the appointor, to whom a life interest only was appointed, became a Christian after the mother's death.

Both Julius and the plaintiff were born after the death of the creator of the power :

Held, first, that the forfeiture clause was not void as against public policy :

Secondly, that it was effectual as to the shares of children marrying Christians or becoming Christians during the lifetime of the appointor, and therefore that the share of Julius was forfeited : .

Thirdly, that the forfeiture clause must be read in conjunction with the gift over, and therefore that, so far as it affected, after the death of the appointor, the share of a child born after the death of the creator of the power, it was void for remoteness, whether such share was appointed for life only or absolutely, and consequently that the plaintiff had not forfeited her share.

MRS. ROSY LYON, widow, who died in 1845, by her will, dated in the same year, gave all her residuary real and personal estate to trustees, and directed them to stand possessed of certain portions of it upon trust to pay the annual produce thereof to her daughter Esther Jacobs for life, and after her death "upon trust for all or any in exclusion of the other or others of them of the children or child of the said Esther Jacobs by her husband Bethel Jacobs as the said Esther Jacobs might, notwithstanding coverture, by her last will and testament give, direct, or appoint."

*Esther Jacobs, by her will, dated in 1874, in exer-   [960 cise of the power of appointment so given to her, appointed that the trustees of the will of Rosy Lyon should stand possessed of the trust funds subject to the power upon trust to appropriate or raise thereout and invest for the benefit of each of her daughters Rosa and Laura the sum of £2,750; and should stand possessed of one of such sums of £2,750 and the investments thereof, upon trust to pay the income thereof to Rosa during her life for her separate use without power of anticipation; and of the other of such sums and the investments thereof upon trust to pay the income thereof to Laura during her life for her separate use without power of anticipation; and, from and after the decease of either of her said two daughters, should stand possessed of both the said sums and the investments thereof upon trust to pay the income thereof to the survivor of them during her life for her separate use without power of anticipation; and from and after the decease of such survivor in trust for such of her (the appointor's) sons Joseph, Henry, Charles, Benjamin, and Julius, and for such of her daughters Maria, Henrietta, and Frances as should be living at the time of the decease of the survivor of her said daughters Rosa and Laura, and if more than one, in equal shares absolutely.

And the testatrix Esther Jacobs directed that from and after her decease the said trustees should stand possessed of the residue of the trust funds subject to the power of appointment in trust for such of her sons Joseph, Henry, Charles, Benjamin, and Julius, and such of her daughters Maria, Henrietta, and Frances, as should be living at her decease, and if more than one, in equal shares absolutely. And the will of the testatrix Esther Jacobs contained a clause of forfeiture and a proviso with reference thereto in the following terms :

"And I hereby direct and declare that if either during my lifetime or after my decease any son or daughter of mine shall marry a person who does not profess the Jewish religion, or shall marry a person not born a Jew or Jewess although converted to Judaism and professing the Jewish religion, or shall forsake the Jewish religion and adopt the Chrstian or any other religion, then and in every such case and as from the occurrence of such event such son or daughter respectively shall absolutely forfeit and lose all share 961] *and participation in and right or power over the principal and income of all and every the trust premises, whether appointed under the powers in that behalf contained in the will of the said Rosy Lyon deceased, or forming part of the property bequeathed to me by my husband or otherwise as aforesaid ; and as to any son of mine or any daughter of mine incurring such forfeiture, his or her share or shares, as well original as accruing by virtue of this provision, and as to the said Rosa Jacobs and Laura Jacobs, if either of them shall incur such forfeiture, the said two several sums of £2,750 hereinbefore directed to be raised for their benefits respectively, and the investments representing the same, and the interest, dividends, and annual produce thereof, shall (notwithstanding anything hereinbefore contained), as from the occurrence of the event occasioning such forfeiture, accrue and go over to the others or other of them my said sons and daughters hereinbefore named who shall be living at the time of such forfeiture, and if more than one, in equal shares, their respective executors, administrators, and assigns, absolutely."

By a codicil to her will dated the 12th of July, 1876, Esther Jacobs recited that she had recently discovered that her son Henry had married according to the rites of the Church of England, and that her son Charles had recently forsaken the Jewish and adopted the Christian religion, and had married a Christian, and that both her said sons, by virtue of the provisions in her will contained, had thus absolutely forfeited all share and participation in the property therein referred to, and their respective shares had accrued and gone over to the other sons and daughters in her said will named, in equal shares ; and in order the better to carry such forfeiture and accruer into effect, and by way of confirming the same, the testatrix Esther Jacobs thereby revoked all the trusts, appointments, and bequests in favor of Henry and Charles, and declared that the shares to which they would but for their conduct have been entitled under her will (whether appointed or otherwise) should accrue, go over to and be divided amongst her sons Joseph, Benjamin, and Julius, and her daughters Maria, Henrietta, Frances, Rosa, and Laura, in equal shares.

Esther Jacobs died on the 19th of September, 1876. Her son Julius during her lifetime but without her knowledge, married a *Christian; and shortly after her death [962 her daughter Laura, who was the plaintiff in this action, forsook the Jewish and adopted the Christian religion, afterwards marrying Mr. Hodgson, who was a member of the Church of England.

Both Julius and the plaintiff were born after the death of Rosy Lyon; and they, with Henry and Charles, were the only children of Esther Jacobs who had either married persons who did not profess the Jewish religion or had forsaken the Jewish and adopted another religion.

Laura Hodgson now brought her action against the executors of the will of Esther Jacobs, who were also the trustees of the will of Rosy Lyon, and against the other beneficiaries under Esther Jocob's will, and claimed to have the rights of parties under both wills ascertained and declared, and the trusts thereof carried into effect under the order of the court.

The questions argued arose with reference to the shares of the plaintiff and Julius Jacobs, and were, whether the forfeiture clause was, as to both or either of them, void either for remoteness or as being contrary to public policy; and by the direction of the Vice-Chancellor the question of remoteness was argued first.

Dickinson, Q.C., and *Bradford*, for the plaintiff: As the plaintiff was not born until after the death of the creator of the power, the forfeiture of her share might take effect at a period remoter than a life in being at that death and twenty-one years afterwards. With respect to the plaintiff, therefore, the forfeiture clause violates the rule against perpetuities, and does not cut down the life interest which is well given to the plaintiff: Lewis on Perpetuities ([1]).

In *Fry* v. *Capper* ([2]) it was held that though an appointor might limit a fund for life to a daughter who was unborn at the creation of the power, inasmuch as she, with those entitled to the fund subject to the life interest, might at any time dispose of it, he could not leave it to her for life without power of anticipation, without infringing the rule against perpetuities, for he would thereby restrict her prob-

([1]) Ed. 1843, p. 173.   ([2]) Kay, 163.

ably during her whole life, from disposing of the fund, and
accordingly, while the appointment was sustained, the re-
963] straint *on anticipation was rejected. Upon this
authority the restriction on anticipation attached to the life
interest of the plaintiff is an infringement of the rule, and
the principle applies by analogy to the forfeiture clause.

W. Pearson, Q C., and *Chadwyck Healey,* for the defendant Julius Jacobs: The fact that Julius Jacobs became a Christian during the life of his mother, the donee of
the power, makes no difference, and all the arguments on behalf of the plaintiff (of which we avail ourselves) apply to
his case.

Hastings, Q.C., and *Byrne,* for the appointor's sons and
daughters, Joseph, Benjamin, Maria, Henrietta, and Frances: First, with regard to the share of the plaintiff. Her
interest has been forfeited under the clause, for the limitation to her gives her a less interest than a life interest,
i.e., a life interest determinable upon an event in her lifetime ; and it being clear that an entire life interest may be
limited to an unborn person without offending the rule
against perpetuities, *a fortiori* an interest determinable before death may be so limited. The rule against perpetuities
is in fact laid down with reference to the commencement and
not to the termination of limitations ; and there is no distinction in principle between a limitation and a clause for
cesser. The gift over is no doubt void for remoteness, but
a clause for cesser such as this is good without any gift over:
Lewis on Perpetuities ([1]); *Joel* v. *Mills* ([2]); *Boughton* v.
James ([3]); *Jee* v. *Audley* ([4]); *Hampton* v. *Holman* ([5]),
overruling *Hayes* v. *Hayes* ([6]).

[HALL, V.C.: When you find a forfeiture clause asso-
ciated with a gift over, is it not reasonable to read them
together.]

Secondly, as to the share of Julius. His share is clearly
forfeited. Under this clause the forfeiture may take effect
in the alternative either during the lifetime of the appointor
or after her death, and as Julius embraced the Christian
faith in his mother's lifetime, the forfeiture was not too
964] remote, and the clause operated : *Allen* *v. *Jackson* ([7]).
These alternatives must in fact be read as if they were
successive limitations taking effect on the two events in
question.

([1]) Page 173.   ([5]) 5 Ch. D., 183.
([2]) 3 K & J., 458.   ([6]) 4 Russ., 311.
([3]) 1 Coll., 26 ; 1 H. L. C., 406.   ([7]) 1 Ch. D., 399, 404 ; 15 Eng. R.,
([4]) 1 Cox, 324.   815.

[HALL, V.C., referred to *Monypenny* v. *Dering* ('); *Doe* v. *Challis* (').

Schloss, for Rosa Jane Jacobs, adopted the same arguments, and referred to the following additional authorities: Lewis on Perpetuities ('); Jarman on Wills ('); *Gooding* v. *Read* ('); *Doe d. Blomfield* v. *Eyre* ('); *Robinson* v. *Wood* ('); *Crompe* v. *Barrow* ('); *Hewitt* v. *Lord Dacre* (').

Robinson, Q.C., and *Solomon*, for the trustees of the will of the appointor.

Dickinson, in reply.

HALL, V.C.: It appears to me that this clause of forfeiture is one single clause applicable to a number of things, not merely to life interests, but also to the capital of the various shares appointed. I do not know why I should split up the clause into two parts, and I cannot in fact so split it up for the purpose of creating a forfeiture, nor can I construe the clause of forfeiture separately from the gift over. I must take the clause as I find it. I do not, therefore, desire any further argument as to the plaintiff's share, but it is worthy of consideration whether, as regards the share of Julius, the forfeiture clause must not be read alternatively.

Chadwyck Healey (*W. Pearson*, Q.C., with him): The clause cannot be read alternatively. The appointment is by will, which takes effect from the death of the appointor, and the words "either during my lifetime" are not applicable. The *condition contemplates operation on a vested [965 interest, and that these children have already got something which they could forfeit and lose.

HALL, V.C.: I am of opinion that the forfeiture clause was effectual as to the share of Julius. In the cases of *Monypenny* v. *Dering* (') and *Doe* v. *Challis* ('), to which I referred during the course of the arguments, there is an intelligible principle which seems to me to be applicable to the present case.

The question whether or not the forfeiture clause was void as being contrary to public policy, was then argued.

Chadwyck Healey (*W. Pearson*, Q.C., with him): The condition which the testatrix has sought to impose by this forfeiture clause is bad in itself, and void as against public policy. It is a condition which the power did not authorize. The exercise of the power must be for the benefit of the ob-

(') 2 D. M. & G., 145.   (⁵) 4 D. M. & G., 510.
(²) 18 Q. B., 231; 7 H. L. C. 531.   (⁶) 5 C. B., 718.
(³) Page 501; supplt., 164.   (⁷) 4 Jur. (N.S.), 625.
(⁴) Vol. i, p. 261.   (⁸) 4 Ves., 681.
        (⁹) 2 Keen, 622.

jects of the power, and not for the purpose of working out some private purpose of the donee of the power. This was held with regard to a condition restricting the residence of an object of the power in *D'Abbacthie* v. *Bizoin* (¹). In *Egerton* v. *Earl Brownlow* (²), the Lord Chief Baron said that the donee of a power could not "make his political principles run 'with the land ;'" again, conditions which lead to the omission of duties, and tend to prevent those upon whom they are sought to be imposed from being good citizens, are void ; and these principles apply with far greater force to a case in which the donee of a power seeks in exercising it to impose a fetter upon the conscience of the objects of the power, and to bribe them into any particular religious opinions: Sheppard's Touchstone (³) ; Hunter's Digest of Roman Law (⁴) ; *Mitchell* v. *Reynolds* (⁵) ; *Wren* v. *Brad-*
966] *ley* (⁶) ; *Wilkinson* v. *Wilkinson* (⁷) ; *Traiton* v. *Trai-*
ton (⁸). Moreover, this condition is bad by analogy to marriage brocage contracts : *Tenant* v. *Braie* (⁹).

HALL, V.C.: I think that every argument that could be urged has been addressed to me in favor of the contentions that this appointment is either unauthorized by the terms of the power itself, or is one which the court ought not to give effect to upon grounds of public policy, or other similar grounds. First, as regards the contention that the appointment is not authorized by the terms of the power. In the absence of any authority to the contrary, I think that a power such as this given to a parent to appoint amongst his children ought not to receive a limited or narrow construction, but ought rather to be construed so as to embrace every ordinary provision which a parent might make, and which might be useful or available for the children amongst whom and in whose favor the power is to be exercised. The power is not a mere power of selecting individuals to take, but a power to appoint amongst all or any one or more of the children.

It is said that this clause of forfeiture is void as being against public policy, and several authorities have been cited in support of that contention. All those authorities, however, were, as it appears to me, cases in which the condition was unquestionably against public morality, and it was on that ground that the court declined to give effect to it. Those cases, therefore, do not establish that for which

(¹) Ir. Rep., 5 Eq., 205.
(²) 4 H. L. C., 1.
(³) 7th ed , vol. i, pp. 117, 132.
(⁴) Page 765 ; citing Ulpian, Dig., book xviii, tit. 7, chap. viii, Preface.
(⁵) 1 P. Wms., 181.
(⁶) 2 De G. & Sm., 49.
(⁷) Law Rep., 12 Eq., 604.
(⁸) Vern., 413.
(⁹) Tothill, 141.

they were cited. The case which comes nearer to the present than any which was cited to me is *In re Dickson's Trusts* ('). There a daughter of the testator was a legatee under his will, and by a codicil the testator provided that that daughter should be excluded from participation under the will if she became a nun, and Vice-Chancellor Lord Cranworth held that to be a perfectly good provision. Still that was throwing out a great temptation, as has been suggested, to the lady not to become a nun; it was a sort of bribe to her not to act according to her conscience—an inducement to her not to profess that which in conscience it may be she ought to have professed. I cannot in *the [967 absence of authority say that a parent or appointor (and for this purpose I see no difference between them) disposing by will either of his own property or of any property over which he has a power of appointment, is not perfectly justified in making a provision in favor of such of his children as shall not embrace a particular faith—Christian, Roman Catholic, Mahommedan, or any other. Therefore the ground on which it is attempted to get rid of the effect of this condition fails.

Solicitors for plaintiff: *Lindo & Co.*
Solicitor for defendant Julius O. Jacobs: *Walter Webb.*
Solicitors for other defendants: *Lindo & Co.*

(') 1 Sim. (N.S.), 37.

See 17 Eng. Rep., 593 note, and other notes there cited.

A condition in restraint of marriage, subsequent and general in its character annexed to a devise or conveyance from parent to child, is void unless there be a valid limitation over. A father conveyed to his daughter with a proviso that the gift should stand if she remained single, otherwise the land to be divided among his three children, the grantee to have fifty dollars the most. Held, that the condition was subsequent, general and void; that a limitation over to one's heirs is of no effect, as a title by descent is the worthier title: Randall *v.* Marble, 09 Me., 310.

A testator devised to his wife, "in lieu of her interest in" his lands, a certain tract of land "during her natural life, or so long as she may remain my widow." Held, the widow having re-married, that she took a life estate, the condition in restraint of marriage being void: Coon *v.* Bean, 69 Ind., 474; S. P., Stilwell *v.* Knapper, 69 id., 558.

In respect to conditions subsequent, there must be a capacity and opportunity and an option, on the part of the legatee, to perform the conditions before a forfeiture of the legacy is or can be incurred. A court of equity, at all times reluctant to enforce a forfeiture or a penalty, will not do so when the victim of it has acted in ignorance of the conditions upon which or with whose non-compliance such forfeiture was involved or dependent.

Where, as in this case, the testator knew that his daughter was separated from her husband, and he had abandoned her, and that she had removed to another State to gain a residence which would enable and qualify her to procure a divorce from such husband, he had paid for her support in such State, and defrayed the expenses of the suit to procure such divorce, and knew that she was entitled to marry again after such divorce, which he knew, before his death, had been granted: Held, that to impose upon her the duty, under the pain of forfeiture of all interest in his estate, to remain unmarried for life, was harsh and cruel in the extreme, when such restriction was contained in a secret will unknown to her, and which she could not know till after his death. In such case the estate, to which the condition contained in such will was annexed, became absolute, to the same effect as if said condition had been fully complied with : Merriam v. Wolcott, 61 How. Pr., 378.

The testator, after making various devises, directed his executors in the eighth clause of his will to pay the residue of the net annual income of the estate to his wife during her life, or until she should re-marry; but in case she should re-marry, she was to have an annual income which was to be readjusted, and she was to receive it during her life for her sole and separate use, free from any debts or control of her husband. In the tenth clause the testator directs that, upon her death or re-marriage, all the estate was to be divided between his children and their issue. Held, that the word "re-marriage," occurring in the tenth clause, was inadvertently and unintentionally used by the testator as an event which would cut off rights in others and hasten the division of the estate, and that the word should be rejected as irreconcilable with the general scope of the will, and as in conflict with the expressed intentions of the testator, both general and special, as shown by the will itself : Lottimere v. Blumenthal 61 How. Pr., 360.

A gift was made by a testator of personalty to his wife, coupled with a subsequent condition which was clearly intended to act in restraint of marriage. Held, 1. If the will had stopped here, this condition would be void as merely *in terrorem*, and the wife would take an absolute estate. But a limitation over in the event of her re-marriage shows that the condition was not intended as a menace, but as the basis of a distinct gift. 2. The bequest over cannot be avoided upon the ground that it is given to a party, upon whom the law itself would cast the property : Hough's Estate, 13 Phila., 279, 14 West. Jur., 27, 9 Weekly Notes (Penn), 475, distinguishing Parsons v. Winslow, 6 Mass., 169.

W. H. C., in consideration of one dime and of natural love and affection, conveyed by deed certain leasehold property to his two sisters M. & E., "to have and to hold the same unto the same M. & E., as tenants in common, so long as they both shall live ; and from and after the death of either of them, then unto the survivor so long as she shall live and no longer, or so long as they both shall remain unmarried, and from and after the marriage of either of them, then unto the one remaining unmarried so long as she shall live and no longer." M. married, and E., who remained unmarried, took exclusive possession of the premises. Upon an ejectment brought by M. and her husband to recover an undivided moiety of the premises ; it was held, 1. That the purpose of the brother evidently was not to restrain the marriage, or promote the celibacy of the sisters, but to give them a small property as a home or support, until they should severally marry and have husbands to maintain them. 2. That there was nothing immoral or illegal in this purpose, and it was carried out by this deed without infringing any rule of law. 3. That the weight of authority fully sustained the validity of the grant : Arthur v. Cole, 56 Md., 100.

A.'s last will and testament provided as follows: "To my beloved Edith I give and bequeath all my estate, real and personal, of which I may die seised, the same to remain and be hers, with full power, right, and authority to dispose of the same as to her shall seem meet and proper, so long as she shall remain my widow, upon the express condition that if she shall marry again, then it is my will that all the estate herein bequeathed, or whatever may remain, should go to my surviving children, share and share alike." A.'s children and Edith survived him. She conveyed the real estate to B. in fee, and subsequently married. Held, that B.'s estate determined on Edith's marriage : Giles v. Little, 104 U. S., 291.

The will of C. gave his estate, real and personal, to executors in trust, to sell, mortgage or lease the real estate, to invest the proceeds, and out of the same to support his children until they respectively attained the age of twenty-one, and until his daughter M. (plaintiff's intestate) should get married, with their consent, and that of her mother. He gave to his said daughter $16,000, to be paid to her on her attaining the age of twenty-one or upon her marriage before that age, with the consent of her mother and said executors. In case of her death, unmarried, before she became of age, the legacy was given to the testator's two sons. In the event of M.'s marrying against the consent of the "said executors and her said mother," it was declared that she should receive but $5,000. To his wife he gave the care and custody of his children during their minority, "as long as she remains unmarried," etc. In case of her marriage, such care and custody was committed to the executors. The executors were directed to pay the debts and legacies, in the first place, out of the personal property; if this proved insufficient, to pay the balance out of the rents and profits of his real estate; and if it became necessary, they were authorized to sell or mortgage the real estate to pay the residue. The testator left personal estate of the value only of about $500. The testator's widow re-married, and after that M. married when about eighteen years of age, with the consent, as the court found, of the then sole executor, but without the consent of her mother.

In an action brought to establish plaintiff's right to the $16,000 legacy, held that M.'s marriage without consent was a breach of the condition; that said condition was a valid one; and, although there was no gift over on breach thereof, as the legacy was not a purely personal one, the land being charged as an auxiliary fund with its payment, and a sale thereof was necessary for that purpose, and there being no personalty out of which it can be paid, that the legacy was forfeited save as to the $5,000 by the marriage of M. without the required consent.

A general gift of a residue is not a gift over within the rule.

It seems that the condition was a condition subsequent; that the gift to M. was immediate, the payment only being postponed until her arrival of age, with a provision for the acceleration of payment, on her marriage with consent before that time, and a revocation of the gift in case of marriage, without consent. The general doctrine of conditions in restraint of marriage considered: Hogan v. Curtin, 88 N. Y., 162, 21 Daily Reg., 905, affirming 47 N. Y., Supr. Ct. R., 250.

[11 Chancery Division, 968.]

Fry, J., May 8, 10, 1879.

*BOLTON V. BOLTON.   [968

[1878 B. 57.]

Way of Necessity—Election—Appurtenances—Exception in Conveyance.

A contract to sell land with the appurtenances does not pass a right to a way to the land sold which the vendor has used over adjoining land of his own.

Where a grantee is entitled to a way of necessity over another tenement belonging to the grantor, and there are to the tenement granted more ways than one, the grantee is entitled to one way only, which the grantor may select.

By an agreement dated the 19th of December, 1877, the trustees and executors of T. J. Bolton agreed to sell to the School Board for London, "First, all those the several messuages or tenements described in the first schedule hereto, with their appurtenances and the inheritance thereof in fee simple free from incumbrances, but subject to the several indentures of lease of the same premises respectively specified in the said first schedule hereto; and all such, if any, interest as the said vendors possess over the yard in Buckingham Mews;" and secondly, certain adjoining leaseholds specified in the second schedule, and called Buckingham Terrace, and which were situated between Buckingham Mews and Lonsdale Road.

The freeholds specified in the first schedule consisted of two rows of houses on each side of Buckingham Mews, to which there was access by two roads, one at the west leading into Portobello Road, the other at the east leading into Lonsdale Road; both roads of access being shown in the plan annexed to the agreement, and both being over land of the vendors.

A draft conveyance was sent by the School Board to the vendors, containing a grant of the lands, "together with all erections, fixtures, ways, lights, rights, privileges, easements, and appurtenances whatsoever to the said pieces or parcels of land and hereditaments respectively or any part thereof respectively appertaining, or with the same or any part thereof now or heretofore enjoyed or reputed as part or 969] member thereof." The vendors *struck out the words "or with the same or any part thereof now or heretofore enjoyed," and added words excepting the right of way into Portobello Road, but expressly granting a right of way into Lonsdale Road.

The School Board objected to the exception of the right of way into Portobello Road, and the vendors took out a summons in a suit for the administration of the estate of T. J. Bolton to have the conveyance settled by the court. Both parties desired to have the point settled by the conveyance.

J. Pearson, Q.C., and *D. Jones*, for the vendors: No doubt both ways have existed over land belonging to the vendors, but the purchasers have not contracted for any right of way, and are only entitled to one right of way, which the vendor will give, and as there are now two ways the conveyance ought to make it clear which is to be the way. Moreover, the School Board are not ordinary purchasers, and must not take from the vendor more than they want. In this case it is doubtful whether they have a right as of necessity to any road, for they must buy the freehold of the leaseholds which we have sold, and then they will have access to a public road over their own land.

Higgins, Q.C., and *Simmonds*, for the plaintiffs in the suit, referred to *Wood* v. *Saunders* (¹).

North, Q.C., and *Kirby*, for the School Board: The purchasers have a right to a conveyance in the ordinary form, and to take such appurtenances as belong to the land sold, without any expressed exception.

(¹) Law Rep., 10 Ch., 582; 14 Eng. R., 805.

[FRY, J.: The vendor often submits to the insertion of general words which include more than the purchaser is strictly entitled to, and I have in settling a draft sometimes struck them out.]

Moreover, all rights of way are included with the appurtenances in the contract: *Langley* v. *Hammond* (¹); *Watts* v. *Kelson* (²). The property must be dealt with as it stood at the time. The plan annexed to the contract showed both roads: *Kay* v. *Oxley* (³); *Denny* v. *Hancock* (⁴). [970 This is not a compulsory purchase, and the School Board have the same rights as an ordinary purchaser: *Clark* v *School Board for London* (⁵).

J. Pearson, in reply: If the board is entitled to a right of way, we give one; but we have a right to give it where we please: Gale on Easements (⁶).

[FRY, J., as to the right of election, referred to Vin. Abr., Election; *Rumble* v. *Heygate* (⁷).]

If the purchaser could choose his way, the vendor would lose his rights over the rest of his land, and could not deal with it.

May 10. FRY, J.: The question which arises for decision on this summons is as to the proper form of conveyance to be executed under a contract between the School Board for London and the trustees of the estate of the late Mr. Bolton.

The contract for the sale of the property does not contain any words with regard to the right of way. In my view, therefore, the contract was for the conveyance of the premises with all that was appurtenant or appendant to them and nothing more. Mr. Bolton's trustees are perfectly willing to grant a right of way over the road which leads into Lonsdale Road; but they decline to grant a right of way over a road which leads into Portobello Road. The School Board contend that they are entitled to the latter right of way.

The first question then is, Was the way into Lonsdale Road, or was the way into Portobello Road appurtenant or appendant to Buckingham Mews, the property contracted for? In my opinion neither of the ways was either appurtenant or appendant. The common words "with all ways thereunto appertaining," strictly and properly speaking, never carry a right of way over another tenement of the grantor; and for this simple reason: When a man who is

(¹) Law Rep., 3 Ex., 161.
(²) Law Rep., 6 Ch., 166.
(³) Law Rep., 10 Q. B., 360.
(⁴) Law Rep., 6 Ch., 1.
(⁵) Law Rep., 9 Ch., 120.
(⁶) 5th ed., p. 149.
(⁷) 18 W. R., 749.

owner of two fields walks over one to get to the other, that
971] *walking is attributable to the ownership of the land
over which he is walking, and not necessarily to the ownership of the land to which he is walking. If authority is
necessary, the two cases of *Harding* v. *Wilson* (') and *Barlow* v. *Rhodes* (') have decided that these words, strictly
speaking, do not carry a right of way over the grantor's
own land. Therefore, in my judgment, the right of way
claimed cannot be claimed as appurtenant or appendant to
the property contracted for.

The next question is, Can the grantee claim a right of way
of necessity? for it is clear that the grantee cannot be entitled to two ways of necessity.

It is objected by the vendors that though a grantee may
in most cases make this claim, yet in this case the School
Board cannot; for the board has purchased for the purpose
of erecting school houses and providing school accommodation, but as they cannot do that until they have obtained
the reversion of the Buckingham Terrace property, it must
be assumed that they will obtain that reversion; and then
they will have a right of way to Buckingham Mews over
their other freehold. That argument does not appear to me
to be sound, and for this reason: The School Board, acting
with perfect propriety, acquire the leasehold interest in the
Buckingham Terrace property, yet it may be that before
they have purchased the reversion they will find that the
land is superfluous, and so may desire to part with their
leasehold interest without acquiring the freehold. I think,
therefore, that the School Board are entitled to one right of
way of necessity over the freehold of Mr. Bolton as incident
to the grant of Buckingham Mews.

Then arises the question, In whom is the right to elect
which of the two rights of way shall be granted? I shall
not in this case go into the general doctrine of election, because it appears to me that the matter is settled by authority.
The authorities determine that the right of election is in the
person who creates the right of way, in other words, in the
grantor. The first case on the subject is *Clarke* v. *Rugge* (').
That case lays down the general rule that where a man
grants a close which is landlocked, and is also the owner of
an adjoining close, the grantee shall have a right of way over
972] the adjoining close as incident to the grant; *for otherwise the grantee cannot have any benefit from the grant.
"And the feoffor shall assign the way where he can best
spare it." The next case which throws light on the subject

(') 2 B. & C., 96.　　　(') 1 C. & M., 489.　　　(') Roll. Abr., 60, pl. 17.

is *Packer* v. *Welsted* (¹). That is the converse case ; that is to say, it is a case in which the owner of two tenements disposed of the outer tenement and retained the inner or land locked tenement. It was held that he would have a right of way over the outer tenement, and that he would have the right of selecting the way. There again the grantor, the person who created the right of way, had the right to select the way. Both these cases were considered in a much more recent case, *Pearson* v. *Spencer* (²). There Blackburn, J., in delivering the considered judgment of the court, after referring to the two authorities I have cited, said : "In each case it seems to have been thought that the person by whose act the way was created was subsequently to select the way subject only to this, that it should be a convenient way." Now, no evidence or argument has been addressed to me to show that the way into Lonsdale Road is not a convenient way. I assume it therefore to be such, and I hold that the right of election was in Mr. Bolton's trustees.

The conveyance, therefore, must contain words to this effect, "Including a right of way for all purposes over the strip of land colored green (at the east end of Buckingham Mews) into Lonsdale Road, but not including any right of way over the strip of land colored brown (at the west end of Buckingham Mews) into Portobello Road."

I think that as this was a very fair question upon the construction of the contract no costs should be awarded on either side. The costs of the trustees will be costs in the cause.

Solicitors for trustees of the will : *Allen & Edwards.*
Solicitors for plaintiff in the suit : *Cronin & Rivolta.*
Solicitors for School Board : *Gedge, Kirby & Millett.*

(¹) 2 Sid., 111.   (²) 1 B. & S., 571, 585; 3 B. & S., 761.

See 31 Eng. Rep., 674 note ; 16 Cent. L. J., 124.

Where a deed conveyed the "farm and plantation given to J. and W. by the will of W. B.," followed by an exact description ; held, that lands situate distinct from that described, and which is not shown to have been a part of the farm of W. B. or in his possession, would not pass under the general words, nor under the word "appurtenances," as land cannot pass as appurtenant to land : Armstrong *v.* Dubois, 15 N. Y. Weekly Dig., 553, 90 N. Y. Rep., 95.

S. P., St. Louis Bridge Co. *v*, Curtis, 103 Ills. 410,

The use by an owner and his tenants of a yard in the rear of his four or five houses, paved and open for all the tenants—the common use of one hydrant on the premises, with city water mains within a few feet of each house for separate connections—the common use of one alley to a certain street between two of the houses, and a footpath to another street, neither of which abutted on the property of the complainant, nor wer essential for the enjoyment of his property as " ways of necessity," cannot be taken to be an apparent necessity and permanent dedication to a common use, in such manner as to subject the property to a continuance of the same condition in the · hands of separate owners.

It was contended by the complainant that it was necessary that the alleyway should pass as an easement, because of the great disadvantage resulting to his property from its loss as a means of access to the yard for the purpose of cleaning the vault or privy on his premises. The only way by which this work could be done without the use of the alley was to pass through the house on complainant's own ground, or perhaps to sink the vault to the gravel. Held, that these difficulties or disadvantages, however great, ought to have been provided for by express grant, if the complainant expected to use other ground than his own to surmount these difficulties: Francier's Appeal, 96 Penn. St. R., 200.

The tangible property of a corporation does not pass as an incident or accession on the sale of the franchise: St. Louis Bridge Co. v. Curtis, 103 Ills., 410.

Where, at the time of purchase of real estate, there is a road or right of way used by the public, such as a public highway or a road used so long that there may be a presumption of a dedication to the public, the purchaser takes the land subject to such rights; and he is not precluded even by a deed of warranty against incumbrances.

Where no private right of way or other easement is reserved in the deed itself, and the purchaser has no notice of any such claim, he takes the property without the burden of any such claim, either from the grantor or any person claiming under him.

Where the deed conveys land without reservation, and the grantee takes all conveyed by the deed unincumbered, unless in some way notice is brought home to him that the land is subject to the incumbrance of some easement or privilege in another person or in the public: Patton v. Quarrier, 18 West Va., 447.

A deed of land contained this: "excepting and reserving" to the grantor, "all the coal underlying," etc., with right of ingress, etc., "for the purpose of mining and conveying away said coal." Held, that the surface owner was entitled to absolute support, and that the mine owner was liable for injury to the surface from a failure to leave such support, and this without regard to the degree of skill and prudence with which he conducted mining operations: Carlin v. Chappel, 27 Alb. L. J., 108, to appear in 99 or 100 Penn. St. Rep.

A "right of way of an alley" included in a deed, implies ex vi termini a passage leading away from the land conveyed.

All grants must be construed reasonably and in the light of the circumstances.

The grantor of a corner lot afterwards deeded an adjoining lot, and included "the right of way of an alley 10 feet wide, on rear end of said 82 feet," the length of the lots conveyed. Such a passageway actually existed from the street, and the land in the rear of both lots was under the grantor's control. Held, that the easement included in the second deed could not be limited to a mere open space behind the lot, and that the subsequent obstruction of the outlet to the alley by persons holding under the grantor would be enjoined: McConnell v. Rathbun, 46 Mich., 303.

A. conveyed to B. a parcel of land bounded on a street, "excepting and reserving" to himself, his heirs and assigns, "a passageway four feet wide, in, through and over said premises," from said street to A.'s house, on an adjoining piece of land. The parties subsequently located the way on the northerly side of the land conveyed. B. dug up the way, and began to build upon and over it:

Held, on a bill in equity by A. against B., that B. was entitled to build over the way, placing no part of the building upon it, and leaving it of a reasonable height: and that A. was entitled to have the soil of the way restored to its former condition: Gerrish v. Shattuck, 132 Mass., 235.

When a wall is erected by the owner of a lot, on the boundary line between his own and the adjoining lot, resting partly upon each, the law imposes no obligation on the owner of the adjacent lot to contribute to its erection; nor will a court of equity enjoin him or a subsequent purchaser from the use of the wall, without making contribution in the absence of a promise to contribute: Preiss v. Parker, 67 Ala., 500.

INDEX.

A.

ACCIDENT.

1. Although the Wreck Commissioner, or other authority, holding a formal investigation into a shipping casualty under the Merchant Shipping Acts, must, if he deals with the certificate of a master or certificated officer, give his decision in open court, yet he may, subsequently in his report to the Board of Trade, state reasons for his decision not mentioned by him at the time when the judgment was delivered.

2. In appeals under the Shipping Casualties Investigations Act, 1879, the Court of Appeal will not permit witnesses to be called to give evidence on questions of nautical knowledge and skill.

3. Where, on an appeal under the Shipping Casualties Investigations Act, 1879, the decision of the Wreck Commissioner, suspending the certificate of a master, was affirmed, but the Court of Appeal recommended that the Board of Trade should shorten the time for which the certificate had been suspended, the parties to the appeal were left to bear their own costs of the appeal. *The Kestrel.* 579

See COLLISION, 186.
NEGLIGENCE.
PRACTICE, 720.

ACKNOWLEDGMENT.

See WILLS.

ADVERSE PARTIES.

1. Notice by a respondent under Rules of Court, 1875, Order LVIII, rule 6, to vary the decision of the court was proceeded upon, though the point was one in which the original appellant had no interest. *Ralph* v. *Carrick.* 856

ADVERSE POSSESSION.

See NUISANCES, 837, 850 *note.*

AGREEMENT.

1. A wife who agrees, or authorizes her solicitor to agree, to stay proceedings in a suit instituted by her for restitution of conjugal rights, on certain terms, will be bound by such agreement, and will not be allowed to set the cause down for hearing. *Stanes* v. *Stanes.* 86

See CHARTERPARTY.

ALIMONY.

1. The court has power under s. 32 of 20 & 21 Vict. c. 85, to make an order for

the permanent maintenance of a wife after a decree absolute has been pronounced. *Bradley* v. *Bradley.* 36

2. When the will of a married woman is tendered for probate on the ground that she had separate property, and the probate is contested, if the court is satisfied that there is separate property, it has power to grant probate of all such property as the testatrix had power to dispose of without deciding what that property is. But it is in general the duty of the court, so far as the evidence and pleadings enable it to do so, to decide judicially of what such property consists.

3. And, *semble*, where the will is made under a power, if the court has all persons interested before it, it ought to decide the question not only whether there is a power, but whether it is well executed.

4. The savings of an annual allowance for her separate maintenance, paid to the wife of a lunatic living apart from her husband, under an order in lunacy, are her separate property, although the order does not expressly state that the allowance is for her separate use. *Tharp* v. *Macdonald.* 51

5. The court in enforcing payment of alimony and costs will authorize sequestrators to receive portions of a civil service pension. *Sansom* v. *Sansom.* 162

6. A wife by a deed of separation, agreed to accept certain sums as a provision for her support, and not to sue her husband for any further maintenance. Subsequently having discovered that he had been guilty of incestuous adultery, she obtained a decree for dissolution of the marriage :
Held, that notwithstanding the deed, she was entitled to the usual order for permanent maintenance. *Morrall* v. *Morrall.* 528, 529 *note.*

7. The provisions of 29 Vict c. 32, do not apply exclusively to the case of a poor man, and the court may order sums of considerable amount to be paid weekly or monthly as permanent maintenance, and may from time to time modify the order. *Jardine* v. *Jardine.* 598

8. A petition for variation of settlements must usually be signed by the petition-

er, but the court will, under special circumstances, allow his solicitor to sign it on his behalf. *Ross* v. *Ross.* 617

9. The provisions of 20 & 21 Vict. c. 85, s. 32, respecting permanent maintenance empower the court to order a gross or annual sum to be secured for the benefit of the wife, but not to make a direct order on the husband to pay a gross or annual or other periodical sum to the wife.

10. The qualification that the maintenance is to be for the wife "dum sola et casta vixerit" is not usually inserted in the order but in the deed of security.

11. The provisions of 29 & 30 Vict. c. 32, respecting the payment of monthly or weekly sums to the wife do not apply to the case of a husband who has property abroad sufficient and available for a security.

12. Per Jessel, M.R., an order for maintenance cannot be made in the alternative for securing a gross or annual sum of money, or else for the payment of monthly or weekly sums by the husband. *Medley* v. *Medley.* 667

13. A husband having committed adultery, disputes arose between him and his wife which led to his committing acts of legal cruelty. A separation deed was then executed, by which he agreed to allow her £250 a year, and to maintain the two youngest children, who were not to be in her custody ; and she covenanted not to take any proceedings to compel the husband to allow her a larger amount of alimony. Subsequently the husband committed adultery, and the wife obtained a decree for judicial separation and an order that she should have the custody of the two youngest children. The husband had since the date of the separation deed become wealthy, and the wife applied for an inquiry as to his means with a view to obtaining increased alimony :
Held, reversing the decision of the president, that increased alimony could not be ordered, for that as the court had not, as it would have had in the case of a decree for dissolution, power to alter the separation deed, the covenant by the wife not to sue for increased alimony was binding on her, and must

the hearing of the appeal. *The Famenoth.* . 738

APPORTIONMENT.

1. A bankrupt had covenanted to pay a life annuity to trustees for the benefit of his wife. The annuity was valued, and proof was made by the trustees for the amount thus ascertained, and a dividend was paid to them. The wife died, and the dividend which the trustees had received exceeded the amount of the payments of the annuity which the bankrupt would have had to make if he had remained solvent :

Held (reversing the decision of the registrar), that the trustees could not be called upon to refund the excess of the dividend above the payments of the annuity which accrued due during the wife's life. *Matter of Bates.* 882

APPURTENANCES.

ARREST.

ASSIGNEE.

ATTACHMENT.

1. Under subs. 8 of s. 25 of the Judicature Act, 1873, the Court of Divorce has power to attach a debt due to a respondent in order to compel obedience to an order of that court for payments of costs. *Whittaker* v. *Whittaker.* 613

2. The rule as to costs in a partnership action is the same as in any other administration action, that is, they are payable out of the assets; " partnership assets" meaning the assets remaining after payment of all the partnership debts, including balances due to any of the partners. If the assets are insufficient for payment of the costs of the action, then such costs must be borne by the partners in proportion to their shares in the profits.

3. Where, however, a partnership action has been rendered necessary by the negligence or other misconduct of a partner, the court will order that partner to pay the costs of the action so far as they have been occasioned by his misconduct, including the costs up to the trial.

4. An order giving a solicitor a charge under sect. 28 of the Attorneys and Solicitors Act, 1860, for his costs as between solicitor and client, on property recovered by him for his client in an action, is sufficient if intituled in the action: it may be obtained either on summons or petition, and need not be intituled either in the matter of the act or of the solicitor.

5. A garnishee in order *nisi* does not create a charge until service of it on the garnishee.

6. A judgment creditor of the defendant in a partnership action obtained a garnishee order *nisi* to attach all moneys in the hands of the receiver in the action appearing to be due to the defendant on taking the accounts. On the following day, and before service of the order *nisi*, the defendant's solicitors obtained, on a summons served on the receiver, a charging order intituled in the action, declaring that they were entitled to a charge for their costs upon all moneys coming to the defendant under the action. On the next day the garnishee order *nisi* was served on the receiver, and was subsequently made absolute :

Held, that the solicitors were entitled to their costs in priority to the claim of the creditor under the garnishee order both under the act and independently of it. *Giles* v. *Hamer.* 909

ATTORNEYS.

1 On a taxation between solicitor and client of the costs of a cause, objections were taken on behalf of the client to charges occasioned by the postponement of the trial and the amendment of the pleadings, on the ground that the postponement of the trial and the amendment of the pleadings had been rendered necessary by the negligence of the solicitor; the registrar refused to disallow the items, on the ground that it was not within his province as taxing master to inquire into the question of negligence:

Held, on motion in court to review the taxation, that the ruling of the registrar was right. *The Papa de Rossie.* 84

2. Lien for services in salvage cases. *The Afrika.* 409

See EVIDENCE, 163, 164 *note*.
SERVICE, 231, 233 *note*.

B.

BANKS.

1. A banking company were employed as agents to collect money and to remit it to their employers. The bank received the money in cash, placed it with the other cash of the bank, and informed their employers that the money had been remitted; but before the money was actually remitted the bank went into liquidation:

Held, that the money was part of the general assets of the bank, and that the employers of the bank were not entitled to be paid in priority to the other creditors. *Matter of West of England Bank.* 810, 816 *note*.

BASTARDY.

See LEGITIMACY.

BIGAMY.

See DIVORCE.

BONA FIDE.

See NOTICE, 830.

BOTTOMRY.

1. A bottomry bond on ship, freight, and cargo provided for payment of a bottomry loan, together with interest at 8 per cent., at or before the expiration of five days after the arrival of the ship at her port of discharge. The bond further provided that an additional premium of 10 per cent. on the loan should become payable if default was made in payment. The ship having arrived at her port of discharge, default was made in payment of the bond, and a suit was instituted by the bondholder against ship, freight, and cargo, to recover the amount of the loan and interest, and the additional premium of 10 per cent. :

Held, that the additional premium of 10 per cent. could not be enforced against the cargo, but that the bondholder was entitled to interest at 4 per cent. from the date when the bond became payable until payment. *The Sophia Cook.* 138
The D. H. Bills. 140

2. Where the holders of a bottomry bond, on ship and freight payable seven days after the arrival of the ship, being apprehensive that her cargo would be discharged forthwith, and their security diminished, instituted a bottomry suit, after the arrival of the ship and before the expiration of the seventh day, and arrested the ship, the court, on the application of the owners of the ship, who had paid the amount of the bond and interest into court, condemned the plaintiffs in costs. *The Eudora.* 239

3. The owner of cargo who ships it on board a foreign vessel, ships it to be dealt with by the master according to the law of the flag, that is, the law of the country to which the vessel belongs, unless that authority be limited by express stipulation at the time of the shipment. Therefore a bond made by the master of a foreign ship hypothecating cargo laden on board such ship, if valid according to the law of the flag of the ship, will be enforced by the

CASUALTY.

See ACCIDENT.

CHARGE.

1. The testatrix by her will directed that her testamentary expenses be paid out of her real and personal estate. The personal estate being insufficient, the court ordered payment of the costs of suit out of the real estate upon conditions assented to by all parties. *Smith* v. *Hopkinson.* 176

See ALIMONY, 757.

CHARITY.

See WILLS, 910.

CHARTERPARTY.

1. Where a vessel is chartered to proceed with cargo to a "safe port .... as ordered, or as near thereunto as she can safely get, and always lay and discharge afloat," the master is not bound to discharge at a port where she cannot, by reason of her draught of water, "always lie and discharge afloat" without being lightened, even if she can be lightened with reasonable despatch and safety in the immediate vicinity of the port or in the port itself.

2. A vessel was chartered to proceed with a cargo of grain from Baltimore to Falmouth for orders, "thence to a safe port in the United Kingdom as ordered, or as near thereunto as she could safely get, and always lay and discharge afloat." The vessel was ordered to Lowestoft. Her draught of water when loaded was such that she could not lie afloat in Lowestoft Harbor without discharging a portion of her cargo, but the discharge of cargo might have been carried on with reasonable safety in Lowestoft Roads. The consignee offered at his own expense to lighten the vessel in the roads, but the master refused to proceed to Lowestoft to discharge, and went to Harwich as the nearest safe port, and there discharged the cargo:

Held, reversing the decision of Sir R. Phillimore, that the consignee could not recover damages against the shipowner for the refusal of the master to discharge at Lowestoft.

3. *Held*, also, that evidence that it was the custom of the port of Lowestoft for vessels to be lightened in the roads before proceeding into the harbor was not admissible. *The Alhambra.* 514

CHATTEL MORTGAGE.

1. Where a beneficial charterparty has been entered into by a mortgagor in possession of a ship, the mortgagee

hole in the barge and caused damage to her cargo. But for the improper position of the anchor neither the barge nor her cargo would have received any damage. In an action of damage by the owners of the barge against the schooner:

Held, reversing the decision of the Admiralty Court, that both vessels were to blame, and that therefore the owners of the barge were entitled to half the damage sustained. *The Margaret*. 521

18. A bark, provided only with a fog-horn, sounded by means of the breath, came into collision, during a fog, with a steamship. The fog-horn was duly sounded before the collision, and was heard by those on board the steamship, and those on board the steamship neglected, for some time after they heard the fog-horn, to stop or reverse the engines. The steamship was held to blame. The bark was held to be deemed in fault for not using a fog-horn, to be sounded by mechanical means, as required by article 12 of the Regulations for Preventing Collisions at Sea, 1879.

19. The circumstance that the bark left port a few days before the regulations came into force was held not to afford any valid excuse for the neglect of those in charge of her to furnish her with a fog-horn, to be sounded by mechanical means, they well knowing, before she left port, that the regulations would come into force in a few days, and there being no evidence to show that they could not have obtained a fog-horn according to the regulations, before she left port. *The Love Bird*. 525

20. The 22d and 23d rules for the navigation of the Thames are not inconsistent, and the intention is that when the 23d rule (as to passing a point) applies, the case for the 22d (as to porting) shall not arise, but if the case does arise the rule will apply.

21. A steam vessel coming down the Thames against tide to a point on the north shore, and being nearer to mid-channel than to the north shore, eased and, then seeing danger of collision with a vessel coming up with tide, starboarded and reversed. The other vessel was coming up with the tide

also near the north shore and rounded the point under a port helm; seeing the other vessel, she ported hard, and stopped, but a collision occurred:

Held, that under the circumstances the 22d rule applied, and that the vessel which had starboarded was to blame.

22. By Jessel, M.R., and Brett, L.J. (Cotton, L.J., doubting), that under the 23d rule the vessel navigating against tide is to wait until she has been passed by the other vessel, and not merely until the other vessel has passed the point. *The Libra*. 559

23. A sailing ship in a gale drove from her anchors across a sand, and her rudder was so damaged as to render the ship unmanageable; in this condition she came into collision after sunset with a brig at anchor. At the time of the collision the ship had her anchor light exhibited and no other light. In an action of damage by the owners of the brig against the ship it was held that the collision was occasioned by inevitable accident, and that the ship in the circumstances of the case was not to be deemed in fault for not carrying side lights or the three red lights prescribed by Article 5 of the Regulations for Preventing Collisions at Sea, and that the suit ought to be dismissed without costs. *The Buckhurst*. 571

24. A ship does not, by carrying a fixed white binnacle light in such a position as to be reflected astern, comply with the provisions of the eleventh article of the Regulations for Preventing Collisions at Sea, which provides that a ship which is being overtaken by another shall show from her stern to such last mentioned ship a white light or a flare-up light. *The Breadalbane*. 720

See COSTS, 70, 386, 733.
　　　DAMAGES, 575.
　　　INTERNATIONAL LAW, 567.
　　　JURISDICTION, 282.
　　　PILOT, 63, 69 *note*.
　　　SALVAGE, 617.

COMMENCEMENT.

See ONUS, 275, 276 *note*.

COMMON.

1. A fold-course is not a several right to the herbage, but a right of common appurtenant of pasture for sheep.

2. Lords of manor can by the Statute of Merton approve against common appurtenant of pasture. The proviso in the Statute of Westminster the Second, c. 46, only prevents derogation from an express grant.

3. A demise of " all that warren of conies in L.:"
Held, by Fry, J., under the circumstances, to pass the soil of the warren and not merely a franchise. *Robinson* v. *Duleep Singh.* 837

COMPROMISE.

See MARRIED WOMEN, 604.

CONDONATION.

1. A husband had been guilty of cruelty and the wife had stipulated in a deed of separation not to take any proceedings against him in respect of that cruelty. He subsequently committed adultery:
Held, following the case of *Gandy* v. *Gandy* (ante, p. 704) that the subsequent adultery did not revive the wife's right to complain of the cruelty. *Rose* v. *Rose.* 755

CONSOLIDATION.

1. In a case where two actions of salvage were instituted, on behalf of plaintiffs having adverse interests against the same vessel, to recover salvage reward in respect of services rendered on the same occasion, the court, on the plaintiffs refusing to consent to a consolidation order, allowed the defendants to make a single tender in respect of the claims in both actions. *The Jacob Landstrom.* 228

CONDITIONS.

1. A testatrix, by will, dated in 1845, limited to a daughter an exclusive power of appointment by will amongst her children. The daughter, by her will, dated in 1874, in exercise of the power, appointed the fund amongst the objects of the power in certain shares, giving to two of her daughters life interests only, and declared that if either during her life or after her death any son or daughter of hers should marry a person who did not profess the Jewish religion, or was not born a Jew though converted to Judaism, or should forsake the Jewish and adopt the Christian or any other religion, then such son or daughter should forfeit all share in the fund, and in case of forfeiture the forfeited share was to accrue and go over to the other or others of the children living at the time of the forfeiture.
Julius, a son of the appointor, married a Christian in his mother's lifetime, but without her consent. The plaintiff, one of the two daughters of the appointor, to whom a life interest only was appointed, became a Christian after the mother's death.
Both Julius and the plaintiff were born after the death of the creator of the power :
Held, first, that the forfeiture clause was not void as against public policy :

2. Secondly, that it was effectual as to the shares of children marrying Christians or becoming Christians during the lifetime of the appointor, and therefore that the share of Julius was forfeited :

3. Thirdly, that the forfeiture clause must be read in conjunction with the gift over, and therefore that, so far as it affected, after the death of the appointor, the share of a child born after the death of the creator of the power, it was void for remoteness, whether such share was appointed for life only or absolutely, and consequently that the plaintiff had not forfeited her share. *Hodgson* v. *Halford.* 918, 925 *note*.

CONDITIONAL WILLS.

See WILLS, 474, 476 *note*.

CO-OWNERS.

See PARTITION, 76, 80 note.

CORPORATIONS.

See STOCKHOLDERS, 778.

CORPUS.

See LIFE ESTATE, 870, 878 note.

COSTS.

1. The defendants in an action for damage, before any statement of claim had been delivered, admitted their liability for the damage proceeded for, and by consent the question of amount was by an order of court referred to the registrar and merchants to report thereon. At the reference before the registrar the plaintiffs claimed as damages £295 18s. 1d. The registrar reported to the court that there was due to the plaintiffs £199 18s. 6d.
    Afterwards the plaintiffs moved the judge to condemn the defendants in the costs of the action and of the reference. Evidence was given on affidavit in support of the motion to the effect that the plaintiffs at the time their action was instituted were liable to a claim for salvage in respect of services rendered to their vessel after the collision, and that subsequently and before the reference £60 had been paid and accepted in settlement of such claim:
    Held, that the court had jurisdiction to certify that the case was a fit case to be tried before it, and that the proper order to be made was that the plaintiffs should have the costs of the action, but that each party should bear their own costs of the reference. The Williamina.   70

2. In a case where the defendants, in two actions of salvage instituted against the same property, were ordered to pay only one set of costs, to be apportioned between the plaintiffs in the two actions, the court directed that the apportionment should be made according

to the amounts of the plaintiffs' respective bills of costs. The Pasithea.   262

3. The costs of the reference as to damages in an action of damages do not follow the costs of the action, but are in the discretion of the judge as the costs of a fresh litigation.

4. Where, therefore, an action had been brought by the owners of a ship and the owners of the cargo against another ship for collision, and both ships had been held to blame, and the judge afterwards gave the plaintiffs the owners of the cargo the costs of the reference, the Court of Appeal refused to interfere with his order. The Consett.   305

5. An action of damage was brought by the owners of the ship V. against the ship S., and the owners of the S. claimed damages by way of counterclaim against the V. At the hearing of the action the court found both ships to blame for the collision, condemned the owners of each ship in a moiety of the damage sustained by the other, referred the question of damages to the registrar and merchants and made no order as to costs. Afterwards the owners of the S. brought their counterclaim into the registry. No tender was made by the owners of the V., and the registrar struck off less than one-ninth of the amount claimed, but made no recommendation as to the costs of the reference:
    The court, on the application of the owners of the S., condemned the owners of the V. in the costs of and incident to the reference. The Savernake.   386

6. In a divorce suit the usual order had been obtained for securing the wife's costs of the hearing, and there had been no appeal from that order and no further costs were asked for at the hearing. Subsequently the case of Robertson v. Robertson (6 P. D., 119) was decided in the Court of Appeal, and the Divorce Court was thereupon asked to order payment of the wife's full costs. Application refused.

7. In future, if in a divorce suit in which a wife is found guilty the court is asked to order payment of her full costs, the court will postpone its decision until after her bill of costs has been taxed. Smith v. Smith.   641

kin being filed, ordered the grant to be made to H. K. L.　*Goods of Hastings.*　168

2. The administrator (with will annexed) of the estate of a married woman does not as such represent an estate of which she was executrix. E. C. S., surviving executrix of W. B., made, while covert, a will, and appointed J. S. her executor. J. S. was also solely entitled to all the estate of E. C. S., of which E. C. S. had no disposing power: *Held,* that J. S., as administrator (with will) of E. C. S., did not represent W. B.—Grant of letters of administration (with will) *de bonis non* of W. B. given to R. F., a residuary legatee under that will. *Goods of Bridger.*　170

3. A testator gave to W. F. B. and H. H. W. all his real and personal estate to apply the same, "after payment of debts," to the payment of legacies.

4. The court granted probate to W. F. B. and H. H. W. as executors according to the tenor. *Goods of Bell.*　170

5. The sole executrix and universal legatee, having died in the testator's lifetime, and the next of kin being abroad, the court granted letters of administration with the will annexed, to the guardian of persons entitled in distribution. *Goods of Lee.*　·　178

6. Administration bond allowed to be executed by foreigners resident abroad, upon proof that the administrator was unable to obtain sureties resident here, that the deceased had no debts unpaid, and that the person on whose behalf the letters of administration were applied for was solely entitled to the estate in this country. *Goods of Fernandez.*　259

7. W. E. died possessed of property of small value in this country, and entitled under the will of J. O. E. to large assets in Scotland, which were being duly administered there. The executors of W. E. proved his will in Scotland only. G. W. H., a legatee under W. E.'s will, applied for a grant of administration of the estate of W. E. in this country, which application was opposed by the executors:

Held, that the court is not bound to make such a grant, but that its power is discretionary:

8. *Held,* also, that it not having been shown that the executors were not doing their duty there was no necessity for any grant in this country. Application refused.

9. A similar application was made by another legatee upon the ground also that such a grant was necessary to substantiate proceedings in chancery.

10. Application refused, on its being proved that the grant was not necessary for the suit in chancery. *Goods of Ewing.*　476

11. A legatee who has propounded a codicil and succeeded is entitled to the same costs as an executor under similar circumstances.

12. The defendant, the executor of the will of R. C., had proved the will only. The plaintiffs propounded a codicil. The court having pronounced for the codicil, condemned the defendant in costs, and gave the plaintiffs also out of the estate such sum *nomine expensarum* as would cover the additional expenses. *Wilkinson v. Corfield.*　483

13. The duties of an administrator and receiver pending suit commence from the date of the order of appointment, and if the decree in the action is appealed from, do not cease until the appeal has been disposed of.

14. Costs of the administrator and receiver pending suit and of his solicitor allowed from the date of the appointment until the dismissal of the appeal. *Taylor v. Taylor.*　485

15. An assignee in bankruptcy of an administrator who is out of the jurisdiction is a creditor within the meaning of 38 Geo. 3, c. 87, s. 1, and 21 & 22 Vict. c. 95, s. 18, and as such may obtain administration *de bonis non* of the intestate limited to the fund to which the assignee is entitled. *Matter of Hammond.*　535

16. J. W., entitled to the property of his wife, E. W., who predeceased him, became indebted to the estate of J. P.

The estate of E. W. afterwards became entitled to a share in the residuary estate of J. P.

The executrix of J. W. refused to take out letters of administration to E. W.'s estate, and a grant was necessary to enable the creditors of J. W. to obtain E. W.'s share of the residuary estate in satisfaction of their debt:

The court granted (under s. 73 of 20 & 21 Vict. c. 77) administration of the estate of E. W. to a creditor of J. W. *Wensley.* 613

See EVIDENCE, 260.
RENUNCIATION.

EXEMPTION.

See ALIMONY, 162.

EXPERTS.

See ACCIDENT, 579

F.

FORCE.

See UNDUE INFLUENCE.

FOREIGN JUDGMENT.

See LIEN, 536.

FOREIGN LAW.

See EVIDENCE, 466, 468 *note.*

FOREIGN VESSEL.

See BOTTOMRY, 680.

FOREIGN WILLS.

See EXECUTORS AND ADMINISTRATORS, 476.
PROBATE, 169.
WILLS, 596.

FORMER SUIT.

1. A collision took place between the ship S. and the C., which was being towed by a tug. The owners of the S. brought an action against the owners of the C., alleging the collision to have been occasioned by the negligence of the C. and her tug, or one of them. The owners of the C. obtained leave to serve notice on the owner of the tug that they claimed to be entitled to indemnity, and the court made an order that the owner of the tug should be at liberty to appear and defend, " being bound as between him and the defendants by any decision the court may come to in this action as to the cause of collision." At the hearing the owner of the tug appeared, but the defendants did not, and the judge of the Admiralty Court pronounced that the collision was occasioned by the default of the master and crew of the C., and condemned the owners in damages and costs, and declared that they were not entitled to indemnity from the owner of the tug :

Held, on appeal, that the order giving the owner of the tug liberty to appear and defend did not put matters in train for trying any issue between him and the defendants, and that so much of the judgment as negatived the right to indemnity by the owner of the tug must be struck out. *The Cartsburn.* 297

See ESTOPPEL, 837.

FRAUD.

See STOCKHOLDERS, 778.

FREIGHT.

1. By the abandonment of a ship by its crew during a voyage, without any intention to retake possession, a right is

given to the owner of cargo on board to treat the contract of affreightment as at an end.

A ship with a cargo of resin in barrels, on a voyage from America to Rotterdam, was, owing to the perils of the sea, abandoned by her crew off the American coast. She was afterwards saved by another vessel, and brought with her cargo by the salvors into a port in England, and there arrested in an action for salvage by her salvors. Before the shipowner had released the ship or cargo, the owners of the cargo applied for and obtained from the Admiralty Court an order for the release of the cargo to them without payment of any freight, upon their giving bail to the salvors :

Held, that the cargo owners were entitled to treat the contract of affreightment as at an end, and that therefore the order of the Admiralty Court was rightly made. *The Cito.*   606

See CHARTERPARTY.

G.

GUARDIAN.

See INFANTS, 763.

H.

HEIRS.

1. Meaning of.   173

HUSBAND AND WIFE.

1. A married woman has the same equity to a settlement, as against her husband or his general assignee, out of property in which she has only a life interest, as out of property in which she has an absolute interest; and the court will make no distinction between the two cases as regards the amount to be settled. In every case the court will exercise its judicial discretion as to the

amount to be settled, having regard to all the circumstances.

A husband became insolvent in 1861 to a large amount, and his estate paid no dividend. In 1876 his wife became entitled to the income of property amounting to £500 a year.

The Court (affirming the decision of Malins, V.C.), ordered the whole income to be settled on the wife. *Taunton v. Morris.*   818

See MARRIAGE.
　　MARRIED WOMEN, 533.
　　SETTLEMENTS, 801.

I.

ILLEGAL RESTRAINT.

See CONDITIONS, 918, 925 *note.*

ILLEGITIMACY.

See LEGITIMACY.

IMPOTENCE.

See DIVORCE, 472.

INCOME.

See LIFE ESTATE, 870, 878 *note.*

INFANTS.

1. When a will is disputed by a guardian *ad litem* on behalf of infants, the Court of Probate has power to inquire whether the suit is for their benefit. *Percival v. Cross.*   763

See MARRIED WOMEN, 604.

INJUNCTION.

1. A petitioner had obtained a decree *nisi* for dissolution of his marriage. Before an order could be obtained to vary the post-nuptial settlement, the respondent was about to sell or otherwise dispose of some of the property. The court granted an injunction to restrain her from dealing with it. *Noakes* v. *Noakes.* 158

See NUISANCE, 837, 850 *note.*

INSANITY.

See LUNATIC, 364, 373 *note.*

INSPECTION.

See DISCOVERY, 85.

INTEREST

1. The master of a Danish vessel being without funds or credit at Hamburgh, in order to obtain necessaries to enable his vessel to proceed on a voyage to Africa and back to London, obtained a loan on the security of instruments by which he pledged his vessel and bound himself for the repayment of the sum advanced within six days after the arrival of the vessel in London. No stipulation was made for interest of any kind:
Held, in an action of bottomry instituted against the vessel, that the instruments were valid bottomry bonds, and that the holders were entitled to payment out of the proceeds of the vessel of the sum advanced together with 4 per cent. interest from the time when the bonds became due. *The Cecilie.* 240

See BOTTOMRY, 138, 141.

INTERLINEATIONS.

1. The initials of a testatrix and the attesting witnesses in the margin of the will opposite interlineations are sufficient to render the interlineations valid. *Goods of Blewitt.* 859

See WILLS, 531.

INTERNATIONAL LAW.

1. As a consequence of the absolute independence of every sovereign authority and of the international comity which induces every sovereign state to respect the independence of every other sovereign state, each state declines to exercise by means of any of its courts any of its territorial jurisdiction over the person of any sovereign or ambassador, or over the public property of any state which is destined to its public use, or over the property of any ambassador, though such sovereign, ambassador, or property be within its territory:
Held, therefore, reversing the decision of the Admiralty Division, that an unarmed packet belonging to the sovereign of a foreign state, and in the hands of officers commissioned by him, and employed in carrying mails, is not liable to be seized in a suit *in rem* to recover redress for a collision, and this immunity is not lost by reason of the packet's also carrying merchandise and passengers for hire. *The Parlement Belge.* 415

2. In an action *in personam*, brought by the owners of a British vessel against the owners of a Spanish vessel to recover damages caused to the British vessel by collision with the Spanish vessel on the high seas, the defendants pleaded that they were Spanish subjects, and that if there was any negligence on the part of those in charge of the Spanish vessel it was negligence for which the master and crew alone, and not the defendants, were liable according to the law of Spain:
Held, bad on demurrer. *The Leon.* 567

See BOTTOMRY, 680.
JURISDICTION, 147.
LIEN, 586.

INTERPRETATION.

See WILLS.

INTERVENERS.

See FORMER SUIT, 297.

INTOXICATION.

See WAGES, 459.

J.

JOINT OWNERS.

See PARTITION, 76, 80 *note.*

JUDGMENT.

See LIEN, 536.
RECEIVER, 439.

JURISDICTION.

1. A vessel of war commissioned by the government of a foreign state, and engaged in the national service of her government, was stranded on the coast of England. She had a cargo of machinery on board her, alleged to belong to private individuals, of which her government had for public purposes charged itself with the care and protection. Important and efficient salvage services were rendered to the ship and her cargo. A suit was instituted on behalf of certain of the salvors against the ship and her cargo. The court refused to order a warrant to issue for the arrest of the ship or cargo, and held it had no jurisdiction to entertain the suit. *The Constitution.* 147

2. A wife's remedy for matrimonial wrongs must be usually sought in the place of her husband's domicile.

3. The English Divorce Court has not jurisdiction against a foreigner, after he has quitted this country, for not rendering conjugal rights to his wife while he was here.

4. The provisions of the 42d section of 20 & 21 Vict. c. 85 (for service out of Her Majesty's dominions) do not apply to suits for restitution of conjugal rights. *Firebrace* v. *Firebrace.* 156

5. In an action of damage between two vessels, the court has jurisdiction, under Order XVI, to determine whether or not the defendants' vessel is entitled to indemnity against a tug by which she was being towed at the time of the collision.

6. A collision took place between the vessels S. and C. The C. at the time was being towed by a tug. The owners of the S. instituted an action of damage against the C., and alleged in their statement of claim that the collision was caused by the negligence of the C. and her tug, or of one of them. The owners of the C. obtained leave to issue a notice to the tug that they claimed to be entitled to indemnity, and the court made an order that the owners of the tug be at liberty to appear and defend, being bound by any decision the court might come to as to the cause of the collision.
At the hearing the owners of the tug appeared, but the defendants did not, and the court pronounced that the C. was alone to blame for the collision, and that her owners were not entitled to indemnity over against the owners of the tug :
Held, on motion on behalf of the owners of the C. to rescind so much of the judgment as pronounced that the owners of the C. were not entitled to indemnity, that the court had not exceeded its jurisdiction. *The Cartsburn.* 282

7. The court has jurisdiction to arrest a vessel in an action of restraint at the suit of a part owner holding a minority of shares, notwithstanding that the vessel is about to proceed on a voyage approved of by a minority of the part owners, and is being employed under a charter entered into by the ship's husband, appointed to act on behalf of all the owners. *The Talca.* 388

8. A court having county court admiralty jurisdiction under the County Courts

Admiralty Acts, 1868 and 1869, has jurisdiction to try and determine an action at the suit of the holder of a bill of lading against a British ship to recover for a breach of the contract of carriage in the bill of lading, notwithstanding that it is shown to the court that at the time of the institution of the suit the owner of the ship proceeded against was domiciled in England or Wales. *The Rona.* 773

> *See* COLLISION, 282.
> DIVORCE, 112, 133 *note.*
> LIEN, 536.

L.

LANDLORD AND TENANT.

See RENT, 879, 881 *note.*

LAW.

See EVIDENCE, 466, 468 *note.*

LEGACY.

See CONDITIONS, 918, 925 *note.*
WILLS

LEGITIMACY.

1. In a petition under the Legitimacy Declaration Act the petitioner may allege that he claims real estate, and may also state how he claims it, but he cannot allege, or pray for a declaration, that he is entitled to such estate to the exclusion of some other person, e.g., by reason of the illegitimacy of the person.

2. A petitioner alleged that he claimed real estate as heir-at-law of his father, and that E. B. M. also claimed to be such heir-at-law. Leave to cite E. B. M.

was refused on the ground that E. B. M. was not interested in disputing the only facts which the court was competent to determine, i.e., the legitimacy of the petitioner or the marriage of his parents.

3. The court has power to amend the pleadings at any time, and, if necessary, to order allegations to be reinserted which it had previously directed to be struck out. *Manuel v. Attorney-General.* 261

LEX LOCI.

See BOTTOMRY, 680.
INTERNATIONAL LAW, 567.
MARRIAGE.
WILLS, 596.

LIABILITY.

See LIMITED LIABILITY, 548, 558 *note.*

LIEN.

1. Of attorney, for services, by agreement in salvage cases. *The Afrika.* 409

2. The plaintiffs, in an action of necessaries against a foreign ship, having at the request of the master advanced money to pay dock dues for the ship at the port of discharge, were held to be entitled to have the amount they had so advanced paid out of the proceeds of the ship in priority to the claim of a bottomry bondholder who had advanced money on bottomry at the port of loading. *The St. Lawrence.* 456

3. The plaintiffs brought an action and obtained judgment in the Tribunal of Commerce at Lisbon against the captain and owners of a British ship for damages for injury caused by a collision with the plaintiffs' ship. The Portuguese courts recognize no distinction between actions *in personam* and actions *in rem.* The defendants' ship having come into a British court the

plaintiffs commenced an action *in rem* against the ship, claiming to enforce the judgment of the Portuguese court against it, and arrested the ship:

Held, reversing the decision of Sir R. Phillimore, that the action in the Portuguese court was a personal action, and that the writ in the present action and all proceedings under it must be set aside, the court having no jurisdiction to enforce a judgment in a personal action by proceedings *in rem*.

4. All civilized nations recognize the validity of maritime lien, and will enforce it when it has been declared by a foreign court; but it is essential that it should appear from the proceedings of the foreign court that the object of the suit was the sale of the ship, and not a personal remedy against the captain or owners. *The City of Mecca*. 536

See ALIMONY, 757.

LIFE ESTATE.

1. A testator empowered his trustees to make demises of his estate for building purposes, and also at their discretion to sell his real and personal estate, and directed them to invest the proceeds, and the rents, issues, and profits of his estate, and to set apart a sufficient part ·of such investments to produce an annuity of £1,200, which he bequeathed to his wife for her life, payable on the usual quarter days; and he gave the entire residue of his said trust estate, and also that part thereof set apart for his wife after her death, upon certain trusts for the benefit of his children. The income of the estate was not sufficient to provide for the widow's annuity of £1,200:

Held (reversing the decision of Hall, V.C.), that the widow was entitled to have the deficiency raised out of the corpus of the trust estate. *Gee* v. *Mahood.*   870, 878 *note.*

See APPORTIONMENT, 882.

LIGHTS.

See COLLISION.

LIMITED LIABILITY.

1. The owners of a German steam vessel instituted an action under the Merchant Shipping Act, 1862, s. 54, to limit their liability for damages occasioned by a collision. The vessel had three decks, and her crew were berthed below the spar deck. By Order in Council, dated the 26th of June, 1873, made under s. 60 of the same act, it was directed that German steamships measured after the 1st of January, 1873, should be deemed to be of the tonnage mentioned in their registers in the same manner, and to the same extent, as the tonnage denoted in the certificate of registry of British ships was deemed to be their tonnage. In the register of this ship the crew space was deducted:

Held, by the judge of the Court of Admiralty, that in estimating the tonnage for the purpose of limitation of liability the crew space must be deducted.

2. *Held*, by the Court of Appeal, that the Order in Council of the 26th of June, 1873, did not make the certificate of registry conclusive evidence of the tonnage or of the propriety of deducting the space solely appropriated for berthing the crew.

3. *Held*, further, that under the Merchant Shipping Act, 1854, s. 21, subs. 4, a closed-in space, solely appropriated to the berthing of the crew, is to be excepted in estimating the tonnage only when it is on the upper deck, and not when it is between the spar deck and the tonnage deck.

4. *Held*, also, that the crew space cannot in the case of a foreign, any more than of a British, ship, be deducted under the "Merchant Shipping Act, 1867," s. 9, unless the provisions of that section as to inspection by a surveyor appointed by the Board of Trade, and the other conditions therein contained, have been complied with; and therefore, that, as in the present case these conditions had not been complied with, the space appropriated for berthing the crew must not be deducted. *The Franconia.*   87

5. A newly built vessel, exceeding fifteen tons burden, on being launched, ran

into and damaged a passing ship. The owners of the 'damaged ship thereupon instituted an action in this court against the newly built vessel to recover for the damage done to their ship, and this court pronounced the vessel proceeded against solely to blame for the collision. Afterwards an action of limitation of liability was instituted by the owner of the newly built vessel, a natural born English subject, who therein claimed a declaration that he was entitled to a limitation of liability in respect of damage occasioned by the collision.

At the hearing of the action it appeared that the newly built vessel, though registered as a British ship at the time of the institution of the action, was not so registered at the time of the collision:

Held, that the vessel was not a "recognized British ship" when the collision occurred, and that her owner was not entitled to have his liability limited. *The Andalusian.* 103

6. In an action of collision in the Admiralty Division, where both ships have been injured and both ships have been held to blame, and have accordingly been condemned to pay the moiety of each other's damage, and either of the parties to the collision has applied to have his liability limited under the Merchant Shipping Act, 1862, s. 54, no set-off is allowed between the two amounts for which they are liable in damages, until the limitation of liability imposed by that statute has been applied.

The S. and V. came into collision, both ships were damaged, but the V. was sunk, with her cargo, and lost. In an action by the owners of the V. and counter-claim by the owners of the S., both ships were held to blame and condemned to pay the moiety of each other's damage. Under this judgment the damage payable by the S. was £14,000, and that payable by the V. was £2,000. The owners of the S. then brought an action in the Chancery Division for limitation of their liability, and paid into court £5,212, the aggregate amount of £8 a ton on her registered tonnage:

Held (Brett, L.J., dissenting), that the owners of the V. must prove for £14,000 against the fund in court, and

must pay the £2,000 in full to the owners of the S.

The judgment of Jessel, M.R., on this point reversed :

7. *Held*, also, by Jessel, M.R., that the owners of the V. and the owners of the cargo, or the underwriters in their place, and the master and crew of the same ship, must prove *pari passu* against the fund in court in respect of the moiety of their respective losses. *Chapman* v. *Royal Netherlands, etc.* 200

8. Although the plaintiff in an action for limitation of liability is ordinarily liable to pay the costs of the action, yet, if the defendants raise unnecessary issues on which they fail, he is entitled to the costs of those issues, and he will not be ordered to pay the costs occasioned by a dispute between rival claimants to the proceeds in court.

9. The master of the ship C., bound from Philadelphia to Antwerp, obtained at Philadelphia from M. a loan of money on freight upon the security of an instrument signed by him, by which it was stipulated that the loan should be repaid after arrival of the C. at Antwerp or other intermediate port at which the voyage should end, and that if there should be no payment of freight the loan should not be paid back.

10. The C., whilst on the course of her voyage to Antwerp, came into collision with another ship and sank, and her cargo was lost. The collision was occasioned by the negligence of those in charge of the other ship, and her owners instituted an action for limitation of their liability. In such action a sum of money was awarded out of the proceeds paid into court to the owners of the C. for loss of freight. M. claimed a portion of this sum in respect of his loan :

Held, that his claim was well founded.

11. *Semble*, where in an action for limitation of liability a sum of money is awarded as compensation for loss of freight to the owners of a vessel run down by the plaintiff's ship, the holder of a bottomry bond on the freight of the vessel run down is entitled to claim, in respect of the loan on bottomry, a

portion of the sum awarded for loss of freight. *The Empusa.*   263

12. The payment into court of £8 a ton under 25 & 26 Vict. c. 63, s. 54, does not place the shipowner in the position of a person who has not done wrong.

13. The owner of a ship sunk by a collision in the Thames admitted it to be his fault, and paid into court £8 a ton in a suit to limit his liability. The Thames Conservators, having powers under the Removal of Wrecks Act, 1877, and the Thames Conservancy Acts, raised the ship and delivered the ship and cargo to the owner, he undertaking to pay the expenses of raising. Part of the cargo was some wool, which was damaged by being sunk:

Held, that the shipowner was bound to deliver the wool to the owner of the wool without claiming from him, by way of contribution to salvage, any part of the expenses of raising the ship and cargo.

14. Where a public body has powers under two acts, it must be taken to have proceeded under that which gave it most advantages. *The Ettrick.*   548, 558 *note.*

15. In a suit of limitation of liability in respect of damage arising from a collision, the shipowners claimed deductions on account of crew space which appeared on the register of their vessel at the time of their application for a decree :

Held, that they were not entitled to the benefit of any deductions not appearing on the register in force at the time of the collision. *The John McIntyre.*   586

LIMITATIONS, STATUTE OF.

See NUISANCES, 837, 850 *note.*

LOG-BOOK.

See EVIDENCE, 80.

LOOK–OUT.

See COLLISION.

LUNATIC.

1. The lunacy of a husband or wife is not a bar to a suit by the committee for the dissolution of the lunatic's marriage.

2. Such a suit may be instituted by the committee of the estate of the lunatic. *Baker* v. *Baker.*   364, 373 *note.*

3. The lunacy of a husband or wife is not a bar to a suit by the committee for the dissolution of the lunatic's marriage.

4. Such a suit may be instituted by the committee of the lunatic. *Baker* v. *Baker.*   471

See ALIMONY, 51.
      EXECUTORS AND ADMINISTRATORS, 168.
      TRUSTS AND TRUSTEES, 870.

M.

MAINTENANCE.

See ALIMONY.

MARRIED WOMEN.

1. A will was made by a married woman who appointed her husband one of the executors. He assented to the making of the will, and after her death expressed his intention to take probate, but died before doing so :

Held, that he had assented to the probate. *Goods of Cooper.*   488

2. A will of a married woman made during coverture, under a power and disposing of real property only, is not entitled to probate, though there is an appointment of executors.

3. The Judicature Acts do not alter the jurisdiction of the Court of Probate in

non-contentious matters. *Matter of Goods of Tomlinson.* 594

4. *Semble.* In an action as to the validity of a will when terms of compromise are agreed to by the parties who are *sui juris,* the Court of Probate will not make an order binding married women or infants to the terms of a compromise. *Norman* v. *Strains.* 604

5. A married woman having a power of appointment over real property executed the power in favor of herself. She afterwards made her will, by which she directed (amongst other things) that a portion of the property should be sold to pay legacies and to erect a memorial window. She also appointed an executor. There were arrears of rent due at the time of her death and subsequently:

Held, that as she possessed the property as separate estate, and had appointed an executor and directed him to pay the legacies, &c., and as the arrears of rent were part of her personal estate, the will was entitled to probate. *Brownrigg* v. *Pike.* 626

See ALIMONY, 51.
EXECUTORS AND ADMINISTRATORS, 170.
HUSBAND AND WIFE, 818.
SETTLEMENTS, 801.

MARRIAGE.

1. The petitioner and respondent, Portuguese subjects domiciled in Portugal, and first cousins to each other, came to reside in England in 1858, and in 1866 they went through a form of marriage before the registrar of the district of the city of London. In 1873 they returned to Portugal, and their domicile throughout continued to be Portuguese. By the law of Portugal a marriage between first cousins is illegal, as being incestuous, but may be celebrated under a Papal dispensation:

Held, reversing the decision of the court below, that the parties being by the law of the country of their domicile under a personal disability to contract marriage, their marriage ought to be declared null and void. *Sottomayor* v. *Sottomayor.* 1, 7 *note.*

2. Two persons domiciled in England arrived in Scotland about 4 A.M. of the 1st of July, 1870, remained there until the 21st following, and between 11 and 12 A.M. of that day contracted a marriage by declaration before a registrar:

Held, that they had not lived in Scotland for twenty-one days next preceding the marriage, and that therefore it was invalid. *Lawford* v. *Davies.* 154

3. The validity of a marriage in England must, though the domicile of one of the parties may be foreign, be decided according to the law of England.

4. Marriage is based upon the contract of the parties, but is a status arising out of the contract to which each country is entitled to attach its own conditions, both as to its creation and duration.

5. G. B., a Portuguese, but domiciled in England, married in England I. S., a Portuguese lady, domiciled in Portugal. They were first cousins, and by the law of Portugal first cousins are, except by dispensation from the Pope, incapable of contracting marriage:

Held, by the English Divorce Court, that the marriage was lawful:

6. *Held,* also, that ignorance of the parties, as to the effects of Portuguese law upon the validity of the ceremony, could not affect the validity of the marriage. *Sottomayor* v. *De Barros.* 336

7. The English Divorce Court will recognize as valid the decree of a Scotch court dissolving the marriage of a domiciled Scotchman and an English woman, although the marriage was solemnized in England, and the marriage was dissolved upon a ground for which by English law no divorce could have been granted.

The question of divorce is not an incident of the marriage contract to be governed by the *lex loci contractus,* but is an incident of status to be disposed of by the law of the domicile of the parties—that is, of the husband's. *Harvey* v. *Farnie.* 489

See CONDITIONS, 918, 925 *note.*
DIVORCE.
LUNATIC, 364, 873 *note.*

MASTER.

See WAGES, 459.

MASTER OF SHIP.

See COUNTER-CLAIM, 301.

MASTER AND SERVANT.

See PILOT.

MISTAKE.

See WILLS, 590, 591, 601, 602 *note*, 633.

MORGUE.

See MORTUARY, 289.

MORTGAGE.

See CHATTEL MORTGAGE.

MORTGAGOR.

1. When may charter ship. *The Fanchon.* 397

MORTUARY.

1. The rector, churchwardens and burial board of an urban parish applied for the grant of a faculty to authorize the erection of a parochial mortuary with a post mortem room attached, in a consecrated burial ground situate in a populous part of the parish, and closed for burials by Order in Council. The court being of opinion that the petitioners had made out their case for the establishment of a mortuary on the site proposed, directed that a faculty should issue for the erection of the mortuary, but directed that certain conditions to be specified in the faculty should be imposed with respect to the manner of using the mortuary. *Rector, etc.*, v. *Hall.* 289

N.

NAVIGABLE RIVERS.

See NEGLIGENCE, 692, 701 *note*.

NECESSARIES.

See LIEN, 456.

NEGLIGENCE.

1. The D. in consequence of the sole default of her master and crew had sunk in the Thames, and had become a wreck obstructing the navigation of the river. Her mate sent a message to the harbormaster at G. to inform him of the accident, who said that he would cause the wreck to be lighted. A few hours afterwards, the wreck not having been lighted, a vessel without any fault on the part of those on board her came into collision with the wreck and sustained damage. An action of damage having been instituted on behalf of the owner of the damaged vessel against the owners of the D., the judge at the trial refused to admit the evidence showing that the mate of the D. had sent a message to the harbor-master, and that the latter had promised to light the wreck:

Held, that the evidence was wrongly rejected, that the collision had not been caused by the negligence of the owners of the wreck, and that they were not liable for the damage done. *The Douglas.* 692, 701 *note*.

2. An error of judgment on the part of the master of a vessel at a moment of great difficulty and danger does not amount to a wrongful act or default, within the meaning of the 242d section

of the Merchant Shipping Act, 1854, so as to justify the suspension or cancellation of the master's certificate. *The Famenoth.* 738, 747 *note.*

NEGLIGENCE.

See ATTORNEYS, 84.
   COLLISION.
   COUNTER-CLAIM, 301.
   JURISDICTION, 282.
   PILOT.
   SALVAGE, 292.
   WATER AND WATERCOURSES, 821.

NOTICE.

1. Disputes having arisen between the plaintiff and W. whether a window in the plaintiff's house overlooking W.'s land was an ancient light, an agreement, not under seal, was signed by which W. agreed that the plaintiff should have access of light to the window, and the plaintiff agreed to keep the window opaque and make it open only in such a way that no person could look out of it. W.'s land was afterwards sold to the defendant, who had no actual notice of the agreement, but knew of the existence of the window:
Held, by Hall, V.C., that the defendant, seeing the window when he purchased, was put upon inquiry, and was affected with constructive notice of the agreement, and therefore must be restrained from interfering with the access of light to the window.

2. *Held,* on appeal, that the mere fact of there being windows in an adjoining house which overlook a purchased property is not constructive notice of any agreement giving a right to the access of light to them. *Allen* v. *Seckham.* 830

   See FORMER SUIT, 297.
   SERVICE, 231, 233 *note.*

NUISANCES.

1 User which is neither physically capable of prevention by the owner of the servient tenement, nor actionable, can-

not support an easement. And this is applicable both to affirmative and negative easements.

2. On this principle the right to make a noise so as to annoy a neighbor cannot be supported by user unless during the period of user the noise has amounted to an actionable nuisance.

3. In considering whether any act is a nuisance, regard must be had not only to the thing done, but to the surrounding circumstances. What would be a nuisance in one locality might not be so in another.

4. A confectioner had for more than twenty years used a pestle and mortar in his back premises, which abutted on the garden of a physician, and the noise and vibration were not felt as a nuisance and were not complained of. But in 1873 the physician erected a consulting-room at the end of his garden, and then the noise and vibration became a nuisance to him. He accordingly brought an action for an injunction :
Held (affirming the decision of Jessel, M.R.), that the defendant had not acquired a right to an easement of making a noise and vibration, and the injunction was granted. *Sturges* v. *Bridgman.* 837, 850 *note.*

O.

ONUS.

1. In a testamentary suit the party propounding the last will is entitled to begin. So also is a party who alleges only undue influence, in opposition to the validity of a will. *Hutley* v. *Grimstone.* 275, 276 *note.*

2. The burden of proving capacity to make a will rests upon those who propound the will, and, *a fortiori,* when it appears that the testator was subject to delusions. *Smee* v. *Smee.* 311, 819 *note.*

ORDINANCES.

See REGULATIONS, 624.

PART OWNERS.

See JURISDICTION, 388.
PARTITION, 76, 80 note.

PENSION.

See ALIMONY, 162.

PILOT.

1. A duly qualified Liverpool pilot having been employed to pilot a ship from sea into the Mersey and take her into dock, piloted her over the bar, but owing to the state of the tide being unable to dock her that day, anchored her in a clear berth in the river. The pilot remained in charge of the ship, and thenext day the state of the weather being such as to render it unadvisable to take her into dock that day, she remained at anchor. In the course of that day, and whilst the pilot was in charge, the ship dragged her anchor and came into collision with a bark. In an action instituted by the owner of the bark against the ship the court decided that the collision was caused solely by the negligence of the pilot in charge of the ship:
Held, that the owners of the ship were not answerable for the damage, for it was occasioned by the fault of a pilot acting in charge of the ship within a district where the employment of such pilot was compulsory by law. The Princeton. 63, 69 note.

2. The master of a vessel belonging to the port of London and bound up the Thames, on a voyage from Australia to London with passengers on board, is required by law to employ a licensed pilot within the limits of the port of London. The Hankow. 235

3. Where a steamtug towing a vessel under a towage contract is so negligently navigated as to come into collision with a vessel belonging to third parties, the owners of the steamtug are liable for the damage done, even if at the time of the collision the vessel in tow was in charge of a duly licensed pilot by compulsion of law whose default solely occasioned the collision. The Mary. 271

4. Where the defendants in a collision suit raise a defence on the merits, and also set up a plea of compulsory pilotage, and the court dismisses the suit on the ground that the plea of compulsory pilotage is established, each party to the suit will, in accordance with the practice prevailing in the Court of Admiralty before the Judicature Acts be left to bear his own costs. Th Matthew Cay. 289

5. Where a collision in the Suez Canal has been caused by the negligence of a Suez Canal Company's pilot compulsorily taken on board the wrongdoing ship, the owner of such ship is not exempt from liability for the damage arising out of the collision.

6. The effect of the Regulations for the Navigation of the Suez Canal is to constitute a pilot taken on board a ship traversing the canal the adviser of the master, and to leave the control of the navigation of the ship solely with the master. The Guy Mannering. 676

7. The 74th section of the Harbors, Piers and Clauses Act, 1847, which act is incorporated with the New Brighton Pier Act, 1864, save and so far as any of the clauses and provisions of the two acts are inconsistent, declares that the owner of every vessel shall be answerable to the undertakers of every pier to which the Harbors, Docks and Piers Clauses Act, 1847, is applied, for any damage done to such pier, but provides that nothing therein contained shall extend to impose any liability for such damage upon the owner of any vessel where such vessel shall at the time when such damage is caused be in charge of a duly licensed pilot whom such owner or master is bound by law to employ. By the 39th section of the New Brighton Pier Act, 1864, it is enacted that if any person having the care of any ship shall wilfully or carelessly cause, permit, or suffer any damage or injury to be done to the New Brighton Pier, then and in every such case the owners of every such ship shall be answerable and liable to make satisfaction to the New Brighton Pier Company for all such damage or injury. A steamship came into collision with

and did damage to the New Brighton Pier, and to recover for the damage so done the New Brighton Pier Company brought an action against the steamship. The owners of the steamship alleged in their statement of defence that at the time the damage was done the steamship was in charge of a pilot employed by compulsion of law; that the collision was not caused or contributed to by the negligence of the defendants or any other persons than the pilot of the steamship, and that the damage was not permitted or suffered by any persons having the care of the steamship within the meaning of the New Brighton Pier Act, 1864. The plaintiffs demurred to these allegations in the statement of defence:

Held, that the provisions of the New Brighton Pier Act, 1864, did not preclude the defendants from setting up the defence of compulsory pilotage and that the demurrer must be overruled. *The Clan Gordon.*   723

8. A bark was at anchor in the Mersey in the way of the C., a vessel about to be launched. The launch was delayed as long as was prudent, but the bark not having been got out of the way in time was struck by the C. in coming off the ways and both vessels were damaged. Reasonable notice had been given of the launch, and a steamtug had been sent by those superintending the launch to tow the bark out of danger, and would have done so in time to have prevented the collision but for the obstinacy of those on board the bark:

Held, that the bark was alone to blame for the collision.

9. The bark had been towed out of dock into the river the previous day in order that she might proceed to sea before daybreak on the morning on which the collision happened. But an accident having happened to the bark she was unable to proceed to sea as intended, and at the time of the collision was waiting in the river to have repairs executed. She had on board of her a duly licensed Mersey pilot:

Held, that she was not at the time of the collision proceeding to sea within the meaning of the Mersey Docks Consolidation Act, 1858, s. 139, and that the pilot on board her was not at the time employed by compulsion of law. *The Cachapool.*   748

10. Sections 353 and 376 of the Merchant Shipping Act, 1854, render foreign vessels trading with cargo and passengers from the port of London to ports between Boulogne and the Baltic subject to compulsory pilotage on their outward passages between London and Gravesend, unless their masters or mates have pilotage certificates from the London Trinity House; and the operation of these sections, so far as such vessels are concerned, is not affected either by the Order in Council of February 18th, 1854, or by the provisions contained in the Harbors and Passing Tolls Act, 1861. *The Vesta.*   767

See COLLISION, 451.
    NEGLIGENCE. 738, 747 *note.*

POST MORTEM.

See MORTUARY, 289.

POWER.

See SETTLEMENTS, 801.

PRACTICE.

See DAMAGES, 575.

PRINCIPAL AND AGENT.

See PILOT, 63, 69 *note.*

PRIVILEGED COMMUNICATION.

See EVIDENCE, 163, 164 *note.*

PROBATE.

1. R., domiciled in Mexico, made a will according to the law of Mexico. The

proper court there decreed probate of a Spanish translation and not of the original:

Held, that the grant in this country must be made upon the production of an English translation of the Spanish copy, and not of a certified copy of the original. *Goods of Rule.* 169

See WILLS, 765.

R.

REAL ESTATE.

See CHARGE, 176.

RECEIVER.

1. The court will appoint a receiver in a co-ownership suit where circumstances exist which in the opinion of the court render such a course just and convenient. *The Ampthill.* 439

REFERENCE.

See DAMAGES, 575.

REGULATIONS.

1. The 22d clause of the by-laws of the river Tees, which provides that no steamship shall be navigated on any part of the river Tees at a higher rate of speed than six miles per hour, is to be construed as prohibiting a steamship proceeding against the tide being navigated at a greater speed than six miles per hour through the water. *The R. L. Alston.* 624

See COLLISION.

REMOTE DAMAGES.

See DAMAGES, 444.

RENT.

1. A lease of a house was vested in a bankrupt as assignee. The trustee in the bankruptcy did not disclaim the lease, but he did not take possession of the property or exercise any act of ownership over it. The bankrupt continued to live in the house, his friends paying the rent for him. After the expiration of the term the lessor sued the original lessee on his covenant to repair, claiming £400 damages. The lessee served a third party notice on the trustee, claiming to be indemnified by him, as assignee of the term, against all breaches of the covenant since the date of the bankruptcy and the trustee's appointment. The trustee then applied to the Court of Bankruptcy for leave to execute a disclaimer in respect of the lease. The lessor opposed the application, and the registrar refused it on the ground that the lease had expired. The trustee appealed, giving notice to the lessor, who did not appear on the hearing of the appeal:

Held, that leave to disclaim might be given, as it could not prejudice the rights of any person who was not before the court. *Matter of Paterson.* 879, 881 *note.*

RENUNCIATION.

1. H. P. W., sole executrix and universal legatee, renounced her rights as such to the grant of letters of administration, which was accordingly made to G. W., one of the next of kin. Upon the death of G. W., intestate and insolvent, H. P. W. was allowed to retract her renunciation as universal legatee, and take a grant of letters of administration *de bonis non. Goods of Wheelright.* 46

RES GESTÆ.

See EVIDENCE, 80.

RESIDENCE.

See DIVORCE.
JURISDICTION.
MARRIAGE.
WILLS, 610, 630.

RESPONDEAT SUPERIOR.

See PILOT.

REVOCATION.

See WILLS.

S.

SAILING REGULATIONS.

See COLLISION.

SALE.

See PARTITION, 76, 80 *note.*

SALVAGE.

1. Under the Harbors and Passing Tolls Act, 1861, the harbor of Ramsgate and the property and powers of its trustees were transferred to the Board of Trade. In a suit for salvage remuneration for services rendered by a vessel belonging to the harbor and vested in the Board of Trade under the provisions of the act:

Held, affirming the decision of the judge of the Admiralty Court, that the vessel was not a ship belonging to Her Majesty within the meaning of the Merchant Shipping Act, 1854. ss. 484, 485; and therefore that the Board of Trade were not precluded from recovering salvage in respect of its services, and that the claims of the commander and crew might be adjudicated upon without the consent of the admiralty. *The Cybele.* 8

2. The C., a Spanish steamship, fell in at sea with the S., an English steamship, with signals of distress flying and entirely helpless from injuries sustained in a collision with a third vessel. The passengers of the S. and a quantity of specie, which had formed part of the cargo of the S., having been taken on board the C., attempts were made by the master and crew of the C. to tow the S. into safety. These attempts were ineffectual, and ultimately, after the master and crew of the S. had gone on board the C. the S. was abandoned, and her passengers, master, and crew were landed in safety at an English port. Afterwards the specie was arrested in an action of salvage instituted at the suit of the owners, master, and crew of the C., who claimed in the action to recover for life salvage and for salvage services rendered to the S. and the specie. The owners of the specie appeared as defendants, and served a notice on the owners of the S. calling upon them to contribute to the remuneration claimed by the plaintiffs. Thereupon the owners of the S. appeared. At the hearing of the action the court awarded salvage remuneration to the plaintiffs for the services rendered, but reserved all questions as to the liability of the owners of the S. The owners of the specie then moved the court to declare that such portion of the sum awarded as was awarded for life salvage ought to be recouped to the owners of the specie.

The court refused the motion on the ground. that no property belonging to the owners of the S. having been salved they could not be held personally liable to pay any portion of the sum awarded. *Cargo ex Sarpedon.* 25

3. Two Norwegian barks, both bound to England, fell in with each other on the high seas, about 3,000 miles from Liverpool; one of the barks was in distress, her first mate having died, and her master, her second mate, and one of the crew being sick with yellow fever. The other bark was shorthanded, but her mate, with the consent of her master, went on board the distressed vessel and succeeded in navigating her to Liverpool. During the voyage, the master, the second mate, and two of the crew died. On the arrival of the vessel at Liverpool an action of salvage was instituted against her. At the hearing of the action, the value of the salved property was taken at £5,135 13s. 2d.

The court awarded £600 to the mate who had gone on board the distressed vessel, £100 to the owners of the salving vessel, £50 to her master, and

£150 amongst the remaining plaintiffs. *The Skibladner.* 21

4. A steamtug, having a vessel in tow, saw a ship ashore and went out of her way to inform, and informed, another steamtug of what she had seen. The other steamtug hereupon proceeded to the stranded ship and towed her into safety. In an action of salvage instituted on behalf of both steamtugs against the ship:
Held, that the owners, master, and crew of both steamtugs were entitled ·to salvage remuneration.   *The Sarah.* 32

5. A vessel constructed entirely for the purpose of conveying the obelisk known ˙ as Cleopatra's Needle from Alexandria to England, was, with the obelisk on board her, abandoned in the Bay of Biscay by her master and crew, and by the steamship employed to tow her to England, and the next day was found floating on her beam ends about ninety miles northeast of Ferrol by another steamship, which succeeded in towing her into Ferrol in safety.
Subsequently an action of salvage was instituted to determine the amount of salvage remuneration to be paid to the salvors for the services rendered, and bail was given in the action in the sum of £5,000. By the consent of all parties, the judge in court fixed the value of the property salved at £25,000.
At the hearing of the action, the court awarded £2,000 as salvage remuneration to the plaintiffs, and on a subsequent application apportioned the award as follow: £1,200 to the owner of the salving vessel; £250 to her master, and the residue to be distributed among her crew according to their rating, and services as salvors. *The Cleopatra.* 70

6. A tug under contract to tow a ship is not entitled to salvage remuneration for rescuing the ship from danger brought about by the tug's negligent performance of her towage contract.·

7. A tug agreed to tow a ship from Liverpool round the Skerries for a fixed sum. The tug imprudently towed the ship in bad weather too near a lee shore, and the weather becoming worse during the performance of the agreed

towage service, the hawser parted, and the ship was placed in a position of danger, and was compelled to let go her anchors to avoid being driven on shore. From this position she was rescued by the tug, having been compelled to slip her anchors and chains, which were lost:
Held, that the tug was not entitled to claim salvage remuneration, and that her owners were liable to pay for the loss of the anchors and chains. *The Robert Dixon.* 191

8. A fishing smack fell in near the Long Sand buoy with a foreign steamship. The steamship had been on the sands near the Kentish Knock light-ship, but had got off with some damage to her rudder, and had a signal for a pilot hoisted. The master of the smack boarded the steamship and piloted her to the entrance of Harwich harbor:
Held, that the owners, master, and crew of the fishing smack were entitled to salvage remuneration.

9. When a person goes on board of a vessel in distress, and pilots her into harbor, he is entitled to salvage remuneration, unless it is established that he has contracted to render the services for pilotage remuneration only. *The Anders Knape.* 243

10. Salvors having by meritorious services rendered at the risk of their lives salved a derelict vessel, her cargo and freight, valued together at £750, the court awarded £360 as salvage remuneration. *The Hebe.* 247

11. A tug under contract to tow a ship is not entitled to salvage remuneration for rescuing the ship from danger brought about by the tug's negligent performance of her towage contract.

12. A tug agreed to tow a ship from Liverpool to the Skerries for a fixed sum. The tug imprudently towed the ship in bad weather too near a lee shore, and, the weather becoming worse during the performance of the agreed towage service, the hawser parted and the ship was placed in a position of danger and was compelled to let go her anchors to avoid being driven on shore. From this position she was rescued by the tug, having been compelled to slip her anchors and chains, which were lost ·

22. In a suit instituted to recover salvage reward in respect of services rendered in towing a disabled vessel into safety, the court awarded a total sum of £4,000, of which £3,000 was apportioned to the owners. *Kenmure.* 622

23. Justices awarded salvage in respect of services rendered to a hopper-barge, which had been found adrift without any person on board of her in the Wash about three miles from Boston. The barge was not furnished with any means by which she could be propelled, and was used for dredging purposes:

Held, that the barge'was a "ship in distress on the shore of a sea or tidal water" within the meaning of the Merchant Shipping Act, 1854, s. 458, and that the justices had no jurisdiction to award salvage. *The Mac.* 671

24. Violent and overbearing conduct on the part of salvors, although it may not amount to such wilful misconduct as to cause an entire forfeiture of salvage reward, will yet operate to induce the court to diminish the amount of the reward. *The Marie.* 735

See COSTS, 262.
TENDER, 731.

SECURITY FOR COSTS.

1. In a petition for dissolution of marriage, the husband, who was an uncertificated bankrupt, claimed damages. Upon application by the co-respondent:

Held, that unless the claim for damages was withdrawn the petitioner must give security for the costs of the action. *Smith* v. *Smith.* 757

2. It is not the practice of the Court of Appeal when ordering an appellant to give security for costs to fix a time within which this is to be done. If the order is not complied with in a reasonable time the respondent may move to dismiss the appeal for want of prosecution; but what is a reasonable time must depend on the circumstances of each case. *Sturla* v. *Freccia.* 799

SEPARATE ESTATE.

See ALIMONY, 51.

SERVICE.

1. Foreign shipowners commenced an action in this country in respect of a collision at sea, and then discontinued the action. An order was made afterwards for leave to serve a writ, in an action respecting the same collision, issued against them at the suit of the defendants in the former action, by way of substituted service upon the solicitors who acted in the former action as the solicitors for the foreign shipowners.

Upon its appearing that the solicitors had ceased to act for the foreign shipowners, the order was set aside. *The Pommerania.* 231, 233 *note.*

SETTLEMENTS.

1. Under a marriage settlement real estate stood limited to H., the husband, for life, with remainder to the use of such of the children or issue of the marriage as he should by deed or will appoint; and in default of appointment, to the use of the children of the marriage equally as tenants in common in fee.

There was issue of the marriage two children only, a son and a daughter. The daughter married, and by her marriage settlement she and her intended husband covenanted with the trustees for the conveyance and settlement of all property which she then was "seised of, or interested in, or entitled to," upon the trusts therein mentioned, including in effect reversionary interests.

The daughter survived her husband, and thereupon H. by deed appointed the real estate comprised in the original settlement, subject to his life estate, to his son and daughter equally in fee, the daughter thus taking the same share as she would have taken in default of appointment:

Held, that inasmuch as the reversionary moiety appointed to the daughter constituted a new interest acquired by her subsequently to the date of her set-

TENANTS IN COMMON.

See RECEIVER, 439.

TENDER.

1. In a case of salvage, in which the defendants pleaded a tender and payment into court of £300, the court pronounced for the tender and condemned the defendants in costs up to the time of payment into court, but made no order as to the costs incurred after that time. *The Lotus.*   731

See CONSOLIDATION, 228.

THREATS.

See UNDUE INFLUENCE.

TOWAGE.

See DEMURRAGE, 441.

TRUSTS AND TRUSTEES.

1. It is the settled practice of the Court of Bankruptcy not to vacate the appointment of a trustee merely because a proof has been improperly rejected.

2. In order to induce the court to vacate the appointment, special circumstances—such as that the rejection of the proof has been procured by fraud—must be shown. At any rate an application for such an order must be made very promptly after the rejection of the proof. *Kimber* v. *Thrift.*   856

3. One of the trustees of an estate which was being administered by the court having become of unsound mind, an order was made under the Trustee Act, 1850, s. 5, appointing a person to concur with the other trustee in transferring into court certain Irish railway stock standing in the names of the

trustees. It being discovered before the order was drawn up that owing to sect. 56 of the act such an order could not be made as to Irish stock, an order was made appointing a person new trustee of the Irish stock in the place of the person of unsound mind, and directing him to concur with the other trustee in transferring the stock into court. *Kenlis* v. *Hodgson.*   870

See BANKS, 810, 816 *note.*
      DIRECTORS, 886, 907 *note.*

U.

UNDUE INFLUENCE.

1. M. A. D., the testatrix, in 1853 made her will, by which she gave her property equally between the plaintiffs, defendants, and interveners. In an action by the plaintiffs propounding this will, it appeared that in 1874 she gave instructions for another will, which would have deprived the plaintiffs of all interest in her estate.
    In the course of the plaintiffs' case some evidence was given tending to show that the testatrix was prevented by force and threats from executing the proposed will.
    The court allowed the pleadings to be amended by adding statements to that effect, and praying for a declaration that the plaintiffs held their shares as trustees for the defendants and interveners. *Betts* v. *Doughty.*   280

See ONUS, 311, 319 *note.*
      WILLS, 311, 319 *note.*

UNREASONABLE DELAY.

See DIVORCE, 762.

USAGE.

See CHARTERPARTY, 514.

V.

VARIATION.

See ALIMONY.
DECREE, 360.

W.

WAGES.

1. A shipmaster who has been habitually
drunk during his employment cannot
maintain an action for his wages. *The
Macleod.* 459

See COUNTER-CLAIM, 301.

WATER AND WATERCOURSES.

1. The defendants, the owners of a mining
property, sunk a shaft by which they
tapped the water which had formerly
found its way into certain old workings on their own ground, and had
thence percolated into the plaintiffs'
mines. The defendants then made a
borehole at the bottom of the shaft.
It was admitted that the making it was
not in due course of mining, but only
for the purpose of getting rid of the
water. The effect of the borehole was
to let off the water into the above-mentioned old workings on the defendants'
ground, whence it percolated into the
plaintiffs' works in the same way in
which it would have done if neither
shaft nor borehole had ever been made :
Held (reversing the decision of Fry,
J.), that the defendants had not by
making the shaft so appropriated the
water as to lay themselves under an
obligation to keep it from coming upon
the plaintiffs' land, and that, as the
effect of the defendants' operations was
not to throw upon the plaintiffs' land
any burden which it had not borne before, the plaintiffs' case failed. *West
Cumberland, etc.,* v. *Kenyon.* 821

WAYS.

1. A contract to sell land with the appurtenances does not pass a right to a

way to the land sold which the vendor
has used over adjoining land of his
own.

2. Where a grantee is entitled to a way
of necessity over another tenement belonging to the grantor, and there are
to the tenement granted more ways
than one, the grantee is entitled to one
way only, which the grantor may
select. *Bolton* v. *Bolton.* 927, 931 *note.*

WILLS.

1. I. D., by his will, gave all his property to A. H. for life, and then "the
whole " . . . . to his "legal heirs and
theirs forever":
The court *held,* that both his realty
and personalty were given to his co-
heiresses, and therefore made the grant
to M. T., one of the co-heiresses, as one
of the residuary legatees. *Goods of
Dixon.* 173

2. A man may be capable of transacting
business of a complicated and important kind, involving the exercise of considerable powers of intellect, and yet
may be subject to delusions so as to be
unfit to make a will.

3. But if the delusions under which a
man labors are such that they could
not reasonably be supposed to have
affected the dispositions made by his
will, the will would be valid. *Smee* v.
Smee. 311, 319 *note.*

4. If upon the face of a testamentary document and the facts known to the testatrix at the time of its execution, it is
doubtful whether the testatrix intended
altogether to revoke a former will, the
court will admit parol evidence to ascertain the intention.

5. In such a case the doubts having been
caused by the condition in which the
testatrix had left her testamentary
papers, the court allowed the costs of
all parties out of the estate, including,
besides the costs of the executors propounding the former will, the costs of
legatees named in it.

6. A testatrix signed a document in the
presence of two witnesses, who twenty

residue, and remainder of her personal estate" to her mother absolutely, and devised her real estate to the same trustees in trust for sale, and directed them to hold the sale moneys and the residue of the said trust moneys, stocks, funds, shares, and securities in trust for the children of C. absolutely.

Part of the property comprised in the bequest to the trustees consisted of impure personalty:

Held, first, that, the church being situate on land already in mortmain, there must be an inquiry to ascertain whether the parsonage house and school, or which of them were or was also so situate, and what sums of money would be required to be laid out in restoring, altering, and enlarging and improving such of the said three objects of the legacy as were or was so situate, and that the legacy was valid, so far as the objects were concerned, to the extent of the money so ascertained to be required:

27. Secondly, that (following *Sinnett* v. *Herbert*) the amount of the legacy required for the objects already in mortmain must be apportioned between the pure and impure personalty, and be paid out of the pure personalty to the extent of its proportion, and, under 43 Geo. 3, c. 108, out of the impure personalty to the full extent of £500:

Held, also, that so much of the £2,000 as failed passed to the legatees of the particular residue of the fund out of which it was given, and not under the general gift of residuary personal estate.

28. The construction of a particular residuary gift is not affected by the presence or absence of a general residuary gift, nor is there any sound distinction between lapsed and invalid dispositions, whether under a power of appointment or in exercise of ownership. *Champney* v. *Davy*.   910

See CONDITIONS, 918, 925 *note*.
EXECUTORS AND ADMINISTRATORS, 177.
INTERLINEATIONS, 359.
MARRIED WOMEN, 488, 533, 594, 626.
PAROL EVIDENCE, 601, 602 *note*.
PROBATE, 169.
UNDUE INFLUENCE.

WORDS.

" Descendants,"	856
" Funds,"	589
" Heirs,"	173
" Issue,"	856
" Money,"	589, 630, 631 *note*.
" Proceed to sea,"	748
" Securities,"	589
" Stocks,"	589

See WILLS.

WORK AND LABOR.

See WAGES, 459.

INDEX TO NOTES.

A.

Divorce—*continued.*
" if decree awards custody of children, cannot be changed collaterally,
32—185.
" though may be in same action, **32**—185.
See *Alimony—Lunatic—Parent and Child.*
Domicile. See *Divorce.*
Dower, when and how barred by ante-nuptial settlement, **32**—580.

E.

Easements. See *Appurtenances—Ways.*
Eaves, when liability for damage, from, **32**—828
Evidence, foreign law may be proved by witnesses instructed therein, **32**
—468.
" as to foreign certificate of protest, **32**—468.
" when common law presumed in force, **32**—468.
" the presumption that foreign law same as that of forum does not
obtain as to penal statutes, **32**—468.
" no presumption common law in force in Russia, **32**—468.
" no presumption statute law of another State same as that of forum,
32—468.
" foreign laws must be proved as *facts*, **32**—468.
" unwritten law of another State to be proven by oral testimony and
reports, not by historical works. **32**—468.
" though statutes of this State relieve from rent, no presumption those
of another do, **32**—468.
" statutes or laws of another State must be pleaded, **32**—468.
" when statutes and books of another State may be read in evidence,
32—468.
" how acts of Confederate Congress may be proven, **32**—468.
" on question of negligence that employed engineer, **32**—829.
See *Parol Evidence—Privileged Communication.*

F.

Foreign Law. See *Evidence.*
Former Suit, fraudulently bring suit in name of insane person, **32**—373.
Fraud, court may declare judgment of another State void for, **32**—134.
" in bringing suit in name of insane person, **32**—373.
Fraudulent Conveyance, a conveyance by husband to defeat wife's claim for
alimony is fraudulent, **32**—530.
Fund, deposited for specific purpose cannot be attached, **32**—817

G.

Grants. See *Covenants.*

H.

Highway, digging in so as to injure adjoining owner, **32**—850.
Husband and wife. See *Alimony—Parent and Child.*

I.

Illegality. See *Privileged Communication.*

Illegal Restraint, legacies in restraint of marriage, **32**—925.

Illegitimacy, testator had two nephews same name, one illegitimate, **32**—603.
See *Parent and Child.*

Income. See *Life Estate.*

Infant. See *Parent and Child.*

Injunctions, when granted in nuisances, **32**—850.
    "   to restrain digging in highway, **32**—850.
See *Covenants.*

Insanity. See *Undue Influence—Lunatic.*

Insurance, when assignment to co-owner does not enable him to recover share of one assigning, **32**—80.

J.

Joint Owners, of vessel, when not partners and when are, **32**—80.
See *Partnership.*

Judgment, of another State may be declared void for fraud, **32**—134.

Jurisdiction, if courts of domicile on obtaining jurisdiction declare marriage illegal, courts of State where marriage performed bound, **32**—8.
    "   after first process, service of papers mere question of regularity, **32**—233.
See *Divorce—Parent and Child—Service.*

L.

Landlord and Tenant, though statute of one State relieve from rent, no presumption those of another do, **32**—468.
See *Rent.*

Law. See *Evidence.*

Legacy, when presumed to be satisfaction, **32**—602.
    "   in restraint of marriage, **32**—925.

Legitimacy, testator had two nephews same name, one illegitimate, **32**—603.
See *Divorce.*

Liability, Limited, of shipowners, **32**—558.

Lien, on sunken vessel or cargo by one raising it, **32**—703.
    "   remedy in such case, **32**—703.

Life Estate, parties to proceedings to determine whether deficiency to be paid out of *corpus* or dividends, **32**—878.
    "   "   . when commissions to be paid out of *corpus* and not income, **32**—878.

Limitations, Statute of, if evidence shows damage within period of, court not bound to submit, **32**—829.
See *Adverse Possession.*

Limited Liability, of shipowners, **32**—558.

Lunatic, at common law marriage with, a nullity, **32**—873.
    "   occasional previous insanity and hereditary taint insufficient for divorce, **32**—873.
    "   statutory rule in *Mississippi* as to insanity at marriage, **32**—873.

T.

U.

W.

Lightning Source UK Ltd.
Milton Keynes UK
UKHW02f0727160818
327336UK00008B/271/P